For Reference

Not to be taken from this room

Handbook of Research on Virtual Workplaces and the New Nature of Business Practices

Pavel Zemliansky
James Madison University, USA

Kirk St.Amant
East Carolina University, USA

INFORMATION SCIENCE REFERENCE

Hershey · New York

Acquisitions Editor:	Kristin Klinger
Development Editor:	Kristin Roth
Senior Managing Editor:	Jennifer Neidig
Managing Editor:	Sara Reed
Copy Editors:	Ashley Fails, Jeannie Porter
Typesetter:	Michael Brehm
Cover Design:	Lisa Tosheff
Printed at:	Yurchak Printing Inc.

Published in the United States of America by
Information Science Reference (an imprint of IGI Global)
701 E. Chocolate Avenue, Suite 200
Hershey PA 17033
Tel: 717-533-8845
Fax: 717-533-8661
E-mail: cust@igi-global.com
Web site: http://www.igi-global.com

and in the United Kingdom by
Information Science Reference (an imprint of IGI Global)
3 Henrietta Street
Covent Garden
London WC2E 8LU
Tel: 44 20 7240 0856
Fax: 44 20 7379 0609
Web site: http://www.eurospanonline.com

Library of Congress Cataloging-in-Publication Data

Handbook of research on virtual workplaces and the new nature of business practices / Pavel Zemliansky and Kirk St. Amant, editors.
    p. cm.
  Summary: "This book compiles authoritative research from scholars worldwide, covering the issues surrounding the influx of information technology to the office environment, from choice and effective use of technologies to necessary participants in the virtual workplace"-- Provided by publisher.
  Includes bibliographical references and index.
  ISBN 978-1-59904-871-0 (hbk.) -- ISBN 978-1-59904-872-7 (ebook)
  1. Virtual reality in management--Handbooks, manuals, etc. 2. Virtual work teams--Handbooks, manuals, etc. 3. Information technology-- Management--Handbooks, manuals, etc. I. Zemliansky, Pavel. II. St. Amant, Kirk, 1970-
  HD30.2122.H36 2008
  658'.05--dc22
                  2007032054

British Cataloguing in Publication Data
A Cataloguing in Publication record for this book is available from the British Library.

All work contributed to this book set is original material. The views expressed in this book are those of the authors, but not necessarily of the publisher.

If a library purchased a print copy of this publication, please go to http://www.igi-global.com/reference/assets/IGR-eAccess-agreement.pdf for information on activating the library's complimentary electronic access to this publication.

Editorial Advisory Board

Table of Contents

Foreword xxvii

Preface xxix

Acknowledgment xxxiii

Section I
Foundations of the Virtual Workplace

Chapter I
Gains and Losses in the Rhetoric of Virtual Workplace 1
  Pamela Estes Brewer, Appalachian State University, USA

Chapter II
Removing Space and Time: Tips for Managing the Virtual Workplace 14
  Christie L. McDaniel, University of North Carolina–Chapel Hill, USA

Chapter III
Communication in Global Virtual Activity Systems.. 24
  Marie C. Paretti, Virginia Polytechnic Institute and State University, USA
  Lisa D. McNair, Virginia Polytechnic Institute and State University, USA

Chapter IV
Successful Communication in Virtual Teams and the Role of the Virtual Team Leader 39
  Jamie S. Switzer, Colorado State University, USA

Chapter V
Foundations and Applications of Intelligent Knowledge Exchange.................................... 53
  S. J. Overbeek, e-Office B.V., The Netherlands
  P. van Bommel, Radboud University Nijmegen, The Netherlands
  H.A. Proper, Radboud University Nijmegen, The Netherlands
  D.B.B. Rijsenbrij, Radboud University Nijmegen, The Netherlands

Chapter VI
Digital Divide Redux: Why the Greatest Gap is Ideological... 70
  Michelle Rodino-Colocino, The Pennsylvania State University, USA

Chapter VII
Parawork 81
  Leah A. Zuidema, Dordt College, USA

Chapter VIII
Impression Formation in Computer-Mediated Communication and Making a
Good (Virtual) Impression 98
  Jamie S. Switzer, Colorado State University, USA

Chapter IX
Telecommuting and the Management of the Human Moment 110
  Alan D. Smith, Robert Morris University, USA

Chapter X
Cultural Implications of Collaborative Information Technologies (CITs) in
International Online Collaborations and Global Virtual Teams... 120
  Bolanle A. Olaniran, Texas Tech University, USA
  David A. Edgell, Texas Tech University, USA

Chapter XI
Explaining Organizational Virtuality: Insights from the Knowledge-Based View............................ 137
  Yulin Fang, City University of Hong Kong, Hong Kong
  Dev K. Dutta, University of New Hampshire, USA

Chapter XII
The Perceptions of Collaborative Technologies Among Virtual Workers 150
  Frankie S. Jones, AT&T, USA

Chapter XIII
Ubiquitous Connectivity & Work-Related Stress 167
  J. Ramsay, University of the West of Scotland, UK
  M. Hair, University of the West of Scotland, UK
  K. V. Renaud, University of Glasgow, UK

Chapter XIV
Employee Privacy in Virtual Workplaces 183
  Robert Sprague, University of Wyoming College of Business, USA

Chapter XV
Accommodating Persons with Disabilities in Virtual Workplaces 196
　　Belinda Davis Lazarus, University of Michigan–Dearborn, USA

Section II
Education and Training for the Virtual Workplace

Chapter XVI
Using Cyberspace to Promote Transformative Learning Experiences and Consequently
Democracy in the Workplace 207
　　William F. Ritke-Jones, Texas A&M University–Corpus Christi, USA

Chapter XVII
Instructional Design and E-Training 223
　　Julia D. Sweeny, James Madison University, USA

Chapter XVIII
Designing the Virtual Classroom for Management Teaching 241
　　Parissa Haghirian, Sophia University, Japan
　　Bernd Simon, Vienna University of Economics and Business Administration, Austria

Chapter XIX
Building Online Training Programs for Virtual Workplaces 257
　　Christa Ehmann Powers, Smarthinking Inc., USA
　　Beth L. Hewett, Independent Scholar, USA

Chapter XX
The Virtual Classroom @ Work 272
　　Terrie Lynn Thompson, University of Alberta, Canada

Chapter XXI
Video Technology for Academic Integrity in Online Courses 289
　　Judith Szerdahelyi, Western Kentucky University, USA

Chapter XXII
Virtual Workplaces for Learning in Singapore 301
　　Kalyani Chatterjea, Nanyang Technological University, Singapore

Chapter XXIII
Using an Information Literacy Program to Prepare Nursing Students to
Practice in a Virtual Workplace 317
　　Mona Florea, University of Rhode Island Library, USA
　　Lillian Rafeldt, Three Rivers Community College, USA
　　Susan Youngblood, Texas Tech University, USA

Chapter XXIV
Preparing for the Virtual Workplace in the Educational Commons..334
    Gary Hepburn, Acadia University, Canada

Section III
Tools and Environments for Virtual Work

Chapter XXV
Technologies and Services in Support of Virtual Workplaces..346
    Alan McCord, Lawrence Technological University, USA
    Morell D. Boone, Eastern Michigan University, USA

Chapter XXVI
Writing Research into Professional E-Mail Communication 364
    Kirstie Edwards, Sheffield Hallam University, UK
    Simeon Yates, Sheffield Hallam University, UK
    Anne-Florence Dujardin, Sheffield Hallam University, UK
    Geff Green, Sheffield Hallam University, UK

Chapter XXVII
New Media and the Virtual Workplace..382
    Matt Barton, St. Cloud State University, USA

Chapter XXVIII
Adoption of Wi-Fi Technologies and Creation of Virtual Workplaces...395
    Ran Wei, University of South Carolina, USA

Chapter XXIX
Using Virtual Worlds to Assist Distributed Teams..408
    Clint Bowers, University of Central Florida, USA
    Peter A. Smith, University of Central Florida, USA
    Jan Cannon-Bowers, University of Central Florida, USA
    Denise Nicholson, University of Central Florida, USA

Chapter XXX
Knowledge Transfer and Marketing in Second Life...424
    Peter Rive, Victoria University of Wellington, New Zealand

Chapter XXXI
Intranets: Interactive Knowledge Management Tools of Networked Communities...........................439
    Goran Vlasic, University of Zagreb, Croatia
    Jurica Pavicic, University of Zagreb, Croatia
    Zoran Krupka, University of Zagreb, Croatia

Chapter XXXII
Instant Messaging (IM) Literacy in the Workplace 455
  Beth L. Hewett, Independent Scholar, USA
  Russell J. Hewett, University of Illinois Urbana Champaign, USA

Chapter XXXIII
Supporting Collaboration with Trust Virtual Organization.. 473
  Aizhong Lin, Macquarie University, Australia
  Erik Vullings, TNO, The Netherlands
  James Dalziel, Macquarie University, Australia

Chapter XXXIV
Augmented Reality and the Future of Virtual Workspaces... 486
  James K. Ford, University of California, Santa Barbara, USA
  Tobias Höllerer, University of California, Santa Barbara, USA

Chapter XXXV
Virtual Writing as Actual Leadership... 503
  James R. Zimmerman, James Madison University, USA

Chapter XXXVI
Business Proces Resue and Standardization with P2P Technologies.. 516
  José A. Rodrigues Nt., COPPE—Federal University of Rio de Janeiro, Brazil
  Jano Moreira de Souza, COPPE—Federal University of Rio de Janeiro, Brazil
  Geraldo Zimbrão, COPPE—Federal University of Rio de Janeiro, Brazil
  Geraldo Xexéo, COPPE—Federal University of Rio de Janeiro, Brazil
  Mutaleci Miranda, Military Institute of Engineering, Brazil

Chapter XXXVII
Collaborative Writing Tools in the Virtual Workplace.. 530
  Norman E. Youngblood, Texas Tech University, USA
  Joel West, Texas Tech University, USA

Chapter XXXVIII
Distance Internships... 544
  David A. Edgell, Texas Tech University, USA

Chapter XXXIX
An International Virtual Office Communication Plan 555
  Lei Meng, Texas Tech University, USA
  Robert Schafer, Texas Tech University, USA

Chapter XL
Design and Managing of Distributed Virtual Organizations 564
    Diego Liberati, Italian National Research Council, Italy

Section IV
Implementation of Virtual Workplaces Across Professions and Academic Disciplines

Chapter XLI
Semi-Virtual Workplaces in German Financial Service Enterprises 570
    Heinz D. Knoell, Leuphana University, Germany

Chapter XLII
Implementing Client-Support for Collaborative Spaces... 582
    R. Todd Stephens, AT&T Corporation, USA

Chapter XLIII
Value, Visibility, and Virtual Teamwork at Kairos... 595
    Douglas Eyman, George Mason University, USA

Chapter XLIV
Plagiarism, Ghostwriting, Boilerplate, and Open Content 604
    Wendy Warren Austin, Edinboro University of Pennsylvania, USA

Chapter XLV
Usability and User-Centered Theory for 21st Century OWLs 614
    Dana Lynn Driscoll, Purdue University, USA
    H. Allen Brizee, Purdue University, USA
    Michael Salvo, Purdue University, USA
    Morgan Sousa, Purdue University, USA

Chapter XLVI
Negotiating Virtual Identity in an Age of Globalization.. 632
    Neil P. Baird, University of Nevada, USA

Chapter XLVII
Virtual Political Office Where Gender and Culture Meet... 641
    Olena Igorivna Goroshko, Kharkiv Polytechnic Institute "National Technical University,"
    Ukraine

Chapter XLVIII
The Benefits of Using Print-On-Demand or POD 668
    Eric Franzén, CFA Institute, USA

Chapter XLIX

Difficulties in Accepting Telemedicine 681

    María José Crisóstomo-Acevedo, Jerez Hospital, Spain
    José Aurelio Medina-Garrido, University of Cadiz, Spain

Chapter L

Reconsidering the Lay-Expert Audience Divide 692

    Michael J. Klein, James Madison University, USA

Chapter LI

Rapid Virtual Enterprising to Manage Complex and High-Risk Assets 702

    Jayantha P. Liyanage, University of Stavanger, Norway

About the Contributors 710

Index 725

Detailed Table of Contents

Foreword xxvii

Preface xxix

Acknowledgment xxxiii

Section I
Foundations of the Virtual Workplace

The chapters in this section address fundamental issues essential for successfully organizing, managing, or participating in a virtual workplace.

Chapter I
Gains and Losses in the Rhetoric of Virtual Workplace 1
    Pamela Estes Brewer, Appalachian State University, USA

Virtual workplaces are information centers in an information age; people within them work at a distance with the goal of knowledge transfer toward specific purposes. What are the communication gains and losses most experienced in virtual workplaces? With rhetoric as the primary unit of exchange, what steps can be taken to ensure its effectiveness? Current research points to planning, face-to-face opportunities, mixed media, boundaries, and metacommunication as most important gains.

Chapter II
Removing Space and Time: Tips for Managing the Virtual Workplace 14
    Christie L. McDaniel, University of North Carolina–Chapel Hill, USA

This chapter compares and contrasts virtual teams with traditional, face-to-face teams. In addition to this analysis, it provides a discussion of tips and suggestions for virtual team managers. This chapter analyzes specific aspects of team relationships when the workplace becomes virtual, including topics such as trust and cohesion. Communication barriers in the virtual workplace are also discussed.

Chapter III

Communication in Global Virtual Activity Systems... 24

Marie C. Paretti, Virginia Polytechnic Institute and State University, USA

Lisa D. McNair, Virginia Polytechnic Institute and State University, USA

This chapter uses activity theory as a lens to understand the implications of virtual collaboration and cross-cultural contact for communication in global virtual teams. Rather than adopting a set of heuristics or guidelines that may readily become dated as cultures and technologies shift in the flat world, we argue that both those who study and those who engage in global virtual teams should critically analyze the entire system. We then provide metacognitive approaches to both distributed work and cross-cultural contact that team managers and team members can use to establish flexible communication practices appropriate to the activity system at hand, and that researchers can use to account for the range of factors that impact team performance.

Chapter IV

Successful Communication in Virtual Teams and the Role of the Virtual Team Leader...................... 39

Jamie S. Switzer, Colorado State University, USA

This chapter provides a general overview of virtual teams and virtual team leadership and discusses specific communication strategies and competencies necessary for virtual team leaders to be effective and successful communicators. Often, organizations have their people perform functional tasks by working in virtual teams, where members use technology to cooperate across geographic and organizational boundaries. As the use of virtual teams in the workforce becomes more prevalent, those involved must have the knowledge to communicate efficiently and effectively, especially the virtual team leaders.

Chapter V

Foundations and Applications of Intelligent Knowledge Exchange... 53

S. J. Overbeek, e-Office B.V., The Netherlands

P. van Bommel, Radboud University Nijmegen, The Netherlands

H.A. Proper, Radboud University Nijmegen, The Netherlands

D.B.B. Rijsenbrij, Radboud University Nijmegen, The Netherlands

This chapter explains the concept of knowledge exchange and how a virtual workplace can support knowledge exchange between workers. A scenario from the field of medicine illustrates how physicians can improve their knowledge exchange by utilizing the virtual workplace models introduced. The intended audience of this chapter is researchers interested in the topic of knowledge exchange and managers who want to improve their organizations' knowledge exchange processes.

Chapter VI

Digital Divide Redux: Why the Greatest Gap is Ideological... 70

Michelle Rodino-Colocino, The Pennsylvania State University, USA

Although the debate on the digital divide has evolved from an analysis of access to skill, scholars have largely neglected the significance of inequalities in the high-tech work force. If the most technically skilled workers face eroding job security and dwindling wages, digital divide research is missing a key source of disparity among today's workers. Overlooking such discrepancies undercuts the practical application of such analyses. This chapter examines the latest developments in digital divide research and the high-tech labor market. The author suggests how scholars and managers can work to create more equitable working conditions for high-tech labor.

Chapter VII

Parawork 81

    Leah A. Zuidema, Dordt College, USA

The term parawork describes spaces and activities that function alongside—yet also outside—of traditional workplaces. In parawork environments, it can be desirable to overlap the personal, social, and professional. This chapter defines parawork by focusing on parawork as enabled by online communication technologies. The author reviews literature that supports an informs this understanding of online parawork. Through case study of one woman's participation in an e-mail discussion list for teacher interns, the practical realities and possibilities of online parawork are considered. The chapter closes with conclusions about conditions necessary for effective online parawork, as well as implications for future research.

Chapter VIII

Impression Formation in Computer-Mediated Communication and Making a

Good (Virtual) Impression 98

    Jamie S. Switzer, Colorado State University, USA

This chapter offers strategies to ensure virtual workers make a good impression on their clients and colleagues when interacting online. In face-to-face interactions, people generally form impressions by focusing on a variety of nonverbal cues. People are now communicating virtually and forming impressions based on mediated interactions. In an online environment the range of nonverbal cues that normally aid in impression formation is drastically narrowed. In the absence of these nonverbal cues, forming impressions via computer-mediated communication places a greater emphasis on verbal (text-based) and linguistic cues.

Chapter IX

Telecommuting and the Management of the Human Moment 110

    Alan D. Smith, Robert Morris University, USA

Telecommuting is a tool that is becoming more and more a way a life for organizations as they strive to recruit and retain employees and assist them in improving their quality of life within the virtual workplace environment. The recurring themes tend to be the need to select the proper employee, training managers to manage remote employees, strong communication (formal/informal) strategies, clear expectations, and a proactive stance in deterring isolation to aid in the development and maintenance of the human moment. Such factors are essential to the psyche and cannot be forgotten regardless of how many other forms of communication are developed..

Chapter X

Cultural Implications of Collaborative Information Technologies (CITs) in
International Online Collaborations and Global Virtual Teams.. 120

Bolanle A. Olaniran, Texas Tech University, USA
David A. Edgell, Texas Tech University, USA

The chapter introduces and explains some critical issues regarding cultural implications of collaborative information technologies (CITs) in international online collaborations and global virtual teams. This chapter attempts to addresses some of the cross-cultural issues in international online collaboration, which include but are not limited to language, culture, trust, and technology along with the implications for organizational virtual collaboration. The chapter also provides useful recommendations and strategies for improving international online virtual collaboration with CMC.

Chapter XI

Explaining Organizational Virtuality: Insights from the Knowledge-Based View............................ 137

Yulin Fang, City University of Hong Kong, Hong Kong
Dev K. Dutta, University of New Hampshire, USA

Based on virtual organization literature and the knowledge-based view of the firm, this chapter develops a working definition of organizational virtuality. The authors do this by conducting a review of existing definitions of a virtual organization, and identifying organizational knowledge-related factors that influence virtuality. More specifically, we propose that (1) an organization's need for knowledge exchange and ability to exchange knowledge jointly determine the level of organizational virtuality that develops in the firm; and (2) the higher the need for and ability to engage in knowledge exchange, the higher this level of resulting organizational virtuality. The contribution that this research makes to academia and managerial practice are also discussed.

Chapter XII

The Perceptions of Collaborative Technologies Among Virtual Workers 150

Frankie S. Jones, AT&T, USA

The purpose of this chapter is to discuss the findings of a qualitative research study which explored how collaborative technologies facilitate or inhibit the work of 12 virtual workers. The chapter first reviews the literature regarding the relationship between virtual work and technology. This is followed by a detailed discussion of the methodology and findings of the qualitative study. The chapter ends with a discussion of the findings and implications for practice and future research.

Chapter XIII

Ubiquitous Connectivity & Work-Related Stress 167

J. Ramsay, University of the West of Scotland, UK
M. Hair, University of the West of Scotland, UK
K. V. Renaud, University of Glasgow, UK

The integration of a number of different communication technologies into everyday life has increased the pace of communication and of everyday life. This chapter considers the ways that e-mail has impacted workers with particular emphasis on the way workplace stressors have changed over the past quarter century.

Chapter XIV
Employee Privacy in Virtual Workplaces 183
    Robert Sprague, University of Wyoming College of Business, USA

This chapter addresses the legal aspects of employee privacy in virtual workplaces. No one has yet examined whether virtual workplaces alter the fundamental assumptions underlying employee privacy rights. By reviewing the current status of employee privacy law and juxtaposing it with virtual workplace environments, this chapter seeks to provide guidance for the privacy issues that are sure to arise with the growth and development of virtual workplaces.

Chapter XV
Accommodating Persons with Disabilities in Virtual Workplaces 196
    Belinda Davis Lazarus, University of Michigan–Dearborn, USA

The chapter discusses the characteristics of persons with a variety of disabilities and the accommodations needed to provide them with access to virtual workplaces. Detailed descriptions of each disability category are provided. The advantages of virtual workplaces for persons with disabilities are described. Also, accommodations that relate to a specific disability are shared along with possible sources of support for employers who wish to hire persons with disabilities.

Section II
Education and Training for the Virtual Workplace

The chapters in this section discuss research on theory and practice of successfully training present and future employees for the virtual workplace.

Chapter XVI
Using Cyberspace to Promote Transformative Learning Experiences and Consequently
Democracy in the Workplace 207
    William F. Ritke-Jones, Texas A&M University–Corpus Christi, USA

This chapter will explain transformative learning and its value and application to corporate training practices by promoting critical reflection on one's "frames of reference." This critical reflection can help one to challenge cultural and social assumptions, potentially leading the person to more democratic ways of thinking and behaving in the workplace. Cyberspace offers a unique and potentially powerful place to employ transformative learning practices, and along with explaining transformative learning, this chapter will explore how cyberspace can be used for this kind of learning. This chapter will also posit that new cyberspace environments such as Wiki's and Second Life hold tremendous promise as transformative learning spaces because they invite small group collaboration.

Chapter XVII
Instructional Design and E-Training...223
    Julia D. Sweeny, James Madison University, USA

The primary focus of the chapter is the importance of instructional design in analyzing the online audience and context, development of instructional strategies, online materials, implementation of a Web-based course, and, finally, the evaluation of an online training course. Future trends and a conclusion complete the chapter.

Chapter XVIII
Designing the Virtual Classroom for Management Teaching...241
    Parissa Haghirian, Sophia University, Japan
    Bernd Simon, Vienna University of Economics and Business Administration, Austria

This chapter discusses the use of virtual classrooms, namely collaborative, information technology-mediated teaching endeavors in management education at universities. The overall aim of this chapter is to provide insights for those who are responsible for the development of management curricula. The chapter also offers specific guidelines to management educators interested in integrating IT-based teaching approaches in their classrooms as well as supporting them to increase teaching effectiveness when designing virtual classrooms.

Chapter XIX
Building Online Training Programs for Virtual Workplaces 257
    Christa Ehmann Powers, Smarthinking Inc., USA
    Beth L. Hewett, Independent Scholar, USA

The chapter provides employers who are interested in developing and implementing Internet-based employee training with key program development principles, ones that have been substantiated by practice and research from various professional fields and that have been successfully used in an Internet-based business that employs hundreds of part- and full-time individuals. The chapter provides: (1) an educational and financial rationale for conducting online human adaptive training for virtual workplaces; (2) an understanding of training/professional development principles and strategies for online employees in virtual businesses via one-to-one and/or group human adaptive settings, and (3) an understanding of how to scale such training processes efficiently and with measurable results gleaned from qualitative and quantitative methods.

Chapter XX
The Virtual Classroom @ Work...272
    Terrie Lynn Thompson, University of Alberta, Canada

Before we can exploit new technologies to realize new ways of working, we must be able to imagine innovative possibilities for learning. In this chapter, findings from a qualitative case study in a geographically dispersed organization are used a springboard to explore the challenges of introducing innovative e-learning initiatives. This chapter delves into two topics: workplace practices that facilitate and frustrate new ways of learning, and notions of online community, informal learning, and blended learning.

Chapter XXI
Video Technology for Academic Integrity in Online Courses 289
    Judith Szerdahelyi, Western Kentucky University, USA

Online students' academic dishonesty combined with faculty's use of performance measures unsuitable for online courses may result in grades that do not represent the students' skills and knowledge. Utilizing multimedia technology, especially video production, in distance learning courses will reduce the possibility of academic dishonesty and improve the quality of teaching and learning.

Chapter XXII
Virtual Workplaces for Learning in Singapore 301
    Kalyani Chatterjea, Nanyang Technological University, Singapore

This chapter defines the term "Virtual Learning Place" as a space or a platform over which learning can be situated without the learners and the facilitator being present face to face. The chapter then examines the background of virtual workplaces and goes on to discuss the issues addressed in three learning scenarios, using the concept of virtual workplaces to recreate a classroom learning situation with teacher supervision, a simulated lab facility, and a virtual teacher-supervised field work session. Finally, the chapter presents an analysis of learner responses that are used to examine the effectiveness of these initiatives in providing a more enriched and more useful learning environment.

Chapter XXIII
Using an Information Literacy Program to Prepare Nursing Students to
Practice in a Virtual Workplace 317
    Mona Florea, University of Rhode Island Library, USA
    Lillian Rafeldt, Three Rivers Community College, USA
    Susan Youngblood, Texas Tech University, USA

The chapter presents healthcare examples of the current virtual working environment and introduces nursing skills necessary for evidence-based practice in a virtual workplace. The authors discuss how the Nursing Information Literacy Program was designed and implemented at Three Rivers Community College to assist nursing students in developing skills such as critical thinking and problem solving, technological literacy, information literacy, and collaborative and cooperative learning. The authors hope that this example will serve as a model for creating other information literacy programs that prepare students for working in a virtual workplace.

Chapter XXIV
Preparing for the Virtual Workplace in the Educational Commons 334
    Gary Hepburn, Acadia University, Canada

This chapter explores the potential of an educational commons to help schools better prepare students for the virtual workplace. Together with the formation of stronger linkages between schools and the business world, making greater use of resources such as open source software in both school and business would greatly reduce costs and enable students to be better prepared to participate in the virtual workplace. With the virtual workplace's emphasis on online communication technologies as a primary tool for completing day to day tasks, schools must acquire the hardware and software as well as explore ways of incorporating these tools into student learning.

Section III
Tools and Environments for Virtual Work

The third section of the book covers the tools available to members of virtual workplaces. These tools range from such traditional ones as e-mail and instant messaging to more recent arrivals on the virtual workplace scene, such as collaborative writing environments and virtual worlds.

Chapter XXV

Technologies and Services in Support of Virtual Workplaces 346

Alan McCord, Lawrence Technological University, USA
Morell D. Boone, Eastern Michigan University, USA

This chapter provides two frameworks—a technology services framework and a virtual services management framework—for evaluating an organization's readiness and capabilities to develop, deploy, and support effective virtual work environments. The elements of the frameworks are explored through examination of real-world issues surrounding the evolution of virtual workplaces. The chapter also proposes two assessment approaches to evaluate virtual work capabilities and the virtuality of enterprise work groups.

Chapter XXVI

Writing Research into Professional E-Mail Communication 364

Kirstie Edwards, Sheffield Hallam University, UK
Simeon Yates, Sheffield Hallam University, UK
Anne-Florence Dujardin, Sheffield Hallam University, UK
Geff Green, Sheffield Hallam University, UK

This chapter discusses research showing the positive influence of a social dimension on team performance and how the lack of unplanned informal exchanges in virtual teams may hinder performance. New research is reported in which adaptations in socio-emotional content of e-mails in academic and commercial writing teams are mapped against a social interactive theory of written communication to interpret the social-task balance in teams, described as the team culture. Based on the results of this and other research within the same program, the authors recommend a more conversational style in professional e-mail writing, encouraging face to face contact, allocating time specifically for social exchanges, and making information about colleagues available to the team.

Chapter XXVII

New Media and the Virtual Workplace 382

Matt Barton, St. Cloud State University, USA

This chapter explores definitions of "New Media," exposing the key concepts and discussing why and how they are relevant for modern business. The goal of the chapter is to show how New Media concepts of play, space, identity, simulation, and collaboration can facilitate professional communication in virtual workplaces. While there is no magical template for building productive virtual workplaces, this chapter will help readers understand and apply some of the principles of New Media to better understand the obstacles and affordances they offer modern business.

Chapter XXVIII
Adoption of Wi-Fi Technologies and Creation of Virtual Workplaces 395
Ran Wei, University of South Carolina, USA

This chapter introduces adoption theory and applies it to examine the use of Wi-Fi, which has the potential to expand virtual workplaces. Research shows that the use of Wi-Fi to access the Internet is low. As understanding users and their needs is a prerequisite for the success of any new information technology, this chapter identifies factors accounting for the low usage of Wi-Fi in organizations and seeks to build a model to increase Wi-Fi usage. The chapter ends with a discussion of future trends in Wi-Fi technology and how increased adoption of Wi-Fi enhances the virtual workplace.

Chapter XXIX
Using Virtual Worlds to Assist Distributed Teams 408
Clint Bowers, University of Central Florida, USA
Peter A. Smith, University of Central Florida, USA
Jan Cannon-Bowers, University of Central Florida, USA
Denise Nicholson, University of Central Florida, USA

This chapter explores the ways in which virtual worlds could support interactive teams at a greater fidelity than that of the previous generation of groupware tools using a popular Virtual World, Second Life as an example. While providing specific examples of how Second Life's current and planned feature sets could already support distributed teams, that is, teams whose members are geographically disbursed. New features that would provide additional support for these types of teams are also discussed.

Chapter XXX
Knowledge Transfer and Marketing in Second Life 424
Peter Rive, Victoria University of Wellington, New Zealand

This chapter explores the context of virtual reality and presence when considering Second Life as a virtual workplace. We examine the requirements of emotional communications and sensory input in order to establish a virtual presence, and the experience of the advertising agency Saatchi & Saatchi with regards virtual workplaces. Knowledge management and marketing remain two of the major drivers for businesses who would like to explore the opportunities of virtual presence and Second Life. In order to achieve creative collaboration intellectual property and digital rights management must be taking into account. Open source software and Creative Commons copyright licenses play an important role in encouraging collaboration in a virtual workplace.

Chapter XXXI
Intranets: Interactive Knowledge Management Tools of Networked Communities............................ 439
Goran Vlasic, University of Zagreb, Croatia
Jurica Pavicic, University of Zagreb, Croatia
Zoran Krupka, University of Zagreb, Croatia

This chapter examines the importance of intranets as knowledge management tools/media enabling efficient knowledge exchange and upgrade within an organization and the "community" of stakeholders. Additionally, communities are analyzed as networked systems of interested parties as related to such tools. In reviewing these topics, the chapter also analyzes possibilities of different approaches to development and management of intranets, and thus of networked people creating a certain networked "community forum." These developments are crucial to virtual workplaces as well as for increasing business efficiency.

Chapter XXXII
Instant Messaging (IM) Literacy in the Workplace 455
Beth L. Hewett, Independent Scholar, USA
Russell J. Hewett, University of Illinois Urbana Champaign, USA

This chapter discusses instant messaging (IM) as a valuable digital tool that has influenced business communication practices at least as much as e-mail. It argues that IM's characteristics of presence awareness, synchronicity, hybridity, and interactivity create a unique set of writing and reading experiences. These functional qualities both require and hone high-level writing and reading skills, which are used powerfully in communicative multitasking. The authors believe that IM should be sanctioned in the workplace and that IM use should be a subject of focused training; to that end, they provide a practical, literacy-based training sequence that can be adapted to various settings.

Chapter XXXIII
Supporting Collaboration with Trust Virtual Organization.. 473
Aizhong Lin, Macquarie University, Australia
Erik Vullings, TNO, The Netherlands
James Dalziel, Macquarie University, Australia

This chapter introduces the trust virtual organization as a means of facilitating authentication and authorization for sharing distributed and protected contents and services. It indicates that sharing institutional protected services and deliverables has proven a hurdle since user accounts are created in many sites. It provides an approach to solving this problem using virtual organizations with cross-institutional Single Sign On, with which users use their existing institutional accounts to login. This chapter also presents the challenges of building trust virtual organizations: manage users from distributed identity providers, manage services from distributed service providers, manage trust relationships between users and services, and authorize the access privileges to users based on the trust relationships. It argues that the trust virtual organization increase the effectiveness of e-learning, e-research, and e-business significantly. Furthermore, the authors hope that the trust virtual organization facilitates not only Web-based authentication and authorization, but also gid-based authentication and authorization.

Chapter XXXIV
Augmented Reality and the Future of Virtual Workspaces...486
    James K. Ford, University of California, Santa Barbara, USA
    Tobias Höllerer, University of California, Santa Barbara, USA

The chapter defines and situates Augmented Reality (AR) technology in common business task-activity contexts. A technology that has been researched and discussed primarily in the computer science world, it is important for business decision-makers, researchers, technical communicators, and workers to be aware of AR, its applications, and possible implications. A definition, brief history of AR, and overview of research projects is provided, along with several examples and a future trends section. The chapter provides a solid base for newcomers of AR and informs experts of business applications of the technology.

Chapter XXXV
Virtual Writing as Actual Leadership..503
    James R. Zimmerman, James Madison University, USA

This chapter suggests how leadership theory can be applied to the daily practice of e-mail composition for new and mid-level leaders who face the challenge of using e-mail productively in large organizations. It advocates that e-mail be a planned, significant part of an overall strategy to communicate the leader's vision, with an emphasis on offering straightforward information and consistent support to subordinates, peers, and even superiors. Included is a simplified but highly-disciplined composition process that facilitates rapid but significant e-mail exchanges.

Chapter XXXVI
Business Proces Resue and Standardization with P2P Technologies...516
    José A. Rodrigues Nt., COPPE—Federal University of Rio de Janeiro, Brazil
    Jano Moreira de Souza, COPPE—Federal University of Rio de Janeiro, Brazil
    Geraldo Zimbrão, COPPE—Federal University of Rio de Janeiro, Brazil
    Geraldo Xexéo, COPPE—Federal University of Rio de Janeiro, Brazil
    Mutaleci Miranda, Military Institute of Engineering, Brazil

Business Process Modeling (BPM) systems are largely used nowadays. However, most process models are started from scratch, not having reuse promoted. Sometimes, large enterprises have the same business process implemented in a variety of ways, due to differences in their departmental cultures or environments, even when using a unique integrated system. A P2P tool is proposed as a way to cooperatively develop business processes models, minimizing the time needed to develop such models, reducing the differences among similar processes conducted in distinct organizational units, enhancing the quality of models, promoting reuse, and distributing knowledge.

Chapter XXXVII
Collaborative Writing Tools in the Virtual Workplace.. 530
    Norman E. Youngblood, Texas Tech University, USA
    Joel West, Texas Tech University, USA

Collaborative writing is an important element of the virtual workplace. While it is sometimes enough to e-mail a document back and forth between authors and editors, users frequently need a more effective solution. Users can choose from system-based or browser-based software and from synchronous and asynchronous editors. These products can vary from the simple to the sophisticated and from free to expensive. This chapter looks at research on the use of collaborative editors, tools currently on the market, and provides guidance as to how to evaluate the appropriateness of the tools, paying particular attention to collaborative features, industry standards, and security.

Chapter XXXVIII
Distance Internships.. 544
    David A. Edgell, Texas Tech University, USA

Traditional internships provide many challenges for students, universities, and industry. Distance internships can provide even more challenges and opportunities. This chapter will initially examine the background and need for traditional internships to situate this model of distance internships and will then give a working definition of a distance internship. In so doing, the chapter will examine a model that represents the need to balance the requirements of the three parties involved within an internship: the student, the company, and the university.

Chapter XXXIX
An International Virtual Office Communication Plan 555
    Lei Meng, Texas Tech University, USA
    Robert Schafer, Texas Tech University, USA

This chapter aims to define a plan for an international virtual office by exploring the problems that hamper communication within a virtual office. Four factors that contribute to miscommunication are explored: linguistics, culture, laws and regulations, and technology. Policies of practice are then offered to mitigate these factors, help increase the productivity, and avoid communication problems, personnel conflicts, and legal liability. Last, different stages of office evolution are discussed and the future trend of office is explored. The purpose of this chapter is to help establish a successful international virtual office as the virtual office is becoming the future trend of the business environment.

Chapter XL
Design and Managing of Distributed Virtual Organizations 564
    Diego Liberati, Italian National Research Council, Italy

A framework is proposed that creates, uses, communicates, and distributes information whose organizational dynamics allow to perform a distributed cooperative enterprise also in public environments even over open source systems. The approach assumes the Web services as the enacting paradigm, possibly over a grid, to formalize interaction as cooperative services on various computational nodes of a network. A framework is thus proposed that defines the responsibility of e-nodes in offering services and the set of rules under which each service can be accessed by e-nodes through service invocation. By discussing a case study, the chapter will detail how specific classes of interactions can be mapped into a service-oriented model whose implementation will be carried out in a prototypical public environment.

Section IV
Implementation of Virtual Workplaces Across Professions and Academic Disciplines

The chapters included in this section cover the different ways in which professions and academic disciplines use, adapt, and appropriate the theory and practice of the virtual workplace.

Chapter XLI
Semi-Virtual Workplaces in German Financial Service Enterprises 570
    Heinz D. Knoell, Leuphana University, Germany

This chapter presents semi virtual workplace (SVWP) concepts in the German financial sector (FS) industry. We give an overview of the German FS market and its recent developments under European Community (EC) legislation. Next we present three German FS companies, who apply successfully semi virtual workplace concepts, followed by detailed descriptions of two semi virtual concepts: strict alternating use of a workplace by two employees (every other day an employee is in his home office) and the concept of the business club, where the employees choose daily their workplace out of a workplace pool when they work on-site. In the last section we compare the concepts and draw some conclusion.

Chapter XLII
Implementing Client-Support for Collaborative Spaces.. 582
    R. Todd Stephens, AT&T Corporation, USA

Deploying collaborative solutions is different than simply implementing traditional enterprise applications which operate over structured data and generally focus on specific business processes. Collaborative environments, moreover, operate over unstructured information and can span several business processes and organizational boundaries. Because the need for virtual workspaces emerges when organizational collaboration occurs, the ability to predict demand is nearly impossible. The objective of this chapter is to lay out a framework for building a self-service environment for provisioning virtual workspaces as well as providing the education to support such technologies.

Chapter XLIII
Value, Visibility, and Virtual Teamwork at Kairos.. 595
    Douglas Eyman, George Mason University, USA

Value, visibility, and infrastructure are key factors in the success and sustainability of any virtual project or workplace. This chapter provides a heuristic for the analysis of virtual workplaces that evaluates the mechanisms for securing or distributing social capital within the organization, exposes the degree to which the tasks and interactions of workers are made visible, and assesses the administrative and technological infrastructure with regard to support of communication and collaboration.

Chapter XLIV
Plagiarism, Ghostwriting, Boilerplate, and Open Content 604
    Wendy Warren Austin, Edinboro University of Pennsylvania, USA

This chapter explains to business people, administrators, and educator/trainers what plagiarism is and is not, and explores authorship ambiguities such as ghostwriting, templates, boilerplate language, collaborative/team writing, and open content. It argues that two key features of plagiarism are the intent to deceive and lack of consent from the original author(s). In addition, the workplace setting—whether it is academic or nonacademic—plays an important part in determining whether plagiarism has occurred because academic settings impose more strict standards on borrowing. A clearer understanding of the standards and expectations of the academic vs. workplace environments will help business people better understand ethical boundaries for acknowledgement and attribution practices.

Chapter XLV
Usability and User-Centered Theory for 21st Century OWLs 614
    Dana Lynn Driscoll, Purdue University, USA
    H. Allen Brizee, Purdue University, USA
    Michael Salvo, Purdue University, USA
    Morgan Sousa, Purdue University, USA

This chapter describes results of user-centered usability research conducted on the Purdue Online Writing Lab (OWL). The testing showed that a user-centered Web site is more effective for OWL users and can be a model for information-rich online resources. In addition to presenting our testing methods, results, and findings, the chapter provides an overview of usability testing and user-centered theory and design.

Chapter XLVI
Negotiating Virtual Identity in an Age of Globalization 632
    Neil P. Baird, University of Nevada, USA

Virtual workplaces are no longer the province of young technophiles, and we must become more conscious of the particular challenges and issues those considered "nontraditional" face in this new environment. Continued globalization, fostered in part by computer-mediated communication, is bringing diverse populations together in virtual spaces; however, because we bring our culture with us when we move online, the default identity of the faceless virtual workplace becomes the young, white male. How do those considered nontraditional then negotiate their identity in order to contribute successfully? This chapter will explore this question with a case study of a Vietnam veteran in the workplace of a freshman writing classroom and, in doing so, will invite educators, employers, and researchers into discussions of virtual identity and interaction, how we perform ourselves in online workplaces, and fostering virtual communities.

Chapter XLVII
Virtual Political Office Where Gender and Culture Meet...641
    Olena Igorivna Goroshko, Kharkiv Polytechnic Institute "National Technical University,"
    Ukraine

This chapter explores the Internet sites of key political figures in the USA and Ukraine focusing specifically on what the content posted to these sites and their structure suggests about gender and cultural peculiarities in constructing political identity on the Web. The personal page is rendered as a virtual political office—a peculiar meeting point between the site's owner and the site visitors.

Chapter XLVIII
The Benefits of Using Print-On-Demand or POD...668
    Eric Franzén, CFA Institute, USA

New technologies blaze new paths for authors and publishers as they try to reach their readers. As a result, traditional publishing business models have been significantly altered. Content creators of the past faced many obstacles in publishing hard copy books, including lack of manufacturing knowledge, high production costs, and warehouse overheads. In response to this, many companies are now offering Print-On-Demand (POD), a technology that allows a book to be produced in small quantities and distributed only after the demand for that book has been proven. Content can be uploaded to vendors' Web sites, stored, and produced at will on digital printing devices. In POD publishing, only minimal production knowledge is required, production costs are covered by the unit's sale, and there is no warehouse to stock. As a result, independent authors, university presses, and commercial publishers have new valuable options

Chapter XLIX
Difficulties in Accepting Telemedicine...681
    María José Crisóstomo-Acevedo, Jerez Hospital, Spain
    José Aurelio Medina-Garrido, University of Cadiz, Spain

This chapter examines the sources of the resistance to incorporating telemedicine. The authors adopt a focus centering on the difficulties that human factors have in accepting the practice of telemedicine. The success of telemedicine projects will be determined by these human factors, as well as by an adequate use of information technology and an appropriate organizational management. This chapter also offers some practical implications in human resource management for managers of telemedicine projects to consider.

Chapter L
Reconsidering the Lay-Expert Audience Divide 692
    Michael J. Klein, James Madison University, USA

This chapter provides educators instructional methods for teaching audience analysis to students in professional writing courses. This rhetorical approach allows students to engage and become members of their audience's discourse community, facilitating improved communication practices.

Chapter LI
Rapid Virtual Enterprising to Manage Complex and High-Risk Assets..702
    Jayantha P. Liyanage, University of Stavanger, Norway

Decentralization of various business activities and the rapid growth in the use of advanced ICT solutions have perhaps induced the greatest commercial impact in the present industrial environment. As the commercial operations around industrial assets get more decentralized, the emergence of new organizational forms is inevitable, compelling conventional organizations to reconsider their formal command-and-control based architecture. Subsequently, important dimensions that apply to business-to-business (B2B) transactions have also been taken up for continuous discussions and revisions. To assess this situation, this chapter examines the rapid enterprising that is emerging on the Norwegian Continental Shelf (NCS) as a new organizational form to manage offshore oil and gas (O&G) production assets. This case, moreover, is a significant one, for the organization begun to break the conventional organizational barriers and has brought an explosive growth in the use of advanced ICT solutions, reflecting the usability of new frontiers in search of commercial excellence.

About the Contributors 710

Index..725

Foreword

The thing about virtual workplaces of any kind is that, thus far, they are always new—or at least, that is my experience.

Twenty years ago, as part of a pilot to determine the efficacy of connecting homes, schools, and retailers, GTE offered all households in West Lafayette, Indiana, a computer and intranet access. I had never used a computer. I had never even heard of an intranet (which to me sounded like something out of outer space, really). And in fact, I didn't know much about the pilot. So I did the perhaps not-predictable thing: I said yes.

I said yes because I like connections, and at bottom or across the horizon, this project was about connections. I would not pursue computer-aided anything for my own purposes, but I would to do so to connect with my child's school. I wasn't planning on any more shopping, but I was not opposed to learning more about what was available or making shopping easier. And I knew that I would learn something in both processes.

Fast forward 7 years: I am a member of Portnet, a group of 10 faculty members from around the U.S. who share an interest in researching the effects of writing portfolios on students. From that project came many presentations, several publications, and at least some of what we know about print portfolios. Interestingly, when we began, we mailed student portfolios to each other, and we seemed more like a collection of individuals than a group. But that changed once we created our own listserv: Portnet as group *and* site *and* research project was born. Because the electronic environment was new, we had to learn new ways of behaving, and because we did not know everyone in the group, initially, we had to be particularly sensitive to that which we could *not* see. When the project concluded—and like many collaborative and virtual projects, it had a lifespan—we had learned more than about portfolios, as important as that research was. We also understood something about how to make such work "work"—the structures that supported it, the rhythms we established and the ways those influenced how our project progressed, the verbal signals we sent each other, and the ways that those were interpreted. It was a learning experience in *many* ways.

Fast forward 7 years and I'm working with Barbara Cambridge on a book on *electronic* portfolios. The book, published in 2001, marked not the end of interest in the topic, but rather an incentive for more information, it seemed, in part because as a concept, electronic portfolios are both robust and flexible. And what we learned, too, is that they are used world-wide. To support and develop this interest, particularly in terms of e-portfolio effects, we created the National Coalition on Electronic Portfolio Research, which has become the *Inter*/National Coalition on Electronic Portfolio Research. Teams from over 40 institutions in several countries have joined the Coalition and work in parallel and in concert on diverse research projects, all of which is being documented in various media and communicated in various channels. Collectively, we are learning how to work across different kinds of projects, across different time zones, across different cultures, and across different spaces—through blogs and f2f meetings, chats and Web meetings, print reports and listservs. In the work, we are widening our understanding of portfolio—and of ourselves.

All of which is to say that on a much larger scale and in much more detail, this volume provides the help I might have used back in 1987 when I was just learning about virtuality, and the help I need now in my current e-portfolio project, when I am often virtual—because if there is one lesson when it comes to virtual learning, it is that we are all learners.

Kathleen Blake Yancey
Tallahassee, Florida

Kathleen Blake Yancey, *Kellogg W. Hunt Professor of English at Florida State University, directs the graduate program in rhetoric and composition studies. Past president of the Council of Writing Program Administrators, she is also a past chair of the Conference on College Composition and Communication. Currently president-elect of the National Council of Teachers of English. She also codirects the International Coalition on Electronic Portfolio Research. She is the author, editor, or co-editor of numerous chapters and articles as well as of 10 books, among them* Portfolios in the Writing Classroom *(1992),* Assessing Writing across the Curriculum *(1997),* Teaching Literature as Reflective Practice *(2004), and* Delivering College Composition: The Fifth Canon *(2006).*

Preface

At one time, the office was a physical place, and employees congregated in the same location to work together on projects. Within this context, one's coworkers were defined by physical proximity and collaborative work generally involved visiting a colleague's office or cubicle to ask questions or discuss ideas. Under this paradigm, the idea of distributing project teams across vast, geographic distances would have seemed the acme of inefficiency—if not downright insanity. The advent of the Internet and the World Wide Web, however, not only made the unthinkable possible, it forever changed the way persons view both the office and work.

Today, online media has transformed the idea of the workplace from a physical location to, essentially, a state of mind. Communication technologies such as e-mail and instant messaging let coworkers in different regions exchange ideas in a fraction of the time it would take to walk from one office to another. Similarly, blogs, wikis, and online chat groups allow entire teams of geographically distributed workers to discuss, debate, and update project plans on a virtually unlimited scale. These same technologies also allow companies to move distribute directly to a global consumer base via a variety of file sharing technologies and software downloads. The result is a workplace—if not an overall work paradigm—in which the office is but a mouse click away.

ADVANTAGES OF THE VIRTUAL WORKPLACE

The ability to transcend physical space means virtual workplaces offer a variety of advantages to organizations that adopt such approaches. To begin, there is the rather obvious advantage that project teams can now be configured based on the expertise of employees vs. the proximity of individuals to a particular office. Similarly, the ease with which information can move from one location to another means virtual work groups can move more efficiently and effectively than could the employees of the pre-Internet era. Moreover, the ability to make quick, easy, and direct contact with prospective clients as well as colleagues means the consumer can actively become a participant in the overall product development process—a factor that was almost unthinkable only a decade ago.

Virtual work environments also offer a range of advantages related to employee attitudes. Certain studies, for example, reveal that individuals involved in some degree of virtual workplace activity seem to display improved employee loyalty to the organization, increased productivity, and decreased absenteeism (Pinsonneault & Boisvert, 2001). Such work environments also seem to enhance an organization's knowledge management activities, and allow for a greater degree of flexibility combined with the ability to respond more rapidly to a variety of situations (Burn & Barnett, 1999; Ruppel & Harrington, 2001).

For these reasons, it is perhaps of little surprise that the use of virtual workplace models is on the rise. Some researchers, for example, have pointed out that almost half of all companies in North America allow their employees to participate in some kind of virtual workplace arrangement (McClosky, 2001; Pinsonneault & Boisvert, 2001). Other researchers have noted that the advantages—particularly in terms of speed and flexibility—of virtual workplaces means that tens of millions of workers currently participate in some sort of virtual work environment (Scott & Timmerman, 1999). In fact, the advantages of such approaches have led some experts to predict that almost one third of the adult workforce will partake in some form of virtual workplace activity by 2020 (Scott & Timmerman, 1999). This expansion, moreover, is taking place on a global scale and is making virtual workplaces increasingly international environments.

PROSPECTS FOR GLOBAL EXPANSION

Participation in virtual workplaces comes down to one key factor: online access. Thus, as more nations gain such access, a broader international range of employees can participate in virtual workplace activities. And while les than one fifth of the world's population currently has online access (roughly 1.1 billion persons), that number is growing at an almost exponential rate (Internet Usage Statistics, 2007). The number of Internet users in Australia, for example, increased by almost 400,000 between June and August of 2004 alone (Active Internet Users, 2004). At the same time, almost half of the adults in Japan have online access while some three fourths of the citizens of South Korea have access to broadband connections (AsiaBiz Tech, 2003; Forsberg, 2005). This increase in access, paired with the rise of multinational organizations and globalization, creates ideal conditions for virtual workplaces to become international entities. Moreover, the growth of international outsourcing—particularly skilled, knowledge-based work—as a core business practice could also mean virtual workplaces will involve individuals from developing as well as industrialized nations (Beyond the Digital Divide, 2004; Relocating the Back Office, 2003).

VIRTUAL WORKPLACES: DECISIONS AND DIRECTIONS

This context brings with it an almost mind-boggling array of choices for organizations interested in using virtual workplaces. It creates a similarly complex situation for employees considering participating in such environments. For example:

- Which technologies should an organization or an individual use for virtual office work and why?
- What are the best uses of these technologies?
- Who should participate in such environments?

Moreover, the pressure to answer such questions quickly and effectively means both organizations and individuals need some sort of resource or reference to help make informed decisions in relation to virtual workplaces. The purpose of this edited collection is to serve as such a reference or resource.

To achieve this objective, this handbook has been divided into three major sections. Each section, in turn, presents information, ideas, and opinions on a particular aspect of virtual workplaces. Through such a three-part approach, the handbook provides individuals with a foundation both for understanding the factors that affect virtual work environments and for making effective decisions related to the effective adoption an the efficient operation of such environments.

OVERVIEW OF THE SECTIONS OF THE BOOK

The book consists of four sections. The first section, entitled "Foundations of the Virtual Workplace," addresses fundamental issues essential for successfully organizing, managing, or participating in a virtual workplace. These issues range from such broad concerns as establishing the right atmosphere for employee collaboration to more specific topics, such as managing stress in the age of "ubiquitous connectivity" or accommodating the needs of virtual employees with disabilities.

The concept of the virtual workplace is still relatively new. Anyone hoping to function in a virtual workplace will have to rethink and adjust some of the basic ideas and assumptions about work. To help with such a transition, competent and timely training of new virtual workers is absolutely essential. In the second section, "Education and Training for the Virtual Workplace," the authors discuss research on the theory and practice of successfully training present and future employees for the virtual workplace. The chapters included in this section will be useful both for practicing virtual workers, such as managers and business owners, as well for college and university faculty and administrators interested in preparing students for success in the virtual workplace.

Despite the relatively young age of the virtual workplace, virtual workers have developed an impressive array of techniques and tools that allow them to accomplish a variety of tasks. The third section of this volume, "Tools and Environments for Virtual Work," covers the tools available to members of virtual workplaces. These tools range from such traditional ones as e-mail and instant messaging to such more recent arrivals on the virtual workplace scene as collaborative writing environments and virtual worlds. We hope that the chapters included in this section will prove useful both for practicing virtual workers and managers and to students of the virtual workplace.

The final section of the book is called "Implementation of Virtual Workplaces Across Professions and Academic Disciplines." It covers the different ways in which professions and academic disciplines use, adapt, and appropriate the theory and practice of the virtual workplace. The fields and professions discussed in this section include business, medicine, politics, education, and others. We believe that this broad scope of disciplines and professions emphasizes the interdisciplinary nature of the study of the virtual workplace. In addition, it stresses the need for any employee, manager, or scholar to keep up-to-date on the topic of the virtual workplace. As editors, we hope that this book will help our readers accomplish that goal. We are sure that the experts who contributed to this collection want to achieve the same goal.

REFERENCES

Active Internet users by country, July 2004. (2004, August 25). Retrieved November 27, 2007, from http://www.clickz.com/stats/sectors/geographics/article.php/3397231

AsiaBizTech. (2003, March 12). *Over 50% of Japanese population online.* NUA Internet Surveys. Retrieved November 27, 2007, from http://www.nua.com/surveys/index.cgi?f=VS&art_id=905358740&rel=true

Beyond the digital divide. (2004, March 11). *The Economist.* Retrieved November 27, 2007, from http://www.economist.com/displaystory.cfm?story_id=2476920

Burn, J., & Barnett, M. (1999). Communicating for advantage in the virtual organization. *IEEE Transactions on Professional Communication, 42,* 215-222.

Forsberg, B. (2005, March 13). The future is South Korea: Technology firms try out latest in world's most wired society. *San Francisco Chronicle*. Retrieved November 27, 2007, from http://www.sfgate.com/cgi-bin/article.cgi?f=/c/a/2005/03/13/BROADBAND.TMP

Internet usage statistics—the big picture. (2007). Retrieved November 27, 2007, from http://www.internetworldstats.com/stats.htm

McCloskey, D. W. (2001). Telecommuting experiences and outcomes: Myths and realities. In N. J. Johnson (Ed.), *Telecommuting and virtual offices: Issues & opportunities* (pp. 231-246). Hershey, PA: Idea Group.

Pinsonneault, A., & Boisvert, M. (2001). The impacts of telecommuting on organizations and individuals: A review of the literature. In N. J. Johnson (Ed.), *Telecommuting and virtual offices: Issues & opportunities* (pp. 163-185). Hershey, PA: Idea Group.

Relocating the back office. (2003, December 11). Retrieved November 27, 2007, from http://www.economist.com/displaystory.cfm?story_id=2282381

Ruppel, C. P., & Harrington, S. J. (2001). Sharing knowledge through intranets: A study of organizational culture and intranet implementation. *IEEE Transactions on Professional Communication, 44,* 37-52.

Scott, C. R., & Timmerman, C. E. (1999). Communication technology use and multiple workplace identifications among organizational teleworkers with varied degrees of virtuality. *IEEE Transactions on Professional Communication, 42,* 240-260.

Acknowledgment

Many people contributed to the success of this book. We wish to thank Kristin Roth and Jessica Thompson at IGI Global for their expertise in organizing and guiding this project. We also thank the development and production staff at IGI Global. We would like to acknowledge the members of the book's Advisory Board and the reviewers who participated in the chapter selection process and provided invaluable revision suggestions to the chapter authors. We thank all the experts who contributed to this project. Without their knowledge and willingness to share it with others, this project would have been impossible. Kirk would like to thank, in particular, his wife Dori for her time, patience, and understanding and his daughters Lily and Isabelle for serving as a continual source of inspiration. Pavel thanks his wife Silvia and son Nikolai for their support, understanding, and humor.

Section I
Foundations of the Virtual Workplace

Chapter I
Gains and Losses in the Rhetoric of Virtual Workplaces

Pamela Estes Brewer
Appalachian State University, USA

ABSTRACT

Virtual workplaces are constructed of people using technology to work at a distance, with the goal of transferring knowledge (both explicit and implicit) toward specific purposes. What are the communication gains and losses most experienced in virtual workplaces? Using an economic frame, this chapter seeks to review literature on virtual workplaces from across professional fields in order to suggest methods for maximizing communication utility and minimizing losses in virtual workplaces. With rhetoric as the primary unit of exchange, what steps can be taken to ensure its effectiveness? Current research points to planning, face-to-face opportunities, mixed media, boundaries, and meta-communication as most important as well as the ability to adapt them to the characteristics of virtual workplaces.

INTRODUCTION

Virtual workplaces provide utility—benefit. They offer unparalleled opportunity for organizations, individuals, and the marketplace. This relatively new paradigm is fast-becoming the norm because of the opportunities it offers to save time and money while crossing boundaries of space, time, and organizations to assemble highly effective teams. Research into virtual workplaces is being done across professional boundaries including technical communication, psychology, anthropology, business, instructional systems, sociology, and others—an indicator of the importance of this model. Because of the importance of virtual workplaces and their potential to contribute to present and future economies, much benefit can be derived from considering the most significant gains and losses experienced in virtual workplaces as compared to the older paradigm of the colocated workplace. Such an economic lens allows us to review the previous literature and ask important questions about the future.

Defining Virtual Workplaces

In his book *The Economics of Attention* (1996), Richard Lanham posits that we live in an age of information. Both he and Drucker (2001) identify our society as one of knowledge—where knowledge of the right information is a key resource. Knowledge, according to Sarker (2005) is made up of both explicit knowing, such as "technical know-how," and implicit knowing, such as management techniques. Within this knowledge society, virtual workplaces are constructed of people using technology to work at a distance, with the goal of transferring knowledge (both explicit and implicit) toward specific purposes. Such purposes might be the exchange of knowledge in order to edit a technical document, to develop a piece of software, or to accomplish any workplace goal. The people participating are workers who might themselves be software engineers, technical communicators, or managers. Communication is conducted almost exclusively via computer or phone with occasional face-to-face meetings.

Consider, for example, the software corporation whose engineers primarily reside in India while the writing and training staff resides in the U.S., and upper management resides primarily in the U.K. At a distance, these co-workers must work intimately and effectively together using technology. Or consider educational institutions who offer online degree programs. A program comprises administrators, educators, and students who conduct day-to-day communication online toward the goal of educating students. Students, and perhaps educators, are dispersed across the globe. The technologies used might be synchronous and asynchronous with a goal of supporting effective learning to the same or greater degree of effectiveness as a face-to-face program. At a distance, students must meet in forums with other students to discuss concepts, they must meet privately with professors to ask questions and receive evaluation, and they must submit projects and receive feedback. When people collaborate in these virtual workplaces, they are often referred to as virtual teams. Teams may work together for a few days or years as their purpose in working together requires.

A number of terms are used when referring to virtual workplaces including "virtual office" (Kishimoto & Suzuki, 1993; Chung, 1995; St. Amant, 2003), "computer-mediated communication" (CMC), "online communication," "distributed teams" (Sarker, 2005), "virtual teams" (Lipnack & Stamps, 1997; Suchan, 2001; Priest, Stagl, Klein, Salas, & Jentsch, 2006), "distributed work," "virtual workplace" (Lee, 2000), "virtual computer-supported teams" (Thompson & Coovert, 2006), "remote project teams" (Larbi & Springfield, 2004), and "computer-supported cooperative work" (CSCW). Additionally, concepts might be referred to by name, abbreviation, or acronym, and they might be used to mean the same thing or different things. Priest et al. (2006) discuss some of the significant differences between "virtual teams" and "distributive teams" but acknowledge that the two terms are often used interchangeably. My purpose is not to present an exhaustive list but to acknowledge the variety and suggest that we construct the rhetoric for virtual workplaces deliberately so that terms have the potential to grow with the field rather than change. Recently, a discussion on the terminology related to computer-mediated communication (CMC) took place on the listserv of the Association of Internet Researchers. CMC is an outdated term for some, and so list members were discussing alternatives. To a very real extent, we are trying to hit a moving target because products and processes change so quickly in response to technology and global distribution (think of the computer that is no longer state of the art by the time you order and receive it), but if we view our terminology as accruing meaning and value over time, we can choose carefully. A rich terminology more effectively focuses attention and filters information.

AN ECONOMIC FRAME

An analysis of virtual workplaces can usefully be framed by the rhetoric of economics. Scholars who write about virtual workplaces often use economic terms to present their arguments. Organizations "capitalize on distributed team performance to cope with the increased complexity of today's operating environments" and virtual environments overcome the "process losses resulting from distribution" (Priest et al., 2006, p. 187). "High-tech teams have a lot to offer, and organizational gains are most likely to occur when technology facilitates the types of interactions that allow team members to share information and capitalize on each other's knowledge skills" (Thompson & Coovert, 2006, p. 213). "One result of such a process could be that products go to market more quickly . . ." (St. Amant, 2001, p. 291). Lipnack and Stamps (1997) refer to "social capital" and to "face-to-face time [that] is increasingly precious, a scarce resource in limited supply" (p. 139). In his study of media choice in a Confucian workplace, Lee (2000) found that the value of showing respect is much more significant than the value of getting things done. This kind of rhetoric abounds in the literature of virtual workplaces. Thus, an economic frame can effectively support an overview of the gains and losses of this workplace model.

In addition to the use of economic terms, common issues regarding virtual workplaces recur over time and profession. Whether a study was done ten years ago and written by a psychologist or done one year ago by a technical communicator, common issues emerge. Virtual workplaces offer a fluid and fertile marketplace—one that gives organizations and people more options for maximizing their utility—that is, making themselves as well off as possible. As people pursue the opportunities of virtual workplaces, what gains and losses are they likely to incur? This chapter will review some of the literature on virtual workplaces in the last ten years through an economic frame identifying the most common gains and losses, suggesting ways to minimize losses, and asking questions about the future of the rhetoric of virtual workplaces.

RHETORIC AS UNIT OF EXCHANGE

Information can be valuable. I say "can be" because undifferentiated information is not valuable—in fact, we have too much of it. Lanham (2006) argues that what we have in today's economy is too much information and not enough time to process it. Thus, he says that attention for processing the information is scarce and valuable. St. Amant (2004) proposes credibility as a significant screen through which information must pass to gain attention. He further identifies two levels of credibility: attention and acceptance. A communication must be credible both in order to draw consideration in the first place and at a deeper level in order to be accepted. I propose that knowledge in the context of virtual workplaces is information that has been perceived as having enough credibility to draw attention; thus it is synthesized with other information to create knowledge that is used.

Information is moved easily within virtual workplaces, saving time and money as well as increasing value. In his edited collection *Market Matters: Applied Rhetoric Studies and Free Market Competition* (2005), Carter writes that rhetorical activity closely resembles free market activity. It is alive and innovative, resisting the status quo, but, he writes, "...we do not generally incorporate any sense of value or value-creation into our theories of language, thereby making it very difficult to teach and comprehend how messages might compete for value in a free market" (p. 2). In order for a virtual workplace to be effective (valuable), rhetoric must be recognized for what it is—the primary unit of exchange. It can be exchanged in units of differing quantity, such as long or short e-mails, and in differing modes, such as e-mails, instant messages, or telephone calls. A unit in this context is a single communication between sender and receiver, what Carter (2005) calls a "single semiotic transmission" (p. 32). A change in sender would signal the beginning of a new unit. For example, a single e-mail or a single send in instant messaging would be a unit of rhetoric. If software developers in India need to provide information to writing and training staff in the U.S., the information (in units of rhetoric) must be exchanged. If a professor wants to encourage a student to analyze a subject from a different perspective, that encouragement is exchanged as units of rhetoric.

Units of rhetoric are exchanged with the goal of transferring knowledge so that it provides utility to organizations and the people who work in them. A unit of rhetoric can be composed of the written or spoken word, but online units of rhetoric can also be composed of other communication such as silences in synchronous forums or emoticons. Rhetoric in virtual workplaces increases value for organizations unless it is corrupted in some way—most often by a misunderstanding. This threatens knowledge transfer and, thus, the value of the information. In virtual workplaces there are many challenges that have the potential to turn a profitable transfer of knowledge into a loss as I will discuss in this chapter.

GAINS EXPERIENCED IN VIRTUAL WORKPLACES

The foremost gain offered by virtual workplaces is their ability to cross boundaries of space, time, organizations, and hierarchies, enabling organizations to assemble teams that are best suited to a task. Virtual workplaces enable teams— powerful teams. Some gains are commonly recognized while others are not. Virtual workplaces have the potential to be open 24 hours a day, seven days a week. They are more democratic and less centralized; like a free marketplace, they are best able

to maximize benefit. As Charles Wheelan points out in *Naked Economics* (2002), "One powerful feature of a market economy is that it directs resources to their most productive use" (p. 12), and so do virtual workplaces. They greatly reduce the cost of moving intellectual property from place to place because no physical movement is necessary. Organizations can hire and retain the best people for a job with fewer constraints, particularly with regard to location. They are literally decentralized as is a decentralized economy. In addition, people can work permanently or temporarily for an organization; indeed organizations that are usually in competition with one another can collaborate on specific goals toward mutual gain because of the fluidity of this model. "In virtual teams, power comes from information, expertise, and knowledge, the foundations of wealth" (Lipnack & Stamps, 1997, p. 73). In addition, innovations and knowledge transfer that are products of virtual teams can be dispersed throughout organizations (Priest et al., 2006). At the heart of these fluid systems is rhetoric as it is exchanged, used, and measured. The rhetorical unit is the most valuable component as it is the foundation for virtual work and all of its utilities.

Virtual workplaces also make more time and resources available. For example, if workers do not have to spend time and money traveling (for work or to work), they can redirect those freed resources to add the utility of flexibility—time they can use elsewhere in their professional or personal lives. Employee productivity and satisfaction can increase. Thompson and Coovert (2006) argue that these benefits increase productivity through a reduction in stress in workers' lives and that workers have fewer distractions when they work apart from company workplaces. Flexibility for organizations means that, like an efficient marketplace, they can swiftly self-correct and redirect resources as needed. In addition, organizations can save money on physical space when there is no need to provide as many facilities as they would for colocated employees.

Finally, consider that virtual workplaces increasingly pump value into organizations. They can add speed and memory as the knowledge transfer is easily recorded and reproduced, offering organizations flexibility and adaptivity.

LOSSES EXPERIENCED IN VIRTUAL WORKPLACES

Certainly, many challenges exist in forming successful virtual workplaces—most of them caused by losses of familiar structures and cues—alterations to rhetorical expectations. This section presents a review of those challenges that are most often identified in the virtual workplace literature including sources from business, psychology, and technical communication.

Trust

The two most commonly raised issues regarding virtual workplaces are trust and social engagement, and, as it turns out, the two issues are closely related for communicators in virtual workplaces. Over and over again, across fields of research and a decade, scholars and the participants in their studies refer to the importance of trust in successful virtual workplaces among virtual teams (Lipnack & Stamps, 1997; Suchan & Hayzak, 2001; Sarker, 2005; Priest et al., 2006; Thompson & Coovert, 2006). Sarker used a four-factor framework (the 4C Framework represents capability, credibility, communication, and culture) to study U.S. and Thai distributed teams. She cites Levin, Cross, Abrams, and Lesser (2004) saying that credibility is composed of trust and reputation and that "trust is the 'magic ingredient' leading to knowledge transfer" (2005, p. 7). Lipnack and Stamps (1997) define trust as "the belief or confidence in a person or organization's integrity, fairness, and reliability" (p. 224). Trust becomes even more important to virtual teams because they operate in a more abstract structure than do face-to-face

teams. It can directly affect the perceived value of the rhetorical unit of exchange in the virtual workplace. If, for example, a group of U.S. writers and trainers can trust that the information they will receive from their Indian colleagues will be reliable, they can schedule for faster turn-around and will experience less frustration and time loss. If, on the other hand, trust is lacking, loss of time and increase in frustration might occur even if the information exchanged is reliable. In addition, Lipnack and Stamps (1997) point out that in many cases "trust has to substitute for hierarchical and bureaucratic controls" (p. 17).

While trust is a key component to successful virtual teams in organizations, we could say that one of the losses of distributed work is a weakening of the cues that create trust. Lipnack and Stamps also point out that "boundary-crossing teams overall need more trust than do colocated teams. Without daily face-to-face cues, it is at once both harder to attain and easier to lose. Mistrust slips in between the slender line of long-distance communication stripped of the nuances of in-person interaction" (p. 224). Once problems of trust have emerged, they may go unrecognized or unresolved for longer periods of time than they would in a face-to-face team and become more detrimental over time.

Social Communication

Trust is key to successful virtual teams and the effective exchange of information, and social engagement is a key to developing trust—distance costs people the opportunity for social engagement (informal communication). People in virtual workplaces do not talk over their morning cup of coffee or while checking their mail, they may not exchange information on the work they are doing, and thus, they do not build trust as easily. In addition, some cultures are more likely to engage in the social interactions online that lay a foundation of trust than others. For example, in their study of students working in distributed teams, Kim and Bonk (2002) found that Korean students displayed much more social interaction than Finnish or U.S. students.

Chung (1995) describes an organization that was transforming from a traditional to an online structure and the importance of putting together a technology package that supports social communication. When interviewed, people were not so concerned about losing their desks as they were about more social problems:

"How do people know how hard I'm working?" "How do I overhear the important things, since no one bothers to tell me anything?" Or simply, "I'm afraid of being out of touch." People were most afraid of disrupting the kind of communication never conveyed by phone, fax, or e-mail: the social interaction that the traditional office, whether by design or convention, seems to encapsulate and support. (p. 8)

Informal communication as rhetorical units underpins roles in organizations, and social isolation makes informal communication more difficult; thus, roles and information exchanged may become more confusing. For example, let us say that informal rhetoric among my colleagues and me in the same building consists of spontaneously stopping in each others' offices and talking in the hallways. Via tone, time spent in chatting, and the pace with which we walk down the hall, I can pretty quickly gage that my boss is very accepting of suggestions for change but only when they pertain to agendas that are the most pressing. Thus, I know his approach to business is low power distance (Hofstede, 1980). That is, he accepts suggestions from those who work for him at all levels, establishing good two-way communication, but he wants to stick with business—not veer off into the personal. People need mutual knowledge and context in order to conduct business, and in a virtual workplace, they must make greater effort to create this context. They must share information and know that the people they are communicating with have received

and understood the information—that "they share the knowledge in common" (Thompson & Coovert, 2006, p. 223). In the example above, it would probably take more time for me to discover these characteristics of my boss if I were communicating with him at a distance through e-mail. It is not likely that he would explicitly deliver his business philosophy to me even if he accurately perceives it himself. In a very thorough analysis, Thompson and Coovert present the likely results of a shortage of mutual knowledge in their chapter "Understanding and Developing Virtual Computer-Supported Teams" in *Creating High-Tech Teams* (Bowers, Salas, & Jentsch, 2006). This lack of mutual knowledge can make it more difficult for team members to retain information and create a trusting foundation.

In addition, the National Research Council (1994) reported that, "Proximity has been linked to informal channels of communication (e.g., the "water cooler") and is vital for disseminating information about organizational norms, socializing new employees, and encouraging collaboration and sharing of information" (in Priest et al., 2006, p. 191). "Social factors above all derail the development of many virtual teams" (Lipnack & Stamps, 1997, p. 168). One can conclude that virtual teams are about people and the exchange of information and that informal communication may serve a meta-communicative purpose enabling people to make implicit knowledge explicit and thus giving important context to rhetoric.

Understanding the Other

Closely related to effective social communication as well as trust, is the concept of other. I use this in the sense of the old business communication literature, where it might have been called the "you attitude" rather than in the post-modern sense of some other that competes with or threatens self. It is the ability, through research and experience, to understand the perspectives of those with whom you are communicating online—to use a commonly understood unit of rhetoric. Because of the increased level of abstraction present in the virtual workplace and the lack of face-to-face cues, communicators are missing some channels of communication that can help them to establish mutual understanding.

Several terms are used to refer to this challenge of perceiving the other in virtual workplaces. Sole and Edmondson (2002) refer to the interpretive barrier (Sarker, 2005) and note that a very explicit structure is needed to overcome it. Fiore et al. (2003) refer to it as team opacity, "the experience whereby distribution decreases awareness of team member actions and may thus alter their interaction" (Priest et al., 2006, p. 192).

St.Amant (2003) explores how Blumer's symbolic interactionism can be applied in understanding and increasing the effectiveness of communication in international virtual offices. Blumer refers to a process of "minding" which means "to indicate to another what he is to do, one has to make the indication from the standpoint of that other" (p. 9). Thus, communication is more likely to succeed when the presenter knows more about the audience so that the rhetorical unit can contain information that is not as vulnerable to misunderstanding. In the previous example with my boss, he or I can research to find out more about the others we work with. I might discover his preference for low power distance and keeping business separate from the personal by talking with other employees. The point is, deliberate attempts to better understand those with whom we communicate increases the effectiveness of communication, and such attempts may need to be more deliberate for online working relationships.

Technology

Another loss in virtual workplaces may be attributed to technology's inability to replicate the richness of face-to-face communication. Though technology provides the tools necessary to support virtual workplaces, no technology to date, despite attempts, has been able to reproduce the same types of rhetoric as face-to-face communication. Perhaps, it neither can nor should. What technology in virtual workplaces needs to do is support the same *utility* as face-to-face communication. That is, it needs to support both the formal and informal as well as product and process rhetoric of doing business. Priest et al. (2006) propose that these spaces be virtual environments that are made up of synchronous tools and virtual reality technology. "...VEs [virtual environments] allow team members to have an alternative common workplace, receive more and richer cues, and meet 'face-to-face' in a virtual space. By virtually colocating teams, organizations can provide better leadership, enrich sense-giving messages, and reduce social isolation" (p. 202).

It was expected that video-conferencing would produce most of the same benefits as face-to-face communication (Chung, 1995), but it has not been able to do so. In Chung's article, now eleven years old, he predicted that video conferencing did not hold all the answers—a prediction that has proved true. In their review of past literature, Thompson and Coovert (2006) argue that limited bandwidth is still a challenge to the use of video and that video may not be effective for newly formed virtual teams because it hinders the ability of participants to make a good first impression.

Each type of media is designed to meet communication needs in a limited way. Overall, those writing about virtual workplaces emphasize the need for a mixture of technologies deliberately chosen (Chung, 1995; Lipnack & Stamps, 1997; Suchan & Hayzak, 2001; Priest et al., 2006). Synchronous and asynchronous tools work in concert; workers can use them as they please to create a rich flow of communication (formal and informal). As packages, these technologies are flexible and help workers adapt to change. They can even offer benefits beyond those of face-to-face communication such as transcripts of conversations and the absence of cues that might, in some cases, be interpreted as noise.

Culture

Whether one is considering intercultural or non-intercultural virtual teams, central issues are similar. A shared context still needs to be created to support the virtual team but is even more important, and complex, for intercultural teams. Decreased awareness due to distance exacerbates the cultural screens that already exist because culture is yet another layer of communication—another screen that the rhetoric must pass through, hopefully without having its value compromised. The study of intercultural communication online is challenging for several reasons. First, languages present a barrier to study, and second, there are very few "intercultural" conclusions that can be drawn from studies. Most conclusions must be drawn for individual cultures, and even that approach is casting a wide net when subcultures are at work within each culture. Nevertheless, scholars have published some very useful findings that can be applied on global or local levels—from the work of Hall and Hofstede to the work of many of the scholars discussed here.

How people create ethos online varies from culture to culture as do variables such as quantity of communication, quantity of silence, face, cues, context, media preference, turn-around time, connotations of words, and willingness to ask questions. Culture affects expectations as to what units of rhetoric should look like. Many scholars point to national culture, and the ability to work with intercultural teams, as being significant to communication in virtual workplaces (Kim & Bonk, 2002; Sarker, 2005). Common sense would tell us this is so. After all, virtual teams operate in the global market, and experience as well as scholarship in face-to-face communication indicates that national culture is a screen that filters communication, modifying context and understanding (Hall, 1989). For example, silences as part of rhetoric have meaning; a silence may allow a coworker to formulate an answer to a question, or a silence may be deliberately inserted to punctuate words of correction. But these silences can be interpreted differently interculturally. In an online synchronous discussion, silences of one to two minutes may mean nothing to some American participants but may leave a German participant wondering what message is being conveyed by those silences. Thus, the German participant may become uncomfortable and perceive a meaning differently than intended by the American. Ulijn's research (1996) indicates that people continue to screen the effectiveness of communication based on the norms of native culture.

Culture has been studied via a number of dimensions, but there is growing opinion by scholars that the individualism/collectivism dimension is most significant for "understanding differences in attitudes, values, norms, and behavior" (Azevedo, Drost, & Mullen, 2002; Thomas, 2002; Triandis, 1995 in Sarker, 2005). An understanding of this dimension may be the key to the exchange of rhetoric that is least corrupted by cross-cultural misunderstanding. According to Hofstede (1980) individualism/collectivism indicate the level of concern for self as opposed to group. Sarker (2005) found that culture affected knowledge transfer in U.S.-Thai teams. She hypothesized that communicators from collectivist cultures would tend to transfer more knowledge in virtual teams than would those from individualist cultures. The results indicated that culture did affect knowledge transfer but in the opposite direction of that hypothesized: communicators from individualist cultures transferred more knowledge than did those from collectivist cultures. This result is consistent with dimensional predictions if you consider that those from individualistic cultures are often low-context communicators who explicitly place all information in the units of rhetoric rather than relying on outside context. Though collectivist cultures may tend to share more knowledge with a group, they may do so by relying heavily on context and the spoken word. Hence, it is the individualist with a low-context style of communication who embeds information most explicitly in online messages. In this study, U.S. participants were dissatisfied with the amount of knowledge transferred by Thai participants, yet individuals from high-context cultures "tend to value those who are likely to engage in implicit and reserved communication" (Sarker, 2005).

In another study, Lee (2000) found that the Confucian tradition in virtual workplaces affected the ethos of technologies like e-mail. For example, e-mail might not be chosen for certain types of communication—like that from a worker to her boss. Cultural perception of face can also be problematic in intercultural virtual communication. Lustig and Koester (2003) describe face as involving a "claim for respect and dignity from others" (p. 274). For example, "From a cultural perspective, directly saying *no* or giving a direct negative answer (*I cannot do that*) can cause face-related problems. In some cultures, directly saying *no* can cause the speaker or the hearer to lose face (creates poor public image)" (St. Amant, 2001, p. 293). Such an offense might also go unrecognized more easily in a virtual work team and cause communication problems that might grow worse over time.

Kim and Bonk (2002) found that "Korean students were more social and contextually driven online, Finnish students were more group-focused as well as reflective and, at times, theoretically driven, and U.S. students more action-oriented and pragmatic in seeking results or giving solutions." Ulijn, Lincke, and Karakaya (2001) used speech act theory and psycholinguistic analysis to explore the affects of culture on non-face-to-face communication and noted that

...non-FTF communication does allow negotiators to employ a cooperative win-win strategy (as recommended by negotiation strategy training), but that the empathy or involvement building required in non-FTF interaction detracts from the win-win strategy by requiring an excessive and perhaps cumbersome use of general and metacommunicative acts to compensate for the lack of the context and nonverbal cues available. (p. 134)

Consider that non-face-to-face communicators must make a strong effort to express pleasure via text or emoticons in place of a smile that they might use with less conscious effort in face-to-face communication. Or they might need to comment on the reason for a silence in online communication while physical context might provide reason enough in a face-to-face encounter. Effective social communication is likely to enable virtual teams to realize their potential value, and more effort is needed to establish effective social communication in virtual workplaces.

Boundaries

Finally, boundaries emerge as an issue of importance in virtual workplaces affecting the meaning, and thus the value, of exchanged units of rhetoric. In the abstract context of virtual workplaces, boundaries are not as obvious as they are in physical space, yet their presence is significant, and they can be used deliberately to promote the success of virtual teams. A listserv that allows access only to those who are registered and who adhere to list protocol preserves that list as a useful space for participants. If every member of an online class has administrative access to a synchronous class tool, the instructor can lose control. Ranking (authority) can also be viewed as a function of boundaries. "According to tradition, authority is highly dependent on access to exclusive places that house special knowledge"—that is, boundaries. (Lipnack & Stamps, 1997, p. 170)

Boundaries are essential to the healthy function of work within these virtual spaces. Because virtual workplaces and teams are highly purpose- (task-) driven with fewer boundaries, they tend to be more egalitarian (Priest et al., 2006; Thompson & Coovert, 2006) and direct (St. Amant, 2002), and roles within these workplaces are often established based on contribution and expertise with regard to task, making leadership a challenge. Thus, the value of a unit of rhetoric may be defined by an ethos that is established somewhat differently than it would be in a face-to-face communication.

9

MINIMIZING LOSSES IN VIRTUAL WORKPLACES

What does the literature on virtual workplaces suggest in order to minimize the losses that are intrinsic to working in virtual offices—to meet the challenges most often identified in research? Many of the suggestions for developing successful virtual teams are the same as those organizations should use in forming any successful team—*just more so*—more planning, more socialization, and so on. And most importantly, all communication needs to be more explicit in order to compensate for the increased abstraction of virtual workplaces. Explicit planning and communication are at the foundation of the suggestions that follow.

Planning

The most common suggestion for creating effective virtual workplaces was thorough planning inclusive of the characteristics of virtual workplaces. Virtual teams need a structure from the beginning—a structure that includes a clear but distributed leadership. Goals need to be communicated explicitly, and incentives need to be awarded to the group based on progress toward those goals. Virtual teams are linked not only by technology but by common purpose. Clear rhetoric that communicates goals is one of the first and most important products necessary in constructing a successful virtual team (Priest et. al., 2006). Lipnack & Stamps (1997) refer to purpose as the "metaphorical campfire" around which virtual teams are built (p. 60). Explicit and well-supported purpose can minimize some of the challenges that face virtual workplaces. That is, the purpose of the virtual team is stated explicitly and communicated to all participants, and participants are rewarded for their contributions to achieving that purpose.

People are working in a more abstract environment lacking in physical cues, so units of rhetoric must form the structure. In their interviews with business professionals who were implementing successful virtual teams, Lipnack and Stamps (1997) found that organizations were using private Web sites to provide the information structure for virtual teams. They "virtually colocate all the information they need to work together and put it all in context" (p. 18). This common document can be a handbook or a Web book and provides a stable rhetorical expectation for communicators.

Planning should include a preparation for cultural differences and is even more important in intercultural virtual teams. Organizations might share specific cultural examples that bring these differences to light (Kim & Bonk, 2002). This will prepare workers to better understand the other before misunderstandings can occur. For example, if connotations of words might be a problem because of a language barrier, organizations should consider a team glossary of important terms that allows for an equivalent understanding. Thus the terms can provide utility for all. If workers will come from both low- and high-context cultures, consider discussing this concept and what it might mean. By acknowledging (naming) some of these differences, team members can keep them in mind so they do not adversely affect the ethos of the other. If members from high-context cultures value more reserved communication while members from low-context cultures value more quantity and detail, a discussion of these differences can result in more effective cooperation and trust. St. Amant (2003) proposes defining specifics of media use, accessibility, timing, and time expression for mutual understanding. Specific planning which accounts for the characteristics of virtual workplaces increases their ability to succeed.

Face-to-Face Meetings

Also common was the suggestion to kick off a new virtual team with a face-to-face meeting and to plan face-to-face opportunities during the life of the team. During face-to-face time, organizations can plan how workers will share information and promote shared mental models (Priest et al., 2006). Time together also enables teams to see each other as people—emphasizes that we are all human, not machines, working together. Methods should be used to enhance social attraction—even photographs can help if a face-to-face meeting is not possible (Thompson & Coovert, 2006). People who will be part of virtual teams need to be encouraged to socialize from the beginning of their contact with one another "wherein their concerns are shared and participation is encouraged" (Kim & Bonk, 2002, p. 26). It takes time for a team to gel, and spending adequate time at the beginning will increase success. Shared mental models and a humanized concept of the "other" contribute to the ethos of communicators and to the rhetoric they exchange at a distance, thus making that rhetoric more effective and more valuable.

Mixed Media & Boundaries

Also important is providing a technology-rich virtual space where workers can choose technologies that support both formal and informal communication. Priest et al. (2006) argue that actual distance is secondary to computer-mediated communication as a factor in virtual team success. Chung (1995) suggests a visual MUD (multi-user domain) "with highly customizable personal and shared spaces" (p. 8) to support social communication; he also suggests extending the system by building "gateways to . . . telephone, e-mail, and voicemail systems" (p. 9). This creates a "palette" of technologies that people can use as they please. Other authors refer to this as a mix of media wherein synchronous communication most supports informal communication. Use of a robust mix of technologies supports critical social connections.

Meta-Communication

Priest et al. (2006) also suggest the importance of meta-communication (i.e, communicating about how we communicate) and self-regulation. By discussing the communication itself, its strengths and weaknesses, teams can make adjustments to their rhetorical expectations before problems arise, thus making knowledge transfer more effective. Richard Lanham (2006) argues that style and substance are both economically important and uses an at-through dichotomy to discuss their interaction. The "through" concept refers to "minimal awareness of an expressive medium" while the concept of "at" refers to "maximal awareness of how we say what we do . . ." (p. 159). It is important that virtual teams look "at" their communication not just "through" it to the task. Consider the online college classroom. If the professor were to focus strictly on the task of criticizing a set of research projects with the goal of helping students become better researchers, she might very well accomplish the task but miss the goal if students misunderstood those comments. While this is true in a face-to-face classroom as well, it is exacerbated by distance, limited context, and limited social cues in the online classroom where the rhetoric stands alone. However, if the professor were to focus on the goal and match the rhetoric to the goal using many of the techniques reviewed in this chapter, the rhetoric is much more likely to accomplish the goal. Where information is everything, communication can derail the accomplishment of task.

CONCLUSION

Virtual workplaces present an opportunity to specialize and decentralize in the global marketplace in a way no other business model can. The gains are tremendous, and careful attention to units of rhetoric, the capital that is traded within virtual workplaces, can minimize losses. While face-to-face teams require careful planning, virtual teams add another layer of complexity, and intercultural virtual teams add yet another layer. Trust, social communication, understanding the other, technology choice, cultural differences, and boundaries present the most significant challenges to effective exchange. Detailed planning, face-to-face meetings, rich technology, attention to boundaries, and meta-communication can minimize losses that are the results of these challenges.

What previous research tells us about virtual workplaces is especially important in the questions it prompts toward future understanding. Important questions emerging from this review include:

- What units of rhetoric has technology enabled that we do not yet recognize?
- What new types of rhetoric will be enabled in future virtual workplaces?
- How might the increasingly global nature of the workplace and the commonality of virtual workplaces affect the speed with which people of differing cultures adapt to online workspaces?
- How can boundaries be configured to promote targeted communication goals?

As Drucker (2001) predicts in his article "The Next Society," "New ways of working with people at arm's length will increasingly become the central managerial issue of employing organizations, and not just of businesses." Toward this end, we can expect new processes and tools that manage the knowledge exchange. The organizations who best address this exchange of rhetoric will gain the most in global virtual workplaces.

REFERENCES

Bowers, C., Salas, E., & Jentsch, F. (2006). *Creating high-tech teams*. Washington D.C.: American Psychological Association.

Carter, L. (2005). Rhetoric, markets, and value creation. In: L. Carter (Ed.), *Market matters: Applied rhetoric studies and free market competition* (pp. 1-52). Cresskill, NJ: Hampton Press, Inc.

Chung, J. (1995, Summer). Social communication in a virtual office. *IEEE*, 7-9.

Drucker, P. (2001). The next society. *The Economist*. Retrieved from EbscoHost.

Hall, E. (1989). *Beyond culture*. New York, NY: Anchor Books/Random House, Inc.

Hofstede, G. (1980). *Culture's consequences: International differences in work-related values*. Beverly Hills, CA: Sage.

Kim, K., & Bonk, C. (2002). Cross-cultural comparisons of online collaboration. *Journal of Computer-Mediated Communication, 8*(1). Retrieved October 13, 2004 from http://www.ascusc.org/jcmc/vol8/issue1/kimandbonk.html.

Kishimoto, T., & Suzuki, G. (1993). Virtual offices. *IEEE Communications Magazine, October*, 36-38.

Lanham, R. (2006). *The economics of attention*. Chicago, IL: The University of Chicago Press.

Larbi, N., & Springfield, S. (2004). When no one's home: Being a writer on remote project teams. *Technical Communication, 51*(1), 102-108.

Lee, O. (2000). The role of cultural protocol in media choice in a Confucian virtual workplace. *IEEE Transactions on Professional Communication, 43*(2), 196-200.

Lipnack, J., & Stamps, J. (1997). *Virtual teams: Reaching across space, time, and organizations with technology*. New York, NY: John Wiley & Sons, Inc.

Lustig, M., & Koester, J. (2003). *Intercultural competence: Interpersonal communication across cultures*. Boston, MA: Allyn and Bacon.

Priest, H., Stagl, K., Klein, C., & Salas, E. (2006). Virtual teams: Creating context for distributed work. In: C. Bowers, E. Salas, & F. Jentsch (Eds.), *Creating high-tech teams* (pp. 185-212). Washington D.C.: American Psychological Association.

Sarker, S. (2005). Knowledge transfer and collaboration in distributed U.S.-Thai teams. *Journal of Computer-Mediated Communication, 10*(4), article 15. Retrieved July 11, 2006 from http://jcmc.indiana.edu/vol10/issue4/sarker.html.

St. Amant, K. (2001). Cultures, computers, and communication: Evaluating models of international online production. *IEEE Transactions on Professional Communication 44*(4), 291-295.

St. Amant, K. (2002). When cultures and computers collide: Rethinking computer-mediated communication according to international and intercultural communication expectations. *Journal of Business and Technical Communication 16*(2), 196-214.

St. Amant, K. (2003). Making contact in international virtual offices: An application of symbolic interactionism to online workplace discourse. *IEEE Transactions on Professional Communication, 46*(3), 236-240.

St. Amant, K. (2004). International digital studies: A research approach for examining international online interactions. In: E. Buchanan (Ed.), *Readings in virtual research ethics: Issues and controversies* (pp. 317-337). Hershey, PA: Idea Group Inc.

Suchan, J., & Hayzak, G. (2001). The communication characteristics of virtual teams: A case study. *IEEE Transactions on Professional Communication, 44*(3), 174-186.

Thompson, L., & Coovert, M. (2006). Understanding and developing virtual computer-supported teams. In: C. Bowers, E. Salas, & F. Jentsch (Eds.), *Creating high-tech teams* (pp. 213-241). Washington D.C.: American Psychological Association.

Ulijn, J. (1996). Translating the culture of technical documents: Some experimental evidence. In: D. Andrews (Ed.), *International dimensions of technical communication* (pp. 69-86). Arlington, VA: Society for Technical Communication.

Ulijn, J., Lincke, A., & Karakaya, Y. (2001). Non-face-to-face international business negotiation: How is national culture reflected in this medium? *IEEE Transactions on Professional Communication, 44*(2), 126-137.

Wheelan, C. (2002). *Naked economics: Undressing the dismal science.* New York, NY: W. W. Norton & Company.

KEY TERMS

Boundaries: Limited access to virtual places, including levels within places.

CMC: Computer-mediated communication. Commonly used to describe the synchronous and asynchronous communication that supports virtual workplaces.

Ethos: Credibility, and essential element to trust which is in turn essential to the effective functioning of a virtual workplace.

Meta-Communication: Communicating about communication.

Social Communication: Informal communication that provides context and mutual understanding.

Team Opacity: Decreased awareness of others due to distance relationships.

Unit of Rhetoric: Can be composed of the written or spoken word, but online units of rhetoric can also be composed of other communication such as silences in synchronous forums or emoticons.

Utility: Perceived benefit.

Value: How much someone is willing to pay for some thing.

Virtual Workplace: Information centers in an information age; people within them work at a distance with the goal of knowledge transfer toward specific purposes.

Chapter II
Removing Space and Time:
Tips for Managing the Virtual Workplace

Christie L. McDaniel
University of North Carolina–Chapel Hill, USA

ABSTRACT

Virtual teams are become more and more popular as the world becomes more connected; furthermore, research is suggesting that virtual teams are as effective as face-to-face teams (Baker, 2002). This chapter compares and contrasts virtual teams with face-to-face teams in order to determine what differences exist as the workplace become virtual. It investigates how relationships between team members change when geographic boundaries are removed and how managers should adjust managerial styles when leading a virtual team. Also, a discussion of team dynamics—including the development of trust, team cohesion, and communication barriers—is included. Tips and techniques for developing an effective team are provided for virtual team managers.

INTRODUCTION

Picture it: you are home sitting in front of your laptop, sipping your coffee, wearing your favorite sweats—and you are *working*. Not only are you working, but you are managing a group of people all over the world who are also sitting in the comfort of their homes, working. You are part of a virtual team. What is a virtual team exactly? It is a traditional team without boundaries, one that uses multiple channels to communicate thoughts and ideas. Zaccaro and Bader (2003) say that it differs from a face-to-face (FTF) or traditional team in two ways:

First, members of these new forms of organizational teams either work in geographically separated work places, or they may work in the same space but at different times. Still other teams have members working in different spaces and time zones, as is the case with many multinational teams. The second feature is that most, if not all, of the interactions among team members occur through electronic communication channels. (p. 377)

The question is: how do these differences translate into changes in the way we work? And do these virtual teams work as well as traditional

FTF teams? Baker (2002) says that virtual teams can be just as effective, and sometimes more effective, than traditional FTF teams. He stated that most of the empirical research on virtual teams reported no difference in the effectiveness between FTF teams and virtual teams; the author concludes that using the right collaborative technology would actually increase the effectiveness of virtual teams. Conversely, Lipnack and Stamps (2000) report that virtual teams have the same problems as FTF teams, only the problems of virtual teams are worse and perhaps more difficult to remedy. Virtual teams have been around since the mid-1980s and have been increasing in popularity over the past few years in industry (Baker, 2002; Zaccaro & Bader, 2003).

With this increase in popularity comes a significant amount of empirical research on virtual teams; however, most of this research has focused on comparing the effectiveness of FTF teams and virtual teams using some form of communication- mediated technology (CMTs) (Maznevski & Chudoba, 2000). While this information is helpful to corporations in making decisions to use virtual teams, little is known about how managers should operate within these teams. As a manager the focus is on getting the job done and keeping team members happy and working effectively. When the manager is physically in a different place, how does their role change? With management in virtual teams, several immediate questions arise: As a manager, how does one deal with troubled (or even troublesome) employees when you cannot sit down and talk it out in a meeting? How do the team dynamics change? How does communication change? How does a manager know if their employees are actually working? Will virtual teams need extra time or warrant extra steps to manage? Finally, how does a manager build trust within a virtual team? All of these questions revolve around the same idea that is the objective of this chapter: what skills or characteristics are needed to be an effective manager in a virtual team?

BACKGROUND

Virtual teams are similar to traditional teams in that they involve a group of people working together toward a common goal. The two teams must both have a certain level of trust between team members, everyone must be committed towards completing the assigned task, and they all must look towards a manager or a leader to guide their process. The differences between the two, however, are tremendous. For one thing, even though a virtual team comprises components similar to those of the traditional team, virtual teams operate differently.

Virtual teams are made up of people potentially working all over the world. The team members work in different places and some may work at different times. This disconnectedness, in terms of physicality, may cause several communication barriers. Team members may easily become confused as to what another team member is saying; this confusion could even lead to conflict between employees. In order to make up for lack of physical connectedness, virtual teams use Communication-Mediated Technologies (CMTs) in order to stay in touch with one another. It is the power of these technologies and their ability to connect everyone at any time, which has guided the way for an increase in the number of virtual teams.

This literature review will assess the components of a traditional team that must exist within the virtual team and how these aspects must change as the team members go virtual. We will begin by discussing the components of a team, and then assess what happens when space is taken away. Next, we will explore the differences between these two teams and how these differences affect team productivity and success. Finally, the role of managers between each team, both FTF and virtual, will be explored.

What Makes a Team?

In *Manager's Toolkit* (2004), Richard Luecke defines a team as "not just a collection of individuals; it is a small number of individuals with complementary skills committed to a common purpose with collective accountability" (pp. 95). Typically, teams are used to complete complex, time-consuming tasks; a task that cannot be completed by an individual. Thus, the idea behind a team is generally 'two heads are better than one'; in the case of most teams, *many* heads are perceived as better than one. With teamwork, businesses get the expertise, innovation, and efficiency of everyone on the team.

In order to be productive, teams must be efficient. Without efficiency, their goal or task may not be reached in an appropriate amount of time, or even at all. Luecke (2004) identifies the following characteristics as important for building 'effective' teams (p. 96):

- *Competence—everyone brings something that the team needs*
- *A clear and compelling goal*
- *Commitment to the common goal*
- *Every member contributes; every member benefits*
- *A supportive environment*
- *Alignment (i.e., coordinating work schedules, milestones, etc.)*

These factors are important aspects of any team, virtual or traditional. In order to be successful, these characteristics must somehow be met.

Analyzing the Effective Team

The first characteristic of Lueke's effective team is competence. The idea behind competence is that each team member is bringing a necessary component to the table. For instance, the team assigned to building the Web site for a public school may include a project leader (who may have an additional role), a usability expert, a designer, and an architect. Each of these members should have expertise within their assigned role in order to move the group towards task completion.

The second aspect of the effective team is having a clear goal. With a clear goal in mind, every team member will understand the purpose of the team and the direction everyone should be headed. Without clearly stipulating a goal (or perhaps several goals), team members will not have the information they need to be productive.

Team members must also be committed towards this goal. By accepting the goal and dedicating one's work time towards it, team members set their team up for productivity. To the same extent, all team members must contribute something towards the goal; likewise, they all must benefit from these contributions. Lueke's (2004) example of this aspect best describes the importance of working together: "Have you ever been on a rowing team? If you have, you know that every member of the team must pull his or her oar with the same intensity and at the same pace as everyone else" (p. 99). Business teams are quite similar; every group member is affected by the productivity and commitment of every other group member.

Effective teams must also reside in a supportive environment. If there are actual barriers prohibiting the team from reaching its goal, one cannot expect efficiency or success. Every team member must be focused on the goal and support the other members of the team.

Finally, the effective team must have alignment. In other words, alignment means coordinating schedules and, generally, working together as one unit. Thus, the team will be *organized* in its endeavors. This organization (or alignment) will ensure that the team is moving together, and coordinating their individual goals with the overall goal in mind.

Other Components of Successful Teams

Intertwined with building an effective team is the need to build a cohesive, trusting team. Benoit and Kelsey (2003) conclude from their research that low levels of trust among team members have a negative affect on the team's ability to produce quality work—they found that the higher the level of trust between team members, the higher the "mark" (pp. 597) the team received for their work. Obviously, organizations want the highest quality of work possible out of their teams; therefore, it is the manager's duty to build trust among team members. Trust is key when working towards a common goal; if even a single team member loses faith in another's ability to complete a task well and on time, the quality of work produced by the entire team is in danger. However, building trust takes time and effort; particularly, if the team members have not worked with each other before. Benoit and Kelsey (2003) go on to report that "good intentions do not build trust; only the ability to perform and actually deliver on commitments (i.e., integrity) will lead to the formation of trust" (pp. 597). Because of this factor, building trust among a new team may be quite difficult and take time.

In opposition to Benoit and Kelsey's work, research by Dirks (1999) says that trust plays an indirect role on team performance and did not affect the outcome of team deliverables negatively or positively. Dirks argues that trust should not be seen as a motivating factor in developing work but rather, it should be seen as a way to keep team members working towards the same goal. Interestingly, working towards a common goal has been identified as the key to building an effective team (Lueke, 2004). Regardless of whether or not trust among team members affects the final product, it is easy to see that trust has a significant impact on maintaining positive group dynamics which directly relates to the emotional state of employees.

The cohesion of a team has also been identified as a factor towards team success and effectiveness. Wellen and Neale (2006) define cohesion as: "the overall attraction or bond amongst members of a group" (pp. 168). Cohesive teams work as one unit with every member's contribution contributing towards the goal. Characteristics of a cohesive team include both social attraction and the ability of individual team members to complete their share of the work (Wellen & Neale, 2006). Notably, contribution towards the work required to reach the goal was identified by Lueke (2004) as part of building an effective team. The social attraction aspect is similar to that of families; they feel as though they are one unit. Cohesive team members seemingly work well together and are thus more productive.

When a team is not cohesive it usually results in a poor working environment. The cohesiveness of a team can be threatened by what Wellen and Neale (2006) identify as a 'deviant' team member. The deviant is the person who does not communicate well with others and often fails to complete work in a timely or acceptable fashion. The deviant has an incredibly negative affect on team perceptions and can bring down performance and production as well as lower trust and cohesion (Wellen & Neale, 2006). A deviant team member can mean the downfall of a productive team. Thus, having effective, trusting, cohesive teams can only translate into better outcomes—something that organizations obviously desire.

What's in a (Virtual) Team?

On the surface, a virtual team is no different from a traditional team—it should comprise a group of people whose skill set works together in a cohesive manner; and who are working towards the same goal. They must have the same set of requirements as an effective traditional team: competence, a clear goal, commitment to that goal, equal team member contribution, support, and alignment (Lueke, 2004). How do the two differ? The main difference is that the team members do not necessarily sit down in the same physical space as a group to discuss problems and pitfalls with their project. They do not meet in a conference room weekly for team meetings; they do not necessarily even live in the same country and they could be working in different time zones. Instead, the team typically uses at least one type of technology for communication: e-mail, instant messaging, phone or video conference—to discuss problems or successes with their project. The basic principles of team building do not change when moving to a virtual team; however, the way team members work together and the methods which they use to communicate change completely. And, the way a team communicates is important to reaching all the aspects of an effective team: trust, cohesion, support, and alignment. In order to understand how communication methods impact team effectiveness, we must first investigate the technologies used to communicate virtually.

CMT: The Difference between FTF Teams and Virtual Teams

Traditional teams are defined as groups of people working together, in a shared *physical* workspace. Virtual teams are very similar except their shared space is *virtual*. These teams must use technological tools to communicate with each other; these tools are known as Communication-Mediated Technologies, or CMTs. CMTs are becoming more and more common in our world; e-mail, text messaging via cell phones, and instant messaging services are all frequently used examples of CMTs. The fact is, these types of technologies are much more commonplace and therefore it is easy to overlook the barriers that they may create.

Teams that cannot have regular FTF meetings must rely on collaborative technologies to provide social interaction (Baker, 2002). These technologies essentially attempt to replace two components of communication: tone of voice and body language. With traditional teams, team members get more than verbal or text-based communication—they get body language and tone of voice to guess their other teammates emotional situation (Baker, 2002). Understanding the emotional aspect of a fellow team member's state of mind is important in remaining a cohesive, successful team.

Baker (2002) identifies four types of CMTs: text-only communication, text communication with video, audio-only communication, and audio communication with video. Each method of communication has its advantages and disadvantages, which will be discussed.

Text only communication is quite common in today's society. There is text messaging, instant messaging, e-mail, wikis, discussion forums, and blogs. Baker (2002) reports that this type of communication works best when one is multitasking and carrying on concurrent conversations—in other words, do not use it for making complicated decisions. This medium has the potential to cause confusion and unnecessary disagreements if it is used for making difficult decisions, or explaining complicated tasks or assignments. However, it is useful for getting quick answers to simple problems.

An example of text communication with video is using one of the aforementioned methods with a Web camera so that you can see the other person(s) involved. Baker (2002) reports that this gives users a higher level of feedback than simple text-only communication; this is because you can read the facial expressions and body language of others involved. This medium should be used when making situations that involve some difficulty or confusion, but not a high degree of it.

One participates in audio-only communication when talking on the telephone. In this situation, you get tone of voice, but not body language or facial expressions. The major disadvantage of this communication medium is that it does not support multiple conversations (Baker, 2002). This CMT should be used when one team member needs to clarify something with one and only one other team member. It is appropriate to use when confusion hits.

Finally, there is audio communication with video. Audio with video is used when participating in a video conference. Baker (2002) found that this method of communication was most effective in performing collaborative tasks. It seems that audio and video communication mediums provide the best quality of communication among team members. In fact, Baker (2002) reports that "video has been found to provide benefits such as: allowing individuals to indicate their understanding, augmenting verbal communications with gestures, conveying attitudes by expressions and posture, and interpreting the significance of conversational pauses" (Baker, 2002, pp. 84). This method of communication is most appropriate when several team members need to understand or assess a particularly difficult situation; it is also useful when the team first convenes as it is an effective way to have team members get to know one another.

Baker found that audio with video was the most effective communication method, followed by text-only communication, text with video, and audio-only communication. Audio with video communication is most similar to working together in the same physical space, at the same time. Apparently the text with video provides no additional functionality than simple text-only communication; however, being able to both see and hear other team members seems to be most comparable to FTF meetings and is highly successful in enhancing the quality of communication among team members.

Remaining Questions

We have seen that the types of interactions in virtual teams differ from the types of interactions in FTF teams. Both types of teams must not only complete their work, but build trust and cohesion as well. The difference between the two is that the methods used for completing these tasks differ.

Virtual team managers are faced with two main tasks: making sure the job gets done and making sure that the team members are mentally satisfied with the team's ability to function successfully. Even with the additional complexity of these tasks, virtual teams remain quite effective; two of their main advantages include the fact that they do not face certain geographical limitations that FTF teams do and thus they can deal with a broader range of customers and stakeholders; also, since they face no geographical limitations they are able to interact with a larger range of customers or clients than FTF teams (Zaccaro & Bader, 2003). Given that virtual teams can be just as effective as and sometimes more effective than FTF teams (Baker, 2002), how should managing styles change when moving from a FTF to a virtual team?

MAIN FOCUS OF THE CHAPTER

Imagine managing a team of people all over the world from your home. Think for a minute of the potential conflicts that could arise: miscommunication could cause one team member to misunderstand the current task and waste valuable time. Another potential problem could occur when tension between team members mounts—disagreements could cause arguments which reduce trust and cohesion not only for the parties involved, but for the entire team. Think of how simple it is to misread an e-mail or an instant message from someone: when tone of voice and body language are taken away from our visual cues, one must judge someone else's attitudes and feelings from words alone. Studying and comparing virtual teams with FTF teams in order to determine how they should be managed could help both types of teams understand these issues.

With FTF teams problems may be easier (though not easy) to solve because technological barriers are less of a factor than in virtual teams. If a problem arises when you are in the same space—both geographically and time wise—as your team, you can walk directly to the source to solve the problem. You will not have to send out an awkward e-mail or instant message or make a phone call, you can solve the problem face-to-face, thus adding in body language and tone of voice. These two additions are physical cues that inform the other party of your emotional state—whether you are angry, frustrated, or happy with the situation. Also, if you physically come in to work everyday with the same people, you likely have deeper personal relationships than you would if you were working virtually. This type of relationship allows one to better interpret the emotional state of other team members and thus make problem-solving easier. When working with people you have never physically met, you cannot make presumptions into how they feel or might react in certain situations. When working virtually, rarely does one have the opportunity to get to know team members well enough to make guesses into their behavioral tendencies.

Tips for Virtual Team Managers

As a virtual team manager, how does one deal with these communication barriers? I believe that the answer lies within creating direct communication channels and setting the tone for the team at the onset of the project. In order to prevent communication difficulties when working virtually, there are several steps that the team manager can take that will help increase team effectiveness.

First, all teams should meet face-to-face at least once, in order to develop social bonds with one another. It is important to attempt to introduce everyone to the project's goal(s) and assign tasks in person. This helps alleviate potential confusion as to what person is assigned to which role and to make sure everyone has a clear concept of what the overall goal is. If it is not possible to meet in person, then the manager should arrange a conference (preferably video, if not then phone) for the team to get to know each other and to learn each other's roles. These people are on your team

for a reason—tell them that and encourage them to get to know each other as both team members and individuals.

However, if the manager can hold a FTF meeting with the team, research shows that this would most likely do a better job of establishing relationships quickly between team members (Zaccaro & Bader, 2003). Zaccaro and Bader (2003) report that it is difficult for virtual team members to build high levels of trust and identification with the team because these emotional states are typically developed in person; virtual teams do not, by definition, provide this environment.

Having a FTF meeting that promotes social activities before the team begins work is a great way to establish personal relationships among team members. These activities promote team cohesion and builds trust, thus helping the team become more productive in the long run. By getting to know each other on a personal basis, the team members will trust each other more and thus perform more productively as a team (Benoit & Kelsey, 2003). With trust and cohesion developed from FTF meetings, virtual teams will perform more efficiently and be equipped with behavioral knowledge about other team members in order to better judge emotional responses.

After attempting to develop social bonds as a team at the onset of the project, the team manager must then attempt to quickly build trust among team members once they are back in the virtual world. One way to do this is to have small deliverables due near the beginning of the team's tenure. This will let the other team members know how their peers work; if every team member gets their portion of the task completed on time, trust will be built among the team members. Benoit and Kelsey's study (2003) concluded that trust is built through learning that other team members are dependable. To prove dependability, the team manager can set short, easy tasks to help develop trust among the team.

A third suggestion for virtual team managers is to not be afraid to redefine roles and reassign tasks within the team in order to ensure better outcomes for the project as a whole. People have different personalities and therefore work in different ways; and as a virtual manager you may not have the insights into your team members' personalities the way a FTF manager does; and this may result in a need to change the organizational structure within the team. In a study by Majchrzak and colleagues (2000), the team managers had to re-structure the organization of their work because of team member differences, which in the end turned out to be beneficial to the team members and the outcome of their work.

Examples of how to change the organizational structure include shifting employees around from their original assignments; re-designing the frequency and duration that meetings are held; or changing the communication-mediated technology through which your team typically communicates. For instance, if there seems to be a lot of misunderstanding after your team's weekly group instant messaging meeting, you could change the technological medium to a video conference in order to reduce conflict. Regardless of the issue, do not be afraid to make changes even after the team has started working together if it means that communication channels might be made clearer.

A fourth suggestion for virtual team managers deals with conflicts. Even though there will always be conflicts when people work together, it is the manager's job to ensure they do not become personal conflicts (Zaccaro & Bader, 2003). Professionals may dispute over aspects of the project or what type of technology to use—that is typical of teams. However, when disputes become petty and people simply are not communicating because of personal disagreements, the team manager should step in and alleviate the problem. The best way to alleviate personal conflicts is to arrange a meeting with all parties involved. From Baker's study (2002) the author concludes that video-conferencing is the best method of communication for virtual team members. In the event of a conflict, the virtual manager should ensure that this communication medium is used. The quicker the conflict is resolved, the faster the team becomes productive again.

The important thing for virtual team managers to remember is that their teams have the same type of conflicts as FTF teams (Lipnack & Stamps, 2000); the difference is in finding a medium to use in resolving the conflict. One thing to always keep in mind is that using video conferencing is best for formal meetings, but one could probably use e-mail or instant messaging for simple tasks. My final tip for virtual team managers is to remember to remain flexible and use the most appropriate method of communication with team members, using whichever technology proves to be most effective for your particular *situation*.

FUTURE TRENDS

Virtual teams have increased in popularity over the past few years as new technologies continue to keep us constantly connected. As the rise of virtual teams continues to increase, it will be important to continue researching this aspect of management. In the concluding chapter of their book Lipnack and Stamps (2000) highlight the importance of trust as more and more virtual teams are created: "Trust is the key to virtual teams" (p. 283). As we continue our quest to work in offices without spatial boundaries and to constantly be connected, we must find new ways of developing trust among team members. It is high levels of trust that will lead to successful virtual teams.

Moore's law tells us that the speed in which computer chips operate increases every eighteen months. With this in mind, imagine how quickly you could be talking to one of your colleagues online 5 years from now? As technology mediums improve and the speed in which they operate increases, more companies will move towards virtual teams. As these teams are created, managers must learn new ways of communicating with and between employees and also feel comfortable using and promoting these skills to others. These communication methods will be directly affected by how well the CMT they are using works and how much contact there is between team members—can you see their face or just watch them type? With the increase of virtual teams we must remember that sometimes it is very important to simply communicate face-to-face, even if it means watching someone over an audio/video connection.

CONCLUSION

Even though virtual teams have been empirically researched over the past fifteen years or so, little effort has been made into researching management differences between virtual teams and FTF teams (Maznevski & Chudoba, 2000; Zaccaro & Bader, 2003). Furthermore, Baker (2002) points out that since virtual teams are increasing in popularity, we must continue to research every aspect of virtual teams. One particular research aspect that should be further explored is developing trust between team members. In fact, Avolio and Kahai (2002) conclude that effective leadership is essential to filling what they call "the voids of trust" (p. 336). If strong managing in virtual teams is a key to their success, then we must identify the changes in managing roles between virtual teams and FTF teams and decipher how managers influence trust-building between these two environments. Bal and Foster (2000) write that "Transforming from traditional teamworking to virtual teaming changes the way work is being carried out and this has considerable effect on people issues" (p. 4025). The people issues are what we, as information professionals, must explore. Communication between people using technology will continue to change and increase in use as the number of virtual teams rise.

ACKNOWLEDGMENT

The author would like to thank Mary Wilkins-Jordan, Ph.D. candidate at the University of North Carolina at Chapel Hill's School of Information and Library Science, for her encouragement and invaluable editing.

REFERENCES

Avolio, B., & Kahai, S. (2003). Adding the "E" to e-leadership: How it may impact your leadership. *Organizational Dynamics, 31*(4), 325-338.

Baker, G. (2002). The effects of synchronous collaborative technologies on decision making: A study of virtual teams. *Information Resources Management Journal, 15*(4), 79.

Bal, J., & Foster, P. (2000). Managing the virtual team and controlling effectiveness. *International Journal of Production Research, 38*(17), 4019-4032.

Beise, C. (2004). IT project management and virtual teams. *SIGMIS CPR '04: Proceedings of the 2004 SIGMIS Conference on Computer Personnel Research* (pp. 129-133). Tucson, AZ. Retrieved from http://doi.acm.org.libproxy.lib.unc.edu/10.1145/982372.982405.

Bell, B., & Kozlowski, S. (2002). A typology of virtual teams: Implications for effective leadership. *Group and Organization Management, 27*(1), 14-49.

Benoit, A., & Kelsey, B. (2003). Further understanding of trust and performance in virtual teams. *Small Group Research, 34*(5), 575.

Dirks, K. (1999). The effects of interpersonal trust on work group performance. *Journal of Applied Psychology, 84*(3), 445-455.

Jarvenpaa, S., & Tanriverdi, H. (2003). Leading virtual knowledge networks. *Organizational Dynamics, 31*(4), 403-412.

Lipnack, J., & Stamps, J. (2000). *Virtual teams: People working across boundaries with technology* (2nd ed.). New York, NY: John Wiley & Sons, Inc.

Luecke, R. (2004). *Harvard business series: Manager's toolkit: The 13 skills managers need to succeed.* Boston, MA: Harvard Business School Press.

Majchrzak, A., Malhotra, A., Stamps, J., & Lipnack, J. (2004). Can absence make a team grow stronger? [Electronic version]. *Harvard Business Review, 82*(5), 131-137. Retrieved July 19, 2006 from Business Source Premier database.

Majchrzak, A., Rice, R., Malhotra, A., King, N., & Ba, S. (2000). Technology adaptation: The case of a computer-supported inter-organizational virtual team. *MIS Quarterly, 24*(4), 569-600.

Maznevski, M., & Chudoba, K. (2000). Bridging space over time: Global virtual team dynamics and effectiveness. *Organization Science, 11*(5), 473-492.

Wellen, J., & Neale, M. (2006). Deviance, self-typicality, and group cohesion. *Small Group Research, 37*(2), 165-186.

Zaccaro, S., & Bader, P. (2003). E-leadership and the challenges of leading E-teams: Minimizing the bad and maximizing the good. *Organizational Dynamics, 31*(4), 377-387.

KEY TERMS

Cohesion: The ability of a team to work together collaboratively. A cohesive team is made up of a well-balanced group of individuals, all working towards the same goal.

CMT: Communication-mediated technologies are the technological tools used by virtual teams to communicate. Examples of CMTs include instant messaging, e-mail, and phone or video conferences. CMT is a common term in empirical research for defining the technologies used by virtual teams.

FTF Team: A face-to-face (otherwise known as traditional) team is a group of people working collaboratively on the same project(s) work in the same geographic location.

Non-Verbal Cues: Non-verbal cues, such as body language and tone of voice, serve as insights into the emotional state of other people. Because virtual teams are made up of people in different geographical locations, team members must learn to communicate differently because the non-verbal cues have been removed.

Team Effectiveness: An effective team occurs when trust and cohesion exist and the team is successfully working towards a common goal.

Trust: In team work, trust occurs when other team members can depend on each other to complete their portion of the project on time. Trust among team members is essential to a team's success, whether the team meets virtually or FTF.

Virtual Team: A group of people working collaboratively on the same project(s) working in different geographic locations; virtual teams use CMTs to communicate across their boundary-less work space.

Chapter III
Communication in Global Virtual Activity Systems

Marie C. Paretti
Virginia Polytechnic Institute and State University, USA

Lisa D. McNair
Virginia Polytechnic Institute and State University, USA

ABSTRACT

This chapter uses activity theory as a lens to understand the implications of both virtual collaboration and cross-cultural contact for communication in global virtual teams. Rather than adopting a set of heuristics or guidelines that may readily become dated as cultures and technologies shift in the flat world, we argue that both those who study and those who engage in global virtual teams should critically analyze the entire activity system. We then provide meta-cognitive approaches to both distributed work and cross-cultural contact that team managers and team members can use to establish flexible communication practices appropriate to the activity system at hand, and that researchers can use to account for the range of factors that impact team performance.

INTRODUCTION

To say that communication is central in team environments is simply to state the obvious. Project failures, from the near meltdown of Three Mile Island Nuclear Plant in 1979 (Herndl, Fennell, & Miller, 1991) to the explosion of the Space Shuttle Challenger in 1986 (Winsor, 1988; Herndl et al., 1991), and more recently Columbia in 2003, all include significant instances of communication breakdowns among team members. Within virtual teams, the lack of both formal and informal face-to-face (f2f) communication widens the potential for such breakdowns. Add an international component, where team members must communicate not only across cyberspace but across cultural space and the problems multiply exponentially.

Yet despite potentially disastrous communication gaps, global virtual teams are an increasingly common feature of the contemporary workplace (Friedman, 2005). As global virtual teams proliferate, however, the need to establish effective communication practices increases. And importantly, the answer is not solely a matter of better technology, attention to time zones, and clear translation guidelines. While developers create increasingly sophisticated software and hardware to facilitate communication, team managers and team members need to grow proficient not only in using this technology adeptly, but in effectively orchestrating the flow of information around the globe.

To identify strategies that foster successful communication in international online environments, we draw on activity theory first to understand the complexity of the problem and second to suggest key areas of meta-cognition for those participating in global virtual teams (GVTs), reporting on classroom case studies to support the theoretical framework. While much has been written about communication in virtual environments and about cross-cultural communication, the success of GVTs requires explicit attention not only to each dimension individually but also to the ever-changing interactions between them. Using activity theory as a framework for understanding those interactions, we describe an analytical approach to establishing and maintaining GVTs built not on a set of soon-outdated heuristics, but on a flexible, context-driven understanding of the system itself. This approach suggests key issues for educators who seek to develop students' abilities to function on GVTs, for managers who oversee such teams, and for researchers who seek to understand more about how such teams operate in the contemporary workplace.

BACKGROUND: ACTIVITY THEORY AS A LENS TO UNDERSTAND VIRTUAL GLOBAL COMMUNICATION

Activity theory has a long intellectual history in psychology as a framework to analyze human behavior not in terms of isolated individuals but in terms of the larger activity system in which individuals operate, including specific settings as well as social, historical, and cultural networks (Cole, Engeström, & Vasquez, 1997; Russell, 1997a; Kain & Wardle, 2005). An activity system is "any ongoing, object-directed, historically conditioned, dialectically structured, tool-mediated human interaction" (Russell, 1997a). Through this lens, human activity is always contextualized, and the system, rather than any single individual or act, is the primary unit of analysis for researchers and practitioners alike (Cole et al., 1997; Russell, 1997a). Within this framework, texts—reports, presentations, e-mails, sketches, meeting agendas, phone calls—are among the "artifacts" or tools that mediate interactions between subjects (members of the team) and objects (the problem or project) to achieve a desired outcome, all resting on a complex contextual foundation. The entire activity system can be represented as a network of triangles, as shown in Figure 1.

In GVTs, as Figure 1 shows, the team members, the project, and the communication activities that mediate the work all exist within an activity system that rests on a dynamic, socially constructed foundation. That is, individuals and groups are shaped by an array of external factors—the rules governing behavior, the personal and professional communities in which the individuals operate,

Figure 1. Workplace Activity System (after Kain & Wardle, 2005)

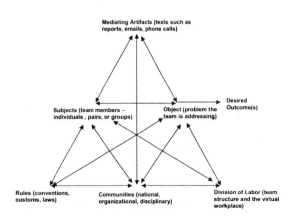

and the ways in which the system divides and organizes the work at hand. These external factors influence the entire system, including the ways in which individuals create, disseminate, and absorb information. As a result, communication practices must adapt to the system to succeed. Treated as a tool in this framework, communication is—to extend the metaphor—less like a hammer, used in the same way on virtually every nail in sight, and more like a drill, where the size, shape, and material of the bit must be changed according to the application at hand.

Activity theory applied to workplace communication can provide a useful theoretical framework to understand the nuances of successful information exchange, as many scholars have shown (Nardi, 1992; Spinuzzi, 1996; Bakhurst, 1997; Russell, 1997a; 1997b; Engeström & Middleton, 1998; Kain & Wardle, 2005). Following Kain and Wardle, who use activity theory as a framework for teaching students to develop transferable communication skills, we draw on it to contextualize communication in global virtual teams, arguing that communication practices cannot simply be a set of static, heuristic-driven guidelines but must instead be treated as flexible tools that respond to the dynamics of the system as a whole. In particular, we posit that developing and maintaining successful communication in global virtual teams requires explicit attention on the part of team members, managers, and educators to two key areas of the activity system: 1) the division of labor as it relates to the dynamics of virtual collaboration, and 2) the communities (national, disciplinary, and organizational) in which participants operate. Effectively analyzing these particular components of the system can help participants define a successful approach to exchanging information throughout a project. Rather than defining this approach via a series of heuristics, we argue for an analytical approach grounded in meta-cognition of the ways in which these factors influence the communication practices of the system—an approach that encourages

teams to consciously examine the dynamics of their own system and develop system-specific conventions and practices.

Division of Labor: Critical Practices for Virtual Teams

Within an activity system, the division of labor encompasses a number of factors, but for this discussion we focus specifically on the physical separation of team members and the nature of virtual rather than co-located work. In particular, in the following subsections, we consider 1) the relational dimension of teamwork that undergirds successful communication and 2) the appropriate technology choices critical to virtual collaboration. We then summarize the implications of division of labor for GVTs.

Relational Space

Successful communication, in both co-located and distributed team environments, requires not simply clear and precise exchanges of information but also an appropriate social space in which this information exchange can occur. Scholars have characterized this space in a variety of ways. Robert and Dennis note, for example, that both attention and motivation are key to successful team communication (Robert & Dennis, 2005). That is, in order for communication to succeed, those on the receiving end must attend to the information they are receiving and be motivated to apply it in meaningful ways to their own work. Jarvenpaa and Leidner, Coppola et al., Tavcar et al., and others posit trust as a critical factor for successful communication (Jarvenpaa & Leidner, 1998; Coppola, Hiltz, & Rotter, 2004; Tavcar, Zavbi, & Verlinden, 2005). This growing body of research makes it clear that for team members to communicate successfully, they must trust one another sufficiently to request and provide the necessary information, as well as to complete tasks competently and appropriately. Particularly important for GVTs is the concept of "swift trust" that operates in groups formed for limited periods around a clear set of goals; it is characterized by a belief or hope in the good will of others, "a willingness to suspend doubt in order to execute the task performance…a willingness to take risks … [and] a positive expectation of benefits" (Coppola et al., 2004, p. 95). In a similar vein, Leinonen et al., in seeking a model to make GVTs aware of the collaborative process, note that teams can only construct new knowledge when they have "a shared cognitive frame that includes awareness of their shared goals and awareness of shared working processes" (Leinonen, Järvelä, & Häkkinen, 2005, p. 303).

Collectively, these studies demonstrate that successful information exchange among team members requires collaborators to establish a social network marked by features such as trust, attention, and shared orientation that makes it possible for them to communicate successfully with each other about the work at hand. Leinonen et al. refer to this as the "relational space" or set of social interactions in which team members operate. That space must, above all, support and sustain relationships among team members that in turn enable successful communication about the project itself (the "object" of the activity system). It includes an understanding of one another's professional identities and expertise, a shared sense of understanding about and commitment to the object and desired outcome, and a willingness to attend to the needs of the system. Kraut et al. adopt a similar approach when they describe the common ground individuals must share to enable successful communication, where "grounding" describes "the interactive process by which communicators exchange evidence about what they do or do not understand over the course of a conversation as they accrue common ground" (Kraut, Fussell, Brennan, & Siegel, 2002, p. 147). Nardi and Whittaker extend the discussion by positing the concept of a "communication zone" that makes complex, project-oriented communi-

cation possible (Nardi & Whittaker, 2002). This communication zone, in which individuals come to understand, trust, and engage with one another professionally and personally, must be in place before collaborators can productively exchange technical information.

This social network—trust, attention, common ground, and the communication zone in which effective information exchanges occur—becomes more difficult to establish and maintain in virtual environments because much of the work associated with establishing it typically occurs unconsciously in informal, face-to-face settings. The process can involve "water-cooler conversations" about popular culture or workplace politics, the ability to see one another's work spaces (and the attendant evidence of personality often present in photographs, calendar choices, and the level of organization of one's desk), and even inquiries about life outside work. The physical distance required for this kind of social development can be as low as 30 meters; beyond that distance, in some scenarios, collaborators could just as easily be separated by miles or oceans (Olson, Teasley, Covi, & Olson, 2002). Nardi and Whittaker, in describing the communication zone that enables complex collaborative information exchange, explicitly associate it with informal face-to-face interactions, not easily replicated in online or virtual environments. Leinonen et al., similarly, note the ways in which virtual collaborators "do not share a common physical environment that provides cues of others' state of work, and so participants do not have common orientations and reference points" (Leinonen et al., 2005, p. 303). Keisler and Cummings, in delineating the challenges of distributed work groups, note that despite sophisticated electronic collaboration tools, physical proximity remains the most effective method for promoting informal, ongoing communication characteristic of successful team communication: "the style of communication in electronically sustained work groups is likely to be somewhat less mutually attentive, less companionable, less frequent, and more effortful than when the team is nearby and talking face-to-face." Underscoring the advantages of physical proximity, Olson et al., in studying what they term the "radical collocation" of all team members in a single room, note the value of ever-present texts collected on a wall or whiteboard to document team activity (Olson et al., 2002). Although collaborative technologies allow team members to create electronic document repositories that can serve similar functions with respect to project tracking, they lack the same physical presence of artifacts taped to a common wall that everyone inevitably looks at daily (if not hourly). Cross, in a study of a collaborative writing project, identified a similar phenomenon: the team seemed to coalesce when it gained a prominent collective physical space with visible physical representations of the work (Cross, 2000). The physical space not only gave team members a sense of collective identity, but it also provided a clear sense of their work and its priority to others in the organization—a sensibility more challenging to achieve in virtual environments where one's work tends to be visible only on one's own computer screen, but key nonetheless to attention and motivation.

Appropriate Technologies

Technology developers provide increasingly sophisticated tools to support virtual collaboration, from decision-support systems to knowledge management databases to interactive video-conferencing, but not every tool is equally effective for every situation. Virtual teams, perhaps more so than co-located teams, must make informed selections regarding communication media. Most discussions of tools for virtual collaboration draw on the theory of social presence first espoused by Short, Williams, & Christie (1976). In social presence theory and its descendent, media richness theory, the most effective media for distance communication are those that establish the highest degree of social presence—those that most closely approximate face-to-face communication, with its cues of voice inflection, facial expression, body language, and personal space. Thus videoconferencing has more social presence than a simple phone call; phone calls have more social presence than e-mail.

However, more recent studies suggest that social presence should not be the only factor governing media choice. In particular, studies by Robert and Denis suggest that media typically considered more "lean" (e.g., e-mail) are in fact often more effective for complex decision-making and information exchanges that require deliberation (Robert & Dennis, 2005). Rich media (those high in social presence) may be necessary for establishing communication zones, but lean media may be more appropriate for knowledge management because of the time required to absorb and evaluate complex information. Hence GVTs need to balance the need for rich media (e.g., video conferences to discuss key issues) to help create the necessary relational space and lean media (e.g., documents exchanged via e-mail) to provide sufficient detail and time for reflection and absorption to support effective decision-making. Tools such as NetMeeting can provide ways for participants to all look at the same documents or drawing spaces at the same time, but individual team members may also need those documents in hand in advance to provide effective feedback.

Summary: Accounting for Division of Labor in GVTs

As the previous subsections suggest, research on the dynamics of virtual teams makes it clear that communicating effectively in these environments involves far more than clear writing or effective PowerPoint presentations. Within activity systems where the division of labor includes a virtual dimension, the challenges of establishing effective social networks and selecting appropriate technologies for information exchange mean that team members must consciously attend to many of the processes that happen unconsciously in co-located settings. This attention, when developed in response to an analysis of the particular system at hand, can lead to conventions and practices ("rules" of the activity system) that directly and explicitly foster effective communication. Managers and collaborators must consider appropriate means to orient all members both to the project and to one another. Possibilities include introductory virtual meetings (with video, where possible) aimed specifically at the process of grounding and establishing communication zones; blogs, wikis, or similar tools that allow collaborators to build an informal virtual dialogue; shared descriptions of each collaborators' work environments and additional projects; and knowledge management systems to create visible representations of ongoing work.

Through such practices, communication becomes a tool not simply to exchange information but also a means to mediate the space in which information exchange occurs. Communication must enable team members to 1) develop swift trust; 2) come to understand one another's professional identities, information needs, and areas of expertise; and 3) develop a common vocabulary as well as a common orientation toward the project at hand. At the same time, the media used for communication throughout the system must not simply be the choice that is most convenient but instead the choice that most effectively accomplishes the goal at hand, be it orienting the team or making complex decisions. By maintaining a level of meta-awareness regarding the impact of virtual collaboration on communication patterns, team managers and team members can take explicit steps to better support the kinds of information networks needed to achieve the desired outcome of the activity system.

Communities: Cultural Complexities in Team Practices

If virtual distributed work environments pose one set of communication problems for team members, cross-cultural environments add another layer of complexity that precludes establishing iron-clad behavioral heuristics that operate across all global virtual teams. Research clearly demonstrates that virtual teams need an effective, appropriate social network among team members to support the collaboration. However, the nature of that network is inflected not only by the distributed nature of the work, but also by the communities or cultures to which members belong, as suggested by Figure 1. Unfortunately, what constitutes an effective communication zone in one culture may not succeed in another culture. The following subsections examine three particular aspects of cross-cultural work (national, disciplinary, and technological communities), then summarize the implications for GVTs.

National Communities

One of the most significant variants GVTs confront, and one that has received extensive attention in the literature on cross-cultural communication, is nationality. As has been well-documented, approaches to team behaviors and practices vary significantly across cultures in everything from information sharing to decision-making to leadership styles (Janssens & Brett, 2006). Janssens and Brett summarize a number of these key differences. They note, for example, that in collective cultures, individuals are often hesitant about putting forth any ideas that would differentiate them from the rest of the group, so information sharing can be severely limited. With respect to decision-making, team members from less hierarchical cultures may make decisions themselves in meetings, while those from more authority-oriented cultures may delay decision-making until they consult with superiors. Some cultures may prefer top-down leadership models, while others operate by more democratic principles (Janssens & Brett, 2006). Other differences include the degree of social interaction expected in work relationships, approaches to learning new information, organizational structures for making and responding to arguments, strategies and expectations for negotiations, understandings of time, and a host of related factors (Varner & Beamer, 2005; Martin & Nakayama, 2007).

These kinds of national cultural differences complicate the process of establishing a productive communication zone, creating trust among team members, and developing a shared set of processes since the approaches that are comfortable for one culture may be completely alien to another. In response, researchers have identified a series of interventions, ranging from a proliferation of textbooks defining cultural variations (e.g., Trompenaars & Hampden-Turner, 1998; Bonvillain, 2003; Harris, Moran, & Moran, 2004; Varner & Beamer, 2005; Barker & Matveeva, 2006; Hart, 2006; Martin & Nakayama, 2007) to more complex approaches such as "cultural intelligence" to describe an individual's awareness of cultural variation (Earley & Mosakowski, 2004).

However, those engaged in GVTs must remember that while such resources are useful starting points for analyzing the national communities associated with a given activity system, all attempts to define cultural variations and prescribe suitable responses remain limited because national cultures are themselves neither monolithic nor static, and essentializing stereotypes can sometimes create as many problems as they resolve (Hunsinger, 2006). At the same time, globalization itself has a profound impact on national culture, and cultures are constantly shifting as fashions, movies, advertising, and music—as well as business practices—migrate around the globe (Hunsinger, 2006). Hence attempts to classify behavior and expectations based on broad categories of national differences remain at best transitory and problematic. Yet those involved in GVTs must

remain alert to potential differences that can arise when creating the social networks needed for effective collaboration, and must continually fine-tune the team's processes to acknowledge and account for those variations.

Disciplinary Communities

In GVTs, however, nationalities are not the sole communities impacting the activity system. National identity is typically only one facet of individual identity, and the degree to which it influences behavior varies from situation to situation (Hunsinger, 2006; Martin & Nakayama, 2007). Corporate affiliation, professional role, gender, class, and other identity markers can influence the ways individuals approach projects and interact with team members, be they co-located or distributed. In many cases, in fact, disciplinary or professional identity in particular can be as sharp a dividing line as cultural difference, as analyses of disasters such as Three Mile Island (TMI) and the Challenger explosion indicate (Winsor, 1988; Herndl et al., 1991). Disciplinary communities, like national ones, often rely on different forms of evidence to determine "truth" and different criteria to shape decisions. During the period leading up to TMI, for example, different approaches to decision-making between the Nuclear Services division and the Engineering division resulted in a failure to implement changes that may have averted the problem. The two groups trusted different forms of evidence and followed different procedures with respect to adopting change, and each side made arguments only in terms of its own approach to the decision process. The result was a failure of understanding, a failure to find common ground, and ultimately, a near-catastrophic equipment failure (Herndl et al., 1991). And such differences are not limited to scientists or engineers; a number of scholars have explored wide-ranging epistemological and practical differences that separate disciplines (Smeby, 1996; Bradbeer, 1999; Perelman, 1999;

Neumann, 2001; Neumann, Parry, & Becher, 2002; Lincoln & Guba, 2003).

Moreover, national identity also impacts disciplinary identity; practitioners in the same profession may approach the activity from an entirely different perspective. Such has historically been the case in engineering; work by Downey and Lucena demonstrates that disciplinary identity and cultural identity construct one another in the engineering field (Downey & Lucena, 2004; Lucena, Downey, & Amery, 2006). They note, for instance, the ways in which French engineers historically adopted an intellectual stance, valuing mathematics and derivations of solutions from first principles, whereas British engineers took a more pragmatic approach, moving up from manual labor and emphasizing practical rather than theoretical knowledge. German engineering represents yet a different historical lineage with its emphasis on precision (Lucena et al., 2006). These cultural differences among professionals in the same discipline mean that in a GVT of engineers from different countries, the kinds of evidence, the approaches to problem-solving, the modes of decision-making—and consequently, the kinds of information that need to be exchanged in pursuit of the outcome—all potentially vary from subject to subject within the activity system.

Technological Communities

Apart from differing approaches to team and work relationships, research by Thorne suggests that even our approaches to technology are culturally mediated (Thorne, 2003). In a study of U.S. students learning French paired with native speakers in France via e-mail, Thorne found that the two cultures had different expectations about the medium, including level of formality, appropriate uses, and response patterns. He thus posits "cultures of use" with respect to electronic communication media, suggesting that technology is not a neutral tool but rather is embedded in cultural practices. Based on field research, he argues that "even something prosaic like e-mail is a variably understood tool, a culturally specific tool, one that may serve a diversity of functions for some, while for others, it conjures up specific associations of may be used for highly restrictive purposes" (p. 40). Moreover, he notes, the ways in which users approach various tools is changing rapidly, influenced by national and regional cultures, economics, educational factors, and social relationships. These uses impact the ways in which various tools do or do not establish social presence, and thus the choices collaborators make when using communication technologies to both shape the relational space and exchange information for decision-making and action.

Moreover, these cultures of use may be generational as well as national. Marc Prensky's work on digital natives versus digital immigrants points to key shifts that may occur in the coming decades. Prensky differentiates between the generation of digital immigrants who grew up before the cyber-revolution, and thus came to tools like e-mail and Blackberries and NetMeeting later in life, versus digital natives, who have been online in one form or another almost since birth (Prensky, 2001a; 2001b). Digital immigrants grew up operating in one arena and made a transition to another set of cultural tools and interactions, whereas digital natives know only this kind of cyber-interaction. Prensky's work, consequently, focuses on the different cognitive processes emerging in digital natives, and the implications of those differences for education (Prensky, 2001b; 2005; 2006). The differentiation is not one of facility—digital immigrants may be just as adept at using the technology as digital natives—but rather of perspective, expectations, and cognition. This shift becomes particularly significant with respect to communication in light of the cognitive dimension of communication preferences. As work by Kock suggests, human beings are psychically predisposed to face-to-face communication; it is part of our evolutionary heritage, and our expectation for both social and professional interactions are mediated by biological preferences (Kock, 2005). But if both Kock and Prensky are right—biology plays a role in media preference, and digital natives are experiencing key cognitive shifts—then any heuristics we might establish about how communication should work in virtual teams or how we might go about establishing effective communication zones are necessarily transitory. Digital natives entering the activity system do so from a different set of cognitive processes, community expectations, and experiences than the digital immigrants who preceded them, and effective communication within the system must take those differences into account as well.

Summary: Accounting for Community Variations in GVTs

As with virtual space, the complexity of cultural differences—be they national, organizational, disciplinary, or gendered— suggest that those engaged in cross-cultural teams need to approach each team project with an analytical eye aimed at identifying, understanding, and ultimately mediating the array of possible differences. Resources regarding the kinds of variations possible across national and regional cultures are certainly helpful starting points when developing guidelines for team processes including decision-making, information sharing, grounding, and related practices. But given the complexity of any activity system, those resources can serve as starting points only. GVT members must remain aware of the kinds of differences they may encounter; however, rather than memorizing a specific set of heuristics that neatly map individuals to prescribed behaviors based on community identity, team members, managers, and educators need to assess each team to understand the particular community identities at work and adapt flexible team practices for approaching communication within a particular system.

GLOBAL VIRTUAL TEAMS IN PRACTICE: CLASSROOM CASE STUDIES

The complexity of global virtual teams became particularly clear in a case study of U.S. engineering students (ENGR) and European literature, culture, and digital media (LCDM) students, as we have reported elsewhere (Paretti, McNair, & Holloway-Attaway, (forthcoming). The study focuses on two specific disciplines (engineering and digital media), but as the previous sections make clear, the challenges and possibilities should prove equally relevant to a full range of fields involved in a GVT. In the first phase of this study, as reported, we sought to understand how digital natives would approach a global virtual team when given minimal instructional scaffolding about collaboration and communication beyond basic course assignments for each group. In this case, the engineering students were completing capstone design projects and the LCDM students were preparing public communication about those projects in the form of white papers and Web sites. Even though these students used technology freely to order their social worlds and, in the case of the (LCDM) students, explicitly focused in their courses on the challenges and possibilities of electronic communication and cyber-identities, our findings suggest that the students were not adept at coming together as a team around a set of shared goals and a shared orientation toward the project at hand. Also, disciplinary differences proved a much larger hurdle to the virtual collaboration than national differences, at least in terms of student perceptions. The resulting process led to significant frustration on the part of all team members and few learning gains (particularly from the engineering students) with respect to successful GVT behaviors.

From surveys and focus groups with the students, we learned more about their anxieties and subsequent barriers to teaming in a virtual workplace. The LCDM students dealt with worries about their lack of technical engineering content, grammatical competency in written English, and tight deadlines that were structured around the ENGR teams' schedules. The ENGR students, on the other hand, did not have a clear understanding of the work required of the LCDM students, and their deadlines were not directly related toward a shared goal (only toward completing their own senior design projects). This setting resulted in a general lack of familiarity and trust between the teams, on levels of culture, work goals and requirements, and understanding of each others' disciplines.

The second phase of this study repeats the collaboration, but adds extensive instructional scaffolding for two new groups of students. Drawing from the previous experience and findings in the literature, we created lectures and exercises to address the various points of networks as formulated in activity systems (and depicted above in Figure 1). In particular, we added structure to the curriculum specifically to develop and maintain successful communication by focusing team members' attention on two key areas of the activity system: 1) the division of labor as it relates to the dynamics of virtual collaboration, and 2) the communities (national, disciplinary, and organizational) in which participants operate. The findings suggest that this attention significantly improved the collaborative process.

Division of Labor: Relational Space, Team Roles and Structure, and Appropriate Technology

In contrast to the first study, students in Phase 2 were required to engage in several specific team communication tasks, and the purpose of those tasks was clearly explained in class. Students were required to send introductory e-mails to establish personal familiarity. This initial communication was then followed up with a videoconference that also focused on introductions and began the question-answer process that the

two teams would need to engage in for the duration of the project (conferences in Phase 1 were audio-only). Based on classroom instruction, the LCDM students planned the agendas and led the videoconference meetings with specific goals for establishing relational space and shared project orientation. We believe that this was a crucial step to take for establishing *relational space* in which team members could work with trust and motivation. By embarking early on a structured question-answer process, students also laid the groundwork for knowledge-finding and feedback cycles that could comfortably be repeated through the project.

To increase competencies, we also introduced instruction on *team roles and structures*. Both groups of students were encouraged to use a rubric to self-evaluate their own team behavior and look at the architecture of their own single-discipline team before engaging in the interdisciplinary GVT. LCDM students assigned roles to themselves in order to organize the tight production schedule. The work and deadline schedule was also mandated from the beginning by instructors, with deadlines dependent on each teams' production. For example, the first major deadline was set for LCDM students to turn in a draft on a Monday at noon, and the ENGR students were required to return the drafts with feedback within 24 hours. This increased awareness of work schedules expanded so that the LCDM students were aware of ENGR holiday and exam schedules. Interestingly, ENGR students, aware of their cohorts' deadlines, voluntarily agreed to contribute feedback throughout their own holiday break, though this feedback was not required by either instructor (no such voluntary support occurred in Phase 1). This supportive step suggests that the initial communications to consciously establish a social network and shared orientation were successful.

In addition to adding video to the conference calls, we also discussed factors students should consider when deciding upon the most *appropriate technology* for tasks throughout the collaboration. We exploited the common space of a courseware application used for the ENGR senior design class. Used frequently for both e-mails and file exchange, this shared workspace became a nearly physical area where documents and other work artifacts (such as video presentations) were constructed. We advised students to use the videoconferencing for tasks that might benefit from real-time exchanges and personal inflection. In addition to the introductory sessions, the students also discuss editorial changes in this more personable medium. E-mails, on the other hand, worked well for the feedback cycles on the works in progress.

Communities: National, Disciplinary, and Technological

The main problem of differing *national and disciplinary communities* involved the LCDM students' anxiety about their competencies in written English and abilities to understand the highly technical subjects that the ENGR students were working on. Again, we do not consider these anxieties unique to the two cultures or the two disciplines involved; language competencies are a common barrier in global teams, and interdisciplinary collaborations are often marked by misunderstandings of disciplinary content. By distinctly separating these two competencies, we believe that both groups of students were able to focus on establishing accurate content in a rhetorically persuasive form. The instructors had purposely made grammatical issues a secondary consideration for both teams. At the same time, LCDM students turned in "pre" drafts to their instructors for clarification, and ENGR students used a review process provided by instructors that encourages students to mark language issues in a non-prescriptive manner. That is, ENGR student editors were told to "underline any sentence they have to read twice," but they were not asked to correct the writing itself.

Unlike the first study, the ENGR students did not complain about their work being over-simplified in the hands of writers from another *disciplinary community*. Instead, they had been involved from the beginning in shaping the written product with an awareness of the goals set for the white paper assignment. These students practiced communicating engineering topics to non-technical audiences in previous courses, and this experience likely contributed to their understanding and valuing the challenge set for the LCDM students.

Interestingly, students' *institutional community* also emerged as an important identifying marker. Students were asked in their introductory correspondence to describe their universities and their academic programs. In addition to the disciplinary difference, this distinction is potentially the most salient, especially since both teams included students from non-U.S. and non-European countries. In fact, this institutional identity has the least "fuzzy" borders; its reliability is perhaps the reason why all the participants (and researchers) defaulted to calling each other by university nicknames rather than their discipline or national culture.

As noted above, the *technological communities* were not a major concern. However, at least one tense moment has occurred as a result of misinterpreted tone in the lean discourse space of an e-mail chain. The solution to this event seems to have been the willingness on both sides to keep adding more communication. In this discussion it was noted that even visual media, such as the video-conferencing, do not completely solve this problem. ENGR students, who in this study received prior instruction in cross-cultural communication, were particularly cooperative throughout these exchanges.

In summary, several key differences may have led to the improved team projects in this study:

- The course instructors added more requirements to the assignments for both groups, including introductory correspondence by each team to describe not only their projects, but also their majors, their universities, and themselves to help foster a relational space in which communication can occur.

- The LCDM students received direct instruction in managing and orchestrating virtual teams, learning to lead meetings and set agendas with specific awareness of the constraints of global virtual collaboration.
- The engineering students received several weeks of instruction in cross-cultural communication prior to the capstone design course to make them aware of the kinds of interaction differences they might expect.
- Over several semesters, engineering students received instruction related to communicating their expertise to a variety of non-technical audiences, including business investors and high school students.

The results from Phase II, which added instruction on how to improve collaborative communication in GVTs, show far different outcomes than Phase I. Students on both sides of the collaboration seem more aware of the constraints and identities of their collaborators, more willing to ask for and provide information about the projects, and more interested in the work of their collaborators. And as noted, although this collaboration looked specifically at team members from engineering and humanities, the implications apply to a full range of cultural differences.

FUTURE TRENDS

Identifying successful communication practices for global virtual teams involves an ever-shifting terrain because the activity systems that shape these teams are constantly shifting. Approaches to team processes, communication media, and rhetorical structures are both infinitely variable and constantly changing. The extent of the variability, documented by both prior researchers

and our own studies of student learners in global virtual teams, suggest key areas for future work to help more fully describe the challenges and practices in this environment:

- Education researchers may explore the development of effective teaching materials to orient students and workplace practitioners to the constraints and limitations of virtual work.
- Communication researchers may investigate the cultures of use associated with various communication technologies.
- Cognitivists may explore the behavior of digital natives as they migrate technologies from social to professional lives.
- Practitioners from a range of fields may develop increasingly sophisticated analytical frameworks rather than static heuristics for successfully negotiating international online workspaces.

CONCLUSION

Approaching the GVT as a dynamic activity system provides a way of looking analytically at the work communication needs to do in terms of both creating and maintaining team relationships and managing the new knowledge created among team members. This heightened awareness of the context-driven nature of collaboration allows all participants to develop a flexible, analytical approach sensitized to possible differences and ready to adapt communication practices to a broad spectrum of settings.

ACKNOWLEDGMENT

This study was supported in part by NSF CMMI 0619263, and by a grant from the Office of International Research, Education, and Development at Virginia Tech.

REFERENCES

Bakhurst, D. (1997). Activity, consciousness, and communication. In: M. Cole, Y. Engeström, & O. Vasquez (Eds.), *Mind, culture, and activity: Seminal papers from the laboratory of comparative human cognition* (pp. 147-163). Cambridge: Cambridge University Press.

Barker, T., & Matveeva, N. (2006). Teaching intercultural communication in a technical writing service course: Real instructors practices and suggestions for textbook selection. *Technical Communication Quarterly, 15*(2), 191-215.

Bonvillain, N. (2003). *Language, culture, and communication: The meaning of messages* (4th ed.). Upper Saddle River, NJ: Prentice Hall.

Bradbeer, J. (1999). Barriers to interdisciplinarity: Disciplinary discourses and student learning. *Journal of Geography in Higher Education, 23*(3), 381-396.

Cole, M., Engeström, Y., & Vasquez, O. (1997). Introduction. In: M. Cole, Y. Engeström, & O. Vasquez (Eds.), *Mind, culture, and activity: Seminal papers from the laboratory of comparative human cognition* (pp. 1-21). Cambridge: Cambridge University Press.

Coppola, N., Hiltz, S., & Rotter, N. (2004). Building trust in virtual teams. *IEEE Transactions on Professional Communication, 47*(2), 95-104.

Cross, G. (2000). Collective form: An exploration of large-group writing. *Journal of Business Communication, 37*(1), 77-100.

Downey, G., & Lucena, J. (2004). Knowledge and professional identity in engineering: Code-switching and the metrics of progress. *History and Technology, 20*(4), 393-420.

Earley, P., & Mosakowski, E. (2004). Cultural intelligence. *Harvard Business Review, 82*(10), 139-148.

Engeström, Y., & Middleton, D. (Eds.). (1998). *Cognition and communication at work.* Cambridge: Cambridge University Press.

Friedman, T. (2005). *The world is flat: A brief history of the twenty-first century.* New York, NY: Farrar, Straus, and Giroux.

Harris, P., Moran, R., & Moran, S. (2004). *Managing cultural differences: Global leadership strategies for the 21st Century* (25th Anniversary ed.). Boston, MA: Elsevier Butterworth Heinemann.

Hart, G. (2006). Sensitivity to other cultures. *Intercom, 53,* 6-9.

Herndl, C., Fennell, B., & Miller, C. (1991). Understanding failures in organizational discourse: The accident at Three Mile Island and the Shuttle *Challenger* Disaster. In: C. Bazerman & J. Paradis (Eds.), *Textual dynamics of the professions* (pp. 279-305). Madison, WI: University of Wisconsin Press.

Hunsinger, R. (2006). Culture and cultural identity in intercultural technical communication. *Technical Communication Quarterly, 15*(1), 31-48.

Janssens, M., & Brett, J. (2006). Cultural intelligence in global teams. *Group & Organization Management, 31*(1), 124-153.

Jarvenpaa, S., & Leidner, D. (1998). Communication and trust in global virtual teams. *Journal of computer Mediated Communication, 3*(4).

Kain, D., & Wardle, E. (2005). Building context: Using activity theory to teach about genre in multi-major professional communication courses. *Technical Communication Quarterly, 14*(2), 113-139.

Kock, N. (2005). Media richness or media naturalness? The evolution of our biological communication apparatus and its influence on our behavior toward e-Communication tools. *IEEE Transactions on Professional Communication, 48*(2), 117-130.

Kraut, R., Fussell, S., Brennan, S., & Siegel, J. (2002). Understanding the effects of proximity on collaboration: Implications for technologies to support remote collaborative work. In: P. Hinds & S. Kiesler (Eds.), *Distributed work* (pp. 137-164). Cambridge: The MIT Press.

Leinonen, P., Järvelä, S., & Häkkinen, P. (2005). Conceptualizing the awareness of collaboration: A qualitative study of a global virtual team. *Computer Supported Cooperative Work, 14*(4), 301-322.

Lincoln, Y., & Guba, E. (2003). Paradigmatic controversies, contradictions, and emerging confluences. In: N. Denzin & Y. Lincoln (Eds.), *The landscape of qualitative research: Theories and issues* (2nd ed., pp. 105-117). Thousand Oaks, CA: Sage Publications.

Lucena, J., Downey, G., & Amery, H. (2006). From region to countries: Engineering education in Bahrain, Egypt, and Turkey. *IEEE Technology and Society Magazine*, 4-11.

Martin, J., & Nakayama, T. (2007). *Intercultural communication in contexts* (4th ed.). Boston, MA: McGraw-Hill.

Nardi, B. (1992). *Studying context: A comparison of activity theory, situated action models and distributed cognition.* Paper presented at the Proceedings East-West HCI Conference, St. Petersburg, Russia.

Nardi, B., & Whittaker, S. (2002). The place of face-to-face communication in distributed work. In: P. Hinds & S. Kiesler (Eds.), *Distributed work* (pp. 83-110). Cambridge: The MIT Press.

Neumann, R. (2001). Disciplinary differences and university teaching. *Studies in Higher Education, 26*(2), 135-146.

Neumann, R., Parry, S., & Becher, T. (2002). Teaching and learning in their disciplinary contexts: A conceptual analysis. *Studies in Higher Education, 27*(4), 405-417.

Olson, J., Teasley, S., Covi, L., & Olson, G. (2002). The (currently) unique advantages of collocated work. In: P. Hinds & S. Kiesler (Eds.), *Distributed work* (pp. 113-135). Cambridge: The MIT Press.

Paretti, M., McNair, L., & Holloway-Attaway, L. (forthcoming). Teaching technical communication in an era of distributed work: A case study of collaboration between U.S. and Swedish students. *Technical Communication Quarterly.*

Perelman, L. (1999). The two rhetorics: Design and interpretation in engineering and humanistic discourse. *Language and Learning Across the Disciplines, 3*(2), 64-82.

Prensky, M. (2001a). Digital natives, digital immigrants, Part I. *On the Horizon, 9*(5), 1-6.

Prensky, M. (2001b). Digital natives, digital immigrants, Part II: Do they really think differently?. *On the Horizon, 9*(6), 1-6.

Prensky, M. (2005). "Engage me or enrage me": What today's learners demand. *Educause Review,* 60-64.

Prensky, M. (2006). Adopt and adapt: 21st-century schools need 21st-century technology. *Edutopia,* 43-45.

Robert, L., & Dennis, A. (2005). Paradox of richness: A cognitive model of media choice. *IEEE Transactions on Professional Communication, 48*(1), 10-21.

Russell, D. (1997a). Rethinking genre in school and society: An activity theory analysis. *Written Communication, 14*(4), 504-554.

Russell, D. (1997b). Writing and genre in higher education and workplaces: A review of studies that use cultural-historical activity theory. *Mind, Culture, and Activity, 4*(4), 224-237.

Short, J., Williams, E., & Christie, B. (1976). *The social psychology of telecommunications.* New York, NY: Wiley.

Smeby, J.-C. (1996). Disciplinary differences in university teaching. *Studies in Higher Education, 21*(1), 69-79.

Spinuzzi, C. (1996). Pseudotransactionality, activity theory, and professional writing instruction. *Technical Communication Quarterly, 5*(3), 295-308.

Tavcar, J., Zavbi, R., & Verlinden, J. (2005). Skills for effective communication and work in global product development teams. *Engineering design, 16*(6), 557-576.

Thorne, S. (2003). Artifacts and cultures-of-use in intercultural communication. *Language Learning and Technology, 7*(2), 38-67.

Trompenaars, F., & Hampden-Turner, C. (1998). *Riding the waves of culture: Understanding cultural diversity in global business* (2nd ed.). New York, NY: McGraw-Hill.

Varner, I., & Beamer, L. (2005). *Intercultural communication in the global workplace* (3rd ed.). Boston, MA: McGraw-Hill Irwin.

Winsor, D. (1988). Communication failures contributing to the Challenger accident: An example for technical communicators. *IEEE Transactions on Professional Communication, 31*(3), 101-108.

KEY TERMS

Activity System: the entire context in which ongoing human interaction occurs, including not only the subjects involved, the problem space they are addressing, and the desired outcome, but also the artifacts (e.g., forms of communication, tools, technologies) that mediate the interactions, the rules (including both laws and customs) that shape behavior, the communities in which individuals operate, and the ways in which work is distributed among members.

Co-Located (or collocated) Work: Teamwork in which the participants occupy the same physical space, such as cubicles or offices on the same floor of a building. The physical limit for proximity for collocation can be as low as 30 meters.

Cultures of Use: The ways in which various cultures or communities use communication technology, including what a given technology should be used for, what kind of tone it requires, guidelines for response, and related factors.

Communication Zone: A social/relational "space" between individuals in which communication is possible or potentially available.

Distributed Work: Work that has been divided up among multiple team members who typically operate in physically separated locations.

Meta-Cognition: Understanding not only of facts, such as a specific set of characteristics associated with a given national culture, but of the context surrounding those facts, the conditions under which they are applicable, and the larger conceptual framework that gives meaning and nuance to the facts.

Relational Space: An alternative version of the communication zone; a social network among collaborators in which effective communication can occur.

Chapter IV
Successful Communication in Virtual Teams and the Role of the Virtual Team Leader

Jamie S. Switzer
Colorado State University, USA

ABSTRACT

The world now lives and works in cyberspace. Often, organizations have their people perform functional tasks by working in virtual teams, where members use technology to cooperate across geographic and organizational boundaries. As the use of virtual teams in the workforce becomes more prevalent, those involved must have the knowledge to communicate efficiently and effectively, especially the virtual team leaders. This chapter provides a general overview of virtual teams and virtual team leadership, and discusses specific communication strategies and competencies necessary for virtual team leaders to be effective and successful communicators.

INTRODUCTION

William Gibson coined the term "cyberspace" in his popular 1984 novel *Neuromancer*, defining it as "a graphic representation of data abstracted from the banks of every computer in the human system...unthinkable complexity" (Gibson, 1984, p. 51). While perhaps not as dramatically as Gibson's vivid portrayal, the modern world now works, lives, and communicates in cyberspace. Geography, borders, and time zones are irrelevant in the way today's business and people's personal lives are conducted. "The death of distance" (Cairncross, 1997) and the ubiquitous role of

communication technologies are profoundly affecting the economy, business, and social existence (Tapscott, 1998).

For many reasons, including the increasing sophistication of communication technologies, corporate mergers, globalization, the need to respond rapidly to changing markets and customer demands, travel costs, and the trend toward flexibility and mobility in the workforce, organizations must change from the old ways of doing business to new ones (Benveniste, 1994; Smith, 1997; Lurey, 1998). Rapid fundamental changes have created new challenges for leadership (Kielson, 1996). To be successful in today's "cyber" work environment requires a new style of leadership.

Part of this operational shift is for organizations to have their people perform functional tasks by working in virtual teams, where members use technology to cooperate across geographic and organizational boundaries (Rutkowski, Vogel, VanGenuchten, Bemelmans, & Favier, 2002; Gibson & Cohen, 2003). No longer is co-location necessary for communication, interaction, and knowledge sharing (Gerber, 1995; Pliskin, 1998). Virtual teamwork is one of the answers to the modern problems of 21st century organizations (Lipnack & Stamps, 1999).

BACKGROUND

The word "virtual" means "existing or resulting in effect or essence though not in actual fact, form, or name" (Websters, 1984). The meaning of "virtual" today has been extended to suggest greatly enhanced effects or actions, physical behavior of non-physical (often electronic) entities, and the use of telecommunications and computing technologies (Grenier & Metes, 1995). The concept of the virtual organization relies on two key factors: new ways of managing people, and communicating by the movement of electronic information across cyberspace to provide new functionality and new capability (Norton & Smith, 1997).

Technologies that facilitate computer-mediated communication (CMC) have transformed the world in several ways. CMC has dramatically increased interconnectivity and has arguably shrunk the world, as people are able to communicate in ways that were once impossible (Olaniran, 2004). Social networks have broadened to include individuals people have not physically met and often those they may never meet in person.

There has also been an increased trend toward globalization practices. The globalization process involves various aspects of contemporary life such as economy, political and international relations, culture, and religion, in which multiple communities become interconnected (Monge, 1998).

With globalization, however, comes the need for organizations to use communication technologies to coordinate their activities in multiple locations and around the globe. Consequently, relationships are cultivated and collaboration on a daily basis is encouraged among individuals who are spatially distant (Olaniran, 2004).

Drucker asserts "changes in concepts will in the end be at least as important as the changes in tools and technology" (Drucker, 1999, p. 101). The virtual worker must have the knowledge and the technological tools to successfully communicate at a distance. Working in virtual teams requires a different skill set, particularly so if the virtual team is to be effective. As the use of virtual teams becomes more prevalent in business and industry, those involved must have the knowledge to communicate efficiently and effectively. This is especially important for the virtual team leaders.

There are still some constants in good leadership practices regardless of the environment, but a new paradigm for leadership is emerging. The virtual environment is changing leadership roles (Montgomery & Clancy, 1994; Harris, 1998). Just because a particular leadership style is effective for communicating in a face-to-face environment does not mean it will work in a virtual setting. Working in a computer-mediated environment requires a "set of traits, skills, abilities, and leadership styles different from those required in the face-to-face communication environment" (George & Sleeth, 2000, p. 303). Many traditional leadership principles apply to virtual teams, but virtual team leaders face additional challenges.

The rest of this chapter will provide a general overview of virtual teams and virtual team leadership, and discuss specific communication strategies and competencies necessary for virtual team leaders to be effective and successful communicators.

VIRTUAL TEAMS

Organizations are encountering situations requiring quick responses to customer needs, flexibility as those needs change, and workers who have unique technical skills and well-developed interpersonal and communicative abilities to complete challenging tasks. These environments require structures supporting communications that promote the speed (customer responsiveness), nimbleness, and adaptability to remain competitive in the demanding environments. Because of this, a number of organizations have turned to virtual teams (Suchan & Hayzak, 2001).

A virtual team is a "group of geographically and/or organizationally dispersed coworkers that are assembled using a combination of telecommunications and information technologies to accomplish an organizational task" (Townsend, DeMarie, & Hendrickson, 1998, p. 18). The power of a virtual team is that it overcomes the "tyranny of distance" (Watson, Bostrom, & Dennis, 1994, p. 38). All virtual teams share certain characteristics: common goals, geographic separation of members, electronically-mediated communication, and loose boundaries (Nemiro, 1998).

It is estimated by 2010, 70% of the U.S. population will spend 10 times longer per day interacting virtually (Emelo & Francis, 2002). This is because virtual teams offer tremendous opportunities for organizations. Well-known companies that embrace the concept of virtual teamwork into their corporate culture include PricewaterhouseCoopers, Whirlpool, Eastman Kodak, Sun Microsystems, NCR Corporation, Intel, Microsoft, and Hewlett-Packard (Bell & Kozlowski, 2002). Kanawattanachai and Yoo (2002) cite a recent survey that found more than 60% of professional employees work in virtual teams.

Electronic communication allows organizations to recruit talent without the constraints of location and to offer more scheduling flexibility such as telecommuting and working from home offices. It also creates the potential for "follow-the-sun" 24-hour workdays and the ability to maintain close contact with employees and customers throughout the world (Solomon, 2001).

Virtual teams can also deal effectively with issues sensitive to diverse cultural contexts, such as designing and introducing new products for specific national markets, by communicating and collaborating with locally-based participants. Growing concerns about the safety and security of international travel are also fueling an interest in virtual teams (Steinfield, 2002).

Even though there are several opportunities with respect to virtual teams, there are also many challenges. It is difficult to effectively communicate with people who must work collaboratively and interactively but may not ever actually see each other. The existence of mediated communication technologies that allows individuals to observe others' responses to situations and to read their facial expressions, gestures, tones, and vocal intonations (Burtha & Connaughton, 2004) can reduce the negative impact of communicating in the absence of non-verbal cues.

Communication in virtual teams is also challenging because group members may be unfamiliar with the different languages, cultures, and behavioral norms present in a global virtual team. Since virtual teams are geographically dispersed, timing becomes an issue because so many different time zones are involved. Another concern is that without effective communication, group members are unaware of remote teammates' availability, current activities, and other information that might influence the effectiveness of their work.

Subgroups may also form within the larger confines of a virtual team (Kayworth & Leidner, 2002). Subgroups reveal a certain level of heterogeneity in team composition as some members will share characteristics that will unify them, while at the same time differentiating them from other members with different characteristics (Gibson & Vermeulen, 2003). There is evidence to indicate that subgroups whose members have exhibited consistency in proposing a position and who have achieved mutual agreement are more likely to exert an influence on final group outcomes (Gebhardt & Meyers, 1995).

Panteli and Davison (2005) found that subgroups had an effect on virtual team cohesiveness, depending on the impact of the subgroup. If the subgroup impact was considered high, communication at the virtual team level was hindered, boundaries were created and social interaction was limited. Accordingly, it became more difficult to communicate effectively to build cohesiveness and team identity. Teams with low subgroup impact were able to work and communicate in a more collaborative fashion, and completed tasks in a more relaxed positive spirit than teams with high impact subgroups.

Virtual teams can be difficult to design, costly and complex to implement, messy to manage, and far less productive than collocated teams (Melymuka, 1997). However, virtual teams address the needs of the new work environment. The office is where the worker is, not the other way around.

To have a successful virtual team, the most important factor is communication. Communication must be constant in order to combat an "out of sight, out of mind" attitude. When team members are geographically dispersed, the challenge is keeping them in the loop as regularly as those who are collocated (Burtha & Connaughton, 2004). To keep team members feeling like they are connected, communication has to happen frequently and effectively. Successful communication occurs when each team member understands the message. One way to achieve effective communication is by facilitating virtual team meetings using communication technologies. In the team meeting, each member should clearly communicate critical information, opinions and concerns.

In order for team members to contribute to the virtual meetings, they have to feel like they trust the other members. Trust is another important factor for successful virtual teams. Trust is developed over time through informal social interaction and sharing of information (Goodbody, 2005). Since virtual teams have nonexistent or limited physi-

cal social interaction, trust is dependent upon the interaction and information communicated within the virtual meetings. To build trust, a virtual team must create and own a simple definition of intent (Wilson, 2003). Members need to establish the virtual team's operating principles, roles, responsibilities, and goals, and any questions should be clarified immediately. Communication must be open and honest and team members must follow through on their promises.

It is important to select the right people for the virtual team. This is critical because the team leaders and members are the ultimate factor in having a functional virtual team. A successful virtual team member is self-motivated and does not need a lot of detailed instruction or structure. However, the most important quality a successful virtual team member can possess is strong communication skills (Solomon, 2001), because the team relies solely on the ability to communicate virtually. Most virtual teams do not have the luxury of relying on non-verbal cues communicated through virtual meeting technologies; therefore, it is imperative that each virtual team member has the ability to communicate successfully through verbal and written communication.

Virtual teams are becoming mainstream in the workforce because there are several advantages to them. Virtual teams allow qualified people to be geographically dispersed throughout the world to collaborate successfully. On the other hand, it is challenging to communicate in virtual teams because there is usually no face-to-face interaction, language and cultural barriers arise, and time zone differences can become a problem. Additionally, virtual teams face particular technological dilemmas around accessibility and compatibility (Dube & Pare, 2001). To meet all of these challenges, effective communication is critical. Successful communication boosts trust among team members, which allows organizational goals to be achieved.

VIRTUAL TEAM LEADERSHIP

Being an effective leader in a virtual environment can be daunting (Kostner, 1994; Lipnack & Stamps, 1997; Solomon, 1998; Duarte & Snyder, 1999). Virtual leaders today are a "collective, networked, virtual force with powers flowing from a jointly created and shared vision" (Tapscott, 1995). Tapscott lists six themes of "internetworked leadership" for the transformation to a digital world where communication is technology-mediated:

- Leadership in a digital economy provides opportunity for everyone.
- The best leadership is leadership for learning.
- Internetworked leadership is born in teams through collective action of individuals working to forge a new vision or solve problems.
- Leadership can and will increasingly be achieved virtually on computer networks.
- A CEO who stewards internetworked leadership can springboard an enterprise into transformation.
- Personal use of technology opens horizons and creates curiosity.

Peters' (1996) five leadership constants (decentralization, empowerment, passion for the product, great systems, and paranoia) that are the trademark of success are now the minimum requirements for running information-rich, dispersed organizations. Organizations must "revisit and rethink leadership in a CMC environment" (George & Sleeth, 2000, p. 288). The nature of business today demands much greater communication skills from virtual leaders than traditional leadership roles; they must adapt or they will not succeed.

Cramton (1997) identified specific communication challenges that are inherent in virtual teams: failure to communicate contextual information, difficulty in communicating and understanding the salience of information, unevenly distributed information, differences in the speed of access information, and difficulty in interpreting the meaning of silence. A strong leader can mitigate those factors and create an environment that stresses clear and precise communication strategies.

"This is the age of the 'accidental' virtual team leader" observe Duarte and Snyder (1999, p. 73). Often people are thrust into leading a virtual team with little or no training and/or support from the organization and are forced to "proceed by the seat of their pants, making up new rules as they go along" (O'Hara-Devereaux & Johansen, 1994, p. 103). Many virtual team leaders report their biggest challenge is an increased sense of burden and responsibility; they feel as if they are the "glue" that holds their virtual team together (Duarte & Snyder, 1999).

Organizations making a long-term commitment to virtual team leaders by providing resources, training, and other types of support will realize extraordinary results (O'Hara-Devereaux & Johansen, 1994; Duarte & Snyder, 1999). Savvy management chooses virtual team leaders more for their "leadership skills and ability to facilitate bringing people together than for their status and rank" (Creighton & Adams, 1998, p. 76). Virtual team leaders in turn can offer specific suggestions to management regarding leadership behaviors such as communicating, establishing expectations, allocating resources, and modeling desired behaviors (Duarte & Snyder, 1999).

As Lipnack and Stamps state, "Virtual teams and networks demand more leadership, not less" (1997, p. 173). To be a successful virtual team leader requires a special set of skills (Montgomery & Clancy, 1994; O'Hara-Devereaux & Johansen, 1994). More than just communication technologies are needed. Virtual team leaders must have the communication tools, techniques, and strategies that work in a virtual environment (Haywood, 1998; Duarte & Snyder, 1999). Leading virtual teams is different from conventional team leadership and requires specific training, particularly in the effective use of mediated communication technologies. As Haywood observes:

For the majority of managers, working with virtual teams is a new experience. The management skills they've developed don't translate well to the virtual world. Most companies have not done an adequate job preparing managers for the shift in the workplace (1998, p. 11).

VIRTUAL TEAM LEADER COMMUNICATION COMPETENCIES

"The only constant that correlates with success is over-the-top leadership" asserts Peters (1996). A virtual team leader must understand the challenges of communication, culture, geography, technology, and organization inherent in distributed teams (O'Hara-Devereaux & Johansen, 1994; Jude-York, Davis, & Wise, 2000). Likewise, virtual team members must clearly understand the role of the leader. A study by Thibodeaux and Yeatts (1991) found the responsibilities of virtual team leaders as understood by team members were spread widely across 46 different roles, with significant differences in rank order of importance.

Duarte and Snyder (1999) have identified seven communication competencies necessary for leading a virtual team effectively: coaching and managing performance without traditional forms of feedback, selecting and appropriately using electronic communication and collaboration technologies, leading in a cross-cultural environment, developing team members, building and maintaining trust, networking across hierarchical and organizational boundaries, and developing team processes. Variations on these specific competencies are found throughout the literature on virtual team leadership (e.g., Suchan & Hayzak, 2001).

Coaching and Managing Performance

"Successful virtual teams have a set of values or principles and operating agreements that carry team members and leaders through the rough spots" observe Henry and Hartzler (1998). It is critical the virtual team leader establish formal communication, organizational authority, and responsibility (Maruca, 1998). The virtual team needs a clear shared vision, mission and strategy based on the organization's values and principles. Objectives and goals need to be discussed, agreed upon, and committed to by all members of the virtual team (Solomon, 1998).

Virtual team leaders often act more as coaches than bosses. They lead through influence, not coercion. Virtual teams can be successful only if people manage the coordination involved in both membership and leadership (Lipnack & Stamps, 1997). It becomes critical, therefore, that clear communication channels exist so each member of the virtual team can be involved in making key decisions.

Communicating exactly where the team is headed as well as its scope and responsibilities provides the link for the virtual members to continue to follow their common agenda (Kostner, 1994). It also determines accountability; clear results-oriented performance measures must be in place. Methods need to be developed to review the virtual team's progress and results. Direct observation is not necessary to verify people are accomplishing their task (Gould, 1997). As Mayer (1998, p. 43) observes, "It is not how many hours, which hours, and from where the work was achieved, but if the deliverable was on time and if it met team and project expectations that are important." Communication and feedback from the virtual team leader to the team must be timely, succinct, and effective.

The leader does not always have all the facts that team members do, and vice versa. Virtual team leaders must be certain to communicate to the team members enough information to know what is expected of both themselves and the rest of the team (Kostner, 1994; Haywood, 1998). They must define the task, the expectations, and the environment so their virtual team members will have a clear understanding of how the work will be done and in what order. According to

Lipnack and Stamps, "A lack of clarity around goals, tasks, and leadership hobbles the team's performance" (1997, p. 145).

Selecting and Using Communication Technologies

Clear lines of communication are essential for the success of a virtual team. Without it, say Lipnack and Stamps (1997), mistakes, mistrust, unexpressed viewpoints, and unresolved conflicts all too easily introduce themselves. Virtual team leaders must "set the drumbeat of communications that the team can count on and come to expect" (O'Hara-Devereaux & Johansen, 1994, p. 147). They need to plan for the use of technology given the virtual team's task and type, the skills and backgrounds of the virtual team members, and the sophistication of the organization.

Different technologies facilitate different types of communication. There is no ideal set of technologies for all virtual teams (Duarte & Snyder, 1999). Communication can be either asynchronous, synchronous, or a combination of both. E-mail, voice mail, calendaring and scheduling systems, whiteboards, discussion/bulletin boards, chat rooms, group decision support systems or other types of groupware, knowledge management systems, Web sites, instant messaging, voice over IP, and file- and application-sharing, in addition to the telephone and fax machine, are standard technologies. The use of videoconferencing and virtual meeting technologies are becoming increasingly popular options. The newest development in communication technologies for virtual teams is peer-to-peer group collaboration systems (Steinfield, 2002). This technology combines several communication and coordination tools (such as e-mail, chat, shared whiteboard, etc.) into one single application.

It is up to the virtual team leader to decide which communication technology or technologies is right for the team and the task at hand. There are several factors the virtual team leader

must consider before making a choice (Duarte & Snyder, 1999):

- Social presence, the degree to which the technology facilitates a personal connection with others
- Information richness, the amount and variety of information flowing through a specific communication media
- Permanence, the degree to which the technology is capable of creating a historical record of team interactions or decisions
- Symbolic meaning, the context over and above the message that is implied by the technology
- Experience and familiarity with virtual operations
- Time constraints
- Organizational and functional cultures
- Access to technological training and support

Studies by Gould (1997) and Gross (2002) found that e-mail and the telephone are the primary communication technologies used by virtual teams. To function effectively, the principle means of communication within the virtual team, including the language, timing, leader and member accessibility, prioritization, and response rate needs to be established. Regardless of the technology used, virtual team leaders must ensure communication flows freely and frequently, and everything is completely understood by all the virtual team members.

Leading in a Cross-Cultural Environment

A virtual team leader needs to understand the cultural differences among virtual team members and use those differences to create an advantage. Different cultural groups require different styles of leadership. How assertively, aggressively, or directly a virtual team member may communicate is governed by cultural norms (O'Hara-Devereaux

& Johansen, 1994). Virtual team leaders must be aware that "a technology can bring out different reactions among participants with different cultural orientations" (Olaniran, 2004, p. 156). For instance, different cultures may be more or less inclined to provide feedback using e-mail. Cultural differences can easily create major misunderstandings within a virtual team.

The virtual team leader must develop a style that fits the mix of communication cultures the virtual team embodies, taking care not to elevate one culture over another. By paying attention to the five fundamental dimensions of culture—language, context, time, power/equality, and information flow (O'Hara-Devereaux & Johansen, 1994)—virtual team leaders can create ways of working and interacting that not only accommodate but also optimize cultural-related communication differences among the virtual team members.

Developing Team Members

Because virtual team members usually do not share a common physical work space, a virtual team leader must find a way to develop and maintain a sense of virtual team identity. Geography should not be a communication barrier; virtual team members should not feel a sense of "out of sight, out of mind" (Kostner, 1994). As O'Hara-Devereaux and Johansen observe:

> Distance teams often fall into the trap of having relationships built only between the leader and individual members. It is equally important for members to establish good working relations with one another. Without these relationships, distributed subteams may find they have no rapport without the trusted leader.

Strong symbols are needed to unite people across time and space. Virtual team leaders must promise as much communication access for their virtual team members as they would offer to colleagues located in the same building. If possible, the best thing a virtual team leader can do is to bring all members of the virtual team together face-to-face at the very beginning to learn more about each other professionally and personally. A short, informal videoconference or virtual meeting would also allow the virtual team to build rapport (1994, p. 147).

Research has shown there are very few teams that are 100% virtual (Gould, 1997). Often, however, a face-to-face meeting or a videoconference is not feasible. It is up to the virtual team leader to facilitate relationships normally created when a team communicates in a shared physical space. This can be accomplished in many different ways:

- Create a symbolic name for the team.
- Design t-shirts with a team name and logo.
- Designate a team historian.
- Create a Web site with the location, photograph, and personal information of each virtual team member.
- Create an "electronic water cooler" (Haywood, 1998, p. 36), a forum where virtual team members can chat, exchange information, or just keep in touch.

BUILDING AND MAINTAINING TRUST

One of the foundations for the success of a virtual team is to build trust. This requires a conscious and planned communication effort on the part of the virtual team leader, because the virtual team members do not operate in a traditional environment with opportunities to meet each other and develop a relationship. Every word, task, action, and initiative builds trust. The only real power and control a virtual team leader has is what the virtual team members exercise over themselves (Kostner, 1994).

The virtual team leader must ensure respect, fairness, and equality of opportunity for all the virtual team members at all times. This can be accomplished by (Kostner, 1994):

- Not favoring one remote site over another
- Getting everyone key information at the same time
- Providing an equal opportunity for input
- Weighing every idea against the vision/mission/task
- Not rejecting an idea outright
- Providing everyone a chance to "shine"
- Rewarding or recognizing contributions
- Socializing with all virtual team members
- Confronting non-performance

Networking Across Hierarchical and Organizational Boundaries

Because virtual teams are geographically dispersed, it is the virtual team leader's responsibility to establish critical communication links with team members, managers, customers, external audiences, and stakeholders. The reporting and administrative relationship between the virtual team and the organization must be clearly established (Townsend, DeMarie, & Hendrickson, 1998). The virtual team leader must effectively communicate to keep management apprised of the virtual team's activities and performance. Planning and creating networking opportunities for the virtual team is also a function of the virtual team leader.

Developing Team Processes

Virtual teams operate in an adaptive, volatile environment. Placing rigid controls and restrictions on the virtual team will destroy the team's ability to perform at its highest level. The virtual team leader must create a communication infrastructure appropriate to the organization, the task, and the team, which allows the virtual team to function to its full capacity.

Virtual team leaders also need to ensure the virtual team has some fun so that work is an enjoyable experience on a personal level. Communicating rewards and recognition, along with celebration of achievements, keep virtual team members connected and convey a sense of progress and team identity.

FUTURE TRENDS

There are four major trends with respect to virtual teams, virtual team leadership, and communication in virtual teams: globalization, the use of new information and communication technologies, the development of the information economy, and the dismantling of hierarchies (Castells, 2000).

As the utilization of virtual teams becomes the standard for conducting business, the makeup of those teams will become more diverse. Maznevski and Chudoba (2000) define global virtual teams as groups that are identified by their organizations(s) and members as a team, are responsible for making and/or implementing decisions important to the organization's global strategy, use technology-supported communication substantially more than face-to-face communication, and work and live in different countries. In addition, global virtual team members represent different cultures and speak different languages. Thus the role of the global virtual team leader in facilitating cross-cultural communication becomes even more critical.

The increasing sophistication of information and communication technologies will also impact communication in virtual teams. New communication technologies are becoming less text-based and more visual with the development of videoconferencing and the advancement of virtual reality technology. As a result, the challenges of communicating in the absence of nonverbal cues are reduced as virtual team members interact in real-time while actually looking at one another, albeit in a mediated fashion.

This is the era of the Information Age, where the exchange of information and services has overtaken that of physical goods. Information is an ideal product for trading virtually (Rasmussen & Wangel, 2007) and therefore is contributing to the global economy by creating a dynamic and fluid environment in which business is conducted.

The rise in the utilization of virtual teams is resulting in the dismantling of hierarchies, as organizations become more flexible and network-oriented and traditional forms of top-down leadership and communication are abandoned. Significant benefits in the areas of innovation, knowledge sharing and response time can be gained by creating infrastructures and cultures that enable virtual teams to communicate effectively (Rasmussen & Wangel, 2007).

CONCLUSION

Leading a virtual team can be much more demanding and difficult than leading a traditional team (Jude-York, Davis, & Wise, 2000). Gross (2002) suggests several strategies for virtual team leaders to help them communicate successfully:

- Communicate continuously
- Use active listening
- Keep communication simple and clear
- Use different technologies to advantage
- Build relationships and trust
- Show respect for other cultures
- Be sensitive to cultural differences
- Check for understanding
- Ask for clarification

The last few years of the twentieth century brought the world into virtual realms that forever changed the way people communicate, work, learn, govern, shop, and entertain themselves (Grenier & Metes, 1995; Norton & Smith, 1997). As the use of virtual teams becomes more and more pervasive, people need to learn to communicate successfully in a virtual environment. In fact, with the use of virtual teams becoming increasingly prevalent in the workforce, with rare exception all organizational teams are virtual to some extent (Griffith & Neale, 2001; Martins, Gilson, & Maynard, 2004).

In a world where time and distance is no longer a barrier, having strong leaders with exceptional communication skills is critical for the success of any virtual team. Huysman, Steinfield, Jang, David, Veld, Poot, and Mulder (2003) found that virtual teams evolve patterns of communication based on what communication technologies are used, how the virtual team used those communication technologies, and why the virtual team used those particular communication technologies. It is the responsibility of the virtual team leader to guide this "media-use," "habitual routine of media-use," and the "purpose and/or consequences of the media-use routine."

Bennis and Nanus believe "the key driver in the twenty-first century is likely to be the speed and turbulence of technological change" (1985, p. 5). New technologies enable leaders to communicate across vast global organizational structures (Sifonis & Goldberg, 1996; Abernathy, 1998). The increasing dominance of information and communication technology demands successful leaders understand the new world order (Liebig, 1994).

Today's new leaders are ethically sensitive, supporters of cultural diversity, consensus-oriented, intuitive, optimists, and global thinkers (Maynard & Mehrtens, 1993; Hickman, 1998). They are "great communicators and networkers... perpetual strategists, capable of leveraging information, knowledge and intelligence" to the organization's advantage (Tyson, 1997, p. 68). Leaders of virtual teams must know how to communicate in order to successfully navigate through today's virtual workforces, and they must also understand the new nature of business practices in the 21st century.

REFERENCES

Abernathy, D. (1998). Four pioneers reflect on leadership. *Training and Development, 52*(7), 38.

Bell, B., & Kozlowski, S. (2002). A typology of virtual teams: Implications for effective leadership. *Group & Organization Management, 27*(1), 14-49

Bennis, W., & Nanus, B. (1985). Toward the new millennium. In: G. Hickman (Ed.), *Leading organizations: Perspectives for a new era* (pp. 5-7). Thousand Oaks, CA: Sage Publications.

Benveniste, G. (1994). *The twenty-first century organization: Analyzing current trends – imagining the future.* San Francisco, CA: Jossey-Bass.

Burtha, M., & Connaughton, S. (2004). Learning the secrets of long-distance leadership: Eight principles to cultivate effective virtual teams. *KM Review, 7*(1), 24-27.

Cairncross, F. (1997). *The death of distance.* Boston, MA: Harvard Business School Press.

Castells, M. (2000). *The information age: Economy, society, and culture, Vol. 1, The rise of the network society.* Oxford: Blackwell.

Cramton, C. (1997). Information problems in dispersed teams. In *1997 Academy of Management Best Paper Proceedings.*

Creighton, J., & Adams, J. (1998). *CyberMeeting: How to link people and technology in your organization.* New York, NY: American Management Association.

Drucker, P. (1999). *Management challenges for the 21st century.* New York, NY: HarperBusiness.

Duarte, D., & Snyder, N. (1999). *Mastering virtual teams: Strategies, tools, and techniques that succeed.* San Francisco, CA: Jossey-Bass.

Dube, L., & Pare, G. (2001). Global virtual teams. *Communication of the ACM, 44*(12), 71-73.

Emelo, R., & Francis, L. (2002). Virtual team interaction. *T+D (Training and Development), 56*(10).

Gebhardt, L., & Meyers, R. (1995). Subgroup influence in decision making groups: Examining consistency from a communication perspective. *Small Group Research, 26*(2), 147-168.

George, G., & Sleeth, R. (2000). Leadership in computer-mediated communication: Implications and research directions. *Journal of Business and Psychology, 15*(2), 287-310.

Gerber, B. (1995). Virtual teams. *Training, 32*(4), 36-40.

Gibson, W. (1984). *Neuromancer.* New York, NY: Ace Books.

Gibson, C., & Cohen, S. (2003). *Virtual teams that work: Creating conditions for virtual team effectiveness.* San Francisco, CA: Jossey-Bass.

Gibson, C., & Vermeulen, F. (2003). A healthy divide: Subgroups as a stimulus for team learning behavior. *Administration Science Quarterly, 48*(2), 202-239.

Goodbody, J. (2005). Critical success factors for global virtual teams. *SCM, 9*(2), 18-21.

Gould, D. (1997). Leadership in virtual teams (Doctoral dissertation, Seattle University, 1997). *Dissertation Abstracts International, 59-07A,* 2602.

Grenier, R., & Metes, G. (1995). *Going virtual: Moving your organization into the 21st century.* Upper Saddle River, NJ: Prentice Hall.

Griffith, T., & Neale, M. (2001). Information processing in traditional, hybrid, and virtual teams: From nascent knowledge to transactive memory. *Research in Organizational Behavior, 23,* 379-421.

Gross, C. (2002). Managing communication within virtual intercultural teams. *Business Communication Quarterly, 65*(4), 22-38.

Harris, M. (1998). *Value leadership: Winning competitive advantage in the information age.* Milwaukee, WI: ASQ Quality Press.

Haywood, M. (1998). *Managing virtual teams: Practical techniques for high-technology project managers.* Boston, MA: Artech House.

Henry, J., & Hartzler, M. (1998). *Tools for virtual teams: A team fitness companion.* Milwaukee, WI: American Society for Quality Press.

Hickman, G. (1998). Leadership and the social imperative of organizations in the 21st century. In: G. Hickman (Ed.), *Leading organizations: Perspectives for a new era* (pp. 559-571). Thousand Oaks, CA: Sage Publications.

Huysman, M., Steinfield, C., Jang, C., David, K., Veld, M., Poot, J., & Mulder, I. (2003). Virtual teams and the appropriation of communication technology: Exploring the concept of media stickiness. *Computer Supported Cooperative Work, 12,* 411-436.

Jude-York, D., Davis, L., & Wise, S. (2000). *Virtual teaming: Breaking the boundaries of time and place.* Menlo Park, CA: Crisp Publications, Inc.

Kanawattanachai, P., & Yoo, Y. (2002). Dynamic nature of trust in virtual teams. *Journal of Strategic Information Systems, 11,* 187-213.

Kayworth, T., & Leidner, D. (2002). Leadership effectiveness in global virtual teams. *Journal of Management Information Systems, 18*(3), 7-40.

Kielson, D. (1996). Leadership: Creating a new reality. *The Journal of Leadership Studies, 3*(4), 104-116.

Kostner, J. (1994). *Virtual leadership: Secrets from the Round Table for the multi-site manager.* New York, NY: Warner Books.

Liebig, J. (1994). *Merchants of vision: People bringing new purposes and values to business.* San Francisco, CA: Berrett-Koehler.

Lipnack, J., & Stamps, J. (1997). *Virtual teams: Reaching across space, time, and organizations with technology.* New York, NY: John Wiley & Sons, Inc.

Lipnack, J., & Stamps, J. (1999). Virtual teams: The new way to work. *Strategy & Leadership, 27*(1), 14-20.

Lurey, J. (1998). A study of best practices in designing and supporting effective virtual teams (Doctoral dissertation, California School of Professional Psychology, Los Angeles, 1998).

Dissertation Abstracts International, 59-04B, 1897.

Martins, L., Gilson, L., & Maynard, M. (2004). Virtual teams: What do we know and where do we go from here?. *Journal of Management, 30*(6), 805-835.

Maruca, R. (1998). How do you manage an off-site team?. *Harvard Business Review, 76*(4), 22-35.

Mayer, M. (1998). *The virtual edge: Embracing technology for distributed project team success.* Newtown Square, PA: Project Management Institute Headquarters.

Maynard, H., & Mehrtens, S. (1993). *The fourth wave: Business in the 21st century.* San Francisco, CA: Berrett-Koehler Publishers.

Maznevski, M., & Chudoba, K. (2000). Bridging space over time: Global virtual team dynamics and effectiveness. *Organization Science, 11*(5), 473-492.

Melymuka, K. (1997). Virtual realities. *Computerworld, 31*(17), 70-72.

Monge, P. (1998). ICA presidential address: Communication structures and process in globalization. *Journal of Communication, 48*(4), 143-153.

Montgomery, J., & Clancy, T. (1994). The latest word from thoughtful executives. *Academy of Management Executive, 8*(2), 7-10.

Nemiro, J. (1998). Creativity in virtual teams (Doctoral dissertation, The Claremont Graduate University, 1998). *Dissertation Abstracts International, 58-12B,* 6854.

Norton, B., & Smith, C. (1997). *Understanding the virtual organization.* New York, NY: Barron's.

O'Hara-Devereaux, M., & Johansen, R. (1994). *Globalwork: Bridging distance, culture, and time.* San Francisco, CA: Jossey-Bass.

Olaniran, B. (2004). Computer-mediated communication in cross-cultural virtual teams. *International and Intercultural Communication, 27*, 142-166.

Panteli, N., & Davison, R. (2005). The role of subgroups in the communication pattern of global virtual teams. *IEEE Transactions of Professional Communication, 48*(2), 191-200.

Peters, T. (1996). Brave leadership. *Executive Excellence, 13*(1), 5-6.

Pliskin, N. (1998). Explaining the paradox of telecommuting. *Business Horizons, 41*(2), 73-78.

Rutkowski, A., Vogel, D., VanGenuchten, M., Bemelmans, T., & Favier, M. (2002). E-collaboration: The reality of virtuality. *IEEE Transactions on Professional Communication, 45*(4), 219-230.

Sifonis, J., & Goldberg, B. (1996). *Corporation on a tightrope: Balancing leadership, governance, and technology in an age of complexity.* New York, NY: Oxford University Press.

Smith, G. (1997). *The new leader: Bringing creativity and innovation to the workplace.* Delray Beach, FL: St. Lucie Press.

Solomon, C. (1998). Building teams across borders. *Workforce, 3*(6), 12-17.

Solomon, C. (2001). Managing virtual teams. *Workforce, 8*(6), 60-64.

Steinfield, C. (2002). Realizing the benefits of virtual teams. *Computer, 35*(3), 104-106.

Suchan, J., & Hayzak, G. (2001). The communication characteristics of virtual teams: A case study. *IEEE Transactions on Professional Communication, 44*(3), 174-186.

Tapscott, D. (1995). Leadership for the internetworked business. *Information Week, 55*(3), 65-72.

Tapscott, D. (1998). *Growing up digital.* New York, NY: McGraw-Hill.

Thibodeaux, M., & Yeatts, D. (1991). Leadership: The perceptions of leaders by followers in self-managed work teams. *Quarterly Journal of Ideology, 15*(3-4), 69-88.

Townsend, A., DeMarie, S., & Hendrickson, A. (1998). Virtual teams: Technology and the workplace of the future. *Academy of Management Executive, 12*(3), 17-29.

Tyson, K. (1997). *Competition in the 21st century.* Delray Beach, FL: St. Lucie Press.

Watson, R., Bostrom, R., & Dennis, A. (1994). Fragmentation to integration. In: P. Lloyd, (Ed.), *Groupware in the 21st century: Computer supported cooperative working toward the millennium* (pp. 28-39). Westport, CT: Praeger.

Webster's II new Riverside university dictionary. (1984). Boston, MA: Houghton Mifflin.

Wilson, S. (2003). Forming virtual teams. *Quality Progress, 36*(6), 36-41.

KEY TERMS

Communication: The exchange of ideas, messages, or information by speech signals, or writing.

Cyberspace: The notional environment in which communication and interaction over electronic networks occurs.

Leadership: Setting a direction for an organization; motivating and inspiring people; aligning people with an articulated vision; ability to effect real changes within an organization.

Virtual: An environment simulated by electronic networks for reasons of economics, convenience, or performance.

Virtual Team Leader: A person who innovates, focuses people, and inspires trust in an electronic environment where people are geographically dispersed.

Virtual Team: A group of geographically dispersed people who have common goals and communicate and interact in cyberspace.

Chapter V
Foundations and Applications of Intelligent Knowledge Exchange

S.J. Overbeek
e-Office B.V., The Netherlands

P. van Bommel
Radboud University Nijmegen, The Netherlands

H.A. Proper
Radboud University Nijmegen, The Netherlands

D.B.B. Rijsenbrij
Radboud University Nijmegen, The Netherlands

ABSTRACT

Exchange of knowledge is becoming increasingly important to modern organizations. In this chapter, it is explained what this elementary knowledge exchange consists of and how a virtual workplace can support knowledge exchange between workers. A scenario from the medical domain illustrates how physicians can improve their knowledge exchange by utilizing the virtual workplace models introduced. Better adaptation to the rapidly changing nature of providing healthcare is a desirable effect of improved knowledge exchange between physicians. Explicit models concerning possible physical, social and digital contexts of knowledge exchange are discussed, as well as models which depict how knowledge relatedness enables intelligent knowledge exchange. Researchers studying virtual workplace models for industry and academic purposes belong to the intended audience of this chapter. Administrators of public sector or other non-profit agencies who wish to incorporate virtual workplace models and methods into their daily operations can also benefit from the contents discussed.

INTRODUCTION

The importance of knowledge and in particular the dissemination of knowledge is becoming increasingly important for organizations. An example can be found in the medical domain, clearly illustrated by Frank (2005) in that today's physicians continue to witness significant change in the nature of healthcare delivery. Practice is changing daily, with literally thousands of medical journals documenting the evolving understanding of biological, social and clinical sciences. Patients are treated in more diversified settings and spend less time in hospitals. In this environment a physician requires to acquire more knowledge than ever before so that the needs of their patients can be met.

Both academia and industry gradually antici-pate on the aforementioned social developments by concentrating on the development of *virtual workplaces* so that knowledge dissemination improves. In this chapter, the general focus is on providing support by means of a virtual workplace so that knowledge exchange between workers improves. Before building such a virtual workplace, in-depth understanding of the support which a virtual workplace can deliver to improve knowledge exchange is necessary, together with comprehension of the reasons of that support. For this matter, it implies a clear understand-ing of knowledge exchange and an elaboration of current computer-based support to improve knowledge exchange.

To better understand knowledge exchange and how a virtual workplace can support that, several models explaining possible contexts of knowledge exchange are depicted. Furthermore, specific support situations are distinguished in which a worker requests assistance from the vir-tual workplace when exchanging knowledge. This chapter will make clear how a virtual workplace is able to facilitate knowledge-sharing using con-textual models and support mechanisms. First, the basics of knowledge exchange and examples of computer-based support for knowledge exchange are introduced. Next, knowledge exchange is de-scribed from a physical, social and digital context. A fundamental model of knowledge exchange is then elaborated, followed by more sophisticated models for improving knowledge exchange. Fur-thermore, future research topics are discussed and the chapter is concluded.

UNDERSTANDING INTELLIGENT KNOWLEDGE EXCHANGE

To be able to better determine what kind of computer-based support is desired and feasible to improve knowledge exchange between workers, a better understanding of knowledge, knowledge exchange, and already available computer-based support for knowledge exchange is called for. Knowledge exchange occurs during organiza-tional knowledge transformation processes and is part of organizational knowledge lifecycles. Both concepts will be discussed in this section to explore various different perspectives on knowledge trans-formation processes and knowledge lifecycles (each possibly taking a specific understanding of what knowledge is as a starting point). We will also stipulate our essential view on knowledge exchange and discuss how this view materializes in each of the discussed transformation processes and lifecycles. First, the basics of knowledge and knowledge exchange are primarily discussed. Readers considering themselves as familiar with these basics, which mainly includes a discussion of common definitions, may skip these sections and may continue reading from the section about software agents onwards.

Definitions of Knowledge

In the literature, many different definitions of knowledge pass in review. Dependent of which interpretation one chooses, our knowledge exchange definition can be specialized using a specific definition of knowledge. Some of the definitions found in the literature are discussed in this section to better understand the notion of knowledge. In many definitions a distinction is made between tacit (or nowadays often denoted as implicit) knowledge and explicit knowledge. There are also definitions which specifically focus on the tacit/implicit part or the explicit part.

Polanyi (1966) is recognized as the one who introduced the term tacit knowledge as a specific form of knowledge. He defined tacit knowledge as complex abstract knowledge that is totally individual, hard to formalize and to communicate, and introspective in nature. However, communication is a necessary prerequisite in order to exchange knowledge and therefore tacit knowledge as defined by Polanyi is also difficult to exchange with another worker. The 'knowledge resource' is often the human brain. So in order to exchange a tacit knowledge item, it must first be distilled from the brain and formulated in a way so that it is suitable for exchange. Dienes and Perner (1999) state that implicit knowledge comprises aspects of knowledge that are not differentiated or articulated. "For example the sentence 'The king is bald' ... presupposes or implicitly represents that there exists a king" (Pinku & Tzelgov, 2005, p. 2). Perhaps the essence of what is meant in literature by tacit and implicit knowledge is concealed in the sentence: 'knowing without telling'.

Explicit knowledge is different in nature than tacit or implicit knowledge. According to Dienes and Perner (1999) explicit knowledge is knowledge which is represented by means of an internal state whose function is to indicate the knowledge. For example the sentence 'The rabbit is brown' explicitly denotes that the rabbit is brown. Nonaka and Takeuchi (1995) also consider tacit and explicit knowledge as two dimensions of knowledge in that tacit knowledge can be characterized by subjectivity, direct personal experience, qualitative nature, simultaneous processing and a practical base. Their definition of explicit knowledge comprises terms as objectivity, rationality, sequential processing and 'quantitative in nature'. Due to its characteristics, explicit knowledge is easier to communicate and hence easier to exchange.

There are obviously many more definitions to discuss in this section, but those already mentioned represent the more fundamental interpretations of knowledge which can be found in the literature. Other definitions can be found in, for example, Barwise (1989) and Siemieniuch and Sinclair (1999).

A Definition of Knowledge Exchange

There is literature discussing the topic of 'knowledge exchange' on itself and also specific ideas to provide computer-based support for knowledge exchange. Kuznets (1962) mentions that knowledge exchange flourishes in dense intellectual settings, and the more intellectual contact flourishes, the more knowledge is added to resources of knowledge. The research of Kuznets focuses on intellectual capital in large cities, while the research discussed in this chapter focuses specifically on exchange of knowledge between workers in an organizational setting.

Heterogeneity (in terms of different types of knowledge) is considered as an important factor in successfully exchanging knowledge (Berliant, Reed, & Wang, 2006). Less knowledge exchange occurs when individuals' types of knowledge are too diverse and when individuals' types are too similar. To determine the efficacy of knowledge exchange, a function is introduced in the research of Berliant, Reed and Wang to measure the ideal 'knowledge distance' between two individuals. Furthermore, their research specifically focuses on the relationships between knowledge exchange and population agglomeration. Cowan, Jonard and Özman (2004) associated knowledge exchange with the arousal of innovation in a community of actors, based on the idea that innovation is largely a result of knowledge exchange among a small group of agents. Cowan, Jonard and Özman specifically took the tacitness of knowledge into account in assessing innovative potential, therefore they indirectly adopted the definition of Polanyi (1966). Our definition is more generic with respect to the concept of knowledge.

In order to define a general view on knowledge exchange, which includes 'software agents' as part of the virtual workplace, we propose that knowledge flows from:

- A worker to another worker
- A software agent to another software agent

- A software agent to another worker
- A worker to another software agent

The term 'software agent' is further explained in the upcoming section. It is assumed that knowledge K can be retrieved from a knowledge resource KR and that knowledge can flow by means of a communication device and a communication medium. A knowledge resource is an entity from which knowledge can be subtracted, for example, a human brain or any suitable hardware device. A communication device is an entity which is necessary to initiate a knowledge exchange event and eventually knowledge can flow by means of a communication medium. The relevant knowledge resources for a knowledge item can be depicted as $R{:}K \to \wp (KR)$, so that $R(x) = \{y_1, y_2\}$ is interpreted as: Knowledge item x is retrieved from knowledge resource y_1 as well as from knowledge resource y_2. Furthermore, it is assumed that a certain worker has a need for knowledge to benefit from a knowledge exchange event. That need for knowledge is influenced by what the worker already has retrieved from another knowledge resource. Weide and Bommel (2006) have already introduced the following function to measure one's need for knowledge: $N{:} \ \wp (K) \times K \mapsto [0,1]$. $N(S,x)$ is interpreted as the residual need for knowledge item x after the set S has been presented to the worker, where $S \subseteq K$. So knowledge exchange involves the broadcasting of knowledge items between workers, or between a worker and a software agent and vice versa, with as specific goal to reduce the need for knowledge of a worker. No more knowledge exchange is necessary if $N(S,x) = 0$. This definition of knowledge exchange is constructed in such a way that at least every one of the definitions of knowledge as mentioned already can be used for the notion of 'knowledge'. The knowledge input and output that a worker consumes respectively generates in the process of knowledge exchange can be depicted as $i,o : T \to (W \to \wp (K)$, where T is the set of worker states (which differ from each other over time) and W is the set of workers. A *worker state* is necessary to keep track of what a worker already has produced in terms of knowledge items and what a worker already has received in terms of knowledge items. The function $i(t_1, w_1)$ for instance determines the input in terms of knowledge items at state one of worker w_1. However, the state aspect will not be relevant for the more basic models of knowledge exchange until support relatedness is introduced later on. For notation simplicity, knowledge input is indicated by the function $i_1(w_1)$ if the worker state is relevant (indicating state one of worker w_1) and the notation $i_1(w_1)$ is used if worker states are not relevant. The character i is replaced by the character o if knowledge output is concerned.

The Term 'Software Agent'

The term 'software agent' has been postulated in our view on knowledge exchange. According to Wooldridge and Jennings (1995), a software agent is an encapsulated computer system that is situated in some environment and that is capable of flexible, autonomous action in that environment. As can be distilled from this definition, software agents are autonomous, which means that they can function on their own, without requiring human support. It has the control over its own actions and internal state and it can decide whether or not to perform a requested action.

Software agents are designed to fulfil a specific purpose and have particular goals to achieve, exhibiting flexible and pro-active behaviour. Software agents are also often capable of 'social' behaviour because they can communicate and cooperate with each other. Eventually, for software agents to be highly intelligent, it is desirable that they are able to learn as they react and interact with their external environment. In this case, a software agent should be able to exchange knowledge with the worker if that is the worker's wish and it should understand the specific need for knowledge which a worker has. A collection of software agents which improve knowledge exchange are part of the virtual workplace we focus on and can assist in improving knowledge exchange between workers. Software agents are further mentioned in this chapter later on.

Knowledge Transformation Processes & Knowledge Lifecycles

Knowledge exchange is part of organizational knowledge transformation processes and organizational knowledge lifecycles. There are many different perspectives on knowledge transformation processes and lifecycles, each taking a specific understanding of what knowledge is as a starting point. This section takes up on the materialization of our essential view on knowledge exchange in each of the discussed knowledge transformation processes and lifecycles.

The research of Siemieniuch and Sinclair (1999) includes such a knowledge lifecycle in which our view on knowledge exchange can be materialized. According to Siemieniuch and Sinclair, knowledge is not uniform and it has a *lifecycle* in a competitive environment. "In other words, if a company is to remain competitive, it must address the issues of new knowledge generation, its propagation across the organization, and its subsequent retirement" (Siemieniuch & Sinclair, 1999, p. 1). A worker's specific need for knowledge, as mentioned before, can cause new knowledge generation to meet that worker's demands. Knowledge input and output is necessary to propagate knowledge across the organization. If the need for a knowledge item x has reached zero and if the need for that knowledge item remains zero long enough, then the knowledge item will eventually deteriorate. Siemieniuch and Sinclair discuss that knowledge will age as the context changes, and humans will be intrinsic components in all processes involving the creation, utilization and retirement of knowledge.

The knowledge conversion model of Nonaka and Takeuchi (1995) is one of the most well-known

models describing knowledge transformation processes within organizations. A knowledge transformation process involves all events which transform a certain knowledge type into another knowledge type, for example, the events to transform implicit knowledge to explicit knowledge which is the case in the model of Nonaka and Takeuchi. Generation and consumption of knowledge is required to distil the knowledge exchange situations that cause a conversion from implicit knowledge to explicit knowledge or vice versa, which are all classified in the model of Nonaka and Takeuchi. To illustrate one of those conversions, assume that a worker pair w_1, w_2 exchange knowledge and that the output of worker w_1 contains explicit knowledge and the input of worker w_2 contains implicit knowledge. This specific transformation from explicit to implicit is classified as 'internalization' by Nonaka and Takeuchi. Internalization is the process of embodying explicit knowledge into a worker's implicit knowledge bases in the form of shared mental models or technical know-how.

Nonaka and Takeuchi (1995) focus on implicit and explicit knowledge when knowledge transformation processes are concerned. Strambach (2001), however, focuses on knowledge transformation processes between organizations by means of knowledge-intensive business services so that new knowledge is acquired by interactions between organizations. An organization on itself can codify or recombine newly gained knowledge and subsequently that recombined knowledge can be disseminated again among client firms causing the birth of new knowledge within the present client firms. In Strambach's model, knowledge exchange takes place on an organizational level, so when a certain organization x has a need for knowledge it can gain new knowledge by exchanging knowledge with client firms. After this inter-organizational exchange process, organization x then exchanges knowledge internally so that the acquired knowledge is codified or recombined. When applying our view on knowledge exchange on Strambach's model, the function $N(S,x)$ expresses the residual need of an organization for knowledge item x after the set S has been presented to the organization due to previous interactions with other organizations. In this case the set S represents the knowledge profile of an organization as a whole.

We have chosen to discuss some examples to illustrate how our view on knowledge exchange materializes in certain knowledge transformation processes and lifecycles. Therefore the list of models discussed in this section is obviously not a complete overview of all existing models.

Examples of Current Computer-Based Support of Knowledge Exchange in the Virtual Workplace

Internet, of course, has allowed the spread of knowledge without frontiers, but intelligent (Web-based) software agents are also utilized when supporting knowledge exchange from a virtual workplace perspective. The research carried out by Li, Montazemi and Yuan (2006) shows an example of how software agents may assist users in the process of searching for acquaintances on the Internet for exchanging musical knowledge. They have developed a Web-based system which allowed users to perform four major tasks: entering music attribute preferences; selecting favourite music at a music site and creating a music collection; communicating with other subjects and manually find buddies; and evaluating the quality of manual- and agent-found buddies. This test system consisted of three major components: a music browser, a message board, and an agent-based buddy-finding system. The agent-based buddy-finding system decreased the burden of searching for the right acquaintances in order to exchange relevant and useful musical knowledge. Time which would be lost in a manual search process for acquaintances can now be used for other purposes and exchange of musical knowledge can be optimized due to the automatically

discovered acquaintances. The focus area 'musical knowledge' does not relate with our research on improving knowledge exchange within the virtual workplace, but the proposed use of agent technology certainly does.

Groth (2004) has proposed a technological framework for supporting knowledge exchange in organizations. The framework depicts that communication (a prerequisite to exchange knowledge), awareness (of others' activities and availability), and information management (how to structure and reuse already existing information) are important aspects to consider when providing computer-based support for knowledge exchange.

Several software applications make use of the technological framework as proposed by Groth (2004) already, however, these applications are not based on agent technology. One of those applications is called 'Mobile Elvin', which involves communication that is mainly synchronous (between desktop and mobile platforms) and from one person to a group of persons. With Mobile Elvin, it is possible to not only pose a question to only one person, but also to a specific group of people within the organization. Depending on the communication device, the worker receives the message on a mobile device or a desktop. Asynchronous communication is supported by means of e-mail applications.

Ordinary *discussion forums* and *news groups* are two successful examples of software applications used for knowledge exchange to improve the quality of learning in organizations. However, these relatively simple mechanisms of cooperation present two main problems (López, Núñez, Rodríguez, & Rubio, 2004): the stimulation to exchange knowledge by answering questions of other users can be weak and professionals may lose their motivation to help others as they can get saturated by a huge amount of questions. The 'market-oriented methodology for discussion forums' by López, Núñez, Rodríguez and Rubio provides a possible solution for these problems.

First, once a user has shown that he adds valuable knowledge to the discussion forum, future questions are shown to more experienced professionals and hence it may enhance the probability that the question will be answered. Second, once a certain user has provided significant valuable additions to the discussion forum, the more easy questions will not be shown anymore to that user. This way, the user will be able to save some effort for those questions that really require the skills of the user. A discussion forum based on the 'market-oriented methodology' might improve knowledge exchange within organizations significantly.

The software applications discussed here show which possibilities are offered to enable intelligent knowledge exchange in a virtual workplace. However, the more fundamental concepts which play a part in both knowledge exchange with or without computer-based support need to be understood. Therefore, possible *contexts* of knowledge exchange are studied in the following section.

KNOWLEDGE EXCHANGE IN CONTEXT

Knowledge exchange will take place in specific contexts. If we expect a virtual workplace to support knowledge exchange, we need to understand these contexts better. The context in which knowledge exchange can take place is regarded from a physical, social and digital perspective. The contexts discussed contain possible concepts which are part of the knowledge exchange situations intended, supported by the definition provided earlier in this chapter. Specific instantiations of the models discussed below are possible when analyzing knowledge exchange situations in practice.

Using Object Role Modelling (ORM) to Model the Knowledge Exchange Contexts

We have chosen to model possible knowledge exchange contexts by means of the modelling language 'Object Role Modelling' or 'ORM' (for details on ORM see e.g., Halpin (2001)). An important role of the conceptual models depicted in the upcoming three sections is to provide a common understanding of the *Universe of Discourse* involved. A Universe of Discourse covers informational aspects of the contexts, while the technical computerized aspects are left out of scope. Thus, the conceptual models introduced in this section cover possible informational aspects when the contexts of knowledge exchange are concerned. It is not our intention to provide a complete representation of knowledge exchange in all its possible contexts (it is assumed that this is not a realistic goal), but to provide more insight in the proposed contexts instead. For clarity, the worker has been positioned within all three contexts.

Knowledge Exchange in its Physical Context

Physical context refers to context about physical properties of knowledge exchange, as can be depicted in Figure 1. At first, a worker requires a communication device to initiate knowledge exchange. A communication device in a physical context can consist of the human vocal cords which can generate verbal signals, but also the head (including eyes and ears) or limbs function as a communication device to communicate non-verbal signals. To exchange knowledge by using a communication device, a transportation medium is required. In case of non-electronic knowledge exchange the air (for transporting vocal sounds) functions as the communication medium. In case of electronic knowledge exchange the hardware

Figure 1. ORM-model of knowledge exchange in its physical context

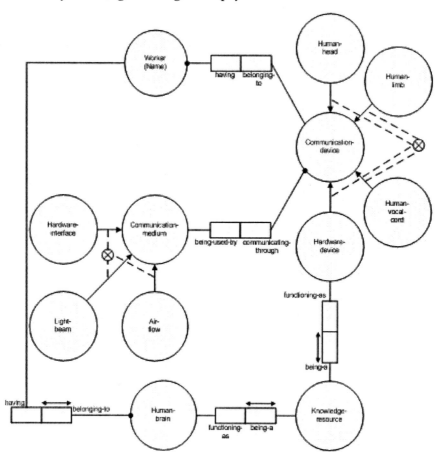

interface serves as the communication medium, at least from a physical point of view. The knowledge resources, such as a hardware device or a human brain, are part of a physical context of knowledge exchange.

Now that a possible physical context has been modelled in Figure 1, it is possible to articulate about the so-called *deep structure sentences* of the ORM-model so that this context can be better understood in practice. Deep structure sentences can be interpreted uniquely if each valid combination **Object-Name Role-Name Object-Name** has a unique interpretation in the information structure. This is called the *Role Identification Rule* or also referred to as a (linear) path-expression. Complex operations on such sentences may reveal parts of the information structure popu-

lation one is interested in. Suppose that we are interested in the workers who communicate at least with worker 'Galileo' through the air using their voice. The following operation is necessary to retrieve the desired results: **Worker having Human-vocal-cord communicating-through Air-flow THAT INCLUDES ALL Air-flow being-used-by Human-vocal-cord belonging to Worker: "Galileo".** The results of this query may be interesting for analyzing the physical communication lines in an organization. By executing a collection of operations certain knowledge about a physical context of knowledge exchange can be gained, dependent of how the ORM-model is populated. This *Role Identification Rule* exercise at least reveals the following aspects in a physical context of knowledge exchange:

Figure 2. ORM-model of knowledge exchange in its social context

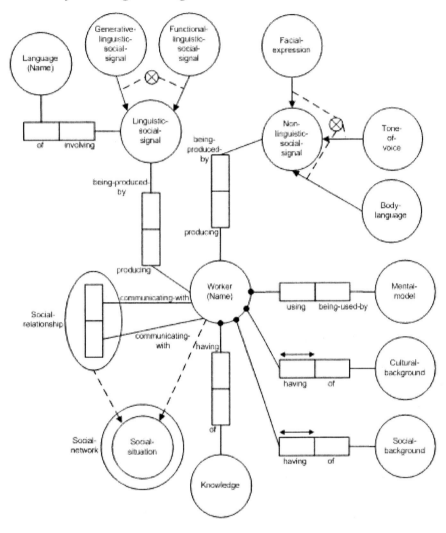

1. Specific physical communication media exist which are used as an interface between workers and physical communication devices.
2. Physical knowledge resources are human brains and hardware devices, which are part of workers respectively used by workers.

Knowledge Exchange in its Social Context

Figure 2 depicts knowledge exchange and the possible objects which play a role in the social context of knowledge exchange. Social context is based

on membership in communities and focuses on the relationships of a worker with others, that is, the social network of a worker (Klein & Giese, 2005). A social situation consists of individual workers on the one hand and social relationships (who communicates with whom) on the other hand. The social network as depicted in Figure 2 consists of the social relationships between groups of workers along with the individual workers involved. In a social context, non-linguistic social signals and linguistic social signals play a role in the knowledge exchange process. Non-linguistic social signals consist of body language, facial expression and tone of voice (Pentland, 2004).

Linguistic social signals have two perspectives: *generative linguistics*, also known as Chomskian linguistics and *functional linguistics*. Research on generative linguistics focuses on the structure of language forms as an isolated topic and functional linguistics aims at describing structural properties of language (both form and meaning) in relation to their function in communication.

Social products are created, institutionalized and made into tradition, into mainstream mental models, by workers in the societies in which they emerge. Mental models are small-scale psychological representations of real, hypothetical or imaginary situations (Craik, 1943). Another aspect in a possible social context of knowledge exchange concerns the different cultural or social backgrounds workers might have, which influences the knowledge a worker possesses.

An interesting operation on the information structure of Figure 2 is to gather the workers who communicate with workers who have at least the knowledge of worker 'Galileo': **Worker communicating-with Worker having Knowledge THAT INCLUDES ALL Knowledge of Worker: "Galileo"**. This is a desirable situation if a certain worker wishes to acquire knowledge which can be provided by at least the worker 'Galileo'. Suppose that a virtual workplace interprets the results of the latter query, it can assist the worker in finding the right person to exchange knowledge with. To provide the worker discussed here with appropriate knowledge, possible workers who possess interesting knowledge must have a knowledge profile which equals the knowledge profile of worker 'Galileo'. So in terms of the function $N(S,x)$ as introduced earlier, the knowledge profile G of worker 'Galileo' must be a subset of a certain knowledge profile S, or formally: $G \subseteq S$. The set G can be interpreted as the personal knowledge of the worker 'Galileo'

(sometimes also called a user profile) during a knowledge exchange session. The set G of already presented knowledge then acts as a *mini-profile* of worker 'Galileo' (Weide & Bommel, 2006). Now several aspects of the proposed social context of knowledge exchange can be determined:

1. A worker possesses specific social properties (knowledge, mental models, a cultural background and a social background).
2. A worker communicates with other workers by producing (non-)linguistic social signals and a social network is formed.

Knowledge Exchange in its Digital Context

Figure 3 shows a possible digital context of knowledge exchange, in which software agents play an important role. A software agent (or agent for short) interacts with other agents or with other workers through software interfaces. When an agent interacts with another agent, an agent relationship is formed. A collection of agents who interact with each other is therefore denoted as an 'agency'. A software agent can make use of a data store for retrieval and storage functions. A data store and a software agent can also function as a knowledge resource if they contain knowledge at a certain moment in time.

An interesting operation on the information structure of Figure 3 is expressed by the following sentence: **Worker interacting-with Software-interface MATCHING ALL Software-interface being-used-by Software-agent: "Agent n"**. This operation leads to the workers who interact with *exactly* the same software interfaces as 'agent n'. Thus, the query returns the workers who communicate with 'agent n', which might be interesting if one wishes to know with whom 'agent n' exchanges knowledge.

Figure 3. ORM-model of knowledge exchange in its digital context

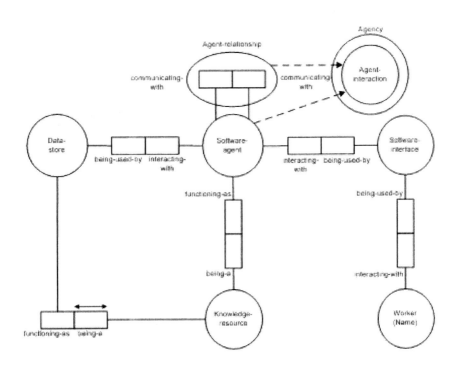

A FUNDAMENTAL MODEL OF KNOWLEDGE EXCHANGE

After discussing possible contexts in which knowledge exchange takes place, a fundamental model for knowledge exchange will be introduced in this section. This fundamental model consists of three parts: basic knowledge exchange, double party knowledge exchange and an overall framework of knowledge exchange.

Basic Knowledge Exchange

Basic knowledge exchange can be considered as knowledge that is exchanged between a worker pair $w_1, w_2 \in W$ using an intervening knowledge set K. We have mentioned that the knowledge input and output consumed respectively generated by a worker during the process of knowledge exchange can be depicted as $i,o : T \rightarrow (W \rightarrow \wp(K))$. For example, the function $o(w_2)$ depicts the output (in terms of knowledge) of worker w_2. A worker's

received respectively broadcasted knowledge items may overlap, which happens if knowledge is exchanged between a worker pair w_1 and w_2. Knowledge overlap may occur on four different occasions:

1. $i(w_1) \cap i(w_2) \neq \varnothing$
2. $i(w_1) \cap o(w_2) \neq \varnothing$
3. $o(w_1) \cap i(w_2) \neq \varnothing$
4. $o(w_1) \cap o(w_2) \neq \varnothing$

However, the intersection of knowledge items which a worker w exchanges only with himself (such that no new knowledge is gained) is considered as an *empty set*. Formally, this can be denoted as: $\forall_{w \in W} [i(w) \cap o(w) = \varnothing]$. These intersections can be left out of consideration.

Double Party Knowledge Exchange via Agents

The above example involved the knowledge exchange between a worker pair. However, it is less trivial to introduce an additional set of *agents* which also interacts with a knowledge set K. To understand how many forms of knowledge exchange are possible if a virtual workplace is used, consider A as a virtual workplace consisting of agents, where an agent $a \in A$ and $A \neq W$. The introduction of a virtual workplace creates a double party model of knowledge exchange, instead of a single party model as was the case with a worker pair interacting with a knowledge set. Apart from the four elementary forms of knowledge exchange as depicted above, there are four additional forms of knowledge exchange between a worker $w \in W$ and an agent $a \in A$ when using a knowledge set K:

1. $i(w) \cap i(a) \neq \varnothing$
2. $i(w) \cap o(a) \neq \varnothing$
3. $o(w) \cap i(a) \neq \varnothing$
4. $o(w) \cap o(a) \neq \varnothing$

An Overall Framework of Knowledge Exchange

In practice, a worker shall deliver knowledge input and output, but agents which are part of the virtual workplace of a worker shall also deliver knowledge input and output. Besides the worker and its virtual workplace, the *external environment* will also provide input and output. In the remainder of this chapter, the focus is on knowledge exchange in which a worker and a virtual workplace are involved. Possible physical, social and digital contexts such as those mentioned before involve objects which are part of the external environment. As a result, it can be concluded that an overall framework of knowledge exchange involves *three parties*.

ENABLING INTELLIGENT KNOWLEDGE EXCHANGE

We have discussed overlap of knowledge items in the process of knowledge exchange. In this section, we will elaborate on that concept and several models for enabling intelligent knowledge exchange are introduced. In this section, input and output relatedness, and *1-*, *2-* and *k*-support relatedness between knowledge items in the process of knowledge exchange are discussed. The models introduced in this section are illustrated with cases from the medical domain.

Input and Output Relatedness

Firstly, the input of a worker w_1 and the input of a worker w_2 may be *input related*. This situation is represented by $i(w_1) \cap i(w_2) \neq \varnothing$. To actually measure the similarities between received knowledge items of workers, the fuzzy logic approach of Jaccard's similarity coefficient can be introduced (Weide & Bommel, 2006). This coefficient normalizes intersection $i(w_1) \cap i(w_2) \neq \varnothing$ with the corresponding union in case both $i(w_1)$ and $i(w_2)$ are non-empty (see Box 1).

The fuzzy logic Jaccard's similarity coefficient expresses the degree in which knowledge items s in $i(w_1)$ and knowledge items t in $i(w_2)$ are similar on a [0, 1] scale. Overlap between output-related knowledge items can also be measured equally. If either $i(w_1)$ or $i(w_2)$ is empty, we have **Jacc** $(i(w_1), i(w_2) = 0$. Finally, **Jacc** $(\varnothing, \varnothing) = 1$. Thus, two possible situations of related knowledge items can be discerned during the process of knowledge exchange: Input-related knowledge

Box 1.

$$\mathbf{Jacc}\ (i(w_1), i(w_2)) = \frac{|i(w_1) \cap i(w_2)|}{|i(w_1) \cup i(w_2)|} = \frac{\Sigma_i \min(s_i, t_i)}{\Sigma_i \max(s_i, t_i)}$$

Figure 4. Input- and output-related knowledge

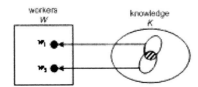
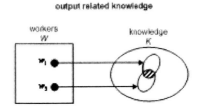

items and output-related knowledge items, as is depicted in Figure 4.

To illustrate the input and output relatedness as shown in Figure 4, suppose that worker w_1 and w_2 are physicians and that worker w_1 is a radiologist and worker w_2 is an assistant radiologist. Assume that the radiologist (worker w_1) shows an x-ray of a tuberculosis patient's lungs to the assistant radiologist (worker w_2). The radiologist asks if the assistant can localize and indicate tuberculosis symptoms on the x-ray and thus he generates knowledge output denoted as $o(w_1)$. Worker w_2 replies with the following output $o(w_2)$: 'Enlarged lymph nodes present in the bottom right of the x-ray indicating possible tuberculosis'. Now assume that this knowledge was not part of the knowledge profile of the radiologist and that the assistant's answer reduces his need for knowledge concerning the x-ray. In this case, we can speak of 'output-related knowledge' between the worker pair, because the assistant produces output which has strong overlap with the output of the radiologist, such that **Jacc** $(i(w_1), i(w_2)) > 0$. A similar example can be given for input relatedness, which is considered trivial.

If virtual workplaces keep track of the input and output relatedness between workers, heuristic patterns of overlap between knowledge profiles of workers can be formed over time. This insight in the knowledge profiles of workers can eventually improve knowledge exchange between them.

Support Relatedness

Besides input and output relatedness between knowledge items, *1*-support relatedness between knowledge items can now be introduced. In a *1*-support-related situation, a virtual workplace supports a worker by receiving input from the worker and then uses that input to deliver relevant support for the worker. Worker states and agent states are also introduced at this point to keep track of a worker's input and output and an agent's input and output. The *1*-support situation includes the functions $o_1(w) \cap i_1(a) \neq \varnothing$ and $o_2(a) \cap i_2(w) \neq \varnothing$. Considering the function $N : \wp(K) \times K \mapsto [0,1]$, the initial need for support at the start of a *1*-support situation by a worker is denoted as $N(\varnothing, i(w))$, where $i(w)$ is the input a worker receives from the virtual workplace. The input which worker w receives as a consequence of output $o_2(a)$ in terms of knowledge items is denoted as $i_2(w)$. This input should contain additional knowledge compared to the knowledge that a worker had at the start of a *1*-support situation, which is expressed by the following function:

$$X \subseteq Y \Rightarrow N(X, i_2(w)) \geq N(Y, i_2(w))$$

Here, X is the knowledge profile of worker w before receiving support from the virtual workplace and Y is the knowledge profile of worker w after receiving support from the virtual workplace. To illustrate a *1*-support situation in the medical domain, suppose that worker w is still the radiologist. At worker state one, the radiologist would like to know which people within his social network have knowledge about 'tuberculosis symptoms on an x-ray of human lungs', which is expressed by $o_1(w)$. The request for knowledge is interpreted by the radiologist's virtual workplace which is denoted as $i_1(a)$. Based on a match between the input $i_1(a)$ and the knowledge profiles which the radiologist's virtual workplace possesses, a selection of profiles are sent (depicted as $o_2(a)$) and eventually absorbed by the radiologist (depicted as $i_2(w)$).

If $N(Y,i_2(w) > 0$, then a *2*-support situation might be desirable. A *2*-support situation, as depicted in Figure 5, complements a *1*-support situation with additional functions $o_3(w) \cap i_3(a) \neq \varnothing$ and $o_4(a) \cap i_4(w) \neq \varnothing$.

Assume the set Z depicts the knowledge which a worker possesses after a *2*-support situation has occurred. To illustrate a *2*-support situation in the case of the radiologist mentioned in the *1*-support situation, assume that the selection of profiles which were sent to the radiologist earlier do not satisfy his need for knowledge. Therefore, he would like to retrieve an electronic handbook on the tuberculosis topic and broadcasts this request which is expressed by $o_3(w)$. The virtual workplace utilizes an agent to scan all available knowledge

resources (including the Internet of course) so that the best suitable handbook on the requested topic can be retrieved. Once an electronic handbook has been retrieved, it is broadcasted to the radiologist (depicted by $o_4(a)$) who receives it (depicted by $i_4(w)$). Eventually, this ends the *2*-support situation if the radiologist is satisfied with the result.

If $N(Z,i_4(w) > 0$, then a *k*-support situation might be desirable. A *k*-support situation simply continues the cycle of providing support to a worker after a *2*-support situation has not resolved certain need for knowledge of a worker. In terms of support relatedness, this can be depicted as:

1. $o_5(w) \cap i_5(a) \neq \varnothing$
2. $o_6(a) \cap i_6(w) \neq \varnothing$
3. ...

If a worker has no more need for knowledge, then the possible *1*-, *2*- and *k*-support situations end.

FUTURE RESEARCH

Verification and validation of the models (which also expands current theory) for intelligent knowledge exchange discussed so far is one of the main challenges of future research. At this stage in the research, a case within the medical domain is sketched to illustrate how a virtual workplace can improve knowledge exchange between physicians based on the theoretical models. The models mentioned earlier are focused on understanding and enabling intelligent knowledge exchange between workers by means of a virtual workplace. There are no models discussed which propose how a virtual workplace can be implemented or how a virtual workplace should be implemented specifically for a certain community of workers. Further research is needed to clarify those issues.

We have chosen to study a community of physicians in order to verify and also validate the models based on their specific needs for better

Figure 5. 2-Support relatedness

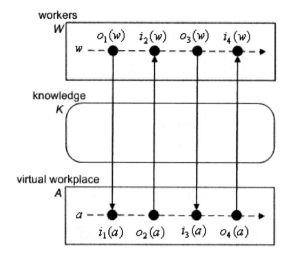

knowledge exchange. Other community studies are planned in the future to find similarities in verifying and validating the models within different communities of workers. Analysis of those similarities may yield reusable parts of the theoretical models which can be used to improve knowledge exchange within a community of workers in general. A collection of those reusable parts may result in a more abstract model for enabling intelligent knowledge exchange for workers in general. Deploying virtual workplaces is then of course proposed as a solution for improving knowledge exchange. The actual development of a possible prototype of an agent-based virtual workplace which enables intelligent knowledge exchange for physicians can be part of the research in the future.

CONCLUSION

An approach to enable intelligent knowledge exchange between workers by means of an agent-based virtual workplace has been elaborated. The approach has been illustrated throughout the chapter by a case from the medical domain. Contemporary physicians witness significant change in the nature of healthcare delivery and the necessity for them to process and disseminate knowledge only increases. After reflecting on the concept of knowledge, a fundamental view on knowledge exchange is elaborated.

Our view is aimed at decreasing a worker's need for knowledge as much as possible and improving the flow of knowledge between workers. It is made clear how the proposed view on knowledge exchange materializes in organizational knowledge transformation processes and organizational knowledge lifecycles. To understand what comprises knowledge exchange in general, insight in possible contexts of knowledge exchange is acquired by introducing several Object Role Modelling (ORM) models. Furthermore, additional theory is introduced to provide a foundation for

the support a virtual workplace can deliver for a worker when exchanging knowledge. A practical case shows how a virtual workplace can provide support for a radiologist's knowledge exchange problems in practice. In this case, the radiologist requires knowledge about tuberculosis symptoms.

Further research is necessary to verify and validate the theoretical models in several practical domains. The verification and validation of the theory causes possibilities for improvements and new additions to existing research results.

REFERENCES

Barwise, J. (1989). *The situation in logic* (CSLI Lecture Notes). Stanford, CA: Stanford University, CSLI.

Berliant, M., Reed, R., & Wang, P. (2006). Knowledge exchange, matching, and agglomeration. *Journal of Urban Economics, 60*(1), 69-95.

Cowan, R., Jonard, N., & Özman, M. (2004). Knowledge dynamics in a network industry. *Technological Forecasting & Social Change, 71*(5), 469-484.

Craik, K. (1943). *The nature of explanation.* Cambridge, MA: Cambridge University Press.

Dienes, Z., & Perner, J. (1999). A theory of implicit and explicit knowledge. *Behavioral and Brain Sciences, 22*(5), 735-808.

Frank, J. (Ed.). (2005). *The CanMEDS 2005 physician competency framework. Better standards. Better physicians. Better care.* Ottawa: The Royal College of Physicians and Surgeons of Canada.

Groth, K. (2004). A technological framework supporting knowledge exchange in organizations. *NordiCHI '04: Proceedings of the third Nordic conference on human-computer interaction* (pp. 381-384). New York, NY: ACM Press.

Halpin, T. (2001). *Information modeling and relational databases, from conceptual analysis to logical design*. California, CA: Morgan Kaufmann.

Klein, F., & Giese, H. (2005). Analysis and design of physical and social contexts in multi-agent systems using UML. *SELMAS '05: Proceedings of the fourth international workshop on software engineering for large-scale multi-agent systems* (pp. 1-8). New York, NY: ACM Press.

Kuznets, S. (1962). Population change and aggregate output. In: R. Easterlin (Ed.), *Demographic and economic change in developed countries* (pp. 324-340). Princeton, NJ: Princeton University Press.

Li, X., Montazemi, A., & Yuan, Y. (2006). Agent-based buddy finding methodology for knowledge sharing. *Information & Management, 43*(3), 283-296.

López, N., Núñez, M., Rodríguez, I., & Rubio, F. (2004). Encouraging knowledge exchange in discussion forums by market-oriented mechanisms. *SAC '04: Proceedings of the 2004 ACM symposium on applied computing* (pp. 952-956). New York, NY: ACM Press.

Nonaka, I., & Takeuchi, H. (1995). *The knowledge-creating company: How Japanese companies create the dynamics of innovation*. Oxford, UK: Oxford University Press.

Pentland, A. (2004). Social dynamics: Signals and behaviour. *ICDL '04: Proceedings of the 2004 international conference on developmental learning* (pp. 263-267). New York, NY: IEEE Press.

Pinku, G., & Tzelgov, J. (in press). Consciousness of the self (COS) and explicit knowledge. *Consciousness and Cognition*.

Polanyi, M. (1966). *The tacit dimension*. London, UK: Routledge and Kegan Paul.

Siemieniuch, C., & Sinclair, M. (1999). Organizational aspects of knowledge lifecycle management in manufacturing. *International Journal of Human-Computer Studies, 51*(3), 517-547.

Strambach, S. (2001). Innovation processes and the role of knowledge-intensive business services. In: K. Koschatzky, M. Kulicke, & A. Zenker (Eds.), *Innovation networks – concepts and challenges in the European perspective* (pp. 53-68). Heidelberg, Germany: Physica-Verlag.

Weide, Th. P. van der, & Bommel, P. van (2006). Measuring the incremental information value of documents. *Information Sciences, 176*(2), 91-119.

Wooldridge, M., & Jennings, N. (1995). Intelligent agents: Theory and practice. *The Knowledge Engineering Review, 10*(2), 115-152.

KEY TERMS

Input and Output Relatedness: Input and output relatedness focuses on the existence of overlap between received knowledge and between broadcasted knowledge.

Knowledge Exchange: Knowledge exchange involves the broadcasting of knowledge items between workers, or between a worker and a software agent and vice versa, with as specific goal to reduce the need for knowledge of a worker.

Knowledge Lifecycle: A knowledge lifecycle provides insight in organizational knowledge generation, the propagation of knowledge across the organization, and subsequently the retirement of knowledge.

Knowledge Transformation Process: A knowledge transformation process causes the properties of (a) knowledge item(s) to change and as a result the knowledge item(s) can be classified differently due to the modified properties.

Object Role Modelling (ORM): ORM is an information modelling language which has a well-defined formal semantics and sufficient expressive power to describe the Universe of Discourse.

Software Agent: A software agent is an encapsulated computer system that is situated in some environment and that is capable of flexible, autonomous action in that environment.

Support Relatedness: Support relatedness comprises theory with as goal to decrease a worker's need for knowledge and to improve the flow of knowledge between workers.

Chapter VI
Digital Divide Redux:
Why the Greatest Gap is Ideological

Michelle Rodino-Colocino
The Pennsylvania State University, USA

ABSTRACT

Although the debate on the digital divide has evolved from an analysis of access to skill, scholars have largely neglected the significance of inequalities in the high-tech labor force. Overlooking such discrepancies undercuts the practical application of such analyses; if the most technically skilled workers face eroding job security and dwindling wages, digital divide research is missing a key source of disparity among today's workers. This chapter examines the latest developments in digital divide research and the high-tech labor market. The concluding section of this chapter discusses what steps workers are taking to close the digital labor force divide and how scholars and managers can meaningfully intervene. By leveraging their unique position as workers who manage other workers, managers can play an important role in creating more equitable working conditions for high-tech labor.

INTRODUCTION

More than ten years after the "digital divide," the gap in access to and skill in computer and Internet technology, has been identified, debated, and rephrased, large gaps in the digital work force remain. Scholarship on the digital divide tends to overlook or minimize the importance of digital labor force divides (Rodino-Colocino, 2006). That negligence is now as glaring as ever, as the captains of digital industry argue for an expansion of the temporary worker visa program (H-1B visas) that enables foreign nationals to work in the U.S. for up to six years, but with little job protection and for less compensation than permanent residents. This chapter examines the latest developments in the digital divide debate and high-tech labor market. The concluding section of this chapter discusses what steps workers are taking to close the digital labor force divide and how scholars and managers can meaningfully intervene.

BACKGROUND: TWO WAVES OF DIGITAL DIVIDE RESEARCH

The digital divide, according to first wave studies from the mid 1990s through the early 2000s, is the gap in access to computer technologies, especially the Internet. First wave divide research took a more determinist stance toward technology than later studies that considered technological skill. First wave studies argued that access to digital technology promised to empower users economically and politically. As the seminal study of the National Telecommunications & Information Administration (NTIA) put it, the U.S. has become "a society where individuals' economic and social well being increasingly depend[s] on their ability to access, accumulate, and assimilate information" and that "while a standard telephone line can be an individual's pathway to the riches of the Information Age, a personal computer and modem are rapidly becoming the keys to the vault" (U.S. Department of Commerce, National Telecommunications and Information Administration, 1995).[1] The NTIA's techno-optimism grew along with the 1990s high-tech investment bubble. In 1999 the NTIA reported, "The Internet is a nascent, rapidly diffusing technology that promises to become the economic underpinning for all successful countries in the new global economy" (U.S. Department of Commerce, 1999).

Although the Bush administration cut funds for various programs designed to close the divide (i.e., the Technology Opportunities Program), the NTIA has continually emphasized information technologies' contribution to economic growth: "The expanding use of new technologies continues to strengthen our economy…As [new electronic] connections open new economic opportunities for more Americans, it is important that all segments of our Nation are included in this ongoing information revolution" (U.S. Department of Commerce, 2002). Starting from the assumption that the Internet, and especially broadband technologies are "transforming the way we live, work, and learn," the 2004 study suggests that the notion of the Internet as vault to Info-Age riches has become accepted wisdom among policy analysts (U.S. Department of Commerce, 2004). Focusing on broadband digital technologies is important, because "now, more than ever before, high-speed connections promise to enhance our Nation's productivity and economic competitiveness, improve education, and expand health care for all Americans. High-speed networks provide the

power to erase geographic, economic, and cultural gaps" (p. i). In addition to providing a means to connect to education and information providers, access to Internet and computer technologies enables a variety of economic transactions from online banking to purchasing products. The report concludes that "As the volume and complexity of the Internet's content has grown, so has the need for high-speed access technologies" (p. 20).

Arguing for the importance of skill over and in addition to access, second wave digital divide research critiques and expands earlier studies. Second wave research faults earlier studies' technological determinism for overemphasizing technological access (i.e., the physical presence of a computer or Internet connection). Examining issues beyond the point of access, titles of second wave research underscore the desire to 'rethink' (Light, 2001; Warschauer, 2003), 'redefine' (Gumpert & Drucker, 2002), and go 'beyond' the digital divide (Jung et al., 2001; Mossberger, Tolbert, & Stansbury, 2003). Research explores different types of 'literacy' (i.e., technical, verbal, and mathematical knowledge), skill, or what Hargittai (2002) calls the "second-level digital divide" (qualitative differences in the use of technologies), and the relationship between use and socio-economic context (Sevron, 2002; Mossberger et al., 2003; Warschauer, 2003).

Second wave scholarship, however, does not entirely jettison the technological determinism it critiques but rather, articulates a "softer" version of it. Hard technological determinists view technology as directly effecting social change; soft determinists consider technology either as influencing social phenomena or as symptomatic of them (Williams, 1974). Examining technologies' effects does not brand one a technological determinist. Neglecting relevant non-technological variables to explain a phenomenon, however, suggests a narrower, determinist view. Second wave divide scholarship constitutes soft technological determinism because it, like earlier studies, overlooks the role the labor market plays in the relationship between computers, the Internet, and work.

This omission has real policy effects, as debates around socioeconomic disadvantage remain relatively disconnected from corporations' efforts to find ever-cheaper labor. As a result, debates about the digital divide develop on a seemingly different track than those around the forging of cheap global labor markets. The two problems, the two divides, are related. As I will discuss later, both are structural issues involving class (and one's class position) and therefore, cannot be solved by merely boosting access to or skill in computer and Internet technologies.

The most recent research on the digital divide moves closer to recognizing the centrality of class not merely as contributing to or resulting from the digital divide, but as constituting it. Like much second wave divide research, van Dijk (2005) calls for expanding the debate to question the assumptions and vocabulary of earlier divide research. Van Dijk contends that the problem involves more variables than the binary referent "divide" suggests. Also arguing that what has been understood as the digital divide is paradoxically closing and deepening, van Dijk's nuanced analysis overlooks the centrality of inequality in the labor market to which digital skills provide access. One chapter looks at "the stakes" of information inequality, and more specifically, considers how lack of skill in and access to information and communication technologies (ICTs) limits job prospects. Van Dijk, however, downplays the determining power of the global IT labor market, which is increasingly defined by inequalities in compensation and security, in addition to segmentation by skill and educational levels.

One study that omits discussion of the labor market at least opens the door to its inclusion. In a review of the literature, Liangzhi Yu (2006) argues that digital divide discourse "may be driven by certain political interests to direct people's attention from the injustice of resource distribution to the imbalanced diffusion of technologies" (p. 243). Yu suggests that debates around the diffusion of ICTs divert critique of class divides that underlie technological and informational

discrepancies. Like other second-wave studies, Yu's piece critiques the grounds and vocabulary of the debate. Her contribution to the literature lies in her argument that two hitherto divergent lines of research, one concerned with "information inequality" (and coming out of library, information, and communication studies), the other focused on the "digital divide" (and coming out an interdisciplinary perspective) should compliment each other in future research and policy efforts. Like much second-wave research, Yu's piece points to the structural, class divides that information inequality and the digital divide metonymize, but does not conduct a structural critique.

Scholars are, however, aware of the limitations of "divide" as a starting point and are introducing new perspectives, such "community informatics" (Gurstein, 2003) and Rawlsian notions of justice (Schement, 2007).[2] I am not sure, however, how useful community informatics are when they are linked to "effective use" of the technologies, an approach that echoes the foci of second wave research.[3] Integrating notions of community, nevertheless, moves the focus of the debate beyond individual uses and effects of technology to groups of people and thus enables a critical analysis of the relationship between media and segments of the working class. Kvasny's (2006) work does such critique, and, as I will discuss under the section "Future Trends," points the way to research sensitive to community and structural issues. Additionally, linking Rawls' theory of justice as fairness to digital divide research points to a moral argument, the development of which complements examination of structural inequalities in the work force. Perhaps these journeys out of a discourse focused on technological access and skill can complement efforts to foreground non-technological problems like exploitation and bifurcation in the digital labor market. Turning now to labor force divides, especially those affecting IT workers, I want to highlight enduring elements and recent developments.

MAIN FOCUS OF THE CHAPTER: A TALE OF "TWO ECONOMIES"

While scholars have worked to expand the debate on its causes and effects, one gap—that between productivity on the one hand and compensation and job security on the other—has grown during the past four decades. From 1973-2003, productivity rose over twice as fast as total compensation for median-income workers (Greenhouse & Leonhard, 2006) and over three times as fast as the median family income (Bernstein & Kornbluh, 2005).[4] Wages have not kept up with the cost of living: the buying power of minimum wage earners plunged to a 50-year low in 2005 followed by a minor recovery in 2006 (Leonhardt, 2006; Greenhouse & Leonhardt, 2006). Work hours, especially women's, rose to fill the income gap left open by falling real wages (Devanas-Walt, Proctor, & Lee, 2006). Hours peaked in 2000, when U.S. families worked 500 hours more annually than they did in 1979 (Bernstein & Kornbluh, 2005). High-tech workers have been among the most overworked, as employers asked them to work eighty-plus hour weeks and unpaid overtime during fat and lean times (Worker Center, 2001; Ross, 2003; Tapia,2004;).

Workers are clearly doing more for less. Following decades of professional and managerial-level downsizing and manufacturing job loss, jobs have continued to disappear.[5] In the first two years after the 2001 recession, the U.S. lost over 2.7 million jobs "for good" (Weisman, 2003).[6] Despite the promise of digital divide discourse that the IT sector would "strengthen the economy" and "erase geographic, economic, and cultural gaps," even for the most skilled users, IT jobs were not spared. The U.S. tech sector shed over 1.1 million IT jobs from 2001-2005, including jobs in software, semiconductors, telecommunications, and Web-related companies (Mandel, 2006). According to the U.S. Department of Labor, between 2000 and 2004 IT workers in the areas of computer programming, computer science and systems analysis, and electrical engineering lost 417,000 jobs. This figure represents a loss of 24% of computer programming positions, 23% of computer science occupations and a 16% drop in electrical engineering employment (Schneiderman, 2005). During the early 2000s, the unemployment rate for Washington's technical workers was nearly twice that of other employees in the state (Doussard & Mastracci, 2003).[7]

Offshoring has exacerbated job loss for IT workers. From January 1, 2000 to May 30, 2007, U.S. corporations offshored 528,478 jobs, and lost about half as many (Offshore Tracker, 2007).[8] One survey of IEEE members found that 15% of respondents attributed their layoff to offshoring (Going Offshore, 2005). According to a survey of 40 Fortune 1000 companies, 80% of real estate executives say they will likely increase offshore call centers and computer services in the five years following the survey (Chittum, 2004). While the majority of respondents claim that their company will not replace U.S. workers, over 42% report that they are moving U.S. jobs overseas (Chittum, 2004). Most state governments offshore work, including the Washington Healthcare Authority and the Washington Department of Corrections (Beckman, 2003; Cook, 2003; Mattera, 2004).

Although offshoring enables companies to employ workers overseas at a fraction of their U.S. wages, the practice has also driven down wages for U.S. workers. The U.S. Department of Labor (2004) found that of the 5.3 million full-time workers laid off due to plant closures or relocations between 2001-2003, 57% were reemployed in full-time wage and salary work that paid less than their previous jobs. Nearly one-third were reemployed in jobs earning wages at least 20% less than their previous positions paid (U.S. Department of Labor, 2004). The IEEE suspects that offshoring partly accounts for the first drop in median salary in 31 years (Incomes of Technical Professionals Decline, 2004; Schneiderman, 2005).[9]

Some argue that offshoring creates wealth by lowering labor costs for countries that send work overseas and boosting wages in countries that receive offshored work (Agrawal, Farrell,

& Remes, 2003). Offshoring's wealth, however, seems to be in the eye of the beholder. Arguing that reduced wages "creates wealth" in outsourcing countries universalizes corporate interests (Levy, 2005). Rather than create wealth, cutting wages in offshoring countries transfers wealth upwards to affluent shareholders and further impoverishes U.S. workers. Although some workers in receiving countries enjoy higher pay, receiving countries also experience heightened wage inequality.

The exploitation of temporary foreign laborers who hold H-1B visas has also aggravated wage and job losses for U.S. workers. By granting temporary work permits to highly skilled foreign workers, the H-1B program ostensibly helps U.S. companies fill jobs left vacant by a shortage of skilled U.S. workers. Employers, however, have used the program to drive down wages and facilitate offshoring (Bjorhus, 2002; Matloff, 2002; Hira, 2007). Estimates of under-compensation vary, but various studies show that H-1B holders are paid 15-33% less than their resident counterparts (Bjorhus, 2002; Matloff, 2002; Hira, 2007) and 50% less than the $100,000 annual wage Microsoft chair Bill Gates quoted in Congressional testimony (Lohr, 2007). Top offshoring companies also make the most requests for H-1Bs, in hopes of sending workers to the U.S. to handle client relations while most of the technical work (i.e., software coding) is done in the country receiving offshored labor (Hira, 2007; Lohr, 2007). Nor are H-1Bs "gateways" to greencards (i.e., permanent resident status in the U.S.) that confer financial and geographical stability that could create wealth for workers. Top H-1B requestors sponsor a fraction of a percent of visa workers for greencards (Hira, 2007). The H-1B labor market is also divided by wage and greencard sponsorship, as new Microsoft H-1B workers earn $82,500, less than the $100,000 Gates claimed, but more than the $50,000 median salary for new H-1B visa holders.[10] Microsoft H-1B workers also enjoy a higher level of greencard sponsorship (26%) than do typical visa holders at Indian outsourcing companies.

Given all of these divides in the national and global labor market, it is no wonder that one analyst described the problem facing U.S. workers as one of "two economies." One economy has been "white hot" for the beneficiaries of the global reorganization of labor, and the other has been stone cold for the "working stiffs" who are doing more for less (Greenhouse & Leonhardt, 2006, A13). What can scholars, activists, and managers, do to create an economy that is neither hot nor cold but beneficial to all workers nationally and globally, and how can research on the digital divide inform such efforts?

FUTURE TRENDS

The depth and breadth of the digital labor force divides suggest that those seeking to realize the ends of digital divide research (i.e., a more egalitarian society) should integrate structural, class-conscious critique with activism. Without secure, living wage jobs waiting on the other side of the skill and access gulf, deep divides and subdivides within the global working class remain.

Digital divide research, particularly recent interest in justice and community informatics, can inform the structural analysis and intervention required to close labor force divides. As Lynette Kvasny argues in her analysis of ICTs as tools of social reproduction, "The benefits that one derives from ICTs are doubly determined by two factors: the conditions in which the individuals acquired their ICT skills and the markets where these skills can be invested to derive profits" (Kvasny, 2006, p. 174). Based on an analysis of underprivileged individuals' use of a new CTC (community technology center) in a large urban area, Kvasny argues that without the jobs, skill in and access to ICTs cannot transform individuals into high-income or living-wage earners. Also, as Kvasny points out, without closing other gaps (in transportation, childcare, and free time), members of economically disadvantaged communities cannot materially benefit from ICT training. Research that explores how to close divides that bifurcate the IT labor force into class fractions of haves and have-nots can usefully address and inform intervention in such structural problems.

What constitutes effective intervention? The most direct route is to support workers' efforts to end their exploitation in U.S. and global labor markets. Activists might join members of unions like WashTech (the Washington Alliance of Technology), the Seattle-based union for high-tech workers, who are working to stem abuse of the H-1B visa program and the job and wage cutting effects of offshoring. Since WashTech's "new model of unionism" depends on members-at-large who are not under contract at specific workplaces, the union encourages IT workers and their supporters to join as paying members or as non-dues paying listserv members. The union serves as a political action group, lobbying for legislation that would protect jobs and workers (van Jaarsveld, 2004; Brophy, 2006; Rodino-Colocino, 2008).[11]

Labor activism and research are complementary projects. Each can inform and improve the other. Scholars can boost the efficacy of a particular union or the labor movement in general by analyzing workers' advocacy in relation to wider social and historical contexts. Participating as activists, likewise, attunes scholars to the real needs, obstacles, and strengths of a union or movement. This process is already underway in community informatics, whose advocacy and participatory efforts inform activism and scholarship (Gurstein, 2003; Clement et al., 2004; Stillman & Stoecker, 2005; Venkatesh, 2006). Considering different forms of activism also helps scholars theorize relationships between research and praxis in interdisciplinary fields like development studies (Fox, 2003) and health communication (Zoller, 2006).

CONCLUSION

In an article I wrote on the digital divide several years ago, I recommended that the largely academic readership of *New Media and Society* should constructively critique digital divide research in ways that communication and new media scholars are uniquely skilled (Rodino-Colocino, 2006). I called for scholars to analyze digital divide research (i.e., doing 'criticism') and to create alternatives that eliminate underlying social disparities (i.e., being 'constructive'). One obvious starting point is to include in our work the voices of workers who have been left out of the debate. Doing so helps us avoid merely producing new marketing for the IT industry and differentiates our work from those in PR departments and firms. Or, as political economist of communication Robert McChesney warned colleagues, 'If we accept the turn to purely market-driven communication as legitimate, we almost certainly undermine any justification for the field's existence' (1997, p. 572). Unless we think and act critically, our work as intellectuals is redundant.

I want to put the same admonition to managers. As buffers between stockholders and workers, executives and managers need to oppose what appear to be purely market-driven forces. In the case of high-tech organizations, this means standing against rampant cost cutting to satisfy investors. Managers are, after all, responsible for their worker's productivity, measured qualitatively and quantitatively, and for their company's end products. Managers are also uniquely skilled, through their professional education and experience, to boost workers' productivity and improve product lines. In the face of declining union membership, following years of union-busting tactics, managers might be the only workers in a company to stand between brain-draining corporate layoffs and a workplace with the skill and experience to produce reliable, innovative products. If managers abandon their responsibilities to their employees and products, they might earn recognition as redundant and be displaced by software programs or workers in cheap labor markets, as have professional IT workers who once appeared irreplaceable. Since managers are workers, perhaps the most significant divide is an ideological one.

ACKNOWLEDGMENT

The author wishes to thank Marcus Courtney, Lynette Kvasny, Jorge Schement, Carol Stabile, and Kirk St.Amant for their quick response to her questions and generosity with their time. Thanks, too, to Stella for the excellent company while writing this chapter.

REFERENCES

Agrawal, V., Farrell, D., & Remes, J. (2004). Offshoring and beyond. *McKinsey Quarterly, 4,* 24-35.

Beckman, D. (2003). The great tech job exodus. *Tech Worker News, TechsUnite.* Retrieved from http://www.washtech.org/news/industry/ display. php?ID_Content=441.

Bernstein, J. (2006). Jobs picture. Retrieved May 29, 2007 from http://www.epi.org/content. cfm/webfeatures_econindicators_jobspict_ 20061208

Bernstein, J., & Kornbluh, K. (2005). *Running faster to stay in place: The growth of family work hours and income.* Washington, D.C.: New America Foundation.

Bjorhus, J. (2002). U.S. workers taking H-1B issues to court. *Mercury News.* Retrieved from http://www.echarcha.com/forum/showthread. php?t=10967

Brophy, E. (2006). System error: Labour precarity and collective action at Microsoft. *Canadian Journal of Communication, 31,* 619-638.

Chittum, R. (2004). Rise in offshore jobs expected. *Wall Street Journal* (Eastern edition), p. B6.

Clement, A., Gurstein, M., Longford, G, Luke, R., Moll, M, Shade, L., & DeChief, D. (2004). The Canadian Research Alliance for Community Innovation and Networking (CRACIN): A research partnership and agenda for community networking in Canada. *Journal of Community Informatics,* 1(1). Retrieved from http://www.ci-journal.net/index.php/ciej/article/view/207/163.

Cook, J. (2003). State jobs moving to workers overseas. *Seattle Post-Intelligencer.* Retrieved from http://seattlepi.nwsource.com/business/152829_ outsource17.html.

Devanas-Walt, C., Proctor, B., & Lee, C.. (2006). U.S. Census Bureau. Current population reports, P60-231. *Income, poverty and health insurance in the U.S.: 2005.* Washington, D.C.: U.S. Government Printing Office.

Doussard, M., & Mastracci, S. (2003). *Uncertain futures: The real impact of the high tech boom and bust on Seattle's IT workers.* Chicago, IL: University of Illinois, Chicago, Center for Urban Economic Development.

Fox, J. (2003). Advocacy research and the World Bank: Propositions for discussion. *Development in Practice, 13*(5), 519-527.

Going offshore cuts technology jobs. (2005). *Manufacturing Engineering, 134*(5), 40.

Greenhouse, S., & Leonhardt, D. (2006). Real wages fail to match a rise in productivity. *The New York Times,* A1, A13.

Gumpert, G., & Drucker, S.. (2002). Information society: The digital divide, redefining the concept. *Intermedia, 30*(4), 8-12.

Gurstein, M. (2003). Effective use: A community informatics model beyond the digital divide. *First Monday, 8*(12). Retrieved May 29, 2007 from http://www.firstmonday.org/issues/ issue8_12/ gurstein/.

Hadfield, W. (2005). Offshoring blamed for salary slump. *Computer Weekly.* Retrieved from http://www.computerweekly.com/Articles/2005/ 10/19/212531/Offshoringblamedforsalaryslump. htm.

Hargittai, E. (2002). Second-level digital divide: Differences in people's online skills. *First Monday,*

7(4). Retrieved May 29, 2007 from http://www. firstmonday.org/ issues/issue7_4/hargittai/.

Hira, R. (2007). Outsourcing America's technology and knowledge jobs. Economic Policy Institute. Retrieved May 29, 2007 from http://www. sharedprosperity.org/ bp187.html.

Incomes of technical professionals decline. (2004). *IEEE-USA, Communications.* Retrieved from http://www.ieeeusa.org/ communications/ releases/2004/ 122204pr.asp.

Kvasny, L. (2006). The cultural (re)production of digital inequality. *Information, Communication and Society, 9*(2), 160-181.

Light, J. (2001). Rethinking the digital divide. *Harvard Educational Review, 71(*4), 709-733.

Lohr, S. (2007). Parsing the truths about visas for tech workers. *New York Times,* section 3, p. 4.

Jung, J., Qiu, J., & Kim, Y. (2001). Internet connectedness and inequality: Beyond the "divide." *Communication Research, 28*(4), 507-535.

Levy, D. (2005). Offshoring in the new global political economy. *Journal of Management Studies, 42*(3), 685-693.

Mandel, M. (2006). What's really propping up the economy?. *Businessweek.* Retrieved May 29, 2007 from http://www.businessweek.com/magazine/ content/ 06_39/b4002001.htm.

Mattera, P. (2004). *Your tax dollars at work...offshore: How foreign outsourcing firms are capturing state government contracts.* Washington D.C.: Corporate Research Project of Good Jobs First.

McChesney, R. (1997). Wither communication?. *Journal of Broadcasting & Electronic Media, 41*(4), 566-572.

Mossberger, K., Tolbert, C., & Stansbury, M. (2003). *Virtual inequality: Beyond the digital divide.* Washington, D.C.: Georgetown University.

Offshore Tracker. (2007). Retrieved from http:// www.techsunite.org/offshore/.

Rodino-Colocino, M. (2006). Laboring under the digital divide. *New Media & Society, 8*(3), 487-511.

Rodino-Colocino, M. (forthcoming). High-tech workers of the world, unionize! A case study of WashTech's "New Model of Unionism." In: C. McKercher & V. Mosco (Eds.), *Knowledge workers in the information age.* Lanham: Rowman and Littlefield.

Ross, A. (2003). *No collar: The humane workplace and its hidden costs.* New York, NY: Basic Books.

Schneiderman, R. (2005). Offshoring, outsourcing, out of work. *Electronic Design,* 65-74.

Sevron, L. (2002). *Bridging the digital divide: Technology, community, and public policy.* Malden: Blackwell.

Stillman, L., & Stoecker, R. (2005). Structuration, ICTs, and community work. *The Journal of Community Informatics, 1*(3). Retrieved May 29, 2007 from http://www.ci-journal.net/index. php/ciej/article/view/216/175

Tapia, A. (2004). The power of myth in the IT workplace: Creating a 24-hour workday during the dotcom bubble. *Information, Technology, and People, 17*(3), 303-326

U.S. Department of Commerce, National Telecommunication and Information Administration. (1995). *Falling through the net: A survey of the 'have-nots' in rural and urban America.* Retrieved from http://www.ntia.doc.gov/ntiahome/ fallingthru.html

U.S. Department of Commerce, National Telecommunication and Information Administration. (1999). *Falling through the net: Defining the digital divide.* Retrieved May 29, 2007 from http://www. ntia.doc.gov/ntiahome/fttn99

U.S. Department of Commerce, National Tele-communication and Information Administration. (2002). *A nation online: How Americans are expanding their use of the Internet.* Retrieved from http://www.ntia.doc.gov/ntiahome/ dn/nationonline_020502.htm.

U.S. Department of Commerce, National Tele-communication and Information Administration. (2004). *A nation online: Entering the broadband age.* Retrieved from http://www.ntia.doc.gov/reports/anol/index.html.

van Dijk, J. (2005). *The deepening divide: Inequality in the information society.* Thousand Oaks, CA: Sage.

van Jaarsveld, D. (2004). Collective representation among high-tech workers at Microsoft and beyond: Lessons from WashTech/CWA. *Industrial Relations, 43*(2), 364-385.

Venkatesh, M., & Owens, J. (2006). Radical praxis and civic network design. *The Journal of Community Informatics, 2*(2). Retrieved May 29, 2007 from http://www.ci-journal.net/index.php/ciej/article/view/344/250

Warschauer, M. (2003) *Technology and social inclusion: Rethinking the digital divide.* Cambridge: MIT Press.

Weisman, J. (2003). Casualties of the recovery: Jobs cut since 2001 are gone for good, study says. *The Washington Post*: E01.

Williams, R. (1992). *Television: Technology and cultural form.* Hanover, NH: Wesleyan University Press.

Worker Center, King County Labor Council, AFL-CIO. (2001). *Disparities within the digital world: Realities of the new economy, A Report for the Washington Alliance of Technology Workers.* Retrieved May 29, 2007 from http://www.WashTech.org/reports/.

Yu, L. (2006). Understanding information inequality: Making sense of the literature of the information and digital divides. *Journal of Librarianship and Information Science, 38*(4), 229-252.

Zoller. (2005). Health activism: Communication theory and activism for social change. *Communication Theory, 15*(4), 341-364.

KEY TERMS

Community Informatics: The study and use of information and communication technologies to construct communities on and off-line.

Digital Divide: The gap in access to and skill in computer and Internet technology that sparked debate and research from the mid 1990s through today.

First Wave Digital Divide Research: The first wave of digital divide research began in 1995 with the publication of the NTIA's report on information "have-nots" in rural America (U.S. Department of Commerce, National Telecommunications and Information Administration, 1995). First wave research focused on access to digital technology and argued that such access promised to empower users economically and politically.

High-Tech Labor: The segment of the workforce concentrated in high-tech industries such as computer software programming, testing, and manufacturing, as well as electrical engineering.

H-1B Visas: Ostensibly, H-1B visas are temporary work permits the federal government grants to highly skilled foreign workers to help U.S. companies fill jobs left vacant by a shortage of skilled U.S. workers. Employers, however, have used the program to drive down wages and facilitate offshoring.

Ideology: The sets of ideas that attempt to legitimize the political and economic power of elites.

Offshoring: The practice of outsourcing work to another company or subsidiary overseas, usually to a cheaper labor market.

Second Wave Digital Divide Research: In response to the access-focused first wave, second wave digital divide research focused on skill in using computer and Internet technologies.

Technological Determinism: Theorizing social phenomena (including technological development) in ways that privilege technological variables while neglecting relevant non-technological ones.

WashTech: Affiliated with the CWA (Communication Workers of America), the Washington Alliance of Technology Workers was founded in 1998 by two temporary Microsoft workers. Today, with 1,500 dues-paying members and 17,000 listserv members, the union represents high-tech workers on issues ranging from unpaid overtime to offshore outsourcing.

ENDNOTES

[1]   The Commerce Department uses 'information haves and have-nots' to describe what it later calls the 'digital divide.'

[2]   Community informatics is the study and use of information and communication technologies to construct communities on and off-line. I would like to thank Lynette Kvasny, for pointing out the relevance of community informatics and to Jorge Schement for discussing growing relevance of Rawls' theory of justice to digital divide research, personal communication, April 19, 2007 and April 24, 2007, respectively.

[3]   Michael Gurstein (2003) defines "effective use" of ICTs as "how and under what conditions ICT access can be made usable and useful" and more specifically, as "the capacity and opportunity to successfully integrate ICTs into the accomplishment of self or collaboratively identified goals." Gurstein argues that examining the usefulness of ICTs helps scholars and activists break out of the haves vs. have-nots binary first wave research constructed and avoid serving as PR for the IT industry.

[4]   At 71.3%, productivity growth outpaced median family income, which grew 21.9% from 1973-2003. In contrast to the three and half decades prior to 1973, median family income growth was robust and outpaced productivity growth 103.9% to 103.5% from 1947-1973 (Bernstein & Kornbluh, 2005).

[5]   The exception was the healthcare sector, which added 1.7 million jobs since 2001 (Mandel, 2006).

[6]   Although average monthly gains in job creation in 2006 was positive, topping 149,000, such growth was the most sluggish of the past five-year periods of economic recovery. Since November 2001, when the recovery began, payroll employment grew a paltry 4.5%, compared to growth rates of 17.3% in 1961, 16.4% in 1982, and 9.5% in 1991 (Bernstein, 2006).

[7]   Washington state's IT workers experienced a double-digit unemployment rate of 10.6%, after high-tech eliminated 9,600 jobs between February 2001 and April 2002.

[8]   Web site operators count jobs "lost" when a source lists the number of layoffs in addition to the number of jobs offshored. Retrieved May 30, 2007 from http://www.techsunite.org/offshore/index.cfm.

[9]   For IEEE members working full time, wages dropped 1.49% between 2002-2003. Similarly, the UK's Association of Technology Staffing Companies attributes the "salary slump" for permanent and contract IT helpdesk workers to offshoring, which has reduced the number of entry level jobs. Pay for UK contract and temporary IT helpdesk workers also fell further than it did for permanent workers. Between 2004-2005 pay

for contract and temp workers saw their pay drop 25%, but pay for permanent workers fell 3% during the same period (Hadfield, 2005).

[10] Data on the median salary for new H-1B visa holders is based on data from the U.S. Citizenship and Immigration Services agency (Lohr, 2007).

[11] I am preaching what I practice, as I have been a WashTech member since 1999. WashTech is affiliated with the Communication Workers of America (CWA) and has 1,500 dues-paying and approximately 17,000 listerv members.

Chapter VII
Parawork

Leah A. Zuidema
Dordt College, USA

ABSTRACT

The term parawork describes spaces and activities that function alongside—yet also outside—of traditional workplaces. Parawork spaces are not regulated by the workplace, but they are available for work-related activities. In parawork environments, it can be desirable to overlap the personal, social, and professional. Participating with others in parawork activities may not "get work done," yet these interactions may facilitate professional identity formation, association with workplace and professional culture, and readiness to accomplish workplace tasks and professional goals. This chapter defines parawork, focusing on parawork enabled by online communication technologies. The author reviews literature that supports and informs understanding of online parawork. Through case study of one woman's participation in an e-mail discussion list for teacher interns, the practical realities and possibilities of online parawork are considered. The chapter closes with conclusions about conditions necessary for effective online parawork, as well as implications for future research.

INTRODUCTION

A few years ago, *The Atlantic Monthly* began running a column called *Word Fugitives*. In this column, and in her book by the same title, Barbara Wallraff identifies phenomena that are familiar to many people and yet have no corresponding name. Wallraff invites readers to propose new words to fill some of English's linguistic gaps, and she features some of the more creative and appropriate monikers in her column. I take up a similar task here—although in a style quite different from that achieved by Walraff. The nameless concept I am interested in is this: the spaces outside of traditional workplaces where people meet with others, and the interplay of personal, social, and professional activities occurring within such spaces that can contribute to a person's ability to accomplish work-related tasks and professional goals. The term I have coined to label these spaces and activities is *parawork*.

As I discuss parawork in this chapter, my objectives are as follows: to explain the parawork concept, to emphasize distinctions between virtual workplaces and online parawork, and to identify through case study some potential benefits of online parawork spaces and activities for workers and their employers. This chapter defines *parawork*, with a focus on parawork enabled by online communication technologies. I review literature pertaining to the parawork concept and then present a case study that illustrates how online parawork occurs through a private e-mail discussion list, Intern-Net. As I analyze e-mail and interview data from one subscriber, a teacher intern, I discuss how she uses the discussion list to construct her professional identity, to ready herself to accomplish workplace tasks and goals, and to improve her association with workplace and professional cultures. The chapter closes with conclusions about conditions necessary for effective online parawork.

DEFINING *PARAWORK*

The definition of *parawork* that I am constructing is built upon the etymology and uses of the prefix *para-*. According to the *Oxford English Dictionary*, the term *para* is a form of an ancient Greek word meaning "alongside of, by, past, beyond." In contemporary English, the prefix is used to give the meaning "analogous or parallel to, but separate from or going beyond, what is denoted by the root word" ("'para-', prefix[1]," 2005). In a general sense, then, *parawork* refers to that which is analogous or parallel to, but also separate from or going beyond, work.

The term *parawork* can refer both to spaces and to activities. If we take *work* to denote a place (as in, "She takes the bus to work"), it becomes apparent how *parawork* can be a spatial referent. When *parawork* is used to indicate place, it describes environments that can facilitate activities related to a person's work, spaces functioning alongside—while also outside the bounds—of traditional workplaces. Parawork spaces are not owned or regulated by the workplace; often these spaces are otherwise associated with personal or social activities. Offline parawork sites include golf courses, restaurants and coffee shops, and planes, trains, and automobiles—places where people may (or may not) choose to engage with each other in work-related talk and activities. In parawork environments, people expect to blend personal, social, and professional roles, to go "beyond' or "alongside of" their work. The tasks they accomplish may be described as "work-related" or seen as somehow contributing to their professional lives, though these tasks are not regarded as precisely the same as the sorts of "work" that people take up at actual workplaces. In parawork spaces, people expect to juggle and perhaps even integrate multiple personal and professional roles. There is an understanding that it is acceptable, even desirable, to use parawork spaces for a combination of social and professional pursuits.

Parawork refers not only to spaces, but also to the intertwined professional, social, and personal activities that people engage in within parawork environments. Given the definition of *para-* that I employ here, these activities are not just ordinary instances of work. Rather, they have unique characteristics that situate them "alongside of" or even "beyond" what is traditionally regarded as work. Specifically, people who participate in parawork activities have opportunities to interact with others in ways that contribute both to their performance of professional tasks and to their ability to manage professional and personal roles. When parawork takes place, the most visible actions may seem distinct from what we tend to think of as work, but the accompanying conversations focus on topics related to work and may contribute significantly to individuals' accomplishment of professional tasks and development.

A brief example: For years I commuted to graduate classes, driving an hour each direction. There were times when my car was a parawork place, and times when it was not; times when parawork activity occurred there, and times when it did not. Parawork was most likely to happen when I carpooled with other graduate teaching assistants (TAs) in programs related to mine.

Conversation would often meander through talk about our family and social lives, our views on the latest news and politics, and our plans for the weekend. But our conversation also included extended talk about what was happening in our teaching and in our work as students, and by the time we reached school or arrived home, my understanding of my roles and work as a graduate student and TA was different from what it had been before we left. Perhaps strengthened or clarified, maybe expanded or complicated, but changed nonetheless. I was contributing to my work (and to my working identity and ability to do my work), though not precisely <u>doing</u> my work. This was parawork.

Carpooling, however, did not inevitably lead to parawork. For a time while I was completing coursework in English Education, I carpooled with two neighbors. One was beginning a program in civil engineering; the other was a medical student. So as far as we knew, we had little in common in terms of professional interests and responsibilities, and our conversations rarely touched on our professional fields or school work. Instead, we talked politics, dissected NPR shows, and chatted about our kids. Our professional roles and tasks rarely came into play in these conversations, and for the most part, we did not engage in parawork.

I share these examples to help clarify the defining characteristics of parawork spaces and activities. Parawork occurs outside of traditional work spaces, in environments where people's professional roles come into play, but away from the places where they typically "get work done"—where they get paid to perform in certain ways or to generate specific products. Parawork happens in places where it can be "good form" to blend or overlap the social and the professional. When parawork takes place, people may not appear to be accomplishing much, and yet they may experience changes to their professional identity and understanding that have significant impact on their work.

LITERATURE REVIEW

Parawork is a new term, but the concept can be connected productively with existing theories and research from diverse fields. This section establishes how online parawork differs from virtual work and then discusses literature that supports and informs ways to understand, apply, and research the parawork concept.

Virtual Work vs. Parawork

To this point I have defined *parawork* in a general sense and have referred only to off-line examples. I now focus on parawork enabled by online communication technologies (OCTs). Today, many terms point to work spaces that are relocated through the use of OCTs (e.g., *homeworking, hybrid workspace, remote work, telework, telecommuting* and *virtual office*). As Hill, Ferris, and Märtinson (2003) point out, any of these terms may take on slightly different meaning from one study to the next, depending on context and authors' preferences. In most cases, though, such terms are used to indicate that tasks normally completed in traditional workplaces are being relocated elsewhere through the use of OCTs (Halford, 2005). The emphasis is on moving the work, usually with the understanding that outcomes and products ought to be much the same as (if not identical to) those that would emerge at corresponding traditional workplaces (Crandall & Wallace, 1998). Additionally, in virtual or "remote" work, there is an expectation that those who telecommute or work from so-called "virtual offices" will keep their personal and professional lives separate. Remote workers, especially women, feel great pressure to prove that they can put in the same number of hours and accomplish the same tasks at home as at the office, and in accounting for their time and efforts, they tend to be "especially scrupulous in separating work time from family time" (Halford, 2005, p. 26). While it is acknowledged that relocation of work through virtual workplaces may impact how workers use their time (Hill et al., 2003; Halford, 2005) and that relocating work may lead to changes in workers' personal and family lives (Halford, 2005; Moore, 2006), virtual work, like traditional work, is still paid labor that is completed in response to stated job requirements or required workplace tasks.

Online parawork activities differ from virtual workplace tasks. Online parawork is not a relocation of work; it is going beyond, alongside, and apart from work. To participate in online parawork, people use e-mail discussion lists, instant messaging chats, interactive blogs, and other OCTs to interact informally with others who share their professional interests. Instead of being paid to complete work-related duties (as in the virtual workplace), people voluntarily use online parawork spaces for their own purposes, often "off the clock," in efforts:

- to find collegial support as they adjust to new professional roles or respond to workplace issues and challenges,
- to learn information or strategies that will help them to succeed professionally,
- to connect with others with similar professional interests.

In online parawork environments, participants are generally accepting of overlaps between social and professional roles, as these overlaps help to promote collegiality and to lend an informal feel to parawork interactions.

An example may be useful in illustrating differences between online ("virtual") work and online parawork. Consider the activities of those who teach in so-called "virtual high schools" (such as the Kentucky Virtual High School). These teachers use OCTs to accomplish many of their workplace tasks: presenting curriculum, facilitating student learning, providing feedback to learners, assessing students' work, and so on. In these instances, we could say that teachers are participating in online work. They are completing

workplace duties, are directly compensated for their efforts, and would face serious consequences for failing to do their work. While these educators *must* participate in the virtual workplace in order to keep their jobs, they may also engage voluntarily in online parawork. Some may elect to subscribe to one of the many discussion lists available for teachers in specific disciplines (e.g., engteach-talk, for English teachers). Others may join online forums for those who teach with OCTs at the high school level. In these parawork conversations, the educator who teaches in the virtual high school may ask other teachers for advice about how to balance personal schedules with time spent giving feedback to students and answering their e-mail and IM questions. The teacher might also circulate work-related humor and anecdotes, share information about professional development opportunities, converse about a current event that affects online education, congratulate others on professional accomplishments or personal milestones, discuss an interesting book or article, and so forth. However the conversation emerges in parawork spaces, it occurs informally and voluntarily in an environment that is not under the jurisdiction of workplace supervisors and evaluators. Participants are not paid to participate in parawork, though they may benefit professionally from parawork activities.

As I suggested previously, the most notable outcome of parawork (online or off-line) is *not* "getting work done" (as it is in the virtual workplace). Rather, what makes parawork significant is its potential for impacting workers: their professional identities, their ability and willingness to adapt to professional cultures, and their readiness to accomplish workplace tasks and goals. Writing about parawork in online environments, then, requires going beyond scholarship on virtual workplaces. This study does so by drawing on literature pertaining to space and online forums, to language and identity construction, and to collegiality in online forums for professional development.

Space and Online Forums

Workplaces are not arbitrary backdrops. Spaces matter; they affect who we are and what we do. In the case of work spaces, Halford (2005) finds that working across multiple types of spaces ("spatial hybridity") "changes the nature of work, organization, and management in organizational space, cyberspace and domestic space, resulting in distinctive practices, experiences and relationships in all three spaces" (p. 25). Likewise, in a study contrasting professional success for women in two different types of "out-of-office" spaces, Morgan and Martin (2006) find that interactions with customers in "heterosocial" and "homosocial" settings impact female salespersons' careers in differing ways (p. 113). Essentially, physical spaces act upon the people who inhabit them by constraining certain types of behaviors while permitting or even promoting other behaviors (see Latour, 1988). But spaces are not static or impervious to change. Gregson and Rose (2000) demonstrate that spaces are complex, uncertain, and unstable; spaces can act upon us, yet they are "brought into being through performances and as a performative articulation of power" (p. 434).

Like physical spaces, cyberspace forums shape and are shaped by the people who inhabit them. Porter (2002) demonstrates that technologies—as well as the *interactions* of humans and computers—affect who people are and what they do. Pointing to the constructive power of technologies, Selfe and Selfe (1994) find that "the maps of computer interfaces *order* the virtual world according to a certain set of historical and social values" (p. 385, emphasis added). In a similar acknowledgement of the importance of technologies as nonhuman actors, Star makes "a call to study boring things" (1999, p. 377). She contends that in order to understand issues such as justice, power, and change, researchers must stop neglecting the impact of "standards, wires, and settings" (p. 379) and start paying attention to reciprocal relationships among technology,

people, and language. Likewise, in "Configuring LISTSERV, Configuring Discourse," Cubbison (1999) argues that it is crucial that e-mail lists be configured carefully, because setting their parameters in particular ways will in turn impact the conversations of subscribers.

In order to fully understand parawork sites, then, it is important to pay attention to the role of space in shaping parawork activities. In off-line environments, the physical spaces themselves are important, as are the ways they shape and are shaped by human inhabitants. In online forums, the technologies that set the parameters of cyberspace interactions are significant, as are the interactions among technologies, people, and language.

Language and Identity Construction

Online parawork is, in large part, accomplished through written language. In the last few decades, substantial energy has been invested in exploring links between language and identity construction, with scholars from a range of fields and disciplines building upon and extending the work of Baudrillard, Derrida, Foucault, and Lyotard (Cerulo, 1997). Much contemporary work on identity construction depends upon an understanding of speech and writing as "performative acts" (Searle, 1969) wherein words are not merely descriptive, but also functional—they get things done through the "elision of discourse and action" (Hodgson, 2005, p. 54). Though theories and research on language and identity construction extend in widely-varied directions, one unifying principle is the tenet that persons' identities shape and are shaped by language.[1]

Links between language and identity formation are evident in scholarship on genre[2] and on stories[3], but the literature most relevant to this chapter underscores relationships between discourse and identity. James Gee (1996), in his sociolinguistic work, writes about discourses in general ("ways of being in the world") as well as about the importance of particular discourses: "A Discourse is a sort of identity kit which comes complete with the appropriate costume and instructions on how to act, talk, and often write, so as to take on a particular social role that others will recognize" (p. 127). The roles that discourses allow people to "take on" may in some cases be professional roles. Hodgson (2005) offers insight into how a discourse identity kit might be used for learning professional roles when he notes that "the processual *enactment* of professionalism" can be equally important to professional knowledge in achieving a professional role (p. 53). Simonsen and Banfield (2006), too, call attention to the importance of discourse in constructing professional identities. Their work to foster mathematical discourse in an online forum for math teachers is built on the assumption that using such discourse will contribute to teachers' professional identities, and therefore to their ability to do their professional work.

The literature on language and identity construction has important implications for study of parawork in online forums. In online forums, the language that contributes to identity construction is most often written language. Study of the written texts that contribute to online parawork helps to make visible the rhetorical actions through which workers construct their professional roles. Whether the focus is on discourse, genre, story, or some other unit of language, textual analysis can highlight the ways in which written online parawork exchanges contribute to workers' efforts to build, transition into, and perform professional identities.

Collegiality in Online Forums for Professional Development

One additional strand of literature that I wish to discuss here is scholarship on the use of online forums to facilitate workers' professional development and continued growth. Much of the literature on this topic emphasizes the importance of collegiality in online forums for professional development. Collegiality is understood as a means for fostering workers' identification with their professional culture and for increasing their willingness to consult with others as they prepare to accomplish workplace tasks and goals. As Wickstrom (2003) describes it, collegiality involves peer relationships based on "openness to the idea of sharing" as well as "a sense of thoughtfulness" (p. 420). Grünberg and Armellini (2004) agree that collegial behavior includes "attending to the work of others, engaging in intellectual reciprocity, providing timely feedback to colleagues, being open to peer review . . . and sharing new ideas and . . . materials" (p. 598). Collegiality may occur as the result of online interactions—though it is not a "given" in online venues (Matsuda, 2002; Swenson, 2003; Wickstrom, 2003; Grünberg & Armellini, 2004). However, when collegiality does occur, it can help workers who write to one another in online forums to identify with one another (Singer & Zeni, 2004), to socialize more personally with one another (Halford, 2005), and "to make sense of their corporate [or organizational] life" (Racine, 1999, p. 170). Furthermore, collegiality can enhance workers' willingness to use each other as resources. While asking for help or advice may be viewed as a sign of weakness or incompetence in some workplace cultures, online forums can be places where participants are committed to sharing and learning with each other (Swenson, 2003; Singer & Zeni, 2004). In parawork environments, which are separate from workplace domains, workers who have escaped the surveillance of supervisors may feel comfortable risking questions that can help them to learn more about their work and how to go about it.

CASE STUDY

In the case study that follows, I examine how an intern I call Leigh uses an e-mail discussion list, Intern-Net, as a parawork site that helps her to construct, transition into, and perform her professional identity as a teacher[4]. In keeping with the literature reviewed above, I am interested in the ways that Leigh's written e-mails function as performative acts. Furthermore, I study the written posts not as isolated texts, but as visible aspects of the interactions of collegial workers, language, and technology-enabled spaces. The case study takes up the following questions: *What online parawork activities are visible through texts? How do people, language, and technology interact to enable parawork online? How can online parawork activities impact a person's professional work?*

To address these questions, I focus on Leigh's use of the Intern-Net listserv as a space for parawork activities. Following principles of rich feature analysis (Barton, 2004), I examine Leigh's e-mail messages from the electronic Intern-Net archives, discussing how Leigh accomplishes parawork through the use of patterned features in the function and structure of her discourse. The analysis also includes data from an interview that I conducted with Leigh. In this text-based, semi-scripted interview (Prior, 2004), I asked Leigh to look back through her Intern-Net posts with me. I used scripted questions to elicit comments related to particular features of her texts, as well as allowing for Leigh to talk open-endedly through memories and reflections that were evoked as she reread her e-mail messages. The scripted questions focused on Leigh's perspective about conditions that may have contributed to her willingness and ability to use Intern-Net for parawork and on the impact of Intern-Net conversations upon her off-line professional life. Using the textual analysis and interview data in tandem, I address the research questions above, exploring the realities and possibilities of parawork in online writing environments.

Background and Participants

The Intern-Net listserv began in 2004, at a time when I was seeking to provide an academic service to teacher interns while also trying to maintain and nurture professional relationships with students who were on their way to becoming secondary school English teachers—and potential partners in school/university service learning and research collaborations. I described it to interns as a list "intended to encourage and support your professional development as a teacher intern…a place to trade ideas, to ask questions, to share about interning experiences, and to reflect on your teaching practices and professional development." When the list began, 36 of the 45 eligible interns signed on. All have continued their subscriptions into this their third year of teaching. The list is private; I approve enrollment for all subscribers. Conversations are electronically archived, but the archives are password-protected to safeguard privacy. As a parawork site, the e-mail discussion list functions outside and alongside the workplace. Neither personnel from the schools nor supervisors from the university have access to the list, but subscribers may use Intern-Net as they choose in order to further their professional work. Conversations emerge informally according to participating teachers' needs and interests.

I began scholarly study of Intern-Net after winning the approval of my university's Institutional Review Board and the informed consent of teacher interns on the list. The work I share here is a small facet of a larger project situated in scholarship related to rhetorical genre studies, teacher learning in English education, and computers and composition. I acknowledge that it is somewhat unusual for a chapter relating to virtual workplaces to present a study of teachers or teacher interns (Grünberg & Armellini, 2004)—unusual, but not inappropriate. In most cases, schools are not businesses or for-profit entities; however, as organizations that are still structured in large part according to principles of Fordism, many contemporary schools have much in common with businesses and corporations (Apple, 1986)[5]. Studies on work and workplaces could and should include more attention to the conditions and contexts in which educators labor. Furthermore, since this study focuses on interns' use of spaces and activities that are outside of (or alongside of or beyond) traditional workplaces, the findings may be informative for a broad range of professions and organizations.

Parawork: Leigh's Case

Analysis of data from my interviews with Leigh and from her posts to the Intern-Net listserv reveals how an online parawork site located outside the bounds of the workplace can facilitate activities that contribute to a worker's professional development and success (and, by extension, to the success of her employing organization). My review of data from Leigh's case highlights the kinds of parawork activities enabled by the Intern-Net list:

Role Overlaps

A prominent pattern in Leigh's e-mails to the discussion list during her intern year is her explicit attention to her many roles and responsibilities. In a message posted during the first week of Intern-Net conversation, Leigh writes:

That's one thing that I have been struggling with as this 'real world' lifestyle takes over - how to maintain composure in the face of so many things going on at one time ([a relative]*passed away last weekend, re-working that* [assignment for Class X]*- does anyone understand that?!?, keeping up on the reading for three different classes and planning for one, trying to maintain friendships, etc.). It is so difficult to stay on top of it all! I have been telling people that student teaching is going well, but that it is extremely challenging to be a 'student' as well as a 'teacher.'*

In this paragraph, Leigh identifies herself as a family member, a student, an observer who must keep up on high schoolers' course readings, a teacher who must plan lessons, and a friend. Roles

are clearly on her mind, and Intern-Net is a site where Leigh can attend to multiple roles at one time. In a message posted the following spring, for example, Leigh uses a numbered list to work her way through items pertaining to three of her differing roles, asking first for information about a university meeting that she had to miss, then inviting discussion about a professional conference for teachers that she and several others on the list attended, and finally, announcing her upcoming musical performance at a local coffee house.

In our interview conversation, which occurred approximately two years after Leigh first began posting to Intern-Net, she emphasized the importance of the discussion list as a place where she could work through the challenges of being "always an intern and a college student at the same time." Offline, Leigh had to alternate between roles, first foregrounding one, and then the next: her role as college student was most important when attending her university classes, but her role as teacher mattered most at the high school where she completed her internship. The parawork environment of the Intern-Net listserv, however, allowed Leigh to overlap roles and freely perform multiple roles within the same time and place.

Role Conflict Mediation

Although an intern may be more of a student or more of a teacher in some contexts than in others, neither of these roles can be conveniently forgotten or made to disappear at a given time. Juggling roles in this complicated way can lead to difficulties, as we see in this message that Leigh posted midway through her internship year:

I have a class-related question for those of you that have [university] *class with* [Instructor A]*. I missed the last class because it was Records Day [at my internship school] and there were way too many papers to grade! I was wondering if anyone could provide me with a clear explanation of what the expectations are for class.*

In many schools and universities, teacher interns are referred to as student-teachers, a label that recognizes their hyphenated identities. As Leigh indicated in an earlier post, it is difficult to balance life on a hyphen. In this case, the two schooling institutions in which she participates are vying for her time; she cannot overlap her roles and successfully complete all of the required tasks in the time available. The teacher role takes precedent in this case. But Leigh does not "drop" her student role; she uses the discussion list to help her catch up so that she can continue to juggle her student and teaching responsibilities.

As a parawork site, Intern-Net literally helped Leigh to *mediate* conflicts between roles during her internship year. Leigh claimed in her interview that "the honesty you can put forth on Intern-Net is like no other place during that year." She explained that interns have to "put on the professional guise" in front of their supervising teachers at their internship sites, and that interns also feel great pressure "to look competent" to the university professors who evaluate interns' work. For Leigh, the discussion list was a safe place to navigate through some of the conflicts that typically occur during internships. She knew that Intern-Net was a supervisor-free zone, that the discussion list was private and password protected, and that her colleagues on the list were going through similar experiences and would therefore be understanding and supportive. In other words, Leigh understood Intern-Net as a space that was both outside and alongside her workplaces. These conditions made Intern-Net a parawork environment where Leigh—without risk of looking incompetent to supervisors and evaluators—could seek others' help as she worked out the glitches in her efforts to manage multiple, sometimes conflicting, roles.

Role Transitions

While the discussion list as a parawork site enabled Leigh to mediate conflicts between her roles, it also assisted in her gradual transition away from the student role and into new professional identities. Leigh's internship year posts show her growing in confidence and acting on values, beliefs, and practices that she believes to be essential to good teaching. In her first messages to Intern-Net, Leigh seems most comfortable in the role of student, acquiescing to her mentor teacher's wishes in order to keep the peace:

I have found myself in a couple of predicaments [with my mentor teacher] *that have made me uncomfortable because I don't want to ruin our relationship, yet I don't want to compromise my beliefs about education. For the time being, I have tended to basically just do what she wants. I want her to learn to trust me as a teacher, and, as time passes, perhaps she will be persuaded into allowing me to do more of what I want to do. At the end of the day, as my field instructor often reminds me, it is my mentor teacher that will be writing my evaluation, so it is good to try to stay on their good side throughout the course of the year, and enjoy the freedom of having my own classroom next year. Have any of you found this balance to be difficult?*

It seems here that Leigh can imagine herself as someday being a peer to her mentor teacher, as someone who can do what she "want[s] to do" when she "enjoy[s] the freedom of having [her] own classroom." Yet for the present, Leigh recognizes that her mentor teacher is in a position of power and authority over her; she remarks that as an intern she is "basically just do[ing] what [the mentor teacher] wants" in order to "stay on their good side."

As time passes, however, and Leigh continues to make posts to Intern-Net, her embrace of her identity as teacher becomes more and more apparent. In an e-mail posted a few months after the message above, Leigh details a conflict with a teacher in her building, asking Intern-Net list members about how to enact the role of teacher in a way that will satisfy several different groups. Just before her closing remarks she writes:

My struggles now are in dealing with the wide range of responses [from the people involved]. *First of all, how do I continue to deal with the students that heard the confrontation? What do I say when they make comments about* [X] *being a mean teacher? Secondly, what do I do about the fact that there is definite tension between the two of us, and we have to work together everyday? What do I do about the fact that she is spreading crap about me around the English department (though [other teachers] have already commented that I did the right thing, and that they are sorry that I took the brunt of* [X's] *insecurity attack)? Finally, what do we as English teachers do about* [students' poor study habits]*? How do we convince kids that they are selling themselves short?*

While this situation was difficult for her, writing about it to her Intern-Net peers seems to have been a catalyst toward Leigh's gaining confidence in assuming more fully the identity of teacher. Whereas in earlier posts Leigh alludes to the overlap and juxtaposition of varying roles and tasks, in this message, Leigh consistently refers to herself as a teacher. Early in the message she remarks, "I had one of the most intense days of my teaching career." Additionally, in her series of questions asking advice of the Intern-Net list, Leigh suggests a set of professional ideals: that she will respond in an appropriate way when students "make comments about [X] being a mean teacher," that she will "work together" with X in spite of "definite tensions," and that she will be prepared to take steps to safeguard her reputation with other teachers. The move that most fully marks Leigh as a teacher, though, is the way in which she circles back to talk about how to instruct students and—in the process—names herself and the other Intern-Net participants as English teachers: "Finally, what do we do as English teachers…?" Instead of merely deliberating about how to be a teacher (as in her first Intern-Net post), Leigh uses the list to step into her teacher skin and prepare for a kind of teaching work. She assesses her students'

learning needs in relationship to her educational goals for them, and then she begins to consider how to meet those needs through curriculum and instruction by asking questions about what can be done. In this way, Leigh begins to use the discussion list not only for identity construction, but also to ready herself to accomplish workplace tasks and goals.

When I talked with Leigh about the professional transition that I observed in the series of posts above, she spoke pointedly about the importance of the Intern-Net listserv for facilitating her transition from student to professional. She commented on the "unique" nature of the discussion list environment and on the ways in which its functions related to, but occurred outside of, her work (and workplaces) as student and teacher. Leigh noted that apart from the Intern-Net listserv, she would not have been willing to engage in transitional conversations like those excerpted above. She was willing to be vulnerable in the Intern-Net space because of her sense that it was a low-risk environment where she could experience collegiality by interacting socially, giving and receiving encouragement and advice, and trading resources, materials, and ideas. These parawork activities were all enabled by the unique nature of the discussion list as parawork space.

Information Exchange

Analysis of later internship-year posts show Leigh beginning to engage in additional parawork activities, employing the discussion list as a resource to gather ideas and expand her repertoire of strategies for carrying out professional responsibilities. Notice the pattern of information brokering that emerges in Leigh's posts over the next few months, as evidenced here in three excerpts from a series of messages requesting others' ideas:

• *Does anyone have a good way to teach writing book reviews? I need to come up with an assignment sheet, and I am having trouble deciding which components are important to assess. Let me know!*

- *Anyone have any great ideas for teaching* [Novel A] *or* [Novel B]*? Let me know.*
- *...our English department is attempting to revamp the curriculum a bit.* [Goes on to describe specific selection criteria and grade levels for use.] *Any great ideas?*

Leigh's posts suggest that for her, Intern-Net can function as a type of English teachers' information exchange. Leigh is not asking others to *do* her work for her; instead, she is asking for information that she can "take to work" with her so that she can successfully perform her teaching duties. She participates not only in requesting information, but also in sharing it. During the same period of time when she begins to ask others for their ideas, Leigh regularly responds to others' requests for assistance by sharing ideas and resources that she has developed. There is no formal trading agreement in place (e.g., "I'll give you a lesson plan on research writing if you'll give me a lesson plan for introducing Shakespeare), but there is evidence of "commitment to collegiality" (Swenson, 2003) and to the values of sharing and thoughtfulness.

When I questioned Leigh about the time and effort required to respond to other interns' requests, her replies shed additional light on the nature and significance of Intern-Net as a parawork site. One essential motivator for Leigh was what she referred to as a "we're-in-it-together mentality." The Intern-Net listserv has been configured to exclude supervisors and evaluators, a setting that can act as a double-edged sword. This setup affords privacy and safety, but it also meant that during Leigh's internship year, I was the only experienced teacher on the list. Since I had positioned myself as a co-learner who would not be "the answer lady" for all questions raised on the discussion list, Leigh felt that she and the other interns needed to pull together in order to make Intern-Net a place that was safe not only for asking

questions, but also for trying out answers. A second motivator that Leigh cited when she discussed her willingness to share ideas and advice also related to the technical configuration of the discussion list. Leigh observed that it has been quick and easy for her to attach documents that she already has, that it takes "very little to help people" when time and space are compressed as they are by online technologies. Additionally, e-mail discussion list technologies allow users either to "reply to all" or to respond privately to a single user. Leigh noted that Intern-Net allows her to pose a question to a large group of subscribers, but then to continue the conversation more privately, only with those who express interest in her initial post. During her internship, Leigh sometimes began exchanges with interns whom she might not otherwise have approached, and she was able to begin and carry on these discussions with a minimal amount of imposition on others who might not be interested in her topic—as well as a minimal amount of "risk" that others would be judging or evaluating the quality of her work. The configurations of the discussion list (along with the collegial habits of the subscribers) made it possible for Leigh, with little effort, to exchange materials, resources, ideas, and encouragement with her peers. These types of exchanges occurred outside of the workplace, yet they heightened Leigh's readiness to engage in workplace tasks and could therefore be characterized as parawork.

Association with Workplace and Professional Culture

Leigh's internship posts also facilitated another type of parawork activity: her association with her workplace and with the professional culture of teaching. A striking feature of Leigh's posts during her internship year is her increasing tendency to use plural rather than singular pronouns. This trend begins in a post excerpted earlier, where Leigh asks her Intern-Net peers what "we as English teachers" ought to do about students' poor study habits and how "we" ought to go about it. This use of *we* (as English teachers) appears frequently in other messages as well, and the pattern that becomes apparent is that Leigh is using the parawork space to try on language that aligns her with her professional culture.

At the same time that Leigh uses the discussion list as a parawork site where she begins to identify with her profession, she also uses list conversations to show that she is associating more closely with the people and activities at the site of her internship. Again, plural pronouns help her to accomplish this parawork task. The messages from early in Leigh's internship typically refer to what "they" do at the high school and to what the mentor teacher ("she") or department chair ("she") wants as opposed to what Leigh ("I") does or expects. For example, in one early post to the list, Leigh describes her relationship with her mentor:

On the one hand, I get along really well with my mentor teacher. She is [X years old and] *lots of fun... However, it is difficult to not step on each others toes when we are in the classroom. She has a very traditional mindset about teaching... She has an obsession with the 5 paragraph essay... I have found myself in a couple of predicaments that have made me uncomfortable because I don't want to ruin our relationship, yet I don't want to compromise my beliefs about education.*

In this post and others like it, Leigh uses pronouns and contrasting descriptions to set herself apart from those at the school where she interns. As time passes, though, she begins to shift her language in order to include herself as an integrated member of her internship school. In her later messages to the list, Leigh frequently refers to what "*we* at [High School X] do" or to what happens in "*our* English department." Through her written parawork posts to Intern-Net, Leigh begins to associate herself with the other teachers at the school, to identify with the culture of her workplace instead of setting herself apart from it.

The language that Leigh used in her internship e-mails not only marked her association with her workplace and professional culture; it also helped to facilitate it. Leigh observed during our interview session that there was an extended period during the first portion of her internship when she felt distinctly separate student and professional identities. Writing to her Intern-Net colleagues, she explained, helped her to find ways to integrate these identities, to become a student of teaching rather than someone who was split between being student and being teacher. "It wasn't until [these identities] merged that I was able to be—or feel—successful," noted Leigh. Her use of written language, including her shift to plural first-person pronouns, was a way for Leigh to begin identifying with her workplace and to include herself as a member of the teaching profession. The opportunity that the discussion list afforded for Leigh to use language in this way is yet another example of the ways in which an online environment like Intern-Net can enable parawork.

CONCLUSION

Leigh's case demonstrates that online parawork sites like the Intern-Net listserv can support parawork activities including mediation of role overlaps, conflicts, and transitions; exchange of work-related information; and association with workplace and professional cultures. These parawork activities are not themselves Leigh's "work" but do impact her professional life in significant ways, making it possible for her to step more fully into her teaching identity and to perform her professional roles and responsibilities with greater skill and confidence. Of course, Leigh is not the only one to benefit from her use of Intern-Net for parawork. Her students, colleagues, and the schools in which she works also gain (albeit indirectly) from Leigh's parawork activities. Any organization can benefit when workers transition smoothly into new roles, respond effectively to workplace issues and challenges, increase their knowledge base, expand their repertoire of skills and strategies, and adapt productively to local and professional workplace cultures.

For Leigh, it is the unique interaction of her written language, her exchanges with collegial peers, and the configurations of the technology-enabled online space that make parawork possible. Her case highlights conditions essential for supporting online parawork spaces and activities that benefit workers in their professional roles:

An Environment that Encourages People to Enact Multiple Roles

The space itself, as well as the people interacting within the space, must send a clear message that it is "good form" to be more than a professional (that is, to be a person who also enacts other roles—professional, social, and personal) within the parawork environment. This message may be communicated explicitly or implicitly, so long as it is sent consistently. A space that allows people to interact with each other while engaging in a variety of roles also allows people to share a variety of interests or common experiences, to relate to each other in diverse ways, and to build trust through multiple connections. Leigh noted during our interview that the times when she felt strong common bonds with Intern-Net subscribers were also the times that she was most likely to post messages to the discussion list and engage in the types of activities that I have identified as parawork.

A Low-Risk Environment

At least three factors relating to safety impacted Leigh's willingness to use the discussion list for parawork. One essential condition that Leigh highlighted repeatedly during our interview was the fact that the list excluded supervisors and oth-

ers whose evaluations of her performance might affect her ability to get or keep work. A second and closely-related condition was the relatively low level of competition among those subscribing to the list. Because of this condition, the interns were more motivated to cooperate and help each other than to withhold information, resources, or ideas. Deliberate safeguarding of privacy was another important condition contributing to Leigh's willingness to use the discussion list for parawork. For Intern-Net, this has meant that the list is closed to new subscribers, that archives are password protected, that names and other identifying information are changed in research presentations and publications about the list (as well as in some messages posted by subscribers), and that there is an explicit agreement that discussion list conversations are not to be forwarded or discussed elsewhere without the permission of the subscribers[6].

A Space that Responds Flexibly to Users' Needs and Interests

It is key that the parawork site be able to support diverse activities that reflect users' needs and interests. For Intern-Net, this has meant that the list has been used to exchange resources and materials, to seek out advice and support, to organize social events, to ask questions, and to provide personal information to the group (updates about moves, weddings, etc.). These needs and interests might vary in other parawork contexts. One constant across parawork spaces, however, is that activities should be driven by users. While the workers who use parawork spaces may choose to take up activities suggested by mentors or even supervisors, doing so must be completely voluntary. A personal e-mail from Leigh illustrates the importance of this kind of voluntary participation. When I was first considering studying the Intern-Net listserv, I asked the interns what they thought about the idea. Leigh wrote to encourage me to proceed with the study. Her supportive message included one caveat: "My only concern with the success of the listserv is that is will become something that is mandatory. . . . The most wonderful thing about the listserv is that it is there for you when you need [it]. . . . It is a fantastic set-up that allows for genuine responses. If this were to ever become required, I think it would lose its authenticity" (personal communication, December 5, 2004). Mandating that anyone use a parawork site—or do so in a particular way—results in an environment that is no longer fully "outside" the workplace, making it impossible for the space to function as an environment shaped by users to support them "alongside of" their professional work. Mandating or regulating participation takes the "para" out of parawork.

IMPLICATIONS FOR FUTURE RESEARCH

Leigh's use of Intern-Net during her internship year demonstrates some of the realities and possibilities of online sites for parawork, but this exemplar case is limited in scope. Further research is necessary in order to better understand the precise nature of parawork, to identify which aspects of parawork spaces and activities remain stable across contexts—and which characteristics change in response to varied contexts. It would be beneficial, for example, to learn how workers' experience levels and the relative stability of their professional roles affect their participation in parawork spaces. Could we expect that experienced workers adapting to new roles and tasks would use parawork spaces much as Leigh has? Would workers with relatively stable professional responsibilities take advantage of parawork spaces in a manner much different from Leigh's approach to the Intern-Net listserv? Similarly, it would be useful to understand more fully the impact of workplace culture on the activities that emerge in parawork spaces. Leigh noted repeatedly that during her internship year, she felt uncomfortable

asking too many questions of (or in front of) her supervisors, so that the discussion list became an important place for her to reflect without risking the appearance of incompetence. How might parawork activities evolve differently for workers who do not feel so vulnerable to the evaluating eye of supervisors?

Investigating the role of other variables in the overall context of the parawork scene would also enhance our understanding of parawork. Leigh's case shows parawork occurring within a discussion list configured in a particular way, with an exclusive and voluntary membership guarded by passwords and other privacy-protecting settings. How might parawork evolve differently on a discussion list with alternate settings, in an "open" discussion list, or even through a different kind of online space such as a discussion board, chat room, or blog? And if an essential quality of parawork spaces is that they exist and function alongside but also *outside* the bounds of the workplace, to what extent could a business or other organization become involved in "sponsoring" a parawork site without also becoming involved in the regulation and oversight of that space and the activities that occur within it? Lastly, I have concentrated here on beneficial aspects of parawork sites and activities. What conditions might contribute to parawork sites having a detrimental effect on workers and their relationships with their workplaces?

These are challenging questions, and they demonstrate that the complex nature of parawork spaces and activities will not be pinned down easily or uncovered through a single study. My hope is that by naming and defining parawork and analyzing one case of parawork in the online world, I will have initiated a productive conversation about alongside-of-yet-outside-of spaces and activities that shape our daily interactions in the ever-changing world of work.

ACKNOWLEDGMENT

Thank you to "Leigh" for permitting a published glimpse into her Intern-Net participation. Thanks also to Jeff Grabill, professor of Rhetoric and Professional Writing and co-director of the Writing in Digital Environments (WIDE) Research Center at Michigan State University, for his insightful and helpful responses to earlier drafts of this work.

REFERENCES

Alsup, J. (2006). *Teacher identity discourses: Negotiating personal and professional spaces.* Mahwah, NJ: Lawrence Erlbaum Associates and National Council of Teachers of English.

Apple, M. (1986). *Teachers and texts: A political economy of class and gender relations in education.* New York, NY: Routledge.

Artemeva, N., Logie, S., & St-Martin, J. (1999). From page to stage: How theories of genre and situated learning help introduce engineering students to discipline-specific communication. *Technical Communication Quarterly, 8*(3), 301-316.

Barton, E. (2004). Linguistic discourse analysis: How the language in texts works. In: C. Bazerman & P. Prior (Eds.), *What writing does and how it does it: An introduction to analyzing texts and textual practices* (pp. 57-82). Mahwah, NJ: Lawrence Erlbaum Associates.

Cerulo, K. (1997). Identity construction: New issues, new directions. *Annual Review of Sociology, 23,* 385-409.

Crandall, N., & Wallace, M. (1998). *Work and rewards in the virtual workplace: A "New Deal" for organizations and employees.* New York, NY: AMACOM.

Cubbison, L. (1999). Configuring LISTSERV, configuring discourse. *Computers and Composition, 16*(3), 371-381.

Gee, J. (1996). *Social linguistics and literacies: Ideology in discourses* (2nd ed.). Bristrol, PA: Taylor & Francis.

Gregson, N., & Rose, G. (2000). Taking Butler elsewhere: Performativities, spatialities and subjectivities. *Environment and Planning D: Society and Space, 18*(4), 433-452.

Grünberg, J., & Armellini, A. (2004). Teacher collegiality and electronic communication: A study of the collaborative uses of e-mail by secondary school teachers in Uruguay. *British Journal of Educational Technology, 35*(5), 597-606.

Halford, S. (2005). Hybrid workspace: Re-spatialisations of work, organisation and management. *New Technology, Work and Employment, 20*(1), 19-33.

Hill, E., Ferris, M., & Martinson, V. (2003). Does it matter where you work? A comparison of how three work venues (traditional office, virtual office, and home office) influence aspects of work and personal/family life. *Journal of Vocational Behavior, 63*(2), 220-241.

Hodgson, D. (2005). Putting on a professional performance: Performativity, subversion and project management. *Organization, 12*(1), 51-68.

Jenlink, P., & Kinnucan-Welsch, K. (2001). Case stories of facilitating professional development. *Teaching and Teacher Education, 17*(6), 705-724.

Latour, B. (1988). Mixing humans and nonhumans together: The sociology of the door closer. *Social Problems, 35*(3), 298-310.

Lingard, L., Garwood, K., Schryer, C., & Spafford, M. (2002). A certain art of uncertainty: Case presentation and the development of professional identity. *Social Science and Medicine, 56,* 603-616.

Matsuda, P. (2002). Negotiation of identity and power in a Japanese online discourse community. *Computers and Composition, 19*(1), 39-55.

Moore, J. (2006). Homeworking and work-life balance: does it add to quality of life?. *Revue Européenne de Psychologie Appliquée/European Review of Applied Psychology, 56*(1), 5-13.

Morgan, L., & Martin, K. (2006). Taking women professionals out of the office: The case of women in sales. *Gender & Society, 20*(1), 108-128.

'para-', prefix[1]. (2005). *OED Online*. Retrieved July 26, 2006, from http://dictionary.oed.com/cgi/entry/50170860.

Paré, A. (2002). Genre and identity: Individuals, institutions, and ideology. In: R. Coe, L. Lingard & T. Teslenko (Eds.), *The rhetoric and ideology of genre* (pp. 57-71). Cresskill, NJ: Hampton.

Porter, J. (2002). Why technology matters to writing: A cyberwriter's tale. *Computers and Composition, 20*(4), 375-394.

Prior, P. (2004). Tracing processes: How texts come into being. In: C. Bazerman & P. Prior (Eds.), *What writing does and how it does it: An introduction to analyzing texts and textual practices* (pp. 167-200). Mahwah, NJ: Lawrence Erlbaum Associates.

Racine, S. (1999). Using corporate lore to create boundaries in the workplace. *Journal of Technical Writing and Communication, 29*(2), 167-183.

Schryer, C., & Spoel, P. (2005). Genre theory, health-care discourse, and professional identity formation. *Journal of Business and Technical Communication, 19*(3), 249-278.

Searle, J. (1969). *Speech acts: An essay in the philosophy of language*. London: Cambridge University.

Selfe, C., & Selfe, R., Jr. (1994). The politics of the interface: Power and its exercises in electronic contact zones. *College Composition and Communication, 45*(4), 480-504.

Simonsen, L., & Banfield, J. (2006). Fostering mathematical discourse in online asynchronous discussions: An analysis of instructor interventions. *Journal of Computers in Mathematics and Science Teaching, 25*(1), 41-75.

Singer, N., & Zeni, J. (2004). Building bridges: Creating an online conversation community for preservice teachers. *English Education, 37*(1), 30-49.

Star, S. (1999). The ethnography of infrastructure. *American Behavioral Scientist, 43*(3), 377-391.

Swenson, J. (2003). Transformative teacher networks, online professional development, and the Write for your Life project. *English Education, 35*(4), 262-321.

Wickstrom, C. (2003). A 'funny' thing happened on the way to the forum. *Journal of Adolescent & Adult Literacy, 46*(5), 414-423.

KEY TERMS

Collegiality: Mutually beneficial disposition of colleagues or peers toward each other, characterized by behaviors such as sharing, thoughtfulness, timeliness, reciprocity, helpfulness, and honesty.

Culture: An ever-emerging social system of values, beliefs, practices, discourses, and constructed knowledge.

Discourse: A system of socially-patterned language practices; discourses continually shape and are shaped by culture, are influential in forming personal identities, and are used as resources as people work within, across, or against cultures.

Identity Construction: The shaping of a person's values, beliefs, practices, discourses, and knowledge; influenced both by cultural systems and by individual actions.

Listserv, or list: When written in lowercase letters, a popular name for any automatic mailing server for e-mail messages; derived from the uppercase name *LISTSERV*™—the registered trademark licensed to L-Soft International, Inc. for the electronic mailing list processor product that it distributes. Each member who subscribes to a discussion list automatically receives an e-mail copy of every message sent ("posted") to "the list." Posts are usually labeled with subject lines that identify the message's theme or topic. A group of messages generated in response to a particular post (and often with identical or related subject lines) is known as a "thread." The Intern-Net discussion list does rely on LISTSERV™ software, and subscribers refer to the space as both *listerv* and *list*.

Nonhuman Actors: Objects, artifacts, or structures that interact in a network with people ("human actors") by constraining, permitting, facilitating, promoting, or responding to human actions; the term is central to Actor Network Theory.

Parawork: Spaces and activities that function alongside—but also outside—of traditional workplaces and work.

ENDNOTES

[1] Note the parallels to space and technology, which can also be said to shape and be shaped by interactions with people, as discussed earlier.

[2] Scholarship in genre studies has consistently shown that participating in professional genres can facilitate a person's assumption of professional roles and their formation of professional identity (Artemeva, Logie, & St-Martin, 1999; Lingard, Garwood, Paré, 2002; Schryer, & Spafford, 2002; Schryer & Spoel, 2005).

[3] Research on a particular type of genre, stories, also points to connections between language use and professional identity construction (Racine, 1999; Jenlink & Kinnucan-Welsch, 2001; Singer & Zeni, 2004; Alsup, 2006;).

[4] Names and other identifying information for the case study have been changed. In quoted excerpts from Intern-Net e-mails, spelling has been "standardized" except where the participant has been deliberately unconventional.

[5] In a treatise that remains relevant for today's educational politics, Apple (1986) criticizes the "commodification of education," complaining that in the popular view, "Good teaching is only that which is demonstrated in competency tests for teachers. Good curricula are only those which have immediately available and easily testable results found in standardized text material. Good learning is only the accumulation of atomistic skills and facts and answering the questions in standardized achievement tests for students" (p. 147). Apple laments that "[t]he language of efficiency, production, standards, cost-effectiveness, job skills, work discipline, and so on" is prevalent in talk, writing, and thought about education (p. 154).

[6] As noted earlier, this study has been conducted with IRB approval and informed consent from Intern-Net subscribers. As part of the informed consent process, drafts of all manuscripts related to the Intern-Net listserv are submitted to subscribers. The subscribers' anonymous responses help to guide my revisions of drafts.

Chapter VIII
Impression Formation in Computer–Mediated Communication and Making a Good (Virtual) Impression

Jamie S. Switzer
Colorado State University, USA

ABSTRACT

In face-to-face interactions, people generally form impressions by focusing on a variety of nonverbal cues. Increasingly, however, people are communicating virtually and forming impressions based on mediated interactions. In an online environment, the range of nonverbal cues that normally aid in impression formation is drastically narrowed. In the absence of these nonverbal cues, forming impressions via computer-mediated communication places a greater emphasis on verbal (text-based) and linguistic cues. This chapter offers strategies to ensure virtual workers make a good impression on their clients and colleagues when interacting online.

INTRODUCTION

As the saying goes, you never get a second chance to make a good first impression. This is especially true when working virtually, where impressions are formed via computer-mediated communication (CMC). As Wallace observes, "Increasingly…the online persona is playing a larger role in first impressions as people rely on email, websites, and discussion forums more for the first contact, and the phone call, letter, or face-to-face meetings less" (1999, p. 14).

The varieties of nonverbal cues that normally aid in impression formation do not exist in an online environment. In the absence of these nonverbal cues, forming impressions via CMC places a greater emphasis on verbal (text-based) and linguistic cues, as well as depending more upon social cues such as shared schema, context, and stereotypes. Indeed, as Tannis and Postmes observe, "communications over the Internet are all but free from influences of the social, the cognitive, and the physical" (2003, p. 692).

It is critical, then, that people working virtually understand how impressions are formed in an online environment and what types of cues aid in forming those impressions, so virtual workers can manage their own online behavior in such a manner that allows others to form an accurate impression.

BACKGROUND

Impression formation is a significant characteristic of communication and a fundamental social-psychological process (Walther, 1993; Liu, Ginther, & Zelhart, 2002). Asch (1946) and Goffman (1959) are generally associated with the earliest scholarly research into impression formation. Regardless of the nature of an interpersonal interaction, as humans "we seem to exit most of our social encounters with some general impression of the other person's characteristics and dispositions" (Hancock & Dunham, 2001, p. 325). It is simply human nature to form impressions of those around us with whom we communicate in a variety of ways and with differing motivations and goals.

Early scholarship into impression formation emphasized how traditional cues and sources of information identified as important in face-to-face interactions were reduced or eliminated in a CMC environment (Short, Williams & Christie, 1976; Kiesler, Siegel & McGuire, 1984; Sproull & Kiesler, 1986). These theories, collectively termed the "cues filtered out" approach (Culnan & Markus, 1987), concluded that a lack of nonverbal cues prevented people from forming impressions in CMC.

However, a growing body of empirical research has since contested the findings of the cues filtered out theories, and instead has shown that people compensate for the lack of nonverbal cues in a variety of ways and do indeed form well-developed impressions in mediated environments (see Sherman, 2001, p. 54). One of the more recent theoretical models that is key to understanding impression formation in CMC is social information processing theory (SIP).

SIP (Walther, 1992) posits that in the absence of nonverbal cues, people adapt. They are mo-

tivated to use whatever information they have available in a particular medium to provide cues to assist in impression formation. According to SIP, while certain nonverbal cues are missing in CMC, other cues needed to form impressions are still exchanged during an interaction. Because of the nature of CMC, the process takes more time and impressions are formed over a more extended period than in face-to-face interactions.

IMPRESSION FORMATION CUES IN CMC

As predicted by SIP, human beings rely on specific types of cues inherent in CMC to form impressions. Categories, stereotypes, schemas, cultural background and preconceived biases all influence the formation of impressions. Studies have shown that the impact of these social cues is considerable in impression formation (Tanis & Postmes, 2003). In CMC, the number of social cues is reduced, but that "does not point to a reduction in the social context of the CMC" (Spears & Lea, 1992, p. 324).

Social stereotypes and exemplars are types of metonymic models (models in which one member of a category is used to understand the membership as a whole) that are commonly utilized when forming impressions in an online environment (Jacobson, 1999). A stereotype is a model where a society or culture recognizes characteristics of an individual or group of people as representing an entire category. For example, some athletes often make headlines by engaging in unruly and unlawful behavior. Thus athletes are often categorized as being rowdy and uncontrollable, which is more likely the exception instead of the rule. There are many, many athletes who devote their time, energy, and money to charitable causes, who are dedicated to their families, and who do not break the law. However, athletes as a whole are often stereotyped according to this commonly held belief that athletes are unmanageable.

An exemplar is a specific individual that a person has encountered, who is then taken as a representative of others who are thought to be in that same category. However, different people have different experiences with different people who serve as exemplars. Using the previous example of athletes, if someone met an athlete at a charity function who was talking and interacting with the crowd, happily signing autographs and taking photos with children, the inference might be that this particular athlete was a nice person. Based on this one encounter, that athlete is an exemplar for all athletes, who must therefore all be nice people. That is certainly not the case, particularly in a few specific sports.

Impression formation in CMC, as in face-to-face interactions, is extremely dependent upon social cues such as stereotypes, along with the context of the communication and shared schema. People tend to fill in their gaps of knowledge about another person with typifications based on stereotypes and exemplars, a concept defined as "idealization" (Goffman, 1959). Within that framework, people need to seek as much information as possible to form an impression.

Impression formation refers to the "interpersonal processes by which people employ all available information and make general judgments of others' personality characteristics" (Liu, Ginther, & Zelhart, 2002, p. 73). In a face-to-face environment, people rely on nonverbal cues like vocal patterns (such as tone or accent), linguistic markers (such as vocabulary and grammar), body posture, gestures and eye contact to glean information. The words that are actually spoken are not as influential when forming an impression (Wallace, 1999). But those nonverbal cues are missing when working virtually—the range of cues available to participants in the interaction is narrowed in mediated interactions (Lyon, 2002).

In an online environment the impressions people form and the judgments they make are based solely on the information available to them. People create a perception of others to the extent that they extensively process available information

(Leyens & Corneille, 1999) within the context of their own biases and culture. However, in an online environment, that information is extremely limited and is usually conveyed mainly via keystrokes, making the keyboard an "unfamiliar and awkward impression-making device" (Wallace, 1999, p. 28). Yet there are many ways—some subtle, some obvious—that information is communicated in CMC.

E-mail addresses and domains can convey a considerable amount of information about someone's personality, character, and status. "John. Smith@mycompany.com" gives the impression of professionalism; "beachluvr@hotmail.com" does not. An e-mail coming from a "dot edu" domain indicates that the person is in some way involved in education, which implies a more intellectual status than a "dot com" domain. However, there is ambiguity within a message received from a "dot edu" domain. Is the sender a teacher or professor? A student? An athletic coach? A maintenance worker? To form an accurate impression of the sender of the message, the receiver must rely on additional textual and linguistic cues.

Linguistic style in discourse has a significant impact on impression formation. Users of powerful language styles are perceived as competent, credible, attractive, and persuasive (Adkins & Brashers, 1995). Likewise, in CMC, additional cues such as language use, word choice, vocabulary, sentence structure, and spelling also provide information about a person.

For instance, in the previous "dot edu" example, if an e-mail included a number of references to a complicated scientific process and long, unpronounceable words, one may conclude the sender was a professor. If the message contained words such as "dude" and "awesome" within short, incomplete sentences with informal or even incorrect spelling (such as "kewl" or "howRU"), the impression is that the sender is an undergraduate student.

Obviously there can be ambiguity within language styles. A professor might very well use the word "awesome" and an undergraduate be well versed in the language of science. In general, however, our shared social schemas lead to forming those particular impressions. According to the stereotype, people believe professors use large words when communicating, and stereotypical undergraduate students use slang.

Likewise, the presence of spelling errors in an online interaction can have multiple meanings. Was the sender just in a hurry and did not closely proofread the e-mail? The impression one might form is that the sender is too busy to be bothered with proper spelling, meaning perhaps it will be difficult to collaborate virtually with this person because they are overworked. Does the sender truly not know how to spell? The impression then might be that the sender would not be a viable partner in a virtual business collaboration.

Vocabulary, word choice, and spelling can also provide information about nationality and/or geographic location. If one of the participants in an online interaction used the word "boot" when referring to the back end of a car, the impression is that the person is from England and not the U.S. (where the term would be "trunk"). Likewise with spelling: the word is spelled "color" in the U.S. and "colour" in England.

Even within countries, linguistic cues can provide geographic information. The term "y'all" is typically associated with the southern region of the U.S. If a message is received containing that term, the impression is that the sender is from the South, which in turn conjures up a host of other stereotypical impressions (usually unflattering) of people who live in the southern U.S.

Information can be communicated in CMC using paralinguistic cues, which can also assist with impression formation. Typographical marks and other textual features such as exclamation points (excitement), ellipses (trailing thought), emoticons (smiley faces), and use of capital letters (SHOUTING) have no lexical meaning per se. The meaning of paralinguistic cues is "dependent on the group or individual context that is pre-established for the communication" (Lea & Spears,

1992, p. 321); to understand them, the meanings must be socially shared among all participants in the interaction. Based on the context, impressions formed using paralinguistic cues can be positive or negative.

Another nonverbal cue utilized when forming impressions in CMC is the use of time, known as chronemics (Walther & Tidwell, 1995). The timing of message sending and receiving, as well as the frequency and duration of online interactions (Liu, Ginther, & Zelhart, 2002), influences impression development in CMC and provides information that can be interpreted in a variety of ways, particularly in the context of a work environment. For example, if a person sends an e-mail late at night, the impression may be that sender is a hard worker who spends many long hours at the computer. If a receiver waits a long time to respond to a message, it may signify superiority of the receiver or a perceived lack of status on the part of the sender. An immediate response implies priority and importance.

However, like all other nonverbal or paralinguistic cues, chronemic cues have their greatest influence in the context of other cues and relationships (Walther & Tidwell, 1995). It may be that the late-night e-mailer works from home and is most productive at night and sleeps during normal business hours. Therefore, the impression of the person as a hard worker may not be correct and other cues are needed to form an accurate impression.

How people present themselves online are types of personal "markers" (Jordan, 2002; Wood & Smith, 2005) that replace nonverbal cues normally present in a face-to-face environment that impact impression formation. Text-based verbal behaviors also play a role in forming impressions in CMC. To ensure that impressions are accurate requires people to engage in impression management.

IMPRESSION MANAGEMENT

Impression management is the process by which individuals attempt to control others' perceptions of them, motivated by the desire for social acceptance and relationship development and maintenance (Becker & Stamp, 2005). People spend a great deal of time on impression management, working to regulate what information is known and not known by others about oneself in order to manage the impression others have of them (O'Sullivan, 2000). Impression management theory posits people are motivated to control the impressions they make on others (Schlenker, 1980), regardless of whether or not the interaction occurs face-to-face or virtually.

Studies by Asch (1946) showed long ago that people tend to leap to conclusions very fast, with few cues to guide them, when forming first impressions. First impressions, however, are "notoriously susceptible to misperception" (Wallace, 1999, p. 15) because people base their impressions on minimal cues and all other assumptions flow from that initial conclusion, regardless of its accuracy.

Additionally, initial impressions often lead people to behave toward another person in certain ways (Sherman, 2001). Sherman gives the example of perceiving someone to be friendly and therefore interacting with him or her in an open and welcoming manner; the other person, then, may respond in a manner even more friendly than perhaps they would normally. This is referred to as the "snowball effect" (Gilbert, 1995), in which a first impression can initiate interactions that gather momentum and become harder to alter and correct if they are indeed inaccurate. First impressions are important because people do not like to admit mistakes. This can lead to confirmation bias, where people ignore evidence that may contradict their first impressions and even actively seek information to confirm the original impression, even though it was incorrect (Wallace, 1999).

Self-presentation is a technique used in impression management. Senders of messages can take advantage of the nature of CMC to carefully craft messages and deliberately enhance the representation of themselves by optimizing self-presentation (Walther, 1996). By engaging in selective self-presentation, people can control what information is revealed during an interaction, thereby influencing what cues are available for the receivers of the message to form impressions.

In some ways, impression management is easier to control in CMC because there are no accidental or unintended nonverbal behaviors or physical cues (Walther, Slovacek, & Tidwell, 2001). Additionally, visual cues may not be present, so there is no preconceived stereotypical perception that can prejudice the interaction.

In other ways, however, impression management in CMC is more difficult than in a face-to-face environment. Research has shown that physical appearance is extremely important in the formation of first impressions (Hatfield & Sprecher, 1986); in most cases that cue is absent in CMC. Words can be construed with different meanings than originally intended in the absence of nonverbal cues. Text-based communications can be wholly misinterpreted by the receiver of the message because there are no additional social cues present to aid in understanding the message more accurately. It is important, then, that virtual workers manage their online behavior in such a manner that others have the information they need to form an accurate impression.

STRATEGIES FOR MANAGING IMPRESSIONS IN CMC

"The desire to form impressions of other people and to manage our own impressions in social settings...does not disappear just because we now do these things on the Internet" (Wallace, 1999, p. 36). Virtual workers must be acutely aware of the nature of CMC in order to make a good virtual impression on their clients and colleagues when interacting online. As predicted by SIP, people form impressions based upon one's online behavior, conveyed using verbal (text-based) and linguistic cues in the context of cultural background and personal biases. In the absence of any "reality checks" (Jacobson, 1999) such as nonverbal cues or visuals, virtual workers must employ a variety of strategies to carefully manage their interactions to gain social acceptance as well as develop and maintain viable relationships.

CMC users employ a variety of uncertainty reduction cues to "give and gain impressions of one another" (Walther, Loh, & Granka, 2005, p. 40). According to Uncertainty Reduction Theory (URT), the exchange and collection of information allows people to predict the attitudes and behaviors of others (Berger & Calabrese, 1975). The more information that is gathered about a person, the more uncertainty toward that person is reduced (Tidwell & Walther, 2002).

URT posits that individuals utilize three different information-gathering strategies as a means of reducing uncertainty: passive, active, and interactive (Tidwell & Walther, 2002). Passive strategies involve the unobtrusive observation of a person to garner information. Active strategies involve targeted efforts to collect information about someone, but without that person's knowledge. Interactive strategies for reducing uncertainty entail direct exchanges among the people involved.

As predicted by URT, people are going to be actively seeking information with which to form an impression of others. In CMC, it is difficult to "observe" a person's behavior, but it is very easy to seek information about someone either actively (by Googling them, for example) or interactively via direct dialogue. Therefore, virtual workers must manage their own behavior in such a way that allows others to form an accurate impression of them in a mediated environment. Below are some strategies to ensure that virtual workers make a good impression on their clients and colleagues when interacting online. While these uncertainty reduction strategies may seem relatively simplistic

and straightforward, they are the most accessible and effective to employ in CMC.

Full Disclosure

One way to reduce uncertainty and prevent idealization of senders and receivers of messages is to voluntarily disclose as much relevant information as necessary in the context of the virtual workplace and the task at hand. The sharing and acquisition of information is a proactive strategy that can significantly reduce any uncertainty present due to the lack of nonverbal cues in CMC (Tidwell & Walther, 2002).

Writing self-descriptions is one way to share information. Introducing oneself to virtual colleagues and customers, providing biographical details relevant to the establishment and development of the relationship (such as years of experience in the field), is an excellent strategy for managing impression formation. People have a tendency to increase the amount of information shared (self-disclosure) when interacting via CMC (Joinson, 2001), thus providing additional cues to aid in impression formation. Research has shown that even minimal cues, such as a few biographical details, can have a drastic impact on the quality of impressions people form of one another (Tanis & Postmes, 2003).

Be Honest

There is considerable uncertainty about the accuracy of information in CMC, particularly with respect to self-presentation and how closely that matches how people really are (Walther & Parks, 2002). Honesty is critical when interacting virtually. It can be tempting when managing impressions to not be absolutely forthright, particularly if there is no chance the virtual working relationship will ever move to a face-to-face environment.

People employ a variety of information-seeking strategies beyond direct online interaction, such as acquiring information from third party sources without the other person's knowledge or using search engines to discover information that is available on the Internet (Ramirez, Walther, Burgoon, & Sunnafrank, 2002). So it is likely that if a person is not honest when communicating virtually, that deception will be discovered. Likewise if an initial impression is inaccurate when it is articulated, if left uncorrected, the "snowball effect" discussed previously can occur.

Research suggests, however, that people do not actively deceive others when trying to form relationships and manage the impression others develop in an online interaction (Albright, 2001). Even "to reveal oneself as clearly and honestly as possible requires individuals to select from a repertoire of self-presentational activities to convey themselves accurately," suggesting that self-presentation is not necessarily manipulative or deceptive, but "should be viewed as a broader concept that includes efforts to present oneself accurately" (O'Sullivan, 2000, p. 406).

Additionally, people who know that the virtual relationship will eventually lead to a face-to-face meeting tend to be more open and honest in the self-disclosure process (Gibbs, Ellison, & Heino, 2006). When that face-to-face meeting does occur and the reality does not match the impression formed from the online interaction, it is usually the result of the participants "filling in the blanks" incorrectly (Goffman's concept of idealization), not because they were mislead or lied to (Albright, 2001). People who meet and interact in a text-based environment are often wildly mistaken when they imagine one another's off-line appearances (Jacobson, 1999), partially because of the impact of cultural stereotypes and personal schema on impression formation.

Ask Questions

Anticipated future face-to-face interaction also strongly impacts CMC participants and promotes the asking of more personal and intimate questions (Tidwell & Walther, 2002). Asking questions aids in self-disclosure and information gathering. If the available information is ambiguous, simply

asking for clarification will ensure that accurate impressions are formed without jumping to incorrect conclusions. Asking questions can also reduce the possibility of the snowball effect or idealization occurring.

Precise Use of Language

The precise use of language is essential to managing impressions in CMC, to ensure that the expression equals the intention (Adkins & Brashers, 1995). Communications in a text-based environment can be extremely ambiguous, particularly because of the absence of nonverbal cues. For example, delivering the words "I hate you" with a smile, a wink, and an embrace make the actual intention of the message clear; paying attention to only the words used in the communication gives an inaccurate impression. Therefore, it is important to take advantage of the nature of CMC by taking the time to construct messages and craft them in the clearest and most comprehensible manner to avoid any misunderstanding.

Be Aware of Cues

Being aware of the verbal (text-based), linguistic, and paralinguistic cues present in CMC is the most important detail to pay attention to when working virtually. As discussed previously, the absence of nonverbal cues in CMC requires participants to use other content and linguistic strategies to gather information that assists in impression formation. Virtual workers must guard against jumping to conclusions based on minimal cues as a guide.

Be aware of the subtle cues communicated by e-mail addresses; a virtual worker's e-mail address should project professionalism. Think about the subtle meanings conveyed by linguistic style when interacting via CMC. Pay attention to details such as language intensity, lexical diversity, and spelling. Be aware of the impact chronemics can have upon impression formation. Paralinguistic cues can also communicate information that is used in impression formation, but only if the virtual workers involved in the interaction share the same framework for assigning meaning to the indicator.

Impression development is significantly dependent upon schema, context, and stereotypes, particularly if they are shared. Participants in a virtual interaction must have the same social context in which to work so communication is clear and understandable. For example, knowing the term "y'all" is associated with people from the southern part of the U.S. If that concept is not shared, the term is meaningless and provides no information that can contribute to impression formation. Impressions are based on the cues provided, in addition to cognitive models and conceptual categories as well as the context in which messages are viewed (Jacobson, 1999). Understanding how those verbal (text-based), linguistic, and paralinguistic cues can be interpreted in light of an individual's cultural stereotypes and personal schema is key to managing impression formation when working virtually.

FUTURE TRENDS

The majority of research on impression formation in CMC has been conducted in text-based environments such as e-mail, bulletin boards and chat rooms. Newer technologies, however, allow for mediated interaction beyond mere text. Virtual workers can now communicate online using a variety of media and channels that permit the exchange of nonverbal cues.

Web cameras and videoconferencing allow real-time mediated face-to-face interaction where people can actually see each other as they engage in a dialogue. They can see the facial expressions, body posture, ethnicity and gender of someone as well as hear the inflections in a person's voice. Digital photographs cannot provide real-time cues, but they still convey information such as the ethnicity, gender, and overall "look" (such as perceived attractiveness, hair color, manner of dress) of a person. Voice over Internet protocol

(VoIP) allows people to talk to each other using a computer, where they can also discern accents, linguistic style and voice inflection.

Each of these "richer" (Daft & Lengel, 1986) communication technologies permits the transmission of nonverbal cues that reduce uncertainty. Common sense dictates that the use of these technologies will facilitate the formation of impressions in CMC. There is scant research into this area, but what little has been conducted has found otherwise.

Studies have shown that seeing a photograph of someone or interacting via videoconferencing does not facilitate and may actually hinder impression formation (Walther, Slovacek, & Tidwell, 2001; Fullwood, 2007), possibly because nonverbal cues may be distorted in a mediated environment, or those cues simply do not have the same impact in CMC versus face-to-face. Additionally, other nonverbal cues tend to be overemphasized in a mediated environment. A photograph may evoke a stereotypical impression, whereas the lack of a picture eliminates that possibility. Indeed, the loss of certain information can have positive consequences (Gilbert & Krull, 1988).

Even though richer communication technologies permit the transmission of nonverbal cues, they may not assist in impression formation. Therefore, virtual workers should still employ the strategies discussed previously to ensure they make a good impression on their clients and colleagues when interacting using newer technologies.

CONCLUSION

Early research suggested a lack of nonverbal cues made CMC feel impersonal and would therefore hinder impression formation. Theories based on further research such as SIP and URT, however, indicate that people interacting via CMC can indeed form well-developed impressions (Sherman, 2001) by simply adapting and using other content and linguistic strategies to aid in impression formation. As Tidwell and Walther observe, "When people want to get to know one another, they overcome the limitations of the medium and do so" (2002, p. 341). Research has also shown that impressions formed in an online environment tend to be less detailed but more intense than those formed in a face-to-face interaction (Hancock & Dunham, 2001), but that impressions formed via CMC become more developed over time (Walther, Loh, & Granka, 2005). As uncertainty about a person is reduced, people form impressions and create mental models that help to understand the environment around them (Srull & Wyer, 1989).

People tend to believe they give the same impression to others regardless of whether the interaction is online or offline (Sherman, End, Kraan, Cole, Campbell, Klausner, & Birchmeier, 2001). As this chapter has demonstrated, that is clearly not the case. The absence of nonverbal cues that normally aid in impression formation drastically impacts how people form impressions in CMC. For virtual workers to gain social acceptance and develop and maintain viable relationships, they must employ specific strategies to carefully manage their online interactions:

- Disclose everything
- Be honest
- Ask questions
- Use precise language
- Be acutely aware of cues

"The impact of CMC on society is still evolving and our understanding of its social, psychological, political, and economic implications is far from complete" (Sherman, 2001, p. 69). As the workplace becomes increasingly virtual and the nature of business practices begins to change, the Internet is transforming how people interact and communicate. While the eventual societal impact of working virtually via CMC is still uncertain, one thing will always remain true: you never get a second chance to make a good first impression.

REFERENCES

Adkins, M., & Brashers, D. (1995). The power of language in computer-mediated groups. *Management Communication Quarterly, 8*(3), 289-322.

Albright, J. (2001). Impression formation and attraction in computer mediated communication. (Doctoral dissertation, University of Southern California, 2001). *Dissertation Abstracts International, 62*(I09), *3199.*

Asch, S. (1946). Forming impressions of personality. *Journal of Abnormal and Social Psychology, 41,* 258-290.

Becker, J., & Stamp, G. (2005). Impression management in chat rooms: A grounded theory model. *Communication Studies, 56*(3), 243-260.

Berger, C., & Calabrese, R. (1975). Some explorations in initial interaction and beyond: Toward a developmental theory of interpersonal communication. *Human Communication Research, 1*(2), 99-112.

Culnan, M., & Markus, M. (1987). Information technologies. In: F. Jablin, L. Putnam, K. Roberts, & L. Porter (Eds.), *Handbook of organizational communication: An interdisciplinary perspective* (pp. 420-443). Newbury Park, CA: Sage.

Daft, R., & Lengel, R. (1986). A proposed integration among organizational information requirements, media richness, and structural design. *Management Science, 32*(5), 554-571.

Fullwood, C. (2007). The effect of mediation on impression formation: A comparison of face-to-face and video-mediated conditions. *Applied Ergonomics, 38,* 267-273.

Gibbs, J., Ellison, N., & Heino, R. (2006). Self-presentation in online personals: The role of anticipated future interaction, self-disclosure, and perceived success in Internet dating. *Communication Research, 33*(2), 152-177.

Gilbert, D. (1995). Attribution and interpersonal perception. In: A. Tesser (Ed.), *Advanced social psychology* (pp. 99-148). Boston, MA: McGraw-Hill.

Gilbert, D., & Krull, D. (1988). Seeing less and knowing more: The benefits of perceptual ignorance. *Journal of Personality and Social Psychology, 54*(2), 193-202.

Goffman, E. (1959). *The presentation of self in everyday life.* New York, NY: Anchor Books.

Hancock, J., & Dunham, P. (2001). Impression formation in computer-mediated communication revisited: An analysis of the breadth and intensity of impressions. *Communication Research, 28*(3), 325-347.

Hatfield, E., & Sprecher, S. (1986). *Mirror, mirror?: The importance of looks in everyday life.* Albany, NY: State University of New York Press.

Jacobson, D. (1999). Impression formation in cyberspace: Online expectations and offline experience in text-based virtual communities. *Journal of Computer-Mediated Communication, 5*(1). Retrieved July 20, 2006 from http://jcmc.indiana.edu/vol5/issue1/jacobson.html.

Joinson, A. (2001). Self disclosure in computer-mediated communication: The role of self-awareness and visual anonymity. *European Journal of Social Psychology, 31*(2), 177-192.

Jordan, T. (2002). Technopower and its cyber-futures. In: J. Armitage & J. Roberts (Eds.), *Living with cyberspace: Technology and society in the 21st century* (pp. 120-128). New York, NY: Continuum.

Kiesler, S., Siegel, J., & McGuire, T. (1984). Social psychological aspects of computer-mediated communication. *American Psychologist, 39*, 1123-1134.

Lea, M., & Spears, R. (1992). Paralanguage and social perception in computer-mediated communication. *Journal of Organizational Computing, (2-4)*, 321-341.

Leyens, J., & Corneille, O. (1999). Asch's social psychology: Not as social as you may think. *Personal and Social Psychology Review, 3*(4), 345-357.

Liu, Y., Ginther, D., & Zelhart, P. (2002). An exploratory study of the effects of frequency and duration of message on impression development in computer-mediated communication. *Social Science Computer Review, 20*(1), 73-80.

Lyon, D. (2002). Cyberspace: Beyond the information society?. In: J. Armitage & J. Roberts (Eds.), *Living with cyberspace: Technology and society in the 21st century* (pp. 21-33). New York, NY: Continuum.

O'Sullivan, P.B (2000). What you don't know won't hurt me: Impression management functions of communication channels in relationships. *Human Communication Research, 26*(3), 403-431.

Ramirez, A., Walther, J., Burgoon, J., & Sunnafrank, M. 2002). Information-seeking strategies, uncertainty, and computer-mediated communication: Toward a conceptual model. *Human Communication Research, 28*(2), 213-228.

Schlenker, B. (1980). *Impression management.* Monterey, CA: Brooks/Cole.

Sherman, R. (2001). The mind's eye in cyberspace: Online perceptions of self and others. In: G. Riva & C. Galimberti (Eds.), *Towards cyberpsychology: Mind, cognition, and society in the Internet age* (pp. 53-72). Amsterdam: IOS Press.

Sherman, R., End, C., Kraan, E., Cole, A., Campbell, J., Klausner, J., & Birchmeier, Z. (2001). Metaperception in cyberspace. *Cyber Psychology & Behavior, 4*(1), 123-129.

Short, J., Williams, E., & Christie, B. (1976). *The social psychology of telecommunications.* London: John Wiley.

Spears, R., & Lea, M. (1992). Social influence and the influence of the "social" in computer mediated communication. In: M. Lea (Ed.), *Contexts of computer mediated communication* (pp. 30-65). New York, NY: Harvest Wheatsheaf.

Sproull, L., & Kiesler, S. (1986). Reducing social context cues: Electronic mail in organizational communication. *Management Science, 32,* 1492-1512.

Srull, T., & Wyer, R. (1989). Person memory and judgment. *Psychological Review, 96*(1), 58-83.

Tanis, M., & Postmes, T. (2003). Social cues and impression formation in CMC. *Journal of Communication, 53*(4), 676-693.

Tidwell, L., & Walther, J. (2002). Computer-mediated communication effects on disclosure, impressions, and interpersonal evaluations: Getting to know one another a bit at a time. *Human Communication Research, 28*(3), 317-348.

Wallace, P. (1999). *The psychology of the Internet.* Cambridge, NY: Cambridge University Press.

Walther, J. (1992). Interpersonal effects in computer-mediated interaction: A relational perspective. *Communication Research, 19,* 52-90.

Walther, J. (1993). Construction and validation of a quantitative measure of impression development. *The Southern Communication Journal, 59,* 27-33.

Walther, J. (1996). Computer-mediated communication: Impersonal, interpersonal, and hyperpersonal interaction. *Communication Research, 23*(1), 3-43.

Walther, J., Loh, T., & Granka, L. (2005). Let me count the ways: The interchange of verbal and nonverbal cues in computer-mediated and face-to-face affinity. *Journal of Language and Social Psychology, 24*(1), 36-65.

Walther, J., & Parks, M. (2002). Cues filtered out, cues filtered in: Computer-mediated communication and relationships. In: M. Knapp & J. Daly (Eds.), *The handbook of interpersonal communication* (pp. 529-563). Thousand Oaks, CA: Sage.

Walther, J., Slovacek, C., & Tidwell, L. (2001). Is a picture worth a thousand words? Photographic images in long-term and short-term computer-mediated communication. *Communication Research, 28*(1), 105-134.

Walther, J., & Tidwell, L. (1995). Nonverbal cues in computer-mediated communication, and the effect of chronemics on relational communication. *Journal of Organizational Computing, 5*(4), 355-378.

Wood, A., & Smith, M. (2005). *Online communication: Linking technology, identity, & culture.* Mahwah, NJ: Lawrence Erlbaum Associates.

KEY TERMS

Computer-Mediated Communication: Interaction that takes place through or is facilitated by mediating technologies, such as a computer.

Exemplar: A specific individual that a person has encountered, who is then taken as a representative of others who are thought to be in that same category.

Impression Formation: Creating an opinion or mental image of somebody or something.

Impression Management: The process by which individuals attempt to control others' perceptions of them, motivated by the desire for social acceptance and relationship development and maintenance.

Linguistic Communication: Interacting and gleaning information using language, both verbal and textual.

Nonverbal Communication: Interacting and gleaning information not using words but by using cues taken from actions such as vocal patterns, linguistic markers, body posture, gestures, and eye contact.

Paralinguistic Cues: Typographical marks and other textual features that have no lexical meaning per se, but the meanings are dependent on group or individual contexts.

Stereotype: Where a society or culture recognizes characteristics of an individual or group of people as representing an entire category.

Working Virtually: Interacting and communicating to achieve set goals or tasks using information and communication technologies, not in a face-to-face manner.

Chapter IX
Telecommuting and the Management of the Human Moment

Alan D. Smith
Robert Morris University, USA

ABSTRACT

Telecommuting is a tool that is becoming more and more a way a life for organizations as they strive to recruit and retain employees and assist them in improving their quality of life. The recurring themes tended to be the need to select the proper employee, training managers to manage remote employees, strong communication (formal/informal) strategies, clear expectations and proactive stance in deterring isolation. Telecommuting is not for everyone or every organization. Extreme care must be taken in preparation; development, implementation and ongoing evaluation must take place to ensure that it is not only a good fit for the employee but also for the organization. Safeguards must be in place to promote the human moment at work that may be lost when there is lack of face-to-face contact with fellow workers. Efforts should be made by management to promote professional development via regularly scheduled meetings with fellow workers, management, and customers.

INTRODUCTION: NEED FOR DEVELOPING THE HUMAN MOMENT

Hallowell (1999), Smith (2005), and Smith and Manna (2005; 2006) discussed the strategically important concept of the human moment, which is the actual interface of two attentive people in physical proximity to each other. Admittedly an elementary idea, it has become a more rare display in many work environments. The proliferation of computers in the ever expanding global commerce, especially in the U.S., almost everyone is within 15 minutes of a home/work PC (Kurland & Bailey, 1999; Kurland & Egan, 1999; Shugan, 2004). The advent of e-mail, cell phones, and more global companies have created more ways to reach co-workers and ways to quickly convey information, but at the same time has made those information transfers very impersonal. Those types of communications are important and have benefited companies, especially as companies expand and coworkers are spread further apart. As far as the limited scope of this chapter, mobile commerce (m-commerce) shall be defined as the transaction of business and other activities resulting in the transfer of capital from one entity to another via the utilization of portable electronic devices including, but not limited to, cell phones (CPs), personal digital assistants (PDAs), and hand-held computers (HHCs). The emphasis of this chapter is on the more widespread and conventional use of wired communications typically found in the virtual workplace. However, these are not replacements for human interface. E-mail and phone calls leave a lot of room for misinterpretation and make clarification very difficult. Face-to-face conversation allows for clarification in real time. There is less chance for misinterpretation. Also mannerisms and physical reactions cannot be duplicated in an e-mail. There is also the human need for social activity that can only be fulfilled through human contact. It leads to more fulfillment and happier relationships. The human moment is essential to the psyche and cannot be forgotten regardless of how many other forms of communication are developed.

In proving his point about the importance of the human moment, Hallowell (1999) uses some real-life examples. One is of a man who mistook an innocent e-mail as threatening and responded in a confrontational manor, which was inappropriate. Incidents like that can burn bridges when neither party had any desire to do so, "An organization's culture turns unfriendly and unforgiving" (p. 60). Without the tone and context of human conversation, it is easy for things to get misunderstood like in this example. A simple situation turned ugly because of reading between the lines that were simply not there. At any point in time during this incident, a brief human moment could have easily solved the problem.

Another unfortunate result of a lack of direct communications is the loss of cohesiveness in an organization. Employees feel less connected to each other as they see each other less. E-mail and phone conversations depersonalize the work relationship. It is easy for a company to loss its identity in this situation. As members feel less connected, they begin to lose an organizational focus and become more individually focused, which is detrimental to the firm. To be a team player, you must work as a team, which means sharing face-to-face conversation. Hallowell states that high tech and high touch must be combined and held in balance. E-mail, cell phones are here to stay. However, firms cannot forget the importance of human interaction. It is essential to the success of the firm that relationships between employees remain real and strong. The combination will provide the speed required in today's business world and the attention required by the human psyche. The balance is hard to maintain and must be a goal of the employees and the top management. It is a smart move to keep the human moment a part of the organization's culture. This chapter specifically addresses the need to maintain this delicate balance between technology and the human moment in a telecommuting business environment.

BACKGROUND

This chapter deals with the benefits, challenges and recommendations of telecommuting in today's world. While focusing on the need for developing the human moment at work, we will discuss how the human moment factor is affected within the world of telecommuting. Advances in technology have allowed telecommuting to become one of the fastest growing fields of employment throughout the world. Telecommuting, telework and teleworking are all used interchangeably and it can be defined in many similar ways. The term telecommuting was credited by Jack Nilles in 1973. He defines it as work conducted via telecommunication instead of in person (Nilles,

1998). Telecommuting can also be described as the use of information and technology to reduce or eliminate the need to commute to a conventional office (Mokhtarian, 2002). The Concise Oxford Dictionary definition of telecommuting is essentially working from home or commuting with a central workplace using equipment such as telephones, fax machines, and modems. According to Nilles, it is considered a work option that reduces dependency on transportation by increasing dependency on information technologies and it can be implemented with no more exotic a technology than a telephone. Also, the employees that are performing a portion of their job from home while still collecting the same salary and benefits they would receive if their job were in an office are described as telecommuters.

Three types of telecommuting can be recognized by location: working at home, working from a telework center (telecenter), and hoteling. The telecenter is where employees use computers and communication technology to connect with a main office, supervisors, co-workers and customers (Gibson, Blackwell, Dominicis, & Demerath, 2002). Hoteling can be described, as telecommuting in, or rather from a hotel room using telecommunications to work in order to satisfy clients and or company needs (Kurland & Bailey, 1999; Kurland & Egan, 1999; Shugan, 2004).

MAIN FOCUS OF THE CHAPTER

There are many reasons why companies and employees choose to telecommute. The benefits can be significant in some cases because it can increase schedule flexibility and productivity, enhance employee satisfaction, attract and retain employees, reduce turnover, and lower costs for the company. In some cases, it can save an average of $10,000 per employee (Manoochehri, 2003). When implemented correctly, telecommuting has the potential to enhance the lives of employees and

aid in achieving competitive advantage. Society, as well as, companies, families, and employees have seen telecommuting become the wave of the next century as the next strategic asset.

Increased Productivity

Employees can schedule their work during their most productive periods. This results in increased performance. Past studies have shown that productivity increases from 20% to 30% when telecommuting is permitted. For example, AT&T also found that "home workers spend an average of an hour more per day on the job due to the high flexibility of their work schedules" (Manoochehri, 2003, p. 10). Typically, a working mother with children can work while the children are in school or at night when they are sleeping. Anyone that has children can understand the time and energy that is spent with taking care of their needs. It is very difficult to focus on work while children are hungry, need a bath, or want attention. Another flexible situation that shows how productivity is increased involves an employee doing their laundry, getting a cup of coffee, or grabbing a cup of yogurt from the refrigerator while a document is downloading. If they were to get a cup of coffee from the donut shop next door, that 5-minute trip to the kitchen can turn into a 40-minute trip through long lines and social interruptions with friends (Hemphill, 2004).

Enhance Employee Satisfaction

Through the ability to balance work and family, telecommuters have been shown to have more satisfaction with their jobs compared to their office counterparts. They avoid the politics and distractions of other coworkers, and produce with lower absenteeism and higher morale. One study demonstrated that "telecommuters had a higher level of overall satisfaction and less likelihood of leaving the company as compared to non-telecommuters" (Manoochehri, 2003, p. 10). When an employee can set their own schedule, increase their performance, spend more time with their family, they tend to appreciate their jobs more.

Attract and Retain Employees

Since telecommuting can eliminate driving to work, a company can expand its recruiting efforts to areas outside of its geographical area. This freedom is not only attractive by potential recruits, but it helps in retaining them as long-term employees. For example, some companies offer 24-hour customer service for their clients. However, many companies find it difficult to hire and retain employees to work graveyard shifts and pay shift differentials. With telecommuting, companies can recruit from a larger geographical area where employees can be set up to take calls from home.

Lower Operating Costs

The savings incurred by companies to provide telecommuting are significant. Major factors contributing to cost reduction include a reduction in required office space, clerical and support staff, and turnover. For example, AT&T freed up $550 million dollars in cash flow since 1991 and continues to save more than $100 million annually (Manoochehri, 2003). The savings are a result of less office space, parking space, the elimination of staff positions, lower operating costs, and reduced training expenses for new employees.

Benefits to Society

With pollution reduction, society has benefited from telecommuting as well. The most obvious reduction in pollution is having fewer cars on the road during high congestion periods. A study conducted in Japan shows that congestion could be reduced by 6.9% to 10.9%. This could mean that there are 9 to 14 million fewer employees driving on the road (Manoochehri, 2003, p. 11).

Therefore, this positive effect can help companies comply with pollution regulations and help keep the air we breathe cleaner.

As a strategic asset, telecommuting can give a company the edge that they need. According to Tim Kane, chief executive office of Kinetic Workplace Inc., enabling their people to work from anywhere at any time has allowed the company to become a more agile company and to effectively compete with larger organizations. In addition, he believed that telecommuting is "coming of age" (Carbasho, 2004). With the technology of the Internet, high-speed connections, video-conferencing, and the telephone line, we will see a growing trend in years to come on the use of this viable option in the workplace.

FUTURE TRENDS

There are several challenges that occur when companies decide to promote the use of telecommuting work arrangements for certain employees. Telecommuting work arrangements are not meant for everyone, since not all employees work the same from their home as they would in a regular office environment. Only certain kinds of work are appropriate to perform from outside the office. The disadvantages of allowing employees to telecommute include: diminished employee morale, lack of supervision, disconnection with fellow employees, home distractions, lack of office services, reduced social interaction and possible neglect from career advancement opportunities.

Diminished Employee Morale

This situation arises within the organization when some employees are permitted to work out of their own home, while others are not. Employees that were not given this opportunity to work from home tend to become jealous and resent the teleworker that did receive special work arrangements. These employees then start to question whether the telecommuter is indeed actually working. This creates a difficult working environment for all employees within the organization (Tan-Solano & Kleiner, 2003).

Lack of Supervision

This challenge may occur when telecommuters do not have direct contact with their supervisor. Since telecommuters work out of their home environments, direct supervision is neither possible nor desirable. Managers expect their employees to work the same amount of hours at home as they would in a normal work environment, but this is difficult to track. Many companies just require the telecommuters to check in periodically, but this does not actually prove that the employee put in a full days work. This makes it very difficult for managers to monitor the performance of their employees that work from home without direct supervision (Cooper 1996; McCune, 1998; Cascio, 2000; Pearlson & Sounders, 2001).

Loss of Direct Communication

This challenge occurs since the telecommuter does not physically work in the office. Telecommuters have the disadvantage of working alone in the home-based office, since they do not have direct contact with their employees. They may be forced to use other means of communication. Unfortunately, all their communication is by memo, e-mail or voicemail, which they exchange often but they almost never meet (Hallowell, 1999; Smith & Faley, 2001). Many employees feel they do not need to have meetings in person, that all-important information can be communicated by either e-mail or voicemail. These companies may not realize that while e-mail and voicemail are convenient, they still need personal contact in order to see how employees react to certain situations. Employees can start to feel discon-

nected when employees work all over the world, not from one central location. It is very important for critical and confidential information not to be communicated through e-mail. Companies need to be concerned about the privacy of confidential information being sent to the wrong people via the Internet. This situation may pose a threat of the information getting into the hands of the wrong person.

Distractions within the Home

Employees may find it difficult to motivate them into getting their work done with constant family and home distractions. Teleworkers may underestimate the impact of home distractions. Telecommuting can often remove boundaries between work and home, which can be an important psychological factor in the motivation to work. There can be distractions from the television, knowing the house needs to be cleaned, and from family members. These distractions make it difficult for the telecommuter to remain focused and get their work completed.

Lack of Office Services

This may pose a threat to the telecommuter working from their homes. Since the telecommuter works out of their home, they must have the right office technology available to do their job, but this is not always the case. This means some office services will be unavailable to the employee. For example, some services available only at the office like services provided by the mailroom, systems personnel when equipment goes down, and corporate library. Difficulty in completing tasks may occur if the services needed are not present at the alternate work site. This creates a concern to both the employer and employee, questioning whether telecommuters have all of the necessary equipment and services needed to do their job effectively.

Lack of Social Contact

This arises when telecommuters do not interact face-to-face with people in the workplace. Employees periodically need a true human-moment experience. These times are difficult enough when the environment is a busy office, but when the face-to-face time is minimal, the chances of true interaction are significantly reduced. Many colleagues enjoy talking to their co-workers. When an employee chooses to work from home, they lose the benefit of 'casual' social interaction. This may make the telecommuter feel isolated and alone (Cooper 1996; McCune, 1998; Cascio, 2000; Pearlson & Sounders, 2001).

Lack of Career Advancement

Employees that do not work in the office find it difficult to become noticed for the work they perform on a regular basis. Telecommuters express concern that since they are not visible in the office, this will damage their career objectives and future promotions. Many fear that on-site workers, being more visible, are more likely to receive raises and promotions (Tan-Solano & Kleiner, 2003). It is very difficult for managers to monitor a telecommuter's performance, since they are not under direct supervision. Therefore, the telecommuter may feel that they are neglected from possible career advancement. Although there are many challenges associated with being some form of a telecommuter, there are many steps that both the organization and the employee can take in order to maximize the telecommuting experience for all. The following includes recommendations that will counteract the disadvantages of telecommuting.

Employee Morale

Companies must take care in establishing a telecommuting program. The program should be one that is established based upon the job and not the employee. By doing this and setting appropriate participation guidelines, organizations can create an atmosphere of equality because everyone is offered an equal opportunity to participate. Employers can be proactive in managing employee morale through its selection. Hence, telecommuters are often portrayed as people who like to work on their own; basically affiliates who dislike working alone do not fit into the ideal telecommuter archetype. In fact, some research evidence suggests that the performance of people with a high need for affiliation that work alone is lower than that of those with a low need for affiliation who works alone. It is expected that people with a higher motivation for social contact will be uncomfortable in a telecommuting situation, which may lead to lower outcomes (Haines, St-Onge, & Archambault, 2002).

Lack of Supervision

The absence of direct supervision can have a negative impact on both the employee and the supervisor. Each party can take steps to minimize or eliminate this impact; hence managers must learn to manage and lead by actual results, not just by observation of the employee working. The optimum profile for a telecommuter is one that is self-motivated, have above average organizational and time management skills, require minimum supervision and have a strong desire to telecommute. Negative traits would include employees who require face-to-face meetings with people in the office every day, require frequent reassurance and positive reinforcement.

Realizing the value of virtual management, Hewlett-Packard (www.hr.com) created an assessment development program for managers called *Managing Remotely*. From this, HP developed a *Remote Managers Strategies Guide*, which contains the best practices and successful strategies for managing remotely. In addition, other forums are held quarterly allowing managers to share experiences and learning (Helms & Raiszadeh, 2002).

Loss of Direct Communication

Employee communication is a critical training issue to address. Essentially, when people do not see one another, everyday socialization or relationship-building communications can be lost. It is a key skill for managers of such remote workers to maintain a balance between task-oriented and relationship-building communications (Helms & Raiszadeh, 2002). If left unchecked, toxic worry, which refers to the widespread result one-way communication methods, may result is worry that prevents workers from completing their tasks in the most productive manner.

While the following tip can be the solution for many of the problems raised, it is best placed in managing communications. In the book 'The Telecommuter's Advisor,' an example is given where an employee gives her boss a weekly status report that shows this week's accomplishments, next week's activities, FYI and "let us talks about" section (Langhoff, 1996). This system provides her boss with her results, plans and the opportunity for the boss to provide feedback. Perhaps only one of the early lessons for managing virtual teams is to walk before you can run. Managers must have already achieved success managing conventional in-house teams before they can be expected to manage an invisible team (Helms & Raiszadeh, 2002). Managers should make a concerted effort to ensure that there is frequent direct contact among the telecommuter and fellow employees and supervisor. In the article 'The Human Moment at Work', an example was given of a "Thursday Pizza" which offered a monthly opportunity for employees to get together informally to enjoy pizza and banter with each other (Hallowell, 1999).

Home Distractions

For the telecommuting experience to work, employees and their family members must become conditioned to the fact that working from the office does not permit the personal activities of the household to interfere with the job. The best scenario is one where the home office is in a separate room away from all other activity in the household. PNC Bank, as an example, requires that all telecommuters have a room with a door and a separate phone line (installed by the bank) to reduce the crossover of personal and business calls on the home line. Family members must be supportive of the telecommuting arrangement and realize that you will not be available during working hours. This includes the willingness of family to minimize distractions and interruptions (D'Innocenzio, 2003)

Lack of Office Services

A high risk to telecommuting is not only the reliability of the technology used to facilitate telecommuting but also the responsiveness of the organization to respond to issues surrounding technology. The response time standard should be the same as those in the traditional office. Organizations must make the commitment to give telecommuters the tools they need in order to perform their job. These tools include, but are not limited to, conditioned phone lines, fax machines, computer hardware and software and a telephone. If the responsiveness is not there, this will negatively impact employee morale.

Lack of Social Contact

Employee morale can suffer for a variety reasons, most prominently the feeling of isolation and thought of limited career advancement. Combining high tech with high touch is not easy; unfortunately technology always seems to take precedence. Organizations should invest in video conferencing. With the proliferation of the Internet and video-cams, this is now becoming a minimal expense with a huge upside. This technology helps overcome isolation that many telecommuters face. This is accomplished by virtually putting the employee in the room with the home base staff and putting a face to the voice. Telecommuters should also make concentrated efforts to get away from the home-office during lunch and seek out non-work social interaction.

Lack of Career Advancement

In a recent study, test results showed that telecommuting was not found to have a direct or indirect effect on career advancement prospects (Weaver-McClosky & Igabaria, 2003). However, the perception does exist among employees who exercise that option and feel that they are left out of the mainstream of promotional activities.

CONCLUSION

Telecommuting employees can follow a few simple tips that employees, not only telecommuters, may follow in perpetuating their career advancement (D'Innocenzio, 2003; Smith & Lias, 2005; Smith, 2006a; 2006b; 2006c):

1. Go out of your way to find opportunities to be involved in projects, special assignments, task teams, that will expose you to greater numbers of people and aspects of the organizations.
2. Schedule a career planning meeting with your manager to lay out your goals, review your plan, outline your strategy, ask for input and obtain your manager's commitment to help you achieve your objective.
3. Develop a reputation for treating people with respect, including the lower level support staff.
4. Most important: Develop a reputation for getting results and consistently doing so with honesty, integrity, and regard for others.

In closing, telecommuting is a tool that is becoming more and more a way a life for organiza-

tions as they strive to recruit and retain employees and assist them in improving their quality of life. In doing research for this chapter, the recurring themes tended to be the need to select the proper employee, training managers to manage remote environments and their employees, strong communication (formal/informal) strategies, clear expectations and proactive stance in deterring isolation. Telecommuting is not for everyone or every organization. Extreme care must be taken in preparation; development, implementation and ongoing evaluation must take place to ensure that it is not only a good fit for the employee but also for the organization. People do require human interaction and in the work place the clarity and fulfillment from the human moment cannot be ignored, especially in telecommuting situations. Management must understand that technology is important and here to stay, and it must be strategically leveraged in order to optimized work performance. However, it is important to remember the value of direct conversation. The human moment is an important key to proper understanding between employees and meeting the needs of individuals in the firm—it is essential for a healthy culture.

REFERENCES

Carbasho, T. (2004). More companies, employees realize the benefits of teleworking. *Pittsburgh Business Times, 23*(32), 25.

Cascio, W. (2000). Managing a virtual workplace. *The Academy of Management Executive, 14*(3), 81-90.

Cooper, R. (1996). Telecommuting: The good, the bad, and the particulars. *Supervision, 57*(2), 10-12.

D'Innocenzio, D. (2003). *101 tips for telecommuters: Successfully manage your work, team, technology and family.*

Gibson, J., Blackwell, C., Dominicis, P., & Demerath, N. (2002). Telecommuting in the 21st century: Benefits, issues, and a leadership model which will work. *Journal of Leadership & Organizational Studies, 8*(4), 75-86.

Haines III, V., St-Onge, S., & Archambault, M. (2002). Environmental and person antecedents of telecommuting outcomes. *Journal of End User Computing, 14*(3), 32-44.

Hallowell, E. (1999). The human moment. *Harvard Business Review, 77*(1), 58-66.

Helms, M., & Raiszadeh, F. (2002). Virtual offices: Understanding and managing what you cannot see. *Work Study, 51*(4-5), 240-253.

Hemphill, B. (2004). Telecommuting productively. If you're so inclined, follow these 10 tips for working successfully at home. *Occupational Health & Safety, 73*(3), 16-18.

Kurland, N., & Bailey, D. (1999). Telework: The advantages and challenges of working here, there, anywhere, and anytime. *Organizational Dynamics, 28*(2): 53-67.

Kurland, N., & Egan, T. (1999). Telecommuting: Justice and control in the virtual organization. *Organization Science, 10*(4), 500-513.

Langhoff, J. (1996). *The telecommuter's advisor: Working in the fast lane.* Newport, RI: Aegis Publishing Group Ltd.

Manoochehri, G., & Pinkerton, T. (2003). Managing telecommuters: Opportunities and challenges. *American Business Review, 21*(1), 9-16.

McCune, J. (1998). Telecommuting revisited. *Management Review, 87*(2), 10-16.

Mokhtarian, P., & Meenakshisundaram, R. (2002). Patterns of telecommuting engagement and frequency: A cluster analysis of telecenter users. *Prometheus, 20*(1), 21-37.

Nilles, J. (1998). Telecommuting. *Transportation Research, 22*(4), 301-317.

Pearlson, K., & Sounders, C. (2001). There's no place like home: Managing telecommuting paradoxes. *The Academy of Management Executive, 15*(2), 117-128.

Smith, A. (2005). Reverse logistics and their affects on CRM and online behavior. *VINE: The Journal of Information and Knowledge Management, 35*(3), 166-181.

Smith, A. (2006a). CRM and customer service: Strategic asset or corporate overhead?. *2006 Handbook of Business Strategy,* 87-93.

Smith, A. (2006b). Exploring security and comfort issues associated with online banking. *International Journal of Electronic Finance, 1*(1), 18-48.

Smith, A. (2006c). Exploring m-commerce in terms of viability. Growth, and challenges. *International Journal of Mobile Communications, 4*(6), 682-703.

Smith, A. (2006d). Supply chain management using electronic reverse auction: A multi-firm case study. *International Journal of Services and Standards, 2*(2), 176-189.

Smith, A., & Faley, R. (2001). E-mail workplace privacy issues in an information- and knowledge-based environment. *Southern Business Review,* 8-22.

Smith, A., & Lias, A. (2005). Identity theft and e-fraud as critical CRM concerns. *International Journal of Enterprise Information Systems, 1*(2), 17-36.

Smith, A., & Manna, D. (2005). Exploring why people love their jobs. *Journal of Business and Economics Research, 3*(3), 21-26.

Smith, A., & Manna, D. (2006). Knowledge-based entrepreneurship: Analyzing a startup. *Journal of Business and Economics Research, 4*(3), 17-22

Shugan, S. (2004). The impact of advancing technology on marketing and academic research. *Marketing Science, 23*(4), 469-477.

Weaver-McClosky, D., & Igabaria, M. (2003). Does "out of sight' mean "out of mind? An empirical investigation of the career advancement prospects of telecommuters. *Information Resources Management Journal, 16*(2), 19-26.

KEY TERMS

Human Moment: The missing element of face-to-face communication in the newer forms of communications, especially voicemail and e-mail, has proliferated. The missing face-to-face communication contributes to loneliness and isolation in the workplace and also to the misunderstanding and the percolation of anxiety. In the extreme, trust and respect deteriorate resulting in a dysfunctional organization and decreased competitive advantage. The term, human moment, refers to face-to-face communication that is real, authentic, and involves the total communication of language; includes boy motion and emotional response.

Remote Environments: Remote or other offsite, nontraditional work environments are rapidly emerging as a preference for productive work environments for both employers and employees.

Telecenter: Telecenters are work environments that centralize telecommuting employees and employers. These environments include sharing office space, compressed work week, working at a satellite center, and establishing a mobile or virtual office through laptop computers or other technology.

Telecommuting: Telecommuting refers to the actual practice of converting a worker's desire to complete their work from their home or other non-office environments, since it usually offers flexibility and reduces commuting costs and hassles. In addition, it allows the opportunity for workers to helping their balance work and their personal life obligations.

Toxic Worry: Toxic worry, as suggested by Hallowell (1999), refers to the widespread result one-way communication methods. A lack of the nuances of personal communication such as facial expression, tone of voice, and body language result in people filling in their own conclusions, which could be either correct or incorrect. This may result is worry that prevents workers from completing their tasks in the most productive manner.

Chapter X
Cultural Implications of Collaborative Information Technologies (CITs) in International Online Collaborations and Global Virtual Teams

Bolanle A. Olaniran
Texas Tech University, USA

David A. Edgell
Texas Tech University, USA

ABSTRACT

This chapter introduces and explains some critical issues regarding Cultural Implications of Collaborative Information Technologies (CITs) in International Online Collaborations and Global Virtual Teams. This chapter attempts to addresses some of the cross-cultural issues in international online collaboration, which include but are not limited to language, culture, trust, and technology along with the implications for organizational virtual collaboration. The chapter also provides useful recommendations and strategies for improving international online virtual collaboration with CMC.

INTRODUCTION

The explosion in computer-mediated communication (CMC) technologies created increased access to information and online interactions that span across the globe. International online collaboration among organizations, institutions and individuals is experiencing significant growth. As international online collaboration grows, there is an increasing need to focus attention on the issue of culture and its effects on communication interactions. This chapter attempts to address some of the cross-cultural concerns in international online collaboration, which include but are not limited to: language, culture, trust, and technology, along with the implications of culture for organizational virtual collaboration. The primary goal of this chapter is to identify key challenges in online and virtual collaborations while attempting to provide some useful recommendations for effective interaction within that context. The chapter also provides useful recommendations and strategies for improving international online virtual collaboration with CMC.

In the age of globalization and a global economy, the idea of international teams and group collaboration are ever present and represent the norm in many organizations. The importance of group work and collaboration has increased considerably as organizational performance and productivity represent the measures for organizational survival (Olaniran, 1994; 2004). Organizations and individuals have come to rely significantly on communication technologies for facilitating communication and coordination activities across different geographical locations (i.e., non-co-located groups). In addition, the resulting globalization trend necessitates virtual collaborations where time and space are no longer mutually exclusive concepts. Computer-mediated communication (CMC) technologies enabled through the Internet allow for global collaboration activities (Davidson & Vreede, 2001; Olaniran, 2001a; 2001b; Solomon, 2001). The term global virtual team refers to the use of collaboration information technologies (CITs) for supporting collaboration among organizational members in international or multinational contexts.

Background and Literature Review

Finding ways to make teams effective is the primary concern facing organizations and teams using communication technologies as their collaborating tools. Added to this challenge is culture, which varies across different geographical locations. Thus, the challenge with groups and virtual collaborations with communication technologies is compounded by cultural differences. Consequently, CMC media represent collaboration information technologies (CITs) that offer both economic and convenient means for groups to collaborate on projects virtually (Jarvenpaa & Leidner, 1999), nevertheless, the members' different cultures and value preferences create challenges for the collaborations (Keenan & Ante, 2002; Olaniran, 2004).

Hofstede (1996) stresses that culture is the "software of the mind," indicating that individuals carry within them certain patterns of thinking, feeling, and behaviors that were learned through their development. People bring with them experiences, expectations, and histories that shape their participation and general communication interactions providing a direct implication for participants in collaborative virtual teams (Cogburn & Levinson, 2003). The next section of the discussion provides an overview of some challenges facing virtual collaboration teams.

Challenges in Online Virtual Group Collaborations

There are problems and challenges in virtual teams using CITs in co-located or non-global contexts. However, cultural challenges, language, trust, and different IT proficiencies are inevitable in virtual groups that span across several countries. These challenges also influence the effectiveness of virtual teams as a whole, along with the usage of CITs (Dube & Pare, 2001; Olaniran, 2004; Munkvold, 2005;).

While the motivation to use virtual teams is often economically driven (i.e., cost cutting, speed, and efficiency), there are some key challenges that hinder their effectiveness and the team's success. Armstrong and Cole (2002) found that while distributed groups sometimes become integrated over time, they nonetheless experience problems due to distance (Olaniran, 1996; Crampton, 2001a; 2002; Solomon, 2001; Walther, 2002). Problems in virtual teams include misunderstandings and confusion from fragmented communication between group members. Armstrong and Cole (2002) found that national cultures and location create a dimension of distance that extends beyond miles and time zones even in integrated groups. Furthermore, they argued that organizational problems are sometimes recreated and can magnify differences within distributed groups. Crampton (2002) contends that working across dispersed locations often reduces the situational information that collaborators have about each other, such as how information is processed, and the development of in-groups vs. out-groups based on location. Consequently, it is concluded that attribution processes bias perception of others' behaviors. For example, attribution of behaviors leans toward dispositional tendencies rather than situational ones. The problem however, can be traced or linked to culture, motivation, and personality factors that influence attribution processes (Olaniran, 2001b; Armstrong & Cole, 2002). In other words, the development of meaningful collaboration in virtual teams calls for greater communication competence that addresses or overcomes distance challenges and cultural boundaries, especially in international online collaboration.

Similarly, Olaniran (2004) argues that virtual team members' intra-cultural communicative competence may not translate to cross-cultural competence. This premise is based on the fact that the dimensions of communication competence involve two factors, effectiveness and appropriateness. Effectiveness focuses on the ability to accomplish goals, while appropriateness emphasizes the contextual suitability of behaviors (Spitzberg & Cupach, 1989; Roy, 2001). However, success is seldom accomplished in both dimensions. Individuals' different cultures have varying beliefs, values, and norms as the foundation of their perception and interpretation of other members' actions (Vroman & Kovacich, 2002). When this is the case, "appropriateness" becomes a difficult dimension to master in cross-cultural settings that are transferred to virtual group communication

interaction (Olaniran, 2004). Research identified that different languages, communication styles, expectations about behaviors, and information processing, create complexities in multinational teams (e.g., James & Ward, 2002; Roebuck & Britt, 2002). Even the choice of virtual team members can create the perception that certain cultures or geographical regions are not valued. Much has been made about the fact that a majority of online content is offered in the English language to the detriment of end users who are non-native English speakers.

Language

It is difficult to talk about language in a virtual context and not discuss English. English has been dubbed "the global language," a status achieved by no other single language (Crystal, 2003; Kayman, 2004). History suggests that English came to achieve a dominant position on the Internet when ARPNET was developed as a national network for disseminating important information and linking American academic and government institutions in a speedy and secure way. English was the language at the inception of the Internet; when other countries and regions of the world began to form and extend links with the network, it was necessary to use English (Crystal, 2003). Eventually, the dominance of the language continued as programmers and content developers created information for use on the Internet when the network was opened to private and commercial organizations in the 1980s. Since the majority of Internet content is in the English language, this threatens nations whose primary language is not English making them feel that their languages need protection. The problem with English as a primary language of communication also emanates from the issue of identity. There are countries that view English as part of their colonial heritage and are trying to move away from it (Kayman, 2004). Furthermore, some view an increase in the use of English in communication technology creates a divide that widens the gap between the "haves" and the "have nots" (Crystal, 2003; Kayman, 2004). Kayman (2004) went on to argue that the association of English with communication technology reinforces its claim as the primary medium of globalization branded as *the* language of interaction. Universally, the reliance on the English language as the vehicle of global communication creates difficulty, especially among those individuals with little competency in the English language which restricts their usage of communication technologies (Gimenez, 2002).

Language difficulty has been attributed to the low participation by the Japanese in e-learning and online education (Kawachi, 1999). Specifically, the Japanese language is targeted at the right brain learning modality of visualization and memorization compared to left brain (i.e., analytic and argumentation skills) required by online content (Kawachi, 1999). The limited English proficiency in Japan is also attributed to how the Internet is used by the Japanese. The Internet is primarily for searching and printing of information for reading, off-line translation, and for games and other entertainment (Kawachi, 1999). In Europe, the language barrier is also seen as a hindrance to the rapid adoption of e-learning and associated technologies. The language barrier results in an increased call for "native-language" content development for local companies who are unwilling to adopt English (Barron, 2000). More importantly, language barriers lead to other issues such as national and cultural pride that affect other communication interactions in the online collaborative environment.

Language differences in virtual teams create misunderstandings based on different assumptions, sometimes fueling ongoing conflicts among office sites. For instance, Roebuck and Britt (2002) offer an instance of e-mail confusion in which a participant from Mexico remarked that a meeting with a client will be "superclassico," which a colleague from the home office in Toronto interpreted as "pleasant," however the intended meaning was rivalry. Another illustration of language difficulty is shown in the account of a cross-cultural transfer

of information technology. A U.S. corporation was in charge of implementing an automated accounting system with two Latin American subsidiaries for a multinational airline company. The company experienced major setbacks because of a lack of participation from the subsidiaries due to language barriers. Specifically, there was a lack of Spanish language training manuals along with other cultural problems regarding managerial power and role requirements (Chang, 2004; Munkvold, 2005).

Language presents difficulty for global virtual teams given that English is the de facto language of most linguistically diverse participants. Furthermore, while it may be typical to have English as a second language in many countries, it is not the case everywhere. Therefore, the fact that one or more team members must speak in a foreign or second language can easily impede interaction and overall team performance. Communication barriers become even more severe in an electronic context with CITs as the communication media. For example, it is difficult to fully participate in a teleconference when one does not speak the language fluently. As a result, a team may lose vital ideas and information or take a wrong direction (Dube & Pare, 2001). In essence, language often creates unintended consequences in virtual environments.

Culture

Given the increased use of virtual group collaboration in the global economy, there is a greater need for organizations to assist their employees in adapting their communicative behaviors in virtual communication environments, and more so in cross-cultural than in co-located (nearby) virtual teams. For instance, the social structure in East Asian cultures shows cultural differences resulting in the suppression of e-mail use in virtual teams (Lee, 2002). The Dutch were found to prefer a more significant level of structure in communication encounters than their U.S. counterparts (Kiser, 1999; Gezo, Oliverson, & Zick, 2000).

In addition, collaboration between Europeans and Latin Americans indicate misunderstandings and confusion due to cultural differences in perception, which impede communication and relegate interaction to strict task orientation (Qureshi & Zigurs, 2001). These examples point to difficulty in the issue of "appropriateness" in cross-cultural communication context. National and organizational cultures affect how people act in any working context. In global virtual teams, cultures and management styles often clash. For example, people from different cultures may have different ideas about what constitutes good performance. Furthermore, notions of accountability can vary according to whether a culture is more collective or more individualistic (Dube & Pare, 2001).

Based on these communication complexities, it is not surprising that an experiment, involving 150 participants located in the U.S., Japan, and Europe, found significant cultural differences in perceptions of communication task-technology fit (Massey, Montoya-Weiss, Hung, Ramesh, 2001). The study indicates that participants from the U.S. perceived less difficulty conveying their opinions than did participants from Asian and European origin. The collaborative technology was seen as conducive to a sender-oriented communication style inherent in individualistic, low-context cultures like the U.S., which exhibits a greater tendency to express and accept communications at the face value. On the contrary, participants from Asia perceived the technology to be a better fit for explaining themselves. Individuals from high-context cultures (e.g., Asia) need to know whether others understand them and whether they can understand others, under the same communication circumstances. Thus, participants from Asia view the asynchronous groupware as allowing enough time to compose messages and explain themselves.

Similarly, the different view of communication interaction influences the overall member participation in virtual teams. For instance, failure to post or respond to messages in a timely manner

when members are geographically distant is a major complaint in online collaboration (Roebuck & Britt, 2002). Massey, et al. (2001) also found that Asian and European participants perceived CITs to be a better fit for convergence-oriented communication than their U.S. counterparts. Specifically, when teams encountered conflict, U.S. members felt it was more difficult to reach agreement. However, Asians from collectivist, high-context, and higher uncertainty avoidance cultures, prefer to reach decisions through indirect communication, with some degree of vagueness, to avoid conflict. Such reliance or comfort with vagueness contrasts with U.S. participants from individualist, low-context, and lower uncertainty avoidance cultures that prefer direct communication, value confrontation, and enjoy intellectual debate which is difficult to accomplish in asynchronous CITs. Consequently, CITs enable certain culturally- driven communication behaviors while hindering others. In other words, CITs are adapted by different cultures to fit the local norms (Davidson & Vreede, 2001).

From a different perspective, Hsieh, Hsieh, and Lehman (2003) examine how Chinese ethics involve relationships. They conclude relationships are defined in terms of father and son, husband and wife, brothers and sisters, teachers and students, superior and subordinates and other hierarchical relations that count and subsequently, influence how they view ethical behaviors. Westerners attend to information ethics from the standpoint of tasks and goals that influence dependence on contracts, to clarify copyrights, loyalty, and intellectual property rights. This observation speaks to the concept of power distance dimension of cultural variability introduced by Hofstede (1980; 2001). First, it needs to be pointed out that the Dimension of Cultural Variability by Hofstede has faced significant criticism for the fact that the individual data collected from a single organization may not be representative of national cultures (McSweeney, 2002; Ess & Sudweeks, 2005). Nevertheless support for the dimension have withstood the test of time (see Ess & Sudweeks, 2005 for summary of studies). Furthermore, Smith (2002) argues that McSweeney ignored "almost entirely" the actual overall pattern of Hofstede's result by focusing only on two countries whose behaviors did not follow expectations. In getting back to the argument at hand, power distance involves the degree to which cultures accept the fact that power is distributed evenly or unequally. Thus, a low power distance culture, such as the United States views power as more evenly distributed, whereas, high power distance cultures such as Asian cultures, accept the fact that power is not evenly distributed. Consequently, the different cultural views influence group member participation in online collaboration (Hsieh et al., 2003; Olaniran, 2004). For instance, in the Chinese culture, the key to interaction involves finding the appropriate individual who has expertise, resources, and authority to act or make decisions (Hsieh et al., 2003). According to Hsieh et al (2003), the emphasis on relationships also identifies how individuals prioritize different relationships. Specifically, in Chinese culture, individuals count the family as the most important, then community, country, and finally, the world, while fostering harmony. The tendency to seek harmony can be linked to communication behaviors that stress indirectness and avoid conflict during virtual collaborations.

Furthermore, Lee (2002) found that in Asian cultures, the value of showing respect is more important than simply getting things done (i.e., performance). This tendency, for example, may explain why Koreans and Japanese employees shy away from e-mail use because of the perception that e-mail may be seen by supervisors to be rude and therefore, they would often use alternative communication media deemed to be more respectful (Lee, 2002). On the other hand, Western cultures do not share the same perception of respect and do not perceive the use of e-mail to be rude. In essence, the role of culture and the complexity that it adds in virtual collaborative projects is crucial as virtual teams work on their respective tasks while they must also negotiate and build relationships with one another.

Such relationship building also relies on different ways of interpreting silence. The idea of silence can be interpreted differently and can alter perceptions. Silence, in reaction to a request or business proposal, would be perceived negatively among Americans, Europeans, and Arab business persons, while it is cherished among listening cultures (e.g., East Asia and West Africa), where silence is considered a part of social interaction and not a "failure to communicate" (Lewis, 2000). Consequently, silence may be intensified in asynchronous CITs, as participants from listening cultures either choose not to use a particular medium (e.g., e-mail) or wait to gather requested information before responding to a request as a show of respect to others (Olaniran, 2004). With asynchronous channels, however, the time lag between messages, when unknown, can result in other participants' attributing "non-communication" to a lack of manners, which can damage relationships (Pauleen & Yoong, 2001; Crampton, 2002). Similarly, certain cultures inhibit individuals from revealing their lack of understanding, considering clarification requests impolite (Lewis, 2000), drastically hindering performance and participation in asynchronous CMC collaboration.

In general, communication technology is believed to decrease sociability, group solidarity, and trust necessary for members to communicate openly (Bal & Foster, 2000; Carleta, Anderson, McEwan, 2002). It stands to reason that culture and a lack of close proximity inevitably interfere with the interactions of virtual groups. People in co-located virtual groups have greater access to multiple communication media and thus, have the benefit of arranging face-to-face (FTF) meetings with ease or can use multiple channels, which in turn permits a broader range of messages, and cues, and at times provides an immediate response to inquiries or issues. However, participants in international online collaborations are relatively limited in their choice of CIT media. For instance, physical time differences restrict the use of synchronous CITs (e.g., videoconferencing, audio and teleconferencing) in certain contexts (Olaniran, 2004). Armstrong and Cole's (2002) study reinforces the effects of proximity in team conflict when they found that managers and facilitators in virtual groups felt that there was as much conflict between sites that were 15km away as those that are 800km away.

Trust

Trust is another major challenge facing virtual teams. Trust is essential to technology- mediated meaning in an attempt to have accurate attribution especially with message intent. Perception of "intent" with CITs is often faced with skepticism, especially when a prior relationship has not been established. Potential CIT users and participants tend to resist adoption of technology when they perceive negative implications on job security (Olaniran, 2004; Munkvold, 2005). Virtual teams are frequently concerned with the temporary and short common history of many geographically dispersed teams, which affect the member's trust and consequently the attribution processes. Members cannot draw on experience with each other in making attributions (Olaniran, 2001b; Crampton, 2002). It seems that when mediated group members in dispersed groups have limited time, they often fail to seek adequate social and contextual information to support their attributions (Olaniran, 1994; Crampton, 2002; Walther, 2002). This may result in dire consequences for participants in maintaining relationship or cohesion in dispersed virtual groups. Therefore, when things go wrong in virtual groups, members tend to blame individuals rather than focusing on assessments of possible situational concerns.

Several past studies focused on addressing outcomes associated with the lack of nonverbal cues that can render mediated communication as being impersonal. Some of these studies conclude that virtual teams need time to adjust to communication technologies and to one another. Differences between FTF and virtual groups reduce with time and more time together allows the development

of trust among participants (e.g., Olaniran, 1994; 1995; Walther, 1994). Furthermore, Vroman and Kovacich (2002) found deadlines to be liberally interpreted in virtual groups. Also, Olaniran (2004) argues that virtual groups emphasize critical incidents, thus, actual timelines are seldom the focus, especially where asynchronous interaction and different time zones are the norm. Notwithstanding, the different interpretation of deadlines influences the level of participation, which affects trust. For example, Cogburn and Levinson (2003) found that the lack of trust between U.S. and South African virtual team collaboration was due to the perception of an uneven distribution of work, infrequent communication among group members, failure to respond to team members' initiatives, and cross-cultural differences in communication.

National culture creates challenges for trust and is responsible for communication problems resulting in different attitudes toward group behavior that is seen as acceptable or unacceptable in virtual groups (Rutkowski, Vogel, Genuchten, Bemelmans, & Favier, 2002). In addition, Rutkowski et al. (2002) found that while group support systems (i.e., CITs) provide structure in group activities, it was found that the perception of the structure is viewed by some as enabling, while others see the structure as a hindrance especially when multiple cultures (i.e., Asian, Dutch, and French) are represented in the group. Similarly, when virtual team participants from different cultures share similar professional cultures, they still perceive each other differently. Specifically, when participants appeared to keep an open mind and change their own perceptions they were less likely to change their perceptions about their co-participants; more importantly, their perceptions are inaccurate in comparison to others' self perception (Rutkowski, Vogel, Genuchten, & Bemelmans, 2002).

Significant attention has been given to the social effects of CMC technologies (e.g., Hiltz, Johnson, & Turoff, 1986; Sproull & Kiesler, 1986) and the capacity to support social cues that serve as a foundation for creating and maintaining relationships otherwise known as media richness (Daft & Lengel, 1986; Daft, Lengel, & Trevino, 1987). The literature is rife with the opinion that different CIT media differ by the bandwidth or numbers of cues they can support. Consequently, FTF medium is considered as the richest medium given its ability to support nonverbal cues, personalization, and language variety (Hiltz, Johnson, & Turoff, 1986; Conolly, Jessup, & Valacich, 1990). CITs, on the other hand, are considered to be less friendly, emotional, or task-oriented (Rice & Love, 1987; Garton & Wellman, 1995). Hence, global virtual teams are challenged with a trust issue, which is compounded by cultural differences. Furthermore, trust within global virtual teams is believed to be fragile and temporal (Jarvenpaa & Leidner, 1999; Holton, 2001). By implication, the perceived lack of multiple "cue-carrying capacity" of CITs hinders trust and lead users to question their suitability for virtual teamwork and group processes that require a certain degree of cohesion through personal and socio-emotional factors.

Technology

The issue of technology usage in virtual groups revolves around the choice of media. At the same time, the hardware and software compatibility issue also accompanies technology discussions. As a matter of fact, the selection of a technology medium has been found to be a way by which globally-adopted identities are imposed by the home office or headquarters and consequently influence the socially-constructed identity sustained by the subsidiary (Gimenez, 2002). Scholars in the past and present have devoted significant attention to the issue of media selection and their implications for communication interaction in virtual environments. Different theoretical perspectives have been proposed to gain a better understanding of the role of technology media. In one particular camp there are those that focus on the media richness—implying that the mechanical and physical characteristics of technology are the primary determinant of communication outcomes (e.g., Daft et al., 1987; Daft & Lengel, 1986; Rice, 1992; Dennis & Kinney, 1998). Another camp focuses on the social influence perspective, which argues that the social contexts in which technology media are used contributes to the communication outcomes by influencing users' perception (e.g., Fulk, Schmitz, & Steifield, 1990; Desanctis, & Poole, 1994; Olaniran, 1995; 1996; Walther, 1995). Despite the views of the two different camps, it has been found that both technology media and the social factors are important and should be taken into consideration when using technology in virtual interaction (Yoo & Alavi, 2001; Olaniran, 2004). At the same time, different media are able to convey different levels of cues through bandwidth.

Similarly, the choice of a particular technology has different implications in different cultural contexts as alluded to earlier. Furthermore, the issue of bandwidth is germane to technological infrastructure, which can restrict or limit the choice or use of a particular medium. For instance, while videoconferencing offers a high degree of social cues, it requires a significant amount of bandwidth and faster connection to make it a reality. Consequently, it may not be a viable option in certain regions where access or high bandwidth connections are not available. Direct software and hardware compatibility can also be an issue where standards and platform formats are not the same.

Solutions and Recommendation

Notwithstanding the challenges in virtual teams, barriers must be overcome to create successful team experiences and allow participants to develop a sense of close ties or cohesion in the process of accomplishing their respective group and personal goals. To achieve optimal communication within virtual groups, solutions and recommendations must address the virtual groups' implicit and explicit requirements.

The issues of language, culture, trust, and technology in online collaboration are complex and intertwined and as such, require the need to address them together. First of all, overcoming the challenges in online collaborations requires a significant level of planning. Adequate planning can help overcome some of the challenges with language, culture, trust, and technology. For instance, one of the first approaches in setting up an effective online collaboration is for organizations and their managers to have a good understanding of the nature of the participants and the level of diversities that participants bring into the group. In essence, it would help to have an appointed moderator who can function as the team leader in assessing the situation, and to make sure all participants work well together. Part of the team leader's responsibilities are to organize a preliminary team meeting, preferably face-to-face but realistically a series of virtual meetings, giving each participant the opportunity to get to know and interact with the other members and to begin a relational development that can be transferred into the virtual context. Olaniran (2004) argues that this process is key to trust development where individuals do not have to second guess one another's intent. From a cultural standpoint, it can be an avenue to allow the members to develop a "new" cultural identity together that is void of "us" and "them."

Moreover, the initial meeting can be used by the virtual team leaders and the organization to assess any language issues and cultural challenges that need to be addressed. The key, however, is that individuals in online collaboration need adequate time to adapt or adjust to one another and the nature of interactions in online meetings and to develop relational bonds. The time to develop relational bond helps individuals in online collaboration groups to overcome attribution errors that occur because of lack of familiarity with one another (Crampton, 2002; Roebuck & Britt, 2002; Olaniran, 2004). At the same time, the choice of a technology medium or media can be made based on the assessment from preliminary meetings.

However, while it is important that a team leader be chosen to mediate the online collaboration, it is equally important that the selected individual be someone who is multi-culturally competent and open to change. In other words, the individuals must have had experience and understanding in working with individuals from each culture or at a least majority of the cultures to be represented in the virtual team.

Furthermore, online teams must establish a memorandum of understanding (MOU)–a normative guide indicating the responsibility and expectations from all participants, the nature of participation, the choice of electronic media and their appropriateness for the task and the context. The MOU helps set the tone for participation and identifies members' responsibilities and more importantly, it signals how to address deviation from established norms. For example, details concerning the frequency of interaction or the numbers of required e-mail in a given week can be specified (Roebuck & Britt, 2002). It is also believed that the normative guide can help address and reduce problems with cultural differences. For instance, the differences between a silent culture and a verbose culture may be overcome by alerting team members to those differences by developing established guidelines for handling them, such that misperception among members can be avoided (Olaniran, 2004). The same can be said about the "power distance" culture effect on communication interaction and technology choice. For example, if South East Asians are members of a virtual team, then members of the team that are guided by low power distance norm can either make allowance by allowing the participants to choose and use a communication medium that does not violate their cultural values. Multiple media use can also prevent the scenario wherein subordinates from a high-power distant culture may be accommodated by agreeing with superiors from a low-power distant culture because of cultural expectations, instead of expressing their true feelings (Oetzel, 1998; Olaniran, 2001). Another approach is to acknowledge the differences and encourage the group to use the selected media while alleviating whatever fear individuals from that culture may have.

Avenues need to be provided for online collaboration in which participants might vent their anger and address any ensuing dispute or conflicts. The online dispute resolution (ODR) may offer some advantages for cross-cultural communication. For instance, Rao (2004) suggests that online venting of frustration or anger can be useful for the upset party because as feelings are written out in e-mail or by posting; which allows the author time to reflect, rephrase, and reconsider the statements before sending them. This is especially helpful in cultures, such as the Thai, where it is considered impolite to show anger, and in the Japanese culture, where harmony is cherished. Rao (2004) offers an example using a negotiation between an American and a Thai, in which an American who may have otherwise shown anger or frustration in a face-to-face negotiation, due to the direct style of communication, may communicate through e-mail and while typing could have time to reconsider the feelings or at least the intensity of the feelings as they are being written, instead of lashing out at the other party. Hence some cultures may find it more comfortable communicating via e-mail or discussion postings where emotions are somewhat diffused or muted (Massey et al., 2001).

In online collaboration, it is important to realize that language can divide participants into the 'in group' of those who speak fluently and understand and the 'out group' of those who do not (Rao, 2004). Therefore, to prevent language differences from increasing "mistrust," "concealment," and "inflexibility," it would help to explain to participants the reason why a particular language is selected over others. More importantly it is essential to clarify that the language selection did not occur to subvert the status of other languages. Effort must be made to offer training and to help participants who may not be at the level of competency required. For instance, members in online collaborations are together responsible for

taking the initiatives to communicate clearly and specifically in a way that minimizes ambiguous expressions or colloquialisms. Gimenez (2002) offers the example of Argentine managers hiring fluent English speaking administrative assistants to help them interpret documents from the head office in the United States. Similarly, it has been suggested that online communication should be done in a way that offers multi-language interaction by making Web sites available in different languages (Rao, 2004) and offering multilingual support to participants.

Learning about national, organizational, and functional cultures can be very useful. Dube and Pare (2001) found that participants want cultural training to address any issue that can affect team performance; such as expected working hours, expected behaviors and involvement, how decisions are made, how tasks or projects will be evaluated, and how to resolve conflicts. The meaning of terms such as accountability, coordination, and collaboration and how they should operate within the team also need to be discussed to ensure all team members share a common understanding. After all, individuals with multicultural experience demonstrate an ability to overcome cultural barriers in virtual teams (Rutkowski et al., 2002). For instance, participants in the Hong Kong and Netherlands (HKNET) virtual teams indicate that the Hong Kong participants, who are accustomed to working in multicultural groups, were less defensive and more capable of coping with situational demands of cultural convergence than their Dutch colleagues who did not share a similar background (Rutkowski et al., 2002).

In regards to trust building and in compliance with facilitating social influence among online collaborators, the creation of a Web page that includes social information about participants in order to allow other members to develop an idea of who the members are, along with their interests, is useful. This approach is especially helpful when virtual team interaction takes place via an asynchronous mode (Holton, 2001; Olaniran, 2004). The existence of a community of interest in global virtual teams also challenges traditional hierarchical organizational and power structures (Maybury, 2001). A similar recommendation is made by Waldir Arevoedo (a research analyst at Gartner Inc.) when he suggests that multiple cues from different media help overcome barriers that are attributable to time, distance, and culture (Solomon, 2001, p. 61). Similarly, occasional FTF meetings are recommended for ongoing virtual groups for complex tasks along with a mix of synchronous and asynchronous CITs (DeSanctis, Wright, & Jiang, 2001; Olaniran, 2004; Saidon & Sitharan, 2004; Bajwa, Lewis, Prvan, & Lai, 2005;). It is essential to train team members in trust building, online communication etiquette, agenda sharing, and timely feedback.

As far as technology is concerned, the selection of an appropriate group of CITs to accomplish tasks is critical because fewer opportunities exist for FTF meetings in global virtual teams. Organizations and their online teams need to determine how and when to use certain technologies, a process that is not always apparent and may require trial and error (Dube & Pare, 2001; Olaniran, 2004). It is ideal for organizations to assign a project coordinator aside from a global virtual team leader who must serve as a liaison for unitizing different locations while diffusing cultural problems as they arise. This approach may also help overcome one of the major disadvantages of a global virtual team, which is the lack of physical interaction, nonverbal cues, and synergies that face-to-face interactions offer (Saidon & Sitharan, 2004). This approach can also help improve trust among team members. For instance, Dube and Pare (2001) found the selection of videoconferencing helpful in alleviating the challenge of the lack of physical interaction.

With videoconferencing, depending on its structure, people can be introduced on a more personal level than through e-mail or teleconferencing (Olaniran, 2004). Notwithstanding, the misuse of videoconferencing can be detrimental as well. For example, unstructured videoconferences can go awry and result in reduced confidence in the project's success and a loss of commitment to the project by team members (Dube & Pare, 2001).

In addition, the role of global virtual team coordinators, along with virtual team leaders, requires the development and management of an electronic workplace that utilizes multiple CITs to support the team's needs. The needs, however, change with the task. Dube and Pare (2001), point to the fact that every technology has its strengths and weaknesses and team members need to learn how to master the technologies that they are using. Furthermore, they suggest that some media will work for some tasks but not for others. A case in point is teleconferencing or videoconferencing, which are much richer than e-mail, but require high levels of commitment, flexibility, and discipline on the part of global virtual team members.

When videoconferencing or synchronous CITs are the media of choice, project coordinators need to communicate that some participants must arise very early in the morning and others must stay up very late to attend e-meetings. The key to making it work, however, is the need for the project coordinator to make the process fair. The coordinator may have to allow different sites to take turns, so that team members do not perceive preferential treatment and hence, destroy team interaction and effectiveness. The coordinators must also be aware that virtual collaboration or meetings interrupt team members' lives, and meetings should be conducted only when necessary, otherwise participation would suffer (Dube & Pare, 2001).

FUTURE TRENDS

Global and international virtual teams face additional challenges when compared to local virtual teams or face-to-face meetings. These challenges include culture, language, trust, and technology in terms of technical hardware and software compatibility, accessibility, reliability, and proficiency. However, organizations and virtual group participants need to recognize that technologies can evoke different reactions among individuals with different cultural orientations. The first step is to acknowledge these differences. The second step is to work toward creating common team norms (Olaniran, 2004). Organizations should require global virtual teams to develop explicit and mutually-agreed-upon operating guidelines (i.e., MOU) for how the team will work. Guidelines need to be in place that define how, when, and which technologies will be used (e.g., when to work separately vs. when to work collectively), and how the team will deal with conflict and make decisions. Establishing norms of behavior regarding communication task-technology use will enhance the performance of global virtual teams separated by space, time, and culture. For instance, CITs that support decentralized networks of communication between participants from different cultural and professional pools offer a potential for encouraging divergent thinking that enhances creativity and innovative ideas. However, the addition of different cultures introduces some challenges. Issues of communication and coordination difficulties must be addressed; otherwise, it may wipe out group creativity opportunities (Rutkowski et al., 2002; Olaniran, 2004).

The studies of global virtual teams emphasize the importance of training group members in order to proactively address issues relating to teambuilding, cultural training, and trust (Qureshi & Zigurs, 2001; Munkvold, 2005). The training, however, must address and specify norms for appropriate behavior with different CITs and general etiquettes. It is stressed that this should be provided in contract form that all team members can adopt (Bostrom, Kadlec, & Thomas, 1998; Munkvold, 2005). However, care must be taken, as alluded to above, that the notion of a "contract" might be perceived negatively by different cultures, thus, the use of the word "contract" may need to be clarified or explained contextually to avoid desensitizing.

Attention in online collaborations has primarily focused on the effects of technology and not enough on the actual and ongoing interaction among collaborators. This interactivity, however, is not a characteristic of a communication medium; rather it is a process in which communication through sequenced messages are related to each other in order to accomplish goals or tasks (Rafaeli & Sudweeks, 1998). This process is not void of culture as some would like to imply. Simply because globalization has increased the influx of people, due to immigration from different cultures, does not imply that all cultures are moving toward universal ideals (Olaniran, 2001b; 2004; Smith, 2002). Gimenez (2002) hypothesizes that "while some corporate differences are disappearing through globalization, local cultures and local meanings are still diverse" (p. 330). Thus, attention must be given to the role of national and local culture and also to the implied changes within a culture in an attempt to understand the essence of interactions taking place in online collaborations, since they vitally influence the negotiation of meaning. Relating to culture is the attitude toward language (i.e., English) in online collaboration. Gimenez (2002) argues that conflicts do not necessarily escalate from the use of English, but from the conflicting cultural realities and the ethnocentric attitudes held by head offices. In other words, organizations where the head offices are insensitive to the views and needs of their subsidiary cultures may be heading for trouble, especially in online interactions. Therefore, to examine the communication process, one needs to have reliable access to simultaneous, ongoing reliable measures of attitudes and behaviors, in addition to the communication content (Rafaeli & Sudweeks, 1998).

Furthermore, attention to the issue of technology adoption should be examined in developing effective online collaboration. The push for adoption of CITs needs to take place at an organizational level instead of at the team level (Munkvold, 2005). This is essential to allow team members to focus on the task at hand rather than having to learn the use of the selected technology. Munkvold (2005) presents findings on the implementation of KINET in Kvaerner, where a decentralized adoption of the system in global virtual collaboration was met with resistance, as some participating companies did not see a need for the technology. Consequently, the level of collaboration with other Kvaerner companies was low. Incentive for adopting CITs must be in place. The incentive does not necessarily have to be tangible; they can be intangible or a combination of both to create intrinsic motivation for participants and potential adopters.

To facilitate intensive intrinsic motivation (drive from within), an essential part of successful virtual communication, encourage active meaningful intrinsic motivation in global virtual team collaboration. Control orientation needs to be developed where participants feel a sense of autonomy (Hargis 2005). Control orientation also implies that participants are allowed to take risks and act as independent thinkers while fostering a sense of community that awakes interdependency among members. For instance, provision of technologies is not enough, given that most individuals can surf the Web on their own volition, but they need a reason to use chosen technology as a collaborative medium.

Technical and human consideration assistance is needed from the local culture to support the adoption process. The selected CITs need to be flexible to accommodate the local cultures of participating companies, especially those of small and distant companies. This flexibility may also enable global teams to have mobility that allows organizations to move projects and operations around, especially in the different stages of a project life cycle. For example, a design project in the oil and gas division of Kvaerner allowed engineers to collaborate in Oslo, Monaco, Abu Dhabi, Korea, Singapore, Perth, and Freemantle (Munkvold, 2005).

CONCLUSION

Organizations involved in global virtual team projects using CITs, must understand that these technologies will not generate overnight success or results. It takes time to adapt to CITs and emphasis must be given to adapting both technologies and communication interactions to local cultures. However, it may be possible for cultural challenges to be overcome and turned to an advantage in global virtual collaboration. Qureshi and Zigurs (2001) illustrate, with the Shell and Monitor case, that when the focus is on tasks and goals, CITs can provide "enduring" and "empowering" ways to develop virtual communities—communities where members' core competencies can be maximized in the process of personalizing interorganizational relationships. Culture presents an incredible challenge for global virtual teams, but it may also offer potential values if organizations proactively seek and develop ways that allow team members to embrace cultural challenges, jointly develop methods for overcoming the challenges, and evaluate concerns with CITs openly.

REFERENCES

Armstrong, D., & Cole, P. (2002). Managing distances and differences in geographically distributed work groups. In: P. Hinds & S. Kiesler (Eds.), *Distributed work* (pp. 167-186).

Bajwa, D., Lewis, L., Pervan, G., & Lai, V. (2005). The adoption and use of collaboration information technologies: International comparisons. *Journal of Information Technology, 20,* 130-140.

Bal, J., & Foster, P. (2000). Managing the virtual team and controlling effectiveness. *International Journal of Production Research, 38*(17), 4019-4032.

Barron, T. (2000). E-learning's global migration. Retrieved on August 26 2005 from http://www.learningcircuits.org/2000/Sep2000/barron.html.

Bostrom, R., Kadlec, C., & Thomas, D. (2003). Implementation and use of collaboration technology in e-learning: The case of a joint university-corporate MBA. In: B. Munkvold (Ed.), *Implementing collaboration technologies in industry: Case examples and lesson learned* (pp. 211-245). London, UK: Springer-Verlag.

Carleta, J., Anderson, A., & McEwan, R. (2000). The effects of multimedia communication technology on non-collocated teams: A case study. *Ergonomics, 43*(8), 1237-1251.

Chang, T. (2004). Transborder tourism, borderless classroom: Reflections on a Hawaii-Singapore experience. *Journal of Geography in Higher Education, 28*(2), 179-195.

Cogburn, D., & Levinson, N. (2003). U.S.-Africa virtual collaboration in globalization studies: Success factors for complex cross-national learning teams. *International Studies Perspectives, 4,* 34-52.

Connolly, T., Jessup, L., & Valacich, J. (1990). Effects of anonymity and evaluative tone on idea generation in computer-mediated groups. *Management Science, 36,* 97-120.

Crampton, C. (2002). Attribution in distributed work groups. In: P. Hinds & S. Kiesler (Eds.), *Distributed work* (pp. 191-212).

Crystal, D. (2003). *English as a global Language* (2nd ed.). New York, NY: Cambridge University Press.

Daft, R., & Lengel, R. (1986). Organizational information requirements, media richness and structural design. *Management Science, 32,* 554-571.

Daft, R., Lengel, R., & Trevino, L. (1987). Message equivocality, media selection, and manager performance: Implications for information systems. *Management Information System Quarterly, 11,* 355-366.

Davidson, R., & Vreede, G. (2001). The global application of collaborative technologies. *Communication of the ACM, 44*(12), 69-70.

Dennis, A., & Kinney, S. (1998). Testing media richness theory in the new media: The effects of cues, feedback, and task equivocality. *Information Systems Research, 9*(3), 256-274.

Desanctis, G., & Poole., M. (1994). Capturing the complexity in advanced technology use: Adapative structuration theory. *Organization Science, 5*(2), 121-147.

Desanctis, G., Wright, M., & Jiang, L. (2001). Building a global learning community. *Communications of the ACM, 44*(12), 80-82.

Dube, L., & Pare, G. (2001). Global virtual teams. *Communications of the ACM, 44*(12), 71-73.

Ess, C., & Sudweeks, F. (2005). Culture and computer-mediated communication: Toward new understandings. *Journal of Computer-Mediated Communication, 11*(1). Retrieved August 26, 2005 from Http://jcmc.indiana.edu/vol11/issue1/ess.html.

Fulk, J., Schmitz, J., & Steinfield, C. (1990). A social influence model of technology use. In: J. Fulk & C. Steinfield (Eds.), *Organizations and communication technology* (pp. 117-140). Newbury Park, CA: Sage.

Garton, L., & Wellman, B. (1995). Social impacts of electronic mail in organizations: A review of the research literature. In: B. Burleson (Ed.), *Communication Yearbook, 18,* 434-453. Thousand Oaks, CA: Sage.

Gimenez, J. (2002). New media and conflicting realities in multinational corporate communication: A case study. *IRAL, 40,* 323-343.

Gezo, T., Oliverson, M., & Zick, M. (2000). Managing global projects with virtual teams. *Hydrocarbon Processing, 79,* 112c-112I.

Hargis, J. (2005). Collaboration, community project-based learning: Does it still work online?. *International Journal of Instructional Media,*

32(2), 157-161.

Hiltz, S., Johnson, K., & Turoff, M. (1986). Experiment in group decision making communication process and outcome in face to face vs. computerized conference. *Human Communication Research, 13*, 225-252.

Hofstede, G. (1980). *Culture's consequences.* Beverly Hills, CA: Sage.

Hofstede, G. (1996). *Cultures and organizations: Software of the mind.* New York, NY: Mcgraw Hill.

Hofstede, G. (2001). *Culture's consequences: Comparing values, behaviors, institutions, and organizations across nations.* Thousand Oaks, CA: Sage.

Holton, J. (2001). Building trust and collaboration in a virtual team. *Team Performance Management, 7*(3-4), 36-47.

Hsieh, Y., Hsieh, C., & Lehman, J. (2003). Chinese ethics in communication, collaboration, and digitalization in the digital age. *Journal of Mass Media Ethics, 18*(3-4), 268-285.

James, M., & Ward, K. (2001). Leading a multinational team of change agents of Glaxo Wellcome. *Journal of Change Management, 2*(2), 148-159.

Jarvenpaa, S., & Leidner, D. (1999). Communication and trust in global virtual teams. *Organizational Science, 10*, 791-815.

Kayman, M. (2004). The state of English as a global language: Communicating culture. *Textual Practice, 18*(1), 1-22.

Kawachi, P. (1999). *When the sun doesn't rise: Empirical findings that explain the exclusion of Japanese from online global education.* Retrieved August 26, 2005 from http://www.ignou.ac.in/Theme-3/Paul%20%20KAWACHI.html.

Keenan, E., & Ante, S. (2002). The new teamwork. *Business Week,* EB 12-16.

Kiser, K. (1999,). Working on world time. *Training, 36*(3), 28-34.

Lee, O. (2002). Cultural differences in e-mail use of virtual teams a critical social theory perspective. *Cyberpsychology & Behavior, 5*(3), 227-232.

Lewis, R. (2000). *When cultures collide: Managing successfully across cultures.* London: Nicholas Brealy Publishing.

Massey, A., Montoya-Weiss, M., Hung, C., & Ramesh, V. (2001). Cultural perceptions of task-technology fit. *Communications of the ACM, 44*(12), 83-84.

Maybury, M. (2001). Collaborative virtual environments for analysis and decision support. *Communication of the ACM, 44*(12), 51-54.

McSweeney, B. (2002). Hofstede's model of national cultural difference and their consequences: A triumph of faith – a failure of analysis. *Human Relations, 55*(1), 89-117.

Munkvold, E. (2005). Experiences from global e-collaboration: Contextual influences on technology adoption and use. *IEEE Transactions on Professional Communication, 48*(1), 78-86.

Olaniran, B. (1994). Group performance and computer-mediated communication. *Management Communication Quarterly, 7*, 256-281.

Olaniran, B. (1995). Perceived communication outcomes in computer-mediated communication: An analyses of three systems among new users. *Information Processing and Management, 31*, 525-541.

Olaniran, B. (1996). A model of Satisfaction in computer-mediated and face-to-face communication. *Behavioural and Information Technology, 15*, 24-36.

Olaniran, B. (2001b). The effects of computer-mediated communication on transculturalism. In: V. Milhouse, M. Asante, & P. Nwosu (Eds.), *Transcultural realities* (pp. 83-105). Thousand Oaks, CA: Sage.

Olaniran, B. (2001a). Computer-mediated communication and conflict management process: A closer look at anticipation of future interaction. *World Futures, 57,* 285-313.

Olaniran, B. (2004). Computer-mediated communication in cross-cultural virtual groups. In: G. Chen & W. Starosta (Ed.), *Dialogue among diversities* (pp. 142-166). Washington, D.C.: NCA.

Pauleen, D., & Yoong, P. (2001). Facilitating virtual team relationships via Internet and conventional communication channels. *Journal of Internet Research: Electronic Networking Applications and Policy, 11*(3), 190-202.

Qureshi, S., & Zigurs, I. (2001). Paradoxes and prerogatives in global virtual collaboration, *Communications of the ACM, 44*(12), 85-88.

Rafaeli, S., & Sudweeks, F. (1998). Interactivity on the nets. In: F. Sudweeks, M. McLaughlin, & S. Rafaeli (Eds.), *Network and netplay: Virtual groups on the internet* (pp.173-190). Cambridge, MA: MIT Press.

Rao. S. (2004). The cultural vacuum in online disputes resolution. Retrieved July 11, 2006 from http://www.odr.info/unforum2004/rao.htm.

Rice, R. (1992). Task analyzability, use of new media, and effectiveness: A multi-site exploration of media richness. *Organization Science, 3*(4), 475-500.

Rice, R., & Love, G. (1987). Electronic emotion: Socioemotional content in a computer-mediated network. *Communication Research, 14,* 85-108.

Roebuck, D., & Britt, A. (2002). Virtual teaming has come to stay: Guidelines and strategies for success. *Southern Business Review, 28,* 29-39.

Roy, M. (2001). Small group communication and performance: Do cognitive flexibility and context matter?. *Management Decision, 39*(4), 323-330.

Rutkowski, A., Vogel, D., Genuchten, M., & Bemelmans, T. (2002). Group support system and vitual collaboration: The HKNET project. *Group Decision and Negotiation, 11,* 101-125.

Rutkowski, A., Vogel, D., Genuchten, M., Bemelmans, T., & Favier, M. (2002). E-Collaboration: The reality of virtuality. *IEEE Transactions on Professional Communication, 45*(4), 219-229.

Saidon, H., & Sitharan, R. (2004). The use of Internet for an international collaborative project. *Leonarno Electronic Almanac, 12*(8). http://mitpress2.mit.edu/e-journals/LEA/Text/Vol_12_n08.txt.

Smith, P. (2002). Culture's consequences: Something old and something new. *Human Relations, 55*(1), 119-135.

Solomon, C. (2001). Managing virtual teams. *Workforce, 80*(6), 60-65.

Spitzberg, B., & Cupach, W. (1989). *Handbook of interpersonal competence research.* New York, NY: Springer-Verlag.

Sproull, L., & Kiesler, S. (1986). Reducing social context cues: Electronic mail in organizational communication. *Management Science, 32,* 1492-1512.

Vroman, K., & Kovacich, J. (2002). Computer-mediated interdisciplinary teams: Theory and reality. *Journal of Interprofessional Care, 16,* 161-170.

Walther, J. (1994). Anticipated ongoing interaction versus channel effects on relational communication in computer-mediated interaction. *Human Communication Research, 20,* 473-501. *Organization Science, 6*(2), 186-203.

Walther, J. (1995). Relational aspects of computer-mediated communication: Experimental observations over time. *Organization Science, 6*(2), 196-203.

Walther. J. (2002). Time effects in computer-mediated groups: Past, present, and future. In:

P. Hinds & S. Kiesler (Eds.), *Distributed work* (pp. 235-257).

Yoo, Y., & Alavi, M. (2001). Media and group cohesion: Relative influences on social presence, task participation, and group consensus. *MIS Quarterly, 25*(3), 371-390.

KEY TERMS

Virtual Team: A collaboration approach in which members interact via communication technologies for the purpose of accomplishing a group goal.

Computer-Mediated Communication: A communication process in which computers and other electronic media serve as the medium of interaction.

Culture: A collection of symbols and norms that affect how humans gather, organize, and process information.

Power Distance: A process that identifies cultural norms or believes where a society comes to accept how power is distributed (either equally or unequal)

Individualism-Collectivism: Individualism speaks to the cultural approach where people look after themselves and their family—in essence, the emphasis is on self. Collectivism emphasizes cultures where people belong to in-groups or collectivities that are supposed to look after them in exchange for loyalty; thus the emphasis is on others.

Globalization: A social, political and economic trend in which denationalization of markets, politics and legal systems occur and from an organizational standpoint, corporations or companies attempt to participate in the global economy by maintaining their presence in foreign markets through incorporation of communication technologies (i.e., Internet) for virtual presence on the international marketplace or e-business.

Virtual Workspaces: Organizational environments in which coordination process and communication activities exist with the aid of electronic mediated technologies.

Chapter XI
Explaining Organizational Virtuality:
Insights from the Knowledge-Based View

Yulin Fang
City University of Hong Kong, Hong Kong

Dev K. Dutta
University of New Hampshire, USA

ABSTRACT

Despite a sizable body of literature on virtual organization, little attention has been paid to defining organizational virtuality and identifying factors that influence degree of virtuality in organizations. Based on virtual organization literature and the knowledge-based view of the firm, we develop a working definition of organizational virtuality. We do this by conducting a review of existing definitions of a virtual organization, and identify organizational knowledge-related factors that influence virtuality. More specifically, we propose that 1) an organization's need for knowledge exchange and ability to exchange knowledge jointly determine the level of organizational virtuality that develops in the firm; and 2) the higher the need for and ability to engage in knowledge exchange, the higher this level of resulting organizational virtuality. The contribution that this research makes to academia and managerial practice are also discussed.

INTRODUCTION

In this century, there is a growing realization that the ways people live, work, communicate with each other, and organize their professional and personal activities are being subjected to an all-pervasive influence of information and communication technologies (ICTs) (Orlikowski & Barley, 2001). Within firms, one of the ways this influence finds expression is through creation and adoption of newer organizational forms such as the virtual organization. A virtual organization (VO) entails employees working outside of the physical central office (Kurland & Egan, 1999; Staples, Hulland, & Higgins, 1999; Neufeld & Fang, 2004), creating virtual teams to work across geographical and temporal boundaries (Lipnack & Stamps, 1996; 1997; Townsend, DeMarie, & Hendrickson, 1998), and working closely with other firms based on ICTs, in order to outsource a large portion of production process outside of traditional firm boundary (Boudreau, 1998;

Kraut, Steinfield, Chan, Butler, & Hoag, 1999; Hoogeweegen, Teunissen, Vervest, & Wagenaar, 1999).

Research on organizing business activities in a virtual manner has its origins in the last decade (Davidow & Malone, 1992) and has been proliferating (Kurland & Egan, 1999; Martins, Gilson, & Maynard, 2004). Correspondingly, we have seen virtual modes of organizing being increasingly adopted in practice too. The Gartner Group estimates that between 2000 and 2010, a typical employee will notice the following shifts in the nature of his/her work: (i) time spent working alone will fall from 40% to 30%; (ii) time spent on working with others (who are based in the same location and thus also in the same time zone) will fall from 15% to 5%; (iii) time spent on working with others (who are based in a different location but in the same time zone) will rise from 15% to 25%; and (iv) time spent in working with others (who are based in a different location and a different time zone) will rise from 30% to 40% (Solomon, 2001). This suggests that there has been and will continue to be an increasing expansion of collaboration across space and time. Similar studies suggest that this change will occur not just in North America but across the world (Edwards & Field-Hendrey, 1996; Russell, 1996).

With proliferation of VOs, it has become fashionable to focus on this phenomenon as part of management research (DeSanctis & Monge, 1999). Yet, to date there has been little consensus not only on defining "virtual" but also with respect to identifying factors that contribute to creation of virtual organizations (Kraut et al., 1999). Extant research on VOs has been concerned mainly with understanding the managerial challenges and consequences that arise *after* such organizations are formed. Issues that have been examined in prior literature include: (i) management dynamics of VOs, such as communication processes (DeSanctis & Monge, 1999), metamanagement (Mowshowitz, 1994; Mowshowitz, 1997; Hoogeweegen et al., 1999), personal relationship on use of virtual networks (Kraut et al., 1999), risk

mitigation (Grabowski & Roberts, 1999), network structure (Ahuja & Carley, 1999) and trustworthiness within VO (Kasper-Fuehrer & Ashkanasy, 2001); and (ii) consequences of VO, such as process improvement (Kock, 2000), flexible and reconfigurable structures (DeSanctis & Monge, 1999) and organizational performance (Davidow & Malone, 1992). With a few exceptions (Fang & Dong, 2006), there has been little research on assessing the circumstances and conditions that lead to creation of VO (i.e., its antecedents and facilitators). Given this backdrop, the following research questions motivate this chapter:

1. What is organizational virtuality?
2. What factors contribute to formation of virtual organizations?

The remainder of the chapter is organized as follows. First, we summarize the definitions of virtual organization based on a review of current literature. Using this summary, we define organizational virtuality. We then explore a plausible reason for why different organizations exhibit varying degrees of organizational virtuality, based on insights from the perspective of knowledge-based view of the firm (Grant, 1996; Spender, 1996). We propose that a potential reason why an organization goes virtual can be associated with related knowledge factors that affect its business and working. The research contributes to our scholarly understanding of determinants of VO, by linking the literature on knowledge-based view with the VO literature. It provides practical implications for managers, by offering insights on how an organization should reflect its form of organizing in response to its emerging knowledge-related challenges and opportunities.

BACKGROUND: ORGANIZATIONAL VIRTUALITY

The study of organizational form is a central issue of concern in organization science. Organizational form is composed of structural features or patterns that are shared across a large number of organizations (McKelvey, 1982). Researchers are concerned with studying a variety of forms. Economists have traditionally focused on two alternative forms, markets versus hierarchies (Williamson, 1975). Sociologists have studied bureaucracy, a form (Weber, 1922) portrayed in contrast to the guild form. Recently, organizational scholars have observed that an alternative to markets and hierarchies seems to be emerging, that of the network (Miles & Snow, 1986; Powell, 1990; Nohria & Eccles, 1992). In the last decade, there has been a growing interest in a number of other "postbureaucratic" forms, one of which is the VO (Davidow & Malone, 1992; Bleecker, 1994; Nohria & Berkley, 1994); yet, there seems to be little agreement amongst researchers on what constitutes organizational virtuality (Kraut et al., 1999).

Virtual Organization

In order to develop a more informed understanding of a virtual organization, we review the prior literature on the topic. The literature search followed the suggestions given by Webster and Watson (2002). First, we reviewed the articles in a special issue of *Organization Science*, edited by DeSanctis and Monge (1999). This was a seminal issue of research papers devoted exclusively to virtual organizations. Second, we went further back in our literature review by identifying other key articles cited by the papers published in the volume edited by DeSanctis and Monge (1999). Third, we went forward by using WebOfScience (www.webofscience) to identify articles citing the key articles identified in the previous steps. This process generated a summary of various definitions of virtual organization (Table 1). For the purpose of this chapter, we adopt DeSanctis and Monge's (1999) definition of virtual organizations as "a collection of geographically/temporally dispersed, functionally and/or culturally diverse entities that work together using information tech-

nology." An essential characteristic embedded in this definition of organizational virtuality is the suggestion of the critical role that information technology plays towards connecting dispersed entities that work together. From Table 1, we notice that prior literature is unanimous with respect to highlighting the central role of information technology in virtual organizations. It is agreed that information technology must be in place before a virtual organization, no matter how geographically dispersed and/or functionally diversified, can exist. Thus, Davidow and Malone (1992) stress that virtual organizations "require taking a sophisticated information network that gathers data on markets and customer needs, combining it with the newest design methods and computer-integrated production processes, and then operating this system with an integrated network that includes not only highly skilled employees of the company but also suppliers, distributors, retailers and even consumers" (p. 6). Underlying this sophisticated information network is the application of information technologies, which integrates the entities within and across organizations. The entities that make up a virtual organization can be individual workers (Clancy, 1994; Barner, 1996), teams and departments (Grenier & Metes, 1995; Lipnack & Stamps, 1997) (i.e., within organization), as well as organizations with external ties (i.e., inter-organizational) (Coyle & Schnarr, 1995). Virtual organizations can arise in either intra-firm or inter-firm contexts (DeSanctis & Monge, 1999; Kasper-Fuehrer & Ashkanasy, 2001). Similarly, duration of existence of a VO can also vary: from satisfying a short-term or temporary goal to fulfilling a long-term or enduring goal.

Organizational Virtuality

Although the idea of VO prevails in both academic and practitioner discourse, few pure virtual forms exist today (Dutton, 1999; Kraut et al., 1999). Instead, aspects of virtuality occur in many business organizations (DeSanctis & Monge, 1999). For example, many firms build some form of the

Table 1. Summary of definitions of virtual organization

Article	Definition of Virtual Organization
DeSanctis, 1999	A collection of geographically distributed, functionally and/or culturally diverse entities that are linked by electronic forms of communication and rely on lateral, dynamic relationships for coordination
Ahuja, 1999	A geographically distributed organization whose members are bound by a long-term common interest or goal, and who communicate and coordinate their work through information technology
Grabowski, 1999	Comprised of multiple, distributed members, temporarily linked together for competitive advantage that shares common value chains and business processes supported by distributed information technology
Staples, 1999	Consists of individuals working toward a common goal, but without centralized buildings, physical plant, or other characteristics of a traditional organization

Kraut, 1999	Defined in terms of the number and importance of cross-boundary transactions.
	    Production processes transcend the boundaries of a single firm
	    Production processes are flexible
	    Parties are geographically dispersed
	    Coordination is heavily dependent on information technologies

Mowshowitz, 1994; 1997	A virtually organized company dynamically links its business goals with the procedures needed to achieve them.
O'Leary, 1997	Defined as one where complementary resources existing in a number of cooperating companies are left in place, but are integrated to support a particular product effort for as long as it is viable to do so… Resources are selectively allocated to the virtual company if they are underutilized or if they can be profitably utilized there more than in the home company.
Hoogeweegen, 1999	Combine core competences of multiple organizations in temporary alignment in response to specific customer preferences
Markus, 2000	New networked organizational forms in which work is conducted by temporary teams that cross organizational lines
Kasper-Fuehrer, 2001	Inter-organizational virtual organization: a temporary network organization, consisting of independent enterprises that come together swiftly to exploit an apparent market opportunity
Boudreau, 1998	A VO operates as "a federated collection of enterprises tied together through contractual and other means. Organizations that are dependent on a federation of alliances and partnerships with other organizations; relative spatial and temporal independence; flexibility" (p. 212)
Kurland, 1999	Virtual organizations are composed of "telecommuters, substitution of telecommunications for physical travel to the organization" (p. 500).

VO based on the external relationships forged with other firms through outsourcing contracts, strategic alliances, and inter-organizational linkages (Mowshowitz, 1994; Nohria & Berkley, 1994; Griffith, Sawyer, & Neale, 2003). More and more firms have deployed telecommuting programs that enable their employees to operate from outside of the physical boundaries of the office (Davenport & Pearlson, 1998; Neufeld & Fang, 2004). Even within the firm, work teams are often geographically distributed (Ancona & Caldwell, 1992). These trends suggest that firms are engaging in and acquiring higher virtuality than before (DeSanctis & Monge, 1999). Even firms that do not appear to be virtual, given the conventional definition of their organizational

forms, do usually conduct certain activities virtually. Thus, for most firms being virtual is a matter of degree (Kraut et al., 1999).

Following from these definitions and characteristics of virtual organizations, we define organizational virtuality as being "the capability of an organization to connect geographically dispersed entities to continuously work together by taking recourse to information system (IS) resources." In our view, even though geographical dispersion, functional diversity and extensive use of information technology comprise the dominant features of most virtual organizations, we cannot define virtuality using these characteristics in a distinct manner. For instance, organizations that have employees based across several countries are more geographically dispersed, but they may not be necessarily more virtual compared to those that have employees dispersed within one city. Again, organizations that have more cultural/functional heterogeneity are more diversified, but not necessarily more virtual, than those with less heterogeneity. Similarly, organizations that have more use of information technology (IT) are more computerized, but not necessarily more virtual, than those with less information technology. In effect, virtuality becomes a state where "individual members of an organization featuring global cross-functional computer-mediated jobs may be considered holographically equivalent to the organization as a whole" (Noharia & Berkley, 1994).

Thus, virtuality is about the ability of an organization and its constituent units to work collaboratively under situations where dispersion, diversity and digitization are essential features. Adopting an integrative view of these three characteristics and the crucial role of IT, we argue that virtuality is the ability of a firm to connect a collection of entities, however dispersed and/or diverse they are, to engage in continuous collaboration through leveraging IS resources. As such, firms can be inter-organizationally virtual when one firm connects some of its own business processes conducted in-house with business processes that are conducted outside the firm's boundaries by its business partners (Kraut et al., 1999). Similarly, a firm is intra-organizationally virtual when its employees are based outside the physical boundaries of the firm and yet connect with some of the central resources within the firm through use of IS, or when a number of virtual teams within the firm but based in multiple locations electronically connect together for teamwork, thus in either case bridging geographical distance.

Having acknowledged that organizations can potentially display virtuality over a continuum, the key thought then becomes identifying specific organizational characteristics that result in differences among organizations with regard to virtuality. To investigate this question further, we take recourse to insights from the knowledge-based view of the firm.

INSIGHTS FROM THE KNOWLEDGE-BASED VIEW OF THE FIRM

The knowledge-based view (KBV) posits that a firm's knowledge is not only valuable, rare, inimitable and non-substitutable, but also strategically *the* most significant resource available to it (Grant, 1996). Therefore, it is knowledge that forms the basis of a firm's sustained competitive advantage. Even though the KBV initially developed as an extension or special case of the more popular resource-based view (RBV) of the firm (Barney, 1991), more recently, several researchers (e.g., Spender, 1996; Cook & Brown, 1999; Orlikowski, 2002) have suggested that rather than the objective knowledge *per se*, it is the idiosyncratic process of "knowing," characterizing ongoing, dynamic social interaction amongst organizational actors, that actually enables the firm to achieve sustained competitive advantage using knowledge. In this expanded view, organizational knowledge is not static but emergent and becomes useful only when it is applied in a context. Thus, "…knowing is constituted and reconstituted every day in practice… [so much so that] capabilities of the organization are not fixed or given properties… Rather, they are constituted every day in the ongoing and situated practices of the organization's members" (Orlikowski, 2002, pp. 269-270). To examine organizational virtuality, we adopt this view of organizational knowledge as "knowing in practice".

Based on four analytically distinct but interrelated streams of discourse in the social sciences, Kakihara and Sorensen (2002) find that organizational knowledge can be viewed from the following perspectives: (i) knowledge as object, (ii) knowledge as interpretation, (iii) knowledge as process, and (iv) knowledge as relationship. As knowledge evolves from being a "…given and stable, as always ready-to-hand" (Orlikowski, 2002, p. 269) objective resource to an emergent entity, reflecting knowing in practice and rooted in organizational interpretation and discourse, it becomes increasingly important to shift the earlier-held understanding of knowledge. Knowledge transforms from being self-contained within the individual to a dynamic exchange occurring amongst two or more organizational actors engaged in a conversation of enduring mutual interest and significance. In the latter case, two attributes of the knowledge that aid this process are: (i) the *need* for knowledge exchange, and (ii) the *ability* to engage in knowledge exchange, amongst interested organizational members. We suggest that both these attributes affect the level of organizational virtuality resulting in the virtual firm. While it is theoretically possible for either attribute to assume an infinite range of values varying from zero (or not at all) to one (or complete), for the purpose of this discussion we categorize either attribute as taking up a value that is either "low" or "high". Therefore, organizational virtuality becomes a function of these two attributes, represented in Figure 1.

Need for Knowledge Exchange

The first attribute or characteristic influencing organizational virtuality is the need for knowledge

exchange that arises amongst a firm's dispersed organizational units and their constituent members. Any knowledge generated and used within an organizational unit can be categorized as being (i) only useful to that unit and only at that point in time, (ii) only useful to that unit but at multiple points in time, or (iii) useful to not only that unit but other organizational units as well, either at a single point in time or for multiple points in time. In case (ii) and/or (iii) prevail over (i), we can say that the firm has a comparatively higher need for knowledge exchange amongst its constituent organizational units and/or their members. For instance, the need for knowledge exchange is certainly higher for (ii) over (i) because knowledge is required at multiple points in time. Given that knowledge is emergent and contextually variant, it will need to be shared and exchanged amongst organizational members repeatedly because the context has changed with time (e.g., some of the organizational members have left the unit) and so the earlier knowledge has lost its partial significance and, therefore, must be renewed. Similarly, between (i) and (iii) as also between (ii) and (iii) the need for knowledge exchange is highest in case (iii) because the knowledge must be shared, enacted and transformed across multiple units and over multiple points in time, before it becomes useful. For instance, McDonald's has thousands of outlets around the world. Every outlet oper-

Figure 1. Organizational virtuality as an outcome of the firm's need for knowledge exchange and ability to engaging in knowledge exchange

Need for Knowledge Exchange	High	*Scenario 3* *Low level of organizational virtuality*	*Scenario 4* *High level of organizational virtuality*
	Low	*Scenario 1* *Non-existent organizational virtuality*	*Scenario 2* *Moderate organizational virtuality, but exists in isolated pockets only*
		Low	High
		Ability to Engage in Knowledge Exchange	

ates independently and the knowledge they have in serving local customers need not necessarily be shared with other outlets; thus, for a specific franchisee the knowledge it holds is only useful to itself. In contrast, Nortel, a global 500 company providing telecommunication and Internet solutions, has many research and development centers (R&D) around the world that engage in global product development. Different R&D centers had different expertise. The R&D centers must necessarily collaborate and leverage each other's unique knowledge. In effect, need for knowledge exchange is very high for Nortel R&D centers.

Ability to Engage in Knowledge Exchange

The second attribute or characteristic that affects organizational virtuality is the ability of the firm to engage in knowledge exchange. Simply possessing a need to exchange knowledge is not enough. What is equally important is an ability to exchange the knowledge amongst the interested organizational constituents (units and/or actors) and at the point in time when the need has been expressed. The ability to engage in knowledge exchange is a function of two parameters: the ability to articulate the knowledge, and the ability to create a shared environment for knowledge exchange, using appropriate technology.

The first parameter is the ability to articulate the knowledge and bring it to a form such that it is amenable to transmission from one organizational member to another. This relates to distinguishing between the two commonly accepted categories of knowledge—tacit versus explicit (Polanyi, 1962). In developing a typology of tacit knowledge, Castillo (2002) suggests that such knowledge can take the following forms: (i) nonepistle tacit knowledge, or knowledge that is based on "gut feelings" and is not or cannot be written in any form or verbalized, (ii) sociocultural tacit knowledge, or knowledge that do not belong to anyone in particular but rather arise in wider social/cultural systems, which learn and make use

of this knowledge, (iii) semantic tacit knowledge, or knowledge that is necessarily abstract, symbolic and can be shared only between individuals who belong to a common professional milieu, and (iv) sagacious tacit knowledge, or knowledge that is perceived only by the sages (i.e., experts) and escapes the notice of novices. From this classification, it is clear that much of tacit knowledge is abstruse, extremely difficult to verbalize, and loses its significance when removed from context. Only a limited proportion of the total tacit knowledge residing within an individual can be made explicit before it is shared with others. In effect, much of the tacit knowledge can be shared only if it is exchanged between individuals on a real-time basis, with the vehicle for sharing sensitive to the context and the dynamic nature of the sharing process.

This is where the second parameter, viz. the ability to create a shared environment for knowledge exchange using appropriate technology becomes crucial. Organizational virtuality enables firms to take recourse to technology and create the requisite infrastructure that provides firms with the ability to exchange technology. Using various expressions of organizational virtuality (such as computer-supported collaborative work, videoconferencing, e-mail, intranet, etc.), it thus becomes possible for firms to create virtual communities of practice that can engage in effective knowledge exchange amongst organizational members and/or unit. For example, Nortel R&D centers located across geographies have developed and deployed a variety of ICT-based applications to facilitate knowledge exchange, including a well-organized/maintained intranet to host contextual information of each site, and distributed defect tracking systems to share and collectively resolve programming difficulties. They also extensively use e-mail, teleconferences for cross-site communication. Having access to this sophisticated information infrastructure certainly makes the company capable, as far as its ability to create a shared knowledge environment for its teams is concerned.

To summarize, Figure 1 depicts the following four situations:

1. **Scenario 1:** both the need for knowledge exchange and ability to engage in knowledge exchange are low.
2. **Scenario 2:** the need for knowledge exchange is low but ability to engage in knowledge exchange is high.
3. **Scenario 3:** the need for knowledge exchange is high but ability to engage in knowledge exchange is low.
4. **Scenario 4:** both the need for knowledge exchange and ability to engage in knowledge exchange are high.

We suggest that a high level of organizational virtuality will be noticed only in Scenario 4 because this is when the conditions within the firm become optimal for both creation and sustenance of a virtual network. In the remaining three scenarios, organizational virtuality will either not be required or if it is set up, will provide sub-optimal benefits to the firm. For example, under Scenario 1 there is simply no requirement to create organizational virtuality. Despite that, if it is created through use of available technology, it will not be used because the firm does not have an ability to exchange knowledge. In effect, the virtual network will fritter away and degenerate over time. Again, under Scenario 2 even though the firm has an ability to engage in knowledge exchange, the need for knowledge exchange is low. Under the circumstances, if a virtual network is created simply because of a fascination with available technology, it will only be partially used. Finally, under Scenario 3 even though the firm has a high need for knowledge exchange, it has only a limited ability to engage in knowledge exchange. Once again, under the circumstances the firm will demonstrate rather low levels of organizational virtuality and fall back upon other traditional methods of knowledge exchange such as face-to-face meetings. Therefore, we suggest:

Proposition 1: Need for knowledge exchange and ability to engage in knowledge exchange jointly determine the level of organizational virtuality that exists in a firm.

Proposition 2: The level of organizational virtuality is highest when both need for knowledge exchange and ability to engage in knowledge exchange are high. Alternatively, the level of organizational virtuality is: (i) non-existent when both need for knowledge exchange and ability to engage in knowledge exchange are low, (ii) low when need for knowledge exchange is high but ability to engage in knowledge exchange is low, and (iii) moderate, but exist in isolated pockets only, when the need for knowledge exchange is low but ability to engage in knowledge exchange is high.

Examples for each category are abundant. For instance, among other major telecommunication device manufacturers, Alcatel is a typical organization fully leveraging its knowledge dispersed across subsidiaries around the world by strengthening its ability to exchange knowledge. Alcatel's strategy of global product development requires that each subsidiary, R&D sites in particular, contribute their location and/or domain-specific knowledge. Depending on products under development, Alcatel dynamically combine knowledge and expertise specific to particular research centers, and hence the need for knowledge exchange among these centers is very high. To facilitate knowledge exchange, Alcatel has built superior IT infrastructure including a variety of IT tools. Hence its ability to exchange knowledge is high. In combination, Alcatel's global product development falls in high-need and high-ability category. In contrast, organizations composed of a number of dispersed "solos" with neither need nor ability to communicate and exchange knowledge via information technology, despite being geographically dispersed, is poor on organizational virtuality. Thus, we note that Alcatel is an example of a company that is currently under Scenario 4.

There are also examples of many firms who fall in one of the other three scenarios, given the unique characteristics of their business. As we already noted, the franchisee network of McDonald's can be taken to be as falling under scenario 1. Scenario 2 would be a company that has invested a lot in IS systems and supporting infrastructure but operates in a rather static industry, where knowledge requirement and rate of change in knowledge are low. Industrial and Commercial Bank of China invested heavily in building its e-Commerce infrastructure, and hence the bank's ability to exchange knowledge is high. However, as banks in China are strictly regulated and influenced by the government, its business applications are limited. This limits the bank's needs to exchange knowledge across different places. Thus, the bank falls into Scenario 2. Similarly, scenario 3 would be the case of a company that is operating in a dynamic industry but has not made much investment in IT to strengthen the ability to exchange knowledge. For instance, K-Mart in the United States failed in responding to the dynamic retailing market, which requires information and knowledge to be extensively shared (i.e., the need to exchange knowledge is high). But K-Mart's investment in information technology infrastructure far lagged behind major competitors such as Wal-mart, and hence its ability to exchange knowledge was low. Therefore, K-Mart falls into scenario 3, whose need for knowledge exchange is high while ability to exchange knowledge is low, leading to a disadvantaged position in comparison to its major competitors such as Wal-Mart.

IMPLICATIONS

This chapter summarizes the extant literature on virtual organizations, proposes a definition of organizational virtuality, and theorizes the reasons for which different levels of virtuality exist in the firm from the knowledge-based view. It makes the following contribution to the literature: First, our research is among the first to define the notion of virtuality based on a unique organizational characteristic, viz. the role of knowledge within the firm. Although research has suggested that organizations' being virtual is a matter of degree (Kraut et al., 1999), the literature has not intensively explored what factors contribute to the variation of virtuality. Our intent here is to relate virtuality in terms of the three major characteristics of virtual organizations (i.e., dispersion, diversity and digitalization) and offer a unified view of virtuality that stresses the capability of continuous operating without face-to-face interactions based on knowledge. This view offers a point of departure for a new venue of research, including determinants and consequence of virtuality and the effects of the three characteristics of virtual organizations on virtuality.

Second, this study is of relevance to researchers who study change of organizational forms, particularly those focusing on the determinants. Organizational change and its enablers have been topics of abiding interest (Huber & Glick, 1993). Developing and adopting an increasing virtual form of organizing is changing the way businesses are run. As such, it is important to study this phenomenon. Previous research only focuses on the influencing factors of virtual organizing on the firm performance. Little research has been conducted to explain why virtual organization comes into being at the first place. Thus, developing an understanding of factors that determine organizational virtuality will enrich the body of research on organizational change. Based on the working definition of organizational virtuality, this chapter contributes to the body of knowledge by adopting the knowledge-based view, suggesting that two factors jointly influence virtuality: need to exchange and ability to exchange.

Third, this research offers opportunities to study the relationship between technology and organizational forms (Fulk & DeSanctis, 1995; Orlikowski, 1996). Virtual organization, as an emerging organizational form enabled by information technology, is of great interest and relevance for IS researchers who study the role of IT in firms (Dewett & Jones, 2001). The knowledge-based view in this study makes the first attempt in linking the knowledge aspect of the firm with organizational virtuality, and thus contribute to the IS literature by linking knowledge management and virtual organizations.

Last but not least, the chapter offers insights to managers who are considering transforming their existing organizations to achieve higher levels of virtuality. We suggest that it is important to review organizational aspects in relation to the need for and the ability to exchange knowledge. It would be a waste of resources to invest in building ability to exchange knowledge (e.g., advanced information technology solutions for collaboration and communication if the need for exchanging knowledge among concerned locations/departments is very low. Alternatively, if the need for exchanging knowledge across sites is high but the ability to exchange knowledge is constrained by the difficulty in articulating knowledge and underdeveloped IT infrastructure and application, the organization's virtuality is seen as limited. Only organizations that maintain a good balance between the need and the ability can achieve a true sense of virtuality.

Our research has a few limitations and thus provides opportunities for future research. First, our discussion of the relationship between the two attributes of knowledge and organizational virtuality still remains preliminary. A more in-depth explanation of how need to exchange knowledge and ability to exchange knowledge individually and jointly affect virtuality is needed. Second, our suggested conceptual framework focuses on defining virtuality and exploring knowledge-related determinants of virtuality for firms. Its generalizability to other virtual forms of organizing, such as virtual communities, is subject to further research. Third, the extent to which the three major characteristics of virtual organization (i.e., dispersion, diversity and digitalization) affect virtuality remains an opportunity for further research.

CONCLUSION

Current literature on virtual organization calls for special attention to understanding "what it means for a firm to become virtual". It also highlights the importance of identifying factors that influence the degree of virtuality in organizations. Based on virtual organization literature and the knowledge-based view of the firm, we develop a working definition of organizational virtuality. We do this by conducting a review of existing definitions of a virtual organization, and identify knowledge-related factors that may influence organizational virtuality. More specifically, we propose that 1) an organization's need for knowledge exchange and ability to engage in knowledge exchange jointly determine the level of organizational virtuality that develops in the firm; and 2) the higher the need for and ability to engage in knowledge exchange, the higher this level of resulting organizational virtuality. We provide several examples from the field of practice that serve to illustrate our framework and the four business scenarios under which the need for and ability to engage in knowledge exchange vary. Our chapter concludes by providing theoretical implications of this research to organizational forms and virtual organizations in particular as well as by indicating practical implications for managers deploying information technologies to deal with organizational virtuality.

REFERENCES

Ahuja, M., & Carley, K. (1999). Network structure in virtual organizations. *Organization Science, 10*(6), 693-703.

Ancona, D., & Caldwell, D. (1992). Bridging the boundary: External activity and performance in organizational teams. *Administrative Science Quarterly, 37*(634-665).

Barner, R. (1996). The new millennium workplace: Seven changes that will challenge managers—and workers. *Futurist, 30*(2), 14-18.

Bleecker, S. (1994). The virtual organization. *Futurist, 28*(2), 9-14.

Boudreau, M., Loch, K.D., Robey, D., & Straub, D. (1998). Going global: Using information technology to advance the competitiveness of the virtual transnational organization. *The Academy of Management Executive, 12*, 120-128.

Clancy, T. (1994). The latest word from thoughtful executives—The virtual corporation, telecommuting and the concept of team. *Academy of Management Executive, 8*(2), 8-10.

Coyle, J., & Schnarr, N. (1995). The soft-side challenges of the 'virtual corporation'. *Human Resource Planning, 18*(1), 41-42.

Davenport, T., & Pearlson, K. (1998). Two cheers for the virtual office. *Sloan Management Review, 39*(4), 51-65.

Davidow, W., & Malone, M. (1992). The virtual corporation. *California Business, 27*(11), 34.

Davidow, W., & Malone, M. (1992). *The virtual corporation: Structuring and revitalizing the corporation for the 21st century* (1st ed.). New York, NY: HarperBusiness.

DeSanctis, G., & Monge, P. (1999). Introduction to the special issue: Communication processes for virtual organizations. *Organization Science, 10*(6), 693-703.

Dewett, T., & Jones, G. (2001). The role of information technology in the organization: A review, model and assessment. *Journal of Management, 27*, 313-346.

Dutton, W. (1999). The virtual organization: Tele-access in business and industry. In: J. Fulk (Ed.), *Shaping organizational form: Communication, and community*. Newbury Park, CA: Sage.

Edwards, L., & Field-Hendrey, E. (1996). Home-based workers: Data from the 1990 Census of Population. *Monthly Labor Review, November*, 26-34.

Fang, Y., & Dong, L. (2006). Going virtual in the e-world - an environment adaptation perspective of organizational virtuality. *International Journal of Information Technology and Management, 6*(2/3/4), 271-28.

Fulk, J., & DeSanctis, G. (1995). Electronic communication and changing organizational forms. *Organization Science, 6*(4), 337-349.

Grabowski, M., & Roberts, K. (1999). Risk mitigation in virtual organizations. *Organization Science, 10*(6), 693-703.

Grant, R. (1996). Toward a knowledge-based theory of the firm. *Strategic Management Journal, 17*(Winter Special Issue), 109-122.

Grenier, R., & Metes, G. (1995). *Going virtual: Moving your organization into the 21st century*. Upper Saddle River, NJ: Prentice Hall PTR.

Griffith, T., Sawyer, J., & Neale, M. (2003). Virtualness and knowledge in teams: Managing the love triangle of organizations, individuals, and information technology. *MIS Quarterly, 27*(2), 265.

Hoogeweegen, M., Teunissen, W., Vervest, P., & Wagenaar, R. (1999). Modular network design: Using information and communication technology to allocate production tasks in a virtual organization. *Decision Sciences, 30*(4), 1073-1103.

Huber, G., & Glick, W. (1993). Sources and forms of organizational change. In: W. Glick (Ed.), *Organizational change and redesign: Ideas and insights for improving performance*. New York, NY: Oxford University Press.

Kasper-Fuehrer, E., & Ashkanasy, N. (2001). Communicating trustworthiness and building trust in interorganizational virtual organizations. *Journal of Management, 27*, 2001.

Kock, N. (2000). Benefits for virtual organizations from distributed groups. *Association for Computing Machinery. Communications of the ACM, 43*(11), 107-112.

Kraut, R., Steinfield, C., Chan, A., Butler, B., & Hoag, A. (1999). Coordination and virtualization: The role of electronic networks and personal relationships. *Organization science, 10*(6), 722-740.

Kurland, N., & Egan, T. (1999). Telecommuting: Justice and control in the virtual organization. *Organization Science, 10*(4), 500-513.

Lipnack, J., & Stamps, J. (1996). *The age of the network: Organizing principles for the 21st Century.* New York, Chichester, Bisbane, Toronto, Singapore: John Wiley & Sons.

Lipnack, J., & Stamps, J. (1997). *Virtual teams: Reaching across space, time and organizations with technology.* New York, Chichester, Bisbane, Toronto, Singapore: John Wiley & Sons.

Martins, L., Gilson, L., & Maynard, M. (2004). Virtual teams: What do we know and where do we go from here?. *Journal of Management, 30*(6), 305.

McKelvey, B. (1982). *Organizational systematics: Taxonomy, evolution, classification.* Berkeley, CA: University of California Press.

Miles, R., & Snow, C. (1986). Network organizations: New concepts for new forms. *California Management Review, 28*(62-73).

Mowshowitz, A. (1994). Virtual organization: A vision of management in the information age. *Information Society, 10*(4), 267-288.

Mowshowitz, A. (1997). Virtual organization. *Communications of the ACM, 40*(9), 30-37.

Neufeld, D.J., Fang, Y., (2005), Individual, Social and Situational Determinants of Telecommuter Productivity, *Information & Management, 42*(7), 1037-1049.

Nohria, N., & Berkley, J. (1994). The virtual organizations: Bureaucracy, technology, and the implosion of control. In: A. Donnelon (Ed.), *The post-bureaucratic organization: New perspectives on organizational change* (pp. 108-128). Thousand Oaks, CA: Sage.

Nohria, N., & Eccles, R. (1992). *Networks and organizations.* Boston, MA: Harvard Business School Press.

Orlikowski, W. (1996). Improvising organizational transformation over time: A situated change perspective. *Information Systems Research, 7*(1), 5-21.

Orlikowski, W., & Barley, S. (2001). Technology and institutions: What can research on information technology and research on organizations learn from each other?. *MIS Quarterly, 25*(2), 145-165.

Powell, W. (1990). Neither market nor hierarchy: Network forms of organizations. *Research in Organizational Behavior, 12*, 295-336.

Russell, C. (1996). How many home workers?. *American Demographics, May*, 6.

Spender, J. (1996). Making knowledge the basis of a dynamic theory of the firm. *Strategic Management Journal, 17*(Winter Special Issue), 45-62.

Staples, D., Hulland, J., & Higgins, C. (1999). A self-efficacy theory explanation for the management of remote workers in virtual organizations. *Organization Science, 10*(6), 758-776.

Townsend, A., DeMarie, S., & Hendrickson, A. (1998). Virtual teams: Technology and the workplace of the future. *The Academy of Management Executive, 12*(3), 17-29.

Weber, M. (1922). *Economy and society: An outline of interpretive sociology.* New York, NY: Bedminster Press.

Webster, J., & Watson, R. (2002). Analyzing the past to prepare for the future: Writing a literature review. *MIS Quarterly, 26*(2), xiii.

Williamson, O. (1975). *Markets and hierarchies: Analysis and antitrust implications.* New York, NY: Free Press.

KEY TERMS

Knowledge: Justified belief for effective action.

The Knowledge-Based View of the Firm: A firm's knowledge is not only valuable, rare, inimitable and non-substitutable, but also strategically the most significant resource available to it.

Knowledge Exchange: Exchange of knowledge between multiple individuals, multiple organizations, or between individuals and organizations.

Knowledge Sharing: Sharing of knowledge among multiple entities to cater to the critical issues of organizational adaptation, survival, and competence in face of increasingly discontinuous environmental change.

Information and Communication Technologies: Any information technologies that enable individuals and groups to communicate, coordinate, and process information, with particular focus on those that facilitate dispersed interaction across time and/or space; Examples include computers, networks, routers, software applications such as e-mail, office applications, and enterprise applications such as accounting information systems, point of sales systems, and so forth.

Organizational Virtuality: The capability of an organization to connect geographically dispersed entities to continuously work together by taking recourse to information system resources.

Virtual Organization: A collection of geographically/temporally dispersed, functionally and/or culturally diverse entities that work together using information technology.

Virtual Work: A particular work arrangement where individuals work outside of traditional centralized offices (e.g., from home or "on the road") and operate remotely from each other and from their managers.

Chapter XII
The Perceptions of Collaborative Technologies Among Virtual Workers

Frankie S. Jones
AT&T, USA

ABSTRACT

This chapter discusses the findings of a qualitative research study which explored how collaborative technologies facilitate or inhibit the work of 12 virtual workers. Overall, participants perceived collaborative technologies as helpful to facilitating their work but mentioned a number of challenges inherent in each. For example, asynchronous technologies afford the ability to respond at one's leisure, but this affordance may generate misconceptions when time lags occur. Synchronous technologies such as online meeting tools with video enhance meetings by affording the communication of visual cues but pose the challenge of coordinating the schedules of virtual team members or clients dispersed across global time zones. Participants also revealed that certain technologies were more appropriate for certain tasks. Finally, the chapter relates the results of this study to previous research on technology-enhanced work and lists implications for future research and practice.

INTRODUCTION

In the developed world, technology has become an essential component of the vast majority of jobs and therefore a fixture in the lives of most workers. Consider the following quote from the Center for Work, Technology, and Organization's (WTO's) Web site (WTO, 2002): "We spend over half of our lives working. Work defines our identity and social status, gives us purpose, and shapes our social network. Work is also the basis for all organizing... In organizations, work gets done through technology." Technology's impact on work is especially powerful for *virtual* work teams, a growing segment of the work population, who depend substantially more on information and collaborative technologies than co-located teams (Gibson & Cohen, 2003).

The purpose of this chapter is to discuss the findings of a qualitative research study which explored how collaborative technologies facilitate or inhibit the work of 12 virtual workers. The chapter first reviews the literature regarding the relationship between virtual work and technology. This is followed by a detailed discussion of the methodology and findings of the qualitative study. The chapter ends with a discussion of the findings and implications for practice and future research.

BACKGROUND: A REVIEW OF RELEVANT LITERATURE

Computer-Supported Cooperative Work

An examination of how collaborative technologies facilitate the work of virtual teams must begin with a discussion of current and future research in computer-supported cooperative work (CSCW). CSCW is a formal area of inquiry "concerned with how technology can help people work together more effectively" whether virtual or co-located (Coovert & Thompson, 2001, p. 2). Since Irene Greif and Paul Cashman coined the phrase during a workshop in 1984, scientists, scholars, and practitioners from such diverse disciplines as anthropology, business, cognition, computer science, ergonomics, human-computer interaction, human factors, information technology, office automation, organizational design, psychology, and sociology have been drawn to CSCW (Coovert & Thompson, 2001). The challenges inherent in such a multidisciplinary field of study, as characterized by Grudin and Poltrock (1997), are the "Tower of Babel" problem and a lack of shared knowledge. Those interested in CSCW often use different terms to describe the same concept and contribute their research and lessons learned to different journals, books, and conferences. What further challenges the field is a split in research foci. While some researchers investigate the technological aspects of CSCW and others focus their investigations on the collaborative aspects, CSCW is "best conceived of as an endeavor to understand the characteristics of cooperative work behavior with the objective of designing adequate technology to support it" (Coovert & Thompson, 2001, p. 6).

The Evolution of CSCW Technologies

Technologies that support cooperative work have evolved over the last three decades and each new generation of technologies has expanded the scope of support available to individuals, groups, teams, and organizations. Research on Group Decision Support Systems (GDSS), an application designed specifically to support cooperative work, began over 20 years ago in business management schools. GDSS was originally intended as an electronic support system designed to facilitate decision-making among high level managers meeting face-to-face (Grudin & Poltrock, 1997). Through a network of computers, managers used GDSS for idea creation and to vote on alternative decisions during ad hoc meetings but not for continuous cooperation (Andriessen, 2003). Originally very expensive, GDSS were only used by high level mangers, but, as costs dropped, lower-level project teams began using these decision support tools.

In the mid 1980s, GDSS researchers began attending CSCW conferences and using the term GDSS more generally to include all technologies that facilitate decision-making including e-mail, and some began to think that GDSS was synonymous with CSCW (Grudin & Poltrock, 1997). Eventually the "D" in GDSS was dropped to reflect the new emphasis on a variety of technologies, not just electronic meeting support systems, and the new acronym became GSS (group support systems). GSS researchers now contribute research to their own journals and focus on project and large group support. They rarely use the term CSCW, since CSCW research tends to focus on small groups or teams composed of ten members or less. Despite their different foci, the GSS and CSCW literatures now both use the term "groupware" (Grudin & Poltrock, 1997).

Groupware is a generic term that can refer to hardware, software, and services designed to support face-to-face or virtual group collaboration (Coovert & Thompson, 2001). According to

Dennis, Pootheri, and Natarajan (1998), groupware enables work in a number of ways by allowing participants to:

- generate, read, and organize information in an archived, structured form
- edit, move, and structure the information in many different formats, so that the structure can add meaning to the comments and reduce the effects of information overload
- use headings and position in the structure to choose what they wish to read
- [make] anonymous comments
- vote on, or otherwise quantitatively analyze, the relative merits of alternatives; vote by ranking or rating alternatives
- [archive] group or organizational memory (p. 68)

In general, groupware products have features that support processes essential to collaborative work such as communication, information-sharing and collaboration, and coordination (Grudin & Poltrock, 1997).

Research findings show that in practice, groupware has not been an overwhelming success in supporting collaborative work (Grudin & Poltrock, 1997; Coovert & Thompson, 2001; Andriessen, 2003). In their book which includes an extensive review of groupware research, Grudin and Poltrock (1997) identified technical and social/organizational challenges to groupware's success. Technical challenges included integration of media, interoperability, and insufficient flexibility. Social/organization challenges included disparity in work and benefit, critical mass, disruption of social processes, exception handling, unobtrusive accessibility, difficulty of evaluation, failure of intuition, and the adoption process. Andriessen's (2003) review identified other factors contributing to the non use or limited use of complex group support systems such as "complexity of the system, lack of user-friendliness, limited advantage over other media, and inadequate introduction of media and training" (p. 21).

Researchers have offered a number of recommendations for improving groupware systems so they better support cooperative work. Grudin and Poltrock (1997) recommended participatory design approaches, reward structures for using groupware technologies, and ethnographic or anthropological research studies that seek in-depth exploration of group and organizational behaviors. They argued the need for such studies because groupware is often designed based on workplace processes found in standard procedure manuals; however, the "masks and myths of smooth, consistent operation" represented in procedure manuals do not capture the truly chaotic and non-routine nature of workplace processes (p. 313). Groupware should be designed to reflect the reality of processes, not the mask/myth.

Coovert and Thompson (2001) criticized groupware because of its inability to support *interrelated* interactions and team processes. Team members operate interdependently while the work of individual *group* members, for whom groupware is designed, is not directly dependent on the work of his or her colleagues. Currently available technologies, they argue, are sufficient for individual or group work but not for *team* collaboration which may explain the results of research studies that indicate computer-mediated teams are dissatisfied with collaborative processes as supported by technology. Coovert and Thompson suggested the design of technologies better suited for the work of teams, called teamware, would allow "coworkers to develop and maintain shared goals, shared understanding, and the coordination of cognitive and physical activities" (2001, p. 39). They discussed two important characteristics of teamware:

The first is the support of cognitive artifacts that are in use by the team—that is, those codifying procedures that make projects (and progress on projects) visible. Secondly, teamware must support member behaviors in a manner that models the natural work practices of those individuals and also cues task coordination among individuals. (p. 39)

The second characteristic supports Grudin and Poltrock's (1997) argument that groupware should reflect natural work practices as opposed to those that are prescribed by procedure manuals.

In summary, a review of the research related to the technical aspects CSCW suggests groupware facilitated the work of virtual team members but improvements are needed. Virtual team members require user-friendly, integrated technological systems that allow them to coordinate tasks and communicate socio-emotional cues. Of course, this body of research has limitations that should be considered. The most important limitation is that researchers have not conducted rigorous, peer-reviewed research about the technical aspects of collaborative technologies in the last five years. Considering the rapid rate at which technologies evolve and are created, the findings of technological research conducted five years ago are mostly likely not generalizable to today's technology. Current research is needed to investigate how collaborative technologies facilitate the work of virtual workers.

In the last five years, researchers have turned their attention from the technical aspects of CSCW to the relational aspects of virtual work. The terminology associated with technology enabling CSCW has also changed from "groupware" to "collaborative technologies." As mentioned previously, Munkvold (2003), who chronicled the history of CSCW technologies, pointed to the recent change in terminology from "groupware" to what he called "collaboration technology". He argued that "collaborative technology" better represents a wider focus to include organization-wide technologies that facilitate collaborative work. He listed the main categories of collaboration technologies and examples; all of which mirrored those considered groupware technologies except one—integrated products—described as collaboration product suites, integrated team support technologies, and e-Learning technologies.

In the next section, I review research that examines the relational aspects of virtual work

mediated by collaborative technologies. Research conducted in this area identifies a number of relational prerequisites, also known as antecedents, which must be in place before CSCW can be successful.

Antecedents to Virtual Team Work

Many research studies related to virtual teams are premised by the theoretical assumption that "social interaction affects both the cognitive and socio-emotional processes that take place during learning, group forming, establishment of group structures, and group dynamics" (Kreijns, Kirschner, Jochems, & Van Buuren, 2004, p. 155). In the next few pages, I spotlight some of these studies in an effort to clarify the affective and co-native structures that research reveals must be in place before work can occur. Those structures include trust, effective communication (as impacted by motivation and self-efficacy), and mutual knowledge.

Trust

Researchers (e.g., Jarvenpaa, Knoll, & Leidner, 1998; Jarvenpaa & Leidner, 1999; Hoag, Jayakar, & Erickson, 2003) have investigated how trust is built by virtual teams via computer-mediated communication systems. In a study that surveyed 350 graduate students who completed a collaborative task in teams of four or five, Jarvenpaa et al. (1998) discovered that high-trust teams exhibited behaviors/strategies via collaborative technologies that were proactive, task output driven, optimistic, dynamic, collectively responsible for clarifying team goals and role division, explicit about time management, and predictable and substantive in providing feedback. In 1999, Jarvenpaa and Leidner reported the findings of a qualitative analysis of the e-mail communications of three high and three low trust teams as identified in the same study's survey results. They found initial behaviors, such as task-oriented communication supplemented by social communication, consistent responses to members, and explicitly expressed enthusiasm and commitment to project goals, were crucial in forming and maintaining trust.

Jarvenpaa and Leidner (1999) suggested future research address ways in which virtual teams learn to dynamically recognize and rectify problems which jeopardize trust in the initial phase of team building and, from an organizational perspective, how virtual teams transfer learning and knowledge from one virtual team to another. I suggest future research also be conducted in actual workplaces instead of with university students. Jarvenpaa and Leidner admitted in their limitations discussion that conducting the study with graduate students instead of employees jeopardized the study's applicability.

Effective Communication

A dominant feature of research literature devoted to relational links between virtual team members is the comparison of virtual and face-to-face teams. Many researchers appear to be fixated on whether or not virtual teams communicate as effectively and/or develop social links as effectively as face-to-face teams. Similar to the results of more than 350 studies on distance education, some researchers have found that no significant difference exists between the two groups (Hoag et al., 2003); while others have found evidence that refutes those results.

Warkentin, Sayeed, and Hightower (1997) questioned whether or not teams using a Web-based discussion board called *MeetingWeb* would develop social links as strongly as would those who worked face-to-face. Relational links, as defined by the researchers, are group dynamics such as motivation and self-efficacy that determine a group member's willingness to contribute information. In their investigation of relational links, the researchers randomly assigned undergraduates to teams—11 three-member teams who

collaborated face-to-face on a problem-solving task requiring communication and 13 three-member teams who collaborated on the same task online using MeetingWeb. The researchers found relational links to be a statistically significant contributor to the effectiveness of information exchange but did not find evidence to support one team's effectiveness over the other. Although the mean for the uniqueness of information items exchanged for face-to-face teams was higher than that of virtual teams, these differences were not statistically significant and thus failed to support the hypothesis that face-to-face groups exchange information more effectively.

The lack of evidence to support the superiority of face-to-face communication over virtual team communication is contradictory to previous studies conducted by two out of three of the same researchers who found face-to-face teams exchange information more effectively than do virtual teams. These earlier studies by Hightower and Sayeed (1995; 1996) were very similar in methodology and task. The difference was in mode of communication. Hightower and Sayeed used a synchronous conferencing system. Regardless of what technology was used, in each of the three studies there was only one tool available to team members. This situation is not realistic to the workplace where virtual workers have a number of tools from which to choose and will switch to another when one is not useful to the task at hand. Future research should reflect the complexity of the workplace by considering the myriad of tools available to teams collaborating on real-world problems.

In yet another comparison of face-to-face and online team interaction, Hoag et al. (2003) employed a pre-test/post-test control group design to measure the effect of the treatment—online interaction—on an experimental group of 28 students who met and collaborated online for a semester in a telecommunications management course. The results of the pre- and post-tests from the control group of 37 students were compared with the experimental group's results. The researchers did not specify what the pre- and post-tests measured or what questions it included, but the study's results were informative. They found no significant differences and declared technology a "neutral" component with respect to enhancing learning (p. 369).

The inconclusive findings regarding the relative effectiveness of face-to-face versus virtual teams reflects similar findings in the research investigating the relative effectiveness of face-to-face classroom instruction and online learning environments (Bernard et al., 2004). Reeves (2005) questions the value of continuing to conduct such comparative studies in the online learning area, and it may be time to question the value of such studies in team communications as well. Hightower and Sayeed (1996) suggested future research be longitudinal to capture how changes in group dynamics impact information exchange among virtual team members.

Mutual Knowledge

The communications literature identifies the problem of "mutual knowledge" or the establishment of "common ground" between members of geographically dispersed teams. Citing research that found "when task-relevant information is distributed among members of a group, there is a risk that they will fail to share and heed uniquely held relevant information," Cramton (2001) raised the question of how new collaborative technologies would affect the mutual knowledge problem (p. 349). By studying the archived e-mail, chat, team logs, and final products of 13 six-member virtual teams engaged in a collaborative task to create a business plan, she found "both physical dispersion of collaborators and frequent use of communications technology tend to negatively affect the means by which people establish mutual knowledge" (p. 364). Failures of information exchange and interpretation impeded mutual knowledge. Technological error and selective distribution caused team members to unevenly distribute critical local information. Team members also experienced uneven feedback cycles, difficulty in interpreting the silence of fellow team members, and the tendency of team members to attend to different parts of the same information. Cramton pointed to feedback lags as an amplifying factor in failures of information exchange and interpretation. Future research, she suggested, should investigate the relationship between mutual knowledge and performance. While she found no clear relationship between the two, she recognized that the task designs in her study were not sensitive enough to detect a connection. She wrote, "…designs should vary the distribution of task-related information across locations and the amount of interdependence required of team members" (p. 366). It was unclear, however, how to do that and how it would help show a clear relationship between mutual knowledge and performance.

The mutual knowledge problem also prompted the research of Sole and Edmondson (2002) who studied how local, situated knowledge of virtual team members influences learning and working in virtual teams. They defined situated knowledge as "knowledge embedded in the work practices of a particular organizational site" (p. 20) and team learning "in behavioral terms as the acquisition and application of knowledge that enables a team to address team tasks and issues for which solutions were not previously obvious" (p. 18). The researchers used the critical incident technique during semi-structured interviews with seven dispersed cross-functional development teams at a multi-national company and captured 44 learning episodes or occasions in which "a team learned something significant that advanced the project" (p. 20). A qualitative analysis of those learning episodes yielded several findings. Knowledge situated in local sites inhibited virtual collaboration, but when that knowledge was identified and leveraged it was a highly valuable source of team learning. In order to overcome the challenge of raising virtual team awareness of relevant situated knowledge, Sole and Edmondson recommended situated knowledge be codified in the form of stories in searchable databases so that virtual team members may become aware of the uniquely held expertise at each local site, but surprisingly they did not specifically mention knowledge management systems in either their conclusions or implications for practice and research.

While research in the relational development and effectiveness of virtual teams using computer-mediated communication has a history of inconsistent results (Walther, 1995; Maznevski & Chudoba, 2000), the combined results of these studies inform researchers and practitioners of antecedents that may affect virtual work. The studies also highlight the importance of investigating and choosing collaborative technologies that support the development of interpersonal relationships and mutual knowledge. A question that remains unanswered by this body of literature is: How do factors such as trust, effective communication, and mutual knowledge affect virtual team collaboration in the context of a work-related project?

Summary of Virtual Team Work Literature

As demonstrated in this section, regardless of the terminology used, technology has barriers to overcome if it is to effectively and efficiently facilitate collaboration among virtual teams. Andriessen (2003) identified five conditions that drive the effectiveness of technology as an enabler of collaboration that should be considered in future design:

- individual acceptance and choice of tools
- match between tool and task
- group and organizational characteristics
- design and implementation
- appropriation, learning, and innovation (p. 39)

Andriessen's conditions are potentially powerful because they appear to address the shortfalls of technology designed to support the collaborative work of virtual teams as identified by research. They provide feasible, but as yet untested, solutions (e.g., individual acceptance and choice of tools) to technology's inability to build virtual team relations such as trust, socio-economic cues, effective communication, and mutual knowledge and to facilitate natural work processes.

This review of the virtual team work literature also reveals the lack of recent, rigorously peer-reviewed research. For example, most of the CSCW literature related to the technical aspects of groupware was published in books and not in peer-reviewed journals. The research was also conducted prior to 2001, limiting the relevance of its findings about technologies that have significantly changed since then. After 2001, researchers turned their attention to the relational aspects of CSCW. One limitation of the relational research is that a number of studies were conducted at universities with students instead of the workplace. Current, rigorously peer-reviewed research about both the technical and relational aspects of virtual work is needed to impact practice and inform future research.

MAIN FOCUS OF CHAPTER: RESEARCH STUDY

The review of literature suggests a need for research that explores how currently-relevant collaborative technologies impact virtual work from the perspective of virtual workers. Specifically, this study sought to answer the following research question: What are the perceptions of collaborative technologies among virtual team members?

Research Design

Basic or generic qualitative studies are those that possess what Merriam (1998) listed as the essential characteristics of qualitative research: "…the goal of eliciting understanding and meaning, the researcher as primary instrument of data collection and analysis, the use of fieldwork, an inductive orientation to analysis, and findings that are richly descriptive" (p. 11). Merriam deemed the generic study the most common form of qualitative educational research and distinguished it from other types of qualitative research by defining it by what it is not. Basic or generic qualitative studies, she wrote, "…do not focus on culture or build a grounded theory; nor are they intensive case studies of a single unit or bounded system…[they] simply seek to discover and understand a phenomenon, a process, or the perspectives and worldviews of the people involved" (p. 11). Other characteristics of the generic study include its theoretical draw from many disciplines, data collection methods such as interviews, and data analysis methods of thematic or categorical identification.

The generic strategy was most appropriate for addressing this study's purpose and research questions for two reasons. First, my goal was to discover and understand virtual work as enabled by collaborative technologies. My purpose was not to build theory, nor did I study a single unit or bounded system. Second, as is characteristic of generic qualitative research, I drew on theories from multiple disciplines, such as instructional technology, human resource and organization development, and educational psychology, to conduct this study. These reasons led me to select the generic qualitative methodology for this study.

Methods

Interviews are a frequently-used qualitative data collection method (Merriam, 1998; 2002; Patton, 2002; Bogdan & Biklen, 2003; Creswell, 2003). I chose interviews as the primary method for gathering data concerning my research questions and used the critical incident technique (CIT) to prepare participants for interviews. Merriam

(1998) advised, "Interviewing is necessary when we cannot observe behavior, feelings, or how people interpret the world around them. It is also necessary to interview when we are interested in past events that are impossible to replicate" (p. 72). Since it would have been impractical and intrusive to observe virtual workers as they engaged in work, I chose to rely on interviews, during which participants could reflect on past incidents of virtual work. I also used the CIT to help participants reflect on past experiences. The CIT is a qualitative research method designed to "…capture the complexity of job behavior in terms of the job's social context" by collecting stories, episodes, or incidents about job behaviors crucial to successful job performance (Stitt-Gohdes, Lambrecht, & Redmann, 2000, p. 59).

Participants

In designing this study, I had hoped to successfully recruit a minimum of 10-15 participants. As Patton (2002) advised, I estimated 10-15 participants as the minimum sample size "based on expected reasonable coverage of the phenomenon given the purpose of the study and stakeholder interest" (p. 246). Of course, the number of participants could have fluctuated depending on when data redundancy occurred (Merriam, 1998). In all, 12 participants participated in the study. Table 1 includes descriptive data for each study participant. Pseudonyms are used in the table and throughout this chapter.

Study participants represent a diverse group of professions. All work from home offices, except Eric, Rita, and Charles. Eric and Rita work from their organizations' headquarters but accomplish work goals daily with globally dispersed team members and/or clients. Charles works from an administrative office, but his team members are distributed across his state.

Table 1. Participant descriptive data

Pseudonym	Current Position	Highest Degree/Major	Years Virtual
Charles	High School Administrator	Graduate degree in Computer Science	6
Michelle	Software Implementer	Business and Information Systems	2
Rebecca	Public Relations Director	B.A. in Political Science; M.A. in Interdisciplinary Studies	4
Andrew	Executive Services Director	Computer Science and Mathematics; Advanced work in Business	10
Kijana	Editor	Graduate work in Literature	9
David	Systems Architect and Software Developer	B.A. in Computer Science	5
Michael	Executive	Applied Physics	15
Victoria	Managing Consultant	Advanced work in Technology with a minor in Business	6
Eric	Senior Technical Recruiter	B.A. in Psychology	8
Gigi	Editor and Project Manager	M.A. in History; M.A. in Library Science	5
John	Executive	Ph.D. in Instructional Technology	7
Rita	Attorney and Case Manager	Law degree	3

Data Collection Procedures

After recruiting and confirming the participation of 12 virtual workers, I sent each of them a reflection guide provoking them to recall critical incidents of their experiences as virtual workers and how collaborative technologies facilitated their work. I scheduled each interview approximately 5-7 days after the participant received the reflection guide to ensure that they had ample time to engage in reflection. I conducted 12 interviews over the course of three weeks ranging from 30-90 minutes.

Data Analysis

In analyzing interview data, I followed Ruona's (2005) step-by-step method for preparing, coding, and cross-analysis using Microsoft Word. Throughout this process, I constantly interpreted interview data and generated meaning as I recognized and made connections between emerging themes. I present themes related to the perceptions of collaborative technologies in the "Findings" section of this chapter.

Study Limitations

This study has several recognized limitations. They are as follows:

- The study generated data related only to technologies used by research participants.
- A small sample size of twelve research participants limits this study's generalizability; however generalizability is usually limited in qualitative studies. Merriam (2002) argued, "A small sample is selected precisely because the researcher wishes to understand the particular in depth, not to find out what is generally true of the many" (p. 28).
- Time per participant was limited to one 60-90 minute interview. Such a time frame limits the depth with which I was able to analyze such a complex topic as informal learning in virtual teams.

Despite these limitations, this study generated useful insights for managers and workers in organizations that employ virtual team members similar to those in this study. The study may also stimulate further research in this area.

MAIN FOCUS OF CHAPTER: FINDINGS

In this section, I discuss this study's findings as they relate to the following research question: What are the perceptions of collaborative technologies among virtual team members? The reported technologies included e-mail, instant messaging, audio and video tools, online collaborative tools, knowledge repositories, desktop sharing, and collaborative systems which integrate these tools. In addition to participants' use and perception of these technologies, I share their opinions about how they should be improved.

E-Mail as a Source of Misconception and Reflection

All participants cited e-mail as a frequently used form of technology, but not all considered it the most useful. E-mail, while mediating communication and document exchange, was a source of frustration for some. The sheer number of e-mails received on a daily basis from fellow team members and clients was cause for contention. Michelle shared:

What I've now learned over the last eighteen months, having been in this group that long, is that people in this group get about sixty to eighty e-mails a day. It is nearly impossible [emphasized] to keep up with it and you're spinning in every direction, you know, this customer, this customer.

Eric concurred, "People get hundreds of e-mails a day." John explained further, "When you're very busy and you get two hundred e-mails a day...So e-mail is not a valuable tool to me anymore. It is a distracter, because people expect...immediate feedback."

The asynchronous nature of e-mail was cited by participants as both a negative and positive characteristic. Time lags between e-mail responses, as alluded to in John's comment, can be a source of misconceptions among team members. Rebecca told of a time when she sent an e-mail and the anxiety she experienced when it was not returned when expected:

I've been wondering and wondering why I didn't get a return and wondering if it was because of this or that or something I did or the way I said it or the fact that she doesn't want to have to do it or something like that...when in actuality that person was traveling or they never got my e-mail or somehow it got sent to their junk file or something like that.

Other participants commented positively about the asynchronicity of e-mail. Kijana recounted an instance when she received an e-mail from a co-worker filled with "frustration" and "concerns." Instead of replying immediately, she waited three days to "get rid of my own emotional response." E-mail allowed her the "luxury of taking time to think about what would be the most useful, helpful way of dealing with this person, so this person felt heard but also could hear what I was saying." She said, "If I had gotten that information face-to-face it would've been much harder for me to pause and think about how I would have responded and probably not as successfully." Eric reported using e-mail with virtual team members when reflection on ideas or issues was required. Michael and Gigi said e-mail was useful because recipients could read and respond to messages on their own time.

The inability to effectively communicate tone through e-mail can also be the cause of misconceptions among team members. Rebecca revealed, "I think e-mails can get really tricky too...There were questions sort of tone. You can't convey a tone in an e-mail, so sometimes things get kind of construed." Eric elaborated, "Some people are more direct and the tone of the e-mail is misconstrued and sometimes that can create some negative feelings." Communicating humor through e-mail is one of Andrew's e-mail "don'ts," because it translates poorly, especially if an established personal relationship does not exist. He said:

Rule number one: humor is never in e-mail. E-mails are one of the most abused electronic areas in the industry...Humor is based on the relationship...When it comes down to e-mail, e-mail is a business tool and it should be viewed as that.

Instant Messaging for Quick Exchanges

Instant messaging (IM), also referred to as chat, is the second most frequently used technology among participants. Charles confirmed, "Internet messaging actually probably gets utilized more than the telephone to be honest. That is something that is going on all the time." In general, participants expressed positive perceptions of IM. Charles offered a theory about this form of communication:

Let's say that you are doing things just through IM. There's generally a conscious understanding of the limitations of that form of communication, so you kind of recognize it as being very different than typical face-to-face communication. And so there's kind of a natural adjusting and kind of moving into the culture and nature of that communication.

Charles' theory may explain why participants reported only using it for short, quick exchanges. Kijana explained:

What I've learned is that in terms of short, short, very efficient, very clear kinds of information that instant message is fabulous. I guess what I would say is when the trust level is high and you really want to just quickly convey short bits of information, IM works really well.

David also remarked about the convenience IM provides: "It keeps the conversation short. You can send a one or two sentence question. You get your answer back then the conversation is over." Eric commented on its efficiency, "It's a lot more efficient to get that movement versus sending an e-mail and waiting for someone to check their box." Similarly, Gigi reported IM as a great tool when you are very busy and need a quick answer to a question.

Drawbacks to IM were that people may interrupt you while you are working and expect you to respond immediately. In some cases, the synchronicity that IM affords is a distraction and may encourage micromanaging. David discussed marking himself as "away" when he needs to work uninterrupted. When team members do not "get the hint," he logs off the IM tool.

Value in the Spoken Word

Participants reported using the telephone for one-on-one conversations when necessary but not as frequently as e-mail and IM. David discussed using it when "it's something I absolutely need answered;" otherwise he prefers IM, because he is not "obligated" to make the call worthwhile by making informal conversation prior to asking for what he needs. Kijana commented that the telephone was useful in helping her understand the enthusiasm an author had for the topic she was writing about, but also admitted to not using the telephone frequently because it does not afford time for reflection. Michael asserted his lack of enthusiasm for the telephone in explaining his preference for using a whiteboard to illustrate meaning.

Participants use teleconferencing, also referred to as audio-conferencing or conference calling, when multi-person audio communication or collaboration is necessary. Michael stressed the importance of staying focused during conference calls:

The problem is when you have ten people and one is distracted after while starts dragging down everybody because people start feeling like somebody isn't present and the level of attention from them starts dropping down so every so often they start doing something else.

John mentioned using a conference call, as opposed to an e-mail, to find out what went wrong on a project. He implied that complexity of the purpose of the meeting required the type of interaction not possible in an e-mail.

Seeing is Believing

Participants reported occasionally using video tools, such as videoconferencing, Webcasting, and Webcams. Video has benefits and challenges. One reported benefit is the ability to see virtual teammates and clients. Rebecca said, "The image of somebody I think is kind of helpful. I mean it is kind of nice to know what somebody looks like." Andrew found video useful in conveying body language during a Webcast where instant messaging was used for question and answer: "When I received the message, they could see me reading the question, but they could see the body language of me answering it. Once again, it's a layer of sincerity to the individual who may never have met." Eric commented that higher levels of attention and professionalism occur when employees are seen, and Gigi stated that her team members expressed their appreciation for videoconferencing, especially during the planning phase of their project. Videoconferencing forced her virtual team members to focus solely on the issues before them and not be distracted as they might be using other collaborative technologies. Rita also credited videoconferencing with facilitating the collaborative work of attorneys and clients at her law firm.

Video tools also pose challenges, because they can be expensive, technically unreliable, and difficult to schedule. Rebecca and David admitted a reluctance to use video tools regularly. Rebecca said, "I'm not just sitting in an office somewhere looking professional." David predicted, "If I ever did use it, I would only turn it on during meetings. I don't know if I would necessarily turn it on for a phone call or a formal kind of meeting that we were having."

Interactive Exchanges

Web-based collaborative tools mentioned by participants included discussion boards, blogs, and wikis. A few participants spoke of using discussion boards for posting personal information about virtual team members and for conducting work-related discussions. Charles described his organization's use of discussion boards, "People posting birthdays, facts about them, you know, things like that to help people to get to know each other better." Kijana uses discussion boards to "archive things like the theme, the big ideas that emerge from the magazine that we're going to use. We want to archive introductions of new members to the group." In David's organization, virtual team members contribute to discussions about resolving technical issues and conduct design discussions online. He said:

Let's say somebody says, 'I entered this value. I expected this result but I got this.' We can have a big discussion thread. We also use that for design discussions when we're working through the initial phases of the requirements.

Kijana expressed interest in using blogs and wikis to collaboratively edit documents and exchange ideas. Michael, on the other hand, objected to the use of blogs, He asserted, "People are going to this blog thing on the internet. Man, people are just spending their life on the internet and writing crap on that."

Knowledge Sharing

Participants discussed their use of knowledge repositories, loosely defined as places where work-related documents or media are stored. Repositories are housed on their organization's shared drive/intranet and on the Internet and are, in some cases, password protected and/or searchable. Michelle, for example, reported that documents are housed and shared on her company's network and that they also use a tool called *Source Space*. She described its function as follows:

It's kind of like a repository that stores and archives our source codes which is kind of how we generate the things that we give to our customers. It stores our source code. It can store our other types of files, so we use that…It's internal and external.

Rebecca's organization posts academic and journalistic articles to their Web site so that chapters within her organization and the public can access them. The purpose of this repository is to educate the public so that individuals can become advocates for themselves. Victoria also reported that knowledge repositories at her company contain media, such as video replays of meetings. When she has to miss an important meeting, she often watches the replay.

Desktop Sharing as a Visual Aid

Desktop sharing was viewed as a helpful collaborative tool among participants who reported using it. David uses it to troubleshoot problems with software applications or demonstrate a prototype with other virtual team members. He commented, "We will use that when we are talking about some more complicated concepts, things where visual aids will help the conversation." John said, "You can surf together simultaneously with all the people that are in your space. Though not termed desktop sharing, attorneys at Rita's law firm use a similar application called Live Note for real-time court reporting. She said:

You can actually see the text as the court reporter types in the text using Live Note. So I can be here in [this city] and the trial can be occurring in [another city] and I can, on my computer through the internet, be able to tap in to the stenographer's typing of the text in court.

Integrating Collaborative Tools

Integrated collaborative systems are those that offer a suite of collaborative technologies that may include any combination of e-mail, IM, video, audio, Web-based collaborative tools, knowledge repositories, desktop sharing, shared whiteboards, project management tools, and multiple team "spaces" for those involved in multiple virtual team projects. Examples of integrated systems cited by participants were *NetMeeting*, *WebEx*, *Groove*, *Notes Buddy*, *Illuminate*, *Tapped In*, and *Microsoft Share Point*.

NetMeeting was most commonly used among participants. Its audio and desktop sharing capabilities fuel virtual meetings. Eric, similar to others, uses it in more formal circumstances when "I would want to have documents available so people could visibly see what I was doing and what I was working on as well as hear *my* voice." Michael reported using *NetMeeting* under similar circumstances: "If we are talking about the document and we want to make sure that everybody sees the same page at the same moment, *NetMeeting* is much better." He added that a synchronous tool like *NetMeeting* can only be used by team members located within certain time zones: "When we work with Japan, Taiwan, India, and you get into a twelve hour difference, it's difficult to pick a time when everybody's available, so this type of conference is more popular over here."

Recommendations for Improvements to Collaborative Technologies

Responses to the question "If you could design a technological system for your organization to help virtual teams collaborate, what would it be like?", inspired different answers. Participants requested that video capabilities be added to their repertoire of tools. For example, Eric suggested, "Maybe something involving some webcams where you can see someone physically and see their facial expressions and gestures. It might make it a little more personal." Other responses included requests for integrated "dashboard" systems with emoticons, cross-platform tools compatible with both PCs and MACs, more technically-reliable tools, the ability to "drop by" as one does in the office, and improvements to e-mail that alert senders when or if their message has been received.

Summary

Overall, participants perceived collaborative technologies as helpful to facilitating their work but mentioned a number of challenges inherent in each. For example, asynchronous technologies afford the ability to respond at one's leisure, but this affordance may generate misconceptions when time lags occur. Synchronous technologies, such as online meeting tools with video, enhance meetings by affording the communication of visual cues but pose the challenge of coordinating the schedules of virtual team members or clients dispersed across global time zones. They also revealed that certain technologies were more appropriate for certain tasks. For instance, IM is appropriate for short, quick information exchanges while videoconferencing is very useful in facilitating more complex tasks such as decision-making.

MAIN FOCUS OF CHAPTER: DISCUSSION

Participants identified a number of technologies as integral to their everyday work. Text-based communication technologies, such as e-mail and instant messaging (IM), were cited as most frequently used when quickly exchanging bits of knowledge, but participants also identified

limitations inherent in text-based technologies. For example, participants attributed miscommunications of humor to the lack of visual cues and to time lags between responses. Similarly, Cramton's (2001) research revealed that uneven feedback cycles and difficulty in interpreting the silence of fellow team members negatively affects the establishment of mutual knowledge.

Participants indicated that other more collaborative text-based technologies, such as discussion boards and Microsoft Word with the "tracked changes" and "comments" features enabled, were integral to their everyday work. These collaborative text-based technologies allow teams to archive personal and work-related discussions and information and to participate equally during collaborative work. Groupware research conducted in the late 1980s and 1990s confirmed that computer-mediated teams participate more equally than face-to-face teams (Coovert & Thompson, 2001). Searchable knowledge repositories housed on the Internet or on intranets are also a good source of information sharing and archiving (Sole & Edmondson, 2002) and participants confirmed having and using them in their everyday work.

Participants also reported audio- and video-based technologies, such as teleconferencing and Webcams, as helpful especially in solving problems or making decisions and in communicating visual cues which, in turn, lessen the miscommunication often experienced when using text-based technologies. Participants suggested that an increase in formality occurs when these technologies are used and that their synchronous nature presents scheduling difficulties. Desktop sharing combined with audio is also powerful for troubleshooting and demonstration. A lack of literature related to the use of audio and video in virtual work exists, but more and better studies should be conducted to further investigate its importance.

According to research (e.g., Grudin & Poltrock, 1997; Coovert & Thompson, 2001) and confirmed by participants, systems designed specifically for virtual teamwork that integrate text, audio,

Figure 1. Technology/task continuum

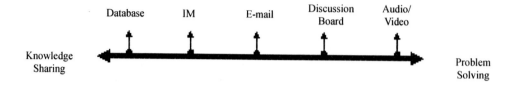

and video technologies have numerous benefits such as asynchronous and synchronous communication, knowledge and document sharing, collaboration, and task coordination. Grudin and Poltrock's (1997) research identified the lack of media integration as a technical challenge to groupware's success. With the advent and adoption of integrated technology suites, such as *Groove*, this challenge should fade. Furthermore, it is interesting to note that participants rarely mentioned ease-of-use or other technical factors as barriers to work. Their discussions of virtual work centered on the work itself and less on the technologies used to facilitate it. It may be that accomplishing work has become the primary focus among virtual workers as technology gradually becomes more transparent and its use more instinctual.

The findings of this study also identify a continuum between technology and task as I have illustrated in Figure 1.

As illustrated, certain technologies are more appropriate for certain tasks—the more complex the task, the more robust the technology. For example, participants cited the appropriateness of certain technologies, such as e-mail and IM, for quick knowledge sharing and certain technologies, such as desktop sharing, teleconferencing, or videoconferencing, for solving problems or making decisions. They conveyed the need to use more robust technologies for complex tasks because of their ability to communicate socio-emotional cues. The task portion of the continuum in some ways mirrors Benjamin Bloom's (1956) hierarchy of learning behaviors within the cognitive domain: knowledge, comprehension, application, analysis, synthesis, and evaluation. Andreissen (2003) made reference to this notion of a match between tool

and task when he named it as one of five conditions which drive the effectiveness of technology as an enabler of collaboration.

Overall, participants perceived collaborative technologies as helpful in facilitating virtual work processes, especially when there is a good match between task and technology. They also identified healthy working relationships built on trust and organizational support as inputs to virtual work.

FUTURE TRENDS: IMPLICATIONS FOR RESEARCH AND PRACTICE

There are a number of implications for research and practice derived from the findings of this study. First, researchers should design and conduct studies that further investigate the context of virtual work. This study was exploratory and therefore did not seek to discover in-depth findings of how contextual factors, such as collaborative technologies, influence virtual work. More in-depth research should be conducted to uncover the nuances of the interaction between technology and virtual work and discover what other contextual factors exist. Second, future research studies might also investigate members of the same virtual team and the impact of various factors such as the level of expertise of virtual workers and the number of virtual projects assigned to a virtual worker. Third, organizations should also dedicate a staff member to researching the use and preferences of technology among virtual team members and recommending upgrades to old technologies or proposing the use of new technologies. Finally, providing integrated collaborative technology suites that include technologies recommended or approved by virtual workers is critical to their success.

CONCLUSION

The success of virtual teams is critical, considering the following conclusion drawn by Duarte and Snyder (2001): "organizations that do not use virtual teams effectively may be fighting an uphill battle in a global, competitive, and rapidly changing environment" (p. 3). The purpose of this chapter was to discuss the findings of a qualitative study of 12 virtual workers and to discuss their perceptions of how collaborative technologies facilitate or inhibit their virtual work. While participants value collaborative technologies, they clearly indicate that there are inherent challenges in their use and identify the need for a match between the technological tool used and the work task.

REFERENCES

Andriessen, J. (2003). *Working with groupware.* London: Springer.

Bernard, R., Abrami, P., Lou, Y., Borokhovski, E., Wade, A., Wozney, L., et al. (2004). How does distance education compare to classroom instruction? A meta-analysis of the empirical literature. *Review of Educational Research, 74*(3), 379-439.

Bogdan, R., & Biklen, S. (2003). *Qualitative research for education: An introduction to theories and methods* (4th ed.). Boston, MA: Pearson Education Group.

Coovert, M., & Thompson, L. (2001). *Computer-supported cooperative work.* Thousand Oaks, CA: Sage Publications.

Cramton, C. (2001). The mutual knowledge problem and its consequences for dispersed collaboration. *Organization Science, 12*(3), 346-371.

Creswell. (2003). *Research design: Qualitative, quantitative, and mixed methods approaches.* Thousand Oaks, CA: Sage Publications.

Dennis, A., Pootheri, S., & Natarajan, V. (1998). Lessons from the early adopters of web groupware. *Journal of Management Information Systems, 14*(4), 65-86.

Duarte, D., & Snyder, N. (2001). *Mastering virtual teams: Strategies, tools, and techniques that succeed.* San Francisco, CA: Jossey-Bass.

Gibson, C., & Cohen, S. (Eds.). (2003). *Virtual teams that work: Creating conditions for virtual team effectiveness.* San Francisco, CA: Jossey-Bass.

Grudin, J., & Poltrock, S. (1997). Computer-supported cooperative work and groupware. In: M. Zelkowitz (Ed.), *Advances in computers* (Vol. 45, pp. 269-320). San Diego, CA: Academic Press.

Hightower, R., & Sayeed, L. (1996). Effects of communication mode and prediscussion information distribution characteristics on information exchange in groups. *Information Systems Research, 7*(4), 451-465.

Hoag, A., Jayakar, K., & Erickson, K. (2003). The role of trust in virtual and interpersonal environments: Implications for team learning & case method pedagogies. *Journalism & Mass Communication Educator, 57*(4), 370-383.

Jarvenpaa, S., Knoll, K., & Leidner, D. (1998). Is anybody out there? Antecedents of trust in global virtual teams. *Journal of Management Information Systems, 14*(4), 29-64.

Jarvenpaa, S., & Leidner, D. (1999). Communication and trust in global virtual teams. *Organization Science, 10*(6), 791-815.

Kreijns, K., Kirschner, P., Jochems, W., & Van Buuren, H. (2004). Determining sociability, social space, and social presence in (a)synchronous collaborative groups. *CyberPscyhology & Behavior, 7*(2), 155-172.

Maznevski, M., & Chudoba, K. (2000). Bridging space over time: Global virtual team dynamics and effectiveness. *Organization Science, 11*(5), 473-492.

Merriam, S. (1998). *Qualitative research and case study applications in education.* San Francisco, CA: Jossey-Bass.

Merriam, S. (Ed.). (2002). *Qualitative research in practice: Examples for discussion and analysis.* San Francisco, CA: Jossey-Bass.

Munkvold, B. (2003). *Implementing collaborative technologies in industry: Case examples and lessons learned.* London: Springer.

Patton, M. (2002). *Qualitative research and evaluation methods* (3rd ed.). Thousand Oaks, CA: Sage Publications.

Reeves, T. (2005). No significant differences revisited: A historical perspective on the research informing contemporary online learning. In: G. Kearsley (Ed.), *Online learning: Personal reflections on the transformation of education.* Englewood Cliffs, NJ: Educational Technology Publications.

Ruona, W. (2005). Analyzing qualitative data. In: R. Swanson & E. Holton (Eds.), *Research in organizations: Foundations and methods of inquiry* (pp. 223-263). San Francisco, CA: Berrett-Koehler.

Sole, D., & Edmondson, A. (2002). Situated knowledge and learning in dispersed teams. *British Journal of Management, 13*(3), 17-34.

Stitt-Gohdes, W., Lambrecht, J., & Redmann, D. (2000). The critical-incident technique in job behavior research. *Journal of Vocational Education Research, 25*(1), 59-84.

Walther, J. (1995). Relational aspects of computer-mediated communication: Experimental observations over time. *Organization Science, 6*(2), 186-203.

Warkentin, M., Sayeed, L., & Hightower, R. (1997). Virtual teams versus face-to-face teams: An exploratory study of a Web-based conference system. *Decision Sciences, 28*(4), 975-996.

WTO. (2002). *Why study work, technology, and organization?.* Retrieved June 26, 2005 from http://www.stanford.edu/group/WTO/gradstudies/why.shtml.

KEY TERMS

Collaborative Technologies: All types of technologies that facilitate communication, collaboration, coordination, and learning at various organizational levels

Virtual Team: An interdependent group of individuals who predominantly use technology to communicate, collaborate, share information, and coordinate their efforts in order to accomplish a common work-related objective

Chapter XIII
Ubiquitous Connectivity & Work-Related Stress

J. Ramsay
University of the West of Scotland, UK

M. Hair
University of the West of Scotland, UK

K. V. Renaud
University of Glasgow, UK

ABSTRACT

The way humans interact with one another in the 21ˢᵗ Century has been markedly influenced by the integration of a number of different communication technologies into everyday life, and the pace of communication has increased hugely over the past twenty-five years. This chapter introduces work by the authors that considers the ways one communication-based technology, namely e-mail, has impacted workers' "thinking time", and become both a "workplace stressor" and an indispensable communications tool. Our research involved both a longitudinal exploration (three months) of the daily e-mail interactions of a number of workers, and a survey of individuals' perceptions of how e-mail influences their communication behaviour in general, and their work-related communication in particular. Initial findings, in the form of individual differences, are reported here. The findings are presented in relation to the way workplace stressors have changed over the past quarter century.

INTRODUCTION

The 19th century citizen inhabited a very different world from the one we know. A discussion of all the differences, and reasons for these differences, is ouside the scope of this chapter, but we will consider the impact of the growth and availability of a variety of communication media. Whereas this growth is almost always perceived to be a positive aid to communication (Walsh et al., 2000), some warning bells are ringing. Cooper and Jackson (1997) found that the use of information technology had had a knock-on effect on work pace and also led to information overload. On the one hand, the potential to be permanently contactable in a variety of ways (phone, e-mail, Web) is well within the reach of most workers of the western world. On the other hand, workplace stress is at record levels (Rudavsky, 2005; Heggy, 2006) and it is just possible that this permanent connectivity is a contributor. Kock (2001) argues that we need to determine the effects of technologies, such as e-mail, on humans. In this chapter, we will consider the question: "Does ever increasing and permanent connectivity, in addition to its obvious benefits, also have a dark side?"

A SHORT HISTORY OF MODERN COMMUNICATION

The face of communication has changed drastically in the last quarter of a century.

The evolution of what is recognised as modern technology-based human-to-human communication has its roots in the 1960s. The Internet grew out of the U.S. defence department's Advanced Research Projects Agency Network (ARPANET), which emerged in the late 1960s. By the early 1970s, ARPANET connected a number of U.S. research institutes working on defence-funded activities. As the network expanded over the years, and with the move to Internet protocol (IP) networks, the global Internet was born. The majority of the emerging *public* technology was still for use *outside of* the office, for example, handheld calculators (classroom), Space Invader machines (gaming arcades), Pac-Man and Tetris games (home) and the arrival of the Sinclair ZX81 in 1981 (home).

Great strides were also made in communications technology. The maintenance of relationships is one of the most basic of human needs (Maslow, 1943). Anything that facilitates or eases the building or strengthening of relationships is bound to succeed.

Up to the first half of the 20th century people communicated either by conversation, letter, or, rarely, by telegram. This is reflected in the books of the era. *Enquire Within Upon Everything*, the

celebrated Victorian self-help guide published in 1884, gives the following social guidance:

If you are not a good writer it is advisable to use the best ink, paper, and pens. For although they may not alter the character of your handwriting, yet they will assist to make your writing look better. (p. 358)

It is doubtful that 21st century employees would aspire to conform to this guideline because the world they inhabit has such different norms and values. A variety of communication media choices is now at our disposal: letter, telephone, fax, SMS or e-mail. Much communication appears to have migrated from traditional conversation or relatively slow letter exchanges, where rigid rules dictate format and language usage, to one of the other, more immediate, more informal, media. Moreover, any letter that *is* sent is unlikely to be handwritten.

In considering the impact of this new era of ambient communication on our lives, it is instructive to go back to the late 19th century to examine the literature of the time to see what kind of nirvana or torment authors were predicting. *Looking Backward*, written in 1887 by Edward Bellamy, and first published in 1888, recounts the tale of a man who wakes up from the 19th Century to find himself in the 21st Century, to witness a world of unprecedented interpersonal accord and harmony.

Although Bellamy may have overstated the case, sufficient material progress *has* nevertheless taken place in the intervening 20th Century to encourage the belief that "the future" might be a harbinger of good things. Instantaneous communications have heralded the advent of the "global village", (a term coined by McLuhan, 1964), where it is possible to engage in real-time communication with others irrespective of their location on the planet. The global village, which emerged with the superseding of visual print, with movable, electronic type, hosted and potentially relayed globally via central servers, has fostered new mechanisms of social interaction and new social paradigms. The methods and timescales by which social groups develop, and the purposes for which they are formed, have undergone significant change. Our perceptions of self and of others have evolved as a function of the new technological platforms currently at our disposal. The impact on our culture has been immense and has led to the erstwhile popular phrase "It's a small world" becoming rather passé.

On the other hand, the 21st century world citizen may well empathise with the irritation evinced by the female protagonist in Forster's tale "The Machine Stops" (Forster, 1909).

There were buttons and switches everywhere—buttons to call for food for music, for clothing. There was the hot-bath button, by pressure of which a basin of (imitation) marble rose out of the floor, filled to the brim with a warm deodorized liquid. There was the cold-bath button. There was the button that produced literature and there were of course the buttons by which she communicated with her friends. The room, though it contained nothing, was in touch with all that she cared for in the world.

Vashanti's next move was to turn off the isolation switch, and all the accumulations of the last three minutes burst upon her. The room was filled with the noise of bells, and speaking-tubes. What was the new food like? Could she recommend it? Has she had any ideas lately? Might one tell her one's own ideas? Would she make an engagement to visit the public nurseries at an early date?—say this day month. To most of these questions she replied with irritation—a growing quality in that accelerated age. (p 5)

With respect to communication media at least, it seems that both Bellamy *and* Forster were right, in their own way, since permanent connectivity and ubiquitous communication has both advan-

tages and disadvantages and whilst it does ease and facilitate communication it also plays a role in the increasing stress experienced by office and other workers today. Since the phone has been replaced by e-mail as the business communication medium of choice (Munter, Rogers, & Rymer, 2003), the rest of this chapter concentrates on e-mail-related research.

THE CHANGING WORKPLACE

In 2006, we inhabit a workplace where it is not unusual for the majority of an individual's day-to-day interactions with others to be indirect or mediated. Developments in the field of human communication are proceeding rapidly and communication technologies are increasingly becoming part of everyday life. Unfortunately, the pace of technology development is outstripping our understanding of how best to deploy that same technology to optimally support human communication and industry.

Against this backdrop of a new and evolving global human communication infrastructure, *the way* in which humans communicate with one another in the workplace is co-evolving. Where online person-to-person interaction had originally assumed the classical one-to-one model, there grew, in parallel, a number of specific communications technologies, such as e-mail, which very quickly became embedded in work and home spheres. What we understand as "social interaction" or "human communication" takes on different characteristics when the interaction is mediated; for this reason it is necessary to identify the circumstances that require synchronous communication, those for which asynchronous is best, how and when to employ 3-D environments and how to determine when the provision of instantaneous "chatting" tools will be optimal. Despite the growth, in the early 1990s, of richer audio-visual-textual communications software, e-mail remains possibly the most ubiquitous workplace communications tool.

Whilst other communications technologies have come and gone over this time, e-mail has retained its position as the most commonly used communications technology—a sign, surely, of its success? Some researchers agree: Buckner and Gillham (2003) have carried out studies that show that e-mail helps maintain social contacts, while Markus argues that e-mail can indeed be richer than traditional media in an organisational setting (Markus, 1994). Car and Sheikh claim that e-mail can revolutionise healthcare by facilitating and easing communication between the patient and the physician (Car & Sheikh, 2004). The Pew Internet and American Life Project (Boase, Horrigan, Wellman, & Rainie, 2006) carried out surveys of American e-mail users and found that e-mail supports social networks and allows people to get assistance when they need it. Many researchers, however, are registering concern about the *negative* effects of e-mail (e.g., Romm, Pliskin, & Rifkin, 1996; Jackson, Dawson, & Wilson, 2003; Rohall, Gruen, Moody, Wattenberg, Stern, Kerr, et al., 2004). Duane and Finnegan (2004), in giving a comprehensive overview of both first and second level effects of e-mail, recommend that organisations have procedures and processes for controlling the negative effects so that e-mail can indeed benefit the organisation. Tyler and Tang (2003) investigated e-mail usage and observed that e-mail exerted pressure on recipients to respond, and they also observed e-mail being used as more of a synchronous than an asynchronous communication mechanism, with occasional almost continuous monitoring eating into uninterrupted working time: a potential stressor. Many researchers are finding that the reservations about ubiquitous technology which caused George Orwell to write his famous book, *1984*, could well be warranted (Orwell, 1949).

For any technology to be successful, it must be usable, useful, safe, effective and pleasurable (Hoffman & Hayes, 2004). The jury is still out

with respect to e-mail. Goffman (1959; 1963) was one of the first to explore communicators' needs to signal their changing levels of availability: in his "dramaturgical" model, communicators are "players" who constantly need to manage an impression of greater or lesser amenability to communications, on a continuing basis. This is true of both physically co-located workers and those inhabiting virtual workspaces. Nonverbal cues such as eye gaze and bodily posture signal accessibility in traditional workplaces. However, the "netiquette" for managing one's own and respecting others' virtual availability is still evolving, and is unfortunately often not respected, which could lead to stress.

Stress is a multi-faceted problem, caused by a multitude of interdependent, independent factors operating individually, cumulatively and in parallel. It can be defined as "a state in which the challenges or demands placed upon an individual are believed, subjectively, to surpass the abilities of that person". The previous discussion went back a century to compare personal communication in different eras but in reality one needs only to go back 25 years to find a very different world of work, when communication media were in their infancy. This kind of study gives us a better understanding of the impact of this technology on "traditional" stress factors, and to identify newly emerging stressors. Historical stress factors differ from current ones (Sapolsky, 1998). The stressors of today tend to be less immediately life-threatening, and potentially endure for longer periods of time, indeed years, in some instances (Kalat & Shiota, 2007). They are often of a second-order, intellectual nature. Common stressors might include ongoing interpersonal difficulties, bullying in the classroom or in the workplace, dealing with increasing demands in the workplace, or financial difficulties. Long-term stress plays a contributory role in conditions such as cancer and heart disease (Sapolsky, 1998) and has been implicated in diabetes development (Landel-Graham, Yount, & Rudnicki, 2003). The "fight or flight" response

(Cannon, 1915), whereby the individual reacts to a perceived threat either by staying and fighting it or by distancing oneself from it, has extreme adaptive value in the wild (e.g., when surprised by a bear). The probability of being surprised by a bear is today, for most individuals, extremely low; we, nevertheless, retain the "fight or flight" response and react to today's stressors, as Kalat and Shiota state (p. 281) "as if we were running or fighting for our lives". This type of response is automatic, and not always appropriate in modern contexts. It is also important to recognise that the extent to which an individual experiences and reports feeling stressed is also a function of an appraisal process (Lazarus, 1991), that is, a personal, subjective judgement of how favourable any particular event is. These appraisals, as Lazarus notes, also take place within the context of a person's plans and goals. Appraisals will therefore differ between individuals, as will the level of stress experienced. The literature identifies a number of pertinent modern-day workplace stressors: resource inadequacy (Gupta & Beehr, 1979), lack of control over daily working hours (Ala-Mursula et al., 2005), effort-reward imbalance (Ala-Mursula et al., 2005), quantitative workload (Spector & Jex, 1998) and interpersonal conflict (Spector & Jex, 1998). Clearly, these stressors differ significantly in nature from historical ones, as previously discussed.

Table 1. Evidence of stress as revealed by the publications of the era

Resource inadequacy (physical)	In nursing (Bailey & Steffen); in academia (Gmelch et al., 1986); in teaching (Green-burg, 1984)
Effort-reward imbalance	Kutash and Schlesinger (1980)
Quantitative workload	Cunningham (1983)
Interpersonal conflict	Matteson and Ivancevich (1982)

Evidence of stress from this group is confirmed by the publications of the eighties, as shown in Table 1.

Increasing numbers of workplaces today are both physical and virtual in form: a combination of a traditional office setting with dedicated desk space for workers, and an electronic environment, allowing individuals to work remotely. This places a new burden upon today's worker—that of being able to move fluently between face-to-face and virtual work-based communications, especially with respect to maintaining the "human moment" to an appropriate degree in virtual communications (Hallowell, 1999). Hallowell defines the human moment as "an authentic psychological encounter that can happen only when two people share the same physical space" (p. 59). Perhaps most crucially, Hallowell states that the human moment requires individuals' "emotional and intellectual attention". In this chapter, we recognise Hallowell's claim, and argue that although e-mail has become an embedded technology, its usage is nevertheless still poorly understood by its users, and, perhaps more crucially, e-mail users are unaware of the extent to which its usage impinges upon their "thinking" time. In other words, e-mail is usable and useful, but there are considerable doubts as to its efficiency and efficacy and potential side effects. Kock (1998; 1999) showed that people took up to 15 times longer to communicate via e-mail than directly, which raises questions as to its perceived efficiency. Rosen recognised this as long ago as 1994 in her call for "RSVP no more"; she called for NRN—"no reply necessary" to be appended to the relevant e-mails, in an attempt to curtail non-essential communications which crowd individuals' working day and may engender stress.

What impact has the emergence of technology-based communications had on stress in the workplace? The traditional utopian notion was that if technology freed up an individual's time, then that time could be used in the pursuit of leisure. However, time that is freed-up is currently filled with more tasks. Where previously a worker might have done one task, they now do multiple tasks, often without training which could help them to manage this constant task-switching behaviour properly. With the move to a knowledge economy, line managers are less likely to have the same skills as their staff; they may be trained in people management, but do not necessarily possess the "technical" skills possessed by their team. Contrast this with the world of 25 years ago, where managers were more likely to have once held the job of their staff members, prior to their being promoted to management.

Decision-making is also much more instantaneous today. Keinan (1987) has illustrated that increasing demands lead to a failure to review all of the available options during decision-making. If every e-mail had to be approved by a line manager, nothing would ever happen. Thus greater responsibility is being placed upon workers, who are dealing with ever heavier workloads. Role ambiguity, conflicting, concurrent demands, working for more than one manager, lack of training and outsourcing all engender workplace stress.

Today's employees are also encouraged to be "lifelong learners", where the spirit of change and development is embraced and rewarded, with individuals typically having a portfolio of job types and a series of career changes in their lifetime. Contrast this with previous times, where it was more common to hold a job "for life". *Status* and *stasis* were aspired to, in complete contrast to today's world of contrasting demands, development and change. One of the key elements of the workplace that has changed over the past twenty-five years, and with which workers have had to come to grips, is workplace technology. The case study in Figure 1 illustrates these changes.

Landau (1979) observed that computers would help society "to achieve radically increased productivity in the office" and in 1982, Zoltan observed (presciently) that the widening availability of computers did not mean that they were acceptable to the people expected to use them.

The issue of the "acceptability" of computers is bypassed; it is an assumed given. DeVaris (1982), echoed Zoltan, in an examination of the effect of computers on workers. What deVaris could not know, in 1982, was that it would not be the technology itself that proved problematic, but rather what the technology might *enable and facilitate*—such as increasing interruptions. Furthermore, e-mail and other technological innovations have made it possible for us to speed up our working day, to be more productive, and to concurrently manage more activities. Unfortunately, increased pace can also have negative health effects (Levine et al, 1989). People are starting to question the flipside of the much-vaunted "benefits" of all this technology. In a recent *Guardian* column, Jonathon Porritt (2005) writes:

Far from improving the quality of our lives, there is growing evidence that this progress is making us more miserable and more stressed." and further down his column: "… the latest study from the Economic and Social Research Council on modern employment trends indicates a rising dissatisfaction with working life over the past decade.

Evidence of stress is, once again, revealed by the publications of the era, as illustrated in Table 2. Raitoharju (2005) discusses the potential of the introduction of technology into the workplace, to place excessive demands upon employee cognitive resources, whilst Halpern (2005) recognises that the inability to exert a degree of control over one's working hours curtails the extent to which an individual can employ stress-related coping strategies, when required. Smith et al. (2005) explored the relationship between effort and perceived reward at work, and witnessed a relationship between effort expended and both "state" anger (situation-specific anger) and cardiovascular indicators. Similarly, Steptoe, Cropley and Joekes (1999) saw greater blood pressure responses in individuals who had jobs that were demanding, but over which they had little control. Dijkstra, van Dierendonck and Evers (2005) cite interpersonal

Table 2. Evidence of stress as revealed by publications since the 1980s

Resource inadeacacy (cognitive)	Raitoharju (2005)
Control over daily working hours	**Åkerstedt and Kecklund (2005); Halpern (2005)**
Effort-reward imbalance	**Smith et al. (2005)**
Quantitative workload	**Steptoe et al. (1999)**
Interpersonal conflict	**Dijkstra, van Dierendonck and Evers (2005)**
Advanced information technologies	**Arnetz (1996); Sankar and Natale (1990)**
Pace of Life	**Arndt (1987); Steptoe et al. (1993); Houtman et al. (1994)**

conflict as a common workplace stressor, whilst Arnetz (1996) showed that the adoption of stress reduction programs by employees lowered stress-related hormones. Finally, Houtman, Bongers, Smulders and Kompier (1994) saw that pace of work influenced musculoskeletal condition.

Note that in the past 25 years, two new stress-ors have emerged: advanced technologies in the workplace, and the increased pace of work life. Of course, new technologies have always been stressful. Consider the following excerpt from "The Diary of a Nobody" written in 1892:

April 8. No events of any importance, except that Gowing strongly recommended a new patent stylographic pen, which cost me nine-and-six-pence, and which was simply nine-and-sixpence thrown in the mud. It caused me constant an-noyance and irritability of temper. The ink oozes out of the top, making a mess on my hands, and once at the office when I was knocking the palm of my hand on the desk to jerk the ink down, Mr Perkupp, who had just entered, called out: 'Stop that knocking! I suppose that is you, Mr Pitt?' That young monkey, Pitt, took a malicious glee in responding quite loudly: 'No sir; I beg pardon, it is Mr Pooter with his pen; it has been going on all morning' (p. 175).

However, it seems that it is only now, at the beginning of the 21st century, that technological advances have invaded all our lives to such an extent (as illustrated in the case study in Figure 1), that the stress this causes has become a specific source of concern for organisations. As a research team, we are particularly interested in the role that e-mail has to play in both of these new kinds of stress, especially in the modern workplace.

E-Mail and Workplace Stress

E-mail's usage etiquette continues to emerge; Suchman (1987) promoted the notion that social practices such as e-mail use are necessarily *emer-gent*, and are interwoven with many other social processes at any one time. The situated cognitive perspective holds that tools, such as communica-tions devices, may only truly be comprehended through their usage, and that their usage is con-tingent upon context. Most contexts, such as the workplace, are subject to interruptions. This is increasingly typical in what McCafferty (1998) terms the "Age of Infoglut", where "analysing transactional data can be like sipping water from a fire hose". Although MacFarlane and Latorella (2002) comment that a person's job performance often relies, to an extent at least, on their ability to monitor constantly changing events and displays and to communicate with others, O'Conaill and Frohlich (1995) and Dismukes, Young and Sum-walt (1998) have shown that many individuals find it difficult to resume tasks after interruptions. In-

Figure 1. A case study illustrating changes in workplace technology in the last 25 years

A quarter of a century ago, in 1980, one of my first jobs after University was to work for one of the London Teaching hospitals. My job title was 'Junior Programmer' but effectively I helped medics with their research, in particular with running the statistical package SPSS. Fast forward to today and, as well as my regular academic role, I am a part-time consultant for a health board where I effectively help medics with their research, in particular SPSS. How has the job changed in the intervening 25 years? The most obvious difference is the PRODUCTIVITY expected in the modern working environment. Back then, I was employed full-time by a single hospital, now I am employed part-time by an entire health board area, extending over hundreds of hectares and comprising many hospitals. This is only possible because of advances in technology that have increased the ease and speed of communication. In 1980 computer resources were heavily centralised. The hospital had a single mainframe housed in the basement which also housed me and a few printers and terminals.

The medics would supply the programs on punched cards which were batch processed, often overnight. Today all the medics have their own PC and printer. SPSS has also become easier to use with the standard GUI interface. The changes in technology have also changed the nature of the job. In 1980 I spent most of my time debugging programs, today I spend most of my time explaining the choice of statistical technique and helping interpret output. The ease of using SPSS has led to an increase in the expectation of what can be achieved. Statistical techniques that were impossible to run twenty five years ago can now be set up and run in a matter of minutes - understanding what it all means however takes a bit longer! And this is where I come in. I used to be somewhat baffled that intelligent folk would pay me good money to advise them on things that they could sort out for themselves. Now I realise that they are paying me because I increase their productivity.

The other major change has been in COMMUNICATION. In 1980 almost all contact with the medics was face-to-face. Firstly, the nature of the technology dictated this. Punched cards and reams of printout, large and heavy, were generally exchanged by hand. Secondly, the slower speed of batch processing meant that telephone communication was not necessary; besides, medics were difficult to reach by phone as they were often on the move. Nowadays all communication can be done by e-mail or text. Moreover, the nature of distributed computing means that not only messages but documents, programs, data and output can all be transferred electronically. This means I am no longer constrained by time and space. Firstly, I can work across a wide geographical area and secondly I can work wherever and whenever it suits. In 1980 my working life was clearly defined: Central London, 9 till 5, Monday to Friday. It is now endlessly and seamlessly entwined with the rest of my life. Curiously, while there is absolutely no need to meet anyone face-to-face I still insist on meeting clients once at least, usually at the start of a working relationship.

terestingly, neither the duration of the interruption nor the perceived control over the source of the interruption facilitates task resumption (Gillie & Broadbent, 1989). Thus it is apparent that e-mail, as a source of interruption, may exert a deleterious effect upon certain individuals' working styles. This is exacerbated by the fact that increasing volumes of e-mail (and hence the number of potential interruptions) does not equate with improved communication (Sarbaugh-Thompson & Feldman, 1998). With this in mind, our own research examined some of the individual differences that might predict the extent to which an individual is negatively influenced by unscheduled e-mail communications.

EMPIRICAL EVIDENCE

In an attempt to gain insight into the manner in which e-mail use is embedded in users' daily lives in the 21st century, the low-level computer behaviours of a series of individuals were (consensually) monitored using the GRUMPS system (Generic Remote Usage Monitoring Production System), (Evans et al., 2003). The investigation was conducted to determine the effects of interruptions. Additionally, a global Web-based survey of individuals' perceptions of their e-mail usage was carried out. The first part of the survey explored e-mail usage behaviours. The second part considered individual differences that might influence the way e-mail interruptions are perceived and then handled. These questions were based on Rosenberg's self-esteem scale, Rotter's (1966) locus of control of reinforcement scale and to a lesser extent upon Turknett's leadership scale (2005). Locus of control of reinforcement refers to the extent to which an individual considers themselves to be able to control events in their life. Some individuals feel that they have greater "internal", or intrinsic control over events. Others believe that "external" events are more responsible for shaping their lives. This might potentially be a factor that influences the way(s) in which e-mail interruptions are handled by different people.

The GRUMPS study found that users spent significant amounts of time checking their e-mails, ranging from 10% to 34% of their online time (Renaud, Ramsay, & Hair, 2006). The other striking finding is that users tend to multitask frequently between their e-mail application and other applications, seldom spending a significant amount of time within any one application. Typically they would switch from e-mail to non-e-mail applications between 30 to 40 times per online hour. Very few e-mail sessions lasted more than a minute, with around half lasting less than 15 seconds. It was clear that much of the e-mail activity was a fairly wasteful monitoring of e-mails. Moreover the knock-on effect of this on other applications was considerable. Only around 15% of non e-mail sessions lasted longer than five minutes.

Analyses from the survey of self-reported e-mail-related behaviour found that while 50% of respondents estimated that they checked e-mails more than once an hour and 35% every 15 minutes, these perceived behaviours did not corroborate the findings from the GRUMPS study. We found there was a massive disparity between what users actually did and what they perceived that they did. This indicates the astonishing extent to which e-mail is embedded in our day-to-day lives.

Respondents also perceived e-mail as a less disruptive medium than, for example, telephone calls. They also generally felt more in control of e-mail communication as compared to other media. However, there was also evidence of pressure: respondents generally felt they had to respond more quickly to e-mails to meet the expectations of senders. Females, in particular, tended to feel more pressure to respond than males.

We also found that while many individuals seem to feel pressured by e-mail, and feel this pressure negatively as stress, some respond positively (Hair, Renaud, & Ramsay, 2006). One key factor

in this difference appears to be the individual's perception of control over the working environment. Those who do not feel in control are more likely to perceive e-mail as stressful. Another factor that seems relevant is ability to deal with distractions. E-mailers less able to ignore distractions were more likely to perceive e-mail as stressful. They also find it more difficult to resume ongoing tasks after an interruption.

Individual differences seem to play a part in this. Those with higher self-esteem feel significantly more in control and hence experience less stress from e-mail. It would appear that they are more likely to treat e-mail as an asynchronous communication medium, a faster form of letter or memo. Those with lower self-esteem tend to feel greater pressure to constantly monitor and respond to e-mail, behaving as if it were more of a *synchronous* communication medium, like a telephone call.

Locus of control was found to be less important. Individuals with an external locus of control of reinforcement found it significantly harder to ignore distractions than individuals with an internal locus of control of reinforcement. This did not seem to relate specifically to e-mails or to e-mail-related stress.

What did seem to matter was how disruptive e-mail was perceived to be compared to other media. Those who perceived e-mail as less disruptive than other media experienced less pressure. More work is required to explain why some employees consider e-mail to be less disruptive. It may be related to other personality factors, such as introversion, that were not measured in the study, or it may be related to situational factors such as level of seniority.

IMPLICATIONS FOR PRACTICE

It is clear, from a review of the literature and from our own empirical work, that practical guidance regarding the appropriate management of virtual workplace communication is urgently required. We suggest the following:

E-mail Senders:

1. Employees need to be encouraged to reflect upon whether a communication is truly essential, and if so,

2. Whether e-mail is indeed the most appropriate form of communication for the content.

3. Once this decision has been made, they should send the e-mail only to relevant recipients.

4. They should never pressure other employees, especially those they supervise, to respond to their e-mails as they would to a telephone call. There are clear exceptions to this, however, such as call centres.

E-mail Recipients:

1. E-mail users must learn to filter and prioritise their handling of e-mail communications.

2. It is neither necessary nor possible to read and respond to each communication immediately; this needs to be accepted and understood at both the organizational and employee level.

3. E-mail should not be polled continuously, since this will negatively affect all other work activities. E-mail reading times should be allocated and all e-mail dealt with in a block of time rather than interspersing with other work activities.

Organizations:

1. They need to recognise the value of Hallowell's "human moment" and develop ways of maintaining it in not only purely virtual workspaces, but in blended ones.

2. E-mail should be promoted as an asynchronous tool, rather than a synchronous one. Employees should be encouraged to meet with other employees face-to-face on a regular basis and not to use e-mail to replace regular meetings.

3. Communicators, as Shea (1995) stated, simply need to "behave", if they wish to observe "netiquette". Hence organisations should have an e-mail use policy for all their employees.

DISCUSSION: THE FUTURE OF NETWORKED COMMUNICATION RESEARCH

So Bellamy and Forster were *both* right—our findings support the hypothesis that mediated communication technologies are proving to be double-edged swords. Such technologies, e-mail in particular, are here to stay, but if office workers (and others) are to truly capitalise upon its functionality, and to minimise its ability to cause stress, further research is urgently required.

What might networked communication look like in another 25 years? We are gradually moving away from a communications landscape where, when one wishes to communicate, one engages in purposeful, explicit, communications activities. In other words, we are living in a world where one sits in front of a computer and logs onto whatever the communications programme of choice might be, or where one picks up the telephone. We are moving to a world where technology-based human communication will be seamlessly integrated into the very fabric of the world around us, that is, it will become ambient and embedded. Ishii and Ulmer (1997) were among the first to refer to ambient communication in their discussion of "tangible objects". A tangible object is an everyday physical object such as a lamp or ornament that has wireless connectivity embedded within it. Beigl and Gellersen's (2001) MediaCup—which they define as "an ordinary coffee cup invisibly augmented with computing and context-awareness"—will support a different form of human communication, namely the communication of abstract, contextual, non-verbal, qualitative, often emotional signals. In the future, rather than being aware that one is explicitly either "online" or "off-line", and available for communication or not, we will be able to take advantage of "always-on" wireless IP networks, ensuring that communication becomes more of a naturally changing human *state* or *condition* than a technology-driven *task*. The definition of communication will change from being action- or task-centric, to being a description of communicator state. We will be able to signal our degree of *interruptibility*.

In order to understand, and hence support and facilitate future technology-mediated human communication, and minimise the deleterious effects of interruptions, we would argue that two principles must be observed.

1. Human communication should be examined and analysed *in situ*, that is within its natural context. Communications contexts of the future will differ significantly from today's; not only will the physical context of device usage need to be ascertained, but more crucially, the psychological, emotional and temporal landscape(s) of the human "communicators". How interruptible or open to communication is the user?

2. Somewhat paradoxically, this requires communications technology developers to appreciate that communication-in-the-raw is often not the primary task that a technology needs to support. Rather, the primary task (for the user) may be of a more subtle and higher order, that is, to monitor, to observe, to watch, to transmit information, to seek information or to influence another's thoughts or emotions. In the case study in Figure 1, it is interesting to note that face-to-face communication is still seen as important despite the plethora of communication technologies available. This bolsters our suggestion that communication "in the raw", as currently facilitated by networked technologies, still falls significantly short of enabling the more naturalistic, rich and organic nature of "higher order" interpersonal interaction. With this in mind, greater attention needs

to be invested in the socio-psychological framework within which the communication takes place.

The point of human communication, whether in the workplace or elsewhere, is, after all, to *meaningfully connect* with others, rather than merely to communicate with them. We suggest that part of the problem in today's world of interruptions is that *communication* is all around us in raw form (e.g., in the countless e-mails in our inboxes) whereas *meaningful connection,* in the more holistic sense, is not. Blunt, raw communication is, we suggest, more liable to "interrupt" than those communications that are sympathetic to the recipient's context, individual traits and general socio-psychological landscape. It is clear from our research—to a certain degree at least—that e-mail users differ in their susceptibility to e-mail interruptions as a function of their level of self-esteem. It is also clear that what e-mail users *think* they do and what they *actually do* is at odds: we found that whereas users said they tended to check their e-mail only once every 15 minutes, the evidence from behavioural tracking suggests that it is actually far more frequent.

CONCLUSION

We are all communicating, but this is not necessarily meaningful. There are potentially many reasons for this. Our research has shown that there is a disparity between e-mail users' beliefs regarding their behaviours and their actual usage behaviour. We have also found that individual differences influence e-mailing behaviour. Although much is already known about how online groups form (Brown, 2000), the mechanisms whereby group cohesiveness is achieved (Lott, 1961), and the dynamics of social synchronisation (Argyle et al., 1968; Argyle, 1969), the practical applications of this knowledge are yet to filter through to the workplace. An understanding of how to *manage* and *appropriately interweave* online and off-line behaviours is a desirable goal. Research into online group development, the role of empathy and the development of behavioural norms or social "etiquette" amongst group members (Preece, 2000) must be encouraged and its insights imported—as an imperative—into the workplace. Technology-based communications tools, such as e-mail, must take account of this, and the other user-driven requirements mentioned in this chapter, if they are truly to prove their worth.

REFERENCES

Åkerstedt, T., & Kecklund, G. (2005). The future of work hours- the European view. *Industrial Health, 43,* 80-84.

Ala-Mursula, L., Vahtera, J., Linna, A., Pentti, J., & Kivimaki, M. (2005). Employee worktime control moderates the effects of job strain and effort-reward imbalance on sickness absence: the 10-town study. *Journal of Epidemiological Community Health, 59,* 851-857.

Argyle, A. (1969). *Social interaction.* New York, NY: Atherton Press.

Argyle, M., Lalljee, M., & Cook, M. (1968). The effects of visibility on interaction in a dyad. *Human Relations, 21,* 3-17.

Arndt, R. (1987). Work pace, stress, and cumulative trauma disorders. *Journal of Hand Surgery, 12,* 866-869.

Arnetz, B. (1996). Techno-stress: A prospective psychophysiological study of the impact of a controlled stress-reduction programme in advanced telecommunication systems design work. *Journal of Occupational & Environmental Medicine, 38,* 53-65.

Bailey, J., Steffen S., & Grout, T. (1980). The stress audit: Identifying the stressors of ICU nursing. *Journal of Nursing Education, 19,* 15-25.

Beigl, M., Gellersen, H.-W., & Schmidt, A. (2001). MediaCups: Experience with design and use of computer-augmented everyday artefacts. *Computer Networks, Special Issue on Pervasive Computing, 35.*

Bellamy, E. (1996). *Looking backward, 2000-1887.* Dover Publications.

Boase, J., Horrigan, J., Wellman, B., & Rainie, L. (2006). *PEW INTERNET & American Life Project.* Retrieved July 20 2006 from http://www.pewinternet.org/pdfs/pip_internet_ties.pdf.

Brown, R. (2000). *Group processes.* Oxford: Blackwell.

Buckner, K., & Gilliam, M. (2003). Using e-mail for social and domestic purposes: Effectiveness in fulfillment of interpersonal communication motives. *International Conference on Home Oriented Informatics and Telematics (HOIT 2003), the Networked Home and the Home of the Future.* University of California.

Cannon, W. (1915). *Bodily changes in pain, hunger, fear and rage: An account of recent researches into the function of emotional excitement.* New York, NY: Appleton.

Car, J., & Sheikh, A. (2004). E-mail consultations in healthcare: Acceptability and safe application. *British Medical Journal, 329,* 439-442.

Cooper, C., & Jackson, S. (1997). *Creating tomorrow's organizations: A handbook for future research in organizational behavior.* Chichester, UK: Wiley.

Cunningham, W. (1983). Teacher burnout—Solutions for the 1980s: A review of the literature. *The Urban Review (Historical Archive), 15,* 37-51.

DeVaris, P. (1982). The impact of electronics on humans and their work environment. *Proceedings of the conference on human factors in computing systems* (pp. 281-286), Gaithersburg, MD.

Dismukes, K., Grant, Y., & Sumwalt, R. (1998). Cockpit interruptions and distractions. *ASRS Directline Magazine, 10*(3), 4-9.

Dijkstra, M., van Dierendonck, D., & Evers, A. (2005). Responding to conflict at work and individual well-being: The mediating role of flight behaviour and feelings of helplessness. *European Journal of Work and Organizational Psychology, 14,* 119-135.

Duane, A., & Finnegan, P. (2004). Managing e-mail usage: A cross case analysis of experiences with electronic monitoring and control. In: M. Janssen, H. Sol, & R. Wagenaar (Ed.), *Proc ICEC'04. Sixth International Conference on Electronic Commerce* (pp. 229-238). Delft, The Netherlands.

Evans, H., Atkinson, M., Brown, M., Cargill, J., Crease, M., Draper, S., et al. (2003). The pervasiveness of evolution in GRUMPS software. *Software-Practice and Experience, 330,* 99-120.

Forster, E. (1909). *The machine stops, from the eternal moment and other stories.* New York, NY: Harcourt Brace.

Gillie, T., & Broadbent, D. (1989). What makes interruptions disruptive? A study of length, similarity, and complexity. *Psychological Research, 50,* 243-250.

Gmelch, W., Wilke, P., & Lovrich, N. (1986). Dimensions of stress among university faculty: Factor-analytic results from a national study. *Research in Higher Education (Historical Archive), 24,* 266-286.

Goffman, E. (1959). *The presentation of self in everyday life.* Garden City, NY: Doubleday.

Goffman, E. (1963). *Stigma.* Englewood Cliffs, NJ: Prentice-Hall.

Greenburg, S. (1984). *Stress and the teaching profession.* Baltimore, MD: Paul H. Brooks Publishing Co.

Grossmith, G. (1892). *The diary of a nobody.* Penguin Books.

Gupta, N., & Beehr, T. (1979). Job stress and employee behaviours. *Organisation and Behavioral Human Performance, 23,* 373-387.

Halpern, D. (2005). How time-flexible work policies can reduce stress, improve health, and save money. *Stress and Health, 21,* 157-168.

Heggy, P. (2006). *New directions. Stressors and the world of work. Mental Health Statistics Improvement Program.* Retrieved July 20, 2006 from http://www.mhsip.org/.

Hair, M., Renaud, K., & Ramsay, J. (2006). The influence of self-esteem and locus of control on perceived e-mail-related stress. *Computers in Human Behavior, 23,* 2791-2803.

Hallowell, E. (1999). The human moment at work. *Harvard Business Review, 77*(1), 58-64.

Hoffman, R., & Hayes, P. (2004). The pleasure principle. *Intelligent Systems, IEEE, 19*(1), 86-89.

Houtman, I., Bongers, P., Smulders P., & Kompier, M. (1994). Psychosocial stressors at work and musculoskeletal problems. *Scandinavian Journal of Work and Environmental Health, 20,* 139-145.

Ishii, H. & Ullmer, B. (1997). Tangible bits: Towards seamless interfaces between people, bits and Atoms. *Proceedings of the ACM Human Factors in Computing Systems Conference CHI 1997* (pp. 234-241). ACM Press.

Jackson, T., Dawson, R., & Wilson, D. (2003). Understanding e-mail interaction increases organizational productivity. *Communications of the ACM, 46*(8), 80-84.

Keinan, G. (1987). Decision making under stress: Scanning of alternatives under controllable and uncontrollable threats. *Journal of Personality and Social Psychology, 52,* 639-644.

Kalat, J., & Shiota, M. (2007). *Emotion*. Thomson Wadsworth.

Kock, N. (1998). Can communication medium limitations foster better group outcomes? An action research study. *Information & Management, 34*(5), 295-305.

Kock, N. (1999). *Process improvement and organizational learning: The role of collaboration technologies*. Hershey, PA: Idea Group Publishing.

Kock, N. (2001). The ape that used e-mail: Understanding e-communication behavior through evolution theory. *Communications for the Association for Information Systems, 5*(3), 1-29.

Kutash, I., Schlesinger, L., & Associates (Eds.). (1980). *Handbook of stress and anxiety - Contemporary knowledge, theory and treatment*. San Francisco, CA: Josey-Bass.

Landau, R. (1979). Productivity, information technology and the office. *Proceedings of the 2nd annual international ACM SIGIR conference on information storage and retrieval: information implications into the eighties* (pp. 59-63). Dallas, TX.

Landel-Graham, J., Yount, S., & Rudnicki, S. (2003). Diabetes mellitus. In: A. Nezu, C. Nezu, & P. Geller (Eds.), *Handbook of psychology, 9, Health Psychology*. New York, NY: Wiley.

Lazarus, R. (1991). *Emotion and adaptation*. New York, NY: Oxford University Press.

Levine, R., Lynch, K., Miyake, K., & Lucia, M. (1989). The type A city: Coronary heart disease and the pace of life. *Journal of Behavioral Medicine (Historical Archive), 12*, 509-524.

Lott, B. (1961). Group cohesiveness: A learning phenomenon. *Journal of Social Psychology, 55*, 275-286.

Markus, M. (1994). Electronic mail as the medium of managerial choice. *Organization Science, 5*(4), 502-527.

Maslow, A. (1943). A theory of human motivation. *Psychological Review, 50*, 370-396.

Matteson, M., & Ivancevich, J. (1982). *Managing job stress and health*. New York, NY: Free Press, Collier Macmillan Publishers.

McCafferty, J. (1998). Coping with infoglut. Retrieved January 5, 2007 from http://www.cfo.com/article.cfm/2990091.

McFarlane, D., & Latorella, K. (2002). The scope and importance of human interruption in human-computer interaction design. *Human-Computer Interaction, 17*, 1-61.

McLuhan, M. (1964). *Understanding media: The extensions of man*. Gingko Press.

Munter, M., Rogers, P., & Rymer, J. (2003). Business e-mail: Guidelines for users. *Business Communication Quarterly, 66*(1), 26-40.

O'Conaill, B., & Frohlich, D. (1995). Timespace in the workplace: Dealing with interruptions *Companion Proceedings of CHI '95*, (pp. 262-263). New York, NY: ACM SIGCHI.

Orwell, G . (1949). *1984*. London: Secker and Warburg.

Preece, J. (2000). *Online communities: Designing usability, supporting sociability*. Chichester, UK: John Wiley and Sons.

Porritt, J. (2005). Too fast, too furious: The 'it's all about me' generation. *The Guardian. 28 September*. Retrieved July 20, 2006 from http://society.guardian.co.uk/societyguardian/story/0,7843,1579354,00.html.

Raitoharju, R. (2005). Information technology-related stress. *IRIS'28 Kristiansand, Norway, August 6-9*. Retrieved July 20, 2006 from http://www.hia.no/iris28/Docs/IRIS2028-1025.pdf.

Renaud, K., Ramsay, J., & Hair. M. (2007). You've got e-mail! Shall I deal with it now? Electronic mail from the recipient's perspective. *International Journal of Human-computer Interaction. 21*(3), 313-332.

Rohall, S., Gruen, D., Moody, P., Wattenberg, M., Stern, M., Kerr, B., et al. (2004). Re-mail: A reinvented e-mail prototype. *Extended abstracts of the 2004 conference on Human factors and computing systems, April 24-29.* Vienna, Austria.

Romm, C., Pliskin, N., & Rifkin, W. (1996). Diffusion of e-mail: An organisational learning perspective. *Information and Management, 31,* 37-46.

Rosen, S. (1994). RSVP no more. *Communication World, 11*(9), 42.

Rosenberg, M. (1965). *Society and the adolescent self-image.* Princeton, NJ: Princeton University Press.

Rotter, J. (1966). Generalized expectancies for internal versus external control of reinforcement. *Psychological Monographs, 80*(609).

Rudavsky, S. (2005). Stress in the workplace. *Daily Record.* 20 December.

Sankar, Y., & Natale, S. (1990). Technological change, technostress, and industrial humanism. *International Journal of Value-Based Management (Historical Archive), 3,* 91-103.

Sapolsky, R. (1998). *Why zebras don't get ulcers.* New York, NY: W. H. Freeman.

Sarbaugh-Thompson, M., & Feldman, M. (1998). Electronic mail and organizational communication: Does saying "Hi" really matter?. *Organization Science, 9*(6), 685-698.

Shea, V. (1995). Miss manners' guide to excruciatingly correct Internet behavior. *Computerworld, 29*(10), 85-88.

Smith, L., Roman, A., Dollard, M., Winefield, A., & Siegrist, J. (2005). Effort–reward imbalance at work: The effects of work stress on anger and cardiovascular disease symptoms in a community sample. *Stress and Health, 21,* 113-128.

Spector, P., & Jex, S. (1998). Development of four self-report measures of job stressors and strain: Interpersonal Conflict at Work Scale, Organizational Constraints Scale, Quantitative Workload Inventory, and Physical Symptoms Inventory. *Journal of Occupational and Health Psychology, 3,* 356-367.

Steptoe, A., Cropley, M., & Joekes, K. (1999). Job strain, blood pressure and response to uncontrollable stress. *Journal of Hypertension, 17,* 193-200.

Suchman, L. (1987). *Plans and situated actions: The problem of human-machine communications.* Cambridge, UK: Cambridge University Press.

Turknett Leadership Group Quiz. Retrieved July 20, 2006 from *http://www.leadershipcharacter. com/eq_quiz2.htm.*

Tyler, J., & Tang, J. (2003). When can I expect an e-mail response? A study of rhythms in e-mail usage. ECSCW 2003. *Proceedings of the Eighth European Conference on Computer Supported Cooperative Work,* (pp. 239-258). Helsinki.

Walsh, J., Kucker, S., Maloney, N., & Gabbay, S. (2000). Connecting minds: Computer-mediated communication and scientific work. *Journal of the American Society for Information Science, 51*(14), 1295-1305.

Zoltan, E. (1982). How acceptable are computers to professional persons?. *Proceedings of the conference on human factors in computing systems,* (pp. 74-77). Maryland.

KEY TERMS

Communication: The exchange of information and meaning between two or more individuals.

E-mail: Electronic communication, usually primarily text-based, but with the capacity to contain sounds and pictures.

Interruption: An unscheduled, temporary cessation of an ongoing activity.

Individual differences: The investigation of behavioural differences between individuals.

Self-esteem: An individual's notion of their own self-worth.

Locus of control of reinforcement: An individual's perceived control over their behavioural outcomes.

Stress: A state that ensues when an individual perceives that they cannot manage the demands being placed upon them.

Chapter XIV
Employee Privacy in Virtual Workplaces

Robert Sprague
University of Wyoming College of Business, USA

ABSTRACT

This chapter addresses the legal aspects of employee privacy in virtual workplaces. The body of law regarding employee workplace privacy that has evolved over the years establishes a minimal expectation of privacy on the part of the employee (meaning employers have been found guilty of violating employee privacy only in rare and extreme cases). No one has yet examined whether virtual workplaces alter the fundamental assumptions underlying employee privacy rights. By reviewing the current status of employee privacy law and juxtaposing it with virtual workplace environments, with a particular focus on communication technologies, this chapter seeks to provide guidance for the privacy issues that are sure to arise with the growth and development of virtual workplaces.

INTRODUCTION

This chapter analyzes whether the growth of virtual workplaces changes the expectations employees may have regarding workplace privacy, and, consequently, whether employers face different legal standards regarding employee privacy. Traditionally, employees have been presumed to have minimal expectations of privacy in the workplace. What has not been addressed is whether these expectations carry over to virtual workplaces.

The focus of this chapter is on employer monitoring of employee communications in a virtual workplace environment. The critical issue is whether the dynamics of the virtual workplace—particularly where employees work primarily from home—are altered with respect to employees' legally protected expectations of privacy and, if so, the potential legal liabilities employers face when monitoring employee communications. While employers have many legitimate reasons for monitoring employee communications, if their monitoring exceeds legitimate business purposes, they may find themselves liable to an employee fired as a result of the content of those monitored communications if the employer has violated the employee's right to privacy.

BACKGROUND

In today's modern workplace, employers find themselves dealing with growing legal concerns over the use of electronic communications. One survey has reported that 24% of companies have had employee e-mail messages subpoenaed by a court or regulatory body, and that 15% of companies have gone to court to defend lawsuits triggered by employee e-mail messages. As a result, more companies, according to the survey, are monitoring employee communications and enforcing company communications policies (*More Workers Fired*). When an employer monitors the communications of its employees, one naturally wonders to what extent do those employees have a legal right of privacy in the workplace.

There is a substantial body of literature reviewing the extent of employee privacy in the modern workplace (Kesan, 2002; Gabel & Mansfield, 2003; Hornung, 2005). While this research factors in the use of the Internet and e-mail communications, for the most part it does not distinguish between physical and virtual workplaces. The nature of the virtual workplace may, however, change the dynamics somewhat. First, because there is reduced physical interaction among virtual coworkers, there are heightened trust issues. Social control based on authority is replaced by self-direction and self-control; therefore, there is concern whether coworkers will fulfill their obligations and behave predictably (Cascio, 2000). This concern can lead to an increased desire to monitor employee communications.

Second, because of the very nature of the virtual workplace—in which employees operate remotely from each other and from managers (Cascio, 2000)—the reduction of face-to-face communication among coworkers creates a greater reliance on electronic forms of communication, particularly by telephone and e-mail messages. Employers are therefore more likely to monitor such communications to monitor the workflow of their employees. Finally, the virtual workplace exaggerates the mingling of personal and professional lives of employees. Their office is also their home in many cases. There is a greater likelihood of eliminating a clear demarcation between using computers, the Internet, and e-mail for personal use and for work.

EMPLOYEE COMMUNICATIONS AND EMPLOYER CONCERNS

Employers have a number of legitimate reasons for monitoring employee communications (particularly e-mail communications). First and foremost, they want to ensure that employees are performing their work according to expectations. Employers have legitimate concerns that employees may be using valuable work time for excessive personal activities, such as sending personal e-mail messages and surfing the Web (Finkin, 2002). In addition, employers may wish to assure that employees are appropriately communicating with fellow employees. For example, Michael Smyth was fired from the Pillsbury Company after sending e-mail messages concerning sales management that allegedly contained threats to "kill the backstabbing bastards" (Smyth, 1996, p. 99).

Employers may also be concerned that trade secrets and confidential information may inadvertently or purposely be disclosed to competitors or other businesses. For example, Shurgard Storage Centers sued Safeguard Self Storage alleging that in late 1999 Safeguard attempted to hire away some of Shurgard's employees and that one of those employees, while still working for Shurgard, had sent trade secrets and proprietary information to Safeguard through Shurgard's e-mail system (Shurgard, 2000).

Employers must also be concerned with communications sent among employees that may be deemed to create a "hostile" work environment. E-mail messages distributed within the workplace that contain obscene, sexually offensive, or racist content may result in the employer violating Title VII of the Civil Rights Act of 1964. Title VII makes it "an unlawful employment practice for an employer… to discriminate against any individual with respect to his compensation, terms, conditions, or privileges of employment, because of such individual's race, color, religion, sex, or national origin." (42 U.S.C. § 2000e-2(a)(1).) The Equal Employment Opportunity Commission (the government agency which enforces Title VII) has determined that conduct that has the purpose or effect of unreasonably interfering with an individual's work performance or creating an intimidating or hostile working environment, based on the target individual's race, gender, religion, sex, or national origin, creates a hostile work environment in violation of Title VII (29 CFR § 1604.11(a)(3)). The concern expressed by the U.S. Supreme Court is that a "discriminatorily abusive work environment, even one that does not seriously affect employees' psychological well-being, can and often will detract from employees' job performance, discourage employees from remaining on the job, or keep them from advancing in their careers" (Harris, 1993, p. 22).

When it comes to e-mail messages that contain offensive material, there is some dispute as to how many such messages must be distributed in order for a hostile work environment to be created. The popular press sometimes indicates that only one offensive or obscene message is necessary (Nusbaum, 2003). The courts, however, have required more. In fact, one court has specifically ruled that a single offensive e-mail is insufficient to create a hostile work environment (Curtis, 1999). In order to establish a hostile work environment, complaining employees must "demonstrate that their workplace was permeated with discriminatory intimidation that was sufficiently severe or pervasive to alter the conditions of their work environment" (Curtis, 1999, p. 213). In addition, a few offensive e-mails sent by co-workers over a period of years will not necessarily create a hostile work environment (Haywood, 2003), nor will a barrage of offensive e-mails sent in a short period of time (Schwenn, 1998).

These court decisions do not mean, however, that employers can ignore what employees are doing with the company's computers, in general, and the e-mail system, in particular. Sending a number of offensive e-mail messages over a period of time to a targeted employee or group of employees can create a hostile work environment (Coniglio, 1999).

An employer will be liable for workplace discrimination if a hostile work environment is created by a supervisor with immediate (or successively higher) authority over the victimized employee (Faragher, 1998). In addition, an employer is liable for co-worker harassment if the employer either provided no reasonable avenue for complaint or knew of the harassment but did nothing about it (Hockeson, 2002). Employers are therefore liable for allowing a hostile work environment to exist if they do not take steps to eliminate the source of the hostile work environment, as well as take reasonable steps in the first place to prevent it. Conversely, employers have avoided liability for racial and sexual harassment claims based on e-mail messages because they properly enforced corporate anti-harassment policies (Gabel & Mansfield, 2003).

The use of the e-mail system to create a hostile work environment may be exacerbated in a virtual workplace environment. Instead of a few employees literally standing around the water cooler trading jokes, relatively private dialogue is replaced by a company-wide communications system. A message intended for just a few recipients can easily transform into a company-wide (as well as world-wide) broadcast. Therefore, employers are well advised to monitor their communications systems to ensure appropriate content within messages.

For the various reasons discussed above, employers have legitimate reasons to monitor employee communications. The reasons become even more compelling in a virtual workplace environment since there may be limited opportunities for direct workplace observation and supervision. Likewise, employers may believe they have, on occasion, a legitimate business interest in searching an employee's workplace (for example, to determine whether the employee is violating the law or company policy). To what extent can employers monitor their employees' communications, or search their workplace, without violating those employees' right of privacy, particularly in a virtual workplace environment?

EMPLOYER MONITORING AND EMPLOYEE EXPECTATIONS OF PRIVACY

There is no single law clearly defining one's right of privacy. The U.S. Constitution does not expressly guarantee a right of privacy, though it has been inferred through the Fourth Amendment, which provides that any unreasonable search and seizure is unconstitutional (Hornung, 2005). "In analyzing the reasonableness of the search, courts often balance the need to search or intrude against the resulting invasion of privacy" (Hornung, 2005, p. 118). While it is generally recognized that the Fourth Amendment provides constitutional protection for employees against unreasonable searches of electronic communications and stored data, the employees must first have a reasonable expectation of privacy—which can be removed if the employer has an e-mail policy which notifies employees that the employer may monitor e-mail or Internet use (Gabel & Mansfield, 2003).

Another limitation of the Fourth Amendment inferred right of privacy is that it applies only to invasions by a governmental entity; as such, it does not directly apply to private employers. Very few states have adopted any form of privacy legislation that would apply to private workplaces (Kesan, 2002). Most state courts have, though, created an individual right of privacy based on the notion of a right to be free from intrusion upon seclusion. However, this right is limited to intrusion which would be "highly offensive to a reasonable person" (Restatement (Second)). As a result, the courts have been reluctant to recognize an employee expectation of privacy in the workplace and have done so only in circumstances where

the intrusion involved intensely private matters (Gabel & Mansfield, 2003).

From a legal standpoint, employers must take steps to avoid violating employee rights of privacy. Although the vast majority of employees are considered "at will" (Sprang, 1994), meaning they can be terminated with or without cause at any time, there are limits to the at-will doctrine. For example, in almost all states an employer cannot dismiss an employee if that dismissal would violate a clear public policy. Most examples of this exception involve employees who are fired because they complied with jury duty or refused to violate a law on behalf of the employer (Ballam, 2000). Courts have recognized that employees may have a limited expectation of privacy in the workplace (principally based upon intrusion of seclusion), and that if an employee is terminated on the basis of information obtained through an invasion of privacy, the employee's discharge may be wrongful (Pagnattaro, 2004) (meaning the employer may have to reinstate the employee and possibly pay damages to the employee).

Physical Searches

Within the workplace context, the U.S. Supreme Court has recognized that employees may have a reasonable expectation of privacy against intrusions by police—meaning the police must have a search warrant in order to conduct the search without violating the Fourth Amendment (O'Connor, 1987). The Fourth Amendment protects individuals from unreasonable searches conducted by the government, even when the government acts as an employer (Leventhal, 2001, p. 72-73). Without a reasonable expectation of privacy, a workplace search by a public employer will not violate the Fourth Amendment, regardless of the search's nature and scope (Leventhal, 2001). It can generally be inferred that a workplace search by a public employer which violates the Fourth Amendment would also violate an employee's right to privacy if conducted by a private employer.

Employees are generally not considered to have any expectation of privacy within the workplace that includes facilities and equipment under the ownership and control of the employer. There are, however, limited exceptions, such as when an employee brings in personal property that remains within the personal control of the employee—such as a handbag or purse (O'Connor, 1987). Personal control does not mean the employee must keep the item within his possession at all times. In the case of *Branan v. Mac Tools* (2004), the court concluded that an employee's reasonable expectation of privacy had been violated when his employer had emptied the contents of the employee's personal briefcase—which the employee had left unlocked in his office after leaving work for the day. The *Branan* court noted that this particular employee's briefcase was not routinely accessed by other employees, so there was no abandonment of an expectation of privacy regarding its contents.

Similarly, in the case of *K-Mart Corporation v. Trotti* (1984), a jury found that the employer's search of an employee's locker and purse (which was inside the locker) was inappropriate where the employer had allowed employees to provide their own locks. In reviewing the jury's verdict, while the appellate court reversed (on a procedural basis) the jury's finding that the intrusion involved an intensely private matter, it did conclude that since the employer allowed employees to provide their own locks, there was a recognized expectation that the locker and its contents would be free from intrusion and interference. In another privacy case involving K-Mart (Johnson, 2000), the court ruled K-Mart had violated employee privacy rights when private investigators hired by K-Mart to investigate employee thefts included in their investigative reports information related to various employees' personal lives.

What has not yet been addressed by the courts is whether an employer has any right to physically search an employee's home regarding legitimate business interests when that employee works exclusively (or extensively) from home. What

the courts have addressed, though, is the level of expectation of privacy an employee may have regarding personal data stored on an employer-provided computer.

For example, in the case of *United States v. Angevine* (2002), the defendant, an Oklahoma State University professor sued, in part, for invasion of privacy after his computer was searched during an investigation of child pornography. The court noted that within the workplace, the U.S. Supreme Court has recognized that public employees' expectations of privacy may be reduced by virtue of actual office practices and procedures, or by legitimate regulation. The *United States v. Angevine* court ruled that the professor did not have a reasonable expectation of privacy regarding data downloaded from the Internet onto his university-provided office computer, in part, because: the University computer-use policy reserved the right to randomly audit Internet use and to monitor specific individuals suspected of misusing University computers; the policy explicitly cautioned computer users that information flowing through the University network was not confidential either in transit or in storage on a University computer; and University computer users should have been aware that network administrators and others were free to view data downloaded from the Internet (2002, p. 1134).

However, in *Leventhal* (2001), the court concluded an employee did have an expectation of privacy regarding personal information he kept on his public employer-provided computer based on the fact that the employee was the only one who used the particular computer and the employer's anti-theft policy (which the employer had accused the employee of violating by using his office computer for personal business) did not prevent the employee from storing personal files on his office computer. In this particular case, the court ruled that "infrequent and selective search for maintenance purposes or to retrieve a needed document, justified by reference to the 'special needs' of employers to pursue legitimate work-related objectives, does not destroy any underlying expectation of privacy that an employee could otherwise possess in the contents of an office computer" (Leventhal, 2001, p. 74). As noted above, though, an individual's right of privacy must be balanced against the need for the search. In *Leventhal*, the court concluded that, despite the employee's recognized expectation of privacy, his Fourth Amendment rights were not violated because the employer's investigatory search for evidence of suspected work-related employee misfeasance was constitutionally reasonable and justified (Leventhal, 2001, p. 75).

In a private employment scenario, one court has ruled that where an employer provided an employee with two computers—one at the office and one to use at home for work—the employee could not have a reasonable expectation of privacy when he used the home computer for personal matters, in light of the fact the employee was aware of the employer's policy which stated that the employer could monitor the computers (TGB Insurance Services, 2002). Of interest to employers may be the court's attitude: it found it difficult for the employee to have a reasonable expectation of privacy in the context of "21st Century computer-dependent businesses" in which "three-quarters of this country's major firms monitor, record, and review employee communications and activities on the job, including their telephone calls, e-mails, Internet connections, and computer files" (TGB Insurance Services, 2002, p. 45).

In a virtual workplace scenario, it would not be uncommon for the employer to provide a computer which the employee uses at home for work. The employee in *TGB Insurance Services* argued that since the computer was used at home, including by his family for personal needs, there was a greater expectation of privacy regarding that computer. The *TGB Insurance Services* court flatly rejected such an argument.

Some courts, however, have recognized that employees may have a reasonable expectation of privacy regarding personal information stored on an employer-provided computer. For example, in the case of *Campbell v. Woodard Photographic*

(2006) the court held that if the employee (suspected of stealing equipment from the employer) could establish that the employer had accessed the employee's personal e-Bay account (using the employee's employer-provided computer), or had reviewed the employee's e-Bay transactions by searching his briefcase, he could establish an invasion of privacy.

Monitoring Employee Communications

When it comes to monitoring employee communication, including e-mail messages, one federal law, the Electronic Communications Privacy Act (ECPA), could possibly be considered to protect employee privacy. The ECPA prohibits the interception of wire, oral, and electronic communications (18 U.S.C. § § 2510-2521) as well as access to stored communications (18 U.S.C. § § 2701-2711) (Kesan, 2002). Underlying the ECPA (which is part of what is generally referred to as the Federal Wiretap Law) is an expectation of privacy in communications. The case of *Dorris v. Absher* (1999) is an example of where an employer can run afoul of federal law in the workplace. In *Dorris*, the employer secretly recorded the conversations of four employees who worked in a common office, and then attempted to fire two of the employees based on those secretly recorded conversations. All four employees then sued the employer for violation of the Federal Wiretap Law, on the basis that the interception of their oral conversations was illegal because they had a reasonable basis (i.e., an expectation of privacy) to believe their conversations would not be intercepted. The *Dorris* court concluded the four employees did have a reasonable expectation of privacy because they thought they were holding private conversations amongst only themselves within the only work area on the premises.

The Federal Wiretap Law (including the ECPA), however, exempts information service providers who monitor communications in their ordinary course of business. Courts have consistently held that when it comes to communications through computer, e-mail, and telephone systems provided by employers, the employers are considered information service providers. Hence, employers may monitor employee communications in the ordinary course of business (Gabel & Mansfield, 2003). In addition, where an employer's monitoring falls within this "business use exemption," employee consent is not required (Watkins, 1983).

"Ordinary course of business" is a key condition. For example, in the case of *Sanders v. Robert Bosch Corporation* (1994), the court concluded that the employer had violated the Federal Wiretap Law by recording (without the employee's consent) all telephone conversations which took place over certain extensions. The court could find no business justification for "the drastic measure of 24-hour a day, 7-day a week recording of telephone calls" (Sanders, 1994, p. 741). The *Sanders* court was following an earlier court decision in *Deal v. Spears* (1992) in which an employer was found guilty of violating the Federal Wiretap Law by surreptitiously recording all telephone calls made over a store's single telephone line.

To a large degree, the extent of the expectation of privacy on the part of the monitored employee has also been based on the extent of the monitoring. While the *Sanders* court considered the employer's monitoring "drastic," it was also somewhat flummoxed by the employer's underlying justification—it monitored all calls made on security extensions because of the fear of bomb threats, yet there had been "scant" evidence of prior bomb threats (p. 741) and the security personnel were not aware of the monitoring. Similarly, in *Deal*, the vast majority of the phone calls recorded by the employer contained "sexually provocative" conversations (p. 1155) the employee had with her boyfriend.

The employee's reasonable expectation of privacy, and, hence, reasonable expectation that certain phone calls will not be monitored, is heightened when the employer allows personal calls. For example, in the case of *Watkins v. L.M. Berry Co.* (1983), sales employees were informed that their phone calls would be monitored to improve sales techniques. However, the employer also allowed employees to use the same phones for personal calls, assuring employees their personal calls would not be monitored beyond the extent necessary to determine whether they were of a personal or business nature. The employer was found guilty of violating the Federal Wiretap Law when its supervisor listened to a phone call an employee was having with her friend during lunch in which the friend inquired about the employee's employment interview with a different company. The employer argued that all employees had consented to having their calls monitored. The court noted though that the consent had been limited—it did not have to be "all or nothing" (Watkins, 1983, p. 582). The *Watkins* court then concluded that the employer's continued monitoring of the employee's personal call when it was clear it was not business-related, was not in the ordinary course of business, and thus not subject to the business use exemption.

Can an employer monitor an employee's home phone when the employee works exclusively (or extensively) from home? Based on current law, yes, if the employee consents to full monitoring. And based on *Watkins*, if the employer agrees to only monitor work-related calls, it must only do so. Without consent, however, it would appear obvious that an employee would have a reasonable expectation of privacy regarding calls made from a home phone, particularly personal (versus business) calls. However, this expectation of privacy may not be all that obvious.

In the case of *Karch v. Baybank FSB*, a bank employee was disciplined based on comments she made during a phone conversation made from her home with a friend that was accidentally recorded by the employee's neighbors on their radio scanner. The conversation took place on a Saturday evening, during non-work hours, and it involved mostly personal matters; however, some work-related comments were overheard. Initially, the neighbors listened to the conversations for amusement, but they later reported them to the employer. The employee eventually resigned as a result of the reprimand and sued the employer, in part, for invasion of privacy. The employee lost her claim of invasion of privacy (specifically, invasion of seclusion) against the employer because, according to the court, it was the neighbors, and not the bank, that had recorded the conversation—the bank had merely acted on information it received.

While the courts have found violations of the Federal Wiretap Law where the employer has been excessive (and secretive) in its monitoring of employee oral communications, courts have yet to find an invasion of employee privacy regarding workplace e-mail communications—at least when the employer provides the e-mail system. For example, in *Smyth* (1996), the plaintiff-employee was fired for transmitting inappropriate and unprofessional comments over the company's e-mail system, despite the company's assurances that all e-mail communications would remain confidential and privileged, and that they would not be intercepted and used by the company against its employees as grounds for termination. The at-will employee in *Smyth* claimed his termination violated public policy because it violated his right to privacy. Applying Pennsylvania law, the court ruled the employee could not have "a reasonable expectation of privacy in e-mail communications voluntarily made by an employee to his supervisor over the company e-mail system notwithstanding any assurances that such communications would not be intercepted by management" (Smyth, 1996, p. 98). In *Smyth*, the court found no privacy interests when an employee voluntarily communicates unprofessional comments over a company e-mail system.

The employee in *Smyth* based his invasion of privacy claim on the tort of intrusion upon seclusion. As to this element, the court noted that liability only attaches when the intrusion is substantial and would be highly offensive to the ordinary reasonable person. The *Smyth* court

ruled, however, that even if an employee had a reasonable expectation of privacy in the contents of e-mail communications over a company e-mail system, a reasonable person would not consider the company's interception of these communications to be a substantial and highly offensive invasion of privacy. The court concluded that "the company's interest in preventing inappropriate and unprofessional comments or even illegal activity over its e-mail system outweighs any privacy interest the employee may have in those comments" (Smyth, 1996, p. 101).

A similar result was reached in the case of *McLaren v. Microsoft* (1999), in which the employee (McLaren) was initially suspended pending an investigation into accusations of sexual harassment and "inventory questions" and subsequently terminated. McLaren brought claims of invasion of privacy (again, based on intrusion upon seclusion) based on the employer (Microsoft) accessing e-mail messages McLaren had initially received through the company e-mail system and then stored on his office computer. The e-mail messages in question had been stored in a "personal" folder on McLaren's computer, protected by a password known only to McLaren.

The court concluded that " McLaren did not have a reasonable expectation of privacy in the contents of the e-mail messages such that Microsoft was precluded from reviewing the messages" (McLaren, 1999, p. 4). Attempting to analogize his situation to *K-Mart* (1984), McLaren argued his situation was similar to one where an employer searches a personal locker (the area where McLaren stored the messages on his computer) secured by the employee's own lock (having access to the messages password-protected). The *McLaren* court recognized that if an employer allowed an employee to store the employee's *personal belongings* in a workplace locker, secured by the employee's own lock, doing so could create an expectation of privacy regarding the personal contents of the locker. The court distinguished the facts in *McLaren* versus *K-Mart* (1984), noting: first, the locker scenario contained only personal items whereas in the instant case the company supplied the e-mail system, so the e-mail messages were not McLaren's personal property; and second, since the e-mail messages were delivered to the company's computers, they were accessible by third parties.

Similar to *Smyth* (1996), the *McLaren* court also concluded a reasonable person would not consider Microsoft's interception of the e-mail communications to be a highly offensive invasion, holding that "the company's interest in preventing inappropriate and unprofessional comments, or even illegal activity, over its e-mail system would outweigh McLaren's claimed privacy interest in those communication." (McLaren, 1999, p. 5). Similarly, in the case of *Garrity v. John Hancock Mutual Life Insurance Co.* (2002), the court rejected dismissed employees' arguments that they had a reasonable expectation of privacy regarding personal e-mail messages because the employer had instructed them as to how to create personal e-mail folders that could be password protected. Relying on *McLaren* (1999), the *Garrity* court rejected the employees' argument.

The *Garrity* court, relying on *Smyth* (1996), also ruled the employees could not have a reasonable expectation of privacy in the e-mail messages at issue because they acknowledged that the recipients of their e-mail messages could have forwarded them to others. The *Garrity* court also weighed the employees' right of privacy (if any) against the legitimate business needs of the employer—the employees in *Garrity* were dismissed for sending and receiving sexually explicit e-mail messages at work; once the employer received a complaint by a fellow employee regarding such messages, the employer had an obligation, under Title VII of the Civil Rights Act, to investigate and take prompt and effective remedial action (Garrity, 2002, p. 2). Finally, the *Garrity* court also ruled that the employer's reading of the employees' e-mail messages would not violate the ECPA because the use of an automatic e-mail back-up system (from which the messages were read by the employer) would be protected under the ordinary business

exemption. The fired employees' case in *Garrity* was also weakened by the fact that the employer had an e-mail policy which reserved the right of the employer to access all e-mail files.

The Stored Communications Act (SCA) (a part of the ECPA and Federal Wiretap Law) may, however, protect an employee's expectation of privacy when e-mail messages are stored on a third party's system. In the case of *Fischer v. Mt. Olive Lutheran Church*, officials of the employer-church accessed a youth minister's personal Microsoft Hotmail account after the officials became concerned over certain conduct of the minister. At the outset, the officials' access of the account without permission would appear to violate the SCA since, as the *Fischer* court pointed out, accessing stored e-mail messages of subscribers without specific authorization would be a violation of the act. Importantly, however, according to the *Fischer* court, there would be no violation of the act unless the church officials also obtained or altered messages, or prevented the youth minister from accessing his account. Unless the youth minister could prove that any of these events took place, the *Fischer* court ruled the church officials would not have illegally accessed his personal e-mail account.

Employer Monitoring Policies

Although one court (TGB Insurance Services, 2002), as noted above, has taken the attitude that employees should assume that modern businesses regularly monitor employee communications, companies should have in place a formal monitoring policy. Indeed, some employees' invasion of privacy cases have been dismissed, in part, because a workplace monitoring policy was in place (Garrity, 2002).

One key trend in workplace privacy analysis is the separation between personal property and employer property. As a general rule, courts find almost no employee privacy expectations in employer property. Therefore, it is important that a workplace monitoring policy remind employees that the telecommunications, computer, and, particularly, the e-mail systems are all property of the employer.

It is usually only when employee personal property is intermingled with employer property that an employee's expectation of privacy may arise. Where the employer, expressly or implicitly, allows its equipment to be used for personal phone calls, e-mail, and Internet use, an employee may have a reasonable expectation of privacy in those personal communications. It is therefore important, as well, that the employer remind employees in the monitoring policy that despite the personal nature of any communications over the employer's systems, all communications remain the property of the employer and are subject to monitoring.

Finally, where some employers have been found liable for violating employee privacy, it is generally where the employer's monitoring has gone beyond legitimate business necessity. "Snooping" is different from monitoring. In actually conducting monitoring, employers must remember to limit the monitoring to legitimate business purposes. And, as the *Leventhal* (2001) court pointed out, selective monitoring for routine maintenance can still leave open a reasonable expectation of privacy on the part of employees. Employers should remind employees in the monitoring policy that monitoring may be focused on the content of communications to ensure compliance with applicable laws, protection of businesses assets, and to ensure workflow productivity.

FUTURE TRENDS

This review of possible workplace privacy indicates that while one can generally assume there are minimal employee expectations toward workplace privacy, there may be exceptions based on various circumstances. It can be assumed these circumstances may become more complex as virtual workplace scenarios expand—one could reasonably assume a greater expectation of privacy

within the home, even when the home is also the workplace.

Two states, Connecticut and Delaware, have enacted legislation requiring employers to give employees notice of a company's monitoring policies (Hornung, 2005). A growing number of states have also enacted employee privacy laws protecting the right of employees to engage in lawful activities or consume lawful products (such as tobacco) without fear of reprisal from employers (Pagnattaro, 2004). However, these laws are specifically limited to off-site, off-duty conduct that is not work-related. These laws do, though, indicate a trend to protect the privacy of employees' personal lives. As virtual workplace practices exacerbate the commingling of personal and work life, one would expect more state legislatures to take notice, and to consider laws that help further distinguish between personal and workplace activities.

CONCLUSION

Historically, employees have been regarded as having a minimal expectation of privacy in the workplace. Public employees are, however, protected from unreasonable searches in the workplace by the Fourth Amendment. Private employees are protected against unreasonable intrusions upon seclusion. As a general matter, though, employee (whether public or private) expectations of workplace privacy are balanced against legitimate business interests for workplace searches or monitoring. In addition, for private employees, any claimed invasion of privacy must be highly offensive. Employers have traditionally been protected against employee invasion of privacy claims, as long as the searches or monitoring are not excessive—going beyond what is legitimately required for business purposes.

A fundamental basis in this analysis, however, is the workplace—usually under the ownership and control of the employer. This is the essential factor in assigning a very low expectation of privacy on the part of the employee. The virtual workplace potentially changes this dynamic. When the workplace is also the home—not only under the ownership and control of the employee, but also a traditionally private refuge—one of the foundations of employee privacy may be substantially altered. As virtual workplaces become more prevalent—that is, as more employees spend more time working from home—one can logically assume they will have a greater expectation of privacy regarding their workplace.

REFERENCES

Ballam, D. (2000). Employment-at-will: The impending death of a doctrine. *American Business Law Journal, 37,* 653-687.

Branan v. Mac Tools, 2004 WL 2361568 (Ohio App.).

Campbell v. Woodard Photographic, Inc., 433 F.Supp.2d 857 (N.D. Ohio 2006).

Cascio, W. (2000). Managing a virtual workplace. *Academy of Management Executive*, 14(3), 81-90.

Coniglio v. City of Berwyn, 1999 WL 1212190 (N.D. Ill.).

Curtis v. DiMaio, 46 F.Supp.2d 206, 212-13 (E.D. N.Y. 1999), *aff'd* 205 F.3d 1322 (2nd Cir. 2000).

Deal v. Spears, 980 F.2d 1153 (1992).

Dorris v. Absher, 179 F.3d 420 (1999).

Faragher v. City of Boca Raton, 524 U.S. 775, 790 (1998).

Finkin, M. (2002). Information technology and workers' privacy: The United States law. *Comparative Labor Law and Policy Journal, 23,* 471-504.

Fischer v. Mt. Olive Lutheran Church, Inc., 207 F.Supp.2d 914 (2002).

Gabel, J., & Mansfield, N. (2003). The information revolution and its impact on the employment relationship: An analysis of the cyberspace workplace. *American Business Law Journal, 40*(2), 301-353.

Garrity v. John Hancock Mutual Life Insurance Co., 2002 WL 974676 (D. Mass.).

Harris v. Forklift Systems, Inc., 510 U.S. 17 (1993).

Haywood v. Evergreen Motor Cars, Inc., 2003 WL 21418248 (N.D. Ill.).

Hockeson v. New York State Office of General Services, 188 F. Supp. 215, 219 (N.D. N.Y. 2002)

Hornung, M. (2005). Think before you type: A look at e-mail privacy in the workplace. *Fordham Journal of Corporate and Financial Law, 11,* 115-160.

Johnson v. K-Mart Corporation, 723 N.E.2d 1192 (Ill. App. Ct. 2000).

Karch v. Baybank FSB, 794 A.2d 763 (N.H. 2002).

Kesan, J. (2002). Cyber-working or cyber-shirking?: A first principles examination of electronic privacy in the workplace. *University of Florida Law Review, 54,* 289-332.

K-Mart Corporation v. Trotti, 677 S.W.2d 632 (1984).

Leventhal v. Knapek, 266 F.3d 64 (2001).

McLaren v. Microsoft Corporation, 1999 WL 339015 (Tex. App.).

More workers fired for misuse of e-mail. (2006).. *Wall Street Journal*, p. B4.

Nusbaum, M. (2003). New kind of snooping arrives at the office. *New York Times*, Sec.3, p. 12.

O'Connor v. Ortega, 480 U.S. 709 (1987).

Pagnattaro, M. (2004). What do you do when you are not at work?: Limiting the use of off-duty conduct as the basis for adverse employment decisions. *University of Pennsylvania Journal of Labor and Employment Law, 6,* 625-684.

Restatement (Second) of Torts § 652B (1965).

Sanders v. Robert Bosch Corporation, 38 F.3d 736 (1994).

Schwenn v. Anheuser-Busch, Inc., 1998 WL 166845 (N.D. N.Y.).

Shurgard Storage Center, Inc. v. Safeguard Self Storage, Inc., 119 F.Supp.2d 1121 (2000).

Smyth v. Pillsbury Company, 914 F.Supp. 97 (1996).

Sprang, K. (1994). Beware the toothless tiger: A critique of the model employment termination act. *American University Law Review, 43,* 849-924.

TGB Insurance Services Corporation v. Superior Court, 96 Cal.App.4th 443 (2002).

United States v. Angevine, 281 F.3d 1130 (10th Cir. 2002).

Watkins v. L.M. Berry Co., 704 F.2d 577 (1983).

KEY TERMS

Electronic Communications Privacy Act (ECPA): A part of what is generally referred to as the Federal Wiretap Law, prohibits the interception of wire, oral, and electronic communications (18 U.S.C. § § 2510-2521).

Employment-At-Will: Legal doctrine under which employment may be terminated by either the employer or the employee, at any time, with or without cause. The majority of employees in the United States are "at will." The employment at will doctrine is not absolute (see "wrongful discharge" below).

Invasion of Privacy: In the workplace privacy context, generally results from an intrusion upon seclusion; an unreasonable and highly offensive intrusion upon an individual's private affairs.

Hostile Work Environment: Created by conduct, such as through offensive or obscene e-mail messages, that has the purpose or effect of unreasonably interfering with an individual's work performance or creating an intimidating or hostile working environment, based on the target individual's race, gender, religion, sex, or national origin. An employer that allows a hostile work environment to exist will be in violation of Title VII of the Civil Rights Act of 1964 (see below).

Privacy: Traditionally, the notion that one has the right to be left alone. Recognized under the Fourth Amendment to the U.S. Constitution as protecting individuals from unreasonable searches and seizures by the government. In the private sector, protects against unreasonable intrusions upon seclusion (see above).

Stored Communications Act (SCA): A part of the Electronic Communications Privacy Act (see above) and the Federal Wiretap Law, prohibits certain access to stored communications (18 U.S.C. § § 2701-2711).

Title VII of the Civil Rights Act of 1964: Federal legislation that prohibits employers from discriminating against any individual with respect to his/her compensation, terms, conditions, or privileges of employment, because of such individual's race, color, religion, sex, or national origin (42 U.S.C. § 2000e-2(a)(1).

Wrongful Discharge: Termination of a worker's employment that violates a law or employment contract. Where an employee is considered "at will" (see above), termination of the worker's employment may be a wrongful discharge if the termination violates public policy, such as terminating the employee because the employee obeyed the law, refused to break the law on the employer's behalf, or, possibly, as a result of information the employer gained by violating the employee's right of privacy.

Chapter XV
Accommodating Persons with Disabilities in Virtual Workplaces

Belinda Davis Lazarus
University of Michigan–Dearborn, USA

ABSTRACT

Virtual workplaces offer persons with disabilities new opportunities in the workplace that may simultaneously accommodate their disabilities while posing challenges in terms of access to the information that they need to perform their jobs. Employers also need information about various disabilities and ways to accommodate the limitations imposed by each one. This chapter provides background and rationale for including persons with disabilities in the virtual workforce, detailed descriptions of each disability category, and common accommodations for each disability category. Resources for employers are discussed.

INTRODUCTION

Over 600 million people worldwide live with a sensory, physical, cognitive, or self-care disability that limits their ability to learn, work, and participate in daily activities (Heumann, 2004). Most people with disabilities wish to pursue careers like their non-disabled peers and many complete post-secondary degrees that provide them with a high level of skills in a wide variety of vocational areas. Many are highly motivated to achieve in the workplace and wish to become productive employees who are able to earn a living and reduce or eliminate their dependence on public assistance. However, a survey conducted by the International Labour Organization (2004-2005) showed that 80% of persons with disabilities in

developing countries are unemployed and 65% are unemployed in industrialized countries. As a result, approximately, fifty countries worldwide have enacted disability anti-discrimination legislation that provides greater access to the workplace for persons with disabilities (Quinn & Degener, 2002).

Prospective employers who fail to hire persons with disabilities either assume that they cannot work or are unable to perform tasks that are required to complete the job. Employers also express concerns that costly special facilities, special safety facilities and procedures, and complicated accommodations will be needed to compensate for limitations that may be the result of disabilities. The sobering labor statistics worldwide and the misconceptions held by prospective employers show that the capabilities of persons with disabilities are often misunderstood or disregarded. In fact, studies show that many employers do not understand disabilities and employment practices that allow them contribute to the workforce (Hendren & Sacher, 1992). Employers need information about disabilities and workplace options that reasonably accommodate persons in all disability categories.

Over a dozen specific disabilities and chronic medical conditions exist and require accommodations that help people become productive employees in both traditional and virtual workplaces. And, although accommodations may require the use of non-traditional approaches to a particular job, a U.S. survey of employers found that most accommodations cost less than $500 and 73% of employees with disabilities did not require any type of structural accommodation. And, in some cases, virtual workplaces may be an accommodation for persons with disabilities (U.S. Equal Employment Opportunity Commission, 2002).

Employers need to understand the capabilities and needs associated with each specific disability, the advantages and disadvantages of the task demands of virtual workplaces, and the specific accommodations that compensate for a variety of disabilities. The objectives of this chapter are to:

1. describe disabilities in general and specifically to enhance employers' understanding of the impact of each disability on the employee's performance
2. explore the demands and advantages of virtual workplaces for persons with disabilities within the context of employment demands
3. provide guidelines for developing appropriate accommodations for disabilities
4. recommend specific accommodations that are commonly used for each disability category.

UNDERSTANDING DISABILITIES IN THE WORKPLACE

According to the United Nations (2006), approximately 10% of the world's populations live with some sort of disability and, due to population growth, improved medical care and ageing, the numbers of persons with disabilities are increasing worldwide. In fact, they represent the largest minority population in the world. General definitions of disabilities vary by country and legislation, however, most of the general definitions focus on the limitations of the disability in terms of independence and daily life functions. For example, the Americans with Disabilities Act (1990) and the United Kingdom's Disabilities Discrimination Act (2005) describe a disability as any physical or mental condition that substantially limits or prevents a person's full participation in major life activities. General definitions also include the caveat that the disability must be viewed by the individual and others as a specific disability.

Specific disabilities have existed for centuries and many have been systematically researched since the mid-nineteenth century. As a result, detailed definitions and common characteristics of most categorical disabilities exist and are widely accepted by professionals in each field. Also, adults with specific disabilities usually understand their disabilities well enough to explain them to others and suggest accommodations for various job tasks. However, virtual workplaces are relatively new environments and accommodations that worked in traditional workplaces may not be useful for tele-workers. So, employers and personnel in human resources need to understand the basic aspects of various disabilities in order to help develop realistic accommodations that offset the impact of each disability

PHYSICAL DISABILITIES

Physical disabilities are more widely understood by prospective employers than sensory or cognitive disabilities because the physical effects of the disabilities may be seen and even experienced through simulations. Orthopedic handicaps, cerebral palsy, multiple sclerosis, and a variety of chronic medical conditions are considered physical disabilities. Although persons with physical disabilities are a heterogeneous population, they have some common characteristics that affect their ability to perform in the workplace. Many have limited mobility, dexterity and stamina, speech that is difficult to understand, and/or low levels of energy due to medications or the extra effort that is required to perform simple tasks. Some persons with physical disabilities may require special transportation to and from work, wheelchairs along with accessible office and building spaces, and even service dogs to fetch items. However, it is important to note that most persons with physical disabilities have average to above average intelligence and excellent academic and vocational skills and, in some cases, virtual workplaces may be the ideal workplace to help them avoid transportation issues.

Sensory Disabilities

Persons with sensory disabilities may be visually or hearing impaired. A small percentage of this population is both blind and deaf. Visual impairments range from low vision that cannot be ameliorated by corrective lenses to blindness. Persons with low vision are often able to perceive large objects and have some sense of spatial relationships, but do not have sufficient visual acuity to read or perceive small objects. On the other hand, persons who are blind cannot perceive objects or spatial relationships well enough to navigate spaces without assistance. They cannot use vision to read, write, learn, or work and may need assistance with self-care.

Hearing impairments are considered "invisible" disabilities, because there are no visual signs that a person may be deaf or hard of hearing. Persons who are hard of hearing have a restricted range of auditory acuity and clarity even with the use of a hearing aid and amplification, however,

may use mid-range sounds to perceive some auditory stimuli. They also have normal speech skills and use language that others can understand. Persons who are deaf cannot perceive auditory stimuli in any range and usually have speech patterns that are difficult to understand. As a result, they often use American Sign Language or writing to communicate.

Cognitive Disabilities

Cognitive disabilities represent the largest segment of persons with disabilities and include learning disabilities (LD), attention deficit/hyperactive disorder (ADHD), emotional impairments (EI), speech/language impairments (SLI), autism (AI), and mental retardation (MR). Persons with cognitive disabilities are also the most diverse disability category. For example, persons with LD, ADHD, EI, and SLI have average to above average intelligence and are often capable of gaining and applying advanced skills in a variety of vocational areas. However, they also may have social, emotional, and/or attention deficits that prevent them from appropriately interacting with co-workers and completing tasks in a timely manner. In contrast, persons with autism and mental retardation may have low intellectual functioning and lack the ability to gain and apply basic skills to problem-solving situations. They are best suited for repetitive tasks that involve assembling objects or materials.

VIRTUAL WORKPLACES FOR PERSONS WITH DISABILITIES

Douglas Kruse, a professor of human resources and the director of the program for disability research at Rutgers University, states that 7% of employed persons with disabilities work 20 hours or more a week from home (Tahmincioglu, 2003). He estimates that in 10 years, 10% of persons with disabilities will be telecommuting, and contends that with new technological advances and efforts to employ persons with disabilities the figure could reach 20% (Schur, Kruse, & Blanck, 2005). Tahmincioglu (2003) relates the story of an NBC network producer who's deteriorating health, due to muscular dystrophy, was accommodated by a partial in-office work week along with a couple of days of telecommuting. Clearly, many variations of the virtual workplace offer employment opportunities to persons with disabilities that did not exist a decade ago.

Virtual workplaces offer the greatest advantages to persons with physical and sensory disabilities. Through telecommuting, persons in these populations may have transportation issues related to poor mobility, communication problems related to poor receptive and/or expressive language and fatigue and self-care that may be related to their conditions. For example, persons with orthopedic disabilities usually need special transportation that is expensive and time-consuming; often taking triple the amount of time to travel from one place to another. The time saved in travel alone that may be devoted to the job at home represents a significant saving for both the employer and employee. Persons who are unable to hear or speak clearly, may use e-mail or instant message systems to communicate with co-workers and complete tasks, and, persons with chronic health conditions or limited mobility may be more comfortable taking rest breaks and handling personal care at home. In their home environments, persons with physical and sensory disabilities often have special equipment, a specially designed environment, and, in some cases, caregivers that facilitate their independence and ability to complete tasks in a more efficient and cost effective manner.

In the area of cognitive disabilities, persons with LD, EI, ADHD, and SLI seldom have mobility or health issues that prevent them from commuting to and from work, however, may be more productive in familiar environments with fewer distractions than those found in the traditional workplace (Hecker, L, Burns, Elkind, Elkind, and Katz, 2002; Rowland, 2004). Poor organizational skills, inability to sustain attention in noisy and fast

paced environments, and the usual interruptions found in traditional workplaces get persons with cognitive disabilities off-task and delay completion of tasks. Use of computers within structured and familiar environments that afford consistency and opportunities to work at a slower and more methodical pace improve their accuracy and task completion rates.

In contrast, telework poses the greatest challenges to persons with AI and MR. Some high-functioning persons with autism or retardation gain the academic skills needed to work in a language-based environment such as the Internet. Family members or caregivers in the home may be able to assist them with work-related tasks and, consequently, provide them with employment opportunities that would otherwise be beyond their skill levels. Low-functioning persons with autism and retardation often obtain jobs that require repetitive, manipulative skills in sheltered workshops. They may assemble simple parts, stuff envelopes, or pack boxes under the close supervision of numerous facilitators. Telework may provide them with the opportunity to work at home under the supervision of existing caregivers or parents who help them use Internet diagrams and telecasts that repeatedly demonstrate the correct procedures to complete tasks.

In spite of the advantages that virtual workplaces offer persons with disabilities, Baker, Ward, and Moon (2005) warn that social isolation may pose special problems for them. Persons with disabilities already have problems fitting into mainstream society and need opportunities to observe appropriate role models and practice social skills. The traditional workplace offers many opportunities for face-to-face interactions that may benefit their social growth and ability to gain and sustain the friendships and supportive relationships that well-rounded adults need. Baker et al. also suggest that the novelty of virtual workplaces poses administrative challenges to employers under ordinary circumstances and contend that most supervisors are struggling to manage non-disabled teleworkers. The special needs of persons with disabilities in the virtual workplaces may impose real or perceived supervision and evaluation problems that supervisors feel are beyond their capabilities. Supervisors and employers are also concerned that if they establish and enforce deadlines, task completion rates, and work standards, that persons with disabilities may file complaints or sue the company. In fact, most persons with disabilities want jobs, not lawsuits, and are no more likely to file employment complaints or lawsuits than their non-disabled colleagues (U.S. Department of Education, 2006). Also, most industrialized countries like the United States, Australia, and Great Britain have legislation that not only protects the rights of persons with disabilities, but also the interests of employers. And, a variety of agencies worldwide offer suggestions for developing practical accommodations.

GUIDELINES FOR DEVELOPING APPROPRIATE ACCOMMODATIONS

Accommodations for persons with disabilities involves modifying a job or the way in which a job is performed in order to give persons with disabilities opportunities to obtain and perform a job commensurate with their non-disabled peers. Accommodations should also give persons with disabilities access to the same "perks" that their co-workers enjoy such as access to employer-owned transportation, computers, cell phones, and so forth. In traditional workplaces, accommodations are often structural and/or ergonomic modifications that give employees with disabilities access to buildings, spaces, and equipment to enable them to perform jobs for which they would otherwise qualify without the disability. In virtual workplaces, accommodations usually involve modifications that give employees access to the information and communication tools needed to perform the job. Companies are responsible for all costs associated with the accommodations; however, the accommodations should not pose an undue hardship on the company and, in some cases, the company may file undue hardship claims to secure funding from rehabilitation agencies and/or the government. Also, persons with disabilities must posses the skills to meet the basic job qualifications required of employees without disabilities. For example, if a person with a visual impairment has the training, skills, and qualifications to be an accountant, but cannot read written text, then accommodations must be provided.

In developing accommodations, several factors should be considered. First, all functions that are needed to perform the job must be identified. Second, the employer must identify the job functions that the employee with disabilities cannot perform without accommodations. Third, the employee's strengths and capabilities pertaining to the job need to be identified. Fourth, the employer must identify reasonable accommodations or alternative functions that may be used to perform the tasks. If the employer or employee cannot identify reasonable accommodations, a rehabilitation specialist may be asked to serve in a consultative capacity. Finally, the employer should develop a method of monitoring the employee's job performance with the accommodation. The monitoring process may be incorporated into the existing employee's evaluation system or an independent assessment that focuses solely on the appropriateness of the accommodation within the context of the company's fiscal capabilities.

Accommodations for Specific Disabilities

The Alliance for Technology Access (ATA), a national network that advocates for the technological rights of persons with disabilities, asserts that all persons with disabilities are entitled the technology needed to foster independence, employment, and leisure activities. The Alliance advances four principles:

- People with disabilities have the right to maximum independence and participation in all environments, without barriers.

- Technology can be harnessed to diminish or eliminate environmental barriers for people with disabilities.
- People with disabilities have the right to control and direct their own choices, and the right to access the information they need in order to make informed decisions according to their goals and interests.
- People with disabilities have the right to employ assistive technologies, strategies for implementation, and necessary training support to maximize their independence and productivity (The Alliance for Technology Access, 2006).

Further, ATA contends that virtual workplaces should be available to all qualified persons with disabilities and may serve a dual purpose: providing equal access to employment while simultaneously accommodating some persons with disabilities. Fortunately, numerous high- and low-tech strategies and devices are available to help persons with a variety of disabilities.

Accommodating Physical Disabilities

Disabilities that limit mobility, involve spasticity, and cause fatigue and weakness require assistive technology and flexible deadlines that foster task completion and success in virtual workplaces. Working from home offers persons with physical disabilities the option to take frequent rest breaks as long as a traditional "9 to 5" work schedule is not required. As a result, employers may assign tasks and set deadlines that allow for a 7-day work week, instead of the traditional 5-day schedule. For example, Judy Johnson, a woman with lupus, rheumatoid arthritis, and a defective hip works as a secretary from home and states, "I can work part of the day, rest and go back to [work]," she says. "That way I can deal with my health." Working from home on a flexible schedule also allows persons with physical disabilities the opportunity to incorporate such things a personal care and physical therapy sessions into their day without interrupting their work schedule.

Persons with physical disabilities may also lack the manual dexterity to use the technology needed to complete jobs in virtual workplaces. Fine and gross motor skill deficits may limit their ability to perform tactile and kinesthetic tasks associated with virtual work environments. Assistive technology such as voice synthesizers, videoconferencing, and keyboards that help people type more quickly without much motor-visual control help compensate for limited fine motor skills. Electric page turners, headwands, and light pointers also help persons with limited manual dexterity to read independently. Prosthetic arms and hands with moveable joints help amputees handle the computer mouse or touchpad and even persons with quadriplegia can telecommute thanks to improved voice recognition and telephone systems.

Accommodating Sensory Disabilities

The needs of persons with visual or hearing impairments are often straightforward. For persons with low vision and blindness, talking pens are available to read words as the person either reads or writes text. Computer keyboards with large letters and monitors with magnified screens help persons with low vision type and read. Kurzweil Omni 3000 Reading System assists persons whose disabilities affect their reading by simultaneously reading text out loud and highlighting each spoken word on a computer display. Users may pause the system at any time and use its pull-down menus to gain instant access to the dictionary, thesaurus, grammar checks, and note taking. Users may also use the system's scanner, voice-output and recording capabilities to create books-on-tape. Braille keyboards and printers allow employees and employers to produce documents that the employ can read and use to perform the job. HumanWare's Maestro assistive technology for the blind and low vision is a portable efficient and reliable accessible PDA with a built-in voice synthesizer.

Persons with hearing impairments need devices that transform sound to visual modes. As a result, the computer is the ideal tool for them to use and virtual workplaces may seem ideally suited for them. However, collaboration among employees in the virtual workplace often involves phone calls and/or videoconferences. Telecommunications Device for the Deaf/TeleTYpewriter (TDD/TTY) telephone relays and closed-captioned television allow persons with hearing impairments to use everyday devices like the telephone and videoconferencing. For persons who are hard of hearing, a variety of amplification devices are available that attach to phones and computers.

Accommodating Cognitive Disabilities

Although most persons with cognitive disabilities have average intelligence, virtual workplaces may pose the greatest challenges to them. Visual or auditory processing problems often prevent them from recognizing words and numbers that they would otherwise understand. Poor organizational skills, problems with attention, and memory deficits affect all aspects of their lives. However, many accommodations have been researched and developed for this population. For all persons in this category, additional training and practice on job skills specific to a particular company are needed. They also benefit from multi-modal training that includes auditory and visual prompts, diagrams, and demonstrations. Web sites and searchable documents that include pictures and diagrams may be an ideal medium to post permanent information that serves as a reminder of job functions.

For persons with poor organizational and time management skills, online calendars, preset e-mail reminders, and networking that allow supervisors to check progress on the employee's computer help keep them on task. Instant messaging systems and scheduled phone conferences provide the employee with the opportunity to ask questions and clarify job assignments while the employer checks the employee's progress and accuracy. Studies have also shown that extended time to complete tasks increases accuracy and productivity for persons with cognitive disabilities (Gerber & Brown, 1997). And, since extended time is an accommodation for a disability, employers usually do not have to pay overtime wages.

The lack of basic reading, writing, and/or math skills common among persons with cognitive disabilities often makes employers reluctant to allow them to work in virtual environments or attempt accommodations for them. However, most persons with cognitive disabilities understand language and numbers at an age-appropriate level. As a result, screen readers, calculators, and voice synthesizers allow them to understand and use web- and text-based medium. Also, captions often help them understand audio tracks and consistent navigational structures help them navigate Web sites and templates needed to perform jobs (Gunderson & Jacobs, 2000; Samuelsson, Lundberg, & Herkner, 2004).

RESOURCES FOR EMPLOYERS

In hiring persons with disabilities, employers may access many sources of information to help them understand their legal obligations and a how to develop accommodations. The Internet contains many Web sites with a wealth of information. In the United States, the Jobs Accommodations Network at http://www.jan.wvu.edu/ contains a wealth of information and connects employers in the U.S. with rehabilitation specialist that help develop accommodations free of charge. The Canadian Web site, the Jobs Accommodations Services, at http://www.workink.com/display. asp?Page_ID=36&State_Province_Code=offers similar assistance to persons in Canada. Through these and similar Web sites, employers, worldwide, have access to information and ideas about employing persons with disabilities.

Although most accommodations cost employers less that $500, employers fear that they may become responsible for major equipment purchases or healthcare costs. However, in the countries like United States, Canada, Great Britian and Japan, public assistance funds pay for items such as wheelchairs, prosthetics, and even caregivers. Rehabilitation agencies often pay for equipment such as hearing aids, Braille printers, voice synthesizers, and screen readers. In fact, some screen readers are available as free downloads from sources such as ReadPlease at http://www.readplease.com, and services like TDD/TTY telephone relays are either free of charge or heavily subsidized. In many countries, employers may also file hardship claims to secure funds for accommodations that are too expensive for the company to afford.

CONCLUSION

Persons with disabilities are entitled to and capable of the same career options as their non-disabled counterparts and increasing numbers of them are taking advantage of virtual workplaces. Many expect their numbers in the telework arena to increase substantially. Employers need to understand the strengths and weaknesses of each specific disability category and the laws that govern their employment. They also need to understand basic accommodations that enable persons with various disabilities to perform job functions. Finally, assistance is available to employers as they strive to help persons with disabilities succeed in the workplace.

REFERENCES

The Alliance for Technology Access. (2006). *Principles*. Petaluma, CA. http://www.ataccess.org/about/principles.html.

The Americans with Disabilities Act. (1990). http://www.usdoj.gov/crt/ada/adahom1.htm.

Baker, P., Ward, A., & Moon, N. *Virtual exclusion and telework: The double-edged sword of techocentric workplace accommodation policy.* Paper presented at the Workplace Accommodations State of the Science Conference. Atlanta, GA. September, 2005.

Gerber, P., & Brown, D. (Eds.). (1997). *Learning disabilities and employment.* Austin, TX: PROED.

Great Britain: Department for Work and Pensions. (2005). *Disability Discrimination Act: Consultation Manual.* The Stationery Office. London.

Gunderson, J., & Jacobs, I. (2000). *User agent accessibility guidelines.* http://www.w3.org/TR/2002/REC-UAAG10-20021217.

Hecker, L., Burns, L., Elkind, J., Elkind, K., & Katz, L. (2002). Benefits of assistive reading software for students with attention disorders. *Annals of Dyslexia, 52,* 243-72.

Hendren, G., & Sacher, J. (1992). Employer agreement with the Americans with Disabilities Act of 1990: Implication for rehabilitation counseling. *The Journal of Rehabilitation, 58,* 481-408.

Heumann, J. (2004). *Disability and inclusive development: Sharing, learning, and building alliances.* Paper presented at the Second International Disability and Development Conference. Washington, D.C.

International Labour Organization. (2004-2005). World Employment Report 2004-05 Employment, Productivity and Poverty Reduction. Released 7 December 2004. http://www.ilo.org/public/english/employment/strat/wer2004.htm.

Noonan, B., Gallor, S., Hensel,-v McGinnis, N., Fassinger, R., Wang, S., & Goodman, J. (2004). Challenge and success: A qualitative study of the career development of highly achieving women with physical and sensory disabilities. *Journal of Counseling Psychology, 57,* 58-80.

Quinn, G., & Degener, T. (2002). *Human rights and disability: The current and future potential of United Nations human rights instruments in the context of disability*. United Nations Publications: New York and Geneva.

Rowland, C. (2004). *Cognitive disabilities. Part 2: Conceptualizing design considerations*. WEBAim. http://www.webaim.org/techniques/articles/conceptualize.

Samuelsson S., Lundberg I., & Herkner B. (2004) ADHD and reading disability in adult males. Is there a connection. *Journal of Learning Disabilities, 37*(2), 155-168.

Schur, L., Kruse, D., & Blanck, P. (2005). Corporate culture and the employment of people with disabilities. *Behavioral Sciences and the Law, 23,* 3-20.

Tahmincioglu, E. (2003). By telecommuting, the disabled get a key to the office and a job. New York Times, July 20, 2003.

United Nations. (2006). *Some facts about persons with disabilities*. Paper presented at the Convention on the Rights of Persons with Disabilities. August, 2006. United Nations Headquarters. New York, NY.

U.S. Department of Education, Office of Special Education and Rehabilitative Services. (2006). *Disability Employment 101*. Washington, D.C.: Author. Available at http:// www.ed.gov/about/offices/list/osers/products/employmentguide.

United States Equal Employment Opportunity Commission. (2002). *Work at home: Telework as a reasonable accommodation*. Fact Sheet. U.S. Printing Office. Washington, D.C.

KEY TERMS

Assistive Technology: Devices that compensate for loss of functioning in persons with disabilities.

Auditory Processing: The ability to perceive, comprehend, and appropriately act.

Braille Displays: Series of raised dots that indicate letters of the alphabet and enable persons with visual impairments to read print and computer screens.

Braille Printers: Printers that transform text into Braille and print documents that may be read by persons with visual impairments upon auditory stimuli.

Cognitive Disabilities: A disorder or condition that affects processing of information and prevents persons from comprehending and using concepts, ideas, and information.

Electromyographic (EMG) Controlled Prostheses: Computer-controlled signals that enable prosthetic devices like arms, hands, and so forth, to move more easily to increase the mobility of the user.

Independent Living Skills:. Basic skills such as self-care, learning and thinking that enable persons to participate in everyday activities.

Manual Dexterity: The ability to use hands, fingers, and toes to complete fine motor tasks.

Physical Disabilities: A physiological disorder or condition that limits a person's mobility, endurance, and/or ability to perform major life tasks.

Spasticity: Inability to control gross motor functions such as arm and leg movements.

Speechreaders: A screen reader is the commonly used name for voice output technology used. Screen readers are used to replace the visual display traditionally viewed on a monitor for those with visual disabilities. Hardware and software produce synthesized voice output for text displayed on the computer screen, as well as for keystrokes entered on the keyboard.

Telecommunications Device for the Deaf/ TeleTypewriter: A user terminal with keyboard input and printer or display output used by the hearing and speech impaired. The device contains a modem and is used over a standard analog phone line.

Section II
Education and Training for the Virtual Workplace

Chapter XVI
Using Cyberspace to Promote Transformative Learning Experiences and Consequently Democracy in the Workplace

William F. Ritke-Jones
Texas A&M University–Corpus Christi, USA

ABSTRACT

This chapter will explain transformative learning and its value and application to corporate training practices by promoting critical reflection on one's "frames of reference." This critical reflection can help one to challenge cultural and social assumptions, potentially leading the person to more democratic ways of thinking and behaving in the workplace. Cyberspace offers a unique and potentially powerful place to employ transformative learning practices, and along with explaining transformative learning, this chapter will explore how cyberspace can be used for this kind of learning. This chapter will also posit that new cyberspace environments such as Wiki's and Second Life hold tremendous promise as transformative learning spaces because they invite small group collaboration.

INTRODUCTION

Sopensky and Modrey (1995) "claim[ed] that in addition to technical communication abilities, technical communicators need procedural or 'how-to' knowledge of how to interact socially within their organizations in order to improve the quality of their written products" (cited in Hovde, 2002, p. 62), but as the workplace becomes more diverse and as corporations stretch into different cultures, social interaction becomes more of a

challenge. The problem would be less severe if everybody in the work place felt secure and as if their voices mattered, especially in collaborative work groups.

Unfortunately, democracy does not rule in the typical Western workplace, a workplace usually organized in a hierarchy; rather, often the ideas of the most powerful dominate because in hierarchal organizations where individuals compete for the recognition that will provide them with more power and money, those with status silence those without. Since people gain status by having their ideas gradually heard and accepted, new hires of the dominant culture may eventually attain a place of prestige, but those not of the dominant culture may never gain that place. When that happens, the corporation loses because valuable ideas and perspectives never get heard.

Hovde (2002) contended that technical communicators in this environment need to mount good, sound arguments in order to be heard, and Moore and Kreth (2005) posited that they need to practice political manipulation in order to survive and thrive. While good arguments could be made for each idea, the former assumes that everyone in the workplace can gain an audience, and the latter assumes that the workplace must be a competitive battlefield. However, no matter how sound one's argument, if nobody listens, the argument has no worth; thus, Hovde's idea may work for people in the dominant culture, but perhaps not for those who do not belong. Likewise, people of a non-empowered culture, race or gender would have a difficult time practicing political manipulation because they have no power at all. Besides, the more employees manipulate one another, the less desirable the workplace. Of these two ideas, Hovde's makes the only sense, but for her idea to work, the workplace must become democratic.

In a democratic environment, all voices have an equal opportunity to be heard. This environment lends itself to the practice of workplace rhetoric as Hovde (2002) apparently envisioned it. In order for this kind of environment to evolve in an organization, however, employees at all stations need to become more democratic minded, and that means that most will have to transform the way they see themselves and others in the workplace, especially those who are of a different race, culture or gender.

To effect these transformations, corporate training practices should include spaces where transformative learning can be fostered. Because of its unique characteristics and because so much collaboration occurs there now, cyberspace offers untapped potential as a place for transformative learning. In this chapter, I will provide an outline of transformative learning and how cyberspace can be an excellent tool for transformative learning within small workgroups and how these smaller transformations can engender transformation in the workplace culture. I will also illustrate how transformative learning strategies could have been applied to two online groups in an effort to show how these strategies could be applied in corporate training practices. Finally, I will propose ideas for fostering transformative learning with wikis, blogs and virtual meeting software as well as with technologies that are on the horizon.

BACKGROUND

Workplace Culture

American workplace culture tends to reflect the European descended, phallogocentric hegemony of American society. While certainly true that white men in junior positions do not have a strong voice in the typical workplace, evidence that women, African and Hispanic Americans, and those from other cultures have even weaker voices certainly exists. For example, stories by Alina Rutten, Steven Jong, and Beth Lee in *Writing a Professional Life* (Savage & Sullivan, 2000) depict the struggles of two women and a Chinese-American as they negotiate the political terrain of three different organizations. Certainly, a young white man starting a new job would have to learn the political landscape just as these three people did, but arguably, the young white man would have enjoyed some status which two white women and a Chinese-American did not.

Writing groups in the workplace often structure themselves in a hierarchy that mirrors this hegemony (Ede & Lunsford, 1991). Studies show that these groups lack the kind of profound creativity that more democratic groups enjoy because members de-voiced due to their lack of status cannot safely express the "feelings, thoughts and questions" necessary for fecund collaborative thought (Morgan & Murray, 1991, p. 71; see also Goddard, 1985; Jones & White, 1985; Souder, 1987; Tjosvold, 1992; Hare & Davis, 1994; Nicotera, 1997; Haslett, 1999; Poole et al., 1999). Never forming the group consciousness that a collaborative group must have (Fischer, 1980; Mabry, 1999; Cross, 2000), these groups generally fall under the direction—or the dictatorship—of one person in the group. Many times these groups produce acceptable products when the rest of the group yields to the one claiming power, but advocates of democratic collaboration would argue that these products are never as good as they could have been if they had been produced by a democratic group. Even if an acceptable product is produced, however, stifled voices create resentment, hurt feelings, and distrust besides costing money and efficiency (Locker, 1992; Cross, 1994; 2001).

Moore and Kreth (2005) offered one way for stifled voices to get heard: "[manipulate] people, events, objects, rules, and the like so that you can get what you want" (p. 307). Not addressing work groups specifically but certainly implicating them, they used terminology reminiscent of war and the competitive "win-at-all-costs" mentality of the current world market place throughout their article, in one instance stating that "we must structure the world so we can win" (p. 303). Clearly, technical communicators as well as all other corporate employees need communicative skills as well as procedural skills, as Moore and Kreth asserted (p. 303), and certainly employees need to skillfully maneuver around "hostile or uncooperative coworkers" (p. 313). Yet the corporate environment as war zone assures that only those trained in war—and who enjoy war—will be heard, leaving a wealth of ideas from the marginalized in the garbage bin.

Although Moore and Kreth would likely criticize her thought as "utopian," Lay (1989) mapped out a much different, more democratic approach to collaboration in the workplace. Instead of lead-ing to political manipulation and hostility, Lay posited that "when collaborators discuss critically all possible approaches to a problem, they often find the best solution" (p. 5), but in a competitive model where all but the strongest voice is heard, only one solution prevails, the one espoused by the strongest person in the group. Besides finding the best solution to a problem, democratic collaborators reap many other benefits, such as increased collegiality and greater job satisfaction (Ede & Lunsford, 1991, p. 64). One could reasonably argue that happy employees, versus those that must constantly be on guard, are more productive and creative.

PERSPECTIVE TRANSFORMATION

Argyris and Schon (1974) marked competitive work groups in which most voices are stifled as those adhering to "Model I" behavior. In Model I, the participant with the most power seeks to "[control] others and prevent him/herself from being influenced by others." Other participants may become defensive and protective and become more concerned with winning or losing than with collaboration (p. 73). Moreover, those in subordinate positions become relegated to menial tasks. Interestingly, as "Jim" illustrated in Locker's (1992) study, those who seek to gain power over others or believe the ideas of others to be inferior often do not realize their behavior. Their "espoused theories-of-action," the values by which they believe they live, conflict with their "theories-in-use," the true assumptions that they hold about themselves, others, their environment, their workplace and so on (Argyris & Schon, 1974, pp. 6-7). For instance, Jim believed that "his ability to listen [was] one of the strengths of his 'management style.' But the other members assigned to the case felt shut out" (Locker, 1992, p. 47). That Jim could not see what others saw indicates an "espoused theory-of-action" that was in conflict with his "theory-in-use."

Jim seemed to be acting out Model I behavior, and if the leaders of an organization act according to Model I behavior, then the organization itself may well be Model I because "organizational cultures are created by leaders" (Shein, 1991, p. 2). About Model I people and organizations, Argyris and Schon remark that "Model I leads to a kind of hybrid world—a pre-civilized, competitive, hostile, defensive, win/lose world onto which the supposedly civilizing safety valves of repression, containment, and deviousness have been grafted" (p. 81). They contrast this kind of behavior with Model II behavior. People—and organizations—acting according to Model II behavior are:

minimally defensive and open to learning, as facilitators, collaborators, and people who hold their theories-in-use firmly... but are equally committed to having them confronted and tested. Defensiveness in interpersonal and group relationships will tend to decrease, and people will tend to help others, have more open discussions, exhibit reciprocity, and feel free to explore different views and express risky ideas. (p. 91)

But Model II behavior usually does not just happen. To attain a personality that exhibits Model II behavior, a person must examine her/his theories-in-use, and in order to do so, that person must not commit to "self-sealing processes" (Argyris & Schon, 1974, p. 76), defined as behavior in which no examination of theories-in-use occurs and which result in the person reinforcing prejudices, bigotries and other negatives by perceiving events to be fulfilling his/her beliefs.

Fundamentally, Model II behavior results from a mind that has become free from its own assumptions, and Argyris and Schon offer some useful suggestions for developing it. However, Mezirow's theory of Transformative Learning provides a more in-depth exploration of how to develop a liberated mind, although his theory has some limitations. Mezirow (2000) defined transformative learning as:

the process by which we transform our taken-for-granted frames of reference (meaning perspectives, habits of mind, mind-sets) to make them more inclusive, discriminating, open, emotionally capable of change, and reflective so that they may generate beliefs and opinions that will prove more true or justified to guide action. (p. 8)

In Mezirow's (2000) definition, frames of reference sound much like Argyris and Schon's "espoused theories-of-action" because he defines a frame of reference as a:

'meaning perspective,' the structure of assumptions and expectations through which we filter sense impressions... Frames of reference are the results of ways of interpreting experience... Many of our most guarded beliefs about ourselves and our world—that we are smart or dumb, good or bad, winners or losers—are inferred from repetitive affective experience outside of awareness. (p. 16)

Thus, when we engage in an encounter, we interpret the encounter and decide how to act within it by drawing on our "frames of reference," usually not being conscious of why we have interpreted the situation as we have.

A person has a perspective transformation when he becomes "critically reflective of [her/his] assumptions and aware of their context—the source, nature, and consequences of taken-for-granted beliefs" (Mezirow, 2001, p. 19). To be more exact, transformative learning can occur when a person engages in a critical reflection of previously held assumptions, values and beliefs that seem to no longer be valid. Sometimes happening as an epoch event but more often incrementally, Mezirow as paraphrased by Cranton (2001) described the critical reflection necessary for "precipitating transformation" as a process by which "uncritically assimilated assumptions about oneself and one's world" are "surfaced and challenged" (p. 231). Thus, in the workplace, the outcome of people having perspective transformations could be an environment where "respect for others, self-respect, willingness to accept responsibility for the common good, willingness to welcome diversity and [willingness] to approach others with openness" (Cranton, 2001, p. 231) would prevail.

CHAPTER FOCUS

The collaborative work group offers fertile territory for transformative learning. By providing a project for the group to complete, the group can be encouraged to engage in a critical reflection of how they interact by keeping journals, having evaluative discussions of their interactions, and so forth. By paying more attention to the process of completing the project than on its actual completion, group members may begin a critical reflection of how their actions in the group may be impeding the group's creativity or even their social cohesion.

The Limitations of Transformative Learning in the Workplace

Particularly for people in authority, some group members not wanting to participate pose the greatest challenge to promoting a transformative learning group in the workplace. Trained to be task-focused and to independently operate in a hierarchy by a patriarchal culture, some people may resist because of the time needed and what they may consider the "touchy-feely" nature of transformative learning. Even worse, some people may "believe their way of being in the world is the only way or the best way [and] it is very difficult for them to see alternative perspectives or to engage in reflective discourse" (Cranton, 2001, p. 196). For instance, "Jim" in Locker's study (1992) fits the description of one incapable or unwilling

to consider the perspectives of the other people in his group, or even people in a position over his. For "Jim" and others, the prospect of challenging their own assumptions and values may be too much of "an intensely threatening [emotional] experience" (Mezirow, 2001, p. 6) because they provide the means by which people make sense of their worlds. Also, because American and other cultures prize the strong, conquering individual, some people may unconsciously fear de-individuation within the group and a subsequent loss of voice. This fear may create significant tension within a transformative group (Smith, 2005, p. 185).

Since Mezirow applied his theory only to the American culture, transformative learning theory may not work as well in cultures where the collective is valued over the individual. Before a transformative group is formed, or at least before the group begins their project, some cross-cultural training may be in order. This training may take the form of high-context cultures such as the Japanese, the Chinese and the Korean learning that more task-focused Americans are not being rude when they dispense with relationship building communication in lieu of being direct and concise and low-context cultures like the American learning that their Confucian culture counterparts have clear motivations for spending so much time on other subjects before they seem to get to the one immediately at hand.

Training such as this could clear the way for transformative experiences in which people from different cultures "[alter their] perspective to effectively understand" people from other cultures (Taylor, 1994, p. 156). To explain how this type of transformation may occur, Bennett (1992) as paraphrased by Kasl and Elias (2001) "suggests that growth in capacity to empathize and experiment with different cultural lenses is a developmental trajectory that moves from ethnocentrism... to ethnorelativism." Within ethnorelativism, he argues that the final stage of development is the integration of "'disparate parts of one's identity into a new whole'" (p. 232).

Besides these issues, to undergo a transformative learning experience requires emotional maturity—awareness, empathy, and control—what Golemen (1998) calls 'emotional intelligence'—knowing and managing one's emotions, motivating oneself, recognizing emotions in others and handling relationships—as well as clear thinking" (Mezirow, 2001, p. 11).

Drawing from Belenky, Clinchy, Goldberger, and Tarule's (1996) description of the "Connected Knower", Belenky and Stanton offer a similar notion to Mezirow's. They (2001) propose that "the more Connected Knowers disagree with another person the harder they will try to understand how that person could imagine such a thing, using empathy, imagination, and storytelling as tools for entering into another's frame of mind" (p. 87).

People engaged in a transformative learning project in the workplace especially need these skills because rarely do the participants in a workgroup enjoy equal power. Thus, those with greater power would need the emotional maturity to allow those with lesser power to have a voice. In fact, Belenky and Stanton's (2001) major issue with Mezirow's theory is that to allow people of lesser power to engage in the reflective discourse necessary for transformative learning to occur "requires the creation of an extremely safe and caring community where people draw each other out and listen to one another with the greatest of care" (p. 83), and as work mentioned elsewhere in this chapter shows, a truly safe, democratic workgroup in any organization is likely very rare.

How Computer-Mediated Communication Can Overcome Limitations

The nature of Computer-Mediated Communication may offer some ways to overcome these limitations and to facilitate transformative learning in corporate and academic workgroups. As some scholars have noted (Lea & Spears, 1992;

Selfe & Selfe, 1994; Pagnucci & Mauriello, 1999; Hum, 2002; Smith, 2005; Jones, 2007), the online environment does not extinguish gender, racial and cultural biases. That these biases are not extinguished, however, is a good thing because asynchronous communication especially makes it easier to archive, confront, and reflect on assumptions and biases as they act to thwart the group's efforts. Thus, for a person who is committed to her or his personal growth and to the success of a collaborative enterprise, CMC provides an outstanding tool for transformative learning.

To effect the perspective transformation that decides whether transformative learning has occurred, Mezirow (2001) stated that the first necessary step is a "disorienting dilemma." A disorienting dilemma occurs when a person realizes that his or her frames of reference are not making her/him successful in the present communicative situation. This occurrence may happen as an epochal event or, more likely, as the consequence of repeatedly bumping into situations where one's normal way of doing things does not work. In an online environment, these "bumps" are easier to see while engaged in collaborative work because communication is in archived print. Moreover, if a person's communication strategies during collaboration display negative assumptions about another person's race, culture, gender or status, the distance that cyberspace affords may make it easier for the offended party or the facilitator to bring the offensive behavior to the attention of the person exhibiting the offensive behavior. This person then has the opportunity to critically reflect on his frames of reference in reflective discourse with the other members of her or his group.

Silent people who do not speak because they unconsciously feel inferior or disempowered may also have more of an opportunity to critically reflect on their assumptions about themselves and their culture in the online environment. When a skilled facilitator confronts a silent person, the facilitator may interview the silent person in a way that will bring feelings of inferiority because of race, gender or culture to the surface. At that point, the facilitator could bring the matter to the group for discussion. This discussion could effect a perspective transformation in the silent person and in people who belong to groups that silence others.

This kind of dialogue requires a safe environment, and people confronting one another on perceived biases also need a safe environment, although an environment as safe as the one described by Belenky and Stanton (2001) may not be necessary. Nevertheless, cyberspace does democratize a workgroup to an extent because at the least a participant can speak without being interrupted in asynchronous discussions. Hawisher and Moran (1993) go further when they argue that e-mail can reduce one's sensitivity to another's status (p. 634), and that argument can be extended to sensitivity about one's gender, race or culture. This reduction in sensitivity flattens the hierarchy somewhat and promotes a "greater equality of participation in CMC groups" (Cross, 2001, p. 206). This characteristic of online groups could provide a safe enough place for transformative learning.

Another characteristic that can be used to foster transformative learning online, St. Amant noticed a "plastic" identity in people working online, and Turkle (1995) argued that one could be whatever she/he wanted to be online. Since a primary goal of transformative learning is empathy, taking on the identity of an online group mate during critical discourse could help that person see things from the other's perspective. Having made the attempt, the person taking on the identity could write a narrative about what it is like to be that person and bring it to the rest of the group. Especially during conflict, this tool could be powerful in effecting transformative learning.

Since communications can be archived, group members have the opportunity to reflect on their collaborative behavior as well as that of their group mates. This reflection could lead to criti-

cal reflection, but not necessarily so. A strategy that could be more effective would be to have people from outside the group and who are perhaps not associated with the class or corporation study the discourse and bring their findings to the group. Discussion should be held online to provide safety.

How Transformative Learning Can be Facilitated Online

Before transformative learning can be facilitated anywhere, the facilitator and the participants must be willing and able to engage in this kind of learning. The participants must possess the emotional intelligence mentioned previously, and Merriam (2004) asserted that transformative learning "mandates an advanced level of cognitive development" (p. 61). The facilitator must possess these qualities as well and should be thoroughly familiar with the principles of transformative learning. Moreover, s/he should have experienced a transformative event and should also be skilled in facilitating collaborative groups in online environments.

A group created to foster transformative learning should address some problem that will be solved collaboratively or some project that will be created collaboratively. Ideally, the completion of the project would be something important to corporate interests. The group will go through the stages of group development as they collaborate on the project, a primary goal being the development of social cohesion so that the members will trust one another enough to make personal disclosures. As Jones (2007) shows, however, the development of social cohesion in online groups has some unique challenges, but these challenges can be met with skillful facilitation (see also Palloff and Pratt, 1999). If the group members have bought into the idea of transformative learning, the task of facilitating them will be much easier.

As the group collaborates on a project, they will have conflicts. The facilitator should encourage the expression of disagreement because it is here that conflict may engender the "disorienting dilemma" that could lead to self-examination and "a critical assessment of assumptions" that are the first three phases of perspective transformation (Mezirow, 2001, p. 22). This could happen as the group negotiates a resolution to the conflict. This negotiation can occur if the group is operating democratically, and the group can operate more democratically in cyberspace, especially if all of the group members have committed to the process.

HOW TRANSFORMATIVE LEARNING COULD HAVE BEEN FOSTERED IN TWO ONLINE GROUPS

To illustrate how transformative learning could work in cyberspace, I will examine two collaborative groups where a facilitator could have seized an opportunity for transformative learning and offer suggestions for what could have been done. Both of these groups were in a course that was conducted solely on the distance learning platform, Blackboard©.

The course in which the two groups were enrolled required the collaborative creation of a manual outlining a process by which a government's education department could help its citizens reach a literacy level that would allow them to fully participate in the world marketplace. While in neither a corporate environment nor in a technical writing course, all of the people in the two groups were working adults between the ages of 25 and 35. Thus, only a short leap would have to be made to apply the ideas here to an upper or graduate level technical writing course or to a corporate course.

Group One

Group one consisted of three females, two white Americans and one Brazilian. These women were 25, 28 and 32, respectively. Their pseudonyms are Martha, Elizabeth, and Victoria. All were highly motivated to attend school, and they all expressed commitment to the collaborative task.

This group encountered a grave conflict during the collaborative process because of their different backgrounds. This conflict caused the group to shatter but could have been used to promote transformative learning. The conflict began because, rather than writing the process manual for which the assignment called, Victoria tried to steer the group towards a more abstract conception of cultural oppression. To accomplish this task, Victoria insisted that the group use Paulo Freire's work as a foundation, remarking in one of her first communications:

One of the things that I would like to explore in this paper are some of the cultural. contexts that would be necessary in other (sic) to deal with literacy. For example you could have a quick ass (sic) manual but if the contents are not meaningful to those who use it, or cultural (sic) sensitive to their needs and where they are at, it will not fly

Later, quoting Freire, Victoria tried to move the essay towards a much more abstract construction than was appropriate for the process manual that the assignment required:

literacy is an active phenomenon, deeply linked to personal and cultural identity' which means that his concept of literacy moves beyond the strict decoding and reproducing of language into issues of economics, health and sustainable development

In response to Victoria's attempt to push the group towards this idea, Elizabeth said: "i (sic) think that [Victoria's idea] is a little deep for beginning literacy. It [basic literacy] is memorizing words and letters to begin with, but I guess some of them can read." Martha tried to bring the discussion back to a more concrete and practical conception of the essay: "letting the people teach the people [literate natives teaching non-literate ones] and in the grassroots development, not only teaching people to read and etc but vocational skills like building and healthcare." Trying to avoid conflict, Martha offered to use the Freirean quotation as a way to begin the essay, but it was too much for Elizabeth and not enough for Victoria.

The culminating moment for this conflict occurred when Victoria attempted to manipulate the posting of her essay instead of the one that the other two women had largely written because, in essence, Victoria had been ostracized from the group. This final event resulted in many angry words being exchanged on the discussion board, Elizabeth accusing Victoria of being crazy and Victoria angrily protesting against what she perceived as cultural insensitivity.

Instead of being the moment that splintered the group, this event could have precipitated a "disorienting dilemma" for all three of these women if the facilitator had managed it properly. Apparently, Paulo Freire was an extremely important national icon for Victoria whose work she wanted to share with the Americans. Showing off Freire as her countryman may also have had an equalizing effect for Victoria because she seemed to exhibit signs of feeling culturally oppressed. That the other two women appeared lukewarm to her attempts to make Freire the foundation of their manual likely created the resentment and hostility that Victoria showed at the last meeting.

Fortunately, the collaboration occurred in cyberspace because Victoria probably felt freer to express her anger there than she would have in a physical space, and her anger as well as that of the other women could have been the precipitating emotion to perspective transformation. To achieve that goal, the facilitator of the group may have opted to do a number of things, the first one

being to intercede and to ask the three women to participate in efforts to more fully understand each other.

The two American women were not familiar with Paulo Freire and his work, so the facilitator may have begun by asking Victoria to write a short report on Freire and to explain to the two Americans why his work is so important to her. Asking the two Americans to do some research on Freire may have been in order, as well. Of even greater importance, the facilitator could have then asked Victoria to explain how she felt when the other two women rejected her ideas, and the two Americans could have been asked to explain to Victoria why they felt manipulated by her. These promptings could have led to deep discussion with the facilitator carefully mediating.

The distance provided by cyberspace would have made these discussions more fruitful because the women would have been less reluctant to be truthful with one another. Truthful disclosures and discussion could have led to a "disorienting dilemma" for all three women. For instance, Victoria could have discovered that she felt oppressed by the Americans and could also have discovered that she was projecting her resentment for her feelings of oppression onto them. This discovery could have led to her critical reflection of her assumptions about Americans. As for Martha and Elizabeth, they could have learned about another culture, and this new knowledge could have begun their movement from ethnocentrism to ethnorelativism.

To make this transformative learning experience deeper, the two American women could have assumed the identity of Victoria and written a personal narrative from her perspective about the group's conflict, and Victoria could have done the same thing from the perspective of Elizabeth because it was she who accused Victoria of being crazy. These narratives could then be posted on the discussion board for discussion, with the person composing the narrative staying in character. While this kind of experiment could be done in a physical space, the online environment makes it easier to assume a new identity and have others believe it.

Group Two

Group two consisted of four people: a 33-year-old Caucasian woman; an African-American woman of 32; a 29-year-old Caucasian woman and a Caucasian male of 25. The pseudonyms for these people are Elizabeth, Donna, Susan and John, respectively. Of the four, the Caucasian woman, Elizabeth, had the most writing skill and seemed the most motivated. She took charge of coordinating the group's efforts, but her superior writing and thinking skills seemed to intimidate the others. The African-American woman, Donna, was also motivated but lacked confidence in her writing skills and in her ability to contribute anything meaningful to the group. The other Caucasian woman, Susan, was engaged in the collaborative project, but she felt intimidated by Elizabeth and left the group. The male, John, wanted to take control of the group, but Elizabeth's strength and maturity prevented it.

Except for Elizabeth, all of the members of this group were silent but for very different reasons. Susan, for instance, apparently went silent because she felt as if her ideas were not as good as Elizabeth's. Her feelings are illustrated by an event in which she expressed ideas that Elizabeth argued against. Elizabeth's argument was not done in a way that should have silenced Susan. In fact, the disagreement could have led to creative conflict. After Susan made a case analyzing the political stability of the country chosen for the manual, Elizabeth said:

The political stability of the country that we chose was important to me as well, otherwise there could be all sorts of barriers to implementation of the program—however, I think this quality may only be relevant to the initial choice of the country & not to the process manual itself. I think this is

what Prof. Jones was getting at. I'm not sure that we have to discuss Kenya much because Kenyans are our audience.

After making this remark, Susan left the class, very effectively silencing herself.

Donna fell silent for a different reason; she felt that her ideas were not valued by the group because she was black, although transcripts do not suggest it. Still, her perception was real and may have been deeply rooted in her being a part of the historically marginalized and disempowered African-American race. Illustrating how she felt in the group, Donna said in my interview with her that she "[didn't] think any of the work or research I did was used at all... which made me feel kind of bad," but in fact her work had been used. For instance, her contributions to an early exercise made the group's completion of the assignment possible. Elizabeth commented to her that:

I think you did a very good job. You gave each sentence clear direction & room to expand into supporting points without being too bold or argumentative (sic). You gave me direction as well. At first glance I wasn't really sure what to do with this assignment. Thanks.

Yet Donna's self-esteem did not increase, proving that her assumptions about herself were much stronger than anything anyone else could say to her.

John remained silent because he wanted to be in control of the group. On an exit survey that he completed, he stated "I admit it was hard and still is hard for me to make compromises. I think I work best if I am the leader (dictator) or if someone assigns me specific work to get done." Clearly, John wanted to work in a hierarchal, male-dominated system. While this evidence alone does not indicate sexism, the fact that he refused to collaborate with the women in the group and tried to dominate the group with his ideas strongly suggests it. When he could not have his way, he detached himself from the group. His detachment may have been the product of his fear of de-individuation, that fear being more pronounced because American culture teaches boys especially to compete and to dominate as individuals.

John, Susan and Donna may not have had the emotional intelligence to engage in transformative learning. Nevertheless, John's and Donna's situation can be used to illustrate how transformative learning can be used to effect perspective transformation in relation to racial and gender issues. As an African-American female, Donna has been trained by American culture to see herself as "less than," and it is necessary for her to achieve a perspective transformation about herself before she can gain her voice. Thus, a skilled facilitator would suspect that her silence may be originating from her feelings of inferiority, as evidenced by her satisfactory work otherwise, and perhaps ask her to adopt the persona of a white person, even a white male, in the online environment.

Assuming this identity may help her to find power that she did not know she had. Finding this power could be a disorienting dilemma that would then lead her to a critical reflection of the assumptions she holds about herself and her race. Concomitantly, others in the group could assume the identity of black females and perhaps create narratives about being a black female that could be posted on the discussion board for discussion. These discussions may lead to a critical reflection of the assumption held by many white people that the oppression of blacks is a myth.

In John's case, a thorough review of the archived collaborations would irrefutably prove that he had not engaged in a democratic collaboration with his group mates and that he had not treated them with respect, especially Elizabeth. While he could deny it, if he were confronted again and again with this kind of behavior in future collaborations, he may eventually have to confront his own cultural indoctrination as an American male and begin the process of perspective transformation.

FUTURE TRENDS

Transformative Learning in New Workplace Technologies

The collaborations of these two groups occurred in a university setting using technology that universities typically use for distance education courses but which corporations do not usually employ. This technology automatically archives threaded discussions, providing an instant way to see who made a statement and what responses it evoked. Additionally, archives can be collected and printed, and chats can be archived, as well. These features make it easy to study communicative events. Moreover, this technology resembles the asynchronous discussion boards, list servs and e-mail that organizations have used for many years to facilitate collaboration among employees; thus, applying principles learned on a distance education platform would transfer well to technologies traditionally used by organizations.

In recent years, however, new technologies such as wikis and blogs have proliferated as corporate collaboration tools. Used with the asynchronous discussion provided by a blog and/or with the synchronous discussion of chat provided by virtual meeting software or telephone, a wiki provides an outstanding tool for collaboration because all members of a group can instantly see what changes are being made to a project (for excellent material on using these new tools for virtual collaboration, see Brown, Huettner, & James-Tanny, 2007).

For the purposes of transformative learning opportunities, wikis used in the thread mode allow for reflection on why changes were made, who made the changes and how those changes may conflict with someone else's vision. Used in conjunction with a wiki, a blog can be invaluable because it displays the presentation and discussion of ideas so that the evolution of a discussion can be readily seen. As easily as distance education platforms, these technologies used together, then, along with virtual meeting software, can reveal silenced voices and biased perspectives created by power differentials.

Potential of Developing Technologies for Transformative Learning

When online communications reveal power differentials, corporate trainers and consultants could elect to use Moodle, an open source distance education platform that incorporates asynchronous threaded discussion as well as having a built-in wiki and Second Life, a virtual, 3-D reality. Moodle could allow for the asynchronous development of social cohesion as employees collaborated on projects on the wiki. Meanwhile, employees could create identities and spaces in Second Life with which other employees could come into contact. For instance, since Second Life allows for the creation of buildings, clothes, furniture and most any other object, employees could create spaces that reflect their personal cultures and social groups. Others entering the space could then learn something about being that person.

As employees collaborate on Moodle and conflicts develop that reveal power differentials, they could be referred to the Second Life environment where they would try to work through the differences by developing empathy and understanding for one another. The distance, consequently safety, provided by Second Life may allow for more intimate disclosures about each person's perspective, thus giving each person the opportunity to know the other in deeper ways. Also, this environment would allow employers to easily adopt the identities of others. It could be reasonably asserted that adopting the persona of the other, perhaps with coaching by the person whose identity has been adopted, would result in fuller democratic habits of mind. For instance, in the case of group one, if Gertrude had adopted Victoria's persona and Victoria had adopted Gertrude's, a richer and

more complete mental representation of each other may have emerged that would have resulted in a healthier democratic workgroup.

The developers of Second Life have proposed a system in which Moodle would be integrated with Second Life, something that they have named "Sloodle" (Kemp & Livingstone, 2007). In this new system, 2-D pages in Moodle would automatically become 3-D objects in Second Life, for instance, "RSS feeds appear in the form of radios or teletype machines" (Kemp & Livingstone 2007, p. 17) in Second Life. These tools promise great things for all kinds of learning, but especially for transformative learning, after challenges such as a steep learning curve for learning how to create and the need for fast computers and graphics cards have been met.

Regardless of the learning space, however, students involved in these learning experiences may develop the critical reflection skills necessary for perspective transformation to occur. Employees will not practice these skills only in limited environments created to foster critical reflection and perspective transformation; they will also take these skills with them into all of their collaborations, in cyberspace and in physical space. Moreover, as critical reflection is practiced on a personal employee level, the nature of the workplace in general may evolve into a more democratic environment.

CALL FOR RESEARCH

At this point, the use of cyberspace as a corporate transformative learning tool is an idea based on sound theories, but it remains only an idea without primary research. In addition to researching personal transformative learning, research should be done to measure how transformative learning in corporate workgroups educates the entire corporate organization. Yorks and Marsick (2001) cited Watkins and Marsick's (1993) "[assertion] that 'teams, groups, and networks can become the medium for moving new knowledge throughout the learning organization' and that such collaborative structures 'enhance the organization's ability to learn because they offer avenues for exchange of new ways of working'" (p. 254). If this assertion is correct, then an organization itself may experience transformative learning, adopting the same democratic habits of mind that the individual worker has.

Because transformative learning projects would take time and money, research also needs to be done to determine if it enhances the health and vitality of an organization by helping to foster the personal development of its employees. It is reasonable to speculate that employees who like themselves and each other would be happier and more productive employees, but top level managers need more than speculation to approve the expenditure of time and money on projects. Once one corporation has success, however, others will likely see the benefit of morphing to a more democratic and collaborative corporate culture.

CONCLUSION

This chapter has explained transformative learning and how it can help people and organizations develop more democratic ways of thinking. The development of democratic ways of thinking will result in more inclusive organizations where diverse voices are heard and invited. With more voices being heard, employees will solve problems more creatively, thus increasing productivity and the value of products. An equal benefit, democratic organizations enjoy an atmosphere that thrives on collaboration and camaraderie rather than on competition and manipulation. Arguably, such an atmosphere will result in happy employees who work hard and joyfully.

This chapter has also argued that cyberspace offers great, untapped potential as a space where transformative learning can be fostered. I have shown how transformative learning could have been fostered in two online collaborative groups using distance education platforms and how these principles could be applied to newer technologies, such as wikis and blogs. Finally, I have shown how technologies currently being developed may have outstanding capabilities as transformative learning spaces.

Many western corporations focus on short-term gains rather than on the long-term health of the organization, and that focus poses the greatest challenge to transformative learning in the workplace. Thus far, corporations may not have seen transformative learning as a valuable endeavor because of the time it would take and because such learning does not seem to be immediately applicable to job performance. Indeed, transformative learning belongs to a more soft skills, process-focused domain than the highly charged, product-oriented focus of most corporations. As organizations increasingly become less white male and more diverse, however, they will need tools to foster the social health of their employees; otherwise, work will not get done or will not get done well. Transformative learning may then become the most powerful tool at an organization's disposal.

REFERENCES

Belenky, M., Clinchy, B., Goldberger, N., & Tarule, J. (1996). *Women's ways of knowing: The development of self, voice, and mind* (2nd ed.). New York, NY: Basic Books.

Belenky, M., & Stanton, A. (2001). Inequality, development, and connected knowing. In: J. Mezirow and Associates (Ed.), *Learning as transformation: Critical perspectives on a theory in progress* (pp. 71-102). San Francisco, CA: Jossey-Bass.

Bennet, M. (1992). Toward ethnorelativism: Developmental model of intercultural Sensitivity. In: R. Paige (Ed.), *Education for the intercultural experience.* Yarmouth, ME: Intercultural Press.

Brown, M., Huettner, B., & James-Tanny, C. (2007). *Managing virtual teams: Getting the most from wikis, blogs and other collaborative tools.* Plano, TX: Wordware Publishing.

Cranton, P. (2001). Individual differences and transformative learning. In: J. Mezirow and Associates (Ed.), *Learning as transformation: Critical perspectives on a theory in progress* (pp. 181-204). San Francisco, CA Jossey-Bass.

Cross, G. (1994). *Collaboration and conflict.* Cresskill, NJ: Hamton Press.

Cross, G. (2000). *Forming the collective mind.* Cresskill, NJ: Hampton Press.

Ede, L., & Lunsford, A. (1990). *Singular texts: Plural authors.* Carbondale, IL: Southern Illinois University Press.

Fischer, B. (1980). *Small group decision making* (2nd ed.). New York, NY: McGraw Hill.

Goddard, R. (1985). Bringing new ideas to light. *Management World, 14,* 8-11.

Goleman, D. (1995). *Emotional intelligence: Why it can matter more than IQ.* New York, NY: Bantam.

Hare, A., & Davies, M. (1994). Social Iiteraction. In:A. Hare, H. Blumberg, M. Davies, & M. Kent (Eds.), *Small group research: A handbook* (pp. 164-193). Norwood, NJ: Ablex.

Haslett, B., & Ruebush, J. (1999). What differences do individual differences in groups make? The effects of individuals, culture, and group composition. In: L. Frey (Ed.), *The handbook of group communication theory and practice* (pp. 115-138). Thousand Oaks, CA: Sage.

Hawisher, G., & Moran, C. (1993). Electronic mail and the writing instructor. *College English, 55*(6), 627-643.

Hum, S. (2002). Performing gendered identities: A small-group collaboration in a computer-mediated classroom interaction. *Journal of Curriculum Theorizing.*

Jones, R., & White, C. (1985). Relationships among personality, conflict resolution styles and task effectiveness. *Group and organization studies, 10,* 152-167.

Jones, W. (2007). Why they don't work: Factors that impede the development of social cohesion in online collaborative groups. *Pennsylvania association of adult and community educators journal of lifelong learning, 16.*

Kasl, E., & Elias, D. (2001). Creating new habits of mind in small groups. In: J. Mezirow and Associates (Ed.), *Learning as transformation: Critical perspectives on a theory in progress* (pp. 229-252). San Francisco, CA: Jossey-Bass.

Kemp, J., & Livingstone, D. (2007). Putting a second life "Metaverse" skin on learning management systems. Retrieved from www.sloodle.com/whitepaper.pdf

Lea, M., & Spears, R. (1992). Paralanguage and social perception in computer-mediated communication. *Journal of Organizational Computing, 2,* 321-341.

Locker, K. (1992). What makes a collaborative writing team successful: A case study of lawyers and social workers in a state agency. In: J. Forman (Ed.), New visions of collaborative writing (pp. 37-62). Portsmouth, NH: Boynton Cook.

Mabry, E. (1999). The systems metaphor in group communication theory. In: L. Frey (Ed.), *The handbook of group communication theory And practice* (pp. 71-91). Thousand Oaks, CA: Sage.

Mezirow, J. (2001). Learning to think like an adult: Core concepts of transformation theory. In: J. Mezirow and Associates (Ed.), *Learning as transformation: Critical perspectives on a theory in progress* (pp. 3-34). San Francisco, CA: Jossey-Bass.

Moore, P., & Kreth, M. (2005). From wordsmith to communication strategist: Heresthetic and political maneuvering in technical communication. *Technical Communication, 52*(3), 302-322.

Morgan, M., & Murray, M. (1991). Insight and collaborative writing. In: M. Lay & W. Karis, (Eds.), *Collaborative writing in industry: Investigations in theory and practice* (pp. 64-75) Amityville, NY: Baywood Publishing.

Nicotera, A. (1997). Managing conflict communication in groups. In: L. Frey & J. Barge (Eds.), *Managing group life: Communicating in decision-making groups* (pp. 104-130). Boston, MA: Houghton Mifflin.

Pagnucci, G., & Mauriello, N. (1999). The masquerade: Gender, identity, and writing for the Web. *Computers and composition, 16*(1), 141-152.

Poole, M., Keyton, J, &Frey, L. (1999). Group communication methodology: Issues and considerations. In: L. Frey (Ed.), *The handbook of group communication theory and practice* (pp. 92-112). Thousand Oaks, CA: Sage.

Savage, G., & Sullivan, D. (2000). *Writing the professional life: Stories of technical communicators on and off the job.* Boston, MA: Longman.

Schein, E. (1992). *Organizational culture and leadership.* San Francisco, CA: Jossey-Bass.

Selfe, C., & Selfe, R. (1994). The politics of the interface: Power and its exercise in electronic contact zones. *College Composition and Communication, 45*(4), 480-501.

Smith, R. (2005). Working with difference in online collaborative groups. *Adult education quarterly, 55*(3), 182-199.

Souder, W. (1987). *Managing new product innovation.* Lexington, MA: Lexington Press.

St. Amant, K. (2002). When cultures and computers collide: Rethinking computer-mediated communication according to international and Intercultural communication expectations. *Journal of Business and Technical communication, 44*(2), 196-214.

Taylor, E. (1994). Intercultural competency: A transformative learning process. *Adult Education Quarterly, 44*(3), 154-174.

Tjosvold, D. (1992). *The conflict-positive organization: Stimulate diversity and create unity.* Reading, MA: Addison-Wesley.

Turkle, S. (1995). *Life on the screen: Identity in the age of the Internet.* New York, NY: Touchstone.

Watkins, K., & Marsick, V. (1993). *Sculpting the learning organization: Lessons in the art and science of systemic change.* San Francisco, CA: Jossey-Bass.

Yorks, L., & Marsick, V. (2001). Organizational learning and transformation. In: J. Mezirow and Associates (Ed.), *Learning as transformation: Critical perspectives on a theory in progress* (pp. 253-281). San Francisco, CA: Jossey-Bass.

DEFINITIONS

Critical Reflection: This refers to the reflection on experience that reveals the underlying assumptions, values, and beliefs that compel a person to act as she/he does in a particular situation and to interpret the actions of another in a particular way; thus critical reflection unveils one's "frames of reference" as Mezirow calls them or one's "espoused theories of action" as Argyris and Schon referred to them. Critical reflection is necessary before transformative learning may occur, but critical reflection does not necessarily lead to transformative learning.

Espoused Theories of Action: This refers to the theory that a person believes s/he operates under. These theories are created by the person according to his or her perceptions of himself/herself and are reinforced by his/her true but often erroneous interpretations of his/her experience and actions. For instance, s/he may believe that s/he does not harbor bias against those of other cultures, but in fact s/he may, a fact the interpretations that others make of his/her actions reveal.

Frames of Reference: These are the "structures of assumptions and expectations through which we filter sense impressions" (Mezirow, 2001, p. 16). One's frames of reference shape how a person perceives, thinks and feels and provides the framework by which one makes meaning of experiences. Frames of reference are "composed of two dimensions, a habit of mind and resulting points of view" (Mezirow, 2001, p. 17) that determine how we will choose to act in a particular situation and how we will interpret the actions or speech of others.

Model I Behavior: This is behavior that is competitive and hostile. Argyris and Schon approach claiming that this kind of behavior is barbaric and uncivilized. In this behavior, individuals compete to get their own needs and wants satisfied with little thought to the collective good. Those practicing this kind of behavior seek to dominate others.

Model II Behavior: This is behavior that is collaborative and inclusive. Rather than seeking to dominate, people who practice this behavior strive to be democratic, inviting and encouraging weaker voices to be heard. Argyris and Schon imply that this way of behaving illustrates more enlightened and emotionally mature people. When conflict occurs in organizations acting from model II, members of the organization seek to understand and empathize with one another even while stating their individual points of view.

Perspective Transformation: This is the outcome of transformative learning. Fundamentally, it is a transformation of a frame of reference that allows a more "democratic" way of perceiving and acting in the world. Perspective transformation implies not just a change of perception but action as well because it is not enough to see the world differently; one must act differently in it. For a fuller definition, see Taylor (2001).

Reflective Discourse: This is the use of dialogue to find "a common understanding and assessment of the justification of an interpretation or belief" (Mezirow, 2001, p. 10). In a group setting, participants challenge each other's assumptions and negotiate alternative perspectives. Arguably, transformative learning cannot occur except in dialogue with one's environment either in a group setting or in acting within the world.

Theories in Use: These are the theories that a person actually uses to interpret a situation and act within it. These theories are often in conflict with a person's espoused theories in those practicing model I behavior. Indeed, often people practicing model I behavior totally deny that they are acting in contradiction to what they say that they believe.

Transformative Learning: This involves a re-framing of assumptions that provide a different perspective on the world. As such, transformative learning leads to "respect for others, self-respect, willingness to accept responsibility for the common good, willingness to welcome diversity and to approach others with openness" (Mezirow, 2001, p. 14). It should be noted that this concept of transformative learning assumes that the aforementioned characteristics are positive, but the pronouncement that these are positive characteristics is a social construct.

Chapter XVII
Instructional Design and E-Training

Julia D. Sweeny
James Madison University, USA

ABSTRACT

Online training or, e-training, can be less expensive, more efficient, and more productive than traditional face-to-face instruction. This chapter reviews why businesses are adopting Web-based instruction, characteristics of exemplary e-trainers and skills online instructors must attain. The primary focus of the chapter is on the importance of instructional design in analyzing the online audience and context; developing instructional strategies and online materials; implementing a Web-based course; and evaluating an online training program. Future trends and a conclusion complete the chapter.

INTRODUCTION

The general perspective of this chapter is that e-training can provide high quality, efficient instruction at a cost savings, if it is well designed and implemented. Like traditional classroom training, Web-based instruction is dependent on the design of the course, the expertise of the trainer, and the support of the administration. Online learning does not work for all businesses, and not all trainers are well-suited for instructing at a distance. The main objectives of the chapter are that the reader will:

1. Recognize that quality training, efficiency, and cost are three reasons that businesses are implementing Web-based instruction

2. Recognize the characteristics of an exemplary online trainer

3. Identify the skills online instructors need to master

4. Identify the difference between synchronous, asynchronous, and blended Web-based instruction

5. Appreciate the importance of sound instructional design to the success of a Web-based course

6. Identify key steps to effectively design an online course

7. Understand that the future of e-learning is unclear

BACKGROUND

Introduction

"A Vision of E-learning for America's Workforce" (2001) is a report by the Commission on Technology and Adult Learning, a committee created by the American Society for Training and Development (ASTD) and the National Governors Association (NGA). The charge for the commission was: "to define and encourage a technology-enabled learning environment that will result in an engaged citizenry and a skilled workforce for the digital economy" (p. 2). The commission found that employees in the 21st Century are faced with challenges of navigating an environment of innovation, customization, contemporary business models, and the latest workplace organizational methods. To thrive on the job, employees have to be trained in new skills and innovative ways of managing knowledge. Businesses, however, are finding that traditional, classroom-based, face-to-face instruction is unwieldy, unproductive, and expensive in providing employees with essential training (p. 11). Therefore, they are turning to well- designed online instruction to train their workforce.

Definitions of Asynchronous and Synchronous Online Instruction

The two primary modes of online instruction are defined according to accessibility. In general, asynchronous instruction can be accessed on the Web at any time and from any place with an Internet connection. Synchronous instruction can also be accessed from any place with the proper connectivity, but participants need to be "logged on" at a pre-arranged time. This mode of communication is synchronous because it occurs at the same time.

Asynchronous instruction can be offered through at least two modes. The first mode is programmed, self-paced asynchronous tutorials or courses offered via the Internet with no inter-vention from an instructor. The learner is asked to perhaps read on or off-line content, perform content-centered activities, and then complete an online assessment. If the assessment results are adequate, a new set of material is presented, and the learner continues through the course. The second type of asynchronous delivery is instructor-led courses offered via the Internet which can be accessed at any time from any place. Instructors in these courses interact with the learner through technologies such as e-mail or discussion boards. The learner can obtain the content on or off-line but performs activities and exercises with the guidance of an instructor, who is sometimes referred to as a facilitator. These activities can also be conducted on or off-line.

Factors Contributing to the Adoption of Online Training

This section examines three key reasons that businesses and corporations are adopting online training: efficient presentation of instruction, quality training, and cost benefits. The chapter first discusses how training online can be more efficient than face-to-face classroom instruction. Quality of online instruction will be discussed second, followed by an examination of the cost benefits of Web-based learning.

Efficient Instruction

Writing for the "Retail Technology" column in the trade journal *Chain Store Age*, Gentry (2005) states that 90% of e-learning in most chain stores is done in-house, so the employees do not have to travel (pp. 2-3). In addition, a report on e-learning was commissioned by W. R. Hambrecht, a financial services company, and written by Urden and Weggen (2000) for the business research firm, SRI Consulting. This report states that e-learning is more efficient since employees can access training on the jobsite: "Workers can also improve productivity and use their own time more efficiently, as they no longer need to travel or fight rush hour traffic to get to class" (p. 9).

Gentry (2005) summarizes how e-learning is more efficient than traditional classroom training. First, the instruction is time-and-space independent. When learning online, the asynchronous classroom is available 24 hours a day, 7 days a week, making it time-and-space independent. Content and instruction are more accessible via the Internet and not dependent on the learner to be present at limited times at prescribed locations. When compared with face-to-face instruction, the problems of a remote location and employee turnover can be avoided.

Most online learning materials are broken into small chunks or modules, thus, allowing employees to spend a few hours a day on training over three or so days, instead of taking several full days off from the job (Urden & Weggen, 2000). According to Gentry (2005), by training in-house, employees can immediately apply newly acquired skills or knowledge to their work. In addition, retention of information is higher and the cost per person is lower (pp. 2-3).

Brian Metcalf, senior vice president of training for Carpet One proprietor, CCA Global Partners, believes that e-learning increases training efficiency:

We can [reduce] eight hours of classroom training by two-thirds in an on-line environment, we've found test scores are higher from on-line training because students can learn at their own pace and review material in the on-line environment. (Gentry, 2005, p. 2)

Fortune Magazine's "E-learning: Harnessing the Power of Knowledge to Maximize Corporate Profitability" (2001) also supports the contention that online learning is more efficient than face-to-face training. This article states that six to nine months of traditional classroom training is reduced to two to three weeks online, which ultimately lessens time to market for products.

In general, corporations find that training online is more efficient, shortens training time, gets workers up to speed more quickly, and is less expensive (A Vision of Learning for America's Workforce, 2001; Singh, 2001a; Adams, 2003; A Flying Start, 2003).

Quality of Instruction

In addition to instructional efficiency, another explanation for businesses implementing e-instruction is that the high quality of well designed, learner-centered Web-based instruction leads to an increase in employee learning and productivity (Vision, 2001). In "Maximizing E-learning to Train the 21st Century Workforce," an article written for *Public Personnel Management,* Pantazis (2002) aligns the quality of Web-based training with the ability to individualize instruction by, "eliminating the one-size-fits-all approach to instruction and customizing content to meet individual needs and learning styles" (p. 1).

"Using E-Learning" (2001), from the trade magazine *Training,* also discusses how providing quality training is one rationale for implementing online instruction. Supervisors at DigitalThink, an e-learning company which provided training for the auditing firm KPMG (KPMG, 2007), found that online instruction was very efficient and effective. Four days after they launched the KPMG online learning program, 60% of 8,500 employees signed up for Web-based instruction. At the end of 3 months, 95% of the audience participated, a much higher percentage than the previous record of 40% for face-to-face instruction. Of those who took the e-courses, 98.6% passed with scores of 94% or higher. These high scores seem to indicate that the quality of online instruction in this case was higher than that presented face-to-face. On the other hand, these results could reflect a novelty effect. In other words, employees may have signed up for and tested well in the Web-based courses because they were motivated by the new delivery mode.

Gentry points out that with programmed, self-paced asynchronous online instruction, content is consistent since it is independent of input from different instructors. In face-to-face workshops, the same content can be presented in a variety of ways from different perspectives. Online, however, the content remains static. E-learning can provide quality instruction since it ameliorates problems such as "inconsistent teaching methodologies that typically result from a 'train the trainer' approach," in addition, "the continuity, flexibility and accessibility of Web-based teaching has inherent appeal" (2005, p. 1).

Cost

High quality training offered efficiently would seem to naturally save corporations money when it comes to instruction. Based on 29 research case studies, an article in *Industrial and Commercial Training* found that, although well designed distance learning training can result in higher learning outcomes, cost savings often appear to be the motivating factor behind the decision to turn to e-training as an alternative to face-to-face instruction (Ettinger, Holton, & Blass, 2006). "A Vision for America's Workforce" (2001) states that, "significant cost savings" are evident when looking at classroom versus online training (p. 2). In addition, this report found that once the admittedly significant start up costs are met through the creation of an infrastructure and course development, "the marginal cost of serving additional students is close to zero" (p. 11). Urden and Wegen (2000) from SRI Consulting found that a 50% to 70% savings can be garnered by replacing live instruction with online learning (p. 9). An example of this type of savings is found by looking at Cisco Systems' e-learning program, which saved the company $1 million per quarter and led to an 80% increase in "speed to competence" (Galagan, 2001, p. 55).

Not all companies, however, find that online learning meets their needs or instructional

philosophy, regardless of costs savings or other reasons which might support the adoption of Web-based instruction. Ramesys Hospitality, which creates and supports Performance Management Software (PMS) for over 4,000 hospitality industries, does not use online learning (Ramesys Increases Options, 2003). In an article for *Hotel and Motel Management*, Andrew Sanders, director of sales and marketing for Ramesys, states that his customers prefer face-to-face instruction over distance learning: "For new installations, customers always prefer us to be on-site to get the kind of feedback you can only get by looking someone in the eye.... There is a cost advantage to online training, but we don't get a demand for it" (Adams, 2003, p. 2).

In conclusion, businesses and corporations are turning to e-training because it is more efficient, provides high quality instruction, and is cost effective. However, any online course is only as good as the e-trainer.

E-Trainers

This section of the chapter addresses characteristics of exemplary e-trainers. It also examines the skills these instructors need to master. Characteristics of successful e-trainers tend to correspond with the traits of quality face-to-face instructors with the addition of feeling comfortable and willing to teach with technology. The context for this discussion is that the instructors would be teaching asynchronous or synchronous instructor-led courses.

Characteristics of Exemplary E-Trainers

For a variety of reasons, not all exemplary face-to-face instructors make good e-trainers. In an interestingly titled article, "Anatomy of a Train Wreck: A Case Study in the Distance Learning of Strategic Management," Crow, Cheek, and Hartman (2003) write about their experiences teaching online. These instructors found that some individuals are better at teaching online than others: "An order and obey instructor and an overly democratic instructor will not fare well in distance learning. One tolerates no flexibility and the other tolerates too much" (p. 4). Instructors who adhere to a lecture-based or "order and obey" philosophy will be less effective teaching online since lecture material rarely transfers well to the online medium. Online students soon lose interest and motivation if they are reading pages of lecture notes or clicking through PowerPoint and then taking a multiple choice test based on the notes. A learner-centered philosophy tends to work best with e-training. In learner-centered instruction, the student bears more responsibility for gathering, assimilating, and applying knowledge. The instructor does not provide information to be memorized and repeated back. For example, in a learner-centered class, instead of reading the lecture notes online, the students could be asked to research the topic or read a chapter which covers the content then work in small groups to answer problem-based questions. Learner-centered instruction encourages students to use self-directed learning to develop an understanding of the content.

A trainer with an "overly democratic" philosophy may encounter difficulties managing lessons and maintaining a sense of order. Self-direction does not imply that the students have total control of the course. Students need structure and clear guidelines in order to function successfully online. Developing the appropriate structure and specific guidelines could be the purview of the instructional designer who often develops and creates the class and then hands it over to an instructor to implement.

"A Vision for America's Workforce" (2001) sees the role of the e-trainer as an extension of the face-to-face instructor. Like traditional trainers, e-instructors must facilitate learning experiences and resources. However, they cannot lecture or act as "outright providers of learning" (p. 20) through the "order and obey" philosophy (Crow,

Cheek, & Hartman, 2003). A distinct requirement for those teaching online as opposed to traditional instructors is that e-trainers have to know the technology and understand the roles of content and service providers (Vision, 2001). They may also need to provide technical support (Salmon, 2001; Vision, 2001; Milne, 2004).

In writing for *Learning Circuits,* the electronic journal for the American Society for Training and Development (ASTD), the leading training and development organization in the world (ASTD, 2007), Hootstein (2002) states that, "…instructors guide self-directed learning in problem-centered environments" (p. 1). The philosophy of e-trainers facilitating learner-centered instruction or acting as a "guide on the side" is common in all modes of distance learning. Hootstein (2002) and others refer to e-instructors as e-facilitators, since one characteristic of these teachers is that they "facilitate" students in making connections and constructing their own learning rather than deliver the instruction via lecture. With the facilitator or "guide on the side" philosophy, learners are often expected to participate in establishing an agenda, defining objectives, and assessing outcomes" (p. 1). All of the following characteristics outlined by Hootstein (2002) in his excellent article, "Wearing Four Pairs of Shoes: The Role of E-Learning Facilitators," reflect the facilitator, learner-centered philosophy. He believes that the three most important tasks for e-instructors are to provide information to help learners complete assignments, suggest ideas or strategies for learning, and help learners connect content with prior knowledge.

Hootstein (2002) lists the characteristics of exemplary online trainers who:

1. Address the needs of adult learners
2. Structure learning where learners make their own meaning
3. Encourage participation and interactivity
4. Provide prompt, informative feedback
5. Demonstrate leadership
6. Help learners feel comfortable with technology

In the article, "10 Ways to Make Your Virtual Classroom Work" published in *Human Resources,* Milne (2004) would add that an online instructor should also be a well established face-to-face trainer.

Essential Skills for E-Trainers

Once individuals are identified as willing to adopt a learner-centered instructional philosophy, they need to master specific skills to teach in the Web-based environment. Not only should they understand the technology, they also need to comprehend the basics of instructional design so they can convert traditional material or create new content for online delivery. They also should consider whether the content is being adapted for instructor-led asynchronous instruction or synchronous instruction, both of which require different approaches. Converting face-to-face content for online delivery is an important skill. It entails re-visioning content, context, materials, activities, and implementation.

An important skill of successful e-instructors is to appropriately apply the principles of instructional design to their educational methodology. If an instructional designer is available for the project, then the facilitator needs to understand the vocabulary and rationale that the designer uses in developing the course. Di Paolo and Patterson (1983) in the journal *Training and Development* state that the trainer and/or designer should be skilled in:

1. Systematically identifying and analyzing training problems and finding solutions
2. Selecting and sequencing content appropriately
3. Analyzing the audience and learning tasks
4. Creating performance objectives and standards

Milne (2004) states that prospective Web-based instructors need to be skilled in online pedagogy: "Once trainers understand the technology, and the principles of online learning, they'll need to think about adapting this style to the web" (p. 2). The instructional designer can be essential in assisting the novice e-trainer in adapting to and understanding principles of teaching online, whether asynchronously or synchronously.

However, statistics from Ryan Ellis (2004), writing for ASTD's *Learning Circuits,* seem to indicate that not all e-instructors are trained in principles of online teaching and learning. Ellis's (2004) findings are summarized in Table 1.

It is encouraging that in 2004, 70.2% of 164 e-trainers had taken an online course so that they can understand the challenges of learning online from the student point-of-view. Unfortunately, it seems that the percentage of e-facilitators having direct instruction on how to facilitate and design courses should be higher than 54.9% and 35.2%, respectively.

Writing for ASTD's online journal, *Learning Circuits,* Mantyla (2000) delineates the skills e-trainers need to master in order to teach through an electronic medium. With the help of an instructional designer or on their own, skilled e-trainers match content with the appropriate technology and select suitable courses to convert using a media selection guide (Web-based, CD-ROM, satellite, video-conferencing). Ideally, the e-instructor or instructional designer on the team develops short (10-15 minute) sequences or blocks of content. In addition, interactive materials account for 30% to 50% of the presentation. Instructional strategies vary from passive to active instruction, implement effective visual aids, such as cognitive maps and tables, and use appropriate technologies. Finally, the instructor or designer often prepares evaluation tools, performs administration and registration functions, and prepares back up plans if a technology fails. Throughout the duration of the course, the instructor also provides learner support.

E-trainers need to have all of the characteristics of a highly skilled traditional instructor, as well as the skills to adjust to teaching online, whether asynchronously or synchronously. When they

Table 1. Percentage of online facilitators receiving relevant training

Training In	Taken Online Course	Multi-Media Design	Online Facilitation	General Web Development	Instructional Design for Online
% n=164	70.2 %	57.7 %	54.9 %;	46.5 %	35.2 %

begin teaching online, they should be trained in converting traditional materials or creating new content for Web presentation, new technologies, and learner-centered instruction. Online trainers also need to be proficient in adult learning theory and practice, planning for instruction, managing instruction, motivating students, and evaluating.

MAIN FOCUS OF THE CHAPTER

The main focus of this chapter is to examine the role of instructional design in the success of instructor-led or programmed asynchronous or synchronous e-training. This section provides a brief introduction to instructional design. It then discusses online instructional specifications and the different modes of asynchronous and synchronous delivery. It also examines navigation, online instructional content, materials, and activities. The final topics of this section cover evaluation and implementation of online training.

Instructional Design of E-Training Courses

Instructional Design

E-instruction can be beneficial if it is well designed, implemented, and supported. To help ensure that an online training course is successful, it is useful to include an instructional designer on the development team. From the initial phase of analyzing learner needs to the final step of evaluation, the designer can assist the e-facilitator or training supervisor in developing effective, learner-based online courses.

The responsibility of the instructional designer is to create training which is instructionally sound

as well as easy to navigate. To accomplish these tasks in face-to-face or online instruction, the designer should follow basic steps of instructional design which according to Gustafson and Branch (2007) include:

1. *Analysis* of the setting and learner needs
2. Design of a set of *specifications* for an effective, efficient, and relevant learner environment
3. Development of all learner and management *materials*
4. *Implementation* of the resulting instruction
5. Both formative and summative *evaluations* of the results of the development [emphasis added] (15)

Instructional Analysis and Specifications

While considering appropriate instructional specifications and materials for online training, the designer should first analyze learner needs and the setting or context. Based on this analysis, the designer decides whether or not the instructional content lends itself to distance learning or face-to-face training. In his discussion in the journal *Quality,* Jacobsen (2002) states that content could be delivered online if it involves, "knowledge, comprehension, understanding and application" (p. 2) (See Table 2). These four levels of knowledge equate to the lower levels of Bloom's (1956) taxonomy of learning categories. Skills requiring knowledge, comprehension, understanding, and application can be delivered through self-paced online instruction. On the other hand, Bloom's (1956) higher level taxonomies: analysis, synthesis, and evaluation, may require face-to-face instruction. Addressing higher learning domains depends on whether the course will be instructor-led or programmed. An online course could address these more challenging domains if an instructor is available to provide appropriate interaction and feedback.

Synchronous or Asynchronous

Once the instructional designer and/or the facilitator determine that the content can be appropriately offered online, the next step is to decide whether to offer the training synchronously or asynchronously. Asynchronous courses are both time-and-space independent; students can access learning materials by logging on at any time from any computer with an Internet connection. If the training is delivered asynchronously, it could be instructor-led or programmed.

In general, programmed or learner-directed online instruction occurs when learners go through self-paced modules, take an assessment, and, depending on their answers to the assessment, are presented with another module that meets their learning needs. A program is said to "branch" when the content presented depends on the learner's input. For example, if an employee chooses choice Z in response to a question, but the answer is A, the program will branch to provide material which focuses on why the learner needed to choose answer A. However, if learners select the correct answer, then they would be presented with different content than the user who chose the incorrect option. Programmed instruction does not involve a trainer. An issue with learner-controlled or programmed instruction is that it does not provide for interaction with an instructor or other students. Lack of interaction can create a sense of isolation, which could result in employee withdrawal from the training.

Synchronous training is conducted at the same time, but from different locales. Programs such as Symposium's *Centra©*, Horizon's *Wimba©*, and Macromedia's *Breeze©* are used to connect learners synchronously using audio, text and, sometimes, video. These Webcasts or "webinars" are popular in business since they do not require that a participant travel. However, it can be difficult to arrange a convenient time for all learners to log on, especially across time zones. Synchronous instruction is always facilitated, although it can be recorded and reviewed multiple times.

As a researcher for Bersin and Associates, a "leading provider of research and advisory services in enterprise learning and talent management" (2007), Karen O'Leonard (2005) wrote the white paper, "Best Practices in Online Customer Training: How to Build a Profitable Online Customer Training Business." The paper was commissioned by WebEx (a synchronous online communications company). In the paper, O'Leonard makes a clear distinction between when content should be offered synchronously and when it should be delivered asynchronously. A course needs to be offered synchronously if the content has a short lifespan or changes often, requiring frequent updates. Synchronous instruction should be specified when it needs to be offered quickly, not allowing time for development of Web-based instruction, and when the instruction involves problem-solving requiring hands-on demonstrations.

On the other hand, asynchronous training can address Just-in-Time (JIT) instruction to immediately provide information addressing a problem on the job (O'Leonard, 2005). Asynchronous courses are also offered "on demand," in other words, no advance technical set up or scheduling is required. The employee registers and begins taking the course. A learner in a synchronous course, however, usually needs to download and test conferencing software and be available at a particular time.

Table 2 summarizes the findings of three different authors who suggest when asynchronous learning should be used versus synchronous learning. This table only addresses what these authors state. For example, although higher level thinking skills can be taught in a face-to-face or hybrid course, none of the authors mentioned this

Table 2. Asynchronous versus synchronous presentation

Characteristic of Learning Content	Asynchronous		Synchronous
	Learner-directed (programmed)	Instructor-directed	
(Jacobsen, 2002)			
Knowledge, comprehension, understanding, application	✘	✘	✘
Analysis, synthesis, evaluation		✘	
(Flood, 2002; Adams; 2003; Gentry, 2005)			
Static information	✘	✘	
O'Leonard (2005)			
Short lifespan			✘
Changes often			✘
Problem-Solving			✘
Needs to be offered quickly			✘
Address an on the job problem	✘	✘	

possibility because these instructional delivery modes were not the topic of their articles. Therefore, face-to-face and hybrid instruction are not covered in the table.

Often, the best implementation of technology is to combine face-to-face and online methodologies in a "blended" or "hybrid" approach. Harvi Singh (2001a) in the *CIO Online Journal* suggests that synchronous instruction be blended with programmed or self-paced online learning. Jim Flood (2002) in "E-Learning: Your Starter for 10" from *COROUS: Corporate Open University Online Resources* delineates three learning strategies to blend e-learning with traditional, classroom-based instruction. First, to promote further study and as a follow-up to a face-to-face class, the designer can implement a short (20-minute) online module or learning object which outlines key concepts. Learning objects, or self-contained chunks of information such as an interactive simulation of how the brain processes alcohol, are often used in distance and traditional learning. Secondly, the designer can create an

online module, pretest, or learning object in order to determine what knowledge the trainee needs to acquire. After trainees take an online course and determine gaps in their knowledge, they can select the appropriate traditional course to meet their learning needs. Finally, designers or trainers in face-to-face courses can incorporate learning objects directly into their instructional strategies and materials in order to individualize instruction. For example, if a trainee has low scores on an assessment about how the production line works at his or her facility, an animated learning object can be presented which visually depicts how the line operates.

Carpet One's training provides an example of hybrid presentation. This training is created by a team of instructional designers and developers. Following the design principle of content specifications matching the delivery mode, asynchronous courses deliever static information, such as product data, that should always be available for new employees and as refreshers for established staff. Face-to-face courses are reserved for new launch sales, which require interaction. Using this blended method, online and face-to-face, Carpet One has found that trainees earn higher test scores (Gentry, 2005).

The concept of content specification matching delivery mode is also exemplified by Microsystems' training program, which uses Web-based courses for "basic" or, in Bloom's (1956) taxonomy, "knowledge" level skills, such as "checking in and checking out guests and housekeeping" (Adams, 2003, p. 1). This Web-based training is designed to be followed up with 4 to 8 days of face-to-face instruction on more complex skills. Employees need to attain a cut-off score in the online class before they can attend follow-up classroom training. Carpet One's Online University (OLU) matches content to delivery mode by offering Web-based courses for static product data information (simple knowledge acquisition), but reserves face-to-face instruction for sales training that requires interaction, for example, launching a new product where an emotional appeal is needed (Gentry, 2005). Hotel management companies which use online instruction for basic skills and then follow up with in-class instruction include Medallion Property Management Systems, Northwind, Pegasus Solutions, La Quinta and Cisco (Adams, 2003). All of these corporations use a hybrid training schedule by combining asynchronous Web-based instruction with traditional face-to-face class time.

Singh (2001a) also suggests the designer consider matching content specifications to online delivery mode. In other words, the instructional designer aligns different learning domains or skills with the appropriate e-learning presentation. Procedures, concepts, facts, processes and principles should each be presented using a unique instructional strategy. For example, a procedure would call for a course that is laid out step-by-step. An online course with content that requires conceptualization would, perhaps, present a definition followed by an example and a non-example.

Navigation

Instructional designers must develop navigation for online courses that is exceptionally clear and intuitive. An article from *COROUS*, states that an online course should be easy to negotiate and content should be located without difficulty (Successful Online Learning: The Five P's, 2004). In *People Management,* Salmon (2001) states that unwieldy navigation leads trainees to feel that they are wasting their time if they struggle to click through an online course. The authors of "Optimizing E-Learning: Research-Based Guidelines for Learner-Controlled Training" in *Human Resource Management* state that "Footprints" or "landmark' links" tell learners where they are in the course, and return links allow trainees to backtrack to earlier items or menus (De Rouin, Fritzsche, & Salas, 2004, p. 155). Icons or learning cues are also helpful in assisting learners in navigating through a Web-based module. To reduce learner anxiety and build confidence, the instructional designer should consider including an "induction phase" of practice activities that include working with navigation and other technical skills before the course starts (Successful Online Learning: The Five P's, 2004). How navigation is developed depends on whether a learning management system (LMS) or content management system (CMS) is being used to implement the course online. In an LMS or CMS, the navigation scheme is predetermined by the system rather than developed by the instructor creating a Web site from scratch using, for example, FrontPage© or Dreamweaver©.

Develop Instructional Materials

In this section, the term "materials" refers to information provided in the online course. For example, in a unit on Return on Investment (ROI), the materials might include several definitions of ROI, case studies, and spreadsheets. Activities are exercises that require the learner to perform an action or demonstrate a skill, for example, being able to calculate ROI given a specific set of data. The combination of all aspects of a course, such as objectives, materials, activities, and evaluation could be defined as the "content" of the training.

In their article for the trade journal, *Industrial and Commercial Training,* Ettinger, Holt, and Blass (2006) posit that an e-training course must include well-designed and appropriate materials in order to produce effective learning outcomes:

... good instructional design is also a key component of quality e-learning materials. Learning materials may have all the video clips and interactive exercises available, but if the learner is not able to follow the structure and glean the key learning points, then all this expensive technology may go to waste. (p. 211)

Learners can more easily follow the instructional structure if content is designed and presented in small chunks or segments, which take approximately ten to fifteen minutes to complete (Mantyla, 2000; Ettinger, Holton, & Blass, 2006). Writing in *Training,* Harvi Singh (2001b) also suggests that learning improves when instructional units are divided into small chunks. David Smith (2004) in *Franchising World,* refers to these chunks or units of learning as "bricks," which have a completion rate of fifteen minutes or less. Training modules should consist of multiple "bricks" through which the employee's progress is tracked and assessed (p. 1).

When developing online training materials, the instructional designer should consider the technological infrastructure, specifically bandwidth capabilities, of the target site. For example, a site with narrow bandwidth capacity should be provided with content containing simple graphics and very small video segments. If more robust bandwidth is needed than the site can provide, CD's of the instruction can be sent to the learners (Gentry, 2005).

In addition to considering navigation and learning cues, the instructional designer of an online course can individualize materials by providing the appropriate level of training for each learner's job requirements and skill level (De Rouin, Fritzsche, & Salas, 2004; Smith, 2004). Harvi Singh (2001a) summarizes this practice: "e-learning content should be linked to the job-specific competencies and skill requirements that are relevant to your organization."

In order to individualize or "personalize" e-learning materials to the learner's skill requirements, the instructional designer can implement a variety of approaches (Singh, 2001a). One method of determining what materials to develop is to pre-test learners in order to identify their learning gaps and entry skills. Singh continues by pointing out that programmed or instructor-led online courses can branch to meet learner needs: "It is also possible to personalize the learning experience at a finer level by embedding rules within the learning content that keep the learners engaged and direct them to suitable activities and resources." At a more granular level, instruction can be individualized based on the learner's job role, media preference, and bandwidth availability (Singh, 2001a).

Fortune Magazine's "Using E-Learning" (2001) covers the e-learning vendor DigitalThink, which implements pre-tests and learner-directed online modules. The company personalizes instruction and meets the design criteria of identifying learner entry skills by administering pre-tests. Pre-tests allow trainers to place users in modules that match their needs. The content of the modules is designed to adapt to the trainee's skills: "To address varying learning styles and skill levels, the team not only develops a careful review process for all content, but also integrated a multimedia platform with a range of materials and methods" (p. 33).

As can be seen in DigitalThink's use of pre-tests, programmed instruction can be individualized for each learner. It should be remembered, however, that individualized learner-directed or programmed instructional materials are difficult to design since this type of training requires an enormous amount of effort on the part of designers and programmers. A programmed, self-paced online course must branch and offer a myriad of instructional materials depending on the learner's choices. It is also a challenge for the instructor of an online course to individualize instruction on-demand with the appropriate exercises and content for every participant.

Research strongly supports that e-learning instructional designers and trainers provide interactive opportunities for instructor-to-student, as well as, student-to-student communication (Mantyla, 2000; Salmon, 2001; Singh, 2001b; Milne, 2004; Ettinger, Holt, & Blass, 2006). Singh (2001a) feels that, "Online learning is more effective when there are frequent interactive activities interspersed with instructional content." In *Learning Circuits*, Karen Mantyla (2000) maintains that along with active learning, interaction should comprise 30% to 50% of the online content (p. 3). "Prompt informative feedback" and interactivity are often hallmarks of successful online instruction (Singh, 2001a ; Hootstein, 2002, p. 3). Hootstein (2002) focuses on interaction when he says, "Some educators believe that the most important facilitator behavior is timely and personal response to learner contributions and questions" (p. 2). "Successful Online Learning: The Five P's" (2004) also encourages online interaction as part of developing a learning community where trainees feel, "Included, Individual, Interested, and Inspired" (p. 2). Singh (2001a) reiterates this point when he states that an online community needs to be created "which encourages and recognizes knowledge sharing, online discussions, and personalized notifications."

In higher education, the importance of interaction to student retention is a common theme. According to Papastergiou (2006) whose article appears in the *International Journal on E-Learning,* "Students show positive attitudes towards CMS-[computer mediated systems] based learning, appreciating the opportunities for online interaction with faculty and peers, and for anyplace/anytime learning." Aalst (2006) in the *British Journal of Educational Technology* admits that providing interaction in online learning is not always easy, but it is essential to the quality of the e-learning experience.

Salmon (2001) cautions, however, that although interaction is "fundamental to learning," these opportunities need to be unobtrusively folded into the online content, not tacked on without a clear connection to the course goals and objectives. In addition, In "10 Ways to Make Your Online Class Work," Milne (2004) wisely notes that if a course provides interactivity, then the number of participants should be smaller than if the class was self-paced and required no interaction between the instructor and students as well as students with students.

Develop Instructional Activities

After the instructional designer has incorporated appropriate materials, interactive activities matching the objectives need to be created. As with materials, the activities should be personalized or individualized for each learner. In addition, the activities also need to be correctly aligned with course objectives and relevant to the workplace (Singh, 2001a)

Activities should be learner-centric such as simulations, role plays, and performance-based assignments (Singh, 2001b). Hootstein (2002) states that e-learning activities should be realistic, problem-based experiences personally relevant to learners. Problem-solving activities could include: small group discussion, simulations, case studies, and collaborative exercises. Activities should include drawing information from technology such as e-mail, Web conferencing, Web databases, groupware, audio, and video-conferencing.

Implementation of Online Training Programs

This chapter has discussed the design process of an online training course, which involves analysis of the learner and setting, instructional specifications, different types of asynchronous and synchronous instruction, navigation, instructional materials and activities. Once the instructional design and development of a course is completed, it needs to be implemented and then evaluated. This section discusses the logistics of putting a course online.

Harvi Singh (2001a) emphasizes that good design and implementation are essential to the quality of an online course:

If designed and implemented appropriately, e-learning can truly deliver ongoing, continuous, personalized, just-in-time, just-enough learning experiences which can be aligned with on-the-job performance measures and business objectives.

Bruce Adams (2003) cites Robin Layman, director of hotel training for Microsystems, which creates documentation, manages productivity and quality control software (Microsystems, 2007). Layman outlines three keys to success when implementing an online training program. First, the administration has to have complete buy-in and support participation in distance learning. Secondly, employees need to be interested in the topic and care about their training. Finally, the trainer has to understand adult education techniques.

David Smith (2004) is more specific in his discussion of how to implement a distance learning program. He outlines five steps to implementation which correspond to Gustafson and Branch's (2007) definition of instructional design stages of analyzing the instructional content and audience. To implement a course online, the instructional designer or e-facilitator should:

1. Identify obstacles
2. Identify hardware needs
3. Identify time constraints
4. Understand the instructional context
5. Consider the age of the audience

The age of the audience is an important consideration since an older audience may need to ease into computer literacy. On the other hand, in designing for a younger audience, the site layout would be more like "*People* magazine than the *Wall Street Journal*" (Smith, 2003, p. 2).

The logistics of implementing an online course can be complicated. Milne (2004) suggests sponsoring a technical "check-in" session prior to the first online meeting. This would be appropriate for either asynchronous or synchronous courses. The trial "check-in" would allow students to practice using the technology and navigation methodology in a low stakes environment. Rather than present necessary introductory material electronically, Le Meridien hotel group mails student information packets about technology and set up. Gentry (2005) discusses other logistical demands, such as consideration of the infrastructure, bandwidth, and hardware capabilities of the target audience. The importance of infrastructure is reiterated by Walker (2003) in *People Management;* e-learning "tends to require extensive IT infrastructure and the standardization of practices" (p. 1). A strong infrastructure ensures "broad and equitable access to e-learning" (Vision, 2001, p. 5). The infrastructure needs to consist of high speed telecommunications, connectivity, and reliable software (Vision, 2001).

In addition to hiring a skilled e-instructor, the success of an online training initiative is also dependent on technical, financial, and content support. The culture of the corporation or business has to be "overtly and institutionally supportive" (Successful Online Learning: The Five P's, 2004, p. 5). Harvi Singh (2001b) points to lack of support and weak company-wide sponsorship as two reasons for learner drop-out. Corroborating this contention is that one factor leading to an unsuccessful online training program was an, "atmosphere of untested technical support" (Crow, Cheek, & Hartman, 2003). The researchers for this pilot program concluded that distance learning can be effective if the instructors and trainees are both technically savvy, consider distance learning as valid, and the "technology framework that supports distance learning is reliable" (Crow, Cheek, & Hartman, 2003).

Evaluation

Almost every instructional design model will insist that assessment instruments align with the goals and objectives determined during the analysis stage of design. Educational credit should be awarded when a trainee can demonstrate skill and knowledge acquisition as measured by the assessment (Smith, 2001; Vision, 2001). Carpet One's Web-based instructional units conclude with a multiple choice and true/false test. The company plans to implement a more informative reporting system that shows the employee's areas of strength as well as knowledge gaps (Gentry, 2005). If the course is new, instructional strategies and materials may need to be revised based on the results of each assessment cycle and on informal feedback from participants (Milne, 2004). The iterative process of evaluation and revising strategies and materials based on evaluation results is a common approach in instructional design. Salmon (2001) states that the true evaluation of training is whether or not the employees can transfer skills and knowledge to the workplace.

FUTURE TRENDS

The future of e-learning is unclear. Some believe that online training has reached its pinnacle or may be in decline. The authors of "E-learner Experiences: What is the Future for E-Learning," believe that the necessity and implementation of distance learning can only increase. These authors make a valid point in recognizing that the new generation of employees beginning to fill the workforce are those who grew up with computers, so they will feel more comfortable and accepting of online learning: "As Generation X and the Millenium Generation become the mainstay of the workforce, the success of e-learning is likely to increase" (Ettinger, Holt, & Blass, p. 211).

"A Vision of E-Learning for America's Workforce" (2001) states that e-learning will continue to be evident in training because of the trend in business and higher education to move from a teacher-centered to learner-centered approach, thus moving from the "institution to individuals" (p. 14). Personalized e-instruction based on an employee's entry skills and needs is becoming accepted practice. In addition, as business methodologies change, distance learning can adapt to meet these new approaches: "Learning is a continuous process of inquiry that keeps pace with the speed of change in business and society, rather than generic instruction based on set curricula" (p. 14).

The future of e-training is dependent on several factors, which hinge on how well the courses are designed and implemented. If online training is boring, difficult to navigate, or unrelated to job skills, then it is not going to flourish. The simplest and, once it is up and running, least expensive type of Web-based training is self-paced, asynchronous, programmed instruction. However, this type of instruction can be un-motivating and tedious if information is offered as rote memorization. Time, effort, and resources, all increasing the cost of providing the instruction, are essential to developing branching and individualized, programmed instruction with appropriate simulations and animations. Offering instructor-led online courses also has its challenges since an instructor must be employed to guide trainees through the modules. The facilitator provides interaction and individualizes instruction. In essence, if online training is to produce learners with updated skills, it may require more than posting self-paced, programmed instruction on the Web. Training supervisors need to consider including instructional designers and well-trained e-facilitators to their team if synchronous or asynchronous instruction is to become part of the training program.

CONCLUSION

Cost savings is the primary reason that businesses and corporations turn to e-training to meet their training needs. Once a distance course is running, the cost to maintain it is a fraction of what it would be for face-to-face training. Some businesses also find that if designed and implemented well, online training can be more effective than traditional face-to-face workshops. An online course could be more effective if it is well developed and leads to high learning outcomes. In addition, distance learning can be more productive than traditional instruction since trainees do not have to travel. If they complete their training on the job, they could immediately implement what they have learned. The possibility of just-in-time (JIT) training with asynchronous courses also increases efficiency because a learner can identify a difficulty on the job, then turn to an online module that directly addresses that issue. After taking the online training, the employee can return to the job having learned how to address the problem.

Just as in face-to-face training, an online course is only as good as the facilitator or instructor. Exemplary online trainers need to have experienced distance learning, possess all of the characteristics of a good face-to-face trainer, be skilled in teaching online, and have a facility for technology. The ideal situation would be to couple an online instructor with an instructional designer in the development, as well as, the implementation of the course. Successful implementation of distance learning is dependent on a well-designed and facilitated course, a well-supported infrastructure, and technical and administrative support.

In choosing the learning strategy for a distance learning course, the instructional designer first needs to decide if the content is well suited for electronic delivery. Some topics which require a great deal of personal interaction or higher-level learning domains, may be best offered face-to-face. However, most content can be offered online. Basic, knowledge level information can be offered in self-paced, programmed asynchronous courses. More advanced skills can be addressed through facilitated online courses. Synchronous courses are well suited to topics that require frequent updates or hands-on demonstrations. Training programs can also incorporate a hybrid approach, combining online learning with face-to-face instruction.

An instructional designer who specializes in online learning is essential to the success of a distance learning training program. The designer can analyze content, learners, learning strategies, methods, and evaluation techniques that are appropriate for an online environment. In addition, the designer can develop a course by matching the appropriate online activities with different types of content. Creating clear navigation and instructions are also areas where an instructional designer is important. An e-instructor should not be asked to perform design tasks in addition to presenting content and interacting with trainees. If e-learning is to produce well-trained employees, then an instructional designer should be included in the development of a distance learning program.

REFERENCES

ASTD. (2007). American Association of Training and Development. Retrieved March 7, 2007 from the ASTD homepage http://www.astd.org/astd.

Adams, B. (2003). Online learning can reduce training costs. *Hotel and Motel Management, 218*(17), 40, 42. Retrieved June 16, 2006 from WilsonWeb database.

Adams, B. (2005). Smooth sailing. *Hotel and Motel Management, 220*(5), 3-5. Retrieved June 21, 2006 from Proquest database.

Berger, C. (1996). *Definitions of instructional design.* Retrieved October 8, 2006 from http://www.umich.edu/~ed626/define.html.

Bersin and Associates. (2007). Homepage. Retrieved March 10, 2007 from http://www.bersin.com/

Bloom B. (1956). *Taxonomy of educational objectives, handbook I: The cognitive domain.* New York, NY: David McKay Co Inc. Retrieved October 8, 2006 from "Bloom's Taxonomy" (n.d.) http://www.nwlink.com/~donclark/hrd/bloom.html

Crow, S., Cheek, R., & Hartman, S. (2003). Anatomy of a train wreck: A case study in the distance learning of strategic management. *International Journal of Management, 20*(3), 335-338. Retrieved June 26, 2006 from Proquest database.

DeRouin, R., Fritzsche, & Salas, E. (2004). Optimizing e-learning: Researched-based guidelines for learner-controlled training. *Human Resource Management, 43*(2-3), 147-162.

Di Paolo, A., & Patterson, A. (1983). Selecting a training program for new trainers. *Training and Development Journal, 37*(1), 96-101. Retrieved July 14, 2006 from Academic Search Premier database.

Dick, W., & Carey, L. (1996). *The systematic design of instruction* (4th ed.). New York, NY: Harper Collins College Publishers.

E-Learning: Harnessing the power of knowledge to maximize corporate profitability. (2001). *Fortune Magazine,* 6.

Ellis, R. (2004). 'Learning Circuits' e-learning trends 2004. *Learning Circuits: ASTD's Source for E-Learning.* Retrieved July 14, 2006 from http://www.learningcircuits.org/2004/nov2004/LC_Trends_2004.htm.

Ettinger, A., Holton, V., & Blass, E. (2006). E-learner experiences: What is the future for e-learning?. *Industrial and Commercial Training,* *38*(4), 208-212. Retrieved October 6, 2006 from EmeraldInsight database.

Flood, J. (2002). E-learning: Your starter for 10. *COROUS: Corporate Open University Sources.* Retrieved June 28, 2006 from http://www.corous.com/who/white-papers/white-paper-02

Galagan, P. (2001). Mission e-possible: The Cisco learning story. *Training and Development,* 46-56. Retrieved August 21, 2006 from LookSmart Find Articles http://www.findarticles.com/p/articles/mi_m4467/is_2_55/ai_70659645

Gustafson, K., & Branch, R. (2007). *Survey of instructional development models* (4th ed.). Retrieved March 10, 2007 from ERIC database.

Gentry, C. (2005) Learning on demand: Flexibility and accessibility lead retailers to Web-based classroom. *Chainstore Age, 81*(6), 58-59. Retrieved March 6, 2007 from WilsonWeb database.

Hootstein, E. (2002). Wearing four pairs of shoes: The role of e-learning facilitators. *Learning Circuits: ASTD's Source for E-Learning.* Retrieved July 14, 2006 from http://www.learningcircuits.org/2002/oct2002/elearn.html.

Jacobsen, P. (2002). Train the e-learning way. *Quality, 41*(6). Retrieved June 26, 2006 from ProQuest database.

KPMG. (2007). Homepage. Retrieved March 15, 2007 from http://www.kpmg.com/About/.

Kirk, J. (2001). A virtual library for instructional systems designers. Retrieved October 7, 2006 from ERIC database.

Learning Circuits Glossary. (2006). *Learning circuits: ASTD's source for e-Learning.* Retrieved October 8, 2006 from http://www.learningcircuits.org/glossary.html

Mantyla, K. (2000). Who wants to be a distance trainer?. *Learning Circuits: ASTD's Source for E-Learning.* Retrieved July 12, 2006 from http://learningcircuits.org/2000/jul2000/mantyla1.htm.

Microsystems. (2007). Homepage. Retrieved March 13, 2007 from http://www.microsystems.com/whatwedo.php.

Milne, J. (2004). 10 ways to make your virtual classroom work. *Human Resources,* 26-38. Retrieved June 21, 2006 from Proquest database.

O'Leonard, K. (2005). Best practices in online customer training: How to build a Profitable online customer training business. 1-31. White Paper sponsored by WebEx for Bersin and Associates. Retrieved July 29, 2006 from http://www.elearningreseach.com.

Overview of Learner-Centered Training, based on the work of Maryellen Weimer. (n.d.).

Retrieved October 8, 2006 from Ferris State University, Center for Teaching Learning, & Faculty Web site: http://www.ferris.edu/htmls/academics/center/Teaching_and_Learning_Tips/Learner-Centered.

Pantazis, C. (2002). Maximizing e-learning to train the 21st century workforce. *Public Personnel Management, 31*(1), 21-27. Retrieved June 26, 2006 from ProQuest database.

Papastergiou, M. (2006). Course management systems as tools for the creation of online learning environments: Evaluation from a social constructivist perspective and implications for their design. *International Journal on E-Learning, 5*(4). Retrieved March 14, 2007 from http://search.ebscohost.com/login.aspx?direct=true&db=eric&AN=EJ747779&site=ehost-live&scope=site

Programmed Instruction. (2006). *HighBeam Encyclopedia.* Retrieved October 8, 2006 from http://www.encylopedia.com.

Ramesys increases options with the addition of entirety PMS- A windows based PMS module within the entirety enterprise suite. (2003). Hotel Online. Retrieved March 7, 2007 from http://www.hotel-online.com/News/PR2003_2nd/Apr03_RamesysEntirety.html.

Salmon, G. (2001). Far from remote. *People Management, 7*(19), 34-36. Retrieved June 16, 2006 from WilsonWeb database.

Singh, H. (2001). Ask the Expert. Message posted to *CIO Online Journal* http://www.cio.com/index.html.

Singh. H. (2001). Keeping learners online. *Training, 38*(2), 100. Retrieved June 16, 2006 from WilsonWeb database.

Smith, D. (2004). Implementing online training. *Franchising World, 36*(8), 124-126. Retrieved June 16, 2006 from WilsonWeb database.

Successful online learning: The five p's. (2004). Retrieved June 28, 2006 from http://www.corous.com/who/white-papers/white-paper-04.

Urden, T., & Weggen, C. (2000). Corporate e-learning: Exploring a new frontier. *W.R. Hambrecht and Company.* Retrieved October 8, 2006 from http://spectrainteractive.com/pdfs/CorporateELearingHamrecht.pdf.

Using e-learning of [sic] enhance e-business skills. (2001). *Training.* Retrieved March 7, 2007 from ProQuest database.

van Aalst, J. (2006). Rethinking the nature of online work in the asynchronous learning networks. *British Journal of Educational Technology, 37*(2). Retrieved March 13,

2007 from EBSCO Research Databases http://search.ebscohost.com/login.aspx?direct=true&db=eric&AN=EJ732774&site=ehost-live&scope=site.

A vision of e-learning for America's workforce. (2001). Report of the Commission on Technology and Adult Learning. ASTD and the National Governors Association, Center for Best Practices. Retrieved June 28, 2006 from http://www.masie.com/masie/researchreports/ELEARNINGREPORT.pdf.

Walker, A. (2003). A flying start. *People Management, 9*(3), 36-38. Retrieved June 16, 2006 from WilsonWeb database.

KEY TERMS

Asynchronous: Learning in which interaction between instructors and students occurs intermittently with a time delay. Examples are self-paced courses taken via the Internet or CD-ROM, Q&A mentoring, online discussion groups, and e-mail (Learning Circuits, 2006).

Content Management Systems: A centralized software application or set of applications that facilitates and streamlines the process of designing, testing, approving, and posting e-learning content, usually on Web pages (Learning Circuits, 2006).

E-Learning (Electronic Learning): Term covering a wide set of applications and processes, such as Web-based learning, computer-based learning, virtual classrooms, and digital collaboration. It includes the delivery of content via Internet, intranet/extranet (LAN/WAN), audio- and videotape, satellite broadcast, interactive TV, CD-ROM, and more (Learning Circuits, 2006).

E-Trainer: Instructor who provides training online via synchronous or asynchronous modes.

Facilitator: The online course instructor who aids learning in the online, student-centered environment (Learning Circuits, 2006).

Instructional Design: Instructional Design is the systematic development of instructional specifications using learning and instructional theory to ensure the quality of instruction. It is the entire process of analysis of learning needs and goals and the development of a delivery system to meet those needs. It includes development of instructional materials and activities; and tryout and evaluation of all instruction and learner activities (Berger, 1996).

Learning Objects: A reusable, media-independent collection of information used as a modular building block for e-learning content (Learning Circuits, 2006).

Learner-Centered Instruction: Being a learner-centered teacher means focusing attention squarely on the learning process: what the student is learning, how the student is learning, the conditions under which the student is learning whether the student is retaining and applying the learning, and how current learning positions the student for future learning. The distinction between teacher-centered and student-centered is made as a way of indicating that the spotlight has shifted from the teacher to the student. In learner-centered instruction the action focuses on what the students are doing not what the teacher is doing. This approach that now features students, accepts, cultivates and builds on the ultimate responsibility students have for their own learning (Overview of Learner-Centered Teaching, 2006).

Learning Management Systems: Software that automates the administration of training. The LMS registers users, tracks courses in a catalog, records data from learners; and provides reports to management. An LMS is typically designed to handle courses by multiple publishers and providers. It usually does not include its own authoring capabilities; instead, it focuses on managing courses created by a variety of other sources (Learning Circuits, 2006).

Programmed Instruction: Method of presenting new subject matter to students in a graded sequence of controlled steps. Students work through the programmed material by themselves at their own speed and after each step test their comprehension by answering an examination question or filling in a diagram (High Beam Encyclopedia, 2006).

Chapter XVIII
Designing the Virtual Classroom for Management Teaching

Parissa Haghirian
Sophia University, Japan

Bernd Simon
Vienna University of Economics and Business Administration, Austria

ABSTRACT

With the modern business environment becoming increasingly dependent on technology, management teaching in higher education faces the challenging task of effectively leveraging technology in diverse learning environments. This chapter discusses the use of virtual classrooms, namely collaborative, information technology-mediated teaching endeavours in management education at universities. The overall aim of this chapter is to provide insights for those who are responsible for the development of management curricula and to give specific guidelines to management educators interested in integrating IT-based teaching to increase teaching effectiveness when designing virtual classrooms.

INTRODUCTION

The business environment within which management education takes place is becoming increasingly competitive. As schools are seeking prestige in terms of research outcomes and teaching evaluations (Armstrong & Sperry, 1994), information technologies (IT) play a crucial role in their pursuits to differentiate service offerings and enhance learning (e.g., Berger & Topol, 2001; Pallab & Kaushi, 2001). On many campuses, this led to "technologically-driven change" (Blake & Jarvenpaa, 1996, p. 38; Green, 1999).

However, the integration of IT into the curriculum is by no means trivial. Traditionally, there was only a loose link between theoretical/conceptual frameworks and their business applications. The bridging of theory and practice was managed by assignment questions, examples in texts, case studies, guest speakers or by integrating business projects into the curriculum. In a technology-oriented world, students are able to switch directly from conceptual and theoretical underpinnings and their application to the real world (Blake & Jarvenpaa, 1996). Thus, the integration of IT into classrooms generates substantial changes to how learning and teaching takes place, and can therefore become an arduous task for educators and education researchers (Webster & Hackley, 1997; Green, 1999).

EDUCATIONAL CHALLENGES OF IT-BASED LEARNING ENVIRONMENTS

Integrating information technology into university classroom confronts educators with numerous opportunities as well as challenges. IT is incredibly powerful in the facilitation of display of information and the access to explicit information. Leidner and Jarvenpaa (1995) argue that this increases the sharing and construction of knowledge in the classroom. The use of information technology (IT) in the classroom therefore creates a rich set of new educational opportunities (Alavi et al., 1997; Webster & Hackley, 1997; Garrison, 2000; Meier & Simon, 2000), especially for management as well as marketing, where real-world examples play an enormous role and student participation is encouraged to enhance team-building skills and marketing competencies (Ueltschy, 2001; Sinkovics et al., 2004).

IT has so become an effective means of enabling intentional changes in teaching and learning process (Leidner & Jarvenpaa, 1995). Following Kolb's (1984) experiential learning theory, IT enables the integration of a greater number of learning experiences into the curriculum. Kolb's view implies that students' comprehension of abstract ideas will be facilitated by immersing them in direct experiences that demonstrate the utility of the concepts taught (Alderfer, 2003). Kolb's (1984) cycle of experiential learning consists of four stages: concrete experience, observation and reflection, abstract conceptualization and active experimentation. The student first is involved with the concrete experience. In the next stage he or she reflects and processes the information received during this experience. In stage 3 these experiences urge participants to create new concepts of their own, and finally the student uses

the generalizations from the stages experienced to develop strategies and guidelines for similar but maybe more complex situations. While doing so, the student gains a clear idea about the experience and also knows how to transform it into activities and strategies. IT-mediated teaching can strongly support these learning processes, by providing actual experience-based learning and assessment and there is every reason to believe that the integration of technology into education will continue to increase with technological advances. It goes beyond the simple provision of computer access and training to faculty and students. IT can play a strategic role. It can be used in a systematic way for designing, carrying out and evaluating the whole process of learning and teaching in terms of specific objectives (Garrison, 2000).

Not surprisingly, the integration of IT into management education has become a topic of interest in education and research. Little emphasis has been placed on the organizational context in which IT-based learning and teaching takes place in traditional higher education institutions (Kerres, 1998). This is an issue of high importance, since using IT is also a risky endeavour for management educators, where many sources of failure do exist. Integrating IT into a university classroom needs a lot of extra preparation and a high degree of interest in modern educational technologies. Students, on the other hand, are also challenged because they may get easily frustrated when IT is not properly introduced into the learning environment. Any meaningful and sensible integration of IT into the modern classroom needs to be guided by the inspiration of instructors about technological possibilities and educational benefits. IT should not and cannot be seen as a solution in its own right, otherwise it will lack pedagogic effectiveness. And IT can, as observed by Alavi, Yoo and Vogel (1997), even offer superior modes of learning and instruction. Yet, guidelines of how to exploit these opportunities will be needed (Smart et al., 1999; Manning et al., 2003).

Consequently, this chapter focuses on the implementation of IT-mediated technology in international management classes. The technology discussed is the virtual classroom, an internet-based technology which makes it possible to broadcast a lecture via a videoconferencing system to a geographically distant location. Two or more classrooms can so be combined, and interactive teaching at several locations at the same time becomes possible.

The objective of this chapter is to describe and analyse a series of virtual classroom events in international management education. It introduces the challenges of setting up this IT-mediated teaching event starting with the instructors' first intentions and subsequently describing the challenges of broadcasting the lecture to other classrooms. Our focus is on the participants of the virtual classroom event, namely instructors, students and IT personnel and their perceptions of the new learning experience. The chapter first presents an overview of the topic of virtual classrooms and shows their potential in enriching management teaching. After this processes and interaction patterns in a virtual classroom experiment are described. Field experiments, involving interactive university lectures at three universities supported by a video-based learning environment, were conducted to gain insight into the organizational and technological design of teaching management in an international context. The discussion focuses on information technology used and the frameworks in which the experiments took place. To provide an analysis of learning effectiveness, a qualitative research design was applied covering the perceptions of instructors, students and IT personnel concerning the costs and benefits of such settings. The final part of the chapter presents the results and recommendations on how to increase effectiveness of virtual classrooms in international management teaching.

MANAGEMENT TEACHING IN VIRTUAL CLASSROOMS

Definition

A virtual classroom refers to two or more higher education institutions that are geographically dispersed and which communicate, for example, via a video conference system. In this chapter, we assume that a virtual classroom has the following properties:

- Two or more student-instructor teams are geographically dispersed.
- Knowledge and content are available from many sources, not just from the local instructor.
- Direct, symmetric interaction is available between all combinations of remote and local instructors and students.
- A combination of media may be deployed. (Multi-site) Video-conferencing supports symmetric, synchronous communication. Additional educational material such as slides, printed case studies, and video recordings may be incorporated into the lecture (Simon et al., 2003).

Such a learning environment allows instructors and students to overcome distance by taking advantage of information technology. Virtual classrooms can too enrich the quality and value of learning environment in an international setting (Alavi et al., 1997; Webster & Hackley 1997; Bell et al., 2001; Pallab & Kaushi 2001).

Enrichment of Management Education

Management course enrichment can be seen at various levels. Dede (1990) states that this learning environment is opening up new opportunities to discover new educational goals and instructional methods that have the potential to reach a wider range of student skills than in the traditional classroom. It also provides opportunities for creating student awareness for international issues and helps understanding the global business environment. International dimensions can be incorporated swiftly by adopting this kind of learning environment (Bell et al., 2001). The virtual classrooms can thus broaden students' perspectives and increase their cross-cultural effectiveness (May, 1997). Students and instructors with different socio-cultural and educational backgrounds bring a host of different ideas, experiences, and distinctive management assumptions and practices to the (virtual) classroom (Ashamalla, 1999). This diversity offers great potential for enriching management courses (Simon et al., 2003).

- **Exploring Cross-Cultural Aspects of Management:** Global dimensions can be easily incorporated by exploring cross-cultural perspectives utilizing the virtual classroom (Bell et al., 2001). Teaching global management in the virtual classroom can thus broaden students' perspectives and increase their cross-cultural effectiveness (May, 1997). It provides opportunities for making students more aware of international issues and for developing a greater knowledge and understanding of the global business environment. Creating international awareness and interest is an important prerequisite for developing knowledge, understanding and skills in the context of business-oriented education.

- **Interaction with International Partners:** Students and instructors with different socio-cultural and educational backgrounds bring a host of different ideas, experiences, and distinctive management assumptions and practices to the (virtual) classroom (Ashamalla, 1999). Differing views and new ideas can be exchanged between students and faculty located in the participating sites.

- **Increasing Students' Skills in Intercultural Communication:** When teaching global management, a learning environment should focus on enhancing communication skills and training cultural sensitivity (Lundstrom & White, 1997). Virtual classrooms can provide a valuable teaching resource for achieving this educational objective (Green & Gerber, 1996). Students learn to read, critique and actively cultivate the ability to determine the relevance of emerging trends; in short, their critical-thinking skills are increasingly challenged and enhanced through interaction with multiple sources (Celsi & Wolfinbarger, 2002).

- **Understanding the Role of Technology in a Global Business Environment:** In the corporate world, management departments increasingly take advantage of IT to perform their communication tasks. Thus, management professors must not only teach these technology-infused topics, they must also model active learning and flexibility by effectively using technology in their own extended classrooms. With video-conferencing increasingly becoming available on everyone's desktop, this technology provides a flexible new tool for communicating with international clients. Hence, management educators need to incorporate these tools into the classroom so that students become familiar with them while they are still studying.

PROCESSES AND INTERACTION PATTERNS

A collaborative, IT-mediated teaching event, such as the virtual classroom involves various actors such as students, instructors and IT personnel (Guth et al., 2001). The following paragraphs outline the stages of a virtual classroom experience and how its actors interact. A summary of these interactions pattern is shown in Figure 1.

Figure 1. Interaction pattern of collaborative, IT-mediated teaching

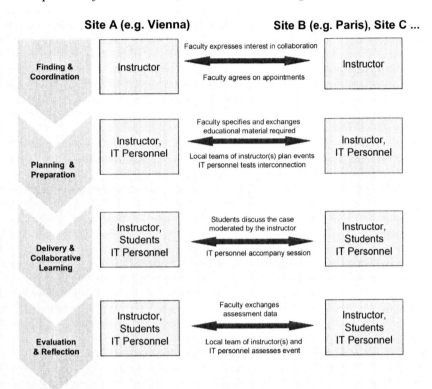

A virtual classroom lecture starts with the expression of interest in undertaking such a IT-mediated teaching event. The formulation of interests should happen a few months before the actual trial, because coordination of time schedules of all participants needs time. This phase is called the *finding and co-ordination phase* and should ideally be supported by the use of new media applications. These technologies can support a number of activities during this first stage, such as support scheduling, maintaining an infrastructure for a community of scholars interested in international research and teaching projects. Media like these can further support the search for suitable partners to conduct the virtual classroom. Finding the right partner is an essential issue. Preparing and conducting a virtual classroom lecture for the first time is extremely time consuming and often accompanied by complications, such as combining class schedules of all participants or different teaching approaches.

It is therefore advisable to find a cooperation partner who has the same interest in IT-mediated teaching as the initiators.

The second phase is the *planning and preparation phase*. During this stage, instructors begin to design the lecture. To do so they need to exchange teaching objectives, specify educational material to be used during the trial and outline the schedule of the lecture. Educational materials which have shown to be very applicable in the virtual classroom are case studies, PowerPoint slides and short videos. Here copyright and intellectual property issues need to be considered as well. Another issue of importance is the decision whether the trial should be evaluated at a later stage. If yes, the evaluation scheme has to be decided on as well. During this stage IT personnel has to inform all participants about the possibilities of the technology used. They need to explain all details of the technology to instructors and students to decrease nervousness and inefficient preparation. During this stage instructors are requested to rehearse the presentations with their students.

By the time *delivery and collaborative phase* starts the technology must be ready and the teaching activity should be fully prepared. At the actual virtual classroom event, instructors hold their lectures in co-operation with other sites according to their prior arranged schedule. Students present their case study results they had prepared during the preparation phase end receive feedback on their ideas from overseas audience.

The delivery phase may optionally be followed by an *evaluation and reflection phase*, during which the parties involved are asked to judge each others' performances: Student presentations are assessed, data on student's perceptions of the event are gathered and reflections on the technology and organizational setting can be made.

REFLECTIONS ON A FIELD EXPERIMENT

Participating Sites and Content

The virtual classroom experiment described in this chapter involved two virtual classroom lecture held by three active European sites (Ecole des Hautes Etudes Commerciales Paris, France; Warsaw University of Technology Business School, Poland; and Vienna University of Economics and Business Administration, Vienna, Austria). The trial took place in the framework of the Universal project, a project aiming at developing an infrastructure for the exchange of learning resources among higher education institutions in Europe (Brantner et al., 2001; Guth et al., 2001). By providing an inter-organizational information system, the still operational Educanext.org Portal, the project served as facilitator for the secure exchange of educational material (e.g., PowerPoint slides, case studies), as well as the organization of collaborative, IT-mediated teaching.

The Virtual Classroom Experiment

At the three active sites the trial was part of courses in the context of a business administration curriculum. All three courses were held independently of each other. The delivery of the discussions on the case studies was carefully planned. The content and structure of the discussion were prepared in advance, to a high level of detail. The faculty in France and Austria were responsible for each of the two lectures and formulated questions to be addressed during the session. Since most of the instructors were inexperienced with the technology the trials were outlined with a instructional scenario, which arranges the order in which all participants are required to ask or answer questions. Developing the scenario was quite time consuming and finally all participants were provided with copies of the cases discussed. They prepared the questions individually and were informed via e-mail or postal mail of which ones to prepare. The whole structure of the experiment was put down in a very precise time schedule, which was distributed to all participants to make sure that there would be no miscommunication during the virtual classroom lecture.

Before delivery, the instructors chose a number of students who were asked to participate actively by presenting their solutions in the trial. The selection of students was different at the various sites. In Austria, where such a trial was taking place for the first time, active students were chosen carefully and personally briefed by the instructor and the teaching assistant. These students prepared PowerPoint presentations and were asked to make them during the trial. More passive students prepared the same questions concerning the case, but no presentation. Thus they only submitted a chapter of five pages summarizing their proposed solution for the trial. In Warsaw, the preparation was based on general guidelines distributed by the instructor beforehand. The students presented solutions before delivery. In the planning and preparation phase the students who would present during delivery were chosen by the instructor. In France, the students and the instructor also discussed the case in advance. Topics related to the case study were assigned to the teams beforehand, but teams had to choose a presenter themselves.

A rigid structure of the trial was a result of insecurity of most participants. Most students presented in front of an international audience for the first time, instructors on the other hand were nervous about the usage of technology and being exposed to their, in some cases, more experienced colleagues.

Information Technology Used

The first trial used standard ISDN-based video-conferencing equipment. France Telecom operated a multicast-unit and the trial was further supported by Universidad Politécnica de Madrid which provided a comprehensive document on setting up a video conference environment.

At the second trial, the IP-based video-conferencing and collaboration system ISABEL (http://isabel.dit.upm.es) was deployed. GEANT (a multi-gigabit pan-European data communications network, http://www.geant.net) was not active at that time. ISABEL therefore required a comprehensive set up of local, national and international networks in order to guarantee a 2 Mbit/s connection between all the participating sites.

METHODOLOGY

After the first attempts using the virtual classroom in international management, teaching an investigation was conducted to examine the benefits and costs of delivering management education in a collaborative IT-mediated environment. Our goal was to find out about perceptions of all participants and to develop ideas on how to improve the efficiency of virtual media in management education.

The investigation was based on a qualitative research design. Patton (1990) defines qualitative

research as follows: "Qualitative methods consist of three kinds of data collection: (1) in-depth, open-ended interviews; (2) direct observation; and (3) written documents. Data from interviews consist of direct quotations from people about their experiences, opinions, feelings, and knowledge. Data from observations consist of detailed descriptions of people's activities, behaviours, actions and the full range of interpersonal interactions and organizational processes that are part of observable human experience" (p. 10).

For this chapter, interviews and personal observations were used to assess the virtual classroom trials. During the process eleven persons were interviewed (3 instructors, 1 teaching assistant, 1 IT personnel, and 6 students) in order to get a comprehensive overview of participants' perceptions. The interviews were transcribed and then analyzed. Dialects, wording and filler words were considered to be of less importance. The analysis itself was based on the question of how participants perceived teaching effectiveness of the virtual classroom. Content analysis was used to determine which aspects of the virtual classroom were considered to be valuable and which were not to generate global insights, by looking for similarities and varieties between the interviews and to recognize major trends (See Lamnek, 1995). The data gathered from the interviews was compared with the personal observations of the instructors. The results of the investigation are presented in the next sections.

ASSESSMENT OF THE TRIALS

Students

Actively Involved Students

The virtual classroom presents not only a technological but also an intercultural challenge for international business students. This increases students' interest to participate but despite this, the first virtual classroom trials did not meet students'

Figure 2. Snapshots of virtual classroom (Simon et al., 2003)

expectations. After the heavy workload during the preparation phase and as stressful perceived presentations during the trial, they did not feel that the trial was providing them with additional knowledge. The technology and the handling of it were overshadowing the actual event. Most students tried to perform well and concentrated on their presentations. During the lecture, students have to address two audiences simultaneously, the local and the remote, a task which is not easy to manage (Figure 2, top row). Students, therefore, mostly concentrated on their presentations and tried to give a very good impression. In doing so, they hardly listened to the content of the lecture or remarks of their counterparts.

On top of this, the time schedule was very tight and each student had only about five minutes to present his or her views. This further increased nervousness among all participants, because they did not want to miss their time slots.

Not surprisingly, students did not judge learning effects in international management very highly, but appreciated the experience in the virtual classroom. Students perceived it as very valuable for their future in an international business setting. As one student put it: "It's like speaking on TV. I was very nervous not to make a mistake." However, they also realize that their learning experience in international management was not increased by using a new teaching technology. Teaching effectiveness was therefore much lower than in a traditional classroom setting.

Passively Involved Students

Students showing a more passive approach towards virtual classroom activities evaluated the lectures in a different way. Since they were not stressed presenting and trying to give a good impression, they concentrated on the performances of their own classroom as well as of other sites. They appreciated the opportunity to gain knowledge from the interaction of all participants so they could observe cultural differences in presentation styles. One student observed: "Our instructor was in the middle of the students; the French instructor was sitting behind a desk and was separated from the students." They also remarked on differences in student—teacher interactions and the language abilities of the participants. In fact, they did not only profit from being exposed to faculty, students and ideas from other countries, they could also gain some intercultural experiences by simply watching the virtual classroom activities.

But they could also see the flaws of the event. They criticized the rigid structure of the discussions and presentations and the fact that there was a general tension in the classroom. The lecture seemed like "a long well-organized presentation" to these students, "which was a bit tiresome to watch."

Instructors

A lecture in an IT-mediated teaching environment differs greatly from a traditional lecture. Instructors interested in teaching technology are generally very enthusiastic about the possibilities arising with the integration of new technologies into their lectures, as information technology brings in a number of teaching opportunities, such as direct exchange with experts all over the world and discussion with overseas experts. However, they often underestimate that these activities also need extra preparation time. Instructors therefore perceived the integration of the virtual classroom into their management class as extremely time consuming. Setting up a virtual classroom for the first time may add an extra 40 hours of coordination for every lecture. Faculty participants have to be very clear about their teaching objectives and their preferred teaching style. All sites have to gain access to the educational material used. Another problem which needs to be considered in this phase is the time differences between participating sites. The farther the geographical distance between the sites the more complicated the arrangements of time schedules become.

Preparation time is decreasing with the number of trials experienced. Instructors do not only feel more confident once they have experienced the virtual classroom for a number of times, they also created some kind of routine with their co-operation partners. In doing so, instructors include more creative elements in the classroom or even start experiments.

Still, less experienced instructors feel often stressed by the fact that they will perform in front of an international audience and tend to prepare the lecture and students' presentation with very great detail. One instructor found the preparation efforts too time consuming and eliminated the virtual classroom event from his lectures after the first attempts. The two other instructors, on the other hand, were enthusiastic about the technology and found the unexpected unique learning effects (i.e., students' intercultural interpretations) very inspiring. Their overall expectations were not really fulfilled due to the structured outline of the lecture, because they had been surprised that the detailed outline did not improve but block communication between sites. Despite this, they started a number of experiments on how to integrate the virtual classroom into their future teaching activities, assuming that as experience with the new technology grows, teaching effectiveness will increase also.

Neither of the instructors got any information on the technology used. However, they felt sufficiently supported during the trial by the IT personnel. Perceptions of technology varied. Instructors who had worked in this context before were enthusiastic about future possibilities for joint teaching. Instructors encountering the technology for the first time perceived the limitations of the media more strongly, whereas more experienced instructors did not. Or, as one instructor put it: "Perfect means the professor forgets that he is teaching in a virtual classroom."

IT Personnel

The virtual classroom is a live event, which gives technical support extra importance. Technical staff is therefore more strongly included in class preparation and teaching activities than before. During preparation phase, instructors will demand detailed instructors on the system used and its applications in the classroom. IT staff also needs to communicate with IT personnel at remote sites, to set up technical systems at all sites and test their interoperability. They therefore need to communicate with two target audiences: Local users (instructors and students) with little experiences using the virtual classroom and their fellow technology personnel at the partner sites. These additional tasks may put additional pressure and work loads on IT personnel supporting the virtual classroom experiences.

DESIGNING THE VIRTUAL CLASSROOM FOR MANAGEMENT TEACHING

The authors conducted a number of virtual classroom trials after the evaluation presented in the last section. Based on these experiences and perceptions of the first trials, the following recommendations for each stage of the virtual classroom experience were developed.

Finding and Co-Ordination Phrase

In the finding and co-ordination phase, instructors interested in IT-based learning environments are searching for partners who are willing to participate in a cooperative class. Preparation should start weeks before the start of the virtual classroom experiences and create additional efforts which are mostly underestimated. During this phase, the level of technology has to be well known and understood by the instructor to make sure there will be no problems connecting the various sites. Universities have to update their video-conferencing equipment frequently to keep up with technological changes. Preparation time usually decreases when experience increases and all participants get to know each other.

Other aspects to be considered are the compatibility of teaching styles and topics between the participating sites. Not every teaching style can be applied in a classroom in which two or more classes and instructors are present. Teaching styles also need to be culturally adapted. Case studies are advisable, because all participants can prepare them beforehand and practice their presentations. Lectures and speeches are suitable for the virtual classroom as well, but in many cases students reported that they felt "like watching TV" and their attention decreased. Discussions with students and presenter cannot be as spontanous as in a "real" classroom, and also need to be discussed before starting the preparations. All instructors and students need to feel comfortable about the teaching style applied in the virtual classroom.

At this stage, respecting intellectual property rights is essential but makes the distribution of materials more difficult. All printed case studies for example need to be placed in good time, all PowerPoint slides need to be converted into pdf files to hinder direct reuse, all non-digital materials need to be sent to all other participating sites.

Planning and Preparation Phrase

Students

Students generally show great interest in participating in the virtual classroom, but need to be carefully prepared before the trial to improve learning efficiency. During planning and preparation phase, the instructor and IT personnel are advised to explain how collaborative, IT-mediated teaching offers advantages on educational but also on personal levels. Being connected to other business schools does not only allow students to experience different teaching styles but also get feedback from faculty with differing cultural and research backgrounds. The virtual classroom also gives them the opportunity to increase their personal skills and gain experience in public speaking.

In any event, the virtual classroom event is perceived as a challenge for participating students. Instead of only 20 or 30 students in a classroom, one more group of students of a differing cultural background has to be integrated in the teaching activity. The instructor therefore needs to handle the class preparation and interaction during the trial with special care. Jackson (2003) reports that students can be divided into two streams: techno-enthusiasts and students who see IT in the classroom with some trepidation. Students who have not participated in virtual classrooms before are generally very curious about the new environment, but also show some anxiety when presenting "live" in front of an international audience. Instructors' empathy plays an especially important role in the application of the virtual classroom. Students need a lot of support and encouragement in highly IT-dependent courses (Rosie, 2000). The classroom is opened to the world, which creates a lot of nervousness, especially when using the virtual classroom for the first time. This leads to intensive preparation of the issues discussed and personal supervision of the materials students are going to present.

When delivery is conducted in a multilingual setting, many participants are forced to present their solutions in a foreign language. Since the virtual classroom is mainly conducted in English, it is important to also involve students whose foreign language skills are not very good (Simon et al., 2003). This may present a stressful situation for the students involved, since some of them may not be familiar or comfortable presenting their results in a foreign language. It may further cause difficulties understanding participants in case they speak with a certain accent or use non-familiar words during their presentation. Spontaneous questions and avid discussions may therefore evolve very slowly if at all.

Instructors

In general, instructors would have preferred a longer and more intensive preparation phase. The first virtual classroom event presents a very stressful situation for them as well, especially for younger faculty not being used to teach in front of more experienced colleagues. It is therefore recommended to discuss questions of course outline, presentation styles, contents and discussion processes with other faculty participating. This helps getting an impression about other participants' expectations of the virtual classroom and improves the quality of the teaching endeavor, especially when a virtual classroom lecture is carried out for the first time. It is further advisable to limit the number of sites to two during the first trials. The higher the number of sites involved the more stressful will the first virtual classroom be perceived.

During the *planning and preparation phase,* instructors must leave enough room for new solutions to be developed spontaneously. During IT-mediated classroom experiences, instructors often tend to push students towards developing a "perfect solution" beforehand in order to guarantee a good performance in front of the international audience. This often puts additional stress on students and may inhibit them from acting in an open and flexible manner during delivery. We therefore recommend a semi-structured teaching scenario without a tight time schedule associated with it. Instructors further need to stress the importance of students' creativity when preparing for the event. For less experienced instructors, a scenario like this may seem very stressful, however, our experience showed that once the number of virtual classroom sessions increases, instructors get more relaxed about the technological environment and

begin to develop a number of ideas on how to increase its teaching effectiveness.

IT Personnel

IT personnel get a new role in virtual classroom. They are not only main actors in the delivery and collaborative learning phase, but also extend their role as technical supporters to technology enablers. At the beginning of the virtual classroom experience, they need to communicate with IT personnel from other participating sites to test the equipment used. Their additional job is to inform the instructors involved about the possibilities and challenges of the new technology. This is especially important, as instructors who are not familiar with the technology may feel insecure about the first trials themselves. As their experiences increases, the ability to outline the virtual lecture is improving as well. At the beginning of the virtual classroom experiences however, IT staff need to be able to instruct and communicate with all participants.

Students should also be familiarized with the technology used, especially how to handle a microphone and how to address to audiences simultaneously. It has also shown to be successful, to provide background information on the technology used to instructors and students. Another aspect that should be considered is to point out the technology's educational and business opportunities. Satisfaction with the virtual classroom also increases if all participants (all instructors involved and in some cases also students) communicate their goals and ideas to each other before the first actual virtual teaching event.

Delivery and Collaborative Learning Phrase

Motivating Students

Students perceive lectures conducted in the virtual classroom as something special, which will remain in their memories. The differing aspects of the topics discussed by students at the remote sites are positively perceived by most interviewed participants (Simon et al., 2003). The new setting and international discussion partners are highly appreciated and discussing with students from other countries via video-based technology is perceived as "very exciting and a new experience". The exposure to different cultures and the opportunities to interact during the lectures on an international basis with universities in foreign countries have a major impact on the positive emotions associated with the lecture.

Despite this positive result, the virtual classroom requires highly motivated students. It is easy to confuse the classroom setting with the passive watching of TV. Seeing colleagues from behind a camera sometimes encourages the tendency to drift off and become even more passive. Involving students in new teaching activities means to identify students who show a strong interest in modern media or teaching technologies. These students should be put on the forefront of the first attempt of virtual classroom teaching and can make the first impression of this technology more appealing to students who feel a bit intimidated about it at first. However, if instructors were to divide classes into active and passive students, they might impose a new two-tier role-distribution, reinforced by technology, with negative effects on overall learning effectiveness (Simon et al., 2002).

Controlling Virtual Classrooms' Interaction

The various instructors at the different sites are a dominant feature of the virtual classroom because they play a vital role in leading the class discussion. Interaction within the classroom may automatically occur, but effective interaction, which aims at promoting learning, does not (Guzley et al., 2001). Technology cannot handle all aspects of group dynamics, which requires instructors to balance IT-based activities and personal interaction (Jackson, 2003). Instructors have to coordinate

contributions from the local audience as well as from the remote sites. The dialogue between the various instructors itself adds to the dynamics of the educational activity and helps to hold students' attention (Tsichritzis, 1999). The need for classroom interaction increases with increases in the number of sites and students participating in the virtual classroom. Teaching simultaneously at more than two sites involved requires a relatively rigid discussion structure in order to avoid chaos in the discussion process. Every participant was given about five minutes to either place a question or answer one based on a very detailed schedule. This inhibited students and instructors to communicated freely and left no room for ad hoc contributions. Free discussion could not develop and most answers were prepared very carefully. Intercultural differences between different sites were therefore only experienced by students who just watched the whole trial, but did not present their results.

Communication including various sites and a high number of students naturally creates challenges for instructors. Not all students can be addressed and it is also difficult to hold the attention of all participants, which may lead to a larger number of students not participating and becoming less interested (Rosenberg, 2001). The quality of the virtual classroom can therefore be enhanced by keeping the group of participating students small (Guzley et al., 2001). The more sites and students participate the more difficult is it to integrate all of them in a discussion. A higher number of participants therefore also implies longer waiting periods and a lot of listening. It is advisable not to rely on an overly-structured design so that interaction between the various participants of the virtual classroom remains fluid and dynamic. In many cases, instructors tend to structure the discussion with the foreign partners too rigidly. This involves designating students to present results and ask prepared questions. However, this also involves a higher proportion of passive students in every site. A more lively and spontaneous interaction design between the various sites proves more satisfying when applying the virtual classroom into the management curriculum. Students listen more attentively and contribute more actively to a lively discussion with culturally diverse participants.

Evaluation and Reflection Phase

After the virtual classroom is conducted, evaluation and reflection of the experience are very important. Especially after the first attempts using video-conferencing technology, instructors and IT personnel need to discuss its effectiveness and possible hindrances when applying it in order to get feedback on their performance by their colleagues from other sites. This may induce critical reactions from colleagues but will improve the future performance of all participants.

Another important aspect is to assess students' perceptions of the virtual classroom. Their feedback does not only enable improvement of the interaction in future virtual classroom activities but also gives them a forum to express their opinions on the experience. For most students presenting via a video-conference system is a rather challenging task; they not only have to speak in a foreign language, but are also exposed to an unknown and sometimes critical audience, whose reactions they can not calculate. Knowing students' perceptions makes it easier to prepare them better and also improves their performance. This is especially important for students who are participating in the virtual classroom for the first time. As time goes by and students and instructors gain more experience, feedback sessions may get shorter. All participants will then have developed a certain routine in video-conferencing.

FUTURE TRENDS

As today's business educators' focus is not only on theory-orientation, but increasingly attempt to prepare students for a future in multinational corporations, practice-oriented teaching approaches become imperative. Technologies, such as the virtual classroom, are not only an interesting feature of every business course focusing on international aspects, but an interesting means to introduce students to technology which are used in modern corporations on a daily basis. Latest developments allow students to implement video-based technology at their personal computers. They can so get used to the technology and its usage, which will improve the efficiency of virtual classroom event, since students will concentrate more strongly on their presentations and the interaction during the trial.

There is a need to develop new applications for the virtual classroom in international management teaching. We implemented a number of new features into our lectures, such as guest speakers from overseas units speaking to the students about their work, company-projects in which students cooperated with corporations via video-based information systems. As technology advances interactive student projects between classes dispersed in various countries will be another future option.

Concluding Remarks

Every new teaching technology needs extensive preparation time, and the virtual classroom is no exception. Both students and instructors need experience in order to begin to feel comfortable with this technology. However, since instructors and students are exposed to the feedback of colleagues from other sites, pressure to perform well increases and overshadows the first experiences with technology.

Technology must therefore be introduced very carefully at the beginning of the teaching experience. For virtual classroom interaction, instructors are encouraged to identify motivated students, focus on their active participation in in-class discussion and provide empathic support when needed. Students should be given clear guidelines on the importance of various issues concerning case study presentation, but at the same time have enough freedom to find solutions for themselves. When preparing the delivery, instructors should list the issues that will be subject to discussion beforehand, so that remote instructors and students can prepare themselves, but desist from a strict schedule.

Students profit from the experience in any case. However, although a one-time virtual classroom experience may stay in students' minds, it does not increase overall teaching effectiveness. It is therefore advisable to implement virtual classrooms on a more regular basis to ensure their teaching effectiveness in international management teaching can be increased.

Numerous challenges remain in the area of deploying collaborative, IT-mediated teaching. In particular, more thorough investigation of several issues is required: how to deal with a larger, international audience, how to avoid losing the attention of passive students and how to integrate other teaching media like presentation slides, videos and speeches into the teaching environment.

Our findings show that a virtual classroom environment is perceived as more successful as faculty gains experience in using it. At their first trial, instructors have difficulties in judging the quality of the technology, and tend to overestimate its challenges and limitations. Hence, virtual classroom teaching needs to be conducted a number of times to establish a routine and confidence among all participants.

ACKNOWLEDGMENT

This work was supported by the Universal Project, a research project partly sponsored by the European Commission (IST-1999-11747). We would like to express our special gratitude to the team from the Universidad Politécnica de Madrid.

REFERENCES

Alavi, M., Yoo, Y., & Vogel, D. (1997). Using information technology to add value to management education. *Academy of Management Journal, 40*(6), 1310-1333.

Alderfer, C. (2003). Using experiential methods to teach about measurement validity. *Journal of Management Education, 27*(5), 520-532.

Armstrong, J., & Sperry, T. (1994). The ombudsman: Business school prestige- Research versus teaching. *Interfaces, 24*(2), 13-43.

Ashamalla, M. (1999). Directed self-learning: The use of student-generated cases in international management training. *Journal of Teaching in International Business, 11*(2), 71-87.

Bell, J., Deans, K., Ibbotson, P., & Sinkovics, R. (2001). Towards the 'Internetalization' of international marketing education. *Marketing Education Review, 11*(3), 69-79.

Berger, K., & Topol, M. (2001). Technology to enhance learning: Use of a Web site platform in traditional classes and distance learning. *Marketing Education Review, 11*(3), 15-26.

Blake, I., & Jarvenpaa, S. (1996). Will the Internet revolutionize business education and research?. *Sloan Management Review, 37*(3), 33-41.

Brantner, S., Enzi, T., Neumann, G., & Simon, B. (2001). *UNIVERSAL- Design and implementation of a highly flexible e-market place of learning resources.* Madison, WI: IEEE Computer Society.

Celsi, R., & Wolfinbarger, M. (2002). Discontinuous classroom innovation: Waves of change for marketing education. *Journal of Marketing Education, 24*(1), 64-73.

Dede, C. (1990). The evolution of distance learning: Technology-mediated interactive learning. *Journal of Research on Computing in Education, 22*(1), 247-264.

Garrison, R. (2000). Theoretical challenges for distance education in the 21st century: A shift from structural to transactional issues. *International Review of Research in Open and Distance Learning, 1*(1), 1-17.

Green, K. (1999). When wishes come true. *Change, (March - April)*, 10-15.

Green, R., & Gerber, L. (1996). Educator insights: Strategic partnerships for global education-Linkages with overseas institutions. *Journal of International Marketing, 4*(3), 89-100.

Guth, S., Neumann, G., & Simon, B. (2001). *UNIVERSAL - Design spaces for learning media.* Maui, HI: IEEE.

Guzley, R., Avanzino, S., & Bor, A. (2001). Simulated computer-mediated/video-interactive distance learning: A test of motivation, interaction satisfaction, delivery, learning & perceived effectiveness. *Journal of Computer-Mediated Communication, 6*(3). Retrieved August 31, 2006 from http://jcmc.indiana.edu/vol6/issue3/guzley.html.

Jackson, P. (2003). Ten challenges for introducing Web-supported learning to overseas students in the social sciences. *Active Learning in Higher Education, 4*(1), 87-106.

Kerres, M. (1998). *Multimediale und telemediale Lernumgebungen.* München: Oldenbourg.

Kolb, D. (1984). *Experiential learning: Experience as the source of learning and development.* Englewood Cliffs, NJ.: Prentice-Hall.

Lamnek, S. (1995). *Qualitative sozialforschung,* (Band II, 3rd ed.). Weinheim: Beltz Psychologie Verlags Union.

Leidner, D., & Jarvenpaa, S. (1995). The use of information technology to enhance management school education: A theoretical view. *MIS Quarterly, 19*(3), 265-291.

Lundstrom, W., & White, S. (1997). A gap analysis of professional and academic perceptions of the importance of international marketing curriculum content and research areas. *Journal of Marketing Education, 19*(2), 16-25.

Manning, R., Cohen, M., & DeMichiell, R. (2003). Distance learning: Step by step. *Journal of Information Technology Education, 2*(1), 115-130.

May, B. (1997). Curriculum internationalization and distance learning: Convergence of necessity and technology. *Journal of Teaching in International Business, 9*(1), 35-50.

Meier, P., & Simon, B. (2000). *Reengineering undergraduate teaching by introducing Internet-based learning information systems.* Vienna: Springer.

Patton, M. (1990). *Qualitative evaluation and research methods.* Newbury Park, CA: Sage Publications.

Pallab, P., & Kaushi, M. (2001). Using information technology for active learning in international business education. *Marketing Education Review, 11*(3), 81-88.

Rosenberg, M. (2001). *E-Learning - Strategies for delivering knowledge in the digital age.* New York, NY: McGraw-Hill.

Rosie, A. (2000). ʹDeep learningʹ. *Active Learning in Higher Education, 1*(1), 45-59.

Simon, B., Haghirian, P., & Schlegelmilch, B. (2002). Case study teaching via collaborative information technology. In: S. Wrycza (Ed.), *Proceedings of the 10th European Conference on Information Systems.* Gdanks, Poland.

Simon, B., Haghirian, P., & Schlegelmilch, B. (2003). Enriching global marketing education with virtual classrooms - An effectiveness study. *Marketing Education Review, 13*(3), 27-39.

Sinkovics, R., Bell, J., & Deans, K. (2004). Using information communication technology to develop international entrepreneurship competencies. *Journal of International Entrepreneurship, 2*(1-2), 125-137.

Smart, D., Kelley, C., & Conant, J. (1999). Marketing education in the year 2000: Changes observed and challenges anticipated. *Journal of Marketing Education, 21*(3), 206-216.

Tsichritzis, D. (1999). Reengineering the university. *Communications of the ACM, 42*(6), 93-100.

Ueltschy, L. (2001). An exploratory study of integrating interactive technology into the marketing curriculum. *Journal of Marketing Education, 23*(1), 63-72.

Webster, J., & Hackley, P. (1997). Teaching effectiveness in technology-mediated distance learning. *Academy of Management Journal, 40*(6), 1282-1309.

KEY TERMS

Computer-Supported Cooperative Learning (CSCL): Any kind of learning process, where cooperation and communication between two dispersed learning sites and their participants are supported by the use of computer-mediated information and communication systems.

Computer Simulation: Training situation in which a real experiment is conducted in form of a computer-supported case study. In business, education simulations are seen as an extension to business case studies.

Educational Mediator: An educational mediator is a service that supports the sharing of learning resources. Examples of educational mediators are Educanext, Merlot or Ariadne. These portals support the exchange of learning resources under open content licenses (e.g., the Creative Commons Licenses). Recent developments in interoperability research have led to a federation of these portals via a protocol referred to as Simple Query Interface (SQI).

E-Learning: Any kind of learning process, which is supported by digital media for presenting and distributing teaching materials or improving or allowing communication between instructor(s) and learner(s), such as simulating a certain situation or allowing access to information which would not be accessible without technology.

Virtual Classroom: A virtual classroom connects geographically dispersed instructors and students, for example via a video conference system. Information and communication technology (ICT) is used to facilitate communication between students and instructors.

Video Conferencing: Video Conferencing Technology provides means for audio and visual communication over telephone lines (ISDN-based) or Internet technology (IP-based). Nowadays, video-conferencing technology is already available at the desktop, provided by Instant Messaging Tools such as Skype, Yahoo! Messenger and Windows Live™ Messenger.

Chapter XIX
Building Online Training Programs for Virtual Workplaces

Christa Ehmann Powers
Smarthinking Inc., USA

Beth L. Hewett
Independent Scholar, USA

ABSTRACT

Companies that conduct their business either in an entirely online setting or in hybrid environments (i.e., online and face-to-face) are in a unique position in today's global economy. They are poised to take advantage of the Internet's flexibility both for assisting their clients and for hiring the best workers available regardless of geographical location. They also are in a unique position when it comes to training and preparing their workers to assist those clients. However, many such companies do not have principle-centered training materials that they can adapt to meet their own institutional needs. This chapter provides employers with such training principles, ones that have been substantiated by practice and research from various professional fields and that have been successfully used in an Internet-based business that employs hundreds of part- and full-time individuals. Specifically, this chapter provides readers with: (1) an educational and financial rationale for conducting online human adaptive training for virtual workplaces; (2) an understanding of training/professional development principles and strategies for online employees in virtual businesses via one-to-one and/or group human adaptive settings, and (3) an understanding of how to scale such training processes efficiently and with measurable results gleaned from qualitative and quantitative methods.

INTRODUCTION

Companies that either conduct their business in an entirely online setting or in hybrid environments (i.e., online and face-to-face) are in a unique position in today's global economy. They are poised to take advantage of the Internet's flexibility both for assisting their clients and for hiring the best workers available regardless of geographical location. They also are in a unique position when it comes to training and preparing their workers to assist those clients. However, many such companies do not have principle-centered training materials that they can adapt to meet their own institutional needs.

The purpose of this chapter is to provide employers with such training principles, ones that have been substantiated by practice and research from various professional fields and that have been successfully used in an Internet-based business that employs hundreds of part- and full-time individuals. Specifically, this chapter provides readers with: (1) an educational and financial rationale for conducting online human adaptive training for virtual workplaces; (2) an understanding of training/professional development principles and strategies for online employees in virtual businesses via one-to-one and/or group human adaptive settings, and (3) an understanding of how to scale such training processes efficiently and with measurable results gleaned from qualitative and quantitative methods.

Although little is written about training employees virtually for virtual work settings, much is written about "e-training" for professional development purposes when "blended" employee teams work remotely *and* face-to-face. Schank (2002), for example, proposes solutions for such business training initiatives and education settings. However, his solutions primarily entail the incorporation of artificial intelligence (AI) into training situations: trainees complete scenarios of various, but generally have low, human interactivity levels (e.g, Aldrich, 2004; Schank, 2005). From practical, financial, and principled perspectives, AI can be appropriate for certain workplace and training circumstances. However, there are numerous situations for which *humans* need to conduct some or all online training interactively with employees who already do or who will work online. Particularly for businesses that involve high-touch, in-depth, consultative client relationships, training methodologies often need to account for human interactions that cannot necessarily be achieved by AI simulations.

Beyond AI, some have addressed human e-learning and training in online educational contexts through adult learning principles (e.g., Salmon, 2002; Hewett & Ehmann, 2004; Cargile Cook & Grant-Davie, 2005; Graves & Twigg, 2006; Hewett & Ehmann Powers, 2007). More work is needed, however, that addresses how such principles and others can be applied to training situations that yield effective, efficient, and scaleable results for virtual workplaces. In their book devoted solely to online training, *Advanced Web-Based Training Strategies: Unlocking Instructionally Sound Online Learning*, Driscol and Carliner (2005) also emphasized the need for continued scholarship in this area.

This chapter, therefore, addresses three primary issues. First, it provides readers with an educational and financial rationale for conducting online human-adaptive training for virtual workplaces. Second, it considers training/professional development principles and strategies for online employees in virtual businesses via one-to-one and/or group human-adaptive settings. Finally, within this framework, it discusses how to scale such training processes efficiently and with measurable results gleaned from qualitative and quantitative methods. For the purposes of this chapter, we focus on online training with specific regard to workplaces that require employees to conduct *all* work with co-workers, colleagues, and supervisors online and at a distance. However, the principle-based e-training that we outline certainly can be valuable for those who interact with employees and clients in blended settings.

This chapter draws on our experiences with Smarthinking, Inc.[1], a business built on the premise of aggregating geographically diverse employees for a 24-7 academic support service. Highlighting design and implementation principles, the chapter focuses on four areas:

- **A Background for Online Training.** The chapter begins with a review of the relevant literature and puts online training in context of other research and scholarship regarding the professional development of virtual teams.

- **Leveraging the Internet for Human Adaptive Training.** Despite being virtual, many workplaces conduct training and professional development in face-to-face venues or online through AI rather than online with other humans. This section provides an overview of educational and financial factors, including effective uses of both trainer and trainee time, that support a decision to conduct online training with human trainers. Unique learning opportunities for trainees and resulting workplace performance and economic benefits are discussed.

- **Design Principles for Online Training.** Having presented conditions under which online training is appropriate, this section examines a five-principle training framework (Hewett & Ehmann, 2004). We will discuss the principles of investigation, immersion, individualization, association, and reflection in relation to their applicability in virtual workplace settings.

- **Future Trends and Implementation Strategies for Online Training.** This section considers future trends in the field of online training relative to the aforementioned principles. Within the context of an ever-changing technology landscape, such trends include conducting training with a disparate group of individuals; conducting training efficiently; producing quality, measurable results; and designing training programs that can be scaled as workplaces grow.

A concluding section then explores areas for development in online training and suggests future research opportunities. Readers will learn both online training principles and procedures for virtual workplaces, as well as steps for addressing such developments.

BACKGROUND

According to Gignac (2005) and Illegems and Verbecke (2003), virtual workplaces in which employees work online from remote locations are increasingly common. Blended work environments that involve some face-to-face as well as online-only employees, or a combination of both, also exist. Merely analyzing the growth of universities that offer predominantly online courses such as the University of Phoenix or University of Maryland University College (UMUC) suggests that in online work environments (both academic and non-academic) more and more employees have opportunities to conduct their work online (e.g., Ruch, 2003; Berg, 2005). The 2005/2006 National Readiness Survey released in July 2006 indicated that 11% of all employees in the United States do some type of work remotely with the potential for 25% of all workers to engage in some form of regular telecommuting (p. 2). By definition, the number of virtual employees who are now required to conduct all of their work online—with co-workers, supervisors, and clients—also has increased. Recent scholarship speaks to the increase in virtual work spaces (Illegems & Verbeke, 2003; Ghaoui, 2004; Gignac, 2005).

The growth and nature of virtual workplaces require that organizations reassess and question their approaches and infrastructures for beginning employee orientation and training, professional development, and management. Organization and development professionals must ask: How do employees transition from traditional face-to-face work environments to online ones? How do supervisors manage employees remotely? How do employees learn to collaborate with one another remotely? How do employees serve clients in an online setting as effectively as in a face-to-face setting?

Indeed, these questions typically revolve around issues of *online training*—for new employee orientation purposes and/or ongoing professional development for employees. Within the context of employee work in virtual business environments, Horton's (2000) defined online training as "any purposeful, considered application of Web technologies to the task of educating a fellow human being" (p. 2). Like Horton, we categorize online training as a form of online learning. Drawing on thinkers like de Leeuwe (2006) and Stockley (2006), such education also is called "e-learning," which we define "as the formal and informal delivery of learning and professional development activities (including training), processes, and associations via any electronic methods including but not limited to the Internet, CD-ROM, videotape, and DVD" (Hewett & Ehmann, 2004, p. xv). Therefore, we can reasonably draw on theories of online teaching and learning in online training situations.

The literature about online training can be grouped into one of three distinctive categories: (1) education-based work that focuses heavily on the "pedagogy" of online training and the learning theory behind it (e.g., Carliner, 2004; Ghaoui, 2004; Bourne & Moore, 2005); (2) scholarship that focuses primarily on the operational and technical mechanisms associated with training (e.g., Horton, 2000; Horton & Horton, 2003; Aldrich, 2004); and (3) those few works that bring together both aspects of pedagogical and operational implications (e.g., Driscoll & Carliner, 2005).

Another characteristic of the literature is that there exists a significant gap regarding online training specifically designed for virtual workplaces. Few pieces, outside of our own, overtly address online training for employees who will exclusively work in virtual business environments, whereas much of the literature discusses online training for employees who eventually will work in face-to-face situations. Interestingly, those texts that do focus on virtual team development (e.g., Gignac, 2005) tend to conceptualize the training implementation as a face-to-face endeavor. Further, the majority of literature relies less on empirical findings regarding training and more on what authors recommend *should* occur in such situations and the philosophical approach that *should* be taken to achieve those presumed goals

(e.g., Horton, 2000; Horton & Horton, 2003).

Within online learning and its subset of online training, this chapter focuses on two primary communication modalities: asynchronous and synchronous. The use of these modalities in online training is what Driscol and Carliner (2005) labelled as "blended learning" (p. 12). The training discussed here also involves asynchronous and synchronous human adaptive training experiences that engage human trainers and trainees, rather than, for example, static contents, self-paced AI modules, or automated multiple-choice tests.

Regardless of the modality and level of human adaptive interactivity, however, many argue that online training cannot yield the kinds of learning that occurs in face-to-face settings. These concerns are well taken; however, we believe that preparing to work in virtual settings requires *online* training. In his on-going meta-analysis of student outcomes and "alternate modes of education delivery," Russell (2001; ongoing) found that the incorporation of Internet-based modalities has no effect on student learning outcomes. In other words, students learn equally "well" online compared to traditional, brick-and-mortar venues. Also acknowledging that student/trainee learning can occur in online contexts, Horton (2000) argued that online training can address "just-in-time training" needs of organizations that have underprepared employees who must learn technology skills and programming. Indeed, online training can be used to help employees develop particular skills in a timely fashion.

We disagree, however, with those like Carliner (2004) who suggested that online learning and training *best* suit the teaching of "rote skills" and "prerequisite material" whereas the traditional training classroom "provides an opportunity to develop higher-order thinking skills and simulate interpersonal exchanges" (p. 36). Rather, we have experienced and researched that online training and, in turn, the work accomplished in virtual workplaces can involve highly complex thinking, tasks, and processes and that it can "work" both for those who may need additional time with certain procedures as well as those who progress rapidly through a training program. Further, unlike Horton (2000) who believed that the incorporation of online technologies into training "does not change how humans learn, but it does change how we can teach them" (p. 6), evidence suggests that there are distinctive outcomes and learning objectives for online work that can only be produced by engaging in *online* training (Ehmann Powers, in progress-a; in progress-b).

Finally, although the aforementioned work speaks to various online training issues, missing from the literature is a comprehensive set of operational and educational principles for training that rises above any one particular venue, situation, business, or technology platform. Also missing is the strategic justification for engaging in online training, particularly with virtual employees. The rest of this chapter, therefore, suggests an online training rationale and principles for the design and implementation of training programs.

MAIN FOCUS OF THE CHAPTER

Leveraging the Internet for Human Adaptive Training

This section provides a justification for training employees online for virtual workplaces. Online training is integral to workplaces that require employees to work with each other and/or clients online rather than in face-to-face settings. Additionally, online training within a business context is driven and necessitated by: (1) a commitment to providing employees with quality learning experiences through which they demonstrate understanding of relevant work material; and (2) a commitment to meeting operational parameters, benchmarks, and efficiencies

To support this justification, we use our early experience developing an online training program for Smarthinking, Inc., an online learning center that was founded on the belief that the Internet could be used to leverage highly skilled and trained

educators to deliver online educational services 24 hours a day, 7 days a week. The company's originators theorized that by aggregating a virtual workforce of educators, the delivery of services across a multitude of educational institutions would be more efficient and of equal or greater quality than organically grown services from any one single institution or program (e.g., Smith, 1999; Maeroff, 2003; Chediak, 2005; Jaschik, 2005; Paley, 2006). By definition, online educators would be staffed around the world to provide the service and could work from any location with computer and Internet access. Although particular management positions were conceived as face-to-face, well over 95% of the workforce would be working with each other and clients remotely. Further, at the company's inception, none of the employees were expected to have online work experience. Within this context, the rationale for online training was clear: online training would be needed for both quality purposes as well as operational efficiencies.

In our early experience with Smarthinking, we saw that for employees the transition from face-to-face to online contexts was complex. Acclimating to a text-based mode of asynchronous and synchronous communication and establishing virtual rapport was not a straightforward process. Employees could not directly transfer their understandings, strategies, and skills about their work from face-to-face to online employment environments. Doing so would necessarily affect their work product and their relationships with co-workers and clients. It did not make sense educationally, therefore, to have trainees undergo exercises in one physical location. Rather, the training that we developed reflected very closely the online duties that employees would perform when working with live, online clients. Some of these specific challenges and complexities have been documented in various publications (e.g., Ehmann, 2000; 2001; Ehmann, Heywood, & Higgison, 2000; Ehmann Powers, in progress-a; in progress-b; Hewett, 2004; 2006).

In addition to such substantive quality standards, we could not overlook operational efficiencies. For the purposes of this discussion, we use Hydro One Inc.'s (2004) definition of operational efficiency as: "reducing costs while providing the same service to customers" (p. 3). The extent to which training for a particular service was delivered efficiently and within operational parameters of Smarthinking's particular business model influenced the decision to conduct training online, or via some other non-face-to-face medium. In other words, it was our fiduciary responsibility to assess and reduce internal expenses as the institution continued to provide and improve the quality of products and services to customers.

In the Smarthinking scenario, it was neither feasible nor financially responsible to coordinate and schedule in-person training. Costs of travel and facilities would be prohibitively high. Additionally, we recruited individuals on an ongoing, rolling basis according to the demand for our service; the composition of our team was never static. As such, defining particular times for employees to engage in face-to-face training simply was not feasible. Further, as the business grew, we expected that employees would continue to work from across the globe and certain business processes would be changeable. Long term, therefore, we needed to implement a system that could accommodate a global workforce as well as the on-going advances of the business.

Interestingly, the academic/educational literature on online training at the time of Smarthinking's inception (and even today) rarely addresses the operational components of online training in this regard. When it does, it often decries the notion of "efficiency" within a learning context (e.g,. Cargile Cook, 2005; Rude, 2005), labeling any discussion of efficiency as antithetical to the learning process. Yet, within the virtual workplace (as well as traditional workplaces for that matter), we continue to contend that the realities of meeting deadlines and operational benchmarks cannot be ignored. Whether in an openly for-profit or non-profit context, efficiencies must be embraced

and considered of equal importance. Indeed, as Hewett (2004) discovered, sometimes attention to efficiency in the workplace actually assists the client (in her case, the student using the learning assistance) by providing a more focused, do-able set of tasks. Within this framework, therefore, we advocate that online training for *both* quality and efficiency objectives is a key rationale for leveraging the Internet to engage in online training.

DESIGN PRINCIPLES FOR ONLINE TRAINING

Working from the premise that *online* employment necessitates *online* training and that technology platforms and innovations are ever changing, we argue that training should be conceptualized within a principle-centered framework (Hewett & Ehmann, 2004). Taking account of the inevitability of technological advances that many individuals like Kilby (2001) and Horton (2000) highlighted, we advocate an approach whereby trainers: (1) identify instructional principles for training that outlive specific technology platforms and (2) then identify training methods adaptable to particular platforms (Hewett & Ehmann, 2004). In other words, whether one uses asynchronous e-mail, synchronous messaging, or particular commercial software for an orientation classroom- or Internet-based networking platform, a training program can engage operational and educational principles that address online business processes comprehensively (also see Covey's (1992) notion of "true north"). The outcome yields a training program that is qualitatively strong, yet "contextually adaptive" in that it will remain structurally sound despite a company's technology changes or upgrades and/or program developments (Hewett & Ehmann, 2004).

Cognizant of action research, adult learning, business-based online "e-training," and experiences as cross-disciplinary educators, we bring together five commonly acknowledged educational principles to ground the development of any online training program: (1) Investigation, (2) Immersion, (3) Individualization, (4) Association, and (5) Reflection. Within this principle-centered framework, we do not advocate any one particular teaching and learning theory for a particular training program. Rather, we believe that different teaching and learning approaches must be driven by the nature of work, project, learners, and task at hand—rather than ideology. In some cases, a strictly "behaviorist"/ "positivist" learning approach might work best; in others, a "constructionist" approach might be most appropriate. Regardless of the ways in which trainers develop their individual training programs, however, particular universal principles that can be applied to their architecture.

Investigation is our first principle in the design of an online training program. Given the lack of empirical research about the effect of the online medium on various work processes, we suggest that employers approach training as a way to strategically and intentionally explore the efficacy of the training processes for the participants involved and, in turn, the company as a whole. We argue that one of the "fundamental aim[s]" of training is "to improve[ing] practice" (Elliot, 1991, p. 49) through systematic investigation, thus improving and refining future versions of the training program. Within training, then, two parallel processes occur. The first relates to the trainee's personal development and learning. The second relates to a broader understanding of how the online medium affects employee work products.

In this regard, we argue that the collection of trainee feedback is of utmost importance to an investigative principle. Such data collection can be undertaken in accordance with the overarching questions the investigator/employer would like to pursue: quantitative and qualitative questionnaires, meta-cognitive exercises, trainer/trainee synchronous online discussions, quantitative and qualitative feedback from individual trainers, and analysis of archived training sessions. Key to this data collection, however, are the following requirements: (1) that these mechanisms are

actually an integral piece of the program and not "busy work" and (2) that trainers have the ability to archive and mine the data according to particular parameters such as by trainee, task, date, and response number. Resulting review of specific feedback informs the periodic revision of organizational training plans, processes, and procedures. Such revision can include training materials with novice trainees and macro-level changes regarding supervision, standards, guidance, technology, instructors, and training to targeted experienced trainers.

Our second principle for training design is *Immersion*. The importance of engaging *firsthand* with a new work circumstance cannot be exaggerated. Experience suggests that this principle is valid in virtual workplaces as well. Grounded in adult learning scholarship (e.g., Knowles, 1990; Apps, 1991; Galbraith, 1991; Galbraith & Zelenak, 1991), online training can be designed to address adult learner needs, who exhibit varying levels of self-directedness, experience in life and teaching, social readiness for work processes and projects, the ability to use relevant learning applications, and the ability to self-diagnose one's learning needs (Knowles, 1990). Practical implications include having all communication done through the online medium with which employees will ultimately interact—whether that be e-mail, synchronous chat, listserv discussions, or reference materials.

Further, all trainer/trainee meetings, schedule-related e-mails and performance reports, asynchronous scheduling and progress reports, and technology troubleshooting are scheduled and conducted via the Web. In exercises or simulations that replicate the work to be accomplished online, the trainer models the learning process and the training material by enacting the online roles of "teacher" (trainer), "student" (trainee), and "client" (recipient of the employee's interaction or work product). Trainees become "students" and enact the role of novice employee to practice skills both privately and online for the trainer, who then assesses the simulated results with respect to the organization's expectations and client needs. Finally, depending on the nature of the work, trainees can conduct additional reading such as theory and other important outside texts. Providing a theoretical framework in which participants operate can enhance understanding, assimilation, and furthering questioning in the virtual workplace.

Our third principle—*Individualization*—suggests that training be tailored to meet the needs of individual participants. Every online employer must reconcile the operational requirement for standardization with trainees' needs for flexibility or individuality as they progress through training. Apps (1991) observed: "Some people learn best by looking at the whole picture first and then examining the pieces. Others want to start with the pieces, add them together, and create a whole" (p. 34). Ultimately, the goal for training programs is to be systematic and efficient, yet fluid enough to account for the trainee's unique emotional and cognitive needs. An integral part of individualization is *human* instruction or mentoring (possibly combined with static content or AI) during the course of training. This process can be achieved by pairing each trainee with an online mentor or individual trainer who then coaches that trainee throughout the program. Within deadlines and time parameters for work products, trainers provide tailored feedback protocols based on trainees' performances on the simulations, referred to in the previous section on "Immersion." Trainee feedback can be embedded locally within the interaction under review, provided via a more global assessment—or both.

Even in settings where some training necessarily is conducted via trainer-to-group, results can be assessed and/or addressed individually, with some aspects of the interaction taking place one-to-one, thus accounting for both employee privacy and unique learning needs. Such methods of individualization also account for individuals' questions and/or problems with various stages of training.

The principle of *Association* targets individuals' need to work "in connection" with others. In virtual workplaces—as well as face-to-face workplaces—employees often seek relationships with co-workers. As such, fostering a sense of "team" with trainers and other trainee participants is important to success, particularly in the online context. Many scholars call a professional and/or educational team that works together toward a common end a "community" (e.g., Hewett, 2004; Cargile Cook, 2005; Rude, 2005). Given the intricacies of the relationships and group dynamics of a community, however, we find many scholars' definitions of community oversimplified. We choose, therefore, a term inspired by Martin Buber (1923): "association." We view training as a means of facilitating "cyber-associations" that are grounded in a *transactional* or *business* purpose—employees developing professional relationships with one another within the context of working toward a shared company mission or goal (Hewett & Ehmann, 2004). Also alluding to the complexities of community and collaboration, Gignac (2005) highlighted the distinction between cooperation and collaboration: "concurrent effort in the pursuit of congruent goals for personal compensation" (p. 62).

In the context of online training, cyber-associations foster that which Renwick (2001) labeled a "facilitator network"—a group that is comprised of fellow trainees/co-workers and supervisors. A cyber-association is not unlike the various special-interest group list servs, or expanded networks, such as the Box Hill Learning Network which affords a "'playground' for experimentation and practice" (p. 5) and allows for scheduled conferences or more impromptu avenues for discussion. Trainees can then air various concerns and exchange particular strategies and approaches that ultimately promote both individual and programmatic growth. In the same vein, creating sub-group list servs or distribution groups amongst trainees helps to create relationships around the "cyber-water cooler" (Hewett & Ehmann, 2004, pp. 18-19). Further, collaborative technology supports group views of training (especially synchronous) and archived training sessions. Such mechanisms help training coordinators provide business-related systems of "lead" and "non-lead" co-workers or trainers who mentor and train online "buddies." This mentoring is key to scaling one-to-one training.

The last principle—*Reflection*—addresses the potential of training to be a reflective and iterative process during which trainees' assumptions about their work product and processes are identified, challenged, and potentially refined. As such, allowing occasions for trainees to alter their practice based on what occurs in the online context is a valuable opportunity for individual as well as programmatic growth. "Reflection" is infinitely more complex than merely "thinking about" one's practice. The emphasis here is that programs can account for how and when trainees consider their practice and then use such accountings to improve both employee practice and training program goals. Highlighting perhaps the greatest advantage of online training, interactions between trainer and trainee, or instructor and student can be saved and archived. As such, online experiences are exceptionally ready for analysis.

In practice, an online employee's recruitment and screening process for an online position can involve a problem-based introduction into the online environment through simulations that demonstrate the applicant's strengths and weaknesses. Transitional communication with the coordinator/recruiter can then set expectations about the type of self-analysis that will be promoted throughout the training program. Follow-up meta-cognitive or evaluative tasks can be positioned at varying stages of the process. Further, static content as well as archives of past training work can be made available for review and reference.

FUTURE TRENDS

Both historic and future trends indicate that technology is never static. Advancements in all areas of communication and network interfacing occur and are, by definition, expected to occur. As such, employees in virtual, hybrid, *and* traditional labor environments must learn and adapt to new ways of working, communicating, and delivering services. Institutions, therefore, must embrace an ever-present need for adapting training and professional development procedures and processes in effective, scaleable, and efficient ways. Given this landscape of change, we argue that future expectations for online training for all institutions—and in particular those institutions that host virtual working teams—hinges more on the transference and application of the principles reviewed in the previous section of this chapter than on any one particular technique, platform, or innovation.

Taking account of the aforementioned principles and mirroring the types of future innovations and expectations outlined by, for example, Driscol and Carliner (2005), Horton and Horton (2003), and Illegems and Verbeke (2003), the rest of this section provides a blueprint of a training program that combines both asynchronous and synchronous modes of working. The key to this example program, however, is that it is embedded within a *principle-centered* training framework. It provides institutions a means of accommodating and leveraging ever-changing work circumstances while still delivering a stable, educationally viable training program in which trainee learning and company profitability remain complimentary foci.

As indicated at the start of this chapter, this training is designed to be conducted with a disparate group of employees located across the globe—an increasingly present characteristic of virtual workplaces in the corporate world (Ghaoui, 2004; Gignac, 2005). Given this trend in virtually expanded relationships, we expect that future online training will have to address more complex ways of working. Within the context of asynchronous and synchronous modalities, therefore, the training framework presented here focuses on high-touch consultative activities.

Although transferable to small-group interactive activities, the core of training involves one-to-one feedback between trainer and trainee on various exercises associated with each modality. With planning, it also meets both quality and operational efficiency objectives.

Specifically, online tasks reflect the online work that employees will ultimately do. While there is some flexibility for retraining at certain stages, each individual progresses through training via the completion of tasks associated with particular deadlines. Individual deadlines for task completion are: (1) negotiated between training pairs, which may save internal administration time and oversight, or (2) imposed by higher-level management. Heeding Gignac's (2005) insight that corporations need to place more and more value in the virtual employee/trainee, the blueprint also positions new employees not just as trainees, but also as strategic partners in a process in which employers analyze outcomes, explore the perspectives of the participants involved, and endeavor to accommodate identified needs—thereby ultimately improving client service and company output. Training, however, is not a static, sequential set of steps. Rather, it is both generative and recursive in that it promotes a culture of observation, reflection, and practice—on the trainee level as well as programmatic level (Hewett & Ehmann, 2004).

Implementation Strategies for Online Training

Presenting a "road map" of different phases of online training, Figure 1 illustrates the union of those principles in practice.

Figure 1 highlights the implementation of learner-centered practical exercises that are complemented by self-evaluation and trainer feedback. Important characteristics are as follows:

- Before the start of training, a head supervisor pairs trainers and trainees. Trainers are then provided with detailed background infor-

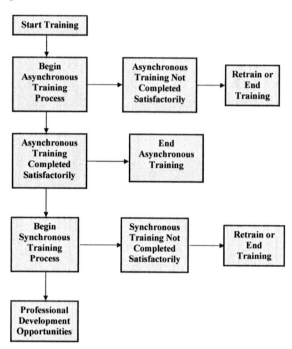

Figure 1. A learner-centered training model. Smarthinking, Inc. © 2003, Used with permission (reprinted from Hewett and Ehmann, 2004, p. 27)

mation about particular trainees including, but not limited to: educational background, experiences, professional characteristics (including strengths and weaknesses) from their screening results during the recruitment phase.

- Once employees embark on the orientation process, they complete a series of tasks including: platform-based technology orientation, asynchronous projects, synchronous projects, and meta-cognitive self-reflection. Most of these exercises are also what Driscoll and Carliner (2005) would label as "problem-based" exercises—in which trainees must focus on the resolution of particular issues with each training task.

- Paired with a direct trainer who reports to one main departmental supervisor/director of training, trainees receive feedback from their trainer with every stage. In such a human adaptive approach, the trainees can stop and retrace steps as needed—but must seek approval for revised timelines from their immediate trainer. Cognizant of overall deadlines, trainers are authorized to grant intermediary extensions at their discretion.

- Given that training occurs online, all trainer and trainee interactions are saved and archived in an individual "orientation portfolio" for each trainee, to which departmental supervisors also have access.

- With each stage, expectations about due dates for particular tasks and response rates are conveyed.

- Throughout the entire orientation process, teacher-trainees may use a variety of tools such as live chat, e-mail, and a listserv to communicate and support their development.

- With each stage of training, trainers also convey their feedback on individual exercises following pre-determined mechanisms that involve both open-ended and closed-ended feedback options. While there is flexibility to individualize responses to a particular trainee, the communications protocols across training pairs are consistent. In many cases, trainers may use quantitative means of describing their assessment of qualitative progress. To that end, progress, pass, and fail rates for trainees are measurable. Final outcomes, however, are accompanied by qualitative critique that is used to actually teach trainees during the course of training.

- After successfully completing the asynchronous phase, for example, those employees who will also conduct work activities in synchronous environments then begin the synchronous segments of their training program—in this case live online teaching (of course, the order of synchronous and asynchronous training should be determined based on the business model and/or mission). Direct trainers, if possible, remain the same

throughout all portions of training.

- Trainees experience the position of "client" explicitly, as they practice role-playing first from a client's position and then from the employee's position as consultant.

- Because training is conducted between individual training pairs, there are options to scale the program quickly. By regulating the deployment of new trainers, the program can grow exponentially or be scaled back as needed (e.g., Sharpe Russo, 2001).

- Finally, all trainers report to a training/departmental supervising head who grants trainees final approval. This individual also reserves the right to overrule, modify, or change any trainer recommendations. Such delegation of responsibilities is not unlike those outlined in scholarship by, for example, Berg (2005), Lechuga (2006), and Ruch (2003), who described the efficiencies gained by separation of teaching/development activities from broader management activities within an organization.

Thus, the online training process inherently recognizes the individuality of the trainee at every point in the process, but remains within the overarching shell of (1) time-sensitive operational guidelines and (2) overall steps of the program, illustrated in Figure 2.

Figure 2. Online training goals. Copyright 2006, Smarthinking, Inc. Used with permission.

Smarthinking, Inc. © 2006

CONCLUSION

As we have described, the general lack of research into online training for virtual workplace settings and virtual employees leaves a substantial gap in online training for business settings. We have described and outlined a principle-based training program that fills this gap. Yet filling a gap is not enough. Given current evidence that suggests the number of virtual workplaces will only increase in years to come, businesses need to test the process of applying such principles to their own settings. Researchers need to know more about their assessments of their companies' unique processes and products—from both qualitative as well as quantitative data. Undoubtedly, more companies will see the potential benefits of leveraging the Internet for their work and for hiring employees. The boundaries from a global economy are more porous and flexible, which will require increased sophistication on the part of those who develop company training programs. Such sophistication will come with built-in data and support from the kinds of principle-centered training programs that we have recommended.

REFERENCES

Aldrich, C. (2004). *Simulations and the future of learning: An innovative (and perhaps revolutionary) approach to e-learning.* San Francisco, CA: Pfeiffer.

Apps, J. (1991). *Mastering the teaching of adults.* Malabar, FL: Krieger.

Berg, G. (2005). *Lessons from the edge: For-profit and nontraditional higher education in America.* Westport, CT: Praeger.

Bourne, J., & Moore, J. (Eds.). (2005). *Elements of quality online education: Practice and direction.*

Buber, M. (1923). *I and thou.* New York, NY: Scribner.

Cargile Cook, K. (2005). An argument for pedagogy-driven online education. In: K. Cargile Cook & K. Grant-Davie (Eds.), *Online education: Global questions, local answers* (pp. 49-66). Amityville, NY: Baywood.

Cargile Cook, K., & Grant-Davie, K. (Eds.). (2005). *Online education: Global questions, local answers.* Amityville, New York: Baywood.

Carliner, S. (2004). *An overview of online learning* (2nd ed.). Amherst, MA: HRD Press.

Chediak, M. (2005). Online tutoring part of growing trend: Market for Web education matures. *The Washington Post,* p. 4.

Covey, S. (1992). *Principle-centered leadership.* New York, NY: Simon.

de Leeuwe, M. (2006). *www.e-learningsite.com.* Retrieved August 1, 2006 from www.e-learningsite.com.

Driscoll, M., & Carliner, S. (2005). *Advanced Web-based training strategies: Unlocking instructionally sound online learning.* San Francisco, CA: Pfeiffer.

Ehmann, C. (2000). *Training online tutors.* Paper presented at the OTiS e-Workshop, Scotland.

Ehmann, C. (2001). Exploring new territory: Developing a research agenda for online tutoring and instruction. *Journal of the National Tutoring Association - Inaugural Edition*(Spring), 69-86.

Ehmann, C., Heywood, I., & Higgison, C. (2000). Quality assurance. In: C. Higgison (Ed.), *Online tutoring e-Book.* Edinburgh: Heriot-Watt University and The Robert Gordon University.

Ehmann Powers, C. (in progress-a). Online writing instruction and faculty attitudes: Influences on theory and practice.

Ehmann Powers, C. (in progress-b). A study of online writing instructor perceptions. In: B. Hewett (Ed.), *Teaching through text: Conferencing with students in online settings.*

Elliot, J. (1991). *Action research for educational change*. Philadelphia, PA: Open University Press.

Galbraith, M. (1991). The adult learning transactional process. In: M. Galbraith (Ed.), *Facilitating adult learning: A transactional process* (pp. 1-32). Malabar, FL: Krieger.

Galbraith, M., & Zelenak, B. (1991). Adult learning methods and techniques. In: M. Galbraith (Ed.), *Facilitating adult learning: A transactional process* (pp. 103-133). Malabar, FL: Krieger.

Ghaoui, C. (Ed.). (2004). *E-Education applications: Human factors and innovative approaches*. Hershey, PA: Information Science.

Gignac, F. (2005). *Building successful virtual teams*. Boston, MA: Artech House.

Graves, W., & Twigg, C. (2006). The future of course design and the national center for academic transformation: An interview with Carol Twigg. *Innovate, 2*(3).

Hewett, B. (2004). Asynchronous online instructional commentary: A study of student revision. *Readerly/Writerly Texts: Essays in Literary, Composition, and Pedagogical Theory,11, 12.1, 2*, 47-67.

Hewett, B. (2006). Synchronous online conference-based instruction: A study of whiteboard interactions and student writing. *Computers and Composition, 23*(1), 4-31.

Hewett, B., & Ehmann, C. (2004). *Preparing educators for online writing instruction: Principles and processes*. Urbana: NCTE.

Hewett, B., & Ehmann Powers, C. (2007). Online teaching and learning: Preparation, development, and organizational communication. *Technical Communication Quarterly Special Issue, 16.1*(winter).

Horton, W. (2000). *Designing Web-based training: How to teach anyone anything anywhere anytime* (Hudson, Theresa ed.). New York, NY: John Wiley & Sons.

Horton, W., & Horton, K. (2003). *E-Learning tools and technologies*. Indianapolis, IN: Wilely.

HydroOne. (2004). *Ontario energy board: Review of further efficiencies in the electricity distribution sector*. Ontario: HydroOne, Inc.

Illegems, V., & Verbeke, A. (2003). *Moving towards the virtual workplace: Managerial and societal perspectives on telework*. Cheltenham, HK: Edward Elgar.

Jaschik, S. (2005). Outsourced grading. *Inside Higher Ed, September 22*.

Kilby, T. (2001). The direction of Web-based training: A practitioner's view. *Learning Organization, 8*(5), 194-199.

Knowles, M. (1990). *The adult learner: A neglected species* (4th ed.). Houston, TX: Gulf.

Lechuga, V. (2006). *The changing landscape of the academic profession: Faculty culture at for-profit colleges and universities*. Boston, MA: Routledge Taylor & Francis Group.

Maeroff, G. (2003). *A classroom of one*. New York, NY: Palgrave MacMillan.

Paley, A. (2006). Homework help, from a world away. *The Washington Post*, p. 1.

Renwick, K. (2001). *Learning to learn online: Box Hill learning network*. Paper presented at the Australian Vocational Education and Training Research Association (AVETRA) Conference, Australia.

Rockbridge, A. (2006). *2005/2006 National technology readiness survey: Summary report*. Great Falls, VA: The Center for Excellence in Service, Robert H. Smith School of Business, University of Maryland.

Ruch, R. (2003). *Higher Ed, Inc: The rise of the for-profit university*. Baltimore, MD: Johns Hopkins University.

Rude, C. (2005). Strategic planning for online education: Sustaining students, faculty, and programs. In: K. Cargile Cook & K. Grant-Davies (Eds.), *Online education: Global questions, local answers* (pp. 67-88). Amityville, NY: Baywood.

Russell, T. (2001). *The no significant difference phenomenon* (5ᵗʰ ed.). Montgomery, AL: The International Distance Education Certification Center.

Russell, T. (ongoing). *No significant difference phenomenon*. Retrieved from http://www.nosignificantdifference.org/.

Salmon, G. (2002). *E-tivities: The key to active online learning.* London: Kogan Page.

Schank, R. (2002). *Designing world-class e-learning: How IBM, GE, Harvard Business School, and Columbia University are succeeding at e-learning.* New York, NY: McGraw-Hill.

Schank, R. (2005). *Lessons in learning: E-learning, and training: Perspectives and guidance for the enlightened teacher.* San Francisco, CA: Pfeiffer.

Sharpe Russo, C. (Ed.). (2001). *Train the trainer, Volume 1: Foundations & delivery.* Alexandria, VA: American Society for Training and Development.

Smith, B. (1999). Higher education: The vision [2015]. *Converge Magazine.*

Stockley, D. (2006). *HRD and performance consulting.* Retrieved August 1, 2006 from www.derekstockley.com.au.

KEY TERMS

Online Human-Adaptive Training: Internet-based training or professional development programs for individuals or employees in various contexts. Such programs require the involvement of person-to-person contact (in, for example, asynchronous or synchronous modes) throughout training activities.

Principle-Centered Training Framework: The overarching operational and/or educational tenets that inform the design and implementation of an online training program. Such overarching principles can be applied to various training modalities—whether a program involves asynchronous e-mail, synchronous messaging, or particular commercial software for an orientation classroom- or Internet-based networking platform. The result is a qualitatively strong, yet "contextually adaptive" training program that will remain structurally sound despite a company's technology changes, upgrades, and/or program developments (Hewett & Ehmann, 2004).

Investigation: An online training principle regarding the need to strategically and intentionally explore the efficacy of the training processes for the participants involved and, in turn, a company as a whole. Investigation also addresses the need for more empirical research about the effect of the online medium on various work processes.

Immersion: An online training principle regarding the process of engaging trainees *firsthand* in the online environment throughout training activities. When training is designed to include immersive Internet-based activities that reflect the online environment in which trainees will ultimately work, employees can transition into their online work more efficiently.

Individualization: An online training principle regarding tailoring training activities to meet the needs of individual participants. Within the online training context, employers can reconcile the operational requirement for standardization with trainees' needs for flexibility or individuality as they progress through training.

Association: An online training principle regarding individuals' needs to work "in connection" with others. Fostering a sense of "team" with trainers and other trainee participants is important to online training success.

Reflection: An online training principle regarding the potential of training to be a thoughtful and iterative process during which trainees' assumptions about their work product and processes are identified, challenged, and potentially refined. More complex than merely "thinking about" one's practice, "reflection" means that programs can account for how and when trainees consider their practices and then use such accountings to improve both employee practice and training program goals.

ENDNOTE

[1] For more information about Smarthinking, Inc., see www.smarthinking.com

Chapter XX
The Virtual Classroom @ Work

Terrie Lynn Thompson
University of Alberta, Canada

ABSTRACT

Before we can exploit new technologies to realize new ways of working, we must be able to imagine innovative possibilities for learning. Organizations seeking to improve the way they work and build knowledge reach for new learning paradigms. Possibilities emerge when exploring learning and working in virtual spaces from social learning perspectives, such as situated learning.. In this chapter, findings from a qualitative case study in a geographically dispersed organization are used as a springboard for exploring the challenges of introducing innovative e-learning initiatives. This chapter adds to our understanding of learning and working in virtual spaces by delving into: (1) workplace practices related to virtual learning and work that facilitate and frustrate new ways of learning; and (2) notions of online community, informal learning, and blended learning which offer promise for re-conceptualizing learning within virtual work spaces. Recommendations are provided to guide the creation of fresh teaching and learning practices.

INTRODUCTION

Salmon's (2000) vision of networked learners demanding "smaller chunks of relevant learning, backed up by connections and explorative opportunities with like-minded others" (p. 91) seems to fit with the needs of the workplace, regardless of how it is configured virtually or physically. Given the prevalence of non-standard work arrangements and our increasingly networked workforce, learners need to slip between informal and formal experiences as learning needs demand, opportunities emerge, and time and tools permit.

However, there seems to be a misalignment between what online communication technolo-gies (OCT) can do in a learning context and what is actually happening. Merely adding OCTs to the organizational technology palette does not automatically foster new approaches. Organizations, worker-learners, and learning practitioners are still mapping expectations and outcomes for virtual learning initiatives. Before we can exploit new technologies or realize new ways of working, we must be able to imagine new possibilities for learning. As organizations seek improvements in the way they work, think, and build knowledge, they reach for new learning paradigms. We must therefore start by looking closely at what assumptions about teaching and learning are embedded within the practices of the workplace.

This chapter builds on a research study that questioned how teaching and learning paradigms influence the design and use of e-learning technologies in the workplace. The setting for this case study was a multi-national consulting firm regarded as innovative in the way it uses e-learning technologies to deliver training. Workers in Consulting Company (a pseudonym) are geographically dispersed, located in a mix of corporate office spaces, home offices, and client sites. Participating in virtual teams for work and learning is integral to the corporate culture. A change-oriented, competitive, and market-driven workplace, Consulting Company (CC) is an organization that defines people as knowledge assets and is dependent on innovative knowledge workers. Employees require a high degree of interpersonal and collaboration skills, technology literacy, and ability to acquire new knowledge and skills as *just-in-time* requirements dictate. The findings illustrate how the workplace context, an eclectic array of assumptions about learning, and technologies in use influence what happens in a virtual classroom.

By drawing attention to the challenges of introducing innovative e-learning initiatives, we add to our understanding of learning and working in virtual spaces as we explore: (1) workplace practices around virtual learning and work that facilitate and frustrate new ways of learning; and (2) the concepts of online community and blended learning which offer promise for re-conceptualizing learning within virtual work spaces. Recommendations are offered for creating innovative teaching and learning practices appropriate for virtual work and learning spaces.

BACKGROUND

New Perspectives of Learning

The parade of Web-based technologies that can be used to create new learning opportunities seems endless. However, we must question whether newer learning paradigms are reflected in the design and delivery of these e-learning experiences or whether we are merely replicating the same teaching and learning practices of the last few centuries. Let us begin by examining two perspectives.

As Rising and Watson (1998) report, a common model of workplace learning is one in which "knowledge is imparted in the fashion of a download: instructors present information and learners are expected to absorb it" (p. 137). The prevailing assumption is that "learning is an individual process, has a beginning and an end, is best separated from the rest of our activities, and is the result of teaching" (Wenger, 1998, p. 3). Based on positivism and behaviorism, this *transmission model* depicts learning as a process of internalizing knowledge; what Freire (1971) refers to as the *banking* concept of education. Numerous research studies and stories from the workplace highlight the ineffectiveness of this learning model (i.e., Knowles, 1980; Brown & Duguid, 1991; Wells, 2000).

What would a new paradigm encompass? Bruner (1996) argues that learning is best when it is "participatory, proactive, communal, collaborative, and given to constructing meanings rather than receiving them" (p. 84). *Knowledge* as an entity is replaced with *knowing* as an action (Sfard, 1998). Increasingly, "our understanding of how 'learning' in the workplace is accomplished expands beyond notions of individual cognition and 'self-direction' to incorporate awareness of situated communities of practice, mentoring, and the role of social participation" (Bratton, Helms Mills, Pyrch, & Sawchuk, 2004, p. 2). This view of learning is based on social learning theory. Offering a way to envision how technology could shape more dynamic learning in virtual learning spaces and workplaces, situated learning and social constructionism offer two compelling socio-cultural learning perspectives.

Situated learning is the work of Lave and Wenger (1991). They state that learning, thinking, and knowing are found in the "*relations* among people *in activity* in, with, and arising from the socially and culturally structured world" (p. 51, emphasis added). Communities of practice sprang into vogue with this work. Wells (2002) explains that Lave and Wenger emphasize that "learning is not a separate activity, but an integral aspect of doing things together in a community of practice that involves individuals with different types and degrees of expertise" (p. 123). Social constructionism is based on the ideas of Vygotsky. Lave and Wenger drew on this work to deepen the social dimension of learning in the everyday. Highlighting how individuals learn within this social perspective, Wells adds that, "the active construction of a personal understanding is an integral part of participating in knowledge building with others" (p. 127). Jonassen and Land (2000) state that adopting a socio-cultural learning perspective entails: (a) learning is a process of meaning-making, not knowledge transmission; (b) learning is a dialogue; and (c) the locus of meaning is found in communities of practice, not the head of an individual.

Differentiating E-Learning Technologies

E-learning initiatives draw on a range of OCTs. One way of distinguishing online learning designs is by the degree of synchronicity. *Synchronous* learning technologies enable same-time collaboration; events and interactions take place in real time. In contrast, *asynchronous* technologies enable any-time, any-place collaboration; learners and facilitators are not necessarily online and interacting at the same time. Both asynchronous and synchronous modes have advantages and neither can address all learning needs. Online synchronicity allows: (a) context to be more easily built and maintained (Ahern & El-Hindi, 2000); (b) more dynamic and natural conversation (Hammond, 2000); and (c) less cumbersome learning (Shotsberger, 2000). In contrast, Berge (1999) suggests that dense content is best managed asynchronously allowing the learner to

mine it from different angles at different times as learning needs change. Haythornthwaite, Kazmer, Robins and Shoemaker (2004) propose that synchronicity contributes more to community building than asynchronous communication and "provides simultaneous many-to-many contact that helps stave off feelings of isolation" (p. 48); an important consideration in a distributed virtual workplace.

Increasingly, learning technologies and the design of online learning experiences use a blended approach that mixes both asynchronous and synchronous technologies along with combinations of e-learning and face-to-face (F2F) learning events. Added to this mix is a new group of OCTs referred to as *social software*. Alexander (2006) explains that social software is a part of the Web 2.0 movement, adding that during the past few years, "a group of Web services became perceived as especially connective, receiving the rubric of 'social software': blogs, wikis, trackback, podcasting, videoblogs and social networking tools like MySpace and Facebook" (p. 33). Anderson (2005) defines educational social software as "networked tools that support and encourage individuals to learn together while retaining individual control over their time, space, presence, activity, identity and relationship" (p. 4).

The Knowledge Worker

Bratton et al. (2004) write that "in response to such economic and political developments as globalization, privatization, and deregulation, both managers and workers realize they must continually focus on learning in the workplace" (p. 1). Increasingly, workers are referred to as *knowledge workers*, characterized as people who continually use knowledge to create new knowledge that offers a competitive advantage to their organization (Romiszowski, 1997). Critical skills for knowledge workers include an ability to: (a) collaborate on teams characterized by greater complexity, diversity, and remoteness; (b) handle vast amounts of information and knowledge (rather than know everything); (c) connect with others cross-culturally; (d) use a variety of technologies to advantage; and (e) become creative and critical thinkers and doers (Salmon, 1999).

Embedded in the workplace are economic, political, social and structural constraints that "complicate the implementation of the learning organization ideal" (Bratton et al., 2004, p. 12). One such constraint is time. Ferraris, Manca, Persico, and Sarti (2000) assert that although time and space constraints are apparently loosened with e-learning, "there is no single time or place *reserved* for learning and this makes it difficult to fit it into the work day" (p. 90). This is especially problematic with asynchronous learning experiences. Wenger (2001) cautions that "the danger of a pure web-based [asynchronous] presence for a community is its timelessness. It is always possible to participate, but by the same token, there is never a special occasion to participate" (p. 48 cited by Gray, 2004). However, asynchronous learning, often promoted as providing "anytime, anyplace" convenience, weaves time and place together in unique ways. The separation of "time and space from place allows for new ways of organizing both" (Anagnostopoulos, Basmadjian, & McCrory, 2005, p. 1701).

The Many Faces of Learning

Learning in the workplace occurs in formal, non-formal, and informal learning settings. Discussions of learning in the workplace are not complete without sorting through the quagmire of definitions surrounding these settings. Livingstone (2001) suggests that primary distinctions are based on whether the directive control of the learning experience rests with educational agents or the learner. Livingstone defines *informal learning* as "any activity involving the pursuit of understanding, knowledge, or skill which occurs without the presence of externally imposed curricular criteria" (p. 5). The objectives, content, learning strategies, duration, and evaluation of outcomes are "determined by the individuals and

groups that choose to engage in it" (p. 5). *Formal learning* entails "formally structured, institutionally sponsored, classroom-based activities" (Watkins & Marsick, 1992, p. 288). Livingstone adds that the teacher has the authority to determine a pre-established body of knowledge and teach this curriculum. In *non-formal education*, learners opt to study voluntarily with a teacher who assists their self-determined interests by using an organized curriculum.

As lifelong learning re-emerged in international and national policy discussions in the 1990s, it set the stage for increased interest in informal learning. Consider The Home Depot's widely proclaimed slogan: *You can do it. We can help.* This slogan exemplifies our interest in do-it-yourself projects, and by extension, informal learning. Also consider the popularity of the *Dummies* book series that released approximately 150 new titles in the first nine months of 2005—everything from *Business Plan Kits for Dummies* to *Meditation for Dummies*. Despite the pervasiveness of our everyday learning and the nod given to it in the lifelong learning discourse, the dominant learning discourse still focuses on formal learning. We need to be wary of attempts to position informal learning as a low-cost learning option, especially in the workplace. Informal learning is a vibrant and essential way of learning, not a second best alternative. It should not be a case of informal versus formal learning: both are essential.

Learning in a Social Context: The Interest in Community

There is much interest in online communities and building community online. The belief is that learning is "enhanced when there is a commitment to the collective good and people engage in learning through and with others" (Thompson & MacDonald, 2005, p. 235). Created over time, a community of practice is a collection of individuals who share a repertoire of beliefs, tools, and discourse and are mutually engaged in the pursuit of a negotiated enterprise (Wenger, 1998). These communities appear to be essential for the worker-learner. As Dede (1996) states, "individual attempts to make sense of complex data can easily fail unless the learner is encouraged by some larger group that is constructing shared knowledge" (p. 21). Trentin (2001) views communities of practice as "self-managing virtual learning groups in which professional growth is based on ... experience-sharing, the identification of best practices, and reciprocal support for tackling day-to-day problems in the workplace" (p. 5).

Although the word, "community", has instant resonance, there is a range of possible understandings. The e-learning discourse is replete with references to online communities often described as virtual communities or learning communities. Creating *communities of practice* is a very fashionable notion. One also reads about communities of inquiry, knowledge communities and communities of interest. Related concepts include networks, learning Webs, and social capital. Trentin (2001) advocates communities of course alumni as an ongoing support mechanism for learners after a formal learning event. Brown and Duguid (2002) introduce the term networks of practice to differentiate more loosely coupled communities from the tightly knit knowledge distributing communities of practice. Prevalent in the business literature are references to peer-to-peer (P2P) networks (Fletcher, 2004). Along with the proliferation of terms, online community is now a marketable commodity. Groove, Groupee, and CommunityZero are just a few of the many community software applications available. Guy Kawasaki (2006) urges companies to create online communities as part of their marketing strategy, which one blogger describes as a product community: "the ecosystem of users and abusers that forms organically around a great product" (Sarkar, 2006, para. 1).

Wenger, McDermott, and Snyder (2002) articulate the essence of a learning community as people "bound by the value they find in learning together" (p. 4). But Rheingold (2000) perhaps best captures the spirit of community as he describes virtual communities as "social aggregations that emerge ... when enough people carry on public discussions long enough, with sufficient human feeling, to form webs of personal relationships in cyberspace" (p. xx).

THE RESEARCH STUDY

A qualitative case study design was used to explore what happens in a workplace e-learning event. The worker-learners, learning professionals (instructors and instructional designers), and software developers form a triad involved in such an online learning experience. The technology in this study is the virtual synchronous classroom (VSC)—Centra Symposium. Using this sophisticated Web-based technology, learners can sit in front of their computers and engage in real-time collaborative learning that mixes text, oral speech, and shared application work. Centra Symposium offers a rich feature set to support live synchronous interaction including voice-over-IP communication, breakout rooms, a multi-user whiteboard, and tools such as online surveys and quizzes. A range of communication and feedback mechanisms are provided. To support content delivery, features enable Web Safaris (visiting and interacting with Web sites), the ability to import multimedia files, and application sharing. According to Masie (2003) the VSC is the fastest growing segment of the e-learning market.

Recognizing that the learning process does not happen in a vacuum, this study probed the critical influences of the workplace as well as the impact of technology and the eclectic array of beliefs about learning that the triad carries with them to their online experience. Workers in Consulting Company (CC) are geographically dispersed. The participants in this study were located in four locations in the U.S. and the UK; some in CC office spaces and others in home offices or at client sites. This multi-national organization was intent on altering traditional learning practices, making substantial investments in distance collaboration tools such as the VSC. The e-learning event was a blended solution that focused on teaching workers how to deliver interactive VSC events. There were three components: an orientation session delivered in the VSC (1 hour), an asynchronous portion which included self-managed learning (1 week), and a second VSC event (2.5 hours). In addition to participating in this event, I interviewed three of the learners as well as both instructors and the business leader influential in how the VSC was being implemented throughout the organization. I also interviewed a VSC project manager because of his significant influence on the design of this e-learning tool. Multiple data collection methods, such as interviews, observation, and document analysis allowed analysis of different perspectives of what unfolded during this virtual learning experience. Direct quotations are used throughout to present the voices of the participants, who have been given pseudonyms.

A central tenet of socio-cultural learning paradigms is collective meaning-making, which is characterized by an "ethos of collaborative inquiry" (Wells, 2000, p. 65) supported by a sufficient "network of conversations" (Ford, 1999, p. 487). By clarifying and altering their beliefs, people attempt to make sense with, and for others, and in the process make sense for themselves (Bruner, 1996). Exploring the collective meaning-making that unfolds in an e-learning experience may provide insight into what influence contemporary socio-cultural thinking has on the design and use of e-learning technologies and events. In this study, the introduction of the VSC did not evoke new paradigms of teaching and learning even though the organization was in the midst of a strategic learning shift. Collective meaning-making was constrained by several factors:

- The workplace created and validated a climate of distracted learning.
- The technology created feelings of being

both close and removed and allowed learners to hide.

- Beliefs and values about teaching and learning permitted learners to be comfortable in a passive role, instructors to assume a teacher-centered role, and software developers to replicate the F2F classroom.

The primary focus in this chapter is on the first factor— the workplace—and an examination of the interdependent relationship between learning and work, a relationship magnified in virtual settings. The findings illustrate how challenging it can be to learn in the workplace. Learning was characterized by a myriad of tensions between individual needs and corporate mandates. Although bite-sized packages of online learning can be slotted into day timers as easily as a meeting, convenience seems to exact a price in terms of distracted learning as workers struggle to multi-task learning and work. Workers are compelled to be self-sufficient in their learning endeavors albeit without much corporate support. As they adjust their learning strategies to each new media that comes along, they make trade-offs—willingly, grudgingly or with trepidation.

Constructing the Place

In a F2F event, learners walk into a ready-made learning setting. In VSC events it is the learners' responsibility to create dual learning climates: within the virtual classroom and within their physical space. Learners struggled to carve out a place and space for learning. Albeit convenient, bite-sized packaging of training presents considerable challenges. The data reveals that most participants were preoccupied during the e-learning session by events happening around them. What emerges is a picture of distracted learning in both their physical and virtual settings. With a constant barrage of telephone calls, people dropping in, e-mails popping up, and work sitting on your desk, the work environment—whether in a corporate space, at home, or on a client site—can work against the learner. Learners found it difficult to stay focused on their learning responsibilities and often wandered out of the VSC to tackle ever present work. This wandering was facilitated by the ease of presenting a façade of attentiveness in the virtual classroom; a façade that enabled the worker-learner to hide behind other learners and the technology.

Making the Space and Time

There seemed to be a tension in this organization between *training* and *learning*. There was decreased time for training as consultants increasingly needed to spend 100% of their time on billable projects. Time reserved for learning was pushed aside at the last minute for more urgent priorities. The worker who planned to take training during a week "off" between projects could easily be shifted to a new project at a moment's notice. With reduced resources allocated to training, the implication is that learning is less valued or at the very least, not to be done on company time. Although workers in this company must take responsibility for their own learning, it could be difficult. Sandy believed that although CC supports continuing education, current practice indicated otherwise: "The result is people rush through training sessions or do not get what they should out of them." With a plethora of learning portals and training options, it can be overwhelming and frustrating, forcing the worker-learner to be flexible and resourceful in how they address their learning needs. The data suggests that the organization and the people it seem to value learning immensely; it is job-critical. I am not sure the same intensity can be ascribed to corporate training sessions—virtual or F2F.

Reaching Beyond the Walls of the Classroom

Given the just-in-time nature of much e-learning, it is debatable whether sufficient time is given to learners or instructors to take part in experiences that ask for more than sitting through a PowerPoint presentation. To some degree the workforce not only tolerates information-push sessions, they expect them. One participant explains:

The classic problem in corporate America is they've got ten times more information they need to get to their employees than they have time for. So they fall back to information push ... get all this information out there very quickly in a one hour session ... throw it out at them and hope some of it sticks. They don't have the time or don't want to spend the effort or resources to really make it engaging or collaborative. Most sessions are just "here's information."

The instructional designers and instructors in this study *wanted* an event filled with dialogue and interaction, not an information-push session. They wanted a learning event that reflected social learning theory rather than the traditional transmission model. However, they were only partially successful in this respect. The data suggests five factors that conspire to perpetuate information-push events: short design cycles, lack of more sophisticated learning models, the ease of *presenting* content in the VSC, the need to impart information quickly, and limited resources.

Cutbacks in formal training and the move to short modular e-learning components put an onus on the learner to rely on informal learning opportunities and engagement within communities of practice. All participants shared stories of rich informal learning activities. Dialoging with colleagues was highly valued and a number of communities of practice were emerging to support collaborative knowledge construction between co-workers. However, several participants were quick to point out the questionable legitimacy of engaging in these activities during their workday without the blessing of the organization. Sandy explained what happens when your manager looks over your shoulder and wonders what you are doing: "If you're on the [CC community of practice] project management website your manager is going to go 'Wow. That's great.' But if I'm just surfing the web looking at other project management stuff they might say 'What are you looking at?'" Participants highlighted how effectively the VSC supported their informal learning activities and one commented that the future of organizational learning is using these kinds of virtual collaboration technologies to enhance informal learning opportunities. Perhaps this renewed interest in informal learning will counteract the current information-push practices.

Evolution not Revolution

There are two intertwined shifts toward more innovative learning practices in this study: (1) the shift from F2F to online or blended learning experiences; and (2) the shift from transmission models of learning to socio-cultural views of learning. While there was evidence of the first shift, the second shift was proving more daunting.

Innovation of e-learning technologies is relentless. This version of the VSC may be just a stepping stone as technology developers strive to leapfrog their own advancements. Yet participants' experiences suggest a progression of corporate learning rather than a transformation. Even though this is an innovative technology in an innovative workplace, much of the current usage reflects replication of the familiar F2F classroom and traditional approaches to teaching and learning.

Participants arrived in their e-learning event with an array of beliefs about learning and a myriad of F2F and online experiences. As employees, they were imbued with the organization's learning philosophy. Despite trendy buzzwords, the data revealed participants were swayed by traditional views of learning. With varying exposure to e-learning, learners inevitably compared this experience to their most familiar learning medium— the F2F classroom. The software developers deliberately used the physical classroom as a model. The instructors and instructional designers borrowed heavily from approaches used in existing F2F courses. Even with an innovative technology, it is difficult to escape the legacy of the transmission model and the legacy of the F2F classroom. Furthermore, participants in this study did not necessarily view these learning traditions negatively. It is possible we impose restrictions on the technology and not the other way around. O'Connor (1998) cautions that:

Deep changes in pedagogy, however well motivated and secured by research, do not easily take hold. While the accoutrements of practice and the terminology may change, teaching practices often stay the same despite attestations by practitioners that they have changed. (p. 43)

Let us look at online interactions as an example. Interactive learning environments make it possible for learners to tap into the expertise of the facilitator, collaborate with other learners, reflect on and apply what is learned to their own work, and obtain hands-on experience supported by coaching. Interaction in a socio-cultural view is not just clicking icons on the computer screen. Instead, learners engage and reflect, annotate, question, elaborate, problem-solve, link, construct, and evaluate (Berge, 1999). Although the functionality of this VSC and the blended design provided a rich opportunity for an array of interactions, it was not realized in this study. It is important to differentiate between interactions designed to keep people on their toes and those meant to foster dialogue and collaboration. Because the instructors cannot read body language, the former type of interactions that prompt people to indicate that they are present and following along are a necessity in a VSC. However, these interactions dominated, perhaps at the expense of more meaningful exchanges. For example, learners were asked what they thought was most important when instructing in a virtual classroom and instructed to place a gold star in the media window next to their choice of either: words, voice quality, or questions you ask. They were not asked to explain their response; nor were they given an opportunity to suggest other ideas. Although the instructors wanted to encourage exploration and discussion of what it is like to teach in this new medium, this type of activity kept learners in a more passive role, clicking rather than dialoguing.

Implications

These findings have implications for two dimensions of workplace learning that are currently the focus of much lively debate: community and blended learning. Woven into the discussion of each of these dimensions is the discourse of informal learning.

Community

In this study, learning in a training session seemed to be regarded as an individual pursuit. Learners decided how much they would invest to create a community with others in their virtual classroom event. Although the organization emphasizes "community" in everyday work, participants did not have this expectation for their learning experience, suggesting that belonging to a community is not necessarily an automatic practice. This study draws attention to the kind of community that the worker-learner sees as useful to their own learning, a preference that is influenced by the organizational setting and the goals of the learning department. Six factors help explain the lack of community in the online event despite the instructors' hopes for creating connections and dialogue: (a) the individual nature of learning, (b) short contact time, (c) lack of emphasis on relationship building, (d) instructor domination, (e) limited focus on co-constructing knowledge, and (f) lack of purposeful design to nurture community.

The research literature suggests that community is an important characteristic of a quality e-learning experience (Preece, 2002; Garrison & Kanuka, 2004; Gunawarenda et al., 2006;). Afonso (2006) writes:

These communities are an important alternative to traditional learning and organizational contexts, and being supported by ICT, they have become more tangible today than they were a decade ago. They represent intellectual, social, cultural, and psychological environments that facilitate and support learning, while promoting integration, collaboration, and the development of a sense of belonging in their members. (p. 148)

However, Thompson and MacDonald (2005) found that learners weigh an array of factors when deciding on their level of participation and the value they derive from a joint learning endeavor, suggesting a need to be clear about how we expect community will enhance the learning experience. It is clear that we are still wrestling with how best to channel the power of this social learning construct in e-learning events.

Blended Learning

There is no consensus on the definition of blended learning. To many, it is simply e-learning combined with F2F learning. Others suggest that it is a mix of F2F training, synchronous and asynchronous e-learning components, and advanced learning support such as assessment tools, e-mentoring, and learning management systems (Fox, 2002; Schacht, 2002). Different elements that can be combined in a dynamic learning menagerie include: F2F and online learning events, synchronous and asynchronous modalities, individual and collaborative activities, formal and informal learning opportunities, and learning events coupled with ongoing knowledge management and action projects (Thompson, 2004). This mix may also include different e-learning media within an online experience and a blend of instruction and coaching. My experiences lead me to believe that the key to designing a successful blended learning experience is creating synergy between elements that are thoughtfully designed to work in concert.

The interest in blended learning reflects growing sophistication in how e-learning elements are being designed and integrated into work and learning practices. Duderstadt (1999) suggests we are seeing a shift from *just-in-case* to *just-in-time* to *just-for you* education, paralleled by a shift to opportunities. He describes ubiquitous learning as a culture of learning in which people are "continually surrounded by, immersed in, and absorbed in learning experiences" (p. 25), a necessity in a world driven by an expanding knowledge base and need for continuous learning. Courtenay, Merriam, and Baumgartner (2003) studied the nature of the learning within a community of practice and discovered an integrated learning process as learners accessed multiple learning formats to meet their goals; a process characterized as a spiral rather than a linear progression. Their study highlights that learners engage in formal learning activities when they realize that their self-directed study (i.e., their informal learning activities such as reading and discussion with others) is incomplete; participants needed the structured environment of formal learning with other people to affirm their informal learning.

Recommendations for Innovative Teaching and Learning Practices in the Virtual Space

The findings of this study, as well as discussion in research and practice circles, suggest that fresh strategies are needed for e-learning initiatives in the workplace. Regrettably, the opportunity to innovate will be missed if we use OCTs only to convey information more efficiently rather than to explore more effective avenues for learning (Dede, 1996; Duderstadt, 1999). Although this qualitative study provides insight into one organization's experience, a number of recommendations emerge that may be useful to other workplaces:

Design and Delivery Strategies

Strong design and delivery strategies and expertise are crucial for creating learning solutions that are effective and enjoyable. Bite-sized pieces of learning, rapid development, and the inevitable technology glitches generated frictions in the online learning session examined in this study. It is not simply a matter of adopting or making a few small adjustments to what worked in the F2F classroom. Barab and Duffy (2000) provide design principles that could be used to guide the development of online learning events: (a) active learning, (b) learner ownership, (c) coaching and modeling of thinking skills, (d) opportunity for reflection, (e) loosely structured dilemmas, (f) learner support, (g) collaboration and social environment, and (h) motivating learning context. Because they are grounded in socio-cultural theory, learning practitioners and business leaders may find that using these principles will help them deliver online learning events more consistent with their desire to foster dialogue and sharing of best practices.

One participant in this study commented that "the need to keep people engaged is more acute online and the consequences of poor instructional strategies more severe". Effective facilitation of online learning events is critical. Although the instructors tried to achieve interactive learning by including a number of activities to keep people busy, it is clear that the social fabric of an e-learning event needs attention to ensure that people are dialoguing, not just clicking. For example, carefully constructed questions can stimulate the type of interactions that help to build the social infrastructure. Such questions are characterized as those that pose dilemmas, challenge canonical beliefs, and surface incongruities (Bruner, 1996). Palloff and Pratt (1999) suggest that to encourage a "volley of views", the art of asking "expansive questions" must be developed (p. 119).

Re-Consider the Role of the Learning Professional Within an Expanded Conception of Blended Learning

A model of community-based learning, in which the worker-learner moves between formal and informal learning experiences as learning needs require, is not happenstance and demands we re-think the role of learning professionals. It reflects what Lave and Wenger (1991) call a learning curriculum—"situational opportunities viewed from the perspective of learners" (p. 97). Imagine the possibilities if we asked, "How can we create a learning community in this content area?" rather than, "What courses do we need to build?" What role does the training department play? Lohman (2000) suggests that a productive focus is to create "organizational environments that do not inhibit individuals and groups ... from learning on their own" (p. 85). However, validating informal learning in the workplace is still a struggle. Studying the informal work practices of workers in a major Canadian bank, Mitchell and Livingstone (2002) found that while workers rely on informal learning, it was compromised by increasing workloads, staff reductions, and supervisors who actively discouraged it.

Four tasks for the learning professional surface: (a) foster an enabling culture that validates informal learning, (b) equip learners with collaboration and meta-cognition (learning how to learn) skills, (c) address personal learning myths, and (d) leverage technology to support a learning curriculum. These tasks mark a new role in creating learning solutions that blend formal and informal learning encounters, asynchronous and synchronous modes, and a variety of technologies. All stakeholders within the workplace—worker-learners, learning professionals, and leaders—need to recognize the unique nature of informal learning as well as online communities. A deft approach is needed in order to *cultivate* these forms of learning rather than smother them with too many top-down mandates and heavy-handed designs.

Allow Workers to Create a Space and Place for Learning

Although the idea of constant immersion in learning experiences (ubiquitous learning) is appealing, learning takes time and demands its own space and place. Without reflection or focused learning efforts, many of our experiences are just that—experiences and not necessarily learning experiences.

Furthermore, the effectiveness of a structured learning event is diminished when people give it only 50% of their attention. Distractions in a virtual learning event are very real. This problem is compounded by a virtual space in which it is easy to hide and wander in and out. The predicament of carving out time for learning warrants consideration of guilt-free *release time* to engage in learning events. Given that many e-learning events are only a few hours in length, not the two-day F2F sessions of old, it should be possible to take a brief time-out for learning.

Even though an organization may be eager to offload responsibility for learning to employees, this study suggests learners require support. To engage meaningfully in collective meaning-making requires sophisticated competencies. Learners are expected to be their own learning self-managers, be adept at collaborating in online contexts as well as they do F2F, be competent with learning technologies, and be able to use advanced thinking skills. Although these skills can be developed, we cannot assume they are present.

Articulate the Meaning of "Building Community"

Wenger et al. (2002) state that communities are "groups of people who share ...a set of problems or a passion about a topic, and who deepen their knowledge and expertise in this area by interacting on an ongoing basis" (p. 4). By bringing diverse expertise and experiences, all members of a learning community can take on a teaching role (Rovai, 2004). The first step for learning leaders is to articulate what is meant by community and how it will enhance the learning process in their workplace.

There is a lively debate on whether virtual communities should to be engineered or are best left to emerge on their own. Wenger (1998) argues that communities cannot be "legislated into existence" (p. 229). Others agree. One blog entry reads: "You can't create community! To say you've created community is like saying you've created a tree. ... A better choice of terms would be 'cultivate'. ...Communities are self-forming: It's an opt-in list" (Martin, 2006). However, Johnson (2001) argues that online communities need to be designed; setting up an infrastructure without a task-oriented reason to work together "will not automatically cause a community to form" (p. 53).

There is a plethora of advice on how to design online community, suggesting that online community has become a desired pedagogical strategy and that we need to learn how to do it. Boyd (2006) offers interesting insights that speak to a design philosophy that exemplifies organic communities and less of a top-down approach. She advises: design conscientiously but plan to react immediately to what's going on; be deeply in touch with what people are actually doing; don't expect users to have the same goals that you have because they won't; and design for reinterpretation. No matter how perfect your design, it will be modified, altered or manipulated in use (pp. 4-6).

Help Develop Skills for Learning in Online Communities and Social Learning Experiences

Adopting a social view of learning gives the worker-learner increased responsibilities. No longer fact sponges, they must be active meaning-makers and invest more than just their time. Although many contextual factors can distract learners in the work space, collective meaning-making is impossible if they do not, or are not, able to participate more meaningfully. Expectations

of the worker-learner can include a willingness to engage in higher order thinking, step out of learning silos and dialogue with peers, learn the online tools well enough to engage collaboratively, and take responsibility for personal learning as well as the development of a community. We should not assume that the worker-learner will automatically be able to use OCTs to leverage social learning opportunities. Gunawardena et al. (2006) emphasize that all participants need to recognize the shift to community focus. Salomon and Perkins (1998) advise that learners need to learn how to "capitalize on the social milieu" (p. 5) by "learning to contribute to the learning of a collective" (p. 21) and mediating the learning of others.

FUTURE TRENDS

Online communities of practice and informal learning within a blended learning milieu offer many possibilities for dynamic learning within virtual spaces. These notions will continue to be key driving forces in workplace learning strategies. Despite the avid interest in communities, informal learning, and blended learning, we are still shaping our understanding of the possibilities. While much of the literature focuses on how we *design* virtual learning experiences to integrate these elements, perhaps we need to pay closer attention to how the worker-learner blends their own learning purposefully and serendipitously, engaging in different communities to construct their own mix of relevant learning opportunities.

Learning practitioners and researchers continue to wrestle with how best to channel social learning especially within an online context. The flexibility of OCTs raises increasingly complex questions. Online discursive practices challenge our ability to become conversant in what is a new and nuanced way of communicating and demands new literacies. These online social spaces also bring questions of inclusion. Jones (1998) writes that "the ability to create, maintain, control space …links us to notions of power … Just because the spaces with which we are now concerned are electronic, there is not a guarantee that they are democratic, egalitarian, or accessible" (p. 20).

Future directions for research include:

- How can synergy and cohesion be created in blended learning experiences that mix asynchronous and synchronous learning in formal and informal venues? What is the impact on knowledge construction when learning events are delivered in short chunks?
- What value do participants in workplace e-learning experiences attach to community and what kinds of community best enhance learning in the virtual space?
- What kinds of learning needs or prior learning experiences drive one to seek out an online community inside or outside the workplace?
- How has the advent of social software created new tools and venues for learning in the virtual space?
- New forms of virtual learning and work experiences engage us in discussions of spatiality, temporality, embodiment, and relationality in cyberspace. Constructing organizational policy within this elasticity of space, time, body, and the other becomes complex. How do we approach these challenges?

CONCLUSION

Although Web-based technologies create opportunities to re-conceptualize learning in the workplace, using new media and trendy buzzwords does not change learning practice. Before we can exploit an e-learning technology we must be able to imagine the possibilities for learning. Without shifting our learning paradigms, any OCT—simple or sophisticated—is just a piece of technology. Perhaps we need to re-consider the language we use. What if we emphasized learning rather than the media? For example, referring to *l(e)arning* instead of *e-learning*?

There is tremendous potential when we move beyond the familiar terrain of formal structured training experiences. More than ever, the ability of tools such as the VSC to support real-time peer-to-peer collaboration signals a shift to informal learning methods, such as communities of practice that better integrate work and learning and support ongoing collective meaning-making.

By exploring notions of community and blended learning within the context of newer socio-cultural paradigms, this chapter highlights the possibilities that emerge when we move beyond traditional views of teaching and learning. Socio-cultural perspectives offer a way to envision how virtual learning spaces could be used to shape more vibrant and dynamic learning in the workplace, learning that extends beyond the walls of a classroom—physical or virtual.

REFERENCES

Afonso, A. (2006). Communities as context providers for Web-based learning. In: A. de Figueiredo & A. Afonso (Eds.), *Managing learning in virtual settings: The role of context* (pp. 135-163). Hershey, PA: Information Science Publishing.

Ahern, T., & El-Hindi, A. (2000). Improving the instructional congruency of a computer-mediated small-group discussion: A case study in design and delivery. *Journal of Research on Computing in Education, 32*(3), 385-400.

Alexander, B. (2006). Web 2.0: A new wave of innovation for teaching and learning?. *EDUCAUSE, 41*(2), 33-44.

Anagnostopoulos, D., Basmadjian, K., & Mc-Crory, R. (2005). The de-centered teacher and the construction of social space in the virtual classroom. *Teachers College Record, 107*(8), 1699-1729.

Anderson, T. (2005). *Distance learning: Social software's killer app?*. Retrieved from July 31, 2006 from http://www.unisa.edu/au/od/aaconference/PPDF2s/13%20odlaa%20-%20Anderson.pdf.

Barab, S., & Duffy, T. (2000). From practice fields to communities of practice. In: D. Jonassen & S. Land (Eds.), *Theoretical foundations of learning environments* (pp. 25-54). Mahwah, NJ: Lawrence Erlbaum Associates.

Berge, Z. (1999). Interaction in post-secondary Web-based learning. *Educational Technology, 39*(1), 5-11.

Boyd, D. (2006). *G/localization: When global information and localiInteraction collide*. Paper presented at O'Reilly Emerging Technology Conference, 2006. Retreived August 1, 2006 from http://www.danad.org/papers.Etech2006.html.

Bratton, J., Helms Mills, J., Pyrch, T., & Sawchuk, P. (2004). *Workplace learning: A critical introduction*. Aurora, Ontario, Canada: Garamond Press.

Brown, J., & Duguid, P. (1991). Organizational learning and communities-of-practice: Toward a unified view of working, learning, and innovation. *Organizational Science, 2*(1), 40-57.

Brown, J., & Duguid, P. (2002). *The social life of information*. Boston, MA: Harvard Business School Press.

Bruner, J. (1996). *The culture of education*. Cambridge, MA: Harvard University Press.

Courtenay, B., Merriam, S., & Baumgartner, L. (2003). Witches way of knowing: Integrative learning in joining a marginalized group. *International Journal of Lifelong Education, 22*(2), 111-131.

Dede, C. (1996). The evolution of distance education: Emerging technologies and distributed learning. *The American Journal of Distance Education, 10*(2), 4-36.

Duderstadt, J. (1999). *Dancing with the devil*. San Francisco, CA: Jossey-Bass.

Ferraris, M., Manca, S., Persico, D., & Sarti, L. (2000). Managing the change from face-to-face to distance training for SMEs. *Computers & Education, 34*(2), 77-91.

Ford, J. (1999). Organizational change as shifting conversations. *Journal of Organizational Change, 12*(6), 480-500.

Fox, M. (2002). Keeping the blended promise: What does it take to make e-learning really pay off?. *e-learning Magazine, March*. Retrieved January 24, 2003 from http://www.elearningmag.com/elearning/article/articleDetail.jsp?id=11689.

Fletcher, K. (2004). Peer-to-peer networks and opportunities for alignment of pedagogy and technology. *AACE Journal, 12*(3), 310-313.

Freire, P. (1971). *Pedagogy of the oppressed*. New York, NY: Herder and Herder.

Garrison, D., & Kanuka, H. (2004). Blended learning: Uncovering its transformative potential in higher education. *Internet and Higher Education, 7*(2), 95-105.

Gray, B. (2004). Informal learning in a community of practice. *Journal of Distance Education, 19*(1), 20-35.

Gunawardena, C., Ortegano-Layne, L., Carabajal, K., Frechette, C., Lindemann, & Jennings, B. (2006). New model, new strategies: Instructional design for building online wisdom communities. *Distance Education, 27*(2), 217-232.

Hammond, M. (2000). Communication within online forums: The opportunities, the constraints and the value of a communicative approach. *Computers & Education, 35*(4), 251-262.

Haythornthwaite, C., Kazmer, M., Robins, J., & Shoemaker, S. (2004). Community development among distance learners: Temporal and technological dimensions. In: C. Haythornthwaite & M. Kazmer (Eds.), *Learning, culture and community in online education: Research and practice* (pp. 35-57). New York, NY: Peter Lang Publishing.

Johnson, C. (2001). A survey of current research on online communities of practice. *The Internet and Higher Education, 4*(1), 45-60.

Jonassen, D., & Land, S. (2000). Preface. In: D. Jonassen & S. Land (Eds.), *Theoretical foundations of learning environments* (pp. iii-ix). Mahwah, NJ: Lawrence Erlbaum Associates.

Jones, S. (1998). Information, Internet, and community: Notes toward an understanding of community in the information age. In: S. Jones (Ed.), *CyberSociety 2.0: Revisiting computer-mediated communication and community* (pp. 1-34). Thousand Oaks, CA: Sage Publications.

Kawasaki, G. (2006). *The art of creating a community.* Retrieved July 25, 2006 from http://blog.guykawasaki.com/2006/02/the_art_of_cre_.html.

Knowles, M. (1980). *The modern practice of adult education: From pedagogy to andragogy* (Rev. ed.). New York, NY: Cambridge, The Adult Education Company.

Lave, J., & Wenger, E. (1991). *Situated learning: Legitimate peripheral participation.* New York, NY: Cambridge University Press.

Livingstone, D. (2001). *Adults' informal learning: Definitions, findings, gaps and future research* (NALL Working Paper #21 – 2001). Toronto, Canada: University of Toronto, Centre for the Study of Education and Work, OISE/UT. Retrieved September 2, 2004 from http://www.oise.utoronto.ca/depts/sese/csew/nall/res/index.htm.

Lohman, M. (2000). Environmental inhibitors to informal learning in the workplace: A case study of public school teachers. *Adult Education Quarterly, 50*(2), 83-101.

Martin, B. (2006). *You can't create community!.* Blog posting to http://caeexam.blogspot.com/2006/02/you-cant-create-community.html.

Masie, E. (2003). The next era of virtual classrooms. *e-learning, 4*(1), 16.

McLoughlin, C., & Oliver, R. (1998). Maximising the language and learning link in computer learning environments. *British Journal of Educational Technology, 29*(2), 125-136.

Mitchell, L., & Livingstone, D. (2002). *All on your own time: Informal learning practices of bank branch workers* (NALL Working Paper #64). Toronto, Canada: University of Toronto, Centre for the Study of Education and Work, OISE/UT. Retrieved September 2, 2004 from http://www.oise.utoronto.ca/depts/sese/csew/nall/res/index.htm.

O'Connor, M. (1998). Can we trace the "efficacy of social constructivism"?. *Review of Research in Education, 23,* 25-71.

Palloff, R., & Pratt, K. (1999). *Building learning communities in cyberspace: Effective strategies for the online classroom.* San Francisco, CA: Jossey-Bass.

Preece, J. (2002). Supporting community and building social capital. *Special Edition of Communications of the ACM, 45*(4), 37-39.

Rheingold, H. (2000). *The virtual community: Homesteading on the electronic frontier* (Rev. ed.). Cambridge, MA: The MIT Press.

Rising, L., & Watson, J. (1998). Improving quality and productivity in training: A new model for the high-tech learning environment. *Bell Labs Technical Journal, 3*(1), 134-143.

Romiszowski, A. (1997). Web-based distance learning and teaching: Revolutionary invention or reaction to necessity?. In: B. Khan (Ed.), *Web-based instruction* (pp. 25-37). Englewood Cliffs, NJ: Educational Technology Publications.

Rovai, A. (2004). A constructivist approach to online college learning. *Internet and Higher Education, 7*(2), 79-93.

Salmon, G. (1999). *The twenty-first century manager.* Retrieved March 23, 2002 from http://oubs.open.ac.uk/businesscafe.

Salmon, G. (2000). *E-moderating: The key to teaching and learning online.* London: Kogan Page.

Salomon, G., & Perkins, D. (1998). Individual and social aspects of learning. *Review of Research in Education, 23,* 1-24.

Sarkar, C. (2006). The art of creating a community [11:54 am]. Blog posting to http://blog.guykawasaki.com/2006/02/the_art_of_cre_.html.

Schacht, N. (2002). Blended learning: Turning the training center into a learning center. *e-learning Magazine, May.* Retrieved January 24, 2003 from http://www.elearningmag.com/elearning/article/articleDetail.jsp?id=18566.

Sfard, A. (1998). On two metaphors for learning and the dangers of choosing just one. *Educational Researcher, 27*(2), 4-13.

Shotsberger, P. (2000). The human touch: Synchronous communication in Web-based learning. *Educational Technology, 40*(1), 53-56.

Thompson, T. (2004). Using e-learning to bridge the global digital divide: Successes and challenges from the international field. In: J. Nall & R. Robson (Eds.), *Proceedings of E-Learn 2004* (p. 87 for abstract; complete paper on proceedings CD). Norfolk, VA: Association for the Advancement of Computing in Education.

Thompson, T., & MacDonald, C. (2005). Community building, emergent design, and expecting the unexpected: Creating a quality eLearning experience. *Internet and Higher Education, 8*(3), 233-249.

Trentin, G. (2001). From formal training to communities of practice via network-based learning. *Educational Technology, 41*(2), 5-14.

Watkins, K., & Marsick, V. (1992). Towards a theory of informal and incidental learning in organizations. *International Journal of Lifelong Education, 11*(4), 287-300.

Wells, G. (2000). Dialogic inquiry in education: Building on the legacy of Vygotsky. In: C. Lee & P. Smagorinsky (Eds.), *Vygotskian perspectives on literacy research: Constructing meaning through collaborative inquiry* (pp. 51-85). New York, NY: Cambridge University Press.

Wells, G. (2002). Dialogue about knowledge building. In: B. Smith (Ed.), *Liberal education in a knowledge society* (pp. 111-138). Chicago, IL: Open Court Press.

Wenger, E. (1998). *Communities of practice: Learning, meaning, and identity.* Cambridge, England: Cambridge University Press.

Wenger, E., McDermott, R., & Snyder, W. (2002). *Cultivating communities of practice: A guide to managing knowledge.* Boston, MA: Harvard Business School Press.

KEY TERMS

Blended Learning: Mixing several elements to create a dynamic learning menagerie: F2F and online learning events, synchronous and asynchronous modalities, different e-learning media within an online experience, individual and collaborative activities, formal and informal learning opportunities, instruction and coaching, and learning events coupled with ongoing knowledge management and action projects.

Collective Meaning-Making: The cornerstone of social learning theory, collective meaning-making is a social activity in which, McLoughlin and Oliver (1998) state, "learning is facilitated through purposeful dialogue, verbalization of thought processes, … and negotiation of meaning" (p. 129).

Community: Wenger, McDermott, and Snyder (2002) state that communities are "groups of people who share …a set of problems or a passion about a topic, and who deepen their knowledge and expertise in this area by interacting on an ongoing basis" (p. 4).

Informal Learning: "Any activity involving the pursuit of understanding, knowledge, or skill which occurs without the presence of externally imposed curricular criteria". The objectives, content, learning strategies, duration, and evaluation of outcomes are "determined by the individuals and groups that choose to engage in it" (Livingstone, 2001, p. 5).

Social Software: "A group of Web services that are especially connective, such as: blogs, wikis, trackback, podcasting, videoblogs and social networking tools like MySpace and Facebook" (Alexander, 2006, p. 33).

Socio-cultural Learning Paradigms: A belief that learning, thinking, and knowing are found in the "relations among people in activity in, with, and arising from the socially and culturally structured world" (Lave & Wenger, 1991, p. 51). Wells (2002) adds that, "the active construction of a personal understanding is an integral part of participating in knowledge building with others" (p. 127).

Synchronous and Asynchronous Modalities: *Synchronous* learning technologies enable same-time collaboration; events and interactions take place in real time. In contrast, *asynchronous* technologies enable any-time, any-place collaboration; learners and facilitators are not necessarily online and interacting at the same time.

Chapter XXI
Video Technology for Academic Integrity in Online Courses

Judith Szerdahelyi
Western Kentucky University, USA

ABSTRACT

In addition to their traditional low-tech repertoire of cheating methods, students are now compromising academic integrity by utilizing sophisticated high-tech innovations to improve their grades. The inexperience of online faculty can also contribute to students' academic misconduct when instructors employ a course design and/or assessment measures that are more appropriate for face-to-face courses. This chapter discusses how easy it is for students to "fake a course" and earn a grade in an online class without acquiring knowledge if a combination of two factors are present: 1) Using pedagogical tools unsuitable for measuring online performance, and 2) Violations of academic integrity. The purpose of the chapter is to present new methods of utilizing multimedia technology, more specifically student video production, to reduce the possibility of academic dishonesty and to improve the quality of teaching and learning.

INTRODUCTION

Academic dishonesty is not a new phenomenon, although "the Internet and other technologies are presenting new opportunities for cheating" (McCabe & Drinan, 1999, p. B7). Since teaching online happens in a computer- and Internet-based electronic environment, "both faculty and students believe it is easier to cheat in distance learning classes" (Kennedy et al., 2000, p. 309). Online instructors deeply care about the academic rigor and academic integrity of their courses, but what can they do to prevent cybercheating (Connors, 1966, as cited in Campbell, Swift & Denton, 2000, p. 728) and grade inflation? The goal of this chapter is to raise awareness of a simple fact: If

technology offers greater possibilities to cheat, it will also offer possibilities for countermeasures to curb cheating. It offers some new technology-based strategies to evaluate students' online performance and to make sure that students do not get credit for work they did not do. It will also throw light on the importance of course design and how well-chosen assessment tools can promote student learning and academic integrity.

BACKGROUND

Based on several recently published studies (Gray, 1998; Olt, 2002; Shyles, 2002; Niel, 2004), it seems that "maintaining academic integrity" continues to be a "challenge in both traditional and online education" (Heberling, 2002). "[A]cademic dishonesty is [not only] a relatively widespread practice" (Campbell, Swift, & Denton, 2000, p. 738), but it has also been "on the rise" (Ridley & Husband, 1998, p. 185) for several decades. Lanier's recent study confirmed that the "rate of cheating for online courses surpassed that of the traditional lecture courses" (p. 258). According to a widely held opinion, the increase in cheating is due to the rapid development of technology and belief that "the possibilities inherent in the Internet mean that engaging in academic dishonesty is easier, faster, and cheaper than in the past" (Campbell, Swift, & Denton, 2000, p. 726).

According to Eisenberg (2004), the number of students violating academic integrity has reached alarming levels (p. 164). "39 percent of students completing the 1963 survey acknowledged one or more incidents of serious test or exam cheating; by 1993, this had grown to 64 percent" (McCabe, 2005, p. 27). "A nationwide poll of 20,000 middle and high school students released last year [1998] by the Josephson Institute of Ethics in Marina del Rey, Calif., suggests the magnitude of the problem: Seven out of 10 high schoolers admitted to having cheated on an exam" (Buschweller, 1999). As anticipated, the problem is not restricted to lower levels of education. "Duke University's Center for Academic Integrity website reports that 75% of students across 21 higher education campuses nationwide admit to some cheating throughout their collegiate careers" (Baron & Crooks, 2005, p. 40). Also referring to the Center for Academic Integrity Web site on, NBC4 reports "that 70 percent of college students admit to some sort of academic cheating. And 37 percent have used the Internet to plagiarize" (2006, para 2). In an international study on cheating, Cizek (2001) found that "3-5% of exam candidates are likely to be cheating" (cited in BBC News, 2000). Davis et al. "reported that between 40% and 60% of their student respondents reported cheating on at least one examination" (cited in Kennedy et al., 2000). Eisenberg (2004) quotes several studies

in which the estimated percentage of cheating U.S. students is between 50% and 90% (p. 164). Equally alarming are the data that Rowe (2004) mentions in his article based on several studies between 1996 and 2003. Dick et al. report that 75% of college students cheated during their college years (Rowe, 2004, p. 1).

CREATIVE EXAM-ROOM CHEATING TECHNIQUES

No matter what type of assignment, students cheat on standardized tests, exams, term papers, and other homework assignments. They use various low-tech strategies and devices during exams, such as the somewhat old-fashioned "crib sheet[s] in [the] pleats of a skirt," or "on [the] underside of [the] brim of [a] baseball cap" (Schneider, 1999; BBC News, 2000), or on the inside label of water bottles (Delisio, 2003). They cheat by communicating through body language, hand gestures, facial expressions, and coughing. They signal to each other by "clicking pens" or by color-coded M&M sweets (BBC News, 2000).

If the above were not proof, Morse's list (n.d.) of "bizarre cheating methods" will surely prove that students' resourcefulness surpasses every stretch of the imagination when it comes to cheating techniques. With the advancement of digital technology, new gadgets such as palm pilots, cell phones, pagers, blackberries, and laser pens have been included in the already sophisticated repertoire of students' cheating devices. Utilizing e-mail and text messaging combined with taking advantage of time-zone differences, students can ensure an easy A on any exam. Hidden video cameras attached to students' bodies and undetectable earpieces connected to cheat stations are noteworthy examples of spy technology that students also take advantage of, not to mention "answer-encoded" pencils and infrared messaging between calculators (Morse, n. d.). Those who need to have access to an even more exhaustive list of cheating techniques might join CheatHouse.

com and read a 32-page article offering additional ideas (The Evil House of Cheat, 1998, as cited in Campbell, Swift, & Denton, 2000).

COMPUTER-BASED CHEATING TECHNIQUES AND PLAGIARIZING

Compromising academic integrity goes beyond test-taking or exam-room situations. When it comes to completing paper assignments or book reviews, the most common form of academic dishonesty is plagiarizing. Not only can students copy and paste chunks of texts or entire papers after Googling some key words, but they can also purchase pre-written or made-to-order essays in any discipline just by signing up with one of the thousands of paper mills (Campbell, Swift, & Denton, 2000; Heberling, 2002). To minimize the chance of detection by a sudden improvement in the quality of the student's previous and current work, some cheat sites allow students to specify the grade they would like to receive on their paper.

In distance education, where there is little or no face-to-face contact between students and instructor and therefore no surveillance in place, students are more likely to use dishonest means to improve their grades. This has serious consequences regarding the validity of grades and the quality of learning in distance-education programs. If students cheat, to what extent do test results reflect their skills and abilities? Or to quote Wade's question (1999), "What do students know and how do we know that they know it?" Can instructors tell if there is any learning taking place at all? If there is no knowledge behind a grade or even a degree, we will soon face a situation that Morse (n.d.) describes thus: "we're going to have accountants who can't add, doctors who don't know an appendix from a gallbladder, and veterinarians who can't tell a Chihuahua from a large rat."

POTENTIAL OF ACADEMIC DISHONESTY IN AN ACTUAL ONLINE COURSE

As I am an online writing instructor, the above questions concern me greatly. When I first started teaching technical writing online several years ago, I realized that my course design allowed students to "fake the course" and earn a grade without internalizing the course material. When I adapted my face-to-face course to suit the online environment, traditional lectures and student-led introductory discussions were replaced by the online student reading the textbook's chapters. The course content which was delivered in presentations and lectures by both the instructor and students in the face-to-face course had no optimal equivalent in the Web course. The only way students had access to content information was through reading.

To monitor students' learning progress, I assigned weekly reflective reading responses to the textbook's chapters. This was a standard requirement in my face-to-face courses, too, but in the online class, journal writing carried more weight. Without face-to-face contact with students, I had fewer opportunities to monitor students' development than I had in the classroom. In fact, journal entries offered the only evidence of whether or not students were reading the course book. Other than providing evidence that they were indeed reading the book, I expected students to use the journal as a tool to help them learn the material in a "writing to learn" mode. However, some journal entries showed no engagement with the material. They were either word-for-word, mechanical copying from the textbook or a summary of the student's personal experience with regards to some idea or concept discussed in the chapter. Composing these journal entries would have been easy for them even if they had not read the book. Feeling that "the rigor of the course [was] being challenged" (Gibbons, Mize, & Rogers, 2002, p. 4) and that I might allow undeserving students to pass the course, I decided on a change of course design and syllabus.

To ensure that learning takes place and that the book's information is retained, I introduced tests and quizzes in the following semester. I used the assessment measures that came with Blackboard (i.e., multiple choice, true or false, fill in the blank, matching, and open-ended essay questions) and followed the theoretical guidelines I learned during my institution's training sessions. The tests and quizzes had a time limit and allowed students only one attempt. They were available for students to take during a period of five to seven days.

Instructions about how to take the test were sent out well ahead of time. To prevent cheating, I reminded students that they were not allowed to use any books, course materials, dictionaries, Web sites, and so forth, to answer the test questions. I emphasized that they were not allowed to use any "outside help" by consulting anything or anybody in person, virtually/electronically, or otherwise. To make sure that students abided by this policy, at the beginning of each test, I included three "honesty questions" that I heard about in an online training course by Sally Kuhlenschmidt, director of the Faculty Center for Excellence in Teaching at Western Kentucky University. They asked students to affirm that they were not going to use any "outside help" while taking the test and that they were not going to reveal test questions/answers to their classmates.

Despite all the preparation, the tests and quizzes did not deliver the results that I had hoped for, and my suspicion that some students could be "faking the course" lived on. The tests only raised further questions about my pedagogy and about students' academic honesty. In a voluntary, anonymous survey I usually administer at the end of each term, I asked students if they thought it would have been easy to cheat on the tests and if they were aware of anybody who actually had. Their responses revealed that it would have been very easy to cheat on these tests although they were not aware that anybody in class had, in fact, cheated. In another course evaluation that was administered by the university and went directly to the department head, two responses were more revealing regarding my tests and quizzes.

One student complained that the "online quizzes [were] entirely too difficult to be completed without using the book. The questions seemed to require word-for-word answers, but the general ideas from the chapters should be what is tested [sic]. It is not realistic to expect students to memorize 7 to 10 chapters at a time." Since my topic here is academic honesty, I am refraining from the discussion of any other teaching/learning issues based on this comment. Although the student does not specifically say that s/he used the book while taking the test, the implication is that violating academic honesty is justifiable if the quiz does not follow students' expectations or if it is perceived to be "too hard."

The other student who mentioned the quizzes in his/her course evaluation seems to repeat the same general idea when s/he says that "it is not realistic to expect things memorized from up to 4 chapters, and then to expect that students in an online class will not use their books. Either make quizzes hard, and allow books, or make the test easier so that we would not need them to pass." Here, too, the difficulty of the test and "unreasonable" instructor expectations seem to justify students' using the book while doing the test. It almost seems that students reserve the right to cheat if that helps them pass the course.

STUDENTS' REASONS FOR ACADEMIC DISHONESTY

When examining the reasons for academic dishonesty in the online classroom, Gibbons, Mize and Rogers (2002) point out that it is usually the busy student who signs up for online classes. These students do not have time to take traditional classroom courses, and they "manipulate their course schedule around work and family obligations" (p. 4). They claim that students who overextend themselves often feel overwhelmed by the online course demands. Since they perceived the course requirements to be unreasonable, their "temptation to use inappropriate resources to complete the course assignments" began to grow (p. 4). There is no way for me to verify whether the two students quoted above would fall under the "busy student" category or whether they had additional reasons to contemplate academic dishonesty. What I can see, however, is that my emphasis was perhaps on the wrong objective in testing: I wanted to make sure that students read the textbook and I was less interested to see if they could apply the ideas discussed in the textbook. This is clearly a course design and pedagogical issue that needed to be reconsidered in future courses.

Examining further reasons why students are tempted to abuse academic integrity, Rowe (2004) lists additional circumstances. The more "distant" a student feels due to lack of interaction between peers and instructor, the more likely it is that s/he will cheat. Students have also been found to cheat simply because cheating is easy and nobody knows about it. Additionally, students' computer skills are usually better than those of their unassuming and often ignorant professors.

STRATEGIES TO PREVENT ACADEMIC DISHONESTY IN AN ONLINE COURSE

What can online instructors do to prevent academic dishonesty? As a first step, instructors should have a well-thought out course design and carefully selected pedagogical tools to assess student performance. When planning a class, instructors need to align course goals, pedagogical tools, and outcomes. Besides reading the literature and participating in workshops, there are several additional professional opportunities to help faculty prepare for online courses. The most obvious places where faculty can seek advice on Web classes are the institution's Teaching and Learning Center and the Distance Learning Office. Instructional designers in charge of distributed learning are great assets to novice online

instructors. Additionally, a simple Google search on "distance education resources" will also offer valuable information about the nuts and bolts of Web-based classes. My personal favorite Web sites are Quality Matters <http://www.qualitymatters. org>, MERLOT <http://www.merlot.org/merlot/ index.htm>, and the TLT Group <http://www. tltgroup.org/>.

The second step is familiarity with when, why, and how students might violate academic integrity. In order to minimize cheating, it is worth looking at the major cheating categories Shyles (2002) created:

1. Impersonation and misrepresentation
2. Copying
3. Communicating
4. Using pre-knowledge

The following list of do's and don'ts contains good advice for online instructors to consider in order to prevent cheating in a Web-based course:

- "Clearly specify the institution's and instructor's policy about academic dishonesty" (Gibbons, Mize, & Rogers, 2002, p. 6).
- Maintain a "high degree of interaction" between students and instructor and among students (Gibbons, Mize, & Rogers, 2002, p. 6).
- Use a variety of evaluation methods (Gibbons, Mize, & Rogers, 2002, p. 6).
- Don't give tests and exams. Use other assessment methods (S. Kuhlenschmidt, personal communication, February 15, 2004).
- Use oral exams in person or over the phone (S. Kuhlenschmidt, personal communication, February 15, 2004). Oral exams at the end of the semester are still a fairly common testing practice in European educational settings.
- If you must give exams, use a proctored testing environment with surveillance cameras (Shyles, 2002, p. 4).

- If you must give exams, create an "open-book" exam.
- Collect samples of students' handwriting and keep their biometrics (photo, fingerprint, etc.) on file in a secure environment (Shyles, 2002, p. 4).
- Learn the students' writing style at the beginning of the semester.
- Use test items that require creative and critical thinking.
- Ask students to sign course agreements with "honesty questions" when they sign up for online classes (S. Kuhlenschmidt, personal communication, February 15, 2004).
- Introduce tests with three "honesty items" (S. Kuhlenschmidt, personal communication, February 15, 2004).
- Hide a "no copy, no print" programming code in the first test item (Brewer, personal communication, February 15, 2004).
- Make students explain why they chose a certain answer in the test (S. Kuhlenschmidt, personal communication, February 15, 2004).
- Create a large system of pools and use random selection of items on tests (Brewer, personal communication, February 15, 2004).
- Have an alternative test with identical first and last few items or change the sequence of test items in the last minute to confuse memorized answers (S. Kuhlenschmidt, personal communication, February 15, 2004).
- Block automatic access to correct answers at the end of the test. Answers should only be available after all students have taken the test (S. Kuhlenschmidt, personal communication, February 15, 2004).
- Use timed testing and warn students about the possibility of being "timed out." This can help prevent the use of unauthorized materials (S. Kuhlenschmidt, personal communication, February 15, 2004).
- Allow students to retake the test with randomized items until they are satisfied with the results (Brewer, personal communication, February 15, 2004).

The above list should not be considered exhaustive, and several of the recommended strategies violate pedagogical principles or have drawbacks, which might make them inappropriate for a given situation. A typical problem with some of these countermeasures is that they increase the already heavy workload that teaching online courses involves. Some of the solutions are time-consuming and complicated. However, new and innovative safeguards are created every day, and ensuring academic integrity will not always be considered virtually impossible.

It is increasingly easier to detect plagiarizing, for example, through the growing number of Plagiarism Detection Services. A library Web site associated with the University of Michigan provides an excellent summary of these services, including their methods used and the cost of service. The list mentions the following sites: Plagiarism.org, Turnitin.com, MyDropBox.com, Jplag, EVE2, CopyCtachGold, WordCheck, MOSS, Wcopyfind, Glatt, and Urkund (Gaither). The most well-known service perhaps is Turnitin.com which was developed to detect exact matches between the student's text and the corpus of student papers compiled in the company's database. When I used Turnitin a few years ago in my face-to-face research writing classes, my goal was to demonstrate to students how the program indicated partial or full matches of text so that students better understand what would be considered plagiarizing and how they could avoid it. The idea was for students to use it as a tool for self-check as opposed to an instructional tool used in anticipation of punitive measures. After using the program, I noticed a welcome difference in students' understanding of citing and documenting sources.

If my emphasis had not been on prevention, students could have walked away with the wrong impression. After doing their self-checks, they reported that the system did not identify all word for word quotes in their texts as perfect matches. This could have sent students the message that it is OK to plagiarize since even this fairly sophisticated software is incapable of catching all thieves. Despite the popularity of the service and the excellent information published on the company's Web site, the program is not without problems. Submitting students' papers without their consent, for example, raises legal concerns. Consequently, being creative with assignments and assessment might provide more suitable alternatives to prevent academic dishonesty.

VIDEO PRODUCTION AND THE LATEST TRENDS IN ASSESSMENT

Some online instructors noticed that there is a discrepancy between the advanced technology used for online course delivery and the old-fashioned, traditionally low-tech assessment methods that instructors are forced to use in order to ensure academic integrity. In other words, assessment tools used in online courses can be far less sophisticated than most other aspects of a Web-based course. This discrepancy is worth addressing and discussing by online teaching professionals. I agree with Kennedy et al. (2000) when they say that "cheating based on technology must be countered by technologically based countermeasures" (p. 4). Using video in and for assessment could be one such effective countermeasure.

Using video cameras and video production offer a wealth of as yet undiscovered opportunities not only to ensure academic integrity, but also to further student engagement. Video can be a useful surveillance tool for exam-room situations to complement or partially substitute the supervision of proctors (Carnevale, 1999; Shyles, 2002; Baron & Crooks, 2005). Monitoring, however, is only one function of video equipment that online instructors could utilize. A more creative way to use video in the context of distributed education would involve students directly in basic video production. My own experiments with integrating technology in the curriculum fall in the realm of video production. What journal writing and tests in my Web course were unable to deliver in my Web-based course, video assignments might just

be able to. Additionally, the impact that video production can have on motivation and active learning should not be underestimated.

The first time I assigned my students a video project was in a face-to-face, upper-level technology and writing course in 2004. In this face-to-face context, preventing academic dishonesty was not the main reason why I assigned students a video project; it was a natural component of the course curriculum. The purpose of the actual assignment entitled "Why English?" was to advertise the major and help the English Department recruit students. The answer to the question "Why English?" was provided by over a dozen English Department faculty members in a series of interviews that were then edited and burned on a DVD. Due to students' enthusiasm and prior technical knowledge of shooting and editing a video, the outcome of the assignment was a successful three-minute trailer.

Although I was aware that the success of this project should not be considered a typical outcome or used to predict the success of video projects I assign other classes, I continued experimenting with it. In academic writing courses, students often show disengagement and resentment towards the class because they consider general education classes a waste of money and a waste of time. By assigning a video project entitled "Why English 300?" I was hoping that they would gain a deeper understanding of the university's rationale behind general education writing courses and the benefits these courses have to offer. The following list contains some ideas for the rationale of incorporating videos in the curriculum in both face-to-face and online classes:

Student-produced video assignments are expected to promote:

- Student motivation
- Active learning and a deepened understanding of course content
- Students' analyzing and critical thinking skills

- Students' creativity and self-expression
- Construction of knowledge and the making of meaning
- Fun for all project participants
- Students' technology and digital literacy skills to meet the demands of 21st century workplace

In their end-of-term course evaluations, some students' comments about the video assignment showed an overlap with the ideas above. This is not to say that all students appreciated all aspects of the assignment, but 64% of those who filled out the evaluation welcomed the project. One student said that the video project "was fun to do" and "[g]ave this course a twist." Others said that it was a "breath of fresh air" and very "de-stressing." Yet others commented that it was a "good way of expressing what [they] think" and that it helped them see "how to make the most of the course" and that it would affect them "later on in life."

During the "Why English 300?" video project, students were working in their workshop groups of three or four. They had great flexibility in deciding which specific aspect of the topic they would focus on, which video genre to work in, and how much time and effort to spend on learning the technical skills necessary to complete the project. They received very little in-class instruction on the theoretical and practical aspect of video production (one class period in a Tuesday-Thursday course). Besides giving them the most basic information about what technical equipment they would need to shoot the video (camera, tripod, external mic, lights, tape, etc.) and what commercially available software packages (Windows Movie Maker, Premiere Pro, Ulead, etc.) they could use to edit the video, I only showed them a collection of video clips demonstrating how not to shoot a video. Otherwise, students were encouraged to take advantage of the services offered by the university's Technology Resource Center at any stage of the production. Those who did not have camcorders or other equipment were able to check these items out of TRC. If requested, they also

received personal training in the use of the equipment and in video editing. In general, students did not complain about technical difficulties.

Although the final products could not be compared to Hollywood quality movies, our emphasis was on the content and not on the technical solutions. Concerning the video genres, most groups produced a documentary type movie that was based on interviews with experts in a certain discipline, with college professors or their fellow students. There was one satirical video game- like animation produced by CS majors, arguing that general education courses are indeed useless. The last and final type of movie was a humorous skit that students wrote, acted out, and taped, while taking turns as members of the production crew and characters in the movie. Other video or TV productions could involve newscasts, "talking heads," trailers, commercials, promotional, or training videos. Seeing the outcomes, I was encouraged to experiment with video in more and more classes, including online ones. In addition to the positive learning outcomes, assigning video projects in an online course has the added benefits of contributing to the prevention of plagiarizing.

So what kinds of video assignments would work in an online course? I assume that probably everything would work that could be used successfully in a face-to-face class. The following list does not even scratch the tip of the iceberg.

In their assignments, students could create a movie to:

- Discover the rationale behind a general education course ("Why English 300?")
- Uncover some assumptions, expectations, or perceptions they or their peers have (If and why students plagiarize in college)
- Make a presentation and explain a concept, process, or assignment solution in the curriculum (What is research?)
- Reflect on what they have learned in the course (Instead of final portfolio cover letter)

- Provide an argument in connection with a debatable course topic (The role of technological knowledge in a research writing course)
- Start a class/group discussion on a certain course-related issue (Should general education courses be required?)
- Describe past experiences or events (Video memoir)

According to the level of technical skills and experience involved, video assignments can range from almost zero knowledge (when all students do is push the "record" button on the camera) to near-professional TV or video production. In one of the more simple types of video assignments, online students would sit in front of the camera and record their thoughts on a given topic. They would be "talking heads," delivering information much like a news anchor on TV. All of the above video assignment categories could be combined with this lowest technical skill level in which the camera is used in a stable recording mode only. More specifically, video reflections could be used to explain the process of completing an assignment, the difficulties students faced, and the solutions they came up with. A good example of this type of assignment would be the "introduction to the writing portfolio," which is essentially the "movie version" of the text-based portfolio cover letter. Video presentations are the equivalent of any kind of presentation assignment normally given in a face-to-face setting. Students can talk about a course topic, a research project, a concept, and so forth.

The completed multimedia assignment would be sent to the instructor via video e-mail, on a DVD, or it could even be published on the Web. In addition to YouTube, Google Video, putfile.com, and similar sites, more and more blogs and wiki sites accept multimedia files with or without space limitation. The instructor can access, watch, and evaluate students' knowledge and/or skills as presented in the video.

The advantage of the visual element in these assignments is that it eliminates the problem of impersonation or misrepresentation in the online class. Except for the rare chance of teaching identical twins, the instructor will see whether or not the person in front of the camera is the student himself/herself, provided that a clear photo of the student has previously been filed. To ensure that the instructor recognizes his/her online students, the following strategies can also be used.

- If the geographical context allows for it, the instructor could organize a face-to-face meeting with the students at the beginning of the semester.
- Students could be asked to create a simple homepage based on the course management system's template, which usually includes posting a photo. When giving this assignment, instructors should specify that students could only upload photos of themselves. Students do not always have a digital photo handy, so occasionally they post a photo of their pets or an everyday object that represents them.
- If the majority of the students come from the same campus, but not one where the instructor is located, a virtual meeting could be arranged via two ITV rooms.
- With Webcams becoming fairly inexpensive, especially in online computer stores, instructors could require that students buy one in order to do video chat using, for example, Yahoo Messenger. To keep the cost of books and supplies down, instructors might consider using reading materials available online instead of books that students have to buy.

Knowing who your students are and recognizing their faces can eliminate a variety of cheating possibilities that the blindness of online delivery presents. Although these video assignments may help to prevent academic dishonesty, they are not entirely without problems either. Besides the usual problems associated with technology, such as lack of sufficient skills or access to video equipment, multimedia assignments cannot guarantee authorship. A friend or relative can write the script for an assignment, which the student then learns and delivers in front of the camera. Teleprompters or cue cards can be used to jog the memory of the students in situations where knowledge should already have been internalized. For all that, video assignments are worth experimenting with for two important reasons: 1) The generally high level of student involvement which ensures active learning and 2) The element of fun that video productions usually offer. If students enjoy what they are doing, there should be no need for them to use illicit sources to complete an assignment.

CONCLUSION

What we need to keep in mind is that the problem of academic dishonesty in distance education will not cease to exist without our continued efforts to look for solutions. If we care about the quality of education, we need to experiment with innovative pedagogy and utilize the potential inherent in technology to ensure academic integrity. It is only through improving our assessment tools and the strengthening of moral standards in our institutions that a grade or a degree will represent what it should: the knowledge that the student has acquired. If we do not pay attention, the situation might have further repercussions. "The literature suggests that students who are academically dishonest often transfer this behavior to the corporate environment after graduation" (Nonis & Swift, 2000; Smith et al., 2002, as cited in Chapman et al., 2004, p. 248). Producing "ethically sound individuals, employees, and leaders" is a crucial part of our professional responsibility (p. 248).

REFERENCES

Baron, J., & Crooks, S. (2005). Academic integrity in Web-based distance education. *TechTrends,*

49(2), 40-45. Retrieved October 31, 2005from <http://www.wku.edu/library/deansoffice/online.htm>.

Buschweller, K. (1999). Generation of cheaters. *American School Board Journal.* Retrieved October 3, 2006 from http://www.asbj.com/199904/0499coverstory.html.

Campbell, C., Swift, C., & Denton, L. (2000). Cheating goes hi-tech: Online term paper mills. *Journal of Management Education, 24*(6), 726-740.

Carnevale, D. (1999). How to proctor from a distance. *Chronicle of Higher Education,* p. A47+. Retrieved October 1, 2005 from http://www.wku.edu/library/ deansoffice/online.htm.

The Center for Academic Integrity. (2006). Retrieved October 10, 2006 from http://www.academicintegrity.org/fundamental.asp.

Chapman, K., Davis, R., Toy, D., & Wright, L. (2004). Academic integrity in the business school environment: I'll get by with a little help from my friends. *Journal of Marketing Education, 26*(3), 236-250.

Cizek, G. (2001). An overview of issues concerning cheating on large-scale tests. Paper presented at the meeting of the National Council on Measurement in Education. Seattle, WA. Retrieved October 1, 2005 from http://www.natd.org/Cizek%20Symposium%20Paper.PDF.

Gaither, R. (2002). Plagiarism detection services. *Resources for Instructors.* The University of Michigan. Retrieved February 23, 2007 from http://www.lib.umich.edu/acadintegrity/ instructors/violations/detection.htm.

Dick, M., Sheard, J., Bareiss, C., Carter, J., Joyce, D., Harding, T., & Laxer, C. (2003). Addressing student cheating: Definitions and solutions. *ACM SIGCSE Bulletin, 35*(2), 172-184.

Eisenberg, J. (2004). To cheat or not to cheat: Effects of moral perspective and situational variables on students' attitudes. *Journal of Moral Education, 33*(2), 163-78. Retrieved October 1, 2005 from http://www.wku.edu/library/deansoffice/online.htm.

Cheats stay one step ahead. (2000). *BBC News* 5 February. Retrieved October 1, 2005 from http://news.bbc.co.uk/2/hi/uk_news/education/631204.stm. Path: BBC Homepage; World Service; Education.

Delisio, E. (2003). Uniting against cheating. *Education World. Wire Side Chats.* Retrieved October 1, 2005 from http://www.education-orld.com/a_issues/chat/chat087.shtml.

Gibbons, A., Mize, C., & Rogers, K. (2002). That's my story and I'm sticking to it: Promoting academic integrity in the online environment. *Proceedings of the 2002 World Conference on Educational Multimedia, Hypermedia, and Telecommunications.* Retrieved October 1, 2005 from http://www.wku.edu/library/deansoffice/online.htm.

Gray, S. (1998). Maintaining academic integrity in web-based instruction. *Educational Media International, 35*(3), 186-188.

Heberling, M. (2002). Maintaining academic integrity in online education. *Online Journal of Distance Learning Administration, 5*(1). Retrieved October 1, 2006 from http://scholar.google.com/scholar.

Kennedy, K., Nowak, S., Raghuraman, R., Thomas, J., & Davis, S. (2000). Academic dishonesty and distance learning: Student and faculty views. *College Student Journal, 34*(2), 309-315. *Project Innovation 2000.* Retrieved February 6, 2006 from http:// findarticles.com/p/ articles/mi_m0FCR/is_2_34/ai_63365187/print.

Lanier, M. (2006). Academic integrity and distance learning. *Journal of Criminal Justice Education, 17*(2).

Lorenzetti, J. (2006). Proctoring assessments: Benefits and challenges. *Distance Education Report, 5-6.*

McCabe, D. (2005). It takes a village: Academic dishonesty. *Liberal Education, summer/fall,* 26-31.

McCabe, D., & Drinan, P. (1999). Toward a culture of academic integrity. *Chronicle of Higher Education, 46*(8), B7.

Morse, A. (n.d.). On campus, cheater ever prosper. *Boundless.* Webzine. Retrieved February 5, 2006 from http://www.boundless.org/2000/departments/ campus_culture/ a0000242.html.

Lanier, M. (2006). Academic integrity and distance learning. *Journal of Criminal Justice Education, 17*(2), 244-261.

Nonis, S., & Swift, C. (2001). An examination of the relationship between academic dishonesty and workplace dishonesty: A multi-campus investigation. *Journal of Education for Business, 76*, 69-77.

Olt, M. (2002). Ethics and distance education: Strategies for minimizing academic dishonesty in online assessment. *Online Journal of Distance Learning Administration, 5*(3). Retrieved October 1, 2006 from http://scholar.google.com/ scholar.

Ridley, D., & Husband, J. (1998). Online education: A study of academic rigor and integrity. *Journal of Instructional Psychology, 25*(3), 184-189.

Rowe, N. (2004). Cheating in online student assessment: Beyond plagiarism. *Online Journal of Distance Education Administration, 7*(2). Retrieved June 1, 2005 from http://www.westga.edu/~distance/ojdla/summer72/rowe72.html.

Shyles, L. (2002). Authenticating, identifying, and monitoring learners in the virtual classroom: Academic integrity in distance learning. Paper presented at the meeting of the National Communication Association, New Orleans, LA.

Schneider, A. (1999,). Why professors don't do more to stop students who cheat. *Chronicle of Higher Education, 45*(20), A8.

Teachers aim to curb online cheating. (2006). *NBC4*. Retrieved October 4, 2006 from http://www.nbc4.com/education/6791215/detail.html.

Wade, W. (1999). What do students know and how do we know that they know it?. *T H E Journal, 27*(3), 94-97. Retrieved June 1, 2005 from http://www.wku.edu/ library/deansoffice/online.htm.

KEY TERMS

Academic Integrity: In an educational context, academic integrity refers to a set of values that support fair and honest student behavior. Students who violate academic integrity are known to plagiarize or cheat on tests and assignments.

Cybercheating: Cybercheating in an educational context refers to one type of academic dishonesty which includes using the information found on the Web without acknowledging the source.

Distance Learning: Distance education refers to a model of structured institutional instruction in which course content is usually delivered asynchronously via electronic means, such as computers, the Internet, and rich multimedia. As the term suggests, there is usually a geographical distance between students and instructor and no face-to-face contact.

Distributed Learning: Although there are numerous similarities between "distance education" and "distributed learning," there is one important characteristic that distinguishes these two models of education. Whereas "distance education" emphasizes the geographical separation of students and instructor, "distributed learning" is usually associated with the relative flexibility of access to course content. Students are able to decide when, how, and where they want to interact or engage the course material.

Grade Inflation: Grade inflation refers to a phenomenon in the world of education in which grades are becoming gradually higher without being backed up by increased levels of student knowledge and skills.

Chapter XXII
Virtual Workplaces for Learning in Singapore

Kalyani Chatterjea
Nanyang Technological University, Singapore

ABSTRACT

The concept of the virtual workplace is used in three initiatives to create an out-of-classroom environment where learners worked on virtual space while engaging in learning activities. The first involves a multi-group field-class working at geographically separated locations, under on-demand supervision from the lecturer on virtual workplace, using Internet, video and text messaging, on-demand file uploads and file transfers. The second involves use of virtual lab, to prepare for complicated laboratory procedures and reduce classroom time by allowing virtual hands-on lab exposure. The third initiative is supported by online learning resources, providing a learning environment on demand, on virtual workplace and hence with the associated freedom of choice. Learner responses to each of these initiatives are discussed.

INTRODUCTION

The virtual workplace, as an alternative working environment has been an issue mostly affecting the employment scenario. Advances in information technology, and people's familiarity of cyberspace almost make it mandatory to look at this very innovative working arena beyond what is deemed as a commercially viable approach. Being virtual in several places and yet not having to be physically there is by itself an extremely useful concept that may unshackle many of the burdens of another very important area of societal development—in the realm of teaching and learning. Many a time

educators lament of having too little time to teach too many things, of having too little time to give customised attention to learner groups. Use of virtual learning place is set to reduce many of these commonly-faced maladies of the teaching environment.

This chapter defines the term 'Virtual Learning Place' as a space or a platform over which learning can be situated without the learners and the facilitator being present face- to-face. From the perspectives defined and delineated in the chapter virtual workplace entails a learning environment where learners and facilitators are situated in physically distant locations but in synchronous remote contact and involved in real-time communication, using technology-supported communication tools. This enables the parties involved to be freed from the confines of face-to-face contacts and yet enables everyone involved to be in contact at all times and on demand. It is argued that this strategy not only optimizes the learning time and space but also encourages learner-centred learning and learner control. Thus technology-assisted virtual workplace can expand the frontiers of teaching and learning, and not just benefit the commercial work environment.

This chapter looks at the background of virtual workplace and goes on to discuss the issues addressed in three learning scenarios, using the concept of virtual workplace to recreate a classroom learning situation with teacher supervision, a simulated lab facility and a virtual teacher-supervised field work session. Finally, learner responses are analysed to examine the effectiveness of these initiatives in providing a more enriched and more useful learning environment.

BACKGROUND

The importance and pervasiveness of the virtual workplace has increased significantly in the work environment. Today's employment market has changed greatly, and many jobs are no longer as rigidly structured in terms of working hours or workplaces as they once were a few years back. Businesses are introducing flexible working arrangements because of the commercial benefits they can bring. This reflects the changing needs of both customers and employees (Department of Trade and Industry, UK, 2006).

Jeremy Zawodny's comments regarding the current work environment, "If someone actually asked me 'how many hours a week do you work?', I'd have no idea how to answer. Living and working this way just seems natural" (Zawodny, 2006), is pervasive in not just one country but everywhere that is touched by Internet connectivity and the concept of a physical boundary of a country or organization or even time seems to disappear with this technologically-connected environment. Quite rightly the comments of Zawodny's visitors, "That's not work—you're just using instant messenger" points to the changing work norms of today's world.

Froggatt (2001) talks about the concept of virtual workplace, which is aimed at professionals working in an organization and trying out new and innovative methods of cooperating with colleagues, customers, and partners using the Internet platform. A secure and shared Internet workplace, sharing documents, discussions, Web links, and even advanced features for booking and having multi-point video conferences are the usual set up requirements for such virtual workplaces. A shared workspace radically improves the efficiency of communication and coordination of work in a project involving several different organizations and has, therefore, been seen as a viable work environment in many forward-looking fields of employment. The virtual workplace, it is argued, gives us the opportunity to liberate ourselves from the traditional constraints of time, space, and infrastructure.

Among the principles put forward by Froggatt (2001) are some very important issues that play a central role in the establishment of a virtual workplace:

- **Initiative:** having the courage to innovate and change
- **Individuality:** helping individuals to discover the work style that suits them best
- **Connectivity:** reducing reliance on face-to-face interaction and using the new technologies to develop a wider sense of community
- **Workplace Options:** shedding the requirement of commuting to the corporate office, increasing choice of workplace and redesigning common work spaces

It is quite obvious from the existing discourses that the establishment and call for institutionalization of the virtual workplace has so far vastly been targeted at the commercial world of work and business. In the education arena, Web-based learning has been around for many years and has made a place for itself as a mode of delivery of learning materials and training. Many training and learning centres have taken the advantage of this virtual workplace and delivered training to learners in geographically distant places. Yet, the advantages of using the virtual workspace in education still remain to be explored and exploited further. The essence of the concept of working in a virtual workplace has not filtered in the same manner to areas of education and training where the student learners may not always be in distant locations and yet may benefit from the concept of virtual workplace. There are some reports of using the virtual environment for some synchronous data updates from remote field locations (Van Boxel & Wentzel, 2003). But this chapter argues that more can be done to explore this new and emerging mode of creating more spaces for learning and training and the concept of virtual workplace can be actually used to extend the areas of training and learning, even in situations where the learners may not always be away from the place of learning.

The three scenarios developed using the virtual workplace concept are actually integrated in some ways, although they can run independently, to create conditions whereby the students are in charge of their own learning but are at every point scaffolded by the facilitator through a virtual workplace and learning resources, providing just the amount of support asked for.

The key points addressed through these initiatives are:

- provisions of simulated learning environment delivered via a virtual workplace to provide enough training time to ensure adequate proficiency in the area

- provisions for extended, customized learning resources delivered via a virtual workplace, with the built-in flexibilities of time and space
- opportunities of multi-group field-based work, with synchronous supervision from lecturer over cyberspace

All of these were developed with an objective of providing learner-controlled learning environment with adequate scaffold, but without the traditional restrictions of time and space. As Thompson (2005) mentions, these ICT-based initiatives provide learner-support through a variety of different channels and hence make interesting use of the available technologies to further educational endeavours. In contrast to Brabazon's (2001) statement that 'technology is framed as a cheaper, more efficient replacement for University teachers', the present development was based on the idea of offering more learner-control and teaching through facilitation and guidance, to use the affordances of technology to initiate learners to work and collaborate remotely, to receive prior training virtually before embarking on complicated procedures at the laboratory. To sum up, the virtual workplace scenario was created to utilize the IT-mediated learning environment to provide greater exposure to the learners. Forbes (2000) mentions how laboratory experience of engineering requires equipment and how supervision is currently not feasible without on-site courses. It is precisely on this issue that the present chapter argues to show that virtual workplace environment can be useful to initiate very critical but complicated laboratory procedures. This can save time and travel to the classroom, while allowing the learner to repeat the procedures, as required, and attain the required degree of proficiency. As Forbes (2000) quite rightly points out, adult learners like to take control of their education and learn at their own pace. Learning over virtual workplace provides just that for the learners, be they adults or young learners, and thus make them responsible for their own learning. From this point, it may be pointed out that the present set of learning modules using the virtual workplace was not developed as a response to 'modalities of crisis and economic rationalism' (Brabazon, 2001), but was more driven by pragmatism and the advantage of pervasiveness of the virtual workplace in a wired learning community. In Singapore, so far, Internet-based learning has not been a response to reduction in government funding. On the contrary, the mandatory in-service upgrading courses as well as the pre-service teacher training courses heavily encourage virtual learning environment as an avenue to incorporate information technology in learning and service. Thus using the virtual workplace was more a choice of an appropriate platform for the specific learning activity than one driven by economic reasons.

Development of the materials in the virtual learning environments had to consider issues of copyright as well as that of customization for specific learner requirements. Instead of looking for available but only marginally suitable virtual courses, efforts were taken to develop customized courses, thus also avoiding copyright issues. The courses are delivered via the University's learning management system to have better control over the distribution of the materials among only registered participants.

ISSUES ADDRESSED IN THE VIRTUAL WORKPLACE DEVELOPMENTS

1. **Procedural:** Whether field-based or lab-based, exercises in procedural training require repetitive exposures to ensure adequate mastery. However, with limitations on curriculum time, and time tabling complications, it is very difficult to allocate classes where students can do repetitive lessons. The result is a hurried exposure which is only enough to demonstrate what is in store. But

this fails to provide a platform for proper training in the procedures. The graduating participant of the course, therefore, is armed with a qualification but is not adequately trained to handle the procedures independently. For professional courses, this lack of adequate exposure may lead to semi-trained personnel whose performance at work may suffer. For the teacher trainees, like in the present study, an inadequate exposure may lead to less than optimum confidence in handling actual classroom situations.

2. **Exposure to field-based experiments:** For the same time constraints as mentioned above, scheduling multiple sessions of field work becomes a luxury no system can afford. The lecturer, therefore, has two options, either to reduce the number of field-based sessions, or to take an entire big group to work together in the field, where due to the large number of students, very few participants can actually benefit from the instructions and demonstrations given by the tutor.

3. **Students of varying abilities and past experiences in the same class:** Such students are a perpetual problem in courses that have intakes from various sources. While the regular lectures provide knowledge on the curriculum-driven topics, different students in such a mixed class often require additional help to align with the course requirements. Bridging courses do not provide customized help, particularly when the source of such student recruitment is very varied. The result might be a less-than-adequate training in the content knowledge.

To address these three very important issues, some integrated courses and course execution were initiated. In the next section, the chapter outlines the development rationale, the actual development as well as some observations on student performances and student feedback on such development. All comments are related to the issue of how learning in the said environment was managed and influenced using some virtual classroom scenarios to suit the requirements of the specific training.

DEVELOPMENT OF VIRTUAL LEARNING ENVIRONMENTS

Virtual Mineral Lab

This initiative involved shortening of actual on-site lab time by the introduction of virtual lab. Usually students doing the first course on mineral and rock identification have to attend multiple lab sessions to master the intricacies of the identification process (see Figure 1). This involves long curriculum time, something that is difficult to allocate. The result is a reduced exposure and limited knowledge on the topic. The present initiative involved development of a virtual lab, available online to students where, after covering the conceptual learning materials both from face-to-face sessions and online resources, the students go through sessions of virtual labs, where the procedures of mineral and rock identification are handled by them, exactly as would be done

in the real lab. With the virtual lab available at all times, the student is free to access it as many times as required before attending the actual lab session. This development reduces classroom time and allows the student freedom to learn at his/ her pace and yet allows the much required lab exposure that is not possible through only learning materials delivered online. The development uses video, audio inputs to simulate lab environment. This virtual learning environment was developed as a preparatory course after the lectures, and before the actual lab sessions. The sequence of activity followed is as shown below:

Sequence #1	Face-to-face session to introduce the topic on minerals and rocks
Sequence #2	Access to online reading resource with learning objects and hyper-linked resources to provide further knowledge, scaffold, when needed, and to provide control over the learning environment
Sequence #3	Online support via Blackboard© LMS
Sequence #4	Access to Virtual Lab session, with video simulations, audio, interactive response features

Figure 1. Some screen shots from the Virtual Mineral Lab

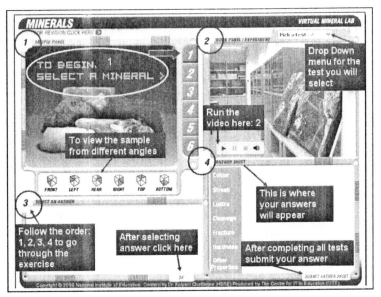

and hyperlinked reading support providing unlimited access to training material. This segment also allows formative learning through self assessment.

This is followed by the actual Lab session for identification of minerals and rocks. By this time, the students are expected to have received enough exposure through the virtual learning space to be able to handle the complicated lab procedures.

Guidance was provided on how to proceed with the Virtual Mineral Lab, to ensure that students get the maximum exposure to the training provided on the virtual workplace.

Field Work Collaboration and Guidance on Virtual Workplace

Introduction of ICT-tools in field work in field-based sciences is not new and equipment such as the GPS, digital tablets, various types of data loggers have been in use for sometime (McCaffrey, et al., 2005; Wentzel, 2006) . Even the use of electronic field notebook, with facilities of data recording for direct upload to a work station back in the lab have been in use for sometime (Brehm, 2002). Use of PDAs has been introduced even in secondary schools in Singapore, with much success and several developments using PDA-based data collection have been around as well (Chatterjea & Ong, 2006). However, the use of wireless technology in a virtual work environment adds a new dimension to this whole array of useful ICT-based field work tools. Wireless technology at NIE was used for teaching a module on Biogeography and Ecosystem Dynamics in the Degree Programme in Geography at NIE. The module involves many sessions of field work where the students require close supervision on the field techniques. Ideally, the same types of soil sampling and other field techniques should be performed in several places to get a good understanding of the processes. Traditionally, this requires several field

sessions for the lecturer as students need to go to several locations on different days. Much time is spent, yet the number of sessions in the field for individual students does not go up.

Through the use of virtual workplace using of wireless technology and video conferencing, all of these requirements could be met easily. The added advantage is an environment where students take charge of their own learning under close supervision of the lecturer and close communication with concurrently working groups at other locations. The entire process is coordinated with the idea of providing the necessary scaffold via a virtual environment.

As preparation for the field sessions, the students were given prior instructions on field procedures and scientific principles. During the actual field sessions, the lecturer stayed in the lab or in her office with a Digital Tablet, Webcam and microphone and a wireless network connection. The students went to the field in groups, with the same set up as the lecturer, plus the field equipment.

The framework of the field sessions was based on the following:

1. Synchronous Remote contact from field sites: with the lecturer on a virtual work space
2. Synchronous Remote contact from field sites: with other groups on a virtual work space
3. Synchronous access to resources using wireless network and creating a virtual workplaces with communication and sharing among all groups

This involved organizing multi-group field exercises where groups gathered field data at physically separated locations, while each being connected at all times wirelessly with all other groups and the lecturer through online video-chat programme. While student groups conducted their field sessions, the lecturer continuously monitored the progress of all groups as well as attended to the queries raised by students. Communication was through video conferencing, text messaging, as well as through the use of electronic notepad on the digital tablet. This last technique was used by the lecturer to draw diagrams to explain issues posed by students, while staying at a remote location. The platform used was MSN Messenger. In all there were three groups working in three different locations and they all communicated with each other while they worked to counter check their field findings. Communication between groups and between groups and the lecturer was maintained through video messaging, text messaging, on-demand file uploads and file transfers. While the experiments were conducted, the groups were able to be guided via video conferencing by the lecturer when the need arose. Groups were also able to ask for supervision and necessary file uploads to facilitate their assigned work and were able to communicate with other groups at different locations. This made the learning very learner-centred, with adequate amount of facilitator assistance, when required via online communication.

The whole class first went through relevant lectures and lab sessions to familiarize themselves with the conceptual framework and knowledge

of operation of the instruments. On the day of the actual field work, three groups were sent to three different locations, with digital tablets fitted with Webcams and microphones. The network connection was made via wireless connection supported by the University (Figure 2).

Figure 2 shows some screen shots from the field sessions, where students are located in remote locations, but are in contact with the lecturer and each other.

The procedures mentioned above were followed for the distributed field work experiment using wireless technology for working on a virtually-guided field work session. The experiment was based on establishing the soil profile of three different locations and analyzing the differences with respect to slope and moisture flow conditions. The three groups had to ascertain the characteristics of the soil profile and compare it with those derived from other field locations and all this was done under virtual supervision from the lecturer. Sometimes additional guidance was sought by the students and the lecturer was in communication with the respective student groups via the wireless, simulating a face-to-face lab situation. Files were uploaded with annotations, using the

Figure 2. Field and lab set ups for the work using virtual workplace

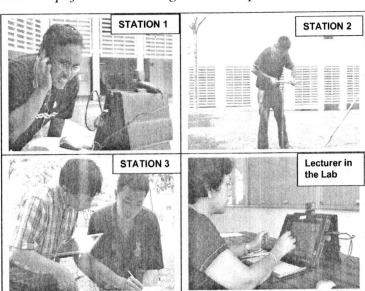

Figure 3. Workflow during one field work session using virtual supervision and online communication

Instructions for conducting experiments on soils on grass-covered slopes, with supervision and communication using virtual space

A total of three experiments will be carried out to investigate Soil characteristics, Soil colour and Infiltration rate on three different locations within NIE campus. Each group will be allocated one site. You will be following the given instructions to conduct the experiments. During the work you will be in contact with the lecturer (Dr. Chatterjea) and the other groups via the wireless network. Given below are the time schedules and instructions to follow:

Please refer to the Handout provided for the objectives of the experiment and the details on the instruments used and the field procedures.

Experiments to be done:

1. Soil profile – create and analyse the texture: Soil Auger and tape
2. Soil colour – determine for all observed layers of the profile: Munsell Colour Chart
3. Infiltration rate – determine the rate / change in rate over a period of 15 minutes: Infiltrometer and water

(Please note that there is only one Infiltrometer – so the groups need to share this equipment during the field work)

Time schedule for the procedures

0900   Each group to assemble at the designated field sites and get the instruments and the Digital tablet ready

0915   Establish contact **using Text messaging** with all groups and the lecturer to get the experiment starting signal

0930   **Groups 1, and 2: Do the Soil profile and Soil Colour tests**

(Follow instructions given earlier)

1. establish text message contact with each other to check if procedures are correct. **Text messaging should be used whever required**
2. Auger a hole and **take out the soil samples** till you reach a depth of about 50 cm
3. **lay the profile** and confirm the depth up to which you have augered, **measure** with tape measure
4. **draw a diagram** of the profile on your note book, with the measurements

5. **write down the description** of the soil at different depths (is it sticky or sandy, gritty, dry or moist, does it have any roots, does it have any other obvious characteristics)
6. **confirm via text message** that you have progressed this far – with all groups (you may ask others if in doubt)
7. **Now determine the soil colour,** using the Soil Colour Chart
8. **If in doubt, call for the lecturer to explain**
9. Write down the soil colour
10. **Confirm with lecturer/ other groups**

Group 3: Start Infiltrometer experiment

(Follow the given instructions: **Establish Video contact with Lecturer** to ensure that you are doing the procedures correctly)

1. **Insert the instrument** in the soil
2. **Pour in the water**
3. **Set the time** to 15 minutes
4. Take **readings every 5 minutes** (if the water seeps in very fast: consult the lecturer)
5. **Record the depression** on the float for every 5 minutes
6. At the end of 15 minutes, stop the experiment, take out the instrument, clean it up and pass it to the next group
7. Continue with the rest of the experiments: follow the instructions given above

electronic whiteboard feature, for explaining some procedures and text messages were used to ensure that students in all groups were in line with the requirements of the field work. Figure 3 shows the step-by-step instructions given to the students for all important steps of work during the field work session. This was necessary to have a well co-ordinated workflow, when the participants were located distantly. Workflow during virtually- connected sessions was organized in a manner similar to what Ruhleder and Jordan (2001) described in their paper on managing complex, distributed environments. One aspect of the present development was the formally determined protocols (Figure 3), while there was also scope for flexible, on-demand virtual collaboration between learners and the lecturer.

Learning Resource on Virtual Space

In today's changing job opportunities and flexible learning opportunities, it is common to get students participating in a certain course coming from diverse backgrounds. In one of the degree courses taught by the author at the National In-stitute of Education (NIE), Singapore students come either directly from the junior colleges (the regular route), or could come from various sources, including various other jobs, as options of changing careers are taken up fairly readily. Table 1 below gives an idea of the diversity of backgrounds of the students who have come to take up the degree course in Geography at NIE this year.

As shown in Table 1, only 50% of the students came with a high school background in Geography. The rest were mostly with diplomas in varied areas. These diverse backgrounds of students lead to very diverse levels of knowledge in the subject area. However, having no definite base level of knowledge is a perennial problem in the smooth and effective running of the undergraduate programmes, since the students have very little time to catch up on their own, if they have any gap in their knowledge base. Some of this problem is sometimes solved by providing bridging courses. But these courses are never ideally situated again because they are not customised and hence fall short of providing the expected upgrading of knowledge. Such problems initiated

Table 1. Student backgrounds in the first year degree course in geography, 2006

Sequence #	Features developed	Purpose
1	Face-to-face lecture session	To introduce the topic of Minerals and Rocks
2	Uploading of Online learning material with learning objects and content materials developed in house, hyperlinked with resources from internet sites	To provide further knowledge on the topic, as well as to provide the required scaffold and bridging course for students who lack prior knowledge of the topic To provide learner control over the learning material, through exposure to varied types of information on the relevant topic through access to the internet
3	Online learning support via Online discussion board on the LMS (BlackBoard)	This provided a platform for discussions and elaborations, as and when required
4	Uploading of Virtual Mineral Lab with video, audio, text and learner response features. This system is also hyperlinked with the learning module, as described in Item 2	This was a simulated lab, developed for the course, to provide opportunities for repeated exposure to near-lab situations. The objective was to allow more time for the learner in handling mineral samples virtually, so that actual lab sessions could be shortened without hampering training quality The hyperlink to the online learning material is to help the learners to revise the topics they may not be familiar with, so that learning from the virtual lab session is more thorough

the development of extensive Web-based courses on areas where students traditionally require some additional academic knowledge.

The Web-based courses, was developed with the objective to provide the pre-requisite knowledge on subject matters to students who have not gone through formal courses in Geography, or even students who feel they lack enough depth in the subject to cope with the undergraduate courses. These courses are delivered online, and are, therefore, available at all times as a virtual knowledge resource, catered particularly to the requirements of the individual learner. The courses are topical, developed specifically to suit the pre-requisites of the undergraduate course in Geomorphology, a strand of Physical Geography. But they have hierarchies of knowledge, to allow more in-depth involvement, if the learner intends to have that. They also allow guided access to relevant information from the Web, so that learners have the choice to decide how far they want to examine any particular topic. This guided access also helps students who require more hand-holding in the subject. The features in the developed course, such as extensive visuals, videos and animations, reference links, formative and summative assessment, non-linear access to materials and resources, are all aimed at providing knowledge resource virtually to bridge gaps in knowledge in learners from diverse backgrounds.

Many of the features developed follow the format described by Chatterjea, (2004; 2005) for an earlier development. For instance, the heavy reliance on visuals, animations, and videos are specifically to engage learners to the course and also to ensure effective learning in the virtual environment which can become somewhat impersonal at times.

USER RESPONSES TO THE USE OF VIRTUAL WORK SPACE

Learner responses for the IT-infused virtual learning environment introduced to facilitate learning,

and to allow greater flexibility in the ways learning is approached, were recorded for all the three types of initiatives for this study.

Response to the Introduction and Usefulness of the Virtual Lab Session

Two groups of students were chosen to use this Virtual Lab environment, after it was launched in July 2006. The first group was doing the Content Upgrading Course on Physical Geography, before embarking on the Post-Graduate Diploma in Education; these are student teachers who did not get the required exposure to Physical Geography while doing their Undergraduate degree, but now faced with the task of teaching Geography in the secondary schools, they are required to attend mandatory courses in Physical Geography. With a limited time allocated and too many topics to cover, having enough time for lab sessions is a big hurdle. The prospect of getting the much-required exposure through the use of virtual learning space seemed like an excellent opportunity. The second group was a first-year undergraduate class, who were given the task of going through the Virtual Lab to prepare for a regular in-campus Mineral Identification Lab session. This was aimed at allowing more time to get familiarized with the mineral identification procedures, without impinging on the classroom schedules.

Both the student groups were given a full two weeks after the initial face-to-face lecture to cover the details through using the Virtual Mineral Lab. Subsequently, they had to come for a session in the lab where they were given a test on identification of minerals. The time given for both the groups was only 30 minutes within which they had to identify six minerals, after going through the test sequences. It was seen that more than 75% students from both the groups picked up at least 8-9 very specific geologic terms that were introduced for the first time in the virtual sessions and all students could identify the mineral and rock samples during the subsequent lab sessions.

These, particularly the use of geologic terms, can be attributed to the exposure the students received from the virtual lab sessions before they came for the actual lab session.

The results show close resemblance and show a very high degree of correct answers, indicating that the students benefited from the Virtual Lab, enough to go through with the processes in a short time, and also do the job well. The other effectiveness of the Virtual Lab is seen on the high percentage of usage of typical geological terms in their submitted lab assignment. There were several geological terms specific to the concepts of mineral and rock identification that were introduced in the Virtual Mineral Lab. These terms are not normally used for mineral description unless they are introduced in a formal class. However, it is believed that because the students were exposed to this simulated environment earlier, they were more proficient in the correct use of specialized terms while doing the lab exercise. Table 2 shows the number of such specialized geological terms used by students in their lab report, which is taken as an indication of the effectiveness of the Virtual Lab in providing a good introductory training before the actual face-to-face lab session.

The responses of both the groups regarding their views on the effectiveness of the Virtual Lab were also sought and the results are shown in Table 2 below.

Table 2 shows that most students from both the courses were impressed by the various approaches using visuals and videos to explain and introduce the materials and thought that the virtual sessions were useful for them to get an introduction on the topic, suggesting that such ventures are useful investments that can help optimize the available time and yet provide the required training to the learners, without straining the infrastructure. The responses were consistent over both the groups, with varied backgrounds and educational levels and hence may be used as guidance for similar development of virtual sessions for training purposes. However, the students realized and appreciated that the exercise on Virtual Mineral Lab was given as an introductory lesson before the actual lab was carried out and all commented that such a development is useful as a good preparatory lesson, delivered with the flexibility of time and space, as long as a face-to-face actual lab session followed. The students were almost unanimous in commenting that the usefulness of such a development lies in the flexibility and repeatability of use and thus gives a good grounding of the subject. Thus the development aims and the results seem to have matched.

Table 2. Compilation of student responses on virtual mineral lab

Sequence #	Work done	Process used	Purpose
1	Pre-fieldwork briefing was given to the entire class and respective roles and responsibilities were assigned	Discussion and familiarization with instruments to be used later	To provide the required information on field procedures, instrument handling, fieldwork management and collaboration
2	On-demand virtual field guidance from the lecturer located at distant lab	Video conferencing	Just-in-time fieldwork guidance is aimed at providing learner-controlled environment, with just adequate scaffolding on-demand
3	On-demand graphic communication, file uploads, and graphic explanations from lecturer	Graphic displays using digital tablet inputs and audio inputs	To provide explanations to questions posed by students in the field To provide students with any required resource through relevant file uploads with required customized annotations by the lecturer
4	On-demand as well as lecturer initiated textual communication between lecturer and one/ multiple group/s	Textual chat format	To allow collaboration and discussion among groups out at different field locations and the lecturer at the lab To provide avenue for advice on procedures, for clarification of queries To allow multiple groups to chat together to clear doubts and queries

Students' Use of the Virtual Supervision During Field Work Session

During the multi-group synchronous field work session, the students sought each others' and the lecturer's views through online text messaging. Several times video-conferencing was also sought for virtual supervision. Students also requested for some explanations for some features observed and were given explanations using the Electronic Notepad. Files were also uploaded for their reference. All groups used the supervision and collaboration features available on virtual platform, with video-conferencing being the most popular, followed by file uploads and sketched explanation via the electronic notepad. This was very much like the face-to-face classroom situations, where the lecturer gives illustrated explanations or demonstrates procedures.

From a class management point of view, this simultaneous multi-group field class using online communication and virtual supervision allowed the lecturer to increase the number of field-based sessions within a given curriculum time as it replaced the traditional field classes where only a limited number of students could be taken out at any one time, necessitating running of repeat sessions on the same topic to allow exposure to all students. This traditional system of running field work sessions, one for each group, with the lecturer dedicated to a single group at any one time meant only a few of those could be arranged in a given term and this could cover only a few topics in the syllabus. Using the virtual supervision system, more frequent field lessons can add relevance and higher comprehension to subject areas that require field experience. It is widely accepted that field work plays an essential role not just for collecting field data and information for subsequent research, but is also an important vehicle for training students in the subject. Field work offers an introduction to the basics of the topic and forms the platform for a solid understanding of the issues at hand. Field work is also

regarded as a perfect vehicle for learning real-life issues. The opportunity to provide more field work experience, therefore, enhances the learning environment for all learners, more so for subjects that require understanding of the environment. The virtual supervision, using technology-supported methods, provides the opportunity for more field experiences to the learners, while also allowing them more control over the degree of assistance and supervision they require for the given task. This way, it allows more opportunities for learner-centred activities and shifts the learning responsibilities to the learners. Similar outcomes of student involvement were also reported by students in the Virtual Mineral Lab session, where the students did mention several times about the usefulness of the system because it offered them freedom of time and action.

Online Knowledge Resource Accessed in a Virtual Classroom Situation

This virtual knowledge resource was made available to the same two groups as in the Virtual Mineral Lab. It served to provide the students with additional knowledge, when they needed additional help, when they required more explanations, and also provided them with immediate feedback on their performance in the integrated quizzes, redirecting them to the required sections if they were wrong in their answers. This is, therefore, a simulated classroom situation, with the lecturer being present to provide the required degree of assistance, when necessary, albeit on a virtual space.

It is apparent that students take to this technology-mediated learning platform to their advantage in today's technology-enriched learning environment. In response to queries regarding their zone of comfort on the use of technology, all students stated that they were very comfortable in the use of technology and obviously they seem to have accepted the use of virtual workplace as a regular platform for knowledge acquisition.

Thus the advantages of freedom of time, travel, space were appreciated and accepted as a norm. It must be mentioned that the students in all the groups have been exposed to the use of IT at every stage of their learning for many years before they came for these courses and this did not add any novelty to their knowledge acquisition, a fact that makes IT-based initiatives easily accepted. But all students (100%) agreed on the issue of having complementary face-to-face sessions, mostly to get clarifications, ready explanations to questions that arise while going through the topics. It is clear that the virtual workplace is well accepted in the presence of supporting face-to-face sessions.

DISCUSSION AND CONCLUSION

Use of the virtual presence of the lecturer over a virtual workplace is the leading theme of all the case studies mentioned in this chapter. The relevance of such a delivery mode comes from the specific requirements in each of these courses involved in the use of such system.

The Virtual Lab development is applicable to all types of training where preparatory training is required but is often cut short due to limited resources and funds and training time available. While development of a 'near-authentic' lab/training situation requires many hours of planning and development, once developed it can be used many times effectively and refined from time to time. From the learner's point of view, this allows the learner to learn the procedures in a 'near-authentic' situation, using no expensive consumables, facilities or infrastructure. Online availability of such training component allows flexibility in terms of learning pace, time as well as a lot of travel time where training facilities are far away. On this count, the virtual workplace provides a plausible complementary additional environment for facilitating learning in widely suitable areas where training of personnel/students is required within a short time frame. Azad and Nadakuditi (2006), taking about a similar devel-

opment in engineering lab work, mention that such developments of virtual labs, developed for specific student use, enable students to perform experiments involving real-life experiments over the Internet and might be cost-effective as well as user-controlled. It must be emphasized, though, that ample assessment of specific training needs and corresponding integration of such training facilities need to be considered in developing such learning systems. But the possible multiple use of the developed system is an advantage in the present requirement of quick yet effective training of people.

With respect to the field-based session under virtual supervision, the best feature, as far as the developer/lecturer is concerned, is the possibility of sending multiple groups of students to more field sessions, while the lecturer can keep track of all the groups' difficulties, queries, using the online communication technologies. While MSN or SKYPE are used in this class, it is not restricted to that and can actually be used with any freely available communication tool, if customised software is not available. Cost-free operation is an added advantage and use of commonly-used tools reduces the learning curve for the learners. The principle can be used for any training sessions where field operations are involved, with limited requirement/demand on training staff. From a learner's point of view, this allows the controls to be shifted to the learner and helps in confidence building while being physically separated from the instructor to conduct any operation but knowing that help/advice is always available, if required.

The use of the virtual learning space to disseminate required knowledge base is another, more commonly found system. But, as mentioned earlier, such upgrading/retraining is useful in today's changing work environment where personnel need to be kept updated at all times and it is not feasible to have physical classes for all phases of the information dissemination.

The current merging of computer and communication technologies and its ubiquitous presence is facilitating the trend towards this virtual workplace. Wireless technology has been able to break the shackles and have given freedom to the learners. Entire regions, if under the wireless umbrella, can be the virtual workplace for training, teaching and learning. Singapore, for instance, has already launched the initiative to provide free wireless net access all over the island by next year (Channel NewsAsia, 2006). This opens up an entirely new package of opportunities for conducting field work from virtual locations, gearing learners with additional training and upgrading via a virtual workplace that allows freedom of choice and time to the learner and thus suits today's dynamic and mobile lifestyle. Already, all tertiary institutions in Singapore like the National Institute of Education, Nanyang Technological University, the National University of Singapore, Republic Polytechnic and several others, provide wide wireless coverage and are using this facility to relieve the desk-bound shackles for teaching and learning. At present, such wireless access is seen as a platform that has freed users in terms of space, with learning environments being distributed all over the campus. Although such facilities are being more and more widely available, use of this new and emerging technological advantage has yet to see a wider application, of greater integrated use in more areas of learning and training than just mere access to the network and the World Wide Web. With the new availability of island-wide wireless network such as in Singapore, teaching and learning in virtual space can be taken to new and higher dimensions.

While world-wide increasing emphasis is placed on working in virtual workplace and related issues, and how the employers need to be aware of the implications (Iqbaria & Tan, 1998), it is felt that using the virtual workplace for learning and training can be just as useful, if not more than the actual work environment. One very feasible future scenario of application of the virtual workplace environment into the education and training arena is through the use of the rapidly expanding mobile technology. In the event of ubiquitous availability of wireless hotspots in many areas, and increasing bandwidth provided by ISPs, extensive physical locations will be suitable for use as virtual workplaces. This could pave the way for development and use of more virtual reality (VR) games. The present generation of learners and technology users are adept at the use of mobile devices. Through these equipment VR games, simulating learning environments, can be made available to capture the imagination of this tech-savvy generation. This can engage the learners while they are on the move but virtually connected. Initial training segments or upgrading courses can thus be delivered via these increasingly popular mobile devices through VR games used in virtual spaces. Initial training and further retraining, thus, can be provided using informal environments over virtual spaces, without impinging on actual training time. The future mobile workforce and the learners can be thus kept connected to the learning loop through this medium of delivery. Pre-service training, upgrading training, as well as mainstream education can all be supported by the use of virtual platforms and enhanced by incorporating mobile devices to deliver learning on demand over virtual workplaces.

Virtual workplace is not just for the post-training workforce, but this new scenario has the capability of revolutionizing the learning and training environment to satisfy the needs of the changing society. With the technological infrastructure being more pervasive in many places, the virtual workplace seems set to make further inroads in more areas than just the working environment.

REFERENCES

Azad, A., & Nadakuditi P. (2006). Internet-based facility for physical laboratory experiments. *Journal of Advanced Technology for Learning, 3*(1), 29-35.

Brabazon, T. (2001). Internet teaching and the administration of knowledge. *First Monday, 6*(6). Retrieved March 15, 2007 from http://firstmonday.org/issues/issue6_6/brabazon/index.html.

Brehm, D. (2002). *Environmental field work gets high-tech boost*. Retrieved October 12, 2006 from http://web.mit.edu/newsoffice/2002/environment-0109.html.

Channel News Asia. (2006). *Free wireless broadband access in Singapore public areas for 2 years*. Retrieved October 10, 2006 from http://www.channelnewsasia.com/stories/singaporelocalnews/view/234742/1/.html.

Chatterjea, K. (2004). Asynchronous learning using a hybrid learning package: A teacher development strategy in geography. *Journal of Organizational and End User Computing, 16*(4), 37-54.

Chatterjea, K. (2005). A blended approach learning strategy for teacher development. In: M. Mahmood (Eds.), *Advanced topics in end user computing* (pp. 301-321). Hershey, PA: Idea Group Publishing.

Chatterjea, K., & Ong, C. (2006). Forest trail monitoring and management at Bukit Timah Nature Reserve using mobile technology and GIS. *Proceedings from NIE-SEAGA conference*. Singapore.

Department of Trade and Industry, UK. (2006). *Benefits of flexible learning* Retrieved November 8, 2006 from http://www.businesslink.gov.uk/bdotg/action/layer?topicId=1073931239.

Forbes, J. (2000). Perspectives on lifelong learning: The view from a distance. *First Monday, 5*(11). Retrieved March 15, 2007 from http://firstmonday.org/issues/issue5_11/forbes/index.html.

Froggatt, C. (2001). *Work naked—Eight essential principles for peak performance in the virtual workplace*. San Francisco, CA: Jossey-Bass.

Igbaria, M., & Tan, M. (1998). *The virtual workplace*. Hershey, PA: Idea Group Publishing.

McCaffrey, K., Holdsworth, R., Clegg, P., Jones, R., Wilson, R., & Imber, J., et al. (2005). Unlocking the spatial dimension: Digital technologies and the future of geoscience field work. *Journal of the Geological Society*. Retrieved November, 8, 2006 from http://www.findarticles.com/p/articles/mi_qa3721/is_200511/ai_n15746308.

Ruhleder, K., & Brigitte, J. (2001). Managing complex, distributed environments: Remote meeting technologies at the chaotic. *First Monday, 6*(5). Retrieved March 15, 2007 from http://firstmonday.org/issues/issue6_5/ruhleder/index.html.

Thompson, D. (2005). *Virtual workplace, where learning brings rewards*. Retrieved October 12, 2006 from http://www.virtual-workplace.com/introduction/index.html.

Van Boxel, P., & Wentzel, P. (2003). Kansen voor de XDA in het onderwijs. Verslag van leerlingen- en studentenpanels in het kader van het onderzoek naar de XDA en mogelijkheden van 'wireless learning' binnen het GIPSY project. Amsterdam, Vrije Universiteit. GIPSY rapport 2003-1 (in Dutch). Retrieved October 6, 2006 from www.geo-informatie.nl/gipsy/.

Wentzel, P. (2006). Mobile learning in The Netherlands: Possibilities of use of real-time database access in an educational field work setting. *Proceedings from mLearn 2005: 4th World Conference on mLearning*. Retrieved October 8, 2006 from http://www.mlearn.org.za/papers-full.html.

Zawodny, J. (2006). *Living and working in the virtual workplace*. Retrieved November 8, 2006 from http://jeremy.zawodny.com/blog/archives/002380.html.

KEY TERMS

Virtual Learning Place: A place 'anywhere', physically remote from traditional physical learning facility.

Online Learning: Learning via the internet platform.

Virtual Lab: A lab facility that is on virtual space, to be accessed through the internet.

Multi-Group Field Work: A fieldwork exercise where multiple groups are operating simultaneously at geographically separated locations.

Lab Procedures Online: Lab procedures that can be carried out on virtual space, using internet platform.

Online Learning Resources: Learning resources that are made available online, not from printed sources.

Learning Scaffold by Lecturer: Facilitation and knowledge support provided by the lecturer.

Synchronous Remote Contact: Simultaneous online contact among multiple groups operating at different locations.

Learning Environment on Demand: Environment supporting student learning initiated and operated upon demand from learners.

Chapter XXIII
Using an Information Literacy Program to Prepare Nursing Students to Practice in a Virtual Workplace

Mona Florea
University of Rhode Island Library, USA

Lillian Rafeldt
Three Rivers Community College, USA

Susan Youngblood
Texas Tech University, USA

ABSTRACT

The chapter presents healthcare examples of the current virtual working environment and introduces nursing skills necessary for evidence-based practice in a virtual workplace. The authors discuss how the Nursing Information Literacy Program was designed and implemented at Three Rivers Community College to assist nursing students in developing skills such as critical thinking and problem-solving, technological literacy, information literacy, and collaborative and cooperative learning. The authors hope that this example will serve as a model for creating other information literacy programs that prepare students for working in a virtual workplace.

INTRODUCTION

The nurse of the 21st century will work in modified virtual environments, such as those that include tele-healthcare. They will access and contribute client data to large healthcare electronic networks and advocate for client access to information through a variety of platforms, thereby ensuring greater health literacy. Workforce training that includes virtual patient simulations will be more efficient. These are givens. What nursing programs now need to do is to develop and implement curricula that give nurses a foundation for functioning in a virtual workforce. In order to function in such a workforce, nurses need curricula that help them develop information literacy and familiarize them with forms of technology similar to those used in the virtual workplace.

This chapter describes just such a curriculum: the Nursing Information Literacy Program (NILP) developed at Three Rivers Community College (TRCC).

Three Rivers Community College, with a student population of approximately 4,000, is located in a rural area of southeastern Connecticut with limited access to educational and research institutions and resources. The associate degree in nursing program prepares students to enter the profession as registered nurses. The nursing students are age eighteen to sixty-two, the average being 29. Students with multiple life responsibilities, who might not have been in school for a number of years, have contact with information technology for the first time and need to be reoriented to academia.

The nursing program is a two-year program. Before being admitted into the program, students have the option of taking Nursing 108, an exploratory course in which twenty to twenty-five students are enrolled each semester. Eighty students are enrolled each semester in each of the core courses of the Nursing Department: Nursing 115 and Nursing 116, lower-level courses, and Nursing 226, Nursing 227, and Nursing 228, upper-level courses. Addressing the TRCC student population's specific characteristics and information needs, the NILP spans the core curriculum to help students develop information literacy that will be essential to their future work.

The growth of the virtual workplace necessitates programs like the Nursing Information Literacy Program. It also addresses the foundations of fostering information literacy within a curriculum and presents in detail the example of the NILP, detailing its three components: information literacy competencies, information literacy activities, and the Nursing Information Gateway Web site.

After completing this chapter, the reader will be able to: (1) define information literacy, (2) discuss critical elements in developing and implementing a plan like the one described below, and

(3) reflect on the potential to develop their own information literacy program in any discipline.

BACKGROUND

Numerous studies (Robertson, 2000; Stough, Eom, & Buckenmyer, 2000; Akkirman & Harrris, 2005; Allan & Lewis, 2006; Quinlan & Hegarty, 2006), professionals, advisory councils, and teachers in 21st century education and workforce development call for changes in preparation of tomorrow's personnel. *The Partnership for 21st Century Skills* identified the following as abilities necessary to succeed as effective citizens, workers, and leaders in the 21st century: "information and communication skills, thinking and problem-solving ability, interpersonal and self-direction skills, global awareness, financial, economic and business knowledge, and civic literacy" (Downey, 2006). Rapid changes in a global community call for new paradigms at all levels. As Barnes notes, "education and training is a cradle to grave process" (2005, p. 7). This holds true for the profession of nursing.

Canton (2004) predicts that some of the top healthcare trends for the 21st century will include many characteristics of virtual environments that will make healthcare more safe and efficient. For instance, healthcare professionals will be part of one large information network. Barriers to healthcare access, like distance from hospitals, will be removed as tele-health and electronic platform information libraries become available, and new technology will help professionals diagnose and treat patients, even from a distance. Furthermore, virtual reality simulations will be used to train professionals.

Virtual Work Environments Are Growing

Visionaries of future healthcare foresee the development of virtual environments. Crandall and Wallace defined the virtual workplace as "networks of people, a workplace where work is done anytime and anywhere, and not bound by the traditional limitations of time, physical space, job description, title, and pyramidal reporting relationships" (1998, p.19). Even the nursing student of today will work in modified virtual environments, such as hospitals with electronic records. In fact, by 2006 in the United States, electronic health records (EHRs) were already at use in about half of all hospitals (Mowry & Constantinou, 2007).

This type of workplace has great potential to solve some of our current problems. The Agency for Healthcare Research and Quality commissioned a meta-analysis of 257 studies of the impact of using health information technology. The researchers found that such technologies (which include EHRs) "increased adherence to guideline-based care, enhanced surveillance and monitoring, and decreased medication errors," as well as improved preventative care (Chaudhry et al., 2006, p. E-12). According to Akkirman and Harris (2005), such technologies could make workplaces more cost-efficient, productive, and competitive. For instance, home healthcare nurses who use electronic record packages can assess clients, document healthcare, synchronize data with the office, and submit work for regulatory review and billing without driving to the office. Supervisors and financial officers within the agency can monitor timely submission of work and ensure that patient records are up-to-date, thereby increasing productivity and revenue. The client can receive accurate information and education with printouts during each home visit or out-of-office communication session. Physicians and primary-care providers can have immediate access to client data. This ease of access facilitates patient care and shortens client stays. Everyone on the home healthcare team benefits.

Although usually seen as new phenomena, virtual health environments were formally put into practice in the 1970s. Navy officers utilized tele-health applications to promote weight loss for crew members at offsite locations. Healthcare professionals assessed and diagnosed conditions via satellite links. Operations were successfully completed via expert direction to a novice healthcare professional who received hospital records for patients (Fyee, 2005). Personnel were able to lose weight and stay in their rank (Fyee, 2005). Undoubtedly, though, the type of virtual workplaces that authors like Crandall and Wallace envision is a much richer outgrowth of these early practices.

The virtual workplace has also been described as "an online forum where members of the team distributed over space and perhaps time can work together" (Turner, Turner, Green, & Mayne, 1998, p. 187). Pat Benner (2001) describes the application of knowledge and the development of new nurses from novice to expert using the Dryfus model of skill acquisition; nurses progress through the five levels of proficiency as they gain experience, making their care less formulaic (rule-bound) and more intuitive, mentally integrating the nuances of complex clinical cases. Online forums and list servs facilitate this growth by providing non-threatening environments where novices can develop their evidence-based practice and experts can continue to share and learn. Thus, this expanded definition of the virtual workplace incorporates environments that allow nurses to continually hone their professional skills.

Nursing organizations and professionals utilize tools and principles of virtual environments such as e-learning, teleconferencing, simulation learning, tele-health, point-of-care tools, electronic records, and network documentation; they do so to facilitate the nursing process, communication, collaboration, and leadership activities. Many nurses work in a blended on-site/virtual environment, while others work entirely in a virtual environment (as in tele-health). Skeptics of virtual workforce environments for nursing state that "the nurse cannot be taken away from the bedside.... we will lose the caring and personalized dimension" (Fyee, 2005). However, supporters have established that nurses can develop telephone skills to convey empathy and develop trust and relationships (Hagan, Morin, & Lepine, 2000).

Nursing personnel and healthcare organizations are diverse in their job descriptions, missions, and goals; therefore, professionals will continue to have multiple opinions of the virtual work environment. Regardless, it is certain that each nurse will use some tools and need skills to operate in a virtual workforce of the 21st century. For instance, some subscribe to e-mail services that provide updates on healthcare practices, such as those offered by the Agency for Healthcare Research and Quality, whose Effective Healthcare Program sends out links to reports about current research. Many nurses use even more tools, particularly in the numerous healthcare settings that have adopted electronic health records (EHRs). We can expect the use of EHRs to grow further because of government intervention: in 2004 the government set a goal to implement a fully networked EHR system—the National Health Information Network—by 2014 (Mowry & Constantinou, 2007).

A Foundation for Virtual Work Environments

Information and Technology Literacy

Understanding the need for a practice-oriented, cross-disciplinary educational environment, nursing educators and librarians identified the need to develop information and technology literacy skills within students. These skills contribute to the foundation of effective participation in virtual work environments and of effective evidence-based nursing practice. Information literacy, involving "the capacity to access information, both physically and intellectually," is essential for the modern nurse (Cheek & Doskatsch, 1998, p. 243). Often, the term *information consumer* is applied to clients who must sift through and assess healthcare information delivered through media such as television and the Internet. Cheek and Doskatsch also view today's nurses as information consumers: nurses must selectively seek and

evaluate information that will help them perform their duties.

To truly be discerning and effective information consumers, nurses must first meet certain information literacy criteria, such as those identified by Cheek and Doskatsch (1998): the ability to use the library and computer technology, the desire to learn, the capability to be a lifelong learner, and the ability to overcome barriers to accessing information. They conclude that nurse educators must provide students with the means to achieve knowledge and the freedom to do one's thinking.

Jacobs, Rosenfeld, and Haber offer a similar outline for competency, one that likewise includes a social dimension. They state that:

competency in information literacy includes an understanding of the architecture of information and the scholarly process; the ability to navigate among a variety of print and electronic tools to effectively access, search and critically evaluate appropriate resources; synthesize accumulated information into an existing body of knowledge; communicate research results clearly and effectively; and appreciate the social issues and ethical concerns related to the provision, dissemination, and sharing of information. (2003, p. 320)

Clearly, information literacy is not something that most nurses master accidentally. This complex set of skills should be carefully nurtured in the professional curricula to ensure that nurses are ready for the ever-changing workplace.

Developing a Systematic Instructional Plan

The first steps in developing an information literacy program are to identify requisite skills and knowledge and to develop an effective instructional plan. Breivik (2000) notes that information literacy competencies "cannot be taught, but must be reinforced with repeated opportunities to use information resources" (as cited in Jacobs et al.,

2003, p. 323). That is not to say that these competencies cannot be nurtured within a class or across an entire curriculum. On the contrary, faculty can help students develop these skills by crafting an instructional plan that carefully introduces these skills and includes ample opportunities for students to apply and hone them.

To be effective, an instructional plan should follow the design of a systematic model of instruction, which consists of a "set of interrelated parts, all of which work together toward a defined goal" (Dick, Carey, & Carey, 2005, p. 1). This model involves ample planning before instruction ever begins. First, the faculty should identify instructional goal(s), conduct instructional analysis, and analyze learners and contexts before writing performance objectives. Then they can develop assessment instruments paired with an instructional strategy and instructional materials. Once the instruction takes place, they should design and conduct formative evaluation of instruction. Finally, based on those findings, they should revise instruction appropriately.

Incorporating E-Learning

A tool of the virtual work environment—e-learning—has changed the face of nursing education. Elliot Massie defines e-learning as "the use of technology to design, deliver, select, administer, support and extend learning" (Sinnet, 2002). The traditional classroom is being enhanced and in some cases replaced by Web-based content; as Tilley, Boswell, and Cannon (2006) point out, "developing effective learning communities is an important component of Web-based courses. Learning communities offer a social context for learning that greatly enhances the knowledge acquisition of all involved parties" (p. 8). Tools like collaborative discussion boards (e-learning tools) help create that context.

Naidu and Oliver (1996) describe an effective project designed to enhance senior nursing students' collaborative problem-solving skills. Some of the project objectives were related to

collaboration, while others were directly related to information literacy. The problem-solving project that they describe also included a critical reflection component using, a collaborative discussion board to nurture some of the competencies that Jacobs et al. outline. Naidu and Oliver identify other situations resembling the virtual workplace in which a collaborative discussion board also could be used successfully, such as "distance education and open learning situations" (Conclusion section, para. 2). True to the systematic model of instruction, the effectiveness of the discussion board was assessed after the project concluded. Students and faculty stated that the discussion board encouraged reflection and the ability to solve problems.

By improving nurses' problem-solving skills and information literacy, the project described above aimed to "facilitat[e]…[nurses'] transitions from the classroom to the workforce" (Naidu & Oliver, 1996, Conclusion section, para. 1). Because part of evidence-based practice is effectively searching and evaluating existing literature, requiring the nurse to be information literate (Jacobs et al., 2003), this type of approach is critical to providing future nurses with the tools they need to later succeed.

MAIN FOCUS OF THE CHAPTER

The Beginning of the Nursing Information Literacy Program

During the past four years, nursing faculty and the reference/instruction librarian at Three Rivers Community College collaborated at creating, implementing, and developing the Nursing Information Literacy Program (NILP). In part the goal is to teach students how to effectively search for and critically evaluate information from online and print sources. Furthermore, the program is designed to teach students how to best use that information in their future roles as practicing nurses.

In their book *The Systematic Design of Instruction*, Dick et al. argue that during the past thirty years "expert lectures" were replaced by "interactive instruction," which emphasizes course outcomes, learner characteristics and needs, and the students' future application of the skills and knowledge being taught (2005). Many graduating nurses will enter virtual or partially virtual workplaces, and preparing students for their workplaces is a goal of the college. Furthermore, as Cheek and Doskatsch (1998) note, nurses in general must be information literate. Thus, Three Rivers Community College set out to enhance these skills in its nursing students by incrementally introducing resources and activities that build student nurses' information literacy competencies. Collaboration, teamwork, critical thinking, and life-long learning are core values that are fostered in the nursing program, and the NILP helps support these values.

The Nursing Information Literacy Program (NILP) was enthusiastically developed in multiple brainstorming and research sessions among a team comprised of engaged faculty, the librarian, and administrators. The team evaluated the skills nursing students had already developed—for instance, they had built up information technology skills in previous course work and independent study modules—and then collaboratively identified specific skills that nurses would need and that could be integrated into the NILP (see Figure 1). In addition, the team reviewed physical and online research resources that might be included in the program.

The team reviewed a number of resources that it could make available to both students and faculty to enhance information literacy. These resources included materials in a variety of media, including print, audio, video, and both library-based and external online materials (such as online

Figure 1. Nursing skills and characteristics

Communicating in electronic format	Presenting	e-Learning	Working Collaboratively / cooperative learning	Working in Teams / virtual teams	Critical thinking and problem solving as applied to information literacy
Sending e-mail w/ attachments	using written format	being motivated to use e-learning	listening critically	working with people from different cultures, countries who may speak different languages and live across time zones	stating information needs
posting to discussion boards	documenting sources	being self-directed	thinking critically		identifying proper resources
participating in chat rooms; instant messaging	delivering oral presentations electronically	using described communication skills	communicating respectfully w/ others		selecting & applying efficient search strategies
using virtual presentations		opening software and efficiently using applications	exchanging ideas	working effectively on a virtual team	evaluating information
using blogs	creating *ePortfolio* presentations	engaging in reflective evaluation with the desire to remediate	being flexible	establishing roles and identities	integrating discovered knowledge into existing knowledge
using professional list serves	using information ethically		working together electronically	resolving ambiguity and uncertainty and taking collective action	presenting & applying in practice
teleconferencing		participating in a virtual learning community	applying electronic social skills *(netiquette)*		becoming a life long learner
using phones & fax machines effectively			transforming disparate knowledge into collective clinical decisions		

databases and general medical Web sites, respectively). They were evaluated using principles of accuracy, authority, currency, comprehensiveness, purpose, objectivity, efficiency, ethics, diversity, and fiscal responsibility. The team also identified nursing and medical associations and organizations that nursing faculty wanted students to become familiar with, linking these Web sites to appropriate course content. The NILP team set out to introduce these resources in incremental modules in order to foster critical thinking and professional development progressively.

The program follows the systematic model of instruction described above. The success of this program is the result of four essential elements: a clear plan, an organizing framework that includes more than one class, the willingness of NILP team to commit to the project over an extended period of time, and effective collaboration.

The Components and Evaluation of the Program

The Nursing Information Literacy Program aims to educate students to use core print and online nursing information resources, to use effective search methods and construct efficient search strategies and techniques, and to critically evaluate information and use it ethically, efficiently, and responsibly in their profession as evidence-based practice nurses. The NILP has three components: information literacy competencies, information literacy activities, and the Nursing Information Gateway Web site.

Component 1: Information Literacy Competencies

The information literacy competencies are designed incrementally and progressively for each course and level of instruction. The competencies include five steps that students must take. First, students need to efficiently formulate an information need related to a class assignment or research

project problem. Second, they must identify quality local and remote sources of information and services. Third, they have to efficiently use search methods, strategies, and techniques in order to retrieve relevant information. Fourth, they must be able to critically evaluate information for accuracy, authority, currency, comprehensiveness, purpose, and objectivity. And finally, students need to use information efficiently, ethically, and responsibly. Detailed information on information literacy competency for specific courses and levels of instruction is available in Table 1.

These information literacy competencies constitute a foundation for the nursing students to develop critical thinking and evaluation skills in order to become informed consumers of information and self-sufficient lifelong learners, characteristics necessary in both today's traditional and virtual workplace environments.

Component 2: Information Literacy Activities.

The information literacy activities consist of introductory physical and online library tours, discussion of the structure of the Library of Congress Classification System Class R, discussion of scholarly versus popular sources of information, demonstrations of nursing and medical online database searches, discussion of criteria for evaluation of print and online sources of information, and course-integrated library instruction sessions.

Furthermore, each course has a library research project:

a. Nursing 108 (the exploratory course) and Nursing 115 students are required to find a current scholarly nursing article on nursing/health/wellness and the learning community research theme of the year (e.g., water, metamorphosis, making connections).

b. Nursing 116 students are required to identify a scholarly nursing article on a medical-

Table 1. Nursing information literacy competencies

	Target Competency	Nursing Course					
		108	115	116	226	227	228
Understanding the Library							
1	Understand the organization of physical and online library collections.	●	●	●	●	●	●
2	Efficiently use library services.	●	●	●	●	●	●
3	Efficiently use the Library of Congress Classification System Class R.	●	●	●			
Articulating of the Information Need							
4	Articulate the information need.	●					
5	State the information need related to assignment or research project.		●	●			
6	Efficiently articulate the information need related to class assignment or research project.				●	●	●
Searching							
7	Identify concepts, key phrases, and keywords and construct a search query.	●	●	●			
8	Use basic search methods: search by subject, author, title, and keyword.	●	●	●	●		
9	Search using Boolean operators.	●	●	●	●	●	●
10	Search using the nesting technique.			●	●	●	●
11	Formulate and refine a search query by identifying concepts, key phrases, and keywords.		●	●	●	●	●
12	Use advanced search methods, wildcards, and proximity operators.					●	●
Identifying Sources							
13	Identify appropriate print and online sources.	●					
14	Identify appropriate local and remote information sources.		●	●			
15	Differentiate between scholarly and popular sources.	●	●	●			
16	Critically identify appropriate local and remote information sources.			●	●	●	●
Evaluating and Using Information							
17	Evaluate information by accuracy, authority, currency, comprehensiveness, and objectivity.	●	●	●	●	●	●
18	Retrieve, manipulate, and transfer information from remote information sources.		●	●	●	●	●
19	Define intellectual property, academic honesty, and use information responsibly.		●	●			
20	Discuss intellectual property and academic honesty.				●	●	●
21	Use information efficiently, ethically, and responsibly.				●	●	●

surgical and maternal-child health topic for presentation in a clinical post conference (a reflection and student presentation time after a student nurse's clinical day) and to also prepare a group presentation related to clinical case studies using evidence-based research data.

c. Nursing 226 students are required to prepare a research paper related to nutritional aspects of specific clinical conditions.

d. Nursing 227 students are required to prepare an evidence-based case study of a complex clinical condition, presenting at a clinical post conference.

e. Nursing 228 students are required to write a research paper on a nursing professional issue or on the history of nursing.

By working on and completing the library research projects, nursing students—organized sometimes into learning communities—develop the communication, collaboration, teamwork, and presentation skills necessary for them as future evidence-based practicing nurses. These skills are crucial to function and succeed in telecommuting, tele-health, and tele-nursing virtual workplace environments. More detailed information about the structure of information literacy activities for each nursing course is available in Table 2.

Component 3: The Nursing Information Gateway

The Nursing Information Gateway is a Web portal composed of six library modules for students (each labeled with the appropriate course number) and one library module for nursing faculty. The Gateway is available on the library's Web site as well as directly linked through the online learning management system (*WebCT Vista*); access via multiple pathways supports successful use. The Nursing Information Literacy Program team began to realize its goal of involving all of the nursing courses and completely integrating the

Gateway when it designed and created the library modules for Nursing 108 (the exploratory course), 115, and 116 between 2003 and 2004. The library modules for Nursing 226, 227, and 228 and the library module for faculty were designed and created between 2004 and 2006. This progressive strategy supported change theory, permitting the team to make iterative changes to the modules, and allowed for "buy-in" from all participants.

Each library module for students contains targeted print resources, such as recommended reference materials, books, videos, and periodicals. It also includes links to the online catalog, the library databases, and general and subject-specific nursing and medical Web resources that have been evaluated by the librarian. Each library module also offers research guides for the CINAHL and PsycINFO databases and the APA citation style guide. Students have access to the services of a virtual librarian 24/7 through the InfoAnyTime service (an online live reference service) and e-mail access to the services of the reference/instruction librarian. See Figure 2 for an example, the module from Nursing 226. Content for each library module within the Gateway was developed from simple to complex, corresponding to the course objectives and curricular content. In addition, the library learning modules promote independent learning and allow students to refresh their skills at any time during their two-year course of study (they can go back to any of the modules available on the Nursing Gateway at their convenience).

Evaluation of and Reflection on Components

Each component of the Nursing Information Literacy Program (NILP) was evaluated in keeping with the systematic model of instruction. The NILP team evaluated the effectiveness of the information literacy activities at the end of the spring 2004 semester by surveying student satisfaction. The great majority of students in both

Table 2. Nursing information literacy activities

Activity	Nursing Course					
	108	115	116	226	227	228
1 **Physical library tour:** physical areas in the library, the research process, and library services.	●	●				
2 **Online library tour:** online catalog, database search demonstrations, Library of Congress Classification System Class R, scholarly versus popular sources, evaluating sources of information.	●	●				
3 **Point-of-need library session:** searching for library print materials, online database articles, and Web materials for library research project; evaluating sources of information.		●	●	●	●	●
4 **Library research project (article):** Find a current nursing, scholarly article on nursing/health/ wellness and the learning community theme of the year (e.g., water, metamorphosis, making connections).	●	●				
5 **Library research project (presentation):** Identify a nursing, scholarly article on medical-surgical and maternal-child health patient care concept for presentation in clinical post conference. Prepare a group presentation related to clinical case studies using evidence-based research data in medical-surgical and maternal-child health nursing.			●			
6 **Library research project (paper 1):** Prepare a research paper related to nutritional aspects of specific clinical conditions.				●		
7 **Library research project (paper 2):** Prepare a complex clinical condition case study for clinical post conference.					●	
8 **Library research project (paper 3):** Prepare a research paper on a nursing professional issue or on the history of nursing.						●
9 *WebCT Vista* **library learning module.**	●	●		●		
10 *ePortfolio* **presentation.**	●	●	●	●	●	●

Figure 2. Nursing 226 Information Gateway Module

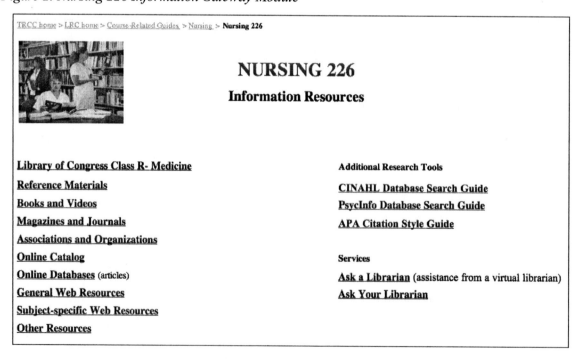

Figure 3. Evaluation of activities and competencies

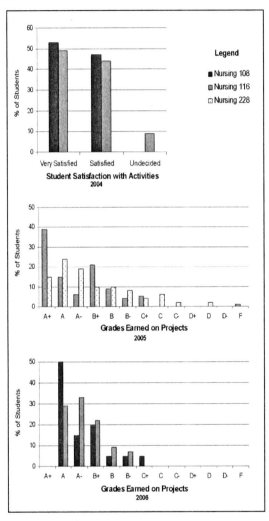

Student Satisfaction with Activities 2004

Grades Earned on Projects 2005

Grades Earned on Projects 2006

first-year courses were satisfied or very satisfied with the activities (see Figure 3). Similarly, student literacy competencies were evaluated from the spring 2004 semester to the spring 2006 semester by examining student grades on the library components of classes. The vast majority of student earned high grades on these projects; student grades, coupled with student evaluations of the Gateway's usefulness, indicate that the program helped most students become competent (see Figure 3 for data from 2005 and 2006).

The usefulness of the Nursing Information Gateway was evaluated during the spring 2004 semester, and student responses indicated that the Gateway was helpful. Ninety-five percent of the Nursing 108 students declared that the Nursing Information Gateway helped them complete the library assignment, and 5% were undecided. The students reported that 24-hour/7-day access to the Gateway allowed them to reinforce their skills. Most nursing 116 students declared that the Nursing Information Gateway helped them complete the class assignments; 9% were undecided, and 9% disagreed. The latter 9% identified *Google* as their search engine of choice. Even so, they did use the search techniques taught and reinforced during the library instruction sessions.

By using the Nursing Information Gateway, nursing students developed effective and efficient research skills, critical thinking, and online information evaluation skills (such as discriminating between fee-based versus free online resources), skills that are necessary in a virtual workplace environment.

Integration with a Learning Management System Fosters Additional Skills

The Nursing Information Literacy Program has been linked to the *WebCT* online course management system since 2003. Each nursing course has a *WebCT* component that provides a link to the Nursing Information Gateway. Within *WebCT*, nursing students acquire and develop skills using the calendar, discussion board, and chat room and mail tools to communicate and collaborate with peers, faculty, and the librarian, who was given the status of teaching assistant in some of the courses. Students could be organized into learning communities to acquire and develop cooperative and collaborative learning skills.

With the upgrade to *WebCT Vista* in 2005, individual library learning modules for the Nursing 108, 115, and 226 courses were integrated into the *WebCT* system, allowing students to work within *WebCT* to access the modules rather than leaving *WebCT* for the Nursing Information Gateway on the library Web site. With this new design, students can access as many of the same resources as they would find on the Gateway, but have direct access from *WebCT* to subject-specific databases such as CINHAL, not just the general access to all library databases that the Gateway provides. Should a student need to expand a search or find additional resources, though, he or she can still visit the Gateway. Furthermore, by giving students the option to visit the modules through either *WebCT* or the Gateway, the NILP reinforces their developing technological skills (see Figure 4).

Other Tools Used to Enhance Virtual Workforce Skills

Between 2005 and 2006, the librarian added blogs to the library learning modules. Blogs are primarily used as a means for the librarian to post instructions and tips. The topics covered might include how to find full-text, scholarly articles in CINAHL database or conduct efficient advanced searches in CINAHL and PsycINFO databases. Blogs are also used to help students to develop online communication and collaboration skills by communicating with the librarian and with their peers.

The content of Nursing 226 *WebCT Vista* library learning module is available in Figure 4.

Electronic portfolios, using the *ePortfolio* software package produced by the Connecticut Distance Learning Consortium (CTDLC), were introduced to the program progressively for Nursing 108 students in 2004, for Nursing 115 and 116 students in 2005, and for Nursing 226, 227, and 228 students in 2006. Today, *ePortfolios* are more than presentations to acquire work or fulfill an evaluation requirement. Students reflect on their work and grow with collaborative interaction between themselves, faculty, peers, the librarian, and college staff. *ePortfolios* demonstrate student growth and skill development over time and are not distorted by bad timing on a hour-long exam. Thus, student outcomes more authentically reflect

Figure 4. Nursing 226 WebCT Library Learning Module

1. **Recommended Nursing 226 Resources**
   - Reference Materials
   - Books and Videos
   - Magazines and Journals
   - Nursing and Medical Associations and Organizations
   - General Web Resources
   - Subject-specific Web Resources
   - Other Resources
2. **Search for Books, Videos, DVD's, CD's**
   - Online Catalog
   - iConn/request Database
   - Library Web site
3. **Search for Articles**
   - CINAHL Dabatase
   - PreCINAHL Database
   - Health Source: Nursing & Academic Edition Database
   - Medline Database
   - Clinical Pharmacology Database
   - PsycINFO Database
   - Psychology & Behavioral Sciences Database
   - JAMA (The Journal of the American Medical Association)
   - Expanded Academic ASAP Database
   - Academic Search Premier Database
4. **Search Tips**
   - Search Tips
5. **Nursing Information Gateway**
   - Nursing Information Gateway
6. **Search Guides**
   - CINAHL Database Search Guide
   - PsycINFO Database Search Guide
7. **Online Library Forms**
   - Request a Library Card
   - Request Materials from Other Libraries
8. **Citing**
   - Citing in APA Format
9. **Ask a Librarian**
   - Get Help From a Virtual Librarian
   - Get Help From Your Librarian

student learning, meaning both students and the program can be more accurately evaluated. The use of the *ePortfolios* within the Nursing Information Literacy Program facilitates continued development of research skills, communication, collaborative learning, and refinement of presentation skills.

Each student can maintain an *ePortfolio* that contains multiple portfolios. The *ePortfolios* are private, but students can send guest views to whomever they choose, and students can opt to send guests views of single or multiple portfolios, thereby choosing what guests are allowed to see. In the fall semester of 2005, students sent guest views to the librarian and career counselor to foster collaborative communication with their peers, faculty, the librarian, and the career counselor.

Nursing 108 students do library research for finding a current scholarly nursing article on nursing/health/wellness and the yearly learning community research theme (e.g., water, metamorphosis, making connections). They are required to place a copy of the article in their *ePortfolio* and create a document describing the library resources and the search methods and techniques that they used in the process. The librarian, who is invited to view this portfolio, evaluates the research work of the students and offers feedback in regard to the quality of the article and the sources of information, search methods, and techniques used by the students. The student invitation to this view of his or her portfolio offers the librarian the chance to reinforce correct research skills and revise how these skills are taught, if necessary. Students make a connection with the librarian for future collaborative work.

FUTURE TRENDS

Both virtual and traditional workplaces already demand a level of information literacy that allows nurses to effectively and efficiently use the many electronic research resources. As virtual workplaces expand, so too will the demand for nurses

who have mastered the associated competencies and other skills, such as the ability to work in virtual teams; communicate in electronic formats; and access, navigate, and update electronic health records (EHRs). In 2004, President Bush set a goal for the U.S. to integrate EHRs into a National Health Information Network (NHIN) by 2014 (Valerius, 2006; Mowry & Constantinou, 2007). The NHIN would, among other things, allow healthcare professionals to access a patient's records from any healthcare facility. The date for implementing such a system will likely be further in the future because of technological challenges (the compatibility of different EHR systems), patient privacy concerns related to rules in the Health Insurance Portability and Accountability Act (HIPAA), and costs. Although the U.S. does not yet have fully networked health records, EHR software is already in use in a number of medical settings, and nurses must be able to respond accordingly.

Medical research will also continue to change as elements of the virtual workplace become more prevalent. According to Mowry and Constantinou, EHRs are already being used by researchers to help doctors refer suitable patients for clinical trials of new treatments; in the case of the University of Cincinnati College of Medicine, this approach has resulted in a "10-fold increase in the number of referrals [to participating studies] generated by physicians" (2007, p. 38). The authors predict that identifying clinical trial participants using EHRs in conjunction with the forthcoming National Health Information Network, or even regional health information organizations, would have several major benefits for clinical research. First, researchers could more easily and efficiently identify participants. Second, pharmaceutical companies could decrease the time and cost of bringing medications to market. Third, by anonymously tracking participants' health, even after a medication is released to the public, researchers could more quickly identify the medication's adverse effects and, if need be, pull the medication from shelves. Nurses in physicians' offices will, of course, participate in this new referral process.

Treatment costs and customer service, too, are driving the industry. Health insurance companies are providing extra Internet and telephone services to customers to minimize unnecessary trips to physicians and emergency rooms. Blue Cross Blue Shield, for instance, has developed a toll-free 24/7 NurseLine program and other phone services, like Special Beginnings®, in which registered obstetrical nurses monitor enrolled mothers-to-be and mothers of newborns over the telephone. They provide these services at no additional cost to members, but these services presumably result in fewer expensive on-site diagnoses.

These changes in nursing are coupled with changes in education: more distance learning in addition to more blended learning, in which students who meet face-to-face also use electronic tools such as *WebCT* and discussion boards. Program outcomes already articulate the need for graduates to be literate in information and technology skills as well as to be capable at critical thinking and quantitative reasoning. Students are preparing to enter the future workforce, one that includes virtual environments, and our edict as educators and professionals is to implement programs that effectively prepare students to enter that workforce efficiently. With the need to prepare information- and technology-literate students who will care for clients in the 21st century, faculty, librarians, administrators, and staff must continue to develop programs to facilitate these ever evolving competencies. If current trends predict the future, we will likely see more programs that use not only traditional teaching materials but also a variety of e-learning tools, including blogs, wikis, discussion boards, and podcasts.

CONCLUSION

Implementing an information literacy program for nursing—or another discipline—requires interdisciplinary collaboration to identify program outcomes and incremental course objectives and to select appropriate content that will prepare students for succeeding in both traditional and virtual workplaces. Like many other educational programs, it should incorporate the best active learning techniques and be tailored to the specific learning environment. Additionally, it requires the commitment to see a pilot program through to completion, evaluating and revising the program along the way. Lastly, if the program is to prepare students for life-long learning in virtual environments, it requires use of a variety of e-learning tools. Although such programs take ample planning and cooperation to develop, the growth of the virtual workplace makes the effort worthwhile.

The Nursing Information Literacy Program (NILP) team continues to evaluate, revise, and develop the program at Three Rivers College. Future goals include acquiring additional nursing library databases, creatively using *ePortfolios,* reinforcing the principles with graduates as they enter advanced programs and healthcare facilities, and creating a culture of information literacy, active learning, and virtual environment processes. Students can transfer their information literacy competencies to evidence-based practice and continue enhancing their *ePortfolios,* fostering the development of a hybrid of traditional and virtual workplaces in the world of nursing. Further research and experimentation with the use of the discussions tool and the chat room in *WebCT* could reveal the tools' potential to help students develop skills necessary in a virtual working environment, such as using network communication or participating in cooperative and collaborative learning. Students engaged with the NILP will be prepared to use the skills and competencies required in the 21st century workplace.

Medical practitioners, metaphorically speaking, are already stepping into the virtual workplace. Their success depends on the medical team's information literacy. For instance, some practitioners allow their patients to e-mail photographs of suspected problems, such as a suspicious looking bump, to save both parties time; some also use digitized x-rays to allow healthcare professionals to easily evaluate conditions, consult with one another from a distance (even from home), and prevent losing the only physical copy of an x-ray (Iaquinta, 2006). These practices require professionals to be able to retrieve information from electronic systems like secure e-mail and electronic health records.

Search skills that nurses develop in an information literacy program will also be put to use in the virtual workplace. Great Britain plans to implement wide use of software that allows practitioners to search for patterns in patient records that might indicate risk factors for cardiovascular disease, then enrolling these patients in a prevention program ("CDV Screening," 2006; Marshall, T., 2006). Furthermore, nurses working in rural areas operate with a smaller network of onsite collaborators and resources than do nurses in urban and suburban areas. Thus, they need information literacy skills to collaborate over a distance and search for and evaluate medical information. The U.S. Navy, because of the isolation of its medical professionals and patients, again leads the way, continuing to develop the digital medical library it began in 1997 for practitioners in the field to use to conduct research to treat their patients (D'Alessandro, M., D'Alessandro, D., Bakalar, R., Ashley, D., & Hendrix, M., 2005). Nurses who do not have the ability to conduct searches and critically evaluate the results leave themselves and their patients at a disadvantage.

Finally, many nurses will apply the skills they develop in programs like the NILP when they receive virtual education in the future. As in many other professions, formal training in nursing does not end with a degree. State boards require nurses to participate in continuing education to renew their licenses. The time commitment and cost of attending on-site training makes training from a distance a good option for many practicing nurses. They must be able not only to critically evaluate new information but also to use Internet and other electronic interfaces to participate in the sessions. And as virtual workplace and training technologies change, a solid foundation in current technologies will help nurses adjust to new ones.

REFERENCES

Akkirman, A., & Harris, D. (2005). Organizational communication satisfaction in the virtual workplace. *Journal of Management Development, 24*(5), 397-409.

Allan, B., & Lewis, D. (2006). Virtual learning communities as a vehicle for workforce development: A case study. *The Journal of Workplace Learning, 18*(6), 367-383.

Barnes, J. (2005). Workforce development and training issues: Testimony to the Joint Commission on Technology and Science's Advisory Committee on Emerging Science and Technology Issues. Retrieved January 19, 2007 from http://jcots.state.va.us/pdf/Training.pdf.

Benner, P. (2001). *From novice to expert: Excellence and power in clinical nursing practice.* Upper Saddle River, New Jersey: Prentice Hall.

Blue Cross Blue Shield. (2008). Plan Information. In *Coverage.* Retrieved March 5, 2007 from http://www.bcbstx.com/ut/select/planinformation.htm.

Canton, J. (2004). Top ten healthcare trends for the 21st century. Retrieved January 19, 2007 from http://www.keynoteresource.com/article8jcanton.html.

CDV screening to be virtual. (2006). *Pulse, 66*(27), 3.

Cheek, J., & Doskatsch, I. (1998). Information literacy: A resource for nurses as lifelong learners. *Nurse Education Today, 18,* 243-250.

Chaudhry, B., Wang, J., Wu., S, Maglione, M., Mojica, W., Roth, E., et al. (2006). Systematic review: Impact of health information technology on quality, efficiency, and costs of medical care. *Annals of Internal Medicine, (144)*10, E-12-E-22.

Crandall, F., & Wallace, M., Jr. (1998). *Work & rewards in the virtual workplace: A "new deal" for organizations & employees.* New York, NY: AMACOM.

D'Alessandro, M., D'Alessandro, D., Bakalar, R., Ashley, D., & Hendrix, M. (2005). The virtual naval hospital: The digital library as knowledge management tool for nomadic patrons. *Journal of the Medical Library Association, 93*(1), 16-20.

Dick, W., Carey, L., & Carey, J. (2005). *The systematic design of instruction* (6th ed.). Boston, MA: Allyn & Bacon.

Downey, G. (Ed.). (2006). Six ed-tech trends to watch in 2007. Service-oriented architecture, 'cloud computing' among the developments sure to have an impact on educational technology in the coming year. *eSchool Newsonline.* Retrieved January 19, 2007 from: http://www.eschoolnews.com/news/PFshowstory.cfm?ArticleID=6781.

Fyee, K. (2005). New frontiers. *23rd Annual International Nursing Computer and Technology Conference.* Atlanta, GA.

Hagan, L., Morin, D., & Lepine, R. (2000). Evaluation of telenursing outcomes: Satisfaction, self-care practices, and cost savings. *Public Health Nursing, 17*(4), 305-313.

Hooks, J., & Corbett, F., Jr. (2005). Information literacy for off-campus graduate cohorts: Collaboration between a university librarian and a master's of education faculty. *Library Review, 54*(4), 245-256.

Iaquinta, S. (2006). The virtual house call. *PC Magazine, 25*(19-20), 141.

Jacobs, S., Rosenfeld, P., & Haber, J. (2003). Information literacy as a foundation for evidence-based practice in graduate nursing education: A curriculum-integrated approach. *Journal of Professional Nursing, 19*(5), 320-328.

Marshall, T. (2006). Estimating the value of information in strategies for identifying patients at high risk of cardiovascular disease. *Informatics in Primary Care, 14*(2), 85-92.

Mowry, M., & Constantinou, D. (2007). Electronic health records: A magic pill?. *Applied Clinical Trials, 16*(2), 36-42.

Naidu, S., & Oliver, M. (1996). Computer-supported collaborative problem-based learning: An instructional design architecture for virtual learning in nursing education. *Journal of Distance Education/Revue de L'Enseignment a distance.* Retrieved January 19, 2007 from: http://cade.athabascau.ca/vol11.2/naiduoliver.html.

Quinlan, N., & Hegarty, N. (2006). Librarians outside the box: Waterford Institute of Technology's library-based virtual learning environment (VLE) training and development programme. *New Library World, 107*(1-2), 37-47.

Robertson, K. (2000). Work transformation: Integrating people, space and technology. *Facilities, 18*(10-12), 376-382.

Sinnet, W. (2002). Ask an FEI researcher about…e-learning. *Financial Executive.* Retrieved January 19, 2007 from http://goliath.ecnext.com/coms2/summary_0199-2220217_ITM

Stough, S., Eom S., & Buckenmyer, J. (2000). Virtual teaming: A strategy for moving your organization into the new millennium. *Industrial Management & Data Systems, 1000*(8), 370-378.

Tilley, D., Boswell, C., & Cannon, S. (2006). Developing and establishing online student learning communities. *CIN: Computers, Informatics, Nursing, 24*(3), 144-149.

Turner, P., Turner, S., Green, S., & Mayne, P. (1998). Collaborative notebooks for the virtual workplace. In: M. Igbaria & Tan (Eds.), *The virtual workplace* (pp. 187-198). Hershey, PA: Idea Group Publishing.

Valerius, J. (2007). The electronic health record: What every information manager should know. Information Management Journal, 41(1), 56-59.

KEY TERMS

E-learning: This is a process of learning that is facilitated by, delivered by, and supported through information and telecommunications technologies.

Evidence-based Practice: This is demonstrated by practitioners who make informed clinical decisions based on the best research evidence available, environment of practice, clinical expertise and the patient's unique characteristics.

Information Competency: This is a set of skills that allows the individual to identify the information need, manipulate information efficiently and make informed, intelligent, ethical decisions in academic, professional, and personal life.

Information Literacy: This is a set of abilities that empowers individuals to understand how the information is organized and to locate, retrieve, evaluate, and use information effectively and efficiently.

Information Literacy Program: This is a planned, systematic process through which information literacy skills are thought and developed incrementally and progressively during a program of academic study.

Nursing Information Gateway: This is a portal that offers access to faculty- and librarian-selected print and online nursing sources of information, research tools, library services and professional organizations.

Technological Literacy: This is the ability to use computers and electronic equipment to meet objectives and goals and improve learning, productivity, and performance.

Tele-nursing: This is the practice of nursing over distance using telecommunications technology (National Council of State Boards of Nursing).

Tele-health: This is the use of telecommunication technologies and electronic information to facilitate access to medical and research information while providing healthcare services to clients across distances.

***WebCT* Learning Module:** This is a structured guide to course content, organized sequentially as a collection of interactive learning tools, assignments, and resources to promote effective learning.

Chapter XXIV
Preparing for the Virtual Workplace in the Educational Commons

Gary Hepburn
Acadia University, Canada

ABSTRACT

This chapter explores the potential of an educational commons to help schools better prepare students for the virtual workplace. Together with the formation of stronger linkages between schools and the business world, making greater use of resources such as open source software in both school and business would greatly reduce costs and enable students to be better prepared to participate in the virtual workplace. With the virtual workplace's emphasis on online communication technologies as a primary tool for completing day-to-day tasks, schools must acquire the hardware and software as well as explore ways of incorporating these tools into the student learning. To reduce the expense of doing so and to ensure that the environments in which students learn reflect that of the workplace, both organizations should consider using more accessible software and working more closely together. Conceptualizing the ideal learning environment as an educational commons, this chapter will explore open source resources and their potential contribution to education and some of the opportunities as well as the challenges that will be encountered as open source resources are introduced to education and business.

INTRODUCTION

As the workplace becomes increasingly virtual in nature, schools are under pressure to provide their students with new types of experiences and skills. Online communication technologies are vital tools in support of knowledge management functions within organizations. These tools can be very expensive for businesses and are often too expensive for schools to acquire. Schools can, however, take an alternative approach to the preparation of their students that will make preparation for the virtual workplace possible, while at the same time creating new opportunities for employers. Employers will gain workers that are ready to take their place in virtual workplaces and have an opportunity to consider more efficient and effective tools to support the virtual activities of their organizations.

In order to prepare students for the virtual workplace, public schools and other educational institutions need to become more familiar with some of the opportunities that are emerging as a result of open source projects. Leveraging the potential of the Internet as a collaborative medium, open source development projects are producing software and other resources that have the potential to meet many needs of schools. As educators become aware of open source resources, they will immediately recognize the advantages of low-cost alternatives to many commercial products that schools currently use and find expensive. They will also notice that open source resources lack some of the usage restrictions that characterize commercial resources. The low cost and flexibility of open source products makes them very attractive, but no less important is the way in which these resources align with some core educational values. In this chapter, I illustrate this alignment by exploring the promise that open source resources hold in supporting the ideal of an educational commons. Specifically, I will discuss (1) the concept of an educational commons, (2) open source resources and their potential contribution to education, and (3) some of the opportunities and challenges that will be encountered as open source resources are introduced to education.

THE EDUCATIONAL COMMONS

The online, collaborative environments associated with virtual workplaces are too often perceived as being out of reach for schools. They are looked upon as expensive add-ons that relate marginally to the curriculum being taught. For employers, the expense of the online environments is considered a necessary cost of doing business. A challenge for employers is finding sources of workers who are prepared to work in these environments. In order to ensure a supply of these workers, schools must realize that a new skill set needs to be developed as students are being educated. Employers also need to understand the importance of supporting schools in their work to prepare workers for the virtual workplace. One serious problem that needs to be addressed is the dependence of employers on expensive technologies that schools cannot afford. One way to do this is to consider the concept of the educational commons as a means of providing rich resources for education and the virtual workplace.

Most of us have at least a passing familiarity with the concept of a commons. According David Bollier (2003), the term refers to "a wide array of creations of nature and society that we inherit freely, share and hold in trust for future generations." Well-known examples of commons that exist or have existed include grazing land, the Internet, fresh water supplies, and roadways. Lawrence Lessig (2001) pushes the concept of a commons further in his book, *The Future of Ideas,* as he describes the role of an *innovative commons* in society:

They create the opportunity for individuals to draw upon resources without connections, permission, or access granted by others. They are environments that commit themselves to being open. Individuals and corporations draw upon the value created by this openness. They transform that value into other value, which they then consume privately (p. 85).

The fact that society has always used the value of that which we hold in common to build greater value allows us to see an important reason why maintaining common resources is good for all. Even private enterprises benefit from that fact that we hold some resources in common. To appreciate this point, all we need to do is consider the value of roadways to individual and commercial activities. Recognizing the importance of common resources is neither anti-private nor anti-commercial. Providing some common resources and seeking a reasonable balance between that which is privately owned and that which is held in common benefits society.

Public institutions, such as schools, can be thought of as a type of cultural commons (Bollier, 2001; 2002; Reid, 2003). Societies around the world recognize the importance of providing education for all and have made substantial investments to do so. Thought of as a commons, schools ideally should be able to provide the resources needed to support optimal learning experiences for students. Our societal investment in education is an attempt to enable this, but we often encounter limitations due to the fact that providing education is complicated and costly. In reality, schools have trouble living up to the ideal of an educational commons. Clearly, schools do not meet some of the criteria Lessig described above for an innovative commons to exist. There are many cases in which schools are not able "to draw upon resources without connections, permission, or access granted by others" (Lessig, p. 85).

Assuming we want to establish an educational commons that supports innovation, we need to reconsider some of the conditions under which education is conducted. Analyzing many current practices through the lens of an educational commons can reveal blind spots as well as future strategies that may lead us closer to an educational commons. Recent technological developments and, in particular the Internet, have provided some ways in which we can draw upon common resources to aid us in our educational activities. Many of these same resources have the potential to directly benefit private industry as well, and using them can indeed become a source of competitive advantage. Before I explore these developments further, I will briefly discuss the principle threat to our ability to realize an educational commons.

MARKET ENCLOSURE

Many current and historical examples can be given of resources that were once held in common being taken over by commercial or private interests. These examples range from the selling of commonly held land in England beginning in the 1400s (Bollier, 2001) to the increased commercialization of the Internet in more recent times (Lessig, 2001). Increasingly, that which is held in common is being sold or given away. It is no different in schools. Schools are being seen as an under-exploited market by corporations, and commercial intrusions into educational spaces are becoming more common. These intrusions are what Bollier (2001; 2002; 2003) calls market enclosure. The concerns the market enclosure of education raise are not going unnoticed (e.g., Apple, 1993; Kunkel, et al., 2004) but many schools find themselves in a difficult dilemma.

Because most schools tend to be under-funded, offers from companies to provide resources or funds in exchange for allowing them to advertise in schools are tempting. Many educators are uncomfortable with the idea of allowing corporations into schools, but they also want more educational resources than schools can currently afford. A well-known example of corporate intrusion has been orchestrated by a company called Channel One. Participating schools are provided with satellite dishes, VCRs, and televisions for each classroom provided they agree to watch a daily, 12-minute, youth-oriented news program. Two minutes of the program are devoted to advertisements. In 1999, Channel One was delivering its services to approximately 12,000 schools which provided its advertisers with access to nearly eight million students in grades 6 through 12 (Hayes, 1999). Schools gain donated equipment that can be used for instruction at times when the newscasts are not being shown and access to the news program, the value of which is a subject of debate. Channel One is just one example of market enclosure impacting schools.

Closely related to the problem of schools feeling pressure to allow a corporate presence is the cost of providing educational resources. Textbooks, computers, software, and encyclopedias are examples of resources for which schools normally pay. After schools have paid operating expenses such as building maintenance and teacher salaries, they often find that there is little money left to purchase these resources. Schools find themselves in the position of having to consider either doing without or taking advantage of alternative sources of financial support, such as corporate funding. Whatever the approach taken to the problem, schools can rarely gain access to the quantity and variety of resources they would like to have available.

Even when a school does manage to obtain some funding for resources, another aspect of market enclosure impacts their ability to use the resources in the ways that will most help students. Resources like software and textbooks are normally protected by copyright. Copyright laws protect the rights of the creators of a work, allowing them to control its use and receive compensation. Copyright law also seeks to balance the rights of the creator with society's right to use the work to create further innovation. Recent changes in copyright laws, however, have increasingly favored the rights of the creator of the work (Lessig, 2001) and this has consequences for schools. After schools purchase the quantity of a commercially produced resource they can afford, they are normally faced with usage restrictions. In the case of educational software, a license is typically required for each computer on which the software is installed. Schools cannot put the software on other computers nor can they provide copies to teachers or students to be used inside or outside the school. The fact that software and other resources are copyright controlled means that a school's use of those resources is largely subject to the conditions set by the corporation or individual that owns them.

The impact of the commercial interests on schools is significant and important. Corporations influence the ability of schools to obtain resources and the ways in which they may use them. For these reasons, there are some substantial limits on the degree to which schools can claim

to be an educational commons. Schools appear to be a commons when we consider that, in most parts of the world, all students can freely attend school and expect to be educated there. A closer examination, however, shows that schools have to negotiate the ways in which they educate students with corporations, and it is the corporations who appear to have the upper hand.

The concept of schools as a commons has appeal, but thinking this way forces us to recognize the threat of market enclosures. We tend to notice recent corporate intrusions into schools because, as Hardin (1968) says, "Infringements made in the distant past are accepted because no contemporary complains of a loss. It is the newly proposed infringements that we vigorously oppose; cries of *rights* and *freedom* fill the air" (p. 1247). There are objections to the emerging enclosures of education, such as that of Channel One, but we must also recognize other types enclosures that we tend to accept without question, such as the purchase of textbooks and software. Because the purchase of copyrighted, commercial products tends to be an accepted educational practice, we generally see it as normal. Given the problems and limitations education encounters that are related to these normal purchases, it may be worth re-examining our practices and options. Recent progress involving the Internet and some of the development models it enables provide a new possibility with which to juxtapose current practices.

OPEN SOURCE SOFTWARE FOR EDUCATION AND BUSINESS

The Internet has become a major resource for education and is used extensively for various purposes, most of which currently appear to relate to research and homework help (Lenhart, et al., 2001). While this role is valuable, there is another way in which the Internet may be able to indirectly bring benefits to schools. Largely due to its potential as a collaborative medium, the

Internet has been able to facilitate a great deal of software development. Of particular note is rapid emergence of open source software.

The open source approach is quite different from that of companies that produce commercial software. These companies normally sell consumers binary versions of their software that can be read by computers but not by people who have programming skills. The companies also use licenses to restrict users from distributing or modifying the software. These measures allow the company to maintain control of the software product and to ensure that anyone who uses it must pay the company. In contrast, open source software development models make the human readable source code of programs available to anyone who wishes to access it and allows for distribution and modification of programs. For software to be certified as open source by the Open Source Initiative (OSI), "the software must be distributed under a license that guarantees the right to read, redistribute, modify, and use the software freely" (OSI, 2007). Open source software can usually be obtained free of cost, although open source licenses do not require this to be the case. When programmers can read, distribute and modify software code, a large community becomes involved in the development effort, allowing bug fixes and enhancements to occur rapidly. Open source software has become more available and successful in the last decade largely due to the growth of the Internet, which has provided the medium for collaboration and sharing on which open source models are built (Lessig, 1999; Goetz, 2003).

Open source development is primarily associated with software production. Most of the desktop software applications that schools and businesses require are available in the form of stable and proven open source software including word processing, spreadsheets, presentations, e-mail, scheduling, Web browsing, and image manipulation, to name a few. One of the widely applicable of these applications is OpenOffice. OpenOffice is a highly developed office suite that is comparable to any serious commercial package, including Microsoft Office (Olavsrud, 2003; Byfield, 2005). The program contains a word processor, spreadsheet, presentation manager, and drawing program. It can be run on the Linux, Windows or Macintosh operating systems. OpenOffice saves documents in its own file formats and can work with others as well, including formats used for Microsoft Office documents. OpenOffice is appropriate for most all school purposes as it has all the functionality that would be required for average and advanced users. The fact that it can be run on a number of operating systems and works with documents that have been created with other office suites, makes it a versatile package that can easily be deployed in schools. OpenOffice can be downloaded free of cost and would be an easy transition for students and staff who are familiar with other office suites.

Operating systems are a basic and necessary part of any computing environment. The emerging challenger to the domination of Microsoft's Windows these days is Linux, the best known of all open source software projects. Linux is recognized as a robust and stable server operating system, and is now demonstrating its potential on the desktop. A number of companies produce their own flavor of Linux and, depending on the precise needs of the school, the Linux operating system can be obtained free of cost or for a modest fee. Ubuntu Linux, for example, has become one of the most popular and education-appropriate Linux distributions. It can be freely downloaded and installed. All Linux users can easily access online community support, but if schools require commercial support, they can pick up various support options from most Linux companies for a modest fee. Linux can be installed on most PC or Macintosh computers. Even older PCs that are unable to run current versions of Windows can often run recent versions of Linux due to its lower hardware requirements. A desktop user who is new to Linux would notice some differences from a Windows environment, but would have little trouble adjusting to some of the more recent Linux desktop environments. In fact, many of the newer Linux desktops are designed to appear very similar to a Windows environment. One important difference that would be immediately noticed with most any Linux distribution is that the package not only provides the operating system but also most of the applications that would be needed.

In addition to more general desktop software, many examples of open source software are available that can be used to directly support virtual learning and work activities. Most of these applications are server-based and can be used by way of a Web browser. Learning and training activities can be supported using a learning management system or an LMS. These are several well- known and well-regarded open source LMS systems available such as Moodle or Interact. Like their far more expensive commercial counterparts, these systems provide high levels of learning interactivity, the ability to post content, assessment tools, and many more features. Open source groupware applications such as WebCollab or eGroupWare allow users to work together on projects and offer a number of management, resource sharing and communication tools. Finally, an exciting new open source application being developed by Sun Microsystems called MPK20 "is a virtual 3D environment in which employees can accomplish their real work, share documents, and meet with colleagues using natural voice communication" (Sun Microsystems, n.d.).

All of this open source software is available to schools and businesses, contributing to a commons from which both types of organizations can draw. If schools were to begin using software, they would have powerful collaboration and learning tools at their disposal to accomplish educational goals. At the same time they would be preparing students for the virtual workplace by giving them experience with the processes and tools they would use there. Making the change to and implementing new software packages is the most difficult part, but once this is done, schools and businesses using open source software would find they have software that is stable and fully functional. The low cost open source software would enable schools to keep pace with the software being used in business, particularly with those businesses that implement the same software solutions. It is not only software that would be provided—open source resources can also be of direct help in providing schools with other cheap and effective learning tools.

MORE OPEN SOURCE SOFTWARE AND EDUCATIONAL RESOURCES

There are many other types of open source projects emerging in addition to those aimed at software development (Stalder & Hirsh, 2002) that can benefit schools. Internet-based collaborative technologies are being used to develop online, text-based materials that are intended for educational purposes. Such projects allow subject experts from around the world to work together to produce materials that are freely available to download, modify, print and distribute. Like software projects, these content development projects are noted for their rigorous review process and ability to be quickly updated as the need arises.

Many examples of text-based, content development projects are emerging. There are initiatives underway to develop online textbooks that can be used in subject areas commonly taught in schools. Wikibooks is a project "dedicated to developing and disseminating free, open content textbooks and other classroom texts." It currently hosts over 1,000 textbooks in varying stages of development. There are many textbooks that are ready to be used in schools now. Along similar lines, Rice University's new open publishing project, Connexions, is in the process of making high quality textbooks available to university and K-12 students (Lyman, 2006).

In addition to textbooks, an encyclopedia development project has proven very successful. Years ago, Wikipedia surpassed the Internet traffic received by the online version of Encyclopedia *Britannica.* Wikipedia has rapidly grown into the largest reference Web site on the Internet. The Wikipedia site claims that the English version of Wikipedia had over 1.8 million articles as of May 2007 (Wikipedia, n.d.).

Schools, in particular, can benefit from these non-software projects as they get the chance to obtain high quality text-based resources, free of cost or usage restrictions. Unlike open source software projects that may prove technically challenging to educators who wish to participate in development, textbook and encyclopedia projects are closely aligned with the expertise of educators. Once educators become aware of these projects as users and contributors, a resource of immense value will be available to schools to be used as they see fit. Open source models can become a revolutionary source of innovation and opportunity for schools. Students become accustomed to finding their learning and information resources on the Internet and this helps prepare them for the virtual workplace.

ADVANTAGES

Returning to the notion of a commons, open source development has the potential to form a commons that will benefit both schools and businesses by placing resources that can be freely used in the hands of students, educators and businesses. One of the advantages of using the products of open source development is that schools and businesses are able to avoid market enclosure. Commercial products are no longer an obligatory passage point (Callon, 1986; Latour, 1987) in obtaining many resources that are required in education and business. With cost being less of a constraining factor, schools and businesses are able to utilize similar software environments, making it easier for each

to address the needs of and cooperate with the other. The money that is no longer required for commercial products that have been replaced by open source products can be used to support other areas of need within the organizations. Businesses stand to save considerable amounts of money on software while, at the same time, gaining access to students who are well prepared for the virtual workforce of the future. Schools also gain a way of preparing students for that workforce that is affordable, flexible, and directly provides the skills and experiences students need.

Interestingly, an important advantage of schools and businesses using open source resources appears to be a reversal of one of the problems that has confronted traditional commons. One of the fundamental problems with most commons is overuse of the resources. Indeed, this concern is the basis of Hardin's (1968) well-known essay, "The Tragedy of the Commons." As more consumers of the resources provided by a particular commons take advantage of it, the resource can become depleted. In order to preserve the resource in a traditional commons, some sort of management strategy needs to be put in place. In contrast to traditional commons, open source projects can actually benefit from increased numbers of users. Software and Web sites are not depleted by those who copy or view the resources. Indeed, users can become co-developers as they provide feedback, suggestions, and improvements (Raymond, 1998). As Raymond (2000) points out, "widespread use of open-source software tends to increase its value.... In this inverse commons, the grass grows taller when it's grazed upon."

As schools and businesses begin to use open source products they will move closer to the ideal of a commons, while solving many problems that have confronted them in the past. As more organizations move in this direction, the value and quality of the resources are likely to increase rather than be depleted. There are, however, several challenges that must be considered in order to begin taking advantage of open source products in a productive way.

CHALLENGES

Beginning to use open source products requires educators and business leaders to revisit some of their basic assumptions about the types of resources we use in schools and from where those resources should come. I am assuming that few educators would object to the concept of an educational commons, but many may have some anxiety about giving up some of the commercial products with which they have become comfortable. Commercial products are often useful and of high quality, but using them in cases where open source alternatives exist tends to lead to many of the problems I have been discussing in this chapter. Knowing this, educators and business leaders need to become familiar with open source resources and explore the appropriateness of using them within their organizations. If the resources are found to be appropriate, they should be used in place of commercial resources. In the case of software, for example, I would challenge organizations to explain why OpenOffice could not replace the commercial office suites that are currently used on most school and business computers. Unless there is an excellent reason, the open source software should be used due to its overall suitability, low cost, and better alignment with core values.

The sort of mindset that would move education and business toward greater use of open source resources is only beginning to emerge. Most educators are not outraged by the corporate intrusion in the educational commons. Education has a long history of such intrusions, although they seem to have intensified in recent times. Educators have become resigned to the fact that corporations seek to profit from in education. From this perspective, it may appear more extreme to consider making use of open source resources as an alternative to commercial ones. The ideal of an educational commons may serve to highlight that which is being lost as more control over the educational enterprise is handed to corporations

seeking to make money directly from the education sector. This point, however, should not be interpreted as a suggestion that schools cut ties with the business community. A transition by schools to open source resources that are similar to those being used by businesses has strong potential to facilitate enhanced linkages between schools and businesses. Educators will become better able to prepare the future workforce that business needs. As this occurs, the efficiencies and cost savings that can be realized by business are highly significant. Education and the business community can formulate a stronger foundation for cooperation and mutual support. Both types of organization can benefit from the new open source fueled commons, but a change of mindset is required for this to happen.

A second challenge faced in implementing open source resources in education and business involves taking on roles in open source development processes. To continue the development of high quality resources that meet educational and business needs, it is important that both groups be willing to participate in the development of various products. It is not uncommon that educators and businesses give feedback to producers of commercial products, particularly when opinions are solicited, but they must be more proactive about participating in open source projects. These projects do not typically have resources to solicit extensive feedback and contributions. Participants must understand the nature of open source development and seek ways to become involved. The development of software and other types of educational resources require a wide variety of contributions and competencies. Becoming an active contributor to projects will ensure that a broad array of resources is produced that are appropriate for the context in which they are being used.

Although educators can contribute to open source projects to an extent and can investigate the sort of preparation students need for the virtual workplace, business needs to take a substantial role in helping schools. Schools will need to make some changes in the way they are preparing students and the sorts of resources they use in doing so. Business can consult with and support schools as they try to make these changes in several ways. They can make research grants available to schools that want to work on implementing open source resources. They can also partner with schools as they consider what preparation students require and what changes are required to implement initiatives. The opportunities to establish a shared mission and a mutually supportive agenda are one of the most exciting possibilities that could grow out of the establishment of a commons, but realizing these opportunities will require a high degree of commitment from both sides.

FUTURE NEEDS

Maximizing the advantages of open source resources and overcoming the challenges associated with their introduction and use requires scholarly support and practical help. The argument for open source resources in pubic education is not one that is well-known to many in education or business. It is important that this message be delivered not only to educators, but also to educational and business leaders, technical leaders and government officials. While the day-to-day changes that the use of open source resources would entail would be felt primarily at the classroom and business level, many of the problems they solve are systemic in nature (Hepburn & Buley, 2006). All stakeholders need to help get the message about open source resources out. Once this is done, stakeholders must look for ways of supporting change and then carefully monitor the impact these changes have in the education and business sectors.

Education, business and government must also consider how avenues can be created for participation in open source projects and implementation efforts. Although there are great advantages to be gained by using open source resources, there

is also a need to consider how contributions can be made to the very projects that produce the resources. Doing so may entail giving teachers or business people release time to work on a project or contributing to projects in other monetary or material ways. Participation will help ensure resources that meet the needs of schools and business while bringing both groups more in line with the ethos of the open source community. Such a partnership would serve, strengthen and reinforce the work of schools, business and the open source community.

CONCLUSION

The vision of an educational commons characterized by easily available resources that are flexible, affordable, and high quality is an appealing one. Further, reducing market enclosure of education at the resource level is desirable. By providing the medium that enables collaborative, open source projects to thrive, the Internet is emerging as a key technological innovation that will allow schools to overcome some significant challenges. Interestingly, this is the same medium that supports the rapidly growing virtual workplace. As schools and businesses forge new partnerships aimed at implementing an educational commons based on open source resources, the benefits to both groups will be exciting. Educators will gain new options and support in preparing students for the virtual workplace. Open source resources that can help get this shared project started are already available. As businesses and educators begin using open source resources and contributing to the projects that develop them, there is likely to be a synergy and insight that develops. This may lead to new ideas and directions, effectively moving beyond the ideal of a commons and toward a true innovative commons.

REFERENCES

Apple, M. (1993). *Official knowledge: Democratic education in a conservative age.* New York, NY: Routledge.

Bollier, D. (2003). *Preserving the commons in the new information order.* Retrieved May 2, 2007 from http://world- information.org/wio/readme/992007035/1078492038.

Bollier, D. (2002). Reclaiming the commons. *Boston Review, 27*(3-4). Retrieved May 2, 2007 from http://www.boston review.net/BR27.3/bollier.html.

Bollier, D. (2001). *Public assets, private profits: Reclaiming the American commons in an age of market enclosure.* Retrieved May 2, 2007, from http://www.newamerica.net/publications/policy/public_assets_private_profits.

Byfield, B. (2005). OpenOffice.org Writer vs. Microsoft Word. *Newsforge.* Retrieved May 30, 2007 from http://software.newsforge.com/article.pl?sid=05/06/14/2137222&from=rss.

Callon, M. (1986). Some elements for a sociology of translation: Domestication of the scallops and the fishermen of St–Brieuc Bay. In: J. Law (Ed.), *Power, action and belief: A new sociology of knowledge?* (pp. 196-229). London: Routledge and Kegan Paul.

eGroupWare. (n.d.). Retrieved May 27, 2007, from http://www.egroupware.org.

Goetz, T. (2003). Open source everywhere: Software is just the beginning. *Wired, 11*(11), 158-167.

Hardin, G. (1968). The tragedy of the commons. *Science, 162,* 1243-1248. Retrieved May 2, 2007 from http://dieoff.com/page95.htm.

Hepburn, G., & Buley, J. (2006). Getting open source software into schools. *Innovate, 3*(1). Retrieved May 27, 2007 from http://innovateonline.info/index.php?view=article&id=323.

Interact. (n.d.). Retrieved May 27, 2007 from http://www.interactole.org.

Kunkel, D., Wilcox, B., Palmer, E., Cantor, J., Dowrick, P., & Linn, S. (2004). *Report of the APA Task Force on Advertising and Children.* Retrieved May 30, 2007 from http://www.apa.org/releases/childrenads.pdf.

Latour, B. (1987). *Science in action.* Cambridge, MA: Harvard University Press.

Lenhart, A., Simon, M., & Graziano, M. (2001). *The Internet and education: Findings of the Pew Internet and American Life Project.* Retrieved May 7, 2007 from http://www.pewinternet.org/reports/toc.asp?Report=39.

Lessig, L. (2001). *The future of ideas: The fate of the commons in a connected world.* New York, NY: Random House.

Lessig, L. (1999). *Code and other laws of cyberspace.* New York, NY: Basic Books.

Lyman, J. (2006). Connexions takes open source approach to education content. Linux Insider. Retrieved May 7, 2007 from http://www.linuxinsider.com/story/51827.html.

Moodle. (n.d.). Retrieved May 1, 2007 from http://moodle.org/.

Olavsrud, T. (2003). OpenOffice.org renews battle for productivity suite. *internetnews.com.* Retrieved May 7, 2007 from http://www.internetnews.com/ent- news/article.php/3085941.

OpenOffice. (n.d.). Retrieved May 1, 2007 from http://www.openoffice.org.

Open Source Initiative. (2007). Retrieved May 10, 2007 from http://www.opensource.org.

Raymond, E. (2000). The magic cauldron. Retrieved April 30, 2007 from http://www.catb.org/~esr/writings/cathedral-bazaar/magic- cauldron/.

Raymond, E. (1998). The cathedral and the bazaar. *First Monday, 3*(3). Retrieved April 30, 2007 from http://firstmonda y.org/issues/issue3_3/raymond/.

Reid, A. (2003). Public education as an education commons. Retrieved May 30, 2007 from www. acde.edu.au/docs/Public%20Education%20as%20a n%20Education%20Commons%20-%2023%20Sep. pdf.

Stalder, F., & Hirsh, J. (2002). Open source intelligence. *First Monday, 7*(6). Retrieved May 3, 2007 from http://firstmonday.org/issues/issue7_6/stalder/.

Sun Microsystems. (n.d.). MPK20: Sun's Virtual Workplace. Retrieved May 28, 2007 from http://research.sun.com/projects/mc/mpk20.html.

WebCollab. (n.d.). Retrieved May 28, 2007 from http://webcollab.sourceforge.net.

Wikibooks. (n.d.). Retrieved April 30, 2007 from http://wikibooks.org/w iki/Wikibooks_portal.

Wikipedia. (n.d.). Retrieved April 30, 2007 from http://en.wikipedia.org/wi ki/Main_page.

KEY TERMS

Open Source Software: Generically, *open source* refers to a program in which the source code is available to the general public for use and/or modification from its original design free of charge. Open source code is typically created as a collaborative effort in which programmers improve upon the code and share the changes within the community. For a more technical definition visit the Web site of the Open Source Initiative (2007).

Commons: A wide array of creations of nature and society that we inherit freely, share, and hold in trust for future generations (Bollier, 2003).

Educational Commons: The idea of an educational system that strives to ensure that resources for teaching and learning are freely available to teachers and students without connections, permissions, or access granted by others. These resources are thought of as a "commons".

Market Enclosure: The process through which resources held in common for all to use are gradually being taken over by corporate interests (Bollier, 2001).

Learning Management System or LMS: A software package that enables planning, delivery, and management of all learning events within an organization, including online, virtual classroom, and instructor-led courses.

Groupware: a Web-based technology designed to facilitate the work of groups. This technology may be used to communicate, cooperate, coordinate, solve problems, compete, or negotiate.

Section III
Tools and Environments for Virtual Work

Chapter XXV
Technologies and Services in Support of Virtual Workplaces

Alan McCord
Lawrence Technological University, USA

Morell D. Boone
Eastern Michigan University, USA

ABSTRACT

Our global business climate is rapidly evolving to require greater use of virtual work tools. This chapter provides an overview of today's virtual work technologies against the backdrop of evolving business needs. The concept of the virtual workplace is discussed from the perspectives of nomadicity, pervasive computing, and globalization. This chapter provides two frameworks—a technology services framework and a virtual services management framework—for evaluating an organization's readiness and capabilities to develop, deploy, and support effective virtual work environments. The elements of the frameworks are explored through examination of real-world issues surrounding the evolution of virtual workplaces. The chapter also proposes two assessment approaches to evaluate virtual work capabilities and the virtuality of enterprise work groups.

INTRODUCTION

Many technologies are available to support virtual work. Sophisticated technologies can fail if deployed by enterprises not ready to use them. Other enterprises may benefit from less complex technologies if they understand how to manage them.

We begin by proposing two frameworks to assess virtual work tools. A "technology services framework" proposes technical capabilities needed to deploy virtual work tools. A "virtual services management framework" proposes organizational capabilities needed to effectively use these tools. We also propose assessment approaches to evalu-

ate virtual work capabilities and the virtuality of enterprise work groups. We conclude with speculations about the future of virtual work and identify research opportunities in the field.

BACKGROUND

A virtual worker is anyone working in a different geographic location from co-workers or supervisors. Some virtual workers are teleworkers—working from home—while others may work in a corporate office without significant interaction with co-located employees. Nomadic workers may regularly work at multiple customer or partner sites, and may not have a permanent office.

Approximately 90% of American workers perform some work away from corporate offices, and over 44 million employees performed some work from home in 2004 (Joyce, 2004). Traditional intermediation factors—physical workspaces and face-to-face meetings—are absent from many of today's work environments.

The American workforce is migrating from production-oriented to "tacit" jobs requiring workers to exercise experiential judgment and collaboration (Johnson et al., 2005). Catalyzed by adoption of quality management systems and enterprise resource planning (ERP) systems, tacit jobs now comprise over 40% of the workforce (Karoly & Panis, 2004). Tacit workers tend to develop original methods for accomplishing their work within "complex, dynamic environments in which prescribed work processes serve only as reference models" (Logan & Muller, 2006). These individualized approaches often evolve into "best practices" and eventually into formalized processes.

Globalization, pervasive technology, and the consumerization of technology provide opportunities for workers to do more of their work from anywhere, for employers to design employee work with less regard for location. Other effects of globalization include large-scale mergers and acquisitions, global supply chain coordination, business responses to fears of pandemics and terrorism, and rising fossil fuel costs.

Our technology environment is evolving from an industrial model to a pervasive model. Gupta and Moitra (2004) describe virtualization and pervasive computing as "an umbrella of IT capabilities…characterized by mobility, wireless connectivity, context awareness, implicit inputs, proactiveness, smart spaces, and the use of natural interfaces for human-device interaction." Leonard Kleinrock, the pioneer responsible for developing packet switching technology, predicted in the late 1960s that the Internet would be ubiquitous as well as invisible, but observes that the TCP/IP protocol

"assumed that end users and their devices and IP addresses would all be found in the same location and would all be tightly coupled" (Kleinrock, 2001). The advent of the commercial Internet in 1995, explosion of cellular telephony, and proliferation of personal computing devices has given rise to "nomadicity," defined by Kleinrock as "transparent virtual networking." Nomadic users access data, programs, and services as they move from place to place in a transparent, integrated, and convenient fashion.

Not long ago, it took years for workplace technologies to find their way into homes. Today, consumers (and employees) often use technologies prior to enterprise adoption. Examples include video capture and editing, peer-to-peer networking, instant messaging, blogging, and portals. Teleworkers can install very capable home technology infrastructures at modest costs. Pervasive technology, nomadicity, and consumerization contribute to a culture of "networked individualism" where individuals interact with the network on their own terms (Boase et al., 2006). The enterprise implications are clear: implement a technology infrastructure capable of supporting virtual work, but support nomadic employees using their personal technologies.

How do these trends relate to the enterprise use of virtual work tools? First, advances in global networking, wireless technologies, and groupware have increased workers' reliance on technology. These same advances result in employee demands to "communicate easily with each other and accomplish difficult work even though they are remotely located or rarely overlap in time" (Olson & Olson, 2000). The perceived effectiveness of virtual work appears to lag its perceived potential: while nearly three-quarters of surveyed business travelers feel that virtual conferencing or collaboration is more efficient than travel, only 37% feel that virtual tools are more effective than face-to-face meetings" (Travel Industry Association of America, 2004).

Second, virtual work is a multi-dimensional phenomenon. Holtshouse (2006) proposes a "four space" model of the future work environment comprised of physical, organizational, informational, and cognitive spaces. Physical space issues and organizational approaches differ for virtual and on-site work. Tacit workers will personalize today's "one size fits all" information space. Virtual workers will have multiple and sometimes conflicting cognitive needs.

Enterprises deploying virtual work tools need to address both technological and managerial issues, and we know that some technologies are implemented without adequate management capabilities. To decide when and how to deploy virtual work tools, we need to understand the global and enterprise technological context, the nature of virtual work tools, and best practices for managing virtual work. This approach is consistent with the definition of computer-supported cooperative work (Wilson, 1991), which "combines the understanding of the way people work in groups with the enabling technologies of computer networking, and associated hardware, software, services and techniques."

OVERVIEW OF VIRTUAL WORK TECHNOLOGIES

We first review enterprise technology decisions made by firms within a global context. Enterprise technology decisions provide the foundation upon which business applications and virtual work technologies are deployed and integrated.

Global and Enterprise Technologies

Internet and cellular services became globally available in the late 1990s, followed closely by broadband wireless services and personal digital assistants (PDAs). With over half of American homes now served by broadband Internet, the potential teleworker population numbers in the tens of millions.

Until the late 1990s, most enterprise applications—even e-mail—used client-server technol-

ogy that required specialized client software on end-user computers. The adoption of the Web browser as a "universal client" has simplified desktop management and promoted software standards but has complicated the delivery of content. Some workers may use a desktop computer with a hard-wired network connection, others use PDAs and cellular network services, and other workers maintain multiple devices and require seamless access to information regardless of which device they choose to use.

Enterprise investments in ERP systems, business process management, Web services, and hardware virtualization provide a foundation for virtual work services. Hardware virtualization promotes rapid provision of new services. Java portlets (Java Community, 2006) enable personalized access to enterprise applications from multiple devices.

Virtual Work Tools

Several trends drive the adoption of virtual work tools. Many industry standards support development of virtual work tools, including SIMPLE (instant messaging and presence awareness), CPIM (common profile for instant messaging), Human ML (human markup language), xCAL (calendar management), iTIP (free-busy time), VideoML (video markup language), SMIL (synchronized multimedia integration), and XMPP (extensible messaging and presence) (Pickering & Wynn, 2004). Internet-based videoconferencing is widely available and no longer requires expensive on-site equipment and support (Topi, 2004).

In addition to using productivity software, e-mail, and calendaring, most employees are familiar with collaboration technologies such as instant messaging, file sharing, and blogging. These employee skills support adoption of groupware and conferencing (Watson-Manheim & Belanger, 2002).

We have grouped virtual work tools into three broad categories—communication, conferencing, and collaboration—as shown in Table 1.

Table 1. Representative virtual work tools

Virtual Work Category	Representative Tools	Applications
Communication	Telephony	Synchronous voice
	Voicemail	Asynchronous voice
	Facsimile	Asynchronous text
	E-mail	Asynchronous text and graphics
	Office productivity suites	Knowledge documentation
	Enterprise file storage	Knowledge storage
	Web sites	Access to documents and processes
	Web browsers and search engines	Knowledge location
Conferencing	Audio conferencing	Synchronous audio
	Video conferencing	Synchronous audio and video
	Webcasting and streaming	Synchronous and asynchronous audio and video
	Web conferencing	Synchronous audio, video, and documents
Collaboration	Project management	Collaboration and control
	Unified communications	Audio, text, and documents
	Shared product and document development	Synchronous and asynchronous collaboration
	Knowledge management	Document repositories and retrieval

Communication tools comprise the least sophisticated set of virtual work technologies and are available to virtually all firms and individuals at relatively low cost. Most employees regularly use these technologies at the office and at home. **Telephony services are** available virtually anywhere as public switched, private switched, voice over IP (VOIP), or cellular services. **E-mail** is widely deployed, and most workers routinely send documents as **e-mail attachments,** although many businesses are not skilled at managing attachments. **Office productivity tools,** including word processing, spreadsheet, presentation, and personal database applications, are used to document tacit knowledge. Most enterprises have deployed **local area networks** or **enterprise file systems** for shared document storage, although document knowledge is usually managed at a departmental or individual level. Most businesses have deployed **informational Web sites** to provide product and service information, and many businesses deploy secure **intranets** to store documentation and process information. This information is access through use of **Web browsers and search engines.**

Many businesses extend their use of communication tools. Some firms use **voicemail notification** to inform employees of new messages via e-mail. Others use office productivity tools for **revision tracking**. Others use **mailing lists and list servs**, maintain **user directories**, support **message boards** for asynchronous discussions, and provide **instant messaging services**.

Conferencing tools comprise more sophisticated virtual work tools supporting real-time meetings between remote workers. Conferencing tools require a more robust infrastructure, greater investment, and better employee training to be effective. **Audio conferencing** connects participants using telephones, cellular phones, or VOIP, and is available from many service providers. **Video conferencing** adds full-motion video to real-time meetings, can be carried over ISDN or Internet connections, and requires specialized equipment for viewing. **Conference bridges** can add audio participants to a video conference session. Video conferences can be **Webcast** in real-time or **streamed** on-demand following the meeting. **Web conferencing** provides participants with an online meeting environment and can be deployed internally or via hosting. Web conferencing provides a presentation area for sharing text or presentations. The meeting leader can stream audio or video to participants. Participants use a chat window to send text messages to the group, and may be authorized to transmit audio or video content. A whiteboard is usually provided to allow participants to mark up a shared workspace.

Many businesses **record Web conferences** and provide on-demand **streams** of prior meetings. Some conferencing tools support **file and application sharing** where participants manipulate a file or application loaded by the leader. Many conferencing tools also provide **survey and polling tools**.

Collaboration tools comprise the most sophisticated virtual work tools, integrating project and document management functions into communication and conferencing tools. Collaboration tools are expensive to acquire and maintain, require ongoing management and employee training, and often require integration with enterprise applications. Collaboration tools support collaborative **document or product development** using productivity or design tools. They include **project management systems** for task and participant assignments, team work areas, and shared calendaring. Many collaboration tools include **unified communications** and **workflow systems** to integrate telephone, facsimile and e-mail messages into the virtual work environment and to route tasks between participants. Collaboration tools provide **participant directories** and **federated contact lists** to help identify participants to address ad hoc problems, and feature **presence indication** to identify who is available within the environment. Collaboration sessions can be initiated within productivity tools or e-mail systems.

Document repositories provide shared access to versioned project documents. Participants can receive **automatic change notification** through e-mail messages, RSS feeds, or voicemail messages. **Project dashboards** aggregate critical project information. Most collaboration tools support **personalization** of screen layout and notification rules. Some collaboration tools support **real-time engineering design**. Businesses may use collaboration tools to provide input to **knowledge management systems**. Some collaboration tools feature **intelligent agents** which take actions on behalf of participants. Some businesses incorporate **social networking** into their collaboration environment.

State of the Virtual Work Technologies Market

There are many providers of virtual work tools including IBM™, Microsoft™, Oracle™, Novell™, Vignette™, WebEx™, Groove™, and Macromedia™. Most providers offer on-site and hosted implementations, and many businesses deploy both solutions. Open source options such as TikiWiki (TikiWiki, 2006) and WebCollab (WebCollab, 2006) focus on communication, document management, and project management. Social networking providers such as Google™, Yahoo! ™, Microsoft™, AOL™, and Skype™ are entering the conferencing and collaboration marketplace with personal applications that may evolve into enterprise services.

Pickering & Wynn (2004) summarize the shortcoming of today's virtual work tools. Today's virtual work tools do not support cross-cultural or cross-language, do not interpreting context and nuance, and lack social networking features. They lack interoperability, suffer from usability issues, are sometimes unreliable, and are often deployed without attention to employee needs.

OVERVIEW OF MANAGEMENT ISSUES

Virtual work should reflect business strategy: value chain, location of work units, and reliance on technology. The nature of work is driven primarily by industry and business value chains. Strategy defines how workers communicate, cooperate, and collaborate to accomplish this work.

The Nature of Tacit Work

Even though most virtual work is tacit, there are many attributes of tacit work which should be considered before determining the best way to organize and support this work using virtual work tools. Table 2 demonstrates the range of challenges associated with tacit work by adapting and extending the attributes of tacit work identified by Logan and Muller (2006).

A virtual work environment will likely consist of a number of tacit tasks, projects, and programs, each of which can be profiled using Table 2. Some tacit work profiles are more appropriate to be supported by the use of communication tools, while others may be more appropriately supported by conferencing or collaboration tools. As the cost of implementing and maintaining virtual work tools varies widely, managers must pay close attention to the allocation of virtual work tool resources to insure that valuable resources are not squandered.

Managing Virtual Teams

Virtual work management must overcome two key challenges: isolation from colleagues and confusion due to inadequate coordination (Brake, 2006). Brake claims that "[w]e can only beat isolation through building community, and we can only

Table 2. Dimensions and attributes of virtual work

Dimension	Attributes	
	Less Challenging	**More Challenging**
Definition	Structured Defined Static	Unstructured Ad hoc Dynamic
Complexity	Single task Repeatable	Project or program Single Use
Talent	Individual General skills Homogeneous skills	Team Specialized skills Heterogeneous skills
Constraints	Not time sensitive Not budget sensitive Not mission critical	Time Critical Budget Critical Mission Critical

beat confusion by promoting clarity." We explore management issues from this perspective. Brake (2006), Barczak et al. (2006), and others summarize key challenges facing virtual and global teams and recommend management actions to meet these challenges. Virtual teams require proactive leadership, project management, and personal attention to team members. Open and frequent communication can build team trust. Team leaders should build clarity and predictability by setting clear objectives and responsibilities, using clear language, and promoting constructive discourse. Team leaders also need to interpret facts and tasks within the larger context of the enterprise.

Managing virtual team members from different companies requires attention to group formation and norming activities. Where possible, team members should possess strong personal networks. Teams should have time to form personal relationships and identify mutual interests, and leaders should provide opportunities for task-related and social interaction.

Managing virtual team members from different countries requires greater communication about work tasks. An initial face-to-face meeting can allow team members to establish relationships. Regularly scheduled status meetings, adjusted for participation across time zones, should be facilitated and documented (Topi, 2004). Team leaders should distribute documentation in advance to insure review by all team members. Team leaders should track team member participation to identify isolated team members.

Managing virtual team members from different cultures requires additional focus on cultural diversity. Team leaders should provide opportunities for team members to discuss cultures and values, and to address cultural communication differences. Some cultures place great importance on face-to-face interaction, so scheduling periodic face-to-face or video meetings is important.

Managing virtual team members who speak different languages requires educating team members about virtual communication and practicing communicating before beginning virtual work.

Team leaders should identify language interventions including translation. Comprehensive written communication is critical to multi-language virtual teams, but team members will need additional time to review documents and interpret context.

State of Management Practices

Team performance is influenced by a number of factors. Doolen et al. (2006) found that team member satisfaction was most influenced by clear goals, team-level training, and team-level feedback and recognition. Term performance, however, was most influenced by team integration and access to technical and business information systems. These findings suggest that effective management practices may be leveraged by the appropriate use of supporting technologies.

Virtual work tools can improve the "connective richness" of interactions or the "collaborative empowerment" of virtual groups (Townsend et al., 2002). Virtual groups may interact at a deeper level due to easier access to colleagues and information, and may feel more empowered to solve problems due to the collaborative nature of virtual work environments.

Virtual team management is influenced by the nature of the work itself, the context within which

the work is performed, and the virtual work tools used. In some cases, virtual work is reorganized in response to technical problems or lack of employee training (Olson & Olson, 2000). The lack of project management and social networking features of many conferencing or collaboration tools exacerbates these problems.

Enterprises may stretch the capabilities of communication or conferencing systems to support collaboration projects. Periodic conferencing may not be effective if the project is not effectively managed. Virtual team leaders may be pressed to start virtual work projects without adequate team member training or relationship building. Businesses may not recognize the overhead of training, project management, knowledge management, or perhaps translation services.

FRAMEWORKS FOR MANAGING VIRTUAL WORK

Based on a review of the literature, we propose two frameworks (Table 3) to describe virtual work tools and management practices: a "technology services framework" and a parallel "virtual services management framework."

Table 3. Technology and virtual services frameworks

Technology Services Framework			Virtual Services Management Framework
TCP/IP Model	*Web Services Model*	*Virtual Work Tools*	
|	Discovery	|	Enterprise Knowledge Practices
|	Business Services	Collaboration	Virtual Group Management
|	Applications	Conferencing	Practices
|	|	|	Enterprise Workgroup Practices
|	|	|	Business Process Decisions
Application	Technologies	Communication	Intellectual Property & Security
|	|	|	Policies
Transport	|	|	Enterprise Architecture Decisions
Internet	|	|	Business Practice Decisions
Net Interface	|	|	Strategic Technology Assessment
|	|	|	|
			|
			Business Strategy Decisions

Technology Services Framework

Our technology services framework aligns the TCP/IP model—an international standard—with a generalized Web services model, which we believe to be the likely future architecture for enterprise technologies.

The TCP/IP reference model is a four-level model where a physical network interface uses Internet standards to transport data generated by applications. TCP/IP is leveraged by telecommunications firms and Internet service providers to establish bundled network interface, transport, and Internet services as commodities to customers. Enterprises need to be aware of the availability, reliability, and costs of these commodities where they plan to conduct business.

The Web services model, adapted from multiple sources, uses a set of underlying technologies and applications to present bundled business services to end-users. A key component of the Web services model is discovery, where intelligent agents identify Web services appropriate to support business process tasks.

We next align virtual work tools—communication, conferencing, and collaboration—against the TCP/IP and Web services models. We consider the evolution of virtual work tools in light of Nolan's (2001) description of technology stages and cycles, where technology evolves in stages and follows a cycle of innovation, contagion, control, and integration. Communication tools are deployed at a relatively low level as TCP/IP applications. Conferencing tools are placed below Web services applications as they do not require application integration. Collaboration tools are placed at the Web services discovery level as collaboration can be improved by presence awareness and discovery.

Globalization de-emphasizes face-to-face communication and can leverage intellectual capital generated by employees and collaborators. Increased and sometimes discontinuous use of communication, conferencing, and collaboration tools can result.

Virtual Services Management Framework

Our virtual services management framework results from a review of expert observations, experiments, and case studies. Akkirman and Harris (2004) state that a successful virtual work environment requires infrastructure, process-focused organization structure, paperless organization, training, and "managing by results." Bharadwaj and Saxena (2005) propose a framework for global team management including a technology platform, norms and project management, processes and knowledge management, knowledge aggregation, and leadership. Olson and Olson (2000) propose measures of "technology readiness" and "collaboration readiness" to support virtual teams.

The virtual services management framework aligns with the technology services framework in recognition of technology readiness issues. However, the virtual services management framework focuses on the enterprise and management issues introduced earlier. Multiple layers of the framework are likely to be active at a given time, but we address the layers individually below.

Business Strategy Decisions

Business strategy decisions focus on how the business will gain competitive advantage. In a global environment where commodity services are available from many providers, businesses may lack competitive focus and may therefore compete only on price and "virtually guarantee a profitless existence" (Carr, 2004).

We know that unique business processes and intellectual capital can yield sustainable competitive advantage (Porter, 1985). Virtual work tools can contribute to competitive advantage by leveraging unique organizational capabilities and proprietary information. Carr (2004) claims that, "new technologies will never conquer cutthroat competition," so strategy decisions must balance the need for free-flowing information with the need to protect proprietary assets.

Business strategy decisions documents core competencies, market positioning, plans to gain competitive advantage, and guidelines for balancing information sharing with protection.

Strategic Technology Assessment

A strategic technology assessment estimates the potential for using technology to support business strategy. The assessment provides a "reality check" link between business strategy, business practices, and virtual work tools.

Global networking trends impact businesses whose strategy dictates global competition and collaboration. If global networking capabilities are not considered, organizations "may be adopting technologies that will limit their potential for global growth by setting their infrastructure requirements beyond the reach of many geographic regions" (Morris & McManus, 2002).

The strategic technology assessment should evaluate evolving technologies from the perspectives of stages, adoption cycles, commoditization, and "buy versus build." An inaccurate assessment of a potential new technology may lead to acquiring a technology that is not used by partners or customers. Predicting the availability and pricing of hosted services has long-term consequences for deploying virtual work tools.

The strategic technology assessment generates projections for network infrastructure and services, a review of emerging technologies, and an approach to buying or building the firm's technology infrastructure.

Business Practice Decisions

Business practice decisions broadly define how business will be conducted. The business should consider its need or centralized versus decentralized operations, and how much tactical and strategic work will be conducted internally or with partners. With more workers employed at remote sites, the enterprise may need to deal with multiple employment regulations in other states or countries (Karoly, 2004).

The business should also consider how much work will be cooperative or collaborative. Cooperative tasks are divided into independent subtasks and managed hierarchically, but collaborative tasks are organized as intertwined layers. Cooperative work requires synchronicity only when assembling partial results, but collaborative work requires continuous synchronicity to focus on emerging products (Dillenbourg et al., 1995). Communication and conferencing tools can support cooperative work, but collaborative work requires collaboration tools.

Business practice decisions generate a philosophy for conducting work, an organizational framework, and descriptions of employee and partner work. These decisions inform the design of enterprise technology infrastructure, intellectual property policies, and business processes.

Enterprise Architecture Decisions

The enterprise technology architecture—networking, operating systems, databases, and application development framework—supports business strategy and practices. International standards and interoperability should guide architecture decisions wherever possible, but most enterprises implement vendor-supplied application systems containing proprietary code.

The technology architecture must address interoperability at the lower levels of the technology services framework shown in Table 1. At higher levels, semantic interoperability insures exchange of knowledge ontologies, process interoperability insures integration of business process transactions, inter-community interoperability insures information sharing between virtual work tools, and international interoperability addresses differences between technologies, working practices, and government regulations (Chinowsky & Rojas, 2003).

At the virtual work tool level, interoperability needs include synchronization, directory information, access rights, security, service partnerships, and distributed resources (Lyytinen & Yoo, 2002). The flexibility required by virtual and nomadic workers conflicts with the "one size fits all" architecture that leverages economies of scale. Virtual and nomadic work may generate unexpected demands for storage, device management, rich media, data security, and physical security.

With more focus on business processes and employee knowledge, technology architecture may focus less on commodity solutions and more on employee data needs. As Carr (2004) notes, "hierarchies ... may outperform markets when it comes to integrating complex information systems, leading to a reemergence of the vertically integrated company." This next-generation vertically integrated company will require an architecture that supports rapid deployment and retirement of virtual work environments (Beardsley et al., 2006).

Architecture decisions define a technology framework on which application systems and virtual work tools are constructed. Communication tools can be deployed once basic architecture decisions are made. Architecture decisions inform the design of business and work processes.

Intellectual Property and Security Policies

Businesses often make intellectual property and security policy decisions in reaction to unforeseen events. We recommend defining broad intellectual property and security policies before deploying virtual work tools.

Protection of patents, copyright, and trade secrets is problematic in virtual environments where multiple partners work within a "collaboration life cycle" of exploration, joint development, and commercialization (Slowinski et al., 2006). Exploration requires significant exchange of information, while joint development and commercialization require tighter controls. An intellectual property policy should address changing protection needs during the collaboration life cycle, recognizing

that employees may concurrently participate in multiple collaboration phases. Nondisclosure agreements, transfer agreements, joint development agreements, licensing agreements, and service level agreements should support each collaboration phase.

Security policies reflect intellectual property policies, statutory requirements, and contractual obligations. Security policies have shorter life cycles than intellectual property policies, and virtual work requires sophisticated use of access control lists as employees work on multiple projects and within multiple project phases. This need for flexibility conflicts with traditional enterprise security control practices.

Intellectual property and security policy decisions define policies for phases of the collaboration life cycle, frameworks for security practices, and a better understanding of business strategy and business practices.

Business Process Decisions

Business processes—detailed specifications for carrying out business tasks—should be designed concurrently with deployment of business application systems. Business processes should integrate requirements for communication, conferencing, and collaboration tools, and should consider the distinction between cooperative and collaborative work.

Business process decisions yield process definitions, business application requirements, and requirements for virtual work tools. The enterprise can now decide how best to design workgroups.

Enterprise Workgroup Decisions

With business processes and application decisions made, enterprises can define how workgroups will operate. On-site, virtual, or nomadic workgroups but should follow common practices for defining tasks, preparing work plans, documenting progress, and communicating results. On-site and virtual workers should receive training in virtual work tools (Baker et al., 2006). A rigid workgroup design will not meet the needs of tacit workers, who "engage in a larger number of higher-quality tacit interactions when ... hierarchies and silos ... don't get in the way" (Beardsley et al., 2006).

Workgroup design yields workgroup processes, training programs, and integration of virtual work tools. The enterprise can now design advanced virtual work and knowledge management systems. Conferencing tools can be successfully deployed at this stage.

Virtual Group Management Practices

Workgroups now use business applications, communication and conferencing tools, and perhaps Web services. Enterprises needing collaboration tools can now effectively plan for their use.

Virtual group management begins with identifying specific skills and individuals for staffing virtual teams. Programs to integrate workers with different languages or cultural backgrounds should be designed. As employees may participate on several virtual work teams, enterprises should anticipate the overhead of managing multiple virtual environments by simplifying and standardizing workgroup processes. Contingency plans should address a range of issues including natural disasters, technology outages, mergers, or acquisitions.

Training plans for virtual team leaders and participants should address use of collaboration tools, goal setting, project management, communication skills, building trust, managing expectations, facilitating virtual discussions, providing feedback, and resolving conflicts (Kirkman et al., 2002; Chinowsky & Rojas, 2003; deVreede et al., 2004). Virtual workers also need training to troubleshoot and independently solve common technological problems (Topi, 2004).

Virtual group management practices prepare the enterprise to use collaboration tools and to harvest knowledge from its virtual work environment.

Enterprise Knowledge Practices

At the highest level of the framework, application systems may feature Web services discovery

capabilities, business processes should be automated, collaboration tools are deployed, and most workers should be engaged in high levels of tacit and virtual work.

Enterprises can leverage knowledge gained from virtual work into new intellectual capital. Knowledge ontologies support knowledge harvesting from on-site and virtual meetings. Knowledge management specialists design and maintain an enterprise knowledge base. A large-scale virtual knowledge initiative may require a coordinating committee to synthesize global knowledge, managers to support the project in the field, and contributors to add knowledge to collaborative environments (Voelpel et al., 2005).

Enterprises at this level can also support self-governing "learning communities" such as those in Hewlett-Package, Xerox, the World Bank, British Petroleum, IBM, and Siemens (Congla & Rizzuto, 2001). Learning communities tend to be national or international in scope, are responsible for a knowledge domain, but are not formal organizational units. Learning communities can be encouraged by incorporating social networking features into virtual work environments.

Enterprise knowledge practices yield competitive advantage derived from alignment of technology architecture, business processes, workgroup practices, and virtual work management practices. This competitive advantage should align to the business strategy defined at the first level of the framework.

APPROACHES TO DESIGNING ASSESSMENT TOOLS

The technologies and management skills needed to support virtual work are still immature. This is due partly to the rapid consumerization of virtual work tools—PDAs, social networking, wikis, and peer-to-peer networking—not yet integrated into enterprise technology architectures (Beardsley et al., 2006). More important is the rapidly changing nature of work itself. These changes are shifting enterprise investments from improving transactional efficiencies to improving employee intellectual productivity.

We know that technology investments contribute to increased productivity where coordinated investments are also made in non-technology areas of the enterprise (Ko & Kweku-Muata, 2006). Tacit work benefits are particularly difficult to define and may include costs savings and/or avoidance from factors such as reducing duplicate projects, improving the quality of coordination between collaborators, reducing travel and relocation costs, and reducing opportunity costs through better time management (Pickering & Wynn, 2004).

It is therefore important for enterprises to use virtual work planning frameworks to better understand their current technology and virtual work capabilities. Most virtual work planning issues should be addressed iteratively using both planning frameworks. Assessment tools can help estimate current technology and management capabilities.

Use of Technology

We propose a four-stage model (Table 4) to assess an organization's technology capabilities in support of virtual work. The model incorporates a technology readiness model (Olson & Olson, 2000) and a four-stage assessment model for pervasive technology (Gupta & Moitra, 2004).

Several survey approaches can assess technology readiness within this model:

- Measuring the frequency of use of business applications and virtual tools
- Matching frequency of use with perceived or measured employee skills
- Measuring employee use versus perceived importance of business applications of virtual tools
- Measuring employee use versus perceived utility of business applications and virtual tools
- Assessment of infrastructure and business applications by internal IT staff or external consultants

Assessors should recognize that organizations may select different virtual tools to perform the same tasks due to factors such as the urgency of communication, organizational culture, individual preferences, quality of training, technology accessibility, and social distance (Watson-Manheim & Belanger, 2002; Sivunen & Valo, 2006).

Organizational Capabilities

We propose a four-stage model (Table 5) for assessing the organization's capability to support virtual work. The framework incorporates a

Table 4. Model for assessing virtual technology capabilities

Stages	Enterprise Technology Infrastructure	Predominant Business Applications	Predominant Virtual Work Tools
Traditional	Servers and desktops	ERP Web-enabled processes	Telephone, fax, e-mail, Voicemail
Mobile	Mobile devices	Customer Relationship and Supply Chain Management	Cellular telephony, e-mail with attachments, audio conferencing
Integrated	Wireless LANs, ubiquitous communication, and personalization	Real-time CRM and SCM	Videoconferencing, Webcasts, repositories, shared calendaring
Pervasive	Ubiquitous access, enterprise integration and abstraction, content management	Automation, knowledge management	Web collaboration, document tracking, and knowledge management

pervasive computing assessment model (Gupta & Moitra, 2004) and three "dimensions of virtuality" (Chudoba et al., 2005):

- Team distribution: degree to which people work on teams that have people distributed over different geographies and time zones
- Workplace mobility: degree to which employees work in environments other than regular offices
- Variety of practices: degree to which employees experience cultural and work process diversity.

The assessment model can be used to assess the extent of virtual work and may predict the need for conferencing or collaboration tools. Several survey approaches can assess technology readiness within this model:

- Measuring the frequency of use of business applications
- Measuring team member and manager perceptions of team distribution
- Measuring team member and manager perceptions of workplace mobility
- Measuring team member and manager perceptions of types of work practices

Furst et al. (2004) applied Tuckman's group life cycle stages (formation, storming, norming, and performing) to virtual teams and identified potential managerial issues requiring interventions at each stages. Assessors should therefore identify the various collaboration and group life cycles within which virtual workers are operating, as survey responses may vary accordingly.

Measuring Alignment

We have presented frameworks for categorizing virtual work tools (Table 1), the nature of tacit work (Table 2), use of technology (Table 4), and organizational capabilities (Table 5). We propose that a measure of alignment between virtual work tasks, selection of virtual work tools, organizational capabilities, and application of virtual work tools can be developed using these principles:

1. The tacit nature of work and the degree of organizational virtuality should drive the selection of appropriate virtual work tools.
2. Organizations should develop a technology infrastructure and virtual work tool portfolio capable of addressing the most complex virtual work contemplated.

Table 5. Model for Assessing Organizational Capabilities

Stages	Organizational Practices	Team Distribution	Workplace Mobility	Work Practices
Traditional	ERP focus, group and individual communication	Work in same time zone, cultural and workplace homogeneity	Most work at one site, little interaction with outside workers	Familiar teams, processes, and tools
Mobile	Customer relationship management, some mobile workers	Some work across time zones, use of audio conferencing, some language differences	Some work at other sites, some interaction with outside workers	Some work with new teams, tools, processes
Integrated	Mobile workforce with collaboration and real-time management	Frequent work across time zones, use of Web and mobile technology, some cultural and language heterogeneity	Frequent work at other sites, common work with outside workers	Regular work with new teams, tools, processes
Pervasive	Automated and flexible processes, routine collaboration	Constant collaboration across time zones, most work with Web and mobile technology, routine cultural and language heterogeneity	Most work at other sites, work groups often temporary and anonymous	Most work with new teams, tools, processes

3. Organizations should develop a set of virtual work management practices capable of effectively implementing and managing all virtual work tools in its portfolio.
4. Managers should apply the least complex virtual work tool to manage a given virtual work task, project, and/or program.

Future Trends in Virtual Work Tools

We expect continued movement toward IP-based voice communications. The rapid deployment of ubiquitous wireless networks and consumerization of wireless technologies will accelerate development of pervasive computing. This discontinuous change will affect the life cycles of some enterprise infrastructure components (Gupta & Moitra, 2004). Most enterprises support more than three instant messaging services (Osterman Research, 2005), but we expect that most instant messaging providers will soon incorporate VOIP, video, and conferencing services.

Future collaboration tools will help manage context for workers and tasks, identifying who is available to collaborate, what virtual work tools they use, when they can meet, and how they wish to receive background information. Context features are tacit and "do not resemble IT systems or reengineered processes that can be copied easily" (Beardsley et al., 2006). They will require considerable integration, training, and support to be used effectively.

We see the maturation of unified communications that integrate telephony, voicemail, e-mail, conferencing, instant messaging, and corporate data. The widespread adoption of video capture and editing will facilitate integration of video content into virtual work environments and knowledge repositories.

Mature knowledge ontologies will facilitate integrating a wide range of objects into the virtual work environment. Individual objects or object collections need to be described in terms of multiple ontologies. Agent technologies will help manage knowledge repositories, objects, and

communications (Marquès & Navarro, 2001).

Virtual work portals will help manage multiple virtual work environments accessed concurrently by workers (Will et al., 2004). A virtual portal will host several logical portlets and enable workers to customize their view of each portlet.

WHERE DO WE GO FROM HERE?

Friedman (2005) proposes a flattening of the global business world based on his belief that existing and future technologies will drive enterprises and individuals to become increasingly collaborative. This will create a global economy that embraces outsourcing, off-shoring, open-sourcing, supply-chaining, in-sourcing, and informing. The future is already with us—for both large and small enterprises—as described by Indian entrepreneur Rajesh: "Already we have in our gaming industry artists and designers working from home ... making their presence no different than the guy in the next cubicle" (Friedman, 2005, p. 188).

Global collaboration is also important to individuals. Virtual work enables employees, partners, and customers to interact on their own terms (Beardsley, 2006), but team leaders and workers need significant training in both technological and team processes (Townsend et al., 2002). Malhotra (1998) describes the behavior of future knowledge workers:

... [K]nowledge workers would also need to be comfortable with self-control and self-learning. In other words, they would need to act in an intrapreneurial mode that involves a higher degree of responsibility and authority as well as capability and intelligence for handling both.

Increasing fossil fuel costs due to global economic growth will cause companies to shift space, energy, and technology costs to partners through virtual work or to employees through telework. Virtual teleworkers need bandwidth, Web services, security, backup, and business continuity services. We see integration between enterprise, home, vehicle, and personal systems as one way of addressing these challenges.

Traditional enterprise technology investments have been necessarily monolithic, with benefits of transactional labor efficiency and some downstream improvements to transformational labor efficiency. The next generation of investments must leverage this efficient transactional base and "make tacit employees better at their jobs by complementing and extending their tacit capabilities and activities" (Johnson et al., 2005). This change can be facilitated by adopting federated approaches to enterprise technology governance where virtual workers participate in setting standards and practices (Ross & Weill, 2004).

There are numerous opportunities for virtual work research focused the intersection of enterprise and individual behavior, as well as on the intersection between technologies and behaviors. Nilan and D'Eredita (2005) propose experimental approaches involving collaboration between information providers and consumers. Voida et al. (2002) propose approaches to investigate how knowledge workers classify information and then act on that information. The agenda for the CSCW 2006 conference includes topics such as managing project team redundancy and interruptions, managing e-mail messages, filtering multiple collaboration alerts, social networking, persistent collaborative relationships, and personal learning spaces (CSCW, 2006).

The frameworks and assessment models presented in this chapter provide enterprises with approaches to assess virtual work needs and capabilities to maximize their return on investments in virtual work tools. The frameworks and assessment models can also be used by individuals to identify personal learning opportunities for success in virtual work environments, and by researchers to extend our understanding of how we will work in tomorrow's virtual environment.

REFERENCES

Baker, A., Avery, G., & Crawford, J. (2006). Home alone: The role of technology in telecommuting. *Information Resources Management Journal, 19*(4), 1-22.

Barczak, F., McDonough, E., & Athanassiou, N. (2006). So you want to be a global project leader? *Research Technology Management, 49*(3), 28-35.

Beardsley, S., Johnson, B., & Manyika, J. (2006). Competitive advantage from better interactions. *McKinsey Quarterly, 2006*(2), 53-63.

Bharadwaj, S., & Saxena, K. (2005). Knowledge management in global software systems. *Vikalpa, 30*(4), 65-75.

Boase, J., Jorrigan, J., Wellman, B., & Rainie, L. (2006). *The strength of internet ties.* Washington, D.C.: Pew Internet & American Life Project. Retrieved August 21, 2006 from http://www.pewinternet.org/PPF/r/172/report_display.asp.

Brake, T. (2006). Leading global virtual teams. *Industrial and Commercial Training, 38*(3), 116-121.

Carr, N. (2004). In praise of walls. *MIT Sloan Management Review, spring,* 10-13.

Chinowsky, P., & Rojas, E. (2003). Virtual teams: Guide to successful implementation. *Journal of Management in Engineering, 19*(3), 98-106.

Chudoba, K., Winn, E., Lu, M., & Watson-Manheim, M. (2005). How virtual are we? Measuring virtuality and understanding its impact in a global organization. *Information Systems Journal, 15*(4), 279-306.

Congla, P., & Rizzuto, C. (2001). Evolving communities of practice: IBM Global Services experience. *IBM Systems Journal, 40*(1).

CSCW. (2006). Retrieved August 21, 2006 from http://www.cscw2006.org/.

deVreede, G., Davison, R., & Briggs, R. (2003). How a silver bullet may lost its shine. *Communications of the ACM, 46*(8), 96-101.

Dillenbourg, P., Baker, M., Blaye, A., & O'Malley, C. (1995). The evolution of research on collaborative learning. In: P. Reimann& H. Spada (Ed.), *Learning in humans and machines: Towards an interdisciplinary learning science* (pp. 189-211). London: Permagon,

Doolen, T., Hacker, M., & Van Aken, E. (2006). Managing organizational context for engineering team effectiveness. *Team Performance Management, 12*(5-6), 138-154.

Furst, S., Reeves, M., Rosen, B., & Blackburn, R. (2004). Managing the life cycle of virtual teams. *Academy of Management Executive, 18*(2), 6-20.

Gupta, P., & Moitra, D. (2004). Evolving a pervasive IT infrastructure: a technology integration approach. *Pers Ubiquit Comput, 8,* 31-41.

Hitch, L., & McCord, S. (2004). Of nomadicity, expectations, campus IT infrastructure and, oh yes, budget. EDUCAUSE Evolving Technologies Committee. Retrieved August 19, 2006 from http://www.educause.edu/LibraryDetailPage/666?ID=DEC0404.

Holtshouse, D. (2006). The future of the future: The future workplace. *KMWorld*, May 26.Retrieved September 8, 2006 from http://www.kmworld.com/Articles/ReadArticle.aspx?ArticleID=15811.

Java Community Process. (2006). Java Portlet API Specification (JSR 168). Retrieved August 19, 2006 from http://www.jcp.org/en/jsr/detail?id=168.

Johnson, B., Manyika, J., & Yee, L. (2005). The next revolution in interactions. *McKinsey Quarterly, 2005*(4), 21-33.

Joyce, A. (2004). Executives leave corner offices behind. *Washington Post*, September 26 (F05). http://www.washingtonpost.com/wp-dyn/articles/A48295-2004Sep24.html.

Karoly, L., & Panis, C. (2004). The 21st century at work: Forces shaping the future workforce and workplace in the United States. Santa Monica, CA: Rand Corporation.

Kirkman, B., Rosen, B., Gibson, C., Tesluk, P., & McPherson, S. (2002). Five challenges to virtual team success: Lessons from Sabre, Inc. *Academy of Management Executive, 16*(3), 67-79.

Kleinrock, L. (2001). Breaking loose. *Communications of the ACM, 44*(9), 41-45.

Ko, M., & Kweku-Muata, O. (2006). Analyzing the impact of information technology investments using regression and data mining techniques. *Journal of Enterprise Information Management, 19*(4), 402-417.

Liang, S., Lee, J., Chen, S., & Shiau, J. (2001). Networked collaborative environment for hydro-engineering. *International Journal of Computational Engineering Science, 2*(4), 557-567.

Logan, S., & Muller, M., Ethnographic study of collaborative knowledge work. *IBM Systems Journal, 45*(4), 759-772.

Lyytinen, K., & Yoo, Y. (2002). The next wave of nomadic computing: a research agenda for information systems research. *Information Systems Research, 13*(4), 377-388.

Malhotra, Y. (1998). Knowledge management, knowledge organizations and knowledge workers: a view from the front lines. Retrieved September 24, 2006, from http://www.brint.com/interview/maeil.htm.

Marquès, J., & Navarro, L. (2001). WWG: A wide-area infrastructure to support groups. *Proceedings of the 2001 international ACM SIG-GROUP conference on supporting group work* (pp. 179-187).

Morris, S., & McManus, D. (2002). Information infrastructure centrality in the agile organization. *Information Systems Management, 19*(4), 8-12.

Nilan, M., & D'Eredita, M. (2005). Organizations as virtual communities: A sense-making approach for uniting knowledge consumers and knowledge workers. *International Journal of Web Based Communities, 1*(3), 262-271.

Nolan, R. (2001). *Information technology management from 1960-2000.* Cambridge, MA: Harvard Business School Press.

Olson, G., & Olson, J. (2000). Distance matters. *Human-Computer Interaction, 15,* 139-178.

Osterman Research. (2005). Critical success factors for deploying real-time collaboration. Retrieved August 21, 2006 from http://www.sitescape.com/whitepapers/pdf/wp001.pdf.

Pickering, C., & Wynn, E. (2004). An architecture and business process framework for global team collaboration. *Intel Technology Journal, 8*(4), 373-382.

Porter, M. (1985). *Competitive advantage: Creating and sustaining superior performance.* New York, NY: The Free Press.

Slowinski, G., Hummel, E., & Kumpf, R. (2006). Protecting know-how and trade secrets in collaborative R&D relationships. *Research Technology Management, 49*(4), 30-38.

Sivunen, A., & Valo, M. (2006). Team leaders' technology choices in virtual teams. *IEEE Transactions on Professional Communication, 49*(1).

TikiWiki. (2006). Retrieved September 24, 2006 from http://tikiwiki.org/tiki-index.php.

Topi, H. (2004). Supporting telework: Obstacles and solutions. *Academy of Management Executive, summer,* 79-85.

Travel Industry Association of America. (2004). Business and convention travelers, 2004 edition. Washington, D.C.: Travel Industry Association of America.

Townsend, A., Hendrickson, A., & DeMarie, S. (2002). Meeting the virtual work imperative. *Communications of the ACM, 45*(1), 23-26.

Voelpel, S., Dous, M., & Davenport, T. (2005). Five steps to creating a global knowledge-sharing system: Siemens Sharenet. *Academy of Management Executive, 19*(2), 9-21.

Voida, S. Mynatt, E., MacIntyre, B., & Corso, G. (2002). Integrating virtual and physical context to support knowledge workers. *IEEE Pervasive Computing, 1*(3), 73-79.

Watson-Manheim, M., & Belanger, F. (2002). Support for communication-based work processes in virtual work. *e-Service Journal, 1*(3), 61-82.

WebCollab. (2006). Retrieved September 24, 2006 from http://webcollab.sourceforge.net/.

Weill, P., & Ross, J. (2004). *IT governance: How top performers manage IT decision rights for superior results.* Cambridge, MA: Harvard Business School Press.

Will, R., Ramaswamy, S., & Schaeck, T. (2004). WebSphere Portal: Unified user access to content, applications and services. *IBM Systems Journal, 43*(2), 420-429.

Wilson, P. (1991). *Computer supported cooperative work: An introduction.* Oxford, England: Intellect.

KEY TERMS

Collaboration Tools: Advanced virtual work tools generally consisting of shared document development spaces, document repositories, project management and calendaring tools, and integrated conferencing and communication tools.

Communication Tools: Virtual work tools including e-mail, telephone, facsimile, and office productivity tools.

Conferencing Tools: Virtual work tools that enable multiple workers to collaborate in real time using audio and video feeds.

Enterprise Technologies: Technologies deployed for use by all workers in an enterprise, generally featuring data or process integration between the individual components.

Governance: The processes established to make investment decisions about the use of technology, including gathering input, weighing options, and making decisions.

Infrastructure: Shared technology components that support deployment of business application systems and virtual work systems.

Learning Community: An informal network of subject matter experts who choose to collaborate with each other to discuss issues, interpret information, and generate knowledge and best practices.

Networked Individualism: A phenomenon where individuals interact with network resources and information on their own terms.

Nomadicity: A phenomenon where individuals perform work from a number of locations and rarely from a central office.

Pervasive Computing: A technology environment that supports nomadic workers using wireless networking, context awareness, personalization, and human-device interaction.

Portal: A gateway to multiple Internet-based services, generally customizable by the end-user.

Tacit Work: requiring workers to exercise experiential judgment and collaboration.

Technology Architecture: A framework for building an enterprise including networking, hardware, operating systems, database management systems, and application development standards.

Telework: A phenomenon where a worker will perform most or all of his or her professional work at home.

Virtual Work: Work performed in a different geographic location from co-workers or supervisors.

Virtualization: The abstraction of enterprise technology resources such as servers or storage devices which support the operation of multiple virtual resources on a single device.

Chapter XXVI
Writing Research into Professional E–Mail Communication

Kirstie Edwards
Sheffield Hallam University, UK

Simeon Yates
Sheffield Hallam University, UK

Anne-Florence Dujardin
Sheffield Hallam University, UK

Geff Green
Sheffield Hallam University, UK

ABSTRACT

A healthy balance between social and task-oriented activities helps teamwork. In virtual teams, e-mail texts must often carry both task-oriented and socio-emotional communication between individuals. While some theories of computer-mediated communication suggest socio-emotional exchange may not be well supported in e-mail communications, research demonstrates that individuals, nevertheless, achieve this. However, the lack of unplanned informal exchanges in virtual teams communicating by e-mail may still hinder team performance. We compared adaptations in socio-emotional content of e-mail communications in academic and commercial team writing contexts. Results suggested a task-oriented focus in the commercial team culture and an even social-task balance in the academic team culture. Our research leads us to recommend a more conversational style in professional e-mail writing. Additionally in virtual team working, we recommend encouraging face-to-face contact, allocating time specifically for social exchanges and making information about colleagues available to each other.

INTRODUCTION

This chapter focuses on semi-virtual team writing projects in an academic and a commercial environment. Team performance peaks and declines with increasing group cohesion, suggesting an optimal balance between sociability levels in the team and dedication to the goal. Socio-emotional communications, which help to develop group cohesion or a sense of team spirit, thus benefit team performance (Argyle, 1994; Hyland, 1998; Barker et al., 2000; Panteli, 2004) and are therefore relevant to virtual team management. Our research has used content analysis of the socio-emotional components of e-mail exchanges during writing projects to explore the teams' task and social orientations, which we describe as the team cultures. Studying adaptations of e-mail behaviour with writing influences such as purpose, receiver and context, describes the team cultures and has the potential to inform on social influences and behavioural norms. Before describing our research, we first review the relevant literature underpinning our approach.

E-MAIL, PERFORMANCE AND SOCIABILITY

Team Culture and Performance

Teamwork requires both task and socially-oriented activities. While task-oriented activities are essential to achieve team goals, it is also important to understand the impact of the social dimension on team performance. We discuss here evidence from the literature suggesting that the balance between task and socio-emotional dimensions in teams affects the welfare of the group.

Kelly and Duran (1985) define group cohesion as "the extent to which members of a group stick together, like and respect one another and feel unified" (p. 186). These researchers studied the cohesiveness and performance of seven groups of students working on problem-solving tasks, for which they had to prepare an oral and written report. Using Bales and Cohen's adjective rating method, they derived a group average score from member scores of perceived behaviour rated on three dimensions: dominant vs. submissive, friendly vs. unfriendly and instrumental vs. emotionally expressive. They interpreted group cohesion from close clustering of scores for members' perceptions of one another and themselves on these dimensions. Groups with either very high or low group cohesion scores did not perform well, from which the researchers concluded that an optimal level of group cohesion might exist; they caution, however, that the study was small in scale.

Evans and Dion (1991) completed a meta analysis of 16 studies on group cohesion and performance. The performance of teamwork in these studies was easily measurable, for example the performance of a sports team. The results may not be applicable, therefore, to real work groups, such as virtual writing teams, where performance is less overtly measurable. The researchers also point out that results may be influenced by different methods used to assess group cohesiveness and by the retrieval bias of only studying published research. However, their results clearly suggest a positive relationship between group cohesion and performance. Mortensen and Hinds (2001) studied 24 teams and found that shared identity was significantly associated with performance, and Timmerman and Scott (2006) have shown that communicative predictors affect virtual team outcomes in terms of perceived cohesiveness, trust and satisfaction. In their study of global virtual teams in a high tech multinational organization, Tucker and Panteli (2003) found that the teams which worked well included a "social and fun element in their computer-mediated interactions, which appeared to have helped in creating stronger relationships" (Tucker & Panteli, 2003; Panteli, 2004 , p. 76).

Also of particular significance to the social dimension of working is the lack of opportunity for informal communication offered in virtual workplaces (Keyzerman, 2003). In their study of collaborations between scientific researchers, Kraut and colleagues (1988) identified the value of informal interpersonal communication in building collaborations, a social interaction missing from dispersed collaborations. The likelihood of collaboration was higher between scientific researchers who were physically located close to one another than between those on different floors or in different buildings, which the researchers attributed to frequency of communications: "The informal contact that results from frequent opportunities for communication often leads to collaboration" (Kraut et al., 1988, p. 5).

Results of further research demonstrated that physical proximity is strongly related to frequency of communication during both the planning stage and writing stage of the research process. The results suggest that co-authors with adjacent offices communicated twice as often as those pairs who were simply co-located on the same floor. Co-location increases frequency of interaction, which in turn increases the likelihood of collaborators liking each other and therefore of further collaboration (Kraut et al., 1988). When Kraut and colleagues (1988) published their research, they were able to draw on earlier research showing that the phenomenon was not restricted to face-to-face (FtF) communication. They present the results of earlier research by Allen (1977 cited in Kraut et al., 1988), whose study focused on industrial research and development engineers, and showed a logarithmic decline in FtF communication frequency with distance between potential communicators. Mayer (1976 cited in Kraut et al., 1988) had shown decreasing communications mediated by telephone with increasing distance between collaborators, and Eveland and Bikson (1987) had shown the same for communications mediated by e-mail.

Reduced communication frequency with distance led Kraut and his colleagues to conclude that "much communication between actual and potential research partners is not planned and would not occur if it had to be planned" (Kraut et al., 1988, p. 9). From interviews designed to explore the effect of quality of communication on collaboration, Kraut and colleagues concluded that "informal communication is important because it allows researchers to develop common interests with their neighbours" (1988, p. 7). Most of their interviewees supervised subordinates and coordinated with peers during casual hallway and lunchroom meetings, just as often as during formal pre-arranged meetings. Kraut and colleagues therefore emphasise not only the lower expenses, for example, travel and telephone costs to maintain dispersed collaborations, but also how "'on the fly" interactions are impossible in collaborations that occur over a distance' (1988, p. 8). Proximity allows people to inexpensively and informally assess how well they might work together. Once they are working together, frequent low-cost communications allow team members to chase work and report to each other informally in casual exchanges, and to share decisions and develop a sense of co-ownership of the work (Kraut et al., 1988).

Virtual working raises the question of whether social presence can match the richness of that in the real world, not for example because social cues visible in FtF scenarios are missing from lean, textual e-mail media, but because the communications are wilful and task-oriented, rather than coincidental and unplanned. "Many of the interactions that make up this feedback over time are damaged by intentionality and simply would not occur if they must be wilfully initiated" (Kraut et al., 1988, p. 9). An interpersonal communication will not arise by chance in the virtual workplace as a result of other human activities, as it might in the real world. The research by Kraut and colleagues (1988) suggests that this type of unplanned informal communication is extremely valuable to teamwork. Textual, computer-mediated interactions such as e-mail, however, preclude such opportunities.

Strong evidence in the literature, therefore, supports the notion that the social dimension in teamwork contributes in a positive way to the performance of the team. This suggests that pro-social behaviour may be as relevant to performance as professional skills (Argyle, 1994; Hyland, 1998; Barker et al., 2000; Panteli, 2004). Damrau (2006) and many other researchers recognize the value of socio-emotional communication in virtual teams (e.g., Nickerson, 2000; Pauleen & Yoong, 2001; Panteli, 2004). Being able to support such communication by e-mail is therefore important to a team's effectiveness. A discussion of how computer-mediated communication (CMC) might influence social behaviour is outside of the scope of this chapter, but relevant however to this research. We therefore discuss briefly the stance from which we developed our research approach.

Theories of CMC tend to fall into two categories: 'deficit theories' (Thurlow et al., 2004, p. 48), and the more social interactive theories. Examples of deficit theories are *media richness* (Daft & Lengel, 1984), *lack of social context cues* (Sproull & Kiesler, 1986) and *social presence* (Short et al., 1976 cited in Walther & Parks, 2002) theories. These are underpinned by technological characteristics of the media, suggesting for example, that lack of audio or visual content in e-mail may inhibit socio-emotional exchanges, and result in more task-oriented exchanges. Here lies a paradox: deficit theories suggest that CMC supporting virtual workplaces may inhibit socio-emotional communication. However, socio-emotional communication helps to maintain the social dimension of team working, which is known to contribute positively to performance. The more social interactive theories, such as social influence (Schmitz & Fulk, 1991), deindividuation (Postmes et al., 1998), social information processing (Walther, 1992) and adaptive structuration (Burke & Aytes, 1998), consider the influences of context, relationships and dynamics. Social information processing and adaptive structuration theories suggest that strategies will be developed with time to achieve similar levels of socio-emotional communication in CMC as in non-mediated communication. Indeed, research has demonstrated this and we now describe some of the strategies being used.

Strategies supporting socio-emotional communication in e-mails include self-disclosure, providing identity information, uncertainty reduction behaviours, politeness and articulations over presence. Self-disclosure and expressions of positive and negative affect represent uninhibited behaviour, and are elements of socio-emotional communication. Sproull and Kiesler (1986) discuss the positive influences of uninhibited behaviour on the task dimension, quoting communication and innovation literature. The structural and social barriers which impede communication and innovation are removed with e-mail, allowing creativity, and leading to new ideas (Sproull & Kiesler, 1986). Taylor (2000) found in her study of e-mail discussions set in a working environment, that there was more self-disclosure in the less anonymous scenario, that is, the more subjects knew about others, the more they tended to disclose about themselves. Providing identity information in this research therefore promoted socio-emotional communication and group cohesion (Taylor, 2000). Taylor's findings thus suggest that an intervention (making information about team members available) is a strategy to promote socio-emotional communication and encourage group cohesion.

Tidwell and Walther's (2002) experimental study with 158 students compared CMC and FtF interaction in first meetings and showed that CMC users adapt to the medium through the modification of uncertainty reduction behaviours. Without nonverbal cues, CMC partners abandoned the socially acceptable questions and answers characteristic among new acquaintances in FtF situations. CMC participants adopted "more direct, interactive uncertainty reduction strategies—intermediate questioning and disclosing with their partners—than did their FTF counterparts. The probes and replies they exchanged were more intimate and led to levels of attributional confidence similar to their offline counterparts" (Tidwell & Walther, 2002, p. 339). In this study, similar to Taylor's (2000) research, e-mail did not appear to inhibit self-disclosure. Tidwell and Walther's work also supports the concept of adaptive structuration playing a role in e-mail communications, in which interactions, rather than technology or individual attributes, are influential.

Politeness strategies are another example of how e-mail communications can present a positive valence contributing to group cohesion. Harrison (2000a) applied Brown and Levinson's (1987) framework of politeness strategies in spoken discourse to an analysis of politeness strategies in 23 consecutive e-mails from a naturally occurring e-mail discussion group. She found many instances of politeness strategies in the e-mail discourse. Of particular note in this study was the fact that participants were using predominantly positive strategies, which reduce social distance and relative power, thus promoting discussion in a safe atmosphere, and strengthening the group (Harrison, 2000a).

Recent work by Panteli (2004) has focused on explicit articulations of presence. In 432 e-mails from a virtual project involving 25 remote team members, Panteli (2004) identified how participants talked about their own and others' presence in the virtual team environment. In such articulations, or absence of such articulations, writers provide a form of self-disclosure and inform on their availability. "Presence was discursively negotiated and renegotiated and constructed even through words and e-mails that were never said" (Panteli, 2004, p. 73). He gives the example of writers talking about their absences, which implies a "do not disturb" message. "The negotiations that they enter into with their team members to define their presence in the shared-mediated environment have contributed to forming and maintaining boundaries between … environments" (Panteli, 2004, p. 75). Panteli thus contributes to the debate over whether boundaries to virtual teams exist, by showing that individuals actively create boundaries between their shared mediated and non-shared environments through the messages they articulate, and also through implied messages articulated through silence.

This aspect is of particular significance to socio-emotional exchange in virtual teams. In FtF or virtual teams, Panteli points out that "members are expected to be present and to develop personally engaging behaviours in role performances …the virtual context, by its nature allows team members to be 'absent' and 'silent'", which can contribute to relationship problems and feelings of isolation (Panteli, 2004, p. 77). Thus, Panteli highlights a separate issue to that of the opportunity of transmitting rich unambiguous information as afforded in FtF scenarios, and that is lack of social restrictions or boundaries to the virtual team construct, which affords the opportunity of absence, not afforded in teams which are physically collocated. This is an interesting issue similar to the topic of informal communication opportunities offered by physical presence—the absence opportunities offered by virtual presence.

Various socio-emotional exchange strategies are thus being used in CMC:

- providing personal information on team members encourages self-disclosure and group cohesion (Taylor, 2000)
- self modification of uncertainty reduction behaviours results in less inhibited behaviour, for example, increased self-disclosure (Tidwell & Walther, 2002)
- positive politeness strategies reduce social distance, contributing to team solidarity (Harrison, 2000a)
- explicit articulations on absence and presence provide an element of self-disclosure (Panteli, 2004) and can inform on social boundaries

Research has shown not only that e-mail can support socio-emotional exchanges, but that specific strategies have developed to achieve this, in support of the social interactive theories of mediated communication. In virtual and semi-virtual teams therefore, where the social interactions are predominantly by e-mail, these

Figure 1. E-mails as social interactions reflecting team culture

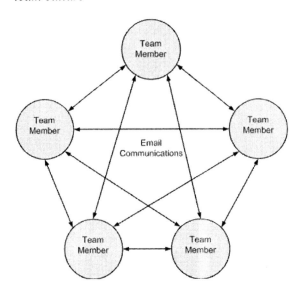

communications provide data for studying team cultures (Figure 1).

E-Mail Style as a Social Interactive Data Source

Before describing our method of e-mail content analysis, we first discuss researchers' views on e-mail style, its evolution and its modality. Many researchers are debating whether the language of CMC veers towards written or spoken discourse, or has perhaps developed a style of its own (e.g., Ferrara et al., 1991; Yates & Orlikowski, 1993; Yates, 1996; Harrison, 2000b; Baron, 2001). Danet (2001) has predicted that e-mail style will become increasingly less formal, particularly regarding greetings, and that the differences between official and personal e-mails will lessen; this style will become expected and therefore accepted as legitimate; variation in public-official e-mail writing will be greater than in traditional letter writing, but certain letter-writing characteristics will persist in certain sensitive scenarios, particularly in first e-mails which represent a virtual first meeting, in upward communications to people of higher status, to strangers, and where there is high risk for the writer. She also predicts that

"as e-mail matures... different text-types will come to have different degrees of normatively approved formality" (Danet, 2001, p. 94), with the more normatively formal style paralleling formal text-types on paper. Her final prediction is that younger people, unaccustomed to traditional letter-writing, will adopt the new style, even in the sensitive scenarios described above. "They will do so with little ambivalence or uncertainty, and will feel comfortable introducing playful material, e.g., a signature file, even when the rest of the letter is in a serious frame" (Danet, 2001, p. 94).

Postmes et al. (2000) studied the evolution of communicative norms in e-mails amongst students. They showed that content and form of communication is normative and defined by group norms, conformity to group norms increases over time and communication outside the group has different social norms. They argue that "the content of communication within CMC will be contextually determined and influenced not only by the general norms of the subcultural milieu ...but also the specific local norms and practices of the communicating group" (Postmes et al., 2000 p. 366). They conclude from their study that the content and form of messages are variable, socially structured, and subject to emergent norms specific to one's social group.

Baron (2001) predicts the likelihood of two styles of e-mail, one formal (edited) and one informal (unedited). She points out that frequent e-mail users may switch off automated editors and may even choose not to manually edit, thus communicating in an informal way, whereas on the other hand "a contract is still a contract" (Baron, 2001, p. 242), requiring accuracy, editing and thereby more formal communication. Crystal (2001) too recognizes the increasing use of e-mail in professional settings in addition to its use for more informal personal communications. "The result will be a medium which will portray a wide range of stylistic expressiveness, from formal to informal, just as other mediums have come to do, and where the pressure on users will be to display stylistic consistency in the same way that this is required in other forms of writing" (Crystal, 2001, p. 128).

Gains (1999) throws a different perspective on the question of whether e-mail leans towards written or oral language, showing a distinction between academic and commercial discourse communities. In a small scale study of 116 e-mails in academic and commercial settings, he found that academic e-mails were less formal with more social chat, that is, more like conversation, whereas e-mails from a commercial environment were more like written business language. From an empirical perspective, Yates (1996) has shown that speech, writing and CMC can be differentiated through type/token, lexical density, pronoun use and modality analyses. Yates and Orlikowski (1993) argue from their quantitative analysis of 1,353 messages between computer language designers using the ARPANET in the early 80s, that e-mail shows "characteristics of both written and spoken discourse, as well as characteristics seemingly unique to electronic discourse" (Yates & Orlikowski, 1993, p. 13).

The debate over whether e-mail has its own style(s), the influences on that style and whether such a style is yet fully developed is thus ongoing. The important point is that there are identifiable traits in e-mail styles, that these traits can be quantified, and that by analysing them, we can explore deeper to understand their significance, influence on, and representation of virtual and semi-virtual team cultures. Researchers of writing and communications support this concept: Faigley writes that "Words carry the contexts in which they have been used" (Faigley, 1985, p. 240). Texts are thus not stand-alone artefacts independent of their context of production and use. "Not only must the text carry the social situation, it must also carry the participants' relationship to the situation, their perception of the relationships between the knowledge and objects under discussion" (Yates, 1996, p. 46). E-mail texts are the social exchange and carry socio-emotional content which represents the relationship between the sender and receiver. This socio-emotional meta-

discourse in e-mail texts allows us to extract and interpret representations (Edwards et al., 2006). Indeed, much research has explored this opportunity, for example, studying e-mail paragraph length (Crystal, 2001), e-mail greeting style (e.g., Sproull & Kiesler, 1986; Sherblom, 1988; Gains, 1999; Nickerson, 2000; Crystal, 2001; Danet, 2001), and use of first person pronouns as indicators of intimacy or solidarity in e-mails (Nickerson, 2000; Vaes et al., 2002). E-mail style, extracted from interpersonal markers in this way can be used to interpret and understand the social-task balance in virtual workplaces.

Although the debate continues as to whether e-mail is more similar to spoken or written communication, Nystrand's (1989) social interactive model of writing recognizes text as a communicative event with a context of production and reception (Nystrand, 1989), and therefore no more autonomous than speech. E-mail text is thus the negotiation of meaning between writer and reader. "We conceptualize text meaning, not in terms of the writer alone, but in terms of interaction between writer and reader purpose" (Nystrand, 1989, p. 76). E-mail authors thus achieve a shared understanding with their receivers by anticipating the reader context and needs and adapting their writing behaviour accordingly (see Figure 2). The team culture is reflected through the team members' adaptations to achieve shared understanding in their team communications, which in virtual teams, are often mediated through e-mails.

Review

In this section, we have explored a number of key concepts which underpin our research approach:

- A social dimension benefits virtual team working;
- Although some theories of CMC suggest that socio-emotional communication is not carried in e-mail texts, research shows that strategies have been developed to achieve this;

Figure 2. Social interactive e-mail communication

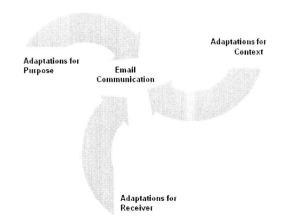

- E-mail texts thus carry a socio-emotional metadiscourse, which can be analysed to describe the social-task balance of teams and interpret team cultures.

Our research has tentatively explored this concept by mapping adaptations in semi-virtual academic and commercial writing projects against Nystrand's (1989) model of social interactive writing. We briefly describe this research and the findings relevant to virtual teams in the following section.

CONVERSATIONAL STYLE: A PERSPECTIVE FROM RESEARCH

Method

Our research studied team culture, described by the balance of task and social dimensions in academic and commercial team writing contexts, by analysing e-mail communications recorded during the writing projects. The commercial project produced manuals for hardware installation and the academic project produced handouts for a postgraduate clinical training course. Researching real-life writing practices introduces many inconsistencies between the projects, of course. For example, the commercial project had six main

team members, whereas the academic project had eighteen. The commercial project was fairly short-term, lasting two months, although the client-supplier relationship was longer term. At the time of writing this chapter, the academic project had been running since 2002 and was ongoing.

E-mail contents were coded to extract *Receiver, Context and Purpose* to interpret adaptations of markers against Nystrand's (1989) social interactive model of written communication. The *Context* variable described the direction either in the client-supplier relationship, for example, an e-mail sent from the client to the supplier, or in the society organization, for example, an e-mail from the president to the course leader. *Purposes* were interpretively coded into distinguishable subtasks of the main project goal. Example purposes are *review discussion, to transfer drafts, courtesy, management,* and so forth.

We studied several markers of pro-social behaviour to help strengthen interpretations: elaboration in body text and greetings of e-mails, style of greetings, use of first person pronouns and social building units. These markers were used to interpret effort and value attributed to communications, formality, involvement, solidarity and sociability. Formality was estimated by summing scores on a scale from (informal) spoken style to (formal) written style for three elements of the e-mail, open and close greeting, and manual signature. Involvement and solidarity were interpreted from frequency of singular and plural first person pronouns respectively. Sociability was interpreted from counts of meaningful expressions representing notions of self-disclosure, humour, apology, courtesy, or other more general social building strategies, such as the good wishes "Happy New Year" or "Looking forward to seeing you". Empirical data derived from the coding were analysed using SAS statistical analysis package and the Kruskal-Wallis test, which is appropriate to compare three or more samples, when the data are not normally distributed. It tests the null hypothesis that samples have identical distribution functions; low p values indicate that two or more of the categories vary significantly. The frequencies and adaptations of socio-emotional markers were used to interpret and compare the social-task orientations in the projects. Pre- and post-analysis interviews were completed with the project leaders to collect information on the project and the team members, to help develop interpretations from the e-mail data.

Results

Pro-Social Behaviour: Marker Frequencies

Frequencies for all the social markers in e-mail communications differed significantly between the two projects, except for close greeting word count (see Table 1). Close greeting length was therefore more susceptible to pervasive norms than group or contextual norms. The remaining markers from these two case studies suggest higher effort and value (in terms of total body text and open greeting word counts), and higher formality, involvement, solidarity and sociability in the academic project than in the commercial project.

Social-Interactive Behaviour: Marker Adaptations

Further, studying the adaptations in pro-social marker behaviour in the project e-mails allows us to search for differences in normative behaviours of the two teams, and reasons for the differences. Nystrand's (1989) social-interactive model of written communication describes meaning or a shared understanding as being achieved by negotiation between the writer and reader, for a particular purpose and context. Table 2 shows the statistically significant adaptations in behaviour. The ticks ($\checkmark$) mean that social marker frequencies varied between two or more of the variable categories, for example, involvement varied between *Context* categories and between *Purpose* categories, but not between *Receivers* on the commercial project.

First person pronouns may represent involvement in the task or involvement in the relation between the writer and receiver. Involvement was adapted for *Purposes*, but not for *Receivers* in the commercial project, suggesting a task-oriented team culture. The fact that involvement adapted with *Context* (which described the direction of the e-mail in the client-supplier relationship) suggests that social and organizational norms may have influenced the team behaviour, and perhaps dominated behaviour, inhibiting adaptations for specific *Receivers* in the team culture. Further in the commercial team, only three of the markers were adapted for *Receivers*: elaboration, formality and sociability. While sociability was adapted for receivers, one component of the social marker, which contributes to the building and maintenance of relationships, self-disclosure, was missing from the data. Greeting length, involvement and solidarity were not adapted for *Receivers*. These were adapted for *Purposes* and all except solidarity were adapted for *Context*, once again suggesting

Table 1. Social marker frequencies in a commercial and an academic project (means for all e-mails on both projects with more than five words in the body text)

	Effort and value/ body text length	Open greeting length	Close greeting length	Involvement % sing. 1st person pronouns	Solidarity % plur. 1st person pronouns	Formality score	Sociability/ notions per e-mail
Pr	<.0001	<.0001	<.1875	<.0001	<.0326	<.0001	<.0001
Commercial	62	1.3	1.5	3.4	1.0	5.0	0.6
Academic	111	1.9	1.7	4.5	1.1	5.4	1.0

Table 2. Significant pro-social adaptations (✓) for Receiver, Context and Purposes in commercial and academic semi-virtual teams

		Effort and Importance/ Elaboration	Open greeting	Close greeting	Involvement	Solidarity	Formality	Sociability
Commercial	Receiver	✓					✓	✓
	Context	✓	✓	✓	✓		✓	
	Purpose	✓	✓	✓	✓	✓	✓	✓
Academic	Receiver	✓	✓	✓	✓	✓	✓	✓
	Context	✓	✓	✓	✓	✓	✓	✓
	Purpose	✓	✓	✓	✓	✓	✓	✓

a dominance of task and organizational-oriented influences (*Purpose* and *Context*) over the social dimension or relational behaviour between the *Sender* and *Receiver*.

In the academic project, writers adapted their communication behaviour for their intended *Receivers* using all the markers. Involvement varied with both the *Receiver* and the *Purpose*, suggesting an even social-task balance in the team culture, despite the fact that the team also adapted behaviour according to the direction of the e-mail in the organizational hierarchy (*Context*).

Task Focus

This difference between the two team cultures, that is, the task-oriented culture in the commercial team and the even social-task culture in the academic team, raises the question of whether the social element in the academic team might not be detrimental to achieving the task. As some of the purposes coded related to task issues and some to team maintenance and sociability, we compared the frequency of e-mails by purpose on the two projects to evaluate whether there appeared to be less focus on task issues in the academic project. First, we needed to assess whether e-mail frequency provided an estimate of relative activity for the different purposes. To answer this question, we used consultancy records available for three of the team members in the commercial team.

For these team members, we compared hours worked with the relative e-mail frequencies of the individuals on the project. Comparing relative hours and relative e-mail frequencies justified the interpretation of e-mail frequencies as representative of relative activity.

Comparing e-mail frequencies by purpose of e-mails between the academic and commercial project thus compares task involvement on the projects (Figure 3). The largest differences were between circulation of information and transfer of documents, for which e-mail frequencies were naturally higher in the project with more team members, and between relative activities for document design. This latter was naturally higher in the commercial context, in which the supplier was commissioned to write the manuals and was therefore more focused on manual design. Otherwise, despite the higher socio-emotional representation on the academic project, relative activity on the social and task oriented purposes varied very little between the two projects.

EMERGING TRENDS AND OPTIMISING E-MAIL STYLE

Our research showed a more task-focused approach to e-mail interaction in the commercial than in the academic setting, which we now discuss in the light of other researchers' findings.

Figure 3. Relative activities by purpose on commercial and academic projects

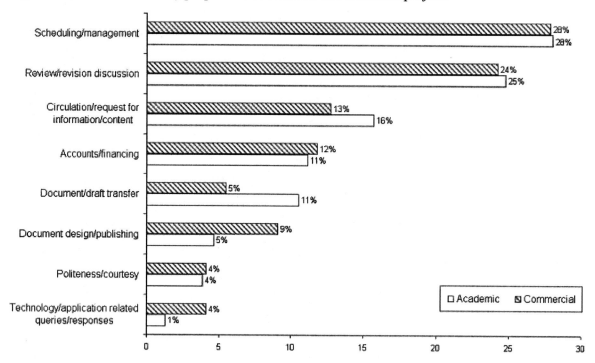

Nickerson (2000) found a "certain amount of relational or non-propositional content, intended to maintain the social system within the corporation, i.e. the patterns of corporate social relations between employees" (Nickerson, 2000, p. 153). Interestingly, also, work on organizational e-mail as early as 1986 by Sproull and Kiesler showed a ratio of work- to non-work-related e-mails of 6:4 (n=1248). Non-work-related e-mails covered personal topics such as recipes, advice on where to get a second mortgage, and so forth (Sproull & Kiesler, 1986). This finding may throw light on why e-mails in our research appeared to have task-oriented foci in the commercial setting and has more to do with the e-mail data collection than the absence or presence of relational communication. It may just be that socio-emotional content, requiring a different style to work-related (more official) content, requires separate communications, and that writers find it difficult to combine different styles for different purposes within a single communication.

However, there is also evidence from the literature to suggest that e-mail style differs between academic and business contexts. Gains (1999) showed a distinction between academic and commercial discourse communities. In a small scale study of 116 e-mails in academic and commercial settings, he found that academic e-mails were less formal with more social chat, that is, more like conversation, whereas e-mails from a commercial environment were more like written business language. He comments that the academics in his study treated e-mails more as "throw-away" communications (Gains, 1999, p. 99). Geisler et al. (2001), however, point out the permanency of e-mails and how they create an organizational memory: "What is recorded in such documents as minutes becomes the official understanding of what has happened or what will happen so that texts are used to shape members' understanding of the organization and its past and future activities" (Geisler et al., 2001, p. 279). They point out that such records may even be used in disciplinary action. This brings us back to Baron's comment that "a contract is still a contract" (Baron, 2001, p.

242). This permanency of e-mail over conversation may inhibit team members in business contexts from including relational content.

Socio-emotional elements in communication contribute to the social dimension in e-mail communication, which contributes positively to performance. The higher social interactive adaptations and pro-social marker frequencies in the academic context thus justified further qualitative exploration to understand how e-mail communication strategies and style varied from the commercial context, and whether this might contribute to knowledge on effective communication in virtual teamwork. This highlighted a mix of task and socio-emotional communication in academic e-mails.

Task and social task dimensions show a parallelism with official and personal e-mail styles. Danet (2001) expects both official and personal e-mails to become more speech-like and the distinction between the two-letter types to become less sharp. Baron (2001) predicts the likelihood of two styles of e-mail, one formal (edited) and one informal (unedited). She points out that frequent e-mail users may switch off automated editors and may even choose not to manually edit, thus communicating in an informal way, whereas on the other hand "a contract is still a contract" (Baron, 2001, p. 242), requiring accuracy, editing and thereby more formal communication. In our research, the merging of personal and professional styles which Danet (2001) has predicted was already apparent in communications from the academic context, and we provide an example in Box 1.

This is a typical example of the mix of personal and task-oriented content in communications on the academic project. Notice in this example that the author twice asks for confirmation that the reader will be able to meet her requests ("Would that be possible?"). The personal content of the e-mail thus does not detract from the focus on the task, but adds a relational component to the communication.

Box 1.

Hi ZZZ,
It is good to see all this work being done. I am a bit overwhelmed at the moment with moving details and paperwork....
Today we brought the boxes with the stuff to take to the [location]. So I spent the last 4 days packing boxes, selecting clothes etc. but that is now over and done...
The visit to [location] was a bit strange in a way that it is different to meet with a group you have not actually worked with before. I think that after the first initial hesitations we agreed on a good workplan. I have to say if only half of the work can be performed the whole trip will be more than worth the effort. Also from a family point of view, we managed to find a house in a very family friendly neighbourhood with a school at the other side of the street. [Spouse] was with me on the trip and is convinced that the location will be ideal for the children.
Your suggestions concerning the clinical exams are great and would be very helpful for me. For the handouts I would only need a description of the patient history and a filled out clinical exam form, conforming to the forms used last year as well as the video observation sheet (I will forward you a form in attach). I need to deliver the handout material by [date] to [course organizer for 2004]. So I would need to receive this as well as the revised text of the handout text of your presentation by [date]. Would that be possible? The video is for the presentation and that can be delayed a bit longer. You can best just send them to the [author's new address].
I think that the [clinical topic] and [clinical topic] would ideally be average [data type] in excel so that I could put them in the same format as agreed for the handouts, last year. Would that be possible?
Thanks again for all you help with the course. I will try to update some handout notes (esp the patient cases of last year) and I will circulate these for your comments beginning of next week.
If you need my brains for productive and inspiring ideas....I have to check if I accidentally packed them. Feels like that.

[First name]

Box 2.

Dear XXX,
Following [Sales Support Manager]'s review and your own comments, I've revised the manual, and attach an updated copy.
Minor corrections were made throughout the document following our conversations, but the main changes are to Section 6 How to Administrate the [Product]. I've removed all the instructions and substituted "Helpful Questions and Answers" in an attempt to pitch the content more appropriately for a System Administrator, and removed duplicated content.
Warnings and important information which were included in the instructions have been included with the Field Descriptions.
Please let me know what you think.
Thanks,
[Abbreviated name]

Box 3.

> [First name],
> For the administration interface I don't think html is the appropriate format. I will come back on this later today.
> [First name]

In contrast, Box 2 and Box 3 are two examples from an earlier (pilot) commercial writing project, also analysed within the same research framework.

In Box 2, the author shows relative informality in the signature and some courtesy in the closing, but there is no true relational content. With the task focus and formality of the main content, it would be quite difficult to incorporate any relational content. Changing to a more conversational style would allow the opportunity to include a query or personal comment not directly related to the purpose of the e-mail and thus contributing towards building the social dimension of the team. Box 3 is a typical e-mail from the previous author's manager. Between them, they appear to have fallen into a communicative behaviour which excluded the possibility of informal exchanges. This behaviour may have been governed by their individual attributes, the manager-subordinate relationship, the organizational culture or other causes, but resulted in a functionally efficient style, which lacked socio-emotional content, an element known to benefit team performance.

Although there were lower frequencies of pro-social markers and fewer adaptations of markers in the commercial project compared with the academic project, there were, however, some good indications of sensitivities to emotional elements in the commercial project. For example, empathy was shown when a subcontractor experienced difficulties, and feelings of anxiety over review were voiced.

The overall differences between the commercial and academic projects may not be underpinned by differences in the openness or communication skills of the team members or even social norms in the client-supplier relationship, but rather a tendency in business settings to separate the task from the social in written communications, to focus on functional efficiency. The task focus of projects may also be nothing to do with deficit theories of mediated communication, which suggest an inherent paucity of socio-emotional communication in leaner media and hyper-communication which focuses on task. Rather it has more to do with the existing social-task balance on the project.

Although this task focus may be deemed the optimal approach in business settings, there may be value in adopting a more conversational style in written professional e-mails. For example, in the commercial case study, a review meeting was suboptimal. In spite of a very successful project, there was also some disappointment in the terminology and this was reported in the final debriefing. Informal exchanges by e-mail between the project leader and the copywriter, and also between the project leader and the client reviewers may have offered the opportunity to exchange ideas on terminology and correct this earlier in the project. An equivalent scenario from the work of Kraut and colleagues (1988) would be the informal exchanges in the corridor between collocated team members.

The very nature of what Danet calls "written conversation" (Danet, 2001, p. 57) in e-mail may provide the informal unplanned communications afforded in collocated teams, which Kraut and his colleagues (1988) concluded is so important to the team's welfare. The academic author in the above example was prompted by task-oriented motivations to contact the addressee, but took the opportunity to inform on personal issues. Opportunizing on the task-motivated exchange to build the social and task dimensions contributes to Walther's social information processing theory (SIP, 1992). SIP predicts that levels of socio-emotional exchange in CMC will reach those possible with FtF communication given time. Walther's research has additionally shown that when interacting in projects over a period of time, CMC participants adopt a more intimate and sociable relational behaviour than their FtF counterparts from the beginning and throughout (Walther, 1995). Our research supports Walther's criticism of deficit theories; he emphasizes the importance of relational communication to job satisfaction, but argues that the deficit theories, (which emphasize the lack of nonverbal communication, social cues and social presence with e-mail communication), assert "that the structure of the medium alters the nature and interpretation of messages, it implies that such effects are inherent and constant whenever people communicate using computers" (Walther, 1995, p. 188). He points out that this precludes the influences of relationships, context or dynamics, such as development and changes occurring with time. Writers from our research are adapting their e-mail style with many different factors and demonstrate socio-interactive writing skills either at an organizational or individual level. The fact that this research has shown many adaptations in communication behaviour with writing influences supports adaptive structuration theory. Writers are not restricted in their communication behaviour by the medium, but adapt using the technology available to them.

However, there is no opportunity for informal unplanned task-checking, for example to check whether a particular term being used in a document is technically correct or socially appropriate. This lack of informal opportunity combined with social norms of behaviour, inhibits our opportunizing on the benefits of e-mail. E-mail is written conversation. E-mail shows a "versatility of discourse styles" (Yates & Orlikowski, 1993, p. 13); this characteristic of e-mail offers opportunities otherwise missed in non-mediated communication; this is the area for exploration in the training of CMC skills. Social and task elements are combined in teams, in individuals and within single exchanges without losing focus on the task. Social dimensions contribute to performance and thus benefit the project. Professional e-mail communications can and must offer more than a traditional business letter or memo. They often provide the social construction of the team and must therefore provide both social and task

dimensions and the opportunities for informal unplanned communication, without inhibition or censure. Walther (1995) points out how the asynchronous nature of e-mail supports this. For example, self-disclose may be considered deviant behaviour in FtF situations, hindering the task which has demanded co-presence, and thus removed individuals from other important work. With e-mail, "...temporal commitments become discretionary, and task versus interpersonal interaction becomes ... de-regulated; both task and social exchange may exist without one constraining the time available for the other" (Walther, 1995, p. 199). This important attribute is what differentiates e-mail from other media, which are perhaps perceived as more sociable, such as video-conferencing or instant messaging, which interrupt workflow and are therefore subject to time constraints.

CONCLUSION

The case studies in this research offer a snapshot of current day e-mail communication behaviour in professional writing contexts. The merging of personal and professional styles which Danet (2001) has predicted is already apparent in communications from the academic context in this research. Social and task elements are combined within single exchanges without losing focus on the task. Workplace e-mail communications can and must offer more than a traditional business letter or memo, because social dimensions and informal exchanges contribute positively to team performance. Conversational e-mail style has the potential to encourage socio-emotional relations, to help overcome social norms in commercial or other virtual workplaces and keep the door open for informal exchange of ideas.

RECOMMENDATIONS

This chapter reports a small part of the analyses conducted within a larger research framework. Premised from our literature review for the entire project, and the full analyses, we make the following recommendations to help support the social dimension in virtual teams:

- Try to arrange FtF meetings, particularly at the beginning of projects (Anawati & Craig, 2006), as FtF meetings benefit team performance (Walther & Parks, 2002).
- Emphasize to team members the long term nature of a project, if appropriate, to encourage the phenomenon of improved relational communication with anticipation of longer term associations (Walther & Parks, 2002).
- Allocate time specifically for socializing and getting to know each other (Anawati & Craig, 2006; Damrau, 2006).
- "Cultural understanding can be obtained via socializing informally with [virtual] team members" (Anawati & Craig, 2006, p. 50).
- "Team socializing is difficult for virtual teams... A few minutes of sociable conversation helps team members feel connected and learn their colleagues' personalities, which can, in turn, lubricate their online communication with each other" (Damrau, 2006, p. 13).
- Encourage team members to provide information about themselves (Taylor, 2000). Self-disclosure contributes to the development of personal intercultural relationships (Gudykunst & Kim, 2003 cited in Bretag, 2006).
- Encourage a more conversational e-mail style to encourage idea and personal exchanges, which contribute to the building and maintenance of the social dimensions of teams.

ACKNOWLEDGMENT

Thank you to all the participants who kindly supported this research, which was part of a Ph.D. research program at Sheffield Hallam University, UK, in collaboration with the Katholieke Universiteit Leuven, Belgium.

REFERENCES

Anawati, D, & Craig, A. (2006). Behavioural adaptation within cross-cultural virtual teams. *IEEE Transactions on professional communication, 49*(1), 44-56.

Argyle, M. (1994). *The psychology of interpersonal behaviour*, 5th ed. London: Penguin books.

Barker, V., Abrams, J., Tiyaamornwong, V., Seibold, D., Duggan, A., Park, H., & Sebastian, M. (2000). New contexts for relational communication in groups. *Small group research, 31*(4), 470-503.

Baron, N. (2001). *Alphabet to e-mail: How written english evolved and where it's heading*. London: Routledge.

Bretag, T. (2006). Developing 'third space' interculturality using computer-mediated communication. *Journal of computer-mediated communication, 11,* 981-1011.

Brown, P., & Levinson, S. (1987). *Politeness: Some universals in language usage*. Cambridge: Cambridge University Press.

Burgoon, J., & Hale, J. (1984). The fundamental topoi of relational communication. *Communication monographs, 51*(3), 193-214.

Burke, K., & Aytes, K. (1998). A longitudinal analysis of the effects of media richness on cohesion development and process satisfaction in computer-supported workgroups. *Proceedings of the Thirty-first Hawaii International Conference* on *System Sciences HICSS, 1* (pp. 134-144). IEEE Computer Press.

Crystal, D. (2001). *Language and the Internet.* Cambridge: Cambridge University Press.

Daft, R., & Lengel, R. (1984). Information richness: A new approach to managerial behaviour and organization design. *Research in organizational behaviour, 6,* 191-233.

Damrau, J. (2006). Managing a virtual team. *Intercom Magazine of the Society for Technical Communication, June,* 12-13.

Danet, B. (2001). *Cyberpl@y: Communicating online.* Oxford: Berg Publishers.

Edwards, K., Williams, N., Dujardin, A-F., & Spaepen, A. (2006). Developing an e-mail analysis tool for writing research. In: S. Carliner, J. Verckens, & C. de Waele, (Eds.), *Recent research in information and document design* (pp.169-190). Amsterdam: John Benjamins.

Evans, C., & Dion, K. (1991). Group cohesion and performance. A meta-analysis. *Small group research, 22*(2), 175-185.

Eveland, J., & Bikson, T. (1987). Evolving electronic communication networks: An empirical assessment. *Office: Technology and people, 3,* 103-128.

Faigley, L. (1985). Non-academic writing. The social perspective. In: L. Odell & D. Goswami (Eds.), *Writing in non-academic settings* (pp. 231-247). New York, NY: Guilford Press.

Ferrara, K., Brunner, H., & Whittemore, G. (1991). Interactive written discourse as an emergent register. *Written communication, 8*(1), 8-34.

Gains, J. (1999). Electronic mail - a new style of communication or just a new medium?: An investigation into the text features of e-mail. *English for specific purposes, 18*(1), 81-101.

Geisler, C. Bazerman, C., Doheny-Farina, S., Gurak, L., Haas, C., Johndan, J-E., et al. (2001). IText: Future directions for research on the relationship between information technology and writing. *Journal of business and technical communication, 15*(3), 269-308.

Harrison, S. (2000a). Maintaining the virtual community: Use of politeness strategies in an e-mail discussion group. In: L. Pemberton & S. Shurville (Eds.), *Words on the Web* (pp. 69-78). Exeter: Intellect.

Harrison, S. (2000b). *The discourse structure of e-mail communications.* Unpublished doctoral dissertation, University of Central England.

Hyland, K. (1998). Exploring corporate rhetoric: Metadiscourse in the CEO's letter. *The Journal of Business Communication, 35*(2), 224-245.

Kelly, L., & Duran, R. (1985). Interaction and performance in small groups: A descriptive report. *International Journal of Small Group Research, 1,* 182-192.

Keyzerman, Y. (2003). Trust in virtual teams. *Proceedings of the IPCC 2003 The Shape of Knowledge* (pp. 391-400). IEEE International.

Kraut, R., Egido, C., & Galegher, J. (1988). Patterns of contact and communication in scientific research collaboration. *Proceedings of the 1988 ACM conference on Computer-supported cooperative work* (pp.1-12). New York, NY: ACM Press.

Mortensen, M., & Hinds, P. (2001). Conflict and shared identity in geographically distributed teams. *The international journal of conflict management, 12*(3), 212-238.

Nickerson, C. (2000). *Playing the corporate language game.* Amsterdam: Rodopi BV.

Nystrand, M. (1989). A social-interactive model of writing. *Written Communication, 6*(1), 66-85.

Panteli, N. (2004). Discursive articulations of presence in virtual organizing. *Information and Organization, 14*(1), 59-81.

Pauleen, D., & Yoong, P. (2001). Facilitating virtual team relationships via Internet and conventional communication channels. *Internet research: electronic networking applications and policy, 11*(3), 190-222.

Postmes, T., Spears, R, & Lea, M. (1998). Breaching or building social boundaries? SIDE-effects of computer-mediated communication. *Communication Research, 25*(6), 689-715.

Postmes, T., Spears, R., & Lea, M. (2000). The formation of group norms in computer-mediated communication. *Human Communication Research, 26*(3), 341-371.

Schmitz, J., & Fulk, J. (1991). Organizational colleagues, media richness, and electronic mail. *Communication Research, 18*(4), 487-523.

Sherblom, J. (1988). Direction, function and signature in electronic mail. *Journal of business communication, 25*(4), 39-54.

Sproull, L., & Kiesler, S. (1986). Reducing social context cues: Electronic mail in organizational communication. *Management Science, 32*(11), 1492-1512.

Taylor, J. (2000). Electronic mail, communication and social identity: A social psychological analysis of computer-mediated group interaction. In: L. Pemberton & S. Shurville (Eds.), *Words on the Web* (pp. 96-78). Exeter: Intellect.

Thurlow, C., Lengel, L., & Tomic, A. (2004). *Computer-mediated communication: Social interaction and the Internet*. London: Sage Publications.

Tidwell, L., & Walther, J. (2002). Computer-mediated communication effects on disclosure, impressions, and interpersonal evaluations. Getting to know one another a bit at a time. *Human Communication Research, 28*(3), 317-348.

Timmerman, E., & Scott, C. (2006). Virtually working: Communicative and structural predictors of media use and key outcomes in virtual work teams. *Communication Monographs, 73*(1), 108-136.

Tucker, R., & Panteli, N. (2003). Back to basics: Sharing goals and developing trust in global virtual teams. In: N. Korpela, R. Montealegre, & A. Poulymenakou (Eds.), *Organizational information systems in the context of globalization* (pp. 85-98). Boston, MA: Kluwer Academic Publishers.

Vaes, J., Paladinao, M., & Leyens, J. (2002). The lost e-mail; pro social reactions induced by uniquely human emotions. *British Journal of Social Psychology, 41*(4), 521-534.

Walther, J. (1992). A longitudinal experiment on relational tone in computer-mediated and face to face interaction. *Proceedings of the Twenty-fifth Hawaii international conference on system sciences (*pp. 220-231). IEEE Computer Society Press.

Walther, J. (1995). Relational aspects of computer-mediated communication: Experimental observations over time. *Organization Science, 6*(2), 186-203.

Walther, J., & Parks, M. (2002). Cues filtered out: Cues filtered in: Computer-mediated communication and relationships. In: M. Knapp & J. Daly (Eds.), *Handbook of interpersonal communication* (3rd ed., pp. 529-563). Thousand Oaks, CA: Sage.

Yates, S. (1996). Oral and written linguistic aspects of computer conferencing: A corpus based study. In: S. Herring (Ed.), *Computer-mediated communication. linguistic, social and cross-cultural perspectives* (pp. 29-46). Amsterdam: John Benjamins.

Yates, J, & Orlikowski, W. (1993). *Knee-jerk anti-LOOPism and other e-mail phenomena: oral, written and electronic patterns in computer-mediated communication.* Retrieved June 2006 from http://ccs.mit.edu/papers/CCSWP150.html.

KEY TERMS

Group Cohesion/Solidarity: Group cohesion describes how socially close team members in a group are, their sense of togetherness or team spirit.

Semi-Virtual Teams: "Semi-virtual" describes the scenario where virtual team members mostly work at a distance from each other, but occasionally have the opportunity to meet face to face.

Socio-Emotional Communication/Relational Messages: Expressions fulfilling a meta-communicative function of interaction, indicating how two or more people regard each other, their relationship, or themselves within the context of the relationship (Burgoon & Hale, 1984, p. 193).

Social Dimension of Team Working: The social dimension of teams is basically concerned with the relationships, whether socio-emotional or organizational. The social dimension of team working is described by communications, activities and behaviours which are not addressed directly towards the group task goal, but rather towards relations, coordination of activities, welfare and maintenance of the team construct.

Team Culture: In this research, the team culture is described by the balance between social and task dimensions of team working.

Team Writing: Team writing can involve two or more professionals working together to create a document. Team membership is not restricted to a particular contributing skill, such as writing, illustrating, administrating, and so forth. If the member is contributing towards creation of the document, they are considered a collaborator or team member.

Virtual Team and Virtual Workplace: Virtual teams comprise people from related disciplines, who work from different locations, and may belong to different organizational contexts, and work at different times. The communications network supported by the Internet in this case becomes their common workplace, or virtual workplace, and is the platform through which they exchange ideas and information, and organize and progress their work.

Chapter XXVII
New Media and the Virtual Workplace

Matt Barton
St. Cloud State University, USA

ABSTRACT

There are few terms in the past decade that have excited the popular imagination more than "New Media," even though few self-described "New Media" scholars agree about precisely what it means or what makes it so new. Nonetheless, New Media has valuable lessons for modern business. The purpose of this chapter is to explore some various definitions of the term "New Media," unlock the key concepts, and discuss how these theories and practices can facilitate professional communication in new virtual workplaces (with a particular focus on 3-D virtual environments). The goal of this chapter is to show how New Media conversations about Play, Space, Identity, Simulation, and Collaboration can help foster more effective virtual workplaces. While there is no magical template for building productive virtual workplaces, this chapter will help readers understand and apply some of the principles of New Media to better understand the obstacles and affordances they offer modern business.

INTRODUCTION

Although the term "new media" is commonly heard in both academic and professional settings, it is not easy to define. Indeed, it may not be possible to offer a definition that any two New Media theorists will accept without substantial qualification. Janet Murray (2003, p. 3) claims that the term "is a sign of our current confusion," and Lev Manovich (2003) acknowledges that it is "not so easy to answer" people who ask him for a definition (p. 15). Perhaps we should not be surprised. Indeed, some wits might quip that

if we could agree on a set of stable criteria to identify and evaluate New Media, we would no longer be talking about something "new." What Fredric Jameson (1991) writes of Postmodernism might well be said for New Media: "The concept, if there is one, has to come at the end, and not at the beginning, of our discussion of it" (p. xxii).

However, rather than dismiss the difficulty of defining "new media" as mere quibbling or inane pedantry, we would do better to accept it as an inevitable (and desirable!) consequence of life in a field so wonderfully fertile and fresh. New Media theorists and artists challenge so many of our oldest and venerated conventions, challenging us always to ponder the unexpected and celebrate the ambiguous. Like its older sibling Postmodernism, New Media is often understood not just as self-conscious and self-reflexive, but self-ironic. If New Media ever takes itself seriously, it is precisely to demonstrate its own playfulness. Finally, New Media theory can help us better understand the phenomenon of the virtual workplace.

One of the central tenets of New Media is the concept of *play*, first elaborated by Johan Huizinga in his *Homo Ludens*. *Play* can be understood in the sense of *playing* a game, *play*-acting, or the *play* of a loose steering wheel. Like so many other aspects of New Media, *play* is flexible and mutable. Surely, videogames are meant to be *played*, but by the same token (or quarter, as it were) these devices allow us to *play* a role and are often said to be *playing* us. Indeed, one of the "holy grails" of computer science is the achievement of truly convincing artificial intelligence, which, among other applications, may one day be sophisticated enough to prevent a human player from distinguishing between human and computer-controlled characters in a virtual environment (the "Turing Test"). Although some of us would probably like to imagine an unbridgeable gap between human and computer intelligence, New Media encourages us to *play* with this "binary" opposition. Rather than view the situation in terms of "us and them," New Media theorists might prefer the metaphor of the *cyborg,* a concept explored by Donna Haraway in her essay "The Cyborg Manifesto."

Another important New Media concept is Space, a category that plays an obvious and critical role in three-dimensional virtual environments. Borrowing from works on architecture and city planning (particularly Kevin Lynch's *Image of the City*), New Media theorists have explored exploration. How does a work of art change when it can be entered and experienced in three dimensions? Although the term "virtual reality" is somewhat outdated in 2007, many of the same concerns raised by the goggles and motion-sensing gloves

also apply to virtual environments represented on a flat screen. We might even consider the Internet itself to be an extended metaphor about the exploration of space. It hardly seems surprising that many of the typical metaphors associated with the net—*Internet Explorer, Netscape Navigator, Safari,* Web "sites"—seem preoccupied with spatial exploration, and one of Microsoft's most familiar catchphrases is "Where do you want to go today?" What is the nature of the relationship between this "you" and the world? Is it possible to "go somewhere" without leaving your computer desk? How do we really experience space anyhow?

Questions like this beg the question of who "we" are anyway, and New Media theorists like Anna Dempsey have long been aware of the inherent difficulty surrounding the concept of "Self." Paradoxes as old as Descartes and Plato return to haunt disembodied minds floating in virtual environments. For example, many virtual spaces—such as the best-selling *World of Warcraft* or the ever-popular *Second Life*—require players to create at least one "avatar," or a character that represents them in the virtual world. Through their avatars, players are allowed to explore, interact, and inhabit a world that could never exist in reality. While some players create avatars that resemble themselves, others delight in exploring different roles. A male player might choose a female avatar, for instance. Other gamers might create and play several different avatars, exploring many different roles simultaneously. Players often become so engrossed (or "immersed") in playing their avatars that they neglect not only their immediate environment, but even their own bodily needs, such as eating and sleeping. Eventually, the boundaries between their "real" Self and their avatars might erode to the point where reality is merely an inconvenience. Can we accurately describe such a person as having a stable, unified consciousness? On a less abstract level, can we still say "I think, therefore I am" in a world of rampant identity theft? Questions about Self and Identity have led New Media scholars into all sorts of intriguing conundrums about gender, race, culture, and authority.

The conversations about Play, Space, and Identity so often heard among New Media theorists come together in discussions of Simulation. It hardly seems mere coincidence that some of the earliest (and best) "Simulations" available on personal computers were games that put players in the role of airplane pilots—literally, people who fly through space. The "flight simulator" may have initially been designed as a training tool for professional pilots, but the underlying technologies—particularly the first-person perspective and fluid movement through a three-dimensional space—paved the way for all sorts of games and virtual reality projects. For instance, the best-selling *Doom* and later "first-person shooter" games derived much of their mechanics from flight simulators, and countless New Media exhibits involve some type of movement through a three-dimensional space. One such work, *The Legible City* by Gideon May and Lothar Schmitt, had participants riding a stationery bicycle through a simulated city composed entirely of text. Although many simulations are based on "real" activities or processes (i.e., piloting a plane), they can also be wildly fanciful. Furthermore, and perhaps most intriguingly, simulations may actually work in reverse. For instance, perhaps an engineer designing a fighter cockpit might borrow liberally from the latest videogames, thereby easing a trainee's transition from simulator to reality. Or, perhaps workers will increasingly earn their living performing simulations that will not have a "real" parallel at all, such as the many hired employees who now patrol the many "massively multiplayer online" games to prevent players from abusing the system (and each other). In any case, it is not hard to imagine the relationship between "Simulation" and "Reality" becoming increasingly blurred.

Finally, New Media theorists like Henry Jenkins have explored the role of collaboration and begun to seriously question the old dichotomies between publishes and authors, authors and readers, directors and viewers, and developers and gamers. Many New Media projects invite some type of direct interaction from the audience, whether that means selecting which links to click in a hypertext or which areas to visit in an online virtual space. New Media "installations" ask participants to literally enter into an artistic space, experiencing rather than simply viewing the art. Quite often, no two people will experience the same exact sequence of events, and are allowed to make critical decisions that were formerly reserved strictly for the author or artist. In the realm of text, this emphasis on interaction and shared authority is called "collaboration," as is perhaps best embodied by the extremely popular and controversial *Wikipedia,* an online encyclopedia authored by thousands and thousands of volunteers. The Internet is fraught with other examples, including Microsoft's *Groove,* a collaborative tool that interoperates with many of Microsoft's other products (including *Office*) to facilitate more robust online collaboration. Meanwhile, many prominent computer games base much of their appeal on "user-generated content." For example, BioWare's best-selling *Neverwinter Nights* game included a powerful editor that allowed gamers to make their own role-playing adventures and distribute them online. In a very similar way, games like *The Sims, Second Life,* and *World of Warcraft* depend much less on premanufactured content by developers, and more on the social interaction among the players themselves. Rather than discuss these games in terms of hand-eye coordination or strategic thinking, New Media theorists are much more interested in the role collaboration plays in identity formation, spatial exploration, and social simulation.

All of these New Media concepts—Play, Space, Identity, Simulation, and Collaboration—provide an excellent framework for thinking about virtual workplaces. After a general overview of the available scholarship in the field, I will show how they can serve as a powerful heuristic for anyone interested in creating, facilitating, or participating in virtual workplaces. My overall objective is to show how these important New Media concepts can be directly applied to foster richer and more productive experiences in these exciting new spaces.

BACKGROUND

One way to think about New Media is as a branch of Postmodernism theory focused on computers and technology. Many of New Media's fundamental issues can be traced back to writers like Walter Benjamin, Jean François Lyotard, Jean Baudrillard, Gilles Deleuze, and Félix Guattari, just to name a few. Likewise, New Media owes a debt to Theodor Adorno and Max Horkheimer, whose essay "The Culture Industry: Enlightenment as Mass Deception" paved the way for Marshall McLuhan's influential (if flawed) analysis of the mass media (e.g., "The medium is the message"). Michel Foucault's and Roland Barthes' critiques of authorship and authority have also proven useful to many New Media theorists exploring online communities. New Media has also been heavily influenced by the work of the psycho-analyst Jacques Lacan, whose division of the psyche into three orders (The Real, Imaginary, and Symbolic) has proven quite useful in discussions of virtuality. While it is well beyond the scope of this chapter to introduce Postmodernism, suffice it to say that it is concerned chiefly with questioning our notions of the "Self" as a stable, coherent consciousness, the relationship between language and the world, and the reliability of any fixed body of knowledge.

Besides a general background in Postmodernism, New Media has also been influenced by a variety of authors interested in the computer as a story-telling medium. Three of these are Brenda Laurel, Janet Murray, and Marie Laure-Ryan. Laurel's *Computers as Theatre* (1993) introduces many insights that are still quite relevant, such as

her admonition to "think of the computer not as a tool, but as a medium" (p. 126). Laurel (1993) argues that software developers and interface designers should look to drama for inspiration. She asks, "When we look toward what is known about the nature of interaction, why not turn to those who manage it best—to those from the world of drama, of the stage, of the theatre?" (p. xii). Laurel stresses that the best way to ensure people will enjoy virtual spaces and find them useful is if they mirror physical reality. People encountering a Xerox machine in a virtual environment will instantly surmise that it will allow them to copy things. However, Laurel (1993) also argues that novel actions can be "effectively represented by establishing causality and probability" (Laurel, 1993, p. 132). Much like a child watching cartoons eventually learns the "cartoon physics" of the Road Runner universe and can predict what will happen when Wile E. Coyote chases the Road Runner over a cliff, a student operating the latest graphic software can soon learn enough to accurately predict the correct way to do any number of sophisticated tasks—assuming that the metaphors of the interface are unified by a coherent "conceptual structure and feel" (Laurel, 1993, p. 132).

In much the same vein is Janet Murray's *Hamlet on the Holodeck* (1997), which begins with the observation that "the birth of a new medium of communication is both exhilarating and frightening" (p. 1). Although many people now view computer technologies primarily in terms of "information overload," Murray (1997) argues that this is only because the computer is still "undomesticated"; the future will see an "increasingly graceful choreography of navigation to lure the interactor through ever more expressive narrative landscapes" (Murray, 1997, p. 83). Much like Laurel, Murray relies heavily on the phenomena of stage drama (particularly a special type called "interactive drama") to conceptualize computer narratives. For Murray, the ideal storytelling technology is "transparent";

the viewer or participant is so immersed in the story that she ceases to be aware of the medium itself (i.e., the singing of the bard or the clicking of the mouse). However, Murray (1997) does not see this process as passive. Rather, the participant must help perpetuate the illusion by using her "intelligence to reinforce rather than to question the reality of the experience" (p. 110). Even in a simulation as sophisticated as the "holodeck" from *Star Trek: The Next Generation,* the users must "play along" to enjoy the program, conversing with the holograms and responding creatively to dramatic situations. Murray's insight should not be lost on designers of virtual workplaces: No matter how realistically a virtual world is depicted on the screen, it is all for naught if the participants are not sufficiently trained and willing to "play along" with the simulation. The successful virtual workplace but is not a tool, but rather a medium for creative and productive expression.

Marie Laure-Ryan's *Narrative as Virtual Reality* (2003) is the most recent and in some ways the most theoretical of the three. Laure-Ryan's (2003) ambitious project is to "rethink textuality, mimesis, narrativity, literary theory, and the cognitive processing of texts" using terms and concepts borrowed from digital culture" (p. 1). While Laure-Ryan's work is perhaps somewhat overwhelming to readers lacking a background in cognitive psychology, analytical philosophy, and phenomenology, many of her classifications are eminently useful for anyone constructing virtual workplaces. For example, Laure-Ryan (2003) defines four features of a world: "Connected set of objects and individuals; habitable environment; reasonably intelligible totality for external observers; field of activity for its members" (p. 91). Each of these features is vital for the construction of a virtual workplace. For instance, rather than construct a series of identical rooms connected in a random or *ad hoc* fashion, designers should consider arranging distinctive rooms in a pattern that can be easily conceptualized, such as a star shape. Furthermore, some type of highly visible

"landmark," such as a tower or mountain in the distance, can help participants maintain a sense of direction. Furthermore, objects in the world should have some clear connection to the environment or the participants: "The user needs a scenario that casts him in a role and projects his actions as the performance of concrete, familiar tasks" (Laure-Ryan, 2003, p. 217). If the goal is to provide a tool that allows participants to record conversations, for instance, an object resembling a cassette recorder will be much more successful than a nondescript cube.

Laure-Ryan (2003) also defines three types of immersion: Spatial, the response to setting; Temporal, the response to plot; and Emotional, the response to character. Again, users will quickly become frustrated if any of these responses are not taken into consideration. For instance, many players of the highly successful *World of Warcraft* find the graphics and quest narratives quite fulfilling, but are turned off when confronted with racist or sexist dialog from abusive players. Likewise, players may be irritated by a computer-controlled character who does not behave as expected given the circumstances, such as a virtual officemate who says "Good morning" no matter what the time of day, or who continues to smile cheerfully despite having his stapler stolen. Characters "need to be real enough that the participant respects them," writes Bryan Loyall (2004, p. 5). Even though such things might seem trivial, they are of the greatest importance when the goal is immersion. "In the fullest type of interactivity," writes Laure-Ryan (2003), "the user's involvement is a productive action that leaves a durable mark on the textual world" (p. 205). In the above example, the secretary should "remember" the stolen stapler and behave differently towards the user afterwards; not simply be "reset" the next day with a brand new stapler and no memory of the incident.

Finally, Laure-Ryan (2003) distinguishes "immersion" from "interactivity/self-reflexivity." Whereas immersion is the "mode of reading of an embodied mind," "interactivity/self-reflexivity is the experience of a pure mind that floats above all concrete worlds in the ethereal universe of semantic possibility" (p. 354). According to Laure-Ryan (2003), a work can alternate between immersion and self-reflexivity, but cannot do both simultaneously: "Language behaves like holographic pictures. You cannot see the signs and the world at the same time" (p. 284). These points may seem rather abstract, but make a good deal of sense when discussing virtual environments. For instance, many immersive videogames begin with a tutorial, which frequently breaks immersion to give the player overt information about the controls or rules of the game. Likewise, players may frequently break the action to view a status or options screen. A good developer of a virtual workplace will balance immersion with interactivity/self-reflexivity, making sure the two complement rather than compete with each other. Once the "tutorial" session is over, the player should not be constantly interrupted by being forced to pay attention to the interface, such as clicking "okay" on a pop-up window.

Taken together, Laurel, Murray, and Laure-Ryan represent a superb introduction to virtual environments and raise many important issues. However, though their work is highly germane to the field, they are not self-described (at least in the books mentioned above) as New Media theorists. I will now turn our attention to three New Media theorists who are recognized as such: Lev Manovich, Jay David Bolter, and Richard Grusin. These writers have achieved significant in a variety of fields, and their texts are often assigned to students as introductions to the field.

Manovich's *The Language of New Media* (2001) is perhaps the most-cited general work on New Media today, and is particularly valuable to anyone struggling to see the "new" in New Media. He reduces New Media to five core principles: numerical representation, modularity, automation, variability, and cultural transcoding. These principles build on each other. For instance, an image of a flower is "numerically represented" in the form of binary code in the computer's memory. Since the image is stored as numbers, the computer can automate procedures by applying mathematical algorithms, such as the many "filters" available in Adobe's *Photoshop*. Likewise, the modularity of programs like Mozilla's *Firefox* allow users to customize and extend their Web browser with a variety of "add-ons" or "plug-ins," which range from cosmetic "themes" to programs like *Zotero*, a citation database. Perhaps the most important concept here, though, is cultural transcoding. Manovich (2001) divides the typical New Media work into two layers: the computer and the cultural. The computer layer is the form that can only be understood by the computer; that is, the machine language that ultimately breaks down into binary code. The cultural layer is the form understood by the humans who operate the program; thus, it is the layer that has some effect on the culture of computer users and eventually to all cultural production (since so much media is currently produced on, and increasingly for, computers).

Manovich's (2001) startling insight is that these layers influence each other in a dialectical relationship. For instance, someone designing a Microsoft *PowerPoint* presentation might base its structure on the included templates. She might even be moved by the template to select certain wordings or images over others, and decide against ideas that do not seem to fit the format suggested by the program (or more generally the constraints imposed by the computer). On the other hand, if enough users complained about the lack of a much-needed feature, Microsoft might very well add it to the next version. A good example of this is the "tabs" feature available in Microsoft's *Internet Explorer 6*. Although originally only available in third-party browsers, tabs proved so useful that many *Windows* users were migrating away from *Internet Explorer* in favor of *Mozilla Firefox*, an "open source" program given away for free by the Mozilla Foundation. Microsoft, long opposed to open source projects no doubt had a strong incentive to add the feature and thus stem the flow (Microsoft favors proprietary software, which places legal restrictions on how users are able to use, modify, and distribute the software).

Although Manovich does not identify as a Marxist, he nevertheless follows Benjamin, Horkheimer, and Adorno by asserting that the means of production determines (or at least heavily influences) the production of cultural goods. Manovich argues that "mass media and data processing are complementary technologies; they appear together and develop side by side, making modern mass society possible" (p. 23). Whereas data processing and automated record keeping were necessary in order to maintain a centralized control over an exploding population, the mass media was needed to homogenize the culture into a "mass society." The concept of a "mass society" is not a flattering one. Manovich portrays movie theaters as "dark relaxation chambers" and film as a "routine survival technique for subjects of modern society" (p. 23). He writes, "All around the world large prisons were constructed that could hold hundreds of prisoners—movie houses. The prisoners could neither talk to one another nor move from seat to seat" (p. 108). However, Manovich sees a massive change in the media underway, a change brought about mostly by the "quite different logic of post-industrial society—that of individual customization rather than mass standardization" (p. 30). The continuing advance of computer and communications technology allow for new innovations in production, such as "production on demand" and "just in time delivery," which Manovich predicts will dramatically alter the cultural landscape.

A handy example of such a change taking place is the "remix" cultural phenomena championed by Lawrence Lessig, author of *Free Culture* (2005). Lessig's (2005) argument is that since the Internet makes it so easy to acquire copyrighted materials and rearrange them into new creative works that we should "rethink the conditions under which the law of copyright automatically

applies" (p. 140). The law should embrace this cultural phenomenon rather than strive vainly to prevent it. Although the "mass media" logic of the recording industry still mandates that every music fan purchase the same set of songs and not be allowed to copy or modify them, the "remix culture," empowered by powerful distribution technologies like Peer-to-Peer Networking, will ultimately prevail. Although Lessig (2005) views this shift as liberating, a less rosy take is that it is simply an inevitable shift caused by a change in production methods, not ethical perspectives. As labor theorist Robert Reich argues in *The Work of Nations* (1991), the future of production belongs to "symbolic-analysts," who do not produce or work with tangible objects but rather manipulate "data, words, oral, and visual representations" (p. 177). Reich (1991) argues that the symbolic analysts will earn their living by "simplifying reality into abstract images that can be rearranged, juggled, experimented with, communicated to other specialists, and [...] eventually transformed back into reality" (p. 178). Perhaps Lessig's (1991) remix culture is but an inevitable and not necessarily desirable consequence of what Reich sees as a general shift of production, and ultimately an example of what Manovich terms "cultural transcoding."

Manovich's principle of cultural transcoding has much in common with what Bolter and Grusin's concept of remediation, which they explore in their book *Remediation: Understanding New Media* (1999). According to Bolter and Grusin, "What is new about new media comes from the particular ways in which they refashion older media and the ways in which older media refashion themselves to answer the challenge" (1991, p. 15). Thus, "remediation" works both ways, and every medium has always already been remediated in some sense. For example, the television brought a challenge to the radio show just as the Internet now challenges television. However, the relationship between media technologies is never one-way or uncomplicated. For instance, magazines and newspapers have greatly altered their format in response to the World Wide Web, and Web addresses regularly appear at the end of television commercials (and almost every television show has a dedicated Web site and online communities of fans).

Much like Laurel, Murray, and Laure-Ryan, Bolter and Grusin (1991) also argue that new media "oscillates between immediacy and hypermediacy, between transparency and opacity" (p. 19). The phenomena is perhaps most clearly perceived in the typical "flashy" Web site, whose brief snippets of text are interrupted by all manner of attention-diverting pop-ups, hyperlinks, and animations. Rather than remain "transparent," the features of these Web sites loudly announce themselves; they are meant to be seen (and perhaps impress upon the viewer the Web designer's technical expertise). Bolter and Grusin argue, however, that viewers or participants do not always desire immersion, and can often appreciate the opaque. For example, devoted fans of Apple's *Macintosh* computer often praise the interface for its aesthetically pleasing icons and windows, to say nothing of the distinctive look of the machines themselves. Far from wishing these aspects to become "transparent," *Macintosh* users are delighted by them. Bolter and Grusin (1991) describe the conflicting impulses towards transparency on the one hand and opacity on the other as the "twin preoccupations of contemporary media," (p. 21).

Perhaps Bolter and Grusin's most useful insight for designers of virtual workplaces concerns the "Self." Instead of claiming that virtual realities offer the possibility of escaping the Self and the body, virtual realities "remediate the Cartesian self. They cannot succeed in denying the body; instead they can only remediate it" (1991, p. 254). However, virtual realities allow us to "occupy multiple points of view" and may very well represent the "major freedom that our culture can now offer" (p. 245). Most intriguingly, Bolter and Grusin (1991) describe cyberspace not as a "parallel universe" but rather as a "shopping mall in the ether; it fits smoothly into our contemporary networks of transportation, communication, and economic exchange" (p. 179). Much as a shopping mall might be designed to resemble a 1940s town complete with bronze statues of barefoot children playing in a fountain or bespectacled gentlemen seated reading newspapers, the Web is crammed with representations of everyday objects and settings. Indeed, modern operating systems encourage users to personalize their settings as much as possible, swapping out generic desktop backgrounds for one's own digital photos and the like. Yet, changing the desktop background ultimately makes no difference to the logic of the software; Andy Warhol's soup cans are just another image file to be swapped in or out at the user's whim.

MAIN FOCUS OF THE CHAPTER

What does New Media theory have to offer modern business? How can abstract concepts like Space and Identity help professionals interact productively in virtual workplaces? Although I alluded above to several points of relevance between New Media and virtual workplaces, I will now make these connections more explicit.

First, let us identify the features of a productive virtual workplace. I suggest the following criteria:

- **Play:** Does the virtual workplace foster creativity and innovation, and promote experimentation? Does the system allow multiple solutions to a given problem? Is playfulness and humor encouraged or stifled?
- **Space:** Is the virtual environment and its physics persistent, consistent, and easy to map mentally? Does it allow participants to determine which parts can be manipulated or explored? Is it a wide-open space or are there areas of subterfuge? Do participants

share the space, or is the "cubicle" concept carried into the virtual? Is there a private space for new participants to learn the interface before entering the workplace?

- **Identity:** Are participants encouraged to create and role-play a diversity of characters, with different roles and abilities? Is participation in the virtual workplace viewed as a creative performance? Or are participants required to use their real names and expected to behave exactly as they would in the office?

- **Simulation:** What range of activities is capable of being simulated in the virtual workplace? Are participants limited to merely operating existing objects, or can they create their own or combine the existing ones to gain new abilities? Are participants encouraged to heighten the effects of the simulation by remaining in character?

- **Collaboration:** Does the virtual workplace encourage collaboration among the participants by requiring them to work together to solve problems, or is the system geared more towards solo operation? Are participants encouraged to converse? To share?

Business leaders should ask themselves these questions before, during, and after the development and implementation of a virtual workplace. No doubt, one of the largest obstacles is the impulse to unnecessarily duplicate limitations of the office world into the virtual workplace, especially the culture of individual responsibility and personal blame, gender or racist stereotypes, the "cubicle" notion of office space, and the idea that professionals must be serious and always "on-task." A successful virtual workplace steers clear of these traps by encouraging playfulness, which is the first step towards nurturing a culture of creativity and experimentation. In the ideal virtual workplace, the opposition between work and play breaks down, and innovation and productivity soars.

Following Laurel's lead, we should think of the virtual workplace not as a tool, but rather as a medium. Furthermore, we should not view the participants in a virtual workplace as passive "users," but rather as creative performers who must be trained to "play along" as a character, actively engaging their imagination to facilitate an immersive experience for everyone. To facilitate this type of immersion, developers should be wary of interrupting the participants by unnecessarily diverting their attention to the interface (i.e., pop-up reminders or references to the mouse or keyboard), or allowing elements into the virtual world that are incapable of behaving realistically (i.e, a virtual dog that does not respond to a bone wagged in its face, or a chair that cannot be sat in). If the developer wishes to introduce a new tool or ability into the workplace, its purpose should be suggested by its appearance. Although each object and activity need not have direct parallels in the physical universe, they should nevertheless obey a common set of design principles.

For example, a virtual workplace might afford the ability for participants to move the furniture in a room to suit their needs. In this case, if a chair can be moved, a desk should also be moveable. If the way to remove a chair is to move it into a trashcan, the same method should get rid of a desk. Arbitrarily deciding which furniture can be moved or deleted will only confuse and frustrate participants and ultimately reduce the coherence of the virtual workplace. Although the virtual workplace need not mirror the physics of our world, it should nevertheless remain consistent with its own physics. The fact that we do not get rid of furniture by shoving it into the small trashcans in our office matters much less than that the virtual workplace operate consistently and predictably, adhering to its own rules.

Secondly, we might wish to follow Reich's (1991) lead in describing the participants in a virtual workplace as "symbolic analysts," and consider how this type of labor is made necessary by new types of cultural and industrial production, particularly the move towards individual customization and away from mass standardization. A prosperous virtual workplace may not actually produce any tangible goods whatsoever, nor must a virtual occupation require skills that have practical correlations in the physical world. To wit, someone who learns how to construct chairs in the virtual workplace may not know even the most basic aspects of real carpentry, yet they are doing "work." The strength of a virtual as opposed to a physical workplace is that the same set of skills that allow a participant to create a chair should also afford the creation of any other object. Consistency is key. However, this is not to say that a virtual world must place no constraints whatsoever on the participants. Indeed, introducing constraints and asking the participants to work around them (or, better, to find ways to use them as assets) is likely one of the most exciting possibilities for virtual workplaces. Instead of merely being told to "think outside the box" to solve a particular problem, participants in a virtual workplace can think inside many different kinds of boxes, each with their own affordances and constraints, until the most efficient solution to the problem is discovered. This is hardly a novel development; for decades engineers have relied on computer simulations to allow them to test variables, states, and conditions that would simply be impossible or impractical in the physical world. *Second Life* and *World of Warcraft* are two of the many available new media applications that implement these principles.

The third feature of a productive virtual workplace is creative role-playing. Much like the problem-solving strategy described above, the ability to create, select, and play different roles and characters in the virtual workplace is eminently useful. The key here is not to insist that virtual participants use their real names and act strictly as they would in the physical workplace. Indeed, one of the greatest values of a virtual as opposed to a physical workplace is precisely the ability to try on a variety of masks, develop multiple characters, and perform social experiments.

For instance, perhaps one of the goals of a virtual workplace is to encourage participants to think creatively and find multiple solutions to a given problem. To this end, individual participants might be assigned different characters to play, such as Einstein, Picasso, Barney Fife, Plato, and Joan of Arc. Alternatively, the roles could be more generic, such as Scientist, Artist, Philosopher, and Jester, each of which would have a unique set of abilities. In any case, the participants would be encouraged to view the problem from different perspectives, including (if not especially) the comical, since one of the goals of comedy is to play with our expectations. Games like *Second Life* and *World of Warcraft* seem particularly fond of this behavior, and comedic gamers like "Leroy Jenkins" from *World of Warcraft* are gaining notoriety even outside the gaming community. Creating opportunities for creative role-playing is one of the reasons why it is so important to avoid the "cubicle" notion; instead of segregating participants into their own private virtual rooms or "cubicles" to perform work, they should be encouraged to work together to solve problems. That said, granting each participant a private, highly customizable work space that others can enter only with permission may help to instill a fuller sense of responsibility and investment in the virtual workplace.

Finally, the ideal virtual workplace is one that fosters a culture of collaboration. As much as possible, participants should be encouraged to interact with each other to identify and solve problems rather than "going it alone." One of the most obvious advantages here is that virtual workplaces can offer a wide variety of communication options to the participants. Perhaps one participant prefers to use a headset and microphone to speak aloud; others might prefer typing, others may say nothing but act in meaningful ways (i.e., "emoting"). We already see this type of collaboration in online games like *World of Warcraft,* where players of diverse characters must band together to defeat the more powerful foes. In many instances, a participant can learn something new simply by observing how another character performs a task; useful activities are constantly being modeled for the benefit of everyone. Meanwhile, the system should keep records of each participants' achievements, both as a way to promote confidence and as a useful log that can be consulted later on, should the participant forget how to do something.

A naïve view is that a virtual workplace can be designed in such a way that all participants will enjoy total equality and collaborate without prejudice. However, virtual workplaces do not eliminate or nullify social and cultural difference. Social categories like gender, race, and ethnicity will still manifest themselves in virtual environments, regardless of the anonymity of the participants. A moment's thought reveals the truth of this claim: If people in our society can be judged on the basis of such fictitious criteria as "racial characteristics," what could possibly prevent these or other prejudices arising from even more arbitrary and baseless criteria in a virtual environment? Indeed, virtual workplaces may very well suffer from even more serious forms of prejudice, since there will be even fewer opportunities to refute unjust claims with empirical evidence. Thus, participants and administrators of virtual workplaces must work hard to ensure that each participant feels welcome, and administrators should take claims about unfair treatment very seriously.

Nevertheless, virtual environments are terrific playgrounds for experimenting with difference, and if participants can experience what it feels like to be subject to a variety of arbitrary constraints on their ability to navigate the space, so much the better. Towards this end, encouraging participants to experiment with playing characters of different genders and orientations might have positive results, particularly if such exercises are combined with outside discussions about difference. Ideally, such activities might help participants understand the performative nature of what is often thought of as a purely biological

construct, or what Judith Butler (1990) means when she writes that "identity is performatively constituted by the very *expressions* that are said to be its results" (p. 25).

To summarize, then, New Media theory has much to offer anyone interested in building, maintaining, or participating in virtual workplaces. Although it is common enough to find postmodern theorists discussing Play, Space, and Identity in the context of printed works, these concepts seem far more obvious and relevant when discussing virtual worlds. The same can be said for the postmodernist claim that reading is far from a passive experience; although we can say that readers "construct" the texts they read as much as the authors who wrote them, the truth of this claim is far from obvious. However, if we are talking about the relationship between developers and participants in virtual worlds, we can easily see how the two work together to create meaning. After all, the developer only creates the interface; it is up to the participants to enact the drama and weave the narrative. What Celia Pearce (2004) says about computer games would seem to apply quite well to virtual workplaces: "Game designers are not so much storytellers as context creators, and what they are doing is nothing short of revolutionary" (p. 153).

FUTURE TRENDS

What is the future of New Media as a field of scholarly inquiry and professional practice? Will it continue to evolve along with computer and networking technology, or will it go the way of the now sadly languishing field of Hypertext theory? Will the term "New Media" survive into the next decade, or fade out of circulation like "Multimedia?" Already, some theorists seem more privy to the term "Digital Media," arguing that it does a better job of describing the type of works they analyze. Of course, the answers to these questions depend on many factors, but, undoubtedly, much rests on how New Media theory results in useful New Media practice. Hopefully, this chapter will serve as a humble contribution towards that goal, but there is a great deal of work to be done in this vitally important area. In any case, as more businesses take the leap into virtuality, there will be a corresponding increase in the demand for individuals with a solid grasp of the concepts I have discussed here. People will need a vocabulary and a theoretical framework for analyzing virtual environments and understanding the type of work performed in them. Whether these terms and theories come from a field called "New Media" is a question that rests, at least in part, on the willingness of theorists to make connections with business and industry leaders.

There are also plenty of opportunities of future research in New Media; indeed, the field is incredibly rich. Grants for purchasing technology and opportunities for publication are booming. Indeed, there is no doubt that promising students who emerge from recognized New Media programs will have little problem securing lucrative employment.

My prediction is the field of New Media will continue to expand both in the academy and in business. Computers and networking technology are becoming more powerful and less expensive everyday, and there is no end in sight. The future of business belongs to the symbolic analyst; the individual most fit for survival in the virtual workplace. Rather than receive training in a particular skill set or work to master a given body of knowledge, the workers of the future will be experts at manipulating symbols and running abstract simulations. The line between "work" and "play" will continue to erode, and the idea of production as the manufacture of tangible products will seem droll or even quaint to the future worker. What will matter far more is the ability to thrive in a virtual environment; to arrange symbols and algorithms in exciting new combinations; to forge new connections and possibilities for collaboration. New Media theory is valuable to business precisely because it is so concerned with these very activities.

CONCLUSION

The concepts of Play, Space, Identity, Simulation, and Collaboration are fundamental to New Media theory. They provide a sturdy theoretical framework for analyzing virtual environments. Although some New Media theory is quite dense and inaccessible to many readers, it has much to offer those who develop, administer, or participate in virtual workplaces. Nevertheless, if this chapter is any indication, there are those willing to work to identify practical applications for these theories. If nothing else, New Media theory can help us understand the challenges and opportunities presented by the virtual workplace. In this chapter, I have worked primarily to introduce some basic concepts of New Media theory and discuss potential applications for modern business. I have shown how New Media theory can help us facilitate a more creative and productive virtual workplace, and why modern business should revisit old dichotomies like "work and play." Although there is obviously still much we could discuss about New Media and virtual workplaces, I hope that this chapter has offered some idea of the breadth and depth of material available, and also suggested possibilities for future research.

REFERENCES

Bolter, J.D., & Grusin, R. (2000). *Remediation: Understanding new media.* Cambridge, MA: MIT Press.

Butler, J. (1990). *Gender trouble: Feminism and the subversion of identity.* New York, NY: Routledge.

Jameson, F. (1991). *Postmodernism: Or, the cultural logic of late capitalism.* Durham, NC: Duke University Press.

Laure-Ryan, M. (2001). *Narrative as virtual reality.* Baltimore, MD: Johns Hopkins University Press.

Laurel, B. (1993). *Computers as theatre.* New York, NY: Addison-Wesley.

Lessig, L. (2004). *Free culture: How big media uses technology and the law to lock down culture and control creativity.* New York, NY: Penguin Press.

Loyall, B. (2004). Response to Janet Murray. In N. Wardrup-Fruin & P. Harrigan (Eds.), *First person: New media as story, performance, and game* (pp. 2-9). Cambridge, MA: MIT Press.

Manovich, L. (2001). *Language of new media.* Cambridge, MA: MIT Press.

Manovich, L. (2003). New media from Borges to HTML. In N. Wardrip-Fruin & N. Montfort (Eds.), *The new media reader* (pp. 13-25). Cambridge, MA: MIT Press.

Murray, J.H. (1997). *Hamlet on the holodeck: The future of narrative in cyberspace.* New York, NY: The Free Press.

Murray, J.H. (2003). Inventing the medium. In N. Wardrip-Fruin & N. Montfort (Eds.), *The new media reader* (pp. 3-11). Cambridge, MA: MIT Press.

Pearce, C. (2004). Towards a game theory of game. In N. Wardrup-Fruin & P. Harrigan (Eds.), *First person: New media as story, performance, and game* (pp. 143-153). Cambridge, MA: MIT Press.

Reich, R.B. (1991). *Work of nations: Preparing ourselves for 21ˢᵗ century capitalism.* New York, NY: A.A. Knopf.

Selfe, C.L. (2004). Students who teach us: A case study of a new media text designer. In A.F.

Wysocki et al. (Eds.), *Writing new media: Theory and applications for expanding the teaching of composition* (pp. 43-66). Logan, UT: Utah State University Press.

Wysocki, A.F. (2004). Opening new media to writing: Openings and justifications. In A.F. Wysocki et al (Eds.), *Writing new media: Theory and applications for expanding the teaching of composition* (pp. 1-42). Logan, UT: Utah State University Press.

KEY TERMS

Collaboration: A task performed by multiple participants.

Identity: A collection of data or characteristics that distinguish one being from another.

Immersion: The state reached when a participant is so actively engaged in a narrative that the mechanism by which that narrative is generated no longer distracts from it.

New Media: (1) A work consisting of at least two inseparable layers, one of which is composed of data in a form capable of being manipulated directly by a computer. (2) A work whose purpose is to draw attention to its own materiality.

Participant: A person performing work in a virtual workplace.

Play: (1) As opposed to "work," a pleasurable activity pursued for its own sake. (2) The free range of movement allowed before work becomes possible.

Simulation: An activity whose purpose is to represent another.

Space: A computer simulation of a physical environment.

Chapter XXVIII
Adoption of Wi-Fi Technologies and Creation of Virtual Workplaces

Ran Wei
University of South Carolina, USA

ABSTRACT

This chapter introduces adoption theory and applies it to examine the use of wireless fidelity (Wi-Fi), which has the potential to expand virtual workplaces significantly. Research shows that the use of Wi-Fi to access the Internet is surprisingly low. As understanding users and their needs is a prerequisite for the success of any new information technology, this chapter identifies factors accounting for the low usage of Wi-Fi in organizations and seeks to build a model to increase Wi-Fi usage. Empirical research reported in this chapter shows that motivations of Wi-Fi use, mass media use, and technology cluster have impacted on the awareness of, interest in, and likelihood to use Wi-Fi. More important, a chain-effect process in the adoption of Wi-Fi was presented: the awareness of Wi-Fi, which was influenced mostly by reading newspapers, had a direct effect on interest in Wi-Fi, which directly affected the likelihood to use Wi-Fi. Thus, to increase Wi-Fi usage, the awareness of and interest in this newer Internet technology must be in place. The chapter also discusses future trends in Wi-Fi technology and how increased adoption of Wi-Fi enhances the virtual workplace.

INTRODUCTION

Wireless fidelity (Wi-Fi) and WiMax represent newer Internet technologies that provide wireless access to the Internet. Wi-Fi uses the 2.4 GHz 802.11 wireless Ethernet standard and with a range up to 350 feet. It is also known as IEEE 802.11b and 802.11g with a data transfer speed up to 11 Mb/s. WiMAX is similar to Wi-Fi, but with a range of 25 to 30 miles (Meadows & Grant, 2006). Both technologies are becoming core architectures of wireless computer networks. A wireless network is an extension of the wired network as it provides broadband access to the Internet via "hot spots" (also called a wireless cloud) built to the edge of the wired network. With this new way of accessing the Internet, users can check e-mail (the most popular online activity), search for information, download files, and access databases on the go. Wi-Fi and WiMax provide a new type of network on which a virtual workplace wirelessly accessible can be built and maintained.

It is noteworthy that wireless Internet networks known as wireless local area network (WLAN) have grown rapidly with the advent of Wi-Fi and WiMAX. Using radio waves, a WLAN allows Internet users to connect to a local area network (LAN) at broadband speed anytime and anywhere within the reach of hot spots. WLANs were deployed at universities, corporate offices, retail outlets, hotels, airports, and downtown areas. In corporate offices, WLANs are installed to serve common office environments offering hot spots. For instance, at its headquarters in Seattle, Microsoft installed 4,000 hot spots. There were 84,000 hot spots in the world in 2005; industry estimates put the total over 100,000 in 2006 (Best, 2005). In addition, municipal Wi-Fi projects for public wireless access are mushrooming in the United States. Young (2006) estimated that 300 cities (including Philadelphia and San Francisco) plan to implement municipal wireless networks for places like parks, libraries, and other public places.

With Wi-Fi, the Internet becomes portable and easily accessible at a low cost. With a wireless card (known as WNIC—wireless network interface card) on laptops, PDAs, cell phones, or game consoles like Wii, users within the range of Wi-Fi or WiMax can go online wirelessly anywhere, anytime. Wireless Internet and mobile computing expand Internet applications (e.g., wireless broadband access on laptops) and services (e.g., live city traffic information). More important, widespread access lets Internet users maintain mobile communication (such as e-mailing) to virtual communities to which they belong. Given these advantages, there is little doubt that Wi-Fi facilitates the expansion of virtual workplaces as a backbone of network infrastructure. With Wi-Fi, employees are able to work in multiple locations, including outdoor areas.

Wi-Fi networks are particularly appealing to organizations that intend to build, maintain, and expand virtual workplaces for employees because of low cost (the cost of Wi-Fi systems has decreased by 70% in the recent years), a seamless connection between Wi-Fi and wired networks, the freedom from wires, and the capacity to offer emerging new applications such as video conferencing and voice over WLAN systems. Deploying Wi-Fi would boost productivity. For instance, Microsoft provided WLAN to its 35,000 employees in the 1990s. Convenience and flexibility drove employees to use e-mail at least 30 minutes per week, which meant a return on $6 million per year on the $9 million invested in Wi-Fi (Microsoft, 2005).

However, existing research shows that use of Wi-Fi in general is low. Only 6% of Internet users surveyed by Jupiter Research in 2002 indicated they ever used it in public places (Villano, 2003). The number of people who accessed the Internet wirelessly increased to only 27% in 2005 (Golvin, 2005). It appears a gap between building a new wireless network and actual use exists in the diffusion of Wi-Fi. Fichman (1995) called it an assimilation gap. That is, a system of new information technology may be built by organizations, but it is only sparsely used within adopting organizations. As understanding users and their needs is a prerequisite for the success of any new information technology, this chapter has three objectives: (1) to explore how user needs account for the low usage of Wi-Fi in organizations where Wi-Fi has become an integral part of the information infrastructure, (2) to build a model that will help organizations increase Wi-Fi usage among employees, and (3) to discuss future trends in Wi-Fi technology and the importance of increased Wi-Fi use in enhancing virtual workplaces.

BACKGROUND: CONCEPTS, HYPOTHESES, AND DATA

An innovation refers to a new idea, practice, or product. With a hardware component (e.g., WLAN) and a software component (e.g., applications), Wi-Fi exemplifies what Rogers (1995) called a technological innovation. Past research on diffusion of innovations in society shows that the adoption of a new information technology is by no means a cakewalk. Adoption, the decision to use an innovation, is influenced particularly by people's intent to use the innovation to fulfill their needs. Thus, this section will examine the role of motivations of Wi-Fi use, technological and personal factors in explaining the low usage of Wi-Fi.

Predictors of Adoption of New Information Technology

Conceptually, adoption refers to "the decision to make full use of an innovation as the best course of action available" (Rogers, 1986, p. 122). The adoption decision is influenced by various factors, which are reviewed next. Moreover, to ascertain if the identified factors hold explanative power over low Wi-Fi usage, hypotheses were developed to test Rogers' (1986, 1995) diffusion of innovation theory.

Demographics

Atkin, Jeffres, and Neuendorf (1998) called demographics, which include age, gender, race, education, income, marital status, and household size, "social locators" of new media adoption (p. 476). Younger, better educated, and upscale males tend to be early adopters (Rogers, 1986, 1995). Numerous studies reported the effects of demographics in adopting personal computers (Dickerson & Gentry 1983; Dutton, Rogers, & Jun, 1987; Lin 1998). Consistent findings were reported in Internet adoption (Atkin et al., 1998; Busselle, Reagan, Pinkleton, & Jackson, 1999; Savage & Waldman, 2005). Accordingly, social locators will account for the low usage of Wi-Fi.

Motivations of Media Use

The benefits of a new media technology to its potential users affect adoption. The generalization is that the more people know about the benefits of an innovation, the more likely they are to consider adopting it (Atkin et al., 1998; Rogers, 1995). Past research further suggests that physical attributes of an innovation (such as speed) are probably less important than people's subjective evaluations of or beliefs about the benefits of an innovation (Agarwal & Prasad, 1997). Most adoption studies focused on testing the effect of Rogers' five perceptual attributes (e.g., relative advantage, compatibility, complexity, trialbility, and observability) on adoption. Though support was found, the support was nevertheless incomplete because the five perceived attributes tended to be empirically undistinguishable.

Several recent studies (Lin, 2001, 2002) included motivations as predictors of Internet use. Results show that user needs were predictors of PC adoption (Perse & Courtrigth, 1993) and use of electronic bulletin boards (James, Wotring, & Forrest, 1995). Others (Lin, 2004) further propose that the uses and gratifications perspective shares a common theoretical thread with perceived attributes in the diffusion of innovations research paradigm. As Lin (2002) argued, perceptions of the attributes of a technology can be mediated by additional perceptual factors such as gratifications sought from using the technology. That is, gratification-seeking motivations have a bearing on adoption likelihood of a new media technology.

Past uses and gratifications research shows that Internet gratifications included information seeking, entertainment and diversion, escape, exploration, and relationship building (Charney & Greenberg, 2002; Eighmey & McCord, 1998; Parker & Plank, 2002). More important, these gratifications were found to be significant predictors of adoption of PCs and the Internet. James et al. (1995) analyzed how subscribers to *Prodigy* and *CompuServe* used the computer to satisfy their various needs such as socializing. Korgaonkar and Wolin (1999) found that those who used the World Wide Web frequently were motivated to seek the gratifications of social escape, information, socialization, and economic features. Other studies on gratifications of Internet use (Papacharissi & Rubin, 2000) found that the more respondents sought entertainment, social interaction, and escape from the Internet, the more time they spent surfing the Internet. Surveying AOL users, Stafford (2003) found that social gratification was the most important motive for early Internet users. Savage and Waldman (2005) found that preferences for attributes of broadband such as reliability, speed, and always-on connectivity predicted adoption of broadband Internet in U.S. households. Thus, the motivations of Wi-Fi use will help explain the low usage of Wi-Fi.

Mass Media

The diffusion of innovations process is conceived as communication-driven via certain channels over time among members of a social system (Rogers, 1986). The role of mass media is underscored in the diffusion research paradigm. At the early stage of adoption, mass media can increase the awareness of an innovation and help get the word out to potential adopters. The generalization is that early adopters tend to use mass media more than later adopters (Rogers, 1995). Empirically, Lin (1998) reported that newspaper reading was a predictor of home computer adoption. Jeffres and Atkin (1996) found that TV viewing was a predictor of Internet use.

Technology Cluster

Rogers (1995) proposed technology clusters as contingent variables to explain adoption behavior. According to him, a technology cluster "consists of one or more distinguishable elements of technology that are perceived as being closely interrelated" (p. 15). Reagan (1987) labeled a set of concurrently diffused new media as functionally similar media technologies or functionally similar technology repertoires. The generalization is that adoption of one new information technology is related to adoption of functionally similar technologies.

Numerous studies reported the effect of technology clusters on adoption of PCs (Dickerson &

Gentry, 1983; Dutton et al., 1987) and the Internet. Using a total of 14 communication technologies, Lin (1998) built a technology cluster index. Lin's (1998) study found that adopters of PCs owned more communication technologies than nonadopters. Moreover, the number of media technologies owned was found as the strongest predictor of home computer adoption. Results of studies on Internet adoption also showed that those owning more technologies were found to be heavier Internet users (Busselle et al., 1999; Lin 2001). In adopting the broadband at home, Savage and Waldman (2005) found that those owning multiple PCs were most likely to embrace broadband. Wi-Fi upgrades and expands existing wired Internet networks. Thus, to use Wi-Fi, technology cluster matters—one must have had laptop computers or mobile devices such as PDAs in place.

Hypotheses make theories like diffusion of innovations empirically testable. Thus, to test the theoretical linkages between demographics, motivations of Wi-Fi use, mass media, and technology cluster and the awareness of, interest in, and likelihood to use Wi-Fi, four hypotheses were stated (see the first column in Table 1). In addition, it is important to find out which predictor is the best in multivariate analyses when all predictors are taken into account. That is, when all predictors (e.g., demographics, motivations of Wi-Fi use, mass media use, and technology cluster) are taken into consideration, their relative contributions to account for the low Wi-Fi usage are explored in a research question (RQ1): Which predictor is the best to account for the low usage of Wi-Fi?

MODELING ADOPTION OF INFORMATION TECHNOLOGY AS A PROCESS

Rogers (1986) characterized adoption as a "process through which an individual passes from first knowledge of an innovation, to forming an attitude toward the innovation, to a decision to adopt or reject, to implementation of the idea, and to conformation of this decision" (p. 163). Thus, knowledge of an innovation and attitudes toward the innovation are considered preconditions for the behavior of adoption. Rogers underscored the important role of mass media at the knowledge stage in creating awareness of and spreading the word about an innovation to a large audience. To examine the underlying mechanisms of Wi-Fi adoption for the purpose of increasing Wi-Fi usage, this study tests a Wi-Fi adoption model, which incorporates awareness of and interest in Wi-Fi. Another research question is raised accordingly (RQ2): How do awareness of and interest in Wi-Fi contribute to the increase of Wi-Fi usage?

Data

University faculty, researchers, and college students were among the earliest users of the Internet prior to its popularity in the general population in the 1990s. It is not a surprise that institutions of higher education outnumbered any other organizations in implementing WLANs at 29% (NOP World Technology, 2003), higher than the manufacturing sector (23%), health care industry (31%), and government agencies (12%). As Jayson (2006) noted, totally-wireless campuses have emerged across the United States. Thus, the data for hypotheses testing were collected in a public university enrolling 24,000 in the Southeast. The university was the chosen site because it started deploying a Wi-Fi powered WLAN in 2004, offering faculty, staff, and students wireless access to the Internet. The wireless network was available in buildings for common use such as the library, the stadium, and buildings designated for teaching and faculty office in addition to all outdoor green space areas. The goal of the Wi-Fi network was to create a mobile computing environment and a virtual workplace by building a seamless wireless network across the campus so that faculty and students would have the flexibility in going online anywhere on the campus.

Multistage stratified sampling procedures were used to draw a probability sample. Respondents

were first selected by department sizes of small, medium, or large. Classes were selected from a stratified list of large, medium, and small classes offered at each of the selected departments with various sizes.[1] Three large, six medium, and six small-sized classes were randomly selected. The number of respondents in the sample totaled 1,280, among which, 774 completed the questionnaires successfully in November 2004, yielding a response rate of 60.47%.[2]

Measures and Scales

Awareness of Wi-Fi was measured by asking respondents to indicate whether they had heard of Wi-Fi technology and the Wi-Fi-powered WLAN on campus (1=yes, 2=no). The two questions were fairly highly correlated ($r = .53, p < .001$) and were combined into a composite scale of awareness of Wi-Fi ($M = .90, SD = .84$, ranging from 0 to 2). Interest in Wi-Fi was measured by asking respondents to indicate how interested they were in Wi-Fi on a 1-5 point scale where 1 meant "not at all" and 5 meant "extremely" interested ($M = 3.42, SD = 1.25$). Likelihood to use Wi-Fi was measured by asking respondents to indicate how likely they would use the newly deployed Wi-Fi in three months. The scale was 7-point, where 1 meant "not likely at all" and 7 meant "very likely" ($M = 4.22, SD = 2.07$). In addition, respondents were asked to indicate their likelihood to use specific applications via Wi-Fi such as e-mail, access courseware, and check class schedules.

Measures of motivations of Wi-Fi use involved asking respondents 14 questions on how Wi-Fi would help them fulfill a variety of needs on a 1-5 point scale (1 meant "not at all" and 5 meant "exactly"). The items were factor analyzed. A 3-factor solution was generated.[3] With six items (Wi-Fi keeps me company; It is a pleasant rest; It allows me to unwind; It relaxes me; When there is on one else to talk to or be with; Wi-Fi is exciting), the first factor was named "social escapist motivation" because it focused on use of Wi-Fi to rest, unwind, relax, and as a companion.

The second factor included five items (You can get immediate knowledge of big news events; It informs me about what is going on in the world; It allows me to keep up with news that is not available elsewhere; It allows me to get info like weather and sports scores; I can find information for homework). They showed the use of Wi-Fi to stay informed and to seek information. The factor was called "information learning motivation." Three items loaded on the third factor (It kills time; When I have nothing better to do; It gives me something to occupy my time). It was named "pass time motivation" as the items focused on using Wi-Fi to fill idle time.

Three motivation subscales were built after adding the items' value and divided by the number of items. Based on means, the information learning motivation was the strongest ($M = 3.45, SD = 1.03$, $a = .94$), followed by the pass time motivation ($M = 3.12, SD = 1.02, a = .90$) and the social escapist motivation ($M = 2.79, SD = 1.10 a = .93$).

To measure mass media use, respondents were requested to report the number of days they read newspapers in a week ($M = 2.64, SD = 2.14$) and the hours per day they watched TV ($M = 2.40$, $SD = 2.25$). Technology cluster was measured by asking respondents whether they owned a desktop, laptop, pocket PC, and PDAs using a dichotomous scale (1=yes, 2=no). Correlation results show that having a desktop was correlated with having a laptop ($r = -.32, p<.001$); also, the correlation between having a pocket PC and PDAs was fairly high ($r= .41, p<.001$). Accordingly, two subscales of technology cluster were constructed after adding the items. The first subscale was called "owning PCs" ($M = 1.32, SD = .53$). The second was named "owning portable devices" ($M = .18, SD = .48$).

INSIGHTS FROM FINDINGS

In terms of awareness of Wi-Fi, 58.3% of the respondents had heard of it, but only one-third (32.3%) had heard of the Wi-Fi powered WLAN on campus. The percentage of respondents who had ever used the newly-deployed wireless system was even lower at 12.9%. Among the users, the wireless devices they used the most were laptops (35.9%), followed by cell phones (6.5%), pocket PCs (5.9%), PDAs (3.9%), and tablet computers (2.1%). They typically spent an average of less than 1 hour going online wirelessly per day. Among the nonusers, their interest in Wi-Fi was high. One third (34.8%) were somewhat and 46.2% were very or extremely interested in accessing the virtual space wirelessly. Regarding the intention to use Wi-Fi, 20% of the respondents were somewhat likely and 45.4% were likely or very likely to use it.

Predictors of Wi-Fi Adoption

Hypotheses provide a means to validate the adoption theory in Wi-Fi diffusion. As summarized in Table 1, the hypotheses developed for testing the linkages between social locators and the awareness of, interest in, and likelihood to use Wi-Fi were partially supported. Female and respondents of ethnicities tended to be less aware of Wi-Fi. Further, the weaker the motivations of using Wi-Fi to learn information, to pass time, and to escape socially, the less the respondents were aware of, interested in, and likely to use Wi-Fi. H2 was supported. The insight out of this result is that the less helpful Wi-Fi was perceived for staying informed, killing time, and unwinding, the less respondents were aware of, interested in, and likely to use this newer Internet technology.

Further, the less often respondents read newspapers, the less they knew about Wi-Fi. Conversely, the more often they read newspapers, the more they were aware of Wi-Fi. H3 was partially supported. The insight generated from these results is that use of the print media contributes to awareness of Wi-Fi. In addition, those respondents who did not own computers were less interest in Wi-Fi and less likely to use it. H4 was basically supported. The insight is that those who did not have the needed hardware tend to be late adopters.

Table 1. Hypotheses regarding the relationships between demographics, motivations of Wi-Fi use, mass media, and technology cluster and awareness of, interest in, and likelihood to use Wi-Fi

Hypotheses	Wi-Fi Awareness	Interest in Wi-Fi	Likelihood to Use Wi-Fi
H1a: The older the respondents, the less they will be aware of, interested in, and likely to use Wi-Fi.	nonsignificant	nonsignificant	nonsignificant
H1b: Female respondents will be less aware of, less interested in, and less likely to use Wi-Fi than male respondents.	$r = .16**$ (gender/female)	nonsignificant	nonsignificant
H1c: The less income respondents have, the less they will be aware of, interested in, and likely to use Wi-Fi.	nonsignificant	nonsignificant	nonsignificant
H1d: Respondents of ethnicities will be less aware of, interested in, and likely to use Wi-Fi than white respondents.	$r = .11*$ (race/white)	nonsignificant	nonsignificant
H2: The weaker the motivations of Wi-Fi use to get information, to pass time, and to escape, the less respondents will be aware of, interested in, and likely to use WiFi.	$r = .17*$ (info-learning) $r = .09**$ (pass time) $r = .08*$ (social escape)	$r = .49***$ (info-learning) $r = .38***$ (pass time) $r = .40*$ (social escape)	$r = .37*$ (info-learning) $r = .34***$ (pass time) $r = .37***$ (social escape)
H3: The less respondents use mass media, the less they will be aware of, interested in, and likely to use Wi-Fi.	$r = .16**$ (reading newspapers)	nonsignificant	nonsignificant
H4: The less computer hardware that respondents own, the less they will be aware of, interested in, and likely to use Wi-Fi.	$r = .09*$ (PCs owned)	$r = .20**$ (PCs owned) $r = .13*$ (Portable devices owned)	$r = .21**$ (PCs owned)

*Notes: N ranges from 695 to 758. *** $p < .001$; ** $p < .01$; * $p < .05$.*

On the other hand, those who had the hardware tend to be early adopters.

Ranking Predictors of Wi-Fi Adoption

To find out which predictor would be the best in predicting the awareness of, interest in, and likelihood to use Wi-Fi, three multiple regression analyses were run. The dependent variables were respectively awareness of, interest in, and likelihood to use Wi-Fi. In the first run, entered in the equation in which awareness of Wi-Fi was treated as the criterion variable were demographics, motivations of Wi-Fi use, mass media use, and technology cluster. As results in Table 2 show (the second column), newspaper reading was the best predictor of Wi-Fi awareness, followed by the motivation of using Wi-Fi for information.

Gender and race were the third and fourth best predictors. The fact that newspaper reading was the best predictor of being aware of Wi-Fi suggests efforts to increase the level of Wi-Fi awareness need to focus on print media.

In the second multiple regression analysis, entered in the equation in which interest in Wi-Fi was the criterion variable included demographics, motivations of Wi-Fi use, mass media use, technology cluster, and awareness of Wi-Fi. As shown in Table 2 (third column), the information learning and the social escapist motivations were the best predictors of interest in Wi-Fi. The awareness of Wi-Fi was the third best, and owning PCs and portable devices were the fourth and fifth best predictors. What these results mean is that interest in Wi-Fi was mostly driven by the motivation to use wireless Internet for information acquisition and social escape. Similarly, a third

Table 2. Summary of multiple regression analyses predicting awareness of, interest in, and likelihood to use Wi-Fi

Ranking of Predictors	Awareness of Wi-Fi (Adj. R^2=4.7%)	Interest in Wi-Fi (Adj. R^2=28.06%)	Likelihood to Use Wi-Fi (Adj. R^2=43%)
The best predictor	Newspaper reading (*Beta*=.13***)	Info-learning motivation (*Beta*=.32***)	Interest in Wi-Fi (*Beta*=.50***)
The 2nd best predictor	Info-learning motivation (*Beta*=.11**)	Social Escape motivation (*Beta*=.19***)	Info-learning motivation (*Beta*=.18***)
The 3rd best predictor	Gender/female (*Beta*=.11**)	Wi-Fi awareness (*Beta*=.14***)	PC owned (*Beta*=.11***)
The 4th best predictor	Race/white (*Beta*=.08*)	PC owned (*Beta*=.13**)	Race/white (*Beta*=.07*)
The 5th best predictor	n/a	Portable devices owned (*Beta*=.08*)	Class standing (*Beta*=-.07*)

Note: *** p < .001; ** p < .01; * p < .05.

multiple regression analysis was performed with these predictors of the likelihood to use Wi-Fi: demographics, motivations of Wi-Fi use, mass media use, technology cluster, awareness of and interest in Wi-Fi. Results (fourth column in Table 2) show that the likelihood to use Wi-Fi was best predicted by interest in Wi-Fi. The information learning motivation and PC owned also mattered, but to a much less degree.

In summary, these multivariate results indicate that demographics and media use variables were most influential in accounting for the low awareness of Wi-Fi. But motivations of Wi-Fi use were the most important factors in explaining the level of interest in Wi-Fi and low usage of Wi-Fi. Specifically, the less respondents felt that Wi-Fi was helpful in fulfilling the need for information-seeking and social escape, the less their interest in Wi-Fi. Furthermore, the less respondents felt that Wi-Fi was helpful in fulfilling the need of information-seeking and the less their interest in Wi-Fi, the lower their intention to use it.

Modeling the Process of Wi-Fi Adoption

The question, then, is how to increase the use of Wi-Fi. Specifically, what are the underlying mechanisms that facilitate the adoption? Informed by the process model of adoption (Rogers, 1986),

a chain-effect process of Wi-Fi adoption was found.[4] As Figure 1 shows, the awareness of Wi-Fi, which was influenced by reading newspapers, had a direct effect on the level of interest in Wi-Fi, which directly affected the likelihood to use Wi-Fi. It is clear that awareness of and interest in Wi-Fi were the preconditions of using Wi-Fi. The insight is that to increase Wi-Fi usage, the awareness of and interest in the newer Internet technology must be in place.

Future Trends

New information technologies play a critical role in building virtual workplaces (Igbaria & Tan, 1998). The telephone gave rise to "telework" (also called telecommuting), which means employees are able to work from a distance away from office. The Internet raised "telework" to an unprecedented level by creating a virtual workplace in which employees are connected not just by telephone lines but also by a network of data and real-time communication. Now, wireless Internet offers expanding applications for all organizations that increasingly rely on local area networks (LANs) for internal and external communications. Wi-Fi powered WLAN enables Internet users to work and maintain communities anywhere, anytime with freedom, mobility, and flexibility. Undoubt-

Figure 1. A chain-process model of Wi-Fi adoption

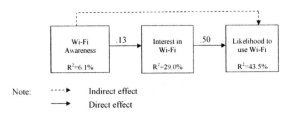

edly, Wi-Fi has enhanced Internet-based virtual workplaces. In fact, fast proliferation of the new generation of Wi-Fi technologies resulted in an increasing number of wireless networks in organizations worldwide. If not already done, it is time for organizations to consider deploying WLAN to expand the virtual workplace.

Several trends shed some light on the future of Wi-Fi and its potential impact on organizations. First, with the rapid diffusion of broadband in U.S. households and the popularity of mobile devices with WLAN adapters such as PDAs, the "always-on" home network has flourished (Meadows & Grant, 2006). WLANs for home networks were estimated to have grown by 103% from 2002 to 2007 (Paolini & Pow, 2002). Wi-Fi offers a novel and efficient way to build and maintain home offices. Second, numerous Wi-Fi networks are being built in public places such as parks, malls, and downtowns. They bridge the gap between office and home networks. As a result, a nationwide wireless infrastructure may emerge. Such a network would allow users to roam among hot spots with continuous wireless LAN access. In the foreseeable future, access to the virtual workplace will be ubiquitous. Business organizations that do not have WLANs will miss the opportunity to be part of this emerging nationwide wireless network.

Meanwhile, with the standardization of Wi-Fi in 1997, Wi-Fi technology has improved rapidly. Under the umbrella term of Wi-Fi (IEEE 802.11) are several types of Wi-Fi technologies. IEEE 802.11b, operating in 2.4 GHz frequency has a data transmission rate from 10 MB/s to 50 MB/s, and

IEEE 802.11g offers higher rates. IEEE 802.11a, which is faster at a speed up to 54 MB/s in the 5 Ghz band, is another alternative. Because of the higher frequency, the inference is minimal for 802.11a (Geier, 2004). Security, a major issue for Wi-Fi networks, is being improved with advances in authentication, authorization, and encryption. For example, virtual private network (VPN) software can be added as a layer of protection. In addition, a new version of Wired Equivalent Privacy (WEP) is being developed to provide more security.

Moreover, newer applications on the horizon will benefit organizations with WLANs. Wi-Fi will be likely to coexist with the emergence of 3G (third generation wireless telephony) in the United States. It is estimated that 10,000 Wi-Fi transmitters will cover the same area as a single 3G transmission tower. Voice over WLANs (VoWLAN) is an emerging application. Because a WLAN takes both cellular phone systems and data traffic, VoWLANs offer mobile telephone communication. Technically, the phone can be used via WLAN and then transit to cellular systems as users roam. This new technology will likely be a killer application because use of the phone is high in organizations. The potential for cost saving is great. Also, the next generation of wireless networks are likely to integrate WiMax with Voice over Internet Protocol (VoIP)(Eccles, 2005). The trend of mobile devices will be convergence. For example, the 3G smart phone offers voice, data, and Internet connection. With high speed, a wider range of coverage, and mobility, newer collaborative applications and tools are likely to be popular. For instance, real-time Web video conferencing will be possible for employees anywhere, anytime within a hot spot.

In short, these newer applications of Wi-Fi to provide mobile access to e-mail and data, VoWLAN, and video conferencing will further expand the virtual workplace. The benefits of enhanced virtual workplaces by Wi-Fi include cost saving and increased productivity, morale, and job satisfaction among employees.

CONCLUSION

The benefits from deploying Wi-Fi should not be taken for granted, however. As the empirical study reported in this chapter shows, even when a wireless network was deployed and the virtual workplace was expanded, low usage was a problem. Slightly over 10% of people had used the newly deployed Wi-Fi network built at the surveyed university. This result is consistent with industry research (Golvin, 2005; Villano, 2003). The point that cries for attention is that building Wi-Fi is not everything; promoting its use should be equally important for management. After all, the ultimate success of Wi-Fi depends on how much employees use it.

The good news is that the interest in Wi-Fi was found high among prospects. To take advantage of wireless networks, understanding the users' needs is critical to the success of virtual workplaces. To convert more employees to Wi-Fi users, management needs to focus on motivating employees to go online wirelessly. As the evidence presented in this chapter shows, the motivations of information learning and social escapism were the best predictors of interest in and likelihood to use Wi-Fi. Thus, the motivations should be based on how Wi-Fi fulfills employees' needs for getting information with mobility, flexibility, and efficiency.

Furthermore, as the empirical research in this chapter shows, lack of awareness constitutes a barrier to Wi-Fi adoption. Awareness of Wi-Fi leads to an increase in interest in Wi-Fi, which in turn results in strong intention to use Wi-Fi. Reading newspapers helps the most with Wi-Fi awareness. The insights out of these results are that before deploying Wi-Fi, increasing awareness about Wi-Fi among employees should be the focus of a publicity campaign to convert highly interested potential users of Wi-Fi. Campaigns to raise awareness should place messages in print media such as newspapers, newsletters, and brochures. Also, signs should be posted around Wi-Fi access points.

In conclusion, a needs-based approach to deal with the low usage of Wi-Fi coupled with suffi-cient publicity is likely to increase Wi-Fi use in organizations. Past research shows that the more employees use the Internet, the more frequently they use it and spend more time online in the office, at home, and on the go. As WLANs are deployed in more offices, homes, and public places, increased use of Wi-Fi will make the success of virtual workplaces more likely.

REFERENCES

Agarwal, R., & Prasad, J. (1997). The role of innovation characteristics and perceived voluntariness in the acceptance of information technologies. *Decision Science, 28,* 557-582.

Atkin, D., Jeffres, L., & Neuendorf, K. (1998). Understanding Internet adoption as telecommunications behavior. *Journal of Broadcasting & Electronic Media, 42,* 475-490.

Best, J. (2005, September). 100,000 for worldwide Wi-Fi this year. *Silicon News.* Retrieved November 6, 2007 from http://networks.silicon.com/mobile/0,39024665,39152752,00.htm

Busselle R., Reagan, J., Pinkleton, B., & Jackson, K. (1999). Factors affecting Internet use in a saturated-access population. *Telematics & Informatics, 16*(1), 45-58.

Charney, T., & Greenberg, B. (2002). Uses and gratifications of the Internet. In C. Lin & D. Atkin (Eds.), *Communication, technology and society: New media adoption and uses* (pp. 379-407). Cress Kill, NJ: Hampton Press.

Dickerson, M. D., & Gentry, J. (1983). Characteristics of adopters and non-adopters of home computers. *Journal of Consumer Research, 10,* 225-235.

Dutton, W. H., Rogers, E. M., & Jun, S. H. (1987). Diffusion and social impacts of personal computers. *Communication Research, 14,* 219-250.

Eccles, R. (2005). The mobile broadband revoluation. Retrieved November 6, 2007, from http://www.twobirds.com/english/publications/articles/The_mobile_broadband_revolution.cfm?RenderForPrint=1.

Eighmey, J., & McCord, L. (1998). Adding value in the information age: Uses and gratifications of sites on the World Wide Web. *Journal of Business Research, 41,* 187-194.

Fichman, R. G. (1995). *The assimilation and diffusion of software process innovations.*

Unpublished Ph.D. thesis, The MIT Sloan School of Management.

Geier, J. (2004). *The state of wireless LANs.* Santa Clara, CA: Intel.

Golvin, C. (2005). *Consumers embrace wireless Internet access.* Forrester Research Report. Retrieved November 6, 2007, from http://www.forrester.com/Research?Document?Except/0,7211,37787.html.

Igbaria, M. & Tan, M. (1998). *The virtual workplace.* Hershey, PA: Idea Group Publishing.

James, M., Wotring, C., & Forrest, E. (1995). An exploratory study of the perceived benefits of electronic bulletin board use and their impact on other communication activities. *Journal of Broadcasting & Electronic Media, 39,* 30-50.

Jayson, S. (2006, October 3). Totally wireless on campus. *USA Today,* p. D1.

Jeffres, L., & Atkin, D. (1996). Predicting use of technologies for communication and consumer needs. *Journal of Broadcasting & Electronic Media, 40,* 318-330.

Korgaonkar, P., & Wolin, L. (1999). A multivariate analysis of Web usage. *Journal of Advertising Research, 39*(2), 53-68.

Lin, C. (1998). Exploring personal computer adoption dynamic. *Journal of Broadcasting & Electronic Media, 42,* 95-112.

Lin, C. (2001). Audience attributes, media supplementation, and likely online service adoption. *Mass Communication & Society, 4,* 19-38.

Lin, C. (2002). Perceived gratification, of online media service use among potential user. *Telematics & Informatics, 19,* 3-19.

Lin, C. (2004). Webcasting adoption: Technology fluidity, user innovativeness, and media substitution. *Journal of Broadcasting & Electronic Media, 48,* 446-465.

Meadows, J., & Grant, A. (2006). Home networks. In A. Grant & J. Meadows (Eds.), *Communication technology update* (10th ed., pp. 295-310). Boston, MA: Focal Press.

Microsoft. (2005). *Improving the wireless network infrastructure at Microsoft: Technical case study.* Retrieved November 6, 2007, from http://www.microsoft.com/technet/itshowcase/content/wirelesslantcs.mspx

NOP World Technology. (2003). *Wireless LAN benefit study.* Retrieved November 6, 2007, from http://newsroom.cisco.com/dlls/prod_111203.html

Paolini, M., & Pow, R. (2002). *Public wireless LAN access: US market forecasts 2002-2007 analysis.* Retrieved November 6, 2007, from http://www.analysis.com/ (News)

Papacharissi, Z., & Rubin, A. (2000). Predictors of Internet use. *Journal of Broadcasting & Electronic Media, 44,* 175-196.

Parker, B., & Plank, R. (2002). A uses and gratifications perspectives on the Internet as a new information sources. *American Business Review, 18,* 43-49.

Perse, E., & Courtrigth, J. (1993). Normative images of communication media: Mass and interpersonal channels in the new media environment. *Human Communication Research, 19,* 485-503.

Reagan, J. (1987). Classifying adopters and non-adopters for technologies using political activity, media use and demographic variables. *Telematics & Informatics, 4,* 3-16.

Rogers, E. (1986). *Diffusion of innovation* (3rd ed.). New York: Free Press.

Rogers, E. (1995). *Diffusion of innovation* (4ᵗʰ ed.). New York: Free Press.

Savage, J., & Waldman, D. (2005). Broadband Internet access, awareness and use: Analysis of United States household data. *Telecommunication Policy, 29*(8), 615-633.

Stafford, T. (2003). Differentiating between adopter categories in the uses and gratifications for Internet services. *IEEE Transactions on Engineering Management, 50*, 427-435.

Villano, M. (2003, November 21). *Wi-Fi is hot, but users still warming to it.* Wi-Fi planet. Retrieved November 6, 2007, from http://www.wi-fiplanet.com/news/article.php/3111721

Young, S. (2006, October 23). Civic lessons: Municipal Wi-Fi networks are moving forward. But not without a few bumps along the way. *The Wall Street Journal*, p. R6.

KEY TERMS

Adoption: This term refers to decision-making about how to best use a technological innovation. Based on the time of adoption of an innovation, adopters are classified as innovators, early adopters, early majority, and laggards.

Diffusion of Innovations: A social psychological theory that describes and explains the patterns, mechanisms and process by which a new idea, product, or technology is communicated through various channels in society.

Hot Spot: A geographic area in which public broadband network access is available wirelessly through a WLAN. It is also called a wireless cloud or access point.

Mobile Computing: A term referring to portable devices run on microprocessors with the capability of accessing computer networks wirelessly.

Radio Networking: Another term for Wi-Fi because it provides seamless connection with a local area network (LAN) via radio waves instead of wires.

Wi-Fi: Short for wireless fidelity, it is a general term for wireless 802.11 Ethernet standard via radio waves rather than wires in the 2.4 GHz frequency range. It is also known as IEEE 802.11b and 802.11g with a data transfer speed up to 11 Mb/s.

Wireless Internet: A network that allows users access to a computer network using a wireless connection within the reach of a hot spot.

WiMax: A term for the newer Wi-Fi technology using the IEEE 802.16 wireless Ethernet standard. Its transmission speed is up to 120 Mb/s in the 10-66 Ghz range.

Wireless Networking: A technology of 802.11b and g that creates a wireless network. A client computer equipped with network interface card can access a LAN with an access point.

WLAN: A wireless local area network that connects computers and servers to share application programs and files.

ENDNOTES

[1]   A large class equaled an enrollment of 180 or more students; a medium-size class, 51 to 179; and a small class, no more than 50 students.

[2]   Of the sample, age ranged from 16 to 58 ($M = 21.5, SD = 4.50$). The gender ratio was about even (48.1% male and 51.9% female). Some 39.5% were freshmen and sophomores, 50.2% were juniors were seniors, and 10.0% were graduate students. The median household income category was $50k to $80k. Most respondents were white (81.6%), followed by African Americans (9.6%), Asians, (4.1%), and Hispanics (1.5%).

3 The 3-factor solution accounted for 73.26% of the variance. *The Eigen value* of the first factor was 4.84, accounting for 34.75% of the variance. The *Eigen value* of the second factor was 3.73, accounting for 26.67% of the variance. The *Eigen value* of the third factor was 2.41, accounting for 17.19% of the variance.

4 The figure was a path model which used the standardized regression coefficients (betas) generated from the three multiple regression runs.

Chapter XXIX
Using Virtual Worlds to Assist Distributed Teams

Clint Bowers
University of Central Florida, USA

Peter A. Smith
University of Central Florida, USA

Jan Cannon-Bowers
University of Central Florida, USA

Denise Nicholson
University of Central Florida, USA

ABSTRACT

Virtual worlds and massively multiplayer online games are becoming a useful tool for distributed teams. From providing a common working place, to allowing members of the team to interact in a physical albeit virtual form, virtual worlds are setting a new standard for tools to facilitate interactions between members of distributed teams. This chapter explores the ways in which virtual worlds could support interactive teams at a greater fidelity then that of the previous generation of groupware tools using a popular virtual world, Second Life as an example. While providing specific examples of how Second Life's current and planned feature sets could already support distributed teams, that is, teams whose members are geographically disbursed. New features that would provide additional support for these types of teams are also discussed.

INTRODUCTION

Due to advances in communications technology over the past 30 years, the use of distributed or virtual teams is becoming more common in the modern workplace. We use the terms "distributed" and "virtual" teams interchangeably to refer to groups of employees who must accomplish their tasks by working with teammates who are physically dispersed. Such teams must rely on a variety of communication technologies to mediate their interactions and enable coordinated effort to occur. Despite the growing importance of virtual teams in the workplace, the mediating technologies that typically support them have been little more than simple modifications of "off-the-shelf" software developed to support individual tasks, such as e-mail and calendar programs. These technologies are not optimized to support true team performance, and often do not respond to the many challenges confronted by distributed teams. However, the emerging field of Virtual Worlds is providing new tools that may support many of the requirements of distributed teams that other technologies do not. To aid this discussion, we will use a Virtual World program called Second Life, developed by Linden Lab, as an example of how virtual world technology can support distributed team performance.

BACKGROUND: A BRIEF BREAKDOWN OF CORE TEAM MECHANICS

Before describing how Virtual Worlds might better support distributed teams, it is important to first discuss the nature of distributed team performance, and the factors that may facilitate or hinder it. Team researchers have identified a number of crucial team processes at the behavioral, attitudinal, and cognitive levels that are believed to be important determinants of effective team performance (see Salas & Cannon-Bowers, 1999). In distributed teams, which must rely on computer-mediated communication channels, these processes must necessarily be modified since the set of cues available to team members is different than in face-to-face teams. In fact, given the nature of distributed teams and the additional coordination demands placed upon team members in such situations, it is not surprising that they are believed to be at even higher risk for coordination breakdowns (Fiore, Salas, & Bowers, 2001). In large part, these coordination decrements can be attributed to the necessary reliance on technology that is incumbent in distributed team performance. Fiore, Salas, Cuevas, and Bowers (2003) have used the phrase "team opacity" to describe the manner in which technology-mediated coordination obscures important team processes such as team mental model development.

The following sections provide an overview of the processes that team researchers have identified as crucial to team effectiveness and the manner in which physical dispersion affects them. We organize these into behavioral, attitudinal, and cognitive processes in keeping with prevailing theories of team performance. Following this, we describe how Virtual World technologies can be used to overcome some of the challenges typically associated with distributed team performance.

BEHAVIORAL DIFFERENCES BETWEEN DISTRIBUTED AND COLLOCATED TEAMS

As noted, the literature in team performance delineates several important behavioral processes that underlie effective team performance, and the potential impact of team opacity is evident in several of them. Powell, Piccoli, and Ives (2004) summarized a number of these effects; we have selected the most salient for this discussion. These include: communication, coordination, adaptability, and leadership. They are summarized in the following paragraphs.

Communication

The most obvious team process affected by physical dispersion is communication. Differences between computer-mediated communication and face-to-face communication have been widely reported. See Bannan-Ritlan (2002) for a review. Given these differences, it is not surprising that distributed teams are subject to disruptions in their ability to accomplish tasks. These disruptions are even more troublesome when teams are composed of a mixture of colocated members and distant ones. In these cases, issues of mistrust frequently arise because it is assumed that the colocated members are having conversations to which the distant members cannot avail themselves (Crampton, 2001).

Coordination

Another critical process for distributed teams is coordination. Coordination refers to the degree to which teams can allocated resources (physical or intangible) in a manner that is timely and efficient. Again, distributed teams are prone to experience difficulties in this regard because they often work with a degraded cue array as compared to their colocated counterparts (Sarker & Sahay, 2002). Essentially, distributed team members have less information available to them about the state of the task and about each other. This may lead to diminished "shared situational awareness" (Salas, Cannon-Bowers, Fiore, & Stout, 2001), an important state that enables team members to coordinate implicitly (i.e., without the need for overt strategizing or discussion). Because distributed team members are less able to assess the needs of their teammates, they are less likely to offer resources before there is an actual request, adding to the workload experienced by the team.

Adaptability

Although not specifically described by Powell et al. (2004), it bears mentioning that adaptability is another construct requiring attention in distributed teams. Adaptability is the ability of the team to notice that a task-relevant change has occurred in the environment, understand the nature of the change, and respond to it accordingly (Campion, Medsker, & Higgs, 1993; Cannon-Bowers, Tannenbaum, Salas, & Volpe, 1995). Adaptability is considered to be one of the features that distinguish effective from ineffective teams (Salas, Sims, & Burke, 2005). Because distributed teams do not have as rich a source of task and team relevant information as colocated ones, they may interpret available cues differently and struggle to respond to changes (Fiore et al., 2004). As such, it might be important to augment the distributed team's environment in some fashion to increase their ability to adapt when necessary.

Leadership

A final category of behaviors that warrants mention is leadership. In the team performance context, leadership refers to the ability to direct the individual member's work, assess team performance, develop and encourage team members, and to plan and communicate effective strategies (Cannon-Bowers et al., 1995; Marks, Zaccaro, & Mathieu, 2000). Leaders of distributed teams clearly have a special challenge in meeting these requirements (Zhang, Fjermestad, & Tremaine, 2005). Specifically, Zhang et al. hypothesize that different leadership behaviors might be required by leaders of distributed teams than by those of face-to-face teams. This is an important notion and more research is required to fully understand the possible differences. It goes without saying, however, that facilitating effective leader behaviors will be an important goal for developers of technologies designed to assist distributed teams.

Attitudinal Differences Between Distributed and Collocated Teams

Team and task-related attitudes have been implicated as important determinants of team performance by a number of researchers (Duffy, Ganster, Shaw, Johnson, & Pagon, 2006). Fiore and his colleagues suggested in this regard that the demands of distributed teams make the effects of attitudes even more salient than in face-to-face teams. In the following paragraphs, we will explore how the distributed environment might affect attitudinal features of the team.

Trust

Several researchers have suggested that distributed teams are likely to have decreased levels of trust among the individual members (Alexander, 2000; Powell et al., 2004). This is important because prior research has demonstrated that low levels of trust are associated with decreased team coordination and cooperation behaviors (Dirks, 1999). Further, groups with low levels of trust have been shown to focus more closely on their own goals and needs rather than the goals and needs of the larger team. Problems establishing trust within the team are especially troublesome when dealing with distributed teams because mistrust may spring from the technology, from the other teammates, or from the interaction of the two. In many cases, development of mistrust by a team member is the result of attributions made about relatively ambiguous and innocuous communication from other members. Thus, there is a need to not only enable communication but to increase the likelihood that the communication will be interpreted correctly and in a way that supports the development of trust among members.

Cohesion

Team cohesion has been shown to be an important determinant of subsequent team performance. In fact, cohesion has been described as "the essential small group characteristic" (Galembiewski, 1962, p. 149). Fiore et al. (2003, p. 349) define team cohesion as "active involvement and commitments driving the willingness to remain, and freely interact, in a group." Higher levels of team cohesion have been related to increased performance in a number of face-to-face teams (e.g., Michalisin, Karau, & Tanpong, 2004; Patterson, Carron, & Loughhead, 2005). Not surprisingly, scientists in this area have expressed concerns that distributed teams might be at risk for lower levels of team cohesion (Driskell, Radtke, & Sals, 2003; Warkentin, Sayeed, & Hightower, 1997). Early data in this area seem to support these concerns (Maznevski, 2000; Strauss, 1996). It should be noted, however, that the cohesion effects observed in distributed teams is likely to be a function of the type of technology used to support the team (Powell et al., 2004). We will have more to say on this issue as we discuss the use of Massively Multiplayer Online Games (MMOGs) to support virtual teams in a later section.

Collective Efficacy

Collective efficacy has been defined as the team's shared belief that it has the resources to accomplish the assigned task (Whitney, 1994). Several researchers have reported a positive relationship between collective efficacy and team performance (e.g., Myers, Feltz, & Short, 2004; Tasa, Taggar, & Seijts, 2007; Watson, Chemers, & Preiser, 2001). Researchers have demonstrated that teams that possess lower collective efficacy are less prone to assist their teammates than teams with higher efficacy (Smith-Jentsch, Kraiger, Cannon-Bowers, & Salas, 2002). In distributed teams, it is likely that the mechanisms team members rely on to develop collective efficacy are different than in collocated teams. Here again, the core issue is the manner in which distributed team members are able to experience and share successes (which builds efficacy) and how accurately they are able to assess the strengths and weaknesses of their teammates and the team as a whole. Although collective efficacy has not been investigated empirically in distributed teams, one would certainly hypothesize that it could be difficult to establish and may affect their performance (Alavi & McCormick, 2004; Fiore et al., 2004). A challenge for scientists in this area is to create enabling technologies to support development of this important construct.

Team Orientation

It has been suggested that a necessary condition for any team to be effective is an overall tendency of its members to believe that teamwork is important, and to be willing to invest energy into teamwork behaviors (Cannon-Bowers & Salas, 2001; Driskell & Salas, 1992). Labeled *team orientation,* this construct has been demonstrated to predict performance in face-to-face teams (Driskell & Salas, 1992). In distributed teams, it is not clear that team members are interpreting themselves as a true team. In other words, the context of distributed team performance may not trigger the mental representations of teamwork (or more precisely, the need for it) that are readily apparent in a face-to-face team. Hence, distributed team members may not recognize that the situation calls for teamwork, even if they are typically effective team members. The challenge is, therefore, to create distributed team environments that cause team members recognize that teamwork is essential.

Cognitive Differences between Distributed and Collocated Teams

As pointed out by Fiore et al. (2004), the nature of information flow in distributed teams causes substantial changes in how team members must think about the data required to do their task. The mixing of synchronous and asynchronous data, information provided through a variety of modalities, and the workload associated with monitoring distant teammates all are likely to impose their own cognitive demands on operators. We review these likely effects briefly below.

Working Memory

Although working memory is a complex, multidimensional process (Baddely, 1986; Baddely & Hitch, 1974), it can be roughly described as the cognitive processes required to perceive and interpret information in complex data arrays. As described above, the demands on working memory imposed by participating in a distributed team environment are likely to be different, and probably greater, than in collocated teams because commonly shared visual and auditory cues are not readily available. This may place distributed teams at risk for degraded performance, especially when dealing with high workload tasks.

Memory Activation

Obviously, the actual memory operations needed to execute complex tasks are of particular im-

portance for this discussion. In describing the role of memory actions in complex task performance, Fiore, Schooler, Whiteside, & Hermann (1997) have focused on two separate memory types: prospective memory and retrospective memory. Retrospective memory refers to "normal" memory; that is, retrieving items that have already been stored. Prospective memory is a special memory task where the operator must remember to do something in the future. The technology associated with distributed teams might make it easy to aid retrospective memory. However, prospective memory might suffer from lack of "cueing" effects. Thus there might be an advantage to creating "reminder aids" for these teammates (Fiore et al, 1997).

Long-Term Memory

Although a number of long-term memory structures have been hypothesized (e.g., Jong & Ferguson-Hessler, 1996), Fiore and his colleagues have suggested that one particular structure, episodic memory, is of particular concern for distributed team performance. Episodic memory usually refers to information about oneself that is coded in the context of specific events (Tulving, 1983). Fiore and his colleagues (2004) have revised this definition for use in considering team performance. They describe episodic memory in this context as being "composed of interactions with teammates and the scenarios or situations engaged by the team" (p. 353). Clearly, because the interactions with team members are likely to be much different in distributed teams than in collocated teams, the long-term memory store is likely to be different as well. It is not clear what the performance implications of these differences are, but the data demonstrates that episodic differences can alter long-term group processes (Moreland & Myaskovsky, 2000).

FOCUS: USING VIRTUAL WORLDS TO ASSIST DISTRIBUTED TEAMS

As noted, the growing importance of distributed teams in the workplace has spawned the development of several technologies designed to assist these groups in coping with many of the demands described above. As pointed out by Driskell and Salas (2004), however, most software developed to assist groups has been developed simply to enable communication among members. There has been little dedicated development that seeks to assist the less overt aspects of team performance noted above. Further, most "groupware" has been simple modifications of "off-the-shelf" software developed for individuals, such as e-mail and calendar programs. While these have the potential to be helpful at some level, they are not likely to respond to the many challenges confronted by distributed teams. Many of these technologies have been reviewed before (Driskell & Salas, 2006), so we will not repeat that information here. Rather, we will attempt to create some hypotheses about how a different type of technology, Massively Multiplayer Online Gaming (MMOG), might be used to respond to these needs more completely.

The Second Life Example

While the application of a "game" technology might not seem appropriate for the workplace at first glance, we hope to demonstrate some of the potential advantages that these technologies offer. There are several MMOG platforms available. For the purposes of clarity, we will provide specific examples in the context of one popular application, Second Life (www.secondlife.com). Second Life is particularly well-suited for this discussion for several reasons. First, it is free and widely available. Second, it allows a greater level of scripting and programming than many of the other platforms. Users can develop a variety of objects with programmed capabilities. Third, it represents each operator as a customizable avatar.

We will discuss the advantages of this capability later in the chapter. Finally, it allows users to "own" and customize specific areas and elements of the virtual world. This allows users to develop virtual yet persistent customized workplaces for use by the team. In the following sections, we will provide suggestions for how this platform might be used to support distributed teams.

Improving Behaviors of Distributed Teams

As discussed previously, "team opacity" describes the manner in which technology-mediated coordination obscures team mental models (Fiore et al., 2003). While conventional groupware introduces substantial encumbrances to the team's mental model as they rely heavily on technology, virtual worlds like Second Life have features that may overcome many of these issues. The discussion that follows is organized around the crucial team processes described earlier.

Communication

As described above, communication is of utmost importance for distributed teams. The geographical distance associated with these teams poses an absolute requirement for effective communication. However, this has traditionally been very difficult for distributed teams to achieve due to the limitations of text as a communications medium, the difficulties associated with asynchronous communication, and the lack of a common frame of reference (Powell et al., 2004). Traditional e-mail based groupware technologies do little to address these issues. However, one might do somewhat better using a Massively Multiplayer Online Game (MMOG) such as Second Life.

Although Second Life is currently text-based (a spoken language version is currently in beta), some of its capabilities may mitigate the shortcomings of more traditional text-based systems. For example, a prime shortcoming of text is the limitation of the stimulus array. Subtleties of language, such as emotion, are often missed or misattributed in these conversations. In Second Life, this might be mitigated by encouraging users to modify their avatar to be consistent with the intended message. This approach is more natural than the "emoticons" that are now used with e-mail. Similarly, scripted behaviors for the avatar might be useful in overcoming the absence of nonverbal cues, a commonly mentioned shortcoming of text-based communication (Sproull & Kiesler, 1991). While effective use of emotional animations comes with a fairly steep learning curve, residents in Second Life have the ability to apply a wide range of emotional states to their avatars in the form of both facial expressions and physical animations.

The use of an MMOG such as Second Life can also overcome the issue of asynchronous communication since communication happens in real-time, similar to Internet chat. These conversations can be easily recorded and stored on the server for other teammates to observe. Additionally, the ability to use objects in Second Life can help to overcome the typical frame-of-reference problem in text-only systems. With a little creativity, users can include any number of real life objects, from PowerPoint slides and spreadsheets, to streaming video and audio from real world events. A recently announced feature will let users import there own three-dimensional objects into the virtual world for use in areas such as design. Users will now be able to highlight the elements of an object or visual to which they are referring, allowing even greater frame-of-reference fidelity.

Finally, one might hypothesize that Second Life could be used to overcome communication differences that have been associated with heterogeneous teams. For example, communication is often less frequent in mixed-gender or mixed-culture teams. Second Life avatars can be customized to look like anything, from different genders and ethnicities to different species. There is a large group of people who call themselves furries, who appear to be a mix between human and animal, as well as people like Linden Lab employee Cube

Linden whose avatar appears to be a large floating cube. In Second Life, people appear how they want to be perceived, not necessarily as who they are. As such, common characteristics or even a common avatar could be used for all teammates, possibly overcoming real world differences that could interfere with communication.

Coordination

Effective distributed team performance depends upon the ability of members to distribute resources effectively. In face-to-face teams, this is done through "explicit" coordination (directly asking for a resource) or "implicit" coordination (sensing that a coworker needs something and giving it to them without being asked) (Kleinman & Serfaty, 1989). Effective teams have been shown to switch to implicit coordination during periods of high workload, while ineffective teams do not demonstrate this behavior (Kleinman & Serfaty, 1991). As noted, because of the limited cue array available to distributed teams, it seems likely that it would be difficult for them to use implicit coordination, especially using traditional text-based software.

However, in Second Life, users have a better opportunity to monitor their coworkers' activity. Indeed, if properly designed, teammates might even be able to observe data on coworkers displays. Second Life monitors the use of residents and changes the state of the avatar based on the actions being taken by the real world user. For example, if the user is actively engaged in tasking, the avatar appears alert. When the user is not interacting with Second Life, the avatar will go into an idle state where it appears to be sleeping. After about half an hour they will be logged off. Members of teams can observe the others' states at all times. Of course, this is highly dependent of the tasking of the user. If most of their work requires them to be in Second Life to complete they should appear alert in Second Life. If they require being on their computers but not in Second Life, they should appear asleep or not logged in at all. That being the case, it is much more likely that users will notice cues of teammates being overwhelmed. In turn, this might enable greater implicit coordination.

Additionally, Second Life allows the creation of "Heads-up Displays." These displays provide information around the periphery of the viewing area without obscuring the main view. It is likely that such a display could be used to provide workers with information about their coworker's activity. This might be another method of increasing the likelihood of implicit coordination.

Finally, as pointed out by Fiore and colleagues (2004), coordination consists of more than just those behaviors that are performed during the period of actual task performance. There are data to suggest that preperformance coordination can be an important determinant of how teams execute their subsequent task performance (Heuze, Raimbault, & Fontayne, 2006; Marks et al., 2000). For example, Marks et al. (2000) shows the relationship between preperformance briefings and a variety of subsequent process and performance behaviors. These types of briefings can be easily accomplished in the Second Life platform. In fact, users can take notes within the software and refer to these notes during task execution if they would like. They can even share their notes with coworkers whether they are present or absent.

Similarly, there seems to be advantages to encouraging teams to gather after performance to provide one another feedback. This "team self-correction" is thought to assist teams in developing a shared mental model of the task and how the team will execute the task (Blickensderfer, Cannon-Bowers, & Salas, 1997; Smith-Jentsch, Zeisig, Acton, & McPherson, 1998). Effective team self-correction approaches emphasize the importance of having each team member focus on specific elements of teamwork. In collocated teams, this is done through PowerPoint slides and handouts serving as aids to focus attention. There are simple equivalents to these in Second Life.

Further, it is relatively easy for team members to capture screen shots during their performance that they can use to show their team members what they were looking at throughout the timeline of performance. They can use these screen shots to test assumptions or to give feedback about co-workers behavior. These stimuli can also be stored to give to absent team members for later reference. It is believed that this opportunity to discuss one another's actions contributes to a "shared mental model" among team members. This, in turn, allows team members to better understand and anticipate their colleague's needs (Mathieu, Heffner, Goodwin, Salas, & Cannon-Bowers, 2000). It should be noted, however, that some researchers have suggested that the nature of effective mental models in distributed teams might be different than those in face-to-face teams (Yanghua, Zhongming, & Zhengyu, 2006). More research is required to fully explicate these relationships.

Adaptability

In complex tasks, it is important that teams can quickly reconfigure themselves to respond to emerging task demands. As noted, distributed teams might struggle to adapt because they do not share the same cue array (Fiore et al., 2004). This can be resolved in Second Life using the data-sharing techniques described above. Further, it has been suggested that adaptability in virtual teams might be hampered because the software that supports these teams is not very flexible (Driskell & Salas, 2006). Oftentimes, the software itself dictates the role that operators must play. This restricts the options that a team has in adapting to new demands. On the other hand, an open virtual world like Second Life might actually increase the ability to adapt. Workers can easily move to different workstations within the virtual environment. They can also give one another resources, watch one another's performance, and even change aspects of their avatar or environment if need be. However, it is unlikely that teams will be able to do this without specific training in adaptive behaviors (Fiore et al., 2004).

Leadership

Leadership poses particular challenges in distributed team, and it appears that leadership in these teams is often less effective than in collocated teams (Bikson & Eveland, 1990). Further, it seems that leading virtual teams requires not only traditional leadership skills, but also some unique ones (Powell et al., 2004; Thompson & Coovert, 2006). For example, it has been suggested that leaders of virtual teams need to be more effective at allowing subordinates to take the lead when necessary (Bikson & Eveland, 1990; Priest, Stagle, Klein, & Salas, 2006). Second Life, compared to traditional groupware approaches, might enable this behavior because the leader can more easily "keep an eye on things" by teleporting around the team's virtual environment. By so doing, the leader is not required to "fly blind," perhaps increasing the comfort he or she would have in releasing control.

Another critical skill for leaders of virtual teams is to establish role clarity (Kayworth & Leidner, 2001). In Second Life, this can be done by developing "notecards" or larger displays that demonstrate the structure of the team and the roles played by each member. The leader can even update these displays in real time to facilitate adaptability. Additionally, Second Life provides specific tools for building groups. Within these tools is the option of setting specific names to roles in the group. These names appear in the same identity tag as the avatars name (a bubble that floats above the avatars head). This allows roles to be explicitly defined within the Second Life environment.

Improving Attitudes of Distributed Teams

As noted, Fiore and his colleagues have suggested that the demands of distributed teams make the effects of attitudes even more salient than in face-to-face teams. In the following paragraphs, we will explore how the MMOG environment might help distributed teams in possessing helpful attitudinal features.

Trust

It has been suggested that the early days of a team's formation are critical in establishing long-term trust (Powell et al., 2004), and specifically that allowing communication and interaction among team members in early days could be effective in building trust (Jarvenpaa & Leidner, 1999). Iacono and Weisbrand (1997) point out that it is important for there to be an appropriate level of feedback and interaction in these early conversations. Traditional groupware makes it difficult for team members to communicate interest in their teammates, but this is much more feasible in Second Life. In fact, a recent study has demonstrated that social eye gaze in Second Life is not substantially different than in real life (Yee et al., 2007). Thus, one might hypothesize that trust would develop in Second Life more readily than text-based environments.

It has also been suggested that informal social contact can be effective in fostering trust (Armstrong & Cole, 2002). Bringing members of a distributed team can be prohibitively expensive in face-to-face teams, but an inexpensive analogue is quite achievable in Second Life. For example, it is not at all difficult to create a virtual picnic, play games, or even attend a concert together in Second Life. Furthermore, Second Life provides many activities for residents to experience. It seems more likely that two team members might find each other in Second Life and have an impromptu interaction. Research is required to investigate whether these virtual social activities are effective in creating trust among teammates.

Cohesion

As described above, cohesion relates to one's interest in being part of a team. Interestingly, it has been suggested that cohesion depends on the degree to which group members perceive that they are similar to the group norm (Hogg, 2004). It might be that one can use the MMOG environment to communicate to members that they are, indeed, similar to the team norm. For example, a limited range of avatars could be used so that the external representation of the operators would all be relatively similar. The team could have the same group name displayed over their heads to show others that they are part of the team. The team could all wear a similar team shirt or uniform.

One of the newer features of Second Life is that teams can purchase a common last name. For example IBM and the Reuters news agency have purchased the last names IBM and Reuters respectively. Also, all members of the Linden Lab staff have the last name Linden. These features might reinforce a notion of cohesion within Second Life.

Additionally, the type of informal meetings discussed above in the context of trust might also be effective in establishing cohesion in virtual teams (Armstrong & Cole, 2002; Thompson & Coovert, 2006). It is likely that the team's leader will have to take an active role to ensure that these early interactions occur (Mannix, Griffith, & Neale, 2002). Leaders of distributed teams might also increase cohesion by explicitly communicating team-level goals (Koch, 1979). Again, these goals can be displayed in the virtual environment to encourage acceptance by the team.

Collective Efficacy

It is important that team members perceive that their team is effective in both task-work and teamwork. As mentioned, it appears that collective efficacy can be achieved by recording and communicating the team's successes (Ronglan, 2007). In Second Life, this can be achieved by placing "reminder objects" in the virtual environment. This might take the form of trophies or other objects that symbolize successes. This might also be accomplished by allowing team members to wear "medals" or other symbols of

success only available to participants who have enjoyed a specific level of success.

It has also been reported that collective efficacy can be maintained when a member who has performed poorly is given feedback and the opportunity to regain his or her confidence (Heuze et al., 2006). This might be difficult in traditional distributed teams, but is easily accomplished in Second Life. Leaders or coaches can meet with the target team member virtually at any time. Further, it might be possible in some circumstances to "replay" the event in which the member did poorly and allow them to retry their performance. This might allow them to increase their personal self-efficacy and, in turn, the team's collective efficacy.

Team Orientation

Complex team performance often relies on large, multidisciplinary teams. Members of these teams often have widely different levels of experience as members of teams, and may value teamwork rather differently. Consequently, they have higher or lower degrees of "team orientation." Fortunately, however, it seems that this psychological state is changeable (Eby & Dobbins, 1997). In fact, these authors argue that team orientation can be improved by providing examples of how team behaviors improved overall team performance. Using screen-recording software, this can be easily achieved with Second Life. In fact, the software allows users to see the task develop from each teammate's perspective so that the benefits of effective teamwork can be illustrated clearly. Further, these attitudes can be changed by communicating about how the software can be used to reduce individual workload. This can be accomplished by showing examples of how individual workers off-loaded their tasking to teammates using the software. A good example of this that was exposed to the public is the Electric Sheep Company's Virtual Aloft blog (Aloft, 2007). The blog uses screen captures from Second Life to document the creation of a virtual Aloft Hotel developed on Aloft Island in Second Life. The Web site not only showed screen captures of the development process, but also explained the more interesting development procedures the team used while building the Island.

Improving Cognitive Performance in Distributed Teams

Distributed team performance is likely to pose serious cognitive demands upon operators, especially in memory systems (Fiore et al., 2004; Malhotra & Majchrzak, 2004). The limited number of modalities tends to tax memory systems in purely text-based systems. In the following paragraphs, we will explore methods to alleviate these demands using MMOG's.

Working Memory

As described above, working memory is likely to be severely taxed in distributed environments, especially in dealing with complex tasks. This is due to the fact that there is a tremendous amount of information presented via one modality. Further, traditional cues (such as intonation) are not available. The reliance on this one, limited modality can severely limit the amount of information that can be processed by the operator (Stanney, et al., 2004). While this is a difficult problem for text-based systems, there are some aspects of Second Life that might serve to reduce working memory load as compared to traditional message-based collaborative work systems. For example, one important advantage of MMOG's like Second Life is the rich visual cue field that can be constructed to augment the text-based communication. This allows any number of memory aids to be placed in the visual environment for easy access. In fact, team members can access frequently-used information without switching screens or accessing files. This is accomplished simply by making displays that are readable in the operator's peripheral vision.

Additionally, the operator can observe the actions of teammates without text (i.e., simply by watching), which is a large advantage over text-based systems. This allows operators to collect a large amount of visual data without invoking the text-processing centers of the brain. This is likely to allow processing of greater amounts of information. This effect is likely to increase when "real" speech is added to Second Life. This might be improved even further through the use of data displays such as Heads Up Displays (HUD's). See Image 1 for an example of an HUD for the NOAA Tsunami Experience built within Second Life.

Memory Activation

Clearly, retrospective memory loads in distributed teams are higher than in face-to-face teams for reasons described above. There is an immense amount of data passed over a limited sensory channel. This might be abated by storing things where they are easy to access using techniques described above. However, as noted, distributed teams might also be at risk for failings of prospective memory (Fiore, Cuevas, Schooler, & Salas, 2006). This is likely due to shortcomings of the "noticing" component that is thought to be critical in this type of memory (McDaniel, 1995). This component is believed to be heavily dependent upon the operator perceiving environmental cues that trigger memory events. Because purely text-based software involves so few cues, it is believed to be a poor supporter of prospective memory (McDaniels & Einstein, 2000). Second Life, however, hosts a much larger cue array. Avatars, for example, can serve as important cues for prospective memory behaviors. By increasing the perceptual saliency of the avatars through unique designs, one might also increase the likelihood that they will cue perceptual memory (Marsh, Hicks, & Hancock, 2000). Additionally, one can send oneself (or the whole team) reminders using the software's messaging system. This could be especially helpful during times of high workload.

Long-Term Memory

In keeping with the assertion of Fiore et al. (2004) that episodic memory is a key driver of distributed team performance, it would seem that MMOGs such as Second Life possess a clear advantage over traditional groupware. The rich visual environment offers many more cues to be used in constructing episodic memory than traditional groupware. It is hypothesized that this, in and of itself, should result in greater long-term memory. However, other aspects of Second Life might contribute additional value to long-term memory. For example, it has been suggested that increasing familiarity with teammates should result in improved long-term memory storage (Rouse, Cannon-Bowers, & Salas, 1992). Second Life offers a number of ways to increase team member familiarity, from customized avatars to detailed profiles of coworkers. These elements might assist team members in forming rich, long-term associations about their fellow teammates.

FUTURE TRENDS

While the field of Virtual Worlds and MMOGs is in its infancy, it is already apparent that it could have great affect on the future of distributed teams. While small companies like The Electric Sheep Company have their corporate headquarters in Second Life, and large companies like IBM are already training new employees in there as well, it is not yet apparent what Virtual World platform will become the clear leader in this space. What is clear is that more and more companies will take the plunge to become part of the virtual business infrastructure that is being laid now. While currently the reasons for this might be to catch the wave of good press, or appear to be cutting edge to investors the end result will be that people use these tools because they support distributed teams in a fashion that no previous technology has been able to accomplish. In the future, people may no longer report to their desk in a large cube farm distracted by the low hum of florescent lights and the constant chatter of the people talking across the room. They may just login to their computers from anywhere in the world and work at a virtual desk in a virtual office in a Virtual World.

CONCLUSION

Virtual Worlds and Massively Multiplayer Online Games are becoming a useful tool for distributed teams. From providing a common working place to allowing members of the team to interact in a physical if albeit virtual form, Virtual Worlds are setting a new standard for tools to facilitate interactions between members of distributed teams. This chapter explored the ways in which Virtual Worlds could support interactive teams at a greater fidelity then that of the previous generation of groupware tools. While this chapter used a popular Virtual World, Second Life, as an example platform, there are likely to be many contenders for the dominant position as an environment that supports distributed teamwork. Our contention is that the most likely of these will take a "team-centered" perspective that begins with the demands of teamwork as its point of departure.

REFERENCES

Alavi, S., & McCormick, J. (2004). Theoretical and measurement issues for studies of collective orientation in team contexts. *Small Group Research, 35*(2), 111-127.

Alexander, S. (2000). Virtual teams going global, *InfoWorld, 22*(46), 55-56.

Aloft. (2008). Retrieved from http://www.virtualaloft.com

Armstrong, D., & Cole, P. (2002). Managing distances and differences in geographically distributed work groups. *Distributed work* (pp. 167-189). MIT Press.

Bannan-Ritland, B. (2002). Computer-mediated communication, elearning, and interactivity: A review of the literature. *The Quarterly Review of Distance Educaiton, 3*(2), 161-179.

Baddely, A. D. (1986). *Working memory.* New York: Oxford University Press.

Baddely, A. & Hitch, G. (1974). Working memory. In G.A. Bower (Ed.), *Recent advances in learning and motivation Vol. 8* (pp. 47-90). New York: Academic Press.

Bikson, T., & Eveland, J. (1990). *The interplay of work group structures and computer support. Intellectual teamwork: Social and technological foundations of cooperative work* (pp. 245-290). Lawrence Erlbaum Associates, Inc.

Blickensderfer, E., Cannon-Bowers, J., & Salas, E. (1997). *Theoretical bases for team self-corrections: Fostering shared mental models.* Elsevier Science/JAI Press.

Campion, M. A., Medsker, G. J., & Higgs, A. C. (1993). Relations between work group characteristics and effectiveness: Implications for designing effective work groups. *Personnel Psychology, 46*, 823-845.

Cannon-Bowers, J. A., Tannenbaum, S. I., Salas, E., & Volpe, C. E. (1995). Defining team competencies and establishing training requirements. In R. Guzzo & E. Salas (Eds.), *Team Effectiveness and decision making in organizations* (pp. 333-380). San Francisco, CA: Jossey-Bass.

Cannon-Bowers, J. A., & Salas, E. (2001). Reflections on shared cognition. *Journal of Organizational Behavior, 22*, 195-202.

Crampton, C. (2001). The mutual knowledge problem and its consequences for dispersed collaboration, *Oranizational Science, 12*(3) pp. 346-371.

Driskell, J., & Salas, E. (2006). *Groupware, group dynamics, and team performance.* Washington, DC: American Psychological Association.

Dirks, K. T. 1999. The effects of interpersonal trust on work group performance. *Journal of Applied Psychology, 85*, 1004-1012.

Duffy, M., Ganster, D., Shaw, J., Johnson, J., & Pagon, M. (2006, September). The social context of undermining behavior at work. *Organizational Behavior and Human Decision Processes, 101*(1), 105-126.

Eby, L., & Dobbins, G. (1997, May). Collectivistic orientation in teams: An individual and group-level analysis. *Journal of Organizational Behavior, 18*(3), 275-295.

Fiore, S., Cuevas, H., Schooler, J., & Salas, E. (2006). *Cognition, teams, and team cognition: Memory actions and memory failures in distributed team environments.* Washington, DC: American Psychological Association.

Fiore, S., Salas, E., Cuevas, H., & Bowers, C. (2003, July). Distributed coordination space: Toward a theory of distributed team process and performance. *Theoretical Issues in Ergonomics Science, 4*(3), 340-364.

Fiore, S. M., Schooler, J. W., Whiteside, D. and Herrmann, D. J. (1997). *Perceived contributions of cues and mental states to prospective and retrospective memory failures.* Paper presented at the 2nd Biennial Meeting of the Society for Applied Research in Memory and Cognition. Toronto, Canada.

Golembiewski, R. T. (1962). *The small group.* Chicago, IL: University of Chicago Press.

Heuzé, J., Raimbault, N., & Fontayne, P. (2006). Relationships between cohesion, collective efficacy and performance in professional basketball teams: An examination of mediating effects. *Journal of Sports Sciences, 24*(1), 59-68.

Hogg, M. (2004). *Social categorization, depersonalization, and group behavior.* Malden, MA: Blackwell Publishing.

Iacono, C. S., Weisband, S. (1997, January). Developing trust in virtual teams. In *Proceedings of the Thirtieth Hawaii International Conference on System Sciences* (vol. 2, pp. 412-420).

Jarvenpaa, S. L. & Leidner (1999). Communication and trust in global virtual teams. *Organization Science, 10*(6), 791-815.

Jong, T., & Ferguson-Hessler, M. G. M. (1996). Types and qualities of knowledge. *Educational Psycologist, 31*, 105-113.

Kayworth, T., & Leidner, D. (2003) Organizational culture as a knowledge resource. In C. W. Holsapple (Ed.), *Handbook on knowledge management: Knowledge matters* (pp. 235-252). New York: Springer-Verlag.

Kleinman, D. L., & Serfaty, D. (1989). Team performance assessment in distributed decision-making. In R. Gibson, J. P. Kincaid, & B. Goldiez (Eds.), *Proceedings of the Interactive Networked Simulation for Training Conference* (pp. 22-27). Orlando Fl: Naval Training Systems Center.

Koch, J. L. (1979). Effects of goal specificity and performance feedback to work groups and peer leadership, performance, and attitudes. *Human Relations, 32*(10), 819-840.

Malhotra, A., & Majchrzak, A. (2004). Enabling knowledge creation in far-flung teams: Best practices for IT support and knowledge sharing. *Journal of Knowledge Management, 8*(4), 75-88.

Mannix, E., Griffith, T., & Neale, M. (2002). *The phenomenology of conflict in distributed work teams*. Cambridge, MA: MIT Press.

Marks, M., Zaccaro, S., & Mathieu, J. (2000). Performance implications of leader briefings and team-interaction training for team adaptation to novel environments. *Journal of Applied Psychology, 85*(6), 971-986.

March, R. L., Hicks, J. L., & Hancock, T. W. (2000). On the interaction of ongoing cognitive activity and the nature of an event-based intention, *Applied Cognitive Psychology, 14*, S29-S42.

Mathieu, J., Heffner, T., Goodwin, G., Salas, E., & Cannon-Bowers, J. (2000). The influence of shared mental models on team process and performance. *Journal of Applied Psychology, 85*(2), 273-283.

Maznevski, M., & Chudoba, K. (2000, September). Bridging space over time: Global virtual team dynamics and effectiveness. *Organization Science, 11*(5), 473-492.

McDaniel, M. (1995). *Prospective memory: Progress and processes*. San Diego, CA: Academic Press.

McDaniels, M., & Einstein, G. (2000). Strategic and automatic processes in prospective memory retrieval: A multiprocess framework. *Applied Cognitive Psychology, 14*, 127-144.

Michalisin, M., Karau, S., & Tanpong, C. (2004). Top management team cohesion and superior industry returns an empirical study of the resource-based view. *Group & Organization Management, 29*(1), 125-140.

Moreland, R. L., & Myaskovsky, L. (2000). Exploring the performance benefits of group training: Transactive memory or improved communication? *Organizational Behavior and Human Decision Processes, 82*, 117-133.

Myers, N., Feltz, D., & Short, S. (2004). Collective efficacy and team performance: A longitudinal study of collegiate football teams. *Group Dynamics: Theory, Research, and Practice, 8*(2), 126-138.

Patterson, M., Carron, A., & Loughead, T. (2005). The influence of team norms on the cohesion—self-reported performance relationship: A multi-level analysis. *Psychology of Sport and Exercise, 6*(4), 479-493.

Powell, A., Piccoli, G., & Ives, B. (2004). Virtual teams: A review of the current literature and directions for future research. *ACM SIGMIS Database, 35*(2), 6-36.

Priest, H., Stagl, K., Klein, C., & Salas, E. (2004). Virtual teams: Creating context for fistributed teamwork. Creating high-tech teams: Practical guidance on work performance and technology (pp. 185-212). Lawrence Erlbaum, Inc.

Ronglan, L. (2007). Building and communicating collective efficacy: A season-long in-depth study of an elite sport team. *The Sport Psychologist, 21*(1), 78-93.

Rouse, W. B., Cannon-Bowers, J. A., & Salas, E. (1992). The role of mental models in team performance in complex systems. *IEEE Transactions on Systems, man, and Cybernetics, 22,* 1296-1308.

Salas, E., Cannon-Bowers, J. A., Fiore, S. M., & Stout, R. J. (2001). Cue-Recognition Training to Enhance Team Situation Awareness. In M. D. Mcneese, E. Salas, & M. R. Endsley (Eds.), N*ew Trends in Cooperative Activities: Understanding System Dynamics in Complex Environments* (pp. 169-190). Santa Monica, CA: Human Factors and Ergonomics Society.

Sarker, S. and Sahay, S. (2002). Information systems development by US-Norwegian virtual teams: Implications of time and space. In *Proceedings of the Thirty-Fifth Annual Hawaii International Conference on System Sciences,* (pp. 1-10), Hawaii.

Sims, D. E., Salas, E., & Burke, C. S. (2005, October). Is there a "Big Five" in teamwork? *Small Group Research, 36*(5), pp. 555-599.

Smith-Jentsch, K. A., Kraiger, K., Cannon-Bowers, J. A., & Salas, E. (2002). *Familiarity breeds teamwork: a case for training teammate-specific competencies*, Unpublished Manuscript.

Smith-Jentsch, K., Zeisig, R., Acton, B., & McPherson, J. (1998). *Team dimensional train-ing: A strategy for guided team self-correction.* Washington, DC: American Psychological Association.

Sproull, L., & Kiesler, S. (1991). *Connections: New ways of working in the networked organization.* Cambridge, MA: The MIT Press.

Stanney, K. M., Samman, S., Reeves, L. M., Hale, K., Buff, W., Bowers, C., et al. (2004). A paradigm shift in interactive computing: Deriving multimodal design principles from behavioral and neurological foundations. *International Journal of Human-Computer Interaction, 17,* 229-257.

Stauuss, S. G. (1996). Getting a clue: Communication media and information distribution effects on group process and performance. *Small Group Research, 27*(1), 115-142.

Tasa, K., Taggar, S., & Seijts, G. (2007). The development of collective efficacy in teams: A multilevel and longitudinal perspective. *Journal of Applied Psychology, 92*(1), 17-27.

Thompson, L., & Coovert, M. (2006). Understanding and developing virtual computer-supported cooperative work teams. In C. Bowers, E. Salas & F. Jentsch (Eds.), *Creating high-tech teams: Practical guidance on work performance and technology* (pp. 213-241). Lawrence Erlbaum, Inc.

Tulving, E. (1983). *Elements of episodic memory.* New York: Oxford University Press.

Watson, C., Chemers, M., & Preiser, N. (2001). Collective efficacy: A multilevel analysis. *Personality and Social Psychology Bulletin, 27*(8), 1057-1068.

Warkentin, M. E. Sayeed, L., & Hightower, R. (1997). Virtual teams versus face-to-face teams: An exploratory study of a Web-based conference system. *Decision Sciences, 28*(4), 975-996.

Whitney, K. (1994). Improving group task performance: The role of group goals and group efficacy. *Human Performance, 7,* 55-78.

Yanghua, J., Zhongming, W., & Zhengyu, Y. (2006). The effect of shared mental model on virtual team's effectiveness. *Acta Psychologica Sinica, 38*(2), 288-296.

Yee, N., Bailenson, J., Urbanek, M., Chang, F., & Merget, D. (2007, February). The unbearable likeness of being digital: The persistence of nonverbal social norms in online virtual environments. *CyberPsychology & Behavior, 10*(1), 115-121.

Zhang, S., Fjermestad, J., & Tremaine, M. (2005). *Leadership styles in virtual team context: Limitations, solutions, and propositions.* Paper Presented at the 38th Hawaii International Conference on System Sciences.

KEY TERMS

Avatar: The digital representation of the user in a Virtual World or MMOG.

Collocated Team: A team in which all of the team members are located in the same location.

Distributed Team: A team in which all the team members are located in multiple locations.

MMOG: A Massively Multiplayer Online Game (MMOG) is a game in which the players all login from their own computers to a persistent environment to play a game with a rule set and specific outcomes.

Resident: The name used to describe the real world player or user in Second Life.

Second Life: Second Life is a popular MMOG developed by Linden Lab. It allows users to edit the world and their own characters to their own specifications.

Virtual World: A Virtual World is a persistent virtual environment in which all users login from their own computers to exist in a world in which there are no specific goals or rules to the world.

Chapter XXX
Knowledge Transfer and Marketing in Second Life

Peter Rive
Victoria University of Wellington, New Zealand

ABSTRACT

This chapter considers the virtual world Second Life as a workplace. It argues that despite its apparent novelty, Second Life is descended from a 2000-year-old tradition of immersive art that informs its popular attraction and its two big business drivers, knowledge management and marketing. To illustrate this, I describe a project by the international advertising agency Saatchi & Saatchi, which shows how knowledge management and marketing can come together in a virtual workplace. The chapter further contends that it is insufficient to simply attain virtual presence in order to achieve knowledge management goals. Instead, intellectual property rights and their management must also be addressed. Because avatars in Second Life own the items they create and can explicitly set permission rights, Second Life users can share virtual goods and knowledge easily, and in the tradition of hacker culture and open source coding. Despite general opposition to Digital Rights Management from some in the open source community, I argue that it is necessary to ensure that the metadata, such as the original creator information, is protected to encourage the sharing and transfer of knowledge in a virtual workplace. The creator of Second Life, Linden Lab, opened up the source code of the client software, thus allowing organizations to further benefit from this virtual workplace.

INTRODUCTION

According to Thomas Friedman's book, *The World is Flat*, the Internet has caused a major shift away from the traditional centers of power and knowledge to a flatter, more decentralized model (Friedman, 2006). Internet convergence has also made online virtual worlds such as Second Life (SL) possible. Operating within these virtual worlds are workplaces that have created equal opportunities for citizens in far-flung zones

to contribute to corporate decision-making and idea generation on an equal footing with their colleagues in other parts of the world.

In this chapter, I will examine the historical context of Second Life and the primary drivers for its "residents," or avatars (virtual representations of the real user, see the key terms), as well as the businesses that use it as a workplace. I look at the deep psychological urge that drives virtual presence and a practical requirement of business to use SL for knowledge management (KM) and marketing. I argue that for KM and marketing messages to be effective they must contain emotional data and extend sensory stimulation beyond sight by itself. However, KM will not simply succeed by addressing these needs alone, it must also take into account intellectual property (IP) rights and digital rights management (DRM) in order to support open sharing and protected knowledge transfer. Despite general opposition to DRM from the likes of the Free Software Foundation, it can ensure the protection of important metadata, such as creation information, contained in virtual goods and knowledge that is transferred. I argue that this is essential in order to build a successful virtual workplace, as it not only has the flexibility to protect sensitive IP and copyright license variations, but also respects the originator and their reputation. This is important because it recognizes a significant motivation behind why individuals share and collaborate, that is, for recognition, and for reputation building. The ability to convey emotional data using sensory stimulation will not only underwrite the necessary trust to ensure creative collaboration, but also be the carrier for tacit knowledge transfer which is notoriously hard to achieve in both real life (RL) and SL. Effective marketing and advertising are also heavily supported by emotional data and sensory stimulation. I later explore how neuroscience suggests some reasons why avatars can engender empathy in SL participants and how that can contribute to trust and sharing (Clippinger & Bollier, 2005).

Second Life is a Massively Multiplayer virtual online world. However, the company that started it, Linden Lab, does not consider it to be a game. Instead, it is closer to a real society, in which resident avatars buy and sell land, houses, and objects that are created. In the parlance of the residents, this "in-world" economy turns over more than $1 million a day, and there is almost every service that you can find in the real world in Second Life. Some of the most successful businesses in SL are real-estate and fashion (Tiffany, 2007).

In 1999, I established a virtual reality (VR) consultancy and reseller business, LaunchSite. The company's expertise builds on my experience in the film and advertising industry and applies it to VR theatres and network enabled virtual workspaces. In this chapter I explore the lessons learned prior to Second Life from my company's experience with the international advertising agency, Saatchi & Saatchi, and argue that there are two main business drivers propelling corporate interest in SL, knowledge management and marketing. The virtual workplace solutions that we explored for Saatchi & Saatchi must be seen in the historical context of the technology available at the time, and as a precursor to virtual worlds such as Second Life. Saatchi & Saatchi Worldwide is an advertising agency that originated in England and is now headquartered in New York. It lists amongst its clients the powerhouse Procter and Gamble, the biggest advertiser in the U.S., and America's number one car company, Toyota. It has approximately 7000 employees and 53 offices in 83 countries. In 2007 it was named "Agency Network of the Year," at the 48th International Clio Advertising Awards (Saatchi, 2007).

In 2000 my company, based in New Zealand, proposed a network of virtual workplaces to Saatchi & Saatchi Worldwide using SGI Reality Theatres. The concept of it was similar to that offered by Linden Lab, the creators of Second Life; however, Second Life goes far beyond our original scope and has the ability to bring together large numbers of dispersed people in a creative and collaborative virtual workplace, and for very little cost. The Saatchi & Saatchi example provides some important points to consider when contemplating virtual workplaces for innovation and creativity. Emotion and sensory stimulation play a central role in marketing to the consumer and in terms of communicating tacit knowledge to coworkers.

Knowledge management has become a popular obsession amongst some of the leading business thinkers (Davenport, Prusak, & Wilson, 2003; Dixon, 2000). Tacit knowledge is that which is locked inside people's heads, according to Polanyi's famous maxim, "We know more than we can tell" (Polanyi, 1967). Tacit knowledge is also an important source of creative ideas, and often corporate improvements. An important goal of KM is converting tacit knowledge into explicit knowledge that can be recorded, so it can be more easily shared. Intellectual property, and the related issues surrounding digital content, are some of the most contentious areas of the knowledge economy. This is brought into sharp focus in a virtual workplace such as Second Life, where people are constantly sharing, selling, and trading ideas and virtual goods. I argue here that an important consideration of KM and creative collaboration in this virtual workplace is fundamentally decided on intellectual property rights and permissions.

Second Life was designed with copyright advice from Stanford law professor, and CEO of the Creative Commons, Lawrence Lessig. This virtual world is almost entirely constructed by its residents, it is a creative hotspot, but it is also social and often involves creative collaboration in real-time. There is an interplay between this social aspect and the business objective of generating new ideas that is important to understand for a successful virtual workplace.

In most virtual worlds, only 2% of all the participants contribute to the content. In Second Life an enormous 65% create everything seen in-world (Purbrick & Ondrejka, 2006). I outline how behavioral economics and cognitive science can explain this creativity within Second Life. In our evolving knowledge economy attributes of emotional intelligence, "right brain" thinking, and a playful approach will all contribute to greater creativity and innovation in our lives and businesses (Pink, 2006).

BACKGROUND

Today, concern over terrorism, the cost and hassle of international travel, and the environmental impact of airlines, have all added to the desire to use virtual workplaces as a knowledge management tool in business. These practical concerns are underpinned by a deeper psychological desire to extend beyond the physical, to attain a virtual presence (Grau, 2003; Heim, 1993; Wertheim, 1999). Thus individuals are predisposed to using virtual worlds such as Second Life, as workplaces. From a pragmatic perspective SL holds out the promise of tacit knowledge transfer through virtual presence, and it is now possible to communicate and collaborate internationally in real-time from your desktop. To many, this communication all seems very new and exciting.

It is often assumed that virtual reality and virtual workplaces are technologies that first appeared in the early 1990s. However, the antecedents date back over 2000 years. Early frescos and paintings were designed to immerse the viewer in a virtual world. The purposes of these art works were often religious and educational; intended to evoke a powerful emotional transcendence in the subject (Grau, 2003; Heim, 1993; Wertheim, 1999). The popular desire to be immersed in a virtual world has an extraordinary lineage descended from the earliest fantasies of religious orders (Wertheim, 1999). This deep-seated yearning not only attracts vast numbers of residents to massively multi player online role playing games (MMORPGs) such as Second Life, but also sits behind the imagination in this virtual workplace. People want to transcend the limitations of the physical world and communicate in the virtual world. This imagination is fuelled by popular science fiction that reinforces the Jungian collective subconscious, or if you would prefer, our shared cultural history. Familiarity with books such as Gibson's *Neuromancer* (Gibson, 1986) and movies like *The Matrix* is common amongst the early adopters of virtual worlds such as Second Life. Many residents of SL are aware of its science fiction roots, and some also know that the "Metaverse" of Neal Stephenson's *Snow crash* is the model for Second Life (Stephenson, 1992).

From its inception, SL has encouraged virtual creative collaboration. Yet, this is not as new and radical as it may first appear. As Grau has pointed out, "The history of technology has always been the history of its myths and utopias, a revelation of human yearnings, and a pre-rational reference base" (Grau, 2003, p. 279). From the Middle Ages through the 16th and 17th Centuries a number of thinkers imagined an "immediate presence at another place, traveling through space, by using mirrors" (Grau, 2003, p. 280). Today, corporations are interested in using virtual presence as a knowledge exchange tool for both explicit and tacit knowledge transfer. Dixon argues that technology cannot replace face-to-face meetings for the transfer of tacit knowledge (Dixon, 2000). She explains that trust needs to be built in face-to-face meetings in order for technology to support it. However, this is precisely the vision virtual presence promises to solve. If people cannot meet face-to-face in the flesh, virtual meetings can attempt to overcome physical distance by using virtual presence to build reputation and trust in order to convey some tacit knowledge. As early as 1989, Scott Fisher, at the NASA - Ames Research Center, was able to foresee the potential of networking VR workstations (Packer & Jordan, 2001, p. 266).

The ability to convey subtle emotional data is the holy grail of virtual presence. Enabling as many sensory communication channels as possible can boost tacit knowledge transfer and heighten emotional response and empathy. This emotional objective is also one aim of advertising and marketing. Sight is the most important sense and has dominated computer interface design, but sound can communicate subtle emotional shifts of pitch and tone. The creators of Second Life have announced they are soon about to introduce voice as part of the client application and are currently testing it on the beta grid.

Virtual Reality (a phrase credited to Jaron Lanier) defined by Michael Heim, "pertains to convincing the participant that he or she is actually in another place, by substituting the normal sensory input received by the participant with information produced by a computer" (Heim, 1993, p. 160). Physical context has been shown to be very important in learning, remembering, and thinking. Cognitive scientists have shown that, "cognition does not take place in brain tissue alone. It takes place in the context of our bodies and the external environment, both of which we constantly use to gather information, draw upon as memory aids, and conduct computations" (Clippinger & Bollier, 2005, p. 270). What this research tells us is that virtual presence can have both an emotional and utilitarian purpose for knowledge transfer and retention. Virtual presence gives the participants, what Tom Furness of the Human Interface Technology (HIT) Lab has called greater "bandwidth to the brain." Other methods of tacit knowledge transfer such as video conferencing, or simply a disembodied voice over the phone, will lack the important physical cues of a virtual space. The importance of our physical environment for thinking is highlighted in research into Alzheimer patients who found a new location made it more difficult for them to think:

Patients with Alzheimer's Disease, ... rely heavily upon a highly structured environment, much of it self-created, in order to recognize things, make mental associations, and reason. Change the patient' physical environment—move them to another location—and they lose large portions of their memory and cognitive capacity. (Clippinger & Bollier, 2005, p. 270)

Because physical presence is hardwired into our cognitive abilities, virtual presence would seem to have an advantage over text or Web-based collaborations.

Virtual reality offers one possible solution to the transfer of tacit knowledge. Going back to the time of Aristotle, "place" has been used as a mnemonic technique to assist with remembering. The corporeal nature of much of human existence means that we learn faster and better moving within physical spaces (Yates, 1966). Thus a virtual space can assist the cognitive processes as an avatar moves around the virtual world. The more real that world appears to be, the more the subject will feel a virtual presence and benefit from the support it gives to their cognitive processes.

The goal of sensory stimulation has informed past research into the human computer interface. In 1948, mathematician, electrical engineer, and communications specialist, Norman Wiener wrote his seminal treatise, *Cybernetics*. He claimed that the quality of human-machine communications would define our inner well-being (Packer & Jordan, 2001, p. 48). Diane Ackerman in her book, *A Natural History of the Senses*, wrote:

Most people think of the mind as being located in the head, but the latest findings in physiology suggest the mind doesn't really dwell in the brain but travels the whole body on caravans of hormone and enzyme, busily making sense of the compound wonders we catalogue as touch, taste, smell, hearing, vision. (Ackerman, 1990, p. xix)

Therefore, in order to convey the optimum tacit knowledge transfer, using virtual presence, the technology must attempt to transmit as much sensory information from the sender to the receiver. Marketers are fascinated by the potential as traditional broadcast media becomes fragmented and ineffectual at reaching consumers, and customized marketing uses vast databases to address niche personal desires (Anderson, 2006).

Saatchi & Saatchi in the Love Cave

Kevin Roberts, CEO of Saatchi & Saatchi Worldwide, developed a concept he called "lovemarks." He claims it is the future beyond brands. Roberts writes this about a product or service that is a lovemark: "Consumers commit beyond price, range, benefit, attribute—beyond the turbo of fads, beyond the machinery of brands. He argues that a lovemark has a deep emotional bond with the consumer that cannot be easily replaced or lost" (Roberts, 2004). Roberts also exhorts his

employees, clients and the world to infuse mystery, sensuality and intimacy into their brands in order to transform them into a lovemark. Roberts (2004) wrote this bit of advice for those trying to market to under 20 year olds. "Sensuality: The five senses are portals to the emotions. Kids want it all: to see, feel, hear, smell, and lick you."

In 2000 it was my company's ambition to provide Saatchi & Saatchi with a powerful portal to the emotions. Roberts has claimed that for a brand to become a "lovemark" it must appeal to as many senses as possible. We conceived the "Love Cave," a virtual reality experience that included sight, sound, feel, and even smell. Theme park ride designers often refer to this as a 4D experience. We intended to incorporate motion control seats, haptic gloves with thermal receptors, 3D vision, 3D interactive sound, and even smell via a clever system that synthesized thousands of scents to provide sophisticated and interactive aromas. The motion control seats were to be mounted on a hydraulic platform that would be synchronized with the motion of the 3D vision. Haptic gloves enable the subject to reach out and hold virtual objects in cyberspace, and thermal receptors could provide a sensation of heat. There is on going research into technology that can give tactile feedback including virtual dental drills and surgical tools. 3D vision can add dramatically to a sense of virtual presence and can be provided by stereo imaging and polarizing shuttered glasses. The 3D scenes were to be projected on a three meter high screen that wrapped around the participants in a 150 degree curve. The 3D audio system can allow the system designer to give realistic perspective to virtual objects as the subject moves around the virtual workplace. In 2000, Digiscent, was a company that offered an interactive scent printer that could generate scents relevant to the virtual scene.

At the turn of the 21st Century much of the developed world were enveloped in the utopian optimism of the dot.com bubble (Abramson, 2005). There was, however, little enthusiasm for virtual reality markup language (VRML), virtual workplaces, and 3D visualization at the time. By the year 2000, the once very successful Silicon Graphics (SGI) was on the ropes. It had made a name for itself with its founder and inventor of the 3D chip, Jim Clark. Its super computers had found homes within the military, in scientific visualization, industrial virtual reality applications, and the studios that created high-end visual effects for movies. However, the end of the Cold War had seen a shrinking of IT spend by the military and a substantial decline in SGI revenue (Abramson, 2006). The concern over SGI's shrinking market in a high tech industry awash with cash extended to its offices in far-flung Australia and New Zealand.

Across town from our offices in Auckland, New Zealand, my small company, LaunchSite, had used my contacts in the advertising industry to establish a dialogue with Saatchi & Saatchi Worldwide. Saatchi's global chief, Kevin Roberts, had charged Geoff Vuleta with the task of transforming the ad agency, into "The Ideas Company." SGI's virtual reality technology was identified as a possible component of that ambition. We proposed a network of virtual workplaces. A radical young team, under Vuleta, set out to initiate the revolution. They stated simply that their objective was: "To be revered as a hothouse of world changing creative ideas that transforms our client's brands, businesses and reputations."

Fundamental to our approach was that the technology was to be a slave to their knowledge management objectives, and the network of virtual workplaces must serve that master. We had perceived that becoming an Ideas Company was primarily about using KM to encourage and manage dialog through out the network. Saatchi's had to maximize the network effect (Sarpiro & Varian, 1999) and facilitate the free flow of creative ideas. Enabling offices with diverse and culturally different origins to "mix it up" has been recognized as a powerful source of innovation (Johansson, 2004; Peters, 1997). The challenge was to unlock the power of the network and manage the knowledge that it contained, in order to produce

world-changing ideas. My business partner, Joe Caccioppoli, and I undertook extensive research into why people did and did not share ideas, and what held back creative collaboration within the organization. We then proceeded to research what was currently available for remote collaboration across the net and for virtual workplaces. Our research uncovered the following reasons for people not sharing their best ideas:

- Fear that they would not get recognition for their idea
- Fear that someone would steal their idea and take credit
- Fear that their idea would be ridiculed or ignored
- Belief that they would not be fully rewarded for their idea
- Ambition to take that idea and develop it on their own

From Nancy Dixon's work we recognized that there were many computer-aided solutions to explicit knowledge sharing and international collaboration (Dixon, 1999). However, we faced the biggest difficulty with tacit knowledge. This also happened to be the most common form of knowledge exchange in creative collaborations. We worked with Dixon to understand the difficulties that companies such as Ford and BP had faced with tacit knowledge. She appreciated the importance that tacit knowledge played in the Saatchi creative environment. We subsequently researched solutions that could simulate face-to-face communication and a virtual physical environment where it was possible to perform virtual show-and-tell sessions. Saatchi's had stressed the importance of communicating emotional information. The virtual workplace that we devised, named the Love Cave, was designed to do just that.

The Love Cave was an expensive high-end virtual environment that was driven by an SGI Onyx 2 supercomputer. We aimed for the highest resolution that we could to enhance the realism and immersion. Inside the Love Cave, creative collaborators could meet, in a virtual workplace, represented as avatars. We determined it was important that the avatars could speak with as much natural animation and emotion as they would in real life. Through the New Zealand Account Manager, Scott Houston, we were introduced to Dr. Peter Hunter who headed Auckland University's Bio-Mechanical Department. Hunter and his team had developed a very interesting application that enabled an avatar to speak with very accurate facial expressions based on the vectors of actual faces. A still of an individual could be turned into an avatar's head and automatically animated in response to their voice, or from written text. Known as LifeFX, this application would have enabled the communication of subtle emotional states that would have made helped to transfer greater amounts of tacit knowledge, and build trust and empathy between remote individuals.

Saatchi's wanted to generate *world changing* and *transformative* ideas. This was upping the ante from being a traditional ad agency. They were interested in what Frans Johannson would later call "intersectional ideas." As Johannson wrote, "Intersectional innovations, …change the world in leaps along new directions" (Johansson, 2004, p. 19). They come from the surprising juxtaposition of diverse people and ideas. We recognized the importance of tacit knowledge transfer throughout the creative process and the challenge we faced of how to communicate emotional information or data between collaborators. Tacit knowledge transfer is a vital part of intersectional innovation and is the knowledge locked away inside people's heads, what Leonard and Swap has called "Deep Smarts" (Leonard & Swap, 2004). This is the gold dust of innovation. In order to transfer tacit knowledge in a virtual workplace, it is important to use as much sensory stimulus and emotional data as possible to replicate face-to-face meetings.

A SECOND LIFE AFTER SAATCHI & SAATCHI

The bombing of the World Trade Center had a dramatic negative affect on the advertising industry around the world. It also signaled an end to the utopian visions of the dot.com era, and saw it replaced by a fearful regime of homeland security and concern (Abramson, 2006). The relationship between Saatchi & Saatchi and SGI failed to eventuate. Our proposal of a network of virtual workplaces, or Love Caves, began to look too expensive and did not fit with the new worldview. By the end of 2001, the dream was over.

Yet, as we had predicted, the deep desire to attain virtual presence has continued to drive the imagination and investment of technologists and visionaries. The popular psychological desire for a virtual presence is supported by the business objectives of knowledge management and marketing. As Ray Kurzweil has shown, despite serious economic and social disruption, technology will continue to evolve and Moore's Law is simply part of a bigger evolutionary trajectory (Kurzweil, 2005). Kurzweil has predicted that virtual presence will become more and more real, and common place (Kurzweil, 2005).

It was no real surprise when a radical new online "metaverse," Second Life was launched. So "what is Second Life?" According to the company, Linden Lab, "Second Life is a 3-D virtual world entirely built and owned by its residents." A number of commentators have mentioned that the rapid growth of SL, and virtual worlds remind them of the early days of the Internet. Many large corporations have flocked to establish an early presence and bought virtual islands to begin experimenting with using SL as a virtual workplace for both knowledge management and marketing. The Chairman of Linden Lab, Mitch Kapor, has described it as the $100 billion opportunity. While many regard the cartoon like avatars, and virtual world of Second Life, as a game, the company does not describe it that way. The connotation and definition of computer games has been problematic for some who have serious intentions in Second Life. However, as Edward Castronova has pointed out, even games can have serious intent (Castronova, 2004). And going further still, Daniel Pink claims that the ability to play is becoming an important career attribute (Pink, 2006). When serious money changes hands in a virtual world the real world takes notice (Dibbell, 2006). The academic industry has been grappling with the importance of both gaming and virtual workplaces; however, there are now many tertiary institutions that teach and have a presence in Second Life. A virtual conference held in SL, Best Practices in Education attracted 850 delegates from a diverse number of institutions. Project examples range from that undertaken by the Stanford Humanities Lab on their virtual island of Neware, to a course I am teaching in-world at the Media Design School at Victoria University in New Zealand. Linden Lab encourages educational organizations to teach in SL, and has a number of supports for it in terms of a wiki, in-world education centers, and islands.

In many ways Second Life has gone way beyond what we had hoped to achieve for Saatchi & Saatchi. For very little cost a company or university could facilitate a virtual presence for all of their employees and students all over the world, direct from their desktops, providing the organizations firewalls allow it. An entire company could be in-world at once even if, like the real world, it is not possible for a big company all to fit in one virtual room together. It only requires a modest broadband connection to connect to Second Life. Philip Rosedale, who had been the CTO of Real Networks, devised a clever method to stream all the 3D objects, and the world itself in real-time. This means that any in-world creation can be observed, at the same time, anywhere in the real world. This is a distinct advantage over the SGI Reality Center that required complicated proprietary software, and hardware, to coordinate virtual presence in two or more locations. The SGI solution also required audio streaming, or a separate phone line for participants to commu-

nicate by voice. By comparison, SL residents are able to immediately experience a shared virtual presence as soon as they log on from their desktop, and can use Skype for free.

Immersion is an effective method of attaining a greater sense of presence and thus providing greater tacit knowledge transfer. SL is currently a far more limited immersive experience than the SGI theatres, yet the greater social opportunities and the ease of creation in-world can provide a compelling virtual presence in Second Life. Residents become immersed through their interaction and the real-time responsiveness of the client application. Hundreds of thousands of residents have contributed over 30 TBs (terabytes) of content in SL (Purbrick & Ondrejka, 2006). Conversely, to build a virtual world for an SGI Reality Center was a daunting process that required highly skilled programmers and designers using SGI's OpenGL Performer. Compared to this esoteric programming, SL is a very easy to use 3D building program. It is based on primitive shapes, with freely available tutorials in-world, and many free in-world classes in building and scripting. In addition to these building tools, there is a thriving economy founded on people selling their services as builders and scripters, including for sale prefabricated buildings and freely available open source and public domain scripts. Second Life has effectively dropped the price of entry into virtual workplaces. It is being used by business as a KM tool including knowledge transfer between both employees and customers and for marketing and public relations purposes. However, for KM to be successful, it must include tools for protecting the individual's investment in idea generation. Without some means of DRM, residents will be reluctant to share truly valuable ideas; fortunately, such a tool is built into the client interface of SL.

WHO'S VIRTUAL IP IS IT?

If employees are to collaborate on innovative and

potentially valuable ideas in SL, their IP must be protected. This protection does not necessarily mean keeping an idea secret, however, the metadata that retains the creator's information must be maintained. IP is central to the success and failure of creative collaboration and knowledge transfer in virtual workplaces. Without a clear understanding of ownership and DRM, collaborators in virtual workplaces can be mistrustful and it can inhibit the transfer of knowledge and the sharing of IP. This is true whether a corporation, or a person ultimately owns the IP, as it remains important that individual contributions are still recognized.

Based on advice by Lessig, Linden Lab took a novel approach to IP and in accordance with copyright law, gave all the residents, the content creators, ownership of their own creations. A DRM tool was built into the client application that allowed the creator to determine who could buy, see, use, and copy their creations. This contrasts with some game developers who have tried to oppose the trade of virtual goods (Dibbell, 2006). In Everquest 2, Sony Online has attempted to segregate players who trade goods for cash, and those that, 'legitimately' earn them in game. From the outset SL has had a vibrant mercantile economy where goods, services and virtual land are bought and sold, living side by side with the hacker culture of the Free Software Foundation and the Creative Commons.

Some examples of corporate involvement in SL includes the car company Pontiac who has a virtual island where it has invited motoring journalists to partake in a virtual car launch, and has also held events, such as game shows, to promote their brands to residents. Calvin Klein fragrance used SL to launch a virtual perfume, CK IN2U that can be sprayed on friends in SL, and offered a million Linden dollars for a photography competition in-world. The news agency Reuters has a permanent journalist living and reporting in SL. IBM is one of many IT companies with a presence and has over 80 groups related to its business there. Virtual objects and land can be purchased with the SL currency, known as Linden dollars; this has a floating exchange rate with American dollars. Micro-payments of less than a $1 are common. Still some residents earn enough money to make a real world living in SL. The virtual land baron Anshe Chung is the first avatar to appear on the front cover of Business Week as the first virtual millionaire.

Any resident of SL can create almost anything imaginable from a few basic 3D shapes, known as "prims," some textures (which are targa picture files converted to JPEG 2000) and an easy to use 3D building tool. As soon as something is created the creator can decide whether to give it away, make it able to be copied, or put a price on it for sale. That object may or may not contain a computer script that can give it functionality, and that script could be copied or written from scratch. Linden Lab has announced its intention to incorporate Creative Commons licensing into the client application.

According to their Web site, Creative Commons is a non-profit organization that "... provides free tools that let authors, scientists, artists, and educators easily mark their creative work with the freedoms they want it to carry. You can use CC to change your copyright terms from "All Rights Reserved" to "Some Rights Reserved." Linden Lab and the Creative Commons believe that the easy ability to identify what rights are reserved will foster greater sharing, mixing and collaborat-

Figure 1. The author's avatar creating and editing an object. The Creative Commons machine was created by Zarf Vantangerloo.

ing in SL. Because the process of content creation is real-time, collaborators can simultaneously work on a project together across continents and time zones. Whether they will or not depends on many of the issues that we identified on the Saatchi project. One of those factors is reciprocity. This has been observed to be a key element within SL and within other online communities who share information outputs (Schultz, 2006). Interviews with SL residents who have discussed their willingness to share information, know-how, objects, and scripts have revealed that, even with friends and business colleagues, if there is not a reciprocal relationship then they are far less likely to share with those people. Reciprocity has been identified as a possible "evolutionary stable strategy." That is, social exchange has been argued by some scientists to be an innate part of the human genome, and this does not only apply to the human species. Clippinger and Bollier point to this research to argue that, "Social exchange is an *evolutionary stable strategy* and thus the critical platform for cognitive development in humans" (Clippinger & Bollier, 2005, p. 266). They cite research by behavioral economists and evolutionary geneticists to argue against the creed of the Free Market Doctrine arguing that people are not rational free agents but fundamentally agents of social contracts (Clippinger & Bollier, 2005, p. 266). Philip Ball, in his book *Critical Mass* also uses science to argue that "...you can devise all the complicated formulas you like, but in the end most of us—including traders—are guided by instinct and impulse, by what (John Maynard) Keynes called *animal spirits*" (Ball, 2004, p. 263). The findings of behavioral economics and the importance of social interaction point to the essential nature of reputation and trust in establishing effective virtual workplaces. Reputation, and peer acknowledgement are seen as an important motivation for sharing knowledge (Goldman & Gabriel, 2005). When you create anything in SL the name of the creator, and the owner are labeled on the object or script, once again the DRM tool built into the program protects this information.

In any social exchange there are important sensory cues that determine the level of empathy, trust, and cooperation. Neuroscience provides us with a possible explanation for why people might feel empathy with another avatar. It has been postulated that empathy and co-operation are hardwired into our brain. In an experiment with macaque monkeys, neuroscientists, Rizzolatti and Gallese identified "mirror neurons" that would fire when the monkeys watched other monkeys perform complex motor actions. These were found to be complemented by "canonical neurons" that were in turn connected to parts of the brain that govern emotions and empathy (Clippinger & Bollier, 2005). Thus it may be that watching your own avatar, interacting with other avatars in a virtual space, could fire "mirror neurons" that result in emotional and empathetic responses. Even the crude facial expressions of an avatar may convey emotional data that results in empathy, and promotes sharing and collaboration. Over time, sharing and reciprocity can help to establish trust. Social networks and reliable behavior between agents reinforce this. The ability to convey emotion is not only important for tacit knowledge transfer but for trust and relationship building. While it is known that there is a real person behind an avatar, there are many aspects of that person that remain hidden. Trust is built on revelations of that person's personality and identity. In SL avatars can illicit empathetic

Figure 2. An Avatar expressing surprise; this was triggered using a built in gesture

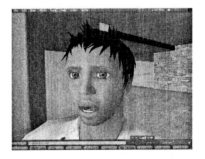

emotions even using only the basic gestures and customized software such as "emotion HUDs," (heads up displays), that attach to an avatar's screen and allow them to select an appropriate gesture. Voice communication assists with this trust building. A successful virtual workplace will include means of expressing emotions and engendering empathy between collaborators in order to build trust, encourage reciprocity and help build reputations.

The ability of a virtual workplace to support social networking is another important aspect of facilitating knowledge transfer. SL has a sophisticated layer of group management built into the client. Anyone can start a group for $L100 (Linden dollars) and appoint officers. These groups can be based on a business associations or simply friendship. Roles and responsibilities can be assigned in a group, and there is the ability to reinforce approved behavior and sanction deviance, both of which are important in encouraging sharing and reciprocity (Schultz, 2006). Groups can jointly own virtual real estate and virtual objects, and can profit from the sale of those jointly owned assets. Those assets can be explicit knowledge such as note cards, that are only accessible to the group, or virtual objects that contain public domain scripts using the built in DRM.

The Un-Secret Source of Second Life

As I have attempted to argue, a virtual workplace requires both emotional and sensory data to communicate knowledge, but it also requires the protection of the creator's metadata to support its success. The DRM tool in SL can be used to protect corporate knowledge or support an open source policy and a mixture of them both. This flexibility is one advantage of SL as a virtual workplace. KM requires DRM tools to facilitate the greatest transfer of knowledge in a virtual workplace, but often under controlled conditions. The requirements of corporate secrecy have to be balanced against the effectiveness of open sharing of knowledge. The findings of behav-

ioral economists and evolutionary geneticists go a long way to explaining the success of open source projects such as Linux. Open source is no longer considered part of the fringe hacker culture, but a valid business model for software development (Goldman & Gabriel, 2005), and it is worth considering that the enormous growth in the Internet has been premised on open source, and open standards (Lessig, 2004).

At the beginning of 2007, Philip Rosedale, announced that the SL client application, the software that residents use to connect to SL, would be going open source. He said it was the company's biggest decision they had made in 7 years. It is fundamental to the Linden Lab philosophy that Second Life is built, shared, and owned by the residents. The President and Chair of the Open Source Applications Foundation, is also the Chair of SL's Linden Lab, Mitch Kapor. He had this to say in an interview with Reuters at the Davos World Economic Forum about SL and open source:

If you look at the history of disruptive technology platforms, like the PC, like the Internet itself, it appears that Second Life, or more properly virtual worlds, are going through that same type of explosive growth that happens when you have a very open platform, in which the barriers to entry and participation are low, in which there's a lot of entrepreneurial incentive, and also a lot of idealism. And when you make the system open the way it is, with the open source client and more opening to come, people will invent fabulous applications of things to do.

Linden Lab has gone from a proprietary closed source code to an open source GPL license for the client. Their servers already run on the open source Linux software and they have extended this through to the SL application and the client software. This gives corporations that want to use it the ability to further shape SL to suit their purposes and to benefit from the many independent developers who can contribute to the code's improvement. As this is explained by Richard Stallman, founder of the Free Software Foundation, open source is free, not as in "free" beer but as in free speech. Open source licenses have been very successful in encouraging hundreds of thousands of unpaid developers to collaborate and contribute to the coding and support of major software projects. A Web site that hosts open source projects, Source Forge, is currently home to 148,087 projects, and 1,581,770 registered users.

The richness of debate and the enthusiasm surrounding the likes of open source, and the Creative Commons, is testament to the belief of many that the time has come to approach intellectual property in a totally new way. Clippinger and Bollier have called this the Renaissance of the Commons (Clippinger & Bollier, 2005). Within Second Life there is a powerful scripting language, Linden Scripting Language (LSL). This is designed to give anyone and everyone who is interested and has the scripting skills the ability to manipulate the world with this programming language. Even those residents who find scripting a challenge regularly open the scripts contained by 3D objects, and tweak the code for their own purposes. Developed by Philip Rosedale, it gives access to avatar and object animation in-world. Linden Lab hosts a wiki to support LSL. To quote the wiki, "LSL is appropriately the stuff of gods in Second Life, though you needn't be a god to master it!" Sharing code and cooperation has long been recognized as an integral part of hacker culture (Levy, 1994). There is a desire to help your fellow hackers, foster friendships, as well build a reputation and acclaim. As SL has some limitations in terms of file sharing, many residents use communications software such as Skype to both talk, and also share files using peer-to-peer protocols. The SL community is self-educating, residents can teach each other how to do things. There are numerous subscriber e-mail lists, and Groups in SL, that are open for all to join, and support their members such as the Scripter group, or Script Class group.

As I have argued, IP and DRM are integral to sharing knowledge within a virtual workplace. The, Digital Millennium Copyright Act (DMCA) (1998) makes it illegal in the U.S. to circumvent copyright protection mechanisms. An example of how important these issues are in Second Life was revealed when a hack removed all protection and ownership metadata and enabled free copying of textures. Without the DRM protection, the SL economy threatened to collapse.

The CopyBot Scandal

In November 2006, a wiki based on the objective of reverse engineering the SL client, www.libsecondlife.com, released code known as CopyBot. This allowed residents to copy prims and textures in-world. This caused a huge concern in SL as it effectively meant that anyone with the CopyBot could copy anything, except protected scripts. Stores throughout SL closed and virtual force fields went up overnight to keep out anyone but the owners. Some thought the entire SL economy would freeze.

Amongst the angry and frightened reactions that ensued on the Official Linden Blog, the point was made that, similar to the Web, it is impossible to completely protect digital assets from copying and duplication. Once the obvious distress and damage of the CopyBot was identified, it was removed from the libsecondlife developer's repository. However, the sensitivity of SL content creators illustrates that in order to encourage knowledge sharing in a virtual workplace, there must be some DRM and IP policy in place.

CONCLUSION

Virtual art and the desire for virtual presence have ancient origins. Saatchi & Saatchi boldly stepped forward to embrace a means of managing the knowledge of their dispersed network only to withdraw after 9/11. The importance of tacit knowledge transfer and communication of emotion are important to both knowledge management and marketing. Sensory stimulation in virtual workplaces is a means of achieving both those business objectives. Second Life is attracting considerable interest because it fulfils both our ancient desires and our pressing business needs to transfer tacit knowledge using virtual presence, and to provide a powerful marketing tool that has emotional resonance.

The success or failure of virtual worlds such as Second Life hinge on their ability to handle not just social networks but the issues of IP, copyright, and new economics. Open source and Creative Commons are some of the solutions to enabling a frictionless new world order. Eventually, there will be no clear delineation between the real world and the virtual. A virtual workplace must have the means to address IP policies using DRM tools that support sharing as well as the protection of the creator's IP.

Today, people are not only more physically mobile they are now more virtually mobile, and this is contributing to the generation of a plethora of intersectional ideas. Frans Johannson wrote. "These three forces—the movement of people, the convergence of science, and the leap of computation—are giving rise to more intersections than ever..." (Johansson, 2004, p. 32). As Tom Peters wrote in, *The Circle of Innovation*, an organization should encourage diversity in order to generate more innovative ideas (Peters, 1997). In Second Life diversity is achieved through connecting geographically dispersed individuals. Our ability to effectively communicate as well in a virtual workplace, as we would in a face-to-face meeting, depends on our ability to communicate subtle emotional states and the gamut of sensory stimulations. When a majority of businesses have a presence in virtual worlds, an effective virtual workplace will become as essential as a meeting room or phone system, yet the virtual water cooler will likely lead to far more world changing ideas and greater innovation as intersectional ideas flourish.

REFERENCES

Abramson, B. (2005). *Digital phoenix: Why the information economy collapsed and how it will rise again.* Cambridge, MA: MIT Press.

Ackerman, D. (1990). *A natural history of the senses* (1st ed.). New York: Random House.

Anderson, C. (2006). *The long tail: How endless choice is creating unlimited demand.* London: Random House Business.

Ball, P. (2004). *Critical mass: How one thing leads to another*: Farrar, Straus and Giroux.

Castronova, E. (2004). Right to play. *New York Law School Law Review, 49*(1).

Clippinger, J., & Bollier, D. (2005). A renaissance in the commons: How the new sciences and the Internet are framing a new global identity and order. In R. A. Ghosh (Ed.), *CODE: Collaborative ownership and the digital economy* (pp. x, p. 345). Cambridge, MA: MIT Press.

Damer, B. (2007). *A brief history of the virtual world.* Retrieved November 10, 2007, from http://news.com.com/A+brief+history+of+the+v irtual+world+-+page+2/2008-1043_3-6134110-2.html?tag=st.next

Davenport, T. H., Prusak, L., & Wilson, H. J. (2003). *What's the big idea? Creating and capitalizing on the best management thinking.* Boston, MA: Harvard Business School Press.

Dibbell, J. (2006). *Play money: Or, how I quit my day job and made millions trading virtual loot.* New York: Basic Books.

Dixon, N. M. (2000). *Common knowledge: How companies thrive by sharing what they know.* Boston, MA:

Friedman, T. L. (2006). *The world is flat: A brief history of the twenty-first century* (1st updated and expanded ed.). New York: Farrar, Straus and Giroux.

Gibson, W. (1986). *Neuromancer.* London: Grafton.

Goldman, R., & Gabriel, R. P. (2005). *Innovation happens elsewhere: Open source as business strategy.* Amsterdam, Boston, MA: Morgan Kaufmann.

Grau, O. (2003). *Virtual art: From illusion to immersion* (Rev. and expanded ed.). Cambridge, MA: MIT Press.

Heim, M. (1993). *The metaphysics of virtual reality.* New York: Oxford University Press.

Johansson, F. (2004). *The Medici effect: Breakthrough insights at the intersection of ideas, concepts, and cultures.* Boston, MA: Harvard Business School Press.

Kurzweil, R. (2005). *The singularity is near: When humans transcend biology.* New York: Viking.

Leonard, D., & Swap, W. (2004). Deep smarts. *Havard Business Review, 13.*

Lessig, L. (2004). *Free culture: How big media uses technology and the law to lock down culture and control creativity.* New York: Penguin Press.

Levy, S. (1994). *Hackers: Heroes of the computer revolution.* New York: Dell.

Packer, R., & Jordan, K. (Eds.). (2001). *Multimedia: From Wagner to virtual reality* (1st ed.). New York: Norton.

Peters, T. J. (1997). *The circle of innovation: You can't shrink your way to greatness* (1st ed.). New York: Knopf.

Pink, D. H. (2006). *A whole new mind: Why right-brainers will rule the future* (1st Riverhead trade pbk. ed.). New York: Riverhead Books.

Polanyi, M. (1967). *The tacit dimension.* London: Routledge & K. Paul.

Purbrick, D. J., & Ondrejka, C. (2006). User creation and scripting in second life. Retrieved November 10, 2007, from http://www.langnet-symposium.com/speakers.asp

Roberts, K. (2004). *Lovemarks: The future beyond brands.* Auckland, New Zealand: Reed.

Saatchi, S. (2007). *Saatchi & Saatchi worldwide named agency network of the year at Clio Ad Festival.* Retrieved November 10, 2007, from http://www.prnewswire.com/cgi-bin/stories.pl?ACCT=109&STORY=/www/story/05-14-2007/0004587573&EDATE=

Schultz, M. F. (2006). Fear and norms and rock & roll: What jambands can teach us about persuading people to obey copyright law. *Berkeley Technology Law Journal, 21,* 651-728.

Stephenson, N. (1992). *Snow crash.* New York: Bantam Books.

Steuer, J. (1992). Defining virtual reality: Dimensions determining telepresence. *Journal of Communication, 4*(24), 73-93.

Tiffany, L. (2007, January 9). Starting a second life business. *Entrepreneur.com.* Retrieved November 10, 2007, from http://www.entrepreneur.com/startingabusiness/businessideas/article172768.html

Wertheim, M. (1999). *The pearly gates of cyberspace: A history of space from Dante to the Internet.* New York: W.W. Norton.

Wikipedia. (2007a). *Digital rights management.*

Wikipedia. (2007b). *Intellectual property.*

Wikipedia. (2007c). *Knowledge Management.*

Wikipedia. (2007d). *Massively multiplayer online role-playing game.*

Wikipedia. (2007e). *Metadata.*

Yates, F. A. (1966). *The art of memory.* London: Routledge and Paul.

KEY TERMS

Avatar: A representation of a real person in a virtual world. Originated from the Hindu philosophy, meaning God's embodiment on Earth. Credited to Chip Morningstar (Damer, 2007)

Digital Rights Management (DRM): "is an umbrella term referring to technologies used by publishers or copyright owners to control access to or usage of digital data or hardware, and to restrictions associated with a specific instance of a digital work or device" (Wikipedia, 2007a).

Explicit Knowledge: Knowledge that is easy to codify, record, and communicate (Dixon, 2000).

Immersion: "The virtual environment submerges the user in the sights and sounds and tactility specific to that environment. Immersion creates the sense of being present in a virtual world, a sense that goes beyond physical" (Heim, 1993).

Intellectual Property (IP): "An umbrella term for various legal entitlements which attach to certain names, written and recorded media, and inventions. The holders of these legal entitlements are generally entitled to exercise various exclusive rights in relation to the subject matter of the IP" (Wikipedia, 2007b).

In-World: A gamer's term to denote inside the virtual world as opposed to the real world.

Knowledge Management: While there is no real consensus on this term a useful definition is that it "comprises a range of practices used by organizations to identify, create, represent, and distribute knowledge for reuse, awareness, and learning" (Wikipedia, 2007c).

Massively Multiplayer Online Roleplaying Game (MMORPG): A genre of online roleplaying video games (RPGs) in which a large number of players interact with one another in a virtual world (Wikipedia, 2007d).

Metadata: This is data or information about data. This could be who wrote something, the date it was published, where, and so forth (Wikipedia, 2007e).

Prim: A Second Life term meaning primitive shape such as a cube, sphere, torus, or pyramid.

Residents: A Second Life term that refers to avatars and agents in the virtual world.

Tacit Knowledge: Credited to Michael Polyani, that knowledge that is in people's heads and therefore hard to access (Polanyi, 1967).

Texture: In Second Life, texture refers to an imported picture file that is mapped to a prim in order to give it appearance eg brick texture on a cube can appear like a wall.

Virtual Reality: Credited to Jaron Lanier, defined by Michael Heim (VR) "pertains to convincing the participant that he or she is actually in another place, by substituting the normal sensory input received by the participant with information produced by a computer" (Heim, 1993, p. 160).

Virtual Presence: In conjunction with virtual reality, it "is based on concepts of *presence* and *telepresence*, which refer to the sense of being in an environment, generated by natural or mediated means, respectively" (Steuer, 1992, p. 76).

Virtual World: "A scene or an experience with which a participant can interact by using computer-controlled input-output devices. Most virtual worlds attempt resemble physical reality …" (Heim, 1993, p. 160).

Chapter XXXI
Intranets:
Interactive Knowledge Management Tools of Networked Communities

Goran Vlasic
University of Zagreb, Croatia

Jurica Pavicic
University of Zagreb, Croatia

Zoran Krupka
University of Zagreb, Croatia

ABSTRACT

This chapter deals with the importance of intranets as knowledge management tools/media enabling efficient knowledge exchange and development within an organization and the "community" of stakeholders. Communities are analyzed as networked systems of interested parties. The importance of intranets is even more stressed today when most company activities are project based—with project members working together from all over the world. Intranets serve as project coordination support as well as organization functioning generalization through combining different project activities into organizational efficiency analysis. This chapter analyzes possibilities of different approaches to development and management of intranets, and thus of networked people creating a certain networked "community form." These developments are crucial to virtual workplaces as well as for increasing business efficiency

INTRODUCTION

This chapter deals with the importance of intranets as knowledge sharing support systems. Virtual communities have become more dynamic than off-line communities making them of great interest for all businesses, especially when internal (company–related) communities are analyzed. The best platform facilitating virtual communities is the intranet—along with the extranet as its extension.

The importance of intranets is even more stressed today when most company activities are project based, with project members working together with no time-space constraints. With worldwide increase in competition, companies' performance (and efficiency) has to be measured and fine-tuned at the smallest possible level of analysis. In such complex situations, intranets serve as project coordination support but also as tracking tools at project component level. By combining project components' individual efficiencies, intranets generate the analysis (later referred to as reporting) on the overall organizational efficiency analysis. They can inductively analyze a company's performance based on the data collected at the project-level intranets.

This chapter also analyzes the virtual communities and their importance in the context of organizational culture. Furthermore, it analyzes the possibilities of different approaches to development and management of intranets and thus of virtual communities. These concepts are crucial to virtual workplaces as well as for increasing business efficiency.

BACKGROUND

Due to the fact that the business environment is more and more volatile and globalized, companies face the increasing problem of effective coordination and efficient work. Requirements for efficiency (concerning time and other resources) have pushed companies' coordination efforts to the limits—making it impossible for "slow" human force to manage it. As a result, intranets have started to be developed mostly to facilitate the growing need for administration management (i.e., document exchange, joint calendars, etc.). Their first feature presented an important improvement, but also served as a type of barrier for greater intranet implementation. The administrative component of intranet was relatively cheaply developed and implemented (especially now that hardware is already available) and thus managers seldom realized the possibility for implementation of more complex intranets, providing extra benefits, but also enduring extra costs. However, with the development of interactive technologies, intranets have become strong powerful tools providing companies (which adequately utilize

them) substantial competitive advantage which could not be ignored. Thus, more and more they have started to be implemented as overall management tools—serving as support systems for knowledge management, process management, project management, and so forth.

In order to analyze this powerful business tool, we provide the following discussion which points out some of the most important concepts surrounding intranets and their implementation.

We define **intranet** as being **the internal network using Internet-like infrastructure and protocols which efficiently facilitates communication, collaborative work, information exchange and strong knowledge development platform providing incontestable competitive advantage** (Baker, 2000; Bland, 2002; Boddendke & Denton, 2006; Chou, 1998; Cumming & Cuthberson, 2001; Damsdaard & Scheepers, 1999; Denton, 2006; Denton & Richardson, 2006; Delarge, 2003; Dolphy & Kala, 2001; Edenius & Borgerson, 2003; Mphidi & Snman, 2004; Siegel, Hartmen, & Quershi, 1998; Standing & Benson, 2000; Stenmark, 2006; Wen, 1998; Wen, Ye, & Lin, 1998; Wen et al., 1998; Vlasic, 2006). As seen here, many authors have recognized these characteristics of intranets.

Before further analyzing intranets, we need to define a closely related concept: the extranet. Some authors see it as a network of intranets (Angeles, 2001). Others view it as an extension of intranets, allowing "outside" users to access data (Bland, 2002). Similarly, Baker (2000) defines extranets as providing secure access to defined (usually vital) data to select outside users. Delarge (2003) stresses the point that extranets enable suppliers and distributors to contribute more efficiently to value adding (Lee-Kelley et al., 2004).

Bernard (1998, p. 363) defines an extranet simply as the "use of the Internet to reach intranet." Likewise, Siegel at al. (1998) indicate that extranet present a "bridge" between the "public" Internet and "private" intranet. O'Shea (2002) points out that extranets enable greater control while completely utilizing all the advantages of Internet. Similar components are mentioned by other authors (Boddendke & Williams, 2002; McCarthy, 1997) defining extranets as being the link between the intranet and the Internet, aimed at sustaining efficient B2B knowledge exchange. With all this in mind, we can state that **extranets present private network of suppliers, vendors, partners, customers, and other relevant stakeholders**.

Based on these key notions, we define extranet as an extension of intranet which allows different levels of access to specific/wider audiences (key stakeholders) based on their identification. Hence, although some authors (Minoli, 2005) point out that extranets have reached the point in development where they need to be analyzed separately from the intranets, in this chapter extranets are analyzed as certain "extensions" of intranets. We have taken this approach due to the fact that similar rules apply to the management of intranets and extranets (Chou, 1998). This is especially so because no extranet can exist without the existence of intranet and access to the information it provides. Thus, we have accounted for the extranets through later presented detailed classification of intranets.

The abovementioned comprehensive definition of intranets points out some of the most important related concepts. The first notion states that it is the fact that intranets are developed (mostly) on Internet protocols. However, intranet could implement some "Internet-like" protocol enabling exchange of knowledge—thus not necessarily use the Internet protocol itself. There is a strict line between the Internet services and the intranet. Baker (2000) stresses that intranet is not just a type of corporate Internet, but one of the key elements of business strategies. Although, usually both use the similar infrastructure, important difference present the "boundaries" (Chou, 1998; Lee-Kelley et al., 2004) defining those who have access.

Another important difference is the security issues (Angeles, 2001; Vlasic, 2006b). World Wide Web (WWW) content is intended for general publics, and thus security issues are of relatively low importance. The content does not present information which should be protected. Most security issues concerning the WWW relate to virus protection and confidentiality issues toward consumers. Intranets present (usually) closed networks which are strictly separated from Internet infrastructure (important: they use similar infrastructure, but the two structures are usually not connected); thus the security issues are related only toward the control of content and use by identified members. Here issues of security should be raised concerning authenticity, privacy, access control, and virus protection. Extranets, among the three, present the most threatened system when privacy issues are analyzed since they include strictly confidential data and are (usually) connected to the Internet infrastructure, thus being protected from unwanted "attacks" by only security protocols. Thus, many security issues need to be addressed (Boddendke & Williams, 2002): authenticity of information and its source, protection from repudiation, integrity of content and system itself, privacy and confidentiality issues, access control (needing to protect system from unwanted users accessing—that is, hackers, while simultaneously allowing for unhindered access by registered users; such protection is done by hardware/software firewalls), and virus protection. Usually extranets are the networks of most interest to hackers (their "warfare attacks") trying to gain access to vital company data, and for all the mentioned reasons truly present the potential privacy pitfalls. Some authors relate intranet to e-commerce, saying that it is a branch of such system (Angeles, 2001; Baker, 2000). However, e-commerce is just one aspect of Internet services which concentrates on transactions. On the other hand, intranets (and its extension—extranets) present completely different concept with strictly different focus. They concentrate on the added value through efficient knowledge exchange.

"Efficiency" is another concept which is often pointed out when intranets are analyzed. It is to expect that beneficial intranet will enable fast and outspread communication (Chou, 1998) enabling much more effective communication and cooperation between all "parts" of business community (Boddendke & Williams, 2002). In stead of having procedures for paper-handling of processes, intranets reduce the cost of needed office supplies as well as enable greater control of who has viewed what, when, and (usually) why. All the information which used to be transferred using regular paper and post can now be posted on intranet sites also enabling intranet signatures. By logging on, every user is identified, and thus, just by "checking the appropriate box" a document could be signed. Of course this implies internal regulations development which will enable and control the use of intranet for such purposes. Intranets can completely substitute all information exchange procedures within a company (which gets even greater importance when the company is doing business world wide). Such change reduces the need (or more importantly the costs) for stationeries simultaneously reducing the time needed for information transfer and search to a minimum (basically momentary information exchange).

Such efficiency is a great motivator for a true use of intranets for communication, collaboration, and information exchange purposes. Members of such intranet community can simultaneously work on the same project with constant up-to-date view of the project progress. It is possible to set up international teams which work on a time shifting basis (they work on the same project during the work time in their time zone). In such situation intranet communities could work closely together and through the exchange of information and automatic knowledge development tools (i.e., artificial intelligence, pattern recognition, etc.); they would be developing new "knowledge." So, intranet serves as a knowledge generation, storage, and management tool providing most recent (most developed) knowledge to any member of the community upon the request. Such queries could have numerous limitators and conditions making intranet also a knowledge filtering tool. All this again strictly points out the usefulness of intranet and its influence on efficiency and profitability—and, thus, on the "competitive advantage"

of a particular company. Companies implementing intranets face higher costs at the implementation phase. However, such costs are usually (if the intranet is well planned and developed) compensated for and profits are soon achieved with every task being done more efficiently. It is important that here we also mention extranets (as extensions of intranets); thus, competitive advantage is obtained also through good cooperation (and possibility of relationship personalization) with suppliers and distributors. Intranets enable momentary exchange of knowledge of all included community members and continuous benchmarking, thus ensuring higher efficiency of knowledge development and modifications of all business processes. It is now obvious that there is a "spill-over" effect present where each community member has increased efficiency, thus the costs of final product are reduced with the multiplicative effects. Intranets and extranets offer brands competitive advantages by working as (Delarge, 2003) brand asset warehouses, enablers of brand communities, and brand-process enablers.

Now, we return to the concept of boundaries as one of the important components characterizing intranets. Boddenke and Williams (2002) define the boundaries based on the focus. Thus, intranets are oriented to members within the organization/project (business-to-"employee" focus). Internet is mainly focused on communication with consumers (business-to-consumer); extranet is focused on those subjects adding value to the final product (mostly business-to-business focus). However, due to developments in technology and increased importance of relationship personalization (conception which assumes relationship development between consumers and companies, based on mutual understanding, developed and continuous knowledge exchange through interactive communication with a goal of achieving added value for all parties involved), even on B2C markets consumers are becoming part of the service/production processes. Thus, they are also becoming important component of companies' extranets (e.g., Internet banking allowing access to internal company information based on more-or-less secure identification).

However, depending on the specifics of the selected group, these targets can be changed. An example is when there are few consumers influencing the company's performance (i.e., on B2B markets), then the focus changes. Internet (more precisely, the WWW—as a service using the Internet as infrastructure) is focused on the general public, while extranet is focused on suppliers, distributors, and (very important) consumers (which have become a part of the value adding system). In some industries (usually of strategic interest) government can present a "member" of extranet (e.g., government institutions, monopolists, etc.). Thus, although very often confused and used interchangeably, the concepts of intranet, extranet, and Internet (WWW) are strictly separated and defined. Further in the chapter we have indicated possible differentiation between the "different" types of intranets.

These boundaries define intranet users thus creating networked type of communities which could be temporary (e.g., project based) or lasting. We have decided to use the term *networked community* for such "groups of people" to separate them from traditional and online communities which are more common. We will define networked community as a group of people with a sense of membership, integration, and fulfillment of needs together with a feeling of shared emotional connections, but with a primary function to achieve the defined goals using interactive technology-supported intranet backbone. Thus, the term *networked* is used to stress that these communities, although having all community characteristics, are primarily goal-oriented networks of individuals.

The traditional/classic perspective on community defines (Zimmerman, 1938) the term *networked* through basic four characteristics which characterize it: social fact, specification, association, and limited area. However, Hillary (1955) argued that the most important components include: social interaction between members of

the community, shared ties, and shared areas, with area being the least important "ingredient." Further, sociologists have argued that "community can be achieved independently of territorial context where social networks exist sufficiently to sustain a *Gemeinschaft* quality of interaction and association" where Gemeinschaft presents a definition of community through intimacy, familiarity, sympathy, interdependence, and reflectiveness of "shared social consciousness" (Almgren, 2000, p. 400). McMillan and Chavis (1986) have further suggested that "a state of community exists when four elements co-exist: membership, influence, integration and fulfillment of needs, and shared emotional connections" defined "either in relational terms or territorial terms as long as these four elements are present together" (Almgren, 2000, p. 400).

This last argument by McMillan and Chavis (1986) allows us to use term community regarding describing a "collection" of people (integration) working together (membership) through interaction and interactive effects on each other (influence) in order to achieve common goals (fulfillment of needs) sharing experiences (shared emotional connections) through intranets. Today theory and practice recognize that even communities that are dispersed worldwide and are closely "interwoven" present a certain networked community concept. Similarity of ideas and values—combined with shared activities/beliefs are the essential components of a community, regardless of the members' geographical proximity (Brint, 2001). People still have the need to be part of a known and recognizable group.

Therefore, these networked communities which have arisen based on the intranets' specificities should be considered as a complement to traditional community. In this sense, companies should act as catalysts for creating and sustaining intranet communities. Although the motives to do so could be different (and should be adequately researched), we are naming several which, in our opinion, play a crucial role: (a) better efficiency and easier problem-solving processes (due to a larger think-tank capacity); (b) more satisfied stakeholders that are, on daily basis, in contact with the people they consider acquaintances, if not friends; (c) certain loyalty effects—stakeholders become integrative parts of the same community and experience some of the "ancient" effects of belonging to a group of socially related people (protection, leadership, differentiation, etc.); and other "more business oriented" motives which are described further in the chapter.

Further analysis in this chapter relates to intranets conceptualization, benefits (and possible pitfalls), and practical suggestions for effective development and implementation of intranets in order to facilitate adequately business processes—but keeping in mind that intranets also need to fulfill expectations set not just by the company but by its users (the community).

CONCEPTUALIZING INTRANETS

Each intranet is supposed to have its "manager"/ "administrator" (of any type) which is identified and responsible for the specific intranet (at least hardware and software aspect of intranets). The manager has the authority to provide access to intranet to other users, as well as to define their authority over intranet usage (or even, to some extent, intranet management). Each (respectable) intranet system keeps track of changes that were made and enables its manager to undo any changes which might not be beneficial to the intranet (networked) community.

One summary of intranet technology use was presented by Damsdaard and Scheepers (1999), who stated that intranets could be used for:

- **Publishing:** Using the technology to publish information (e.g., home pages, newsletters, technical documents, product catalogues, employee directories);
- **Transactions:** Using the technology for transactions (especially important for extranets);

- **Interacting:** Using the technology to interact with other individuals and groups in the organization (e.g., via discussion groups, collaborative applications) regardless of location of the interaction participants;
- **Searching:** Using the technology to search for organizational knowledge (e.g., via search engines, indexes, search agents);
- **Recording:** Using the technology to record the computer-based *organization memory* (e.g., best practices, business processes, frequently asked questions) which will be used for the development of future knowledge.

Although intranets provide numerous benefits for managing the abovementioned tasks, they can provide much more. Intranets, as administrative tools, are readily available and rather inexpensive tools. However, it is beneficial to implement artificially intelligent protocols in intranets in order to raise their functionality to a new dimension—where they fulfill the basic "administrative" functions but also enable true knowledge development and management. This intranet "upgrading" requires relatively large investments due to the fact that it very company-specific and must be individually deployed.

In order to efficiently plan and develop intranets, we propose the classification of intranets based on the several different variables: time span, audience, goal, range of additional services, interconnectedness (with other intranets), and management style. Although one can argue that there are many more intranet attributes to be analyzed, based on the research (Vlasic et al., 2007), we believe that defining these elements will drastically reduce the unnecessary expenses of intranet implementation.

Time span presents the length of time for which intranets are going to be managed. This is especially important to define in the case of development of temporary project based open source intranets. So, according to *time span*, intranets could be divided into:

- **Short term:** which duration is expected to be less than one year (i.e., intranets developed for particular projects: event organization, MBA lectures, and so forth_;
- **Long term:** which duration is expected to be longer than one year, but finite (i.e., intranet set up for a certain long term project such as research project or apartment contraction);
- **Eternal:** which are usually more general (i.e., company intranet, or intranet for discussion and analysis of scientific work regarding interactive technologies).

Intranets' audience presents a type of very lively virtual community which is automatically concentrated on exchange processes. According to *audience,* intranets could be targeted at:

- **Team members:** where each user is identified by a username and password (or any other identification device, i.e., biometrics) and could include: employees, investors, suppliers, distributors, and even consumers;
- **General audience:** where each user (even unidentified) has a right to view/comment intranet elements (i.e., a Ph.D. student interested in interactive technologies wants to view some ideas relating to his subject area and wants to share his opinions on existing intranet content. The student, in this case, cannot add or change content but just view it);
- **Unlimited general audience:** where intranet becomes very similar to being a portal relating to a particular topic.

According to *goals* the intranet is supposed to achieve, we could divide intranets into:

- **Predefined goals:** intranet topic is clearly predefined (i.e., particular project management intranet);
- **Moderated goals:** intranet has general "overall" goal but its structure (goal particles) can be developed according to needs (i.e., intranet of a particular company which

is then developed into project-based and/or functional organization);
- **Unconstrained goals:** intranet is open to general discussions/knowledge sharing with no considerable constraints.

Besides, providing general administrative services, intranets could provide a wide range of extra services extending its usefulness and having further strong effects on cost reductions. Thus, according to *services* they provide, intranets could be:

- **Administrative:** intranets used only for communication and administration purposes;
- **Extended administrative:** intranets enable different extra services to its users (i.e., blogs of users, e-mail automation, Internet searches, etc.)
- **Knowledge management:** intranets are used to exchange knowledge developed through information exchange;
- **Artificially intelligent:** intranets are capable of exerting human-like behavior developing knowledge automatically and "intelligently" self-administrating the intranet (i.e., system is capable of forwarding and handling orders).

Further, important aspect of intranets presents the interconnectedness (with other intranets). It could be expected that, more and more, intranets will be connected into a larger "interest" network providing extra benefits for all involved. Different intranets could collaborate on developing knowledge, on R&D projects, and so forth. Thus, according to *interconnectedness,* intranet could be:

- **Island:** intranet is separated form other intranets and serves strictly defined purpose (i.e., certain company, project, etc.)
- **Interconnected:** intranet is connected into a network of intranets dealing with related content, either through certain touch points

(i.e., financial results) or through multiple connection points;

- **Incorporated:** where a intranet is incorporated into a "larger scale" intranet (i.e., in groups of companies each subsidiary has its own intranet which are built into an overall parent company's intranet).

As stated, managers/administrators of intranet need to develop strong support for all the implemented procedures in order to ensure long term sustainability of intranet components. However, *management of content* could be differently managed (Tredinick & Tilly, 2001):

- **Laissez-faire:** decentralized model with no hierarchy so every participant is allowed to publish any material (usually either for intranets targeted at two "extreme" segments: open to unlimited general audience where usually no particular goal is defined, and those open to team members which are identified and trust exists among them along with the tracking mechanisms);
- **Centralized model:** where all the intranet content is controlled by an "overall" supervisor in charge for intranet development;
- **Mixed model:** where intranets are under limited control enabling relatively free participation under certain general rules which the coordinator is in charge of controlling;
- **Support services model:** where the organization provides support for intranet contributors through the development process.

Classification of intranets is crucial to its further development because it requires different interface, structure, content, and security level. Thus, in the planning period of intranet it is important to define it according to all of the mentioned aspects. Only if well planned, can intranets provide benefits to the organizations that they promise.

Benefits Provided by Intranets

Stenmark (2006) has presented some conflicting views on intranet usage. He states that those who oppose intranets stress that the central information staff can provide the organization with relevant information. Also, opposers believe that once that information is published, the employees can search for the information themselves; thus there is no need for "automated" knowledge management system such as intranet. In addition, they believe that people are much more inclined to ask others for information rather than search for information using intranets themselves. However, Stenmark (2006) responds to such statements stating that the information staff cannot possibly know what every single individual finds relevant and that not even the individuals themselves are of their information needs. Intranets, as knowledge warehouses, are useful. Intranets reduce bottlenecking because central staff can manage one request at a time and are more efficient. Intranets enable more contributors regardless of their geographical position. Thus, the benefits of intranet implementation are numerous.

Intranet presents a foundation for data, communication, marketing, and management purposes enabling users to make queries based on which they receive up-to-date information (Chou, 1998). Many authors have analyzed benefits that intranets offer (Baker, 2000; Chou, 1998; Lynch, 1997; Ruikar, Anumba, & Carillo, 2005; Vlasic et al., 2007). First, intranets enable information exchange and sharing instantaneously. There are no more information gatekeepers which control the information flow. Information is ready available to all authorized users and is constantly kept on the server—thus intranet serves as a bank of documents and knowledge. If well interconnected, intranets enable strategic communication between companies and their offices and mobile workers (networked community) and access to different application processes (i.e., order entry, production tracking, etc.). Furthermore, intranets provide extra security to companies by control of access and keeping track of logs. Thus, vital documents do not need to be printed; rather they could be kept on the intranet server and available. It is obvious that intranet can act as an enabler for information retrieval, sharing and management, communication and collaboration, and access to databases and applications.

In addition, a more comprehensive analysis of intranets' benefits clearly shows its influence on shortening the learning curve since knowledge is easily transferred and implemented. Intranets enable many-to-many communication simultaneously enabling faster knowledge development and dissemination. When analyzed just at the administration level, intranets:

- enable handling many users simultaneously, which no human-handled process could manage;
- provide timely and readily accessible information;
- save printing costs;
- communicate corporate identity and influence corporate culture through "branded" interface/content/structure/reporting.

When further analyzed, intranets actually present a comprehensive corporate network which is scalable, standardized, and cost efficient, having powerful data management and knowledge development capability through supporting dynamic workgroup exchange (Chou, 1998). They present a truly remarkable tool useful for all size projects combining advantages (in its fully developed shape) that are offered by all Internet services with extra capabilities of security, community management, and documentation handling (approval).

Ruikar et al. (2005) have provided a different perspective on intranet benefits through the analysis of end users and their perspectives on possible benefits of project intranets. They have extracted the following main benefits:

- **Improved value adding process management:** Intranet enables faster and more efficient value adding system which is fostered by all involved subjects (suppliers, company, distributors, consumers, etc.);
- **Reduced response time across the supply chain:** Intranets have enabled real time approval system where each involved subject can approve their specific part of the project through intranet (i.e., company can make an order through intranet and can "sign" a contract with the suppliers just by digitally approving it). However, for this system to work properly all intranet participants have to adopt adequate procedures which honor these practices;
- **Faster and cheaper document processing:** Documents can be transferred and managed without any need for formal paper transactions or (even) e-mail exchanges. Intranets have enabled automatic document processing where document author just specifies who has to check the document and what is their role. The intranet manages the rest;
- **Eliminated manual rekeying;**
- **Created a grater level of trust among its members due to possibility of momentary control and tracking:** Since intranets keep track of all the changes its participants have greater trust in doing transactions which are registered in detail and can be thoroughly analyzed;
- **Increased involvement of all the members:** Intranet members' activity can also be tracked. But, more importantly, intranets enable equal opportunity to all its members to innovate and connect with the company;
- **Improved service to client:** clients can be one of the intranet's (extranet's) publics and as a result get better services or even services which have never before existed (i.e., online banking and mobile banking which

use computers / cell phones as interface for accessing the intranet);

- **Knowledge database and preservation of corporate memory:** which has been thoroughly discussed;
- **Avoid disputes:** creates an audit trail including details such as meeting minutes, actions, comments, requests, approvals, and notifications; also maintaining records of information such as who has published what, when information was viewed and by whom.

Besides those mentioned, Mphidi and Snman (2004) stress consistency of the procedures and the treatment of members (according to authorization levels). In addition, intranets enable interactivity and easy and cost effective system update. Also, intranets utilize user-friendly and personalized interface for communication with the system. Further, they centralize all the knowledge, they provide extra services (especially in comparison to human-handled administration), they enable easy access and publishing, and they ensure accuracy and responsibility for provided information and increases efficiency. Although providing so many advantages, intranets are rather simple to be developed and maintained (given that planning was done properly)

Usually, the main benefits that motivate companies to implement intranet include (Cumming & Cuthbertson, 2001): the improvement of communications within the organization, and expected increase in efficiency and productivity. In addition, main motivators present the IT and information management capabilities and reduced printing and distribution costs.

An increasingly important element of intranets is reporting. It can be viewed as a possibility to instantaneously and clearly report any needed information in any format desired. Reporting has to enable numerous filters and combinatorial explanations. Using these filters users define the knowledge which they require which is then derived from a vast amount of data, information

and knowledge, in order to provide true benefits to its users. In these reports knowledge needs to be systemized and developed through automatic comparative systems enabling management of great number of input to provide output (reports). Reports (in any form) present the final result/need of intranets. All the data in the intranets is useless if it cannot be viewed and used efficiently. Thus, more and more, intranets present interface between the user and the knowledge management "apparatus" behind it.

POSSIBLE PITFALLS

Several concerns on the growing use of intranets include (Chou, 1998) the growing need for management, management of bandwidth, security control, and the management of data transfer and knowledge development speed. With greater implementation new elements need to be controlled. As the number of users and information increases, the infrastructure has to be developed to sustain the extra traffic simultaneously pursuing the most recent security checks to ensure the confidentiality of communication and data transfer and storage. We believe that the development of the whole ICT is going to the direction to enable greater and more secure data transactions, and thus intranets will benefit.

Besides these aspects which could be said to view the possible intranet flaws from the user side, Ruikar et al. (2005) have defined some of the most important barriers to implementation of project intranets from the company side. In their classification of barriers, they stress the security issues which increase with a need for "virtualization" of workspaces. With such developments intranets are no longer closed networks, but most often they present a network of networks—"simulating" real-life relationships and procedures. Thus, they require the ability for users outside physical network to access the intranet content through Intranet infrastructure. This again raises the security problematics which needs to fully protect the system from unwanted entries, at the same time enabling predefined access level to the selected individuals.

Also, they point out the problem of costs in the implementation stage—which could be substantial due to needed investments in hardware, software, and lifeware. Great problem, often omitted when intranets are analyzed, present the legal issues. The most interesting legal aspect is contracting: is it possible to use the intranets for formal contract management. In order to enable interorganizational approving by intranets, the legislature needs to define and operationalize concepts like digital signature and authorization procedures.

STEPS FOR INTRANET DEVELOPMENT AND IMPLEMENTATION

When developing intranets one needs to be aware of the important concepts concerning the implementation of intranet technology (Damsdaard & Scheepers, 1999):

- Intranet presents a rich multipurpose networked technology;
- Intranet depends on supporting technologies such as communication protocols and network infrastructure;
- In the development of IT, usage level should be taken into account and interface personalization enabled;
- In the case of intranets the clear distinction between developers and users become blurred;
- Intranet requires a critical mass of both users and content to provide mentioned advantages;
- Intranets may be implemented centrally in the organization as a corporate intranet, but units (such as divisions, departments or functional groups) can also implement the technology; also, intranets can be developed

for other purposes (other than business);
- Intranet is as good as is its worst component (infrastructure, content, interface, and so forth)

In order to develop high quality and utilizable intranet, certain steps need to be followed (Bland, 2002; Mphidi & Snman 2004; Spoolstra, 1999; Vlasic et al., 2007):

1. **Planning the intranet/establishing a vision**. In this stage, the goals that intranet needs to fulfill have to be defined. To ensure its true usability, goals need to be defined on a general level (what will it concentrate on), but also developed down to actions (methodology presented at Vlasic et al., 2007). It is important to envision long term goals and not just define intranet to fulfill current needs. It has been proven many times that intranets develop efficiency—and by doing so they foster further growth. The vision of intranet has to include these expected mid-term and long-term developments resulting from efficiency of intranets.

2. **Get the support of senior management**. Intranets present a type of new communications and knowledge/material exchange channel. Thus, senior management needs to be involved to ensure obligatory use of developed intranet by all participants. Since it is a new channel, it requires new skills and procedures—and thus requires education of all involved. Management needs to ensure that there are no parallel lines of command and information exchange existing. Otherwise, advantages of intranets will not be achieved, rather, intranet will present just another "unnecessary" cost.

3. **Classify the intranet**. In order to plan and develop it adequately, it is important to classify it correctly according to above-mentioned: time span, audience, goal, range of additional services, interconnectedness (with other intranets), and management style. According to the selected elements, it

is possible to define intranet requirements more easily.

4. **Research the processes and needs**. Based on the selected classification, requirements of each aspect need to be analyzed. Thus, planned time span will influence the structure of the intranet as well as the acceptable investment level. Audience (accurately defined) will strongly influence the content, the procedures and the interface. Range of additional services will influence the intranet structure. Interconnectedness will raise security issues and investments as well as influence the audience structure. Management style will influence the procedures applying to intranet management; however, in formalized intranets, usually the management of intranets is rather formalized. For this process to continue all the defined aspects need to be researched and defined to ensure different requirements are taken into consideration.

5. **Attention to detail**. Researched elements need to be defined down to the most detailed level and re-researched if needed. In intensive knowledge management tool like intranet, it is important to handle all the elements, because any problem (in interface or knowledge management itself) could cause serous long term problems due to the possibility of providing incorrect knowledge on which business decisions will be based.

6. **Define budget**. Budget for intranet is rather substantial. It cannot be developed as a casual activity. Intranet development needs investment of time and resources, thus such investments need to be planned with respect to amount and time.

7. **Specify content**. Only after everything has been thoroughly done, is it possible to specify the content which will satisfy all the predefined and expected requirements. Research points out that usual content includes: news, directories, budget handling, reports, agreements and contract management, archives, policies, letters, training materials, forms management, discussion forums, bulletin boards, and points of interest.

8. **Develop an intranet plan**. Intranet plan has to include all the main aspects along with a clear plan for its future development.

9. **Build it from small toward the overall intranet**. Develop intranet and test it on some smaller projects in order to spot its limitations and eliminate them. Than, based on the testing period, generate an overall intranet management tool.

10. **Define user problems and possible problems**. The goal is to enable user friendly interface (with personalization possibilities) for analysis and development of knowledge;

11. **Ensure reliability**. Reliability is indeed an important concept regarding intranets especially with the broadening of target groups. Since intranets contain crucial information and present true knowledge database, it is important to protect it from unwanted entries, but also to ensure that data will not

12. **Enable long-term sustainability of intranet**. Intranet has to incorporate efficient growth strategy and adaptation of content and form to new/future requirements of its stakeholders.

It is important that once developed, intranet should be managed carefully so that it contains always up-to-date information and that it concentrates on sharing the best practices (Mphidi & Snman, 2004).

FUTURE TRENDS

Information and communication technologies (ICTs) have influenced the "traditional" notion of community-building and development (Preece, Maloney-Krichmar, & Abras, 2003), with communities being "unbounded" from the geography and moving toward virtual networks, bringing together "individualized" social entities into "person-to-person" social relationships. Although this process is usually discussed within the context of the social consequences of the Internet (and related "mass" technologies), that is, introduction and development of the "information society" (Martin, 2005), it can also be analyzed from the viewpoint of an individual organization.

Namely, multinational and globalized organizations also need to leverage their neglected knowledge resources, in order to put social capital into use (Stewart, 2001; Krupka, 2006), which also applies to small organizations, for which the online communities represent a vast resource of relevant contacts, sources, skills, and so forth. In this context, Communities of Practice (CoPs) represent a specially useful approach/tool, as they provide shared "virtual" spaces to the members of a peer group, focused on a specific problem, issue, discipline, and so forth (see, for example, the seminal work of Brown & Duguid, 1991), in order to produce tangible business benefits. Those are designed according to the social principles of information-seeking and, by using the IT-based collaboration tools, provide opportunities for organizational learning and re-use of valuable knowledge resources (Langer, Alfirevic, & Pravicic, 2005; Lesser & Everest, 2001).

We expect that intranets will develop further and in the future, present one of the most important services running on Internet-like infrastructure. No longer will e-mail represent main means of business communication. Intranets developed around specific projects will present information source. They will be combined with other interactive services which consumers find useful (Vlasic & Kesic, 2007) such as online news, e-mail services, VoIP, and so forth. However, intranets will no longer be "isolated islands" each working independently. We expect that a consistent, highly content/goal/initiator related structure will evolve enabling wider range cooperations. Members of particular intranets will be able to participate in other intranets according to individual (or group) affordances by other intranets' coordinators—all bringing about greater knowledge sharing, and thus knowledge development.

Each intranet will present a particular business unit capable of online cooperation in virtual communities. It is possible that such developments will influence new services arising—providing specialization services for virtual communities. Different intranets (projects/organizations) will be able to develop their ideas to have effects in traditional business setting ("off-line world") using specialized agencies which will handle, that is, ordering, press-cutting, and building news components of intranets, publishing, distribution, and so forth, on behalf of the virtual (or better yet, intranet) community.

However, we propose a bit more "far fetched" vision of intranet future developments. It could mean "the doom" of the Internet services as they are currently perceived. The need for information will be satisfied through intranets and related services—so people will have less need to turn to World Wide Web for information seeking. Internet will develop into infrastructure which enables (and presents) a certain interface for intranet use and holds the information (knowledge) available for intranets to report on depending on the user set filters.

CONCLUSION

In conclusion, we can say that intranets could become virtual presentations of certain communities with common goals—that is, employees of a company working together to achieve each other's goals. People will reduce regular types of work. They will increase their efficiency by multitasking through "simultaneous" work on several different intranets—that is, on several different projects. Such participation is independent of location and time and thus can be performed more efficiently. By doing so, human capital will (at least in the more professional sphere) present a commodity which can be bought and paid based on their involvement. However, if intranets are to become an overall accepted tool, appropriate legislature needs to be passed recognizing intranet "contracting" and regulating different aspects of its usage. Future trends and conclusions we have defined present ideas based on experiences with intranet development and management envisioned in practice, but need yet to be researched, thus presenting interesting possible future research areas.

REFERENCES

Almgren, G. (2000). Community. In E. F. Borgatta & R. J. V. Montgomery (Eds.), *Encyclopedia of Sociology* (pp. 362-369). New York: Macmillan Refference Books.

Angeles, R. (2001). Creating a digital marketspace presence: Lessons in extranet implementation. *Internet Research: Electronic Networking Applications and Policy, 11*(2), 167-184.

Baker, S. (2000). Getting the most from your intranet and extranet strategies. *The Journal of Business Strategy, 21*(4), 40-43.

Bernard, R. (1998). *The corporate intranet.* New York: John Wiley & Sons.

Bland, V. (2002). The expanding world of the extranet. *New Zealand Management, 49*(6), 45-49.

Boddendke, S., & Williams, M. C. (2002). *Extranets and information warfare.* Paper presented at 3rd Australian Information Warefare and Security Conference, Brisbane.

Brint, S. (2001). Gemeinschaft revisited: A critique and reconstruction of the community concept. *Sociological Theory, 19*(1), 1-23.

Brown, J. S., & Duguid, P. (1991). Organizational learning and communities of practice: Toward a unified view of working, learning, and innovation. *Organization Science, 2*(1), 40-57.

Chou, D. C. (1998). Developing an intranet: Tool selection and management issues. *Internet Research: Electronic Networking Applications and Policy, 8*(2), 142-148.

Cumming, M., & Cuthbertson, L. (2001). Wired in whitehall: A survey of Internet and intranet use in government. *Aslib Proceedings, 53*(1), 32-38.

Damsdaard, J., & Scheepers, R. (1999). Power, influence and intranet implementation. *Information Technology & People, 12*(4), 333-358.

Delarge, C. A. (2003). The role of the intranet in brand knowledge management. *Design Management Journal, 14*(1), 55-61

Denton, K. (2006). Strategic intranets: The next big thing? *Corporate Communications: An International Journal, 11*(1), 5-12.

Denton, K., & Richardson, P. (2006). Intranets for implementing strategic initiatives. *Competitiveness Review, 16*(1), 3-11.

Dolphy, M. A., & Kala, C. S. (2001). Classic: Collaborative layered system using intranet capabilities. *Logistics Information Management, 14*(1/2), 99-106

Edenius, M., & Borgerson, J. (2003). To manage knowledge by intranet. *Journal of knowledge management, 7*(5), 124-136.

Hillary, G. A. (1955). Definition of community: Areas of agreement. *Rural Sociology, 20,* 111-123.

Krupka, Z. (2006). *Relationship between parent company and subsidiaries in business internationalization of groups of companies.* Master thesis, University of Zagreb, Zagreb.

Langer, J., Alfirevic, N., & Pavicic, J. (2005).

Organizational change in transition societies. Aldershot, UK: Ashgate

Lee-Kelley, L., Kolsaker, A. & Karadimas, G.(2004), The role of extranets in delivering customer service; The *Journal of Computer Information Systems, 44*(4), 78-84.

Lesser, E., & Everest, K. (2001). *Communities of practice: Making the most of intellectual capital.* IBM Corporation white paper. Somers, NY: IBM.

Lynch, G. (1997). Intranets – just another band-wagon? *Industrial Management & Data Systems, 97*(4), 150-152.

Martin, B. (2005). Information society revisited: From vision to reality. *Journal of Information Science, 31*(1), 4–12.

McCarthy, S. P. (1997). Internet, intranet, or extranet? *Logistics Management, 36*(11), 59.

McMillan, D.W., & Chavis, D.M. (1986). Sense of community: A definition and theory. *Journal of Community Psychology, 14*(1), 6-23.

Minoli, D. (2005). Preparing for next-gen extranets. *Network World, 22*(24), 39.

Mphidi, H., & Snman, R. (2004). The utilisation of an intranet as a knowledge management tool in academic libraries. *The Electronic Library, 22*(5), 393-400.

O'Shea, D. (2002). Building a better extranet. *Telephony, 243*(4), 20.

Preece, J., Maloney-Krichmar, D., & Abras, C. (2003). History of online communities. In K. Christensen & D. Levinson (Ed.), *Encyclopedia of community: From village to virtual world* (pp. 1023-1027). Thousand Oaks, CA: Sage Publications.

Ruikar, K., Anumba, C. M., & Carillo, P. M. (2005). End-user perspectives on use of project extranets in construction organisations. *Engineering, Construction and Architectural Management, 12*(3), 222-235.

Siegel, J. G., Hartmen, S. W., & Quershi, A. (1998). The intranet and extranet. *The CPA Journal, 68*(2), 71-73.

Standing, C., & Benson, S. (2000). Irradiating intranet knowledge: The role of the interface. *Journal of Knowledge Management, 4*(3), 244-251.

Stenmark, D. (2006). Corporate intranet failures: Interpreting a case study through the lens of formative context. *International Journal of Business Environment, 1*(1), 112-125.

Stewart, T. A. (2001). *The wealth of knowledge.* London: Nicholas Brealey Publishing.

Tredinnick, L., & Tilly, B. (2001). Building an Intranet content management strategy. *VINE, 30*(3), 20-26.

Vlasic, G. (2006a, June). Factors influencing development of interactive personalized relationships. In L. Galetic (Ed.), *An enterprise odyssey: Integration and disintegration conference proceedings.* Zagreb: University of Zagreb, Faculty of Economics and Business.

Vlasic, G. (2006b). The power of information and communication control in ICT environment – what information collection/use practices should companies implement to gain consumers' confidence? *Management - Journal of Contemporary Management Issues, 11*(2), 9-27.

Vlasic, G., Mandelli, A., & Mumel, D. (2007). *Interactive marketing – interactive marketing communication.* Zagreb, Croatia: PeraGO.

Wen, H. J. (1998). From client/server to intranet. *Information Management & Computer Security, 6*(1), 15-20.

Wen, H. J., Ye, D. C., & Lin, B. (1998). Intranet

document management systems. *Internet Research: Electronic Networking Applications and Policy, 8*(4), 338-346.

Whiting, R. (2002). Extranets go the extra mile. *Information Week, 889,* 72-76.

Zimmerman, Carle C. (1938). *The changing community.* New York: Harper and Brothers.

KEY TERMS

Intranet: Internal network using Internet-like infrastructure and protocols which efficiently facilitates communication, collaborative work, information exchange, and strong knowledge development platform providing incontestable competitive advantage.

Extranet: An extension of intranet which allows different levels of access to specific/wider audiences (key stakeholders) based on their identification.

Community: A social category which exists when membership, influence, integration, and fulfillment of needs, and shared emotional connections are simultaneously present either in relational or in territorial terms.

Reporting: Possibility to instantaneously and clearly report any needed information in any format desired enabling use of custom-made filters and combinatorial explanations.

Relationship Personalization: Conception which assumes relationship development between consumers and companies, based on mutual understanding, developed and continuous knowledge exchange through interactive communication with a goal of achieving added value for all parties involved

Gemeinschaft: A definition of community through intimacy, familiarity, symphaty, interdependence, and reflectiveness of shared social consciousness.

Networked Community: A group of people with a sense of membership, integration, and fulfillment of needs together with a feeling of shared emotional connections, but with a primary function to achieve the defined goals using interactive technology-supported intranet backbone.

Chapter XXXII
Instant Messaging (IM) Literacy in the Workplace

Beth L. Hewett
Independent Scholar, USA

Russell J. Hewett
University of Illinois Urbana Champaign, USA

ABSTRACT

This chapter discusses instant messaging (IM) as a valuable digital tool that has influenced business communication practices at least as much as e-mail. It argues that IM's characteristics of presence awareness, synchronicity, hybridity, and interactivity create a unique set of writing and reading experiences. These functional qualities both require and hone high-level writing and reading skills, which are used powerfully in communicative multitasking. The authors believe that IM should be sanctioned in the workplace and that IM use should be a subject of focused training; to that end, they provide a practical, literacy-based training sequence that can be adapted to various settings.

INTRODUCTION

Instant messaging (IM) is a primarily one-to-one text-based communication platform that also enables group interactions; it is highly popular among many Internet users and is ubiquitous among young adults. Currently businesses are hiring members of the "IM generation" as their newest, most computer-savvy employees, who are transferring their social IM skills to business settings. Flynn and Kahn (2003) projected that as many as 530 million people would use IM by the year 2006 (p. 187); many of these would be teenagers (Pew Internet and American Life Project,

2005). Although not included in these statistics, IM also can be accessed via some cell phones and personal digital assistants—increasing its use, popularity, and impact.

Not surprisingly, then, many businesses use IM through both enterprise-level and Internet-based IM clients. The International Data Corporation estimated there would be 229 million corporate IM users by 2005 (Miller, 2001, p. 208), and much IM use is practical and work-based. In their research, Isaacs, Walendowski, Whitaker, Schiano, and Kamm (2002, pp. 17-18) found that the primary use (62%) of IM in the workplace was for conversations about work, which included work talk, doing work, and work-related talk, while simpler tasks of scheduling and coordination (31%) were a secondary use (see also Handel & Herbsleb, 2002). Alarmingly, however, some businesses actively ban IM use in the office, ignoring or not understanding its benefits in terms of connecting employees. In particular, employees benefit from IM in settings where workers are dispersed geographically, within a building, or across a corporate structure. In both traditional and virtual workplaces, IM is versatile and interpersonally interactive, supplementing the telephone and e-mail and providing inexpensive, accessible communication.

These predictive statistics for IM usage are staggering, and they suggest how powerfully a digital tool like IM can change communication practices in the workplace. In fact, IM has enabled remarkably complex communication skills that belie its seemingly simple technology and uses. Baguley (2002) claimed that: "IM will not fundamentally change the way we work like e-mail did." We disagree. IM has already produced fundamental changes to the workplace, comparable to e-mail, by virtue of the literacy skills and communicative multitasking capabilities of each person who uses it. Such capabilities, which we will define and describe in this chapter, represent skills that employers can leverage for contemporary workplace practices. We argue that employers not only should sanction and provide IM connections, but also should train employees to use IM more effectively for their workplace settings. Thus, we also present practical training material for engaging IM's communicative functionalities and conveying the business's communication priorities to its employees.

BACKGROUND

Historically, IM has existed in one form or another for over 30 years, which has implications for the number of users who have developed the unique IM literacy skill sets described in this chapter. IM has its natural home in the workplace as it initially was developed in a work setting to meet early computer programmers' needs for one-to-one communication. Indeed, one primitive form of IM called *write* existed on large mainframe UNIX computers as far back as 1975. The protocol enabled computer operators to inform each other of operations that might affect the entire mainframe, but most likely they also used it for social chat.[1]

Most contemporary IM clients also provide a variety of new media affordances like voice and visual communication, personal calendars, Weblog interfaces, and such Web services as newsfeeds, weather, and current events—any of which may be valuable for workplace settings. However, in this chapter we focus primarily on text-based, default one-to-one, and selective one-to-group "chat." Text-based chat is IM's most basic, oldest, and most commonly used feature for interactive communication from which all its other features derive or diverge. IM users are connected through a common server via client software, and they "find" each other through their registration or user-supplied nicknames. Any IM software produces text boxes through which participants "talk" to one another. Upon logging into the IM client through an intranet or Internet connection, an IM user can see others who are logged-on and part of their acquaintance or "buddy" network.

An IM platform is like a telephone in that it enables one-to-one synchronous conversation;[2] yet it also is like e-mail in that it can be answered at one's convenience. Like a telephone call, IM requires two people who are simultaneously connected to engage an initiated interaction. If the recipient of the IM message is online and logged onto the IM client, but temporarily away from the computer or busy with other tasks, the "call" is on hold. The initiating text message—now asynchronous as it awaits the recipient—becomes like telephone voice mail, where the caller's message signals an attempt at contact (see also Huang and Yen, 2003, p. 66). Like e-mail, however, the message can be returned immediately upon contact or later when it is more convenient. IM technology provides a connection similar to the telephone in its capacity for interactive conversation between and among speakers. More like e-mail in its textual form, however, IM employs text for message creation, which offers it "persistency" and archival quality (Leuf, 2002, p. 143). Because an IM is delivered to the recipient's computer immediately, there is a negligible time lag between message sending and reception, making it a synchronous tool, whereas e-mail is asynchronous. The rest of this section briefly defines IM's key functionality through a discussion of presence awareness, synchronicity, hybridity, and interactivity.

Presence Awareness and Synchronicity

IM chat can be "socially less demanding than a real-time conversation" (Leuf, 2002, p. 143; see also Huang & Yen, 2003; Wood, 2000), a characteristic partially due to presence awareness. Presence awareness, one key to IM's popularity as a business tool, is a feature that exists in both physical and virtual spaces. IM chat can occur physically in collocated spaces, where participants are visible to each other in the same room, such as an office suite. In such cases, IM users both can *visually* see each other for physical and verbal contact and can *virtually* "see" each other through their IM service, enabling private online conversation outside of their surroundings and public interactions. Virtual presence awareness also transcends distributed space (e.g., through a local area network of a business server) and distance space (e.g., across state and national borders).

Beyond accessibility, however, presence awareness offers other, more crucial advantages by way of social interaction and human connectedness (Huang & Yen, 2003, p. 65; see also Agnew, 2000). According to Hard af Segerstad and Ljungstrand (2002), "[a]wareness of presence increases the more synchronous the communication" becomes (p. 155). In other words, presence awareness is not only a technical feature of IM, but it also reflects a genuine sense of one's physi-

cal or virtual presence—the immediacy of one person's awareness of another using computer-mediated communication (CMC). For example, some people may find e-mail, which can be like the modern phenomenon of "telephone tag," unsatisfying because of the time-lag associated with asynchronous communication. One person sends a message and the recipient eventually responds—or does not respond. Asynchronous writing activities, thus, are "monomodal" (Hard af Segerstad & Ljungstrand, 2002, p. 154).

With a more synchronous exchange like oral speech in a face-to-face or telephone communication, people can speak and control the message simultaneously. With such synchronicity, they can exchange and overlap ideas or words in a rapid-fire manner. Oral speech, therefore, is a "multi-modal" activity (Hard af Segerstad & Ljungstrand, 2002, p. 155), produced in a relatively effortless manner as compared to writing. Speakers remain aware of each other both as recipients and creators of the message. Unlike asynchronous communication where the written words are likely to become the focus through a rhetorical drafting process, synchronous communication like oral speech and IM chat push the focus toward the real-time interaction of the interlocutors and the messages they are conveying. Using IM, people communicate in quick, natural exchanges—much like oral speech. When they engage in IM, people become speakers and listeners, as in an oral conversation, but they also are readers and writers who depend on context and who negotiate meaning.

Hybridity

Whether asynchronous or synchronous, CMC is commonly understood to use a "hybrid" form of oral speech and written language (Faigley, 1992; Hult & Richins, 2006). Computer-mediated talk, of which IM chat is but one form, is neither the opposite of spoken talk nor simply a typed version of spoken talk. Any computer-mediated talk has elements of both spoken and written language. It is like oral language in that instead of being monologic, as writing traditionally has been, it attempts to connect dialogically with other participants and to engage them in the open-endedness of oral talk. However, computer-mediated talk has tendencies toward being closed and finite, characteristic of written language. It also is like oral language in that it is context-dependent. Interlocutors cannot understand one another *as* interlocutors without knowing the background and conditions of the conversation.

IM's hybrid nature, when combined with presence awareness and synchronicity means that people who communicate via IM can write much like they would speak in person or on the telephone—in short, spontaneous utterances, with quickly shifting points of focus, and without regard to surface correctness or perfection. Misunderstandings that occur because of this hybridity are similarly correctable, allowing participants to check out their understanding or impressions almost immediately. Indeed, small textboxes and character limits in some IM clients encourage a communicative habit of chatting in short phrases and brief or fragmented messages; such characteristics are further encouraged by small cell phone text message spaces. Indeed, these messages may actually deepen chat's hybridity by compressing talk into IM-ular slang.

Interactivity

Register theory (Halliday & Hasan, 1976) can illuminate the interrelationship, or interactivity, of speakers engaged in IM conversations because register provides useful language for discussing the social aspects and situational variables inherent in any discourse. Register variables consist of *field* (what the language is being used to talk about), *mode* (the role the language plays in the interaction), and *tenor* (the role relationships between the interactants). Here we use the concept of *mode* and a continuum based on the work of Eggins (1994) to examine the distances between spoken and written situations of language use, and for placing IM within a continuum of interactivity.

In a workplace setting, for example, distance is both spatial and interpersonal, which enables judging the possibilities for "immediate feedback between the interactants" (Eggins, 1994, p. 53). Eggins explains this distance through an interpersonal continuum ranging between casual conversations (whereby speakers communicate orally) and writing a novel (whereby the writer/speaker's listener/reader cannot respond interactively to the novelist) (1994, p. 53). The continuum represented in Figure 1 shows the most interpersonal interaction on the left and the least interpersonal on the right; not coincidentally, the interactions on the left side also are the most synchronous in nature. We have placed IM between the telephone and e-mail given the level of interactivity it affords. Notice that *e-mail* and *IM* represent asynchronous and synchronous digital communication respectively; both are located mid-continuum because they are similar in their hybrid, interpersonal natures.

As becomes evident in this model, human interactivity emerges from the potential for feedback or response, and it is intimately connected to interpersonal distance among speakers. The degree to which the speaker can offer feedback suggests the degree of interactivity. IM is slightly more interactive than e-mail, and it clearly is far more interpersonally interactive than the solitary experience of, for example, reading any text such as a novel or a Web page.

Figure 1. IM-inclusive communication interactivity continuum

Casual Conversation ↔ Telephone ↔ IM ↔ E-mail ↔ Fax ↔ Radio ↔ Text

MAIN FOCUS OF THE CHAPTER: IM LITERACY AND THE WORKPLACE

Literacy Skill Sets

Traditional literacy in terms of reading and writing has taken new forms in the digital world—leading to new literacy skill sets. There are adjustments that readers and writers make when they move from a traditional print (linear) reading style to a digital hypertextual or threaded (associative) chat (Bolter, 2001; Bolter & Gruisin, 1999). As a hybrid, IM has led to new syntactic habits regarding word and phrase abbreviations, and participants may need some contextual knowledge, however slight, of IM dialects for both reading and writing IM. It is this feature of IM about which some corporate managers and educators worry; some express fear that the abbreviated and speedy language of IM will "change young people so much" that they will lose their ability "to think in proper grammatical sentences" (Carpenter, 2006; Guernsey, 2003, p.E1; Worley, 2003). Others, however, suggest that given a background in appropriate genres, such as those of business communication practices, IM communicators are fully capable of strong writing.[3]

Indeed, just as Graham (2006) argues for global collaboration and citizenship among distance-based businesses, we argue that IM-ular language contributes to a need for shared language and "universal literacy" (Worley, 2003). Our observations of IM and its users suggest that widespread IM communication—a sort of universal connectivity—fosters a universal literacy of IM communication through user-developed skills in associative, recursive writing and reading. As opposed to a pessimistic view that literacy skills decline with IM chat, we think that IM both requires and develops more sophisticated—if less standardized—writing *and* reading skills. Businesses can take advantage of these literacy skills to improve communication among its employees and clients.

Writing IM Messages

Traditional literacy requires skillful writing, yet people might not see a similar skill set as necessary for IM chat. Because IM chat tends to retain the structure of spoken language—quick, short, spurts of talk with abbreviated language and slang—it encourages interactivity and open-endedness, and it brings to written communication a more dynamic and interactive quality. Thus, IM chat reveals certain language choices that stem directly from its synchronous, hybrid, interactive nature: informal, spontaneous expression; non-standard grammar, punctuation, and spelling; fragmentary statements (e.g., neither "complete" sentences nor lengthy paragraphs); and shorthand language choices that include abbreviations and phatic utterances. The text also reveals mistypes and self-repairs, which indicate the speakers' rapid speech and a focus on the message over the text itself. These qualities comprise an atmosphere of give-and-take and circumlocution similar to that of oral speech (Ong, 1982). Yet, these same qualities concern those who critique IM, fearing that such a writing style necessarily interferes with writing in standard situations, such as a formal business memo or e-mail. Figure 2 demonstrates these qualities as an example IM exchange between coworkers Jamal and Christina.

This short, but contextually rich, message occurs over nearly 10 minutes, and it demonstrates a wide range of writing skills. Jamal and Christina were multitasking during their conversation, which accounts for some of the time lag between messages. In particular, Jamal was involved in an apparently more formal IM conversation with Daryl, the team leader, while he was chatting less formally with Christina. When conversing online, spontaneity often reveals itself in everyday language like speech, making the conversation "sound" like street talk. Phrases like "got a sec?" and "what's up?" are greetings one might hear in passing through an office. Nonstandard grammar, spelling, and punctuation are also hallmarks of IM chat that often are attributable to rapid typ-

Figure 2. IM chat

[1] **Jamal (1:57:50 PM):** hey, got a sec?

[2] **Christina (1:58:01 PM):** sure; what's up?

[3] **Jamal (1:58:32 PM):** I've got Daryl on IM. She's concerned about whether the team can get the McMurtry order done on time. How r the numbers going?

[4] **Christina (1:58:48 PM):** ...I'm catchin up; Jack didn't get the data to me until yesterday after 5

[5] **Jamal (1:58:59 PM):** did he let you know he would be late?

[6] **Christina (1:59:14 PM):** he didn't call until 20 min late and I had other calls to take, so I didn't get the message and all the info til this morning

[7] **Jamal (1:59:47 PM):** did you set up something else while you were waiting? Daryl wants to know how the drawings are going on the rest of the project...

[8] **Christina (2:00:05 PM):** didn't waste time while I was waiting, got the call lists finished. But I did feel like I was just filling in time...

[9] **Christina (2:00:18 PM):** I don't have a good read on the drawings. Only saw one from Ed; looked like a really rough draft.

[10] **Christina (2:00:37 PM):** Would you ask Daryl if we'll be able to adjust the due date if needed?

[11] **Jamal (2:00:50 PM):** k; sounds to me like the team needs a push –

[12] **Jamal (2:00:57 PM):** sec brb

[13] **Jamal (2:04:35 PM):** so, just told Daryl that we're doing ok on the Smithson project but this one has us a little batty. She seems concerned

[14] **Christina (2:04:40 PM):** hmmm

[15] **Jamal (2:04:56 PM):** Here's what she wants. We'll have a conference call as a team today at 4:00 – she'll have the agenda in the e-mail soon.

[16] **Christina (2:05:32 PM):** think we could get our ducks in line with a quick group chat w/o Daryl just to figure out where we all are before getting on phone?

[17] **Jamal (2:05:45 PM):** sounds good; I'll invite you, Jack, and Ed to the chat. btw thanks

[18] **Christina (2:05:58 PM):** huh? For what?

[19] **Jamal (2:06:03 PM):** for the assist here

[20] **Christina (2:06:19 PM):** Oh, I got it, okay... welcome. ☺

[21] **Christina (2:06:34 PM):** bye then; I need to finish this reporte. I'll look for your invite.

[22] **Jamal (2:06:39 PM):** k; bye

ing. However, the combination of standard ("I don't have a good read on the drawings") with nonstandard ("Only saw one from Ed") written English in many IM chats suggests that the speakers are purposefully choosing the language in their conversations and that they have control of standard usage when they want to use it, which is a sign of linguistic competence.

Similarly, meaning would be clear to most literate writers despite inaccuracies of capitalization, punctuation, and spelling. When nonstandard and standard words are combined in a chat, as in this example, they demonstrate each speaker's proficiency, as well as indicate some type of regularity or pattern to the nonstandard forms (Shaughnessy, 1977). Certain regularities of punctuation, such as the dash (–) or use of ellipses (...), also provide relatively clear indicators of continuing thought even where the sentence is fragmentary. Besides regularizing and signaling the beginning or end of a thought, such punctuation helps to manage the almost inevitable interruptions and overlaps that can occur with IM talk. These nonstandard language uses lend the written chat an air of spontaneity and speed.

IM chat does not simply mimic talk through typographical symbols; rather, it *facilitates* such talk through specialized shorthand language. IM shorthand can be as common as "sec" for "second," "min" for "minute," or "bye" for "goodbye," which are typical to contemporary written and spoken English. On the other hand, some shorthand, such as "brb" for "be right back" and "btw" for "by the way," reflect a specialized discourse particular to IM chat. Sometimes cited as corrupted English (Brown-Owens 2003; Eason, & Lader, 2003; Worley, 2003), these abbreviations stem partially from small text boxes provided for writing a message; however, they also are related to IM's inherent loss of visual and aural cues, helping to keep the chat on track and making it a recognizable conversation.

When people communicate orally, nonverbal gestures and signals (e.g., moving eye contact from one speaker to the next, clearing the throat and other nonverbal noises, head nods, and smiles or frowns) combine with orality to signify intention, action, qualification, and phatic connection. In IM chat, "brb" acts as a qualifier, signaling action and the writer's intention to return to the conversation; similarly, "btw" and "afaik" ("as far as I know") also are qualifiers. Other shorthand language signals ownership of action and emotion, such as "ooops" and "<blush>" to acknowledge a mistake or embarrassment, and emoticons like smileys "☺." Finally, phatic-like language such as "hmmm," "uh huh," "thinking," and "k" (for "okay") provide backchannel cues that help speakers to convey that, despite a break in typing, they are still present and participating.

Clearly, IM-ular writing is not simplistic or corrupted, as some suggest. Instead, IM seems to have developed its own dialect comprised both of systematic and irregular "rules" or customs. To communicate fluidly with other IM users, people both adapt their writing to these customs and develop new ones as needed, which are abilities that mark able writers rather than illiterate ones. In the workplace, these abilities can help to get the job done by opening communication with writers of varying skill levels, to include nonnative speakers of English in both national and international settings.

Reading IM Messages

Reading IM chat is a similarly complex affair that develops sophisticated, if specialized, literacy skills useful to readers and writers of any online text. Slatin (1991) suggested that successful hypertextual reading requires an intuited sense of its nonlinear and associative process, which is much like the thinking process. Because IM speakers can talk interactively and synchronously, the likelihood of overlapping talk is high, creating a challenging environment for reading comprehension while simultaneously forming a response and/or beginning a new thread of ideas. The ability to contextualize information is important to making sense of threaded chat. Just as talking through IM requires conscious steps in the

writing (talking) process, it also tasks literacy in the reading (listening) process. Participants must read individual comments and choose whether and how to respond to them.

Because IM chat may be used to negotiate sophisticated, complex collaborations, multiple topic threads can occur in any one conversation, where either participant might lag behind the other's chosen or "hot" topic (Faigley, 1992, pp. 180-181). The threaded nature of such synchronous chat itself requires speakers to associatively read, respond, search out pertinent messages, read, and respond again recursively—often rapidly (Hewett, 2000, p. 270). The process of unthreading messages requires conscious steps different from oral communication, and in synchronous communication like IM, such unthreading must occur somewhat rapidly. Indeed, unthreading IM chat seems substantively different from reading any asynchronously written message, even a complex e-mail, for example.

In Figure 2, one can see this recursive reading process occur as speakers Jamal and Christina greet each other, discuss the McMurtry project, reconcile their team leader Daryl's questions with their own and coworker Jack's progress, make an action plan for a group chat prior to a required conference call, and close the chat. While the chat begins in the turn-taking manner common to asynchronous communication, it quickly spins into multiple threads of talk. Thus, for example, in line 7 Jamal asks what Christina was doing while waiting for Jack's part of the project and immediately thereafter conveys Daryl's question about the project drawings. Christina uses two separate lines to answer these questions. Then, at the same time as he acknowledges Christina's question for Daryl about deadlines, Jamal offers his own opinion that "the team needs a push." There is a 4 minute time lag while Jamal concludes his talk with Daryl and then he returns to his chat with Christina; presumably, she addressed other tasks while waiting for his response.

Undoubtedly, like writing IM chat, reading it taxes literacy skills through the need for constant contextual thinking; in effect, reading IM chat creates a fluency of associative skills similar to those of speech that many other writing situations do not require. Good IM chat requires attentiveness, memory, follow-through, and recognition of turn-taking that is quite different from e-mail correspondence. As we discuss below, the literacy skill set connected to avid IM usage already has affected contemporary workplace communication beyond the concerns of syntax and grammar that we have already discussed. Given that the IM generation is fluent in multiple digital literacies, readers should wonder to what degree reading IM influences literacy skills necessary for other digital communication forums used in the workplace.

Communicative Multitasking

Many IM speakers conduct multiple conversations at one time, a phenomenon that we call "communicative multitasking," which requires participants to keep various channels of communication and topic threads straight and to keep the different chats going in a sensible manner (see also Abel, 2003; Cohn, 2002; Yuan, 2003). Communicative multitasking is the process of having more than one communicative exchange with one or more interlocutors at the same time. It is analogous to multitasking in a generic sense. For example, one who simultaneously eats lunch, prints a document, and IMs a coworker is multitasking, which certainly can use time profitably (Hult & Richens, 2006; Isaacs et al., 2002).

However, communicative multitasking, which is at once a complex communicative activity and an adaptive social act, involves participation in more than one communicative action at a time and is an important dimension made possible by synchronous CMC like IM. In the common terminology of communications and rhetoric studies, an exchange would be a single topic or thread, and the link between the two communicators would be a channel. For example, as Figure 3 reveals, in a single channel, single thread interaction, the exchange (A) is a single topic or *thread*, and the

link (1-2) between the two communicators is a *channel*. This interaction does not represent communicative multitasking because only one thread of talk is occurring over one channel: Jake talks only to Drew about one issue at a time.

Rather, communicative multitasking can be understood in three forms: (1) single channel, multithread, (2) simple multichannel, and (3) complex multichannel.[4] When users communicatively multitask, their literacy skills are flexed and strengthened contextually and responsively.

The first form of communicative multitasking is shown here in Figure 5, where A and B are the interwoven topics threads over the channel (1-2). When two people write to each other about two or more interwoven topics during the course of one IM chat, their talk is a single channel communication because it is only between them. Their subject matter is multithreaded because they are talking about more than one issue simultaneously. A single channel, multithread IM communication occurs when, for example, Tom and Paul write to each other about two or more interwoven topics during the course of one IM chat. Tom might write about a new project at the same time that Paul writes about a conference during which they will copresent an older project. While Tom responds to Paul's message, Paul is responding to Tom's message. They continue in this manner for several posts, discussing both topics simultaneously.

The second form of communicative multitasking is shown here in Figure 4 (and exempli-

Figure 3. Single channel single, thread interaction

Figure 4. Single channel, multithread interaction

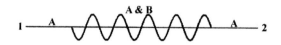

Figure 5. Simple multichannel interaction

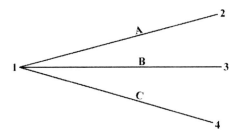

Figure 6. Complex multichannel interaction

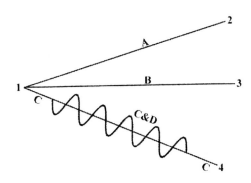

fied in Figure 2) where A, B, and C represent different conversation threads with different people over different channels, 1-2, 1-3, and 1-4 respectively.

Jamal's conversation with Christina and Daryl represents a simple multichannel chat because he is IMing to both Christina, whose chat we can see, and to Daryl, whose chat we cannot see. It is simple because in each channel only one topic is being discussed at one time. The interlocutors are working over multiple—two—channels, as Jamal talks both with Christina and with Daryl. If Jamal was using the telephone instead of IM to talk with Daryl, it still would be a simple multichannel communication with the telephone as the second channel; if Jamal had yet another IM chat going, the additional channel would increase the communication's complexity. For example, an IM user in a work setting might use IM chat to discuss with her colleague the due date for a joint project, help a junior employee troubleshoot a problem, and keep her supervisor informed about the problem, both explaining the situation and receiving guidance; at the same time, she might keep an IM window open to joke with another coworker with whom she shares a more social relationship. Undoubtedly, while it takes skillful communication skills to keep even two chats going sensibly, some IM communicators have more than five chats open at once.

Such intricacy is increased in complex multichannel communicative multitasking, the third type relevant to IM, as Figure 6 shows.

A complex multichannel interaction is much like the second form (Figure 5) except that at least one of the channels follows the pattern of the simultaneous multithread found in the first form (Figure 4). Thus, in a complex two-channel interaction, one channel might be used for a normal, single threaded chat while the other would be used for a simultaneous, multithreaded chat. Arguably, this kind of interaction might be less common than the other two forms, yet the reality of even one channel following the pattern of the first form in a multichannel series of communications adds to the challenge of communicating in general and of reading and writing the IM messages in specific.

A good deal of communication certainly takes place in these scenarios. Multiple types of interaction occur, a broad spectrum of work gets done, and one becomes somewhat skilled in juggling a number of communicative tasks simultaneously. However, particularly in multichannel IM communications where different chats occur quickly and concurrently, we acknowledge that one's focus also shifts among the various communications—sometimes, we suspect, for the worse in terms of precision, politeness, appropriateness, or attentiveness to the interlocutor and/or message. The very synchronicity of IM may make it harder to ignore than e-mail, for example (Herbsleb, Atkins, Boyer, Handel, & Finholt, 2002, p. 171).[5] Highly interactive IM users might become cognitively stressed, possibly showing some mental fatigue during the day. Imagine the embarrassment of responding to one person's message in another recipient's textbox—especially when one speaker is a peer and the other a supervisor. Yet, also likely, an individual chat that occurs concurrently among several chats might quickly and easily resolve a question or concern while not interfering significantly with one's attention to the other chats (see, for example, Isaacs et. al., 2002, p. 12).

The relative importance of IM chat-based communicative multitasking should not be underestimated. Because of sheer volume, communicative multitasking is likely to be or to become dynamic in work settings where IM is sanctioned. Depending on the setting, users may be linked only at the enterprise level or nationally and internationally by widely available IM protocols. These links to other users can vastly increase the company's reach in terms of distance-based employees and contact with clients. As the usage statistics at the beginning of this chapter suggest, there are millions of people connected via IM protocols—any of whom can become essential to one's business.

The importance of IM-based communicative multitasking, therefore, is that in the increasing numbers of IM communicators, the incidence of multitasking is increasing exponentially and its consequences—positive or negative—also are on the rise. The literacy skill sets that make communicative multitasking possible are introduced to computer users at a relatively young age, honed through adolescence and young adulthood, and brought to workplace settings where the users can adapt social and school practices to meet the needs of their daily work. Undoubtedly, then, IM users have brought to the workplace fundamental literacy and communication changes—comparable to the business practice changes resulting from e-mail—leading to potentially increased productivity.

An IM Training Sequence

In empirical research conducted at AT&T Labs, Isaacs (2003) analyzed over 21,000 IM conversations among 437 workplace users. Her research indicated that business-based IM use focuses on "working collaboratively to address complex, work-specific problems" (see also Isaacs et al., 2002). Contrary to common anecdotal studies, she found that most workplace IM use is primarily for "complex, work-specific interactions" and that such users tend to complete their conversations via IM rather than moving to another medium from IM. In the workplace, the implication is that workers can be efficient, creative, and productive when they have IM on their computers, which suggests that employers would be well served to harness IM technology and to develop IM policies that engage both workers' and the technology's strengths. In light of the complexity of literacy and communicative multitasking skills inherent to IM use, as well as IM's popularity among young adult workers, we argue that business settings can benefit from sanctioning its uses for inter- and intra-office communications. However, there are potential challenges that accompany such an action. Encouraging IM usage does not come without its difficulties. Thus, we offer the following suggested training materials that employers can sequence and adapt to their own work settings.

In these materials, we have been influenced particularly by Cargile Cook's (2002) concept of "layered literacies" as a framework for technical communication instruction: "Today, technical communicators need to be multiliterate, possessing a variety of literacies that encompass the multiple ways people use language in producing information, solving problems, and critiquing practice" (pp. 5-6). Assuming that "workplace writers need a repertoire of complex and interrelated skills to be successful" (Cargile Cook, 2002, p. 7), Cargile Cook developed a framework of six inter-related literacies for a college-level technical communication curriculum: basic (writing and reading), rhetorical (focusing argument to audience, purpose, occasion), social (working and communicating with others), technological (using technologies for social, collaborative, and business interactions), ethical (understanding decision making, personal responsibility, and workplace ethics), and critical (understanding power structures, ideologies, and stakeholders' needs).

This chapter has already addressed the basic literacies of writing and reading IM; to these, we add the other framework elements. Our purpose is to enable technical communicators "both to promote and assess the increasingly complex range of knowledge and skills" necessary for using IM successfully in business communication (24). Cargile Cook's (2002) layered literacies provide a heuristic for determining other workplace goals for IM training. Table 1, developed from these layered literacies, advances some outcomes for training in IM usage, which can be sequenced according to a particular workplace's training needs.

What implications arise as IM moves into business environments? Such implications both *will affect IM users,* who are in the workforce, and *will be affected by these users.* In this next section, we describe five training scenarios that can be used in training. Discussion can be framed using the layered literacies and/or in terms that most concern a particular corporate setting. One useful way to conduct this training, particularly for distance-based employees, is through a form of group IM chat. The act of responding about IM chat using chat enables a metacognitive and reflective experience about IM that will prove helpful on various cognitive and practical levels.

Training Scenario 1: Presence Awareness

When employees can connect remotely to each other for collaborative activities, administrators can use IM to note and monitor employee presence. Presence awareness provides supervisors with a way of virtually seeing employee activity. Since some IM clients offer information such as how long the user has been online or whether a user's keyboard has been idle, the technology may assist employers in judging effective or, at least, attentive work practices—particularly in distance work arrangements. How might such monitoring affect users who know how to employ IM for social

settings, but who otherwise might be unfamiliar with workplace restrictions and accountability? If IM is used both for communication and accountability in the workplace, could the latter lead to misuse and should workers be notified as to such aims for the technology (see also Selber, 2004, p. 85)? In a workplace setting, has the employer purchased the employee's time and gained the right to monitor it electronically? What practical and legal regulation policies should be developed to address IM chat as it might be used for social, as well as business, activities (Flynn & Kahn, 2003, pp. 189-191)?

Training Scenario 2: Transferring social skills to business settings

Young or inexperienced workers who are skillful social users of IM need to transfer such social skills to professional settings. The hybrid nature of IM chat may enable or support some potentially confusing practices when social and workplace uses blend. Conventional IM practice, for example, allows people simply to ignore a message until a convenient time arises, which typically would not offend the sender. In professional settings, where expedient communication is one of IM's benefits, there may be a general understanding that one participant is busy or temporarily away from the computer whether or not a formal "away" message has been posted (Leuf, 2002). Users know that the message has been received because connectivity requires an online presence. However, when one finally does respond, how can one construct a contextually and rhetorically appropriate message to the audience and relationship? What are the rhetorical, social, and ethical consequences of, for example, ignoring a supervisor or failing to post an away message?

Additionally, although IM chat invites shortcuts and abbreviated language, it also conveys tone, which requires thoughtful and knowledgeable communication habits. How does one develop an understanding of formality levels in IM settings? Is that understanding different in IM

Table 1. Layered literacies for IM in workplace settings

Basic Literacy	Learn how to write and read IM so that users of all skill levels can understand the communication.
	Assist coworkers and supervisees with appropriate, literate IM use.
	Adopt consistent IM talk strategies relative to associative language and threaded messages.
	Use communicative multitasking purposefully to achieve company goals.
Rhetorical Literacy	Understand the nature of an IM relationship (e.g., employer, supervisor, peer/coworker, client, outside contact).
	Practice respectful IM talk with each of the above audiences.
	Use the IM chat for specific purposes and in particular communication situations (e.g., schedule meetings, ask questions, make social connections that smooth business).
	Evaluate language level (e.g., formal, informal, familiar/slang) for the setting and the participant/s in the chat.
Social Literacy	Know when to focus on work, when to socialize with coworkers, and how to move between these goals..
	Know how and when to shift roles from supervisor to coworker to help the work progress.
	For supervisors and team leaders, learn how to use IM to gain adherence to a policy or task, and when and how to use IM for mentoring, praise, and admonishment.
	Take personal responsibility for the message that an IM can send about participants and the company regarding word choice; tone; IM name; and personalization of icons, type/font size, color, and away messages.
Technological Literacy	Learn how to use the technology to all capacities sanctioned by the workplace (e.g., text messaging, group meetings, file transfer, video/voice capability, and message saving).
	Understand how to follow security protocols for whether and how to download files obtained through IM or using hyperlinks.
	Determine how IM technology can best assist with particular tasks, especially those requiring real-time collaboration.
	Balance IM use with other available technologies like e-mail to the advantage of the task, workplace, and interpersonal relations.
Ethical Literacy	Determine the ethical implications of using IM for particular interactions, to include archiving them.
	Make decisions about ethical issues, such as of monitoring presence awareness for worker activity, based on professional ethical principals.
	Recognize personal responsibilities in using IM for completing tasks and interacting with clients.
	Understand the company's policies for social uses of IM in varied situations.
Critical Literacy	Consider how others are affected by workplace IM messages.
	Determine how different stakeholders might define and/or understand an effective IM interaction.
	Recognize how corporate and personal stances might be different and similar in various IM use scenarios.
	Evaluate the effects of communicative multitasking and use these as guides to producing ethical and effective IM interactions.

than in a chat room, through a message board, or during face-to-face talk with the same people? If so, how? How does one know to adjust register and switch from language like "how goes?" to "Hi, Bob. How are you today?" When is "Hey Bob" or "hey bob...you there?" appropriate in professional settings? Are social and workplace rules more or less forgiving in an IM chat environment than, perhaps, in e-mail or other asynchronous forums?

Training Scenario 3: IM and Individual Responsibility

IM is not a neutral tool. Its intention is to enable users to communicate with each other; communication always goes beyond writing and reading skills to carry overtones relative to rhetorical purpose, social levels, technological choices, ethical issues, and critical thinking. One non-neutral dimension of IM is its personalization capabilities and how users in particular might actually use them (see, for example, Selber, 2004, pp. 86, 90). The artifacts of personalization may show that some IM users are less savvy about the visual, aural, and textual rhetoric of their interactions than employers would prefer. In the workplace setting, are personalized icons, wallpaper, sounds, and emoticons marketed as "smileys" considered appropriate? Why or why not? Under what conditions? Under what conditions, if at all, is it acceptable in particular work environments to create personalized messages and profiles? What rhetorical, social, or ethical considerations should guide such creations? When, if at all, is it acceptable to link to outside Web sites or to prompt other users to access those sites?

Training Scenario 4: Saving and Archiving IM Messages

IM clients often enable either automatic or user-based saving of completed interactions. Different from telephone calls or conferences, these saved chats can be archived to create useful text-based records of decision processes, tasking, and other communications. Where laws require e-mail but not telephone conversations to be archived, how should IM which is a hybrid, be treated? Who needs to be informed that a particular chat is being saved? Does being informed constitute giving permission, or is permission not an issue when communicating in a business environment? When is it ethically permissible to save an IM in which a client or subcontractor has participated? Do individual participants have any legal or ethical say over whether their words can be saved? What can be done legally and ethically with such archived interactions? How long should they be saved? Should all participants have access to the archived interaction?

Training Scenario 5: Encouraging Communicative Multitasking

By its nature, communicative multitasking that involves IM requires an active user who is capable of shifting awareness and cognition to a wide variety of communicative tasks. For certain kinds of jobs, one might find employees switching focus rapidly and often with a variety of interlocutors and alternating single channel, simultaneous multithreaded with simple and complex multichannel communicative multitasking. Many IM users seem to have developed these skills without any formal prompting or training. When does communicative multitasking represent a positive series of interactions? At what point does a worker need to slow down or focus on a single communicative task? Is this a personal or corporate decision? In what scenarios would the kinds of communicative multitasking described in this chapter be helpful or harmful to the corporate goals? What kinds of cognitive distress or physical fatigue might an overuse of this skill set create? What are the warning signs? Who would benefit from training in communicative multitasking and why? How can supervisors best assist employees in developing and/or moderating their own communicative multitasking skills?

FUTURE TRENDS

We expect that IM use will continue to grow in workplace settings—not because it is a trendy digital tool, but rather because the youngest workers are bringing well-honed IM literacy and communicative multitasking skills to bear on the workplace. IM is a natural fit for many employees and a potentially powerful assistant to group-based, collaborative tasks and enterprises. Nonetheless, businesses would benefit from talking with employees—either through formal training or informal opportunities—about the benefits and detriments of IM chat in their particular settings.

Additionally, there is a need for technical communication specialists to collaborate with business leaders and computer scientists in considering the ramifications for human communication that digital communication technology like IM seeks to enable. Take, for example, presence awareness needs. Because presence awareness is a feature that technology researchers consider important to effective CMC, research into presence awareness and development of presence awareness tools similarly address a key question: "What other cues of activity should collaborators share to help coordinate their work?" (Tang & Begole, 2003).

Some awareness services innovations have already been developed to this end. For instance, awareness services innovations that use and increase presence awareness include "Awarenex" (a prototype for understanding the context of user availability for initiating contact and negotiating conversation), "Rhythm Awareness" (an analytical system for predicting future availability of IM users based on past usage), and "Lilsys" (a sensor-based sign system that infers when colleagues who are present at the computer may not be "mentally receptive to being interrupted") (Tang & Begole, 2001). Because social interaction and human connectedness appear to be linked inherently to presence awareness via synchronicity, innovations such as these may be the future of IM chat. Yet, is it a valid practice to use digital indicators as to whether someone can talk, such as with "Awarenex" and what does such use mean in terms of business communication practices? Or, as with "Rhythm Awareness," if the technology predicts whether one is available for interaction based on past usage, what does that mean for users who remain connected online whether or not they are physically present to the computer?

If users maintain a "false" presence, whether purposefully or not, how would such a technology interpret their availability and how would that interpretation influence different audiences like professional supervisors? Indeed, if "Lilsys"-type technology appears to produce realistic and/or reliable signs that a user is "mentally receptive" to a message, what does that mean for reading and writing literacy or for communicative multitasking? Of what different IM characteristics should users then become critically aware and how will such awareness translate into different communi-

cation practices when using future iterations of IM technology or in varying communicative contexts? Finally, in what ways have the users themselves defined presence awareness as necessary to their IM communications? Indeed, how have these users inspired the thinking of technologists as they develop new presence awareness innovations? A collaborative effort at answering questions such as these will become more necessary as IM takes its place among other digital tools adapted to business communication.

CONCLUSION

We have argued that IM is an important communication tool that businesses can and should sanction and prepare their workers to engage. The unique qualities of IM in terms of presence awareness, synchronicity, hybridity, and interactivity have created a unique literacy skill set, as well as the phenomenon of communicative multitasking in its various forms. A first step toward using IM technology to its fullest advantages in business settings involves training of the kind outlined in this chapter. Another step involves thoughtful discussions among business leaders in terms of using IM and taking advantage of the IM-based literacy and communicative skills that their employees bring to the table. Yet another step addresses the need for researchers in technical communication to collaborate with computer scientists, technologists, and corporate managers in creating future versions of IM that respond to rapidly changing business communication practices and requirements while attending to the nature of successful and thoughtful interactions. From our perspective, technical communication educators and researchers should join with business representatives to jointly research questions that address the intersections of synchronous communication and IM technology.

REFERENCES

Abel, K. (2003). *Teens and talk: The lure of instant messaging.* Retrieved November 14, 2007, from http://familyeducation.com/article/print/0,1301,68-11432,00.html?obj_gra. ()

Agnew, M. (2000, July 10). Collaboration on the desktop: Web conferencing and instant messaging bring people together. *Information Week, 794,* 87.

Baguley, D. (2002, October 22). Instant messaging finds its way to the enterprise. *Computerworld Today.* Retrieved November 14, 2007, from http://www.itworld.com/App/299/021022im/

Bolter, J.D. (2001). *Writing space: Computers, hypertext, and the remediation of print* (2nd ed.). Mahwah, NJ: Erlbaum.

Bolter, J.D., & Grusin, R. (1999). *Remediation: Understanding new media.* Cambridge, MA: MIT Press.

Brown-Owens, A., Eason, M., & Lader, A. (2003). *What effect does computer-mediated communication, specifically instant messaging, have on 8th grade writing competencies?* University of South Carolina at Aiken. Retrieved November 14, 2007, from http://www.usca.edu/medtech/courses/et780/may03/groupprojects/cmc-im.html

Cargile Cook, K. (2002, Winter). Layered literacies: A theoretical frame for technical communication pedagogy. *Technical Communication Quarterly, 11*(1), 5-30.

Carpenter, D. (2006, December 14). Writing around the problem. *Daily Herald.* Retrieved November 14, 2007, from http://www.dailyherald.com/search/printstory.asp?id=259963

Cohn, E.R. (2002). *Instant messaging in higher education: A new faculty development challenge.* University of Pittsburgh. Retrieved November 14, 2007, from <http://www.ipf2.edu/as/tohe/2002/Papers/cohn2.htm>

Czerwinski, M., Cutrell, E., & Horvitz, E. (2000). Instant messaging and interruption: Influence of task type on performance. In *Proceedings of the OZCHI 2000.* Retrieved November 14, 2007, from <https://research.microsoft.com/~cutrell/OzCHI2000.pdf>

Eggins, S. (1994). *An introduction to systemic functional linguistics.* London: Pinter Publishers Ltd.

Faigley, L. (1992). *Fragments of rationality: Postmodernity and the subject of composition.* Pittsburgh, PA: University of Pittsburgh Press.

Flynn, N., & Kahn, R. (2003). *E-mail rules: A business guide to managing policies, security, and legal issues for e-mail and digital communications.* New York: AMACOM.

Graham, A. (2006, February). Collaborating virtually in the global workplace: Practical ideas to measure your global team effectiveness. *Link&Learn™ eNewsletter* (originally in *Link & Learn*). Retrieved November 14, 2007, from <http://www.linkageinc.com/company/news_events/link_learn_enewsletter/archive/2006/02_06_Article_Collaborating_in_Global_Workplace_Graham.aspx>

Guernsey, L. (2003, August 14). A young writers' roundtable, via the Web. *The New York Times,* pp. E1, E6.

Halliday, M.A.K., & Hasan, R. (1976). *Cohesion in English.* New York: Longman.

Handel, M., & Herbsleb, J.D. (2002, November 16-20). What is chat doing in the workplace? In *Proceedings of the 2002 ACM conference on computer supported cooperative networks* (pp. 1-10). New Orleans, LA, NY: ACM Press.

Hard af Segerstad, Y., & Ljungstrand, P. (2002). Instant messaging with Web who. *International Journal of Human-Computer Studies, 56,* 147-171. Retrieved November 14, 2007, from http://www.idealibrary.com.onIDEAL

Herbsleb, J.D., Atkins, D.L., Boyer, D.G., Handel, M., & Finholt, T.A. (2002, April). Introducing instant messaging and chat in the workplace. In *Proceedings of the SIGCHI Conference on Human Factors in Computing Systems: Changing Our World; Changing Ourselves,* Minneapolis, Minnesota (pp. 171-178).

Hewett, B.L. (2000, December). Characteristics of interactive oral and computer-mediated peer group talk and its influence on revision. *Computers & Composition, 17,* 265-288.

Holmevik, J.R. (2004). *TraceBack: MOO, open source, and the humanities.* Doctoral dissertation, University of Bergen. Retrieved November 14, 2007, from http://lingua.utdallas.edu/encore/?

Huang, A.H., & Yen, D.C. (2003). Usefulness of instant messaging among young users: Social vs. work perspective. *Human Systems Management, 22*(2), 63-72.

Hult, C.A., & Richins, R. (2006, Spring). The rhetoric and discourse of instant messaging. *Computers and Composition Online, Theory into Practice.* Retrieved November 14, 2007 from http://www.bgsu.edu/cconline/hultrichins_im/pages.htm

Isaacs, E. (2003, November). A closer look at our common wisdom. *ACM Queue, 1*(8). Retrieved November 14, 2007 from http://www.acmqueue.com/modules.php?name=Content&pa=showpage&pid=91

Isaacs, E., Walendowski, A., Whittaker, S., Schiano, D.J., & Kamm, C. (2002, November 16-20). The character, functions, and styles of instant messaging in the workplace. In *Proceedings of the 2002 ACM conference on computer supported cooperative networks.* New Orleans, Louisiana (pp. 11-20). NY: ACM Press.

Leuf, B. (2002). *Peer to peer: Collaboration and sharing over the Internet.* Boston: Addison-Wesley.

Miller, M. (2001). *Discovering P2P.* San Francisco: Sybex.

Ong, W.J., S.J. (1982). *Orality and literacy: The technologizing of the word.* New York: Methuen.

Pew Internet and American Life Project. (2005). Retrieved November 14, 2007, from http://www.pewinternet.org/PPF/r/162/report_display.asp

Selber, S. (2004). *Multiliteracies for a digital age.* Carbondale, IL: Southern Illinois University Press.

Shaughnessy, M. (1977). *Errors and expectations: A guide for the teacher of basic writing.* New York: Oxford University Press.

Slatin, J. (1991). Reading hypertext: Order and coherence in a new medium. In P. Delany & G.P. Landow (Eds.), *Hypermedia and literary studies* (pp. 153-169). MI: MIT Press.

Tang, J.C., & Begole, J. (2003, November). Beyond instant messaging. *ACM Queue, 1*(8). Retrieved November 14, 2007, from http://www.acmqueue.com/modules.php?name=Content&pa=showpage&pid=90

Wood, C. (2000, November 13). A mania for messaging. *Maclean's, 113*(46), 58.

Worley, B. (2003, November 16). The changing face of language. *TechTV.* Retrieved November 14, 2007 from http://www.techtv.com/news/print/0,23102,3420263,00.htm

write. BSD General Commands Manual. (1993, June 6). Retrieved from http://mirror.cc.vt.edu/pub/projects/Ancient_Unix/PDP11/Trees/V6/usr/source/s2/

Yuan, Y. (2003, June). The use of chat rooms in an ESL setting. *Computers and Composition, 20*(2), 194-206.

KEY TERMS

Channel: The link between the two communicators—IM, telephone line, e-mail.

Communicative Multitasking: The process of having more than one communicative exchange (for example, IM, telephone, or face-to-face) with one or more interlocutors at the same time.

Computer-Mediated Communication (CMC): Any communication that occurs through computer technology, such as IM or e-mail.

Hybridity: The nature of computer-mediated talk, which has elements of both spoken and written language; people who communicate via IM can write much like they would speak in person or on the telephone.

Interactivity: The degree to which a reader or listener can respond interpersonally with the writer or speaker.

Phatic: Oral and typed language such as "hmmm," "uh huh," "thinking," and "k" (for "okay") that provides backchannel cues to help speakers convey that they are present and participating in the conversation.

Presence Awareness: Both a technical feature of IM that indicates the availability of another person a chat and a genuine sense of one's physical or virtual presence—the immediacy of one person's awareness of another using CMC.

Synchronicity: The quality of being synchronous, or "real-time" in communication; for example, an IM requires two people who are simultaneously connected to engage an initiated interaction, whereas an e-mail, which is asynchronous, does not require the recipient's immediate presence and participation.

Thread: The exchange between two communicators; each topic of discussion is a separate thread.

ENDNOTES

1   Two popularly accessible forms of chat were established in the 1980s: Internet Relay Chat (IRC) and AOL's closed network system (Holmevik, 2004; Miller, 2001). In 1996, IM was introduced to the Internet as *ICQ* (literally "I seek you"), a protocol that most contemporary users would recognize (Miller, 2001, pp. 210-211), and it found increasing popularity in both social and workplaces—as well as increasing digital sophistication—in no-cost clients like AOL's *AIM* and *ICQ*, Microsoft's *MSN Messenger*, Yahoo's *Yahoo! Messenger*, *Pidgin*, *Trillion*, and *Jabber*.

2   Because an IM is delivered to the recipient's computer immediately, there is a negligible time lag between message sending and reception, making it a pseudo-synchronous tool. Using such a distinction, a genuinely synchronous technology is an electronic whiteboard where both interlocutors can view the text as it is being typed or see graphics as they are being drawn without clicking a "send" icon; having made this distinction, for the purposes of this chapter, we treat IM as a synchronous tool.

3   In a small study of four students' essay writing, Christine Hult and Ryan Richins (2006) found that even though the writing showed some linguistic characteristics of IM language, the students stated their awareness of "the needs of a certain writing genre" and believed that they would "employ the appropriate tools for that genre." However, there were too many variables to attribute the IM-like attributes of the writing to IM alone, and the researchers concluded that helping student writers to become "conscious of the written genres they are using and the differences among them and to help them to question and to probe" beyond surface issues in writing would assist them to circumvent potential negative effects from IM.

[4] For a more complete discussion of communicative multitasking, contact the authors to see "A Theory of Communicative Multitasking" (in progress).

[5] In research into the effects of IM interruptions on various tasks, which is aimed at assisting IM developers, Czerwinski, Cutrell, and Horvitz (2000) found that IM interruptions interfere more with particular, "stimulus-driven search tasks" than those of "effortful, cognitively taxing search tasks." Nonetheless, they suggest "that experience handling the interrupting tasks reduces their harmful effects over time."

Chapter XXXIII
Supporting Collaboration with Trust Virtual Organization

Aizhong Lin
Macquarie University, Australia

Erik Vullings
TNO, The Netherlands

James Dalziel
Macquarie University, Australia

ABSTRACT

This chapter introduces the trust virtual organization as a means of facilitating authentication and authorization for sharing distributed and protected contents and services. It indicates that sharing institutional protected services and deliverables has proven a hurdle since user accounts are created in many sites. It provides an approach to solving this problem using virtual organizations with cross-institutional Single Sign On, with which users use their existing institutional accounts to login. This chapter also presents the challenges of building trust virtual organizations: managing users from distributed identity providers; managing services from distributed service providers; managing trust relationships between users and services, and authorizing the access privileges to users based on the trust relationships. It argues that the trust virtual organization increase the effectiveness of e-learning, e-research and e-business significantly. Furthermore, the authors hope that the trust virtual organization facilitates not only Web-based authentication and authorization, but also grid-based authentication and authorization.

INTRODUCTION

Complex problems often require multi-disciplinary collaborations. The benefits of collaborations across organizations include (Kürümlüoglu, Nøstdal, & Karvonen, 2004): sharing knowledge, resources, and services among partners; reducing development time to market; spreading costs and risks with partners; accessing to new markets through partnerships; improving capacity utilization, and

gaining access to global networks. Virtual organizations (VOs) are the new paradigms to support collaborations among semi-independent partners using communication tools and information technologies. In virtual organizations, partners with separate core competencies can band together temporarily to achieve business objectives. With virtual organizations, the collaborations among partners can break out the time and geographic limitations.

The increasing complexity of e-learning, e-research, and e-business leads to collaboration across multiple disciplines and multiple institutions. Virtual organizations with cross-domain single sign-on that focus on facilitating multiple discipline and multiple institution collaborations are becoming increasingly more predominant. In order to support the collaboration across multiple disciplines and multiple institutions, virtual organizations are required to (1) deal with the new user authentication mechanism in which users are authenticated by distributed user identity management systems (identity providers or IdPs) rather than the local user authentication mechanism; (2) deal with the new resource and service (R&S) protection mechanism in which resources and services are protected by distributed resource and service management systems (service providers or SPs) rather than protected by the local resource and service management system; (3) provide the trust-based authorization mechanisms in which temporary trust relationships between identity providers and service providers are managed and authorization processes that define which user can access which resources or services are based on these trust relationships; and (4) provide a single sign-on (SSO) mechanism to enable users from different identity providers access resources and services from different service providers with only one time sign-on. The benefits result from the new functionalities in virtual organizations and will include: saving the administrators' time and reducing the administrators' costs for identity management and R&S management, reducing the users' sign-on time for accessing R&Ss, and improving the effectiveness of users accessing R&Ss.

The requirements of new functionalities in virtual organizations cause the research and development of new VO authentication and authorization mechanisms that are not found in existing virtual organization systems. Our research provides a trust virtual organization, which extends functionalities of existing virtual organizations, to facilitate the management of

distributed users, distributed R&Ss, temporary trust relationships, and access controls. A *Trust Virtual Organization (TVO)* is a virtual organization in which users are authenticated by distributed trusted identity providers, R&Ss are protected by distributed service providers, service providers and identity providers can be set to trust mutually in a certain level, authorization processes are based on the trust relationships, and a single sign-on mechanism enables users access resources and services with one time sign-on. This chapter introduces the trust virtual organization, its motivation, functional model, conceptual models, management components, and an implemented prototype.

BACKGROUND

Since computer-supported cooperative work was proposed in network computing a dozen years ago, Web-based collaborations are widely applied in various areas. Virtual organizations such as Sakai (Sakai, 2007), Moodle (Moodle, 2007), LiveNet (Hawryszkiewycz, 1999), eRoom (E-Room, 2007), and Groove (Rensink, 2003) have become the popular tools supporting Web-based collaborations for learning, research, or businesses.

While many virtual organization systems have been implemented, substantially little is known about the development of virtual organizations with single sign-on and trust-based authorization. In authentication (including single sign-on) aspect, a research project Shibboleth provided by Internet2 (Erdos & Cantor, 2002), however, addressed the design and implementation of a Web-based authentication (including single sign-on) and authorization system. With the Shibboleth, identities of users are managed in distributed identity providers; R&Ss are protected in distributed service providers. That which user can access which R&S is determined by the trust relationships between the identity providers and service providers. Shibboleth project is developed based on the Security Assertion Markup Language (SAML, 2007) assertions that specify the user identities, which are appended to the header of the Web page the user is going to access. Another research project by Liberty Alliance (Liberty Alliance, 2003) provides the authentication and authorizations mechanism based on the Web service technologies. Shibboleth supports only the Web-based applications. Liberty Alliance can be applied to larger application areas. In addition, Microsoft CardSpace (Windows CardSpace, 2007) could be the first commercial product supporting the distributed authentication and authorization in Windows systems. On the other hand, in authorization aspect, most virtual organizations are developed with role-based access control (Ferraiolo, Cugini, & Kuhn, 1995). Signet (Signet, 2006), for example, focuses on the management of distributed R&S access privileges. The Signet privilege management system provides critical information functions needed to support enhanced authorization control. The software enables consistent application of policy and business access rules across managed services and resources and puts the control of the resources in the hands of the decision makers.

Only recently, research projects that explore the combination of virtual organization and single sign-on are found. Project MyVocs (MyVocs, 2007) is developing virtual organization system as essentially a bridge between a federation of Shibboleth identity providers and a federation of Shibboleth service providers. Using MyVocs, the SPs (called VO SPs) are aggregated into virtual organizations. Using open source software components Shibboleth, MySQL, and Sympa, MyVocs provides the "glue" that permits the VO SPs to be grouped into logical VOs. However, it is unable to set temporary trust relationships between users and R&Ss in MyVocs.

TVO MODELS, COMPONENT, AND PROTOTYPE

This section presents the design and implementation of the trust virtual organization, including its functional model, conceptual model, components, and prototype.

TVO Functional Model

The trust virtual organization plays two roles in supporting collaboration. On the one hand, it is a collaborative environment that supports the sharing of distributed protected resources and services by remote distributed users, groups, and IdPs. On the other hand, it is a scalable and flexible federation that manages the trust relationships between users or groups or IdPs and R&Ss or SPs. Figure 1 illustrates the TVO conceptual model. The concepts are defined as follows:

- An *identity provider* is a service that asserts the identities of users who are local to an institution running the provider. An identity provider can release the identities to some targets based on attribute release policies.
- The *identity provider manager* is a service that maintains and provides the detail information of multiple identity providers.
- The *user & group (U&G) manager* maintains and provides the detail information of users who are authenticated by the trusted IdPs and groups organized for specific purposes.
- A *service provider* is a service that provides and protects resources and services. Those resources and services can only be accessed by the users who are authenticated by trusted identity providers.
- The *service provider manager* is a service that maintains and provides the detail information of multiple service providers.
- The *resource & service (R&S) manager* maintains and provides the detail information of resources and services that are protected by the trusted SPs.
- The *trust relationship manager* maintains and provides the trust relationships between IdPs and SPs, and U&Gs and R&Ss.
- The *trust-based access control manager* is a service that maps the trust relationships

Figure 1. The functional model of the trust virtual organization

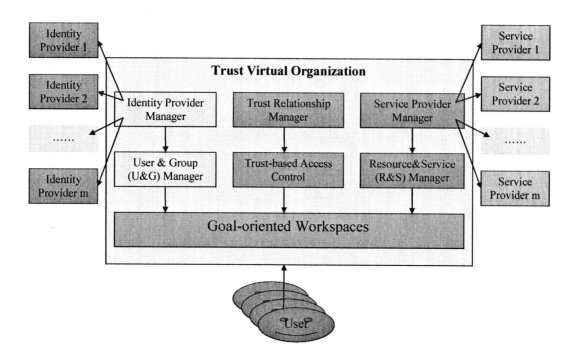

between U&Gs and R&Ss to the access behaviours.

- The *goal-oriented workspace* is a virtual place for distributed users to work together for a specific goal via sharing R&Ss and workflows.

The trust virtual organization provides goal-oriented workspaces that can be dynamically created and removed. Users enter the trust virtual organization system via single sign-on. After a user logs in the TVO, the identities of the user is released from her identity provider to the TVO and managed by the U&G manager component. In the meantime, R&Ss protected by distributed service providers can be collected into the TVO. If a user plays a role in a workspace, she enters the workspace and shares the R&Ss. When a user in a workspace accesses a resource in the workspace, the identities of the user are passed to the resource based on their trust relationships and the identity release policy. In addition, trust relationships between U&Gs or IdPs and R&Ss or SPs can be established or destroyed in some purposes.

TVO Conceptual Model

As illustrated in Figure 2, the trust virtual organization conceptual model is a two layers model: VO layer and workspace layer. The concepts in this model are defined as following:

- **User:** The authenticated actor who works in the trust virtual organization
- **Group:** a collection of users
- **R&S:** a resource or a service
- **Workspace:** a virtual workplace for groups of users to work together
- **Goal:** the objective of a workspace
- **Role:** a position to be taken with assigned permissions to do tasks in a workspace
- **Participant:** a user from a group, joining a workspace, and taking a role in the workspace

In VO layer, a user can create and manage groups, R&Ss, and workspaces. In workspace

Figure 2. The TVO conceptual model

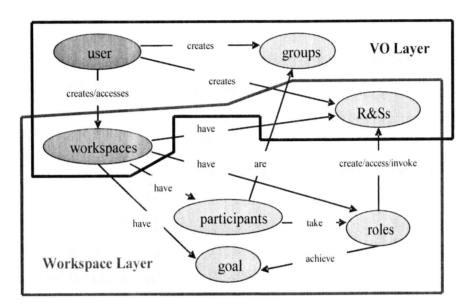

layer, a workspace has a goal, roles, participants, and R&Ss. The workspace goal is achieved by roles. A role is taken by one or more participants. In contrast, a participant can take one or more roles in a workspace. A participant comes from a group. Roles can create, manage, or access R&Ss in terms of the permissions assigned to them.

TVO Components

As presented in the conceptual model, the TVO contains seven major components that are separated in four categories. The first category maintains and provides the identity providers, users, and groups. The second category maintains and provides the service providers, resources, and services. The third category manages the trust relationships and trust-based access control policies. The last category deals with the goal-based workspaces.

IDENTITY PROVIDER, USER, AND GROUP MANAGEMENT COMPONENT

This section describes the first category components: the identity provider manager; the user and group manager.

Identity Provider Manager

The identity provider manager maintains the identity providers, provides the user authentication mechanism, and releases the identities of users. An identity provider maintains and manages user identities in a User Identity Repository (UIR). The UIR is managed by the UIR management function. A single sign-on service in an identity provider receives the login request, performs the authentication process, and responses the user identities.

The IdP manager manages the detail information of identity providers in a IdP Repository

(IdPR). The IdPR is managed by the IdP management function. A "Where Are You From" (WAYF) service provided by the IdP manager accepts the login request, retrieves the IdP information, and provides the SSO service URL of an IdP.

User and Group Manager

When a user becomes a TVO member, more attributes representing TVO member properties will be added to the user. The user manager provides the storage and management functions to manage TVO member attributes. A TVO member has not only the basic identities from an IdP but also the member identities in the TVO user repository (VOMR). When a trusted service provider in the TVO is accessed, the user manager will release both the identities from the IdP and from the VOMR to the trusted service provider.

When a TVO member joins to a TVO group, more attributes will be added to the user to represent the user's group attributes. The group manager provides the storage and management functions to manage TVO member groups. A TVO group member has the basic identities from an IdP, the member identities in the TVO user repository, and the group identities in TVO group repository (VOGR). A group creator or administrator manages group attributes of users via the group service by sending a group management request and then receiving the management results from the service. The group attributes such as the group identifier are also kept in the VOMR. When a user accesses a trusted service provider, the user's basic attributes, member attributes, and group attributes are released from the VOMR to the service provider.

SERVICE PROVIDER, RESOURCE, AND SERVICE MANAGEMENT COMPONENT

This section describes the second category components: the service provider manager; the resource and service manager.

Service Provider Manager

The service provider manager maintains the service providers and releases the identity consumer services of the service providers to the users who access the services. A service provider maintains and manages resources and services in a Resource and Service Repository (R&SR). The R&SR is managed by the R&S management function. A user identity verification service in a service provider receives the R&S access request and redirects the request to the WAYF. After the user identities are received from the proper IdP, the user identity verification service verify the user identity, perform the authorization, and deliver the resource or service to users.

The SP manager manages the detail information of service providers in a SP Repository (SPR). The SPR is managed by the SP management function. A metadata service provided by the SP manager accepts the login request retrieves the SP information and releases the metadata to the service provider.

Resource and Service Manager

Resources are one category of the most important objects to be shared by users for goals. A resource could be a URL link, a text paragraph, or a particular format file. The detail information of the resource is stored in the resource repository (VORR) and managed by the VORR management component. A service provided in the resource manager receives the resource access request. If the resource to be accessed is a URL link, the service redirects to the link with the user attributes. If the resource is a text paragraph or a file, the service delivers the contents to the user.

Services are another category of the objects to be shared by users for goals. A service is a Web application or component that is activated by a URL in the HTTP protocol. The detail information of the service is stored in the service repository (VOSR) and managed by the VOSR management component. The service manager provides a particular service that receives the user request and then responses the proper service URL to the user.

TRUST RELATIONSHIP AND ACCESS CONTROL MANAGEMENT COMPONENT

This section describes the third category components: the trust relationship manager and the trust-based access control policy manager.

Trust Relationship

Trust, as defined in dictionaries, is "firm reliance on the integrity, ability, or character of a person or thing." It describes a specific relationship between parties. Trust relationships are normally established between parties after they have a certain time of communications and collaborations. For example, that a person Alice trusts another person Bob means that "from a certain time of observation, Alice understands and acknowledges the behaviours of Bob." Once a trust relationship is established in two parties, it will determine the future behaviours of their interactions. When parties trust each other, they like to share services and resources in a certain level. Trust relationships between parties have some noticeable properties which will considerably affect the generation of trust models:

- First, trust is a subjective and individual judgment between parties. Alice trusts Bob does not mean that Bob is trust worthy to all other parties. Therefore, when forming the trust relationships in a group of people, each person has its own judgment to each of other persons in the group.
- Second, a trust relationship is unidirectional, that is, that Alice trusts Bob does not mean that Bob also trusts Alice.
- Third, trust relationships are levelled. In different situations, trust relationships may be changed. For example, that Alice trusts Bob when sharing documents does not mean that Alice trusts Bob when sharing money.
- Next, trust relationships between parties can be accumulated or decremented when more interactions happened between the parties.
- Finally, a trust relationship is easier to destroy.

TVO Trust Model

Previous VO systems exploit role-based access control mechanism to assign the privileges to users. In TVO, we intend to provide another access control mechanism—trust-based access control. First, we define five categories of parties:

- **user:** An individual has identity attributes, can access R&Ss
- **group:** A group of users, can access R&Ss
- **IdP:** An identity provider. A large pool of users who can access R&Ss
- **R&S:** A resource or service can be accessed by a user, a group of users, or users in an IdP
- **SP:** A service provider. A large pool of resources and services can be accessed by a user, a group of users, or users in an IdP

Table 1. Possible existence of trust relationships between parties

	User	group	IdP	R&S	SP
user				x	x
group				x	x
IdP				x	x
R&S	x	x	x		
SP	x	x	x		

Trust relationships can be established between these parties. Table 1 shows the possibilities of trust relationships between parties, in which "x" means a possible trust relationship. In this table, we define that the column parties trust the row parties. And in Table 2, we define the trust relationships and its access behaviours.

Certificate and Trust Relationships

In principle, trust relationships are subjective judgments that are defined by the users. However, for the security reason, when a party A sets up a trust relationship to party B, party A has to provide its certificate signed by a public acknowledgeable authority to party B. The signed certificate includes the public key of the party A. When party B receives the public key from party A, it can decode the messages from party A to obtain the identities of party A.

Goal-Based Trust and Global Trust

A *goal-based trust* is a local trust relationship established in a workspace for achieving a specific goal. Its scope is the workspace. From parties start to live in the workspace, their access privileges are controlled by the trust relationships. If the workspace is removed, all the goal-based trust relationships related to this workspace are destroyed. A *global trust* is a trust relationship established in the creation of a party in the TVO system. It is used to control the behaviours of all workspaces.

Access Behaviour, Access Mappings, and Access Policy

The basic behaviours that can be assigned to a trusted party to access a specific R&S are:

- **list:** The party can list the R&S
- **read:** The party can read the R&S
- **execute:** The party can execute the R&S

Table 2. Trust relationships and accessible behaviour explanations

Trust relationship	Explanations
user A trusts R&S B	The attributes of user A can be released to R&S B
user A trusts SP B	The attributes of user A can be released to all R&Ss in SP B
group A trusts R&S B	The attributes of all users in group A can be released to R&S B
group A trusts SP B	The attributes of all users in group A can be released to SP B
IdP A trusts R&S B	The attributes of all users in IdP A can be released to R&S B
IdP A trusts SP B	The attributes of all users in IdP A can be released to the SP B
R&S A trusts user B	The R&S A can be accessed by user B
R&S A trusts group B	The R&S A can be accessed by all users in group B
R&S A trusts IdP B	The R&S A can be accessed by all users in IdP B
SP A trusts user B	All R&Ss in SP A can be accessed by the user B
SP A trusts group B	All R&Ss in SP A can be accessed by all users in group B
SP A trusts IdP B	All R&Ss in SP A can be accessed by all users in IdP B

Figure 3. The TVO prototype architecture

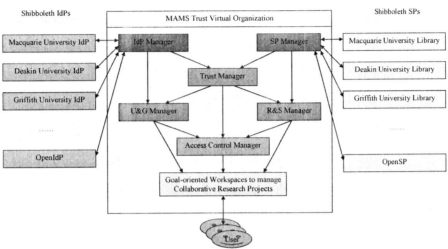

- **modify:** The party can modify the R&S
- **write:** The party can write the R&S
- **grant:** The party can grant privileges to other parties

The access mapping function generates the behaviours from the levelled trust relationships based on the following rules:

- **level_0:** can do nothing
- **level_1:** can *list* R&Ss
- **level_2:** can *list* and *read/execute* R&Ss
- **level_3:** can *list, read/execute*, and *modify* R&Ss
- **level_4:** can *list, read/execute, modify*, and *write* R&Ss
- **level_5:** can *list, read/execute, modify, write,* and *grant* R&Ss

In TVO, it is more flexible to specify the permissions from trust relationships to access behaviours in an access policy file rather than the trust levels. The access policy file is a XML-based file containing a collection of trust rules wrapped by the tags *<AccessPolicy>*, *<Rule>*, and *<Behaviors>*:

```
<?xml version="1.0" encoding="UTF-8"?>

<AccessPolicy   xmlns="mams:tvo:trust:tp:1.0"
                xmlns:xsi="http://www.w3.org/2001/XMLSchema-instance"
                xsi:schemaLocation="mams:tvo:trust:tp:1.0
trust-tp-1.0.xsd">
    <Rule id="rule-00382" type="global" name="Role Access
Policy" user_identity="role">
        <IF role="mams_member">
            <Behaviors service="Autograph">
                <Behavior name="search">
                    <Permission access="permit"/>
                </Behavior>
                <Behavior name="list">
                    <Permission access="permit"/>
                </Behavior>
                <Behavior name="read">
                    <Permission access="permit"/>
                </Behavior>
                <Behavior name="execute">
                    <Permission access="deny"/>
                </Behavior>
                <Behavior name="update">
                    <Permission access="permit"/>
                </Behavior>
                <Behavior name="create">
                    <Permission access="deny"/>
                </Behavior>
                <Behavior name="grant">
                    <Permission access="deny"/>
                </Behavior>
                <Behavior name="delete">
                    <Permission access="deny"/>
                </Behavior>
            </Behaviors>
        </IF>
    </Rule>

</AccessPolicy>
```

Figure 4. The interface of the TVO overview

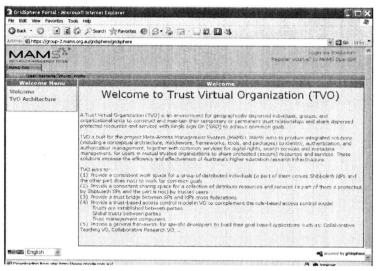

Figure 5. The interface of the TVO trust manager

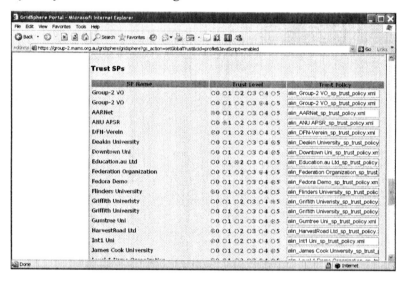

Trust Combination

The TVO trust-based access control mechanism maps the trust relationships to access behaviours. If an R&S is controlled by a global trust relationship as well as a goal-based trust relationship, the final behaviours are the logic "or" operation of the behaviours based on the global trust relationship and the behaviours based on the goal-based trust relationship.

An example will explain the trust combination. Suppose we have two parties: user A and resource B. Resource B is set to trust user A in level_2. The trust-based access control function maps the level_2 trust to the access list {*list, read/execute*}. In the meantime, in a workspace C, resource B is set to trust the role the user A plays a member in level_5. Based on the level_5 trust, user A can get another access list {*list, read/execute, modify, write, grant*} to the resource B. Then the final access behaviours that user A get from the global level_2 trust and the goal-based level_5 trust is the logic "or" of two subsets, that is, {*list, read/execute*} or {*list, read/execute, modify, write, grant*}

= {*list, read/execute, modify, write, grant*}.

TVO Prototype

The TVO prototype was developed for the MAMS project (MAMS, 2007) to improve the effectiveness of Australia education and research. It was implemented based on the open source project: Shibboleth Identity Provider and Shibboleth service provider, LDAP (Howes & Smith, 1997), Fedora (Payette & Lagoze, 1998), and GridSphere (Novotny, Russell, & Wehrens, 2004). The Shibboleth project provides the components to construct individual IdPs and individual SPs. The LADP is used to build the OpenIdP that provides the identity management for users who are not in any Shibboleth IdP. The Fedora is used to build the OpenSP, which provides the management functions for resources and services that are not been protected by any Shibboleth SP. The GrisSphere is a portlet framework employed to build the Web-based and portlet-based TVO System.

Figure 3 shows the system architecture of the TVO prototype. First, a number of Shibboleth IdPs are installed for universities (such as Macquarie University, Deakin University, and Griffith University) to manage the identities of their staff members. Secondly, a number of Shibboleth SPs are installed for university libraries (such as Macquarie University Library, Deakin University Library, and Griffith University Library) to manage the resources including technical reports, university regulations, subject examination papers, and so on and so forth. As introduced in the TVO conceptual model, the TVO prototype consists of the following components: IdP manager, SP manager, trust manager, user and group manager, resource and service manager, access control manager, and goal-oriented workspaces.

The human interfaces show the implemented TVO prototype. It can be accessed and tested via the URL: https://group-2.mams.org.au/gridsphere. Figure 4 shows the overview of the TVO. It lists the TVO main components in the menu bar: U&G management, R&S management, Workspace management, and Trust management. The menu items shown on the top-right of the interface allow users to login via Shibboleth IdP or register themselves to the TVO open IdP.

The components IdP manager and SP manager is automatically appended to the TVO menu bar after a user is successfully signed in the TVO and the role of the user is the TVO administrator. The IdP manager maintains the IdPs registered to the TVO system. Users can choose a sub set of the whole IdP set to be displayed in the TVO WAYF. The SP manager facilitates service providers becoming the TVO trusted parties. Trust relationships will be established between the registered IdPs and registered SPs.

Figure 5 shows the detail work of the trust manager. Using the trust manager, a user, a group leader, or an IdP administrator can choose resources, services, or SPs to be the trusted parties. Mutually, the owner of a resource, a service, or an SP can select users, groups, or IdPs to be the trusted parties. When a user trusts an SP, the identities of the user can be released to the resources or the services protected by the SP. When a resource trusts an IdP, the resource can be accessed by all users of the IdP. The access behaviours are defined by trust relationships and access control policies.

FUTURE TRENDS

The trust virtual organization prototype, at the moment, accepts the identities of the users who are authenticated via Shibboleth IdPs, that is, the user identities come from the HTTP header. Meanwhile, the TVO prototype can only support the Shibboleth SPs. In the future, this project will extend these functions to enable the TVO system to accept user identities and deliver resources and service from other IdPs and SPs respectively.

Another focus of the TVO project will be on developing the TVO system to a collaborative environment framework. This framework can be employed to develop collaborative systems for different domains. For example, it can be used to build collaborative learning system or collaborative research system to support online learning activities or online research activities respectively. The domain collaborative systems inherit the TVO functionalities to support single sign-on, accept distributed user authentication, maintain distributed protected resources and services, and manage trust relationships and trust-based access controls to achieve goals of specific domains.

CONCLUSION

This chapter introduces the trust virtual organization developed for MAMS projects. It extends the functionalities of classic virtual organizations. On the one hand, like those virtual organizations, it provides the functionalities to support collaborations within goal-oriented workspaces to achieve common goals. On the other hand, unlike the previous virtual organizations, it provides new functionalities to organize the remote distributed user identities, maintain distributed protected resources and services, manage their trust relationships, and authorize access privileges to users based on the access control policies.

REFERENCES

Erdos, M., & Cantor, S. (2002). *Shibboleth architecture DRAFT v05*. Retrieved November 14, 2007, from http://shibboleth.internet2.edu/docs/draft-internet2-shibboleth-arch-v05.pdf

E-Room Web site. Retrieved November 14, 2007, from http://www.eroom.net/

Ferraiolo, D., Cugini, J., & Kuhn, R. (1995, December 11-15). Role-based access control (RBAC): Features and motivations. In *Proceedings of the 11th Annual Conference on Computer Security Applications*, New Orleans, LA (pp. 241-248).

Hawryszkiewycz, I.T. (1999, September). Supporting teams in virtual organisations. In *Proceedings Tenth International Conference, DEXA'99*, Florence.

Howes, T., & Smith, M. (1997). *LDAP: Programming directory-enabled applications with lightweight directory access protocol*. Indianapolis, IN: Macmillan Technical Publishing.

Kürümlüoglu, M., Nøstdal, R., & Karvonen, I. (2004). Base concepts for virtual organization. In L.M. Camarinha-Matos, H. Afsarmanesh & M. Ollus M.. (Eds.), *Virtual organization systems and practices* (p. 21). Boston: Spinger.

Liberty Alliance. (2003). Liberty alliance complete specification. Retrieved November 14, 2007, from http://www.projectliberty.org/index.php/liberty/specifications__1

MAMS: Meta Access Management System. Retrieved November 14, 2007, from https://mams.melcoe.mq.edu.au/zope/mams

Moodle Web site. Retrieved November 14, 2007, from http://moodle.org/

MyVocs: A collaborative environment. Retrieved November 14, 2007, from http://myvocs-box.myvocs.org/

Novotny, J., Russell, M., & Wehrens, O. (2004). GridSphere: An advanced portal framework. In *Euromicro, 30th EUROMICRO Conference (EUROMICRO'04)* (pp. 412-419).

Payette, S., & Lagoze, C. (1998). Flexible and extensible digital object and repository architecture (FEDORA). In *Proceedings of ECDL 98* (pp. 41-59).

Rensink, A. (2003). GROOVE: A graph transformation tool set for the simulation and analysis of graph grammars. Retrieved November 14, 2007, from http://www.cs.utwente.nl/groove

Sakai Web site. Retrieved November 14, 2007, from http://www.sakaiproject.org/

Security Assertion Markup Language (SAML). (2007). Retrieved November 14, 2007,

Signet: Privilege Management. (2006). Retrieved November 14, 2007, from http://www.internet2. edu/pubs/200612-IS-Sig.pdf

Windows CardSpace. (2007). Retrieved November 14, 2007, from http://msdn2.microsoft. com/en-us/netframework/aa663320.aspx

KEY TERMS

Goal-Oriented Workspace: A virtual place for distributed users to work together for a specific goal via sharing R&Ss, calendars, and workflows.

Identity Provider: A service asserts the identities of users who are local to an institution running the provider. An identity provider can release the identities to some targets based on attribute release policies.

Identity Provider Manager: A component maintains and provides the detail information of multiple identity providers.

Resource & Service: A resource or service provides the detail information of resources and services that are protected by the trusted SPs.

Service Provider: A service provides and protects resources and services. Those resources and services can only be accessed by the users who are authenticated by trusted identity providers.

Service Provider Manager: A component maintains and provides the detail information of multiple service providers.

Trust Relationship Manager: A component maintains and provides the trust relationships between IdPs and SPs, and U&Gs, and R&Ss.

Trust-Based Access Control: A function maps the trust relationships between U&Gs and R&Ss to the access behaviours.

User & Group Manager: A component maintains and provides the detail information of users who are authenticated by the trusted IdPs and groups organized for specific purposes.

Chapter XXXIV
Augmented Reality and the Future of Virtual Workspaces

James K. Ford
University of California, Santa Barbara, USA

Tobias Höllerer
University of California, Santa Barbara, USA

ABSTRACT

Until recently, Augmented Reality (AR) technology has rarely been discussed outside of the computer science world. It has taken years for this technology to become closer to a stable existence, and will most likely take several more years before it will be used by average citizens. However, the technology does exist, it has been applied in several areas, and research is being done to create even more stable systems that are adaptable to various environments. For this reason, it is necessary for decision-makers in establishments where education and training, knowledge distribution, and individual and collaborative task completion are essential to be aware of this technology, its abilities, and the possible impacts to common workspaces and workers. The purpose of this chapter is to inform decision-makers of AR's history, the completed research and current applications of AR, possible impacts to managers and workers, and the future trends of the technology.

INTRODUCTION

As humans we have an amazing ability to use whatever items available to complete a task, and if an appropriate item does not exist, we attempt to invent a technology to assist us. For example, we understand that, although possible, it is not practical to memorize the name and location of every body of water on Earth or every mountain range. Instead, we create a drawing that represents the location and name of every body of water or mountain range. We place this information on a large piece of paper that may be displayed on a wall, or smaller versions that may be rolled or folded for travel purposes. Then, during a task-solving situation where it is necessary for us to recall a specific locale, we check the inscription on the map for an appropriate answer. Here, the map works as a mnemonic device for solving a simple task. In the case of using a map for travel, we open our map, check our location, envision our place on the map in contrast to the destination, possibly take a few notes to assist our memory, and plan our voyage with a higher level of understanding of our location in comparison to our destinations. A document with inscribed symbols has allowed us the ability to simply recall information, or more importantly as a task-solving traveler, it has shown us multiple ways to envision our path to our destination. The information needed to solve our task, the location and possible routes, has been enhanced, and thus, so has our mind. The microscope, telescope, and x-ray machine are other examples of technologies that enhance information and allow us to better understand and conceptualize our world. Without them, we would struggle to envision solutions or possible pathways to solutions in scientific and medical applications. With Augmented Reality (AR) technology, enhancement of information in a variety of workspaces is possible.

Great technological inventions allow us to not only complete tasks in more efficient and less error-filled ways, they also allow us to "see," categorize, and understand the task at hand in multiple new ways that we were once unable to envision. Engelbart (1963, p. 1) explains his plan for a program aimed at developing means to augment the human intellect. These methods or devices can include many things, all of which appear to be but extensions of those developed and used in the past to help man apply his native sensory, mental, and motor capabilities.

Engelbart's (1963) view was to develop technologies, namely computer technologies, that assisted in augmenting the human mind. Personal computers and the Internet have followed. Technologies that augment of this sort are needed in the workplace, and this chapter discusses Augmented Reality as such a device that as Engelbart (1963) believed, can be used for "increasing the capability of a man to approach a complex problem situation, gain comprehension to suit his particular needs, and to derive solutions to problems" (p. 1).

It is imperative for those of us that research the interactions of humans, technology, and communication, or manage in industry those complex interactions, to be at the forefront of advanced technological equipment information. Augmented Reality Systems hold promise of impacting workplace environments as drastically as the Internet did in the 1990s and continue to do so today. Similarly to early publications that explained and defined the possibilities of the Internet, its impacts on education, workplace settings, and information distribution for humans worldwide, this chapter takes similar aim.

It is true that information on Augmented Reality has been contained mainly in computer science journals and in editorials forecasting new technologies in popular tech-related magazines. Because of the limited number of stable systems, the lack of widespread use in industry, and the lack of collaboration across academic departments on most campuses, information on this technology has yet to find its exit from computer science literature. However, Augmented Reality systems are being used in several areas. The military has used Heads Up Displays in fighter jets for years assisting pilots in finding targets and providing additional information. BMW is likely the most popular car manufacturer that has conducted research into how the systems may be used to assist while driving and in engine repairs. There are several examples of systems designed for use in the field of medicine. These systems provide doctors additional information overlayed on a patient's body to assist in surgery, and provide a type of x-ray vision into the patient's body. This chapter discusses similar examples in a variety of fields and how AR can be used in the average office setting.

It is because knowledge of Augmented Reality has stayed within such a narrow audience and because it is an immerging technology that we find it necessary to provide information so that researchers in social sciences, human computer interaction, writing studies/technical communication and similar fields will begin to apply methods of research to this technology. We also wish to inform managers and workers in industry of the technology and the possible impacts on workplace environments to better prepare decision makers for when the technology becomes readily available.

This chapter will:

1. Define Augmented Reality (AR), situate it amongst similar technologies, and provide a brief history of research conducted.
2. Explain how workers can use AR as an Online Communication Tool (OCT) for:
    *   Organizational Knowledge Management
    *   Workplace Training/Education
    *   Conceptual Design and Display
    *   Advanced Concept Understanding
3. Provide an outlook for the future of AR systems, including an explanation of Mobile Augmented Reality (MARS), the inclusion of voice, sound, and an authoring system.
4. Discuss appropriate workplaces for AR and the potential impact on workers.

Augmented Reality Defined and Situated

In 1965, Ivan Sutherland, a pioneer computer scientist, coined the term, "The ultimate display," and in 1968 he published a paper on his invention of the first Head Mounted Display (HMD). His invention provided a user of the HMD with additional three-dimensional information only the user could see while wearing the HMD. This invention is accepted amongst augmented reality (AR) researchers as the first attempt at creating what is now the modern day AR system. An AR system "supplements the real world with virtual (computer-generated) objects that appear to coexist in the same space as the real world" (Azuma et al., 1997, p. 34). Thus, the world around the user becomes augmented in real time, and the real world with the virtual information becomes the user's interface.

To better understand AR, we can define it within what Colquhoun and Milgram (1999) call the Reality-Virtuality (RV) Continuum. Within the continuum there are five terms: Real Environment (RE), Augmented Reality (AR), Mixed Reality (MR), Augmented Virtuality (AV), and a Virtual Environment (VE). The two polar opposites are the RE and VE. The RE contains no computer assistance or modeling, and the VE is completely computer assisted and modeled. MR encompasses both AR and AV because in both of those worlds the computer assisted and modeled portions of what the user encounters, thus creating a mixture of virtual and real information in an environment. In the case of AV, the base environment in which the presentation takes place is predominantly virtual. A few real objects, plus 2D and 3D photographs, add more realism to such an AV. AR, the topic of this chapter, is closer to the RE side of the spectrum, because it is concerned with augmenting a user's RE with virtual information. The base environment is the physical world itself. Figure 1 is a graphical representation of the Reality-Virtuality Continuum.

This definition is based on the affordances of the technology, and not based on the user's perception, or feeling of presence or telepresence as described in Steuer's (1992) work. However, in regard to Steuer's (1992) explanation where he rightly argues

Figure 1. Definition of mixed reality and augmented reality within the context of the reality-virtuality continuum (as introduced by Milgram & Colquhoun (1999))

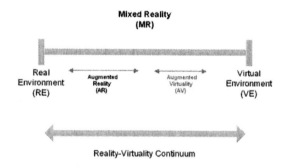

that the virtualness of the environment is based on the user's perception, it is the goal of AR systems to keep the user within the realm of reality and to simply augment that reality with unobtrusive and purely assistive virtual information.

Another commonly held definition for AR presented by Azuma (1997), which does not limit AR by the technological hardware, is that an AR system contains the following characteristics:

1. Combines real and virtual
2. Interactive in real time
3. Registered in 3-D

This definition works well because it separates those technologies that do provide much needed enhanced information like a map, the dashboard of a car, a digital wristwatch, and television (even with the enhanced information provided for sporting events) from a pure AR technology.

Augmented Reality History as a Research Field

Although a version of AR can be traced back to the time of Sutherland (1965), AR was not a field of study itself until the early 1990s. Realizing that although VR was a powerful technology with many applications, VR technologies provided only virtualized representations, or engulfed a user fully in virtuality, and there are many applications where a user needs to remain in synch with reality while receiving augmented information via a virtual image, text, or sound. Thus, AR branched off from VR and researchers began to create what was once only theorized into actual working AR environments.

AR visionaries began to see the potential use of the technology in many areas of life. Azuma's (1997) *A Survey of Augmented Reality* outlines ways that AR can be a powerful tool in medicine, architecture, assembly and maintenance, teleoperation of robots, entertainment, and the military. It is safe to add to this list the areas of education, industry train-

ing and communication, and tourism. Through the 1990s computer scientists concentrated on simply creating AR systems that worked. Although still difficult, creating an AR system in a controlled, indoor environment can today be done routinely. Computer scientists are currently tackling the issue of creating stable AR systems in uncontrolled, outdoor environments where tracking is difficult, displays are not as clear, and computer failures are common. The Mobile Augmented Reality System (MARS) (Feiner, MacIntyre, Höllerer, & Webster, 1997) created at Columbia University is the first functional example of a mobile outdoor system. (The difficulties of mobile AR system applications and implications are discussed in the *Future Trends* section.)

Of the major projects in AR, most have been Industrial Augmented Reality (IAR) projects. One of the first attempts of using AR in industry as a workplace assistive tool, was conducted at Boeing in 1992. This project attempted to provide a, "*see-thru* virtual reality goggle to the factory worker, and to use this device to augment the worker's visual field of view with useful and dynamically changing information" (Caudell & Mizell, 1992, p. 660). The idea was to provide information that would assist the worker who was responsible for complex wiring tasks in the 747 aircraft. Another, ARVIKA, was "designed to implement Augmented Reality system(s) for mobile use in industrial applications" (Friedrich, 2002, p. 3). ARVIKA, sponsored by BMBF (German Federal Ministry of Education and Research) and carrying a consortium holding such companies as Daimler Chrysler, Volkswagen, Audi, Ford, and Siemens (amongst many others), began in 1999 and ended in 2003. The project created "about 30 application-specific prototypes ...and have been evaluated in usability tests" (Friedrich, 2002, p. 3). Another very large, but non industrial AR project was the Key Technology Research Project on Mixed Reality Systems (MR Project) (Tamura, Yamamoto, & Katayama, 2001) which was launched in 1997 and backed with funding from Canon and the Japanese government. The project lasted until March of 2001 and yielded several major advances in the areas of image-based rendering, registration, HMD's, mobile AR, and collaborative MR.

While computer scientists are working hard at creating new stable systems and publishing their results in the computer science world, very few researchers are looking at potential information distribution and communication impacts in the workplace and on workers.

AUGMENTED REALITY IN WORKSPACES

The affordances of an AR system are numerous. As a training/education tool, it can be used to direct a user through a series of steps to complete a task, in place of a technical manual. As a persuasive/rhetorical tool it can be used to assist in the design or display of a 3D object that has yet to be modeled with real materials. As a collaborative tool, an AR system allows multiple users to view the same 3D material, and it allows real time communication among collaborators distributed across geographical locations. As a knowledge management tool, AR may record and document the viewpoint of the user at all times, and then replay the interactions for educational/training/safety/legal purposes. As a conceptual display tool, AR works as an advanced schematic of a concept in that it can display all of the inner workings and connections of a system to a user.

Augmented Reality as a Knowledge Management Tool

In Wensley and Verwijk-O'Sullivan's (2000) work, *Tools for Knowledge Management,* AR was not included in the list of possible Knowledge Management (KM) tools. This is because AR is usually seen as a technology that is used to display or augment information. However, AR technology

does have the ability to assist in what Schwartz, Divitini, and Brasethvik (2000) call the "three tenets of Internet-based knowledge management" (p. 10). Acquire, Organize, and Distribute, the AOD model, are the overarching actions required in a KM system dealing with digital information. In fact, AR technology is based as a system for documenting (with an authoring system), saving/recording, retrieving and creating information in both a 2D and 3D text, visual, and sound based environment.

"Acquisition relates to how we collect knowledge from members of the organization or other resources, and store them in an organizational memory" (Schwartz et al., 2000, p. 10). An AR system can record the actions of a user interacting with virtual and real information, the communication amongst users surrounding the activities, and with an authoring system that allows users to document, via digital text, voice, or image, information for other users. Thus, an AR system is acquiring new organizational information each time a user works with the system, and this information can be stored in a database. Also, each time an AR system environment is authored, knowledge of the environment, the virtual information involved, the virtual objects that have been created, and so forth, are being time stamped in the system and can be retrieved, analyzed, or relived by future users. Acquisition of information refers to not only the way in which we acquire needed information for a database system, but also the time and space in which that information or knowledge is understood. When information is acquired by a worker, that information must be logged in some form and then acquired in another form by the recording system. An AR system allows, for instances when the information is 3D or not, the worker to immediately document organizational knowledge and physically place that information in a 3D environment.

"Distribution is the ability to get the relevant knowledge to the person who needs it at the right time" (Schwartz et al., 2000, p. 11). As a distribution technology, an AR system could be programmed to provide a user with the relevant virtual information, overlayed on the real world, in 3D, and that is interactive, in the time period when the user requires it most. Thus, a worker could be solving a task using the AR system, pertinent virtual information that is applicable to the situation could appear, the user can choose to use the information or disregard it, or, the worker can add to the current database of knowledge for future workers involved in a similar task at a later date. As with the system described by Ayatsuka, Hayashi, and Rekimoto (1998), users of an AR system are able to leave virtual notes, instructions, or directions for coworkers throughout a workspace and throughout time. Those special pieces of organizational information can be saved in a database system as well, and then redistributed at later dates for other employees during the completion of a similar task. This would be similar to leaving a sticky note on a copy machine that is not working properly, only it is possible for the information to be only retrieved by a certain employee using the AR system with an appropriate password (if needed). The system can even decide if the information is relevant to the specific task of the user at that time.

These examples are not meant to glorify AR as a technology that somehow can read a user's mind, or create new organizational "knowledge" for a worker. Hislop's (2005) distinction between data, information and knowledge is valuable here. He explains the three by defining data as "raw numbers, images, words, sounds…", information as, "data arranged in a meaningful pattern…where some intellectual input has been added", and knowledge, "can be understood to emerge from the application analysis, and productive use of data and/or information" (p. 15). We also understand that AR is similar to Internet information in that, "to assume that the Web can *deliver* knowledge is as naive a belief as the idea that knowledge can be *extracted* from individual experts and embedded in computer programs" (Wensley & Verwijk-O'Sullivan, 2000, p.120).

Managers and workers must somehow interact and use all of this data, and AR is a system similar to other KM tools in that it can save data, with the interaction of workers acquire information, organize it in a database, and provide retrieval of that information in new ways possibly allowing for the making of knowledge for workers. The obvious benefit to this is that the information being stored and retrieved is not based on a top-down system, but closer to Fischer and Ostwald's view of KM as a cyclic process where workers are reflective practitioners and, "workers, not managers, create knowledge at use time [and]…knowledge is a side effect of work" (2001, p. 60). In this AR KM system, the information is dynamic, interactive, virtual, 3D, overlayed on the real environment, and is not attached to a particular time and space.

AUGMENTED REALITY AS A WORKPLACE OCT FOR TRAINING, EDUCATION, DESIGN AND DISPLAY

In light of the above examples explaining AR as a KM technology, it is easy to imagine how an AR system could assist workers as an OCT for workplace training, education, design, and display.

AR Workplace Training and IAR's

One of the first attempts at creating an Industrial Augmented Reality (IAR) system would be the Knowledge Based Augmented Reality for Maintenance Assistance (KARMA) printer created by AR researchers at Columbia University in 1993, which was a "testbed system for exploring the automated design of augmented realities that explain maintenance and repair tasks" (Fiener, Macintyre, & Siligmann, 1993, p. 54). Basically the KARMA printer, with the use of a HMD, provided the user with additional 3D information about the printer itself. It could show the user simple information like how to remove a tray or which handle to lift by showing virtual 3D arrows or virtual trays located inside the printer. These virtual cues were intended to be used to assist a user in completing a simple task of opening a tray or lifting a handle.

The technology has advanced since 1993 with projects such as the ARVIKA initiative that, along with other AR tools, created systems allowing users to work with 3D information that provided step-by-step instructions for task completion. Unlike a paper or online training manual, an AR system places the information on top of the object so the user does not have to move away from the task, interact with the help system, and then return to task. Prototype systems have been created that take a trainee through simulations where the user may interact with 3D models containing the augmented information. The technology also allows communication and collaboration with expert trainers who may work with their trainees across any distance. Distributed AR,

enables users on remote sites to collaborate on the training tasks by sharing the view of the local user equipped with a wearable computer. The user can interactively manipulate virtual objects that substitute for real objects, try out and discuss the training tasks. (Boulanger, Georganas, Zhong, & Liu, 2003, p. 7)

The major advancement in AR here is that the system is now being used as a Computer Supported Collaborative Work (CSCW) technology. "The combination of Augmented Reality, mobile computing and CSCW produces a new technology, called Mobile Collaborative Augmented Reality (MCAR)" (Boulanger, 2004, p. 321). Because, "training costs are a considerable part of expenses for many industries..." and, "the problem is compounded when the trainers are far from the would-be trainees" (Boulanger, Georganas, Zhong, & Liu, 2003, p. 2). "The trend is to provide on-the-job training, giving learners performance support by integrating computer-

based guidance and information into the normal working environment through augmented reality technology" (Boulanger et al., 2004, p. 2).

Spatial Augmented Realty (SAR) and the Office of the Future

Raskar, Welch, Cutts, Lake, Stesin, and Fuchs (1998, p. 179) described their version of the office of the future" and the technology required to create such a space. Their office consisted of using "real-time computer vision techniques to dynamically extract per-pixel depth and reflectance information for the visible surfaces in the office including walls, furniture, objects, and people, and then to either project images *on* the surfaces, render images *of* the surfaces, or interpret changes *on* the surfaces.

This is what Bimber and Roslear (2005) define as Spatial Augmented Reality (SAR). SAR refers to the application of AR in non-mobile environments, like a traditional office workplace, by displaying interactive 3D objects for the user without the need of a HMD.

A similar type of "smart" display technology has been put into practice in the "Augmented Reality Kitchen" (Bonanni, Lee, & Selker, 2005). The MIT Media Laboratory undertook the complex workspace of a kitchen and "built a series of discrete context-aware systems to monitor and inform the most commonly performed tasks in a residential kitchen. These five systems collect information from the environment and project task-specific interfaces onto the refrigerator, cabinets, countertop, and food" (Bonanni et al., 2005, p. 2). In this kitchen a virtual recipe is displayed on a wall, food temperature is calculated by an infrared thermometer, food inside the refrigerator is displayed, cabinets contain an inventory system that lights up the item needed in chorus with the current step of the virtual recipe, and a sink colors its water depending on its temperature. A system like this built for a kitchen could easily be adapted for use in task completion in a traditional office setting.

These types of displays may be used to enhance office communication during the planning stages of a project, presentation, or during deliberations. Maintaining the idea of projected AR displays, Pinhanez (2001) described how Everywhere Displays Projectors (ED-projector) can be used to "provide computer access in public spaces, facilitate navigation in buildings, localize resources in physical space, bring computational resources to different areas of an environment, and facilitate reconfiguration of the workplace" (p. 93). This type of system is particularly advantageous because it provides an AR environment, but it does not require a HMD. In a traditional office setting this type of display would assist presenters by providing 3D object display for all attendees to view and discuss. MagicMeeting (Regenbrecht, Wagner, Baratoff, 2002), is a collaborative AR system "designed to support a scenario where a group of experts meet to discuss the design of a product" (p. 151). Such a system would be of particular value to those in architecture, or other design fields where 3D interactive models are necessary to fully explain concepts. Workers can collaborate on a design by displaying the informa-tion anywhere that is suitable, and that design is now an interactive and dynamic display ready for manipulation by local or telepresent observers.

AR Videoconferencing

Not all workplace meetings revolve around a 3D designed artifact. However, these meetings do revolve around workplace information. AR-based videoconferencing systems exist to assist in the communication practices usually found in a traditional office meeting. A system, "cAR/PE!" allows

three participants at different locations to communicate over a network simulating a tradi-tional face-to-face meeting. Integrated into the AV environment are live video streams of the participants spatially arranged around a virtual table, a large virtual presentation screen for 2D display and application sharing, and 3D geom-etry (models) within the room and on top of the table. (Regenbrecht, Lum, Kohler, Ott, Wagner, & Mueller, 2004, p. 338)

Barakonyi, Fahmy, and Schmalstieg (2004) describe a similar AR videoconferencing system

Figure 2. A collaborative AR conferencing example: This picture shows one meeting participant's view of an architectural scene, a reminder of a meeting agenda, and some information on a particular building, all overlaid on top of a meeting table to create a common shared scene with other meeting participants, such as the colleague in view, or remote collaborators

that is a "remote collaboration tool combining a desktop-based AR system and a videoconferencing module" (p. 89). This system merges the advantages of face-to-face communication in a videoconferencing environment and AR's technological affordances with virtual objects. Billinghurst, Furness, Kato, and Weghorst (1999), describe a system where "users can easily change the arrangement of Virtual Monitors, placing the virtual images of remote participants about them in the real world and they can collaboratively interact with 2D and 3D information using a Virtual Shard Whiteboard" (p. 1).

Although similar to a Webcam display in that participants can discuss information in real time while viewing each other, an AR videoconferencing system allows for the display of 2D and 3D information in the space of each worker taking part in the meeting, and thus workers have access to shared virtual information that each participant may manipulate.

AR in Workplace Design and Display

In workplaces that require workers to create 3D models, as in engineering and architecture, and for jobs that require workers to explain, discuss, and sell ideas based on 3D models, an AR system can work well as an assistive design/rhetorical tool because of its ability to show 3D models of advanced designs, interactive in real time, and available for numerous observers to view. Often, it is necessary for designers to create models to sell their project ideas. In certain situations a paper or digital diagram, built-to-scale model,

or a computerized 3D virtual tour may be the appropriate design/selling medium. However, there are instances where a diagram may not be augmented enough, a model does not provide enough detail, and a virtual tour is too separate from the real environment. An AR system like ARTHUR may be an alternative as it "aims to put virtual 3D models on the designer's meeting table alongside conventional media" (Penn et al., 2004, p. 220). Wearing HMD's, users can collaboratively create 3D architectural designs complete with pedestrian simulations. The benefit of this technology is that users are present in their current work desk locations, and maintain access to other design tools, like pencil and paper, a computer, tangible models, and so forth. Users are able to see and interact with the virtual design creations and changes of other users.

Whether a designer is selling the idea to a superior in the workplace or potential outside buyers, an AR system can be used as a powerful rhetorical tool, or it may be used earlier in the design process as a participatory design tool.

The technological affordances of AR as an OCT for training explained in the above examples allow workers to be trained with virtual 3D objects, images, text, or sound in conjunction with completing their task, with the option to collaborate with a trainer who is physically or virtually present. As an OCT for education in the workplace, AR allows for enhanced design and discussion strategies, enhanced displays for presenting 2D or 3D content, and as a CSCW system, AR is excellent because enhanced collaboration across vast distances, with the ability

Figure 3. An image sequence documenting an interactive augmented reality presentation of a planned building (UCSB California Nanosystems Institute) in its future location before construction has started

to interact with tangible tools in the same virtual space is possible.

As valuable as these tools are, the future of AR research is looking to expand on these affordances by using ubiquitous computing technology and Mobile Augmented Reality Systems (MARS).

FUTURE TRENDS OF AUGMENTED REALITY

The true potential of AR as an enabling technology for virtual workplaces will likely be reached only when it can be applied in truly arbitrary, dynamic, and mobile settings; that is, away from the carefully conditioned environments of research laboratories and special-purpose work areas. Several technologies must be combined to make this possible: global tracking technologies, global wireless communication, location-based computing and services, and wearable computing. From the pace of development and improvement of these communication and information technologies over the past decade, we can safely predict that the basic technological needs for what we may want to term "anywhere augmentation" will be met in the not-too-distant future, but research will have to focus on a few key concepts. Possible scenarios include:

An architect stands in front of a future construction site, discussing his ideas with the owner. Both carry tablet-shaped Anywhere Augmentation devices, which allow them to visualize, modify, and jointly review the design for a new nine story building that they want to blend in with the neighborhood as much as possible. Since it will be the tallest structure around, they carefully simulate the shadowing and light reflection effects at different weather conditions and times of day. They often use the tablet display, which has a camera on its back, as a magic lens that they hold up and "see through" to observe the construction site with the simulated building appearing directly on top of the filmed physical world.

A field scientist assesses a natural reserve to determine where to place a sensor that will report data critical to an evolving model of erosion and runoff phenomena. She dons her augmentation glasses, overlaying several measured and simulated data distributions of relevant variables on the landscape: humidity, percentage of daily sunlight, slope angle, vegetation index, and the anticipated degree of erosion. Despite imperfect localization, she is quickly able to align the contours of the virtual 3D elevation model with the outline of the hill in front of her, establishing registration for overlaying the landscape and data values behind the hill directly in her field of view, in the fashion of Superman's X-ray vision. The system helps her to get an overview, spot anomalies, and lets her pinpoint exactly where to place the new sensor.

A schoolchild is on a field trip to learn about botany. Distinguishing different orders and families of trees has never been his strength, but help is at his fingertips. His small electronic companion allows him to see labels of already classified trees directly overlaid on his view and allows him to add tentative new classifications and take pictures for later verification by the teacher or field guide.

What all these scenarios have in common is the idea of having computational resources available anytime and anywhere, and, moreover, being able to form a link between the location-specific information and the physical world by direct vision overlays. The term Anywhere Augmentation emphasizes the necessity for such a system to work in arbitrary workspaces in order to become adopted by users and make life easier for them.

One approach that pursues the goal of Anywhere Augmentation is Ubiquitous Computing (Want et al., 1995), but despite 15 years of strong research contributions in this field, the overall vision of a pervasive infrastructure of interconnected and inter-functioning computing engines, sensors, and displays, remains elusive. Even though computing, sensing, and display equipment has become orders of magnitude more powerful

Figure 4. Different examples of anywhere augmentation hardware platforms: (a) a research prototype mobile AR system, (b) ruggedized tablet computer (camera and GPS and orientation sensor not in view), (c) a handheld AR prototype from an Austrian-German 2003 research collaboration, based on two PDAs and sensors, (d) hypothetical smart-phone platform and user situation for dominant hand pointing and nondominant hand framing

and cost-effective while shrinking in size, the cost and effort to integrate vast interconnected networks of this equipment with architectural and urban developments is very high, and maintenance and upgrades for such deployed infrastructure is difficult and expensive. Apart from these problems, there will always be scenarios where deployment of an infrastructure will be prohibitive or where the user could be prevented from using an infrastructure deployed by non-cooperating parties. Privacy issues would also be harder to handle because personal data would have to flow through a common central infrastructure in order to be useful to an individual.

For all these reasons, the more user-centric combination of wearable computing and augmented reality (Barfield & Caudell, 2001) appears to be a more promising approach to Anywhere Augmentation. Mobile and wearable computing technologies have found their way into mainstream industrial and governmental service applications over the past decade. They are now commonplace in the shipping and hospitality industries, as well as in mobile law enforcement, to highlight a few successful examples. However, current mobile computing solutions outside of research laboratories do not sense and adapt to the user's environment and they do not link the services they provide with the physical world.

If the computer cannot make sense of arbitrary new environments all by itself, the idea must be to enable the human to achieve this task together with the computer. The overall task is easy to describe: The computer has access to a wealth of information about a specific physical environment, and has approximate knowledge of the user's current location, orientation, and interests with regard to that environment, but it lacks the capabilities to link the information accurately to the physical world. Consequently, the human should be empowered with efficient computer-assisted interaction techniques to manage the different data sources that the computer has access to, and to help establish the link and registration with the physical world. After this necessary semi-automatic initialization step for the new environment, the user will be able to reap all the benefits of a directly coupled AR interface.

Humans will have to drive the task of pairing the available digital information with locations in the physical environment, and in order to be able to benefit from grassroots activities, the user interfaces for doing this should be simplified and smartly assisted by computers. A standard access method needs to be in place for retrieving location data from databases responsible for the area the augmented worker is currently passing through. This requires mechanisms such as automatic service detection and the definition of standard exchange formats that both the database servers and the mobile AR software support. It is clear from the history of protocol standards that without big demand and money-making opportunities on the horizon, progress on these fronts can be expected to be slow. On the other hand, the World Wide Web, HTML, and HTTP evolved from similar starting conditions. Some researchers see location-aware computing on a global scale as a legitimate successor of the World Wide Web as we know it today (Spohrer, 1999).

In general, *AR authoring*, the process of generating content for augmented environments, is a key software technology that will have a big impact on the possible success of AR in workplaces. The process can be compared with data entry for today's standard computer-assisted workspaces, in which a set of databases and a business-wide network, a so-called intranet store, distribute information for a large set of decision makers in a company. Because of improved user interface technologies, data entry was shifted from a task that required a computer specialist to a more distributed task that could be performed by the very employees who encountered new data in their daily work processes. Workers on many different levels of the employment hierarchy were enabled to enter, view, analyze, and update business data directly. The same goal holds for AR systems, only that the task is far more complicated, since all information has a very specific positional and contextual component and the data presentation will potentially involve a much more flexible interface than the fairly standardized 2D desktop environments of current office computers. This is why it is of utmost importance to keep the authoring system simple and detached from implementation details. Nonprogrammers need to be enabled to add computer annotations to arbitrary environments to bring about all the benefits we have discussed so far.

In AR, information presentation is not limited to the visual sense. Interaction with a portable or wearable computer can benefit significantly from multimodal interfaces (Cohen et al., 1998) which allow for direct and robust user input, employing the input and output resources most practical in a specific user context. Valuable input and output modalites for AR interfaces include audio, and in particular speech input and output, and also gesture-based input, either using a pen on a display surface, or through free-form hand motion. The goal is for the worker to operate as unencumbered by technology as possible. This, however, means that computers need to be enabled to infer information by simple observation rather than by interpreting specific learned input sequences using particular input devices. The multimodal requirements for convenient computer access also differ substantially depending on the current user activity. A user who is surveying a terrain from an elevated observation point with the goal of getting an overview of a larger area's geographic properties has very different computer access needs than, for example, a field scientist who is using both hands to deploy a sensor in a carefully selected location (Krum, Omoteso, Ribarsky, Starner, & Hodges, 2002).

Appropriate AR Settings and Possible Effects on Workers

Not every workspace or worker necessitates a technology like AR. Paper, pencil, computer, and an online training manual are proven tools to complete many tasks, especially in office environments. However, because of the affordances of AR in that it combines the real with the virtual, there are situations where an AR system may be used to enhance the task completion process, or display and/or communication of information in conjunction with traditional technologies.

We have provided numerous examples of workplace conditions where AR would be applicable such as when:

- communication at a distance with enhanced visualization and interaction of 2D and 3D material is imperative;
- training and education while interacting with tangible objects and communicating with a trainer either in shared physical space or by distance is needed to enhance communication, increase safety and efficiency and reduce errors;
- recording, distribution, and recollection of information in 2D and especially 3D environments is needed as in a KM tool; and
- collaborative design and interaction of 3D models is necessary.

An even more important discussion involves the possible impacts of this technology on the workers who interact with AR. On the positive side, as with the affordances of the Internet, workers will now have access to a wealth of information pertaining to specific job tasks. Unlike the Internet, where information is found in particular linked Web pages, and users must use search engines in order to locate pertinent information, AR technology allows managers and workers the ability to author their own environment by embedding the relevant information needed for task completion. This allows trainers and workers to create, track, and peruse an information database that is displayed on top of the real world. Expert knowledge is now embedded in the artifacts with which the users interact. An issue here is that although the expert knowledge used to assist a worker may be greatly beneficial to an expert, that knowledge does not simply transfer to a nonexpert worker. The advantage of AR in this regard is that the information embedded is dynamic in that each worker may tailor that information specifically for individual task completion. This provides a worker with freedom to complete work with important idiosyncrasies intact. The effect on the worker here is that the AR system is not an imposing piece of technology, but as technological tool available to assist

the worker. However, even with a user friendly authoring interface, it is likely that information specialists, like technical communicators and graphic designers, will be needed to mediate the flow of information from expert to novice.

Although AR may not be imposing on how a task is completed, the system does have capabilities to be imposing because each step a user completes, and the way in which that task is completed, may be recorded and reviewed. From a managerial standpoint this is an excellent feature because expert work may be presented to other workers as an educational and training piece. But this may have a negative effect on the worker because it may limit a worker's sense of freedom for fear of mistakes being recorded and reviewed by superiors. And, since the technology can assist a worker by providing accurate directions, a sense of error-free task completion may be felt by the worker.

The effect of information overload, especially in a real-time, interactive, and 3D environment will most likely be an issue for some workers. Having the ability to control the amount of information being displayed will help workers, but a worker must also know which information is relevant for task completion of his specific job, and which information he may already understand. The strain on the literacy level of the worker will be great and the adaptation to such an environment is a place for future research.

In the future, AR systems, unlike any static information source, actually could counteract the problems of information overload if the condition is recognized in time. If the human reaction to information overload was better understood and the computer was equipped with the right sensors, the AR interface could be made adaptive to the worker's stress and confusion level. Information would be presented at different speeds and in a clearly prioritized manner. Adaptive user interfaces have a great potential to enhance their own usefulness under non-optimal circumstances, but they are exceedingly hard to program. Basically, the programmer's task is to provide practical solutions to the unexpected and unforeseen. The only viable solution may be a machine-learning approach where a device accepts after-the-fact user recommendations for previous crisis situations, and attempts to infer future strategies from that data. Such systems are still in their infancy today.

In indoor or mobile AR systems where users must wear a HMD, the weight of the equipment, along with the goggles that must be worn can be cumbersome. In tasks where a worker must be precise while interacting with a tangible object it is possible that the weight of the HMD, or the strain placed on the head or neck may impede precision. In outdoor, mobile environments, workers will have to carry, along with the HMD, a significant weight of equipment equal to that of a backpack full of books.

CONCLUSION

Marshall McLuhan (1964) argued that technology and media are an extension of our bodies, and the message is in the media. If he is correct, then McLuhan would also argue that AR is the technology extended just beyond our skin and clothing, and the message that needs to be researched is how this technology will impact the distribution of information in society, the training and education of workers, and the traditional workspaces where information and knowledge are routinely created, interpreted, acted upon, or dismissed. Possibly AR is the "Ultimate Display" for certain workplace environments, but it may also be the Ultimate Information Communication Tool in the years to come. If this is the case, then researchers in both social science and computer science will need to collaborate in order to create the most efficient and usable AR technology. Education, tourism, entertainment, and medicine, along with the employment fields mentioned in this chapter are all possible locales for AR use.

Specialists in these areas will need to make their information known to designers of AR systems, and AR system developers would be wise to seek out their expertise. The rise of the Internet is a prime example of an information technology where once only experts were able to design how information would be distributed. Now average citizens, with the help of editing software, are able to publish their information. AR technology is similar in that authoring systems will be developed to allow the worker who does not have advanced programming skills the ability to author her own AR environment.

The fields of technical communication, graphic design, interface development, and human-computer interaction will be impacted and their specialties are currently needed to ensure highly usable displays of information including virtual texts, images, icons, and video playback. Research on the symbol systems used to provide information, the interaction of the user and the computer, and the impact of the technology and the information display on the user are extensions of research niches for scholars in the above fields. The research that has been conducted in these fields thus far is valuable and needs to be applied and researched in the AR environments. That information needs to be used as a basis for design and study of AR systems where the information is no longer on paper or on an online help system, but provided interactively in 3D space combining real and virtual information displayed on the real world. The empirical evidence and theories grounded in earlier technologies needs to be adopted and tested by researchers interested in enhanced display systems.

As humans, we do have an amazing ability to use or create what we need in order to be successful. Creating, researching, hypothesizing, theorizing, and testing those technologies to learn more about the success of that technology as a tool for humans is a natural part of that process. AR is a next step in the evolution of human technology. It holds with it many of the technologies we have used in the past. However, it is not simply the inclusion of multiple technologies that make a new technology great; it is the ability of humans to use that technology successfully to the point that the technology disappears, and its interactions with us become blurred with our natural surroundings and reality. AR is a technology that comes with a learning curve. It is up to the decision-makers in industry as to whether AR is the appropriate tool for their workers, and it is up to AR designers and all of us as researchers to keep producing and testing those technologies that have the ability to enhance the human mind.

REFERENCES

Ayatsuka, Y., Hayashi, K., & Rekimoto, J. (1998). Augment-able reality: Situated communication through physical and digital spaces. In *Proceedings of the 2nd IEEE International Symposium on Wearable Computers* (pp. 68-76). IEEE Society.

Azuma, R. T. (1997). A survey of augmented reality. *Presence: Teleoperators and Virtual Environments, 6*(4), 355-385.

Barakonyi, I., Fahmy, T., & Schmalstieg, D. (2004). Remote collaboration using augmented reality videoconferencing. In *ACM International Conference Proceeding Series: Vol. 62 Proceedings of the 2004 conference on Graphics interface* (pp. 89-96). London, Ontario, Canada: Canadian Human-Computer Communications Society.

Barfield, W., & Caudell, T. (2001). *Fundamentals of wearable computers and augmented reality.* Mahwah, NJ: Lawrence Erlbaum Associates.

Billinghurst, Furness, T. A., M., Kato, H., & Weghorst, S. (1999). *A mixed reality 3D conferencing application* (Tech. Rep.). Seattle, WA: Human Interface Technology Laboratory, University of Washington.

Bimber, O., & Raskar, R. (2005). *Spatial augmented reality: Merging real and virtual worlds.* Wellesley, MA: A.K. Peters, Ltd.

Bonanni, L., Lee, C., & Selker, T. (2005). CounterIntelligence: Augmented reality kitchen. In *Proceedings, Conference on Computer Human Interaction (CMI)* (pp. 373-376), Portland, Oregon.

Boulanger, P. (2004). Application of augmented reality to industrial tele-training. In *Proceedings of First Canadian Conference on Computer and Robot Vision* (pp. 320-328).

Boulanger, P., Georganas, N., Zhong, X., & Liu, P. (2003). A real-time augmented reality system for industrial tele-training. In S. El-Hakim, A. Gruen & J. S. Walton (Eds), *Videometrics VII: Vol. 5013, Proceedings of The International Society for Optical Engineering* (pp. 1-13).

Caudell, T. P., & Mizell, D. W. (1992). Augmented reality: An application of heads-up display technology to manual manufacturing processes. In *Proceedings, IEEE Hawaii International Conference on Systems Sciences* (pp. 659-669).

Cohen, P., Johnston, M., McGee, D., Orviatt, S., Pittman, J., Smith, I., et al. (1998). Multimodal interaction for distributed applications. In *Proceedings of The Fifth ACM International Multimedia Conference* (pp. 31-40).

Colquhoun, H.-Jr., & Milgram, P. (1999). A taxonomy of real and virtual world display integration. In Y. Ohta & H. Tamura (Eds), *Mixed reality—merging real and virtual worlds* (pp. 5-40). Chiyoda, Tokyo: Ohmsha, Ltd.

Englebart, D. C. (1963). A conceptual framework for the augmentation of man's intellect. In P. W. Howerton & D. C. Weeks (Eds.), *Vistas in information handling (Vol. 1)* (pp. 1-29). Washington, DC: Spartan Books.

Feiner, S., MacIntyre B., Höllerer, & Webster, A. (1997). A touring machine: Prototyping 3D mobile augmented reality systems for exploring the urban environment. In *Proceedings of ISWC '1997 First International Symposium on Wearable Computers* (pp. 74-81).

Feiner, S., MacIntyre, B., & Siligmann, D. (1993). Knowledge-based augmented reality. *Communication of the ACM: Special Issue on Computer Augmented Environments: Back to the Real World, 36*(7), 53-62.

Fisher, G., & Ostwald, J. (2001). Knowledge management: Problems, promises, realities, and challenges. *IEEE Intelligent Systems, 16*(1), 60-72.

Friedrich, W. (2002). ARVIKA – augmented reality for development, production and service. In *Proceedings of the International Symposium on Mixed and Augmented Reality (ISMAR'02)* (pp. 3-4).

Hislop, D. (2005). *Knowledge management in organizations.* Oxford, NY: Oxford University Press Inc.

Krum, D. M., Omoteso, O., Ribarsky, W., Starner, T., & Hodges, L. F. (2002). Speech and gesture multimodal control of a whole Earth 3D visualization environment. In *Proceedings of VISSYM (Joint Eurographics and IEEE Symposium on Visualization* (pp. 195-200).

McLuhan, M. (1964). *Understanding Media: The extensions of man.* New York: McGraw Hill.

Penn, A., Mottram, C., Schieck, A. F., Wittkamper, M., Storring, M., Romell, O., et al. (2004). Augmented reality meeting table: A novel multiuser interface for architectural design. In J. P. VanLeeuwen & H. Timmermans (Eds.), *Recent advances in design and decision support systems in architecture and urban planning* (pp. 213-231). Kluwer Academic Publishers.

Pinhanez, C. (2001). Augmenting reality with projected interactive displays. In B. Fisher, K. Dawson-Howe & C. O'Sullivan (Eds.), *Proceedings from virtual and augmented architecture* (pp.

93-100). London: Springer-Verlag.

Raskar, R., Welch, G., Cutts, M., Lake, A., Stesin, L., & Fuchs, H. (1998). The office of the future: A unified approach to image-based modeling and spatially immersive displays. In *Proceedings of SIGGRAPH 98* (pp. 179-188). ACM Publications.

Regenbrecht, H., Lum, T., Kohler, P., Ott, C., Wagner, M., & Mueller, E. (2004). Using augmented virtuality for remote collaboration. *Presence, 13*(3), 338-354.

Regenbrecht, H. T., Wagner, M. T., & Baratoff, G. (2002). MagicMeeting: A collaborative tangible augmented reality system. *Virtual Reality, 6*(3), 151-166.

Schwartz, D. G., Divitini, M., & Brasethvik, T. (2000). On knowledge management in the Internet age. In D. G. Schwartz, M. Divitini & T. Brasethvik (Eds.), *Internet-based organizational memory and knowledge management* (pp. 1-23). Hershey, PA: Idea Group Publishing.

Spohrer, J. (1999). Information in places. *IBM Systems Journal, 38*(4), 602–628.

Steuer, J. (1992). Defining virtual reality: Dimensions determining telepresence. *Journal of Communication, 42*(4), 73-93.

Sutherland, I. E. (1965). The ultimate display. *IFIPS Congress, 2,* 506-508.

Tamura, H., Yamamoto, H., & Katayama, A. (2001). Mixed reality: Future dreams seen at the border between real and virtual worlds. *IEEE Computer Graphics and Applications, 21*(6), 64-70.

Want, R., Schilit, N., Adams, I., Gold, R., Petersen, K., Goldberg, D., et al. (1995). An overview of the PARCTAB ubiquitous computing experiment. *IEEE Personal Communications 2*(6), 28-43.

Wensley, A. K. P., & Verwick-O'Sullivan, A. (2000). Tools for knowledge management. In D.

Chauvel & C. Despres (Eds.), *Knowledge horizons: The present and the promise of knowledge management* (pp.113-130). Boston, MA: Butterworth-Heinemann.

KEY TERMS

Augmented Reality: AR supplements the real world with virtual (computer-generated) objects that appear to coexist in the same space as the real world. An AR system has 3 characteristics:

1. Combines real and virtual worlds
2. Information is interactive in real time, and
3. Registered in 3-D

Head-Mounted Display: AR equipment worn on the head which houses a display technology (goggles). Displays may either be projected on the lens of the goggles or projected directly on the retina of the user.

Hand Held Display: A display technology that allows a user to see an AR world only when the display technology is held in reference to specific authored environments. This is an alternative to a Head Mounted Display and includes technologies like a portable flat screen monitor or a cellular telephone.

Mixed Reality: An all-encompassing term that includes the spectrum of worlds modeled by computers from Augmented Reality to Virtual Reality.

Mobile Augmented Reality: Refers to AR use, either indoor or outdoor, where users are able to use the system in unauthored environments either by carrying the AR equipment or by remotely accessing the virtual information. Head Mounted Displays are usually worn for mobile AR, but other displays like a hand held device or portable LCD screen may be used to display virtual information.

Spatially Augmented Reality: AR displayed in non-mobile environments like a traditional office space by projectors. Displays may be on walls, desks, ceilings, people, other tangible objects, and so forth.

Virtual Retina Display: A type of display technology that works with Head Mounted Display goggles that projects an infrared ray onto the retina of the user. This projection theoretically provides clearer virtual images.

Chapter XXXV
Virtual Writing as Actual Leadership

James R. Zimmerman
James Madison University, USA

ABSTRACT

This chapter applies the evolving principles of electronic communication rhetoric and recent leadership theory to the daily practice of e-mail composition by leaders in large organizations. It articulates principles and techniques for new and midlevel leaders who most need to use e-mail. This analysis specifies opportunities and pitfalls and recommends that e-mail be a planned, significant part of an overall strategy to communicate the leader's vision while offering support and information to peers and superiors. The discussion addresses rhetorical principles and practices as they apply to the advantages and disadvantages of leadership via e-mail, and it advocates a composition process to increase effectiveness and reduce inefficiency for all levels of leadership in large organizations.

INTRODUCTION

Our use of e-mail, like that of automobiles and firearms, can be hazardous to our own health. Great leaders tend to avoid driving their own cars and carrying their own guns—they have people who do those things for them—and they tend not to send e-mail because of its inherent, highly-publicized risk factors. The obvious alternative to the challenge of using e-mail for leadership purposes is to delegate the task, but this safer path means missed opportunities, and it insulates leaders from key information and rich relationships even as it removes them from the many distractions, complications, and hazards that e-mail entails. Nevertheless, for leaders not absolutely at the very top of the organizational food chain, e-mail is the proverbial necessary evil, and it is instructive to explore its typical uses and how it can be leveraged most effectively for leadership purposes.

Contemporary leadership theory articulates a set of fairly standard general principles, but these are often inapplicable to e-mail—at least at first glance. Everything in 21st Century leadership literature indicates that each person in an organization is expected to assume some kind of leadership role, and that role presumably includes the judicious use of carefully calibrated electronic messages that are distinct from purely informational content. Given the gray areas and the high stakes involved, leadership through e-mail is a risky but required art form with ill-defined rules and rewards that stand in need of clarification, and it is crucial for the most vulnerable leaders, the newly-promoted or recently-hired, those identified as "high potential," and middle managers throughout large organizations who are expected to build and lead teams during periods of rapid change.

Leadership, when it succeeds, makes everyone better; in the presence of good leadership, the organization, the associates, and the leaders themselves thrive. E-mail, when it is at its best, is an essential component in the lifeblood of fast-paced organizations that allows them to collaborate creatively in the identification and exploitation of competitive advantages. But leadership theory and e-mail practice both include gray areas of ambiguity, uncertainty, and unreliability. Communication is the means by which leaders work their magic in person and otherwise, but, despite books and seminars devoted to the secrets of leadership, there are still mysteries about the way successful leaders communicate. Although these mysteries apply to all forms of communication, they particularly apply to electronic communication, with its odd shelf-life nature that combines the usually ephemeral with the possibly permanent. Two questions present themselves: "What can we say for sure about how leaders use e-mail effectively?" and "What aspects of e-mail composition can be learned, practiced, and improved upon?"

Often, we do not notice the little things that make leaders stand out. We are well aware of the big things, like the way the leader's image is projected, what his or her reputation is, and how a charismatic CEO can change the atmosphere in a room or an entire company. Yet it is usually the little things that set us up for noticing the larger ones. Great leaders are masters of the fine points of audience-and-purpose consciousness and, especially, message delivery (or per-

formance). In other words, leaders consciously "model" productive attitudes and behaviors in the details of their daily professional life. Subordinates presumably watch and learn. But one of the "little" things in leadership communication today is the use of e-mail, and top leaders avoid using it, except for formal, carefully-crafted, and usually lengthy announcements. Instead, it is the leadership levels below the very top rung of the executive world where we find the most useful modeling of creative and productive e-mail, but these midlevel and emerging leaders lack the usual master models to guide them. They must find their own way—and they are. A careful look at the quality of the electronic communication of a successful midlevel leader reveals a judicious use of electronic mail, with careful attention to tone, content, consistency, clarity, brevity, and audience-and-purpose precision.

MATURATION OF A FORM

Now that the novelty and freshness of e-mail is a thing of the past century, the mode is established as a routine form of *business communication*, and its consequent ubiquity is now decried much more than celebrated. Magazine articles, Web sites, and even books are now devoted to tips on e-mail, most of them obvious to everyone who has learned the hard way since the form began rearing its timid little subject lines over three decades ago. Norms of etiquette and appropriateness have converged with opportunities to transcend the traditional hard copy memo to leave us with something both more and less. For new and midlevel professionals aspiring to leadership roles, e-mail is an essential and continuous form of communication, but it can be particularly problematic and even downright dangerous. Immediacy and interactivity are obvious characteristics of the new form that give it distinct advantages, while casualness (even to the point of reckless impulsiveness), frequency, and length are obvious hazards. One thing to consider carefully and often before the unforgiving instant of touching "Send" is what many former employees of companies have learned the hard way: the best e-mail is quickly acted on and forgotten, while the worst is maliciously remembered (even immortalized), and can lead to litigation or termination.

Tina the Tech Writer in Dilbert's *Random Acts of Management* (Adams, 2000, p. 126) provides a cautionary tale that caricatures the psychological complexity of the form. Tina both resists writing and resists thinking, a terrible combination. She thinks, "Every time I send e-mail I get a stomach ache and an urge to flee the country." Her paralysis is debilitating. Ironically, her unfortunate solution is to avoid the anxiety by quickly sending an impetuous message that she immediately regrets, causing her to approach Mordac, "the preventer of information services" because she needs him "to delete it from the server." Clearly, Tina the Tech Writer would have been better off thinking more productively before she sent her message. Every author of e-mail has had this moment, but it is a moment most dramatically connected to leadership behavior.

In fact, there are worse consequences than embarrassment for leaders and their organizations when the legal environment is ignored or unclear. The American Management Association (AMA) (2004) reports that 20% of the respondents in a 2004 survey of 840 U.S. businesses "had employee e-mail or instant messages (IM) subpoenaed in the course of a lawsuit or regulatory investigation." In addition, "Another 13% have battled workplace lawsuits triggered by employee e-mail." Because of statistics like these developed by the AMA, professionals in every field are wary of committing sensitive information to e-mail. Not surprisingly, most attorneys recommend that their physician clients use e-mail only very carefully, if at all. Obviously, there are the legal issues associated with "putting something in writing," but it is more than that; time-sensitive information—especially urgent information—is not a good subject for e-mail.

E-mail is harder than it looks because it is so easy to compose and send to dozens of people, with ramifications that the sender failed to imagine. Worse still, good e-mail excites little notice, while bad e-mail can turn an organization inside-out. Like anything else involving high performance, it looks easy when it is done right, but that apparent ease belies the difficulties underneath and hides a great deal of craft and no little art. A writer can get better, but a hurried writer can also make both minor mistakes and conceptual howlers even at the stage of expert competence. In fact, one of the easiest mistakes to make is the distribution of a rash e-mail that can have the same impact as yelling "Fire!" in a packed theater. The innocent audience, absorbed in events of a typical day, can be startled into an electronic stampede. Substantial forethought and deliberate composition must precede every e-mail, however seemingly innocuous the occasion.

As Dumaine (2004, p. 1) points out, "Besides the difficulties of leading successfully in face-to-face situations, today's leaders face the additional obstacle of leading from afar. They have the task of clearly communicating their leadership and inspiring their team through writing." Bolter (2001) notes that the "implicit model" for e-mail "is not written or printed text at all, but face-to-face conversation or perhaps conversation on the telephone" (p. 73). In the case of the highest-ranking executives, however, the initiative and control is obviously one-sided, and many characteristics of traditional written text still obtain. Top leaders literally "lead" the dialogue, pre-empting all response, simply by the tone and content of their messages.

Electronic communication is already providing fascinating opportunities for highly technical research. For example, Hewlett-Packard's Tyler, Wilkinson, and Huberman investigate "the identification of leadership roles within communities" in an article entitled, "E-Mail as Spectroscopy: Automated Discovery of Community Structure Within Organizations" (Ball, 2003). Their work identifies patterns among lower-level leaders as proven by their writing roles in "communities of practice," the effective working groups in large organizations that often overlap formal departments. This is evidence of what every professional in a large organization knows: a lot of midlevel leadership is operating via e-mail dialogue, including mentoring, coaching, collaborating, and being generally supportive and encouraging with colleagues within departments and across departmental (and even organizational) lines.

Given the frequency and variety of leadership writing, it is useful to apply the principles of writing in general to the genre of the formal, semiformal, and informal professional e-mail message. In every communicative act, there is of course a presence of some sort, constituted by both content and character. In terms of the classical notion of *ethos*, the best we can do as leaders is to achieve something brief and deft, dignified yet energetic, and specifically purposeful. A vigilant consciousness of our values in terms of both the overall mission of the organization and the ethics of communication itself should ideally inform every e-mail communication.

The realm in which e-mail operates is quasipublic and semiprivate. It is a minipublic-sphere-subset that can at any moment be expanded for the inadvertent "howler" that strikes a rebellious chord somewhere among the many members of the unlucky leader's audience. More often than not, effective e-mail is more likely to occur at the one-on-one level, a much more personal venue akin to handwritten communication. Writing to a large group of recipients is often more successful in a more traditional form. The traditional memo genre still exists, and the author of an e-mail memorandum must make a conscious decision concerning the effects of embedding the memo in the body of an e-mail message or by use of an attachment. In most cases, the mechanism of the attachment provides a more formal setting, usually complete with letterhead. The embedded e-mail memo is less formal and therefore more personal, while seeming "shorter and sweeter" because of the ease of access.

With more than one audience member for an e-mail communication, a particular dynamic intrudes, which is the possibility of the other two audience members communicating, comparing notes, expanding the circle. This is much more likely than one-on-one because, with exclusive e-mail, the boss (or the sender) knows it just went to one person. And with every additional audience member the dynamic increases geometrically. President Thomas Jefferson "kept full meetings of the cabinet to a minimum to avoid argumentative debates" (Ellis, 1998, p. 225). Similarly, the use of e-mail must take into account the interpersonal and group dynamics. The decision to have a one-on-one exchange (in person, on the phone, or on e-mail) can sometimes prevent the undesirable ramifications attendant on a large recipient list. "The method of separate consultations," as Jefferson put it, "prevents disagreeable collisions" (Ellis, 1998, p. 225).

This early American example of leadership consciousness points up an enduring requirement for leaders: a pragmatic approach that is also ethical. What one might call the metapurpose of communication is always "intellectual and emotional adherence" (Perelman, 1982, p. 162). No leader should shy away from the essential act of leadership, which is the bold attempt to show their audience the way. But showing others the way has two parts: the matter and the manner. Warren Bennis observes in *On Becoming a Leader* that "integrity is the most important characteristic of a leader, and one that he or she must be prepared to demonstrate again and again" (2003, p. xiv). What this has to do with what might seem like a trivial category for a leader—the use of e-mail—may not be immediately obvious because so few top executives risk using the form. For those leaders who do take the risk, however, the reward is great—if they can express their character effectively through their e-mail messages. Personal and organizational integrity (or a suspicion of the lack thereof) permeates a leader's communicative actions. It is, simply put, the repetitive consistency as embodied in every expression or behavior. The problem with e-mail is that it can erode perceived character instantly while it can build it only in increments.

E-mail has evolved, and we have evolved with it, accumulating habits and styles and approaches as we go. Bennis (2003, p. 157) warns that we tend to be "creatures of our context, prisoners of the habits, practices, and rules that make us ineffectual" (p. 30). In *Seven Life Lessons of Chaos*, Briggs and Peat (1999) argue for an entirely new and different way of looking at organizations, dominance, and power. They urge a vision that abandons the notion of individuals functioning as "disconnected fragments" (p. 164) in favor of a point of view that moves from "an obsessive focus on control and prediction to a sensitivity toward emergence and change" (p. 165). E-mail communication, especially that inviting thoughtful dialogue, can nurture a holistic view of leadership that may well be more in tune with the interconnectedness created by the Internet.

Bennis (2003) further emphasizes the leader's "voice" as a powerful influence that can even transform the culture of an organization: "Leading through voice, inspiring through trust and empathy, does more than get people on your side." He adds, "It can change the climate enough to give people elbow room to do the right things." Ultimately, a leader's e-mail messages can add up to a powerful stream of motivation, combined of equal parts encouragement, guidance, prodding, stimulation, and teaching. To paraphrase Kennedy's definition of rhetoric, e-mail takes the form of a *dis*continuous exposition (Aristotle, 2007, p. 28). Because it can be very well-thought-out and precisely targeted—and because it can facilitate quick and convenient exchanges of ideas and information—e-mail offers leaders a tool of optimal communicative effectiveness.

RISK AND REWARD

Many top leaders in large organizations rightly view e-mail as hazardous and leave it to their subordinates. This is not an unreasonable attitude or practice, but it is a cautious approach that has its own drawbacks and potential costs, especially if a reluctance to express oneself in e-mail trickles down into the organizational ranks. Middle management can begin to perceive the lack of e-mail coming from above as evidence of a vacuum at the top. This can, in effect, model over-cautiousness, and it can engender the feeling of being left out of the loop, ignored, forgotten, or just generally shortchanged.

E-mail communication can appear very risky indeed for many reasons, including an organization's internal political dynamic that could make an electronic trail useful to a leader's detractors, opponents, or enemies. Often, out of caution, top leaders avoid e-mail entirely but find other ways of using *electronic communication*. Copies of speeches or news releases with brief introductory statements by public relations staff writers can be offered in lieu of conventional e-mail. Blogs, sometimes authored by staff writers, are appearing above the signatures of CEOs with greater and greater frequency. Invitations to send e-mail to the top executive (with standard, form-letter response and subordinate follow-up) are also becoming more popular. These tactics do not conceal the absence of an e-mail strategy completely; they merely mask it. They are carefully calibrated hedges that speak to the tremendous downside of organizational e-mail.

In the governmental realm, Richardson and Cooper write, "There is considerable debate over whether e-mail makes the job of a legislator easier…or whether e-mail has negative impacts by creating demands the legislator cannot meet" (2006, p. 116). This research identifies different target audiences, something every leader should be adept at. In this case, "insiders" and "outsiders" are the obvious general categories, with a category in the middle the authors call "intermediary groups," such as "journalists and interest groups." Richardson and Cooper (2006) find that an incentive to use e-mail varies with target groups (p. 117). The authors note that legislators have legitimate fears about using e-mail for various reasons (including confidentiality and "the expectation of an immediate reply"). They conclude, not surprisingly, that "e-mail is much more useful to communicate with some audiences than others" (p. 126). This invites the obvious and crucial question: Which audiences are more useful, and for what purposes?

One audience that is always relevant and often urgent is the general category of those who need and want to learn from a leader, and need that teaching on an ongoing basis. In terms of the greatest opportunities for leadership in general, Tichy emphasizes "the teachable point of view" (2002, p. 51). If leadership is, as the contemporary literature claims, mostly about developing leadership qualities in the very people with whom the leader is communicating, the first act of an e-mail is exemplary modeling of the process of this highly specialized form of electronic communication.

Everyone in an organization has the potential to contribute leadership when it comes to writing e-mail. This can take the form of "leading up" as well as directing subordinates, and it can be leading one or leading many. Transformational notions of leadership speak to the principles of self-expression and encouragement, if not outright inspiration. Bennis warns against a typical "supervisor's role," which tends "to limit the potential of the people who work for him" (2003, p. 45). In fact, every leadership act is an act of expanding the potential of the intended audience. It is an act of service, in other words.

In order to serve an audience, writers must of course be self-aware and self-critical about the text they generate. Dumaine (2004) offers a very helpful, if brief, overview of the importance and power of writing, but there is more to say about how e-mail for leadership purposes can be most efficiently and effectively composed. Her approach is indicative of the seriousness with which substantive e-mail communication is now treated in corporate settings.

The *tone* problems associated with e-mail are notoriously troublesome. Of all the hazards of sending e-mail, the greatest one after legal exposure is that of unreadable or misreadable tone. In order to avoid problems with tone, it is advisable to test the draft with every audience involved and any who might be shown it, even inadvertently or inappropriately. With e-mail, more than with most representative communicative actions, the Scottish proverb applies: "Every man can make a contribution, for even a fool can set an example for others" (Torricelli, 2001, p. 155). The harsh reality of unfiltered, unedited, or uncensored e-mail is something we all know about but something leaders are especially unable to afford. What might seem pertinent to one subset of an audience might strike a top leader as completely wrongheaded.

Perelman's (1982) warning about the equivocal nature of language—he says ambiguity is "the rule" (p. 44)—is one of the many cautionary guidelines that writers of important e-mail must note. Ambiguity is not, in most cases, a good thing, even if it is a condition of 21st Century organizational experience. Although leadership theorists often highlight the tolerance of ambiguity as one of the prerequisites of a successful leader, the paradox is clear: a leader has the daily, often hourly, duty to clarify matters for peers and subordinates. This is exaggerated when it comes to e-mail because of the tonal imprecision so characteristic of the medium. Any doubt felt by the composer of an e-mail is worth honoring, especially when the writer senses certain telltale warning signs. Among these are the awareness of intended boldness, a temptation to send unrevised text, an inclination to hit "Send" immediately, a desire to write at great length, or an unusual sense of pride in the product. E-mail is not the place where the expressive leader should attempt to articulate visionary thoughts or respond with the full force of the leaderly character to rapidly-developing events.

Above all, if a writer is thinking (with Tina the Tech Writer), "My derogatory and condescending e-mail will set things right" (Adams, 2000, p. 126), that writer needs to think again. Furthermore, the importance of reading and rereading a draft is impossible to overemphasize. Spell checks are the first and last order of business (and they are advisable for every draft in between), but even correct spelling cannot save a misconceived e-mail. Trusted advisers are essential; perhaps even a trusted ghost writer, who then allows the leader to take the more rational role of editor.

A further paradox of the genre is that it can be a terrific waste of time, both for the writer and the recipient. "Work expands so as to fill the time available for its completion" wrote Parkinson in the first sentence of his classic work (1957, p. 1). An awareness of the relativity of time spent to time available is an admirable approach to all forms of communication, but it applies to e-mail at two levels. First, it warns against the unnecessarily long, unedited composition; second, it warns against unending rewriting and editing. Two rules that writers who successfully exploit e-mail for leadership purposes follow are, "State the most important thing first," and, "Stop as soon as possible after stating the most important thing." Just as composing a single e-mail can consume hours of the unsuspecting (subsequently hapless) leader's time, so can the leader's boss note that the author has too much time on their hands. Dumaine (2004) promises that any leader can learn to write effectively, in e-mail and other forms, but that effectiveness comes with practice, discipline, and any number of minor failures along the way.

Ultimately, the leadership challenge with e-mail is one of technology meeting human nature, given rapidly changing technical and cultural situations. Text messaging is the telegrammatic version of e-mail, and it appears—at this writing—less useful for leadership purposes because of its extreme compression and rapid rhythm. Bennis (2003) asks, rhetorically, "What problems can technology solve, unless the users of that technology have first grappled with the primary questions?" (p. 73). This suggests that the "primary question" involved in the case of e-mail

is the core question of human communication, particularly written communication. Unless the user understands what leadership communication in general (and writing in particular) can do in the first place, that user cannot effectively employ electronic communication as a means of leadership. This comes back to the basics of classic rhetoric; audience and purpose is everything. In the case of e-mail for leadership purposes, it is important to identify the range of possible purpose even before a specific audience is targeted.

CHOOSING E-MAIL PURPOSES AND AUDIENCES

The range of communication *purposes* is broad, but the overall set of purposes appears to remain constant. Leadership purposes, on the other hand, are evolving. Instead of issuing a command, a directive, or an ultimatum, today's leaders are more likely to be powerful persuaders, energetic motivators, and generous mentors. However, old habits die hard, and the supervisory, the managerial, and the administrative inclinations of leaders persist. The most troublesome confusion nowadays may well be with leadership and administration. Leadership is different from administration—more complex, more delicate, less certain, and much more important. Leadership power can be easily eroded even after it is painstakingly built. Sustaining leadership is a job in itself because of the inherent suspicions of the self-perceived underling in all of us. The effective power of a leader in the contemporary American organizational setting is tentative, provisional, and contingent. Careless use of e-mail can undermine a lot of patient, painstaking work.

Significant purposes for a leader's e-mail communication include persuading, motivating, inspiring, guiding, directing, correcting, evaluating, recognizing, thanking, informing, reminding, agenda-setting, prioritizing, provoking responses, planting ideas, and asking questions. In each case, the conscious awareness of purpose is crucial during the composing process of the e-mail. Whatever choice a leader makes for a given purposeful communication, that choice is likely to have a more powerful result if it is dedicated to a specific, limited point. In e-mail communication, a single important point is the best approach. Rather than a laundry list, one or two powerfully articulated points will have more impact than any five or ten carefully enunciated points. It is clear that one source of confusion when it comes to purpose is the tendency to settle for a term or phrase that is in fact a topic or subject rather than a purpose. Robbins, writing in the "Harvard Business School Working Knowledge for Business Leaders Archive," makes the point very powerfully: "Use a subject line to *summarize*, not *describe*" (2007). This is harder than it sounds, but it is a principle and a practice that turns out to be tremendously effective when it comes to day-to-day e-mail leadership.

One of the most important generic leadership purposes is encouraging subordinates to speak up. E-mail is especially suited to this kind of personal encouragement. Pressure for unanimity in meetings can be stifling (Perlow& Williams, 2003, p. 54). High-level leadership is often about encouraging (or giving the courage to) lower-level leaders to make the most of their opportunities within the organization. It is about motivating in some deep sense, not just cheerleading. Trust is involved, and something substantive in the way of attitude, vision, and long-term strategic thinking. As Noel Tichy (2002) emphasizes, strong and effective leaders have a "teachable point of view." One approach to teaching is to raise significant, compelling questions. A relevant question that could be profitably answered by an individual or a group of people offers a useful e-mail leadership purpose, as long as that question is phrased in a manner that does not threaten or induce low-level anxiety.

The best e-mail leadership purposes—and often the least used—involve any inclination to encourage, motivate, guide, praise, thank, or in some way affirm and re-affirm the leader's support

for and confidence in the recipient. Ultimately, as all leadership literature worth reading will remind us, the fundamental job of the leader is the job of developing people in the workplace. Great leaders, we are told over and over, make the people around them better by encouraging them to learn, be proactive, take risks, and help others in the organization and even in the community at large. Because of the unremitting stress associated with the faster and faster pace of business communication, leaders, like anyone else, need to remind themselves from time to time that they sincerely care about the members of any given audience they address, in person or otherwise. E-mail, like interstate traffic, can become a blur of activity that seems to involve faceless, nameless, unrelated strangers.

A COMPOSITION APPROACH

Mastering the realm of e-mail requires discipline, and most leaders have discovered their own methods of confronting their jammed inboxes. Typical of top leaders who actually use e-mail is Jim Estill (2005), the CEO of Synnex Canada Limited, who follows a "two-minute rule" when it comes to e-mail: if he can deal with it in that time, he does—otherwise he ignores it. This representative executive audience suggests the importance of brevity and precision in terms of the message, and it is a necessary compositional principle, especially for lower-level leaders aspiring to "lead up."

For new and aspiring leaders without a consistent, reliable approach to composing e-mail, the following description of a process adapted from the work of Rodgers and Zimmerman (2007) will provide considerable help if it is assiduously applied over a one- or two-week period. The essence of the method is the fundamental rhetorical analysis of audience-and-purpose calibration augmented by a precise awareness of limited and specific message content and further supplemented by a final check in the form of a brief series of questions. The key to using this approach is a hard-headed awareness of the limits of any purposeful communication. An accurate assessment of human nature in the context of workplace realities will always come up against the extremely modest capacities that message recipients will have regarding their understanding, acceptance, retention, and motivation.

One way to maximize the chances that e-mail communication will be both appropriate and powerful is to embrace "communication points," sometimes called key or core messages, takeaways, or simply main points. Essentially, the question to ask is, why send an e-mail? In other words, what action are you trying to stimulate, what attitude are you trying to inspire, or what information are you trying to impart?

Estelle Rodgers, President of Estelle Rodgers and Associates, has coached top corporate leaders for 25 years and helped guide them through various technological transitions, including e-mail. She observes that e-mail is an especially difficult problem for leaders because it is so easy to use, so difficult to use well, and so permanent (Zimmerman, 2006). However, she situates it in a broader context of leadership challenges. "Leadership is primarily about great communication, which is guided by the discipline of knowing your audience and committing to a purpose," she says. "People in new leadership positions may make mistakes using e-mail, sometimes because they've reacted too quickly, or too tersely." Rodgers notes that new leaders sometimes fail to ask enough questions to understand the complexities of the issues. Often, she suggests, new leaders are better off relying on face-to-face meetings or, failing that, relying on telephone conversations, in order to take full advantage of the broader range of verbal and non-verbal communication these forms offer.

Once e-mail is determined to be the certain preference, Pascal's famous observation about needing more time to write a shorter letter applies to e-mail, but the good news is that the time involved is not substantial, and, better yet, it diminishes with practice. The process of com-

posing communication points, explained below, looks like this in outline:

1. Brainstorm all possible messages for the designated audience and purpose.
2. Combine the related elements in the list.
3. Rank order the elements.
4. Convert them to brief communication points.

By listing all of the possible goals a leader is trying to achieve with a given e-mail, and then matching them to all of the sub-audiences and secondary audiences addressed or potentially reached, a leader can identify the whole spectrum of the leadership inclination. This is best accomplished by a brainstorming session of a few minutes in which every conceivable message is listed, including everything the writer wishes the audience to understand, accept, remember, or do. Often, such a list can reach two dozen items. Next, these quickly-and randomly-generated items can be combined wherever possible; typically, a list of a dozen or two can be reduced by combination to as few as three or four groupings of clearly-related thoughts.

At this point the exercise becomes one of limiting and ranking. The most useful question is, "If I had only one point I could make to my audience, what would it be?" This becomes the raw material for the first communication point, and the ranking continues in this fashion. Once ranked, the raw material can be composed into brief memorable sentences that embody the messages inherent in the ranked groupings. The spoken word and the written word, though distinctly different in sentence structure, tone, and word choice, are related closely enough so that this exercise generates what might be called message concepts. These are of great use to the resourceful leader because they can be almost endlessly varied in performance. In person, by phone, on paper, and in e-mail, these message concepts can be delivered repeatedly without being repetitive.

The final stage of the composition process is the revision. Every sophisticated writer revises, and the writer of e-mail is no different. This is a fundamental revision effort, not just a proofreading and machine-based spelling check. In order to maximize the effectiveness of the communication points, however, one significant stage remains: "anticipated audience reactions."

The first part of the final stage involves a role-playing exercise that lists every conceivable reaction—spoken or unspoken, positive or negative, trivial or significant—that any of the audience members might have to the composed message and its embodied communication points. Following that exhaustive list, which will take no more than 1 to 5 minutes, the writer must consider the possible revisions necessary or desirable. This is no different from the exacting discipline required of any leadership communication in principle, but different in form and dynamic (time frame, setting, occasion). By brainstorming a list of all the conceivable reactions to the draft communication points, the leader learns to listen to the audience in advance, in order to develop a deep sense of the effects of the draft communication. Rodgers refers to what she calls "anticipated audience reaction" as "the single most important principle embodied in the single most effective technique" that corporate leaders learn from her. After the list of reactions is completed, the loop continues: revise, retest, revise again, retest. Within days, leaders master this process and begin to perform it routinely upon all of their communicative actions, including voice mail, leading meetings, speeches, one-on-one negotiations, and, of course, e-mail.

When it comes to multiple communication points, in the case of a speech, Rodgers recommends that all of the ranked items can be included, but in the case of e-mail, it is advisable to restrict the communication to only the first, or at most, the first and second. At this point, the opportunity involves choosing the language in which to communicate the core message. By writing the message in appropriate and memorable terms, the writer has achieved a draft of a communication point.

William Faulkner is sometimes credited for a well-known dictum familiar to thinking people concerned with communication: "I don't know what I think until I read what I said" (Bennis, 2003, p. 42). It is a phenomenon too familiar to be false. The most important thing for the writer to remember is never to send a composition until the writer has taken the time to read and understand what it is that that the writer has evidently thought, based on what is on the screen.

Many e-mail drafts will properly go unsent. Fortunately, there is an upside to drafting e-mail that goes unsent. Leaders can learn from the composition process. Just like a good journal, e-mail drafts can be sources of insight that may reveal emotions, hidden agendas, obscure patterns, and new opportunities for problem-identification and problem-solving. For leaders, the primary job is to express themselves only after they fully understand who they are, what they think, and how their audiences will perceive them and their message.

CONCLUSION

The combination of easy access, *tonal indeterminacy*, and the potential for permanence is a volatile one. Discretion is the better part of valor, and leadership and e-mail are a mixture that tempts the valorous but rewards the discreet. Too many actual and potential leaders fail to distinguish discretion and non-participation, or confuse encouragement with Frankfurt's (2005) memorable technical term, "bullshit." Even though the contemporary philosopher ultimately equates "sincerity" and "bullshit," leaders must seize the proverbial bull by the horns and be bold enough to offer sincere and even general encouragement when it is called for by the intensely pressurized atmospheres now prevalent in large organizations. E-mail is a uniquely valuable, expressive tool if used in the frequency, length, and audience-orientation for which it is best suited. Generally speaking, there is a curious symmetry at work:

top leaders, whose challenge it is to control the climate of an organization, and low-level associates, who are interested in "leading up," should both use e-mail sparingly and more formally, with greater attention to composition, detail, and polish. Midlevel leaders involved in traditional organizational efforts or informal communities of practice ought to feel free to express themselves with greater frequency and informality.

The paradox in formal leadership applications of e-mail, then, is that, too often, the higher up the chain of command, the less visible the leader, and the less directly present to those being led. The lower the leaders, the more safely present they can be in e-mail, and the more frequent and direct the probability of uncomplicated, productive contact.

Great leaders help shape the careers of their subordinates, in every sense, and then get out of the way. But leadership is not a short-term venture; changing people's minds and behaviors takes time and perseverance. Gardner (2006) notes that "most mind change is gradual," and when it happens it is often not conscious within the individual, with a "pronounced tendency to slip back to earlier ways of thinking." Because of these factors, e-mail offers a special opportunity for repetition, amplification, and re-inforcement of key points during times of intense organizational change.

Often, for everybody who finds e-mail a continuous presence in their professional day, the best leadership use of e-mail may be in thoughtfully drafting it and deliberately deciding *not* to send it. Future studies of leadership e-mail will no doubt rely heavily on anecdotal evidence, as do most studies of the art of leadership, but they will also continue to find evolving patterns of contact among similarly situated midlevel leaders. E-mail applications must be used sparingly, if only as an act of respect for the tremendous burden of electronic messages every professional employee confronts.

As everyone engaged in leadership endeavors eventually comes to understand, a communication strategy is essential to any meaningful, sustainable success. E-mail, as a potentially flexible, powerful, highly focused tactical communication mode, must fit into the overall strategy. For every individual leader, the question about electronic communication in general—and e-mail in particular—becomes, "What are the most effective strategic and tactical uses of messages of this kind?" The use of e-mail should be part of an overall communication strategy; every e-mail should fit into that design, and every commitment to e-mail communication should be deemed sustainable at the outset. E-mail that is not easily and immediately understood or not essential to the overall vision of the leader's communicative character is e-mail best left unsent. Sometimes writing and not sending is an important, if unseen exercise in leadership. Indeed, the higher the ratio of composed and unsent messages is to the total of sent messages, the more likely it is that the writer is on the way to optimizing the use of e-mail for leadership purposes. Ultimately, the highest level of e-mail performance for leadership purposes is achieved when the writer can rapidly consider and reject unnecessary compositions, on the one hand, while learning to quickly compose brief and effective messages, on the other. E-mail for leadership purposes is an art characterized by precision and simplicity, and its most adept practitioners frequently are known more for their character than their compositional skills.

REFERENCES

Adams, S. (2000). *Dilbert: Random acts of management.* Kansas City, MO: Andrews McMeel Publishing.

American Management Association. (2004). 2004 Workplace e-mail and instant messaging survey summary. Retrieved November 16, 2007, from http://www.amanet.org/research/pdfs/IM_2004_Summary.pdf

Aristotle. (2007). *On rhetoric: A theory of civic discourse* (2nd ed., G. Kennedy Trans.). New York: Oxford University Press.

Ball, P. (2003, March 20). *Email reveals real leaders: Network analysis maps companies' informal structure.* Retrieved November 16, 2007, from http://www.nature.com/news/2003/030317-5.html

Bennis, W. (2003). *On becoming a leader* (Rev. ed.). Cambridge, MA: Perseus Publishing.

Bolter, J. D. (2001). *Writing space: Computers, hypertext, and the remediation of print* (2nd ed.). Mahweh, NJ: Erlbaum.

Briggs, J., & Peat, F. D. (1999). *Seven life lessons of chaos: Spiritual wisdom from the science of change.* New York: Harper.

Dumaine, D. (2004, December). Leadership in writing. *T+D, 58*(12), 52-55. ProQuest. Carrier (James Madison University) Library, Harrisonburg, Virginia. Retrieved November 16, 2007, from http://proquest.umi.com/pqdweb?index

Ellis, J. J. (1998). *American sphinx: The character of Thomas Jefferson.* New York: Vintage.

Estill, J. (2005). *2 minute rule and slush folders.* Retrieved November 16, 2007, from http://www.jimestill.com_2005_09_01_archive.html

Frankfurt, H. G. (2005). *On bullshit.* Princeton, NJ: Princeton University Press.

Gardner, H. (2006). *Changing minds: The art and science of changing our own and other people's minds.* Boston: Harvard Business School Press.

Parkinson, C. N. (1957). *Parkinson's law.* New York: Ballantine.

Perelman, C. (1982). *The realm of rhetoric.* Notre Dame, IN: University of Notre Dame Press.

Perlow, L., & Williams, S. (2003, May). Is silence killing your company? *Harvard Business Review, 81*(5), 52-58.

Richardson, L. E.-Jr., & Cooper, C. A. (2006). E-mail communication and the policy process in the state legislature. *The Policy Studies Journal, 34*(1), 113-29.

Robbins, S. (2004). Harvard Business School working knowledge for business leaders archive. Retrieved November 16, 2007, from http://hbswk.hbs.edu/archive/4438.html

Rodgers, E., & Zimmerman, J. R. (2007). *The communication effectiveness seminar handbook* (4th ed.). Columbus, OH: Estelle Rodgers & Associates.

Tichy, N. M., & Cohen, E. (2002). *The leadership engine: How winning companies build leaders at every level.* New York: Harper Collins.

Torricelli, R. G. (Ed.). (2001). *Quotations for public speakers: A historical, literary, & political anthology.* New Brunswick, NJ: Rutgers University Press.

Zimmerman, J. R. (2006, September). Interview with Estelle Rodgers, President of Estelle Rodgers & Associates, Columbus, OH.

KEY TERMS

Anticipated Audience Reaction: A method of testing drafts of a composition that depends on the writer's ability to imagine what any audience member might say or think in response to the draft.

Brainstorming: A rapid-fire free-associational listing of items according to a specific purpose.

Communication Point: A single-sentence meta-statement of a core message composed in memorable terms that can be adaptable and richly, productively repeatable.

Community of Practice: An effective working group that transcends traditional organizational lines.

Leader: Anyone with formal or informal power or influence over the attitudes and behaviors of others in an organization.

Leadership: the art of setting standards, creating a community and climate, and developing short- and long-term plans for an organization and its employees, especially in times of rapid organizational change.

Chapter XXXVI
Business Process Reuse and Standardization with P2P Technologies

José A. Rodrigues Nt
COPPE—Federal University of Rio de Janeiro, Brazil

Jano Moreira de Souza
COPPE—Federal University of Rio de Janeiro, Brazil

Geraldo Zimbrão
COPPE—Federal University of Rio de Janeiro, Brazil

Geraldo Xexéo
COPPE—Federal University of Rio de Janeiro, Brazil

Mutaleci Miranda
Military Institute of Engineering, Brazil

ABSTRACT

Business Process Management (BPM) brings together the idea of effectively managing organizations and properly using Information Technology to fulfill organizations' needs. For this purpose, BPM systems are largely used nowadays. However, most process models are started from scratch, not having reuse promoted. Sometimes, large enterprises have the same business process implemented in a variety of ways due to differences in their departmental cultures or environments, even when using a unique integrated system. Additionally, although technology plays an important role in actually improving organizations, the human factor is still fundamental, since any improvement attempt goes through cultural changes. In this chapter, a peer-to-peer (P2P) tool is proposed as a way to cooperatively develop business processes models, minimizing the time needed to develop such models, reducing the differences among similar processes conducted in distinct organizational units, enhancing the quality of models, promoting reuse, and distributing knowledge.

INTRODUCTION

Business Process Management (BPM) brings together the idea of effectively managing organizations[1] and properly using Information Technology to fulfill organizational needs. Although technology plays an important role in actually improving organizations, the human factor is still the fundamental one, since any improvement attempt goes through cultural changes. Organizational culture is a very complex subject. It is usual to find organizations that have the same activity performed differently in each of their units. Although BPM can help standardize such behaviors, a brute force approach is not always effective or advisable.

We believe that a cooperative approach for creating and sharing business processes can greatly reduce differences among organizations' units and promote reuse. In addition, using a distributed implementation, we can provide the organizations with a low cost tool. These characteristics, besides being beneficial for large organizations, can make BPM accessible for small and medium businesses (SMB) where the cost of traditional BPM tools can make it impossible for them to accrue such benefits.

Additionally, the approach proposed here also allows for the creation of modeling communities inside and outside organizations. Finally, since modelers can work independently of any organization, the tool may also be used on an individual basis, as an open repository and reuse promotion mechanism.

Addressing these issues, we propose the use of a peer-to-peer (P2P) tool to exchange processes models, promoting a "natural" standardization. The proposed tool also allows for the enhancement of existing models, through an evolutionary approach that helps in organizational learning (Liebowitz, 1999).

The chapter is organized in the following sections: Background, with an overview of business process management and some general related concerns, including some social and human aspects;

Business Process Collaborative Modeling Issues, where we present an overview of technologies closely related to BP modeling and collaboration; A Tool for Collaborative Modeling, which presents a tool that can help in collaborative modeling and discusses some important aspects of virtual collaboration; and Future Trends and Conclusion.

BACKGROUND

BPM has gained popularity and strength in the last few years. The factors that have most contributed to this have two different origins. On the management side, the failure or saturation of previous approaches to optimize work on organizations, and, on the Information Technology (IT) side, the inefficiency of traditional approaches for systems modeling in fully addressing the needs of most organizations, especially on aligning the development's final product with business objectives (Chan, 2002), have contributed to this picture.

On the Management side, efforts that begun with Taylor works have evolved through statistical techniques, as viewed by Deming and others, and Total Quality Management (TQM), to Business Process Reengineering (BPR). BPR, not focused only on production itself, later turned out to be the motivation for workforce reduction, labeled as process optimization. Considering that the human factor is the main force for any organization improvement or cultural change, it did not take long to show BPR weaknesses (Jeston & Nelis, 2006). Recent changes have taken some organizations to the last hype—Six Sigma—another statistical approach to reaching process perfection, or "zero defects."

BPM, independent of any specific methodology or technique, brings to the scene a more holistic approach. In a sense, it considers the essence of the above-mentioned approaches—process management—and the need for a broader view to improve organization effectiveness and efficiency. To implement BPM, we will find the need for business process modeling.

In most situations, either it is unfeasible to test new ideas in existing systems due to risks and cost, or the system does not exist and so does not allow for direct test of new ideas. In the first case, system modification can have a great impact on the organization, and, in general, the risks should be avoided. On the latter, it is usually not worthwhile to build a new system and later discover that it was built the wrong way. Therefore, models come into place as a way to test, with low cost, modifications in existing systems or the various alternatives to build a new one (Law & Kelton, 1982).

Considering a business process perspective, models allows for the understanding, control, and adjustment of organization processes. In the framework of BPM, such activities are oriented towards the alignment with the organization's strategy and objectives. A lack of such an approach may take the organization to "local optimums," losing the big picture (Harmon, 2003).

Despite the great benefits process modeling can bring to management (Harmon, 2003), IT is considered a fundamental factor for implementing BPM. Considering the IT side, modeling the business process can greatly facilitate requirements gathering, still viewed as the source for most problems with projects (Hofmann & Lehner, 2001). Moreover, the work on Model Driven Architecture (MDA) (Miller & Mukerji, 2003), enhancing the value of Platform Independent Models (PIM), also contributes to leveraging the importance of process modeling. MDA focuses on automating application construction from application's conceptual model.

Since we can understand the modeling activity as a creative process, we shall recognize the importance of the relationship of the modeler with its environment and with others peers. More specifically, complex design processes require more knowledge that is usually possessed by any single designer. Designers can use books, articles, and so forth, to acquire knowledge. Nonetheless, this can also be done by looking at previous solutions devised by other peers (Arias, Eden, Fischer, Gorman, & Scharff, 2000).

There exist several common, or similar, processes in organizations. For instance, most organizations have their own procurement and acquisition processes. Sometimes, large organizations have this same process defined in different ways among their units. We believe a cooperative approach to modeling can drastically enhance standardization and reduce models' development time. However, this cooperative approach may be achieved through the participation of known or unknown modelers in the virtual model-sharing network. In such a scenario, mechanisms for preventing misuse of the network and to guarantee the quality of the shared resources are essential.

This is especially the case when there is not a community of practice (Wenger, 1998) supporting the model-exchange network. In this case, there ought to be some means to attest the reputation of a participant and the quality of its shared work. Reputation and ranking methods may be used to do so.

BUSINESS PROCESS COLLABORATIVE MODELING ISSUES

A large amount of common business processes do exist among organizations. Due to the increase of attention to business process management (Smith & Fingar, 2003a), organizations tend to fully model their processes. Many times, though, models are developed from scratch, with little attention to reuse or process standardization (Rodrigues Nt., Souza, Zimbrao, Xexeo, Neves, & Pinheiro, 2006).

In large enterprises, where several nonintegrated systems exist (May, 2003), differences among their units or departments can be reduced if there is some way of standardizing their common processes. Process standardization may be achieved through cooperative modeling and design. A cooperative approach can also ease the modeling task among different enterprises, where process integration may be needed.

The adoption of standardized processes is expected to enhance efficiency and performance, for example, streamlining the supply-chain process (May, 2003), while facilitating reuse and reducing modeling costs. In the networked economy, flexibility and reuse deserve special attention (Smith & Fingar, 2003b).

The Modeling Scenario

Making organizations adopt a standard process is not an easy task. This task gets even harder if these organizations are part of different companies. Cross-organizational business process modeling, besides demanding special care, especially due to privacy and competitive constraints, can be a complex job (Lippe, Greiner, & Barros, 2005).

The Business Process Cooperative Editor (BPCE) (Rodrigues Nt., Souza et al., 2006) focuses on the improvement of models, the optimization of modeling activities, the reuse of models among organizations, and the promotion of organizational learning.

UML for BP Modeling

There exists many modeling notations/languages available that can be used for process modeling. Some of them are developed in the context of proprietary tools and others are published as standards. In the latter case, the Business Process Modeling Notation (Business Process Modeling Notation, 2006) and the Unified Modeling Language (UML 2.0 Superstructure, v2.0 Formal, 2005), are at the center of the stage. Although the earlier may provide some advantages for representing model semantics and mapping to execution languages, such as the Business Process Execution Language for Web Services (BPEL4WS), (Business Process Execution, 2005), the latter is widely adopted for software modeling and suitable for business process modeling. For business process modeling, the UML Activity Diagrams are usually chosen. Therefore, we decided to use

Activity Diagrams for business process modeling due to the following reasons:

- Being a standard;
- Wide use of XMI for model interchange in CASE tools; and
- IT background of targeted users.

For the purpose of BPCE, we handle whole diagrams or fragments as models. This way, a user who wants to develop a new model can do it by assembling existing diagrams or parts of existing diagrams to compose a model that suits the established requirements.

Model Exchange

Model exchange can be accomplished in a variety of ways. Actually, the lack of one widely adopted standard format is still recognized as a problem for the advancement of BPM. It is desirable that an interchange format presents the following characteristics: readability, ease of implementation, platform independence, efficiency, free availability, and support of standards (Mendling, Neumann, & Nuttgens, 2005).

The XML Process Description Language (XPDL) (Workflow Process Definition, 2005) would be a good choice. Besides being supported by a number of tools, it is capable of handling both UML models (based on the Meta Object Facility—MOF) and Business Process Modeling Notation (BPMN) models.

However, the XML Metadata Interchange Format (XMI), proposed by OMG (MOF 2.0/XMI Mapping Specification, 2005) is adequate for the purpose of our tool and appears as a natural choice. XMI was chosen, mainly, for two reasons:

- The modeling media was the activity diagram, from UML; and
- Extensions of the work to deal with software models or other XMI based tasks would be facilitated (Rodrigues, Rodrigues Nt., Mello, & Porto, 2003).

Although restricted to interchanging diagrams based on MOF, also from OMG, it is absolutely platform independent (MOF 2.0/XMI Mapping Specification, 2005). It also shall be noted that BPMN has not yet defined a language for diagram interchange (Business Process Modeling Notation, 2006).

The P2P Approach

A Peer-to-Peer (P2P) system is a computational network application in which each node is autonomously managed and can contribute with its resources to the distributed execution of tasks requested by other nodes.

The properties expected from an ideal P2P system are decentralization, fault-tolerance, and scalability. Decentralization means that no specific node is entirely responsible for essential system functions. However, in practice, some real systems accept a certain degree of centralization to improve their performances. Fault-tolerance is a consequence of decentralization, once the distributed responsibility for system's functions precludes that a small number of individual failures impair the system behavior as a whole. Finally, scalability can be obtained because each node that enters the network can offer additional computational resources to increase system capacity overall.

The three main application areas for P2P systems are resource sharing, collaboration, and hive computing. Resource sharing occurs when each system's node uses data storage space, storage data, processing power, or bandwidth from other nodes to reach its individual goals while, at the same time, offering its own resources to those other nodes.

Collaboration occurs when users' groups are composed to execute tasks of common interest and employ the system to share resources and perform communication and coordination, possibly in a synchronous manner.

In hive computing, a single complex computational problem, whose treatment in a centralized fashion is not viable, is partitioned and distributed to the system's nodes.

To evaluate the adequacy of a P2P approach, an analysis of the proposed system was conducted, based on the work of Roussopoulos, Baker, Rosenthal, Giuli, Maniatis, and Mogul (2005). An evaluation, considering their proposed decision-tree, led us to the conclusion that a P2P approach was suitable to our problem.

Summarizing, the use of a P2P approach is justified, in this case, by the following.

- Budget constraints: the low cost entry of P2P systems allows for its use in any organization and also by independent modelers, starting their own cooperation network;
- High relevance of the resources being shared, to the participants;
- Noncritical nature: the shared models are used as basis for the development of new models and, consequently, the system is not considered critical, since the modeled business is not actually running on it;
- Abundance of process models on different and, sometimes, unrelated sources, which could jeopardize a centralized approach; and
- The possibility of an independent, sometimes "unknown" modeler, to participate autonomously in such a cooperation network, posting its contributions was considered.

Bearing in mind that a P2P system depends on the actual participation of its peers, the reuse of someone's models builds up his reputation, and cooperation in the form of models' evaluation adds up to the evaluator's reputation, we believe that introducing a formal reputation mechanism would motivate the cooperation of peers. However, free riders might well exist in this scenario (Parameswaran, Susarla, & Whinston, 2001).

A TOOL FOR COLLABORATIVE MODELING

BPCE is a P2P tool that allows modelers to share their models freely. It is implemented as a four-layer architecture, as described:

1. Infrastructure layer: implemented by COP-PEER (Miranda, Xexeo, & Souza, 2006), it is responsible for the P2P primitives;
2. Repository layer: responsible for storing local models;
3. Searcher layer: has the mechanisms for finding models—the Searcher—which can be aggregated to build a new model, using COP-PEER resources. It also includes a simple tool for visualizing model elements—the Viewer—prior to being selected for use in the Editor; and
4. Editor layer: holds the graphical environment with resources to modeling—the Editor—including assembling obtained model elements collected from the network of agents.

Figure 1 shows the conceived architecture.

Published models are stored in local repositories—the search space for COPPEER. Whenever a user wants to build a new model, a search can be performed on the Searcher, which uses COPPEER for it. The search returns pointers to model elements.[2] Basic information about found elements is based on their XMI and additional attached data. That basic information is displayed to the user in

Figure 1. BPCE architecture

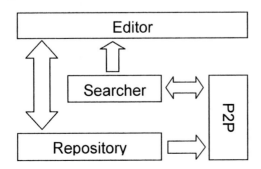

Figure 2. Modeling cycle

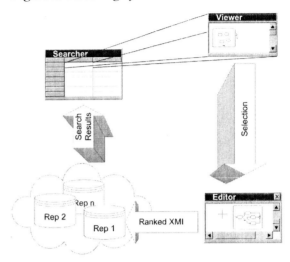

the Searcher window, where model visualization can be requested. As soon as the local repository receives enough data to display graphically any information about the selected model element, a Viewer, which is part of the Searcher, may be started.

The user can briefly check the found model, using the Viewer. If the user decides to use a model, it can be transferred to the Editor, either to a new Editor window or to an already open one.

On the Editor, the user can modify the received element, by editing it or by aggregating it to other existing elements. A new version of the same element, or a new one, can then be directly added to the repository, through a publishing mechanism.

An overview of a basic modeling cycle is shown in Figure 2.

COPPEER: A P2P Framework

The bottom layer, which COPPEER (Miranda et al., 2006) provides, takes care of model exchange and allows for the search of models or models' elements related to desired subjects.

The COPPEER framework is an environment for developing and running P2P applications. It is a research project developed at the Database Lab of the Federal University of Rio de Janeiro

Graduate School and Research in Engineering (UFRJ/COPPE). It implements a P2P environment under the Complex Adaptive Systems (CAS) paradigm (Tan, Wen, & Awad, 2005).

Thanks to emergence, complex systems with adaptive behavior can be composed from a number of simple software agents, which are inexpensive to develop and maintain. In COPPEER, the key to achieve this property is the use of shared spaces (Eugster, Felber, Guerraoui, & Kermarrec, 2003), to implement agents' communication. COPPEER offers as communication infrastructure a network of shared spaces, which alleviates developers from caring about program's objects hierarchy, management of local or remote references between agents, and multithreading programming intricacies. Each shared space stores data items written by agents, and notifies other agents interested in data matching these items. Besides that, COPPEER supports mechanisms to exchange data among shared spaces without agents' intervention.

The Model Editor

The Editor provides resources to assemble and edit model elements. Models prepared on the Editor are published as XMI files.

Since the appraisals of imported models are done after building a new model, the Editor has a function to publish a model. The published model becomes available on the model repository for use by other peers. Publishing includes the creation of a Model Object (MO), by the Editor, which aggregates a small image of the published model, its score, and its information vector. Such a vector is produced by the XMI representation of the model, discarding the header, common to all published files.

Additionally, when a model is published, the evaluation of the models used to compose it is done. Later on, if the user wants to evolve a published model, the Editor asks for a new evaluation, only if new models are imported and added to the model.

Retrieving Models

Searching the Models' Space is performed using a simple search mechanism, based on the vector model (Baeza-Yates & Ribeiro-Neto, 1999). Each new model has its vector calculated, inserted on an inverted index, and preserved, in MO's, created to later use by the Searchers and Viewers.

Since XML's tags are also used when calculating vectors, the search can further be directed to specific types of elements, according to activity diagram schema. For example, it can be constrained to *ActivityGroup* (UML 2.0 Superstructure, 2005), by simply adding the term to the query.

Considering the search space can be populated by a large amount of models, user can specify the maximum distance allowed from the query vector, for retrieved models. Retrieved models are presented, ordered by similarity to the query, with their respective scores.

Ranking Models

In an environment with an expected growing number of choices, ranking turns out to be helpful in optimizing user's work. When there are several models dealing with the same subject, it is to the benefit of the users that some kind of ranking exists, to facilitate the choice of any particular option. The idea of cooperatively filtering the available models can be applied to such a context (Goldberg, Nichols, Oki, & Terry, 1992; Resnick, Iacovou, Suchak, Bergstrom, & Riedl, 1994).

A model's score is an indicator of the usefulness of the model, based on its usage. Since we believe that, at least at the beginning of the model's life, the reputation of the author is a good indicator of model's quality, to calculate the score, an assessment of the author's reputation is required. The reputation indicator used in BPCE tries, through tracking models usage, to indicate the quality of the models produce by each user. The rationale behind this is that if models produced by an author are always well used, this information can be used as an indicator of his capacity as a modeler.

While maintaining scores or reputations on a traditional distributed system could be done using a central server, this is not the case in a P2P environment. Some approaches have been already explored (Aberer & Despotovic, 2001) and show that in P2P environments, the maintenance of evaluations is not trivial. We assumed, for the sake of reducing complexity, that minor differences among peers' local values are acceptable.

Most P2P reputation systems have two kinds of problems:

- Reputation is based on just a few peers evaluations, losing the big picture; or
- Reputation is based on all peers' evaluations, unnecessarily raising the traffic on the network (Kamvar, Schlosser, & Garcia-Molina, 2003).

The proposed algorithm is not susceptible to the above problems, since the reputation is build up considering all uses of a modeler's model and just this, that is, it does not require the participation of all peers on the network, but just the peers that actually manipulated the model.

Models are ranked according to their utilization by other modelers. When a retrieved model is used, that is, the user decides, when using the Viewer, to export it to the Editor, it receives points. Those few points granted, mean that the model has, at least, gotten the attention of the user; however, this mechanism is not actually a way to reward the model, but to discard the ones that are not even looked at by users. Later, when a new model is created on the Editor, the user is presented with a list of the models imported by him, where he marks the models that were actually used to derive the new one. Those selected models receive some additional points, to leverage their ranking, according to their utilization on the new model, that is, the user can state that an imported model had low, medium, or high influence on the new developed model. The imported models' received points are weighted by the appraising

modeler's reputation. Again, we believe that the capacity of the modeler can stand as a measure of his ability to judge others' models.

Synthesizing, a new model has its initial points, based on the score of the models used in its composition and the reputation of its author. Then, it keeps receiving points during its life, according to its utilization on the development of new models.

A modeler's reputation is calculated based on the reutilization of his models and on his collaboration to the overall ranking process. The modeler receives points each time one of his models is selected and additional points when it is actually used, as stated for the model ranking explained above. Points are also granted when he decides to collaborate on the appraisals of the imported models. This is done to motivate the participation of users in the ranking system, fundamental to the overall effectiveness of the tool. We apply a simplified version of the HYRIWYG reputation system (Garcia, Ekstrom, & Björnsson, 2004).

So, let:

- I be the set of modelers;
- M be the set of models, $J \subset M$ be the set of models from modeler i, and $K \subset M$ be the set of imported models in model m;
- ps_{ijm} be the points for selection (0 if not selected, 1 otherwise), by modeler i, when building model j, of model m;
- pu_{ijm} be the points for use, where not used = 0, low = 1, medium = 2 and high = 3, given by modeler i, when building model j, to model m;
- pe_j be the points for evaluation, where $pe_j=0$ if the modeler does not evaluate imported models, and $pe_j=1$ if he does evaluate, when building his model j;
- R_i be the reputation of modeler i;
- wi be the weight of memory, ws be the weight of selection, and wu be the weight of use;
- PI_m be the initial points of model m;
- PS_m be the points received by model m for being selected;

- PU_m be the points received by model m for being for the development of a new model;
- PM_m be the total points accrued by a model; and
- PR_i be the modeler's cumulative points.

The evaluation system can then be expressed by:

Model's Initial Points

$$PI_m = \frac{\sum_K \left(PM_k * \frac{pu_{imk}}{3} \right)}{|K|} \quad (1)$$

The initial points factor evaluates a model, based on the reputation of the models used in its composition. This is done by considering that if a model is an evolution of other models, it must carry some of their reputation. It can be understood as the model's DNA.

Model's Selection Points

$$PS_m = \sum_I \sum_J \left(R_i * ps_{ijm} \right) \quad (2)$$

The selection points factor accounts for the points accrued by the model due to its selection by other modelers when building new models. A model receives a reward for being, at least, interesting.

Model's Use Points

$$PU_m = \sum_I \sum_J \left(R_i * pu_{ijm} \right) \quad (3)$$

The use points factor accounts for the points the models receives from other modelers, when appraised due to their use on composing other models. It is the reward for the actual utilization of the model for building models.

Model's Total Points

$$PM_m = wi * PI_m + ws * PS_m + wu * PU_m \quad (4)$$

Total points are calculated by the formula above. The weights are used to balance the factors. We believe that different organizations or scenarios may require different customizations of the system, manipulating how ranking shall be affected by each of these factors. It is important, though, to understand that these weights must be set for once and for all, since each specific evaluation is episodic, computed at the time a model is built or used and never more, that is, the system keeps no evaluations' history. Points then are changed by use and not by reevaluation of past utilizations.

Modeler's Reputation (R)

$$R_i = \frac{PR_i}{\sum_I PR_i} \quad (5)$$

The modeler's reputation introduces the reputation of the modeler into the scenario. It is defined as above, based on the modeler's points.

Modeler's Points

$$PR_i = \left[\frac{\sum_J PM_j}{|J|} \right] + \left[\sum_J pe_j \right] \quad (6)$$

The first factor is the average points the modeler's models. It is the actual score of the modeler.

The second factor is the motivating factor—a reward, given to the modeler, each time he builds a new model, and contributes to the whole system evaluating the models used to compose his new model. This feature enhances the cooperation among modelers, improving the effectiveness of the collaborative filter.

A Brief Example

Just to give an idea of how simple it is to use BPCE, we provide a brief description of a typical utilization.

A modeler in ACME wants to model the procurement process of the Sales Department. The modeler shall then open BPCE and start a search for *procurement* keyword. The search interface will show all available models that have *procurement* in their structures (title or activities descriptions). Then, the modeler can do a basic inspection on the models returned, just looking at the pictures of the models, which are also made available by the searcher.

Having decided what models the modeler wants to use as a basis for building the new model, the modeler marks the chosen models and press the button *Export to New Model,* which will open the modeling editor and show all imported models.

The modeler builds his new model cutting and pasting from the imported models or just using the ideas presented by them. When done with the new model, the modeler closes it. The Editor then pops-up a window, asking the modeler to evaluate the contribution of each imported model for its new model. After that, the modeler can also choose to publish his new model, what is automatically done by the tool.

According to the evaluations provided by the modeler, BPCE will automatically update models' points and build all the necessary mechanisms for publishing the new model.

FUTURE TRENDS

BPCE, as presented in the preceding sections, is currently under implementation and we intend to deploy it in a large company where part of the problems stated do exist. Enhancements, where some are still subject of research, and shall be implemented on next versions, are described below.

Looking at the tool itself, several issues have appeared during the development. Due to the time constraints of the project, we intend to consider them on the next versions of the tool. A list of the most important issues is provided.

- **Ontology based search:** besides optimizing search, it allows for customization, including partitioning the search space onto business areas, which have proper ontologies;
- **XPDL:** support of XPDL and related technologies;
- **Security mechanisms:** avoiding fraud and selecting what information can be viewed by other users are desired functionalities of an application of this kind. Indeed, this deserves special care when conducting cross-organizational modeling. Additionally, the need for anonymity must be studied, since social barriers, in a large sense, may difficult sharing; and
- **Ranking:** the present implementation just considers the modeler participation on the ranking process as a binary function, on each new developed model. This can be changed into a system where points received are also based on the quality of the judgment made by the modeler (Garcia et al., 2004). In addition, proper experiments shall be conducted to allow for the assessment of the advantages and disadvantages of the proposed algorithm when compared to the other existing ones.

Looking at the big picture, we understand that BPM is a natural move for most enterprises. It helps enterprises to optimize their processes, facilitates the interface between business and IT and adds the needed transparency to enterprise governance. However, we believe the large adoption of BPM depends on several factors, where some of them may automatically occur due to BPM market grow, as

- Reduction of associated costs: BPM tools and implementation are still expensive for some enterprises;

- Standardization: we still miss modeling and execution languages standardized and widely adopted;
- Cultural change: IT is still learning how to streamline the process of deriving systems from business processes specifications. New trends such as Service Oriented Architecture and MDA can contribute to optimize it.

CONCLUSION

Considering the growth of BPM and the need organizations have to implement it and streamline their business processes, we believe BPCE can facilitate the development of new business process models through knowledge reuse. This is done using the P2P paradigm, hiding model exchange complexities from users, and providing them with an easy to use, low cost, and simple interface. We believe that, especially for low-budget enterprises, BPCE can be a handy tool.

We also claim that while it facilitates the adoption of BPM practices, it promotes knowledge sharing. In this sense, it may be seen as a distributed knowledge management tool, supporting organizational learning in the enterprise. Additionally, when used by different enterprises, it can help organizations tune-up their processes and better understand each other.

However, there exist some negative aspects of the approach. While some of them may be mitigated with some effort, some may require some extra effort. The list below is a basic assessment of the cons:

- **Trust:** while in a controlled membership scenario the problems associated with trustiness may be minimized, as inside an organization or in a community of practice, this turns out to be much harder in an open environment;
- **Participation:** heavy dependence on peer's availability, since models are stored on authors' peers, may develop as a problem.

Although the natural complexity of model building may encourage users to establish a cooperation network, and reputation build up may work as a motivating factor, promoting model sharing by users, the unavailability of a node, while not critically compromising a modeler's work, may act as a demotivating factor. We believe that replication can address this problem, reducing its impact;

- **Diversity of modeling languages:** the system's effectiveness is based on the use of a common standard or, at least, compatibility among shared models. Translators, although feasible, may not be practical; and
- **Diversity of tools:** even assuming the existence of a unique exchange mechanism, as XMI, our assessment has shown that each modeling tool has some particularities when preparing their XMI files. While BPCE, as a plug-in, can be adapted to work with several existing tools, the wide use of nonstandard resources in XMI files can affect system's effectiveness.

Despite the downside of the coin, we understand that through BPCE, the organization can share, adapt, and evolve its processes. As a result, in the long run, we expect the best-fitted processes to survive, contributing to the evolution and standardization of the organizations' processes and helping the BPM initiatives.

REFERENCES

Aberer, K., & Despotovic, Z. (2001). Managing trust in a peer-2-peer information system. In *Proceedings of the 10th International Conference on Information and Knowledge Management* (pp. 310-317). New York: ACM.

Arias, E., Eden, H., Fischer, G., Gorman, A., & Scharff, E. (2000). Transcending the individual human mind—creating shared understanding through collaborative design. *ACM Transactions* on *Computer-Human Interaction (TOCHI), 7*(1), 84-113.

Baeza-Yates, R., & Ribeiro-Neto, B. (1999). *Modern information retrieval* (pp. 27-29). ACM Press.

Business process execution language for Web services version 1.1. (2005). Retrieved November 17, 2007, from www-128.ibm.com/developerworks/library/specification/ws-bpel/

Business process modeling notation specification, v1.0. (2006). Retrieved November 17, 2007, www.omg.org

Chan, Y. (2002, June). Why haven't we mastered alignment? The importance of the informal organization structure. *MIS Quarterly Executive, 1*(2), 97-112.

Eugster, P. T., Felber, P. A., Guerraoui, R., & Kermarrec, A. M. (2003). The many faces of publish/subscribe. *ACM Computing Surveys, 35*(2), pp. 114–131.

Garcia, A. C., Ekstrom, M., & Björnsson, H. (2004). HYRIWYG: Leveraging personalization to elicit honest recommendations. In *Proceedings of the 5th ACM Conference on Electronic Commerce - EC '04* (pp. 232–233). ACM Press.

Goldberg, D., Nichols, D., Oki, B. M., & Terry, D. (1992). Using collaborative filtering to weave an information tapestry. *Communications of the ACM, 35*(12), 61-70.

Harmon, P. (2003). *Business process change—a manager's guide to improving, redesigning, and automating processes.* USA: Morgan Kaufmann.

Hofmann, H., & Lehner, F. (2001). Requirements engineering as a success factor on software projects. *IEEE Software, 18*(4), 58-66.

Jeston, J., & Nelis, J. (2006). *Business process management - practical guidelines for successful implementations.* UK: Butterworth-Heinemann.

Kamvar, S., Schlosser, M., & Garcia-Molina, H. (2003). The eigentrust algorithm for reputation management in P2P networks. In *Proceedings of the 12th International Conference on World Wide Web, Budapest, Hungary - WWW '03* (pp. 640–651). New York: ACM Press.

Law, A. M., & Kelton, W. D. (1982). *Simulation modeling and analysis* (2nd ed.) (pp. 4-5). McGraw-Hill.

Liebowitz, J. (1999). *Building organizational intelligence: A knowledge management primer.* CRC Press.

Lippe, S., Greiner, U., & Barros, A. (2005). *A survey on state of the art to facilitate modelling of cross-organisational business processes.* Paper presented at the meeting of Second GI-Workshop XML4BPM XML for Business Process Management.

May, M. (2003). *Business process management - integration in a Web-enabled environment.* UK: Pearson Education Limited.

Mendling, J., Neumann, G., & Nuttgens, M. (2005). A comparison of XML interchange formats for business process modelling. In L. Fischer (Ed.), *Workflow handbook 2005* (pp. 185-198). USA: Future Strategies Inc.

Miller, J., & Mukerji, J. (Eds.). (2003). *MDA guide, version 1.0.1.* OMG.

Miranda, M., Xexeo, G. B., & Souza, J. M. (2006). Building tools for emergent design with COPPEER. In *Proceeedings of the 10th International Conference of CSCW in Design - CSCWD 2006* (pp. 550-555). USA: IEEE.

MOF 2.0/XMI mapping specification, v2.1. (2005). Retrieved November 17, 2007, from www.omg.org

Parameswaran, M., Susarla, A., & Whinston, A. (2001). P2P networking: An information-sharing alternative. *IEEE Computer, 34*(7), 31-38.

Resnick, P., Iacovou, N., Suchak, M., Bergstrom, P., & Riedl, J. (1994). GroupLens: An open architecture for collaborative filtering of netnews. In *Proceedings of the 1994 ACM Conference on Computer Supported Cooperative Work - CSCW 94* (pp. 175-186). USA: ACM.

Rodrigues, E. M., Rodrigues Nt., J. A., Mello, R. N., & Porto, F. (2003). Mapping OO applications to relational databases using the MOF and XMI. In *ECOOP 2002 Workshop Reader* (LNCS 2548, pp. 184-191). Springer-Verlag Heidelfeld.

Rodrigues Nt., J. A., Souza, J. M., Zimbrao, G., Xexeo, G. B., Neves, E., & Pinheiro, W. (2006). A P2P approach for business process modeling and reuse.In *Business Process Management Workshops* (LNCS 4103, pp. 297-307). Austria: Springer-Verlag Heidelfeld.

Roussopoulos, M., Baker, M., Rosenthal, D., Giuli, T., Maniatis, P., & Mogul, J. (2005). 2 P2P or not 2 P2P? In *Proceedings of the 3rd International Workshop on Peer-to-Peer Systems* (LNCS 3279, pp. 297-307). Springer-Verlag Heidelfeld.

Smith, H., & Fingar, P. (2003a). *Business process management - the third wave.* Meghan-Kiffer.

Smith, H., & Fingar, P. (2003b). *IT doesn't matter - business processes do.* Meghan-Kiffer.

Tan, J., Wen, H., & Awad, N. (2005). Health care and services delivery systems as complex adaptive systems. *Communications of the ACM, 48*(5), 36-44.

UML 2.0 superstructure, v2.0 formal 05/07/04. (2005). Retrieved November 17, 2007, from www. omg.org

Wenger, E. (1998). *Communities of practice: Learning, meaning, and identity* (pp. 45-49). UK: Cambridge University Press.

Workflow process definition interface—XML process definition language (XPDL) (2005). Document Number WFMC-TC-1025: Version 1.14. Retrieved November 17, 2007, from www. wfmc.org

KEY TERMS

Business Process Management (BPM): Activities performed by organizations to manage and continually improve their business processes.

Collaborative Filtering: The process of recommending of information based on the analysis of the similarity between the opinions of one user and a group of users in a system.

Communities of Practice (CoP): Groups of individuals sharing information, ideas, or experiences on a common domain.

Distributed System: A system where different parts of a program run simultaneously on two or more computers that are communicating with each other over a network.

Knowledge Management (KM): A range of practices used by organizations to identify, create, represent, and distribute knowledge for reuse, awareness, and learning across the organizations; also referred to as organizational learning or organizational intelligence.

Model Reuse: Total or partial use of a model in the construction of a new model.

Peer-to-Peer (P2P): A computational network application in which each node is autonomously managed and can contribute with its computational resources to the distributed execution of tasks requested by other system nodes.

Reputation System: A type of collaborative filtering algorithm which attempts to determine ratings for a collection of entities, given a collection of opinions that those entities hold about each other.

ENDNOTES

[1]   The term organization is used here with a generic sense, that is, it can be a company or a company unit.

[2]   Model and model elements are sometimes used interchangeably in the chapter. In the case of activity diagram, model element means a fragment of a model, eventually just an atomic action.

Chapter XXXVII
Collaborative Writing Tools in the Virtual Workplace

Norman E. Youngblood
Texas Tech University, USA

Joel West
Texas Tech University, USA

ABSTRACT

Collaborative writing is an important element of the virtual workplace. While it is sometimes enough to e-mail a document back and forth between authors and editors, users frequently need a more effective solution. Users can choose from system-based or browser-based software and from synchronous and asynchronous editors. These products can vary from the simple to the sophisticated and from free to expensive. This chapter looks at research on the use of collaborative editors and tools currently on the market and provides guidance as how to evaluate the appropriateness of the tools, paying particular attention to collaborative features, industry standards, and security.

INTRODUCTION

Over the last 20 years, many businesses have gradually, and sometimes not so gradually, moved towards a virtual work environment, bridging barriers of time and space. This relatively new environment encompasses many aspects of our lives. A radiologist in India may be responsible for reviewing an x-ray from Boston. A taxi cab driver from Boston may earn a Bachelor's degree online from a college in Texas. Writers from across the country may collaborate on a magazine article or report. At the heart of much this progress is the Internet and the World Wide Web, which have increasingly provided a way not only to share information, but a way to collaborate on creating documents.

Not surprisingly, many of the electronic tools for the brick and mortar office have evolved into tools for the virtual office, particularly the word processor, which has evolved from a replacement for a typewriter to a tool for collaborative writing. Collaborative writing tools generally fall into one of two categories: synchronous and asynchronous. These tools can also be divided another way: system-resident and Web-based. While both versions often use servers as part of the editing process, the latter moves the actual software away from the local system into the Web browser. This trend, still in its early stages, is considered by many pundits to be the future of software. This chapter sets out to examine some of the collaboration tools and technologies available for use in the virtual workplace. This chapter also offers insights into the pros and cons of each type of tool, provides guidance as to how to evaluate the appropriateness of the tools for different work environments, and suggests some best practices for using the tools.

BACKGROUND

The word processor, an electronic tool for composing written documents, has changed how people write and how they think about writing (Heim, 1987). Academic research on the tool began as early as 1962, and commercial computer-based word processors were available by the mid-1970s (Myers, 1998). Those fortunate few who had access to these tools were suddenly freed from the horror of making a spelling mistake in a document and then having to retype the page or struggle with correction fluid to hide their error. With Michael Shrayer's 1976 release of Electric Pencil, word processing moved to the burgeoning realm of the personal computer. By the mid-1980s, writing tools such as WordStar and WordPerfect were playing a major role in the business environment and developers began to look at leveraging nascent networks to create tools to let people edit in a collaborative environment (Malcolm & Gaines, 1991; Myers, 1998).

In their discussion of how they designed their collaborative writing system, GroupWriter, Malcolm, and Gaines (1991) laid out the basic requirements of a collaborative authoring system as:

- allowing simultaneous editing
- allowing comparison of versions
- allowing reversion to older versions when needed
- allowing insertion of comments

- being compatible with other software
- being similar enough to existing word processors to be easy to use
- having no need for users to manage the system
- incorporating e-mail
- providing reliable and secure data storage

While this rubric is 16 years old, it is still very much a viable way to evaluate collaborative writing software.

Although electronic collaborative writing tools have become a common and important part of business and academic communication, they have not been accepted uncritically. A number of researchers have examined the use of technology to help mediate the collaborative writing process. These studies have taken a variety of approaches ranging from observational studies (Forman, 1991) to experimental (Galegher & Kraut, 1994). Forman identified a number of problems among novice collaborative writers. These problems included group process issues such as coordinating group and individual efforts, leadership issues, and resolving conflicts; writing issues such as not meeting the reader's needs and not understanding the need for revisions or the difference between editing and revising; and computing issues such as lack of voluntary standardization of equipment and software or basic computing practices. In short, many of the participants experienced "cognitive overload" and found the new technology stifling and hard to master rather than an efficient management tool.

One of the concerns raised early on was that an over reliance on computers in collaborative writing might hinder the writing process, particularly if all communication between the writers was computer-mediated. Kraut, Galegher, Fish, and Chalfonte (1992) identified the needs among collaborators to resolve three types of complexities—social, intellectual, and procedural—when collaborating electronically. Authors must establish goals, divide tasks, resolve issues of authority, decide on the document's structure, and determine the workflow. An experimental study by Galegher and Kraut (1994) conducted with graduate students in the early 1990s found that while the end products produced by computer-mediated groups were of a similar quality to those produced by groups that communicated face-to-face, the computer-mediated group encountered more problems with coordinating their project than the face-to-face group and reported less satisfaction with their social interactions. A third condition, computer-mediated groups that included telephone discussions, fell somewhere in between the other two in terms of coordination and social interaction issues. In their conclusions, the authors state that there will be a "recurring need for face-to-face interaction" until a better technology comes along (Galegher & Kraut, 1994, p. 136).

Computer-mediated collaborative writing can pose a challenge even in a business environment in which hardware and software have been standardized and employees are already used to writing collaboratively. Tammaro and Mosier (1997) studied the adoption of such a system with the engineering company MITRE. Despite a relatively homogeneous computing environment and training on the software, users had mixed reviews of the collaborative tool (Instant Update), in part because of a lack of advanced features such as spell check and poor integration with Microsoft Word—a violation of Malcolm and Gaines (1994) aforementioned maxim. In addition, the researchers found that a user's level of experience or if they "were just plain more cooperative than others" often played a major role in the success or failure of a project (Malcolm & Gaines, 1994, p. 49).

More than a decade later, researchers still express concerns that while collaborative writing efforts are common, the process is still not well understood and can suffer from subpar performance. One option that has proved effective, particularly for asynchronous collaboration, is establishing standard procedures as to how the collaborative process should work. This can improve the quality of the overall work, as well as work relationships and overall satisfaction with the writing process

(Lowry, Nunamaker, Curtis, & Lowry, 2005). In addition, best practices articles still encourage occasional face-to-face meetings and/or conference calls, particularly for initial brainstorming and for finalizing a document (Knipstein, 2007).

SYSTEM-BASED COLLABORATIVE TOOLS

Removing the barrier of geography is perhaps the single most important advantage of a network among workers in a modern office, and the process of collaboration on documents has been aided by a number of proprietary groupware packages, such as Lotus Workplace, to help manage documents. This section takes a look at a few off-the-shelf software solutions available to workers today.

Collaborating on documents in a remote or virtual office environment can be as simple as e-mailing a quarterly sales performance assessment to a supervisor for review and revisions. Workers tend to view e-mail as a reliable form of bidirectional communication (Adler, Nash, & Noel, 2006) and their familiarity with the protocol allows them to use it for collaboration. But collaboration through e-mail, something for which e-mail was never intended, is cumbersome at the least and potentially hazardous at the worst. Even with Rich Text Formatting HTML-based e-mail, limitations in the formatting options available to a user soon become apparent. As a workaround to the comparatively sparse formatting features of an e-mail client, users can attach a Microsoft Word or other word processor document to the e-mail, preserving formatting while permitting such necessities as creating headers, footers, tables, charts, and page-numbering.

As discussed above, however, problems may soon arise if there is not a clearly thought-out and articulated workflow. As documents circulate and users make contributions and revisions, users can become confused as to which version is the "correct" master version. Additionally, if multiple copies are disseminated for individuals' input, then someone must ultimately undertake the laborious, time-consuming task of manually compiling the changes for the final version of the document. Finally, although some of the features work between the various platforms and there exists within each package a reasonable level of backward compatibility, it is advisable that writers collaborating use the same software package, preferably the same versions, to ensure the most seamless workflow possible.

Asynchronous Collaborative Text Editors

Perhaps the most commonly used method of collaborative editing is a feature available in the more robust word processing packages called "track changes." Microsoft Word, Corel's WordPerfect, and the open-source OpenOffice's Writer provide tools for the user to track changes, or "redline." Authors are able to edit documents in normal fashion but can still view the text as it originally appeared.[1] Users are then able to accept or reject changes made by others or provide further editing. Each of these programs also allows a user to compare two versions of a document and merge them into a single document.

Writers may e-mail documents or disseminate them to co-authors using removable media, such as "flash" or "thumb" storage devices. This process is straightforward and allows collaborators to freely refine the document while providing reasonable assurance that changes made to the document can be reversed should a collaborator elect to do so. Writers can tell who made each change by hovering their cursor over a tracked change. Again, however, it is worth noting that if multiple people are reviewing the document at the same time using this distribution technique, one person needs to keep a master document and be responsible for merging the revised versions into it as they are returned.

While tools such as track changes and compare documents facilitate collaborative writing, these tools can prove a liability when the final version of a document is released. Users need to exercise particular caution when collaborating on documents that include privileged or sensitive information,

such as those dealing with employees, company strategies. As the track changes feature preserves material from previous draft, that material is available to anyone who opens the document and turns the feature on unless the document has been finalized. Several stories about a document's "history" have become a source of embarrassment for organizations and even countries when documents were not finalized. The following are but three of many examples:

- In 2004, a reporter reviewing the filing of a lawsuit by SCO against DaimlerChrysler determined that the original recipient of the lawsuit was to be Bank of America. (Wildstrom, 2004)
- A 2005 United Nations report on the assassination of the Lebanese prime minister implicated Syria as being involved in the plot but did not provide the names of those involved. The official version released to the media had not been finalized and still contained information related to the involvement the Syrian president's brother (Young, 2005)
- In 2007, a blogger's 8-year-old son accidentally turned on track changes while his father was reading a Coalition Provisional Authority report, revealing that the report had not been finalized and contained material that was not meant for public consumption (Moore, 2007)

Collaborating using standard word processors can unfortunately prove cumbersome sometimes. Documents must be either disseminated through e-mail, removable media, or retrieved through a server. The latter option usually prohibits more than one person from editing a document at any given moment unless it is opened and then resaved as a new version. In addition, the more people involved in editing a project, the more work that may be required later to consolidate the changes into a single, unified document. At the same time, having multiple versions of the document in circulation means that there is a backup system of sorts in place if something happens to the original document. Still, this asynchronous method of collaborative writing is not usually the most efficient way to collaborate, particularly early on in the process of creating a document.

SYNCHRONOUS COLLABORATIVE TEXT EDITORS

Though collaborative computing editing systems have been employed in science and academia since the 1980s with document management systems such as revision control system (RCS) and products such as GroupWriter, only since the decentralization of computing systems (Malcolm & Gaines, 1991, p. 147) and the ubiquity of the Internet have we seen synchronous collaborative text editors in mainstream use. Collaborative synchronous (real-time) text editors, which are applications dedicated to editing documents over LANs, WANs, and the Internet, offer users true simultaneous collaboration on text documents. Users, who are usually granted permission in the form of an invitation from the document's creator, are able to write and edit on the same document at the same time while immediately seeing changes made by collaborators in a What You See Is What I See (WYSIWIS)-style environment. Even though most collaborative writing is performed with writers working alone (Tammaro, & Mosier, 1997, p. 47), there are times when collaborating in real time, in a "tightly coupled" manner may be more productive. For example, it can shorten the time from draft to final approval status if team members can make revisions to the document simultaneously, reviewing and revising each others' work "on the fly" rather than individually marking up a document and sending it to the next reviewer.

SubEthaEdit, a real-time collaborative editor for Apple's Macintosh OS X operating system, is a good example of a basic synchronous collaborative writing tool. Released in 2003 as a freeware product called Hydra, SubEthaEdit allows a user to write a document and announce its availability for editing over a local network and make provisions for users to access the document over the Internet. Each co-authors' edits appear in a separate color, making it easier to tell what each person is doing. It does not, however, support comments in the traditional sense. Other packages in this category that are platform-independent include Gobby and A Collaborative Editor (ACE). Both of these programs are offered in versions that run on Microsoft Windows, Mac OS X, and Linux. It is worth noting that SubEthaEdit and ACE rely on Bonjour, Apple's implementation of Zero Configuration Networking (Zeroconf), whose use may not be supported in some corporate networks. Many collaborative real-time text editors are not intended to replace advanced word processors, and their feature set is closer to that of general purpose text editors. While this simplicity makes them easy to use, it does mean that users who need fine control of layout, pagination, charting, and other advanced formatting features will have to import the copy into another software package. One possible solution to this is a product like CoWord.

CoWord is a freeware product that adds real-time collaboration features to the Windows versions of Microsoft Word (2000, XP, and 2003), using "transparent adaptation" approach (Xia, Sun, Sun, Chen, & Shen, 2004) designed to leverage single-user, proprietary software packages for use in a collaborative environment. CoPowerPoint, developed by the same group, is another example of how a single-user, proprietary product (Microsoft PowerPoint) can be turned into a collaborative application. Both of these products allow users to work in an environment they are already familiar with and access most of the primary application's features, reducing training time. CoWord includes track changes, allowing users to see the changes in real-time and to accept or reject changes on the fly. CoWord requires the use of a "repository" server, either stand alone or on one of the collaborators' systems, to share documents among collaborators. Users log on to the system with usernames and passwords established by the repository's administrator and are presented with a list of directories and/or documents that are available for collaboration. Collaborators work in a synchronous environment in which they can see other people's changes to a document as the changes are entered. At the moment, documents on the server are not encrypted nor are they currently protected by individual permissions. As Malcolm and Gaines (1991) suggest, this may be an issue for some users.

Workers already familiar with Word's interface and features are not forced to learn another word processing package. Additionally, writers are able to use a subset of Word's comparatively more powerful formatting and pagination features typically not available in other real-time collaborative writing applications. CoWord does, however, require collaborators to have both CoWord and Microsoft Word installed on their systems.

Adobe Acrobat and PDFs

Although most may use collaboration to facilitate the writing process, collaboration also can be achieved in fields where concern for aesthetics and design are as much of the process as the writing itself, particularly in fields where design is inherently important, such as advertising, marketing, publishing, and packaging.

Compared to word processing, graphic design and page layout software are quite complex. In most cases, both of the latter types of software require the fonts and images used in the design of a document be present on a computer that is used to view the file. The Portable Document Format (PDF), released by Adobe in 1993, addresses many of these problems. This cross-platform solution provides users a common file format that can be viewed using a free reader on a wide variety of operating systems and devices. PDFs can be created directly within the full version of Adobe Acrobat or other dedicated PDF software, or files can be exported to PDF from another software package. Regardless of how a PDF is created, it

retains the visual integrity of the original document without requiring the presence of system fonts. In contrast, a Microsoft Word document created on one computer may or may not appear identically on another system or printer. At the very least, both systems must have the same fonts used to create the document and, in some cases, compatible versions of the software installed.

Commercial printers, publishers, and advertisers were quick to recognize the value of the PDF in their workflows because of the format's ability to retain all the elements of design in what is known in the industry as a "soft" or "e"(lectronic) proof, a digital version of the work that is as close as possible to the final, printed version of the work. Even the most elaborate of layouts and typographically complex designs appear the same on any system, making PDFs an ideal way for those who use commercial printing to review files, such as advertisements, brochures or even a magazine, exactly as it will be printed. These e-proofs can sometimes eliminate a step and significantly lessen the time required in the proofing process to make hard-copy proofs, such as bluelines. PDFs have become a standard document format for many industries and there are ISO PDF standards for use in commercial printing, graphic arts, engineering, archives, and government agencies.[2]

As mentioned above, PDFs can be generated a variety of ways. In addition to the full version of Adobe Acrobat, there are a number of third-party packages, including Bluebeam PDF Revu, Inceni Infix, and Foxit PDF Editor, that can be used for authoring PDFs. Most of these programs also install special printer drivers that can be used to export PDFs from almost any program with a print option. Windows users can also take advantage of programs like CutePDF, a simple, freeware printer driver that gives users the option of "printing" to PDF. Mac users have had a built-in, print-to-PDF feature since the release of Mac OS X 10.0 in 2001.

Like MS Word, Adobe Acrobat includes the ability to add comments and make changes to a document, as well as to track which author made a specific change. It also allows users to markup text in ways similar to the way an editor works on paper—items can be circled and highlighted, comments can either be typed directly into the text or into the equivalent of a sticky note. Also like Word, however, users should make sure documents are finalized before releasing them to the public. Users concerned with security should be aware that Acrobat also has security options that allow the user to restrict documents from being opened, printed, or from material being copied from within document.

GROUPWARE SYSTEMS

The peer-to-peer collaboration software discussed above will meet the needs of a variety of users. Larger organizations, particularly corporations, however, may need an integrated suite that supports a wider variety of collaborative efforts than just writing. These suites typically fall into the category of Groupware.

IBM Lotus Domino/Notes and Workplace suites, Oracle's Collaboration Suite, EMC Software Documentum eRoom, Microsoft SharePoint, and Microsoft Groove are all current examples of robust, enterprise-level groupware. Built around databases, these proprietary systems are powerful, customizable, and scalable. They do, however, tend to be relatively complex and may require significant training for users to fully take advantage of their capabilities. Some of the services a groupware suite might offer include:

- real-time document collaboration and revision control systems
- permissions-based file repositories, allowing different team members to work on only those documents pertinent to them
- e-mail
- instant messaging
- calendaring
- voicemail and fax services
- discussion/message boards

- screen-sharing/whiteboarding
- voice, video, and Web conferencing.

Groupware excels in contextual collaboration—merging collaborative features within applications that allow users to instantly communicate or share information with each other.

Groupware systems are much more expensive to purchase, install, and configure than peer-to-peer systems. Some groupware systems require a license to be purchased for each user, and some may require the purchase of an annual maintenance fee—sometimes based on user numbers. Many systems may require the purchase of hosting services through a third-party if the client does not have its own server. Groupware is not considered off-the-shelf software, so companies exploring their options may want to get advice from a consultant to help evaluate the company's needs and recommend the most-appropriate solution. Companies should also take customization and system administration into account when planning to implement a groupware product.

While groupware vendors may offer similar services, they often differ in how they implement their products. For example, users access almost all of SharePoint services through a Web interface, meaning a user must have a persistent network connection and access to the SharePoint Portal Server. In contrast, Groove allows users to work online or off-line—for example, a worker using the Groove client can synchronize all of the latest versions of documents and spreadsheets before leaving the office for a business trip. The user can review and revise documents and then synchronize them the next time they access the server, propagating the changes throughout the system.

Another advantage to enterprise-level groupware solutions is security. These systems typically offer means to encrypt all data traveling to and from the servers and among connected team members to help ensure information transferred remains the property of the company.

WEB-BASED COLLABORATION TOOLS

The move to Web 2.0—the Web as a computing platform—has opened the doors to Web-based applications, and not just database front ends for registering for a hotel room (O'Reilly, 2005). An increasing number of developers are building browser-based office tools such as word processors, spreadsheets, and presentation tools. Others have put together browser-based tools for editing photographs, drawing pictures, and even editing video. One of the key technologies behind many of these projects is Asynchronous JavaScript and XML (AJAX). This programming technique allows items to change on the page without the page having to reload—one of the prerequisites for having a usable word processor running in a browser (Mahemoff, 2006). To a great extent, browser-based office software has its origins in browser-based e-mail applications, as once there was a way to write a letter inside of a browser and store it offsite, the leap towards trying to implement a word processor was not too far off.

Writely, introduced by Upstartle Software in August 2005, was an early browser-based AJAX word processor. It offered users a basic What You See is What You Get (WSYWIG) word processor that could work with OpenOffice documents as well as save documents to a variety of formats, including Open Document Format (ODF) and PDF. Documents were saved to Upstartle-run servers, and users could download them as needed. It also, and perhaps most importantly, allowed multiple people to work a document at the same time. The program garnered a tremendous amount of attention, in large part because many pundits considered it as leading the charge in what Web 2.0 had to offer. In March 2006, Google purchased the company and used Writely as the core of Google Documents, a service which, while still in beta at the time of this writing, is a leading example of one of the directions the virtual workplace can take.

The Google Docs word processor, like its predecessor, can open and save to a variety of document types including Word, OpenOffice, RTF (Rich Text Format), HTML, and text documents. It supports most basic word-processing features, including basic text formatting functions such as bold, italics, underline, super and subscript, strike-out, font face, and font color. It allows the user to create hyperlinks, create bulleted and numbered lists, and align paragraphs. It also has a built in spell-check module. The editor also allows the use of non-English characters and can be set to edit right-to-left, an option that is particularly helpful for users needing to incorporate Arabic or Hebrew text. Users can also insert and resize images and tables, as well as add special characters, page separators, and comments. This last option is critical for using the editor in a collaborative environment, though the comments are not included in exported documents. The product does, however, have some limitations for users who are accustomed to the more refined features of programs like MS Word. As an example, while styled text is not changed on import, the markup for the style is not imported and cannot be reused or modified. The styles that are available within the editor are currently limited to Header 1 (huge), Header 2 (big), and Header 3 (standard). The editor also lacks the ability to double space a document, control margins, or deal with footnotes. That being said, Google Documents may well be sufficient for many users, particularly for initial drafts.

Allowing another user to view or edit the document is relatively easy as long as the user has a G-mail (Google's e-mail service) account: all one has to do is click on the share or publish tab. When a document is shared for editing or viewing with someone, he or she receives an e-mail invitation to edit or view the document. The editor includes a window at the bottom of the screen that notifies the user if the document is currently being edited by another user. Up to 10 people can work on a document simultaneously, and as many as 200 users can view the document at once. Overall, the program seems to handle simultaneous editing fairly well, though not with the elegance of SubEthaEdit because a user cannot readily see what has changed while editing. The editor does let users review versions of a document as well as compare two versions of the document—it does the latter by making the edits by each author visible in one document, something that would be helpful if it did automatically during synchronous editing. Google Docs works with most current browsers, though some versions of the Macintosh browser Safari are know to have trouble with it.

Google Spreadsheets offers similar features to its sibling. It can work with .csv, .ods, .txt, and .xls as well as being able to export the PDF and HTML. As with the document editor, the spreadsheet allows up to 200 users to view a spreadsheet at the time, and increases the number of those who can simultaneously edit to 50. As this chapter was being written, Google announced its purchase of Tonic Systems, producers of TonicPoint, a series of Java-based software packages that allow Web-based creation of PowerPoint presentations (Schillace, 2007). Google has also released Google Apps Premier Edition, which allows an organization to integrate Google Apps, including Google Docs, into an existing IT infrastructure, which is particularly helpful for managing users. Premier Edition also includes calendaring, e-mail, and instant messaging. One of the advantages of this solution is that it allows a company to use G-mail with addresses based on the company's own domain rather than @gmail.com. Yet another advantage is the ability to create a custom company portal with targeted news and information as well as password restricted access.

Google Documents is, of course, not the only choice in browser-based office packages. It is, however, supported by a major player in the Web and as such is likely to have staying power. One of the missing features in Google Documents as it exists now is the lack of an off-line editing capability. While Internet access has certainly become more ubiquitous in the last few years with the proliferation of always-on home Internet, Internet hotspots, and Internet enabled phones, these technologies do fail from time to time. In addition, in 2007, Google had some hiccups that

kept G-mail and Google Home off-line for up to a day. While some users may be able to afford this downtime, this type of problem inevitably occurs in the midst of an important project. Zimbra, another AJAX browser-based open-source office solution, has demonstrated a solution. Zimbra's solution to off-line editing is to cache the remote data locally and then resynchronize the data once the user is back online. It would be surprising if this solution does not appear in other browser-based software (Taking Zimbra Off-line, 2006).

One of the advantages of online collaborative tools for many users is the cost—often free or relatively inexpensive. This is particularly helpful to organizations such as libraries that are trying to keep down cost. From a public access perspective, these programs also solve the problem of where a user should store information. In this case, remote is better (Singer & Stephens, 2007). Web-based collaborative tools are also being well received in educational circles, where they are used to facilitate group writing and the peer review process (Borja, 2007). Some businesses are also likely to consider adopting these tools as they can provide an inexpensive or free collaborative environment, particularly as more and more products are added to the online office tools. Options such as Google Premier Edition make this all-in-one virtual intranet particularly appealing as it gives companies the option of bypassing, to at least some degree, the need for dedicated servers and some of the IT support staff, or to minimize the hardware requirements by integrating these products into their existing IT infrastructure. In addition, companies such as Google open the door to affordable offsite storage/backup.

While offsite storage may offer users a safety net of sorts, it also opens them to new threats, including the aforementioned possibility of not being able to access your documents due to a lack of connectivity. In addition, and potentially more serious, having an offsite-only storage strategy leaves one at risk for losing all of one's documents in the event of a catastrophic failure at the other end, though companies such as Google do build in a tremendous amount of redundancy into their storage systems. Users relying on offsite storage as their primary repository for documents must take the responsibility of backing up their documents to another location, probably onsite, much like users storing documents locally should be sure to back up important documents offsite.

In moving to offsite storage, be it for e-mail or documents, one runs the risk of exposing documents to people outside of the company, particularly when combined with a relatively public system. As Google uses the first part of the e-mail address as the log in name, potential hackers begin with half the battle already won—if they know someone's e-mail address, they know the log in. When using a service like Google Docs for mission-critical documents, it is vital to get those involved with the project to harden their passwords by including upper and lower case letters as well as numbers in their passwords.

Relying on an outsider for managing your documents may raise document retention issues for some users, particularly those in business. Delete, as many of us know, frequently does not mean delete. Having multiple revisions of a document available for review is often helpful, but users need to be aware that the snarky comment, or worse, bad/illegal idea that was typed into a draft and then deleted, may still be hanging around in a saved revision when the authorities investigate.

Yet another potential problem comes in the way much of the software itself is designed. Both Java and JavaScript have been know to have security problems, though so have systems developed by Microsoft and others, including both open- and closed-source. Additionally, one should be careful about "free" programs from unknown developers. Trojan programs have been around for decades and, while the authors are unaware of any cases in which an unscrupulous developer has embedded malicious code in an office-like product, it is always a concern. Related to this, in some corporate and educational environments, local IT may limit the use of Java-based tools on the LAN

or restrict traffic considered "personal."

In many ways, collaborative authoring using browser-based tools is not that much different from using local-based tools, though there are differences that are worth pointing out as well some similarities that bear repeating. The most important difference, of course, is that your documents are likely to be located on some else's server. The temptation is likely to trust that company, particularly a large company such as Google, to maintain your files. As discussed above, this is a bad idea. Establish a plan to back up your files locally and follow it with religious-like devotion. This not only protects you from catastrophic failure on the other end, but also protects you against the possibility that a company might suddenly go out of business. It is bad enough to lose software support because of vendor lock in. It is an entirely different issue to lose your data to lock in. Second, decide on a workflow. Several strategies for working in a collaborative environment have already been discussed. Moving to a browser-based application adds one more step, deciding who will make the final set of changes. This issue is particularly important if the document needs to be modified outside of the original editor, that is, if you need to move a document into a word processor to implement formatting options that are otherwise unavailable.

FUTURE TRENDS

The need for effective collaborative software, particularly for word processing, will continue to grow with the move toward virtual workplaces. There are a number of options currently on the market, and the options are likely to increase. This will raise a number of difficult-to-deal-with issues, some of which have already reared their heads in other parts of the Internet. One of the concerns for anyone doing business across international borders is that countries have different legal systems. This issue has already cropped up in eCommerce—just ask eBay, Yahoo, or

Amazon about problems selling World War II related artifacts and French anti-Nazi legislation (Charney, 2000). It put Google in the position of having to decide to make a censored "government approved" version of its search engine available if it wanted to provide information quickly inside of the "Great Firewall of China." Microsoft has deleted information on one of the blog services it runs—the servers were housed outside of China. More seriously, Yahoo turned over account information for a Chinese business journalist who leaked information on Chinese government press restrictions—the journalist was sentenced to 10 years in jail. Google has tried to avoid this issue and has intentionally avoided offering e-mail service in China (Thompson, 2006). Users and decision makers need to be aware of the laws in the countries they plan to do business with and how the companies they do business with handle government and court demands for access to client information and client data. They also need to be aware of differences in the treatment of intellectual property.

The rise and fall of software companies is another issue that is likely to plague collaborative software users, particularly those that rely on Web-based tools. This is not a new issue. Companies have always been concerned about a developer going out of business and leaving them with abandonware, software that is no longer supported. While this can certainly pose a problem for users as software ages, it is nothing compared to the potential horror of waking up to discover your Web-based applications are no longer available because the company went out of business or was taken over. Not only is your software no longer available, there may be important documents that need to be retrieved. Decision makers should pay particular attention to the financial health of the companies providing these services and, as discussed above, implement a plan to backup of documents, regardless of whether the documents are stored locally or remotely. Despite the saying "just because it is free does not mean it may not cost you anything,"

decision makers need to be just as concerned about services they pay for as they are with free services. Closely related to the above concerns, security will continue to be a major issue, both in terms of preventing people from outside the company looking at documents and controlling who inside the company can look at documents. Questions that should be of particular concern include:

- Can access to documents be restricted to specific users?
- For documents edited via a browser-based product, is the data encrypted (i.e., is https or SSL used)?
- Is there are a way to delete revisions and to finalize documents?
- How secure are the local/off-site/remotely hosted servers being used?
- Are there security flaws in the software, and when there are, does the developer patch them quickly?

Not long after there was more than one word processor on the market, people began to need to move document between them. This is still an issue and should be a concern for decision makers involved in selecting collaborative writing programs. One of the trends to look for over the next few years is the development of an open standard for electronic documents. There are currently two major contenders for this standard. The Organization for the Advancement of Structured Information Standards's (OASIS) OpenDocument Format (ODF) is based in part on eXtensible Markup Language (XML) and provides a nonproprietary way of storing document that allows editing software to be improved on without rendering documents created in older versions of the editor (or possibly other editors) unreadable (Eisenberg, 2005).

The other contender is Office Open XML (OOXML), a standard backed by Microsoft and others, which offers many of the same features as well as an "open and royalty-free specification" (Ecma Office OpenXML, n.d.).

There have, however, been concerns raised that OOXML will lead to vendor lock-in and will not be interoperable with ODF. There are also concerns about patented portions of OOXML. The debate between the two standards has entered the legislative realm, and a number of governments have announced their adoption of ODF, including Denmark, Belgium, and Massachusetts. Numerous individual government agencies have followed suit (Barrionuevo-Garcia, 2006; Hiser & Edwards, 2006; Marcich, 2006). Whatever the result of this debate, these standards open the possibility of more transportable documents that include such vital features as style sheets. Finally, look for an increase in collaborative software for a variety of purposes, particularly using browser-based products. As mentioned earlier, a number of these products are already on the market ranging from office tools to tools for creating multimedia projects such as audio, images, and video. While many of these tools are in beta form now, be prepared for the introduction of these tools to change how people collaborate, particularly in the virtual workplace.

CONCLUSION

Computers have evolved from devices that only a privileged few organizations such as universities, governments, and major corporations had access to into tools that are available to the masses. In a similar vein, collaboration software is beginning to go mainstream. Standards for network protocols, the ubiquity of the Internet, and overall affordability of computers have merged to make collaboration a fairly trivial task. Relatively simple-to-use tools, such as Google Docs and Spreadsheets, track changes in Word, and markup in PDFs, allowing users from around the world to collaborate on a project. At the same time, enterprise-level groupware provides larger organizations an even more powerful means to collaborate, share information, and communicate.

Malcolm and Gaines's (1991) rubric is still

valid. This chapter was a collaborative writing effort. The authors wrote most of it using Google Documents, though small portions were written using other collaborative editors. With the initial draft completed, the document was moved into Microsoft Word for formatting and then shared by e-mail with reviewers and editors with track changes and commenting turned on. Once the document is finalized, it will be converted to a PDF and sent to the typesetter, where it may be integrated into yet another system. The writing process for this chapter would have broken down, or at least been more complicated, if the authors had not been able to edit at the same time or been able to review and reverse changes. Commenting features were critical, particularly for asynchronous editing. Finally, and it is difficult to stress this enough, having a tool for synchronous communication, either voice or chat, and setting aside time to take advantage of it, made a tremendous difference. Rather than relying on the phone, the authors used the text-based chat program Google Chat (which works in a Web browser) and iChat, a video/audio-based chat program that is installed on the local computer.

The importance of planned implementation, emergency workarounds, and exit strategies should be neither overlooked nor underestimated when adopting a collaborative environment. What will happen if information is temporarily unavailable or if the vendor abandons its product? Are you locked into a vendor with proprietary document formats that cannot be accessed by other companies' software? How will that affect your ability to switch to a different solution should you want or need to change products? How will backups be handled, who has access to them, and who is ultimately responsible for making them? What would happen to the data if a person were incapacitated or suddenly left the company on bad terms? How securely is the information stored or transmitted? What are the policies for releasing finalized files internally to employees or externally to the media or a legal team? These are all issues that decision makers need to carefully consider before selecting or implementing a collaborative writing environment.

REFERENCES

Adler, A., Nash, J. C., & Noël, S. (2006). Evaluating and implementing a collaborative office document system, *Interacting With Computers, 18*(4), 665-682

Barrionuoevo-Gacia, A. (2006). ISO-26300 (OpenDocument) vs. MS-Office Open XML. *UPGRADE: The European Journal for the Informatics Professional, 7*(6), 29-38.

Borja, R. R. (2007). Teaching assistants. *Education Week, 26*(30), 18-22.

Charney, B. (2000, November 19). *E-Bay, Amazon avoid French knot.* Retrieved November 18, 2007, from http://news.zdnet.com/2100-9595_22-525752.html

Ecma office open XML file formats overview. (n.d.). Retrieved November 18, 2007, from http://office.microsoft.com/en-us/products/HA102058151033.aspx

Eisenberg, J. D. (2005). *OASIS OpenDocument essentials: Using OASIS OpenDocument XML.* Airlie Beach, Australia: Friends of OpenDocument Inc.

Forman, J. (1991). Novices work on group reports: Problems in group writing and computer-supported group writing. *Journal of Business and Technical Communication, 5*, 48-75.

Galegher, J., & Kraut, R. (1994). Computer-mediated communication for intellectual teamwork: An experiment in group writing. *Information Systems Research, 5*(2), 110-138.

Heim, M. (1999). *Electronic language: A philosophical study of word processing* (2nd ed.). New Haven: Yale University Press.

Hiser, S., & Edwards, G. (2006). Interoperability: Will the real universal file format please stand up? *UPGRADE: The European Journal for the Informatics Professional, 7*(6), 38-46.

Knipstein, S. C. (2007). Bringing geographically dispersed people together: Collaborative writing is still key to success. *Public Relations Tactics, 14*(2), 19.

Kraut, R., Galegher, J., Fish, R., & Chalfonte, B. (1992). Task requirements and media choice in collaborative writing. *Human Computer Interaction, 7*, 375–407.

Lowry, P. B., Nunamaker, J. F., Jr., Curtis, A., & Lowry, M. R. (2005). The impact of process structure on novice, virtual collaborative writing teams. *IEEE Transactions on Professional Communications Series, 48*(4), 341-364.

Mahemoff, M. (2006). *AJAX design patterns: Creating Web 2.0 sites with programming and usability patterns.* Sebastopol, CA: O'Reilly.

Malcolm, N., & Gaines, B. R. (1991). A minimalist approach to the development of a word processor supporting group writing activities. *ACM SIGOIS Bulletin, 12*(2-3), 147-152.

Marcich, M. (2006). ODF: The emerging document format of choice for governments. *UPGRADE: The European Journal for the Informatics Professional, 7*(6), 47-49

Moore, P. (2007, May 18). The secret Iraq documents my 8-year-old found. Retrieved November 18, 2007, from http://www.salon.com/news/feature/2007/05/18/cpa_documents/

Myers, B. A. (1998). A brief history of human-computer interaction technology. *ACM Interactions, 5*(2), 44-54.

O'Reilly, T. (2005). *Web 2.0: Compact definition.* Retrieved November 18, 2007, from http://radar.oreilly.com/archives/2005/10/web_20_compact_definition.html

Schillace, S. (2006, April 17). *We're expecting.* Retrieved November 18, 2007, from http://googleblog. blogspot.com/2007/04/were-expecting.html

Singer, R. S., & Stephens, M. (2007). Promoting productivity. *Computers in Libraries, 27*(5), 30-31.

Taking Zimbra Off-line. (2006, November 9). Retrieved November 18, 2007, from http://www. zimbra.com/blog/archives/2006/11/taking_zimbra_offline.html

Tammaro, S. G., & Mosier, J. N. (1997). Collaborative writing is hard to support: A field study of collaborative writing. *Computer Supported Cooperative Work: The Journal of Collaborative Computing, 6*(1), 19–51

Thompson, C. (2006, April 23). Google's China problem (and China's Google problem). *New York Times Magazine.* Retrieved November 18, 2007, from http://www.nytimes.com/2006/04/23/magazine/23google.html

Wildstrom, S. (2004, April 28). Don't let word give away your secrets. *BusinessWeek.* Retrieved November 18, 2007, from http://www.businessweek. com/magazine/content/04_16/b3879047.htm

Xia, S., Sun, D., Sun, C., Chen, D., & Shen, H. (2004). Leveraging single-user applications for multi-user collaboration: The CoWord approach. In *Proceedings of the 2004 ACM Conference on Computer Supported Cooperative Work* (pp. 162-171). New York: ACM Press.

Young, M. (2005, October 28). Assad's dilemma. *International Herald Tribune.* Retrieved November 18, 2007, from http://www.iht.com/articles/2005/10/27/opinion/edyoung.php

KEY TERMS

Asynchronous Editing: Editing in which users are not able to edit the same document at the same time.

Asynchronous JavaScript and XML (AJAX): A programming technique that allows items to change on a Web page without the page having to reload.

Browser-Based Software: Software that runs inside of a Web-browser rather than as a stand alone program. Browser-based software is frequently run from a remote server.

Groupware: An integrated suite of applications that supports a wide variety of collaborative efforts. These efforts can include writing, calendaring, instant messaging, and data basing, as well as fax, voice, and video services.

Office Open XML (OOXML): An open standard for electronic documents developed in large part by Microsoft for its Office 2007 suite. OOXML is based in part on XML

Open Document Format (ODF): An open standard for electronic documents developed by the Organization for the Advancement of Structured Information Standards (OASIS). ODF is based in part on XML.

Synchronous Editing: Editing in which users are able to edit the same document at the same time and changes are reflected in the document in real time.

ENDNOTES

[1]   The pros and cons of using open-source is a major topic of discussion in the information technology (IT) field. This topic and open-source in general are handled in another chapter of this book.

[2]   Readers interested in looking at ISO specifications should visit the Adobe Web site at http://www.adobe.com and the Web site for the International Organization for Standardization (ISO) at http://www.iso.org.

Chapter XXXVIII
Distance Internships

David A. Edgell
Texas Tech University, USA

ABSTRACT

Academic internships and cooperative programs exist so that students can build a bridge between their academic learning and their professional lives. These programs exist primarily for the student, but also serve a purpose for the university as a way to promote their academic program and for industry to become familiar with the talents and knowledge of new graduates. In a global economy where industries distribute work around the world, internship students may need a chance to become acculturated and familiar with this new professional environment. Distance internships may also provide opportunities for students that are not available locally.

INTRODUCTION

Academic internship programs provide students an opportunity to work outside of a university setting in a real workplace environment and achieve some measure of university credit. Depending on the school, these internships can vary between paid and unpaid positions, between 1 and 12 hours of credit and can be either undergraduate or graduate level courses. Internships are a requirement for the fulfillment of a degree at some institutions and are not a requirement at other institutions; some institutions pay their internship directors to negotiate positions for impending graduates and others give no benefit to faculty for performing this service for their students and for the univer-

sity. The nature of internship programs varies greatly depending on the academic department and the importance placed on this pivotal step in the career of students.

As industries and companies open multiple offices around the world, the importance of working in this global setting increases for practitioners who want to compete for jobs in this marketplace. Skills in working at a distance during an internship can give practitioners more opportunities for placement in this global economy. Distance internships can also give students options with regard to the type of work they want to do, work options that might not be available to them locally.

Traditional internships provide many challenges for students, universities, and industry.

Distance internships can provide even more challenges and opportunities. This chapter will initially examine the background and need for traditional internships to situate this model of distance internships and will then give a working definition of a distance internship.

This chapter will examine a model that represents the need to balance the requirements of the three parties involved within an internship: the student, the company, and the university. The student requires acculturation into the profession, transition from consumer of education to provider of services, and work experience. Companies require competent workers familiar with the needs of industry who are able to bring the latest academic ideas into the marketplace. Universities send students out into industry as representatives of their academic program, students who should be able to demonstrate the skills they have learned during their time in school.

To balance the needs of these three groups, some safeguards to prevent problems need to initially be put in place so that each group has a concept of the requirements of the internship. With distance internships, these safeguards become more important. There are also ways to increase the productivity of the internships by bringing together industry and the university. Finally, this chapter will examine trends that could make distance internships more feasible and relevant for future practitioners.

BACKGROUND

Internships have a place in many professions. A number of engineering students each year find cooperative work during the summers between their academic semesters and these internships often lead to permanent positions. In 1932, the Society for the Promotion of Engineering Education suggested that a college program laid the foundation for a career that would be built by experience (Silva, 2000). Engineering internships

and cooperative programs provide the beginning of that experience. Journalism has a history of valuing first-hand experience gained through internships and apprenticeships (Silva, 2000). Medical interns gain a knowledge of patient interaction and hospital dynamics that is unavailable to them while they are in medical school. Education programs frequently place teachers in classrooms with more experienced teachers to guide them in the management of the classroom and their lessons. Many trades have systems that allow experienced workers to oversee new members of their trade.

The ubiquity of these training programs speaks to their necessity and effectiveness in the workplace. However, many academic programs do not prepare students for the workplace by giving them adequate experience in managing projects and operating in a business environment. In studies conducted with the cooperation of industry and practitioners, there is a chasm between what students are taught and the skills they need in industry (Southard, 1988). Whiteside (2003) found that "over 50% of managers also rated project management, problem solving skills, and business operations knowledge as areas these employees lacked" (p. 311). Whiteside (2003) also found that "60% of technical communicators that graduated with an undergraduate degree in technical communications between 1999 and 2001 felt initially uncomfortable with their knowledge of business operations as they transitioned into business and industry" (p. 310). Effective internships can provide students exposure to business operations and the politics of the workplace. As Freedman (1996) relates concerning internships, "students were inducted into the ways of thinking, that is, the ways of construing and interpreting phenomena, valued in that discipline" (p. 405).

The modern global economy also requires students to have aptitude in intercultural workplaces because "work and jobs move rapidly and frequently from one continent to another" (Doerry, Doerry, Bero, & Neville, 2004). Doerry et al. (2004) also suggest that core engineering skills are not enough, "modern engineers must possess cross-cultural communication skills, team management skills, and the ability to perform on geographically-distributed teams" (p. 1). Distance internships can provide practitioners experience working with technologies and dealing with the challenges inherent in virtual workspaces. An employer might see a distance internship as an advantage for an applicant who will work with team members across the world (Ross, personal communication, 2007).

Distance internships can be defined as a program where a student receives academic credit for work completed outside the university within their discipline that contributes to their experience in that discipline, but where they do not maintain a physical presence in the work environment. Examples of these internships could include students editing manuscripts for publishers located in other cities, novice programmers structuring databases for remote companies, student writers proofreading documentation for international companies, and future practitioners who want to learn skills that are not available to them locally because they are in an area of the country without companies that employ that discipline. In all of these examples, distance internships would provide students the relevant experience in their discipline that that would otherwise be unavailable to them.

RESEARCH METHODS

A number of papers have examined the efficacy of academic programs, the usefulness of internships, and service learning. Whiteside (2003) interviewed recent graduates and managers of technical communication departments and analyzed the curricula of the programs to find where students need more preparation to meet the needs of industry. Whiteside (2003) found that students need more preparation in business operations,

project management, problem solving skills and technical knowledge. Sutliff (2000) finds that academic programs must teach theory only if it can be applied in a market-driven world and recommends students have opportunities to shadow and be mentored by current practitioners and participate in internships. English and Jereb (1995) examined academic programs from an industry perspective and found that programs need to give students training in actual job assignments to understand the challenges that face practitioners. Service learning provides some experience with real-world problems that exist in their community, but it is useful only up to a point because it will always be a classroom experience (Southard, 1988; Tovey, 2001). Wilson and Ford (2005) interviewed seven practitioners 10 years after their Master's programs and found that alumni expected their jobs to be like their internships. One graduate who went into academia found that to include all the training, including project management, business politics, changing technology, and interacting with difficult subject matter experts (SMEs) needed to adequately prepare a practitioner for their career, this training would have to be part of their internship experience (Wilson & Ford, 2005).

However, very little has been published concerning virtual, telecommuting, or distance internships. My interest in this field started when I worked with the editor of a medical journal to research the process of using XML to tag its content for submission to online search engines. As a Masters student in a Technical Communication program, I wanted to gain experience with a medical journal, but there were no opportunities available locally. The internship director of this university had a contact with a journal published in another state. During my time working for the journal, I never met the editor but I talked to him on the phone and communicated with him via e-mail. I personally experienced the rewards and difficulties of a distance internship. I interviewed a former technical communication practitioner who is now a Ph.D. student. She had completed both traditional undergraduate and graduate internships and a graduate distance internship.

I interviewed internship directors from the English department of Texas Tech University, the Engineering Professional Development Department at the University of Wisconsin, and the Communications Media Department at Fitchburg State College. I also interviewed Marjorie Davis, Professor and Chair of the Department of Technical Communication at Mercer University's School of Engineering and Professor David Farkas from the University of Washington's Department of Technical Communication. With about 60% of the technical communication programs in the United States governed by English departments, my interviews were primarily with programs that were affiliated with engineering departments. I believe that engineering departments have more of a historical precedent in using internship programs as a capstone to their academic programs and they are therefore more apt to see the value of internships. Programs located outside the humanities also have more experience with the challenges of the internship process.

BALANCING NEEDS

Robinson and Courter (1989) stated that if an internship program is "well done, it can serve not only to enhance the student's academic experience, but also to forge closer ties between the engineering college and industry, which can only benefit engineering education in general. These ties and the necessary balance between the needs of the student, the university, and industry leads to a model of internships:

The simplified model (Figure 1) illustrates the links and dependence between the interested parties in an internship program. Each group has their needs and each group can benefit from a well run and well funded program, whether it is a traditional or a distance internship. To examine the needs of the individual parties in an internship program,

Figure 1.

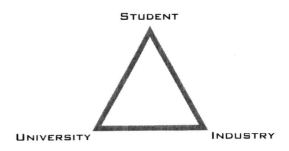

this section will first examine those requirements traditionally and then compare how a distance internship might meet those needs.

Needs of the Student

Giving a student basic experience and an exposure to the student's field of study is one of the primary functions of an internship program. This experience can be thought of as a type of acculturation. The students have gained knowledge about the discipline and understand some fundamental theories, but have not become part of the culture surrounding the profession. They need to understand how to start building working relationships. Freedman and Adam found that "social and political relations in the workplace context are considerably more complex. Tensions among employees must be discerned and then navigated" (1996, p. 44). Interns also need to work with difficult SMEs, managers reported that this was not a skill that students had after graduation (Whiteside, 2003). The need to learn workplace negotiation skills, dealing with people outside their chosen field and the politics of the workplace; these are skills that are difficult to teach in a classroom but are important for students' success.

Another part of an internship is the transition from consumer of educational services to provider of expertise (Freedman & Adam, 1996). Sutliff (2000, p. 1) recognized that teachers should remember "that their students will not be students forever but must eventually compete in a market-driven society where they will be paid to *do*, not merely to *think*." Internships place students into this social structure and guide them through this transition. One of the graduate students I interviewed found the restriction of their schedule and the lack of freedom a regular job placed on their life as valuable lessons they gained from their internship experience (Schroer-Motz, personal communication, 2007). In a well-guided internship, one lesson students can learn is how to become a useful member of their profession, guided by its principles and practices, rather than merely a receiver of information (St. Amant, personal communication, 2007).

While distance internships may not provide some of the physical interactions available in a traditional workplace environment, with new communications technologies many people do not function in a traditional workplace but interact with clients, vendors, and supervisors via e-mail, voicemail, Web cameras, videoconferencing, and many other communication technologies. Students also need to be prepared to work in this environment. Contract workers may never physically meet their client, although Charles Sides (Sides, personal communication, 2007) maintained that many professions were still accustomed to face-to-face meetings. Office workers now call help centers located in India order expensive systems without going to a showroom and work with nationally or globally located teams. Distance internships can provide students with the experience and the responsibilities of working in a modern global environment.

Distance internships may also provide opportunities to students that would not be available to them locally. Dr. Farkas at the University of Washington has sufficient businesses in the Puget Sound region that can provide positions for their students, but many schools are not located where there is an established base of industry in the student's field of study. A survey of managers found that students needed "lots of internship choices"

(Whiteside, 2003, p. 311). Many forms of work require a physical presence, but with broadband capabilities, modern communication technology is quickly eliminating those barriers. However, trust is still a major factor in initiating distance internships (St. Amant, personal communication, 2007). In many cultures face-to-face interaction forms the basis of a working relationship and without some initial interaction, this trust can't be constructed. Dr. St. Amant (personal communication, 2007) challenged the idea of video-conferencing making distance internships easier because cultural factors can become an issue. If an intern is unknown to a manager except by the reputation of the school and the internship director then there would be no prejudice regarding their age, race, sex, or other factors. However, when a sponsor views an intern via a videoconferencing link, seeing the intern might prejudice the manager against an effective working relationship with the intern. Those prejudices might also manifest in a face-to-face internship; participants must be ready to deal with similar challenges involved in both types of internships.

Needs of Industry

Industry needs capable, experienced, well-trained, and socially adept workers. Students who have little work experience need jobs. In her article, Lurkis (2001) illustrates the difficulties a new graduate faces in getting a first job and recommends an internship program. Industry uses internship programs to build necessary structures of trust before hiring new graduates. The students get an understanding of the performance of their profession and the company, and the company sees if the student could fit with lessened risk. "Employers use internships to evaluate potential future employees as well as to let students evaluate them as potential employers" (English & Jereb, 1995, p. 66). The student can work for the length of their internship and have a deeper interaction with employees; job interviews simply cannot achieve this broad a level of interaction.

After their internship within a company, the new graduate provides a company with an employee familiar with their procedures and processes. This familiarity does not change with a distance internship; distance can still provide an indication of whether the student performs within norms and deadlines specified by the company. A distant employee or intern must hone their communication skills to function with fewer feedback cues. They also have experience working with remote colleagues, newer groupware and interactive communication technologies, if these technologies are available at both the company and the university.

Needs of the University

Interns become the representatives of university programs to industry. They become the personification of the theories and curriculum of the university program. If the intern shows up late, it reflects on the intern, but it also reflects to a certain extent on the university. If the intern is untrained in the latest technology or tools, then the academic program is at fault, not the student.

In the past, internship programs have usually not been concerned with the intern as a representative of their internship program (Farkas, personal communication, 2007), but it may become more important in the future. In 1990, 7.2% of the population in the United States held advanced degrees (above a Bachelor's) and in 2000, that percentage had risen to 8.9% (Bauman & Graf, 2003). With rising numbers of practitioners returning to school to supplement their education, universities have to maintain their academic reputation. If the interns they place in jobs in industry and the graduates they produce are not able to function in the workplace, then practitioners will not seek out those schools to further their education or their children's and thereby reduce the university's income in tuition.

Distance education provides more choices to all students, but especially practitioners. The Master of Science in Technical Communication Management at Mercer University is comprised of practitioners with an average of 8 year of experience in their field (Davis, personal communication, 2007). As more people further their education from a distance and work at a distance, getting an internship at a distance becomes more reasonable if the needs of the student, industry, and the university can be maintained.

Safeguards

Industry and the university can balance these needs by using certain safeguards including contracts, long-term commitments, and real-life projects to make any internship, including distance internships, work for all concerned. All parties also have to maintain a high level of dedication to the processes to make internships fruitful. Students have to communicate with their sponsors and ask for help from the university to negotiate problems with their sponsors, if the student is not able to work out the problems themselves. Industry has to provide mentors to interns, invest in tools, dedicate time and establish links with universities to find talented employees. Universities have also forge links with industry so they are familiar with industry's needs and the tools and software they use. Interns and well-run internship programs can provide these links.

Many universities use some form of contract or agreement outlining the responsibilities of the intern, the company supervisor and the internship director. Mercer University's document gives the benefits of hiring an intern, the responsibilities of the employer and the student, and details the procedure for formalizing an internship (Mercer University). Fitchburg College's Communication Media Department utilizes a comprehensive booklet that details the role of the student. The student section outlines eligibility for the internship, certification, interview and interview preparation, and internship preparation and execution. The internship organization section describes how to become an internship site, how to set up internships and the on-site supervisor's obligations. The role of the educational institution is detailed in four phases. Phase 1: screening the students and sites. Phase 2: placement of students. Phase 3: internship supervision. Phase 4: evaluation of students and the internship site. The nine appendices contain all the documents required for the internship including agreements and letters (DeNike & Sides).

Miami University's Master's Degree Program in Technical and Scientific Communication Regulation booklet contains a contract, discussion of proprietary information and requirements of a student's final internship report (Miami University, 2004). Additionally it contains guidelines for telecommuting internships, which include the requirement that "the sponsoring organization will provide the intern with an on-site orientation to the organization including meetings with the subject matter experts, and when appropriate, the user." The document also covers the requirement that the writing mentor have weekly meetings with the intern via phone, e-mail, or in-person. Detailing requirements for everyone is important under normal circumstances, but these details can be especially helpful in distance or telecommuting internships.

Real-life projects can pose a challenge to companies who may not trust student employees and therefore be unwilling to assign them to real work tasks and projects. However, "a key criterion of success in an internship relates to the degree to which the learner sees the task as authentic—that is, one that has consequences in its context" (Freedman & Adam, 1996, p. 411). Students need real-world projects to give them experience. In Whiteside's (2003) study, one respondent stated they needed "project management because everything I do is a project. Now I am a lone writer and I have no idea where to start." All technical employees can use some basic knowledge of project management and while some may see this as a task of the university, it is more useful for interns

to see the consequences of missed deadlines and the frustrations of negotiating agreements to keep work on schedule.

Dedication

Maintaining dedication to the internship may be difficult but dedication is a key part of its success. Students need to feel that they are contributing and they need to be able to make the transition from educational consumer to a provider of solutions for their employer. Regular work hours and fixed schedules may be a problem for some students and some younger students without work experience may find regular internships difficult. Distance internships require even more dedication and motivation from the student, since their sponsor is not prodding them to produce and since distance internships may be more product driven, rather than process driven. Most of the individuals I interviewed for this chapter indicated that many undergraduates would be too inexperienced in the workplace to be able to successfully complete a distance internship. Distance internships require the student to have some skills in managing their own time: such as setting their own deadlines and knowing their own work habits. Some students also confuse the concepts of an internship and an independent study program (St. Amant, personal communication, 2007). A course of independent study permits a student to investigate an area of their discipline not covered in their normal coursework and the deliverable usually consists of a research report. Internships require the student to produce a meaningful product for their sponsor. Internships force the student to transition from the consumer of an education program into someone that can produce a product that meets the needs of their sponsor. Communication, contracts, and supervision would solve many of the problems involved with any type of internship program, but especially those problems involved in a distance internship. Regular meetings with the internship director and the supervisor, keeping a diary that becomes part of the deliverable for the course, and an interest in the project could maintain the student's dedication.

Industry needs to have dedication to the internship program. Companies must invest time in nurturing workers so that they can become either capable company employees or experienced members of their profession. This requires companies to encourage experienced professionals to mentor interns. Companies also have to maintain ties with universities to give them feedback on the education interns have received from the university and how it is applicable at their company. This feedback loop can improve the training students receive and it can improve the quality of employees, as long as the education of the student is not restricted to the needs of a single company, preventing that student from finding job placement anywhere else in their field. For distance internship programs, companies may also want to invest or upgrade their conferencing and collaborative technologies. This can be a significant investment for smaller companies, but the technology can be used for other projects; it would not be restricted to internships.

Universities need to maintain a dedication to their internship programs. Fitchburg State College probably demonstrates a level of dedication to their internship program that is unmatched by most programs. Dr. Charles Sides is the Internship Director and he keeps his focus on improving the program by regularly meeting with corporate sponsors around the country, meeting with interns on the job and by promoting the program. The college does not require him to teach classes. Fitchburg has found that this investment in their program has given them substantial returns. About forty percent of the students they place in internships are hired by their sponsoring company, and they have received glowing responses from their industry contacts concerning the program. The internship program is one of the main reasons communication students attend Fitchburg College (Sides, personal communication, 2007).

Their program does not fit a model of a distance internship, but many of their students complete their internships while working full-time for sponsors that are not located near the college. In this case, the physical distance lies not between the student and the worksite, as is usually the case in a distance internship, but the distance lies between the school and the sponsor.

FORGING ALLIANCES BETWEEN INDUSTRY AND ACADEMIA

Creating trust and working with companies located in the same area provides many challenges, but working with companies in other states and other countries magnifies those challenges. It is difficult for an internship director in this country to build trust and make contacts with industry in other countries, so that students can serve international internships. There has been some success in building alliances and trust between universities in different countries and then requesting the university in the remote country to act as a liaison between companies in the remote country and the home university (St. Amant, personal communication, 2007).

Northern Arizona University (NAU) has difficulty with students wanting to expend the effort and expense to find overseas internships when there are sufficient opportunities locally (Doerry et al., 2004). Finding internships, comfort with foreign cultures, and integrating internships into an academic schedule are all problems with international internships, but NAU is trying to solve this problem by creating a database of internship opportunities.

Dr. St. Amant (St. Amant, personal communication, 2007) conceives that the solution to companies finding interns and interns finding projects that suit their needs might be accomplished through a national colloquium where university internship directors could meet with company representatives to learn about internship openings and companies could learn more about the universities' programs. Companies could pass this information to mentors within the company and universities could relay the information to their potential interns. This solution could also build the trust relationships that are necessary for successful internships of any kind.

FUTURE TRENDS

Increased bandwidth and decreasing costs of conferencing technology should permit the proliferation of interactive solutions for collaborative workplaces, which would permit the placement of conferencing technologies in more locations, including small businesses and universities. The proliferation of these technologies and the bandwidth to support them could change the current concept of the workplace, altering the necessity for interns to travel to their work, in most cases. Just as cellular telephones enabled the possibility of a mobile office, cheap and efficient communication technologies may permit practitioners and students to bring the workplace anywhere. With a ubiquitous workplace, distance internships become more of a necessity to prepare students to work in this new environment.

To maintain ties with industry faculty might need to participate in internships also. Davis (2000, p. 72) suggests that internship directors, "While working with industry to secure meaningful internships for students, extend the efforts to include work experiences for faculty." Distance internships might serve as both a research opportunity for faculty and as a source of additional income. Distance internships would allow faculty to gain industry experience and sample new workplace communication technologies without the need to leave their university setting.

CONCLUSION

Internships require a bond and trust between industry and the university to create viable internship programs. Distance internships require increased levels of trust. Industry has to believe that the university is training interns to use the tools and techniques required on the job, and the university needs to know that its students will receive a positive work experience. Distance internships also require more motivation and communication skills on the part of the student. While distance internships may not be suitable for all disciplines or types of work, they do serve a necessary function in a world where teams work together around the world.

REFERENCES

Bauman, K. J., & Graf, N. L. (2003). *Educational attainment: 2000.* U.S. Census Bureau.

Davis, M. T. (2000). *Technical communication degrees for the 21st Century.* Paper presented at the Professional Communication Conference.

DeNike, L., & Sides, C. *Communications media internship handbook.* Fitchburg State College.

Doerry, E., Doerry, K., Bero, B., & Neville, M. (2004). *The global engineering college: Lessons learned in exploring a new model for international engineering education.* Paper presented at the American Society for Engineering Education Annual Conference & Exposition.

English, K., & Jereb, B. (1995). Communication and the internship: The roles of program directors, teachers, and corporate supervisors in facilitating change. In *Proceedings of the Society for Technical Communication*, Washington, D.C. (pp. 66-67). Arlington, Virginia: Society for Technical Communication.

Freedman, A., & Adam, C. (1996). Learning to write professionally. *Journal of Business and Technical Communication, 10*(4), 33.

Lurkis, E. B. (2001). The technical writing internship. *Intercom Online.* Retrieved from http://www.stc.org/intercom/PDFs/2001/200111_21.pdf

Mercer University, S. o. E., Department of Technical Communication. *Information for employers: Interns from the technical communication department.* Retrieved November 18, 2007 from http://www.mercer.edu/Engineering/undergraduate_pgms/tco/realworld/employer_info.pdf

Miami University. (2004). Regulations governing internships. Retrieved November 18, 2007, from http://www.units.muohio.edu/mtsc/intern-regsempl.pdf

Robinson, P. A., & Courter, S. S. (1989). A new kind of internship: Technical writing for engineers. *IEEE Transactions on Professional Communication, 32*(3), 4.

Silva, M. K. (2000). *Accreditation, knowledge, and strategies of professionalizing occupations.* Pennsylvania State University, University Park.

Southard, S. (1988). Experiential learning prepares students to assume professional roles. *IEEE Transactions on Professional Communication, 31*(4), 3.

Sutliff, K. (2000). *Academe/Industry Relationship: Balancing Academic Principles and Marketplace Demands.* Paper presented at the 47th Annual Society for Technical Communication Conference, Orlando, FL.

Tovey, J. (2001). Building connections between industry and university: Implementing and internship program at a regional university. *Technical Communication Quarterly, 10*(2), 14.

Whiteside, A. L. (2003). The skills that technical communicators need: An investigation of technical communication graduates, managers and curricula. *Journal of Technical Writing and Communication, 33*(4), 15.

Wilson, G., & Ford, J. D. (2005). The big chill: Seven technical communicators talk ten years after their master's program. *Technical Communication, 50*(2), 4.

KEY TERMS

Acculturation: The process of becoming a part of another culture. In this context, when students are employed and work in their chosen profession they start to acquire knowledge, practices, and experience that can only be obtained through the process of working with other professionals in their field.

Cooperative Program (Coop): Usually used to refer to semester long jobs where engineering students work for engineering firms on projects similar to projects and problems they would encounter in the profession.

Discipline: A field of study.

Geographically-Distributed Teams: Teams that work together on projects but are separated by distance. This distance could be different offices in the same town or different offices in different countries.

Independent Study: A course where the student works with the instructor to construct a course that meets the needs and interests of that specific student. The student usually works alone and completes a final paper summarizing their research and study.

Internship: A scholastic program for course credit that places a student in a work environment to learn the nature and practices of their profession.

Internship director: Usually a position held by a faculty member who matches the needs of students for work experience and the needs of industry for new practitioners.

Mentor: Usually an experienced professional who gives direction and guidance to interns and new practitioners.

Practitioner: Someone who practices a profession.

Service Learning: A process where students are asked to work on projects for organizations outside the academic community; frequently these projects are for not-for-profit or government organizations.

Subject Matter Expert (SME): An expert in the field; someone who has specific knowledge concerning a subject.

Chapter XXXIX
An International Virtual Office Communication Plan

Lei Meng
Texas Tech University, USA

Robert Schafer
Texas Tech University, USA

ABSTRACT

This chapter aims to define a plan for an international virtual office by exploring the problems that hamper communication within a virtual office. Four factors that contribute to miscommunication are explored: linguistics, culture, laws and regulations, and technology. Policies of practice are then offered to mitigate these factors, help increase the productivity, and avoid communication problems, personnel conflicts, and legal liability. Last, different stages of office evolution are discussed and the future trend of office is explored. The purpose of this chapter is to help establish a successful international virtual office as the virtual office is becoming the future trend of the business environment.

INTRODUCTION

As worldwide connectivity through the Internet becomes pervasive, more companies are adopting virtual organizational structures that allow teams of workers to operate across geographic boundaries and apart from a local, central office. More professional workers find themselves members of virtual teams "consisting of members in remote locations who work together primarily through computer-mediated communication" (Robey, Huoy, & Powers, 2000, p. 51). Members of virtual teams often collaborate to construct documentation for technical information products such as computer software, customer service, and pharmaceuticals.

Practitioners of technical communication anticipate that they will soon work in a multicultural, global work environment (Hill, 2006; Murphy, 2007; Nesbitt & Bagley-Woodward, 2006), but are uncertain as to how to adapt current skills and practices within a traditional office environment to a new context: "the international virtual office" (St. Amant, 2001, p. 80). This international virtual office is comprised of the following components:

- Virtual team in which members of various functions work together to bring their respective skills and perspectives to a common work output (Robey et al., 2000, p. 51)
- Virtual team consisting of people who are assembled to accomplish a task via information and telecommunication (Anawati & Craig, 2006, p. 45)
- Virtual teams that work on a specific project that has a beginning and an end (Anawati & Craig, 2006, p. 45)
- Virtual team members that will most likely consist of persons from different geographical locations and cultures that operate within the umbrella of one company or virtual organization (Robey et al., 2000, p. 52)
- Virtual office or work environment that is shared by team members (Harrison, Wheeler, & Whitehead, 2004, p. 57)

Online communication across office contexts has helped to change the traditional concept of the office to include coworkers from varied national and cultural backgrounds. This new telecommuting work environment has the potential to increase productivity while reducing cost (Fritz, Watson, Narasimhan, & Hyeun-Suk, 1998, p. 8) through content sharing (Hill, 2006, p. 12) mediated by collaborative technology (Nesbitt & Bagley-Woodward, 2006, p. 28) resulting in lower overhead.

Although an international virtual office environment may promise low-cost benefits, this new workscape also presents unique challenges. Problems that can hamper communication—and consequently, productivity—in the international virtual office generally originate from factors in four primary areas: linguistics, culture, laws and regulations, and technology. This chapter first analyzes the influences of those aspects that might cause confusions or problems in international virtual offices, and then, based on the analysis, it provides a series of policies that could help us avoid those potential problems in international virtual offices.

BACKGROUND

Linguistic Factors

The fact that individuals from different cultures usually speak different languages presents a basic challenge within the international virtual office because communication among team members is primarily completed through use of spoken and written human language. Without a "universal language" that all members of the international virtual office can understand, communication cannot take place (Kilpatrick, 1984, p. 36). Fortunately, English is helping to bridge the communication gap because it is becoming a global language (Thrush, 1993, p. 273).

Even though English is often used in the international virtual office, linguistic factors will still present unique challenges for team members. Edmond Weiss (1998) demonstrates that even if universal writing practices for simplifying English are used, documents can contain lapses such as "wordiness, ostentation, clumsy links, tense problems, jargon, nominalization, and passives" (p. 255). Although simplified English is intended to be univocal, univocal language may be a barrier to satisfactory communication between the Western and the Asian language speaking people in particular (Weiss, 1998, p. 258), and lead to stereotyping and condescending tolerance (Weiss, 1998, p. 260).

Kirk St. Amant suggests that English-as-a-second-language (ESL) speakers may not understand all of the "nuances and intricate uses of the language" (St. Amant, 2001, p. 82) for reasons such as "limited access to native English speakers, limited access to good teaching materials and effective and competent instructors, or the nature of a given educational system" (St. Amant, 2001, p. 82). In addition, English has different dialects, which may cause misunderstanding about the information being conveyed (Thrush, 1993, p. 273). Considering these issues of encultured and embedded knowledge (Williams, 2006, p. 591), ESL team members may misunderstand some information exchanged in English. As a result, problems caused by linguistic factors in the international virtual office still remain, even if all of the team members do speak a "universal language," such as English (Weiss, 1993, pp. 257-259).

Cultural Factors

Because the practice of information communication varies among cultures, cultural factors will influence the intercultural communication process in the international virtual office. Among the factors that pose communication problems for coworkers, those problems that arise from cultural differences can be the most challenging. The fact that different cultures generally hold different values affects how individuals shape their own attitudes, which in turn guides their communication behaviors.

The contemporary research demonstrates that individuals from various cultures often have different rhetorical expectations in communication: they hold different perspectives toward ethos, logos, and pathos (Williams, 2006, pp. 590-592). As a result, a pattern of communication that works best for a particular culture might not be effective for another. Specific cultural issues that affect communication and pose problems for the international virtual office include whether individuals come from a culture that Edward T. Hall (1989) identifies as predominantly low-context or high-context (p. 128). This relationship is often seen as a continuum (Beamer, 2000, p. 112) along which a particular culture can be placed (See Figure 1).

Hall (1989) uses Japan as his example of the highest-context culture and German Swiss as his example of lowest-context culture. High-context cultures value relationships, are homogeneous, and use forms of communication that are implied

Figure 1. Low context/high context continuum

Low-context   High-context

and implicit (p. 113). Low-context cultures value results, are heterogeneous, and use forms of communication that are explicit (p. 166).

When coworkers in the international virtual office are from both low-context and high-context cultures, those team members from low-context cultures may be confused by the implicit way in which the other person is communicating because the members from low-content cultures prefer conveying the background information clearly and explicitly, while their coworkers from high-context cultures tend *not* to verbalize all of the background information.

For example, suppose your international virtual team consists of team members from a country in Asia where many cultures are considered to be high-context and team members from Western Europe, which are generally understood to be low-context cultures. In an exchange between such team members, the Western European coworker may expect considerable details such as the exact specifications for the customer's deliverables or the precise timelines. Differently, the team members from Asia may communicate based on the assumption that such information is already known or understood or that certain words or phrases the team member has used already provide, through implication, the information the other team member needs. In such cases, the best practice is for all team members to discuss their expectations for the level of background information that is necessary to complete the project.

Directness and indirectness will also pose problems for the international virtual office. In his presentation "Intercultural conflict patterns and intercultural training implications for Koreans," Professor Yun Hee Choe of the University of Suwon, Korea, describes how supervisors might use direct or indirect communication to react to similar situations:

If a North American supervisor is unsatisfied with a subordinate's sales proposal, the response will probably be explicit and direct: "I can't accept this proposal as submitted, so come up with some better ideas." A Korean supervisor, in the same situation, might say: "While I have the highest regard for your abilities, I regret to inform you that I am not completely satisfied with this proposal. I must ask that you reflect further and submit additional ideas on how to develop this sales program." (Choe, 2003, p. 5)

This example demonstrates that how the individual from the indirect culture may feel uncomfortable if the team member from the direct culture uses an imperative and direct tone.

In addition, because the communication in the international virtual office is heavily computer-mediated and often asynchronous online communication, the problem posed by directness and indirectness is exacerbated as the speaker and the receiver of the information will not be in a position to grasp the tone or see the facial expression of the other person.

Legal Factors

Legal issues that may arise in the international virtual office can also affect the quality of communication. Such issues are typically complex since laws are often promulgated based on cultural values and therefore few, if any, laws can be applied to every culture. A more complicating factor is that since communication in the international virtual office usually occurs electronically, borders of countries become blurred. Therefore, it may be difficult to determine which laws govern the behavior and communication of the team members, who are from various countries, in the international virtual office.

According to St.Amant (2004), this "fuzzy situation" poses specific problems regarding copyrighted material and privacy issues. He indicates in "Legal and Ethical Aspects of Globalization," for example, that if the team members from two different countries in the international virtual office have both a strict copyright law and another more liberal copyright laws, then potential legal problems will arise if the colleague governed by the liberal law uses copyrighted material (St.

Amant, 2004). Use of such material may be legal in that team member's country but against the law in the colleague's country. Similarly, conflicts and even legal sanctions can result if one team member fails to protect and discloses information deemed to be private according to the laws of another team member's country, since two nations may not share the same laws and ethics on privacy.

Technical Factors

Because the international virtual office relies heavily on technology such as Internet and computer-mediated technology, communication cannot succeed if the technology infrastructure does not support the free and rapid exchange of information. For this reason, obsolete technology poses significant problems for the communication in international virtual offices.

For example, when the network of an organization goes down on one side of the virtual office, the exchange of information will most likely be truncated or be delayed. This, in turn, might delay the important information transfer to other team members of the virtual office. In addition, if coworkers in an international virtual office do not have sufficient knowledge as to how to use e-mail, how to use file transfer programs to upload or download files, or how to encrypt important data, communication in such a virtual office is hindered, unsafe or, worse, impossible.

MAIN FOCUS OF THE CHAPTER

By putting into place some basic policies to address the issues confronting international virtual offices, organizations can increase productivity, improve the flow of information among team members, and avoid personal conflicts and legal liability. The following section will discuss the main focus of the chapter—proposed practices for the International Virtual Office.

Practice for Linguistic Aspects

To avoid the potential problems caused by linguistic factors in international virtual offices, a key practice that organizations can adopt is to require team members to convert culturally specific wording into more general wording and to use a standard vocabulary so that the international audience can easily understand the information. Specific practices that can be put into place in the international virtual office:

- Avoid culturally specific wording such as idiomatic expressions and metaphoric expressions. In his article "Designing for Translation," St. Amant explains that the meaning of such expressions "is linked to a particular cultural pattern of use" (St. Amant, 2003, p. 6). Regardless of how fluently an international coworker speaks English, it is unrealistic for that individual to know and stay current on all of the idiomatic or metaphoric expressions present in the English language, because such expressions are largely culturally dependent and understanding them requires that the individual have regular contact with the culture. Therefore, coworkers in the international virtual office should avoid idiomatic and metaphoric expressions to preclude the possibility that the receiver of the information will skew the speaker's intended meaning.
- Use standard, simple English in communication. A large number of coworkers in the international virtual office are ESL speakers who are taught standard English grammar and usage; as a result, they may not know the subtle nuances of the language. To help ensure that ESL speakers will not be confused by a particular expression, using the simple word and standard sentence structure is recommended. For example, team members should avoid using demonstrative pronouns such as *this* or *that*, should use parallel structure when listing individual items, and should avoid long or overly complex sentences.
- Attach glossaries to written materials when both the sender and receiver of the information are communicating in a written pattern. An organization may also take the additional step of building a standard glossary for use to explain terms, abbreviations, and uncommon words so that the information can be communicated correctly and consistently among team members.

Practice for Cultural Aspects

To avoid the potential problems that cultural factors bring to the international virtual offices, organizations should consider implementing the following policies for international virtual office team members:

- Show respect for and appreciation of other cultures. St. Amant (2001) suggests in "Success in the International Virtual Office" that this practice is essential because it not only creates "a positive first impression," but also demonstrates the "commitment to the overall relationship" (p. 88). Showing respect for other cultures is a crucial step we can take to ensure the successful communication in the international virtual office because team members from one cultural background will see that their colleagues from another cultural background have actually made efforts in studying and understanding a different culture. Therefore, even if one team member may not behave in a manner that is considered appropriate in the culture of another team member, another team member will be tolerant with it and the inappropriateness will not compromise the business relationship.
- Workers in the international virtual offices should acquire basic knowledge about intercultural communication and their colleagues' cultural backgrounds. Simply showing respect and appreciation will not

be enough to resolve the problems caused by cultural differences in the international virtual offices; it simply weakens the possibility to ruin a business relationship. In order to avoid or solve the problems, individuals need to be sensitive to where the cultural differences might result in a different behavior and understanding. In addition, they also need to know how they could adjust their behaviors to adapt to another group of culture. The team members do not necessarily have a degree in intercultural communication, but special training about the basic concept on directness/indirectness, low/high context or individualism/collectivism should be offered by the company to the team members who will work in the international virtual offices. The company might also assign a special expert for intercultural communication to help the common workers resolve any problems with communication in the international virtual office.

- Policies for conflict resolution between team members should be established and defined in such a way as to allow for an open and respectful exchange that is sensitive to cultural context. Research conducted by Pei-Wen Lee (2006) indicates that conflict management between workers from different cultures can often result in friendship between both parties involved (pp. 17-18). In Lee's (2006) study, participants from different cultures who were friends "often chose to emphasize their shared similarities rather than be concerned about their differences" (p. 16). Cultural sensitivity in conflict management can result in stronger, more cohesive teams.

Practice for Legal Aspects

Legal factors in international virtual offices are complex, but can be more easily resolved because the law is low-context and seldom generates various meanings. As long as a law or a policy could

be made, all team members can simply follow the rules due to law's low-context nature. Therefore, the key lies in the agreement all team members in the virtual office could have agreed. The organization can adopt a "strictest law" policy—the set-up of a law or a policy in the virtual office based on the "minimum" policy, which means to ensure the minimum possibility to break a law among all international team members. For example, if two nations have both liberal copyright law and the strict copyright law, the law practiced in the virtual office should meet the expectation of the nation with the strict copyright law.

Practice for Technical Aspects

Obsolete technologies also pose problems for the successful international virtual office. For this reason, companies should pay close attention to the technical factors that can impede communication among team members and be prepared to invest in the infrastructure that will foster collaboration and productivity of team members.

As Suchan and Hayzak (2001) suggest in their article "The Communication Characteristics of Virtual Teams: A Case Study," companies need to "invest in technologies and networks" (Suchan & Hayzak, 2001, p. 177) and "recruit talented technical support staff" (Suchan & Hayzak, 2001, p. 177) so that the technologies used in the international virtual office could be maintained at a level that can meet the work requirements for all team members. Also, once technical problems are raised, they should be resolved quickly and efficiently by the technical support staff so that the communication among team members is not delayed.

In addition to hardware limitations, software deficiencies may also occur. Pamela Nesbitt and Elizabeth Bagley-Woodward (2006), in their *Intercom* article "Practical Tips for Working with Global Teams," identify three basic categories of collaboration software necessary for an international virtual office (p. 28):

- Electronic communication tools that send information between different people to review at different times, such as e-mail, fax, and voice mail.
- Electronic conferencing tools that allow the simultaneous sharing of information between different people, such as telephone and video conferencing, discussion boards, and chat rooms.
- Collaborative management tools that manage group activities, such as electronic calendars, workflow systems and knowledge management systems.

Together, these three categories of collaboration software provide the software tools necessary to manage a geographically dispersed team and companies should ensure that virtual team members have access to these technologies.

Companies should also provide appropriate training to their employees so that team members can make full use of the technologies that work best in the online environment for online communication purpose. In some situations, technical problems occur at the individual level. In such cases, training to enhance the individual's technical knowledge of an application or device can also save technical support staff time in resolving the issue.

FUTURE TRENDS

Tomio Kishimoto and Gen Suzuki (1993), in their article "Virtual Offices," elaborate three stages of office evolution. In the first stage, they believe the main role of the office "was thought to be that of a physical communication environment in which people and paper (in other words, communication and information) were gathered together" (p. 36). In the second stage, the office "offer(s) a comfortable and productivity-enhancing environment for the business people who work there and make full and frequent use of electronic tools" (Kishimoto & Suzuki, 1993, p. 36). This is the most common module of office nowadays, where

people are achieving business purposes with the help of various types of electronic devices such as telephones, computers, software applications etc. that are actually installed in the offices. And Kisimoto and Suzuki (1993) believe we are entering the third stage of the office evolution, where the office is "an intelligent building within a computer network," rather than "a computer network within an intelligent building" (p. 36).

Under this concept, the role of the physical office building and that of the computer network have actually switched. The computer network, rather than the physical building, becomes the infrastructure of the business environment (i.e., office), which leads to the new trend of alternative work arrangement such as telecommuting and homeshoring.

U.S. Department of Labor statistics (2003) say "some 13 million to 19 million workers telecommute in the United States." And homeshoring is "the transfer of service industry employment from offices to home-based employees with appropriate telephone and Internet facilities," according to Macmillan English Dictionary. Homeshoring is also considered to be a combination of telecommuting and outsourcing and it is becoming the most popular business module for freelancers. To adapt to the trend of telecommuting and homeshoring, many companies have updated their IT infrastructure such as the use of virtual private network (VPN), e-fax, Webinar, and so forth. For example, with a VPN, the employees do not need to come to the office in a snow day and can easily control his own office computer at home. With an e-fax, an individual freelancer does not need to purchase a traditional fax machine or tons of paper and can accomplish the same business activity as with the traditional way. More interestingly, Fritz et al. have showed that "telecommuters were more satisfied with overall office communication than were conventional office workers" (p. 19) in their research, but they have also concluded that the satisfaction heavily depends on "the satisfaction with IT support" and the "availability and use of IT by workers" (p. 21).

The advanced technology facilitates the shape of the new forms of virtual offices, but in turn the new trend of virtual offices also requires the continuous development of IT infrastructure to best meet the communication purposes.

CONCLUSION

With the advent of high technologies, the virtual office is the future trend of business environment, which changes the conventional concept of office environment. This shift exists at a local level, a national level, and an international level, as well. As analyzed in this chapter, successful communication at the international level/in the international virtual office is closely related to linguistic, cultural, legal, and technical factors. By being aware of these factors and proactively putting policies in place to address them, companies will be able to increase their productivity and avoid communication problems, personnel conflicts, and legal liability. Among the proposed practices, an awareness of cultural difference and a willingness on the part of both organizations and employees to adapt are keys to the success of the international virtual office.

REFERENCES

Anawati, D., & Craig, A. (2006). Behavioral adaptation within cross-cultural teams. *IEEE Transactions on Professional Communication, 49*(1), 44-56.

Beamer, L. (2000). Finding a way to teach cultural dimensions. *Business Communication Quarterly, 63*(3), 111-118.

Choe, Y.H. (2003). *Intercultural conflict patterns and intercultural training implications for Koreans.* Retrieved November 18, 2007, from http://segero.hufs.ac.kr/library/iar/9-6.pdf

Fritz, M.B., Watson, Narasimhan, S., & Hyeun-Suk, R. (1998). Communication and coordination in the virtual office. *Journal of Management Information Systems, 14*(4), 7-28.

Hall, E.T. (1989). *Beyond culture.* New York: Anchor Books/Double Day.

Harrison, A., Wheeler, P., & Whitehead, C. (Eds.). (2004). *The distributed workplace: Sustainable work environments.* London and New York: Spoon Press.

Hill, N. (2006, July/August). Going global with technical writing. *Intercom, 53,* 11-13.

Kilpatrick, R.H. (1984). International business communication practices. *The Journal of Business Communication, 21,* 33-44.

Kishimoto, T., & Suzuki, G. (1993). Virtual offices. *IEEE Communications Magazine, 31*(10), 36-38.

Murphy, M. (2007, February). Protecting yourself from offshoring: Advice for U.S.-based technical communicators. *Intercom, 54,* 4-7.

Nesbitt, P., & Bagley-Woodward, E. (2006. June). Practical tips for working with global teams. *Intercom, 53,* 25-30.

Pei-Wen, L. (2006). Bridging cultures: Understanding the construction of relational identity in intercultural friendship. *Journal of Intercultural Communication Research, 35*(1), 3-22.

Robey, D., Huoy, M.K., & Powers, C. (2000). Situated learning in cross-functional virtual teams. *IEEE Transactions on Professional Communication, 43*(1), 51-66.

St. Amant, K. (2001). Chapter V: Success in the international virtual office. In N. Johnson (Ed.), *Telecommuting and virtual offices: Issues and opportunities* (pp. 80-99). Hershey, PA: Idea Group Publishing.

St. Amant, K. (2003). *Designing for translation. The internal graduate class course material.* Lubbock, TX: Texas Tech University.

St. Amant, K. (2004). *Legal and ethical aspects of globalization. The internal graduate class course material.* Lubbock, TX: Texas Tech University.

Suchan, J., & Hayzak, G. (2001). The communication characteristics of virtual teams: A case study. *IEEE Transactions on Professional Communication, 44*(3), 174-186.

Thrush, E.A. (1993). Bridging the gaps: Technical communication in an international and multicultural society. *Technical Communication Quarterly, 2*(3), 271-283.

U.S. Department of Labor statistics (2003). *CTA: US Telework Scene - stats and facts* (2003 onwards) Retrieved January 5, 2008, from http://www.ivc.ca/studies/us/index.htm

Weiss, E.H. (1998). Technical communication across cultures: Five philosophical questions. *Journal of Business and Technical Communication, 12*(2), 253-269.

Williams, A.M. (2006). Lost in translation? International migration, learning and knowledge. *Progress in Human Geography, 30*(5), 588-607.

KEY TERMS

E-Fax: refers to E-mail/Internet fax by which people can get a real fax number tied to their e-mail and can receive and send faxes using the e-mail and the Internet without the fax machine and fax modem required.

International Virtual Office: refers to a setting where people from various cultures are working together through online communication.

Low-Context Culture: refers to a culture in which cultural behavior, beliefs, and so forth, need to be spelled out explicitly; for example: German culture.

High-Context Culture: refers to a culture in which less is spelled out explicitly and much more is implicit or communicated in indirect ways because people have a great deal of commonality of knowledge and views; for example: Japanese culture.

Idiomatic Expressions: the expressions used in everyday language in a specific culture, which is hard to understand by people from different cultures since the idioms cannot be translated word by word.

Metaphoric Expressions: the expressions in which a figure of speech is used so that a word or phrase that ordinarily designates one thing is used to designate another, thus making an implicit comparison.

Telecommuting: refers to the working module where people work away from the office workstation with the use of telecommunication technologies such as Internet, computers, telephones, and other advanced network technologies.

Virtual Teams: teams of workers consisting of members in remote locations who work together primarily through computer-mediated communication (Robey et al., 2000, p. 51).

VPN: Virtual Private Network, which is a private communications network to communicate confidentially over a public network on top of standard protocols. A VPN can send data across secured and encrypted private channels between two points. It is commonly used by telecommuters when they are away from the office.

Workscape: refers to the work environment in which people are expected to perform tasks and produce goods and services related to their profession.

Chapter XL
Design and Managing of Distributed Virtual Organizations

Diego Liberati
Italian National Research Council, Italy

ABSTRACT

A framework is proposed that creates, uses, communicates, and distributes information whose organizational dynamics allow it to perform a distributed cooperative enterprise in public environments even over open source systems. The approach assumes Web services as the enacting paradigm, possibly over a grid, to formalize interaction as cooperative services on various computational nodes of a network. A framework is thus proposed that defines the responsibility of e-nodes in offering services and the set of rules under which each service can be accessed by e-nodes through service invocation. By discussing a case study, the chapter will detail how specific classes of interactions can be mapped into a service-oriented model whose implementation will be carried out in a prototypical public environment.

INTRODUCTION

Science is nowadays more and more a question of a critical mass of skilled people—often with complementary backgrounds—becoming a unique global organism in pursuit of a substantial common goal. This was true last century in physics, and it is going to hold true now in biology. A particular difference is worth mentioning: while traditional specialized workforces have historically been concentrated in unique sites with special instruments in physics, the availability of ICTs enables full networks to be built in remote sites, together with the absence of the need of a big site for many of the problems faced in biology, or even natural distribution, like, for instance in geology,

makes it interesting to resort to a possible network of experimenters, physically not necessarily together, but logically co-present in the framework of the same cooperative big experiment involving all their complementary competences. In the paradigmatic bioinformatics application domain dealt with in this chapter within the framework of e-science (Hey & Trefethen, 2004), collaboration may be even more needed than in other areas such as financial transactions (although any ICT-assisted business interaction could be described in the same way).

A proper virtual organisation is thus required in order to manage the workflow of information over a given network in order that cooperation among the nodes does not deteriorate into an absence of competition among potential partners with the same competence but at a different level of capability. Flexibility is essential, due to fast-developing competences and technologies, and will ensure that any redesign(s) will not have to be done "from scratch" every time. Proper orchestration would allow a better exploitation of every component. Interoperability among components is another important characteristic. A networked organisation such as this may be logically defined through workflows acting over Web services, possibly in a grid context, and made as public as the contributing actors agree—not just among them but also to a wider community—by exposing data and/or results while keeping reserved within the cooperating group the workflow. The technology addressed in this chapter would thus allow the most competent scientist to design the workflow even if he is not at a very high level of competence in IT issues (which are, in a sense, logically embedded), as is common in application contexts like the bioinformatics faced here, as well as in other application domains, where the proposed tools can also be applied. It is worth noting that such an approach is also a way to overcome a certain form of digital divide, if encompassing not just extremes being able or not to access to Information and Communication Technologies, but including also not homogeneous situation of partial access, provided that minimal requirements such the one here proposed are satisfied. In such a sense, approaches like the proposed one could provide a tremendous improvement in the capability to easily recruit a higher portion of the human capital not yet fully involved in global research.

BACKGROUND

Grid computing (Foster, Kesselman, Nick, & Tuecke, 2002) has facilitated the growth of virtual organizations: the basic idea is to have a framework, unbound to a specific technical solution (Foster & Kesselman, 2004), where people (not at the same location, but having direct access to linked ICT heterogenic resources) can achieve a common goal through collaboration with each other.

To do this, every resource shared across the network has to be associated with a sufficiently high-level interface in order to allow the corresponding service to be remotely controlled, locally granting a sufficient quality of service with respect to the usual problems of (say) faults, handling of exceptions, security, and so forth.

Web services (Booth et al., 2004; Christensen, Curbera, Meredith, & Weerawarana, 2003; Graham & Treadwell, 2004) are among the proper technologies to address such resource virtualisation problems, which form the local part of the whole networking problem.

The global side is, instead, the proper orchestration (Peltz, 2003) of the whole subset of the possibly heterogeneous and probably delocalised needed resources. Workflows (van der Aalst & Hofstede, 2003) address the orchestration of such a distributed process.

NETWORKED EXPERIMENTS

An easy way to face a complex problem is a divide-and-conquer strategy, aiming to decompose a set of simpler subproblems. In this case, the workflow is an orchestrated set of virtual procedures, each of them defined by the core computation on input data in order to produce output data related to a single activity. Such orchestration can easily be described as a way of reminding the classical general schema of petri net as being useful to define at an abstract level of sequenced interaction among actors.

Every single procedure—even if software-modeled—also usually involves human experts, adding specific value to the automatic capabilities of the integrated tools, whose geographical location is impacted, if not bounded, by the standard live(s) of the human actors, whose quality is usually of paramount importance in sophisticated applications such as e-science.

Human actors, skilled in the application domain (but not necessarily in the details of every single part or location of the implementation of every single procedure), define the workflow(s) by selecting the distributed resources needed in order to compose them in the desired task.

To this aim, the system has to support the human actor in automatically discovering and localizing the resources, as well as offering a spectrum of already defined procedures and workflows that can be, at least partially, reused. The actor will not merely exploit the system for the actor's own interests, but will also contribute to the workflow(s) designed in order to contribute to the library available to the peers.

The paradigmatic distributed experiment presented in this chapter refers to a process of DNA-microarrays clustering, based on two techniques: the first proposed by Garatti, Bittanti, Liberati, and Maffezzoli (2007), with feature selection; the second based on the Adaptive Bayesian Network presented by Bosin, Dessi, Fugini, Leberati, and Pes (2006).

In order to simplify the workflow design, a workflow graphical particular editor, Taverna (http://taverna.sourceforge.net/) may be used to discover, select, and link Web services in order to define and execute workflows, and then to analyse their outputs.

The defined workflow can then be instantiated in the form of Simple Conceptual Unified Flow Language (Oinn, 2004), which is similar to (the more diffused) Business Process Execution Language (Andrews et al., 2003).

The data requested by the designed workflow may belong to one or more different organisations with respect to the one(s) to whom the workflow designer belongs, provided that they have exposed all the data necessary for the experiment as a Web service and identified it through an URL. If many sources are available, parallels could be exploited by several instances of the same workflow.

Particular care has to be posed in interfacing the format of data with the one of the computational tools that will be used in the next processing phase: full standard is far from being a rule in scientific domains, both for data and for processing software, which is understandable due to the rapid modifications of experimentation even in the same single context, when its complexity and novelty are of the kind of the bioinformatics one. For the DNA-microrrays data in this example, there are at present three quasi-standard repository formats. The relative data extraction module may thus be designed in Java as able to express all the different kinds of format in a unique intermediate representation that is exposed as a Web service and could be used even in other workflows in order to convert the data in the proper format for the computation. A useful URL may be one where a wide number of data is available, that is, for instance, the Cancer Program Data Set of the Broad Institute (www.broad.mit.edu/cgi-bin/cancer/datasets.cgi), where the data used in the example are both presented and stored.

The computation may then be executed on one or more adequate machine(s). In principle, they are different from both the ones in which either the Taverna or the data do reside, in order to satisfy both computational and/or software and/r supervision needs. In the example presented here, unsupervised clustering associated with principal component analysis (Garatti et al., 2007) may be performed under Matlab (www.mathworks.com), while Adaptive Bayesian Networks with Minimum Description Length feature selection (Bosin et al., 2006) may be performed under Oracle (www.oracle.com) data mining procedures. It is worth noticing that, even in such simple examples, each of the two processing options is again composed of a couple of associated procedures. Both of them are thus worth being examined alone in order to enable another designer to reuse only the smaller module at the designer's convenience. Such a refinement also enables a more easily split computation on a number of machines, if needed, without the need of resorting to parallelisation, the management of which can be troublesome.

In the case of Matlab, the experiment engine needs to interface with the Matlab environment to execute the relative code through the Matlab functions that cannot be directly exposed, and thus made active, by Java script through the interface JMatLink (jmatlink.sourceforge.net). The whole of the Java code can thus be exposed as Web service. Single Matlab functions, or a group of them, can then be selected as different Web services to enable their re-use. Apache Axis can be used to build Web services, once installed on the Web container Apache Tomcat (tomcat.apache.org).

The results can then be visualised either or both at the same site where the experiment is launched, to let the designer appreciate them, or at a different site, where a demo or a report is expected. Finally, the whole experiment can be saved through the additional tool myGrid (www.mygrid.org.uk) in order to be able to reuse it.

FUTURE TRENDS

On the technological side, an extension of the proposed framework is expected to migrate over the emerging support of the Grid technology, in order to gain, at least, automatic load balancing from the connection grid of distributed computers.

On the application side, other e-science applications would benefit from the proposed approach. In geo-informatics, for instance, data are often intrinsically distributed and sometimes of non homogeneous nature; moreover, some research groups may have novel or different analyzing techniques at the forefront of the discipline. The capability to share data and processing tools in a simple friendly network like the one proposed in this chapter would increase the efficacy of a naturally distributed system of research and monitoring. In a less widely known context, like neuro-informatics, where a few centres in the world have the structures and the skills to not invasively deeply investigate the pathophysiology of the human brain, a similar framework helping to share data and techniques would help to reach a critical mass in order to further improve the state of the art.

Besides such quite peculiar scientific approaches like the one exemplified in this chapter, it is worth stressing that a wide area of business

interactions is open to be addressed with the proposed approach, after appropriate tuning, not excluding e-marketplaces.

Such extensions make the proposed framework a quite general tool in order to easily exchange information and processing tools in a peer-to-peer network, which is one of the appealing modalities in the public information context addressed by the present book.

CONCLUSION

A virtual organisation for e-science has been proposed here by resorting to paradigmatic bio-informatics examples. This proposal is based on workflows rooted in Web services through a tool called Taverna. At present, it is not yet implemented on a grid service. However, it is designed in order to be able to migrate when it is required. The approach is designed at a very abstract level. Thus, it is easy to generalize it to almost any area of science (and more widely business) interaction, after appropriate tuning.

REFERENCES

Andrews, T., Curbera, F., Dholakia, H., Goland, Y., Klein, J., Leymann, F., et al. (2003). Business process execution language for Web services version 1.1.

Booth, D., Haas, H., McCabe, F., Newcomer, E.I., Champion, C., Ferris, C., et al. (2004, February 11). Web service architecture W3C specification (W3C Working Group Note). Retrieved November 18, 2007, from http://www.w3.org/TR/ws-arch/

Bosin, A., Dessì, N., Fugini, M.G., Liberati, D., & Pes. B. (2006). *Applying enterprise models to design cooperative scientific environments* (LNCS 3812, pp. 281-292). Springer-Verlag.

Christensen, E., Curbera, F., Meredith, G., & Weerawarana, S. (2003, June 24). WSDL Web service definition language version 1.1. W3C Recommendation.

Foster, I., & Kesselman, C. (2004). *The GRID2: Blueprint for a new computing infrastructure* (2ⁿᵈ ed.). San Francisco: Morgan Kaufmann.

Foster, I., Kesselman, C., Nick, J., & Tuecke, S. (2002, June 22). The physiology of the GRID, an open GRID services architecture for distribuited system integration. In *Open Grid Service Infrastructure WG, Global Grid Forum.*

Garatti, S., Bittanti, S., Liberati, D., & Maffezzoli, P. (2007). An unsupervised clustering approach for leukemia classification based on DNA micro-arrays data. *Intelligent Data Analysis, 11*(2), 175-188.

Graham, S., & Treadwell, J. (2004, June 10). Web service resource framework W3c specification (Working Draft). Retrieved November 18, 2007, from http://docs.oasis-open.org/wsrf/2004/06/wsrf-WS-ResourceProperties-1.2-draft04.pdf

Hey, T., & Trefethen, A. (2004). *E-science and its implications.* UK: E-Science Core Programme, Engineering and Physical Sciences Research Council, Polaris House, Swindon SN 1ET.

Oinn, T. (2004). Xscufl language reference. European Bioinformatics Institute. Retrieved November 18, 2007, from http://www.ebi.ac.uk/~tmo/mygrid/XScuflSpecification.html

Peltz, C. (2003). Web services orchestration and choreography. *IEEE Computer, 36*(10), 46-52.

van der Aalst, W.M.P., & Hofstede, A.H.M. (2003). Workflow patterns. *Distributed and Parallel Databases, 46*(6), 5-51.

KEY TERMS

Adaptive Bayesian Networks: Conditional probabilistic trees describing the relative importance of each relevant variable to determine a classification.

Bio-Informatics: The application of information technology to advanced biological problems, like transcriptomics and proteomics, involving huge amounts of data.

E-Science: The cooperative work of scientists with various competences at different sites over an ICT connection in order to achieve a common scientific goal.

Grid Computing: A computing paradigm that enables the sharing, selection, and aggregation of a wide variety of geographically distributed computational resources.

Micro-Array: Technology providing biologists with the ability to measure the expression levels of thousands of genes in a single experiment.

Minimum Description Length: Information Theory principle stating that the best model is the one that minimize the number of bits needed to codify both the model and the data, here used in order to quantify the number of relevant features.

Principal Component Analysis: Rearrangement of the data matrix in new orthogonal transformed variables ordered in decreasing order of variance.

Unsupervised Clustering: Automatic classification of a dataset in two or more subsets on the basis of the intrinsic properties of the data without taking into account further contextual information.

Workflow: The automation of a business process, in whole or part, during which documents, information, or tasks are passed from one participant (human or machine) to another for action, according to a set of procedural rules.

Web Services: Software paradigm enabling peer-to-peer computation in distributed environments based on the concept of "service" as an autonomous piece of code published in the network.

Section IV
Implementation of Virtual Workplaces Across Professions and Academic Disciplines

Chapter XLI
Semi Virtual Workplaces in German Financial Service Enterprises

Heinz D. Knoell
Leuphana University, Germany

ABSTRACT

In this chapter we will present semi virtual workplace (SVWP) concepts in the German financial sector (FS) industry. We give a short introduction into the problem and an overview of the German FS market and its recent developments under European Community (EC) legislation. In the next sections we present three German FS companies that apply successfully semi virtual workplace concepts, followed by detailed descriptions of two semi virtual concepts: strict alternating use of a workplace by two employees (every other day an employee is in his home office) and the concept of the business club, where the employees choose daily their workplace out of a workplace pool when they work on-site. In the last section we compare the concepts and draw conclusion. Further we outline our future research.

INTRODUCTION

In the need to keep pace with competitors, enterprises have to find new ways of saving costs and speeding up their business processes (Igbaria, 1998, p. 5). Syler and Schwager (2000) cite Christie and Levary (1998, p. 1699):

Organizations today must constantly adapt to the ever-changing, fiercely competitive business environment not only to be successful but also to survive. There is a host of external and internal forces that make constant change almost a necessity. Rapid changes in customers' tastes and needs, incredible advancements in technology, phenomenal growth in the internationalization of businesses, volatile capital markets, varying employee attitudes, and changing customer demographics are all part of the fluid scenario.

In the same paper, Syler and Schwager (2000, p. 1699) argue that "it (i.e., the virtual organization) is not an organization, but rather it is a strategy for organizing the elements of the value chain or a characteristic of an organizational approach."

As we can learn from their research, there is a great variety of definitions of virtual organizations, virtual teams, virtual enterprises, and virtual workplaces. An excellent overview of literature concerned with these terms can be found in Syler and Schwager (2000) and Li (2004).

Virtual workplaces are a promising concept which arose in last decade of the 20th Century. As Christie and Levary (1998) stated, there are three major reasons for the installment of virtual workplaces: saving costs, gaining flexibility, and speeding up processes. But what can these goals achieve using virtual workplaces?

Cascio (2000, p. 81) lists the common benefits of virtual workplaces (VWP) as follows:

- reduced real estate expenses (see also O'Connel, 1996, p. 1),
- increased productivity,
- higher profits,
- improved customer service,
- access to global markets, and
- environmental benefits.

Cascio (2000, p. 82) names also the risks of virtual workplaces:

- set up and maintenance costs,
- loss of cost efficiencies,
- cultural issues,
- feelings of isolation, and
- lack of trust.

O'Connel (1996, p. 2) addresses one more major problem of VWPs: "Overcoming the resistance of middle managers, on the other hand, is a tougher challenge. As new demands are placed on the remote manager, the corner office becomes a thing of the past."

Besides the technical aspects, the psychological, sociological, and managerial problems are the most important ones (see Riemer & Klein, 2003; Townsend, DeMarie, & Hendrickson, 2000). In order to overcome these latter problems, semi virtual workplaces (SVWPs) may be the answer.

In this chapter, we deal with SVWPs and other new types of workplaces in the German Financial Sector (FS) industry. Fritz, Narasimhan, and Rhee (1998, p. 2) call that type of workplace design "part time telecommuting" if the virtual workplace is at home. We call these work places "semi virtual work places (SVWPs)," as they are designed in a way that the employee spends a part of his work time on site and another part off site elsewhere, maybe at home.

THE FINANCIAL SERVICES MARKET IN GERMANY IN BRIEF

Overview

This section gives an overview of the German financial services market in order to improve the background understanding of the problems presented in Chapter 3 and concepts presented in Chapters 4 and 5. The German financial services market is unique in Europe: There are 92,080 enterprises active in this market (Pohle, 2004) with a total of 472,200 employees. Compared to the other European nations, this figure is more than 10 times higher compared, for example, to the UK with a similar population.

The financial service (FS) market in Germany is represented by banking companies, insurance companies, and building societies. In addition, there are brokers, agents, and service enterprises, which supply the FS companies with IT services and more. According to their ownership (see Table 1), German financial service companies are subdivided into

- private, mainly owned by shareholders,
- cooperatives, and
- owned by municipal authorities and state owned.

Each category has its own characteristics and problems, partly due to EC legislation. Due to the enforcement of competition and deregulation by the EC commission, mainly the cooperatives

Table 1. German financial sector enterprises with their sector and ownership (BaFin, 2004)

Financial Sector Enterprises	Number (2003)	Total (2003)
Banking (Total)		2295
Retail banking companies	5	
Regional private banking companies	231	
Subsidiaries of foreign banking companies	121	
State banks	13	
Municipal saving banks	491	
Cooperative banks	1394	
Real estate banks	25	
Special banks	15	
Building Societies (Total)		27
Private building societies	16	
Public building societies	11	
Insurance (Total)		633
Life insurance	105	
Pensionkassen	158	
Death benefit funds	41	
Health insurance	54	
Property/casualty insurance	231	
Reinsurance undertakings	44	
Total	**2955**	**2955**

and public sector owned FS companies encounter dramatic changes since the 1990s. The private banking sector is also affected, but not to such tremendous scale: there are only five retail banking companies in Germany, one of them the Postbank, formerly owned by the federal government. The remaining four private banks are global players, in particular the Deutsche Bank. Also Dresdner Bank (the major shareholder is Germany's biggest insurance group Alliance), Commerzbank, and Vereins-und Westbank are operating internationally (Bundesbank, 2006).

Banking Companies

Table 1 shows the distribution of banking companies in Germany. You can easily recognize the vast majority of cooperative banks, followed by the municipal savings banks. These banks are predominantly small banks with a limited regional market. Since the deregulation of the FS sector by the EU, they have no longer their safe regional harbor; they have to compete with national competitors and European market players.

Figure 1 shows how the municipal saving banks and the cooperative banks reacted to the market pressure. In 2005, less than a half of the cooperative banks were left, compared to 1991. The situation of the municipal saving banks is better, as they are still owned by the municipal authorities. In addition, they do not need to secure their business with a deposit at the central bank of Europe nor by insurance, because their business is guaranteed by the local authority which will take the money from the tax payer if necessary. Nevertheless their number has decreased from 1991 to 2005 by approximately one third. The decrease of German banking companies is nearly compensated for by the appearance of international banking companies, whose number increased from 1991 to 2002 from 85 to 318. Until now they have not played a big role in the German market, but they increase their market share every year (BaFin, 2003).

Like every merger, the merger of cooperative banks and municipal savings banks is frequently wrenched: Many jobs considered to last forever have been eliminated, increasing the number of unemployed and early retired people in Germany. Even worse, a large number of politicians lost their additional income, being members of the supervising board of one of these banks. This concentration process is still ongoing. The EC commissioners insist on equal chances for all competitors in the market, especially for the municipal savings banks and the state banks.

Building Societies

The municipal savings banks are related to state owned building societies, which are related to

Figure 1. Number of cooperative and municipal banking companies from 1991-2005 (Bundesbank, 1990, 1995, 2000, 2002, 2006)

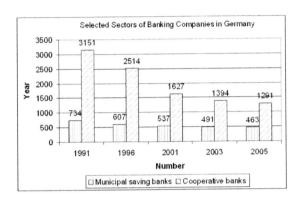

Figure 2. Number of insurance companies from 1996-2005 (GDV, 1996, 2001, 2003, 2005)

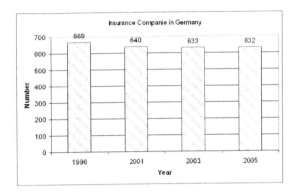

the German state banks. Close to these state banks are also state insurance groups, related to the municipal savings banks. As these insurance companies are already serving a larger market, there was only little concentration in the past.

The cooperative banks have shares of one building society (Schwäbisch Hall) and of one insurance company (RuV) to which they are related in their daily business.

Insurance Companies

A similar concentration process is taking place in the German insurance market. This market has not had as tremendous a concentration process as the German banking market. In contrast, the concentration process started earlier in the 1990s. One big difference is that the branding of the insurance companies stayed the same (in contrast to the banks); even following a merger they are independent companies. So the statistics don't show the correct picture (BaFin, 2005). In a way, not visible to the customer insurance companies like Aachen-Münchener and Volksfürsorge are owned by the Italian global player Generali (BaFin, 2005). In addition, cross-domain mergers become more common, whereby an insurance company, like Allianz AG, takes over a bank, for example the second largest private bank, namely Dresdner Bank AG.

The German insurance market is dominated by Allianz AG, a company owned by private shareholders. The private shareholder-owned insurance companies are about one half of all, followed by small and local operating cooperatives, which are about one third of the enterprises. About 14% are cooperative insurance companies, independent from cooperative banking companies and the rest, are private owned or from abroad (GDV-Statistics, 2005).

In the German insurance market, like in the banking sector, the cooperative and the public sector companies are under severe market pressure. So they are more encouraged to develop new models for savings costs than other market participants. The privately owned banks had their business reengineering projects already in the early 1990s and they are still working on it. Also since that time there was a big wave of mergers and acquisitions.

PORTRAIT OF FS COMPANIES WITH SVWP CONCEPTS

The companies selected in this section are two cooperative companies and a company from the public sector banking. As mentioned in the previous section, especially the cooperative and the public sector FS enterprises are under strong market pressure in Germany. Here are short portraits of these companies.

LVM Insurance Group

LVM (Landwirtschaftlicher Versicherungsverein a.G. Münster = farmers cooperative insurance Münster) Insurance Group located in Münster, is one of the cooperative insurance companies with a steady growth since it was founded as a farmers agricultural cooperative insurance in 1896. Since 1969, the insurance has been opened to the public. Every customer becomes automatically a member of the cooperative. Since that time the number of policies have grown from 560,000 to 5.3 million, and the headcount of the staff grew from 300 to 2,400 in 2006. By using Information Technology in a clever way and by having only one centralized administration, the group was able to keep costs, as well as insurance premiums, low. Therefore, a steady growth in a competing market was possible. The LVM insurance group has now (December 2005) 2.8 million customers and is in the top three of the German car insurance market according to the number of policies (LVM, 2006).

This growth was limited in the 1990s by the company's office space and the restrictions of the local authority, which would not permit extensions of the existing buildings to a complex of skyscrapers. At that time, nearly 2000 persons were employed in the central administration (Keller, personal communication, August 24, 2006).

At first the executives tried to purchase a monastery in the neighborhood from the Roman Catholic Church. Since this was the only lot of land of interest it was considered to relocate the entire enterprise or a part of it to the outer rim of the city of Münster. It soon turned out, that this would cause tremendous costs, endangering the competitive position in the market (Busch, personal communication, August 24, 2006; Balthasar, 1999).

The cost benefit analysis led to new ideas, which made these ideas obsolete. The solution was the SVWP concept, with which we will deal in the next section.

GAD

GAD (Gesellschaft für automatische Datenverarbeitung) in Münster is an IT-provider for cooperative banking companies in northern Germany. It dominates the northern German market. GAD was founded in 1963 in an era dominated by mainframe computers. The locally operating cooperative banks recognized that they needed to use data processing in order to satisfy customer needs and provide services customers demand for. The cooperative banks in Westphalia started a cooperative computer center in the Westphalian capital Münster. It now serves 476 (2005) cooperative banking companies and has a staff of 1,327 (GAD, 2006).

GAD competes with LVM in the employment market and sometimes hires specialists from LVM's IT services department, and vice versa; therefore, it was easy to learn about LVM's semi virtual workplaces, and GAD implemented it in nearly the same way (Keller, 2006).

FinanzIT

FinanzIT, Hannover, like GAD in Münster, is an IT-provider for the banking sector. The main difference of this company is that it offers its services to municipal savings bank companies in northern Germany. It shares the German market with one larger competitor, Sparkassen Informatik Ltd. in Frankfurt. FinanzIT was founded in 1970 to serve local municipal saving banks with IT-services. Like GAD, it was founded in an era dominated by mainframe computers. The locally operating municipal saving banks were in need to use data processing in order to satisfy customer needs and provide services customers demand for; therefore, the municipal saving banks in the

Hannover area started a cooperative computer center in Hannover. It now serves 170 (2005) municipal saving banks and has a staff of 2,700 (FinanzIT, 2005, 2006).

In the need for a new office building for the Hannover headquarter, the company management choose the Office 21 concept developed by Fraunhofer Institute, a federal research institutes group in Germany.

THE SVWP CONCEPT OF LVM AND GAD

In this section, we will describe the SVWPs of LVM cooperative insurance. As mentioned in the previous section, LVM insurance group is a steady growing enterprise since its opening for the whole German market instead of restricting itself for regional farmers.

No one knows who had the idea of sharing an on site workplace with another person in the same working group, but this idea spread within the company and started in 1995. Now, July 2006, the total number of participants of SVWPs was 643, which is nearly 27% of the whole staff.

How does this concept work? Every participating employee shares an on-site working place with another employee. It follows a strictly day-by-day scheme, where the off site employee works at his home office with the same equipment like the on site office: desk, chair, PC, printer, and telephone.

The main difference of SVWP and on site is that in the SVWP an employee's computer and telephone are connected via a Virtual Private Network to the head quarters.

The technical environment at LVM insurance and GAD are quite similar (GAD, 2004), as shown in Figure 3.

LVM insurance started in 1997 in cooperation with E. Jehle from the University of Dortmund Business School (Balthasar, 1999) with an assessment of productivity, employee satisfaction, and quality of work. In addition, the requirements for managers of SVWP employees was assessed. A second assessment was done in cooperation with Czeschinski (2002) from the University of Münster Medical Center. Both reports gave surprisingly encouraging results:

- the SVWP employees judge their working environment partly better than the on-site employees. Nearly no one thinks the SVWP working environment is worse than purely on site.

- there are more positive job features (or at least equal) judged by the employees with SVWP compared to purely on-site employees.

- the existence of worse job features is assessed by employees with SVWP and employees purely on-site as essentially similar.

Figure 3. Technical configuration of an off site working place

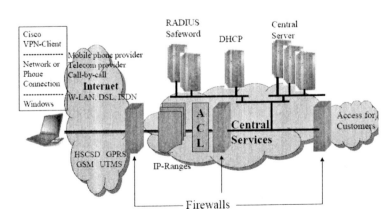

- the qualification opportunities and job security are assessed similarly, namely very highly both by employees with SVWP and by employees purely on-site.
- the internal job development opportunities are assessed badly by employees with SVWP as well as by employees on-site to a high quota.
- the effects of the job on their social environment are judged more positively by employees with SVWP. The social consequences by the professional changes are judged better than by employees purely on-site.
- the negative reactions to the job workload are represented by employees with SVWP as lower compared with employees purely on-site.
- the job satisfaction is assessed by all employees equally well.
- the health complaints are reported by all employees to a similar extent.
- the psycho vegetative complaints are reported by employees with SVWP to a considerably smaller extend compared with employees purely on-site.
- the annual savings of LVM insurance group are nearly 2.8 million euros per year, not counting omitted costs for relocation of the company and omitted new buildings.
- the SVWP employees save commuting costs and time.

In summary this is consistent with the findings of (Broadfoot, 2001).

The HR department has estimated that 700 employees occupy jobs which are SVWP capable. This is nearly 30% of all jobs. They aim to realize 80% of them, which is 280 workplaces or 560 jobs. With this percentage the yearly saving for LVM will be 3.4 million euro per year. At present, this goal is more than achieved, as in 2006 there are 640 SVWP jobs realized.

The Office 21 Concept of Fraunhofer Institute at FINANZIT

In this section we will demonstrate a different concept of shared virtual workplaces in a company, which is comparable to GAD. The differences to the concept dealt with in the previous section are: there is no strict rule, when and where to work off-site, and the employees have no designated workplace—they choose any empty desk if they work on-site.

Here is a brief history: Because of the merger with several competitors FinanzIT was in need for more office space in order to accommodate the new acquired staff. It decided to construct an entirely new building in a radically new design at the rim of the city of Hannover, Germany.

The design was done in cooperation with the Fraunhofer Institute for Labor Management and

Figure 4. Pattern of the different areas of the business club

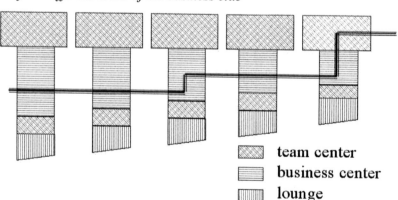

team center
business center
lounge

Organization (IAO) within the framework of the office 21 project (Wincor-Nixdorf, 2000; IAO, 2006a, 2006b). In 1999 the new 112.5 million euro building was ready for 1,850 of the 2,744 staff. It offers 1,350 (72% of 1,850) workplaces considering that there is a bandwidth of 45-90% of workplace usage with an average of 61%: Investigations have shown that the maximum occupation of workplaces was 76%. Those members of staff who are not using their on site desks have various reasons: meetings, working at customers, trainings, vacations, and sick leave. So the new building was designed to provide a work place to 72% of the staff (FinanzIT, 2005; Lange, 2005; Thiele, 2001).

The design was radical new in two ways:

- effective use of energy (Plesser et al., 2004) and
- design of the workplaces as so called "business club."

Within the building there are several designated areas allocated:

- business centers,
- team centers, and
- lounges for creative phases (Thiele, 2001).

Business Centers

The business center is the area where the workplace desks are allocated. The staff can store their personal belongings and personal files in a central container storage, which is located in the center of the building. When a member of staff arrives at the office building, his first way is entering the container storage and with his personal container he goes to an empty desk. There he can plug in his laptop computer or use one of the desktop computers in the area (see Figure 4).

Team Centers

The team centers aim to support meetings in order to discuss projects or to set schedules, or whatever is necessary in an IT service company. These team centers are located close to the business centers, so that the staff involved into a meeting have short distances to the team center. Everything needed for presentations and discussions is provided in these center, so the meeting can start immediately upon arrival of the participants.

Lounges

The third designated area type in the business club are lounges for creative work. Lounge chairs enable a relaxed body position and quietness helps to concentrate on the subject.

Survey of Workplace Satisfaction

An HR survey covering the staff working in the business club gave a good overall satisfaction with the new concept (Thiele, 2001). The pros from the staff were:

- the workplaces correspond better with the work tasks
- many well equipped meeting rooms (team centers)
- modern ergonomic workplaces
- easy communication
- bright and friendly atmosphere of the building.

Cons from the employees' point of view:

- too dense placement of the desks
- no chance to choose a special workplace
- demand for more team centers
- demand for teleworking
- start up at the workplace takes too long
- hard to find a coworker
- e-mail substitutes personal communication
- too high noise level.

Pros from the management point of view:

- improved business processes
- improved communication
- less costs for the office building.

Cons from the management point of view:

- staff is harder to manage.

FinanzIT's business club project found a multiple echo in the German press, who praised it as the office of the future. Beside of the savings in construction by nearly 30%, the press pointed out the energy saving features of that building by the use of natural airflow for cooling and the green house effect for heating. These aspects were out of the subject area of this chapter.

CONCLUSION

In this chapter we presented two different concepts of semi virtual workplaces (SVWPs). Whereas LVM and GAD have a strict alternating use of the on site working place in the headquarter's office building, preventing a construction of an additional office building, FinanzIT constructed a radical new office building with 72% of the work places compared to the one to one assignment of staff to workplaces.

FinanzIT's so-called business club office building is praised by the press, not only for the functionality, but also for its energy saving construction features.

Conclusions for the LVM insurance group's SVMP concept: it is hard to find a workplace and time design that balances the aims and advantages of the enterprise and those of the employees in a perfect way (Schmidt, 2005). That is the reason why no one is forced into SVWP; the employees have to apply to the HR department to be assigned to SVWP.

The reports form GAD give a similar picture (Gaetjen, personal communication, August 24,

2006), however, compared with LVM, a less scholarly assessment took place there.

We note without further comment that in July 2001 FinanzIT started an LVM like SVWP project, in addition, starting with 75 members of staff (FinanzIT, 2001).

The SVWP apparently combines the advantage of saving office space and commuting costs with the advantage for managers and staff of not being cut off the social network of the enterprise. The LVM concept of SVWP has two advantages in addition: there is no need for a new office building construction and the employees and managers stay in tight connection, despite of SVWP everyone has kept his/her on-site workplace.

In the near future we plan to assess the overall workplace satisfaction of the FinanzIT staff, as they have the choice of both SVWP models presented in this chapter.

REFERENCES

BaFin. (2003). *Jahresbericht.* Bundesaufsichtsamt für Finanzdienstleistungen, Frankfurt, Germany.

BaFin. (2004). *Jahresbericht.* Bundesaufsichtsamt für Finanzdienstleistungen, Frankfurt, Germany.

BaFin. (2005). *Jahresbericht.* Bundesaufsichtsamt für Finanzdienstleistungen, Frankfurt, Germany.

Balthasar (1999). *Abschlußbericht der Arbeitsgruppe "Bewertung streng alternierender Telearbeit im Hinblick auf Arbeitsverhalten und Arbeitsergebnisse".* Münster, Germany, LVM.

Broadfoot, K.J. (2001). When the cat's away, do the mice play? Control/autonomy in the virtual workplace. *Management Communication Quarterly, 15,* 110-114.

Bundesbank. (1990). *Bankenstatistik, Statistisches Beiheft,* Frankfurt, Germany, Deutsche Bundesbank.

Bundesbank. (1995). *Bankenstatistik, Statistisches Beiheft,* Frankfurt, Germany, Deutsche Bundesbank.

Bundesbank. (2000). *Bankenstatistik, Statistisches Beiheft,* Frankfurt, Germany, Deutsche Bundesbank.

Bundesbank. (2002). *Bankenstatistik, Statistisches Beiheft,* Frankfurt, Germany, Deutsche Bundesbank.

Bundesbank. (2006). *Bankenstatistik, Statistisches Beiheft,* Frankfurt, Germany, Deutsche Bundesbank.

Cascio, W.F. (2000). Managing a virtual workplace. *Academy of Management Executive, 14,* 81-90.

Christie, M.J., & Levary, R.R. (1998, July-August). Virtual corporations: Recipe for success. *Industrial Management, 7,*11. Cited by Rh.A. Syler & P.H. Schwager (2000).

Czeschinski, P.A. (2002). *Arbeitsmedizinische Untersuchung zu gesundheitlichen Auswirkungen streng alternierender Telearbeit bei Mitarbeiterinnen und Mitarbeitern des LVM- Vergleich der Ergebnisse Balthasar 1 - Balthasar 2.* Presentation on December 9, 2002 to LVM Insurance Group, Münster, Germany, Institut für Arbeitsmedizin / Arbeitsmedizinischer Dienst des Universitätsklinikums und der Westfälischen Wilhelms-Universität Münster

FinanzIT. (2001, July 27). *dvg schafft 75 mobile Arbeitsplätze* (press release). Retrieved November 19, 2007, from http://www.finanzit.com/

FinanzIT. (2005). *Geschäftsbericht 2005.* Retrieved November 19, 2007, from http://www.finanzit.com/publikationen/geschaeftsberichte/index.html

FinanzIT. (2006). *FinanzIT.* Retrieved November 19, 2007, from http://www.finanzit.com/

Fritz, M.B., Narasimhan, S., & Rhee, H.-S. (1998). Communication and coordination in the virtual office. *Journal of Management Information Systems, 14,* 7/28.

GAD. (2004). *Basis 21 Mobiler Arbeitsplatz.* Münster, Germany.

GAD. (2006). *Geschäftsbericht 2005.* Retrieved November 19, 2007, from http://www.gad.de/

GDV. (1996). *Jahresbericht.* Gesamtverband der Deutschen Versicherungswirtschaft, Berlin, Germany, GDV.

GDV. (2001). *Jahresbericht.* Gesamtverband der Deutschen Versicherungswirtschaft, Berlin, Germany, GDV.

GDV. (2003). *Jahresbericht.* Gesamtverband der Deutschen Versicherungswirtschaft, Berlin, Germany, GDV.

GDV. (2005). *Jahresbericht.* Gesamtverband der Deutschen Versicherungswirtschaft, Berlin, Germany, GDV.

GDV-Statistik. (2005). *Statistisches Taschenbuch.* Gesamtverband der Deutschen Versicherungswirtschaft, Berlin, Germany, GDV.

IAO. (2006a). *Projektbeschreibung zur Innovationsoffensive Office 21 – Zukunft der Arbeit.* Stuttgart, Germany, Fraunhofer-Institut für Arbeitswissenschaft und Organisation IAO. Retrieved November 19, 2007, from www.office21.de/Projektbeschreibung/index.htm

IAO. (2006b). *Fraunhofer Office Innovation center OIC.* Stuttgart, Germany, Fraunhofer-Institut für Arbeitswissenschaft und Organisation IAO. Retrieved November 19, 2007, from www.office21.de/forschung/icl.htm

Igbaria, M. (1998). Managing virtual workplaces and teleworking with information technology. *Journal of Management Information Systems, 5,* 5-6/2708-2715.

Lange, J. (2005). *Die FinanzIT GmbH.* Presentation at the University of Hannover, Germany. Retrieved November 19, 2007, from www.iwi.uni-hannover.de/lv/2005_11_24_Vortrag_Lange.pdf

Li, H. (2004). Virtual community studies: A literature review, synthesis and research agenda. In *Proceedings of the Americas Conference on Information Systems.*

LVM. (2006). *LVM-Versicherungen.* Retrieved November 19, 2007, from http://www.lvm.de/

O'Connel, S.E., (1996). The virtual workplace moves at warp speed. *HR Magazine, 41,* 50-56.

Plesser, St., Bremer, C., & Fisch, M.N. (2004). EVA – forschungsbericht zur Evaluierung von Energiekonzepten: Auf dem Prüfstand II. *Intelligente Architektur, 01,* 52-55.

Pohle, A. (2004). *Nichts als die Wahrheit.* Presentation to the Employers Association of Financial Services Providers, Frankfurt, Germany. Retrieved November 19, 2007, from www.experten.de/archiv/104819_2659.ppt

Riemer, K., & Klein, S. (2003). Challenges of ICT-enabled virtual organizations - a social capital perspective. In *Proceedings of the 14th Australasian Conference on Information Systems* (pp. 1-12).

Schmidt, W. (2005, February). *Flexible Arbeitsformen durch Alternierende Telearbeit Erfahrungen aus 9 Jahren Praxis bei den LVM-Versicherungen.* Paper presented at LVM Versicherungen, Münster, Germany.

Syler, R.A., & Schwager, P.H. (2000). Virtual organization as a source of competitive advantage: A framework from the resource-based view. In *Proceedings of the Americas Conference on Information Systems* (pp. 1699-1704).

Thiele, F. (2000, November 11). *Kombi-Büro und Business-Club – Bürokonzepte der Zukunft?* Paper presented at School of Business, University of Applied Sciences Lüneburg, Lüneburg, Germany.

Townsend, A.M., DeMarie, S.M., & Hendrickson, A.R. (2000). Virtual teams: Technology and the workplace of the future. *IEEE Engineering Management Review, 28,* 69/80.

Wincor-Nixdorf. (2000, May). Weniger Büro – Mehr Leistung/less office – more performance. *report, Retail and Banking Solutions,* Paderborn (pp. 11-14).

KEY TERMS

Business Process: A business process is a set of linked activities that create value by transforming an input into a more valuable output. Both input and output can be artifacts and/or information and the transformation can be performed by human actors, machines, or both (Wikipedia, 2007).

Financial Sector Enterprise: A financial sector enterprise is an enterprise serving the financial sector, that is, banking companies, insurance companies, building societies, and so forth. The commonality of all these enterprises is that they provide a service based on their customers financial assets.

SVWP: Semi virtual workplaces (SVWP) are workplaces which do not fulfill the criteria of a virtual workplace in full. Workplaces where the workers fulfill duties partly on site and partly in a home office workplace are called SVWPs

Virtual Enterprise: A virtual enterprise (VE) is a temporary alliance of enterprises that come together to share skills or core competencies and resources in order to better respond to business opportunities, and whose cooperation is supported by computer networks. It is a manifestation of collaborative networks and a particular case of virtual organization (Wikipedia, 2007).

Virtual Organization: A virtual organization comprises a set of (legally) independent organizations that share resources and skills to achieve its mission/goal, but that is not limited to an alliance of for profit enterprises. The interaction among members of the virtual organization is mainly done through computer networks (Wikipedia, 2007).

Virtual Workplace: A virtual workplace is a workplace that is not located in any one physical space; rather, several workplaces are technologically connected (via the Internet) without regard to geographic boundaries. Employees are thus able to interact and work with one another in a collaborated environment regardless of where they are in the world. A virtual workplace decreases unnecessary costs by integrating technology processes, people processes, and online processes (Wikipedia, 2007).

Workplace Satisfaction: Workplace or job satisfaction describes how content an individual is with his or her job. There are a variety of factors that can influence a person's level of job satisfaction; some of these factors include the level of pay and benefits, the perceived fairness of the promotion system within a company, the quality of the working conditions, leadership and social relationships, and the job itself (the variety of tasks involved, the interest and challenge the job generates, and the clarity of the job description/requirements) (Wikipedia, 2007)..

Chapter XLII
Implementing Client–Support for Collaborative Spaces

R. Todd Stephens
AT&T Corporation, USA

ABSTRACT

This chapter examines the critical task of providing client support for virtual environments. The vast majority of information workers are not familiar with virtual solutions and need guidance on how to best utilize and integrate this technology into their day to day operations. A company's ability to manage information effectively over its life cycle, including sensing, collecting, organizing, processing, and maintaining information, is crucial to the long term success in a global economy. Over the past few years, the case study organization has been actively engaged in building, deploying, and managing the procurement, education, and strategic direction for a Fortune 500 company. The success of the studied organization can be seen by reviewing the metrics as the collaborative content continues to grow by an average 28.08% per month and the usage rates have grown by 21% per month. This growth rate was accomplished by focusing on building communities of practice, physical and electronic training programs, promotional road shows, self-service procurement processes, templates, pattern libraries, and an evolving online environment that supports the business user every step in the learning process.

INTRODUCTION

The boundaries of the workplace are shifting and are frequently less defined by organizational structures than by the value added to the business. As the work force becomes mobile, businesses embrace globalization and the speed to market becomes a better determinate of competitive advantage, collaborative solutions will play a more strategic role. Collaborative technologies can be defined as any application that allows more than two people to interact. Baltzan, Haag, and Phillips (2006) describe collaborative systems as a technology-based set of tools that support the work of teams by facilitating the sharing and flow of information. Most organizations collaborate with other businesses or customers through a variety of applications including Electronic Data Interchange (EDI) and the World Wide Web (WWW). Collaboration tools create virtual workplaces and include of a wide variety functional information categories including: knowledge management, content management, online meetings, discussion groups, Weblogs, wikis, and so forth. Collaboration tools are actually a subset of a much larger tool palate denoted as the tools of the information worker. This expanded tool collection includes: security tools, enterprise applications, portals, office suites, client applications, process automation, and enterprise knowledge stores. Deploying collaborative solutions is different than simply implementing traditional enterprise applications which operate over structured data and generally focus on specific business processes. Collaborative environments operate over unstructured information and can span several business processes and organizational boundaries. Since the need for virtual workspaces emerge when organizational collaboration occurs, the ability to predict demand is nearly impossible. More importantly, when the business need arises for a virtual workspace, the technology cannot wait or the competitive advantage may be lost. In this environment, self-service or self provisioning is an imperative. The objective of this chapter is to lay out a framework for building a self-service environment for provisioning virtual workspaces as well as providing the education to support such technologies. After reading this chapter, you should be able to:

- Describe the components of the information worker portfolio;
- Define the requirements for developing a client-support organization;
- Distinguish between management, measurement, and governance of the information technology portfolio;
- Explain the role of self-service in deploying virtual work spaces.

BACKGROUND

Virtual workspaces are generally designed for distributed teams which can be defined as groups of people that interact through interdependent tasks guided by common purpose, and work across space, time, and organizational boundaries primarily through electronic means (Chudoba & Maznevski, 2000). In order to be effective in sharing information and working in an online environment, end users need to understand and develop knowledge sharing practices (Becerra-

Fernandez & Sabherwal, 2001). The background section will establish the foundational elements of information worker, virtual workspaces, and the criteria for success.

Knowledge or Information Worker

Peter Drucker was one of the first people to use the phrase "Knowledge Worker" to describe individuals that work with information instead the physical objects of labor. Today, many people use the term information worker in a similar reference to people that work with information vs. manual type activities. The value of information workers to an organization is their ability to gather and analyze information and make decisions that will benefit the company. They are able to work collaboratively with and learn from each other; they are willing to take risks, expecting to learn from their mistakes rather than be criticized for them (Rogoski, 1999). Information workers now account for as much as 70% of the U.S. labor force and contribute over 60% of the total valued added in the U.S. economy (Apte & Nath, 2004). Unlike the information worker of the 1970s, today's expert has a much large collection of tools available. While most of these tools are not semantically connected, they do fulfill the basic functional requirements such as office automation, business intelligence, collaboration, e-mail, elearning and search. Over the past few years, a collection of integrated applications are emerging to connect people, processes, and environments. Virtual workspaces or collaborative environments provide enormous value to the business by reducing the barriers of information flow. The new economy thrives on producing, collaborating, and passing knowledge between partners, employees, and customers.

Virtual Workspaces

Virtual workplace environments allow people to work separately while still experiencing a mutual sense of presence. Working collaboratively over networks is ultimately about real communication enhanced by a virtual presence. The tools for these virtual communities include threaded discussions, e-mail, calendaring, surveying, instant messaging, customizable interfaces, document management, and real-time conferencing (Chignell, Ho, & Schraefel, 2000). Virtual workspaces provide historical reference, enhance situation awareness, and facilitate multichannel interactions (Hinds & Baily, 2003). In addition, virtual workspaces are provided for distributed teams where the physical constraints of time and presence of removed. Distributed team can be defined as groups of people who interact through interdependent tasks guided by a common purpose, and work across space, time, and organizational boundaries primarily through electronic means (Maznevski & Chudoba, 2000).

While traditional workflow management systems have proven useful in supporting well-defined organizational processes, they are less suitable for the support of less well-defined and emergent processes. The early efforts of computing focused on the structured side of systems. Specifically, these efforts resulted in transaction processing system as well as data warehouses and data marts. Knowledge and content management emerged as disciplines due to the needs of the business to ease the partnering aspects of the organization, manage expertise turnover, and decentralize decision making (Applehans, Globe, & Laugero, 1999). Both these two efforts focused on standardized and well defined processes. Virtual workspaces realize that speed to market and innovation are key to the emerging business models where standards may not be set or even defined. Virtual workspaces are temporal since there existence is determinate on the existence of the team itself. Once the value or utility of the team is gone the workspace will dissolve.

Success Criteria

While there is a large amount of research on virtual workspace, e-learning, and collaboration, very little rigor has been applied to the actual

implementation and servicing of the environment. Traditionally, success has been defined by the acquisition of the software and hardware with little attention has been paid to the actual content and usage of the environment. The content represents the amount of structured and unstructured information within the virtual workspace while usage focuses on the actual metric of utility. Content metrics should be able to answer the following questions:

- How many end users are members of this workspace?
- What type of knowledge is represented in the workspace?
- When was this information updated and by who?
- Who is librarian or steward of the workspace?

Usage is the measurement of information use or reuse within the organization. The majority of collaborative environments are created in a way that we can easily track the number of times someone visits the information asset page. Usage metrics allow us to answer questions such as:

- What workspace element was viewed most often?
- What is the most downloaded artifact?
- How many people subscribe for updates to the virtual workspace?
- How many first time visitors viewed the workspace?
- How long does the average information worker visit the workspace?

Success of virtual workspaces must revolve around the actual usage, not simply the availability and reliability of the application. When managers begin to review the measurements of success, they will begin to understand how the commoditization of hardware, software, and open source is creating an environment where the differentiation comes down to client-support and the customer experience. Barufaldi and Reinhartz (2001) identify four main components essential to the collaboration process, namely, shared vision, interconnectivity among the organizational units, recognition of a multitiered process, and client support.

The success of collaboration requires three primary elements. The first and most important is a collaborative culture that recognizes the value of collaboration and rewards those who model collaborative behavior. The second is the establishment of a solid collaboration technology foundation that minimizes choices among similar products but provides the widest range of channels to accommodate varying communication needs within and between business processes. The third is the presence of processes for aligning investments with the business, discovering collaborative opportunities, methodologies for modeling collaborative behavior, and integration with planning, to provide perspectives and priorities for investments in collaborative work (Rasmus, 2003). While collaborative software may come with manuals, documentation, and some form of training, this type of content represents information. Over the past decade, organizations have shifted from a focus on information to a focus on knowledge. The client-support consultant assists with the end user's comprehension of the information which represents knowledge (Mojta, 2002). Collaborative environments create an environment where knowledge is exchanged vs. simply information or data.

Figure 1. Customer perspective client-support framework

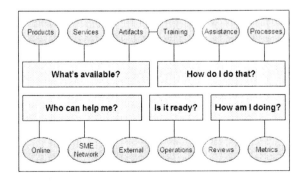

CLIENT-SULIENT-SUPPORT FRAMEWORK

The previous section focused on defining the foundation for implementing a Client-Support Framework (CSF). In order to deploy and service a large scale environment of virtual workspaces, client-support is a basic requirement that must be addressed. This section of the chapter will lay out the CSF currently in use by a Fortune 500 company where annual growth rates of adoption are above 200% and continue to average double digit growth every month. The CSF is not built from an architecture, technology, or functionality perspective. Rather, the framework comes from the point of view of the customer. Figure 1 provides the basic foundation of a solid client-support environment built to enable virtual teams get the most value from the environment.

Focusing on the middle section, the CSF asks five basic questions of the collaborative environment:

- What collaborative products and services are available to me?
- How can I utilize these products and services within my environment?
- Who can help me in case I need some professional guidance?
- Are the collaborative applications ready for enterprise usage?
- How am I doing in comparison to others or against best practices?

In order to address these questions, organizations should look toward developing a support group that can enable the end user rather than hindering their understanding of a collaborative environment. Meeting the needs of the customer may vary depending on the level of knowledge the user brings to the environment. Customers who are new to technology expect a high level of reliability and support in order to gain the greatest value possible (Johnston & Supra, 1997). Customer service should not be homogeneous and both the online and physical support environments need to take into account the experience level of the end user (Dutta & Roy, 2006).

Support Portfolio

The customer wants to know what products, services, and documentation are available to them within the collaborative environment. The content of an online environment is not limited to the product or services provided. Rather, content includes the solutions and strategies employed to make it easy for the user to accomplish important tasks, such as information retrieval, search, and obtaining feedback (Calongne, 2001). Support information or content should include the product and service quantity, quality, and relevance to the customer (Palmer, 2002). Technologists often make the mistake of assuming a certain level of expertise with the user community. Unlike e-mail or Office products (Word Processing or Spreadsheet), virtual tools are fairly unknown to the end user.

Products

While there are many products in the world of collaboration, most organizations will implement a single product and then add additional components as the business demands new functionality. The collaborative tool defines how the information will be stored, presented, and integrated into the environment. The virtual workspace design will emerge from the various artifacts already produced which include the user requirements, research from the business case and the architectures described by the technical community. The workspace should be based on solid design principles and subjected to usability studies. Remember, virtual workspaces are not just a single function but rather a collection of utilities or applications. Knowledge management, information architecture, content management, search engine technology, and portalization are just a few of the evolutionary benefits of implementing collaborative solutions at the enterprise level. Collaborative products like Microsoft's SharePoint, WebEx, and

IBM's WorkPlace deliver a set of solutions which include many of the following:

- E-mail, Task Management and Calendar
- Document Management and Publishing
- Intranet and Extranet Environments
- Discussions
- RSS Feeds
- Taxonomy and Information Domain Constructs
- Personalization
- Wiki and Weblog (Blog) Functionality
- Form Management
- Workflow

Services

The natural progression of any organization is to move beyond the product and into value-add services. Services are what make the difference between doing the job and creating a "Collaborative" cause. Collaboration is more than products and procedures; collaboration is a philosophy that must be supported by a service-oriented staff and value offering. In the vast majority of implementations, organizations identify a support group that can offer additional services like domain management, term inventories, and taxonomy design. Value-add services can also be added to the portfolio like PDF conversion, metadata standardization, subscriptions, reservations, inventory management, and records management methodologies.

Services are not always physical; many services are more subject matter expertise (SME) oriented. How do you ensure that content can be located within the corporate search engine, how do you manage informational assets within the technical communities, or how do you enable reuse in a nondevelopment oriented organization? Sarbanes-Oxley (SOX,), Service Oriented Architecture (SOA), and Enterprise Application Integration (EAI) continue to ask the question of how enterprise ready are the services delivered by the collaboration application.

The quality of the business process around the technology is the key indicator of the perception of service. Organizations must manage the results of the collaborative technology by enabling services that support and enhance the virtual experience. As defined by Heskett, Sasser, and Schlesinger (1997), service value emerges from service quality, capability, satisfaction, loyalty, and productivity.

Artifacts

Artifacts include the associated documentation for the product or services defined in the prior section. Documentation may include user guides, documented best practices, templates, disaster recovery plans, and backup strategies. Artifacts like information models, mappings, vocabulary definitions, and policies for data administration may also be added but should not necessarily be made available to the general audience. Artifacts are critical to the virtual environment since they can add context to the organizational purpose, business processes, and team member knowledge.

Instructional Support

While the products and services focus on what is available, users also want to know how business functions can be executed within the tool environment. All users are different in their needs and knowledge background. Figure 1 provided a dotted line link between training and the artifact section since many of these elements are generally closely related. The key for instructional support is to provide multiple methods of getting the "how to" information to the end users. This information may be delivered in a virtual setting, digitally archived, or direct communication.

Training

Training allows the organization to move the methodology of collaboration to each and every person within the organization. There are vari-

ous models for delivering training as defined by Cohen (2001) beginning with on-site, synchronous communications that take place at single location. This type of education is generally delivered in a presentation or lab environment. The second type includes synchronous communication where communication occurs at different locations and would utilize teleconferencing and shared space. Emerging today is more of an asynchronous methodology where education can be delivered anytime and anywhere.

Online training provides many benefits over in-class type training programs including being accessed without time or resource constraints. Online training is becoming the dominant delivery method in e-learning settings across organizations of various sectors and of varying sizes. Although many organizations are recognizing the potential of online training to bring learning closer to employees, there appears to be some issues to be addressed in delivering content. Learners still face some barriers to online training, such as situational, organizational, and technical barriers (Bonk, Kim, & Zeng, 2005). In the past few years, e-learning has emerged as a promising solution to lifelong learning and on the job work force training. E-learning can be defined as technology-based learning in which learning materials are delivered electronically to remote learners via a computer network. Effective and efficient training methods are crucial to companies to ensure that employees and channel partners are equipped with the latest information and advanced skills (Nunamaker, Zhang, Zhou, & Zhou, 2004). The vast majority of online offerings are self-paced which allow users with different experiences to take the same class. Although the initial cost of developing online training may be higher, the long term cost is much lower since users have unlimited access. Providing reoccurring classes on a consistent schedule is important and can help rolling out the collaboration message.

Most training is aimed directly at the end user where they can return to the office and apply the new techniques. Other options in training include train the trainer, developing a subject matter expert program, books, articles, and other items of interest. All of which support the program and expand the body of knowledge.

Assistance

All users need help and even advanced users will push the technology into new areas that the average user may not. Assistance may come in the form of a help desk or a simple contact phone number that assures the customer that someone is available. In a recent study done by the Princeton Survey Research Associates (2002), 81% of the respondents indicated that it is very important for organizations to provide e-mail address, street address, and phone number in the development of trust. Users need to believe that if they have problems, they will have the opportunity to speak to someone to resolve the problem quickly. Over one third of the respondents indicated that information like company address, phone, staff, and policies are critical in the development of trust. The Web should serve as a strategic information center for the organization. Key information, such as physical locations, key agents, new products, and services should be posted on the site as well. The content will build the customer's knowledge of the company and provide a level of relationship management for the organization (Gilbert, Powell-Perry, & Widijoso, 1999).

Consulting services are also a form of assistance where the supplying organization implements, customizes, or provides hands-on guidance to the customer. Consulting services is the ultimate service where organizations can not only demonstrate their expertise but build consistency in the base product. Collaborative consulting services bring the best practices, technologies, and business models that help the organization to adapt quickly in a technology environment that is under rapid change. Shneiderman (2000) discusses the concept of accelerating action by clarifying responsibility. As soon as a user begins the process of investigating the purchase of a product or service, the support

environment Web site should begin to address the emerging resistance by clarifying the responsibilities and obligation.

Processes

When researchers think about virtual workspaces, the concepts of business processes are rarely associated with client support. Yet, virtual workspaces cannot be created unless an initial "top" level site exists. Large organizations will have a collection of top tiered workspaces based on organizational structure or business function. While organizations want the free flow of information and ideas, they still want to control the growth and govern the environment. In the reviewed organization, every "top" level site has a storage limit which must be managed by the owner. This forces the owner to ensure that virtual workspace information is critical to the business since the storage will be reduced from the overall allocation for every element of content. This leads to one example of a business process that should be automated; the procurement process of a "top" tier site. Other business process like workspace retirement, storage utilization, and traffic analysis should be automated as much as possible.

Support Network

The customer does not want to feel alone and without support. The customer support model provides three specific areas where the support team can provide help and assurance. The areas include an online environment, SME networks, and external resources.

Online Environment

Everything is going online; all business and applications are going to be made available online in the near future. This same approach needs to be taken into account by the collaboration support organization. The Web allows customers to access information at any time during the day or night. Automating processes by utilizing the Web creates an environment of self-service where the vast majority of business and application functions are accessible 24 hours a day. When you start a collaboration business initiative you will need to review your business processes that impact customers. This is a great time to determine how you can simplify those processes or interactions and at the same time provide new services over the Web. This could include incorporating impact analysis program, pattern libraries, self-service procurement, search, taxonomies, and other customer-focused initiatives. The Internet lends itself to direct interaction with each and every customer. As the online environment design and development evolve, organizations will be continually refining them, expanding the programs that have been successful and curtailing efforts regarding the ones that have generated little bottom-line Return on Investment (Ruud & Deutz, 2002).

External Resources

An external resource is any knowledge or information developed outside of the organization. Bringing in external resources can add substance to the implementation by adding the element of credibility. Many organizations utilize industry experts like Gartner or Forrester to simply verify their strategy or support the implementation plans. The academic world publishes an enormous amount of research as well. Organizations such as IEEE and ACM publishes credible research on the topics of collaboration, virtual workspaces, and Web 2.0 technologies. Other external resources like books, online articles, subject matter experts, and industry leaders are excellent resources for the collaboration implementation environment.

Subject Matter Expert Network

User groups are independently run and meet on a regular basis to discuss and share information on a variety of technology topics. Joining a developer or collaboration user group is an excellent, inex-

pensive way to receive technical education and meet with your peers to get more out of the latest platforms, products, technologies, and resources. Collaborative environments, blogs, wiki, community of practice (CoP), and discussion groups are also forms of SME networks. CoPs contrite to the groups overall understanding of the utility of cooperation, knowledge management, and collaboration (Klamma, Rohde, & Wulf, 2005). The basic purpose of collaboration is the creation of value in a manner that involves shared efforts. In order for collaboration to be successful, it must address common objectives, shared resolve, and partnership behaviors. This, for most companies, is much harder than it looks. Creating strategic and economic value through collaborative programs requires a balancing act of concepts, processes, resources, and behaviors that are tendered by special leadership.

Production Ready

Information technology routinely engages in project work, skunk works, and pilot type projects where the customer is not really sure if the application is production ready. Collaboration groups need to ensure they communicate that the products and services are operationally mature, covered under Service Level Agreements (SLA), and supported from hardware and software perspective. Two key areas emerge as value-add from the customer's perspective: operations and technical support. These two areas ensure a message that the virtual environment is production ready and not a pilot program.

Operations

Operations consist of many different areas including hardware support, operating system support, licensing, backups, disaster recovery, application support, networking, and security audits. In a virtual environment, the operations generally go unnoticed by the end user. Methodologies, like Six Sigma, are creating operational environments that are expected to be 99.73% defect free (Ferrin, Miller, & Muthler, 2002). Support groups need to ensure that maturity of the environment is communicated to the end users in order to create a sense of stability with the application.

Technical Support

Technical support provides a user interface that can answer any question a user may have about the collaborative environment. Collaboration services should provide an extensive list of customer support options, including Web-based, telephone access, and product updates so that issues can be resolved quickly and effectively. The content of a technical support site should not be limited to the subject, product or services provided. Rather, content should include the solutions and strategies employed to make it easy for the user to accomplish important tasks, such as information retrieval, search, and navigation required in making a purchase, and obtaining feedback (Calongne, 2001). The technical support group may offer a range of products, industry knowledge and hands-on experience which can be made available 24 hours a day. This allows the end user to take advantage of the online support services and receive product documentation, updates, application notes, and access to the searchable knowledge base.

MONITORING SUCCESS IN THE COLLABORATIVE SPACE

People want to know how well they are doing in comparison to other groups or against industry standards. Is the organization utilizing the virtual applications correctly? Is the organization getting enough value from the program to defend the ongoing investment? Are the virtual environments growing in both content and usage?

Reviews

One service that can be offered is that the collaborative services group can review how an organization is actively utilizing the workspaces within their environment. The collaborative environment should be integrated into the day to day functions of the business. Is the working knowledge of the organization being captured and reused during the normal process of business? Organizations may want an expert review of how they have organized their data or documents within the workspace. Routinely, when organizations deploy collaborative solutions from the bottom up, information overload will follow.

Metrics

Metrics have always been an important part of information technology; unfortunately metrics is generally an after thought to the implementation. Anderson, Larsen, and Pererson (2006) describe metrics as the central element of control that impacts organizational audits, current and historical reporting, and daily validation of the enterprise strategy. The natural progression of a system that moves from innovation, incubation, and migration is to eventually measure the impact and value the system brings to the technology portfolio.

In the world of collaboration, there is any number of possible metrics to be reviewed and captured. Two key metrics that focus on the success and integration of the virtual environment is content and usage. Content is basically the metrics around what information you have inside the virtual workspace. Without considering how the information is used, content focuses on the inventory of knowledge assets. Perhaps the most obvious example of content metrics is the object count. Collaborative workspaces can be a collection of documents, lists, surveys, Web pages, or social type software. Having an understanding of how many assets are within the space will help determine the value and utility for the organization.

The other key metric is usage which is the key to delivering long term value-add to the organization. Many Web-based applications utilize three high-level classifications for user traffic: user behavior, page metrics, and downloads. Assuming the virtual environment can be monitored by a traffic application, the user behavior can be monitored. This allows the support organization the ability to evaluate the information architecture and navigation structure. The page view indicates that an end user has loaded the content into their browser which in turn indicates a transfer of knowledge. Other usage metrics can track the number of artifacts downloaded or the amount of time spent reading the information. These simple usage metrics can alter the way information is organized within the workspace and ultimately enhance the value.

Results

Does the CSF work within a large scale organization? That question can be easily addressed in the growth rate of virtual workspaces. Prior to implementing the CSF, the studied organization had only implemented 100 virtual workspaces over a period of 2 years. While some of the elements of the CSF were started, there was not an over arching strategy or implementation plan. In December of 2004, the Collaboration and Online Services Group was established with a mission of extending the collaborative and virtual toolset to the entire

Figure 2. Active virtual workspace inventory

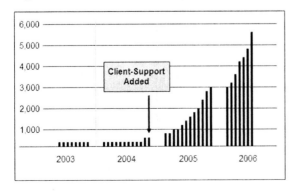

organization by utilizing the CSF presented in this chapter. The results to date are that the average monthly growth rate exceeds 29.08% with a total of 5,598 active virtual workspaces as of August 2006. Figure 2 presents the inventory of virtual workspaces captured on a monthly basis.

More impressive to this research is that prior to the implementation of a client support group, 95% of the virtual workspaces were developed for the technology community. By the middle of 2006, the percentage of virtual workspaces for the business had risen to 65% of the total inventory. In addition, customer satisfaction scores have risen dramatically over the past few years. Customers report that they are able to get up and running faster, obtain greater value, as well as experience better communications.

THE FUTURE OF CLIENT-SUPPORT WITHIN VIRTUAL WORKSPACES

Basic e-mail, spreadsheet functionality, and word processing have been around for 20 years and have had plenty of time to become part of the organizational culture. Much of the early designs done by Apple and Microsoft are still in use today. Virtual workspaces are a more recent technology and will need time for the vast majority of users to become familiar with the basic utility and functionality. Until then, a solid client support organization will be a requirement for long term success.

Extended Beyond the Organizational Border

With the success of the Internet and business to business exchanges, it is hard to believe that organizations do not have an extended presence in cross organizational virtual workspaces. Part of the issue is with the mindset of the traditional organization that wants to protect its intellectual property. In the future, organizations must move beyond the closed door mentality and develop open communications to their suppliers, partners, vendors, and customers. These new cross organizational workspaces will need client support just as the internal ones did. Cross organizational communication may introduce new challenges with the culture differences which could indicate a lack of trust. The word trust has been active in human language throughout written history. Although the concept of trust is vital to our daily lives, most people have trouble defining trust in specific terms. Arceneaux (1994) defines trust as the dependence of sources such as reliability, genuineness, truthfulness, intent, competence, and other similar factors. These factors can be applied to situations that either enable trust or destroy it. Bhattacharya, Devinney, and Pillutla (1998) define trust as an expectancy of positive outcomes that can be received from another party. Trust can be based on the expected actions within an interaction characterized by uncertainty. Knowledge-based trust is based on the predictability created through information collected between parties (Sabherwal, 1999). This trust is the most common form of trust in business as well as personal relationships. Over time, numerous interactions with the other party and our knowledge of them lead us to associate a certain level of trustworthiness. Based on this type of research, collaboration across organizational boundaries will be critical in developing competitive advantages in the future.

Integrated Intranet, Applications, and Virtual Workspaces

One of the most frequent requests is that the virtual workspaces integrate with the organizational Intranet and business applications. In many organizations, the technology group implements three different solutions that are rarely integrated. The most common form of integration problem is the search engine. Each technology may have its own internal search engine which requires the end user to decide before hand if the information is located on the company portal, corporate Intranet, knowledge stores, or virtual workspaces. Part of

the issue is technology, but politics and usability also come into play, which make it difficult to integrate the various knowledge environments.

Conclusion

In this chapter, we have laid a framework to support the implementation of virtual workspaces. As discussed, users come to this technology with a wide variety of experience levels which cannot be assumed by the technology community. Client-support must be implemented if the business wants universal adoption and a high degree of business value. The different components of the framework address the concerns of the end user which can put them at ease and create a more open environment for integrating this new technology. Perhaps in the future, these support components can be moved online and limit the number of employees dedicated to serving the user community. Organizations like ours focus on creating as much of a self-service environment as possible, which helps in giving the end user perceived control if not full control over their information and knowledge.

REFERENCES

Anderson, K., Larsen, M., & Pedersen, M. (2006). IT governance: Reviewing 17 IT governance tools and analyzing the case of novozymes A/S. In *Proceedings of the 39th Hawaii International Conference on System Sciences*. Kohala Coast, HI: Institute of Electrical and Electronics Engineers, Inc.

Applehans, W., Globe, A., & Laugero, G. (1999). *Managing knowledge: A practical Web-based approach*. Reading, MA: Addison-Wesley.

Apte, M., & Nath, H. (2004). *Size, structure and growth of the U.S. information economy* (Working Paper). Huntsville, TX: Sam Houston State University.

Arceneaux, C. (1994). Trust: An exploration of its nature and significance. *Journal of Invitational Theory and Practice, 3*(1), 35-45.

Baltzan, P., Phillips, A., & Haag, S. (2006). *Business driven technology*. Boston, MA: McGraw-Hill Irwin.

Barufaldi, J., & Reinhartz, J. (2001). *Models of science teacher preparation-theory into practice*. Norwell, MA: Kluwer Academic Publishers.

Becerra-Fernandez, I., & Sabherwal, R. (2001, Summer). Organizational knowledge management: A contingency perspective. *Journal of Management Information Systems, 18*(1).

Bhattacharya, R., Devinney, T., & Pillutla, M. (1998). A formal model of trust based on outcomes. *Academy of Management Review, 23*(3), 459-472.

Bonk, C., Kim, K., & Zeng, T. (2005, June). Surveying the future of workplace: E-learning: The rise of blending, interactivity, and authentic learning. *E-Learn Magazine, 5*(6), 2-3.

Calongne, C. (2001, March). Designing for Web site usability. *Journal of Computing in Small Colleges, 16*(3), 39-45.

Chignell, M., Ho, J., & Schraefel, M. (2000). Building virtual communities for research collaboration. In *Proceedings from the International Working Conference and Industrial Expo on New Advances and Emerging Trends in Next Generation Enterprises*. Buffalo, NY: Institute of Electrical and Electronics Engineers, Inc.

Chudoba, K., & Maznevski, M. (2000, September). Bridging space over time: Global virtual team dynamics and effectiveness. *Organization Science, 11*(5), 473-492.

Cohen, D. (2001). Transitioning to teaching online: Factors that can help or hinder the process. In *Proceedings of the 29th Annual ACM SIGUCCS Conference on User Services*. Portland, OR: The Association of Computing Machinery.

Dutta, A., & Roy, R. (2006). Managing customer service levels and sustainable growth. In *Proceedings of the 39th Hawaii International Conference on System Sciences*. Kohala Coast, HI: Institute of Electrical and Electronics Engineers, Inc.

Ferrin, D., Miller, D., & Muthler, M. (2002). Six sigma and simulation, so what's the correlation? In *Proceedings of the 2002 Winter Simulation Conference*. San Diego, CA: Penn State University.

Gilbert, D., Powell-Perry, J., & Widijoso, S. (1999). Approaches by hotels to the use of the Internet as a relationship marketing tool. *Journal of Marketing Practice: Applied Marketing Science, 5*(1), 21-38.

Heskett, J., Sasser, W., & Schlesinger, L. (1997). *The service profit chain*. New York: The Free Press.

Hinds, P., & Bailey, D. (2003). Out of sight, out of sync: Understanding conflict in distributed teams. *Organization Science, 14*(6), 615-632.

Johnston, B., & Supra, J. (1997). Toward an integrated approach to information services support. In *Proceedings of the 25th annual ACM SIGUCCS conference on User services*. Monterey, CA: The Association of Computing Machinery.

Nunamaker, J., Zhang, D., Zhao, J., & Zhou, L. (2004, May). Can e-learning replace traditional classroom learning? Evidence and implication of the evolving e-learning technology. *Communications of the ACM, 47*(5), 75-79.

Princeton Survey Research Associates. (2002). *A matter of trust: What users want from Web sites*. Retrieved November 20, 2007, from http://www.consumerwebwatch.org/news/1_abstract.htm

Rasmus, D. (2003). Enterprise collaboration: Time to consider a platform (Research Report). Forrester Research.

Reichheld, F., & Schefter, P. (2000, August). Loyalty-your secret weapon on the Web. *Harvard Business Review*.

Rogoski, R. (1999, January). Knowledge workers top company assets. *Triangle Business Journal, 19*, 21.

Ruud, M., & Deutz, J. (1999). Moving your company online. *Management Accounting Montvale, 80*(8), 28-32.

Sabherwal, R. (1999). The role of trust in outsourced IS development projects. *Communications of the ACM, 42*(2), 80-86.

Shneiderman, B. (2000, December). Designing trust into online experiences. *Communications of the ACM, 43*(12), 57-59.

KEY TERMS

Client-Support: Client support reflects the efforts of an organization that provides "customer" oriented services, such as, training, best practices, documentation, and user guides.

Collaborative Environment: Collaborative Environments are designed for distributed teams which can be defined as groups of people that interact through interdependent tasks guided by common purpose, and work across space, time, and organizational boundaries primarily through electronic means.

Content Metrics: Content Metrics are measurements of the amount of information held within the collaborative environment or knowledge store.

Information Worker: Information Workers are individuals who work with information instead the physical objects of labor. Information workers are individuals who create, manage, share, receive and use information in the course of their daily work, including those who act and react to information.

Self-Service Collaboration: Self service environments allow the end user to gain access to the client-support information through the Web browser. Information and training can easily be pushed to the end user for consumption.

Usage Metrics: Usage Metrics are measurements on the amount of usage which may include page views, downloads, memberships, or subscriptions of content.

Chapter XLIII
Value, Visibility, Virtual Teamwork at Kairos

Douglas Eyman
George Mason University, USA

ABSTRACT

This chapter proposes an analytic for the assessment of sustainability and success of virtual workplaces. This analytic considers value, visibility, and infrastructure as key factors required for success, and suggests that an assessment of sustainability must include methods for evaluating current and possible mechanisms for securing or distributing social capital, exposing the degree to which the tasks and interactions of workers are made visible, and assessing the administrative and technological infrastructure with regard to support of communication, cooperation, and collaboration. This analytic is applied through a case study of the virtual workplace of the online scholarly journal Kairos: Rhetoric, Technology, Pedagogy.

INTRODUCTION

The editors, editorial staff, and editorial board of *Kairos: A Journal of Rhetoric, Technology, Pedagogy* have successfully produced a well-regarded peer-reviewed academic online journal since 1996. The production work for the journal takes place almost exclusively online, with geographically distributed authors, editors, and editorial board members working as, in effect, virtual teams. Over the decade of experience we have had producing the journal, we have learned the importance of constructive autonomy for distant workers and the requirements for developing a

sustainable enterprise. This chapter will discuss three key aspects of virtual workplace practices that have played important roles in the success of the journal: providing mechanisms for associating work with value (operating through the accrual and distribution of what Pierre Bourdieu calls "cultural capital," rather than solely through wage compensation), making sure that the work that takes place is made visible to all of the actors in the workplace (because, especially for virtual workplaces, the work the gets done is often invisible, and thus either misunderstood and/or undervalued by other team members), and developing technological and administrative support structures that both facilitate and privilege cooperation, collaboration, and the sharing of both responsibilities and resources by all of the stakeholders in the institution.

The approach taken in this chapter assumes that the kinds of work that take place in virtual environments are representations of knowledge work and that, as Deborah Brandt (2005) notes, "writing is at the heart of the knowledge economy" (p. 166), as well as understanding that the knowledge economy is associated with "processes of learning, communication, and social networking, almost always technology enhanced" (p. 167). The production of an online journal like *Kairos* represents an ideal case study for examining the practices of knowledge work both because that is its explicit purpose (to develop, distribute, and circulate knowledge) and because the core processes of production are tied to writing, learning, communication, and social networking.

KAIROS: RHETORIC, TECHNOLOGY, PEDAGOGY

Kairos is a refereed online journal exploring the intersections of rhetoric, technology, and pedagogy. Each issue presents varied perspectives on special topics such as "Critical Issues in Computers and Writing," "Technology and the Face of Language Arts in the K-12 Classroom," and "Hypertext Fiction/Hypertext Poetry." *Kairos* was specifically conceived as a venue for the publication of academic "Webtexts," which are texts authored specifically for publication on the World Wide Web. These Webtexts include scholarly examinations of large-scale issues related to special topics, individual and collaborative reviews of books and media, news and announcements of interest, interactive exchanges about previous *Kairos* publications, and extended interviews with leading scholars.

In 1996, the journal had an average monthly readership of 1,447 individuals who visited the

site, but since the first issue, overall readership has steadily risen; the journal currently serves over 45, 000 readers per month. In addition to the increase in readership, there has been a shift from a primarily U.S. audience to a much more international audience. A little over 80% of our readers come from the U.S., which means that about 20% come from elsewhere—the logs have recorded visitors who hail from 190 different country codes, from Belize, Belarus, Botswana, and Brazil; from Vietnam, Venezuela, and the Ukraine. And that 20% is now over 9,000 readers per month, thus establishing *Kairos* as an "international" scholarly publication venue.

Mick Doherty (1996), the first editor and publisher of *Kairos*, explains that the name of the journal was selected after careful consideration: "Kairos, the ancient Greek term that can roughly be interpreted as a rhetorical combination of understood context and proper timing, carries exciting new implications in our developing rhetorics of hypertext and online communication" (start.html). In a knowledge economy, finding the opportune moment and the appropriate processes to meet the needs of users as they develop at specific intersections of cultural practice and technological capability greatly contributes to the success or failure of Internet ventures; however it is not simply recognizing the right moment that is important—selecting the right media and networks for user interaction are equally critical. Eric Charles White (1987) explains the relationship of time and action embedded in the notion of "kairos":

Kairos is an ancient Greek word that means "the right moment" or "the opportune." The two meanings of the word apparently come from two different sources. In archery, it refers to an opening, or "opportunity" or, more precisely, a long tunnel-like aperture through which the archer's arrow has to pass. Successful passage of a kairos requires, therefore, that the archer's arrow be fired not only accurately but with enough power for it to penetrate. The second meaning of kairos traces to the art of weaving. There it is "the critical time" when the weaver must draw the yarn trough a gap that momentarily opens in the warp of the cloth being woven. Putting the two meanings together, one might understand kairos to refer to a passing instant when an opening appears which must be driven through with force if success is to be achieved. (p. 13)

The notion of "kairos" is a particularly useful construct for the examination of the virtual workplace: in order for virtual work to be both productive and sustainable, the institution of the virtual workspace and the productive activity that results from virtual teamwork both need to take into account timing (opportunity) and infrastructure (the technologies that provide the necessary degree of force for a successful enterprise).

KAIROS AS VIRTUAL WORKPLACE

Currently Senior Co-Editor of Kairos, I have worked as a *Kairos* author, reviewer, interviewer, CoverWeb Editor, and Co-Editor of the journal. Although I am not one of the founding editors, I have been a part of the journal since its first year of publication (I contributed a news article and a review in the first issue). I joined the staff as CoverWeb Editor in 1997, beginning with issue 2.1, although I worked alongside managing editor Michael Salvo on issue 1.3 as I learned the ropes of editorial work for a peer-reviewed online journal whose staff, distributed across the country, worked almost exclusively via online communication, only meeting in person at annual professional conferences.

Work at the journal takes place at three distinct locations: the development of Webtexts by authors, the review and assessment of those texts by the editorial board members, and the shepherding of the texts through the review and publication process by the editorial staff. When an author submits

a query, the editorial staff responds with a link to our author's guide and with suggestions; when the initial draft of a Webtext is presented for review, the entire editorial board is provided with access to the text and then an open discussion about its merits, shortcomings, and potential value takes place on our editorial board listserv. Editorial staff coordinate the response to the author(s), and if the text is provisionally accepted for publication, the staff also facilitates the revision and review process, and finally the copyediting and coding that is necessary for the work to be included in the published issue.

Like many virtual workplaces, the primary product of the journal is textual, and the primary activity is digital communication about the development and deployment of these texts. Thus, the parameters I have identified as contributing to the success and sustainability of the journal are easily generalizable to any virtual workplace whose primary production is textual. The three key elements that I see as contributing to the success of *Kairos* as both academic journal and virtual workplace are the value interactions that take place for all of the parties involved (authors, reviewers, and editors), the care with which we make sure that the actual work being done is made visible throughout the organization, and the development and deployment of both technological and administrative infrastructure that is designed to encourage and support cooperation and collaboration.

THE VALUE OF VIRTUAL WORK

The value of work can be assessed in a fairly straightforward and traditional manner by linking productivity and earnings and by determining the appropriate level of material gain for the labor that is provided by the workers. But there is another way of seeing the value of work as related to the nonfiduciary benefits that may accrue to the worker through the work activity. *Kairos* is a particularly well-situated case for examining this second form of value because the journal's economics work solely through what might be called "academic capital" rather than through the distribution of profit in the form of wages: *Kairos* is both nonprofit and does not engage in monetary accounting at all because our infrastructure is donated and the work that produces the journal is rewarded with both intrinsic value and the accrual of a form of social capital that I refer to as "academic capital," but not with wage earnings. The best way to describe how this social/academic capital functions within the economics of digital production is to contrast it with traditional Marxist representations of capital derived from material production.

Because Marx's work is concerned with material production, his framework includes consumption as an integral (and cyclical) component of the production process (and also required for the establishment of value). Consumption, however, becomes useful only at a metaphorical level when the object of the exchange is digital: exact reproductions can be made that do not consume the original products. Consumption can be described in terms of external resources (such as the living expenses of the workers who create and edit digital texts), but it no longer plays a direct role in the economies of the virtual workplace (although one might substitute "use" for consumption in order to fulfill all of the requirements of production in Marx's theory). This is not to say that digital objects are immaterial; they have material value by virtue of use and exchange. But it is useful here to depart from a strictly Marxist interpretation of capital and consider the role of what Bourdieu calls "cultural" and "social" capital in the economies of digital production.

The production of digital objects endows them with use-value, but the motivation for production is grounded in the subjective exchange-value that is garnered through the distribution and publication (and ultimately circulation) of the texts. Because digital production does not function in the same way as material production, it is better to approach the question of exchange-value not through Marxist theory, but via Bourdieu's theory of cultural capital. Particularly in terms of virtual teamwork and knowledge management ecologies, digital objects are not typically traded for material or monetary gain; instead, the exchange-value of the work comes from the accrual of cultural or social capital.

Bourdieu's (1977) project began as an attempt:

to extend economic calculation to all the goods, material and symbolic, without distinction, that present themselves as rare and worthy of being sought after in a particular formation—which may be "fair words" or smiles, handshakes or shrugs, compliments or attention, challenges or insults, honour or honours, powers or pleasures, gossip or scientific information, distinction or distinctions, and so forth. (p. 178)

In a sense, the Marxist perspective can be used to consider the production of digital texts as capital that requires labor, production, and distribution, while the Bourdieu-ian perspective is concerned less with the objects of circulation and more with the composers and appropriators of those texts.

In "The Forms of Capital," (1983/1986), Bourdieu extends Marx's notion of capital beyond material production in order to develop an economic theory that more ably explains "immaterial" products and that can describe the tight relationship between the social and the economic in terms of distribution of capital. Bourdieu (1983/1986) posits two new forms of capital: cultural capital and social capital. Cultural capital can take the form of cultural goods (the expression of accrued cultural capital) or it can be institutionalized, in the forms of educational credentials. In this second form, cultural capital represents a "certificate of cultural competence which confers on its holder a conventional, constant, legally guaranteed value with respect to power" (Bourdieu, 1983/1986, p.

248). While the collection of cultural capital is at its core an individual undertaking, Bourdieu describes "social capital" as residing in the relationships that develop in and around social networks: social capital is "the aggregate of the actual or potential resources which are linked to possession of a durable network of more or less institutionalized relationships of mutual acquaintance and recognition" (p. 248). Social capital can take the form of group membership and identity—it is possible, therefore, to delineate various types of social capital based on their fields of production. In considering the circulation of scholarly texts, for instance, one might describe the textual networks embodied in citation and reference interconnections as academic capital. The exchange-value of scholarly work then is the acquisition of academic (social) capital. James F. English (2005) calls this process of exchange the economy of symbolic cultural production, which might also be considered the economy of prestige (p. 75). Social and cultural capital operate at the level of activity: although it is possible to exchange social and cultural capital for material capital, gaining social capital is not as simple as purchasing material goods. Social capital—academic capital in particular—is, like material capital a product of labor. The difference here is that the labor is intellectual and self-motivated, rather than physical. The circulation of rhetorical objects is part of the process of production that leads to greater or lesser degrees of social capital for the composer (as well as for others who appropriate and use the compositions as the basis for further production).

In the case of *Kairos*, social/academic capital is linked to the circulation of the work we publish—authors gain academic capital through the publication of rigorously peer-reviewed research and scholarship (which is valued in the tenure and promotion process), and editoral board and staff gain academic capital via the service and research-based work that we do that insures the success and sustainability of the journal. This kind of capital is then exchanged for material economic benefits in the form of fellowships, job offers, tenure, and promotion—this is the link between the accrual of social capital and more traditional forms of remuneration. But without the operation of social capital, the continued sustainability of the journal as a viable enterprise would be radically diminished; even a shift to a monetary economy, I suspect, would engender a negative impact unless the social capital and the motivation to use it continued to be the primary economic system.

Social/academic capital works as a motivational force in part because it is visible—in an academic setting, publications and networking improve an individual's visibility as a productive member of the discipline; in the same way, social capital can be a motivator for individuals who work in other knowledge domains as well. Visibility is not just an outcome of the distribution of social capital; visibility of work practices and processes is also a key factor in the continued sustainability of any virtual work practice.

MAKING WORK VISIBLE

Professional and technical writers often find themselves in the position of developing products whose appearance does not reflect the amount of time or energy invested in the process of production. Nardi and Engström (1999) argue that "understanding the nature and structure of invisible work is crucial to designing and managing organizations" (p. 1). The editors of *Kairos* also agree with Nardi and Egström's (1999) suggestion that "invisible work also occurs in the case of workers' input to continuous improvement and development of practices, products, and technologies" (p. 2).

For *Kairos*, the communication between editors and authors and between editors and editorial board members represent a great deal of invisible work, as does the production of the issue itself. Because, as professional writers, we are sensitive to the fact that knowledge work often encompasses significant labor that may be unobserved and unacknowledged, we have developed two primary mechanisms for surfacing the research, supporting processes, and communication activities that have no explicit representation in the final products (the articles, reviews, and whole journal issues): process-based documentation and opportunities to take on different organizational roles during the production of each issue. These mechanisms help to make our virtual workplace into what Erickson and Kellogg (2000) term a "socially translucent system" (p. 59)—we have attempted via these mechanisms to build in "visibility, awareness, and accountability" (p. 61) into our processes and to use these practices to develop our organization as a knowledge community, "within which people would discover, use, and manipulate knowledge, and could encounter and interact with others who are doing likewise" (Erickson & Kellogg, 2000, p. 67).

Documenting both processes and outcomes has been a very useful way that the overall work on any given aspect of production for the journal can be explicitly represented and made visible. The kinds of documentation that we support do not focus exclusively on accountability so much as they are expected to provide insight into successful practices as well as avenues and approaches that were less appropriate to achieving particular production outcomes. Documentation as record keeping also provides a view of the communication activities involved in the development of each element of the journal for each issue; these documentation processes are public documents, and thus are particularly useful for fostering awareness and visibility, in addition to the accountability function inherent in documentation. *Kairos* is particularly supportive of this kind of surfacing of labor and activity in ways that make it accessible to others: we are instituting a new feature in the journal that documents and explicates the work (and work processes) that goes into the creation of new media scholarship with the aim of producing both heuristics for other new media producers and of supporting an argument that the intellectual work that goes into new media development is at least equivalent to the kind of work that is required of traditional scholarly textual production.

The other mechanism that we have to make work visible is the practice of taking up different organizational roles within the editorial structure; in essence, we encourage editors to work on different projects and in different roles in order to best understand the overall processes that lead to the production of each issue and to also provide a shared experience base for developing and implementing new methods aimed at improving the work-flows or communication networks engaged in each area of production. Allowing for (and encouraging) flexibility in organizational roles means that each of the editorial staff members has had the experience of working on a section different from the one for which they are responsible; this practice allows the staff to see the connections that must exist between the work flows of each section and the overall journal structure and allows them to both see and experience the otherwise invisible work that goes into the production of each section. This practice has arisen organically from the typical movement through staff positions over time; for instance, I began as the editor of the CoverWeb section, which produced collaborative and interconnected hypertexts based around a particular topic or theme. I later moved into the role of overall editor and publisher and although I am still involved with the management and production of each issue, as senior editor I currently focus my work on projects that support or promote the journal rather than on content production. I have also had the opportunity to work with each of the sections and to take on the roles of system administrator, copyeditor, communications manager, and site designer.

The practice of working across the organization in different roles is obviously constrained by the prior experience and skills of each staff member; because no one should take on roles for which they are unprepared, a related practice of shadowing or assisting across organizational roles (as appropriate and commensurate with the strengths of the individual workers) also provides a view of the work that takes place within and across the various departments and tasks within the overall organization. It is also important to acknowledge that this role-switching activity is in some ways more difficult to enact in virtual workplaces than in face to face environments. Successfully working together, either within or between work groups, can be supported by the online tools that are available, or they can be hindered by a lack of useful and accessible tools. Both tools and the administrative structures that support such collaborative work constitute the overall infrastructure of the virtual workplace.

INFRASTRUCTURE FOR COLLABORATIVE AND COOPERATIVE WORK

Adequate and appropriate infrastructure—providing the networks and tools that support work—is critical for the success of any labor-intensive enterprise, and particularly so for knowledge work (in both material and virtual workplaces). Infrastructure is not only the systems, networks, hardware, and software that facilitate knowledge work; infrastructure includes the operational frameworks that support or derail particular practices within the workplace. Infrastructure, then, includes the "often invisible issues of policy, definition, and ideology" (DeVoss, Cushman, & Grabill, 2005, p. 16). Thus the overall infrastructure of a virtual workplace also needs to be made visible in order to best assess its capacity to support collaborative and cooperative work. As DeVoss et al. (2005) note, "the concept of infrastructure itself demands an integrative analysis of these visible and invisible issues" (p. 16). Infrastructure is also

not a static environmental presence: one of the moves that contributes to *Kairos* as a successful virtual workplace is a constant evaluation of the efficacy of our infrastructure for supporting the work that we do.

Perhaps the most obvious (and visible) elements of infrastructure relate to the software tools and information computing technologies that are engaged in the practices of knowledge work. These tools can often become embedded in workplaces in such a way that they become unquestioned (and unquestionable) tools of the trade. But *Kairos* is acutely aware of the opportune moment as always open to reinvention; thus, we ask our editorial staff to routinely engage in usability studies of the processes we use when producing the journal. We also allow the various teams and departments to determine the best communication technologies and practices for their particular work: some teams use synchronous chat and instant messaging to a much greater degree than others (although everyone uses email as the main mode of communication). We are also building our own tools and systems, tailored to our specific needs. Seeing infrastructure as a developing and ongoing process of support and assessment allows us to constantly improve our communication and documentation opportunities, which in turn contribute to the overall visibility of the work done by each team.

Kairos also habitually assesses the administrative infrastructure—the organization chart, the increase or reduction of authority in various domains, and the protocols that govern work practices within the organization. As with technical infrastructure, we find that a high degree of flexibility is beneficial for the smooth operation of interpersonal communication in our virtual workplace. The different departments are each led by coteam leaders (co-editors) who are granted a high degree of autonomy in the day-to-day production tasks. Infrastructure in this sense is tied to value, as this authority requires a degree of trust (developed in part through the accountability of our visibility mechanisms) and also confers increased social capital within the organization. This sense of autonomy and trust allows for good ideas to circulate freely; because we also see infrastructure as malleable, we are also willing to engage these ideas in a spirit of entrepreneurial experimentation (which also reinforces the social capital granted to those workers who generate good ideas, often regardless of whether those suggestions are ultimately successful). Although the organizational structure is ostensibly hierarchical, bottom-up activity is privileged over top-down declarations—a model supportive of the workers in ways that strictly demarcated lines of communication and responsibility typically cannot provide. Of course, because of our operational model, we are positioned to experiment to a much greater degree than most other businesses that provide and rely upon activities that take place in virtual workplaces.

ASSESSMENT OF SUSTAINABILITY AND SUCCESS WITHIN VIRTUAL WORKPLACES

Because *Kairos* does not have the constraints that typical businesses do, it presents a case study of what could be; we have taken risks and engaged in experimentation in ways that traditional knowledge production-oriented systems cannot. Through the examination of the factors that have enabled the success of the journal and that have contributed to its visibility and sustainability, I would like to propose an analytic for the assessment of sustainability and success for virtual workplaces. This analytic considers value, visibility, and infrastructure as key factors required for success, and suggests that an assessment of sustainability would include methods for evaluating current and possible mechanisms for securing or distributing social capital, exposing the degree to which the tasks and interactions of workers are made visible, and assessing the administra-

tive and technological infrastructure with regard to support of communication, cooperation, and collaboration.

REFERENCES

Austin, W. W., Bowie, J. L., & Jones, B. (2001). Hypertext and pedagogy: Strategies, techniques, ideas. *Kairos: Rhetoric, Technology, Pedagogy, 6*(2). Retrieved November 20, 2007, from http://kairos.technorhetric.net/6.2/binder2.html?coverweb/hypertext/jonesbowieaustin/index.htm

Bourdieu, P. (1986). The forms of capital (Richard Nice, Trans.). In J. G. Richardson (Ed.), *Handbook of theory and research for the sociology of education* (pp. 241-258). New York: Greenwood P. (Original work published 1983)

Bourdieu, P. (1977). *Outline of a theory of practice* (Richard Nice, Trans). Cambridge, MA: Cambridge UP.

Brandt, D. (2005). Writing for a living: Literacy and the knowledge economy. *Written Communication, 22*(2), 166-197.

DeVoss, D. N., Cushman, E., & Grabill, J. T. (2005). Infrastructure and composing: The *when* of new-media writing. *College Composition and Communication, 57*(1), 14-44.

Doherty, M. (1996). Layers of meaning. *Kairos: Rhetoric, Technology, Pedagogy.* Retrieved November 20, 2007, from http://kairos.technorehtoric.net/layers/start.html

English, J. F. (2005). *The economy of prestige: Prizes, awards, and the circulation of cultural value.* Boston, MA: Harvard UP.

Erickson, T., & Kellogg, W. A. (2000). Social translucence: An approach to designing systems that support social processes. *ACM Transactions on Computer-Human Interaction, 7*(1), 59-83.

Kairos: Rhetoric, Technology, Pedagogy. (1996-2007). Retrieved November 20, 2007, from http://kairos.technorhetoric.net/

Nardi, B. A., & Engeström, Y. (1999). A Web on the wind: The structure of invisible work. *Computer Supported Cooperative Work, 8,* 1-8.

Star, S. L., & Ruhelder, K. (1996). Steps toward an ecology infrastructure: Design and access for large information spaces. *Information Systems Research, 7*(1), 111-134.

White, E. C. (1987). *Kaironomia: On the will-to-invent.* Ithaca, NY: Cornell UP.

KEY TERMS

Academic Capital: Academic capital is a form of social capital particular to academia; it is accrued through the activities and recognition of publications and presentations within a particular scholarly discipline.

Cultural Capital: Pierre Bourdieu (1977) coined the term "cultural capital" as a reference to the material goods that are collected and displayed by the cultural elite (such as paintings by famous artists, extensive libraries, or collections of fine wines). The goods that represent cultural capital reference elite cultural values (and are thus not simply a display of wealth, but a display of the owner's knowledge).

Infrastructure: Infrastructure includes both the material support systems that make virtual work possible (such as computers and computer networks) and the embedded practices of communication that have been established within a particular community of workers. Star and Ruhleder (1996) argue that infrastructure is transparent to use, but becomes visible when it breaks down and is linked with conventions of practice (p. 113).

Social Capital: Unlike cultural capital, social capital is primarily not material; rather it is the network of *who you know* rather than *what you have.* Social capital is accrued through the acquisitions of awards or other recognition of an individual's value, as well as the exchange of social indebtedness between individuals who belong to the same social networks.

Visibility: Visibility is the degree to which the labor of individuals working in virtual workplaces is both available and acknowledged by management or other administrative roles within the work institution.

Webtexts: In the most basic sense, Webtexts are texts that reside on the Web. These texts are distinguished both from hypertext (because their structures may be linear rather than hypertextual) and from print texts that have been placed on the Web (such as PDF copies of journal articles). Jennifer Bowie (qtd. in Austin, Bowie, & Jones 2001) notes that while:

some [W]ebtexts are hypertext, ... many others just incorporate a few of the multilinear and hypertextual possibilities. Webtexts are found on the World Wide Web and, like hypertext, can be multimedia. They will have links between different nodes, however the text may be designed to be read more linearly than hypertextually. (definitions.html)

Chapter XLIV
Plagiarism, Ghostwriting, Boilerplate, and Open Content

Wendy Warren Austin
Edinboro University of Pennsylvania, USA

ABSTRACT

This chapter explains to business people, administrators, and educator/trainers what plagiarism is and is not, and explores authorship ambiguities such as ghostwriting, templates, boilerplate language, collaborative/team writing, and open content. It argues that two key features of plagiarism are the intent to deceive and lack of consent from the original author(s). Furthermore, whether the environment is an academic or work environment plays an important part in determining whether plagiarism has occurred, because academic settings impose stricter standards on borrowing. However, if both the original author and the borrowing author are aware of the origination of words and consent to their re-use, and the issue involves template or boilerplate language, or incorporates acknowledgement of influences, help, or collaborative contributions, it does not constitute plagiarism. Clarifying differences in standards and expectations of the academic and workplace environment will help business people better understand the ethical boundaries for practices of acknowledgement and attribution.

INTRODUCTION

The workplace thrives on transforming the ideas of others into a new-and-improved version of the old. Without imitation and influence, society would never advance. Yet the line between acceptable and unacceptable borrowing, as is the case with plagiarism, has become more and more blurred. Today hardly a day goes by when the news does not include some reference to plagiarism. The purpose of this chapter is to explain to business managers, administrators, educators, trainers, and executives what plagiarism is and is not, and to explore the nature of this highly public issue and business-related ambiguities in authorship such

as ghostwriting, use of templates, boilerplate language, viral marketing, "rubber stamp" correspondence, collaborative/team authorship, and open content. Clarifying the differences between the academic and the workplace environment and the standards and expectations that each encounter will help business people better understand the ethical boundaries for practices of acknowledgment and attribution.

BACKGROUND

Plagiarism has come to be such a trigger word for the media that it comes close to murder or kidnapping in the sense of outrage that the accusation conjures up. This may be because the word "plagiarism" comes from the Latin word "plagiarius" meaning "kidnapper, seducer, or plunderer," in the sense of a literary thief. However, the concept developed its roots in an age when the idea of the solitary author took on an almost mystical importance in the late Renaissance, fed even more in the centuries to follow by the pervasive philosophy of John Locke's theory of "possessive individualism," applied to property law, and extending the idea of property to written products. Copyright law had its origins at the same time that such legal and philosophical theories developed, and since the lawmakers deemed a writer's written work product as physical property, the two realms of law became intertwined. Several good sources for examining the development of this phenomenon are Woodmansee and Jaszi's (1993) compilation of essays, *The Construction of Authorship: Textual Appropriation in Law and Literature*, and Eisenstein's (1980) seminal work.

Copyright Infringement vs. Plagiarism

Although copyright infringement is not the same thing as plagiarism (one is strictly a legal violation, the other an ethical and/or moral violation that incurs academic censure), the two terms take on the same sinister dimensions in media exposure. Since the latter term carries the more menacing connotation, even though it is not actually even a crime, *plagiarism* seems to get the most press. This is unfortunate, because notions of writing as a solitary activity have changed, notions of copyright law are being challenged, and certainly, the idea of a written product as a fixed and permanent piece of property has changed. These changes are hardly more apparent than in the virtual workplace. Nevertheless, to compete in global society, we must be aware of the current notions that are prevalent, even if they are not ideal or outdated.

"Plagiarism" in the most common sense of the word, means to claim some piece of writing is one's own when it is not. The Council of Writing Program Administrators (WPA) (2003) developed a statement that includes a definition of plagiarism to help teachers of writing in colleges. They define plagiarism in this way: "In an instructional setting, plagiarism occurs when a writer deliberately uses someone else's language, ideas, or other original (not common-knowledge) material without acknowledging its source. (p. 1)" This definition, developed in 2003 by writing program administrators well aware of the changes in writing practices, copyright law, and nature of written products, represents a current understanding of how plagiarism is viewed among writing teachers and intellectual property scholars in academia. Plagiarism is a deliberate act intended to deceive others of its originality.

Common Knowledge

The WPA statement on plagiarism specifically exempts material that is common knowledge from having to be cited. However, the term "common knowledge" is open to interpretation, and determining whether something is common knowledge depends in large part on context, purpose, genre, and audience. Within academic circles, common knowledge may be one of two types:

1. general cultural knowledge of which anyone in that cultural context with a high school/secondary school education is expected to be aware, or
2. discipline-specific knowledge, knowledge that anyone in a specific discipline, discourse community, or organization would be expected to know, such as typical jargon, common metaphors, seminal works or breakthroughs in the field.

General cultural knowledge is generally the same thing as "commonsense-expert knowledge" (Elin-Door, 2006), while discipline-specific knowledge refers to the body of knowledge and/or tasks that one is expected to know for a certain job or within a discipline (Carter, 1990).

Several researchers/scholars (Brandt, 2005; Lunsford & Ede, 1990) in the composition studies field reported in their findings that in the workplace authors frequently share knowledge more freely than in the academic realm, collaborate in varied ways, and do not always give as much importance to who wrote what in a company's document, as much as they concentrate on ending up with a coherent, well-written finished document on time. In the workplace, the organization tends to take precedence over the individual author. In addition, it is extremely common to have teams with sometimes shifting membership serve as a collective author for a firm's written product. By virtue of an employee's work assignment and goals, team managers expect writers to share their written work product with the team and firm. No intent to deceive is operating here; managers expect consensual collaboration and workers contribute voluntarily on a written product that may or may not have every contributor's name on the finished product.

Borrowing Poorly or Unconsciously

Another composition/rhetoric scholar (Howard, 1993, 1999) has developed a more thorough understanding of the concept of plagiarism by coining and explaining the idea of "patchwriting." She defines patchwriting as "copying from a source text and then deleting some words, altering grammatical structures, or plugging in one synonym for another" (Howard, 1999, p. xvii), and sees patchwriting as a positive stage in the novice writers' development during which they "try on" the language of the discourse community to which they aspire to belong. The problem with this sort of paraphrasing, she believes, is that it is inherently trial and error in its success, and the errors become noticeable. When the novice writer leaves enough of a trace of the original language or structure for professors and more

expert writers to notice, the expert writers often cry "plagiarism!" and insist that the plagiarizer has intended to deceive them, when often no such intent existed.

In everyday situations, as well as in the workplace, people often think they have an original idea but really have heard it from somewhere else previously but just do not remember they do (Defeldre, 2005). Psychological researchers call this phenomenon "cryptomnnesia," and, like the patchwriting Howard (1993) describes, the unconscious borrowing also lacks the element of intent. People in advertising and creative fields who develop slogans may be likely to have this happen to them frequently.

MAIN FOCUS

The definition from writing program administrators indicates that intent to deceive is one of the key defining features of plagiarism. When students enroll in college classes, they essentially enter into a contract with the instructor that claims that whatever they produce, written or otherwise, for course requirements will be solely their own (with the exception of explicitly designated collaborative projects), for which they will get something in return, a grade, (Hurlbert, 1988). No one is allowed to "ghostwrite" essay exams or research papers for other students; not that this cannot be done. It happens all too frequently, especially with term paper mills charging $8 per page to do the students' work for them. These sites may facilitate plagiarism, but the writers of these papers are ghostwriters, not themselves ethically at fault, except perhaps in enabling students to commit unethical acts.

Ghostwriting and Institutionalized Plagiarism

Ghostwriters produce a written product for others and are paid for that work product. They have no intention to deceive, but simply have a skill and a product for which they wish to be paid. A publishing company specializing in ghostwriting services clarifies the distinction:

You can make a very successful career for yourself as a ghostwriter. You can be expelled from school or given a failing grade for plagiarizing. In both cases "the author of record" and the "real" author are two different people. Why is one a serious offense and not the other? The difference is one of knowledge and permission. (Griffith Publishing, 2003, p. 2)

Some ghostwriting services believe, like this one, that if a book is ghostwritten, it should somehow state that it is, if not on the cover of the book, then in the acknowledgements section. Others believe that ghostwritten works are best when the result is a "smoothly written mirage" (Crainer & Kleiner, 1998). Political candidates have long had speechwriters ghostwriting their speeches for them. The public, though they will attribute the speaker's words to the person speaking them, also understands that these public figures do use speechwriters. Organizational and business leaders also rely on units within their firms to create public statements, and as such whatever they say or produce on behalf of the company is a collaborative effort. Seeger (1992) and Einhorn (1981) provide good overviews of this ghostwriting debate.

Moodie (2006), writing about college administrators, puts a name to the practice of speaking for an organization: "nominal authorship." Nominal authorship, according to Moodie (2006), comes in three forms: ghostwritten, rubber stamp, or nominal direction. Ghostwriting public affairs staff members may author college presidents' speeches, opening remarks, and newsletter columns, while the "rubber stamp" method of authoring often prevails with such documents as invitations, holiday cards, donation requests, and questionnaires. Discussion papers and proposed policies or procedures may be written by "nominal direction," by college officials working at the directives of the head administrators, as may the college Web site, annual report, viewbooks, or any other officially sanctioned college document. These documents may or may not be signed by their authors, but each one had one or more authors at some point. However, while Moodie (1996) may see problems with not listing authorship either directly or at all, calling it "bureaucratic plagiarism." Martin (1994) refers to it as "institutionalized plagiarism," more or less business as usual in bureaucracies. A case in September 2006 involved such a situation of "bureaucratic plagiarism," where the person doing the borrowing, the chancellor of Southern Illinois University at Carbondale, Walter V. Wendler, was fired as a result of using similar material from work done at a former job to his (then current) job as chancellor of SIU (Smallwood, 2006). While the situations and tasks at both jobs were similar, the wording borrowed from the previous school's institutional documents, their strategic plan, was deemed too alike, that is, too plagiarized, for SIU's strategic plan, and Wendler's job as chancellor was traded for that of a professor (Lederman, 2006). Many employees do similar work at different jobs, taking with them their ideas, their habits of wording, turns of phrase, but in this case, it is possible that Wendler did not differentiate carefully enough between his own intellectual property and work for hire. Lederman (2006) reports that "Wendler had said that he was using his own intellectual property, but a faculty panel, while defending his character, criticized Wendler for not being more careful about identifying the source of his work." (http://insidehighered.com/news/2006/11/09/siu).

Many of the actions employees do fall under the category of "work for hire," a special term used by the United States Copyright Act and the copyright laws of most countries. Works for hire are works created by employees within an organization that are specifically within the scope of the employees' job responsibilities. In these cases, the organizations hold the copyright, not the individuals, because they are specifically being paid to create such works on an ongoing basis.

In the case of the SIU chancellor, the wording of the previous school's strategic plan stayed at the previous school, despite its author having moved to a new institution. It is not an easy task for any author to do, to keep his or her written words compartmentalized within the context of their creation, but what probably would have mitigated the former chancellor's situation would have been his sharing where he had originally conceived of and used the words. Then his colleagues would have been fully informed. Even if that had been the case, the fact that the business environment happened to also have been an *academic environment*, may have clouded the issue, causing academic standards to be applied to a bureaucratic (albeit academic bureaucratic) context or vice versa. Another case, reported in January and February of 2000, describes a professor and communication department head who, in the rush of finishing a lecture on time, failed to cite one 64-word sentence he quoted, after which a student reported this to the dean. When this was called to his attention, the professor resigned as chair, but retained his teaching post, admitting it as an "ethical lapse" ("Department Chair," 2000).

The motive of deception, whether actively seeking to deceive or passively doing so, by not informing the readers, is a critical one in determining whether something is plagiarized or unethically ghostwritten. For example, Greenbaum (1993) reports that some marketing research companies are using junior or part-time employees to ghostwrite focus group research reports, even when they were not present at the focus group. When the client is not told that the reports are written by someone other than the moderator present, this constitutes deception (Greenbaum, 1993) and becomes troubling.

A recent practice of ghostwriting in science (Krimsky, 2003) and medical journals has stirred major concerns because its readers are not immediately aware that there may be a potential conflict of interest between a sponsoring agency and the writer of an article. Pharmaceutical companies may finance an individual or company to write a seemingly unbiased article about their new drug or medical method, who will then submit it (or *the sponsoring company will arrange for the article to be submitted*) to a peer-reviewed medical journal for publication (Laine & Mulrow, 2005; Fugh-Berman, 2005; Tierney & Gerrity, 2005). The journal's editors and/or peer reviewers may not know that the article, frequently praising a drug or criticizing its competitor, was underwritten by the same company whose drug or treatment method the article itself is promoting. Unsuspecting readers, perhaps doctors deciding to adopt the drug, certainly are not told about the underwritten articles, and thus are deceived. This type of ghostwriting, one that breaches the basic trust between academic journals and their readers, is deceptive, akin to the deception practiced by some student plagiarists.

Boilerplate and Templates

D. Jameson (1993) has pointed out that "plagiarism is a relative, not absolute matter." An essential determining factor, especially in business environments, is genre, in addition to context, audience expectations and writer intentions. The media tend to view all "copying" as plagiarism, regardless of the context or genre of the documents. Jameson (1993), who defines plagiarism as "the misappropriation of materials (ideas, facts, word structures) that were created, originated, or discovered by someone else (p. 19)" has emphasized that "misappropriation is the key word in identifying whether something is plagiarized, because it connotes a sense of impropriety in the taking of an idea, word, or document. Using an example of a consulting firm report that a team of four employees collaborate on over a period of months, the writers of the final report may start with some "boilerplate" sections from reports written years before by other, perhaps unknown employees. Since the entire report comes from the same company, the material is not plagiarized, even when the original writer of the boilerplate section is not acknowledged. It is the collective organization who is responsible for the report, not individuals. Jameson (1993) has noted that "word-for-word lifting [without attribution] from a company's past written records is common" (p. 25).

Attorneys use boilerplate contract language in their work all the time, although Isaacs (2006) explores the extent to which litigation documents can be copyrighted. Boilerplate language is a form of standard language that functions much like a document template, except that the former is language, while the other refers to the design of a document. Obviously, many offices nowadays could not function very efficiently if the employees did not have access to multiple forms of templates.

FUTURE TRENDS

Usually the genres that use borrowed material without attribution can be found within the realm of business and industry, rather than in the academic realm. One exception, noted by J. D. Alexander (1988), besides the ones dealing with college administration and marketing, is the college professor's lecture. Frequently, in the process of delivering a lecture, professors may not fully mention the sources from which they draw their material. Perhaps this trend will change with the growing numbers of online lectures and podcasts; lectures delivered in these ways are captured and memorialized, and may fall under greater scrutiny than in the past, pressuring more professors to include specific attribution within their lectures.

Creative Commons Licensing and DRM

However, more fundamental changes have been taking place regarding the concept of copyright itself, particularly in the creation of the Creative Commons license, begun in 2002, and spearheaded by Stanford lawyer and intellectual prop-erty specialist Lawrence Lessig and like-minded individuals. The Creative Commons license (see http://creativecommons.org) borrowed from the model of the open-source code movement and establishes a copyright-like license based on the idea of giving automatic consent to share while still requiring attribution of the original source. The numbers of Web pages and other works that carry a Creative Commons license are rising astronomically, and at last count (in 2006) on the similarly named Web site, listed 140 million pages using this model. Bailey (2006) cites the swiftly changing nature of copyright, along with two other critical issues that are becoming more volatile every day of which we should remain aware: the growing use of technologies in affecting Digital Rights Management (DRM) and the concerns over Internet neutrality. DRM refers to the techniques used by vendors, publishers, and manufacturers of various technologies that prevent or restrict copying of digital content. Using a variety of encrypting and encoding schemes and technical controls, some companies, like Apple, sell products that will only play on their other products. For example, if a person buys a song on the iTunes store, the music formats a certain type of audio files (called ACC), and encodes them with an encrypting technology (called Fair Play) only supported by iPods, and includes within the technology the capability to play only on a certain number of computers at one time (See Dilger, 2007, for an in-depth explanation of this technology). As new technologies are created and adopted, just as often, ways to get around those technologies are also found. One case in point and interesting consequence is the fate of audio CDs' DRM technologies. Starting in 2002, the big music companies tried to put technical controls against copying on audio CDs; by January 2007, no major companies had anticopying protection on their audio CDs any longer.

Net Neutrality Debate

The "net neutrality" issue, as it has been called, is hotly debated by lawmakers, especially after the even election years when Congressional partisanship has the potential to shift emphasis and vote patterns, and as telecommunications companies seek to secure stronger economic footholds in the industry. Meanwhile, powerful opponents and popular entities, such as Amazon.com, Google, and Yahoo, as well as many Internet pioneers and a groundswell of grassroots support remain highly vocal in the efforts to keep the Internet free. As Crowcroft (2007), writing from the technical standpoint, explains, "the net neutrality argument is a debate between radically different stakeholders, and the one thing the reader must recall when reading any contributions, is that the goals of different stakeholders are very different" (p. 54).

Open Content

A related idea on the horizon is the concept of Open Content—free digitized information available to all without restrictions. The Open Content movement is mainly focused in the areas of opening access to educational resources (see http://opencontent.org/googleocw/ for more information), but the trend in open content also creates such go-to staples on the Web as the Wikipedia, an online encyclopedia that can be authored by anyone and everyone. Although it has no formal oversight editorial board, Wikipedia's contributors actively scan its nodes for mistakes, and do a remarkable job in keeping its entries as accurate as possible. Durno (2003) explains the concept of open source well for those new to it, referring to Raymond's (1998) likening of the traditional model of information and the open model to the cathedral and the bazaar.

Remixing

"Remixing" appears to be a new buzzword for the act of creating new thing by taking bits and pieces of previous creations and adding, subtracting, changing, and rearranging the parts. The word is taken from disc jockeys' "remixing" different combinations of CD tracks to play them in a new sequence, and now is often applied to creating any new thing out of an old one, an action made exponentially easier by digital means. If the term remixing is not used, one might run across other phrases to represent acceptable form of plagiarism: recombinant writing, for example (Critical Arts Ensemble, 2006).

CONCLUSION

Key elements in determining whether a work has been plagiarized include intent, consent, and context. When someone uses a work with an intent to deceive the reader into thinking the work is his or her own, then plagiarism has occurred. Whether the environment is an academic or work environment also plays an important part in determining whether plagiarism has occurred. Academic environments impose stricter standards and expectations on "original" work, while many work environments do not. A third important factor in determining whether a work has been plagiarized involves consent. If both the original author(s) and the borrowing author(s) are aware of the origination of the words, and consent to their re-use, generally the issue involves template or boilerplate language or incorporates acknowledgement of influences, help, or collaborative contributions, and do not constitute plagiarism.

In a conference presentation about writing and digital knowledge, Porter and DeVoss (2006) ask the most important question about the connection between original information and the workplace: "Is there any practical connection between the digital composition practice of remixing and economic development of the digital economy—or are these simply two widely different, unrelated areas? (p. 4)" They conclude that we are not ready to answer that question adequately yet, but invite scholars and researchers to continue making it possible for the workplace to thrive by transforming the old into the new.

REFERENCES

Alexander, J. D. (1988). Lectures: The ethics of borrowing. *College Teaching, 36*(1), 21-24.

Bailey, C. W. (2006, Sept.). Strong copyright + DRM + weak net neutrality = digital dystopia? *Information Technology and Libraries, 25*(3), 116-139.

Brandt, D. (2005). Writing for a living: Literacy and the knowledge economy. *Written Communication, 22,* 166-197.

Carter, M. (1990). The idea of expertise: An exploration of cognitive and social dimensions of writing. *College Composition and Communication, 41,* 265-86.

Council of Writing Program Administrators. (2003). WPA statement on plagiarism. Retrieved November 21, 2007, from http://www.wpacouncil.org/node/9/

Crainer, S., & Kleiner, A. (1998). Who wrote these books? *Across the Board, 35*(10), 22-27.

Critical Arts Ensemble. (2000). *Utopian plagiarism, hypertextuality and electronic cultural production. In the electronic disturbance.* Brooklyn, NY: Autonomedia.

Crowcroft, J. (2007). Net neutrality: The technical side of the debate: A white paper. Editorial. *ACM SigComm Computer Communication Review, 37*(1), 49-56.

Defeldre, A. (2005). Inadvertent plagiarism in everyday life. *Applied Cognitive Psychology, 19,* 1033-1040.

Department chair steps down over attribution question. (2000, Summer). *Public Relations Quarterly, 45*(2), 23.

Dilger, D. E. (2007, February 26). How FairPlay works: Apple, iTunes DRM dilemma. Retrieved November 21, 2007, from http://www.roughly-drafted.com/RD/RDM.Tech.Q1.07/2A351C60-A4E5-4764-A083-FF8610E66A46.html

Durno, J. (2003). Open content: Open source, hold the software. *Feliciter, 2,* 69-71.

Einhorn, L. J. (1981). The ghosts unmasked: A review of literature on speechwriting. *Communication Quarterly, 30*(1), 41-47.

Eisenstein, E. L. (1980). *The printing press as an agent of change.* Cambridge, UK: Cambridge UP.

Elin-Dor, P. (2006). Taxonomies of knowledge. *Encyclopedia of Knowledge Management.* In D. G. Schwartz (Ed.), Hershey, PA: Idea Group.

Fugh-Berman, A. (2005). The corporate coauthor. *Journal of General Internal Medicine, 20,* 546-548.

Greenbaum, T. L. (1993). Using ghosts to write reports hurts viability of focus groups. *Marketing News, 27*(19), 25.

Griffith Publishing. (2003). *All about ghostwriting.* November 21, 2007, from http://www.griffith-ghostwriting.com/ghostwritingbook.pdf

Howard, R. M. (1993). A plagiarism pentimento. *Journal of Teaching Writing, 11*(2), 233-246

Howard, R. M. (1999). *Standing in the shadows of giants: Plagiarists, authors, collaborators.* Stamford, CT: Ablex.

Hurlbert, C. M. (1988). Rhetoric, possessive individualism, and beyond. *Writing Instructor, 8*(1), 8-14.

Isaacs, D. (2006, Spring). The highest form of flattery? Application of the fair use defense against copyright claims for unauthorized appropriation of litigation documents. *Missouri Law Review*, 392-446. Retrieved November 21, 2007, from http://online.wsj.com/public/resources/documents/Davida05052006.pdf

Jameson, D. A. (1993, June). The ethics of plagiarism: How genre affects writers' use of source materials. *The Bulletin for the Association of Business Communication, 56*(2), 18-28.

Krimsky, S. (2003). *Science in the private interest: Has the lure of profits corrupted biomedical research?* Lanham, MD: Rowman & Littlefield.

Laine, C., & Mulrow, C. D. (2005, October 18). Exorcising ghosts and unwelcome guests. *Annals of Internal Medicine, 143,* 611-612.

Lederman, D. (2006). Southern Illinois chancellor forced out. *Inside Higher Education.* Retrieved November 21, 2007, from http://www.insidehighered.com/layout/set/print/news/2006/11/09/siu

Lunsford, A., & Ede, L. (1990). *Singular texts/plural authors: Perspectives on collaborative writing.* Carbondale, IL: Southern Illinois University.

Martin, B. (1994, Fall). Plagiarism: A misplaced emphasis. *Journal of Information Ethics, 3*(2), 36-47. Retrieved November 21, 2007, from http://www.uow.edu.au/arts/sts/bmartin/pubs/94jie.html

Moodie, G. (2006). Bureaucratic plagiarism. *Plagiary: Cross-Disciplinary Studies in Plagiarism, Fabrication, and Falsification, 1*(6), 1-5. Retrieved November 21, 2007, from http://www.plagiary.org/bureaucratic-plagiarism.pdf

Porter, J. E., & DeVoss, D. N. (2006, July 12). Rethinking plagiarism in the digital age: Remixing as a means for economic development? (WIDE Paper #6). Retrieved November 21, 2007, from http://www.wide.msu.edu/widepapers/devossplagiarism

Raymond, E. S. (1998, Feb. 16). The cathedral and the bazaar. *First Monday* Retrieved November 21, 2007, from http://www.firstmonday.org/issues/issue3_3/raymond/

Seeger, M. W. (1992). Ethical issues in corporate speechwriting. *Journal of Business Ethics, 11*(7), 501-504.

Smallwood, S. (2006, Sept. 6). Plagiarism hunters at Southern Illinois U. say campus's strategic plan was lifted. *The Chronicle of Higher Education.* Retrieved November 21, 2007, from http://chronicle.com/daily/2006/09/2006090802n.htm

Tierney, W. M., & Gerrity, M. S. (2005). Scientific discourse, corporate ghostwriting, journal policy, and public trust. *Journal of General Internal Medicine, 20*(6), 550-551.

Woodmansee, M., & Jaszi, P. (1993). *The construction of authorship: Textual appropriation in law and literature.* City, Duke UP.

KEY TERMS

Boilerplate: Language that is able to be used over and over again with consent and without attribution for similar purposes, especially in generic business documents, such as trial briefs, quarterly reports, mastheads, rubrics, forms, and releases, without liability as to copyright infringement.

Common Knowledge: Cultural knowledge that a literate adult in society would be expected to know or knowledge within a specific discipline or field that most members in that field would be expected to know.

Copyright Infringement: A civil legal violation in which one copyrighted work uses information from another copyrighted work without permission of the original author(s), or when some entity improperly copies, performs, or distributes copies of an existing work, either in whole or in part.

Cryptomnesia: Inadvertent plagiarism, having an idea, creating a word, song, or solution to a problem for which a person assumes originality, but is actually drawn from the person's subconscious memory from some earlier source.

Ghostwriting: A practice that involves someone or some group that writes, usually for monetary gain, for some other person or group, with the latter taking the credit for the product of the former. Essentially, it is the practice of writing for money for someone else without getting the credit.

Institutional Plagiarism: Also may be called bureaucratic plagiarism, a practice of using junior employees to write material for which senior employees take credit. This practice may also be referred to as nominal authorship.

Open Content: An initiative based on the concept of the IT industry's Open Source Move-

ment, this type of content refers to future or current freely available information on the Internet. Wikipedia and MIT's Open Courseware are good examples of open content.

Plagiarism: To claim some piece of writing that is not considered common knowledge to be one's own with the intent to deceive the recipient otherwise.

Patchwriting: A stage of writing in which (usually novice) writers substitute their own words and/or sentence structures of an original source in an unsuccessful attempt to paraphrase.

Work for Hire: Works created by employees of a company (or a contractor with a company) that is specifically within the scope of their employment to do, for which the employer gains copyright, while the employee receives compensation in the form of a salary, commission, or contract rate.

Chapter XLV
Usability and User–Centered Theory for 21st Century OWLs

Dana Lynn Driscoll
Purdue University, USA

H. Allen Brizee
Purdue University, USA

Michael Salvo
Purdue University, USA

Morgan Sousa
Purdue University, USA

ABSTRACT

This chapter describes results of usability research conducted on the Purdue Online Writing Lab (OWL). The Purdue OWL is an information-rich educational Web site that provides free writing resources to users worldwide. Researchers conducted two generations of usability tests. In the first test, participants were asked to navigate the OWL and answer questions. Results of the first test and user-centered scholarship indicated that a more user-centered focus would improve usability. The second test asked participants to answer writing-related questions using both the OWL Web site and a user-centered OWL prototype. Participants took significantly less time to find information using the prototype and reported a more positive response to the user-centered prototype than the original OWL. Researchers conclude that a user-centered Web site is more effective and can be a model for information-rich online resources. Researchers also conclude that usability research can be a productive source of ideas, underscoring the need for participatory invention.

INTRODUCTION

Universities have been leaders in developing virtual workplaces. Campus-based research has led to the development of remote information access, telecommunication, and the infrastructure research that supports the emerging 21st Century virtual workplace. Indeed, in *Datacloud*, Johnson-Eilola (2005) presents studies of a number of campus-situated offices as places of information-age literacy practice. One conception of campus situates academics in ivory towers separated from the realities of the working world, a romantic representation of a detached life of the mind. Contrary to this idealization/criticism, which represents the university and its knowledge workers as out of touch with the working world, universities have been leaders in developing cutting-edge flexible and virtual workplaces. Similarly, college campuses have been sites of the first realizations of emerging problems that accompany postindustrial knowledge work—cubicle farms and boundary-blurring between work and home, business and family.

Envisioning the university as a site of change should not be surprising, as campuses began as a center for knowledge-making, for research and development, and then for dissemination of these findings. Knowledge-making is the basis for land grant universities (see the NASULGC history). And recently, corporations have used college campuses as models for a substantial number of corporate worksites. That these emerging 21st Century business architectures are modeled after college campuses should not come as a surprise. Corporate universities, designed as educational institutions, emerge from an earlier model of collection, organization, and dissemination of knowledge. Faber and Johnson-Eilola (2003) write about corporate educational structures built in imitation of universities. Their investigation of corporate knowledge creation demonstrates how reliant these organizations were on their academic precursors, and also how corporations quickly shifted from a model of replacing universities to one of cooperation, collaboration, and strategic augmentation. Knowledge-making requires intensive investment and long-term commitment.

Indeed, the Purdue Online Writing Lab, or OWL, described in this chapter is built on the model of an institution built for 19th Century information dissemination: the land grant university. The OWL started as a group of filing cabinets filled with handouts about classroom-based writing instruction. Literacy educators began by imitating their colleagues in the agricultural extension program, which was designed to bring practical knowledge from campus to farmers working their fields. The OWL was originally designed to bring best teaching practices to the classrooms of Indiana. As this chapter describes the OWL's development, keep in mind how its technological

practices closely follow the development and dissemination of information, from paper- and mail-based dissemination to digital communications technologies, from file cabinets (early databases) from which documents were copied and mailed, to e-mail and early digital formatting, to Web-based browser searches and always-accessible digital warehousing of online information resources. And notice how the scope expands from a local (state) resource to increasing spheres of influence with global reach and dissemination.

This chapter presents the results of two generations of usability research designed to support creation of user-centered taxonomic and navigation structures. The technological development closely follows that described by Rosenfeld and Morville (2006) in *Information Architecture for the World Wide Web*, in which isolated "archipelagoes" of information are gathered together and formalized under increasingly complex organizational schemes and centers of institutional control. User-centered design, which could also be represented as citizen-centered design, also informs the research.

Each successive generation of OWL information design reflects the commitment to timely dissemination and integration of applications of research, following the collaborative spirit of the land grant University. The University of Wisconsin-Madison has, not surprisingly, named this commitment to citizen participation the Wisconsin Idea, reflecting Wisconsin's progressive history by bridging participatory design with information architecture. Often referred to as Scandinavian Design because of its northern European roots, the Wisconsin Idea brings Participatory Design together with Information Design. Key to this collaborative relationship between the University and the citizens it serves is mutual respect and two-way communication, or according to Wisconsin's Center for Integrated Agricultural Systems (2004): experts were "on tap, not on top."

This chapter describes two steps in an ongoing commitment to user-based research to improve the usability and accessibility of Purdue's OWL. Embedded in a history of citizen access, integration and collaboration, the OWL can be understood as a virtual workplace that specializes in providing timely and tested literacy materials as well as best practices in workplace communication and the teaching of writing. As a member of an elite group of land-grant institutions that support democratic processes, OWL research supports the efforts of Indiana's citizens by making research findings available. Purdue's OWL may be a unique virtual workplace. However, each virtual workplace is embedded within a unique context of historical and technological development. This chapter is one attempt to articulate the current context of Purdue's user-centered development. Please visit the OWL's research page at http://owl.english.purdue.edu/research/ to read more about this continuing project.

HISTORY OF THE PURDUE WRITING LAB AND THE PURDUE OWL

Writing labs, also known as writing centers, are collaborative spaces where writers and writing tutors work together. Many writing labs also have a strong online presence, offering writing-related materials, interactive media, and online consultations.

In 1976, Purdue University established its Writing Lab, a campus-based service designed to assist learners in their writing processes. Outreach from the Writing Lab began with a collection of paper-based resources physically mailed to users as they contacted the Writing Lab requesting information on writing, citation, or research. In 1993, these resources became available electronically through GOPHER, a FTP precursor to the World Wide Web. The Writing Lab launched its OWL on the Internet in 1995 (found at owl.english.purdue.edu). Having made its library of resources available electronically, the Purdue OWL is now accessed by users worldwide.

The Purdue OWL was the first of its kind and is still one of the leading online writing labs in the world. Every year, millions of users access resources available on the OWL. The following is a breakdown of usage patterns from May 1, 2006 through April 31, 2007 (Purdue Writing Lab Annual Report, 2006-2007):

- **Web site:** 84,863,489 visits from over 125 countries
- **Data:** 6,363 gigabytes
- **E-mail tutoring:** 5,404 e-mails answered
- **Pages Linked to OWL:** 2,520 added during this time

Data reveal that OWL users fall into the following categories:

- Primary and secondary teachers (grades K-12)
- English as a Second Language (ESL) teachers and ESL students
- English as a Foreign Language (EFL) teachers and EFL students
- Purdue faculty, staff, and students
- Non-Purdue college instructors and students, including other writing lab personnel
- Professionals seeking writing assistance
- Professional and corporate trainers
- Government trainers
- Active duty, retired, and transitioning military personnel
- Parents of students, including home-schooling educators.

In order to improve accessibility and usability of the original OWL—to organize and present its large library of resources in a more efficient way—the Writing Lab redesigned the OWL according to Web accessibility and Web development standards. The OWL launched its redesigned site on August 26, 2005. The new site boasted improved access, resource sustainability, and a cutting-edge database-driven content management system. The goals for this redesign included:

- Maintain writing support for all users
- Develop library-like features
- Achieve a more interactive environment
- Ensure accessibility of materials and navigability of the site, including 508 compliance
- Transition from a print-based to an electronic medium (the Web)
- Utilize advantages of Web-based material
- Ensure scalability—management of over 200 handouts
- Develop multiple identities appealing to a wide variety of users
- Provide solid pedagogical material
- Remain committed to the mission of the OWL and the Purdue Writing Lab
- Create a flexible design so users can navigate and read information in their preferred way
- Attract new users.

Despite the success of the redesign, user response and an initial pilot usability test indicated that users were still confused by the OWL. Therefore, the Writing Lab, in collaboration with other programs within the English Department, launched the Purdue OWL Usability Project to research the OWL and improve its usability. This chapter examines our findings relating to user-centered design excerpted from the results of our first two generations of usability tests.

THE PURDUE OWL USABILITY PROJECT

The purpose of the Purdue OWL Usability Project is to help the Purdue Writing Lab fulfill its goals for the Purdue OWL, as outlined. In addition, the project works to ensure the best possible accessibility and usability of the Purdue OWL. Finally, the project helps scholars and professionals dedicated to the usability of online learning resources by providing access to data, research, conclusions, and recommendations through the OWL research site. Ensuring the success of such a complex project is challenging; a number of

staff, students, and scholars work together in a unique multidisciplinary space to contribute to OWL usability research.

Multidisciplinary Cooperation

The Writing Lab faces many challenges in its OWL redesign: testing and redesigning, appealing to and assisting a huge global user base, creating and posting a large number of writing resources in diverse media, and organizing resources developed over 10 years into a usable online architecture. Compounding these obstacles is, of course, rallying the available resources to handle the challenges. Fortunately, the Purdue Writing Lab has a rich history of overlapping, dynamic programs to assist in this project: Writing Lab staff, Professional Writing students (graduate and undergraduate), Rhetoric and Composition students (graduate), and junior and senior faculty in all these disciplines. Although we recognize that members of our audience may not be able to pool the same resources, we would like to outline the multidisciplinary cooperation that makes this project a success and hope this information acts as a model for future work. Importantly, we base our cooperation in theory.

Blythe's "Wiring a Usable Center: Usability Research and Writing Center Practice" (1998) is instructive, providing not only guidance to Purdue's process of OWL redesign but advice for all those concerned with maintaining electronic writing resources. Blythe (1998) advocates local research that analyzes writers and technology. Specifically, Blythe (1998) asserts, "We need ways to gather meaningful data that will yield insights into how people interact with sophisticated technologies. Moreover, we need to develop productive research strategies that bring about change" (p. 105). Blythe views usability research as an effective vehicle for this type of work and a way to bring stakeholders together to build knowledge, learn about human-technology relationships, and to help users (1998, p. 106). Blythe also stresses usability research as a means of developing students' professionalization:

Usability research offers several promising methods not only because they engage students at various points in a design and decision-making process, but also because they can empower participants; they are theoretically informed; and they can yield data that is not only locally useful but potentially publishable. (1998, p. 111)

The OWL usability project fulfills many of these goals. The project provides data on how users find Web-based writing resources. The tests provide information OWL designers can use to improve the usability of the interface and the efficiency of the content management system. And, the research builds knowledge collaboratively as a focused activity where students, staff, and faculty work together outside a traditional classroom. While we are testing the usability of the OWL, we are also fulfilling the needs of many other stakeholders: the users, the undergraduate and graduate professional writing programs, the faculty, and the Writing Lab staff. Figure 1 illustrates how these stakeholders negotiate the usability research space and interact to build knowledge.

While this figure is static, the relationships between users, faculty, the Writing Lab, and the

Figure 1. Usability research relationship between stakeholders

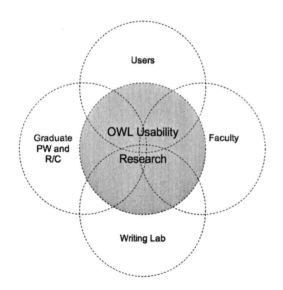

graduate programs in professional writing and rhetoric/composition are overlapping and fluid. We present the diagram in order to clarify the interaction in areas of collaboration. Once again, we recognize that not all programs may be able to collaborate as we have. But by outlining the theory and multidisciplinary structure framing our work, we hope to provide a guide for those interested in adapting this information to create similar projects situated in different contexts. In addition to multidisciplinary cooperation, vital to achieving the goals of the OWL redesign was integrating user-centered theory and usability research into the iterative and ongoing work associated with the Purdue OWL.

USER-CENTERED THEORY AND USABILITY RESEARCH

In the past 50 years, issues in user-centered theory and usability have reemerged as important elements of technology and design. In addition, scholars in rhetoric and professional writing have embraced user-centered theory and usability in their study of the relationship between computers, composition, and workplace literacy. As such, these ideas played fundamental roles in the Purdue OWL Usability Project. This section builds historical context for user-centered theory and usability research and outlines the definitions and theoretical approaches we are using in the Purdue OWL Usability Project.

Histories and Foundations

Inquiry into the relationship between user-centered theory, usability and technology is not new; in fact, we can trace the relationship to ancient Greece. In Book Three, Part XI of *Politica* (350 B.C.E.), Aristotle reminded us that:

there are some arts whose products are not judged of solely, or best, by the artists themselves, namely those arts whose products are recognized even by those who do not possess the art; for example, the knowledge of the house is not limited to the builder only; the user, or, in other words, the master, of the house will be even a better judge than the builder. (Politica, para. 36)

Aristotle's impact on user-centered theory and usability has been noted by professional writing scholars. In his seminal work, *User-Centered Technology: A Rhetorical Theory for Computers and Other Mundane Artifacts*, Johnson (1998) included a discussion of Aristotle's (350 B.C.E.) *Politica*; Johnson recognized Aristotle's attention to "the basic human right to take part in the decision-making activity of a culture...who, Aristotle asks, is the better judge—the one who makes the product or the many who must use it?" (p. 11). Johnson's discussion is important because it helps us consider the broader influence of user-centered theory and usability in democratic societies and democratic processes of design.

In contemporary business contexts, usability and user-centered work was conducted as early as the 1950s and 1960s when IBM's Federal Systems Division and Advanced Systems Development Division and Research Division began studying human factors and ergonomics related to their computers, System 360 and System 370 (Ominsky, Stern, & Rudd, 2002). And since 1998, the Nielson-Norman Group has raised awareness of user-centered design and usability through their work with cognitive psychology and customer-oriented consulting services.

With the large amount of work conducted in user-centered and usability theory, it is not surprising that different theoretical approaches and definitions exist. Therefore, before we discuss the details of the OWL Usability Project, it is important that we explain the theoretical framework for our research. In short, what follows are the definitions of user-centered theory and usability with which we work.

User-Centered Theory

The work of Ehn (1993) is important for our project because it aligns with our theoretical approach to building knowledge *with* users rather than *for* users. Put another way, we believe the most effective approach to designing a usable online literacy resource is to work collaboratively with users and research participants rather than consulting them during late stages of design.

Also important for our work is Johnson's (1998) *User-Centered Technology: A Rhetorical Theory for Computers and Other Mundane Artifacts.* In his text, Johnson has provided—through the work of Draper and Norman (1986)—an effective definition of user-centered theory we see aligning with our project: "the emphasis is on people, rather than technology, although the powers and limits of contemporary machines are considered in order to...take that next step from today's limited machines toward more user-centered ones" (p. 12). Importantly, though, Johnson (1998) moves beyond the technological scope addressed by Draper and Norman to interrogate the "discursive, or nonmaterial, aspects of technology and

Figure 2. User-centered technology applied to the OWL

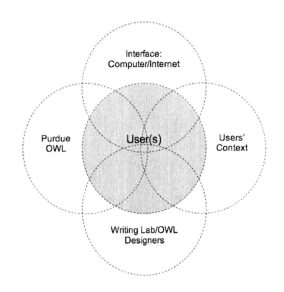

technological use" (p. 14). Figure 2, adapted from Johnson's (1998) book and contextualized for the OWL Usability Project, illustrates the user-centered view of technology.

Just as important as centering the user in the ideological approach to design is the user-centered development process. A user-centered design process integrates users' input at all stages of development, not just the final stages.

System-Centered Approach

Johnson's (1998) text also helped us define and avoid what he calls the system-centered approach to designing technology: "[a] view…based upon models of technology that focus on the artifact or system as primary, and on the notion that the inventors or developers of the technology know best its design, dissemination, and intended use" (p. 25). Despite its long history and reemergence in academe and business, user-centered theory often plays little or no role in contemporary design and technology, thus propagating a system-centered ideology. The pervasiveness of system-centered design was one element that sparked interest in composing a user-centered OWL.

User-Centered vs. User-Friendly

User-friendly design is often confused with user-centered design. Johnson's text helped us distinguish the difference between the two approaches, and his explanation helps us build an argument for the collaborative, participatory research we conduct. Specifically, Johnson states

interfaces can be merely complimentary or flattering to the user and therefore create an illusion of the greater workings of the system. These interfaces are commonly referred to as being user-friendly, and are not to be confused with user-centered designs. User-friendly can describe a technological interface that is easy to use but may not necessarily be in the best interest of the user. (p. 28)

We believe that both the design process and the assessment of design and technology should be user-centered, and so we resist the system-centered notion of developing user-friendly technology. We believe the usability of technology should be determined by the *users*. Table 1 illustrates how we integrated certain aspects of user-centered theory into our work.

Table 1.

User-Centered Theory and the OWL Usability Project	
User-Centered Theory	**OWL Usability Project**
"take action to counter the powerful, but ultimately controllable, force of technology" (Johnson, 1998, pp. xi-xiv)	Based in theory, usability test designs and usability research work to make the OWL a more usable technology
"The act of defining these limits [of technology] and then governing them is…the responsibility of the populace, not something that should be left to the institutions that currently control the direction of technology, development, and dissemination." (Johnson, 1998, pp. xi-xiv)	The OWL Usability Project involves a diverse set of stakeholders: Writing Lab staff, the Professional Writing program (graduate, undergraduate), Rhetoric and Composition (graduate), junior and senior faculty in all these disciplines, as well as OWL users
User-centered design "works toward the empowerment of users: the audiences of technology…I am arguing for an audience-centered, not a writer-centered, approach to technology" (Johnson, 1998, pp. xi-xiv).	User-centered theory informs all aspects of the OWL Usability Project to empower OWL users; empowering users even includes the composition and accessibility of the project's open-source OWL Report designed to empower audiences, such as writing center staff and usability researchers
"Help your readers find the key information quickly…state your main point at the beginning rather than the middle or end of your communications…use headings, topic sentences and lists to guide your readers to the specific information they want to locate." (Anderson, 2007, pp. 18-19)	These elements formed the framework and design goals for user-centered recommendations supported by data from the two generations of usability tests. The usability team continually focuses on OWL users' needs and expectations and use this information to develop a keen sense of the situation

Usability

We take as an important guide for our project the work of Joseph S. Dumas and Janice C. Redish in *A Practical Guide to Usability Testing* (1999). In the first section of their text, Dumas and Redish (1999) construct what we see as an effective definition of usability:

Usability means that the people who use the product *can do so* quickly and easily *to accomplish* their own tasks. *This definition rests on four points:*

1. *Usability means focusing on users.*
2. *People use products to be productive.*
3. *Users are busy people trying to accomplish tasks.*
4. *Users decide when a product is easy to use.* (p. 4)

Also important are the guidelines Dumas and Redish (1999) provide on the process of achieving usability: "Usability is not a surface gloss that can be applied at the last minute. Usability is deeply affected by every decision in design and development. Therefore, usability has to be built in from the beginning" (p. 8). Usability research conducted at all stages of development aligns with our ideas of user-designer collaboration.

Usability Testing vs. Usability Research: In his influential article, "Wiring a Usable Center: Usability Research and Writing Center Practice," from *Wiring the Writing Center*, Blythe (1998) explains the differences between usability testing and usability research, a point we see as vital to our work:

I use the term "usability testing" to refer to a range of tests often conducted near the end of product development. Such tests are designed to ensure that a product is "usable" for clients and consumers. "Usability research," on the other hand, need not be tied so directly to product testing; rather, it is intended to yield insights into how people use

tools in specific situations. The immediate goal of usability research is insight into human-computer interaction, while the immediate goal of usability testing is making humans fit with, or accept, a technology. (p. 113)

We are advocating an iterative, sustained participation between users and designers so that work *throughout* the development process fosters a space for research and innovation as well as a process for measuring traditional usability benchmarks, such as mouse clicks and time to complete tasks. Overall, "usability research" most accurately reflects the work we complete. What follows is an explanation of our usability research.

METHODS: GENERATION ONE (G1)

We conducted usability testing on the Purdue OWL (2005 version) in two iterative generations of testing. The methods and results provided here are only part of our larger usability study.

We conducted a short pilot test prior to our first generation of testing to refine test materials and train test leaders. Following the pilot test, we conducted two different generations of usability tests. Our first generation (G1) included a demographic survey, paper prototyping activity, site usability test, and an OWL feedback survey. Our second-generation (G2) tests replicated our first generation but also added user-centered scenarios. The methods and results described here are part of our research from a larger series of usability tests.

Participants

Our first generation tests involved 18 participants including 5 females (or 27.7%) and 13 males (or 72.2%). Although our participants were all faculty, staff, and students at Purdue University, they represent a range of ages, class levels, ethnicities, languages, and computer proficiencies.

Site Usability Test

Our site usability test was designed to assess the live OWL site and gather feedback on participants' experiences. Part one of our site usability test asked participants to use the OWL to answer four writing-related questions presented in a randomized order. This task asked participants to mimic behaviors of site users—not only finding the correct page on the OWL, but also finding information within that page to answer a writing-related question.

The test began with participants at a computer screen displaying the OWL home page. Each test question was read aloud to each participant. Time was recorded beginning at the end of the question and ending when the participant answered the question correctly. Each navigational click and navigational path was recorded to track the flow and success of participant navigational courses.

During test sessions, leaders described to participants the tasks they would be asked to complete and led them through each task. Test leaders followed a script but often adlibbed questions based on participants' responses and behaviors. Test recorders monitored participants and typed observations and participant comments on laptop computers.

After the site usability task was completed, participants were asked to complete a feedback survey rating their experiences. A summated rating scale (1-5) was used to rate participants' responses on a number of areas including ease of use, navigation, organization, and impressions while using the site. Two open-ended qualitative questions were also asked at the end of the survey to triangulate our quantitative results.

Results and Conclusions: Generation One (G1)

Time and Clicks

Although participants were able to complete most of the tasks during the site usability test, they required much more time than expected to complete an alarming number of tasks. A total of 71 tasks were run with our 18 G1 participants (approximately 4 tasks per participant). While many tasks took participants 1 minute or less to complete, some tasks took participants up to 2 minutes or more to complete. Ten tasks took five-plus minutes to complete, and four participants could not finish their tasks. While some tasks required 3 clicks or fewer to complete (the industry standard), many tasks took participants more than 3 clicks to complete. Some tasks even took participants 6 or more clicks to complete, with the highest being 29 clicks. The mean number of clicks per task was 5.56, and the mean number of clicks per user for all tasks was 23.34. Participants took an average of 117.16 seconds to complete each task and spent approximately 452.67 seconds in the completion of all four tasks. We had a click range of 1 to 24 clicks per participant per task and a range of 45 to 600 seconds per task.

After-Test Feedback

Some of our most interesting results came from our after-test feedback survey of the participants' experience while navigating the site. Participants rated their experiences as slightly above average in most cases. Overall, participants had a large range of answers, demonstrating that they ranged in their opinions of their experiences. When asked to rate their experiences while finding specific information, participants reported scores ranging from 1 to 5.

The wide range of our responses revealed to us that not all participants were comfortable finding information on the OWL site; although on average, participants the OWL site slightly above neutral in the "ease of finding information." When calculating the mean of participant responses, participants indicated that finding information on the site was between "neutral" and "easy" for them (mean 3.6 out of 5). Participants also indicated that the information was not buried in pages (mean 3.61 out of 5). In addition, participants reported a 1-5 range of answers relating to the overall organization of the homepage and a 3-5 range of overall site organization. Again, the wide range of answers demonstrates that not all participants had positive experiences with the OWL homepage organization, a primary goal of the OWL redesign.

Overall, our participants rated the OWL site slightly above average in most areas. The range of scores in the overall organization area was troubling because at least some users were experiencing great difficulty in understanding the site organization. Surprisingly, we found no significant correlation between the amount of time and clicks it took participants to complete the tasks and their rating of the OWL site.

When asked about what features could be improved or included in the OWL, participants suggested moving the navigation bar to the left side of pages and adding a search function. Participants preferred to see more user-centered information on the homepage, such as links for different types of visitors (teachers, students, ESL learners) and a box with the site's most popular resources. Also, participants wanted fewer steps involved in finding what they needed.

Conclusions for Generation One Testing (G1)

The site usability test showed that while some users were able to complete their tasks in three or fewer clicks, an alarming number of users clicked six or more times. Three clicks to destination is currently considered the commercial standard for navigation; however, no such standards have been determined for informational resources like the OWL. The average amount of time users spent on tasks was also troubling because of the documented short attention span of Web users.

Results from the OWL feedback survey show that participants liked and found useful content and design elements of the OWL. However, the survey results also reveal that participants did not respond in the positive manner expected of the OWL. While we did not receive negative responses from participants on the feedback survey, we are concerned about the number of neutral responses.

The high number of clicks and the long amounts of time participants required to complete tasks, as well as the number of neutral responses on the feedback survey, justified a second generation of testing with one notable modification—the addition of a user-centered prototype. The user-centered prototype test took direct feedback from users and combined it with user-centered theory. The mockup allowed us to compare a user-centered OWL prototype and the OWL Web site for performance and ease of use. The user-centered OWL prototype usability assessments were designed to test whether the user-based navigational taxonomy would be more beneficial for participants over the current OWL navigation system.

METHODS: GENERATION TWO (G2)

Our second-generation test replicated our original testing scenario and added user-based prototypes. Each participant was asked to complete both our user-based prototype test and the site usability test from G1 for comparison. Ordering of tasks and questions was random for participants, and all participants completed the same number of questions.

Participants

Our second generation of tests included 14 participants (8 females, 6 males). Our participants again represented a range of ages, class levels, ethnicities, languages, and computer proficiencies. The participants collected for G2 brought our total number of participants for both generations to 32 (n = 32).

User-Centered Prototypes

In our second generation of testing, we developed a user-centered OWL prototype and added four tasks to our site usability test to measure the prototype's effectiveness. Each task required participants to find writing-related information on the OWL prototype, such as information about punctuation handouts for K-12 teachers and APA format. We measured the amount and type of information participants found and used on the OWL prototype, as well as the amount of time and number of mouse clicks participants required to access this information. Finally, we asked participants to reflect on their experience in a feedback survey. These procedures are unchanged from first generation testing. Figure 3 is a screenshot of the OWL splash page during testing (top image) and a screenshot of the user-based prototype used during testing (bottom image).

During the user-centered prototype test, participants were asked to assume a fictitious role (that of a K-12 teacher, parent of a student, or a student from a University other than Purdue) to match the categories of users upon which we based our link taxonomy in the OWL prototype. Participants were given new use scenarios with the user-centered OWL prototype. The order of the paper prototyping and site usability tasks were randomly altered to decrease the chance that participants were influenced by the order of tasks they completed during the test.

Results: Generation Two (G2)

Time

Participants found the user-centered prototype much easier to navigate than the current OWL site, and they took less time to complete tasks with the user-centered prototype than with the OWL site. Also, participant's times for the first tasks were significantly lower for the prototype than for the OWL site. Table 2 provides an average breakdown of the time required to complete each task. The time is measured in seconds.

When we compare average times for individual participants, we find that participants overall located information in less time using

Figure 3. Screenshots of the OWL Web site (top) and the user-centered prototype (bottom). Copyright 2007, the Purdue Online Writing Lab. Used with permission.

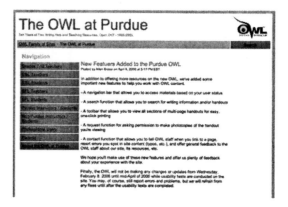

the user-centered prototype. Out of the nine participants who were timed, four (44%) found information in less time while two participants (22%) required more time to locate information. Three participants' average times on tasks were within 10 seconds of each other, and hence, had negligible results either way.

Clicks

Participants also had a lower average number of clicks using the user-centered prototype (4.89) than the OWL redesign (6.09 clicks). When comparing the tasks in the order participants completed them, we again see the most pronounced difference in the first tasks. Table 3 provides a detailed break-

Table 2. Task times for OWL and user-centered prototype

	OWL	**User-centered prototype**
Task 1*	176.87	75.14
Task 2	73.33	71.25
Task 3[a]	56.67	100.56
Task 4	105	123.7
Average	105.5	97

*   p <0.002

[a]   *Several subjects may have perceived question #3 in ways that were not intended, which can account for the widely varied scores on this item. Fours scores in this set were four standard deviations away from the mean; if these four scores are removed, the numbers become: OWL: 94.86 and User-centered prototype: 75.19.*

down of mouse clicks per question (averaged for all participants).

Question three of the user-centered prototype test seemed to be difficult for participants. One participant in this group registered a number of clicks that were nearly four standard deviations from the mean. If we remove this user, the mean prototype clicks for question three becomes 4.15. A second participant registered a number of clicks that were two standard deviations from the mean. If we remove this participant, the mean number of clicks becomes 3.58. While we do not suggest that these two participants' scores are invalid, removing these two outliers allows us to see that even for a question that caused two participants significant difficulty, the prototype performed well for the remaining 12 users.

When we compare the average number of clicks for each participant while using the OWL redesign and the user-centered prototype, we find that 42.86% (6 participants) out of our 14 participants required fewer clicks with the user-centered prototype. Three participants (or 21.46%) required higher amounts of clicks, while 5 participants (37.14%) were within two clicks of each other, and hence, had negligible results either way.

Table 3. Average mouse clicks of participants

Task Question	Redesigned OWL	Prototype
First question*	10.15	4
Second question	4.79	5.43
Third question[a]	3.5	6.07
Fourth question**	5.71	4.07

**   Approaching significance at p<0.05

[a]   Again, participants had trouble with the third question. One score was four standard deviations away from the mean.

Feedback Survey

The amount of time and number of clicks represents only part of the participants' experiences while navigating the redesigned OWL and the user-centered prototype. Participants were also asked to rate each site at the end of each respective set of tasks. Table 4 provides a list of means based on participants' feedback from the redesigned OWL and user-centered prototype tests.

Participants still rated their experiences using the prototype more positively as a whole. In particular, participants rated the user-centered prototype's organization, a targeted focus of the prototype, significantly higher.

Much of the G2 participant feedback mirrored feedback from G1 testing (requests for search bars, visual issues, etc.); however, some feedback was specific to the organization and navigation of the site. In general, participants seemed very interested in the hierarchical relationship and organization of the site as well as how information from the site is described.

Seven of our eight comments from our G2 feedback survey related to the taxonomy of the navigation system or its naming practices. Participant feedback includes:

- "More obvious headings and hierarchies within individual pages."
- "Avoiding Acronyms like EFL/ESL. The navigation links a bit more prominent + organized."

Table 4. Participant means from feedback survey

Question	Redesigned OWL	User-Centered Prototype
Ease of Finding Information	3.31	3.64
Effectiveness of Homepage	3.71	3.93
Accessibility of Information	3.43	3.57
Effectiveness of Organization*	3.29	4.07
Effectiveness of Site Navigation	3.71	3.86
Feelings When Finding Information	3.43	3.57
Feelings When Using Site**	3.43	3.86

* $p < 0.02$
**   Approaching significance

- "Concise design on the main page. Category clarity."
- "User's menu or just "how to use the Web site" / "help." Online helper."
- "I thought that the organization of the columns and boxes was not very professional looking, but the information was well organized."
- "Adding icons like paper writing help/thesis writing etc…"
- "Highlight the direction. For example. When I looked for: when use words or numbers. I skipped the first sentence (the answer) and looked at the subtitles."

And finally, this comment has a bearing on the redesigned OWL navigational system:

- "I like that the info is broken down at the right side of the page but there is so much info put there maybe that could be done differently some how."

DISCUSSION

User-Centered OWL Prototype

We designed the user-centered OWL prototype based on data-driven hypotheses drawn from the pilot test, G1, and user-centered theory. Overall, the user-centered prototype proved effective in reducing the amount of time and the number of mouse clicks participants required to complete tasks. In addition, most participants reflected favorably on the user-centered OWL prototype in their feedback surveys.

User-Centered OWL Design

Based on combined data from the pilot test, G1, and G2, we believe the user-centered prototype should guide—and form the basis of—future OWL redesigns and can be a guide for similar information resources. Figure 4 shows screenshots of the OWL Family of Sites homepage as it looked during G1 and G2 testing (top image). Figure 4 also illustrates the user-centered changes made for the OWL Family of Sites prototype (bottom image).

Figure 5 illustrates the layout changes we recommended for the redesigned OWL homepage (top image) based on the user-centered prototype layout (bottom image).

The prototypes based on user-centered design will help ensure a more accessible, usable OWL and, hence, will help fulfill the goals of the OWL redesign as outlined by the Purdue Writing Lab. In addition, we find that participants value information architecture, site navigation, and taxonomy. We believe users' expression of positive feelings for the redesign supports our recommendations to shift from the organization reflected in the OWL to a more user-based organization.

While users would not use such language as *information architecture, user-centered design, ease of navigation,* or *improved organizational taxonomy,* these technical terms accurately represent the feelings users expressed through two

Figure 4. The OWL splash page (top) design and the OWL Prototype design (bottom). (Copyright 2007, The Purdue Online Writing Lab. Used with permission.)

Figure 5. Recommendations for OWL redesign

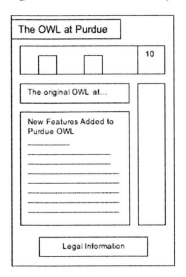

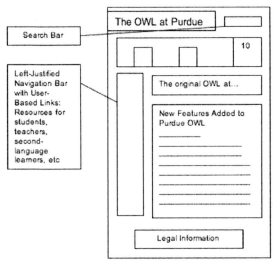

generations of usability testing and offer a clear set of guidelines for OWL revision and improvement. We recommended the Writing Lab do the following:

1. Design links/pages around the types of visitors using the OWL (user-based taxonomy)
2. Move the navigation bar from the right side to the left side of the OWL
3. Add a search function
4. Incorporate graphical logos in the OWL Family of Sites homepage
5. Continue testing to measure usability and to generate new ideas for design and content.

Purdue's OWL is an important and valuable catalogue of writing-related information and deserves its devoted following and global reach. These usability conclusions are intended to improve the overall user experience and to retain the interest of returning OWL users as well as to inspire commitment from a savvy group of students, teachers, faculty, and administrators whose expectations are established by use of the Web. Purdue has an outstanding brand in the OWL, as demonstrated by its increasingly impressive Web statistics. Therefore, this information is intended to maintain and increase the leadership of an outstanding resource.

FUTURE TRENDS

The future of usability studies seems to reflect several trends: a commitment to methods and analysis of usability practices; development of theoretical models of usability theory; merger of usability models in education with that in industry; further exploration in the area of remote testing.

Researchers in usability studies advocate iterative collection and examination of usability data. Particularly, they assert that the field's systematic investigation of fundamental mechanisms driving user behavior warrants better and more critical measures of examining the data involving user tasks, problems and achievement, and changes in environment (Davis, 1989; Dieli, 1989; Gerlach, 1991; Norberg, Vassiliadis, Ferguson, & Smith, 2006).

The field of usability studies also seems to be moving toward the creation of and distinction between various theoretical models. Byerley and Chambers (2002) call for a distinction between the terms *accessibility* and *usability* and assert that accessibility within a site does not equate with one that is user-centered (p. 177). Meurer (2001) encourages the future of design to be both critical and analytical. He appears to be pushing for a field that questions existing practices and critiques contexts, and in response, develops alternatives and more comprehensive problem-solving strategies. Ultimately, he calls for design to be liberated from its one-dimensional concentration on completing tasks so it can focus on the constant creation of new tasks (Meurer, 2001, p. 53). Norberg et al. (2006) invites designers to seek out more effective ways to consider audiences' cultures, heritages, and experiences when constructing user-centered sites (p. 295). And Davis (1989) encourages a reflexivity within the fields of design and usability; this reflexivity, he claims, will promote sustainable progress (p. 335).

We see *Opening Spaces: Writing Technologies and Critical Research Practices* by Sullivan and Porter (1997) as influential in achieving many of the goals outlined above. Important to the future of usability research are the practices Sullivan and Porter (1997) outline for postmodern empirical work: theory-methods-practice = *praxis*. In addition, Sullivan and Porter (1997) help guide the ethical and situated knowledge building, research mapping, project management, and multidisciplinary cooperation important for usability research. Sullivan and Porter (1997) provide a detailed and graphical plan for integrating theory, methods, and practice to form a *praxis*. In doing so, they establish a framework (though shifting and necessarily conflicted) for some of the core principles and practices of contemporary and future usability research: projects grounded in relevant theory, projects informed by critical, empirical research, and projects connected to pedagogy and engagement.

The fields of design and usability studies are also undergoing a more collaborative shift. Roth (1999) argues that collaboration with industry professionals in the fields of engineering and computer science can provide new and compelling material for growth in both fields (p. 25). Gillan and Bias (2001) assert that organizations must recognize the value of usability science. To do this, they argue that usability experts must communicate the importance of usability so that products can withstand the transition from design to use (Gillan & Bias, 2001, p. 368). And from an educational standpoint, many new doctoral programs in design are in development at a number of institutions (Roth, 1999), further promoting a dedication within higher education to design and usability.

Finally, remote testing has become a cost-efficient alternative to conducting traditional laboratory-based usability testing. McFadden, Hagar, Elie, and Blackwell (2002) point out that traditional usability testing scenarios are costly. To circumvent this issue, many usability evaluators have begun conducting remote testing to complement more traditional methods of usability research. Remote testing is less expensive and can be conducted with a larger, global number of participants (McFadden et al., 2002, p. 489).

To read more about—or contribute to—remote testing of the Purdue OWL, please visit Purdue OWL Usability Testing Survey site at http://owl.english.purdue.edu/survey/. Additional generations of testing are planned for Purdue's OWL as much to maintain and strengthen the relationship we have built with our users as to improve the site's usefulness and effectiveness. Here, as with other emerging virtual workplaces, we have established connections and good will with our users by interacting with them and learning to listen to their concerns.

CONCLUSION

Usability research can serve multiple purposes for writing centers and their online counterparts. First, usability research can provide systematic and specific feedback on writing center and OWL services, which contributes to the continuing improvement of those operations. Second, usability research leads to dynamic workspaces, which foster new research questions while maintaining a balance of power and potential gains between participants and researchers. Finally, usability research provides unique opportunities for collaboration with individuals in multiple disciplines and research experience for students.

Writing centers and online writing labs can benefit from usability research. Our findings have provided a clear trajectory for revision of the Purdue OWL rooted in research. Blythe (1998) found that usability methods can offer writing labs avenues for critical reflection and can generate data useful for reporting to administration, for producing scholarly publication, and for incorporating student and tutor voices into decision-making processes about writing labs and OWLs. Usability is a type of research, and although it may be more practical than other types of basic research, scholarly questions can still be asked and answered throughout its duration.

Work with participants and research findings can lead to new questions and research ideas while avoiding ethical pitfalls. In their introduction to *Ethics and Representation in Qualitative Studies of Literacy*, Kirsch and Mortensen (1996) ask the following questions of research: "Who benefits from the research? Whose interests are at stake? What are the consequences for the participants?" (p. xxi). Usability studies and participatory design circumvent potential ethical issues by providing more usable services and products for research participants. Moreover, participants can work with researchers and designers to generate new ideas, thus forming a participatory relationship between user and developer.

Usability research can provide another benefit through its collaborative nature. During our testing, writing center personnel worked with research methods specialists and professional writing experts to design and administer the tests and to analyze results. Collaboration between professional writing faculty, writing center administrators, and graduate and undergraduate professional writing students fostered an educational atmosphere while invigorating professionalization.

The development of new technologies sparks opportunities for the evolution of online literacy resources. In turn, usability research ensures that writing labs and OWLs keep pace with these changes and continue to address the needs of users, writing lab staff, faculty, and student researchers. We have found that usability research and user-centered theory are critical for developing a 21st Century OWL. We hope this project and its findings will form a framework of continuing research on Internet-based usability that ensures premium services for OWL users and users of other online literacy resources.

REFERENCES

Anderson, P. (2007). *Technical communication: A reader-centered approach* (6th ed.). Boston, MA: Thomson-Wadsworth.

Aristotle. (350 B.C.E.). *Politica* (B. Jowett, Trans.). Retrieved November 21, 2007, from http://classics. mit.edu/Aristotle/politics.html

Blythe, S. (1998). Wiring a usable center: Usability research and writing center practice. In *Wiring the writing center* (pp. 103-118). Utah: Utah UP.

Byerley, S. L., & Chambers, M. B. (2002). Accessibility and usability of Web-based library databases for non-visual users. *Library Hi Tech, 20*(2), 169-178.

Center for Integrated Agricultural Systems. (2004). Retrieved November 21, 2007, from http://www.cias.wisc.edu/citizen.php

Davis, F. D. (1989). Perceived usefulness, ease of use, and user acceptance of information technology. *MIS Quarterly, 13*(3), 319-340.

Dieli, M. (1989). The usability process: Working with iterative design principles. *IEEE Transactions on Professional Communication, 32*(4), 272-278.

Dumas, J., & J. Redish. (1999). *A practical guide to usability testing* (pp. 4-8), revised edition. Portland, OR: Intellect Books.

Ehn, P. (1993). Scandinavian design: On participation and skill. In D. Schuler & A. Namioka (Eds.), *Participatory design: Principles and practices* (pp. 41-77). Hillsdale, NJ: Lawrence Erlbaum Associates.

Faber, B., & Johnson-Eilola, J. (2003). Universities, corporate universities, and the new professionals: Professionalism and the knowledge economy. In T. Kynell-Hunt & G. Savage (Eds.), *Power and legitimacy in technical communication volume I: The historical and contemporary struggle for professional status* (pp. 209-234). Amityville, NY: Baywood.

Gerlach, J. H., & Kuo, F. (1991). Understanding human-computer interaction for information systems design. *MIS Quarterly, 15*(4), 527-549.

Gillan, D. J., & Bias, R. G. (2001). Usability science I: Foundations. *International Journal of Human-Computer Interaction, 13*(4), 351-372.

Johnson, R. R. (1998). *User-centered technology: A rhetorical theory for computers and other mundane artifacts.* Albany, NY: State University of New York Press.

Johnson-Eilola, J. (2005). Datacloud: Toward a new theory of online work. In C. Selfe & G. Hawisher (Eds.), *New dimensions in computers and composition.* Cresskill, NJ: Hampton Press.

Kirsch, G., & Mortensen, P. (Eds.). (1996). *Ethics and representation in qualitative studies of literacy.* NCTE. XXI.

McFadden, E., Hagar, D., Elie, C. J., & Blackwell, J. M. (2002). Remote usability evaluation: Overview and case studies. *International Journal of Human-Computer Interaction, 14*(3/4), 489-502.

Meurer, B. (2001). The transformation of design. *Design issues, 17*(1), 44-53.

Morville, P., & Rosenfeld, L. (2006). *Information architecture for the world wide Web: Designing large-scale Web sites* (3rd ed.). Cambridge: O'Reilly & Associates.

National Association of State Universities and Land Grant Colleges (NASULGC). (1999). The land-grant tradition. Retrieved November 21, 2007, from http://www.nasulgc.org/publications/ Land_Grant/Land_Grant_Main.htm

Norberg, L. R., Vassiliadis, K., Ferguson, J., & Smith, N. (2006). Sustainable design for multiple audiences. *OCLC Systems and Services, 21*(4), 285-299.

Norman, D., & S. Draper. (1986). *User-centered system design: New perspectives on human-computer interaction* (p. 2). Hillsdale, N.J.: Lawrence Earlbaum Press.

North, S. (1984). The idea of a writing center. *College English, 46,* 433-446.

Ominsky, M., Stern, K., & Rudd, J. (2002). User-centered design at IBM consulting. *International Journal of Human-Computer Interaction, 14*(3/4), 349-368.

Roth, S. (1999). The state of design research. *Design Issues, 15*(2), 18-26.

Sullivan, P., & Porter, J. (1997). *Opening spaces: Writing technologies and critical research practices.* Greenwich, CT: Ablex Publishing Corporation.

Trenner, L., & Bawa, J. (1998). *The politics of usability: A practical guide to designing usable systems in industry.* Springer, NY: Springer-Verlag.

KEY TERMS

Engagement: Meaningful communication between users and designers.

Online Writing Lab (OWL): A Web-based environment that provides writing-related assistance and resources; it can include online tutorials, handouts on writing-related topics, and interactive writing exercises.

Participatory Design: A design practice that asks users to contribute to the development of designs for new products, services, or Web sites. It differs from usability testing because it asks users to contribute ideas during all stages of development rather than providing feedback on nearly completed or completed technologies and products.

System-Centered Theory: An approach to development that places the designer or technology at the center of the process. Users are not consulted at all or they are consulted in the late stages of design.

Usability Research: The integration of usability work into all areas and all stages of design so that users are contributing to development. Acknowledges and fosters a space of professionalization for graduate students and a space for ongoing, critical practices that benefit everyone involved in the project, including researchers, faculty, staff, and so forth.

Usability Testing: The quantitative and qualitative process of determining how well a Web site, product, or service works for users. It can include user testing based on scenarios and collecting users' opinions and feedback. For the purposes of our work, we differentiate between usability testing and usability research.

User-Centered Theory: A theory of design that places users at the center of technology development in an iterative, recursive, and collaborative process.

Web Accessibility: Access to Web technologies by any number of users regardless of physical, cognitive, or emotional disabilities. For more information on Web accessibility, please see the Web Accessibility Initiative (WAI) sponsored by the World Wide Web Consortium (W3C) on the Web at: http://www.w3.org/WAI/.

Writing Lab or Writing Center: A place, often situated on an educational campus, where individuals can go to receive one-on-one tutoring about their writing. Writing labs often provide other types of writing-related services such as online consultations, writing workshops, resource libraries, and ESL services.

Chapter XLVI
Negotiating Virtual Identity in an Age of Globalization

Neil P. Baird
University of Nevada, USA

ABSTRACT

Virtual workplaces are no longer the province of young technophiles, and we must become more conscious of the particular challenges and issues those considered "nontraditional" face in this new environment. Continued globalization, fostered in part by computer-mediated communication, is bringing diverse populations together in virtual spaces; however, because we bring our culture with us when we move online, the default identity of the faceless virtual workplace becomes the young, white male. How do those considered nontraditional then negotiate their identity in order to contribute successfully? This chapter will explore this question with a case study of a Vietnam veteran in the workplace of a freshman writing classroom and, in doing so, will invite educators, employers, and researchers into discussions of virtual identity and interaction, how we perform ourselves in online workplaces, and fostering virtual communities.

NEGOTIATING VIRTUAL IDENTITY IN AN AGE OF GLOBALIZATION

We find ourselves working more and more in virtual spaces these days. Even so, while many of us are compelled, in both senses of the word (i.e., drawn to and forced), to work in this new environment, we expect those who work in these settings and share these spaces with us to perform and behave in the ways they regularly do in traditional workplace environments. We expect them to stay focused and on task. We expect them to communicate efficiently and effec-

tively with each other. We expect them to remain professional and courteous in their interactions with us. We expect them to cooperate in order to collaboratively produce innovative ideas and new products. This chapter defines virtual workplaces as any virtual space where two or more people come together to accomplish some sort of task. As virtual workplaces in this sense became more and more popular to work and exist within, many scholars argued that the disembodied, faceless nature of this environment promoted and fostered the above values more than traditional settings (Butler & Kinneavy, 1991; Cooper &

Selfe, 1990; Flores, 1990; Selfe, 1990). However, these technophilic, almost Utopian conceptions of online environments are being challenged by a number of researchers (Forman, 1994; Hawisher & Selfe, 1991; Janangelo, 1991; Matheson, 1991; Takayoshi, 1994).

What many of these studies are discovering is that we bring our culture with us when we move online, and the same issues of race, gender, and class that plague us in the "real" world also plague us in online environments. For example, we make certain assumptions about an other when all we see is a name on a screen, and the assumptions we make are fostered partly by the culture we live within. How many of us have made the assumption when working with a faceless name in a virtual workplace that the other person was white, male, and probably between the ages of 18-25, only to discover an identity very different when we finally meet that person face-to-face? More importantly, how does someone who is not white, male, and between the ages of 18-25 experience working in an environment where these assumptions are being made?

While the research challenging Utopian notions of virtual environments is doing so through the lenses of race, gender, and class, very few are examining the intersections of age and the online environment. Virtual workplaces are no longer the province of young technophiles, and we must become more conscious of the particular challenges and issues those considered "nontraditional," who are drawn to or being forced to work in virtual workplaces, face in this new environment. Continued globalization fostered in part by computer-mediated communication is bringing diverse populations together in virtual spaces. The default identity of many online workplaces can be difficult for them, many of whom are over the age 30, to negotiate. When the default identity of the faceless virtual workplace is the young, white male, how do those considered nontraditional present themselves in order to contribute successfully in the ways we value in traditional workplace settings?

This chapter will explore this question with a case study of a Vietnam Veteran in the virtual workplace of an online freshman writing classroom. A 60-year-old Vietnam veteran began my fully online course as a student who had no desire to share personal details of his life in order to begin fostering an online community. As the course progressed, he began to bear witness to his wartime trauma and experiences as a paramedic after the war, significantly altering his relationship with other members of the class. An e-mail he wrote to me shortly after the course came to an end expressed his gratitude at being able to come to an acceptance of himself and his trauma, an acceptance, he argued, that would not have happened in a traditional classroom. By exploring the way this student presented himself in a virtual workplace dominated by young freshman just out of high school, this chapter will invite educators, employers, and researchers into discussions of virtual identity and interaction, how we perform ourselves in online workplaces, and fostering virtual communities.

We expect those who work in virtual workplaces to perform and behave in the ways they regularly do in traditional workplace environments. We expect them to remain focused and on task in order to collaboratively produce innovative ideas and new products. Many who are compelled to work in virtual spaces, especially for the very first time, experience the disembodied and faceless nature of the online environment in ways that work against these values. Some may feel isolated and utterly alone in an environment that does not allow face-to-face communication and subsequently do not participate. Some may perceive an absence of authority and act out in ways that disrupt an online community's ability to function. Palloff and Pratt (1999) argue that making people conscious of the ways they contribute to building an online community is vitally important to offsetting the feelings of loneliness and alienation many of them will most likely experience. My first activity then is for students to post short introductions to each other, a seemingly risk-free task that begins to foster community while allowing them to try out the software that will be so vital to their learning. The third student posted an introduction that read as follows:

I find that revealing personal information to complete strangers over an unsecured public forum odious at best. I am not in the habit of disclosing to anyone anything I do not wish them to know. For me, unsolicited information about others is just trashcan fodder, as the chances that I will ever know any of you personally are unlikely. Foremost, I don't care to know. I hold no illusions that some readers will find this offensive to a degree, but in my estimation, this type of assignment is an infringement on my right to privacy. Being required to complete this writing task, I have unwillingly disclosed a transparently biased indignation and opinionated view which is part of, however by no means remotely indicative, of who I am... It is not the business of anyone of whom I do not choose to inform concerning my age, what I do or what I have done, what I like or dislike (other than previously stated), where I live or have lived, where I was born, my goals or direction, anything about my family, military experience, or any other aspect of my life. Having expressed my disinclination to unmask my personal self to strangers over the Internet, I have fulfilled the requirement of 250-300 words for this assignment.

My reactions to this post ran the gamut. Indignation: Who does this student think he is, challenging my deeply held assumptions and my newly developing philosophy of teaching in the virtual classroom? Fear: I had 19 other students who would read this introduction before posting their own. How would they respond? Would this outright resistance to community be a detriment to the sense of community this activity was designed to foster? Would this set up a pattern of resistance I would struggle with throughout the course? Helplessness: From reading, for example, Cogdill (2000), I was familiar with the horror stories concerning the ways some students respond

to the decentered nature of virtual classrooms. Despite this and having taught two successful semesters in the virtual classroom, I began to sympathize with Faigley's (1995) experiences, even though I was familiar with Cooper's (1999) rereading of his chatroom transcripts. Awe: I was delightfully surprised and somewhat awed by this introduction. I love its sophistication, especially the way it reads, and found myself reading it to my colleagues who had similar reactions, asking me what I was going to do. This seemed to paralyze me the most. What should I do? Should I private message this student about the importance of community to virtual classrooms? Should I say something publicly? What would be the consequences of doing nothing at all? I ultimately decided to do nothing, and the course progressed, with this student contributing thoughtfully to discussions, never offering any substantial details about himself; that is, until Week 8.

In order to understand how this student performed in Week 8, which stands in stark contrast to his opening introduction, it is necessary to explain the context of this course. At the University of Nevada, Reno, we are invited to teach our second-semester composition courses focusing on argument and research around a theme of our choosing. For some time, my attention had been drawn to my students' uncritical use of cultural memory in their arguments. Arguments about terrorism or the war in Iraq, for example, were based on 9/11, but seldom would students acknowledge that for many of us the way we remember 9/11 was created by the media. It was my hope then that a theme of cultural memory and the formation of identity would make them aware of how people use cultural memory as warrants when making arguments.

By Week 8, my students have read several studies of cultural memory. They have read and discussed Barbie Zelizer's study of the effects of early American photo-journalism on the way we remember the Holocaust, Roberta Pearson's application of commodified public memory to five disparate documentaries about Custer's

Last Stand, and Liliane Weissberg's study of the material rhetoric of the United States Holocaust Memorial Museum. By this time, my students have proposed and are diligently researching and composing similar investigations of cultural memory and identity of their own choosing. One of the most important features of the virtual classroom is that every utterance is recorded, and it is at this time that I invite students to return to earlier discussions we have had to reflect on the ways we were drawing on cultural memory to make arguments even in our online discussions. In order to prepare students to do so, I have them read the first chapter of Kali Tal's *Worlds of Hurt: Reading the Literatures of Trauma*.

This seminal work focuses on the individual and cultural representations of three traumatic events: the Holocaust, the Vietnam War, and the sexual abuse of women and children. Her research questions explore what it means to be a "survivor" and to "testify" when individual trauma is adapted to fit within dominant social, cultural, and political discourse. Tal (1995) offers three strategies cultures use to cope with traumatic events—mythologization, medicalization, and disappearance—noting that all three strategies work in combination to codify individual trauma (p. 6). Once my students have struggled with and begin to own these concepts, many begin to see these strategies at work in earlier posts when Week 8 returns them to online discussions held at the beginning of the course.

It is during Week 8 that this student offered the following contribution to our discussion. It is presented in full so that the enormous contrast from his post that began the course can be seen:

I am one of the oldest people enrolled at UNR and as such have had many experiences throughout my existence that may be classified under trauma, both physical and mental. As a kid, my brother and I were regularly beaten by our father, every day, for trivial matters. Neither I nor my brother were disciplinary problems in the least. On the rare occasion that our family had company, the main

event was for my dad to take his 2-inch leather belt, grab me by one arm, and swing me around in circles while hitting me on the back, butt, and legs. My ensuing yelps seemed to bring some joy, as that was the entertainment for company. When dad was in a playful mood, he would snap his belt like a whip, leaving great red welts. The funny thing was that my brother and I laughed along with him not knowing any different. That all stopped when I was about 12 and no longer made any sound or movement when he was expressing his aggression. The day I graduated from high school, I came home to find my dad in the driveway working on a piece of wood. He looked up with no congratulation for achieving successful completion of twelve years of classes. He only uttered "get a job or get out." I joined the military within the hour...

My time in the military began just as the war in Vietnam was beginning. Needless to say there were many opportunities to experience trauma both personally and with others. As a Navy Corpsman attached to a Marine division (Marines are part of the Navy), I not only was put in harms way with everyone else, but my job was to keep the wounded alive until evacuated and to another's care. Screams, burning flesh, body parts, horrendous wounds, the dead, the dying all around. Somehow I was able to see only what had to be done, to render the best care possible under the conditions, and move on to the next victim.

After an honorable discharge a couple of re-ups later, I became an EMT for a major ambulance service in Los Angeles. I was in the Harbor Division, one of the nastiest of all. Again it was a matter of seeing what had to be done and doing it. Everything the city, county, or state police rolled on we were there and often times arrived before they did. It wasn't much different, just got to go home after 24 hours duty...

How do you put aside or forget walking onto a fresh scene where an estranged husband bringing

Christmas gifts to his children and wife had gotten into an argument, shot his wife, his 8 year old son, his four year old and 18 month old daughters and finally himself? The baby died in my arms as I resuscitated her, the wife died at the scene, and the son and older daughter died at the hospital.

I began to worry about this student. He defined himself as a survivor of child abuse and combat trauma and a witness to unspeakable tragedy as a paramedic after the war. In addition, he began to express his difficulty with the course readings in subsequent posts:

These projects have re-stirred unwanted memories for me, very unpleasant, horrifying experiences that have occurred during the six plus decades of my existence... I have spent far more than half my life trying to cage these past demons and keep them in control. These reading, writing, and responding tasks have stirred up these evil memories that have taken so long to contain."

Had my course retraumatized this student in some way? What was my responsibility? Should I leave him alone and allow him to work through the support system he must have set up in order to cope with his trauma before this course? Should I direct him to some of the counseling services provided by the university?

After the semester ended, I sent this student an e-mail. Why did he reveal these deeply intimate details about himself when he worked so hard to conceal his identity at the beginning of the course? What prompted him to bear witness to his trauma at that particular moment in Week 8? Would he have witnessed his trauma in a traditional, face-to-face classroom? His response surprised me by thanking me for his experiences in the course:

I think I learned to appreciate who I am in this class. That was tough to say. This class gave me an opportunity to see more clearly who I have been in the past and envision who I can be in my somewhat limited future.

His response suggested that this acceptance of himself could not have happened in a traditional, face-to-face classroom.

What this student revealed about himself suggests that a brief definition of trauma is needed in order to understand his experience in my online course. Herman (1992) argues that "The core experiences of psychological trauma are disempowerment and disconnection from others" (p. 133). Those who experience traumatic events are disempowered because these events overwhelm ordinary human adaptations to life. Herman notes that "At the moment of trauma, the victim is rendered helpless by overwhelming force... Traumatic events overwhelm the ordinary systems of care that give people a sense of control, connection, and meaning" (1992, p. 33). Because survivors are rendered helpless in the face of overwhelming force, their faith and trust not only in themselves but other people are shattered. According to Herman (1992),

Traumatic events call into question basic human relationships. They breach the attachments of family, friendship, love, and community. They shatter the construction of the self that is formed and sustained in relation to others. They undermine the belief systems that give meaning to human experience." (p. 51)

Because the core experiences of trauma are helplessness and isolation, "Recovery, therefore," notes Herman, "is based upon the empowerment of the survivor and the creation of new connections" (1992, p. 133). My student's ability to come to some kind of acceptance of himself suggests our virtual classroom provided him with empowerment while at the same time allowing him to connect with others.

Empowerment begins with safety. One of the things my students tell me they value the most about virtual classrooms in end-of-the-semester reflections and course evaluations is the sense of safety they felt. They appreciate not having to hold the floor while 20 other students gaze at them while they speak. They also appreciate the ability to think and revise before they contribute to a discussion that asynchronous discussion affords. However, there is a sense that the safety my course provided this student went far deeper than easing the fear of public speaking. In response to my questions at the end of the course, this student argues,

I have no doubt that a traditional, face-to-face class setting would have produced very different reactions from other students. My countenance is grim. I rarely smile, laugh, or talk to anyone... My appearance is that of a brutish biker. Reactions, at least initially, from other students, as experience has taught, is to stay away... I would have revealed practically nothing about myself, stoically non-communicative until forced by necessity to speak, this only exacerbating any proclivity to uneasiness in the situation. I would have felt backed into a corner, as it were.

There is a strong sense that meanings attached to his body prevented him from making connections with other students in traditional classrooms, thus preventing him from contributing in ways that he wanted to. In contrast, the faceless nature of the virtual classroom allowed this student to "open up and be more like who I really am."

Safety is also created by establishing a sense of autonomy. One of the patterns that appears in his contributions to our online discussions is a strong dislike of his experience in his first-semester composition course. Commenting on the opening activity requiring him to introduce himself to the class, he says,

I can only hope (that this course) does not continue to follow in this direction but will have some real composition value, unlike English 101 that taught absolutely nothing and, for me, was extraordinarily juvenile, a complete waste of time, money, and energy.

At first, I thought that his feelings toward English 101 were a result of the personal writing required in that course; however, upon further reflection, I am not so sure. Now, I think his feelings might be more a result of issues concerning autonomy. In one post, he mentioned being removed from his English 101 course near the end of the semester and placed into another to finish because he said the word "shit" in class. While I think that there is more to this story than he conveyed, what he revealed in that post and generally in others, especially in his introduction to the class, is a strong distrust and aversion to authority imposing itself upon him.

In a virtual classroom, I am as faceless as my students. Many of my students have problems with the autonomy that this offers them. One of the main complaints of virtual classrooms whenever I ask students to reflect on the differences between traditional and virtual classrooms is that the instructor is not "present" to explain the assignments. I find this interesting given that I provide a space that simulates asking questions in class, have online office hours, and am available for face-to-face and phone conferences. While many students struggle with this autonomy, there is a sense that this student thrived given the autonomy he experienced because it empowered him. The post in which he bears witness to the trauma that makes up so much of who he is suggests that he does not feel that personal writing is juvenile, which I originally thought. What I will argue is that his use of personal writing came at a rhetorically appropriate moment. What might have been juvenile to him was the loss of autonomy he experienced at being *forced* to writing about the personal details of his past in English 101.

I had originally wanted to focus all of my energy on what it must have meant for this student to write the story of the trauma itself. It is, after all, through the discursive telling and retelling of the trauma story that it ceases to become an extraordinary memory but one memory among others. According to Herman (1992), "It occurs to the survivor that perhaps the trauma is not the most important, or even the most interesting, part of her life story" (p. 195), and once this happens, the traumatic event has less hold over the survivor and reconnection with others can begin. However, what I think is most important is not the reconstruction of the traumatic story itself but its rhetorical appropriateness.

Herman notes that "knowledge of horrible events periodically intrudes into public awareness but is rarely retained for long. Denial, repression, and dissociation operate on a social as well as an individual level" (1992, p. 2). Few scholars have examined this phenomenon more rigorously than Kali Tal. Her book presents survivors of concentration camps challenging the seemingly sacred nature of the Holocaust, Vietnam veterans working against the simplistic image of the combat soldier as merely victim, and rape/incest survivors bearing witness to make their trauma real and visible. Having encountered Tal's three strategies of culture coping, my student perceived them at work in our online discussions, which prompted him to bear witness to the traumatic experience of his past:

I do not recall any specific response that influenced my reaction. I believe it to be the result of the reading assignments in addition to the build-up of student interchange. During our discussions, especially those of Kali Tal, I perceived a distinct lack of understanding for a large percentage of the class, a kind of TV cartoon conception. I think it upset me to some extent, forcing me to reveal myself a little at a time... Perhaps I was trying to say wake up, look to other sources, gather more information, step outside the boundaries of what you are told, and then come to an educated, informed conclusion.

Perceiving that his experiences were being appropriated by the surrounding virtual community, this student offered personal details from his past, and as members of the class were made to witness his trauma, two interesting things happened.

First, the choice to bear witness at this particular point in the course allowed him to experience the sense of empowerment that comes when writing affects change. In his e-mail to me, he notes that:

After revealing some information about myself during the Kali Tal discussion, I did see a change in the way other students responded to me... Interpersonal communication to my contributions appeared to have more thought behind them rather than the "I agree" pattern so prevalent in the class.

In addition to experiencing ways his testimony could persuade others to be more critical of what they say, he also experienced a change in the ways other students interacted with him on a personal level, noting that others seemed to "open up about themselves, their thoughts, and perspectives as they reflected in writing." His testimony enabled other students to come forward and bear witness to traumas that they had experienced. One student, for example, wrote about the death of her husband in the September 11th attacks. Herman (1992) notes important differences between bearing witness publicly vs. privately: "As each survivor shares her unique story, the (community) provides a profound experience of universality. The (community) bears witness to the survivor's testimony, giving it social as well as personal meaning" (p. 221). Not only did my student discover a sense of empowerment, his traumatic experiences became ordinary, just one experience among many as students came forward. In other words, he discovered that he was not alone and references connecting with two other students on a deeply personal level in his final e-mail to me.

Herman's (1992) conception of identity is postmodern. For instance, once the survivor's story has been told and has become just one ordinary memory among others, she notes that the survivor "has mourned the old self that the trauma has destroyed; now she must develop a new self" (Herman, 1992, p. 196). Elsewhere, Herman argues that healing requires that "Compassion and respect for the traumatized, victim self join with a celebration of the survivor self" (1992, p. 204). Many scholars argue that this protean, postmodern self is central to the way we experience life in online environments. Turkle (1995) argues that "When we step through the screen into virtual communities, we reconstruct our identities on the other side of the looking glass" (p. 178), and these identities become "objects-to-think-with" (pp. 47-49). The empowerment my course provided through safety and autonomy allowed this student to create an object-to-think-with closer to who he felt he truly was, and as he was able to watch how this object interacted with other members of our virtual community, he was able to come to an appreciation of this self. "Although I did create an online persona, as we all did," he argues, "this class allowed me to be who I am inside, without all the pretense and posturing."

In a virtual workplace of mostly young freshman, the disembodied, faceless nature of my classroom allowed this Vietnam veteran to assert his identity in ways that not only benefited him but the community and the work we were doing as a whole. The default identity of many virtual workplaces, however, can and often does have adverse affects on those who do not share that default identity. They may find it hard to establish their presence or establish it in ways antithetical to the goals of the community. This student's experience suggests that one of the ways to help those who are experiencing struggles negotiating their identity is through conscious self-reflection on how they contribute to building the online community. Reflecting on past discussions through the framework Kali Tal provides, this student found ways to use who he was to connect in meaningful ways with other members of the virtual workplace.

Even though this narrative focuses on a virtual composition classroom, it raises an awareness of the complexities inherent in any virtual workplace, especially when it comes to the influx of those considered nontraditional into this new environment. For me, it was only through my consideration of a body in pain that I came to a fuller understanding of this student's performance in my course, and perhaps our identities and being conscious of how virtual spaces work on them are more important to contributing successfully in virtual workplaces than the often bodiless virtual environment would have us believe.

REFERENCES

Butler, W. M., & Kinneavy, J. L. (1991). The electronic discourse community: God, meet Donald Duck. *Focuses, 4,* 91-108.

Cogdill, S. (2000). Indiscipline: Obscenity and vandalism in cyberclassrooms. In S. Harrington, R. Rickly & M. Day (Eds.), *The online writing classroom* (pp. 81-103). Cresskill, NJ: Hampton Press, Inc.

Cooper, M. (1999). Postmodern pedagogy in electronic conversations. In G. E. Hawisher & C. L. Selfe (Eds.), *Passions, pedagogies, and 21st century technologies* (pp. 140-60). Logan, UT: Utah State UP.

Cooper, M., & Selfe, C. L. (1990). Computer conferences and learning: Authority, resistance, and internally persuasive discourse. *College English, 8,* 847-869.

Faigley, L. (1995). *Fragments of rationality: Postmodernity and the subject of composition.* Pittsburgh, PA: University of Pittsburgh.

Flores, M. J. (1990). Computer conferencing: Composing a feminist community of writers. In C. Handa (Ed.), *Computers and community: Teaching composition in the twenty-first century* (pp. 106-117). Portsmouth, NH: Boynton/Cook.

Forman, J. (1994). Literacy, collaboration, and technology: New connections an challenges. In C. L. Selfe & S. Hilligoss (Eds.), *Literacy and computers: The complications of teaching and learning with technology* (pp. 130-143). New York: Modern Language Association.

Hawisher, G. E., & Selfe, C. L. (1991). The rhetoric of technology and the electronic writing class. *College Composition and Communication, 42*, 55-65.

Herman, J. L. (1992). *Trauma and recovery.* New York: BasicBooks.

Janangelo, J. (1991). Technopower and technoppression: Some abuses of power and control in computer-assisted writing environments. *Computers and Composition, 9*, 47-64.

Jessup, E. (1991). Feminism and computers in composition instruction. In G. E. Hawisher & C. L. Selfe (Eds.), *Evolving perspectives on computers and composition studies: Questions for the 1990s* (pp. 336-355). Urbana, IL: National Council of Teachers of English.

Matheson, K. (1991). Social cues in computer-mediated negotiations: Gender makes a difference. *Computers in Human Behavior, 7*, 137-145.

Palloff, R. M., & Pratt, K. (1999). *Building learning communities in cyberspace: Effective strategies of the online classroom.* San Francisco: Jossey-Bass Publishers.

Selfe, C. L. (1990). Technology in the English classroom: Computers through the lens of feminist theory. In C. Handa (Ed.), *Computers and community: Teaching composition in the twenty-first century* (pp. 118-139). Portsmouth, NH: Boynton/Cook.

Takayoshi, P. (1994). Building new networks from the old: Women's experience with electronic communications. *Computers and Composition, 11*, 21-35.

Tal, K. (1995). *Worlds of hurt: Reading the literatures of trauma.* New York: Cambridge UP.

Turkle, S. (1995). *Life on the screen: Identity in the age of the Internet.* New York: Simon & Schuster.

KEY TERMS

Computer-Mediated Communication: A broad term used to describe any means by which a computer serves as a medium of communication between two or more people. Common examples include listservs, chatrooms, and blogs.

Decentered Classroom: Considered a common characteristic of online learning, this term describes a classroom in which power and authority is not centered solely with the instructor but is dispersed or entrusted to students.

Globalization: This term typically means to extend to other or all parts of the globe or make worldwide. In the context of this chapter, the term is used to argue that diverse populations of people are brought together as computer-mediated communication extends into other parts of the globe.

Nontraditional Student: A term used to label a student that is not attending college right out of high school. Synonymous with adult student and re-entry student, the term is typically used to describe a much older student attending college for the first time or returning after an extended period of time.

Postmodern: A term used to describe a number of trends or movements in the arts and literature developing in the 1970s in reaction to or rejection of modernism. In the context of this chapter, the term is used to define identity as fluid and many rather than stable and unitary.

Technophile: A term used to describe someone who has love or enthusiasm for technology, especially computer technology. The term often has a negative connotation, often used to describe someone who is blinded by their enthusiasm for computer technology and uncritical of its uses.

Chapter XLVII
Virtual Political Office Where Gender and Culture Meet

Olena Igorivna Goroshko
National Technical University "Kharkiv Polytechnic Institute", Ukraine

ABSTRACT

Based on the underlying assumption that gender is a social construct, this chapter explores the World Wide Web home pages of key political figures in the USA and Ukraine focusing specifically on what the content posted to these sites and their structure suggests about gender and cultural peculiarities in constructing political identity on the Web. The personal page is rendered as a virtual political office—a peculiar meeting point between the site owner and its potential audience, electorate, and citizenry providing an excellent working place to be constantly in touch with the electoral body from anyplace and in anytime. All data are analyzed according to four parameters: male, female, Ukrainian, and American. The main result highlights the intersection across culture, gender, and computer-mediated communication (CMC) influencing the virtual identity formation. The intersectional approach towards viewing gendered virtual identity is proposed. The data obtained lead to suggestions for the creation of sites that are more in line with the potential provided by the Net to facilitate political communication.

INTRODUCTION

CMC and Virtual Office

The notion of Computer-Mediated Communication (CMC) is the term that covers popular applications of the network, including electronic mail, electronic bulletin boards, Web pages, and so forth. CMC presents the class of computer-based technologies (including the Internet) to assist people in getting in touch with each other. The Internet is more versatile than any other interactive medium currently available to us. The net enables us permanently to communicate with closed friends or with total strangers, with individuals or with large groups, using our real names or remaining totally anonymous. Jennifer Carpenter declares that:

the Internet is not simply a medium, like the telephone or snail mail system—it is also a place, a virtual environment where people meet, engage in discourse, become friends, fall in love, and develop all of the relationships that are developed in physical communities. (Carpenter, 1998, p. 1)

Nevertheless the ways that people work and communicate via the Web destabilizes a great number of conventional social categories. For example, one can refer to "social lives at work and at home" as if ones apply to distinct places as well as webs of social relationships. However virtual offices and activities realized through them enable people to work routinely while they are in their homes, and blur the boundaries between office and home, private and public, virtual and real (Kling, 1996). It has raised the additional problematic area for the Web research about the boundary renegotiations provoked by the net.

There are four fragmentations as it is claimed in CMC theory viewing the Internet as a new social domain "where physical-world boundaries or those of prior domains of convention have not yet been developed" (Katz & Rice, 2002b, p. 268). They cover the public-private distinction as revealed in online self-presentation, since the boundary between *private* and *public* on the net is rather blurring. Simultaneously the boundary between *professional* and *personal* on the Web also does not pronounce intensively. The *social* and *technical* boundary initiates the critical distinction between the priority of construction and social understanding and the individual construction and extension of self as an artifact of technology (Katz & Rice, 2002b, p. 269). The fourth boundary issue lies between the *real* and the *virtual*. It initiates the disappearance of conventional reality from the world outside the computer into the virtual world expressed within computer (Katz & Rice, 2002b, p. 270). The Internet presents a boundary-shifting medium that carries over into physical domains. Nowhere are the social challenges of the Internet so pronounced as in the virtual workplace. The Internet breaks down a lot of different social barriers. As a result, subordinates acquire nearly as much communicative power in the "virtual workplace" as their own superiors. Virtual workplaces are beginning to replace the traditional office environment of cubicles and office buildings. Individual virtual workplaces vary in how they apply existing technology to facilitate common activity. There are three approaches prevailing in this area:

- **Telecommuting** (the availability and use of communications technologies, such as the Internet, to work in an offsite location);
- **Hot desk environment** (individuals are not given separate desks; rather each day employees are allocated to a desk where they can access the Internet, e-mail, and computer network files);
- **Virtual team** (the collaboration of individuals working closely together and in constant contact who are physically located in different parts of the world).

Virtual workplaces are advantageous in an information age where technology is expanding rapidly and people need to meet across the globe. A virtual workplace enables individuals to work from anyplace at anytime in the world. Virtual workplaces streamline systems from multiple facets of work into a single unified unit easily accessible. They decrease costs as well as increase efficiency, due to the single system, is an instantaneous advantage. A virtual workplace is easier for individuals because of opportunities to travel without restrictions, consolidates services, and assists in the communication processes. Simultaneously "there are many challenges associated with the implementation of virtual workplaces, and if not carefully analyzed, organizations can be threatened by not fully realizing the enormous benefits that can be achieved through virtual workplaces." More and more CMC gurus argue the lack of human contact and increased sensitivity to communication, and interpersonal and cultural factors present the main pitfalls for effective functioning of virtual working places and offices. However many of these challenges can be overcome by having good management applied to the virtual workplace. Good workplace management has been said to increase the probability of success in virtual workplaces and within virtual community whatsoever.

The personal pages of politicians are rendered in this study as their virtual political offices. These offices provide all logistics to sustain professional online activity: managing political impression online, sustaining a necessary and constant feedback with their electorate and citizenry, and supporting effective political communication for days and nights. Coincidentally these pages develop a unique platform for building virtual identity including the political one. Many CMC theorists point out that the Web page generates also a more solid backup for the problematic claims of identity, gender, or expertise that are made on the net (Chandler, 1998). Thus, the personal Web page presents a platform that offers a challenging object for study about gender differences in self-presentation techniques as well as diverse ways of building virtual identities at large.

I want to stress that the topic of building gender identity on the English-speaking Internet is rather well researched but there are no comparative studies across languages and cultures. A culture consists of structures and practices that uphold a particular social order by legitimizing certain values, expectations, meanings, and patterns of behavior. To explore this supposition, it is helpful to consider how culture creates, sustains, and promotes more basic values, democracy, and then how it upholds the gender practices (Wood, 2003, p. 28), off- or online as in this research.

Thus the main objective of study is to analyze the peculiarities of building virtual personae on the political office across cultures and genders. All data are to be analyzed according to four key parameters: male, female, Ukrainian, and American.

BACKGROUND

Building Virtual Identity through Home Pages

In CMC theory, the personal page usually is defined as Web site that is typically maintained by one individual or family or an organization (Dominick, 1999, p.646). Personal home pages enable people to create their own content and distribute it globally. Currently the Web permits for page creation to use graphic, sound, animation, and visual objects to present your virtual personae in all diversity. Usually the start or the home page presents the first document that users encounter when entering the site. The home page orientates the user to the site, informs about its purpose, states about what type of information can be obtained, and provides links to other relevant sites or documents. Barnes argues that namely the personal Web pages represent the Web at its most basic and eclectic way (2003, p.80).

Haas and Grams (2000), who outline a useful approach to classify and describe the methodological tools for personal Web pages research, and Doring (2002), who provides a valuable overview of current practices in this area, make it clear that personal home pages are not always defined the same way. Some scholars studying cyberspace compare personal Web pages to an open house where the owner is never present or to informal resumes that sometimes contain very personal information (Rubio, 1996). Chandler (1998) declares that personal home pages are the best self-advertisement for personality. Other definitions border on the pejorative: "Burns said they are the business cards of the twenty first century while Plotnikoff likened them to electronic refrigerator doors (taking in mind a "motionless," nonanimated picture of self on the Web—insert added)" (Dominick, 1999, p. 646). Erickson (1996), summing up these debates, declares that:

personal pages and the World Wide Web are not being used to publish information; they are being used to construct identity—useful information is just a side effect. A personal page is a carefully constructed portrayal of a person. Personal pages are something like informal resumes, except that in addition to professional material they often contain personal information. Hobbies, research interests, pets, professional publications, children, politics, friends, colleagues, all are grist for the personal page. I believe that this seemingly frivolous blending of the professional and the personal is the key to why the Web is becoming a fundamentally different thing from the systems of information servers that preceded it. (p. 16)

Miller and Mather (1998) claim that no other forms of CMC—both chat, e-mail, and even forum permit such manipulations with our identity as home page. To their thinking, the creation of a personal Web page is rendered as a systematic answer to the critical reflection of the self. By accommodating personal views about the self, the Web page sustains its homogeneity and effectiveness.

Since personal pages, as some scholars argue, are being used to construct identity (which is socially mediated and much of that mediation is realized through language and culture), hence namely cultural and language environment affects greatly this process. It follows that as new social processes and new ways of using language emerge, like CMC, it may be possible to develop new aspects of identity and exactly the culture might play first fiddle in it.

Simultaneously, more and more researches speak about virtual identity and virtual personae as new phenomena of post-modernity and informational society: the developing communication technologies of the last 20 years have had a profound implication for our sense of self. CMC research has paralleled the shift in the understanding of identity from Erickson's (1996) idea of a stable personal identity to the pluralities of identity in postmodernist interpretations as *patchwork, narrative, collage identity,* and *multiple selves* (Erickson, 1996; Wynn & Katz, 1997). Doring regards that postmodern identity is comprised of independent and partially contradictory, alternative subidentities. These are subsequently used to construct any new identity, and this new identity in turn is seen as a *puzzle* that is possible to deconstruct and then construct again. In everyday life, these subidentities support a sense of coherence and consolidate personality (Doring, 2002, p. 6). To the notion of off-line postmodern identity the CMC space adds such properties as *virtuality,*

spatiality, disembedding, and *disembodiment.* Each of these characteristics emphasizes a radical disjuncture between online and off-line communications, relations, and identities (Slater, 2002, p. 534). The progress over the last two decades in social discourse emphasizing the cultural and social context in the structure of identity has also enabled a significant move in approaches to the study of online self, identity, and personhood (Burnett & Marshall, 2003). This notion of the CMC postmodern self is clearly embodied in personal Web pages, which can be constantly updated and transformed. Always "under construction," these items reflect the latest ideas of their authors about their personality. Web pages thus make it possible to bring together various subidentities quickly and easily, thereby establishing a particular social hypertext as the latest iteration of the personal self. Rather frequently in CMC theory, the online self is coined as a *social hypertext* (Chandler, 1998).

Overall researchers of this segment of the Internet agree on a number of points: the personal Web page presents the best place for a meeting of its owner with a virtual audience, being an original advertisement board for the personal self. Home pages attempt to construct a unified presentation or at least to pull together diverse aspects of the self so that browsers can follow paths that attract them. Thus the homepage is a pulled-together presentation of self and this presentation must be either totally consistent or provides the mixing of styles and features from multiple conventions being a more architectural metaphor of postmodernism (Winn & Katz, 1997). Nevertheless a question "Are we what we post?" challenges new opportunities to situate the net in a broader and more continuous social environment.

Currently home pages are used not only as a means of self-advertisement, image-promotion, or to consolidate virtual identity, but they present a helpful communicative tool for professional communication of any kind (Schau & Gilly, 2003). On the Web, they are rendered as virtual offices—convenient working places in profes-

Figure 1. The virtual office of Congresswoman Jane Harman

sional or business surroundings. It is necessary to emphasize that namely personal pages' owners, not CMC theorists', view home pages more and more frequently as their virtual offices.

Gendered Identity Online

There is a huge flow of research concerning gender aspects of CMC: gender biases in Internet access and use, gendered interaction styles online, gendered e-language, and so forth. Many social scholars now render gender as a social, symbolic category that reflects the meanings that society confers on biological sex:

These meanings are communicated through structures and practices of cultural life that pervade our daily existence, creating the illusion that they are the natural, normal ways for women and men to be. What gender means varies across cultures and over time in a particular culture, and how we conceive each gender is related to our views of the other. (Wood, 2003, p. 28)

Gender provides the meaning that a particular culture attaches to sex: What our society defines as feminine and masculine may seem natural to us but there is nothing necessary about any particular meaning given to gender. By extension, this insight suggests we have more choice than

we sometimes realize in how we define ourselves as men and women (Wood, 2003). The meanings of gender are reflected and promoted by social structures and practices. One of the primary practices that structures society is communication including through the Net. Wood asserts: *"We are surrounded by communication that promotes social gendered images and seeks to persuade us these are natural correct ways for men and women to be and to behave"* (Wood, 2003, p. 29). Socially endorsed meanings are also communicated through structures such as institutions, which serve to announce, reflect, and perpetuate gendered cultural views. Because gender is important in our society, its institutions uphold preferred meanings and encourage individuals to conform to what is collectively endorsed as appropriate masculine and feminine behavior, they often reinforce established cultural prescriptions for gender. Through its structures and practices, especially communication practices, societies create and sustain perspectives on what is normal and right.

There is a great debate in gender studies and in social sciences generally about the nature and perception of gender. One of the latest approaches in this area is based on the notion of *intersectionality*. This approach supposes that gender lies on the crossroads of many social factors: power, class, race, nation, and so forth. It presents a conventional product stipulated greatly by these factors (Cranny-Francis, Warning, Stavropoulos, & Kirkby, 2003). These views on gender influence the latest ideas about virtual gendered and cultural identity.

The previous research indicates a number of gender traces in this area. Some scholars fix gender differences into the social purposes of personal Web page production. Gender does not influence the male and female priorities much, except that women more often use Web pages to establish and maintain relationships and less for self promotional purposes. The same research also reveals that larger differences were impacted by the age of Internet-users (Petric, 2006).

There are differences between the kinds of identity presented by men and women and in the ways the identity is presented. Females include more information about personal topics than do males. Further, females are more likely than males to include information about their family and spouse or romantic partner. Women and men do not differ in the frequency with which they speak about their likes and dislikes with the exception of sport topics. Females are far more likely than males to include statements about their outlook or philosophy on life. Also female pages significantly more than male pages contain some examples of poetry, stories, or artwork. However there are no differences in the type/number of links that each page contains. Nor is there a difference in feedback mechanisms and usage of visual images (Dominick, 1999, pp. 652-653). The results obtained in other studies of personal pages run counter to these data (Goroshko, 2006; Miller & Mather, 1998). The research of a random sampling of 70 male and female Yahoo! homepages by Miller and Mather (1998) and Miller and Arnold (2001) indicates a lot of gender differences concerning the site interactivity, the number of links and visual images, and the volume of text messages. Women's pages are sometimes longer, contain more guests-books, links, e-mail addresses, and show more awareness and responsiveness to their reader (Miller & Arnold, 2001; Miller & Mather, 1998). When women and men represent themselves visually in their pages, only men use joke images and only women use symbolic representations (Miller & Mather, 1998, p. 4). The questionnaire conducted by Miller and Arnold (2001) on building individual identity within an institutional Web page framework testifies that women academics often feel certain vulnerability to present themselves online as private persons and cancel their photos and intimate information from their Web sites as undermining their academic status.

The research of randomly selected RuNet (Russian segment of the Internet) homepages confirms also the data obtained by Miller and Mather (1998): women appear to be more experienced and more skillful communicators than men. Women are more interested in feedback whereas male communicative behavior concentrates more on self-presentation, that is, an original PR of their self (Goroshko, 2006). Larisa Kompanceva obtains the same results researching the political space of UaNet (Ukrainian segment of the Internet) (Kompanceva, 2004).

The study conducted by Joseph Dominick shows very curious thing though:

the page designation is the most frequently used by both genders, but among those who chose to describe their personal sites with another metaphor, females seemed more likely to use a metaphor that was associated with power or dominance while males chose more familiar, less formal descriptions of their pages. (Dominick, 1999, p. 654)

It can probably be stipulated by a certain female compensation for the existing biased power-balance in modern society (Prino, 2003).

Given that personal and social aspects of identity are combined in CMC, it is easy to see that the structure of gender relations can be viewed through the juxtaposition of "individual I" and "I—as a representative of gender group" (Klecina, 2004, p. 335). Gender identity is not fixed, however, and can be impacted greatly by social transformations. Simultaneously, gender identity is considered the most stable among the other forms of identity. When the individual as a subject of gender relations is inserted into the system of external evaluations by his/her social surrounding that corresponds with the norms of "femininity/masculinity." The opposition of "femininity/masculinity" becomes a marker for performing gender identity (Klecina, 2004, p. 30). As a venue for self-presentation and self-disclosure, personal Web pages provide a fertile ground for the study of gender identity. The opportunity to make a complex, multi-layered, but controlled presentation—the hypertext self does provide new possibilities for how people can think about themselves, and get others to think about them as *men* or *women* (Burnett & Marshall, 2003, p. 79).

Cultural Identity Online

Many investigations concern the cultural aspects of CMC. Luc Pauwels argues that "disembodied" CMC environment may provide much significance for getting to someone's personal and cultural identity or self (Pauwels, 2003, p. 605). The issue of interrelation between cultural identity and CMC is probably the most ambiguous in the area of Internet research and often viewed as something nonscientific and relating more to popular prejudices than to positive knowledge. The net as a global communicative environment is often rendered as a means of effacing differences between local cultures and even it can be used as a tool of coercive global unification in accordance with the American or Western values (Gauntlett, 2000, p. 538). Simultaneously, the opposite tendency can be observed: nationally or ethnically defined cultures are resistant to the unification and globalization impacts of CMC and preserve their individuality. Due to the dominance of text-based communication on the net it is the language that plays first fiddle not only in off-line and online identity building but it is connected toughly with cultural values and patterns of behavior. It helps to keep the original cultures within the net. There are no borders on the net except the language ones. Languages trace new maps across the Internet (Crystal, 2001; Danet & Herring, 2007; Gorny, 2006). However, the language being a key factor in enhancing cultural accommodation online influences very ambivalently on preserving local peculiarities of CMC. Some scholars explain this ambivalence by the global widespread of practically only one language on the net: The English sites prevail in cyberspace (Danet & Herring, 2007, p. 10).

Trying to provide a new dimension toward cultural aspects of CMC, Ess and Sudweeks (2005, pp. 8-9) review different frameworks for study from

Hall's and Hofstede's approach towards high and low context cultures (Hall, 1976; Hofstede, 1990) to more complex critical culture theories: from presumption of culture as fixed and essentialist to its interpretation as a *fluid* and *dynamic* cultural community where culture is rendered as series of practices and habits that are also fluctuated and changing. Pauwels (2005) analyzing opportunities and issues of online media research also asserts that Web pages have been definitely received far less scholarly attention in this area than other forms of CMC (chats, e-mails, virtual games, and blogs). Nevertheless some CMC theorists render Web pages as visual and multimodal cultural expressions.

Personal Homepages on the Political Web

Politics in a democratic country depends on some form of communication. Participating in the political process is a privilege of any democratic society. Moreover, citizen participation is vital to maintaining a healthy democratic society. Barnes declares that "central to political participation is political communication, and the Internet provides a new communication channel for sending political messages and receiving citizen feedback" (Barnes, 2003, p. 298). The Internet becomes more and more popular for online political activity. A great variety of Internet genres are used for their purposes, including e-mail, discussion groups, Web pages, blogs, and online news groups (Katz & Rice, 2002). In 1992, a number of political campaigns began to use e-mail to connect campaign strategists, and candidate Ross Perot suggested using electronic town hall meetings in the election process. Later both of these techniques have become part of political campaigns (Barnes, 2003, p. 299). Dutton (1999) argues that the Internet could counterbalance the influence of television on political discourse, and even could surpass its value because the Internet is an interactive medium that facilitates the development of connections between people and information. It extends government decision-making by involving more people in the political life and moving politics away from centralized representation (Vershinin, 2001). Cyber-politics is a new type of political communication. Whillock says that in its most simple form "cyber-politics involve information dissemination, communication exchange, and the formation of electronic political coalitions across the Internet" (1997, p. 1208).

My own investigation of the RuNet personal home pages indicates that sites of famous political figures occupy a rather voluminous space on the Net (Goroshko, 2006). We failed to find the proper information to the peculiarities of building gendered political identity on the Web sites except one paper describing gender aspects of political communication on the UaNet (Kompanceva, 2004). However the comparative cross-cultural context is missing in this research. Simultaneously, there are a lot of studies exploring the key political figures' homepages in the USA and Europe. Basically they focus on how the content posted to these sites and their structure speaking about their audiences, effectiveness of political communication realized through them, their role in political campaigning, and so forth (Bykov, 2006; Jarvis & Wilkerson, 2005; Kern, 1997; Norris, 2003). Currently, home pages are specified within CMC theory as the most popular and effective tools supporting the political communication online (Bykov, 2006, p. 106; Xenos & Foot, 2005, p. 173).

Within all communicative platforms used in cyber-politics, Web sites present very cheap and convenient tools for keeping, disseminating, and updating useful information. A Web site is operated as a platform sustaining practically all forms of political activity. Xenos and Foot propound that campaign Web sites are recognizable genre with stable prevalence of particular kinds of features and content (2005, p. 174). An online survey of frequent Web users conducted by the Annenberg Public Policy Center of the University of Pennsylvania indicates that there are a lot of reasons for getting news and information about politics from the Web

pages: the convenience of the Web in itself, the ability to search a variety of news sources, the ability to obtain the data from the Web that was not available elsewhere, and the multimedia capabilities of the Net (Schneider, 2000). The surveyed Web users want candidates to provide comparative information, contributor lists, and archives of campaign materials, as well as the issues positions and candidate biographies (Schneider, 2000). Political sites frequently can be used for advocacy: to make people aware of impending congressional votes and to ask people to phone or e-mail their representatives. The site can provide information about fund-raising services, lobby for legal action, identify potential party members, or consolidate the political audiences and partisans (2004 Presidential Campaign Sites, 2005). Currently practically every famous politician has own site serving as a powerful tool for a political career and promotion. It is rather useful to keep in touch with the electorate. It supports intensively in community building and political networking activities (Barnes, 2003, p. 308). I consider that the notion of *virtual working place* or *virtual office* can be easily "removed" from the organizational communication area and "be inserted" to the cyber-politics' discourse. Homepages of political actors can be also viewed as their virtual political offices not only by them (see Figure 1) but also CMC researchers.

Some studies reveal that structural designs of political sites are linked directly with the motivation for their creation. One suggests that Web sites perform three major functions: *information*, *persuasion*, and *solidarity* (Erickson, 1996). Certain scholars argue that although a great variety of political topics could be explored in this analysis, three subjects appear particularly valuable for study as they are central for the Web's role in reenergizing, for example, American politics: *information, identification,* and *participation* (Jarvis & Wilkerson, 2005, p. 3). The information block covers the following items: *biographies, photos, press releases, speeches,* and so forth (16 items); the identification is connected with *party cues* and the participation block contains *con-*

tacts, counter, update and *polls/surveys* rubrics (Jarvis & Wilkerson, 2005, pp. 8-9). The definite structural site features' review and "the content analysis allowing to classify items objectively and systematically according to explicit rules and criteria" are used for these purposes" (Jarvis & Wilkerson, 2005, p. 3). Sometimes to measure Web sites' effectiveness, the following list of factors are examined: *accessibility* (including ease of navigation and access to information); *interactivity, content,* and *presentation* (covering the use of multimedia and imagery) (Yates & Perrone, 1998).

One can argue that the political site, unlike the personal Web page, is mediated not only through the computer channel of communication but also through the team of professionals engaged into the maintenance of various site activity: design, development, promotion, operation, and so forth. Site owners at best only enable us to supervise, approve, or disapprove the thematic filling of our own site, probably the logic architecture of its context and design, pick out certain color palette, and so forth.[1] Some politicians participate in interactive online activity with their audiences through specially organized site-forums, e-mails, and so forth. Hence, to research the political Web means to study partly the gendered and cultural mediated features in online identity building: certain constructs influenced greatly by two principal factors—technical (the Web) and human (the team). One can assert that it *must* provide an additional dimension to *gender practices* researched online.

VIRTUAL POLITICAL OFFICES: GENDER ACROSS CULTURES

Comparative Study of Ukrainian and American Political Webs

According to the latest statistics, the total number of Internet users in Ukraine exceeds 6 million people (http//index.bigmir.net). More than 15% of Internet users in CIS Countries live in Ukraine. The UaNet shows the stable and dynamic growth. Kompanceva provides rather perfunctory description of the UaNet political sector (Kompanceva, 2004, pp. 113-114). To her data, political Web occupies a modest place within the Ukrainian segment of the net (nearly 300 sites). Personal sites of politicians and parties cover only 8% of this "territory." Almost all sites are hosted in Kiyv; 66% of sites are presented in Russian, 30% (in Ukrainian and 3% in English. Among the Ukrainian "Verkhovna Rada" representatives, there are only 10% of members with their personal sites. Kompanceva (2004) also attributes them more as fashion items than political tools, but I think that for 2 recent years their importance in local cyber-politics has increased dramatically (Bykov, 2006; Vershinin, 2001). Unfortunately it lacks data concerning the involvement of Ukrainian citizens in online political activity. However practically everyone could observe the role of UaNet in providing of unbiased information about the Orange Revolution. Namely the UaNet consolidated the Ukrainian community greatly at that time. It has been generating trust to the political events and its leaders for ordinary people in Ukraine being a powerful alternative to local newspapers, TV, radio, and so forth. Just like the U.S. Presidential Campaign gave the tremendous boost to blogging, the Orange Revolution changed the nation attitude towards the Web.

In those times millions of people all of a sudden realized that the classic media they got used to ...[ ] are either not trustworthy (because almost 100% were controlled by the regime) or very slow in reacting on the situation (which did change dramatically literally every minute). To them knowing the real situation was not just a matter of curiosity but sometimes a one personal safety for themselves and the loved ones. (Yefetov, 2006, p. 2)

As for American segment of the political Web, it is much more spacious and diverse. Every U.S. House of Representatives member, civic organizations, heads of major, minor, or fringe political parties, and parties themselves have their own sites. Currently 23% of American eligible citizens who can vote visit Web sites with political information (Norris, 2003).

Experimental Design

The conducted literary analysis reveals also that the gendered facets of identity on the political Web present no-go areas for study as well as there being very scarce research of cyber-politics across cultures (Norris, 2003). Therefore, the primary aim of this study is to analyze Ukrainian and American political sites from structural and communicative perspectives. The impacts of gender and culture on identity construction, self-presentation, and image-impression on the Web are traced in this study presenting a qualitative research of twenty specially selected home pages retrieved from the congressional home page of U.S. House Representatives (http://www.house.gov/house/MemNameSearch.shtml) and the list of Ukrainian Supreme Council "Verkhovna Rada" people's deputies (http://gska2.rada.gov.ua/pls/site/p_deputat_list?skl=5#top). The selective criteria are based on political ratings and positions occupied in political system (speaker, head of party or congress chamber, future nominee to the presidency, or leaders of opposition). The total number of sites for this study comprises 20 items (see Appendix 1).

One can hypothesize that gender being a social and cultural construct impacts the way people communicates through the political Web. Simultaneously, not only gender but also culture and local political environment might influence the gender identity in CMC and these peculiarities can be intersected. Thus the approach towards gender as a product of intersectional interaction provides the theoretic foundation for this research (Cranny-Francis et al., 2003).

A lot of criticism of focusing on quantitative analysis of differences (including the gender ones) can be found currently in methodological reviews

of CMC research (Miller & Arnold, 2001; Pauwels, 2005). Looking for gender differences is labeled as being sexist in itself. Some feminist scholars argue why they should establish differences unless it is for the sake of validating discrimination (Miller & Arnold, 2001, p. 11). Pauwels criticizes the recent CMC studies of Web pages for their focus on a rather limited operationalization of the phenomena researched, simplification of approaches (e.g., "more links" means "more democratic"), prevalence purely descriptive level (listing typical categories of content and their potential role in identity construction), the textual bias research to the detriment of cultural and ethnographic methods for analyzing analysis of the hybrid media). Pauwels asserts that the hybrid multi-layered space as a Web site requires hybrid research methodology (e.g., to perform a detailed analysis of the form, content and organization of the imagery: the selection of moments and subjects, their posture, the anchoring with verbal parts, etc.) (Pauwels, 2005, pp. 609-610).

Considering all this criticism, the items for research are selected according to this *hybrid principle*. The selection criteria for research items are stipulated by certain CMC theories in the area of gender and culture. First the hypothesis about *male-orientated instrumental* and *female-oriented expressive* cognitive styles by Bem provides a useful methodological tool for also for CMC research (Bem, 1981; Miller & Mather, 1998). According to Miller and Mather, "A more expressive style would focus on feelings, people, and relationships, while the instrumental style might show itself in reference to abilities and achievements, material goods, and organizations and products rather than people" (Miller & Mather, 1998). Dominick also agues that people use links on their home pages as a means of social association, so that by providing a set of links to other sites, people indirectly define themselves by listing their interests (Dominick, 1999). More boldly Miller declares: "Show me what your links are, and I tell you what kind of person you are" (Miller, 1995). Hence the qualitative analysis of links is proposed. Then the thematic filling of Web pages as an inventory of topics, issues (including significantly absent items) are researched for study of online identity construction. As a powerful means for political networking and advocacy, Web sites may contain guest-books, rant-pages, and mailing lists permitting their hosts to seek positive reinforcement through inviting visitors to subscribe to the informational letter or e-mail question to the site owner or to sigh plainly their "guest-books" (Norris, 2003; Xenos & Foot, 2005). Consequently the number of guest-books, rant-pages, blogs, counters, and all elements in Web design providing interactivity for homepages (e-mail addresses, invitations to chats and forums, discussion lists, appeals to visit this home page again, etc.) is analyzed.

I also separately scrutinize the graphic objects located on the sites: pictures of the owner, party symbols and images, cultural and national symbolic presented on sites. Additionally, the number of basic colors on personal Web pages and the choice of color palette are reviewed on the assumption that the female choice of colors must be more diverse and exquisite. Women more often than men choose rare rather than commonly widespread colors (Steckler & Cooper, 1980). More colorful Web page may speak also about the more pronounced emotionality of its owners (Jan'shin, 1996). At the same time within the Hall and Hofstede framework (Hall, 1976; Hofstede, 1990) towards cultural analysis of CMC high-context cultures (HC) are likely to use more imagery and less text than low-context cultures (LC). LC Web sites are more consistent in layout and use of color than HC Web sites and images chosen for HC Web sites reflect HC cultural values (family, kids), while LC Web sites represent the individualistic values (personal hobbies, interests, leisure activity, etc.) (Pauwels, 2005, p. 4). Therefore the analysis of the site imagery including their semantics is organized.

The latest information drawn from CMC theory indicates that language provides the powerful tool for gender and culture identities'

formation not only off-line but also online (Crystal, 2001; Danet, 1996; Danet & Herring, 2007; Gorny, 2006). Atabekova (2003), having studied the linguistic design of Russian and American corporative Web pages, agues that namely the linguistic peculiarities reflect the different cultural and cognitive domains. Web pages written in English are more individually oriented and interactive than the Russian ones. Their design is more targeted at the dynamic aspects of the data presentation, embodied in more intensive usage of verbs, interrogative and incentive syntax constructions, personal plural pronouns, used in hyperlinks titles. They also combine various genres supporting the dialogue between the site owner and visitor: interviews, questionnaires, quizzes, and so forth. They contain much more incomplete sentences reducing the social distance between the site host and guests, as Atabekova declares. The Russian sites lack these features very often (Atabekova, 2003, pp. 176-177). She also declares that English sites are more *interactive* and Russian pages are more *informative* (Atabekova, 2003). Thus some linguistic peculiarities are analyzed regarding to gender and culture. The following items are chosen to trace on the sample home pages: the usage of personal pronouns (which would probably show the difference between HC and LC cultures on the Web), imperative verbs (that can appeal directly to the site's visitors and provide the imitation of the shared virtual space between the site owner and its visitor), incentives, exclamatory and interrogative sentences, and the means of politeness manifested on the sites (*behahitives* like: *sorry, we apologize, thank you, welcome* which can indicate the gender peculiarities in speech styles).

This chapter looks at 19 Web sites (see Appendix 2), all of which are analyzed according to four parameters: male, female, Ukrainian, and American. In addition, the number of male and female American representatives and Ukrainian people's deputies having their own personal sites is counted.

RESULTS AND DISCUSSION

Gender Impact

The study—surfing the political Web—reveals that male political pages dominated as in real life one can observe a prevalence of male-dominated political discourse both in the USA and Ukraine. The research also reveals that the information on political sites is organized *in a dialogic way.* The addressing is actively used to provide a two-way communication and stimulate the visitors' response and feedback. The results indicate that female sites are more dialogic. Women are trying to sustain networking very intensively beyond "national" boundaries and culture does not touch greatly this female networking. One can assert that interactivity and dialogism are intertwined on the female Web site: here are more counters and guest-books, appeals to comment on the site, rant-pages, and so forth. Female Web pages provide more opportunities for instant online communication such as *chats* and *forums.* The Julija Tymoshenko's Site can be set up as a model *how to interact online.* However, this difference between male and female samples is not so striking as in the research by Miller and Mather (1998) or Miller and Arnold (2001).

The content analysis of the rubrics' titles reveals that 70% of male and female titles are identical. However there are more different rubrics' titles namely located on the female Web. Also their fillings are more diverse. It might indirectly show that female virtual identity is more dispersed and not so homogenous as the male one, but this question requires additional examination. It is interesting that sample female pages contain rubrics presenting their owners in different social-roles indicating clearly their group identity. The start page of Inna Bogoslovskaja's site demonstrates clearly its owner's group identity associations: Inna Boboslovskaja describes herself through such rubrics as *Sponsor, Business Lady, Political Leader,* and *Social Activist.*

The study of thematic fillings and imagery located on the Web sites shows that the male political Web exploits more self- and member-centered approaches towards the information posted online. Male sites seem to be more conceptual whereby mission and objectives, principles of social activity, and comment and analysis concerning everyday political and public events are formulated more clearly and efficiently as well. However they are comparing with the female Web yet more boring as excessively politicized. Information on male pages recalls the motto, "It is more important to present yourself instead of lending an ear to somebody." Males underscore the distance between the elected official and the visitor. This pattern is particular evident in their biographies, description of activities tended to focus on the accomplishments and professional successes of members in very reserved and formalized ways, and the selection of photos located on the Web where the male figure of site owner occupies the biggest space against the national landscapes or ordinary electorate. Sometimes other VIPs can surround this figure. My data confirms completely the results by Jarvis and Wilkerson (2005, p. 10).

The conducted research indicates that women are more open to the public. On the female Web more personal (even intimate information) can be exposed globally. One can observe that *private* and *individual* easily can be intermingled with *public* and *professional.* The results obtained on Russian personal pages reveal the same (Goroshko, 2006, p. 116). The Barbara Mikulski's site containing *Senator Barb's Favorite Crab Cake Recipe* demonstrates rather clearly the blurring of boundaries between the *public* and the *private* on the nt.

As for graphic objects, both women and men insert the same number of their photos. There is no difference in usage of avatars containing complicated Web-design, party cues, logos, and so forth. Only party cues are registered through this research and this feature is more pronounced on female sites. This fact can be attributed either to higher emotionality of female Web or a female incline for more pronounced party identification but it is only preliminary supposition requiring further research.

Cultural Impact

One can observe also the difference between two political Webs—American and Ukrainian. As a whole , the structural analysis of home pages shows that site rubrics as a rule include the following items: *News, Biography, Photo Gallery, Speeches, My Position, Elections, Hot Topics, More about Me,* and so forth. Frequently the number of rubrics exceeds 20 items. American pages contain more rubrics. They also include more rubrics concerning legislation, state and political concerns, and constituent services. The information content analysis of American Web reveals: it stands to reason that the site audience must understand the inner workings of Congress. This assumption stands in sharp contrast to the Ukrainian political Web and might be explained by the influence of national political culture or the peculiarities of local cyber-politics. Ukrainian Web looks much more user-friendly. Nevertheless the further research must be conducted to this point.

As for different communicative platforms used on the sites, there are a lot of various means supporting interactivity online: chats, forums, guest-books, and so forth. It is remarkable that only American sites maintain blogs as a tool for communication. There are no blogs on the Ukrainian political sites. It enables to testify that blogging has not become the popular social practice as in the West.

It is common for the political American sites, in contrast to the Ukrainian Web, to contain a block *Kids' Page* with entertaining and educational information for children and their parents. Locating this rubric on the site its owner obviously makes an original PR-move that must emphasize eternal values: family, home, children, and provide positive image of its owner as a respectable member of certain community. This rubric also helps to attract much more age-differentiated audience including kids and teenagers.

Ukrainian sites lack this information altogether. It is also surprising that in contrast to the Ukrainian political Web, the American Web reveals great sensitivity to different age groups and their problems on the whole. Hillary Clinton's site presents the brightest example how to care about their generations from young to old. Ukrainian sites do not contain social care information at all. There are not *Kids' Pages* on the Ukrainian sites. I consider that this finding contradicts greatly with the supposition that only HC Web sites can provide such information.

At the same time, the Ukrainian sites keep not only the officially approved information as the American ones do. In such a way Victor Medvedchuk's site maintains the rubric *Rumors about Medvedchuk.* This site keeps the unique feature missing on the rest of sample sites. It contains negative information about its owner. The rest of the sites promote only positive information about their bosses. This feature is observed only on the UaNet.

My research and other CMC studies show that Ukrainian politicians are more sincere with their virtual audience. For example, the same Victor Medvedchuk's site contains the following passage:

One can not always win. A person involved in politics shall ever remember that triumphs are alternated with defeats. Otherwise, progress would have been impossible. I have already experienced it in my life, as an outbreak of the parliamentary struggle has forced me to leave the Deputy Speaker's chair. But even then I was not shocked, having been prepared to be in and out of office. One should be able to live an ordinary life, where the family, love and whole-heart devotion are of much more importance than any other thing.

It is also an unexpected revelation for us that only Ukrainian politicians are permitted to locate anti-Semitic and *politically incorrect* information on their sites. Thus Stepan Khmara's site exposes the owner's article with the title "President Kuchma is the Father for all Jews in Ukraine" or the site owing to Natalija Vitrenko (Leader of Progressive Socialist Party of Ukraine) abounds in insulting and derogatory remarks, words, and cartoons for her political opponents. One must consider inadmissible to promulgate this stuff within any civilized discourse at all including the political Web.

As for links investigating their qualitative research shows that American visitors must be informed beforehand about the running of Political Office. There is a vast number of links to press releases, constituents' services, state problems and concerns, legislation issues, and so forth. Their primary goal is to direct to the required recourses not to interpret or clarify them. The data posted on the Web is located usually without any interpretation, background description, editorial input, or legislator commentary. This research confirms almost the study by Jarvis and Wilkerson (2005) arguing that all information located on the political congressional homepages "is not anchored by an authorial voice…the information presented is more meaningful for visitors who already have a through understanding of current events, the duties of federal government, and the organization of the House of Representatives" (Jarvis & Wilkerson, 2005, p. 12).

Figure 2. Congressman Chris Cannon's site working only for advanced users

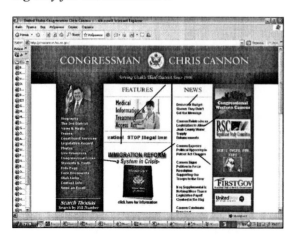

The Ukrainian political Web is more arranged and prepared for fresh netizens (*newbies*) and inexperienced users. It looks *interpretative* and *user-friendly* as mentioned earlier. The low level of IT development in Ukraine stipulates partly these results.

The study reveals that both American male and female sites are more colorful and imagery diverse than the Ukrainian ones. On almost every site, there are many pictures of local geography, slides of the representative's state and U.S. sightseeing generally. On these sites, cutting edge multimedia opportunities (streaming video and audio) are realized to a large extent, which is probably explained by the leading position of this country in IT and digital technology.

As for color design, Ukrainian sites are more laconic and reserved in their sense. Ukrainian male sites are presented mainly in *blue* and *gray* shades. Female sites' palette includes such colors like *pink, gray, yellow,* and *blue*. These data are in conflict also with the HC/LC theory of Web-design mentioned earlier (Pauwels, 2005).

With regard to language, all sites are primarily written in state languages (80%). However, if the site is hosted in Ukraine, the issue of local context arises immediately. Usually those sites are bi- and/or trilingual (the state language along with Russian and/or English). However, one faces the situation that two language versions of sites are only declared on the home page and in reality (even in virtual) only one version is located on the Web (see Natalija Vitrenko's or Olexandr Moroz's sites). Sometimes there are a lot of differences between the versions written in the state language and in English (see Raisa Bogatyriova's site). The English version is not also such frequently updated as the Ukrainian. The sites by American politics from my research sample (with the exception by Hillary Clinton's and Nancy Pelosi's sites (they are in English and Spanish)) are written only in English demonstrating again the global, all-permitting nature of the English language, especially on the Web.

Concerning the linguistic peculiarities of the sites, currently researchers more and more frequently emphasize a consolidating role of pronouns in the language system and speak about global meaning they express "pronouns are notions about time, space, creature, subject, phenomenon… about elementary bounds and relationships between the realities of the world and its knowledge" (Shvedova, 1998, p.45). Analyzing American and Ukrainian political sites, one notices that the owners of Ukrainian sites are represented by a deictic sign, expressed by a personal pronoun *we (us)* or possessive pronoun *our*, whereas creators of American sites use a personal pronoun *I (me, my)* with the same aim. "I'm committed to looking out for your day-to-day needs" (Barbara Mikulski's site). "I am able to provide assistance to you… If you have had a problem and have not successful resolving it through normal channels, my staff and I would be pleased to see if we can be of any assistance" (Hillary Clinton's site). "I hope you will find it very useful for you" (Steve Pearce's site). Using a personal pronoun *I (my, me)* emphasizes personal nature and individualistic essence brightly expressed in American LC culture. The pronoun *we*, to the contrary, expresses a sense of participation and community. The politician associates himself directly with community or society and identifies interests and views with the interest of the whole nation. It can be regarded as the heritage of the Soviet past. Moreover, using a deictic pronoun *we* in *promising sentences* contributes to creating future prospect. "All of us know what we should expect" (Stepan Chmara's site). "We must give results without waiting for elections and changes of power structures" (Julija Tymoshenko's site). These findings go in line with the idea of HC and LC cultures manifested through the Web and confirmed by Atabekova's comparative research (2003).

Research of political personal pages reveals the existence of recurring texts on Web pages of Ukrainian politicians. Their usage is not acciden-

tal but a stable feature of e-language of politics. These statements have authority over the people, and their usage actualizes concepts having social significance and importance for site visitors: *duty, justice,trust*. The recurring texts are met mainly on Ukrainian sites and absolutely missed on the American Web. It can be attributed to the collectivistic HC Slavonic culture. The Luydmila Suprun's site even maintains the specially organized questionnaire about the level of trust in certain political leaders.

The Intersection of Gender and Culture

Usually political male sites contain thematic blocks covering global political events, demonstrating main principles of their owners' political platforms, hot topics and publications, interviews, and so forth. All bio information, descriptions of activities, speeches on male sites, are arranged to the principle "promoted the boss." It manifests more brightly on the U.S. Web. I suppose these featuring cues underscore the distance between the elected official and the visitor. All male biographies tend to focus on the accomplishments and professional success of members in very formalized ways. The site by Ukrainian Speaker Olexandr Moroz illustrates these findings rather precisely—only officially approved biography is located on it: there are no other rubrics at all on this page. All interaction elements supporting the feedback or reducing social distance between the Speaker and his audience are drastically missed on this page. It is the only site in Ukrainian sample containing its boss image against the Verkhovna Rada Building (Ukrainian Parliament). Visually this image layout emphasizes merely Moroz's position in political hierarchy and just deepens a huge social "gap" already existing between Speaker and his citizenry. In contrast to the Moroz's site the Pelosi's page covers a great variety of topics from *Personal Data* to *Health Care* and *Environment Issues* not to mention *News Room, Photo Gallery,* and *Audio/Video Postcards.* The

Figure 3. The start page of Olexandr Moroz's site during the political crisis escalation in Ukraine

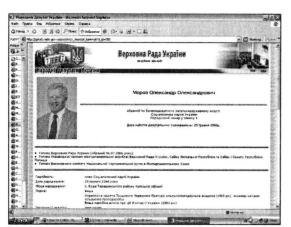

Figure 5. Kay Bailey Hutchison's and Earl Pomeroy's images against national American flag

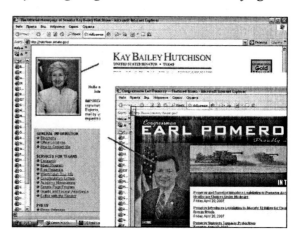

Olexandr Moroz's site demonstrates strongly the trappings of the office, signifying the position of the Speaker rather than his relationships with constituents. It is especially striking difference at the period of political crisis in Ukraine: The site of one of the key figures in this crisis is frozen, inactive, and silent.

This comparison between two sites shows clearly that culture may increase and strengthen or neutralize and diminish the gender performance on the Web.

The analysis of site owners' photos reveals both cultural and gender peculiarities in this type of imagery. The attributes of national and state identification are very persistent on the American

Figure 4. Barbara Mikulski's image against the capitol

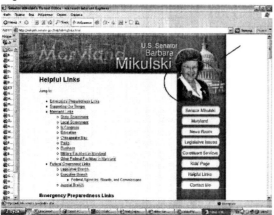

political Web. They provide the constant background for the images of site's owners.

The Ukrainian politWeb practically lacks this dimension with the exception of Olexander Moroz's site. As for female and male photos, almost all American male photos are suit-and-tie headshots in front of U.S. flags or the Capitol. One might consider that this tendency on American Web stresses more distance from their audience rather than a connection with.

All Ukrainian photos are less official and the female images are not so static and reserved. They are vivid, more colorful and emotional striving for the immersion of virtual visitors into the site virtual environment. As it appears these female photos are appealed to disclose the inner personal life of their owners to cut the social barriers between the site owner and its virtual audience. This feature is much more pronounced on the Ukrainian female Web. It can be explained by not only the gender, but also the impact of more HC local culture. Again one can mention that culture emphasizes gender meanings or blurs and even covers them in virtual reality quickly and effectively.

As for gendered style in CMC discourse, female sites, both Ukrainian and American, contain more polite expression confirming again the Lakoff highly criticized hypothesis about more polite women speech: "Thank you for visiting my online office. I appreciate your interest in the issues before the United States Senate. Please let me hear from you…" (Hillary Clinton's site). "Hello and welcome! I am pleased to make this Web site available for Texans and others interested in my activities as a U.S. Senator. I hope you find the Website helpful" (Kay Bailey Hutchinson's site). "Dear Visitors! I'm very glad to welcome you on the site. I'm sure that your decision to communicate with me online was not accidental. It's the evidence for me that you are not indifferent to this information and my work. Your friendly support is very important for me. Thank you for your trust! Yours faithfully, Lyudmila Suprun" (Lyudmila Suprun's site). However some American politicians also exploit very polite forms of expressions: "Thank you for visiting my online U.S. Senate office. It is an honor and privilege to represent you in the United States Senate. As your Senator, I want to be your voice in Washington, but first I need to hear your thoughts and concerns. So I hope that you will consider my U.S. Senate Web site your link to me and that you find it a useful tool to help me better serve you. Please visit often, since I will regularly post the most up-to-date Senate news and information on important events going on across the state. Here, you will also find information about the constituent services my office can provide. Again, thank you for visiting my online office. Sincerely," (Barack Obama's site). This tendency on the American male Web demonstrates again instable character of gender—gender-performance, gender-mask covering our virtual self.

This research does not fix any serious gender differences concerning links' number and usage as the previous studies declared (Goroshko, 2006; Miller & Mather, 1999). The inner links (inside the body of site) are prevailed over the outer links directing to other Web resources practically on all sample pages. All sample sites are updated on permanent base and rather regularly (it was traced on the fresh *Press-releases* or *News* rubrics with the indication of exact date and time). There are

neither cultural nor gender differences to these parameters on the political Web. Probably the cyber-political discourse might differ greatly from everyday life practices particularly to these dimensions but additional research is required to clarify this supposition.

Limitations

This research possesses a number of limitations. However, this is the size of the sample presenting the main one. Future research on gender influences in CMC may wish to adopt a different approach to understanding political Web. It may be useful to examine the impact of all aspects of identity formation (social background, ethnicity, age, etc.) in CMC through the use of more qualitative and quantitative approaches basing on ethnomethodology and statistics analysis' use. This may be the more effective way for understanding the complex processes underlying the formation or construction of virtual identities such as gender and culture in cyber-politics.

The research also reveals the longitudinal observations are required to examine more deeply the political Web. Thus the current results concerning the sites of Ukrainian politicians differ greatly from the results obtained by Kompanceva in 2004. According to her data male sites practically lack interactivity. Some key political figures haven't got any personal sites: "Hi, guys! Mr. Janukovich (recently elected Prime-Minister of Ukraine) doesn't have his personal site, does he?" (http://slavonic.ipt-elecom.net.ua/forum/messages.php?id=baz1830). There are no salutations on the male Web sites (Kompanceva, 2004). My findings received in a 3-year gap stand in sharp contrast to her data. The cyber-politics changes very quickly.

The results obtained over the sites written in the same languages (Russian and English) but hosted in different countries (Ukraine and the USA) do not go in line with Atabekova's declaration that English sites (hosted in UK) are more *interactive* and Russian pages (hosted in Russia) are more *informative* (2003, p. 177). According to my data, Ukrainian sites written in Russian are more interactive and American sites in English are more interpretive and gender only emphasizes this difference between two samples. This issue also requires additional observation concerning the influence of other factors on the political Web.

The CMC theory indicates that a growing body of research on political Web sites is being conducted in other countries but little of this adopts a comparative cross-cultural design covering a wide range of established and new appeared democracies. Further comparative and longitudinal investigations are needed (Norris, 2003, p. 25).

The conducted study shows that the Hall and Hofstede framework towards cultural analysis of CMC does not work effectively on the political Web providing rather discrepant, contradictory results, and resembles the naïve cultural simplification. Thus, this theory declares that HC cultures use more imagery and less text than LC cultures. This declaration absolutely runs counter with my results. This theory asserts that LC Web sites are more consistent in layout and use of color than HC Web sites, and images chosen for HC Web sites reflect HC cultural values (family, kids), while LC Web sites represent the individualistic values (personal hobbies, interests, leisure activity, etc.). The obtained results practically show the opposite: Ukrainian (HC) sites are more consistent in layout and reserved in color usage. Only the sites of American politicians (attributed as representatives of LC culture) maintain *Kids' Pages*, and so forth. It is just the linguistic design of homepages that confirms the idea about the existence of LC and HC cultures on the Web. Maybe through language practices LC and HC cultural ideas are more pronounced.

The descriptive character of studies also does not facilitate the more thorough understanding of cyber-politics, including the political Web pages. More research is needed to study not only the site structure and posted information, but also the use of sites by the electorate.

FUTURE TRENDS

The study clearly shows that the owners of virtual offices pay less attention to the visitor "*than other related forms of communication that aim to profit politically and economically by flattering the needs of the audience*" (Jarvis & Wilkerson, 2005, p. 10). Culture and gender can only emphasize or cover this arrangement. The homepage which is literally a visual model of political office with the primary aim of thinking about their people in virtual reality cares more about its owner, not the visitor.

After this research one question remains unanswered "How are we to facilitate the running of the virtual political office?" These findings reveal some weak points in virtual political office functioning and the problem is arising as to how to answer them.

One solution could be that male site-owners think more about narrowing the distance between their personae and the audience online and providing more networking through these sites. American homepages' designers, producers, and owners should think how to develop more user-friendly virtual surroundings not only for their clients but also for ordinary people without special training in political office functioning. The Ukrainian political Web needs to become more professional and socially and age sensitive to the everyday common people's problems and exploit more cutting-edge media opportunities provided by the Net.

Many CMC researches testify that the majority of site visitors mention the convenience of the Web, the ability to search new sources, and "*the fact that they could obtain information from the Web that was not available elsewhere, indicating that being able to give either their opinion, and the multimedia capabilities of the Net as factors in their decision to use it*" (Schneider, 2000, p. 2).

One more aspect of Web site research must be concentrated on the site producer since the Web site can be viewed from the triangular perspective: *owner—visitor—producer*. The factor of site producer who acts not only just a content-provider but primarily he acts as a Web architect and supervisor of all activities running through the site. He may play a definite role in the process of social meaning-making (as a gate-keeper or co-producer). *"He can be involved into the broader social and political infrastructure that surrounds the definite representational practices as well as technical standards and defaults"* as Pauwels asserts (Pauwels, 2005, p. 611). Viewing homepages as symbolic social texts and querying about their intended virtual audience and potential changes over times, genders, and cultures would allow to better interrogate these sites and gather insights as to their primary purposes how to communicate better through the Web and be more in line "with the potential of the medium to serve the online public" (Jarvis & Wilkerson, 2005, p. 19).

Deliberate political identity construction, articulary the virtual one trying to present very often the polished image of oneself, *"not telling a blatant lies but by offering a selective amount of data is a widespread practice in most forms of human exchange, only the means and degree may vary according to medium, purpose and circumstance"* (Pauwels, 2005, p. 609) and this research can add to this list two other words *country* and *gender*. The Web forms both a unique subject and tool for cultural and gender expressions and a more culturally and gendered focused analysis of a hybrid media as the Net is permits to become more culturally and gender *"savvy and expressive when using the Web as a tool to communicate their insights"* (Pauwels, 2005, p. 612).

However, the cyber-politics' perspective is in the hands of all political stakeholders who are to develop new ways to reinvigorate social capital through exploring new possibilities of super-highway environment that the Internet presents. *"Whether or not the promise of this new medium is fulfilled depends on access to the medium beyond the upscale citizens who predominantly use it"* as Kern argues (1997, p.1248) although many problems, of course, remain unresolved in this area and tendencies of this development are not predicted so easily.

CONCLUSION

The study shows that the female online identity appears more dispersed, individualistic, and akin to a collage, whereas, for males, greater homogeneity and integrity are noted. It also highlights the fixed notions of individual and group characteristics, including the gender ones.

The selective study of political personal Web pages provides a set of characteristics peculiar to the gendered CMC: judging from their personal Web pages, women appear to be more experienced and more skillful communicators than men. For example, women are more interested in feedback and networking whereas male communicative behavior concentrates more on self-presentation and promotion, that is, an original PR of themselves. Women are more inclined to employ an expressive way of information gathering and processing while men adopt a more instrumental approach towards information retrieving, which is useful for Web-design of sites and preparation of any kinds of advertisements. This research confirms the idea that boundaries between *private* and *public* are rather stable on the political Web and only the female political Web reveals more intensive blurring between the *private* and the *public* online.

There are a lot of factors influencing online identity. The theoretic approach towards viewing and analyzing of virtual identity as a product of intersectional interaction is very promising (Cranny-Francis et al., 2003). In essentialist notions of identity a regulatory normative force, even where the identity being addressed is not a socially influential one. Another important feature of postmodernist (*multiple, split, fractured*) identity relates to its political function, and is perhaps the way past the concern that postmodernist interrogations devalue shared experience and shared identity. "Postmodern culture with its *decentered subject* can be the space where ties are severed or it can provide the occasion for new and varied forms of bonding" (Hooks, 1990, p. 31). If identity is seen as *fluid*, rather than *fixed*, but as capable of points of (temporary or conditional) stasis, then the political force is not lost but enhanced. In the postmodern scenario, identity is not an essentialist attribute of an individual but a *strategy* which individual (complex, multiple) subject can use to create new and varied alliances and this strategy can be very well exploited for building virtual political personae on the Web. Rosi Braidotti, a famous feminist scholar, uses the notion of *nomad* to explore this strategic use of identity (Braidotti, 1994). The nomadic subject, says Braidotti, is fiction which enables her to think about and beyond well-known categories such as class, race, ethnicity, gender, age and so on, without being confined or limited by those categories. It enables to think of the individual subject in relation to many of these categories at once, even where they sometimes contradict. Braidotti argues about "blurring boundaries without burning bridges" (Braidotti, 1994, p. 4).

In 1990, Giddens declared that globalisation paradoxically carried with it a trend towards local concerns (Giddens, 1990). The global and the domestic, even the personal, are becoming intertwined. With Internet use rising, the domestic, private sphere becomes intimately connected with the global. As well as bringing the world of politics into the local virtual office, the play between the local and the global may accommodate also the play between the cultural and the gendered.

ACKNOWLEDGMENT

The author would like to thank Professor Jill M. Bystydzienski, Former Director, and Julie Snyder-Yuly, Program Coordinator, Women's Studies Program, Iowa State University, Ames, IA, USA, for drawing her attention to the study of American Political Office, and of her understanding of the American political system, gender, and cultural issues. Also she is deeply thankful to her colleague and member of Cross-Cultural and Modern Languages Department NTU "KhPI" Larisa Pavlova for her kind help in Internet research for this chapter.

REFERENCES

Atabekova, A. A. (2003). *Linguistic design of Web pages (comparative analysis in English and Russian).* Moscow, Russia: RUDN.

Barnes, S. B. (2003). *Computer-mediated communication: Human-to-human communication across the Internet.* Boston, MA: Pearson Education.

Bem, S. L. (1981). Gender schema theory: A cognitive account of sex typing. *Psychological Review, 13*(88), 354-364.

Braidotti, R. (1994). *Nomadic subjects: Embodiment and sexual difference in contemporary feminists theory.* New York: Columbia University Press.

Burnett, R., & Marshall, D. (2003). *Web theory: An introduction.* London, UK: Routledge.

Bykov, I. (2006). Internet-sait kak instrument politicheskoj kommunikacij *Kommunikacija i konstruirovan'je socialnykh realnostej.* Part 2. Saint-Petersburg, Russia: SpB SPU, 102-107.

Carpenter, J. L. (1998). *Building community in the virtual workplace.* Retrieved November 24, 2007, from http://cyberlaw.harvard.edu/fallsem98/final_papers/Carpenter

Chandler, D. (1998). *Personal home pages and the construction of identities on the Web.* Retrieved November 24, 2007, from http://www.aber.ac.uk/media/Documents/short/Webident.html_

Cranny-Francis, A., Warning, W., Stavropoulos, P. & Kirkby, J. (2003). *Gender studies: Terms and debates.* New York: Macmillan Palgrave.

Crystal, D. (2001). *Language and the Internet.* Cambridge, UK: Cambridge University Press.

Danet, B. (1998). Text as mask: Gender and identity on the Internet. In S.G. Jones (Ed.), *Cybersociety 2.0* (p. 102). Thousand Oaks, CA: Sage.

Danet, B., & Herring S. (Eds.). (2007). *The multilingual Internet: Language, culture, and communication online*. New York: Oxford University Press.

Dominick, J. (1999). Who do you think you are? Personal home pages and self-presentation on the World Wide Web. *Journalism and Mass Communication Quarterly, 76*(4), 646-658.

Doring, N. (2002). Personal home pages on the Web: A review of research. *Journal of Computer-Mediated Communication, 7*(3). Retrieved November 24, 2007, from http://jcmc.indiana.edu/vol7/issue3/doering.html

Dutton, W. (1999). *Society on the line*. New York: Oxford University Press.

Erickson, T. (1996). The world wide Web as social hypertext. *Communications of the ACM, 39*(1), 15-17.

Ess, C., & Sudweeks, F. (2005). Culture and computer-mediated communication: Toward new understandings. *Journal of CMC, 11*(1). Retrieved November 24, 2007, from http://www.jcmc.indiana.edu/vol11/issue1/ess.html

Gauntlett, D. (2000). *Web.studies: Rewriting media studies for the Digital Age*. London, UK: Arnold.

Global'naja statistika ukrainskogo Interneta (2006). Nojabr' 2006. Retrieved November 24, 2007, from http://www.sputnikmedia.net

Gorny, E. (2006). Russian LiveJournal: The impact of cultural identity on the development of virtual community. In H. Schmidt, K. Teubener & N. Konradova (Eds.), *Control + shift. Public and private usages of the Russian Internet* (pp. 73-90). Berlin, Germany: Norderstedt.

Goroshko, O. (2006). Netting gender. In H. Schmidt, K. Teubener & N. Konradova (Eds.), *Control + shift. Public and private usages of the Russian Internet* (pp. 106-119). Berlin, Germany: Norderstedt.

Haas, S. W., & Grams, E. S. (2000). Readers, authors and page structure: A discussion of four questions arising from a content analysis of Web pages. *Journal of the American Society for Information Science, 51*(2), 181-192.

Hall, E. T. (1976). *Beyond Culture*. New York: Random House.

Hofstede, G. (1980). *Culture's Consequences: International Differences in Work-Related Values*. Newbury Park, CA: Sage.

Hooks, B. (1990). *Yearning: Race, gender and cultural politics*. Boston: South End Press.

Jan'shin, P. V. (1996). *Emocional'nyjj cvet*, Samara, Russia: Izd-vo SamGPU.

Jarvis, S., & Wilkerson, K. (2005). Congress on the Internet: Messages on the homepages of the US House of Representatives, 1996 and 2001. *Journal of CMC, 10*(2). Retrieved November 24, 2007, from http://www.jcmc.indiana.edu/vol10/issue2/jarvis.html

Katz, J. E., & Rice, R. E. (2002a). Political involvement: Survey results. *Social Consequences of Internet Use* (pp. 135-151). London, UK: MIT.

Katz, J. E., & Rice R. E. (2002b). Interaction and expression: Self, identity, and homepages. *Social Consequences of Internet Use* (pp. 265-283). London, UK: MIT.

Kern, M. (1997). Social capital and citizen interpretation of political ads, news, and Web site information in the 1996 presidential election. *The American Behavioral Scientist, 40*(8), 1238-1249.

Klecina, I. S. (2004). *Psikhologija gendernykh otnoshenijj*, SPb, Russia: Aletejjja.

Kling, R. (1996). Social relationships in electronic forums: Hangouts, salons, workplaces and communities. *CMC Magazine.* Retrieved November 24, 2007, from http://www.december.com/cmc/mag/1996/jul/kling.html

Kompanceva, L. F. (2004). Diskurs-analiz ukrainskogo politicheskogo Interneta (gendernyi aspect). *Aktualnij problemy teorij kommunicaci,* Saint-Petersburg, Russia: SpB SPU, 112-134.

Miller, H. (1995). *The presentation of self in electronic life: Goffman on the Internet.* Retrieved November 24, 2007, from http://www.ntu.ac.uk/soc/psych/miller/goffman.htm

Miller, H., & Arnold, J. (2001). Breaking away from grounded identity? Women academics on the Web. *CyberPsychology & Behavior, 4*(1), 95-108.

Miller, H., & Mather, R. (1998). The presentation of self in WWW home pages. In *Proceedings of the IRISS'98 Conference,* Bristol, UK. Retrieved November 24, 2007, from http://ess.ntu.ac.uk/miller/cyberpsych/millmath.htm

Norris, P. (2003). Preaching to the converted? Pluralism, participation and party Websites. *Party Politics, 9*(1), 21-45.

Pauwels, L. (2005). Websites as visual and multimodal expressions: Opportunities and issues of online hybrid media research. *Media, Culture & Society, 27*(4), 604-613.

Petric, G. (2006). Conceptualizing and measuring the social uses of the Internet: The case of personal Web sites. *The Information Society, 22,* 291-301.

Prino, N. (2003). Gender digital divide. *Gender Issues in Information Society.* Paris, France: United Nations Educational, Scientific and Cultural Organization (UNESCO*).*

Rubio, S. (1996). *Home page. I am nobody.* Retrieved November 24, 2007, from http://www.hss.cmu.edu/bs/24/rubio.html

Schau, H. J., & Gilly, M. C. (2003). We are what we post? Self-presentation in personal Web space.

Journal of Consumer Research, 30, 385-404.

Schneider, M. S. (2000). Congressional candidate Web sites in Campaign 2000: What Web enthusiasts wanted what candidates provided. *NetElection.org. The Internet & Campaign 2000.* Retrieved November 24, 2007, from http://Net.election.org

Shvedova, N. U. (1998). *Mestoimenie i smysl.* Moscow, Russia: Nauka.

Slater, D. (2002). Social relationships and identity online and off-line. *Handbook of New Media: Social Shaping and Consequences of ICTs* (pp. 533-547). London, UK: Sage.

Steckler, N., & Cooper, N. (1980). Sex differences in color naming in unisex apparel. *Anthropological Linguistics, 22,* 371-373.

Vershinin, M. S. (2001). *Politicheskaja komunikacija v informacionnom obshchestve.* Moscow, Russia: Izd-vo Mikhailova.

Whillock, R. K. (1997). Cyber-politics. The online strategies of '96. *The American Behavioral Scientist, 40*(8), 1208-1225.

Winn, E., & Katz, J. E. (1997). Hyperbole over cyberspace: Self-presentation and social boundaries in Internet home pages and discourse. *Information Society, 13*(4), 297-327.

Wood, J. T. (2003). *Communication, hender and culture.* Canada: Thomson-Wadsworth.

Xenos, M. A., & Foot, K. A. (2005). Politics as usual, or politics unusual? Position taking and dialogue on campaign Websites in the 2002 U.S. elections. *Journal of Communication, 1*(3), 169-185.

Yates, S. J., & Perrone, J.L. (1998). Politics on the Web. In *Proceedings of the IRISS'98 Conference.* Bristol, UK. Retrieved November 24, 2007, from http://ess.ntu.ac.uk/miller/cyberpsych/millmath.htm

Yefetov, A. (2006). *Internet usage in Ukraine: UaNet audience survey.* Retrieved November 24, 2007, from http://www.internetworldstats.com

2004 Presidential Campaign Sites. (2005). Retrieved November 24, 2007, from http://www.politicalWeb.info/2004/2004.html

KEY TERMS

Computer-Mediated Communication (CMC): This is the term that describes popular applications of the network, including electronic mail, electronic bulletin boards, Web pages, and so forth. The CMC is the class of computer-based technologies to assist people in getting in touch with each other. In this chapter, I review how key political actors through their personal home pages use all possibilities provided by the net and how CMC has found its way into the political office routine activity.

Culture: This refers to the set of attitudes, values, beliefs, and behaviors that are shared by a group or people but that differ for every individual and that are communicated from one generation to another. Culture, like gender, affects virtually every aspects of life. A culture consists of structures and practices that uphold a particular social order by legitimizing certain values, expectations, meanings, and patterns of behavior. To explore this supposition, it is helpful to consider how culture creates and sustains more basic values, democracy, and then how culture upholds the gender practices (Wood, 2003, p.28).

Cyber-politics: This involves information dissemination, communication exchange, and the formation of electronic political coalitions across the Internet. This includes a variety of media including e-mail, Web pages, discussion groups, online databases and research, and online news.

Gender: This is rendered as social and cultural construct. Gender is viewed as a set of male and female behavioral and mental potentials that are shaped and developed by particular societies. Studying gender across cultures also allows us to appreciate and perhaps to refute arguments about the essential differences between women and men. At the same time, such comparative studies permit us to identify and celebrate any true universals about men and women.

Identity: This is rendered differently during the various historical periods. In premodern societies, an individual identity was fixed, solid, and stable. Identity was based on predefined social roles and traditional societal systems with established beliefs and behavior patterns. Identity was not a subject of reflection or negotiation. Identity theories traditionally assume a notion of identity as homogeneous and stable; however, postmodern identity is understood as a patchwork or pastiche of independent and partially contradictory subidentities, which are to be constructed anew in everyday identity work and related to one another to support a sense of coherence.

Intersectionality: This is a new approach in gender studies based on the supposition that gender lies on the crossroads of many social factors: power, class, race, nation, and so forth. It presents a conventional product stipulated greatly by these factors. Intersectionality is considered as a paradigmatic approach, especially applied to activism and social activities. It argues that the classical models of oppression within a society, such as those based on race/ethnicity, gender, religion, sexuality, class, disability, and other markers of difference do not act independently of one another. Instead, these forms of oppression interrelate, based on which markers apply to a given individual (and intersectionality derives its name from this intersection of forms of oppression). Intersectionality thus holds that knowing, for example, that a woman lives in a sexist society is insufficient information to describe her experience; instead, it is also necessary to know her race, her sexual orientation, her class, and so forth.

Personal Web page: This is defined in CMC theory as a Web site that is typically maintained by one individual or family or an organization (Dominick, 1999, p. 646). Personal home pages enable people to create their own content and distribute it on the net. Usually the start or the home page presents the first document that users encounter when entering the site. The home page orientates the user to the site, informs about its purpose, states what type of information can be obtained, and provides links to other relevant sites or documents.

Political Communication: Participating in the political process is a privilege of any democratic society. It is vital to maintaining a healthy democratic community. Central to political communication is political communication. It involves the public, the mass media, the government, and the interest groups providing the link among them. It initiates the models of relations between political institutions and individuals. The Internet makes it easier for people to communicate with their government representatives, politically organize, debate topics, and educate each other about political issues. In its turn, main political actors are able to communicate effectively through the Web with their citizenry. Thus the net provides a new communication channel for sending political message and receiving citizen feedback (Barnes, 2003, pp. 291-311).

Virtual workplace: This is a workplace that is not located in any one physical space. Rather, several workplaces are technologically connected (via the net) without regard to geographic boundaries. Employees are thus able to interact and work with one another in a collaborated environment regardless of where they are in the world. A virtual workplace decreases unnecessary costs by integrating technology processes, people processes, and online processes. In this chapter, personal pages of politics are rendered as peculiar virtual political offices for their owners providing great opportunities to communicate with their target audiences.

ENDNOTE

[1]   O. Goroshko obtained this information during her personal interview with the Head of Julia Tymoshenko's Personal Site Design Team.

APPENDIX A: LIST OF SAMPLE PAGES

Ukrainian Male Sites:	Title and URL	Position in Political Structure
1.	Viktor Medvedchuk—personaln'yj informacijnyj server http://www.medvedchuk.com.ua	Former Head of President Administration, Leader of
2.	Viktor Yanukovych. Personal'nyj infor-matsijnij server http://www.ya2006.com.ua/	Prime Minister of Ukraine, Leader of Party of Regions, opponent to the acting president of Ukraine
3.	Volodymyr Seminizhenko—personal'nyj sait http://www.semynozhenko.net	Former Vice Prime Minister of Ukraine. Since 1997 – Deputy Head of Committee of Science and Techniques of Ukraine, Advisor to the President
4.	Sait Oleksandra Moroza http://gska2.rada.gov.ua/pls/site/p_depu-tat_kerivnyk?d_id=381	Speaker of the Supreme Council of Ukraine
5.	Oficijnij sait Stepana Ilkovich Khmary, narodnogo deputata Ukrajny http://www.hmara.com.ua	People's Deputy from Our Ukraine Party (Nasha Ukraina) backed by President of Ukraine (former Head of this party)

Ukrainian Female Sites:	Title and URL	Position in Political Structure
1.	Oficijnij sait Raisy Bogatyriovojj http://www.bogatyrova.org.ua	Deputy Head of Party of Regions (Partija Regioniv)
2.	Inna Bogoslovskaja—personal'nyjj sait http://www.inna.com.ua	Head of Popular Assembly Party (Veche), former people's deputy
3.	Sait N. Vitrenko—lidera Progressivnoj socialisticheskoj partij Ukrainy http://www.vitrenko.org/	Head of Progressive Socialist Party of Ukraine, former people's deputy
4.	Personal'nyjj sait Julii Timoshenko http://ww2.tymoshenko.com.ua/eng	Leader of Opposition, Head of Our Motherland Party (Bat'kivshchina), Leader of Oppositional Block "B'UT"
5.	Suprun Ludmila Pavlivna Verkhovna Rada Ukrajny, narodnij deputat http://www.suprun.com.ua/	The president of the Ukrainian peace fund, vice speaker of "The Civil Parliament of women of Ukraine" and the president of the Figure-skating Federation of Ukraine. The head of the People's Democratic Party.

American Male Sites:	Title and URL	Position in Political Structure
1.	Edward Kennedy (D-MA) Elected 1962 http://kennedy.senate.gov/	Senator Edward M. Kennedy has represented Massachusetts in the United States Senate for 43 years, elected in 1962 to finish the final 2 years of the Senate term of his brother, Senator John F. Kennedy, who was elected President in 1960. Since then, Kennedy has been re-elected to 7 full terms, and is now the second most senior member of the Senate.
2.	Barack Obama (D-IL) Elected 2005 http://obama.senate.gov/	Nominee to the Presidency, United States Senator from Illinois. Barack Obama has dedicated his life to public service as a community organizer, civil rights attorney, and leader in the Illinois State Senate. Obama now continues his fight for working families following his recent election to the United States Senate.
3.	Chris Cannon (R-UT) Elected 1996 http://chriscannon.house.gov/	Chris Cannon was elected to Congress on November 5, 1996. Congressman Cannon was named Chairman of the House Judiciary Subcommittee on Commercial and Administrative Law at the beginning of the 108th Congress in January of 2003. He also serves on the Judiciary Subcommittee on Courts, the Internet, and Intellectual Property. Additionally, Congressman Cannon is a member of the House Government Reform Committee. He serves on the Subcommittees on Criminal Justice, Drug Policy, and Human Resources as well as Regulatory Affairs. Congressman Cannon is also a member of the House Resources Committee, serving on the Energy and Mineral Resources and Forests and Forest Health Subcommittees. In January of 2003, Congressman Cannon was elected chairman of the influential Western Caucus, an organization of over 50 Congressmen leading the debate for rational, balanced, and sound resource management.
4.	Steve Pearce (R-NM) http://pearce.house.gov/	Steven E. "Steve" Pearce (born August 24, 1947) has represented New Mexico's 2nd Congressional District (map) as a Republican in the United States House of Representatives since 2003. He is an Assistant Minority Whip. Steve is a leader on the House Natural Resources Committee where he is the Ranking Member on the Subcommittee on Energy and Mineral Resources and is a member of the Subcommittee on National Parks, Forests, and Public Lands. Steve also serves on the House Financial Services Committee, where he is the Deputy Ranking Member on the Subcommittee on Housing and Community Opportunity and is a member of the Subcommittee on Financial Institutions and Consumer Credit.
5.	Earl Pomeroy (D-ND) http://www.pomeroy.house.gov/	Earl Pomeroy was first elected in 1992 as North Dakota's only Member of the House of Representatives, and in the decade since then, has emerged in Congress as a substantive leader with common-sense solutions for everyday problems.

American Female Sites:	Title	Position in Political Structure
1.	Elizabeth Dole (R-NC) Elected 2003 http://dole.senate.gov/	Elizabeth Dole has had a remarkable public service career, serving five United States Presidents and winning 54% of the vote in November 2002 to serve the people of North Carolina in the United States Senate. She serves on the Senate Armed Services, Banking, Small Business, and Aging Committees.
2.	Barbara Mikulski (D-MD) Elected 2001 http://mikulski.senate.gov/	The people of Maryland elected Senator Barbara A. Mikulski to be their U.S. Senator because she's a fighter—looking out for the day-to-day needs of Marylanders and the long-range needs of the nation.
3.	Hillary Clinton (D-NY) Elected 2001 http://clinton.senate.gov/	Hillary Diane Rodham Clinton is the junior United States Senator from New York, and a member of the Democratic Party. She is married to Bill Clinton, the 42nd President of the United States, and was the First Lady of the United States from 1993 to 2001. She is a lawyer and a former First Lady of Arkansas. Clinton was elected to the United States Senate in 2000, becoming the first First Lady elected to public office and the first female senator to represent New York. She was re-elected in 2006. As senator, she sits on the Committee on Armed Services, the Committee on Environment and Public Works, the Committee on Health, Education, Labor, and Pensions, and the Special Committee on Aging.

4.	Kay Bailey Hutchison (R-TX) Elected 1993 http://hutchison.senate.gov/	In 1993, Texans elected Kay Bailey Hutchison to the United States Senate in a special election, making her the first, and to date, the only, woman elected to represent the state in the Senate. One year later, she was re-elected to a full 6-year term. And in 2000, more than four million Texans voted for her re-election to a second full term; no other Texas candidate has ever captured more votes. In 2006, she was again re-elected by an overwhelming margin. She serves in the Senate leadership, having been elected by her colleagues to be chairman of the Republican Policy Committee in the 110th Congress, making her the fourth-highest ranking Republican senator.
5.	Nansy Pelosi (D-) Elected 2006 http://www.speaker.gov	On January 4, Nancy Pelosi made history, breaking the marble ceiling to become the first woman to serve as Speaker of the United States House of Representatives. For the last four years, Nancy Pelosi has led House Democrats with remarkable effectiveness as House Democratic Leader. Elected in 2003 as the first woman to lead a major political party in Congress, Pelosi has built consensus and unified the Democratic caucus.

APPENDIX B: LIST OF RESEARCH OBJECTS

	Site Owner:
1.	Names of rubrics
2.	Their numbers
3.	The presence of forum, e-mail, guest-book, mailing list, blog, rant-page, navigational site search, and so forth.
4.	The ratio of text volume to the images' volume
5.	Number of images and their content
6.	Number of languages
7.	Color palette, number of basic colors
8.	The general site design
9.	The Number of inside links
10.	The Number of outside links
11.	The Presence of negative information
12.	Photos (number and quality) pictures of owner, party symbols and images, cultural and national symbolic presented on sites
13.	Informational content
14.	Presence of Multimedia
15.	Invitations to chat and forum, discussion list, appeals to visit this home page again, and so forth.
16.	Pronouns (number and character),
17.	The linguistic means of expressing politeness
18.	Number of verbs and their voice
19.	Number of exclamation and question marks
20.	UPL and Recent Update and its frequency
21.	Comments

Chapter XLVIII
The Benefits of Using Print-On-Demand or POD

Eric Franzén
CFA Institute, USA

ABSTRACT

The Internet and other new technologies have made possible an ever-growing availability of distribution channels. New paths are being blazed for independent book authors to reach readers and business models have been notably altered for traditional book publishers. Content creators of the past faced many obstacles in publishing hard copy books including lack of manufacturing knowledge, high production costs, and warehouse overheads. Only large publishers with demonstrated business plans could survive the marketplace to produce works at the quantities required to maintain viability. This is rapidly changing. Many companies are surfacing that offer Print-On-Demand (POD), a technology that allows a book to be produced in quantities as low as one book, and distributed only after the demand for that book has been proven (the book has already been sold). Because most content is already in digital form, it can be uploaded to vendors' Web sites, stored, and produced at will on digital printing devices (upgraded copiers). The companies then can bind and professionally finish the work before shipment to the buyer. Books can be listed on numerous Web sites and found by related topic area Web searches. Links to Amazon or a POD vendor's Web site can complete the transaction. The author simply takes his cut once demand has been shown. Not much knowledge is required of the mechanical process of producing the book, production costs are covered by the unit's sale, and there is no warehouse to stock. Independent authors, university presses, and commercial publishing houses all have new options and these options are proving valuable.

INTRODUCTION

The objective of this chapter is to demonstrate why content providers, either individual or corporate, will be required to use Print-On-Demand (POD) technology to survive in the publishing industry. POD will save time printing a book, offer certain financial benefits, and at the same time require little in the way of resources or industry knowledge. The POD process will be described which includes both a *virtual front-end* and a *digital back-end*. In the *virtual front-end*, content is uploaded, stored, and used to market the book on the Internet. In the *digital back-end* step, files stored in the front-end stage are used to directly create printed materials using digital printing devices, essentially high-end copiers. Independent authors, university presses, and commercial publishing houses all will be users of this technology. Advantages and disadvantages for each will be examined and the necessity for using POD demonstrated.

BACKGROUND

Nicholas Negroponte, best known as the founder and Chairman Emeritus of Massachusetts Institute of Technology's Media Lab, predicted in 1996 that in the future, content would flow more easily from creator to end consumer. He also argued that middlemen would be "disintermediated" in the process. Negroponte's prediction has proven accurate as evidenced by the digital music revolution (Negroponte, 1996). The consumer is able to acquire the desired content on demand and, in a lot of cases, directly from the artist. Technology revolutions in many other content industries are following the digital music's prototype. Movies are now available on-demand at movie rental stores and online "movies-on-demand" are now available from Amazon.com and other vendors. Television shows are also available for purchase on the Web without commercial interruption.

If this trend continues, written content will also be made more directly available to consumers as technology progresses. Traditional book publishers may soon lose the ability to select and bundle content in the traditional format of the printed book, which, over the centuries, has proven to make them the most money. Many in the publishing industry have worried that books will go the way of music and would be freely pirated on the Internet. More importantly, however, the vehicles for distributing new, original content in hard copy format could completely bypass the publishers (Pfund, 2002). After all, it was not long ago that printing methods were so cumbersome that only larger companies with substantial resources and knowledge of the publishing industry could create a book, print it, and offer it for sale. Printing small quantities of books was possible, but there were many limitations. With recent advances in publishing technologies, the situation has changed. Just about anyone with content can publish it in a variety of formats, including hard copy. Print-on-Demand services (POD) are constantly becoming cheaper and more efficient.

Traditional Publishing Methods

Economic forces used to encourage traditional publishers to manufacture as many copies of a book as possible to achieve better economies of scale and lower per-unit costs (Snow, 2001). A good portion of the cost in printing a book was in the setup stages of the press run. In conventional "offset" printing, negatives needed to be made to image large metal plates that were fastened to large printing devices filled with ink. Skilled laborers would make the press ready, and this process took a long time to unfold before ink actually hit the paper. Once printed, the pages were collated and fastened together. The more copies of a book a printer produced, the cheaper each copy became. Ink and paper were variable costs but other fixed costs needed to be stretched out to be covered by higher quantities. Graph 1 represents the quantity to cost curve in traditional publishing.

Graph 1.

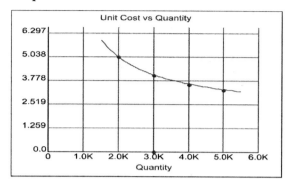

Until recently, the effects of this curve put the decision of what gets printed in the hands of publishers who had the resources and the expertise to manage the publishing process. If there was enough anticipated demand, publishers would splurge for the printing and marketing costs necessary to print the book and make a profit. Any books which did not sell enough copies were not reprinted, and their content was buried as "out of print," only to be available to consumers on the used market (Snow, 2001).

Once sold to distributors and wholesalers, books produced using this method took up shelf space and could sit for long periods of time depending on demand. Books lived inside the supply chain and carried their costs with them. If there were ever any problems with sales on the retail side, options for returns all the way back up the supply chain were available. Returns are a way of life in publishing and therefore books could live in perpetuity being sold and returned at will (Wallace, 2004). Returns put a lot of pressure on publishing houses to be shrewd in predicting demand.

Early efforts were made to try to alleviate some of the guess work. Printing only to match demand and even just-in-time inventory has been around for awhile. Publishers and authors alike sought to fight the traditional methods to be able to see what really would be in demand and sell but their efforts were not heavily rewarded. Digital reproduction offered one way to circum-

vent the large printing runs required from offset printing. However, digital printers were usually limited to books with few images and could not handle books full of pictures and illustrations, such as a book on architecture. Rapid changes in technology have helped but traditional printing is not going away, at least for now, experts say (Carnevale, 2005).

Early Print-On-Demand

Printing based on demand began in the 1990s. Initially, the technology suggested a potential revolution in the way books were produced. Customers could place an order for any title ever written and get a hard copy made especially for the buyer. "No title would ever be *out of print* again" (Wallace, 2004). Unfortunately, it was simply not profitable to produce one book at a time in response to *actual* demand so books were usually manufactured in small print runs. Even then, a sizable initial investment was still required. Many saw the movement as just another form of vanity publishing, a form of publishing in which a publishing house usually just takes your money for printing costs and does not help you sell any books (Hall). There was a stigma associated with these short run books, too. Often there was little regard to quality, design, or marketing and books were rarely found in customary bookstores (Wallace, 2004).

Sometimes new technology does not necessarily drive adoption of that technology. Thus has been the case with POD. The technology to digitally print books was available; however, the process change itself has been slow (Peck, 2007). Entrenched practices in the industry have simply not been completely altered yet. There are still those that frown upon books that are not "published" in the usual sense of having fixed print runs (a problem shared in a sense with electronic publishing, which does not involve physical copies at all) (Wallace, 2004). Some may see an opportunity here. The industry will eventually catch up with the technology. Recent activity suggests that POD is gaining momentum. Observation of the increasing comfort levels book readers have with online book ordering, payment, and online book repositories like Google Book Search should inspire further investigation (Neubauer, 2007).

PROGRESSION OF POD

Advancements in POD technology will mean different things to different users. Independent authors, university presses, and larger publishing houses will all have different motivations to use the technology in the marketplace. Independent authors will benefit from improvements in submission, marketing, digital storage, and printing quality. University presses will benefit slightly more from being able to store more content in a digital format for ready use in printing. Finally, commercial publishing houses will see most improvements in the quality of printing and binding finished works.

New Technologies

In his book *The Long Tail,* Chris Anderson argues that products that are in low demand or have low sales volume can collectively make up a market share that rivals or exceeds the relatively few current bestsellers and blockbusters, if the store or

distribution channel is large enough (Anderson, 2006). The Internet is such a large distribution channel that a lot of narrow or even obscure titles can be sold to relatively few customers and still be profitable. Book resellers such as Amazon have long realized this strategy to be successful demonstrated by their extraordinary collection of titles. While sales for any one title may be low, aggregate sales of all titles allow for profitability.

Many large distributors such as Amazon and Ingram (a large national distributor to major retailers) have bought or started their own POD companies which offer online transactions with publishers. Other POD sites have sprung up as well. These sites are fully automated and easy to use. The only costs for publishers are in digitizing content and administering the POD Web site transactions. The libraries become fully available in print format and the publishers do not have to carry inventory costs as once was a necessity.

The process, in which, publishers upload, store, and market can be referred to as the *virtual front-end.* This is where digital libraries are kept and all of the processes of getting the images ready to go on to paper are automated (see Figure 1). Lightning Source, a division of Ingram claims that 500,000 titles are housed in its digital library and that they have a customer base of more than 4,500 publishing partners, including booksellers (Jeffrey, 2007). This allows them to produce 1 million books every month (Peck, 2007).

Figure 1. Automated virtual front-end

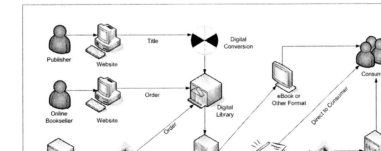

Virtual front-end solutions also include offering a selection of distribution models. Lightning Source's distribution models allow fulfillment in a number of ways including direct mail to the end user. They pay publishers for each book sold, less the cost of printing, and send detailed sales reports monthly to the publisher (Jeffrey, 2007). They are also able to use already established distribution channels allowing publishers to maintain presence in markets. This simplifies the logistics of ordering numerous books from a conventional printer, deciding how many to print, and arranging for shipment.

While many independent authors and academics can benefit from *virtual front-end* solutions, POD has opened up the door for traditional publishers, especially academic publishers, to republish many of their old works in low volumes, taking advantage of the Long tail curve of selling few books each of many titles. The big publishers and booksellers have also mastered the on-demand model. Many of them are quite secretive about how they are using it, but POD is working to their advantage (Jeffrey, 2007).

Improvements in the *digital back-end* have also made POD a more viable solution. The biggest improvements are in quality. The quality of books being produced now is better than it was 15 years ago when POD began. Other machine improvements have come in speed. Digital presses can now deliver quantities from 50 to 5,000 at economical speeds. Continuous paper feed copiers, as opposed to cut sheet copiers, aid in the alacrity. The sheets going through them are also wider, allowing more images to be produced at one time. However, the biggest improvements in the POD realm come with binding capabilities now available. Once, only flimsy bindings made sense at small quantities. Advances in adhesive binding have allowed for professionally bound books whether producing 1 book or 100. At Lightning Source, the average number of books per title printed is just 1.8 and they look like traditionally produced books (Jeffrey, 2007).

The *virtual front-end* and the *digital back-end* make POD accessible by independent authors, university presses, and commercial publishing houses alike. All can benefit from the advancements made. Some things still warrant caution, like the ability to reproduce certain graphics with many screens in them, but the technology is better than it ever has been.

POD for Independent Authors

In the past, authors who wanted to self publish could do so if they could maneuver through the expensive setup costs. There were basically two ways to self-publish: to start your own publishing company (requiring thousands of dollars) or to go through a vanity press (also requiring thousands of dollars) (Hall). Vanity presses received their name from the fact that most of the sales of their books were to the authors themselves or to their friends and family. Most of the time these outfits simply charged encouraged authors to print their books without ever offering any guidance in the way of sales or marketing. When sales did come about, the prospect of making any money was unrealistic. The offsetting costs of returns, warehousing, shipping, and the lost costs of money invested usually caused the project to become a money losing experience (Rosenthal, 2007). In effect, the printing part of the process was the easy part; the not so easy part was in selling the book (Spors, 2006). The result being that a small percentage of authors would ever get published and most of them that did were writing for narrow markets. These books would seldom be of interest to traditional publishers (Clopper, 2005).

New technologies in both the *virtual front-end* (transmittal, storage, setup, and online marketing) and on the *digital back-end* (improvement of digital print devices) now allow independent authors to print and distribute their works with a lot less initial investment. Online distribution channels offer consumers ways to find titles by keywords or topics and inexpensive online marketing tools like Google's Adwords program make it easier than ever for an author to get exposure and retain a good portion of any profit made on his work. Online bookstores like Amazon and Barnes & Noble also make it easy to list self-published books and special order with any online bookstore is possible using hyperlinks. Even if authors are unable to get a book physically stocked on bookstore shelves, the book can still sell. The author still needs to do his own marketing or pay someone else to market his product. This process can take a lot of time (Hall). However, any margins that once went to publishers now are directed to the bank accounts of the authors instead. Booksellers and readers both have greater choices of what to sell and read (Clopper, 2005)

Improvements in quality, ease of use, and considerably lower costs have led to an upswing in those designated "publishers." Bowker, the book number registry service, shows the number of publishers has swelled to over 78,000 through 2004, more than double the number two decades earlier (Clopper, 2005). Does this mean the authors are "published" in the traditional way? This is an issue being debated since being "published" used to carry with it a testament of validity. An editor at a publishing house had vetted several manuscripts and chosen just a few that were considered worthy of investment. In the new world of POD, there will likely be new indicators of success. If an author makes his books available for sale and there is significant demand, a publisher might see the consumer demand and rush to buy the rights for the book and publish it as a reprint. On the other hand, an author may feel his work is validated simply from selling 200 copies online. The classification of being "published" becomes indistinct.

University Presses and POD

Academics usually seek the reputation associated with being published by a university press. The approval of a manuscript signifies that their content is worthy of being produced at the university's expense. The printing of a scholar's book is sometimes thought of as the "gift economy" of the academic world. Thousands of hours of scholarly work are rewarded with self-effacing print runs, some reviews, and perhaps a shot at tenure. University presses, however, are businesses and thus are charged with selling the many different titles produced (Pfund, 2002). The high cost of printing a book used to require higher volume runs than the modest sales could cover. This conundrum forced many books to sit in warehouses while orders from libraries, facing budget constraints themselves, decreased (Peck, 2005).

POD has been used very effectively by university presses who embody the Long Tail theory put forward by Anderson (Anderson, 2006). University presses that use POD say it saves them tens to hundreds of thousands of dollars per year. University presses are quick to point out though that using on-demand printing is not a reason to publish books that otherwise would be rejected. The presses want to make sure they distinguish themselves from vanity publishers (Carnevale, 2005). The benefits are not necessarily in making money but in furthering reputation, sharing principles, and fulfilling a mission. At little cost, a lot of historical content can be made available worldwide, in print, to anyone who wishes to use it.

One of the most important advantages that POD offers university presses is in the *virtual front-end*. Data can be stored digitally, indefinitely, allowing for immediate reprints (Carnevale, 2005). University presses can make many books accessible, sell few of each title, and not have to maintain vast catalogs. Because of this, deep backlist titles have seen increases in print sales. Content is now obtainable by more people, in more formats, than ever before (Albanese, 2007). POD works particularly well with publishers who require certain economics to be in place before making content available. POD can make the entire library available at little to no risk.

Another advantage POD offers university presses is in the elimination of warehouse costs incurred. POD books are stored in digital format. This avoids overstocks of books that would otherwise be costly to house and further destroy. POD also avoids any inventory taxes and insurance required to store books and POD makes returns to a warehouse less likely. The demand for the books is already proven and does not have to be tested at the end of the supply chain.

Further, POD offers test marketing abilities where books can be tested for adoptability by professors and the like. POD offers the ability to regionalize content or even customize it for use by university classes since the chapters are all in digital format. If so desired, foreign language editions could be easily created without incurring large costs for each version offered.

Quality, while improving rapidly in POD, is best suited for university presses, too. Much of the research printed is text or line art which is better suited for the *digital back-end*. There are not as many screens or pictures which are often compromised by POD. Because many books at the university level are favored for their content rather than their formatting or marketing, quality is a little more forgivable. Plus, if demand is already present, the publisher knows that the content is what the buyer is after and does not require marketing aesthetics.

Distribution through the Internet is also an aid to university presses. Most buyers already know that the books are niche books and likely will use the Internet to search for the limited copies available. Researchers are most likely to be Internet-savvy as well since in all probability they do much of their research online. POD allows easy sales through online channels and has completely changed the topography of the academic-publishing supply diagram.

University presses face some disadvantages too when using POD. Other costs related to editing, formatting, and distribution are still required. These costs can still be substantial. University

presses also need to have the right people who know how to turn the content into the proper formats. POD systems also allow anyone to publish, which waters down the market. Vanity presses that have sprung up to print books with little or no editorial review worry some academic publishers (Carnevale, 2005). Finally, POD will not force university presses to market books heavily and drive up sales. The motivation caused by financial risk is no longer present. Authors who count on high print sales will not be compensated as well. Being able to use the content at will in multiple formats or over long periods of time will only benefit the university press and not the authors who may depend on print sales as a main source of income.

Many university presses are now using POD and reviews are mixed. Harvard University Press was one of the first academic publishers to use digital printing and John F. Walsh, assistant director of Harvard University Press has said that "in some ways it democratizes the whole publishing process" (Carnevale, 2005). This, no doubt, refers to the ability of anyone to publish who has the small sum required. The door has been opened to all kinds of content with little or no standards applied.

Jane Bunker, editor in chief at the State University of New York University Press, says they experienced a lot of trepidation about moving to POD. The biggest issue was quality and they were afraid of getting pages that looked like copier pages. They were pleasantly surprised to find that thanks to recent improvements in the technology, digital printing comes out nearly as crisp as a traditionally printed book. Eric Rohmann, director of sales for Princeton University Press believes quality is so good that the process is transparent to the consumer. It allowed them to immediately publish books (Carnevale, 2005). In research, sometimes speed to market is everything.

Cost savings and making money are also important to university presses. Doug Wilcoxen, inventory manager at the University of California

Press, states that the press earns an additional $250,000 per year by digitally reprinting 600 titles it could not make available otherwise Niko Pfund, Vice President and Publisher of Oxford University Press, believes Oxford has probably saved hundreds of thousands of dollars, too (Carnevale, 2005). Oxford University Press has been involved with Lightning Source Inc., a subsidiary of Ingram Industries, Inc., and made over 6,800 titles available for POD. They have digitized much of their old content and created a new separate department for POD believing it to be an effective way to distribute their content going forward. Sales for POD were over $3.5 million in 2007 (N. Pfund, personal communication, May 4, 2007).

Whatever changes lay ahead, publishers, particularly university presses, are unlikely to find themselves endangered and POD has most likely played a significant part in helping them to carry on. There are more benefits in using the technology than risks in its adoption.

Commercial Publishing Houses Use of POD

Many of the advantages and risks that apply to university presses also apply to publishers as well. Trade, professional, and commercial publishers are able to use POD to increase sales, save dollars on inventory, and eliminate out-of-stock and out-of-print situations. POD book manufacturing has a significantly lower amount of risk (Peck, 2007). Many commercial publishing houses are turning to POD. Large publishers now account for 63% of Lightning Source's business (Jeffrey, 2007). According to John Conley, vice president, publishing, Xerox Corp., Rochester, N.Y., "Digital is now part of the everyday platform and ... publishers' ... everyday decision process. We're starting up that curve" (Carnevale, 2005).

Many publishers are even buying their own digital equipment and setting up in-plants for actual production runs bringing the *digital back-end* in house (Carnevale, 2005). However, there is still

an effort to conceal that they are using digital technology and they use it as a supplemental method, not as their main means of printing books. Many argue that POD is not merely a different way to print a book—it changes everything to do with the book business (Clopper, 2005).

Some of the many advantages that POD offers publishers are the ability to:

- get a book to the marketplace quickly
- keep more books in print, including regional sellers;
- bring back out-of-print titles;
- test-market new titles;
- facilitate the market for foreign language publications;
- reach customers anywhere in the world;
- avoid costly overstocks;
- avoid warehousing expenses and inventory taxes; and
- be more cost-efficient than offset printing for many modest-selling titles.

Shorter runs also mean far less in the way of returns. Publishers can limit or even curtail the number of books returned by book stores using POD (Clopper, 2005). Returns are currently a way of doing business in the publishing industry and publishers get hit with huge costs of books that retailers and wholesalers down the supply chain could not sell. Typical return policy in the industry allows for open returns, meaning there is no time limit on when they are accepted.

POD is very well-suited for public domain titles, reference volumes, and other books whose warehousing expenses would make them impractical for traditional publishers to keep in print (Wallace, 2004). Books go out of print for the reason that generally only the feverish buying pace of a newly-published book can bring enough profit to make it worthwhile. After awhile publishers will allow the book to go out of print and remain out of print for 10 or 20 years so that a new base of readers can develop (Hall). If they used POD, they could manage supply and demand more efficiently, thereby reducing the costs of printing, inventory, shipping, and returns and thereby keep books in the marketplace (Carnevale, 2005). One publisher, Rowman & Littlefield, put more than 500 titles back into print and generated more than $1 million in revenue for books that would have otherwise been dead. "Digital printing on demand has allowed Rowman & Littlefield to capture revenue we used to walk away from due to the economies of traditional manufacturing," says James E. Lyons, Rowman & Littlefield president and publisher ("Turn End-of-Life Titles," 2004).

Challenges to using POD for commercial publishing usually relate in some way to cost-per-unit and quality which are apects of the *digital backend*. Per-unit production costs are often high. Many publishers and, more importantly, buyers believe the quality to look like Xeroxed copies where ink density is light or dark and pages are crooked. The quality of finishing is also in question. Many do not believe POD books can be bound to look like professionally printed books. POD books are rarely found on bookstore shelves. These press and postpress issues are being considerably improved every day. Digital printers now print books so well that if a consumer were to hold one up to one done on an offset press they would not be able to tell the difference (Carnevale, 2005).

Something to be considered with bringing back titles is rights management. Sometimes content that is reused may not be licensed for additional print runs. Publishers need to check permissions carefully or risk legal action. When one edition of a book is printed at larger volumes, it is much easier to make sure any required permissions are in order.

The benefits to publishers in using POD are many. Some risks still require attention. However, intense growth in technology is radically changing the industry. A report, "Trends in Print-On-Demand: A Transitional Technology Hits its Stride," published in late 2006 by book publishing software and solutions provider Vista International

(2006) predicts, "Those offering print-on-demand services should be in for a period of extremely rapid (and presumably profitable) growth" (Carnevale, 2005).

FUTURE TRENDS

A paradigm shift is taking place in the book publishing industry. POD is changing the way independent authors get materials to readers and ways in which publishers manufacture books. Publishers can save costs by using POD, and the current technology allows them to produce high-quality products. Even if publishers do not completely adopt the technology, they will continue to integrate and supplement traditional methods of printing with POD methods. Economic pressures will mandate that they consider these innovative processes.

The next steps in this evolution will be the availability of custom books. Digitization of the content in books allows for tagging material with metadata. Eventually, users will be able to produce hard copy books with chapters from many original works, all dealing with the same topic area. These books can be used by professors, seminar leaders, and businesses and will free them from the cost of having to buy many different books when they only need a portion of a book's content. The original books could be expensive when bought separately. Traditional high quantity print runs forced publishers to have higher costs which they passed on to consumers.

Niko Pfund, Vice President and Publisher of Oxford University Press, refers to the new ways content can be delivered as "format agnosticism." This means that content is now stored in ways that make it easily usable in many formats—print, online, audio. On April 12, 2006, Matthew Wayne Selznick was the first person to release an original fiction book titled "Brave Men Run - A Novel of the Sovereign Era" as a print publication, an e-book in five formats, an MP3 audio-book, and a free podcast ("Indie Author Releases Fiction," 2006). As Mr. Pfund has commented "more people can access your works in more ways from more places than ever before. And that does translate to dollars" (Albanese, 2007).

It is an exciting time if you are an author or publisher because the next generation of the Internet will be all about content and its availability. Content will be free of format and continue to fragment. The book as a vehicle of transmission is also fragmenting, but this can be seen as an opportunity for authors and publishers. Indeed, publishers will need to learn to multiformat their content but the book itself is not dying (Albanese, 2007). Last year's page count, approximately 20 billion book pages, is predicted to grow to approximately 38 billion book pages by 2009 (Beisser, 2007). The printed work also becomes better with advancements in technology.

Future research in the publishing industry will substantiate the growth of on-demand printing systems that work right in a bookstore at the moment of purchase. Machines exist today that take in a computer file on one end and create a finished book at the other end. Such machines will soon be found in bookstores (Clopper, 2005) Industry observers predict a significant number of bookstores may someday begin to produce books on-site in less than an hour (Snow, 2001).

Other research may focus on the environmental impacts of switching to systems that only produce books that are wanted. The Energy Information Association (EIA) says that the number one material that is thrown away in landfills is paper. For every 100 pounds of trash, 34 pounds are paper (http://www.epa.gov/epaoswer/non-hw/muncpl/pubs/msw06.pdf). Much of this paper is undoubtedly in the form of books that publishers cannot sell and therefore simply dump and write off as expenses. Many publishers may be environmentally conscious enough to at least recycle some of these but there is still waste. In addition, the energy required to make the materials and manufacture all of these books that are never used is wasted. As more and more small to mid-sized presses use POD to their advantage, especially when bringing back out-of-print titles and test marketing new releases, they will not only limit their financial risks but also minimize their environmental impact (Snow, 2001).

CONCLUSION

Independent authors as well as large publishing companies can use POD to save time printing books, reaping certain financial benefits, and at the same time requiring little in the way of resources or industry knowledge. Improvements in the *virtual front-end* technologies where content is uploaded, stored, and used to help in distribution make POD quite attractive. In addition, the advancements in the *digital back-end,* where the files stored are used to create printed books on digital printing devices, reduces many of the risks once associated with POD. For example, the risk that the book may be poorly reproduced or feebly bound together is being mitigated quickly. Although industry practices seem entrenched in traditional book manufacturing practices, POD is racing ahead. Eventually, the industry will catch up with the technology.

REFERENCES

Albanese, A. (2007, February 6). LJ talks to Niko Pfund. *Library Journal*. Retrieved November 25, 2007, from http://www.libraryjournal.com/index.asp?layout=articlePrint&articleid=CA6413419

Anderson, C. (2006). *The long tail: Why the future of business is selling less of more.* New York: Hyperion.

Beisser, P. (2007, February 1). Ready to print. *Book Business, 10*. Retrieved November 25, 2007, from http://www.bookbusinessmag.com/story/print.bsp?sid=45779&var=story

Carnevale, D. (2005, December 9). Books when you want them. *The Chronicle Review, 52*. Retrieved November 25, 2007, from http://chronicle.com/weekly/v52/i16/16a02701.htm

Clopper, L. (2005, August 1). Cavemen, Gutenberg and the "new" stone tablets. *Book Business, 8*. Retrieved November 25, 2007, from http://www.bookbusinessmag.com/story/print.bsp?sid=12224&var=story

Hall, J. (2007, November). *Self-publishing, POD technology and author mills.* Retrieved November 25, 2007, from http://www.jh-author.com/self-publish.htm

Indie author releases fiction title in multiple media. (2006, April 15). Retrieved November 25, 2007, from http://www.printondemand.com/MT/archives/008182.html

Jeffrey, N. (2007). Electrified book production. *Printing Impressions, 49*(10), 22-24.

Negroponte, N. (1996). *Being digital.* New York, NY: First Vintage Books.

Neubauer, B. (2007). An on-demand book boom? *In-Plant Graphics, 57*(1), 8.

Peck, G. A. (2007, February 1). An on-demand world. *Book Business, 10*. Retrieved November 25, 2006, from http://www.bookbusinessmag.com/story/print.bsp?sid=45795&var=story

Pfund, N. (2002, June 28). University presses aren't endangered. *The Chronicle Review, 48*. Retrieved November 25, 2007, from http://chronicle.com/free/v48/i42/42b00701.htm

Rosenthal, M. (2007). *Print on demand.* Retrieved November 25, 2007, from http://www.fonerbooks.com/pod.htm

Snow, D. O. (2001, January 1). Print-on-demand: The best bridge between new technologies and established markets. *BookTech.* Retrieved November 25, 2007, from http://www.bookbusinessmag.com/story/print.bsp?sid=45779&var=story

Spors, K. (2006, August 29). Small talk. *The Wall Street Journal*, p. B4.

Turn end-of-life titles into profit. (2004, August 1). Retrieved November 25, 2007, from http://www.bookbusinessmag.com/story/print.bsp?sid=12255&var=story

Vista International. (2006, November). *Trends in print-on-demand (POD): A transitional technology hits its stride.* Retrieved November 25, 2007, from http://www.vistacomp.com/about_us/Trends_in_POD_Research_by_VISTA.pdf

Wallace, S. (2004, March 10). Publishing in the future: The potential and reality of POD. *LOCUS online.* Retrieved November 25, 2007, from http://www.locusmag.com/2004/Features/03Wallace_PODEssay.html

KEY TERMS

Academic Publisher: A publisher created to produce academic works. Traditional methods of printing made low quantities unattractive so academic publishers formed as a means to concentrate content and back the costs for printing, which were often high.

Author: Someone who originates content and records it for use by others. Typically done for pay but also done for recognition. An author usually does not understand how to publish.

Backlist Titles: List of books that are still available from a publisher. Usually publishers do not hold many backlist titles in stock because they take up warehouse space and there is little demand for them. With print-on-demand, many titles can be held available without storing physical copies in a warehouse.

Digital Back-End: The physical process of creating an image on paper and the associated manufacturing required to turn it into book format.

Digital Printing: Process for printing that does not use a plate for printing but rather uses digital data to put an image on paper. Faster and less expensive, this process is almost always used in POD. Relatively new, the process is not as quality controlled as offset printing.

Disintermediated: A buzzword used to describe Internet-based businesses that use the Internet to sell products directly to customers instead of going through traditional retail channels. This eliminates the middleman and allows companies to sell their products cheaper and faster. Many people believe disintermediation is a driving force behind a revolution in how products are sold.

Distribution Channel: The route a product moves through to get from original creator to final consumer. The channel includes all of the intermediaries: distributor, wholesaler, and retailer, that move the product along through the process.

Distributor: An agent or business that buys books from a publisher to resell, at a higher cost, to wholesalers, retailers, or individuals. Distributors often have a financial incentive to actively market books and generate orders from buyers further down the supply chain.

Format Agnosticism: Content that is free of format discrimination. It can be used in print, online, or other formats without requiring manual manipulation. Print is considered just another vehicle for transmission. Publishing in the 21st Century is fragmenting, and content needs to be easily channeled into many formats. POD can be one such format.

Offset Printing: The most common commercial printing technology in use today. The process utilizes a lithographic plate to place ink on paper. A large part of production cost is in the time it takes to set up the press for work, making higher quantity production runs more cost efficient per unit.

Print-On-Demand: Referred to in the trade as POD, print-on-demand is the ability to short-run manufacture books or magazines in relatively low numbers, from one copy to many, to meet already proven demand.

Publishing House: Any of the large commercial publishers that purchase manuscripts through agents or from authors and then make all editorial decisions regarding content and style, pay all production and distribution costs to make it into a hard copy book, and own the copyright. Proceeds from sales of books go to the publisher, who then pays royalties to its authors if a contract warrants it.

Retailer: Sells books directly to end users. Often offers much in the way of utilities to the consumer, including online views of books, perusal in book stores, and easy return policies.

Self Publishing: Self publishing is when the creator of the content also publishes the content in book format. This includes designing the book, printing it, and marketing it.

Short Run Printing: Printing using offset printing or digital printing to produce quantities of books from very few to over 1,000. Content is usually the focus rather than form. Books produced in this fashion are much more expensive per unit and extremely complicated charts, graphs, screens, and colors raise the print costs exponentially.

University Press: A publisher owned and controlled by a university. Works produced are more likely to be scholarly in content. University presses are often used as vehicles for publishing research, and are more important for author recognition than mass sales. University print runs are much lower than consumer titles.

Vanity Press: A publisher that manufactures books only at the authors' expense. A vanity press' intended market is not a general audience but rather the author himself or his friends, thus, appealing to the author's vanity.

Virtual Front-End: The processes by which content is prepared for physical manufacture as well as the surrounding marketing activities that make it available and attractive to consumers.

Wholesaler: A company that buys books from distributors, usually in large volume, then sells them to bookstores or libraries. Because of long established return policies in the industry, the wholesaler can return large numbers of books at any time. This often results in wholesalers who just stock books for orders without actively selling any particular title.

Chapter XLIX
Difficulties in Accepting Telemedicine

María José Crisóstomo-Acevedo
Jerez Hospital, Spain

José Aurelio Medina-Garrido
University of Cadiz, Spain

ABSTRACT

Telemedicine requires a new type of worker: the health care teleworker. Nevertheless, physicians remain wary of adopting telemedicine. This work examines the sources of the resistance to incorporating telemedicine. We adopt a focus centering on the difficulties that human factors have in accepting the practice of telemedicine. Employees' resistance to change comes mainly from the inertia that perpetuates traditional routines and methods of working. The success of telemedicine projects will be determined by these human factors as well as by an adequate use of information technology and an appropriate organizational management. This work also offers some practical implications in human resource management for managers of telemedicine projects to consider.

INTRODUCTION

Information technology (IT) can improve aspects of both medical care and of the underlying administrative infrastructure. Thus, as in any other industry, we are seeing a proliferation of specialist applications and systems such as hospital information systems (HIS), medical decision support systems, interpretation of biomedical signals and medical images, integration of knowledge-based systems with HIS, and telemedicine.

Telemedicine enables the provision of health care services or the exchange of health care information across geographic, temporal, social, and cultural barriers (Chau & Hu, 2004). Telemedicine makes use of a wide range of technologies to overcome distances, such as radio, analog landlines, e-mail, the Internet, ISDN, satellites, telesensors, and so forth, for the transmission of medical information (data, voice, and video) and provision of medical services from a distance.

Thanks to telemedicine, health care centers can offer diverse specialty services to other centers, to other physicians, or directly to the patient, such as, for example, telecardiology, teledermatology, teleendoscopy, telemedicine, telemonitoring, telenursing, telepathology, teleradiology, and telesurgery (Tachakra, 2003).

The concept of telemedicine does not actually require the use of information technologies. Indeed, it was common in the past to exchange medical opinions and prescribe treatments using mail, the radio, or even visual signals. People living in remote areas of Australia at the beginning of the 20th Century used radio to communicate with the Royal Flying Doctor Service of Australia. At this time, physicians on dry land also used the radio to communicate with ships suffering from medical emergencies (Wootton, 2001). Some African villages used smoke signals to warn outsiders not to approach the village during an epidemic. Similarly, ships used flags to warn that they were in quarantine (Darkins & Cary, 2000). Nevertheless, modern IT has given new meaning to the practice of telemedicine (Bladwin, Clarke, & Jones, 2002).

Telemedicine requires a new type of worker: the health care teleworker. Indeed, telemedicine can be seen as a pioneering activity in the field of teleworking. But unlike in other types of telework, the human factor is much more important for the success of projects in telemedicine. Nevertheless, physicians remain wary of adopting telemedicine. Most experts agree that the major barriers to implementing telemedicine are known but that the solutions are complex and require cooperative efforts.

This chapter examines the sources of the resistance to incorporate telemedicine. We adopt a focus centering on the difficulties that human factors have in accepting the practice of telemedicine. Employees' resistance to change comes mainly from the inertia that perpetuates traditional routines and methods of working (Pardo & Martinez, 2003; Rumelt, 1995). The success of telemedicine projects will be determined by these human factors, as well as by an adequate use of IT and an appropriate organizational management (Bruque-Cámara, Vargas-Sánchez, & Hernández-Ortiz, 2004; Khatri, 2006; Melville, Kraemer & Gurbaxani, 2004; Powell & Dent-Micallef, 1997).

The rest of this chapter is organized as follows. The second section discusses the relationship between telemedicine and human resource management. The third section tries to identify the obstacles in the way of an adequate acceptance and development of telemedicine. This section also offers some practical implications in human resource management for managers of telemedicine projects to consider. Section four suggests some future research opportunities within the domain of the telemedicine and human resource management topics.

BACKGROUND

There has been a considerable amount of work on telemedicine in the scientific literature (Demiris & Tao, 2005; Roine, Ohinmaa, & Hailey, 2001), but academics have focused mainly on technical questions—to do with what technologies are available for the practice of telemedicine (Rao, 2001)—or on health care issues: to what medical fields telemedicine can be applied (Fishman, 1997; Tachakra, 2003).

Researchers have shown rather less interest, however, in questions concerning the organization and management in the adoption and implementation of telemedicine projects. In particular, few studies analyze the impact of telemedicine projects on the management of the human resources participating in such projects (Croteau & Vieru, 2002; Hu & Chau, 1999; Hu, Chau, Sheng, & Tam, 1999).

Health care staff's reluctance to accept the new technology or collaborate on it is one of the main causes of the failure of such projects, these professionals being the proposed end-users of the system (Gagnon, Lamothe, Fortin, & Cloutier, 2005). The rejection of telemedicine by the health care workers involved is often a result of the resistance to change generated by inertias in the existing organizational routines (Pardo & Martinez, 2003; Rumelt, 1995). These routines are threatened by the need to redefine traditional professional roles and by the professionals' loss of status, since IT blurs the functional and hierarchical boundaries in health care organizations (Aas, 2001; May, Gask, Atkinson, Ellis, Mair, & Esmail, 2001).

Apart from the problem of acceptance, there are problems due to the fact that the staff involved are not only teleworkers—their work is also based on the possession, application, and exchange of knowledge. In this sense, telemedicine collaborations can be mutually beneficial exchanges of knowledge to develop partner absorptive capacity and access to unique learning experiences and data (Robinson, Savage, & Campbell, 2003).

There is a common misconception that investing in IT leads to a reduction in costs and enhanced efficiency in the production or services delivered. This belief led to what some have called the productivity paradox, or technology paradox, whereby productivity is negatively associated with investment in IT. As in other sectors, investment in telemedicine and its advantages have been exaggerated. Clearly, not all investments in telemedicine projects satisfy initial expectations, and some even fail. Explanations for the productivity paradox include (Bruque & Medina, 2002): organizations need to learn how to use new technologies efficiently, which takes time; the strategic necessity hypothesis, whereby organizations invest in IT to match other companies competitively rather than to achieve advantages over them; savings in production and transaction costs are achieved, but they are outweighed by the investment made in IT; and when the social and technical systems do not have the same interests, format, or structure. With regard to the latter, a mere change in the information systems is not enough to change the culture of the organization. Technology cannot transform a company by its mere presence. The necessary transformation requires a fundamental change in habits, attitudes, values, expectations, and incentives relating to information management.

DIFFICULTIES IN ACCEPTING TELEMEDICINE

There is no doubt that telemedicine offers considerable advantages. Physicians can gain by accessing digital information that can help them in their diagnoses and treatments, as well as use the technology to exchange opinions with expert colleagues. Nevertheless, the use of telemedicine is advancing only slowly, and health care professionals have shown some reluctance to embrace it (Audet, Doty, Peugh, Shamasdin, Zpaert, & Schoenbaum, 2004; Parente, 2000; Sands, 2004; Wilson, 2005).

This section analyzes the main factors that may explain practitioners' resistance to accept telemedicine. The most important obstacles to the development of telemedicine are as follows: inertias in the existing organizational routines, problems inherent to telework, lack of time, opposition from professional organizations, limitations of the technologies, difficulty in using the technologies and understanding their utility, lack of training, and lack of trust.

The most common inertias, or obstacles to change, in the specific case of telemedicine projects, are those that arise either from the management of the telemedicine project or from organization members' resistance to change (Arjonilla-Domínguez & Medina-Garrido, 2002). Project managers may fail due to lack of leadership, lack of top management support, lack of adequate training, the failure to adapt the project to the organization's strategy or to the available organizational resources, or the failure to adapt the structure of the organization to the proposed changes.

Employees' resistance to change may be a result of their lack of participation in the project, the failure to consider their interests or needs, the fear that their jobs or status are under threat, lack of training and information, fear of uncertainty of what will happen when the new system is launched, the perception that change is unnecessary, the tendency to concentrate on short-run problems, the refusal to believe that past successes may end unless things change, group pressure on the individual to continue with what has been normal up to now, the risk of failure, the effort required when adopting something new, a lack of strategic vision throwing doubt on whether the right path has been taken, a lack of consensus with regard to the decisions taken, the difficulty in breaking with the established routines, and waiting for others to act so as not to run the risk of changing unilaterally.

The essence of telemedicine is to move the medical knowledge and experience rather than move the patient physically. For this, telemedicine involves rather more than just taking medical services to where they did not exist before. It has also become a practice of transmitting and handling knowledge. It enables medical practitioners to exchange their knowledge (Robinson et al., 2003) so that others can apply it in specific situations.

Health care professionals who practice telemedicine can therefore be said to be knowledge teleworkers. Nevertheless, the nature of the work of a knowledge worker is inconsistent with the flexibility associated with telework (Bentley & Yoong, 2000). In this respect, there are various problems with the development of telemedicine with regard to its consideration as telework (Arjonilla-Domínguez & Medina-Garrido, 2002):

- Telework is mainly an after-hours' activity, and thereby extends the normal working day (Bentley & Yoong, 2000). But this activity tends to be measured by results rather than by the time dedicated, so it frequently leads to overworking.
- The figure of teleworker is not as legislated in most countries as other contractual labor figures. This can generate some labor and economic insecurity, as well as fewer social security benefits.
- Teleworkers, depending on where they are located, can feel isolated from their firm or from their profession and may perceive a lack of status. Their location may often provide an inadequate working environment.

- Often, not of the technical resources necessary to do the work are available due to insufficient planning. A telemedicine project is often validated by implementing a small-scale pilot project, only for the full-scale project to be denied the equivalent resources when it is launched.
- Telemedicine teleworkers, being knowledge workers, can easily feel isolated, making it difficult for them to work in a team and resolve operational problems.

Some possible solutions to the above problems include:

- Establish areas and timetables requiring teleworkers' presence. Mix telework with presential work. Create telework centers and networks of teleworkers. Develop contact mechanisms (meetings, discussion forums, etc.).
- Offer clear contractual conditions, and conditions for promotion and training. Offer competitive economic incentives (Ahern, Kreslake, & Phalen, 2006).
- Offer continuing support from the firm, and provide the necessary resources.
- Communicate a feeling of being in a team, and develop group training.

In addition, these problems of health care teleworkers make it necessary to develop the right human resource policies to retain valuable personnel in the telemedicine projects. Such policies include notably: offer telemedicine as a flexible working environment, that is, as a chance to reconcile working life with family life; retain valuable personnel who wish to retire or work part time; offer recognition and status visible to others; and since the work processes are not always observable in telemedicine, it is useful to link incentives with the measurable results obtained (Ahern et al., 2006; Arjonilla-Domínguez & Medina-Garrido, 2002; Bentley & Yoong, 2000).

Physicians often argue that they do not have time to attend to patients remotely, as they are too busy with the consultations and medical services they provide to the patients who see them in person. This is a shortsighted view from the strategic perspective, since they would be able to attend to more patients if they saved time on traveling and if they automated medical services wherever possible. By using technology to automate existing routine tasks, performance can be optimized (Kirsch, 2002). Better efficiency is driven by better use of information, and this is where telemedicine can be utilized. In this respect, many of the services provided to patients are routine and repetitive, and by definition, are capable of being automated. For example, it is possible to automate the process of dispensing prescriptions to patients, if the physicians establish the treatment requiring them in the computer system, or if they have diagnosed a chronic illness. But automating this process would lead to a loss of power on the part of these professionals.

The power that professional colleges hold over health care professionals is well known. This is particularly true in the case of the medical colleges. Telemedicine projects need broad institutional support to gain legitimacy. This institutional environment is made up of the public authorities, legislators, labor unions, the population, and the above-mentioned professional colleges. Nevertheless, some medical colleges are drawing up ethical codes of conduct that make it difficult to do telemedicine properly. Such colleges have even criticized the practice of medicine realized exclusively by mail, telephone, radio, press, or the Internet (Ferrer-Roca, 2001).

One of the arguments used by the organizations of health care professionals to reject telemedicine concerns privacy. Although this is a legitimate concern, patient data can be more vulnerable in physical files in a medical filing room than in electronic records in a well-designed information system. Despite this, many interest groups resist change in the name of the right to privacy (Kirsch, 2002).

One of the most reasonable concerns of telemedicine professionals is the doubt about whether telemedicine can really substitute properly for face-to-face care. For example, in a videoconference-based telemedicine project involving Hope Hospital, in Salford (UK), and the University of Salford, nurses tried to monitor the neonatal intensive care unit from a distance. Many participants complained that the image quality made it impossible to detect the subtle color changes in the infants' pallor, and that the sound quality made it impossible to correctly hear their breathing (Qavi, Corley, & Kay, 2001). On the other hand, physicians' acceptance of telemedicine is strongly influenced by psychological and perceptual factors. Thus, physicians' acceptance of telemedicine depends on: their attitude towards the use of technologies in general, their previous experience in using technologies (Qavi et al., 2001), and their perception that the technologies are easy to use, and that they will prove useful in their work (Hu et al., 1999).

These psychological factors suggest some useful conclusions for the management of human resources in telemedicine projects. Managers need to cultivate a favorable attitude towards the general use of technologies among health care staff (Hu et al., 1999). To achieve this objective, the health care organization that is promoting the telemedicine project should communicate clearly and to all concerned the utility of the technologies in medical work. Technical and informational sessions need to be organized to communicate their utility for medical practice. It will not always be possible to reduce the perception that some technologies are difficult to use, but this problem can be alleviated through intensive training courses. To encourage acceptance of change, these courses should focus on how the new technologies can make patient care and the services provided to patients more efficient, rather than on how they should support the already existing organizational routines.

The need for training and preparation in the use of the technologies supporting telemedicine is not reflected in the syllabuses of university medical departments (Ferrer-Roca, 2001). This is why many health care professionals fail to see the connection between their work and the technical issues (use of applications and databases, electronic interchange of data and image files, standards to use, etc.) or legal issues (IT security, data protection and privacy, international practice of telemedicine, etc.) that concern telemedicine.

Trust plays a key role in all collaboration relationships (Gefen, 2000), and this is particularly true in virtual relationships. Telemedicine projects that do not inspire trust among the physicians do not tend to encourage team working (Paul & McDaniel, 2004). Nevertheless, telemedicine brings its own additional problems in creating and maintaining trust. This is because telemedicine involves the participation of multidisciplinary teams, and in virtual processes that are different from the ones health care professionals are used to. Launching a telemedicine project can also be seen as a threat—as the first step in the replacement of the health care professionals by other professionals delocated geographically, even in other countries.

From the practical perspective, managers need to foster confidence in the telemedicine projects they are implementing if they wish the professionals to work together successfully in teams (Paul & McDaniel, 2004). For this, they should be aware that telemedicine depends on a social context in which the professionals may be reluctant to work together and may distrust the management's intentions. The most practical way of improving this confidence is by training, information sessions and meetings involving the participating professionals. At the same time, the management of the health care institution needs to make it clear that the intention is not to substitute the staff participating in the project, and offer incentives (salary, social, status, professional, quality of working life, etc.) to the participants (Ahern et al., 2006). Managers also need to emphasize the professional advantages possible from using telemedicine, and the improved service quality it can provide.

The most significant advantages of telemedicine for health care professionals are (Robinson et al., 2003; Wilson, 2005): quick access to information anytime, anywhere; real-time access to specialty consultations; access to continuing training; platform for learning specific medical techniques; fast diffusion of information, knowledge, and skills; generation of professional contact networks, useful for collaboration in work and in research; better communication and coordination between physicians; specialist support for primary care physicians treating patients; less traveling and loss of time spent reaching remote areas, working in teams, receiving training or learning specific techniques, and so forth.

Health care professionals also need to be informed about the benefits telemedicine can bring to their patients. These benefits include: fast access to health care services; specialty care under the supervision, or not, of the family physician; freedom to choose or switch hospitals and physicians; staying close to home and to relatives whenever possible; convenience for the patient; continuous improvement in the health care services; more information about the illness suffered and the prescribed treatment; less traveling and concomitant time wasted; prescription of over-the-counter (OTC) medicines, and so forth.

Some authors ask why some companies encounter difficulties and yet others prosper when using the same IT, and why IT-based advantages dissipate so quickly. Their response is that integration should be produced between the IT, complementary human resources, and business capabilities (Bruque-Cámara et al., 2004; Khatri, 2006; Melville et al., 2004; Powell & Dent-Micallef, 1997). The integrated management of IT and complementary resources and capabilities can be regarded as the most feasible path towards attaining IT advantages. A list of these complementary resources and capabilities is shown in Table 1.

The benefits of IT lie in its capacity to free up information throughout the organization. An artificial culture or structural constraints devalue

Table 1. Complementary human resources and business capabilities (Source: Adapted from Powell and Dent-Micallef (1997))

Human resources	Business capabilities
• Open organization	• Strategic planning and IT
• Open Communication	• Relationship with suppliers
• Consensus	• Connect IT with suppliers
• Commitment of managers	• IT training
• Flexibility	• Redesigning processes
	• Orientation towards teamwork
	• Benchmarking

the technologies. The philosophy of having an open organization and an open communication permits access to operational information and promotes informal and frequent communication across functional and project boundaries.

Consensus is not necessarily always positive for performance in a technological project—a low level of conflict enriches and enables innovation—but a high level of conflict is dysfunctional. Consensus reinforces the capacity of IT to expand communications and disseminate information. Conflicts rooted in territorial disputes or between health care professionals frustrate this consensus and inhibit the functionality of the technologies.

Management commitment increases the success of telemedicine projects, making resources available for their implementation, integrating IT into the organization's strategies and processes, and ensuring that the investment in IT will continue over time.

Another requirement for the adequate implementation of a telemedicine project is organizational flexibility. Implementing a telemedicine project provokes significant changes in the organization's structure, communication models, and power relationships. But individuals tend to show resistance to change (Pardo & Martinez, 2003; Rumelt, 1995). This resistance is even stronger if the changes imply the need to acquire new knowledge or to modify work routines.

The management capabilities listed in Table 1 include the need to take investment decisions regarding the technologies for telemedicine that are consistent with the organization's strategic planning. The technologies used in telemedicine cannot be chosen to meet operational health care needs in an improvised way; they must be adequately planned. At the same time, managers need to integrate the choice of the most appropriate technologies for the telemedicine projects being implemented into the strategic planning of the entire organization.

The technologies used to connect with the health care service providers and suppliers, although not regarded as telemedicine, are contained within the concept of e-health. As in other industries, specific standards of electronic data interchange (EDI) systems are put in place to facilitate electronic interaction with the providers. But such a system is of little use unless there is a relationship of open communication and trust with the provider. Thus, connecting electronically with the providers should be preceded by the establishment of mutual trust that creates a favorable environment for making investments in specialist technologies. This trust is essential because these specialist investments cannot always be used for interchanges with other providers. All this, of course, does not preclude the necessary contractual guarantees.

Implementing any technology is sure to fail if the individuals that are to use it do not have sufficient technical training. But the majority of university courses in the health care area do not include this training in their syllabuses. Although extrapolating traditional health care practice to the electronic universe may seemingly be immediate, in fact this is generally not the case. Some authors estimate that it takes about 2 years for health care staff to be trained to use telemedicine properly in medical practice (Ferrer-Roca, 2001). They need to relearn how to manipulate and interpret patient information (for example, from their electronic medical records), images (such as radiographs, high-resolution medical images, computer tomography scans, magnetic resonance imaging pictures, ultrasound images, electrocardiograms or echocardiograms, video images of endoscopic cameras, etc.), or sounds (for example, from electronic stethoscopes) (Rao, 2001).

Supporters of process reengineering argue that the traditional functional structure of organizations can mask the best way of conducting some processes at work. The organization's management should not invest in IT that immortalizes its current processes, but should instead find a new, more rational design for the processes. Indeed, the access to information and the support IT provides to communication dissolve traditional hierarchical and departmental boundaries, and enable work processes crossing these boundaries to be designed. In the case of telemedicine, it is essential to design new processes that meet the technical and health care needs of each telemedicine service (telenursing, teleradiology, telepathology, teledermatology, telecardiology, telesurgery, etc.), eliminating or automating many of the bureaucratic and administrative activities that clog up the process without adding any value to the traditional health care services.

One of the most important uses of IT lies in the support it offers for working in teams. Technologies such as e-mail, voice mail, conference by computer and videoconference make it possible to coordinate the asynchronous and geographically-separated tasks that normally hinder team working. Telemedicine frequently implies that there is an exchange of health information, without personal contact, between two physicians. Thanks to telecommunications technologies, telemedicine enables the exchange of health care information across geographic, temporal, social, and cultural barriers (Chau & Hu, 2004).

In telemedicine, as in other innovative applications of IT, benchmarking the best practices of other health care organizations is a fundamental tool. This procedure allows managers to precisely evaluate the characteristics, functionalities, benefits, applications, and costs of the technology. All telemedicine projects should avoid the mistake of "reinventing the wheel." Thus, when planning the telemedicine project the strategic analysis stage should carry out an in-depth study of the characteristics of other, similar telemedicine projects carried out in other organizations and countries.

FUTURE TRENDS

Implementing and managing IT cannot be undertaken independently of the management of other elements in the organization. The human resources and business capabilities of the managers are two vital factors for the success of any technological project, and, by extension, of any telemedicine project. In this respect, managers of telemedicine projects would be recommended to develop human resource management practices centering on: (1) the existence of a fluid communication between technical staff and the management; (2) the absence of any organizational conflict; (3) flexibility in the procedures and decision-making; (4) the use of inter-departmental working groups; (5) the explicit leadership of the top management in the process of technological renovation; (6) the dedication of efforts in training for the new technologies; (7) an inclination towards change of the organization members; and (8) the fit between the technology used and the socio-economic system of the organization (Bruque-Cámara et al., 2004).

Future research should examine whether these human resource practices have the same positive impact on the performance of IT-based projects in the health care sector as in other industries. In this respect, some particular characteristics of health care professionals should be considered, such as their feeling of professional autonomy, perception of a high social and professional status, and strong professional corporatism, the existence of protocols and organizational work routines that are difficult to change, the fact that the results of the work are not always easily observable, and the possession of knowledge that is difficult to structure and automate.

CONCLUSION

Now in its early years, telemedicine will have to overcome the same legal, financial, personal, and cultural obstacles that have confronted every other technological change in the history of medicine (Jarudi, 2000).

In this chapter we have analyzed various factors leading health care staff to reject telemedicine. Chief among these have been the obstacles to change generated by inertias in the current organizational routines, problems inherent to their nature as teleworkers, the irrational excuse of lack of time, the influence of the professional organizations' opposition, the impossibility of these technologies substituting for personal contact with the patient, the perception of the ease of use and utility of the technologies to be applied, the lack of training and preparation in the use of the technologies, and problems of trust for working in virtual teams.

Analysis of these obstacles to acceptance allows us to offer some practical implications for managers of the human resources involved in telemedicine projects. They would be advised to promote the trust of the participants, inform professionals about the benefits of telemedicine both for the professional and for the patient, and correctly manage the complementary human resources and business capabilities of the managers.

Many authors have forecast the rapid diffusion of telemedicine for supporting health care services provision, but in fact the new markets being created by these technologies are growing very slowly, rather like the acceptance of such technologies by health care professionals. The first thing that really needs to be done to ensure that a telemedicine project will work—and be accepted by the health care staff—is to combine the real and current needs with user-friendly technologies, so that current processes can work better, more quickly, and more cheaply (Kirsch, 2002).

REFERENCES

Aas, I.H.M. (2001). A qualitative study of the organisational consequences of telemedicine. *Journal of Telemedicine and Telecare, 7*(1), 18-26.

Ahern, D.K., Kreslake, J.M., & Phalen, J.M. (2006). What is e-health: Perspectives on the evolution of e-health research. *Journal of Medical Internet Research, 8*(1), e4.

Arjonilla-Domínguez, S.J., & Medina-Garrido, J.A. (2002). *La gestión de los sistemas de información en la empresa.* Madrid, Spain: Pirámide.

Audet, A.M., Doty, M.M., Peugh, J., Shamasdin, J., Zapert, K., & Schoenbaum, S. (2004). Information technologies: When will they make it into physicians' black bags? *Medscape General Medicine, 6*(4), 2.

Bentley, K., & Yoong, P. (2000). Knowledge work and telework: An exploratory study. *Internet Research, 10*(4), 346.

Bladwin, L.P., Clarke, M., & Jones, R. (2002). Clinical ICT systems: Augmenting case management. *Journal of Management in Medicine, 16*(2/3), 188-198.

Bruque, S., & Medina, J.A. (2002). The technology paradox: Characteristics, causes and implications for information technology management. *International Journal of Information Technology, 8*(1), 75-94.

Bruque-Cámara, S., Vargas-Sánchez, A., & Hernández-Ortiz, M.J. (2004). Organizational determinants of IT adoption in the pharmaceutical distribution sector. *European Journal of Information Systems, 13*(2), 133.

Chau, P.Y.K., & Hu, P.J. (2004). Technology implementation for telemedicine programs. *Communications of the ACM, 47*(2), 87-92.

Croteau, A.M., & Vieru, D. (2002, January 7-10). Telemedicine adoption by different groups of physicians. In *Proceedings of the 35th Hawaii International Conference on System Sciences*, IEEE, Big Island, HI.

Darkins, A.W., & Cary, M.A. (2000). *Telemedicine and telehealth: Principles, policies, performance, and pitfalls*. New York: Springer Publishing.

Demiris, G., & Tao, D. (2005). An analysis of the specialized literature in the field of telemedicine. *Journal of Telemedicine and Telecare, 11*(6), 316-319.

Ferrer-Roca, O. (2001). *La Telemedicina: Situación Actual y Perspectivas*. Madrid, Spain: Fundación Retevisión.

Fishman, D.J. (1997). Telemedicine: Bringing the specialist to the patient. *Nursing Management, 28*(7), 30-32.

Gagnon, M.P., Lamothe, L., Fortin, J.P., & Cloutier, A. (2005). Telehealth adoption in hospitals: An organisational perspective. *Journal of Health Organization and Management, 19*(1), 32-56.

Gefen, D. (2000). E-commerce: The role of familiarity and trust. *Omega, 28*(6), 725-737.

Hu, P.J., & Chau, P.Y. (1999). Physician acceptance of telemedicine technology: An empirical investigation. *Topics in Health Information Management, 19*(2), 20-35.

Hu, P.J., Chau, P.Y., Sheng, O.L., & Tam, K.Y. (1999). Examining the technology acceptance model using physician acceptance of telemedicine technology. *Journal of Management Information Systems, 16*(2), 91-112.

Jarudi, L. (2000). Doctors without borders. *Harvard International Review, 22*(1), 36-39.

Khatri, N. (2006). Building IT capability in health care organizations. *Health Services Management Research, 19*(2), 73-79.

Kirsch, G. (2002). The business of e-health. *International Journal of Medical Marketing, 2*(2), 106-110.

May, C., Gask, L., Atkinson, T., Ellis, N., Mair, F., & Esmail, A. (2001). Resisting and promoting new technologies in clinical practice: The case study of telepsychiatry. *Social Science and Medicine, 52*(1), 1889-901.

Melville, N., Kraemer, K., & Gurbaxani, V. (2004). Review: Information technology and organizational performance: An integrative model of it business value. *MIS Quarterly, 28*(2), 283-322.

Pardo del Val, M., & Martinez Fuentes, C. (2003). Resistance to change: A literature review and empirical study. *Management Decision, 41*(1/2), 148-155.

Parente, S.T. (2000). Beyond the hype: A taxonomy of e-health business models. *Health Affairs, Chevy Chase, 19*(6), 89-102.

Paul, D.L., & McDaniel, R.R., Jr. (2004). A field study of the effect of interpersonal trust on virtual collaborative relationship performance. *MIS Quarterly, 28*(2), 183-227.

Powell, T.C., & Dent-Micallef, A. (1997). Information technology as competitive advantage: The role of human, business, and technology resources. *Strategic Management Journal, 18*(5), 375-405.

Qavi, T., Corley, L., & Kay, S. (2001). Nursing staff requirements for telemedicine in the neonatal intensive care unit. *Journal of End User Computing, 13*(3), 5-12.

Rao, S.S. (2001). Integrated health care and telemedicine. *Work Study, 50*(6/7), 222-228.

Robinson, D.F., Savage, G.T., & Campbell, K.S. (2003). Organizational learning, diffusion of innovation, and international collaboration in telemedicine. *Health Care Management Review, 28*(1), 68-92.

Roine, R., Ohinmaa, A., & Hailey, D. (2001). Assessing telemedicine: A systematic review of the literature. *Canadian Medical Association, 165*(6), 765-771.

Rumelt, R.P. (1995). Inertia and transformation. In C.A. Montgomery (Ed.), *Resource-based and evolutionary theories of the firm: Towards a synthesis* (pp. 101-132). Kluwer Academic Publishers.

Sands, D.Z. (2004). Help for physicians contemplating use of e-mail with patients. *Journal of the American Medical Informatics Association, 11*(4), 268-269.

Tachakra, S. (2003): Telemedicine and e-health. In *Business briefing: Global health care 2003.* World Medical Association.

Wilson, P. (2005, September). *My health/my e-health. Meeting the challenges of making e-health personal.* Paper pesented at ICLM9, Brazil

Wootton, R. (2001). Telemedicine. *British Medical Journal, 323,* 557-616.

KEY TERMS

E-Health: The provision of any health care service that is supported by electronic processes and communications.

Electronic Medical Records: Computer-based patient medical records. Patient medical records are a systematic documentation of a patient's medical history and care.

Over-the-Counter (OTC) Medicine: A medicine that can be bought without a doctor's prescription, such as some analgesics.

Telecardiology: The digital transmission between health care professionals of information relating to electrocardiograms, echocardiograms, angioplasty, and cardiac pacemaker monitoring.

Teledermatology: The digital transmission between health care professionals of images of the skin using a dermascope.

Teleendoscopy: The digital transmission between health care professionals of the results of endoscopic examinations.

Telemedicine: The use of information and communications technologies to exchange information between practitioners, or to deliver medical services to a patient remotely.

Telemonitoring: The remote monitoring of patients' state of health. It is fundamentally used to control and treat chronic patients.

Telenursing: Health care services provided by nurses remotely, such as monitoring patients in their homes or referring patients to the appropriate medical services through the processing of patient data.

Telepathology: The digital transmission between health care professionals of high-resolution images of, for example, microscope slides, photographs of injuries or smears, and so forth.

Teleradiology: The digital transmission between health care professionals of electronic radiology images such as X-rays, computerized axial tomography scans, or magnetic resonance images.

Telesurgery: Remote surgery using robotics and audio/video devices.

Virtual Health Care Teams: Teams made up of health care professionals that share information about patients electronically in order to improve their knowledge and decision-making.

Chapter L
Reconsidering the Lay-Expert Audience Divide

Michael J. Klein
James Madison University, USA

ABSTRACT

This chapter provides educators instructional methods for teaching audience analysis to students in professional writing courses. It argues that a rhetorical approach to the teaching of professional writing, focused on audience analysis, allows students to learn how to engage and become members of their audience's discourse community. This engagement allows the writer to better conceptualize the audience and their needs, facilitating improved communication practices. The author hopes that such an approach will prepare professional writers for their future careers, be it in a traditional or virtual workplace, by gaining a recognition of the different levels of expertise of audience members.

INTRODUCTION

Over the past decade, corporations have increasingly integrated aspects of the virtual workplace into their daily routines (St. Amant, 2002). Alford (1999) describes how ARC International, a company that provides trainers and consultants to the business community, went virtual by eliminating their headquarters. While doing so required the adoption of new technology, it also required the employees to reconceptualize the way the company did business. Changing from a brick-and-mortar company to a virtual company forced the employees of ARC to evaluate their strengths and weaknesses in doing business. The transition ARC underwent had as great an impact on the

cultural elements of their business as it had on the technological ones.

Aware of the way culture changes in a virtual environment, educators have adopted new methods of providing a virtual experience for their students. Carnegie (2003) used an assignment incorporating a virtual teaching environment in her traditional professional writing course. Students responded positively to the activity, but demonstrated stereotypical notions of the workplace before engaging in the online environment (Carnegie, 2003, p. 60). Students felt that face-to-face meetings provided the best practice of interaction for employees. After participating in online discussions, the students had a better sense of what working a virtual environment entails, including "greater individual responsibility, motivation, and self-discipline" (Carnegie, 2003, p. 61).

Academia has also begun utilizing distance-education classes that take place in a completely virtual environment. Educators teaching in such environments have found that the culture of an online course evolves distinctly from that of a traditional course (Duin, 1998). The successful online course must make accommodations for the lack of face-to-face interaction by providing assignments that stimulate the creation of a sense of community amongst the participants (Klein, 2007).

In this chapter, I discuss the methods of taking a rhetorical approach to teaching audience to teachers and practitioners of professional writing. This approach introduces students to the norms and values of the discourse community for which they will be writing. Such an approach leads to better training for their students and colleagues in writing in virtual settings. This training promotes better job performance and allows for the creation of documentation suited to an evolving audience. I offer an example of how I teach audience in a professional writing class that takes into consideration the new technologies available and explores the ramifications this has on writers in the business community. I hope that this example will facilitate further conversations about training writers for their future careers in the workplace.

RHETORIC AND THE NEW MEDIA TECHNOLOGIES

The introduction of new media technologies into the workplace has occurred a number of times in recent decades. Halpern (1985) describes her surprise in learning that the "new" communication technologies of her time would lead her to focus her attention on something ancient, classical rhetoric. Halpern's (1985) essay, which deals with the requirements of students in learning to compose in the writing classroom, emphasizes the application of rhetorical theory to the teaching of writing:

My research showed the need for a rhetoric of electronic composing that emphasized planning (which I consider one aspect of rhetorical invention), arrangement, style, memory, and delivery.... Students who had not mastered these five arts in college would find it increasingly difficult to succeed in an electronic work environment, an environment dominated by written and oral communication. (p. 157)

Halpern (1985) rightly believes that while new technologies transform the workplace in which writers compose and edit, these technologies do not markedly change the *way* professional writers compose and edit. The technologies she describes—"audio mail, dictation systems, electronic mail, teleconferencing, and word processing"—seem rather mundane to us two decades later. However, they proved just as challenging to the previous generation of writers as the more recent "new communication technologies"—wikis, Weblogging, the World Wide Web, and wired networks of computers—challenged us (Bartell, 2002). We must step back and reflect upon the nature of writing and the teaching of writing with these new technologies in mind.

Just as Halpern (1985) looked toward classical rhetoric as a way to better teach and learn about writing for the workplace, I also turn to classical rhetoric to deal with the challenges—and untapped potential—of the changes taking place in the classroom and workplace. The need to focus writers and companies on the people they produce documentation for requires an adequate conveyance of information, especially complex and technical information, to a growing and diverse audience.

Such a notion reflects the findings in previous studies which noted that "at work, writers typically must address a variety of kinds of readers, not just one or two kinds" (Anderson, 1985, p. 56). To properly write to all of these audiences (the study continues), teachers of writing, especially nonacademic writing, must consider this variety of audiences when designing courses:

Teachers can gain important insights into ways to design their courses by learning the purposes writers at work try to achieve, the circumstances under which these writers write, the expectations and conventions that pertain to writers at work, the features that distinguish communications that succeed in that environment, and composing processes writers customarily rely on there. (Anderson, 1985, p. 75)

Teaching students proper techniques to assess audience and produce quality writing remains key to subsequent positive performance in the workplace. Especially now, writers in the workplace need to consider a broader and more diverse audience for most of the documentation and materials they produce.

RECOGNIZING THE NEED FOR RHETORIC

Individuals from both the academic and business communities have begun to recognize the role for rhetoric in training new professional writers. Spigelman and Grobman (2006) discuss their involvement in the creation of a professional writing program at their institution based on rhetorical theory and professional discourse (p. 49). Spigelman and Grobman's (2006) agreement with the belief that in the past, "technical writing programs have inadequately served their graduates and the technical and commercial fields in which they are employed" (p. 51), served as an impetuous for this combination. Technical writers traditionally only have a limited set of skills at their disposal, skills that may not translate easily to new situations. If writers receive training to write a letter but not instruction to address a rhetorical situation (including situation, audience, and purpose), then they will be limited to writing letters for very similar occasions. While students must understand the modes of a given discourse, they also need to understand the rhetorical significance of

different situations, situations that will inevitably arise when they write professionally.

Spigelman and Grobman (2006) chose rhetoric as a component of the new professional writing program to "instill in them [students] a sense of responsibility for the power and complexity of language in order to complicate their understanding of their future roles as professional writers" (p. 53). If teachers instruct students to rhetorically analyze a situation and then pick a form of communication appropriate to it, the students become far more flexible in dealing with a variety of writing circumstances. The business world, replete in shifting discourses across national borders and cultures, needs and values such a skill.

Reinsch and Turner (2006) of the McDonough School of Business at Georgetown University argue in a similar fashion for the need for rhetoric in education, but from a business rather than professional writing perspective. Reinsch and Turner (2006) recognize that "today's environment calls for us [business scholars and educators] to intensify our efforts to help students think rhetorically and understand business practitioners as rhetoricians" (p. 341). Such an action will help students to think more critically and be more aware of just how business shapes communities. Reinsch and Turner (2006) outline their beliefs about the need for the incorporation of rhetoric into the business curriculum:

Business communication pedagogy should focus, therefore, on helping students think more deeply and systematically about the opportunities and challenges offered in rhetorical situations that have been shaped by technology...and recognize that each rhetorical option helps shape a community. (p. 345)

Technology became a key component for their teaching because new technologies lead to new ways of doing things, not just doing things more efficiently (Reinsch & Turner, 2006, p. 342).

Of course, by understanding the communities they shape and interact with, business practitioners will understand just how a new technology functions or how it does not. Just because a new technology becomes available does not mean people should use it. Teaching students about the norms and values of a discourse community can help them assess how, when, and even if a community should or would employ a new technology.

RHETORICAL APPROACHES TO AUDIENCE

In looking to rhetoric to train professional writers for the workplace, I specifically focus on the need for teachers to emphasize audience in the classroom. Rhetoricians' examination of audience has a long tradition. Much of Book 2 of Aristotle's (1991) *On Rhetoric* (*Ars Rhetorica*) examines the audience in rhetorical situations. However, as Porter (1992) points out, Aristotle had a very limited view of audience. For Aristotle, audience existed outside the scope of the rhetorical discourse (Porter, 1992, p. 17). In other words, while a rhetorician might tailor a speech to a specific audience, the audience existed as something apart from the rhetorician. The rhetorician assumed the audience's ignorance of the topic and educated the audience by teaching them the "truth" about the subject. Only in the more philosophical method of debate called *dialectic* would the audience and speaker interact as equals.

To a certain extent, this concept of audience carried through to the 20th Century. While audience analysis has been an important part of rhetoric, only recently has such an analysis broken with the Aristotelian tradition. With the advent of poststructuralism, analysis of audience shifted from a passive to active element of the speaking/writing experience (p. 82). Accordingly, the writer does not so much write to an audience, but become a member of it through socialization (p. 115). Thus, the writer becomes aware of the norms and values of the discourse community and shares in them. Such a step becomes essential for the writer to effectively communicate with

members of that community.

While such norms do include items directly related to writing, norms not related to writing might also impart information to the writer, making her job easier to carry out. For example, certain members of a discourse community might be educated differently than others. While nurses, nursing assistants, physician assistants, and emergency medical technicians all serve as members of the medical field, their training varies. Thus, their knowledge of terms or procedures might differ. A writer would need to know that these differences exist (if not the nature of the differences), and adjust her writing depending on which specific audience she addresses.

Early researchers in nonacademic writing learned of the effects of norms on writers working within their community. In his essay on the social context of writing in the business community, Odell (1985) discusses surveys of analysts/writers he conducted. Odell's (1985, p. 252) data consisted of interviews he had with the analysts to determine their rationale for altering a specific piece of text and his findings concluded that:

The analysts in this study frequently referred to elements of the culture in which they worked. Specifically, they referred to:

- Widely shared attitudes or values...
- Prior actions or previously held attitudes.
- Ways in which the agency typically functioned.

The writers based more of their choices on the norms of their community they operated within than on the norms of their audience's community (which they did not even mention). While this would be understandable if their audience happened to be a member of their own community, it would be problematic if their audience came from a different community.

One needs to assess how much the norms of their environment affect the way writers compose texts. Certainly, they should not hold too much sway because their audience (especially in this new electronic age) will not be aware of the values (or necessarily share them). The use of new media technologies means that writer and audiences do not necessarily come from the same discourse communities; indeed, their aims/goals/values may be at cross-purposes.

PROBLEMS WITH ACCOMMODATION

Odell's (1985) research findings above reflect what may happen when science and technical writers write for the public or when writers in an institution write for an audience outside of their organization. In such cases, writers might consider those audiences unfamiliar with the information they transmitted; thus, they would label the audiences as lay, or amateur, in the field.

Rhetoricians of science first examined the way experts communicated scientific and technical information to a lay audience over 20 years ago. In one instance, Fahnestock (1986) looked at the way scientific "facts" change as they move from one genre of discourse to another (p. 277). Fahnestock explains the change as one in which the type of rhetorical discourse shifts. While scientific papers are forensic in nature, dealing with the impact of past events, "scientific accommodations [the transfer of information from expert to lay audiences] are overwhelmingly epideictic; their main purpose is to celebrate rather than validate" (Fahenstock, 1986, pp. 278-279). Clearly, a shift of this nature (from explanation to celebration) would have significant consequences for the character of the information transmitted to an audience.

Science writers use this celebratory tone, according to Fahnestock (1986), because they assume that lay audiences cannot recognize important or significant information on their own (p. 279). To better explain the subject to this "uninformed" audience, science writers appeal to audiences in one of two ways. The first uses deontological methods, whereby the writer attaches the scientific fact to some other significant event

("this is the greatest discovery since Einstein's Theory of Relativity"). The second utilizes teleological methods, whereby the writer links the discovery to potential future applications ("this new knowledge could lead to a breakthrough in cancer research") (Fahenstock, 1986, p. 279).

The shift in genre, thus, leads to a shift in information. Statements that would often be hedged by scientists with terms like "perhaps," "maybe," or "possibly," become much more certain in the journalists' writing (p. 279-280). This transformed information, now more definite and associated with significant events, sets up false expectations in the minds of the audience members (Ryan, 2005, p. 624). If the information turns out to be wrong, or the research does not prove to be as promising as the article had indicated, the audience might very well blame this inconsistency on the scientists themselves.

Subsequent examinations of science writing have identified further misconceptions, mostly due to the assumptions made by researchers in textual studies. The theory of the "dominant view" postulates that the transmittal of scientific information moves only from expert to lay audience and that audience members resemble a blank slate without prior scientific knowledge (Myers, 2003, p. 266). This, however, does not accurately represent the nature of a lay audience. Very often, individuals have knowledge about specialized fields. For example, when doctors first diagnosed AIDS and began research in earnest in the late 1980s and early 1990s, some people with AIDS informed themselves about the disease to engage in dialogue with scientists from the Centers for Disease Control and Prevention about research protocols for new AIDS drugs (Epstein, 1996). In this case, these individuals, while otherwise lay people about most medical matters, functioned as quasi-experts, if not outright experts, about certain aspects of AIDS and its treatment.

With the continuing fragmentation of disciplinary studies and the subsequent move towards interdisciplinary examinations of topics, the lay-expert divide becomes more blurred. The anatomist does not fully comprehend what the molecular biologist across the hall researches. Thus, the anatomist represents an amateur or lay audience member when discussing molecular biology. However, this should not suggest that the anatomist functions as a blank slate when it comes to other information they might share, such as adherence to the scientific method or basic biological information. At other times, the opposite may be true, and the molecular biologist might have a hard time understanding research and theories governing anatomical development in organisms.

In other words, we all transition between the roles of expert and amateur every day. Whether at home or in the workplace, we spend periods discussing and listening to familiar, unfamiliar, or even commonplace information. The boundaries between these states often change and become indefinable. The teacher must articulate this to the technical writing student as he or she trains to become a professional.

LEARNING TO ENGAGE THE DISCOURSE COMMUNITY

The broad field of medical writing encompasses many distinct types of writing: physicians' articles published in medical journals, scholarly books about the field, the notes taken down by a nurse or physician's assistant during a patient history, and a newsletter published by a hospital's communications department. While all these examples involve medical writing, they include very different writing styles and cover a wide range of writing genres.

In order to train professional writers to consider audience, I used an immersion method of teaching in a medical writing course at James Madison University in the spring semesters of 2005 and 2006. The course makes up part of the curriculum for the Bachelor's Degree in technical and scientific communication, with most students majoring in the field. Students demonstrated an

unfamiliarity with the medical community except for their role as patients. While most did not intend on becoming professional communicators in a medical-related field, a few did have that interest and subsequently participated in internships in medical writing.

Examining the Norms and Language of Medicine

I started the course with a discussion of the history of the field of medicine so that they could understand the norms and values of the field. The students read a history of medicine structured as a series of minibiographies of famous doctors such as Linaeus and Hippocrates (Nuland, 1988). While reading the text, discussion focused on the nature of medicine as an art or a science. At the end of this section of the course, I asked the students to submit a theory statement in which they argued for a definition of medicine, drawing upon readings and class discussion in justifying their positions. I did not want the students to come up with one definition but to start thinking about the various facets of knowledge medicine comprises.

In the second unit, I focused on the role language plays within the field of medicine using a text and film. The text (Hunter, 1991) examines how various documents (charts, reports, case narratives, etc.) function within the medical field and help produce and transmit knowledge. The film *Wit* (Nichols, 2001) deals with a professor of Renaissance literature dying of cancer and undergoing radical chemotherapy. The film highlights not only the role language plays in the field of medicine (such as when doctors examine the protagonist during grand rounds and she laments that one who has analyzed books for a living now displays her body like a book), but also the hierarchy that exists between physician, nurse, and patient.

The two initial course units served three purposes. First, they introduced the students to the field of medicine from a perspective beyond that of being a patient. Second, the readings and assignments exposed the students to the way practitioners used language within the field, including terms particular to the field. Finally, topics such as these provided students with a better understanding of the values of the medical community and the ways members of the community communicated amongst themselves and with patients. This examination often provided the students their first glimpse into the medical discourse community.

While many of these norms appear in the type of writing that occurs in medicine, other values outside of communication remain relevant when trying to write medical literature. For example, while reports written by doctors and nurses may contain a great deal of information, these medical personnel gather that information from patients as quickly as possible. Verbal interactions between patients and medical professionals transpire more succinctly than documents describing these interactions indicate. While medical practitioners value thoroughness in gathering patient information, they also value brevity in recording the information.

EXPLORING GENRES OF MEDICAL WRITING

After the students had examined the field as a whole, I needed to decide just what types of documents I should cover in the course, both as models and as topics for assignments. While my students would probably never be in the position to write a journal article for a medical journal or a scholarly work on the history of a disease, I thought it important to expose the students to these genres of medical writing. Such an introduction provided the students with a view of the field from a historical context so that they could see how the field developed and changed over time.

Thus, I asked my students to analyze an editorial published in *The New England Journal of Medicine*. I instructed them to determine the author's argument, analyze the way the author constructed the argument using the three types of persuasion—*logos* (logic), *pathos* (emotion), and *ethos* (character of the speaker)—and determine the author's intended audience for the piece given its rhetorical context (in this case, an editorial against human cloning).

In another assignment, students read a book about medicine and wrote an analysis of it. Again, they took a rhetorical approach in determining the argument the author laid out for the audience and analyzing the nature of the support the author utilized. Specifically, students focused on the use of primary and secondary sources as a means of justification for the author's perspective.

For a final project, the students created documents usually produced by professional writers in the medical field. Working in groups, students prepared a proposal for a community health project, researched and created materials for the project, and presented the work to the class at the end of the term. In some cases, they prepared this work specifically for use in the community. In other cases, they offered it to health care professionals for their potential use. The documents the students created included flyers, brochures, and Web sites, among others. A professional writer could potentially create all of these documents with their intended audience for each document being different subgroups within the community (at both the local and national levels).

Students' Response to the Course

Students generally reacted favorably to their experiences in the course, stating in course evaluations that they had learned a great deal and had a new view of medicine. More importantly, a few secured internships in medical writing, usually in writing for the communications department of a hospital. I view these as good results, especially given that most of the students indicated they had signed up for the course initially not because they wanted to learn about medical writing, but because they wanted to avoid taking another class offered that term.

In exposing students to the field of medicine through an examination of its history and its rituals, students better understood what the field valued in terms of communication and how writers communicated to a varied audience of clients. As individuals who had once been members of a lay medical audience (one with no knowledge of medicine outside of trips to the doctor), but who now had a better conception of the field, the students could appreciate the subtle distinction between expert and amateur. They translated this experience into the production of documents that did not insult their audience, but rather treated the audience members as individuals who needed accurate information about medical topics.

While this example dealt with the medical field, I believe that teachers can apply these lessons to other types of professional writing. Teachers should expose their students to a discourse community by providing them with a history and sense of values of a discipline before the students can start writing within that field. This will make it easier for the students to produce documents that both reflect the goals of the field in communicating information, while at the same time communicating that information in a clear and accurate fashion. The subsequent transition from lay to quasi-expert will be especially beneficial to the students so they can understand the needs of both the community producing the information and the communities receiving it. I envision an immersive technique such as this being especially valuable in courses teaching business and science writing to the professional writing student.

APPLICATION FOR THE BUSINESS COMMUNITY

Ultimately, a professional writing program turns the student technical writer into a working technical writer, both during the course of internships and finally through permanent employment. These new writers will need to adapt themselves to a professional writing community that will be using newly developed technologies to provide information to a variety of audiences. Writers trained to understand and address audience in a sophisticated way will be beneficial to the companies that employ them.

First, the writers' previous training will lead them to expect to learn the culture of the firm in which they work. While the students always encounter a bit of a learning curve, the new writing professionals will have already experienced this type of initiation a number of times before. This will make it easier for them to transition once again, leading to less time spent in training and more time spent working in their intended roles.

Second, these writers will be aware that audiences shift and change, especially in a world where information remains one click away via the Internet. Because of their training with a focus on audience, they will be able to transition amongst a company's audiences more readily, producing documents appropriate for each situation they encounter. This will lead to more efficiency on the part of the writer and less time their supervisor will need to edit and change their work.

Finally, the writers will be able to envision better and new ways of employing new technologies to communicate, both within, and outside of, the organization. Their previous training will have prepared them to integrate new technologies, when appropriate, into the creation and dissemination of information. Such a familiarity with technology will allow them to learn new technologies quicker and better.

As Halpern (1985) noted 20 years ago, the more technologies become commonplace in the workplace and the classroom, the more writing and speaking come together (p. 160). This becomes even more true today with the advent of technologies like instant messaging, which, though conducted by typing on a keyboard, resembles the spoken word more than the written. It makes sense to train the next generation of technical communicators to deal with the various modes of discourse available to them. An emphasis on audience provides one way of accomplishing this. In doing so, the technical communicators, the professional writing programs that train them, and the businesses that employ them will benefit.

REFERENCES

Alford, R. J. (1999, January). Getting real. *Training & Development, 53*(1), 34-44.

Anderson, P. V. (1985). What survey research tells us about writing at work. In L. Odell & D. Gaswami (Eds.) *Writing in nonacademic settings,* (pp. 3-83).

Aristotle. (1991). *On rhetoric: A theory of civic discourse* (G. A. Kennedy, Trans.). Oxford: Oxford University Press.

Bartell, S. (2002). Rhetorical shifts in author/audience roles on the world-wide Web. *Orange Journal, 2*(2). Retrieved November 26, 2007, from http://orange.eserver.org/issues/2-2/sbartell.htm

Carnegie, T. A. M. (2003). Teaching a critical understanding of virtual environments. *Business Communication Quarterly, 66*(4), 55-64.

Duin, A. H. (1998). The culture of distance education: Implementing an online graduate level course in audience analysis. *Technical communication quarterly, 7,* 365-388.

Epstein, S. (1996). *Impure science: AIDS, activism, and the politics of knowledge.* Berkeley, CA: University of California Press.

Fahnestock, J. (1986). Accommodating science: The rhetorical life of scientific facts. *Written Communication, 3,* 275-96.

Halpern, J. W. (1985). An electronic odyssey. In L. Odell & D. Gaswami (Eds.), *Writing in nonacademic settings* (pp. 157-201).

Hunter, K. M. (1991). *Doctor's stories: The narrative structure of medical knowledge.* Princeton, NJ: Princeton University Press.

Klein, M. J. (2007, March). *Online instruction: Creating student e-identity in an academic environment.* Paper presented at the Conference on College Composition and Communication Conference, New York, NY.

Myers, G. (2003). Discourse studies of scientific popularization: Questioning the boundaries. *Discourse Studies, 5,* 265-279.

Nichols, M. (2001). *Wit* [Motion Picture]. United States: HBO.

Nuland, S. B. (1988). *Doctors: The biography of medicine.* New York: Vintage.

Odell, L. (1985). Beyond the context: Relations between writing and social context. In L. Odell & D. Gaswami (Eds.), *Writing in nonacademic settings* (pp. 249-280).

Odell, L., & Gaswami, D. (Eds.). (1985). *Writing in nonacademic settings.* New York: Guilford.

Porter, J. E. (1992). *Audience and rhetoric: An archaeological composition of the discourse community.* Englewood Cliffs, NJ: Prentice Hall.

Reinsch, N. L., Jr., & Turner, J. W. (2006). Ari, R U there? Reorienting business communication for a technological era. *Journal of Business and Technical Communication, 20,* 339-356.

Ryan, C. (2005, July 10-13). *The ethical implications of accommodating audiences: Some lessons for engineers entering the workplace.* In Proceedings of the IEEE Professional Communication Conference, Limerick, Ireland (pp. 624-630). Piscataway, NJ: Institute of Electrical & Electronics Engineers, Inc.

Spigelman, C., & Grobman, L. (2006). Why we chose rhetoric: Necessity, ethics, and the (re)making of a professional writing program. *Journal of Business and Technical Communication, 20,* 48-64.

St.Amant, K. (2002). Integrating intercultural online learning experiences into the computer classroom. *Technical communication quarterly, 11,* 289-315.

KEY TERMS

Audience Analysis: The writer's determination of the intended or perceived audience.

Discourse Community: Individuals who use a particular form of communication that contributes to shared values.

Distance Education: The delivery of course materials in a virtual environment.

Rhetoric: The technique of persuasion through written or spoken language.

Scientific Accommodation: The transmission of scientific information from expert to nonexpert audiences.

Virtual Workplace: A workplace not located in a physical space.

Web Log: An electronic publication of thoughts and links whose entries appear in reverse chronological order (also known as a Blog).

Wiki: A collaborative technology for organizing Web site information.

Chapter LI
Rapid Virtual Enterprising to Manage Complex and High-Risk Assets

Jayantha P. Liyanage
University of Stavanger, Norway

ABSTRACT

Operational enterprising is gradually emerging as a new solution to manage offshore assets on the Norwegian Continental Shelf (NCS). This is seen as an inevitable step-change with respect to obvious commercial challenges in the immediate future, and thus has become an integral component in the new efficiency leap of oil and gas (O&G) production business. This rapid enterprising solution in principal is based on the use of advanced ICT solutions, and active integration of technical disciplines, experts, and organizations to establish Smart assets. This would eventually allow the offshore assets to be supported and managed on a 24/7 online real-time basis irrespective of the geographical location. It has already begun to break the conventional organizational barriers and has brought an explosive growth in the use of advanced technologies. Current rapid enterprising practice on NCS exemplifies the usability of robust technologies blended with innovative organizational solutions as new frontiers in search of commercial excellence.

INTRODUCTION

Decentralization of various business activities and the rapid growth in the use of advanced ICT solutions have perhaps induced the greatest commercial impact in the present industrial environment (Dyer, 2000; Hosni & Khalil, 2004; Lipnack & Stamps, 1997; Wang, Heng, & Chau, 2006). As the commercial operations around industrial assets get more decentralized the emergence of new organizational forms is inevitable compelling conventional organizations to reconsider their formal command-and-control based architecture. Subsequently, important dimensions that apply to business-to-business (B2B) transactions have also been taken up for continuous discussions and revisions. The current trend by far insists on smarter B2B solutions to manage business activities in a relatively more open commercial landscape where trust, relationships, equal opportunity partnerships, win-win solutions, and so forth, have a specific role play for sustainable competitive advantage. However, the need to open up the commercial landscape to enable joint efforts to realize a common objective has been challenged, on the other hand, by unknown risk factors. It implies that while traditional organizations are subjected to a wave of integration effort through some form of fusion of tasks and responsibilities, an acceptable level of security, reliability, dependability, and so forth, are also demanded within the new organizational models.

In the constant search for novel solutions, to retain commercially critical operations secure and intact, many organizations today are more and more inclined to enhance their technology-based capabilities. Among various forms of technologies available, integrated information platforms, Web-based networking solutions, mobile technologies (such as smart phones), portable video communication devices, and so forth, have already become the technologies of the decade. An effective and efficient use of them has a substantial potential to facilitate not only the establishment of new form of organizations but also to enhance connectivity and interactivity among those who are jointly engaged in managing commercial activities on a daily basis. In fact advanced online communication technologies (OCTs) have contributed much in setting a new basis and an informal standard for commercial operations allowing the gradual formation of a very dynamic virtual environment.

This chapter briefly elaborates on the rapid enterprising that is emerging on the Norwegian Continental Shelf (NCS) as a new organizational form to manage offshore oil and gas (O&G) production assets. Since it has been deemed as an integral and an inevitable component in the new efficiency leap, in the presence of new commercial risks yet with substantial value creation potential, the new setting has drawn Norwegian currency (NOK) billions of investments from Norwegian O&G industry for developmental work. It has already begun to break the conventional organizational barriers and has brought an explosive growth in the use of advanced ICT solutions, reflecting the usability of new frontiers in search of commercial excellence.

BACKGROUND

The report number 38 (2003-2004) to the Norwegian Parliament on the petroleum activities on the Norwegian Continental Shelf (NCS) directly addressed and underlined that there is a critical need for an immediate long-term development scenario to reduce the risk and to improve value creation. The main focus has been on reducing operating costs and improving recovery efficiency, and other simultaneous positive impacts, for instance on health and safety. Subsequently, NCS today has stepped into a completely new integrated scenario to manage offshore oil & gas (O&G) production assets. This new scenario is termed *Integrated E-Operations* (OLF, 2003), and is dedicated to establish *Smart offshore assets* based on advanced ICT solutions, technology-embedded support centres, integrated operational networks, and collaborative partnerships. The re-engineering process that has gradually gathered momentum, slowly commenced its early activities in the year 2005 and is expected to be in fully functional operational status towards 2015 or so.

Interestingly, in this context, it has become very clear that the conventional work practices, organizational forms, B2B operational landscape, and so forth, pose considerable challenges to the dedicated change process. However, at the same time, the organizational effects of new technologies have also been more apparent with explicit indications that formal boundaries and limits for interorganizational exchanges and transactions need to be re-evaluated for effective use of the potential presented particularly by the online communication and data management technologies (OCDMTs). In fact, this has induced a clear opportunity for O&G producers to capitalize on the new potential brought by the change processes for commercial advantage leaning towards an enterprising solution that is deemed critical for 24/7 online real-time operational mode (Liyanage, n.d.; Liyanage & Langeland, n.d.; Nathan, Dagestad, Lilleng, & Pedersen, 2006; Unneland & Hauser, 2005).

RAPID VIRTUAL ENTERPRISING IN NORTH SEA OFFSHORE ASSETS

Drivers of Change

Major changes within organizational environments, in most cases, need to be driven by commercial incentives of significant scale. The industry and the major actors need to be adequately convinced about the true need for change and that their following-up commitments have a clear business case towards its commercial advantage. There are also certain other cases where a step-change cannot be completely avoided due to specific situations that are of less or no control to the business in question. The present accelerated change within the O&G production business on NCS is in fact a combination of both, that is, indications of immediate threats in the near future that has shown some trends towards gradually declining commercial activity level, and O&G prospects that are left untapped and the remaining value creation potential of significant scale. The threats brought about by maturing assets ageing equipment were very clear in the first place. A good number of assets both in the North and Norwegian Seas have been reaching the maturity level in their life cycle raising some concerns about the higher probability for declining production from the Continental Shelf within the next 10-15 years. On the other hand, the volatile oil price has contributed substantially to a reduction in the activity level due to lack of investments for further development of existing assets or to find new prospects. Adding to the same situation has been the increased production costs due to inherent complexities and economical risks associated with O&G recovery from maturing assets. The O&G recovery efficiency has mostly been in a range of 30-35% of the production capacity. It implies that a substantial proportion of O&G prospects have mostly been left untapped due to technological challenges or economical risks. While the need for new solutions to increase the O&G recovery factor became very clear in 2003-2004, some innovative solutions were also deemed necessary to reduce capital expenditures and operational costs. Through a revision of current practices and assessment of technology-based options, it became very clear that the industry needs some restructuring challenging the conventional mode of operations. At the same time, the availability of advanced technologies has been catalytic and the major O&G producers have begun to incline more towards a search for integrated technology solutions as they map the future options for commercially feasible assets operation strategies.

Furthermore, the industry has not been so successful in attracting the talent of the new generation. This situation, in conjunction with the ageing workforce within organizational premises of O&G producers, has raised some early warnings regarding the growing competency gaps. Subsequently, the industry in general became aware that serious measures are necessary to make the O&G production an attractive business to work for, and at the same time major producers began to pay attention on various options to manage competency gaps. While experience and knowledge management gradually emerged as a strategic issue, there have been some additional concerns such as the need for more effective communication modules with, for instance, drilling service providers and external experts due to growing complexities in drilling activities, reservoir monitoring, data interpretation issues, and so forth. Simultaneously, better time, resources, and activity management methods drew major interests with a focus on making the operations more cost effective. Moreover, as the challenges and bottlenecks in the conventional operational practices became more and more convincing, issues pertaining to the traditional decision-making, work management, use of IT and data warehousing, supply chain issues, and so forth, have also been brought into discussions.

As the future challenges on NCS to O&G production activities became more and more clear, the industry-wide understanding about the timely need for a mass-scale re-engineering became a true strength. It does not imply that all the parties have equally agreed on specific set of implementation solutions, but that it is the right time to make a major change to the conventional mode and that it is absolutely necessary. Moreover, the accelerated growth in application technologies and their usability potential, commitments from sociopolitical sources such as Norwegian Oil Industry Association (OLF), growth in online application solutions, higher oil price, and so forth, brought additional positive impacts on the situation creating a fertile landscape to adapt some new thinking.

Enterprising Solution and Key Features

The enterprising task primarily involves opening up centralised conventional organizational boundaries within and without, and some initiatives to allow a strategic fusion between different technical processes and organizations; not only specific operational tasks and responsibilities that provide a basis for the fusion, but also data and work flow structures. The emerging enterprising solution on NCS, allows such a fusion primarily between offshore assets, onshore support system of the operator, and the external support environment. Figure 1 illustrates this basic organizational foundation of the enterprising termed "enterprising triangle."

Figure 1. The enterprising triangle on NCS

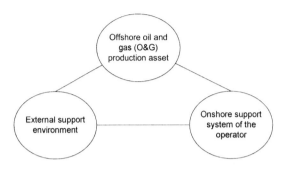

Table 1. Nature of technological setup in use for rapid enterprising task on NCS

There are dedicated centres equipped with large VDU terminals, smart boards, video conferencing facilities, CCTVs, and so forth. Furthermore, the offshore crew is also equipped with portable video communication devices to provide direct image access (DIA) to onshore experts. Diagnostic technologies (e.g., or vibration monitoring) have been installed in some of the critical equipment with real-time data acquisition and transfer capabilities to onshore expert centres. In addition to fixed-technologies, portable communication devices such as portable digital assistants (PDAs), smart phones, and so forth, are also gradually appearing as integral components of the operational workspace. Such robust ICT solutions not only provide the necessary technical infrastructure to support dynamism within the enterprise, but also provide the capabilities to establish a virtual environment within the commercial partners.

Furthermore, dynamism is a critical success issue for asset operations on NCS today for many underlying reasons, particularly inclusive of urgent and emergency response. In fact, the level of dynamism within a complex enterprise is dependent largely on the access to robust net-based ICT platforms. The need on NCS for such a solution is addressed by a specific networking solution termed "Secure Oil Information Link" (SOIL). Today, SOIL provides a high-secure, reliable application service with a higher bandwidth to more than 170 organizations involved in O&G business both in North and Norwegian Seas. It covers both Norwegian and UK Continental Shelves though its technical configuration built on a large fibre-optic network laid on the seabed, satellite communication facilities, and Web-based remote access solutions.

SOIL, together with other fixed and mobile ICT solutions, establish the legs of the triangle providing the support to enable authorised connectivity to different segments within the virtual enterprise. This is largely a matter of specific tasks and responsibilities assigned to each party (i.e., internal process owners or external organizations) involved and the nature of exchange and transaction activities.

Figure 2. The triple stages of rapid virtual enterprising' on NCS

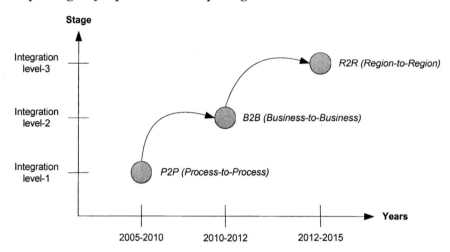

Each node of the triangle has its own data management and communication module with built-in state of the art technologies. A brief description of the technological setup that is used for enterprising efforts is given in Table 1.

The "rapid virtual enterprising" in principle involves a major effort for integration of technical processes and organizations. Given the complexity of this task, this is known to take a longer time-period, and at three separate levels, as shown in Figure 2.

In fact, parallel activities at each integration level is in progress to a certain extent, but the limitations imposed on the progress appears to be considerable if integration tasks at each level cannot be realized at least to a reasonable scale.

Functional Characteristics

The new enterprise setting, in fact, has already made a significant impact by redefining and re-engineering the conventional practices (Nathan et al., 2006; Unneland & Hauser, 2005). The most salient functional feature is the 24/7 online real-time capabilities to support and to manage offshore assets through a dynamic network of experts and organizations. Table 2 illustrates some of the specific functional characteristics of the new enterprising setting (also see Liyanage, Herbert, & Harestad, 2006).

Table 2. Some specific functional characteristics of the enterprising solution on NCS

• 24/7 connectivity and interactivity through tightly integrated offshore-onshore environment, technical disciplines, and organizations
• online and real-time collaborative activities with the knowledge industry by means of advanced ICT solutions
• ready access to skills, experience, and expertise based on systematic and strategic integration of onshore support environment independent of the location
• common data access, joint data interpretations, information and knowledge sharing, and agile response capabilities to specific needs
• joint pursuit of data-to-decisions and decisions-to-action processes
• virtual instructions based guidance to technical tasks and remote problem solving

In brief, ongoing developments mainly target a highly reliable enterprise that has dedicated experts and organizations where active information and knowledge sharing takes place between the nodes of the network. In addition to SOIL, the potential for the use of mobile communication devices allows quick expert localization capabilities with direct payback in terms of fast yet effective decisions and time-to-actions to manage offshore assets on an interactive basis. This implies an interdependent virtual workplace and a novel business practice realized by means of both physical and virtual configurations for commercial advantage.

FUTURE TRENDS

The progress of enterprising efforts has been quite slow during 2004-2006 time period, but now appears to be gradually gaining momentum. The re-engineering process on NCS relies largely on new forms of value-driven partnerships, B2B strategic cooperation, and integrated competencies to realize targeted commercial benefits. However, there are numerous organizational and technological challenges yet to overcome.

From a purely technological perspective, smart instruments with built-in self-assessment capabilities, electronic gadgets, equipment with advanced functional capabilities, 3D and simulation technologies, virtual training modules, and so forth, will have a larger impact on the immediate future. Also, the real-time usability of such smart devices as PDAs, Smart phones, RFIDs, and so forth, would also be improved in due time, enabling more effective localization of specific technical expertise to solve specific technical problems. Apart from various potentials that the current technologies are presented with, perhaps the biggest impact will occur in the use of cooperate networks. As the current digital infrastructure on NCS gradually grows in terms of number of organizations and dynamisms between authorised partners, the coverage and the accessibility features will be widened, raising some concerns on the systems vulnerability. Hence, much effort will have to be made to ensure security and safety around enterprise boundaries.

Developments within organizational structures, on the other hand, depend largely on the change absorption capacity of both internal and external organizational settings. Breaking the conventional organizational boundaries and extending it to allow strategic fusion still takes place at a slow pace, since one has to define and implement effective interfaces without inducing chaos or unwanted complexities. An integral component of organizational interfacing is also risk sharing formulae and incentives for resource commitments and improved performance.

The enterprising task, in fact, has already started to bring various forms of complex solutions and technologies into the operational landscape. An issue of major concern is that the increasing complexities may lead to unforeseen vulnerabilities with considerable loss potential. Thus the authorities such as Norwegian Petroleum Safety Authority and R&D institutions have paid much attention to the proper blend of human and organizational factors with the novel solutions. Much work in this particular area of interests has already begun to appear particularly from health, safety, and environmental perspectives (see, for instance, Liyanage & Bjerkebæk, 2007).

Given the nature and scale of innovative change processes, the ability of the sociotechnical system to adapt plays a very critical role. Organizations have to ensure that necessary internal mechanisms are there to facilitate effective change absorption capabilities and that the system's response is well below the acceptable risk levels. This implies that implementation of systems error preventing barriers, more support tools and techniques, and reliable mechanisms to ensure quality and standard of decisions and activities within the enterprise setting.

In fact, the results that have been achieved so far has also brought optimism to the industry, and various R&D efforts, new technology testing and implementation tasks, organizational development programs, regulatory revisions, and so forth, are in gear to achieve the fully integrated operational status by the year 2015 or so.

CONCLUSION

This chapter brought a brief overview on the *rapid virtual enterprising* effort around offshore O&G production assets that is central to establish Smart assets on NCS. This is emerging as an integrated solution to managing offshore O&G assets challenging the conventional organizational forms leading the O&G industry towards a new era with 24/7 real-time online connectivity and interactivity. In the new setting, effective technological and organizational interfacing is a critical issue to reduce vulnerabilities particularly owing to the sociotechnical complexity of the new business practice. Moreover, safety and security issues today have gathered attention due to organizational exposure through Web-based networking solutions that are under implementation. The progress so far has brought good optimism to achieve fully-functional *Integrated E-Operational* status during the targeted time period.

REFERENCES

Dyer, J.H. (2000). *Collaborative advantage: Winning through extended enterprise supplier networks.* Oxford University Press.

Hosni, Y.A., & Khalil, T.M. (Eds.) (2004). *Management of technology – Internet economy: Opportunties and challenges for developed and developing regions of the world.* Elsevier.

Lipnack, J., & Stamps, J. (1997). *Virtual teams: Reaching across space, time, and organizations with technology.* John Wiley & Sons.

Liyanage, J.P. (n.d.). Integrated e-operations-e-maintenance: Applications in North Sea offshore assets. In P. Murthy & K. Kobbacy (Ed.), *Complex systems maintenance.* Springer.

Liyanage, J.P., & Bjerkebæk, E., (2007). Key note paper: Use of advanced technologies and information solutions for North sea offshore assets: Ambitious changes and socio-technical dimensions. *Journal of International Technology and Information Management (JITIM) 15*(4), 1-10. International Information Management Association (IIMA).

Liyanage, J.P., & Langeland, T. (n.d.). Smart assets through digital capabilities. In M. Khosrow-Pour (Ed.), *Encyclopaedia of information science and technology (IST).* Idea Group, USA.

Liyanage, J.P., Herbert, M., & Harestad, J., (2006), Smart integrated e-operations for high-risk and technologically complex assets: Operational networks and collaborative partnerships in the digital environment. In Y.C. Wang et al., (Eds.), *Supply chain management: Issues in the new era of collaboration and competition* (pp. 387-414). Idea Group, USA.

Nathan, E., Dagestad, J.O., Lilleng, T., & Pedersen, T. (2006). *Proven commercial implementation of second-generation integrated remote drilling operations centre* (IADC/SPE paper number 99066). Retrieved November 26, 2007, from www.spe.org

OLF (Oljeindustriens landsforening/Norwegian Oil Industry Association). (2003). E-drift for norsk sokkel: Det tredje effektiviseringsspranget (E-operations in the Norwegian continental shelf: The third efficiency leap). Retrieved November 26, 2007, from www.olf.no.

Unneland, T., & Hauser, M. (2005). *Real-time asset management: From vision to engagement – an operator's experience* (SPE paper number 96390). Retrieved November 26, 2007, from www.spe.org

Wang, W.Y.C., Heng, M.S.H., & Chau, P.Y.K. (Eds.). (2006). *Supply chain management: Issues in the new era of collaboration and competition.* Idea Group, USA.

KEY TERMS

Direct Image Access: Provision of access to a physical image online real-time to a remotely located expert using advanced technological capabilities.

Enterprising: Establishing a large scale extended organizational form involving a number of distinctive organizations through fusion of a specific set of tasks and responsibilities dedicated to achieve a set of common objectives.

Expert Localization: Locating an expert for his or her expert assistance to a given problem that occurred elsewhere regardless of the actual location of physical presence with the purpose of closing the physical gap between the problem and the expert.

Integrated Information Platforms: Information systems solution with an integrated architecture for compiling and sharing of information across different technical disciplines, experts, and organizations to facilitate active collaboration.

Rapid Virtual Enterprising: Enterprising effort dedicated to establishing a functionally very dynamic setting with no geographical barriers to work more or less in a virtual mode through robust technical solutions for enhanced interactivity and connectivity.

Technology-Embedded Support Centres: Support centres built with advanced information and communication technology solutions and other capabilities, to provide necessary expert assistance in managing a production plant or facilities.

About the Contributors

Pavel Zemliansky is an associate professor of writing and rhetoric at James Madison University where he also directs the first-year composition program. Dr. Zemliansky teaches courses in composition, visual and digital rhetoric, and methods of teaching writing. He has published several books and numerous book chapters and journals articles on rhetoric and the teaching of writing.

Kirk St.Amant is an associate professor of technical communication in the Department of English at East Carolina University. He has a background in anthropology, international government, and technical communication and his research interests include intercultural exchanges via online media and international outsourcing. He has taught online and conventional courses in technical and professional communication and in intercultural communication for Texas Tech University, Mercer University, and James Madison University. He has also taught courses in e-commerce, distance education, and business communication in Ukraine as a part of the USAID-sponsored Consortium for the Enhancement of Ukrainian Management Education (CEUME).

***

Wendy Warren Austin is an associate professor in the English and Theatre Arts Department at Edinboro University of Pennsylvania, and has taught technical writing, business and professional writing, and first year composition there since 1988. She has a PhD in rhetoric and linguistics from Indiana University of Pennsylvania, an MA in rhetoric and composition from Purdue University, in addition to her BA in humanities from University of Houston. Her research interests are in plagiarism, emerging technologies, and computers and composition.

Neil P. Baird is a PhD student concentrating in rhetoric and composition at the University of Nevada, Reno, where he teaches traditional and online writing courses as a lecturer. His dissertation is a series of case studies that examine how the embodied literacies of collegiate football players function in upper-division, writing-intensive courses across the disciplines.

Matt Barton is an assistant professor of English at St. Cloud State University in St. Cloud, Minnesota. His research interests are video games, wikis, new media, rhetoric, and computers and writing. He has published in the journals *Text and Technology*, *Computers and Composition*, and *Kairos,* and has chapters in three forthcoming edited collections. Currently, he is serving as an assistant editor of *Kairos* and an associate editor of *Kairosnews*.

Morell D. Boone serves as dean of the College of Technology at Eastern Michigan University. Boone also served EMU as professor and dean of learning resources and technologies from 1986 to 2001. He provided the leadership for visioning, design, and implementation of the Bruce T. Halle Library. Prior to coming to EMU, Boone was dean of learning resources at the University of Bridgeport. He is a frequent contributor to academic publications and a presenter at national and international meetings regarding the impact of information technologies on library design and services. Boone holds a PhD in instructional design, development, and evaluation from Syracuse University.

Clint Bowers is a professor of digital media at the University of Central Florida. He is also chief scientist of the university's Augmented Cognition for Training in Virtual Environments Laboratory (ACTIVE). Dr. Bowers' research interests include team training, team performance, and the use of technology in complex workplaces.

Pam Estes Brewer lectures in the English & Philosophy Department at Murray State University and coordinates the Professional Writing program. She is completing her doctorate in technical communication and rhetoric at Texas Tech University. Her research interests include intercultural virtual workplaces and related studies. She has presented at the Society for Technical Communication, the Association of Teachers of Technical Writing, and Computers & Writing conferences. In addition, she was part of a research team that won a $10,000 STC grant for their work concerning authors' preferences in editing, and served on the organizing committee for the 2006 Computers & Writing Online Conference.

H. Allen Brizee, Purdue OWL coordinator, is a PhD candidate in rhetoric and composition at Purdue University with secondary areas in professional writing and public rhetoric. He has been teaching writing in labs and classrooms since 1996. He earned his AS (cum laude) from Northern Virginia Community College while working as a technical writer for the Department of Defense at Ft. Belvoir, Virginia. He earned his BA in English (summa cum laude) and his MA in English (composition and professional writing) from Virginia Tech. Mr. Brizee continues to work as a professional writer with the Editorial Cooperative at Purdue.

Jan Cannon-Bowers recently left her position as the U.S. Navy's senior scientist for training systems to join the Institute for Simulation and Training and Digital Media Department at the University of Central Florida as an associate professor and research scientist. Her research interests are in technology-enabled learning and synthetic learning environments. To date, she has been awarded several grants to support this work, including two awards by the National Science Foundation. Dr. Cannon-Bowers has been an active researcher, with over 100 publications in scholarly publications. She is on the board of directors of the Society for Simulation in Health Care and Advisor to the national Serious Games Initiative.

Kalyani Chatterjea is an associate professor of geography at the Nanyang Technological University, Singapore. Her specialization is in geomorphology, geography education, and IT in geography education. She has developed many Web-based in-service training packages for teachers in Singapore, has developed several learning packages and used the new strategies such as mobile technologies and virtual environments for teaching physical geography at university level and her own research, and has also published in journals and books on topics related to her areas of specialization, in geomorphology and in geography education.

María José Crisóstomo-Acevedo is a physical therapist at Jerez Hospital, in southern Spain. She earned a BS in physical therapy, University of Seville, and a master's degree in sports physical therapy. Her research interests include the enabling role of information systems for telemedicine and telerehabilitation. She has contributed to several books on IT and telemedicine. Her papers have been published in *Encyclopedia of IS&T 2nd Edition, Research on E-Health and Telemedicine, Thematic Health Network TM-64, Encyclopedia of Physical Therapies, Encyclopedia of Rehabilitation*, and *Encyclopedia of Human Resources Information Systems: Challenges in E-HRM*.

James Dalziel is professor of learning technology and director of the Macquarie E-Learning Centre of Excellence (MELCOE) at Macquarie University in Sydney, Australia. James leads a number of projects including: LAMS (Learning Activity Management System—www.lamsfoundation.org); MAMS (Meta Access Management System—www.federation.org.au); RAMP (Research Activityflow and Middleware Priorities—www.ramp.org.au), and ASK-OSS (the Australian Service for Knowledge of Open Source Software—www.ask-oss.mq.edu.au).

Dana Lynn Driscoll is a PhD candidate in rhetoric and composition at Purdue University with concentrations in research methodologies and writing program administration. She holds an MA in linguistics from SUNY Stony Brook and a BA in English from California University of Pennsylvania. As the Webmaster of the Purdue OWL, she has worked to implement many usability changes and continues to guide the OWL with sustainable, accessible information design. She is interested in mixed methods and participatory research methodologies, information literacy, human-language-technology interaction, and disciplinary knowledge making.

Anne-Florence Dujardin is senior lecturer on the MA course in technical communication at Sheffield Hallam University. Her research interests are in information design and e-learning.

Dev K. Dutta is a final year PhD candidate at the Richard Ivey School of Business at the University of Western Ontario. He came to Canada for his doctoral studies after working for over 12 years in the Indian IT industry as a strategy and organizational process consultant. Dev's two main areas of research focus are strategic management and entrepreneurship. Within these broad domains, he is interested in studying different competitive contexts of firms, for example, multimarket competition, competition across geographies and national boundaries, and competitive contexts of pre-organization and nascent organization. Dev's research has been published in the *Journal of Business Venturing* and *Entrepreneurship Theory and Practice*. In the Fall 2007, Dev will join as a full-time faculty member at the Whittemore School of Business and Economics at the University of New Hampshire.

David A. Edgell has over 10 years experience as a technical communication practitioner in the health care and information technology professions in New Mexico and Wisconsin. He graduated with a BS degree from the University of Wisconsin and currently is working towards a master's degree in the Technical Communication and Rhetoric program at Texas Tech University. His research interests include communication structures surrounding medically informed consent and patient education. He is also concerned with integrating and informing technical communication programs to meet the needs of industry and the future.

Kirstie Edwards is an independent scientific and technical editor. She has been researching communications at Sheffield Hallam University for the past 6 years, where she has also been teaching a postgraduate course in editing and collaborative work since 2004. Her particular fields of interest are computer mediated communication in professional contexts and scientific writing.

Christa Ehmann Powers is vice president of education for Smarthinking, Inc., a Washington, DC-based online learning company. She has developed online training and quality control programs for hundreds of online instructors and currently manages a growing operations department of over 600 online employees. She recently co-authored *Preparing Educators for Online Writing Instruction: Principles and Processes* (NCTE, 2004) and co-edited a special issue of *Technical Communication Quarterly* (16.1, Winter 2007). Christa's current research focuses on online teaching, learning, and employee training, empirical research methods for online settings, and distance management strategies.

Douglas Eyman is senior editor of *Kairos: A Journal of Rhetoric, Technology, and Pedagogy* and is completing a PhD in professional writing and digital rhetoric at Michigan State University. He has accepted a position as assistant professor of English at George Mason University. He has served on the board of directors of the Alliance for Computers and Writing and as a member of NCTE's Instructional Technology Committee; he is currently a member of the CCCC Committee on Computers in Composition and Communication. Eyman's research interests and publications address digital literacies, new media scholarship, electronic publication, teaching and writing in digital environments, and digital rhetoric.

Yulin Fang is an assistant professor at Department of Information Systems, City University of Hong Kong. He earned his PhD at Richard Ivey School of Business, the University of Western Ontario. His current research is focused on knowledge management, virtual team, and open source software projects. He has published papers in major journals such as *Strategic Management Journal, Information & Management, Communications of the Association for Information Systems, The DATA BASE for Advances in Information Systems,* and *Journal of Information Systems Education.* He had extensive business experience in the consulting industry.

Mona Florea is the education & curriculum materials librarian at the University of Rhode Island Library. She previously worked for Yale University Medical Historical Library, Landmark College Library, and Three Rivers Community College Library. Her interests concentrate on reference, library instruction, designing information literacy programs, and on using online course management programs to enhance library services.

James K. Ford is a doctoral student in education at the University of California, Santa Barbara. His general research interests are in writing studies, technical communication, and rhetoric. More specifically, he is interested in the way technology (namely enhanced display systems) impacts literacy practices, not only in education settings, but also in the workplace, and in common societal practices such as in political campaigns, tourism, and entertainment. His background is in technical communication and writing studies. He received his master's degree in technical communication from Texas Tech University in 2001 and began his studies at UCSB in 2004.

Eric Franzen works for CFA Institute in Charlottesville, Virginia where he manages printing and distribution of publications. CFA Institute is a global membership organization that awards the Chartered Financial Analyst® (CFA®) designation. CFA Institute publications provide investment management research to investment professionals. Eric has a masters degree from the University of Virginia in managing information technology. Eric also holds a masters degree from George Mason University in telecommunications management. He has 15 years of experience in publishing and printing with a focus on publications technology.

Olena Igorivna Goroshko holds a PhD in linguistics. She is professor of linguistics and head of Cross-Cultural Communication and Modern Languages Department at National Technical University "Kharkiv Polytechnic Institute." She is also affiliated with the Kharkiv Center for Gender Studies. Dr. Goroshko's professional interests include gender and Internet studies, forensics, and distance education. She is the author of three books and more than 100 articles on communication and gendered linguistics. Her most recent book is on gender trends in the Russian-language Internet.

Geff Green is the course leader for the MA Professional Communication Programme at Sheffield Hallam University, where he teaches technical and professional communication, hypermedia design, and visual communication. His PhD research focused on South East Asian cultural history and he has extensive professional experience designing, programming and maintaining multimedia applications for organizations such as Epic Media Group PLC in the UK.

Parissa Haghirian received her master's degree in Japanese Studies from Vienna University (1998) and was awarded a master's degree (2000) and PhD in international management (2003) from Vienna University of Economics and Business Administration. Since 2006 she has been an assistant professor of international management at the Faculty of Liberal Arts at Sophia University, Tokyo, Japan. Her research and consulting interests include market entries into the Japanese market, intercultural knowledge transfer, and Japanese consumer behavior.

Mario Hair is a fellow of the Royal Statistical Society. He is a lecturer and a member of the Statistics Consultancy Unit at the University of Paisley. His special interests are in the psychology of survey design and the analysis of survey datasets.

Gary Hepburn obtained his PhD from the University of British Columbia in 1997 and he is currently a faculty member in the School of Education at Acadia University. He teaches at the graduate and undergraduate levels in the area of technology integration into education. His research interests are the use of open source software in education and online learning. Dr. Hepburn is interested in how educational software environments can be improved by using open source software as well as some of the related policy, financial, philosophical, sociological, and technical issues. Dr. Hepburn is also involved in the design and development of online courses. He studies the way in which emerging and established online technologies have the potential to shape learning.

Beth L. Hewett consults in online and traditional writing programs and writing center development, and she is a writing coach for graduate and post-graduate writers. She is co-author of *Preparing Educators for Online Writing Instruction: Principles and Processes* (NCTE, 2004), co-editor of *Kai-*

ros: A Journal of Rhetoric, Technology, and Pedagogy, co-editor of a special issue of *Technical Communication Quarterly* (16.1, Winter 2007), and co-editor of *English Studies: Innovative Professional Paths* (Erlbaum, 2006). She recently has completed a book manuscript regarding asynchronous and synchronous conference-based online writing instruction for secondary and post-secondary English and WAC online educators.

Russell J. Hewett is a graduate student in the Scientific Computing Group, in the University of Illinois Computer Science Department. He is a co-author of "Solar Activity Monitoring" in *Space Weather: Research towards Applications in Europe* (2007, Springer) and lead author of "Multiscale Analysis of Active Region Evolution" (under review). He has spent the past 8 years working as an intern and a contractor with NASA's Goddard Space Flight Center, and he recently held a visiting scholarship at Trinity College Dublin, in Dublin, Ireland.

Tobias Höllerer is an assistant professor of computer science at the University of California, Santa Barbara, where he leads a research group on Imaging, Interaction, and Innovative Interfaces. A computer science graduate from Technical University of Berlin in Germany, Höllerer did his PhD work on mobile augmented reality systems at Columbia University. Höllerer co-organized several conferences and workshops on augmented and virtual reality, including the 2006 IEEE and ACM International Symposium on Mixed and Augmented Reality. His main research interests lie in augmented and virtual reality, 3D displays and interaction, visualization, mobile and wearable computing, and adaptive user interfaces.

Frankie S. Jones completed her PhD in instructional technology with a concentration in human resource and organizational development at The University of Georgia in 2006. She currently works as a learning and development manager at UPS in Atlanta, Georgia. Her professional interests include virtual collaboration, learning technologies, informal learning, and international human resource development.

Michael J. Klein, PhD, is an assistant professor of writing and rhetoric studies at James Madison University where he teaches courses in first-year composition, technology and writing, visual rhetoric, and rhetoric of science. He holds advanced degrees in science and technology studies from Virginia Tech, in technical communication from Rensselaer, and in rhetoric and composition from the University of Arizona. His research interests include an examination of the role of rhetoric in the dissemination of scientific information to the public and the use of popular cultural in public policy debates on science and technology.

Heinz D. Knoell is currently visiting professor of IS at the German Department of IS of the Marmara-University in Istanbul. In the academic year 2004/2005 he was a visiting scholar at the UCLA Anderson School where he pursued a research project on the outcomes of ERP systems. He is a professor in information systems at the University of Lueneburg, Germany, and a visiting professor at the University of Wolverhampton, UK. His research interests include software project management, business process optimization and software quality assurance. Knoell received his PhD, MSc, and BSc from the University of Muenster, Germany. He is a member of AIS and the German Chapter of the ACM.

Zoran Krupka is working at the Marketing Department of University of Zagreb—Faculty of Economics and Business, teaching International Marketing and Brand Management. His research areas include: international marketing, brand management, and mergers and acquisitions. He has published several papers in the area of his interest and has been working as a consultant to several Croatian companies. Currently he is enrolled in on the PhD program at University of Zagreb.

Belinda Davis Lazarus earned a PhD in special education and applied behavior analysis from the Ohio State University. She has conducted studies and published articles in the areas of inclusion strategies for students with disabilities, virtual environments and disabilities, and assessment. Dr. Lazarus is the Director of the Master of Education in Special Education and the Special Education Distance Learning Program at the University of Michigan-Dearborn.

Diego Liberati, earned his PhD in electronic and biomedical engineering at the Milano Institute of Technology. He is the director of research, Italian National Research Council, and author of 50 papers on ISI journals. He is the editor and author of books and chapters, secretary of the Biomedical Engineering Society of the Italian Electronic Engineering Association (and Milano prize laureate in 1987), and he has chaired scientific committees for conferences and grants. He was a visiting scientist at Rockefeller University, New York University, University of California, and International Computer Science Institute, and he has directed joint projects granted by both private and public institutions and mentored dozens of pupils toward and beyond their doctorate

Aizhong Lin is currently a research coordinator at the MELCOE (Macquarie E-Learning Center of Excellence) at Macquarie University in Sydney. His research interests include Web and Grid authentication, authorization, and collaboration, virtual organization, trust management, Peer-to-Peer service integration, and software agent. His research and development achievements include IAMSuite (Identity and Access Management Suite), AbWSIP2P (Agent-based Web Service Integration on Peer-to-Peer network), AbEPMS (Agent-based Emergent Process Management System), and about 20 published papers and book chapters.

Jayantha P. Liyanage is an associate professor of industrial asset management at the University of Stavanger (UiS), Norway. He is also the chair and a project advisor of the Center for Industrial Asset Management, and a member of the R&D group of the Center for Risk Management and Societal Safety (SEROS), at UiS. Dr. Liyanage is the Co Organizer and Coordinator of the European Research Network on Strategic Engineering Asset Management. He has earned BSc in production engineering (First Class Honours), MSc in human factors (Distinction), and PhD in offshore engineering. Dr. Liyanage is actively involved in joint industry projects both at advisory and managerial capacities, and also currently serves as the principal and external advisor for a number of PhD projects. He has published more than 75 publications in various books, international journals, and conferences over the last few years. For his performance, he has received a number of prestigious awards inclusive of University of Peradeniya Award for the Best Performance in Engineering (1995), Colombo Dockyard Award for the Best Performance in Production Engineering (1995), The Overall Best in Masters (1999), Lyse Energy Research Award for Excellent Research and Academic Contributions (2001), Society of Petroleum Engineers Best PhD Award (2003), and the Emerald Literati Club Award for Excellence (2004). He is active as a member of a number of international societies and networks. He also serves as an editorial reviewer and a member of international editorial boards of a number of international journals, and actively involves in national and international conferences as a member of International steering committees and program chair. His R&D interests include technology and engineering management, human-technology-organization, value added processes, decision quality and work processes, risk based decisions, asset operations, maintenance technology, sustainable industrial systems and processes, knowledge management and process intelligence, total quality, information systems, performance measurement and management, and so forth.

Jose-Aurelio Medina-Garrido is lecturer at the University of Cadiz, Spain. He has contributed to several books and articles on IT. He is a member of the GEM (Global Entrepreneurship Monitor) international project, developed by Babson College and the London Business School. He participates in several Research Groups on "Dynamic Capabilities and Strategic Change," "Strategic Management and Human Resources," "Global Entrepreneurship Monitor," and "Creation of Cultural Firms." Dr. Medina-Garrido has been a consultant for several firms.

Alan McCord serves as executive director of LTU Online, and College Professor in the College of Management at Lawrence Technological University. His teaching responsibilities focus on the University's Doctor of Management in Information Technology program. Prior to LTU, he held senior information technology positions at the University of Michigan and Eastern Michigan University. He has consulted for several private sector businesses and higher education institutions, is the author of book chapters and articles on IT infrastructure, IT outsourcing, online learning programs, and information systems education. McCord holds a PhD in Instructional Technology from Wayne State University.

Christie L. McDaniel has a BSIS with honors and an MSIS from the School of Information and Library Science at the University of North Carolina at Chapel Hill. She is currently an adjunct assistant professor of Practice at SILS at UNC and will begin working as an associate systems engineer at Cisco Systems in fall 2007. Her research interests include gender and technology, virtual management, and networking.

Lisa D. McNair is an assistant professor of engineering education at Virginia Tech. She is co-director of the Virginia Tech Engineering Communication Center (VTECC), where she is developing communications curricula and assessment methodologies for engineering students and faculty, and conducting on-going research. Her research interests include using linguistic analysis to study cognitive design and interdisciplinary and intercultural collaborations.

Lei Meng, a native Chinese, is currently working as a localization project manager for a translation company. Lei has 4 years of localization experiences and received her MA degree in technical communication and rhetoric from Texas Tech University in 2004. She is interested in research in intercultural communication and localization.

Mutaleci Miranda, born May 3, 1971, Rio de Janeiro, Brazil, holds a bachelor's degree in computer science (1993) and an MSc in database systems (1999), from the Military Institute of Engineering (IME/RJ). He is a Brazilian Army Officer, Engineer Corps, and has worked with combat simulation systems and electronic document management systems development. He is currently a teacher at IME and is enrolled in the PhD Program at COPPE/UFRJ, in the Computer and Systems Engineering Program.

Denise Nicholson is the director of the Applied Cognition and Training in Immersive Virtual Environments Laboratory (http://active.ist.ucf.edu/) at the University of Central Florida's Institute for Simulation and Training. She is also a faculty member in UCF's Modeling and Simulation Graduate Program, a Research Scientist in the College of Optics and Photonics/CREOL, and a certified modeling and simulation professional. Dr. Nicholson's research focuses on human systems modeling, simulation and training includes virtual reality, human–agent collaboration, and adaptive human systems technologies for Department of Defense and Duel-Use Applications. She has authored/co-authored more than 40 technical publications and given numerous invited lectures/presentations.

Bolanle A. Olaniran (PhD, University of Oklahoma, 1991) is a professor in the Department of Communication Studies at Texas Tech University, Lubbock, Texas. His research areas include: computer-mediated communication, cross cultural communication, and organization communication. His works have appeared in international, national, regional journals, and several book chapters.

S.J. Overbeek, MSc is pursuing a PhD in the area of knowledge discovery and exchange in collaboration with the Radboud University Nijmegen, The Netherlands. He works at E-Office, a Dutch IT company specialized in developing virtual workplaces by using portal technology. He received the MSc in information science from Radboud University Nijmegen in 2005.

Marie C. Paretti is an assistant professor of engineering education at Virginia Tech and codirector of the Virginia Tech Engineering Communications Center (VTECC). Her work addresses the role of communication in engineering design, communication across disciplinary and cultural boundaries, and the integration of communication into engineering curricula.

Jurica Pavicic is working at the Marketing Department of University of Zagreb—Faculty of Economics and Business, teaching Marketing Strategy and Marketing for Nonprofit Organizations. His research areas include interdisciplinary interwoven approach(es) to: strategic marketing, social change, sociological concepts of communities, and nonprofit institutions. He has published widely in the abovementioned areas and (co)authored books and chapters with several distinguished publishers: Ashgate, Lawrence Erlbaum, CAB International, and Masmedia. When he is not "absorbed" with international academic challenges and consultancies for firms and nonprofits, he travels and spends time with family and friends.

Prof. Dr. H.A. (Erik) Proper is a professor in information systems science at the Radboud University Nijmegen, The Netherlands. Erik has co-authored several journal papers, conference publications, and books. His main research interests include system theory, system architecture, business/IT alignment, conceptual modelling, information retrieval, and information discovery.

Lillian Rafeldt teaches prenursing and nursing content online and onground. Her areas of expertise include curriculum development, gerontologic and medical surgical nursing. Her professional experience includes caring for clients in multiple care settings. She also is facilitating implementation of computerized charting in a nonprofit Visiting Nurse Association as a member of the Board of Directors. Lili celebrates the nursing profession and its future!

Judith Ramsay is a chartered psychologist, specialising in the psychology of human-computer interaction. She is a lecturer in psychology at the University of Paisley, UK.

Karen Renaud is a computer scientist, specialising in various aspects of human interaction with facilitating technologies and applications. She is a senior lecturer in the Computing Science Department of the University of Glasgow.

D.B.B. (Daan) Rijsenbrij is a Professor in Digital Architecture at the Radboud University Nijmegen, The Netherlands. Digital architecture is the architecture of the digital world. He firmly believes in the similarities between physical architecture (the architecture of cities, landscapes, buildings, and the interior architecture) and digital architecture (the architecture of digital business services, information provisioning, information traffic, applications, and technology infrastructures). As an independent guru in the field of digital architecture he displays his ideas under the label of "(Enterprise) Digitecture" covering the phases of architecture and design in the digital world.

William F. Ritke-Jones is Haas professor of English at Texas A&M University—Corpus Christi where he teaches courses in teaching ESL composition, technical communication, teaching composition, rhetorical theory and computers and composition. His research focuses on intercultural communication, especially in electronic environments, online technical communication education, computer mediated communication and adult education. He has also examined the dynamics of online collaborative groups extensively, focusing on how instructors can foster the emergence of dialogically collaborative online groups, especially in those composed of diverse people. With that goal in mind, his research currently focuses on how transformational and liberatory learning theories can be applied to online groups.

Peter Rive is a PhD candidate at the School of Design located at Victoria University of Wellington, New Zealand. He will be teaching New Zealand's first university course in the virtual world, Second Life based on the School's virtual island, MediaZone. Peter is a professional film and TV editor who has worked in almost all areas of production for the past 20 years. His company, LaunchSite, was established in 1999 as a consultancy in virtual reality and virtual worlds. It specializes in high impact VR, machinima, marketing, and knowledge management.

Michelle Rodino-Colocino is assistant professor in the College of Communications at Penn State University, where she teaches courses on media and culture. Her research explores the relationship between media, technology, gender, and labor. Her work has appeared in *Critical Studies in Media Communication*, the *Journal of Computer-Mediated Communication, Feminist Media Studies, New Media and Society*, and *Workplace: A Journal of Academic Labor*.

José A. Rodrigues Nt. is a PhD student of the Computer and Systems Engineering Program, at the Graduate School of Engineering (COPPE) of the Federal University of Rio de Janeiro (UFRJ–Brazil). He received his bachelor's degree in systems engineering (Brazilian Naval Academy–1982) and holds am MSc in computer science and an MSc in operations research (U.S. Naval Postgraduate School–1994). He has prior experience in robotics, software engineering, C4I systems, decision support systems, distributed systems, and business processes. He currently researches KM, BPM, CSCW, and distributed systems. He is also an experienced consultant for major Brazilian companies.

Michael J. Salvo is assistant professor of technical and professional writing at Purdue University, where he teaches usability and user-centered design. He has been a usability consultant for the Purdue Online Writing Lab since 2003. He is interested in usability testing and research, and is particularly intrigued by opening spaces for user participation in technology deployment and design.

Robert Schafer is a doctoral student in the Technical Communication and Rhetoric program at Texas Tech University. Robert has 10 years experience writing, designing, and marketing for ecommerce Web sites. Currently, his research interests include intercultural communication, research methods, and cultural anthropology.

Bernd Simon, a graduate of Wirtschaftsuniversität Wien and the International Management Programme at New York University's Stern School of Business, is a researcher at the Institute for Information Systems and New Media of Wirtschaftsuniversität Wien. As a member of the Prolix project he is leading cutting-edge research on learning management solutions. In 2005 he cofounded Knowledge Markets, a university spin-off providing consulting services for knowledge-driven organisations. As an active contributor to the EducaNext Portal he works at the frontier of IT-supported, academic knowledge exchange. Bernd's research on the effectiveness of educational systems and system interoperability has been disseminated through top journals and conferences.

Alan D. Smith is presently university professor of operations management at Robert Morris University, located in Pittsburgh, PA. Previously he was chair of the Department of Quantitative and Natural Sciences and coordinator of Engineering Programs at the same institution, as well as associate professor of business administration at Eastern Kentucky University. He holds concurrent PhDs in engineering systems/education from The University of Akron and in Business Administration from Kent State University. He is the author of numerous articles and book chapters.

Peter A. Smith is currently visiting research faculty at the University of Central Florida's Institute for Simulation and Training. As part of the Augmented Cognition for Training in Virtual Environments (ACTIVE) Lab, Peter fills the role of resident games expert through his previous experience in Serious Games working with the Navy's NETC Experimentation Lab. Peter is also an avid blogger, with experience writing for the Serious Games Initiative blog and AOL's Second Life Insider.

Morgan Sousa is a PhD candidate at Purdue University in rhetoric and composition with a concentration in professional writing. She completed her MA in professional writing and editing at West Virginia University in the summer of 2005. Prior to her MA work, she graduated from Assumption College in 2003 with a BA in English and a minor in management. Morgan has been a member of the Purdue OWL Usability Research Team since the spring of 2006. Her research interests include usability and accessibility, OWLs, gendered patterns of searching and learning, and information design.

Jano Moreira de Souza is a professor of computer science at the Graduate School of Engineering (COPPE) and Mathematics Institute of the Federal University of Rio de Janeiro (UFRJ) (Brazil). His area of specialization is databases, and he is involved in research in fields such as CSCW, DB, DSS, KM, and GIS. He received his bachelor's degree in mechanical engineering (1974) and his master's degree (1978) in system engineering from UFRJ, and his PhD in information systems (1986) from the

University of East Anglia (England). He has published more than 200 papers in journals and conference proceedings and supervised around 50 theses and dissertations.

Robert Sprague, JD, MBA, teaches undergraduate business law courses in the University of Wyoming College of Business. Sprague's research interests focus on the convergence of law, business, and technology. His recent publications include an article concerning the impact of business blogs on commercial speech rights, as well as an article examining the legal consequences of employees being fired as a result of content in their personal blogs. Sprague has also recently had accepted for publication an article regarding the recent, growing phenomenon of prospective employers using Web-based social networks to preview job applicants. Prior to becoming a professor on a full-time basis, Professor Sprague held senior management positions with Internet-related companies in Silicon Valley. He has several years of experience consulting in the area of legal automation, as well as practicing law, primarily representing clients in the computer industry.

R. Todd Stephens is the technical director of the Collaboration and Online Services Group for the AT&T Corporation. Todd is responsible for setting the corporate strategy and architecture for the development and implementation of the enterprise collaborative and metadata solutions. Todd has over 130 professional and academic publications including three patents, six patent pending filings, and he writes a monthly column for *Data Management Review.* Todd holds degrees in mathematics and computer science from Columbus State University, an MBA degree from Georgia State University, and a PhD in information systems from Nova Southeastern University.

Julia Diedrich Sweeny received her BA, MA, and MEd at James Madison University. Her PhD is in curriculum and design with a concentration on instructional design from Virginia Tech. Her dissertation was on "Online Learning: The Student Point-of-View" (written under last name Harbeck.) She was the instructional technologist at the Center for Instructional Technology at James Madison University from 2000-2006. She is currently an assistant professor in writing and rhetoric studies at James Madison University. She lives in Virginia with her daughter and dog.

Jamie S. Switzer is an assistant professor in the Department of Journalism and Technical Communication at Colorado State University. She received her doctorate in educational technology from Pepperdine University, and also holds degrees in technical communication from Colorado State University and radio/TV/film from Texas Christian University. She has over 18 years of experience in new media technologies and mediated communication. Dr. Switzer conducts research on computer-mediated communication, new media technologies, and online mentoring. She has published in *The Internet Encyclopedia, The Encyclopedia of Distance Learning, Teaching, Technologies, and Applications, Interactive Educational Multimedia, Innovative Higher Education, THE Journal, the Journal of Educational Technology Systems,* the forthcoming *Encyclopedia of Multimedia Technology and Networking,* and the forthcoming *Encyclopedia of E-Collaboration.* Dr. Switzer is the founder and director of the Online Mentoring Program in the Journalism Department at CSU. She also founded the Center for Innovation in Learning Technologies in the CSU College of Business.

Judith Szerdahelyi is assistant professor of English at Western Kentucky University where she teaches multilevel composition courses, including technical writing and technology and writing, both face-to-face and online. Her teaching and research interests include composition theory and pedagogy, computers and writing, digital literacy and multimedia writing, digital video production in higher education, and distance learning. Her publications include a co-authored textbook on writing and various academic articles published both in the U.S. and in Europe.

Terrie Lynn Thompson, a telecommuter for 10 years, is familiar with the virtual workplace. Her background includes research, management, facilitation, and curriculum design in higher education, high tech, not-for-profit sport, and international social development. She was a global e-learning strategist, authored an international e-learning bulletin, and awarded a WebCT Exemplary Course Award (2004). As the learning director for a Canadian NGO, she developed technology-based learning experiences focused on social development for youth and community members in developing countries. Current research interests include self-employed workers' engagement in online communities for informal learning and quality standards for e-learning initiatives in the health care sector.

P. (Patrick) van Bommel received his MSc degree in computer science in 1990, and his PhD in mathematics and computer science from the Radboud University Nijmegen, The Netherlands in 1995. He is currently assistant professor at the Radboud University Nijmegen. Patrick has co-authored several journal papers, conference publications, and books. His main research interests include information modelling and information retrieval.

Goran Vlasic is working at the Marketing Department of University of Zagreb—Faculty of Economics and Business, teaching marketing communications, interactive marketing and marketing innovation. He presented many papers at international conferences, published 3 papers in international journals, published 18 case studies, a textbook on interactive marketing, and a book on new media management. He works as a consultant to several Croatian companies. He is researching areas of interactive marketing, relationship personalization, innovations, and high-tech marketing. Currently he is on PhD in Business Administration and Management program at Bocconi University.

Erik Vullings recently started working as Senior Systems Architect at TNO in the Netherlands, the third largest research organization in Western Europe. From 2004-2007, he was program manager at Macquarie University in Sydney, Australia, of several DEST-funded projects (total value $8m) in identity and access management. These projects laid the foundation for the Australian Access Federation, providing single sign-on between all 39 Australian universities, as well as providing practical open source solutions for virtual organizations. Between 1999 and 2004, he worked as systems engineer at Philips R&D and was the programme manager of a €24m FP6 Integrated Project in assembly equipment.

Ran Wei (PhD, Indiana University-Bloomington, 1995) is an associate professor at University of South Carolina's School of Journalism & Mass Communications. His current research interest focuses on the adoption, use and impact of new media technology in national, organizational, and individual contexts. His publications include 32 refereed journal articles, 3 book chapters, and 1 co-authored book. Two of his papers received national awards. Dr. Wei also serves on the editorial board of 3 journals.

Joel West is the director of the Center for Communications Research at Texas Tech University, where he also teaches courses in advertising and public relations. His professional experience includes

7 years of prepress systems management for a commercial printer, overseeing a transition from an analog/conventional to a 100% digital workflow.

Geraldo Xexéo received his bachelor's degree in electronic engineering from the Military Institute of Engineering (IME/RJ) in 1988 and received his doctor of Computer and Systems Engineering degree from COPPE, Federal University of Rio de Janeiro (UFRJ – Brazil), in 1994. Since 1995, he has been a professor of computer science at UFRJ. His research is on distributed applications, information retrieval and extraction, and fuzzy logic. He is also an experienced consultant for major Brazilian companies.

Kathleen Blake Yancey, Kellogg W. Hunt professor of English at Florida State University, directs the graduate program in rhetoric and composition studies. Past president of the Council of Writing Program Administrators, she is also a past Chair of the Conference on College Composition and Communication. Currently president-elect of the National Council of Teachers of English. She also codirects the International Coalition on Electronic Portfolio Research. She is the author, editor, or co-editor of numerous chapters and articles as well as of 10 books, among them *Portfolios in the Writing Classroom* (1992), *Assessing Writing across the Curriculum* (1997), *Teaching Literature as Reflective Practice* (2004), and *Delivering College Composition: The Fifth Canon* (2006).

Simeon Yates is director of the Cultural, Communication, and Computing Research Institute at Sheffield Hallam University. Current and previous research topics include sociolinguistics of online interaction, science in the media, and gender and new media use.

Norman E. Youngblood is an assistant professor in the Department of Electronic Media and Communications at Texas Tech University where he teaches courses in digital media production and the interplay of electronic media and society. Prior to teaching, he worked for 3 years as an IT professional in an academic environment and was the graduate-fellow and Interim Director of the CNN World Report Television Archive at Texas Tech University. His research areas include interface design and issues related to the adoption of electronic media technology.

Susan Youngblood is a PhD candidate in Technical Communication and Rhetoric at Texas Tech University. Her research areas are risk communication and rhetoric of science and technology. She is particularly interested in how the Internet is used by subject matter experts to communicate with the public. Her professional experience includes private and public sector work in environmental science and public health.

Geraldo Zimbrão is an assistant professor of computer science at the Graduate School of Engineering (COPPE) and Mathematics Institute of the Federal University of Rio de Janeiro (UFRJ – Brazil). His area of specialization is Databases, and he is involved in research in fields such as spatial databases, GIS, query optimization, data warehouses, and database cluster. Professor Zimbrao received his bachelor's degree in computer science (1992), his master's degree in applied mathematics (1993) and his PhD in computer and systems engineering (1998) from the Federal University of Rio de Janeiro (Brazil).

James R. Zimmerman received an AB from The University of Michigan and worked as a reporter, press secretary, cable TV anchor, news director, and Editor of Warner Communications' Qube Program Guide. He earned the MA and PhD from Ohio State University, taught at Case Western Reserve University and Richard Stockton College, and was affiliated with West Virginia University's Center for Executive Education. Zimmerman has served as consultant to Fortune 500 companies, is the cocreator and cofacilitator of "Communication Effectiveness Seminars," and is a member of the Writing and Rhetoric Studies faculty at James Madison University.

Leah A. Zuidema recently joined the English Department at Dordt College in Sioux Center, Iowa, where she teaches courses in English education, business and technical writing, and composition. Her chapter is based on research that she conducted as a doctoral candidate at Michigan State University while in the Critical Studies in the Teaching of English program.

Index

A

academic dishonesty 289, 290, 291, 292, 293, 295, 290, 289, 293, 290, 291, 292, 293, 294, 295, 296, 297, 298, 299, 300

academic dishonesty, prevention strategies for 289, 292, 293, 294, 295, 297

academic dishonesty, reasons for 292

academic dishonesty, technical countermeasures against 289, 294, 295

academic integrity 289, 290, 291, 293, 294, 295, 298, 299, 300, 292, 289, 299

access policy 481

activity system 24, 25, 26, 27, 29, 30, 31, 32, 33, 35, 38

activity theory 24, 25, 26, 36, 37, 38

Adobe Acrobat 535, 536

adoption theory 395, 400

alienation 633

Aloft 417, 418

Amazon.com 668, 669, 671, 673

American Management Association (AMA) 505

Anderson, Chris 671, 673, 677

anywhere augmentation 495, 496

Aristotle 618, 619, 630

ARPANET 168

assistive technology 201, 204

asynchronous communication 456, 457, 458, 461, 466, 471

asynchronous editing 541

asynchronous JavaScript and XML (AJAX) 537, 538, 542, 543

attribution 604, 609, 611, 612

audience 692, 693, 694, 695, 696, 697, 698, 699, 700, 701

auditory processing 202, 204

augmented reality

(AR) 486, 487, 488, 489, 490, 491, 492, 493, 494, 495, 496, 497, 498, 499, 500, 502

authentication 473, 474, 475, 477, 484

authorization 473, 474, 475, 478

authorship 604, 607, 612, 613

authorship, nominal 607, 613

autonomy 637, 639

avatar 413, 414, 415, 428, 430, 432, 433, 434, 435

B

banking 571, 572, 573, 574, 572, 573, 580

Bennis, Warren 506, 507, 508, 509, 512, 514

blended learning 272, 273, 279, 280, 281, 283, 284

blogs 208, 217, 219, 220, 322, 328, 330

Blythe, Stuart 617, 621, 629, 630

Bollier, David 335, 336, 343, 344

Bourdieu, Pierre 595, 598, 599, 602, 603

Bowker 673

Braille displays 204

Braille printers 204

Brandt, Deborah 596, 602
browser-based software 530, 538
building society 573
business-to-business (B2B) 702, 703, 707
business capabilities 686, 687, 688, 689
business process 516, 517, 518, 519, 526, 527, 528, 580
business process management (BPM) 516, 517, 518, 519, 525, 526, 528
business process reengineering (BPR) 517
business strategy 350, 354, 355, 356

C

capital, academic 598, 599
capital, cultural 595, 598, 599, 603
cheating. *See* academic dishonesty
chunks. *See* learning objects (LO)
client-support 583, 584, 585, 594, 585
Cogdill, Sharon 634, 639
cognitive disabilities 197, 198, 199, 202
collaboration 384, 390, 391, 474, 583, 393, 475, 585, 584, 586, 587, 588, 589, 590, 592, 593
collaboration tools 350, 351, 352, 353, 354, 355, 356, 358, 359, 362
collaborative discussion boards 321
collaborative information technologies (CITs) 120, 121, 123, 124, 125, 126, 127, 126, 127, 130, 131, 132
collaborative learning 327, 329, 330
collaborative technologies 150, 151, 153, 155, 156, 157, 158, 159, 161, 162, 163, 164, 165, 166
collaborative technologies, e-mail 151, 153, 155, 160, 161, 162, 163, 164, 167, 168, 170, 169, 170, 181, 167, 159, 171, 159, 172, 173, 174, 175, 176, 177, 178, 179, 180, 181, 168
collaborative technologies, instant messaging (IM) 159, 160, 161, 162, 163, 164
collaborative work groups 207
collaborative workplaces 552
collegiality 84, 86, 90, 91, 95, 96
colocated work 1, 4, 5, 10, 26, 38
commons, cultural 336

commons, educational 334, 335, 336, 337, 341, 342
commons, innovative 335, 336, 342
commons, open source as 339, 340, 341
commons, schools as 336, 337
commons, traditional 340
communication, ambient 168, 176
communication, barriers to 14, 15, 20
communication, informal 365, 366, 368
communication, pro-social 366, 371, 372, 373, 375, 376
communication, socio-emotional 364, 365, 367, 368, 370, 371, 372, 373, 374, 375, 376, 377, 381
communication, written 370, 371, 372
communication-mediated technologies (CMTs) 15, 18, 22, 23
communication points 511, 512
communication technologies 548, 549, 552
communication tools 362
Communication Workers of America (CWA) 78, 79, 80
communication zone 27, 29, 30, 38
communicative multitasking 455, 456, 462, 463, 464, 466, 467, 468, 472
communities of practice 273, 274, 276, 278, 283, 284, 285, 286, 287
communities of practice(CoPs) 589
community 439, 442, 443, 444, 445, 446, 447, 450, 451, 452, 453, 454
community informatics 72, 74, 75, 76, 77, 78, 79
community of practice (CoP) 528
computer-mediated communication (CMC) 2, 13, 99, 100, 101, 102, 98, 40, 104, 43, 103, 104, 98, 104, 105, 106, 107, 108, 120, 121, 125, 126, 457, 462, 468, 471, 555, 558, 563
computer-mediated communication theory 641, 661
computer-supported cooperative learning (CSCL) 256
computer-supported cooperative work (CSCW) 151, 153, 156
computer mediated communication (CMC) 367, 368, 369, 370, 376, 377

conferencing 551, 552

conferencing tools 350, 354, 356, 362

content analysis 365, 369

content metrics 590

cooperation 707

copyright 425, 426, 432, 435, 436, 437, 607, 605, 438, 609, 607, 609, 611, 612, 613

copyright law 337

CoWord 534, 535, 543

creative collaboration 425, 426, 427, 429, 432

Creative Commons (CC) 609

creative commons (CC) 432

critical incident technique (CIT) 157

critical thinking 317, 322, 323, 327, 330

cross-cultural communication 25, 29, 34, 35

Cube Linden 414

cultural differences 557, 560

cultures of use 31, 35, 38

cybercheating 289, 300. *See also* academic dishonesty

cyberspace 39, 40, 51, 52, 207, 208, 212, 213, 214, 215, 218, 219

D

deception 608

Dent-Micallef, Anne 687

diffusion of innovation 397

digital divide 70, 71, 72, 73, 74, 75, 76, 77, 78, 79

digital divide, first wave research 70, 78, 79

digital divide, second wave research 71, 72, 79

digital immigrants 31, 32, 37

digital natives 31, 32, 35

digital rights management (DRM) 425, 431, 432, 433, 434, 435, 436, 438, 609, 611

disciplinary communities 34

discourse community 692, 693, 695, 698, 699, 700

distance education 700

distance learning 223, 224, 225, 226, 227, 228, 229, 231, 232, 233, 234, 235, 236, 237, 235, 231, 236, 238, 239, 236, 237, 238, 239, 240, 289, 291, 293, 298, 299, 300

distributed learning 300

distributed team 409, 410, 411, 412, 414, 416, 419, 420

distributed work 2, 5, 12, 24, 27, 29, 37, 38. *See also* virtual workplace

documentation 600, 601

dominant culture 208

E

e-learning 319, 321, 322, 330, 332, 584, 587, 593. *See* distance learning

e-mail 503, 504, 505, 506, 507, 508, 509, 510, 511, 512, 513, 530, 531, 532, 533, 536, 537, 538, 539, 540, 541

e-mail style 369, 373, 374, 377, 378

e-training 258, 262

educational commons 344

educational mediator 256

electromyographic (EMG) controlled prostheses 204

Electronic Communications Privacy Act (ECPA) 188, 191, 194

electronic health records (EHRs) 319, 320, 329

employment at will 194

empowerment 636, 638, 639

English-as-a-second-language (ESL) speakers 556, 559

English language, the Internet and the 122, 123, 129, 131, 133, 134

enterprise 705, 706, 707, 708

enterprise applications 348, 350

enterprise knowledge 356

enterprise technologies 348, 353, 363

evidence-based practice 317, 319, 321, 323, 330, 332

extensible markup language (XML) 537, 540, 542, 543

extranet 439, 440, 441, 442, 443, 447, 452, 453

F

face-to-face (FTF) teams 125, 126, 127, 130

face to face (FTF) team 14, 15, 18, 19, 20, 21, 22, 23

financial sector 570, 572, 580

full disclosure 103

G

Gemeinschaft 443, 452, 454
generic remote usage monitoring production
    system(GRUMPS) 174, 175, 179
geographically dispersed 139, 140, 141, 144,
    149
Gibson, William 39, 40, 41, 49
globalization 121, 123, 131, 133
global language 122, 134
globally located teams 548
global village concepts 168
global virtual team 121, 130, 132
Google 537, 538, 539, 540, 541, 543
grade inflation 289, 300
Groove 536
group cohesion 365, 367, 368, 381
group support systems (GSS) 151
Groupware 536, 543
groupware 339, 344
GroupWriter 531, 534

H

H-1B visas 70, 74, 75, 76, 78, 80
Hewlett-Packard 505
hierarchal organizations 207
hierarchy 207, 208, 211, 213
high-context (HC) cultures 651, 653, 654, 655,
    656, 658
high-tech labor 70, 78
homeshoring 561
hostile work environment 185, 194
hot spot 403, 406
human moment 110, 111, 117, 118, 119, 116,
    119
human resource policies 684
hybridity 457, 458, 459, 465

I

identity 383, 384, 392, 393
identity construction 84, 85, 86, 90, 96, 97
image-impression theory 650
immersion 386, 387, 389, 390
impression formation 98, 99, 100, 101, 103,
    104, 105, 106, 108, 99, 108
impression management 101, 102, 108

independent living skills 204
industrial augmented reality (IAR) 489, 491
informal learning 272, 275, 278, 279, 280, 281,
    282, 283, 284, 286, 287
information and communication technologies
    (ICTs) 137, 149
information competency 333
information consumer 320
information design 615
information evaluation 327
information literacy 317, 318, 320, 321, 322,
    323, 325, 329, 330, 331, 333
information system (IS) resources 140, 141,
    145, 146
information technologies (IT) 241, 242, 243,
    244, 245, 246, 247, 248, 249, 250, 251,
    252, 253, 254
information technology (IT) 141, 144, 145,
    146
information worker 582, 583, 584
infrastructure 595, 597, 598, 601, 602, 603
Ingram book publisher 671, 675
instant messaging (IM) 455, 456, 458, 459,
    460, 461, 462, 457, 456, 463, 464, 458,
    460, 462, 464, 465, 466, 467, 468, 471,
    472
institutional documents 607
instructional design 223, 227, 228, 229, 230,
    233, 235, 228, 236, 232, 233, 234, 235,
    237, 238
instructional design, learner-centered 225, 227,
    228, 229, 236, 240
insurance 571, 572, 573, 574, 575, 576, 578,
    580
integration 702, 703, 706
intellectual property 354, 355
intellectual property (IP) 425, 431, 432, 435,
    436, 438
intercultural communication 557, 559, 560
intercultural virtual communication 9
intercultural workplaces 545
international management 243, 247, 248, 253,
    254
international virtual office 555, 556, 557, 558,
    559, 560, 562
Internet 440, 441, 442, 443, 445, 447, 451,

452, 453, 454

internship 544, 545, 546, 547, 548, 549, 550, 551, 552, 553

internship director 546, 548, 549, 550, 551

internships, distance 545, 546, 548, 549, 550, 552

interruptibility 177

intranet 439, 440, 441, 442, 443, 444, 445, 446, 447, 448, 449, 450, 451, 452, 453, 454

invasion of privacy 186, 187, 188, 190, 191, 192

IT-based teaching 241

J

JavaScript 537, 539, 543

Jefferson, Thomas 506, 514

Johnson, John 614, 615, 619, 620, 630

K

Kairos (Journal) 595, 596, 597, 596, 597, 598, 599, 600, 601, 602, 603

knowledge 439, 440, 441, 442, 444, 445, 446, 447, 448, 449, 450, 451, 452, 453, 454

knowledge, definition of 54, 56

knowledge, explicit 54, 55, 57, 67, 68

knowledge, implicit. *See* knowledge, tacit

knowledge, input related 56, 57, 63, 64, 65, 66

knowledge, organizational 137, 141

knowledge, output related 56, 57, 63, 64, 65, 68, 65

knowledge, tacit 54, 55, 57

knowledge-based view (KBV) 137, 141, 149

knowledge community (KM) 600

knowledge exchange 53, 54, 55, 56, 57, 58, 59, 60, 61, 62, 63, 64, 65, 66, 67, 68, 137, 142, 143, 144, 145, 146, 149

knowledge lifecycle 57, 68

knowledge management (KM) 424, 425, 426, 429, 431, 434

knowledge transfer 4, 5, 8, 11, 13

knowledge transformation processes 54, 57, 58, 67, 68

knowledge work 596, 600, 601

knowledge workers 273, 274

L

Laure-Ryan, Marie 385, 386, 387, 389, 394

Laurel, Brenda 385, 387, 389, 390, 394

leadership 503, 504, 505, 506, 507, 508, 509, 510, 511, 512, 513, 514

learning community 363

learning environment scaffold 303, 305, 306, 309

learning management system (LMS) 339, 344, 339, 344

learning objects (LOs) 225, 231, 233, 225, 230, 233, 236

learning professionals 276, 282

Lessig, Lawrence 335, 336, 337, 338, 343, 388, 394, 426, 432, 434, 437

Linden Lab 409, 414, 417, 423, 424, 425, 430, 431, 432, 434, 435

linguistic communication 108

listerv 97

LISTSERV™ 96, 97

locus of control of reinforcement 174, 175

long tails 677

low-context (LC) cultures 651, 654, 655, 658

M

management education 241, 242, 243, 247, 254, 241, 243, 253, 254

Manovich, Lev 382, 387, 388, 394

manual dexterity 201, 204

market enclosure 336, 337, 340, 342, 343, 344

marketing 424, 425, 427, 428, 430, 431, 435, 436, 424

massively multiplayer online game (MMOG) 413, 414, 416, 417, 418, 423

massively multiplayer online role playing game (MMORPG) 438

mass media 395, 398, 399, 400, 401, 402

McLuhan, Marshal 499

media richness theory 28

memorandum of understanding (MOU) 128, 131

memos 504, 506

meta-cognition 25, 26, 38

meta-communication 1, 11, 12, 13

metadata 424, 425, 432, 434, 435

Mezirow, Jack 210, 211, 212, 214, 219, 220, 221, 222

Microsoft Word 532, 533, 534, 535, 536, 537, 541

modeling 504, 508

modules. *See* learning objects (LOs)

Moodle 218

motivation 399, 400, 401, 402

multidisciplinary cooperation 617, 618, 628

Murray, Janet 382, 385, 386, 387, 389, 394

mutual knowledge 153, 155, 156, 163, 165

N

Negroponte, Nicholas 669, 678

net neutrality 610, 611

network 705, 706

networked individualism 347, 363

nomadicity 346, 347, 361, 363

non-empowered culture 208

non-verbal cues 23

nonhuman actors 85, 97

nonverbal communication 108

Nursing Information Gateway 318, 323, 325, 327, 328, 333

O

object role modelling (ORM) 59, 60, 61, 63, 67, 69

objects-to-think-with 639

Office Open XML (OOXML) 540, 541, 543

offshoring 73, 74, 75, 76, 77, 78, 79

online communication 558, 561, 563

online community 272, 273, 276, 283, 284

online human adaptive training 257, 258, 270

online instruction, asynchronous 223, 224, 225, 226, 228, 229, 230, 231, 232, 235, 236, 237, 239, 240

online instruction, synchronous 223, 224, 226, 228, 229, 230, 231, 235, 237, 240

online interactions 120, 131

online learning. *See* distance learning

online learning resources 301

online training principles, association 263, 264, 268, 269, 270

online training principles, immersion 259, 263, 264, 270

online training principles, individualization 259, 263, 264, 270

online training principles, investigation 259, 263, 270

online training principles, reflection 259, 263, 265, 266, 271

online workplaces 632, 633

online writing lab (OWL) 614, 615, 616, 617, 618, 619, 620, 621, 622, 623, 624, 625, 626, 627, 629, 631

open document format (ODF) 537, 540, 541, 542, 543

OpenOffice 533, 537

Open Source Initiative (OSI) 338

open source software 334, 335, 338, 339, 340, 341, 342, 343, 344

organizational learning 517, 519, 526, 528

organizational virtuality 137, 138, 139, 140, 141, 142, 143, 144, 145, 146, 147, 149

Organization for the Advancement of Structured Information Standards (OASIS) 540, 542, 543

P

Palloff, Rena M. 633, 640

paralinguistic cues 101, 104, 105, 109

parawork 81, 82, 83, 84, 85, 86, 87, 88, 89, 90, 91, 92, 93, 94, 97

participatory design 615, 629

peer-to-peer (P2P) 516, 517, 520, 521, 522, 523, 521, 523, 526, 527, 528

pervasive computing 346, 347, 358, 359, 362, 363

physical disabilities 197, 198, 201, 204

plagiarism, bureaucratic 607, 613

plagiarizing. *See* academic dishonesty

play 383, 386, 390, 391, 393

portable document format (PDF) 535, 537, 538, 541

postmodern identity theory 644, 660, 663

Powell, Thomas C. 682, 686, 687, 690

PowerPoint 534, 538

Pratt, Keith 633, 640

Prensky, Marc 31, 32, 37

presence awareness 455, 457, 458, 466, 467, 468

principle-centered training framework 265, 270

print-on-demand (POD) 668, 669, 670, 671, 672, 673, 674, 672, 673, 674, 675, 676, 677, 678, 679

Privacy 183, 188, 194

process models 516, 517, 518, 519, 520, 521, 522, 523, 524, 525, 526

productivity paradox 683

professional development 84, 86, 87, 88, 95, 96

professional writing 692, 693, 694, 699, 700

Purdue OWL usability project ix, xxiv, 614, 615, 616, 617, 618, 621, 624, 626, 627, 629

Q

qualitative research 150, 157

R

ranking system 518, 522, 523, 524, 525

reality-virtuality continuum 488

Reich, Robert 388, 390, 394

relational space 26, 27, 28, 31, 33, 35, 38

relationship personalization 442

remote environments 117, 119

remote testing 628, 629

reporting 440, 447, 448

reputation system 518, 520, 522, 523, 524, 526, 527

Research on Group Decision Support Systems (GDSS) 151

resistance to change 681, 682, 683, 687

resource-based view (RBV) 141

rhetoric 693, 694, 695, 700

rhetorical unit 4, 5, 7, 13

S

safety 636, 637, 639

Second Life 414, 207, 409, 408, 415, 413, 415, 218, 416, 417, 415, 418, 419, 423, 424, 425, 426, 427, 430, 431, 434, 435, 436, 438

second life 220

self-presentation theory 642, 643, 646, 650, 659, 661

self-reflexivity 386, 387

self-service 582, 583, 589, 592

SharePoint 536

Silicon Graphics (SGI) 425, 429, 430, 431

simulated classroom 312

simulated environment 311

simulated lab facility 302

simulated learning environment 303

simulation 384, 386, 390, 394

single sign on (SSO) 474, 478

situated learning 273

social capital 595, 598, 599, 602, 603

social communication 5, 6, 9, 11, 13

social constructionism 273

social information processing theory (SIP) 99, 103, 105

social learning theory 273, 278, 288

social presence theory 28

social software 274, 284

software agent 55, 56, 62, 68, 69

space 383, 384, 389, 390, 391, 392

spasticity 201, 204

spatial augmented reality (SAR) 492

speechreaders 204

stakeholders 617, 618, 620

stereotypes 98, 99, 100, 101, 104, 105, 109

Stored Communications Act (SCA) 191, 194

stress, work-related 168, 169, 170, 171, 172, 173, 175, 176, 178, 179, 180, 181

SubEthaEdit 534, 537

support relatedness 56, 64, 65, 66, 69

sustainability 595, 597, 599, 602

Sutherland, Ivan 488, 489, 501

swift trust 27, 29

synchronous communicaton 456, 457, 458, 459, 461, 462, 468, 471

synchronous editing 538

synchronous remote contact 302

system-centered approach 620

T

tacit knowledge 425, 426, 427, 428, 429, 430, 431, 433, 435, 436

tacit work 351, 363
tangible objects 176
team cohesion 14, 20
team culture 365, 381
team effectiveness 14, 16, 17, 18, 20, 23
team opacity 13
team performance 364, 365, 376, 377, 378
teams, semi-virtual 368, 373, 381
teams, virtual 364, 365, 368, 370, 379, 380, 381
team trust 14, 15, 17, 18, 19, 20, 21, 22, 23
team working, social dimension of 381
team writing 381
technological determinism 71, 79
technological literacy 317, 333
technology, asynchronous 150, 163
technology, synchronous 150, 163
technology architecture 354, 355, 356, 363
technology assessment 354
technology cluster 395, 398, 400, 401, 402
technology literacy 320
technology services framework 346, 352, 353, 354
tele-health 317, 318, 319, 325, 333
tele-nursing 325, 333
telecardiology 681, 688
telecenters 112, 118, 119
telecommuting 83, 111, 112, 113, 115, 116, 115, 116, 117, 118, 119, 546, 550, 556, 561. *See also* virtual workplace
teledermatology 681, 688
telemedicine 681, 682, 683, 684, 685, 686, 687, 688, 689, 690, 691
telenursing 681, 688
telepathology 681, 688
teleradiology 681, 688
telesurgery 681, 688
telework 83, 359, 362, 363, 682, 683, 684, 689. *See also* virtual workplace
teleworkers 346, 348, 359
The Electric Sheep Company 419
Tichy, Noel 508, 510, 514
Title VII of the Civil Rights Act of 1964 184, 194
TonicPoint 538
toxic worry 116, 119

traditional teams 15, 18. *See also* face to face (FTF) teams
trust 473, 474, 475, 476, 477, 479, 480, 481, 482, 483, 484, 485
Turkle, Sherry 639, 640

U

ubiquitous computing (UC) 495, 501, 495
underwritten articles 608
usability research 614, 615, 617, 618, 620, 621, 628, 629, 631
usability testing 621, 627, 628, 631
usage metrics 591
user-based research 615
user-centered design 617, 619, 620, 626
user-centered theory 618, 619, 620, 623, 626, 629

V

video conferencing 243, 247, 256
virtual 703, 705, 706, 707, 709
virtual classroom experiment 243, 246
virtual classrooms 243, 244, 245, 246, 247, 248, 249, 250, 251, 252, 253, 254, 256
virtual classrooms, instructors and 242, 243, 244, 245, 246, 247, 249, 250, 251, 252, 253, 254, 256
virtual classrooms, IT personnel and 243, 244, 245, 247, 249, 250, 251, 253
virtual classrooms, students and 241, 242, 243, 244, 245, 246, 247, 248, 249, 250, 251, 252, 253, 254, 255, 256
virtual collaboration 120, 121, 130, 132, 133, 135
virtual communities 632, 633, 639
virtual education 331
virtual environment 692, 693, 701
virtual identity 632, 633
virtuality 39, 40, 41, 42, 43, 44, 45, 46, 47, 48, 49, 50, 51, 570, 571, 574, 576, 578, 579, 580, 581
virtualization 363
virtual office 2, 12, 83, 95. *See also* virtual workplace
virtual organization 139, 140, 149

virtual organization (VO) 137, 138, 139, 140, 145, 146, 147, 148

virtual organization
 (VO) 474, 475, 476, 479

virtual presence 424, 426, 427, 428, 430, 431, 435, 436

virtual reality (VR) 425, 427, 438

virtual services management framework 346, 352, 353

virtual supervision 307, 308, 312, 313

virtual synchronous classroom (VSC) 276, 277, 278, 279, 284

virtual team 351, 356, 361, 423

virtual team leaders 39, 40, 43, 44, 45, 44, 45, 46, 47, 48, 52

virtual team leadership 39, 40, 44, 47

virtual team managers 20

virtual teams 14, 15, 19, 20, 21, 22, 23, 39, 40, 41, 42, 43, 44, 45, 47, 48, 49, 50, 51

virtual work 98, 100, 104, 105, 106, 109, 149, 346, 347, 348, 349, 350, 351, 352, 353, 354, 355, 356, 357, 358, 359, 360, 362, 363

virtual worker 346

virtual workplace 2, 3, 5, 6, 7, 12, 13, 84, 301, 302, 303, 306, 307, 312, 306, 313, 13, 95, 304, 314, 313, 314, 315, 317, 318, 319, 321, 323, 325, 327, 329, 330, 331, 332, 333, 366, 381, 395, 399, 402, 403, 404, 405, 570, 571, 578, 579, 580, 581

virtual workplace models 53

virtual workplaces 54, 65, 67

virtual workspaces 546

virtual work tools 346, 347, 348, 349, 350, 351, 352, 353, 354, 355, 356, 358, 359, 360, 362

virtual world 409, 413, 414, 415

virtual worlds 424, 425, 426, 430, 434, 436, 438

visual impairment 200

W

Washington Alliance of Technology Workers (WashTech) 75, 77, 78, 79, 80

web-based instruction. *See* distance learning

Web accessibility 616, 631

WebCT learning module 333

White, Eric Charles 596, 603

Wi-Fi 395, 396, 397, 399, 400, 398, 396, 401, 400, 401, 402, 403, 404, 406

Wikipedia 610, 613

wikis 208, 217, 219, 220

wireless technology 306, 307

WLAN 396, 399, 400, 402, 403, 406

workplace 570, 571, 575, 576, 577, 578, 579, 580, 581

workspace 476, 477, 480, 482

Writely 537

writing lab 616, 629

writing practices 605

wrongful discharge 194

Y

Yahoo 539, 540

Z

Zimbra 538, 543